MIDDLE EAST CONFLICTS FROM ANCIENT EGYPT TO THE 21ST CENTURY

MIDDLE EAST CONFLICTS FROM ANCIENT EGYPT TO THE 21ST CENTURY

An Encyclopedia and Document Collection

VOLUME 2: G–N

Dr. Spencer C. Tucker
Editor

An Imprint of ABC-CLIO, LLC
Santa Barbara, California • Denver, Colorado

Copyright © 2019 by ABC-CLIO, LLC

All rights reserved. No part of this publication may be reproduced, stored in a retrieval system, or transmitted, in any form or by any means, electronic, mechanical, photocopying, recording, or otherwise, except for the inclusion of brief quotations in a review, without prior permission in writing from the publisher.

Every reasonable effort has been made to trace the owners of copyright materials in this book, but in some instances this has proven impossible. The editors and publishers will be glad to receive information leading to more complete acknowledgments in subsequent printings of the book and in the meantime extend their apologies for any omissions.

Library of Congress Cataloging-in-Publication Data

Names: Tucker, Spencer, 1937– editor.
Title: Middle East conflicts from Ancient Egypt to the 21st century : an encyclopedia and document collection / Spencer C. Tucker, Editor.
Description: Santa Barbara, CA : ABC-CLIO, [2019] | Includes bibliographical references and index. |
Identifiers: LCCN 2019020655 (print) | LCCN 2019021604 (ebook) | ISBN 9781440853531 (ebook) | ISBN 9781440853524 (set : alk. paper) | ISBN 9781440853548 (volume 1 : alk. paper) | ISBN 9781440853555 (volume 2 : alk. paper) | ISBN 9781440853562 (volume 3 : alk. paper) | ISBN 9781440853579 (volume 4 : alk. paper)
Subjects: LCSH: Middle East—History, Military. | Arab countries—History, Military. | Middle East—History, Military—Encyclopedias. | Arab countries—History, Military—Encyclopedias.
Classification: LCC DS63.15 (ebook) | LCC DS63.15 .M53 2019 (print) | DDC 355.020956/03—dc23
LC record available at https://lccn.loc.gov/2019020655

ISBN: 978-1-4408-5352-4 (set)
     978-1-4408-5354-8 (vol. 1)
     978-1-4408-5355-5 (vol. 2)
     978-1-4408-5356-2 (vol. 3)
     978-1-4408-5357-9 (vol. 4)
     978-1-4408-5353-1 (ebook)

23 22 21 20 19   1 2 3 4 5

This book is also available as an eBook.

ABC-CLIO
An Imprint of ABC-CLIO, LLC

ABC-CLIO, LLC
147 Castilian Drive
Santa Barbara, California 93117
www.abc-clio.com

This book is printed on acid-free paper ∞
Manufactured in the United States of America

To Laurent Boetsch:
Gentleman scholar, linguist, university president,
leader in international education, and esteemed friend.

About the Editors

Spencer C. Tucker, PhD, has been senior fellow in military history at ABC-CLIO since 2003. He is the author or editor of 66 books and encyclopedias, many of which have won prestigious awards. Tucker's last academic position before his retirement from teaching was the John Biggs Chair in Military History at the Virginia Military Institute. He has been a Fulbright scholar, a visiting research associate at the Smithsonian Institution, and, as a U.S. Army captain, an intelligence analyst in the Pentagon. His recently published works include *World War I: The Definitive Encyclopedia and Document Collection, Wars That Changed History: 50 of the World's Greatest Conflicts,* and *Enduring Controversies in Military History: Critical Analyses and Context,* all published by ABC-CLIO.

Priscilla Roberts, PhD, is an associate professor of business at the City University of Macau and codirector of the university's Asia-Pacific Business Research Centre. With Spencer C. Tucker and others, she has coedited and contributed the documents volumes to 11 ABC-CLIO encyclopedias on the Korean War, World War I, World War II, the Cold War, the Arab-Israeli conflict, and Middle East wars. Roberts is the editor of *Cuban Missile Crisis: The Essential Reference Guide, World War II: The Essential Reference Guide, Voices of World War II: Contemporary Accounts of Daily Life, Arab-Israeli Conflict: The Essential Reference Guide, Arab-Israeli Conflict: A Documentary and Reference Guide,* and *The Cold War: Interpreting Conflict through Primary Documents.* In addition, she is the author of numerous other books and articles in international history. Roberts spent 2003 at George Washington University as a Fulbright scholar and has received numerous other academic awards for research in the United States, Great Britain, Australia, Canada, Hong Kong, and Macao. She earned her PhD at King's College, Cambridge, England, and specializes in 20th-century diplomatic and international history.

Contents

Volume 1: A–F
List of Entries   ix
List of Maps   xxiii
Preface   xxv
Introduction   xxvii
General Maps   xxxv
Entries   1

Volume II: G–N
List of Entries   ix
List of Maps   xxiii
General Maps   xxv
Entries   441

Volume III: O–Z
List of Entries   ix
List of Maps   xxiii
General Maps   xxv
Entries   901
Chronology   1383
Glossary   1389
Selective Bibliography   1391
Editors and Contributors   1397

Volume IV: Documents
List of Documents   ix
Documents   1405
Index   1775

List of Entries

Abadi, Haider al- (1952–)
Abbas, Abu (1948–2004)
Abbas, Mahmoud (1935–)
Abbasid Caliphate (750–1258, 1261–1517)
Abbasid Revolution (747–751)
Abbas Mirza (1789–1833)
Abbas I the Great (1571–1629)
Abd Allah ibn al-Zubair (624–692)
Abdel-Rahman, Omar (1938–2017)
Abdulhamid II (1842–1918)
Abdullah I (1882–1951)
Abdullah II (1962–)
Abizaid, John Philip (1951–)
Aboukir, First Battle of (July 25, 1799)
Aboukir, Second Battle of (March 8, 1801)
Aboukir Bay, Battle of (August 1, 1798)
Abu Abbas (1948–2004)
Abu Ghraib
Abulustayn, Battle of (April 15, 1277)
Abu Muslim Khorasani (718?–755)
Abu Nidal (1937–2002)
Achaemenid Empire (550–330 BCE)
Acre, Battle of (November 3, 1840)
Acre, 1189 Siege of (August 28, 1189–July 12, 1191)
Acre, 1291 Siege of (April 6–May 28, 1291)
Acre, 1799 Siege of (March 17–May 20, 1799)
Actium, Battle of (September 2, 31 BCE)
Adan, Avraham "Bren" (1926–2012)

Adana Massacre (April 1909)
Aden Emergency (1963–1967)
Adrianople, Battle of (August 9, 378)
Adrianople, Crusades Battle of (April 14–15, 1205)
Adrianople, 1444 Treaty of (June 12, 1444)
Adrianople, 1713 Treaty of (June 24, 1713)
Adrianople, 1829 Treaty of (September 14, 1829)
Aegospotami, Battle of (405 BCE)
Ager Sanguinis, Battle of (June 28, 1119)
Agha Muhammad Khan Qajar (1742–1797)
Agranat Commission (November 18, 1973–January 30, 1975)
Ajnadain, Battle of (July 30? 634)
Akkad
Akroinon, Battle of (740)
Al-Adil (1145–1218)
Al-Afdal (?–1122)
Alam el Halfa, Battle of (August 31–September 7, 1942)
Al-Amin, Muhammad (787–813)
Al-Anfal Campaign (1987–1988)
al-Aqsa Martyrs Brigades
Al-Aqsa Mosque Massacre (October 8, 1990)
al-Atrash, Sultan (1891–1982)
Alawites
Aleppo, Battle for (July 19, 2012–December 22, 2016)
Alexander I Balas (ca. 173–145 BCE)
Alexander III the Great (356–323 BCE)
Alexander III's Invasion of the Persian Empire (334–323 BCE)

Alexander Severus, Roman Emperor (ca. 208–235)
Alexandria, Bombardment of (July 11, 1882)
Alexandria, Sack of (October 9–12. 1365)
Alexandropol, Treaty of (December 2, 1920)
Alexios I Komnenos (1048–1118)
Alexios III Angelos (ca. 1153–1211)
Alexios V Doukas Mourtzouphlos (1140–1204)
Algiers Agreement (March 6, 1975)
Algiers Declaration (November 15, 1988)
Ali, Ahmad Ismail (1917–1974)
Ali Bey al-Kabir (1728–1773)
Ali ibn Abi Talib (ca. 600–661)
Aliya Bet
Allawi, Ayad (1944–)
Allenby, Sir Edmund Henry Hynman (1861–1936)
Allon, Yigal (1918–1980)
Allon Plan (July 26, 1967)
Al-Mamun, Abd Allah (786–833)
Al-Nusra Front
Alp Arslan (ca. 1030–1072)
Al Qaeda
Al Qaeda in Iraq
Al Qaeda in the Arabian Peninsula
Al-Sabah, Jaber al-Ahmad (1926–2006)
al-Sannabra, Battle of (June 28, 1113)
Altalena Incident (June 23, 1948)
Amalric of Jerusalem (1136–1174)
Amara, Battle of (June 3, 1915)
Amasya, Treaty of (May 29, 1555)
Ambush Alley
Amer, Abdel Hakim (December 11, 1919–September 14, 1967)
Amiriyah Shelter Bombing (February 13, 1991)
Amman Campaign (March 21–September 25, 1918)
Amr ibn al-As (ca. 585–664)
Anbar Awakening Movement
Anglo-American Committee of Inquiry (1946)
Anglo-Egyptian Treaty (August 26, 1936)
Anglo-Egyptian War (1882)
Anglo-Iranian Oil Crisis (1951–1953)
Anglo-Iraqi Treaties of 1922 and 1930
Anglo-Jordanian Defense Treaty (March 15, 1948)
Anglo-Ottoman Treaty (1838)
Anglo-Ottoman War (1807–1809)
Anglo-Persian War (1856–1857)
Anglo-Sudan War (1883–1899)
Ankara, Battle of (July 20, 1402)
Ankara, Pact of (October 19, 1939)

Ansar al-Islam
Anti-Arab Attitudes and Discrimination
Antigonus I Monophthalmus (382–301 BCE)
Antioch, Principality of
Antioch, Sieges of (1097–1098)
Antioch on the Meander, Battle of (1211)
Antiochus I Soter (ca. 324–261 BCE)
Antiochus III Megas (ca. 241–187 BCE)
Antiochus IV Epiphanes (ca. 215–164 BCE)
Antiochus VII Sidetes (ca. 159–129 BCE)
Antiochus Hierax (ca. 260–226 BCE)
Anti-Semitism
Aoun, Michel (1935–)
Aqaba, Capture of (July 6, 1917)
Aqaba, Gulf of
Arab Economic Boycott of Israel
Arabi, Ahmed (1841–1911)
Arabia, Roman
Arab-Jewish Communal War (November 30, 1947–May 14, 1948)
Arab League
Arab Legion
Arab Liberation Army
Arab Nationalism
Arab Oil Embargo (October 17, 1973–March 18, 1974)
Arab Revolt in Palestine (1936–1939)
Arab Revolt of World War I (June 5, 1916–October 31, 1918)
Arab Riots, Jerusalem (April 4–8, 1920)
Arab Spring (December 17, 2010–Mid-2012)
Arafat, Yasser (1929–2004)
Ardashir I (180–240)
Arif, Abd al-Salam (1921–1966)
Armenians and the Armenian Genocide
Army of Islam
ARROWHEAD RIPPER, Operation (June 19–August 19, 2007)
Arsuf, Battle of (September 7, 1191)
Artah, Battle of (August 11, 1164)
Artaxerxes I (?–424 BCE)
Artaxerxes II (435 or 445–358)
Artaxerxes III (359–338 BCE)
Artemisia I (5th Century BCE)
Artuqid Dynasty (1101–1408)
Asabiyya
Ascalon, Battle of (August 12, 1099)
Ashkenazic Judaism
Ashurbanipal (ca. 693–627 BCE)
Assad, Bashar al- (1965–)

List of Entries

Assad, Hafez al- (1930–2000)
Assassins
Assyrian Empire
Ataturk, Mustafa Kemal (1881–1938)
Auchinleck, Sir Claude John Eyre (1884–1981)
Aurelian, Emperor (214–275)
Auspicious Incident (June 15, 1826)
AUTUMN CLOUDS, Operation (November 1–8, 2006)
Ayn Jalut, Battle of (September 3, 1260)
Ayyubid Dynasty

Baath Party
Babylon, Siege of (539–538 BCE)
Babylonian Empire, Neo- (626–539 BCE)
Babylonian Empire, Old (ca. 1894–911 BCE)
Badr, Battle of (March 15, 624)
Badr al-Jamali (1015–1094)
Baghavard, First Battle of (June 14, 1735)
Baghavard, Second Battle of (August 9, 1745)
Baghdad, Capture of (March 11, 1917)
Baghdad, 812–813 Siege of (August 812–September 813)
Baghdad, 1258 Siege of
Baghdad, 1401 Siege of
Baghdad, 1638 Siege of
Baghdad, 1733 Battle of (July 19, 1733)
Baghdad, 2003 Battle of (April 5–10, 2003)
Baghdadi, Abu Bakr al- (1971–)
Baghdad Pact (February 4, 1955)
Bahrain
Bakhchisarai, Treaty of (January 3, 1681)
Bakr, Ahmad Hassan al- (1914–1982)
Balak ibn Bahram ibn Ortok (?–1124)
Baldat al-Shaykh Massacre (January 31, 1947)
Baldwin I of Constantinople (1171–1206)
Baldwin I of Jerusalem (ca. 1061–1118)
Baldwin II of Constantinople (1217–1273)
Baldwin II of Jerusalem (1060–1131)
Baldwin III of Jerusalem (1130–1163)
Baldwin IV of Jerusalem (1161–1185)
Balfour Declaration (November 2, 1917)
Balkans, Ottoman Conquest of the (1350s–1593)
Balkan Wars (1912–1913)
Balta Liman, Convention of (May 1, 1849)
Baltim, Battle of (October 12–13, 1973)
Bapheus, Battle of (July 27, 1301)
Barak, Ehud (1942–)
Barkiyaruq (1079/1080–1105)
Bar Kochba Revolt (132–135)

Bar-Lev Line
Basian, Battle of (1203)
Basil II Bulgaroctonos (958–1025)
Basra, Battle for (March 23–April 7, 2003)
Bassorah, Battle of (November 7, 656)
Baybars I (1223–1277)
Bayezid I (1360–1403)
Bayezid II (1447–1512)
Bedouins
Beersheba, Battle of (October 31, 1917)
Begin, Menachem (1913–1992)
Belisarius (ca. 505–565)
Ben-Gurion, David (1886–1973)
Bernadotte, Folke (1895–1948)
Beth-Horon, Battle of (October 66 CE)
Bible
Bin Laden, Osama (1957–2011)
Bithynia
Black September (September 6, 1970–July 1971)
Black September Organization
Bohemund I of Antioch (ca. 1054–1111)
Bohemund VI of Antioch-Tripoli (ca. 1237–1275)
Bohemund VII of Antioch-Tripoli (1261–1287)
Bonaparte, Napoleon (1769–1821)
Boniface I of Montferrat (ca. 1150–1207)
Border War (1949–1956)
Bremer, Lewis Paul, III (1941–)
Bubiyan Island, Battle of (January 29–30, 1991)
Burqan, Battle of (February 25, 1991)
Bush Doctrine
Byzantine Empire (330–1453)
Byzantine Empire Civil War (1341–1347)
Byzantine-Muslim Wars (629–1035)
Byzantine-Ottoman Wars (1280–1479)
Byzantine-Sassanid War (602–628)
Byzantine-Seljuk Wars (1048–1308)

Caesar, Gaius Julius (100–44 BCE)
Caesar's Campaign in Egypt (48–47 BCE)
Cairo Accord (May 4, 1994)
Cairo Agreement (November 3, 1969)
Cairo Declaration, Palestine Liberation Organization (November 7, 1985)
Cambyses II (?–522 BCE)
Camp David Accords (September 17, 1978)
Camp Speicher Massacre (June 12, 2014)
Carrhae, Battle of (June 9, 53 BCE)
Carter Doctrine (January 23, 1980)

Caucasus Front, World War I
Cezayirli Gazi Hasan Pasha (1713–1790)
Chaldiran, Battle of (August 23, 1514)
Chamoun, Camille (1900–1987)
Chancellor, Sir John Robert (1870–1952)
Chemical Weapons and Warfare
Chesma, Battle of (July 5–7, 1770)
Chinese Farm, Battle of the (October 14–18, 1973)
Cleopatra VII (69–30 BCE)
Clermont, Council of (1095)
Climate of the Middle East
Cold War in the Middle East
Cole, USS, Attack on (October 12, 2000)
Conrad III, King of Germany (1093–1152)
Constantine I (ca. 277–286–337)
Constantine XI Palaiologos (1405–1453)
Constantinople, Crusader Siege and Capture of (April 8–13, 1204)
Constantinople, Latin Empire of (1204–1261)
Constantinople, Muslim Siege of (August 15, 717–August 15, 718)
Constantinople, 1590 Treaty of (May 21, 1590)
Constantinople, 1700 Treaty of (July 3, 1700)
Constantinople, 1720 Treaty of (November 16, 1720)
Constantinople, 1832 Treaty of (July 21, 1832)
Constantinople, 1913 Treaty of (September 29, 1913)
Constantinople, Ottoman Siege of (April 6–May 29, 1453)
Constantius II, Emperor (317–361)
Copts
Corupedium, Battle of (281 BCE)
Crassus, Marcus Licinius (ca. 115–53 BCE)
Cresson, Battle of (May 1, 1187)
Croesus of Lydia (ca. 595–547 BCE)
Crusades in the Holy Land, Christian (1096–1291)
Ctesiphon, 363 Battle of (May 29, 363)
Ctesiphon, 1915 Battle of (November 22–25, 1915)
Cunaxa, Battle of (401 BCE)
Cunningham, Sir Alan Gordon (1887–1983)
Cyprus
Cyprus, Athenian Expedition to (450–449 BCE)
Cyprus, Ottoman Conquest of (1570–1571)
Cyrus II the Great (ca. 601/590–530 BCE)
Cyrus the Younger (ca. 423–401 BCE)

Damascus, Allied Capture of (October 1, 1918)
Damascus, Siege of (634–635)
Damascus Agreement (December 28, 1985)

Damietta
Danishmendid Dynasty (1071–1178)
Daoud, Abu (1937–2010)
Dar al-Islam and Dar al-Harb
Dardanelles Campaign (February–March 1915)
Darius I (ca. 549–486 BCE)
Darius II (?–404 BCE)
Darius III (ca. 380–330 BCE)
Dawud Pasha (1767–1851)
Dayan, Moshe (1915–1981)
Debecka Pass, Battle of (April 6, 2003)
DEFENSIVE SHIELD, Operation (April 3–May 10, 2002)
Definitive Treaty (March 14, 1812)
Degania, Battle of (May 20, 1948)
Deir Yassin Massacre (April 9–11, 1948)
Demetrius I Poliorcetes (336–282 BCE)
Demetrius II Nicator (ca. 160–125 BCE)
DESERT FOX, Operation (December 16–19, 1998)
DESERT THUNDER I, Operation (1998)
DESERT THUNDER II, Operation (1998)
Devshirme System
Dhahran, Scud Missile Attack on (February 25, 1991)
Dhofar Rebellion (1962–1976)
Diadochi, Wars of the (323–275 BCE)
Diaspora
Djemal Pasha, Ahmed (1872–1922)
Doha Agreement (May 21, 2008)
Donkey Island, Battle of (June 30–July 1, 2007)
Dorylaion, Battle of (July 1, 1097)
Druze-Ottoman Wars
Druzes

EARNEST WILL, Operation (1987–1989)
Edessa, County of
Edward I, King of England (1239–1307)
Egypt
Egypt, Ancient
Egypt, Arab Conquest of (640–642)
Egypt, Athenian Intervention in (460–454 BCE)
Egypt, British Invasion of (1807)
Egypt, French Invasion and Occupation of (1798–1801)
Egypt, Ptolemaic and Roman Periods
Egyptian-Arab Wars (1811–1840)
Egyptian-Ottoman Wars (1831–1833 and 1838–1841)
Egyptian Revolution of 2011
Egyptian-Soviet Arms Deal (Summer 1955)
Egypt under British Rule (1882–1936)
Eilat, Israel

Eilat, Sinking of (October 21, 1967)
Eisenhower Doctrine (1957)
Eitan, Rafael (1929–2004)
El Alamein, First Battle of (July 1–27, 1942)
El Alamein, Second Battle of (October 23–November 11, 1942)
Elazar, David (1925–1976)
Entebbe Hostage Rescue (July 3–4, 1976)
Enver Pasha (1881–1922)
Erdoğan, Recep Tayyip (1954–)
Erzincan, 1230 Battle of (August 10–12, 1230)
Erzincan, 1916 Battle of (July 25–26, 1916)
Erzurum, First Treaty of (July 28, 1823)
Erzurum, Second Treaty of (May 31, 1847)
Erzurum Offensive (January 10–March 25, 1916)
Eshkol, Levi (1895–1969)
Eumenes of Cardia (ca. 361–316 BCE)
Eumenes I of Pergamum (r. 263–241 BCE)
Eumenes II of Pergamum (r. 197–159 BCE)
Euphrates River
Eurymedon, Battle of (ca. 468–466 BCE)
Eustace III of Boulogne (ca. 1058–1125)
Evagoras I (ca. 435–374 BCE)
Exodus Incident (July 11–August 22, 1947)
Expellees and Refugees, Palestinian

Fahd, ibn Abd al-Aziz al-Saud (1922–2005)
Faisal I, King of Iraq (1885–1933)
Faisal II, King of Iraq (1935–1958)
Fallujah, First Battle of (April 4–May 1, 2004)
Fallujah, Second Battle of (November 7–December 23, 2004)
Fallujah, Third Battle of (May 23–June 28, 2016)
Fao Peninsula
Farouk I, King of Egypt (1920–1965)
Fatah, al-
Fatimid Dynasty (909–1171)
Fatwa
Fedayeen
Finckenstein, Treaty of (May 4, 1807)
Forbie, Battle of (October 17, 1244)
Franco-Lebanese Treaty (November 13, 1936)
Franco-Syrian Treaty (September 9, 1936)
Franco-Turkish War (1920)
Franks, Tommy (1945–)
Frederick I or Frederick Barbarossa (1122–1190)
Frederick II, Holy Roman Emperor (1194–1250)
Frederick V, Duke of Swabia (1167–1191)

Gabiene, Battle of (316 BCE)
Galerius, Roman Emperor (ca. 250s–311)
Galilee
Gallipoli Campaign (April 25, 1915–January 9, 1916)
Gamaat Islamiya
Ganja, Treaty of (March 10, 1735)
Gaugamela, Battle of (October 1, 331 BCE)
Gaza, Battle of (November 13, 1239)
Gaza, First Battle of (March 26–27, 1917)
Gaza, Second Battle of (April 17–19, 1917)
Gaza, Third Battle of (October 31–November 7, 1917)
Gaza Raid (February 28, 1955)
Gaza Strip
Gaza Strip Disengagement (August 15–September 12, 2005)
Gaza War of 2006 (June 27–November 26, 2006)
Gaza War of 2008–2009 (December 27, 2008–January 18, 2009)
Gaza War of 2012 (November 14–22, 2012)
Gaza War of 2014 (July 8–August 26, 2014)
General Treaty of Peace (1820)
Geneva Accord (December 1, 2003)
Geneva Peace Conference (December 21, 1973–January 9, 1974)
Geography of the Middle East
Georgian-Seljuk Wars (11th–13th centuries)
Ghazi
Ghulams
Giddi Pass
Glubb, Sir John Bagot (1897–1986)
Godfrey of Bouillon (ca. 1060–1100)
Gog and Magog
Golan Heights
Golden Horde–Ilkhanid Wars (1261–1323)
Goltz, Wilhelm Leopold Colmar von der (1843–1916)
Gordian III, Emperor (225–244)
Gouraud, Henri Joseph Eugène (1867–1946)
Granicus, Battle of the (May 334 BCE)
Greco-Persian Wars (499–479 BCE)
Greco-Turkish War (1919–1922)
Green Line
Green Zone, Iraq
Grivas, Georgios (1898–1974)
Gulf Cooperation Council
Gulistan, Treaty of (October 24, 1813)
Gulnabad, Battle of (March 8, 1722)
Guy of Lusignan (ca. 1150–1194)

Haditha, Battle of (August 1–4, 2005)
Hadrian, Emperor (76–138)
Haganah
Haifa Street, Battle of (January 6–9, 2007)
Hama Massacre (February 3–28, 1982)
Hamas
Hammurabi (ca. 1810–1750 BCE)
Hanit, Attack on the (July 21, 2006)
HARD SURFACE, Operation (June 12, 1963–January 1964)
Haredim
Harim, Battle of (August 12, 1164)
Hariri, Rafik (1944–2005)
Harran, Battle of (May 7, 1104)
Harun al-Rashid (763–809)
Hashemites
Hashomer
Hasidic Judaism
Hasmonean Tunnel Incident (September 23–28, 1996)
Hattin, Battle of (July 3–4, 1187)
Havlaga
Hayreddin Barbarossa (ca. 1483–1546)
Hebron Massacre (August 23–24, 1929)
Hebron Mosque Massacre (February 25, 1994)
Hejaz Railroad, Attacks on (1916–1918)
Hellespont
Hellespont Campaign (411–410 BCE)
Henry of Constantinople (ca. 1178–1216)
Henry VI of Germany (1165–1197)
Heraclius (ca. 575–641)
Herzl, Theodor (1860–1904)
Hezbollah
Holocaust (1941–1945)
Homs, First Battle of (December 11, 1260)
Homs, Second Battle of (October 29, 1281)
Homs, Third Battle of (December 23, 1299)
Hormuz, Strait of
Houthi, Hussein Badr al-Din al- (?–2004)
Houthis
Hrawi, Elias (1925–2006)
Hulegu (1218–1265)
Hunkar Iskelesi, Treaty of (July 8, 1833)
Husaybah, Battle of (April 17, 2004)
Hussein, Saddam (1937–2006)
Husseini, Haj Amin al- (1895–1974)
Hussein ibn Ali ibn Mohammed (1856–1931)
Hussein ibn Talal, King of Jordan (1935–1999)
Hyksos

Ibelin, Battle of (May 29, 1123)
Ibn Saud, King (1875–1953)
Ibrahim Pasha (1789–1848)
Ikhwan
Ilghazi ibn Artuq, Najm al-Din (ca. 1062–1122)
Ilkhan Dynasty (ca. 1261–1353)
IMMINENT THUNDER, Operation (November 15–21, 1990)
Improvised Explosive Devices
Inab, Battle of (June 29, 1149)
INHERENT RESOLVE, Operation (August 8, 2014–)
İnönü, İsmet (1884–1973)
Intifada, First (1987–1993)
Intifada, Second (2000–2004)
Ionian Revolt (499–493 BCE)
Ipsus, Battle of (Spring, 301 BCE)
Iran
Iran, Islamic Revolution in (1978–1979)
Iran Air Flight 655, Downing of (July 3, 1988)
Iran Hostage Crisis (November 4, 1979–January 20, 1981)
Iran Hostage Rescue Mission (Operation EAGLE CLAW, April 25, 1980)
Iran-Iraq War (1980–1988)
Iran Nuclear Deal (July 14, 2015)
Iraq
Iraq, Sanctions on
Iraq Insurgency (2003–)
Iraq No-Fly Zones
Iraq War (March 19, 2003–December 15, 2011)
Irgun Tsvai Leumi
Isfahan, Siege of (March–October 23, 1722)
Islamic Army of Aden
Islamic Civil War, First (656–661)
Islamic Civil War, Second (680–692)
Islamic Radicalism in the 20th and 21st Centuries
Islamic State of Iraq and Syria
Ismail, Khedive (1830–1895)
Ismail Ali, Ahmad (1917–1974)
Ismail I, Shah (1487–1524)
Ismailis
Israel
Israel-Egypt Peace Treaty (March 26, 1979)
Israeli Air Strikes Beginning the Six-Day War (June 5, 1967)
Israeli Air Strike on Presumed Syrian Nuclear Facility (September 6, 2007)
Israeli Security Fence
Israeli War of Independence (1948–1949)

Israeli War of Independence, Truce Agreements (February 24, 1949–July 20, 1949)
Israel-Jordan Peace Treaty (October 26, 1994)
Issus, Battle of (November 333 BCE)
Italo-Ottoman War (1911–1912)
IVORY JUSTICE, Operation (July 24–August 1990)
Izz ad-Din al-Qassam Brigades

Jabotinsky, Vladimir Yevgenyevich (1880–1940)
Jadid, Salah al- (1926–1993)
Jaffa, Battle of (August 5, 1192)
Jaffa, Treaty of (September 2, 1192)
Jam, Battle of (September 24, 1528)
Janissaries
Jarring Mission (December 9, 1967–October 1973)
Jassy, Treaty of (January 9, 1792)
Jawhar (?–992)
Jeddah, Siege of (February 10–December 17, 1925)
Jenin, Battle of (April 3–11, 2002)
Jericho Conference (December 1, 1948)
Jerusalem, Capture of (December 9, 1917)
Jerusalem, Crusader Siege of (June 7–July 15, 1099)
Jerusalem, Latin Kingdom of
Jerusalem, Roman Siege of (70 CE)
Jewish Brigade
Jewish Legion
Jewish-Roman War, First (66–73 CE)
Jihad
John of Brienne (ca. 1170–1237)
Jordan
Jordan River
Joscelin I of Edessa (?–1131)
Jovian (331–364)
Judaea
Judas Maccabeus (ca. 190–130 BCE)
Julian, Emperor (331–363)
Justinian I the Great, Emperor (483–565)

Kabakchi Incident (May 25, 1807)
Kadesh, Battle of (1274 BCE)
Kafr Qasim Massacre (October 29, 1956)
Kafur, Abu al-Misk (905–968)
Kapikulu Corps
Karameh, Battle of (March 21, 1968)
Karbala, Battle of (October 10, 680)
Karbala, First Battle of (March 31–April 6, 2003)
Karbala, Second Battle of (August 27–29, 2007)

Karbala Gap
Karbugha (d. 1102)
Karim Khan Zand, Muhammad (ca. 1705–1779)
Karlowitz, Treaty of (January 26, 1699)
Kars, Battle of (August 9–19, 1745)
Kars, Treaty of (October 13, 1921)
Kassites
Khadairi Bend, Battle of (December 13, 1916–January 29, 1917)
Khafji, Battle of (January 29–February 1, 1991)
Khalid bin Sultan, Prince (1949–)
Khalid ibn al-Walid (ca. 592–642)
Khanaqin, Battle of (June 3, 1916)
Khandaq, Battle of the (January–February 627)
Khan Yunis
Kharijites
Khartoum Resolution (September 1, 1967)
Khirokitia, Battle of (July 7, 1426)
Khobar Towers Bombing (June 25, 1996)
Khomeini, Ruhollah (1900–1989)
Khosrow I Anushiravan (496?–579)
Kirkuk
Kobanî, Siege of (September 27, 2014–January 26, 2015)
Kobanî Massacre (June 25–26, 2015)
Konya, Battle of (December 21, 1832)
Köprülü Abdullah Pasha (1694–1735)
Köprülü Fazil Ahmed Pasha (1635–1676)
Köprülü Mehmed Pasha (1583?–1661)
Köse Dağ, Battle of (June 26, 1243)
Kress von Kressenstein, Friedrich Sigismund Georg (1870–1948)
Kuchuk Kainardji, Treaty of (July 21, 1774)
Kurdan, Treaty of (September 4, 1746)
Kurds
Kurds, Massacres of
Kutahya Convention (May 4, 1833)
Kut al-Amara, Siege of (December 7, 1915–April 29, 1916)
Kuwait
Kuwait, Iraqi Invasion of (August 2, 1990)
Kuwait, Iraqi Occupation of (August 2, 1990–February 27, 1991)
Kuwait, Liberation of (February 27, 1991)

Lahoud, Émile Jamil (1936–)
Latakia, Battle of (October 6, 1973)
Latrun, Battles of (May 25–July 18, 1948)
Lausanne, First Treaty of (October 18, 1912)

Lausanne, Second Treaty of (July 24, 1923)
Lavon Affair (July–December 11, 1954)
Lawrence, Thomas Edward (1888–1935)
League of Nations Covenant Article 22
Lebanon
Lebanon, First U.S. Intervention in (July 15–October 25, 1958)
Lebanon, Israeli Operations against (July 13–August 14, 2006)
Lebanon, Israeli Security Zone in
Lebanon, Second U.S. Intervention in (August 24, 1982–February 26, 1984)
Lebanon Civil War (April 13, 1975–August 1990)
Lebanon-Israeli War (June 6–September 1982)
Leilan, Battle of (November 9, 1733)
Leo III the Isaurian (ca. 680–741)
Leopold V of Austria (1157–1194)
Lepanto, Battle of (October 7, 1571)
Liberty Incident (June 8, 1967)
Libyan-Egyptian War (July 21–24, 1977)
Liman von Sanders, Otto (1855–1929)
LITANI, Operation (March 14–21, 1978)
Lod Airport Massacre (May 30, 1972)
Lohamei Herut Israel
London, 1840 Treaty of (July 15, 1840)
London, 1913 Treaty of (May 30, 1913)
London Round Table Conference (February 7–March 17, 1939)
London Straits Convention (July 13, 1841)
Long Campaign in Hungary (1443–1444)
Long War in Hungary (1593–1606)
Louis VII, King of France (1120–1180)
Louis IX, King of France (1214–1270)
Lucius Verus (130–169)
Lydia
Lysimachus (ca. 355–281 BCE)

Ma'an, Siege of (April 17–September 28, 1918)
Maccabean Revolt (167–160 BCE)
MacMichael, Sir Harold (1882–1969)
Madrid Conference (October 30–November 1, 1991)
Magnesia, Battle of (December 190 BCE)
Mahmud, Muhammad Sidqi (1923–)
Mahmud II, Sultan (1785–1839)
Majid al-Tikriti, Ali Hassan al- (1941–2010)
Makarios III, Archbishop (1913–1977)
Maliki, Nuri Muhammed Kamil al- (1950–)
Malik Shah I (1055–1092)

Mamluk-Ilkhanid Wars (1260–1323)
Mamluk-Ottoman Wars (1485–1491 and 1516–1517)
Mamluk Sultanate (1250–1517)
Mandates, League of Nations
Mansurah, Battle of (February 8–11, 1250)
Manuel I Komnenos, Emperor (1118–1180)
Manuel II Palaiologos, Emperor (1350–1425)
Manzikert, Battle of (August 26, 1071)
Marcus, David (1901–1948)
Marcus Aurelius, Emperor (121–180)
Marj Dabiq, Battle of (August 24, 1516)
Maronites
Marsh Arabs
Martyrdom
Masada
Mashal, Khaled (1956–)
Massacre at the Citadel (March 1, 1811)
Maududi, Abul A'Ala (1903–1979)
Mawdud (?–1113)
Maysalun, Battle of (July 24, 1920)
McMahon-Hussein Correspondence
Medina, Siege of (1916–1919)
Medina Ridge, Battle of (February 27, 1991)
Megiddo, Ancient Battle of (1479 BCE)
Megiddo, Battle of (September 19–21, 1918)
Mehmed Ali (1769–1849)
Mehmed II, Sultan (1432–1481)
Meir, Golda Mabovitch (1898–1978)
Mersa Matruh, First Battle of (June 26, 1942)
Mersa Matruh, Second Battle of (November 7, 1942)
Mesopotamia
Mesopotamian Theater, World War I
Michael VIII Palaiologos (1223–1282)
Miletus, Battle of (411 BCE)
Mithridates VI Eupator Dionysius (ca. 134–63 BCE)
Mithridatic Wars (89–84, 83–81, and 73–63 BCE)
Mitla Pass
Mizrahi Judaism
Mongol Invasion of the Middle East (1256–1280)
Montenegrin-Ottoman Wars (1852–1913)
Mont Giscard, Battle of (November 25, 1177)
Montgomery, Bernard Law (1887–1976)
Morrison-Grady Plan (July 31, 1946)
Morsi, Mohamed (1951–2019)
Mosul, First Battle of (November 8–16, 2004)
Mosul, Second Battle of (October 17, 2016–July 9, 2017)
"Mother of All Battles"

Moudros, Armistice of (October 30, 1918)
Mount Lebanon Civil War (1860)
Muawiyah I (602–680)
Mubarak, Hosni (1928–)
Müezzinzade Ali Pasha (?–1571)
Mughal-Safavid Wars (1622–1623 and 1648–1653)
Muhammad, Campaigns of the Prophet (622–632)
Muhammad, Prophet of Islam (ca. 569–632)
Multinational Force and Observers in the Sinai
Multi-National Force–Iraq (2004–2009)
Murad II, Sultan (1404–1451)
Murray, Sir Archibald James (1860–1945)
Muslim Brotherhood
Muslim Wars of Expansion (623–732)
Mutla Ridge (February 25–27, 1991)
Mwawi, Ahmad Ali al- (1897–ca. 1979)
Mycale, Battle of (479)
Myriokephalon, Battle of (September 17, 1176)

NACHSHON, Operation (April 5–20, 1948)
Nadir Shah (1688–1747)
Naguib, Mohammad (1901–1984)
Nahr al-Bared Refugee Camp, Siege of (May 20–September 2, 2007)
Najaf, First Battle of (August 5–27, 2004)
Najaf, Second Battle of (January 28, 2007)
Nasar, Mustafa bin Abd al-Qadir Setmariam (1958–)
Nasiriyah, Battle of (March 23–29, 2003)
Nasser, Gamal Abdel (1918–1970)
Nasuh Pasha, Treaty of (1612)
Nebuchadnezzar II (ca. 634–562 BCE)
Nelson, Horatio (1758–1805)
NEMESIS, Operation (1920–1922)
Netanyahu, Benjamin (1949–)
Nicaea, Empire of (1204–1261)
Nika Uprising (January 13–18, 532)
Nikopolis, Crusade in (1396)
Nile River
NIMBLE ARCHER, Operation (October 19, 1987)
Nineveh, Battle of (December 12, 627)
Nisibis, Battle of (217)
Nissa, Treaty of (October 3, 1739)
Nixon, Sir John Eccles (1857–1921)
Nixon Doctrine (November 3, 1969)
Nizip, Battle of (June 24, 1839)
Norfolk, Battle of (February 26–27, 1991)
NORTHERN WATCH Operation (January 1, 1997–March 17, 2003)

Nur al-Din (1118–1174)
Nuri al-Said (1888–July 15, 1958)

O'Connor, Richard Nugent (1889–1981)
Odenathus (ca. 220–268)
Olmert, Ehud (1945–)
Oman
Organization of Petroleum Exporting Countries
Osiraq Raid (June 7, 1981)
Oslo Accords (September 13, 1993)
Osman I (ca. 1254–1324/1326)
Osman Nuri Pasha (1832–1900)
Otlukbeli, Battle of (August 11, 1473)
Ottoman Empire (1299–1922)
Ottoman Empire, Entry into World War I
Ottoman Empire, Post–World War I Revolution in
Ottoman-Habsburg Wars (1529–1791)
Ottoman-Hungarian Wars (1437–1526)
Ottoman-Persian Wars of the 18th and 19th Centuries
Ottoman-Polish Wars of the 17th Century
Ottoman-Safavid Wars (1526–1639)
Outremer

Palestine, British Mandate for (1922–1948)
Palestine, Partition of
Palestine, Pre-1918 History of
Palestine and Syria Campaign, World War I (1915–1918)
Palestine Liberation Army
Palestine Liberation Front
Palestine Liberation Organization
Palestinian Islamic Jihad
Palestinian National Authority
Palmach
Palmyra
Pan-Arab Congress (September 8, 1937)
Pan-Arabism and Pan-Arabist Thought
Paraetacene, Battle of (317 BCE)
Parthian Empire (247 BCE–224 CE)
Passarowitz, Treaty of (July 21, 1718)
Patria, Destruction of (November 25, 1940)
Patrona Halil Revolt (September 28, 1730)
Peel Commission (August 1936–July 7, 1937)
Pelagius of Albano (ca. 1165–1230)
Pelekanon, Battle of (June 10–11, 1329)
Pelusium, Battle of (525 BCE)
Perdiccas (365–321 BCE)
Pergamum
Persia, Arab Conquest of (642–671)

List of Entries

Persia, 18th-Century Wars of Succession
Persian Cossack Brigade
Persian Front, World War I
Persian Gulf
Persian Gulf War, Air Campaign (January 17–February 28, 1991)
Persian Gulf War, Cease-Fire Agreement (April 6, 1991)
Persian Gulf War, Ground Campaign (February 24–28, 1991)
Persian Gulf War, Naval Operations (January 17–February 28, 1991)
Persian Gulf War, Overview (January 17–February 28, 1991)
Peshmerga
Peter the Hermit (1050?–1115)
Petraeus, David Howell (1952–)
PHANTOM STRIKE, Operation (August 15, 2007–January 2008)
PHANTOM THUNDER, Operation (June 16–August 14, 2007)
Pharnabazus (?–ca. 370 BCE)
Phase Line Bullet, Battle of (February 26, 1991)
Philippe II, King (1165–1223)
Philomelion, Battle of (1116)
Phoenicia
Pompeius Magnus, Gnaeus (106–48 BCE)
Pontus (281 BCE–62 CE)
Popular Front for the Liberation of Palestine
Popular Front for the Liberation of Palestine–General Command
Popular Front for the Liberation of the Occupied Arabian Gulf
Portuguese Colonial Wars in Arabia (1507–1650)
PRAYING MANTIS, Operation (April 18, 1988)
PRIME CHANCE, Operation (1987–1989)
PROVIDE COMFORT, Operation (1991)
Pruth, Treaty of (July 23, 1711)
Ptolemaic Kingdom (305–30 BCE)
Ptolemy Ceraunus (ca. 320–279 BCE)
Ptolemy I Soter (367–282 BCE)
Ptolemy II Philadelphus (308–246 BCE)
Ptolemy III Euergetes (r. 246–221 BCE)
Ptolemy IV Philopator (ca. 244–205 BCE)
Ptolemy V Epiphanes (ca. 210–180)
Ptolemy VI Philometor (ca. 186–145 BCE)
Pyramids, Battle of the (July 21, 1798)

Qaboos bin Said al-Said (1940–)
Qadisiyya, Battle of (November 16–19, 636)
Qalawun (ca. 1222–1290)
Qarmatians
Qasim, Abdul Karim (1914–1963)
Qassam, Izz ad-Din al- (1882–1935)
Qatar
Qawuqji, Fawzi al- (1890–1976)
Qibya Massacre (October 14, 1953)
Qilij Arslan I of Rum (1079–1107)
Qilij Arslan II of Rum (ca. 1115–1192)
Quran
Qurna, Battle of (December 4–9, 1915)
Qutb, Sayyid Ibrahim Husayn Shadhili (1906–1966)
Quwatli, Shukri al- (1891–1967)

Rabat Summit (October 26–29, 1974)
Rabin, Yitzhak (1922–1995)
Rafah Tunnels
Ramadi, Fall of (November 21, 2014–May 17, 2015)
Ramadi, First Battle of (April 6–10, 2004)
Ramadi, Recapture of (November 25, 2015–February 9, 2016)
Ramadi, Second Battle of (June 17–November 15, 2006)
Ramesses II the Great (ca. 1303–1213 BCE)
Ramla, First Battle of (September 7, 1101)
Ramla, Second Battle of (May 17, 1102)
Ramla, Third Battle of (August 27, 1105)
Raphia, Battle of (June 22, 217 BCE)
Reagan Plan (September 1, 1982)
Red Sea
Reform Judaism and Zionism
Regime Change, Iraq War
Religious Sites in the Middle East, Christian
Religious Sites in the Middle East, Jewish
Religious Sites in the Middle East, Muslim
Republican Guard, Iraq
Resht, Treaty of (February 1, 1732)
Revisionist Zionism
Reza Shah Pahlavi (1878–1944)
Rhodes, Demetrius's Siege of (305–304 BCE)
Rhodes, Suleiman's Siege of (July 28–December 21, 1522)
Richard I, King (1157–1199)
Richard of Cornwall (1209–1272)
Ridda Wars (632–633)
Right of Return, Palestinian
Rogers Plan (December 9, 1969)
Rognvald Kali Kolsson (ca. 1099–1158)
Romani, Battle of (August 4–5, 1916)
Roman-Parthian Wars (53 BCE–215 CE)

List of Entries   xix

Roman-Sassanid Wars (232–440)
Rommel, Erwin Johannes Eugen (1891–1944)
Rum, Sultanate of (1080–1307)
Russo-Ottoman Wars (1676–1911)
Russo-Persian Wars (1722–1911)

Saadabad Pact (July 8, 1937)
Sabra and Shatila Massacre (September 16–18, 1982)
Sadat, Anwar (1918–1981)
Saddam Line, Persian Gulf War
Sadeh, Yitzhak (1890–1952)
Sadr, Muqtada al- (1973–)
Sadr City, Battle of (March 26–May 11, 2008)
Safavid Dynasty (1501–1722 and 1729–1736)
Saif al-Dawla (926–967)
Sakarya, Battle of the (August 23–September 13, 1921)
Saladin (1138–1193)
Salafism
Saleh, Ali Abdullah (1942–2017)
Samawah, Battle of (March 30–April 4, 2003)
Samita Incident (December 1972–April 1973)
Samu Raid, West Bank (November 13, 1966)
Sanchez, Ricardo S. (1951–)
San Remo Conference (April 19–26, 1920)
San Stefano, Treaty of (March 3, 1878)
Saracen
Sargon of Akkad (ca. 2350–2279 BCE)
Sarikamish, Battle of (December 22, 1914–January 17, 1915) in pages.
Sassanid Empire (224–651)
Saudi Arabia
Saudi-Hashemite War (1919–1925)
Saudi King as Custodian of the Two Holy Mosques
Saudi-Kuwaiti War (1921–1922)
Saudi-Ottoman War (1911–1913)
Saudi-Rashidi Wars (1887–1921)
Saudi-Yemeni War (1934)
SCATHE MEAN, Operation (January 17, 1991)
Schwarzkopf, H. Norman, Jr. (1934–2012)
SCORPION, Operation
Seleucid Empire (312–63 BCE)
Seleucus I Nicator (ca. 358–281 BCE)
Selim I, Sultan (1470–1520)
Selim III, Sultan (1761–1808)
Seljuk Dynasty (1016–1153)
Seljuk War of Succession (1092–1105)
Sennacherib (?–681 BCE)
Sephardic Judaism

September 11, 2001, Attacks on the United States
Septimius Severus, Emperor (ca. 145–211)
Serbian-Ottoman War (1876)
Settlements, Israeli
73 Easting, Battle of (February 26, 1991)
Sèvres, Treaty of (August 10, 1920)
Shakur, Yusuf bin Raghib (1928–)
Shallah, Ramadan Abdullah Mohammad (1958–)
Shamir, Yitzhak (1915–2012)
Shapur I the Great (ca. 215–270)
Shapur II the Great (309–379)
Sharia
Sharm El Sheikh
Sharon, Ariel (1928–2014)
Shatt al-Arab Waterway
Shaw Commission (August 1929–March 31, 1930)
Shazly, Saad el- (1922–2011)
Shia Islam
Shiqaqi, Fathi (1951–1995)
Shishakli, Adib al- (1909–1964)
Shomron, Dan (1937–2008)
Shultz Plan (March 4, 1988)
Siffin, Battle of (July 26–28, 657)
Sinai Campaign of 1916–1917 (March 1916–January 1917)
Sinai Campaign of 1956 (October 29–November 6, 1956)
Sinai I and Sinai II Agreements (January 19 and September 4, 1974)
Sinai Peninsula
Siniura, Fuad (1943–)
Sinope, Battle of (November 30, 1853)
Sisi, Abdel Fattah el- (1954–)
Sistani, Sayyid Ali Hisayn al- (1930–)
Six-Day War (June 5–10, 1967)
Smyrna Crusade (1344–1348)
SOUTHERN WATCH, Operation (1992–2003)
South Lebanon Army
South Yemen Civil War (January 13–24, 1986)
Special Night Squads
Special Republican Guards
Stark Incident (May 17, 1987)
STEEL CURTAIN, Operation (November 5–22, 2005)
Stern, Avraham (1907–1942)
St. Petersburg, Treaty of (September 12, 1723)
Strait of Tiran Crisis (1956–1967)
St. Sabas, War of (1256–1270)
Suez Canal

Suez Canal, World War I Ottoman Operations against
Suez Canal and Egypt, World War II Campaigns for Control of (1940–1942)
Suez Crisis (July 26, 1956–March 6, 1957)
Suicide Bombings
Suleiman I (1494–1566)
Sumer
Sunni Islam
Sunni Triangle
Sykes-Picot Agreement (May 16, 1916)
Syria
Syria and Lebanon Campaign (June 8–July 14, 1941)
Syrian Civil War (March 25, 2011–)
Syrian-Egyptian Wars (274–168 BCE)
Syrian-Roman War (192–188 BCE)

Taalat Pasha, Mehmed (1874–1921)
Tahmasp I, Shah (1514–1576)
Taif Accords (October 22, 1989)
Taji Bunkers, Attacks on (January 17–February 27, 1991)
Talmud
Tamerlane (1336–1405)
Tammuz I Reactor
Tancred (ca. 1076–1112)
Tanzimat
Task Force Normandy (January 17, 1991)
Tehran Treaty (November 25, 1814)
Tel el-Kebir, Battle of (September 13, 1882)
Ten Thousand, March of the (401–399 BCE)
Terrorism
Thani, Khalifa bin Hamad al- (1932–2016)
Theodore I Laskaris (ca. 1174–1221)
Thutmose III, Pharaoh (ca. 1504–1425 BCE)
Thymbra, Battle of (546 BCE)
Tiglath-Pileser I (?–1077 BCE)
Tiglath-Pileser III (?–727 BCE)
Tigris and Euphrates Valley
Tigris River
Titus, Emperor (39–81)
Townshend, Sir Charles Vere Ferrers (1861–1924)
Trajan (53–117)
Transjordan Campaign (1918)
Trebizond, Empire of (1204–1461)
Tripartite Declaration (May 25, 1950)
Tripoli, County of
Troop Surge, U.S., Iraq War

Troy, Siege of (1194–1184 BCE)
Turan Shah (?–1250)
Turcopoles
Turkey
Turki ibn Abdullah, Campaigns of (1823–1833)
Turkish-Armenian War (1920)
Tutush I (1066–1095)
Tuwaitha Nuclear Facility
Tyre and Gaza, Sieges of (332 BCE)

Umayyad Caliphate (661–750)
Umm Qasr, Battle of (March 21–23, 2003)
United Arab Emirates
United Arab Republic (1958–1961)
United Nations Palestine Partition Plan (November 29, 1947)
United Nations Special Commission on Palestine (May 13–August 31, 1947)
Uzun Hasan (1425–1478)

Valens, Emperor (ca. 328–378 CE)
Valerian, Emperor (ca. 193–260/264)
Valley of Tears, Battle of the (October 6–9, 1973)
Varna Crusade (1444)
Vasvár, Treaty of (August 10, 1664)
Venetian-Ottoman Wars (1416–1718)
Vespasian, Emperor (9–79)
VIGILANT WARRIOR, Operation (October 8, 1994–December 8, 1994)
VIKING HAMMER, Operation (March 28–30, 2003)

Wadi al-Batin, Battle of (February 26, 1991)
Wahhabism
War of Attrition (July 1969–August 1970)
Wauchope, Sir Arthur Grenfell (1874–1947)
West Bank
White Paper of 1922 (June 3, 1922)
White Paper of 1930 (October 31, 1930)
White Paper of 1939 (May 17, 1939)
Wingate, Orde Charles (1903–1944)
Woodhead Report (November 9, 1938)
World War I, Impact on the Middle East
World War II, Impact on the Middle East
Wye River Agreement (October 23, 1998)

Xenophon (ca. 431–ca. 354 BCE)
Xerxes I (519–465 BCE)

Yarmouk River, Battle of (August 15–20, 636)
Yazidis
Yemen
Yemen, Civil War in the North (1962–1970)
Yemen, Civil War in the South (May 4–July 7, 1994)
Yemen Civil War (2015–Present)
Yemen Hotel Bombings (December 29, 1992)
Yemenite War (February 24–March 19, 1979)
Yom Kippur War (October 6–25, 1973)
Young Turks
Yudenich, Nikolai Nikolaevich (1862–1933)

Zab, Battle of (February 26, 750)
Zangi, Imad ad-Din (1084/1085–1146)
Zanj Slave Revolts
Zarqawi, Abu Musab al- (1966–2006)
Zayed bin Sultan Al Nahyan (1918–2004)
Zenobia (240–274?)
Zionism
Zoroastrianism
Zsitvatorok, Peace of (November 11, 1606)
Zuhab, Treaty of (May 17, 1639)
Zuravno, Treaty of (October 16, 1676)

List of Maps

General Maps
Ancient Near East, ca. 1400 BCE
The East, ca. 600 BCE
Middle East, 1945–1990

Entry Maps
Battle of the Nile, August 1, 1798
Naval Battle of Actium, September 2, 31 BCE
The Empire of Alexander the Great
Drive on Baghdad, March 20–April 12, 2003
Bahrain
Byzantine Empire, 1355
Siege of Constantinople, April 6–May 29, 1453
The Crusades
Cyprus
Egypt
Ancient Egypt
Gallipoli Campaign, April 25, 1915–January 9, 1916
Persian Empire, ca. 500 BCE
Greece during the Persian Wars

Iran
Iraq
Israel
Israeli War of Independence, 1948–1949
Jordan
Kuwait
Lebanon
Expansion of Islam, 814
Oman
Expansion of the Ottoman Empire, 1361–1571
Asia Minor in 189 BCE
Israel and Phoenicia, 860 BCE
Qatar
Saudi Arabia
Balance of Forces, May 14–24, 1967
Syria
Battle of Tel el-Kebir, September 13, 1882
Turkey
United Arab Emirates
Yemen

General Maps

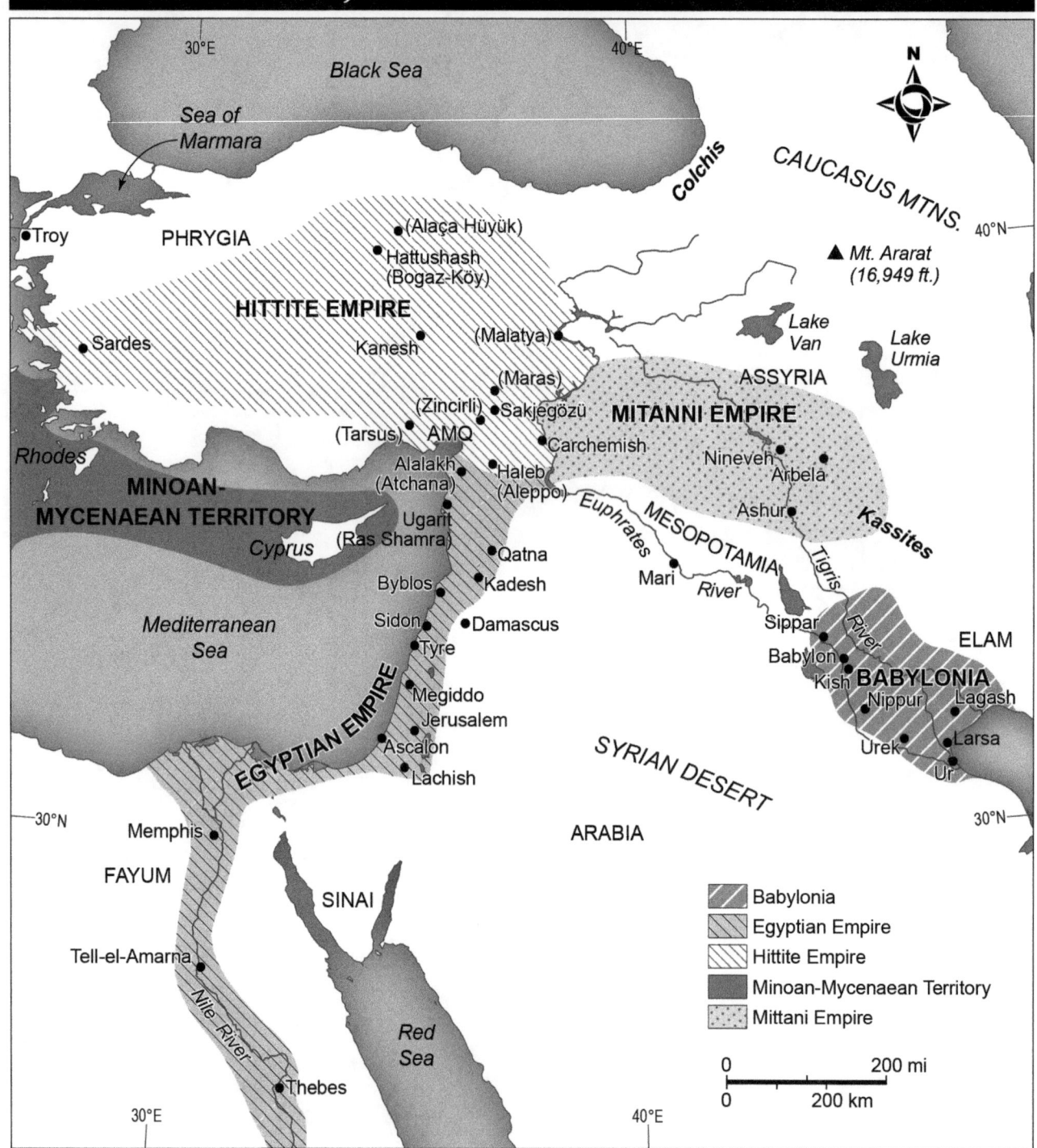

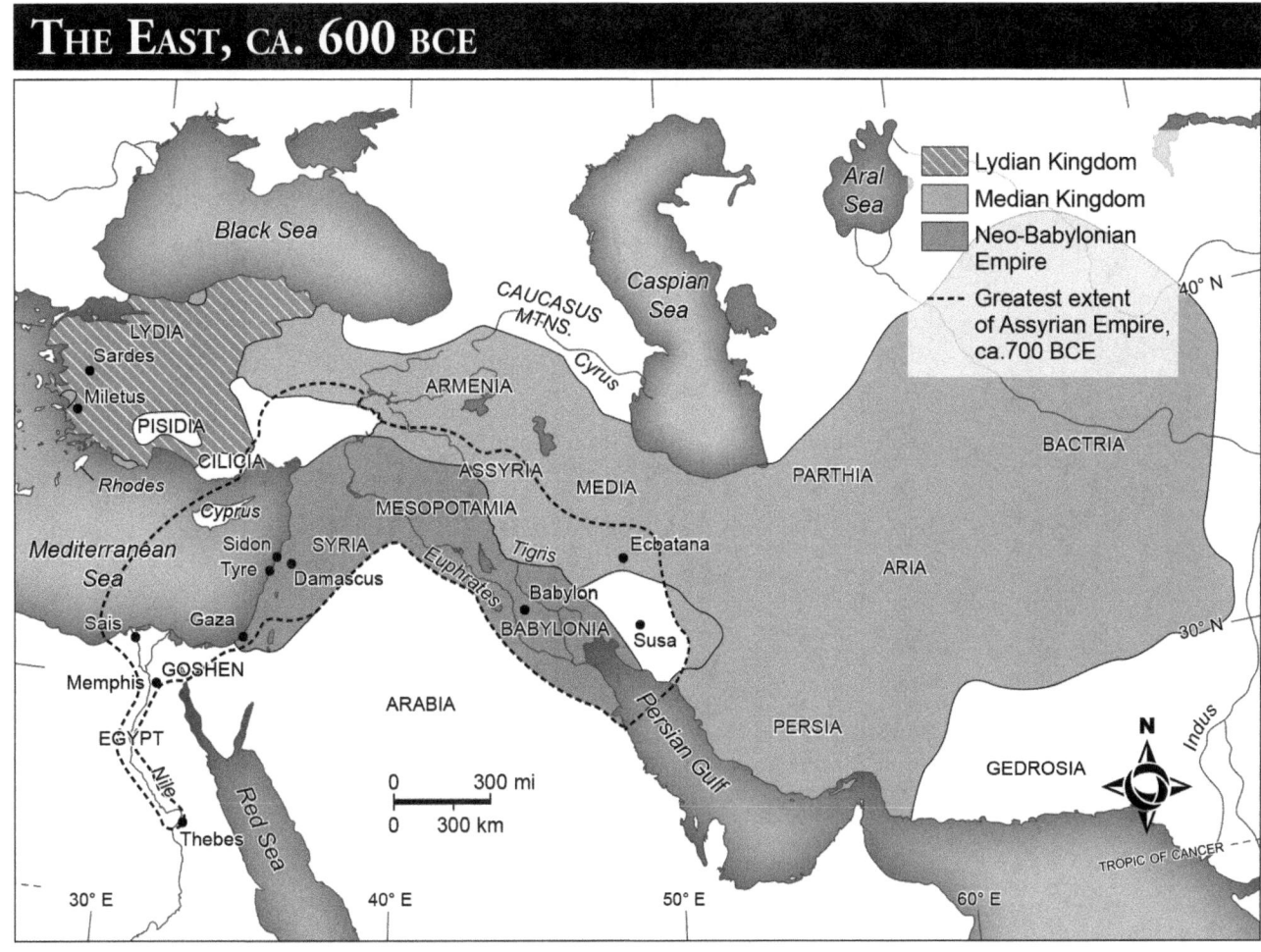

xxviii General Maps

Middle East, 1945–1990

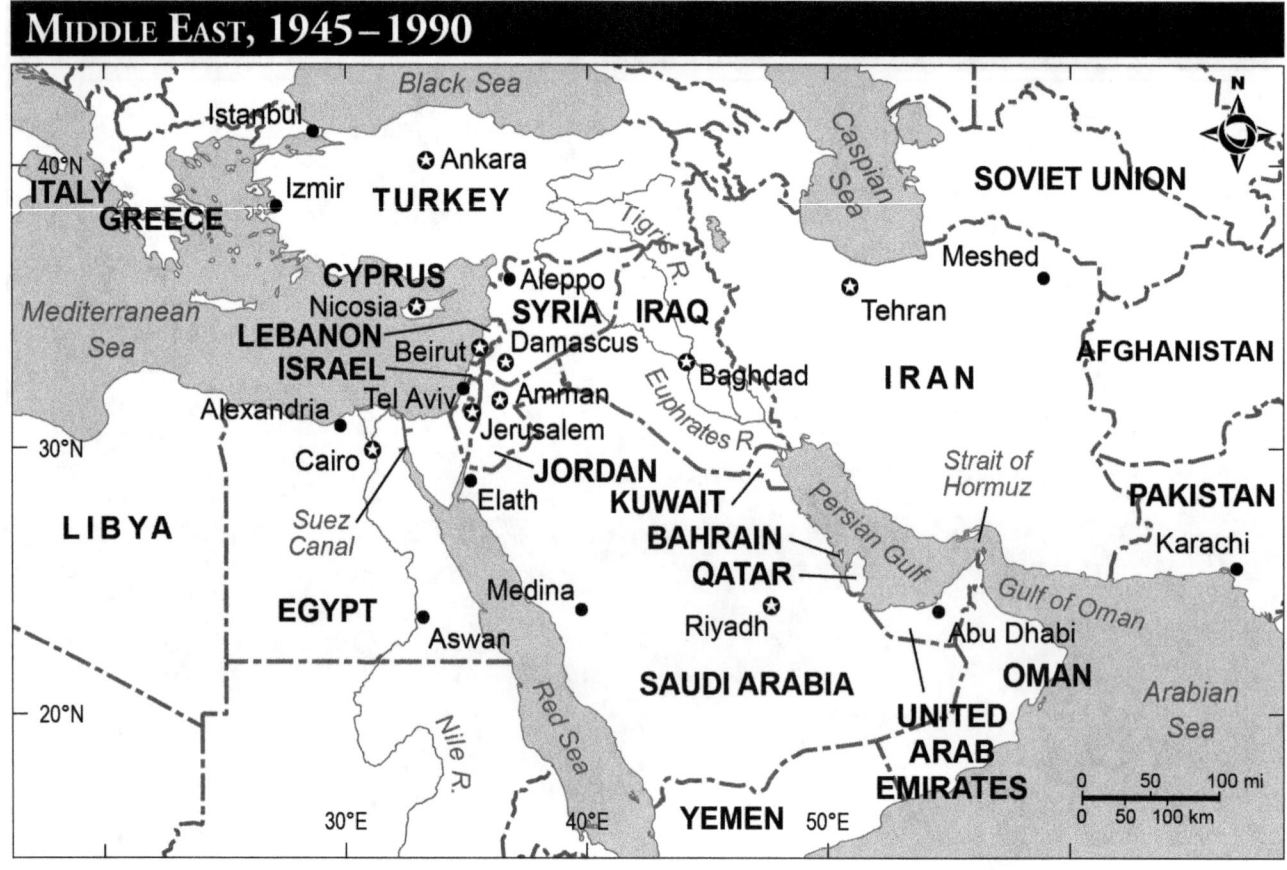

G

Gabiene, Battle of (316 BCE)

Decisive battle of the Second War of the Diadochi (319–315 BCE). Diadochi is Greek for "successors." The Diadochi Wars were fought following the death in 323 of Alexander III of Macedon (Alexander the Great) by his warring generals seeking to control the territory he had conquered. The battle occurred northwest of Persepolis in Asia Minor in the winter of 316 between the armies of Eumenes of Cardia and Antigonus I Monophthalmus ("The One-Eyed," so called because he had lost an eye in battle). The Battle of Gabiene followed the inconclusive Battle of Paraetacene of the year before.

Antigonus had some 41,000 men: 10,000 light infantry, 22,000 heavy infantry, and 9,000 cavalry. He placed his phalanx in the center, cavalry on the wings, and elephants and light infantry in front of the whole line. Eumenes had some 43,000 men: about 37,00 infantry and 6,000 cavalry. Seeing Antigonus's deployment, Eumenes stationed his best cavalry on his left flank opposite Antigonus's better cavalry, with his war elephants *en echelon* as a left-flank guard, hoping to repeat his success at Paraetacene. His phalanx was in the center, and his weaker cavalry and remaining elephants were on the right. Eumenes intended to hold back his weak right wing until the battle was decided elsewhere, while Antigonus intended to overwhelm Eumenes's elite left wing.

The battle opened with an advance by Eumenes. The elephants and light troops in front of both armies began a sharp combat, and the cavalry followed. Antigonus then personally led a second wave of cavalry into the melee. Eumenes's flank guard of elephants entered one at a time, however, neutralizing their numerical superiority. The battlefield was very dry, and the fighting soon raised great clouds of dust. Seeing this, Antigonus sent a detachment, hidden by the dust clouds, to capture Eumenes's camp. Meanwhile Peucestas, one of Eumenes's commanders, withdrew with about a third of Eumenes's cavalry. Eumenes moved his remaining cavalry to the other wing to join his reserve troops. In the center Eumenes's phalanx routed that of Antigonus. Eumenes tried to rally Peucestas's cavalry, but when they refused to rejoin the battle he withdrew from the field. As at Paraetacene, the battle had been inconclusive.

That evening Eumenes tired to convince his commanders to renew the fight the next day. Many of his commanders were anxious to return to their satrapies and were opposed, but some of the soldiers took decisive action. Learning that Antigonus had captured their camp, along with many of their wives and families as well as baggage, they secretly opened negotiations with Antigonus. In return for surrendering Eumenes, Antigonus promised to return their families and baggage to them. The men then handed over Eumenes and his senior officers to Antigonus.

Although reluctant to do so because he admired his generalship, in 315 Antigonus was persuaded to execute Eumenes. Several of Eumenes's senior commanders suffered the same fate.

Graham Wrightson and Spencer C. Tucker

See also

Antigonus I Monophthalmus; Diadochi, Wars of the; Eumenes of Cardia; Paraetacene, Battle of

References

Devine, Albert M. "Diodorus' Account of the Battle of Gabiene." *Ancient World* 12 (1985): 87–96.

Hackett, John. *Warfare in the Classical World.* London: Sidgwick & Jackson, 1989.

Pietrykowski, Joseph. *Great Battles of the Hellenistic World.* Barnsley, UK: Pen and Sword, 2009.

Galerius, Roman Emperor (ca. 250s–311)

Caesar during 293–305 and Augustus in 305–311, Gaius Galerius Valerius Maximianus won a notable victory over the Sassanid Persian Empire.

Probably born in the 250s in eastern Illyricum, Galerius may have been a Dacian. His mother may have been a priestess, influencing him to hate Christians. Galerius entered the army and advanced rapidly in the ranks. He was raised to caesar in 293.

As caesar, Galerius took command of the Roman war with Sassanid Persia, which had broken out afresh in 296 owing to the accession of a new ruler, Narses. Galerius lost his first encounter with the Persians, somewhere between Callinicum and Carrhae, angering Emperor Diocletian, who nonetheless let him try again. In 297 Galerius invaded through Armenia with great success. The next year he advanced down the Tigris and captured the Persian capital of Ctesiphon. He then returned up the Euphrates. In 299 the Romans negotiated peace with the Persians at Nisibis on very favorable terms to the Romans. Galerius had restored Roman control of the East up to the Tigris River and avenged the defeat and capture of Emperor Valerian in 260. When not fighting the Persians, Galerius assisted Diocletian in campaigning against Germanic peoples and Sarmatians on the Danube.

According to one account, Galerius may have influenced Diocletian to persecute the Christians, begun in 303 and lasting to 311, based on his personal hatred of Christians and Diocletian's fear of Galerius, who had become arrogant following his Persian victory.

On Diocletian's abdication in 305, Galerius was proclaimed Augustus, together with Constantius I. Apparently Galerius influenced Diocletian to name his own friend Severus and his nephew Maximinus Daia as caesars.

On the death of Constantius I in July 306, Galerius automatically became senior Augustus, and Constantine I revolted at York. The revolts of Maxentius and the ex-Augustus Maximian followed. For his part, Galerius attempted to hold the Second Tetrarchy together. Severus, now Augustus in the West, lost to Maxentius and was captured and executed. Galerius invaded Italy, but this did not save the situation. He called a conference of all the emperors (including Diocletian, in retirement at Spalato) at Carnuntum in November 308. Here Maximian was induced to retire, and Licinius (a friend of Galerius) was made Augustus; Constantine and Maximinus became caesars, and Maxentius did not get even that. Subsequently, Galerius recognized Constantine and Maxentius as having the status of Augustus. Galerius became ill and died in 311 following a painful illness. On his deathbed he rescinded the persecution of the Christians. His wife, Diocletian's daughter Valeria, attended by her mother Prisca, fled from Maximinus (whom the widowed Valeria refused to marry) and Licinius and were eventually caught and killed by Licinius's men.

Sara E. Phang

See also

Constantine I; Roman-Sassanid Wars; Valerian, Emperor

References

Leadbetter, W. L. *Galerius and the Will of Diocletian.* New York: Routledge, 2013.

Potter, David S. *The Roman Empire at Bay: AD 180–395.* New York: Routledge, 2004.

Rees, Roger. *Diocletian and the Tetrarchy.* Edinburgh, UK: Edinburgh University Press, 2004.

Williams, Stephen. *Diocletian and the Roman Recovery.* New York: Routledge, 1985.

Galilee

A region of northern Israel. Galilee has been traditionally subdivided into three geographic areas: Upper Galilee, Lower Galilee, and Western Galilee. Galilee encompasses more than one-third of present-day Israel's entire landmass. Upper Galilee runs from the Beit HaKerem Valley in the south to the Lebanese border in the north and borders the Sea of Galilee. Lower Galilee runs from Mount Carmel and the Gilboa Ridge in the south to the Beit HaKerem Valley in the north, and its eastern border is Jordan. Western Galilee covers the area from just north of Haifa to Rosh HaNikra. The region's principal towns include Nazareth, Tiberias, Akko, Nahariya, Karmel, and Safed. Although not technically part of Galilee, Haifa, on the Mediterranean coast, is the major commercial center for much of the region.

Galilee has a varied climate and an abundance of different geographical features, including mountain ranges, plains, and rivers. The area's largest industries are agriculture and tourism.

Galilee has been inhabited for several thousand years. It is mentioned repeatedly in the Old Testament, and Jews inhabited the land for many years prior to the diaspora. In the New Testament, Galilee takes center stage as the primary area of Jesus Christ's ministry. The area and places within it are frequently referenced in the New Testament. Nazareth and Capernaum—both in Galilee—are said to be areas in which Jesus spent much time. Among other miracles, Jesus is said to have healed a blind man in Galilee.

Following the diaspora, the region was ruled successively by larger states, some with few prior connections to the area. For almost 500 years, Galilee was controlled by the Ottoman Empire, with its capital at Constantinople (present-day Istanbul). As the Ottoman Empire slowly imploded in the early years of the 20th century, the population of Galilee was made up chiefly of Arabs and Druzes, with a small population of Jews. As Jewish immigration to the area accelerated, the Jewish population in Galilee swelled considerably. Israel took control of Galilee during the 1948–1949 Israeli War of Independence. Although many Palestinian Arabs fled, a relatively large number remained in Galilee.

Since 1948, Upper Galilee has been the scene of many military conflicts either with Syria, the Palestine Liberation Organization (PLO) operating from Lebanon, or Jordan. In the late 1990s the militant group Hezbollah, based in Lebanon, launched frequent Katyusha rockets into Israeli towns in Upper Galilee. Since then, the area has seen numerous military confrontations. During Israeli operations against Lebanon in the summer of 2006, Hezbollah guerrillas launched a flurry of longer-ranged Katyusha rockets that hit targets throughout Galilee.

Galilee is unlike other parts of Israel in that it has a large Arab population. And despite the best efforts of the Israeli government and the Jewish Agency before it, not many Jews have chosen to settle in Galilee. Roughly half of Galilee's population is Jewish, while the remainder includes Arabs, Christians, and Druzes.

PAUL G. PIERPAOLI JR.

See also
Druzes; Hezbollah; Israel; Lebanon; Lebanon, Israeli Operations against

References
Garfinkle, Adam A. *Politics and Society in Modern Israel.* Armonk, NY: M. E. Sharpe, 1997.
Horsley, Richard A. *Archaeology, History, and Society in Galilee.* New York: Continuum International Publishing Group, 1996.

Gallipoli Campaign (April 25, 1915– January 9, 1916)

The Gallipoli Campaign was the unsuccessful Allied ground effort during World War I to secure the Turkish Straits (Dardanelles) and drive the Ottoman Empire from the war. Although the naval effort to force the Dardanelles during February–March 1915 had failed, much had been invested, and political pressure to continue the campaign meant the belated injection of land troops.

London had actually taken the decision to send out land forces even before the naval bombardment of March 18, 1915. While First Lord of the Admiralty Winston Churchill exhorted naval commander Vice Admiral Sackville Carden to greater action, first sea lord Admiral John Fisher and secretary of state for war Field Marshal Horatio Kitchener came to the conclusion that troops would have to be landed on the Gallipoli Peninsula at the northern entrance to the Dardanelles. Rear Admiral John de Robeck, who replaced Carden as Allied commander on March 16, concluded, after meeting with ground force commander General Sir Ian Hamilton on March 22, that army support would be necessary before the naval assault could continue.

Kitchener arranged to send the untrained Australian and New Zealand Corps of two divisions, then in Egypt. He also decided to send the crack British 29th Division and the Royal Navy Divisions. The French also agreed to send a division. Kitchener appointed General Sir Ian Hamilton to command the force of 75,000 men. There was little preliminary planning for the troop landing on Gallipoli. Maps were few and inaccurate, and intelligence about Ottoman forces was virtually nonexistent. Hamilton also lost valuable time by deciding to concentrate his forces in Egypt.

Alerted by the naval bombardment, the Ottomans prepared for Allied landings. Inspector general of the Ottoman Army German general der kavallerie Otto Liman von Sanders took charge of the defenses, with the Ottoman Fifth Army of six widely dispersed divisions. The hilly and rocky Gallipoli Peninsula was ideal defensive terrain, and Liman organized strong positions in the hills immediately behind likely invasion beaches. He was ably assisted by Ottoman colonel Mustafa Kemal.

An armada of 200 Allied ships gathered for the landings, which were supported by 18 battleships, 12 cruisers, 29 destroyers, 8 submarines, and a host of small craft. On April 25, 1915, Allied troops went ashore at five beaches around Cape Helles (the extremity of the peninsula) and on the southwest side of the peninsula to the north near Gaba Tepe, at a beach still called Anzac. Ottoman opposition was

Gaba Tepe, also known as Anzac Cove, was the location of the amphibious landing of the Australian and New Zealand Army Corps (ANZAC) on April 25, 1915, during the Gallipoli Campaign. (Bettmann/Getty Images)

fierce and Allied casualties were heavy, but by nightfall the invaders were established ashore. French troops landed on the Asiatic side of the straits at Kum Kale, where they met a larger Ottoman force. With advance impossible, on April 27 the French were evacuated and transferred to Helles.

The Allied troops were in two lodgements about 15 miles apart, controlling only small pieces of territory. The fighting took the form of trench warfare, with opposing lines often only a few yards apart. The Ottomans could easily detect any Allied moves to drive them from their almost impregnable positions. Ottoman artillery was ideally situated to shell the beaches.

Early in May the Allies sent out two additional divisions and a brigade from India. Although some ground was gained, stalemate soon followed. The British then supplied five additional divisions, monitors for shore bombardment, more naval aircraft, and armored landing barges, but Ottoman strength increased apace, to 16 divisions.

A new naval attack was abandoned in mid-May after the Ottomans sank the British battleship *Goliath*. Only submarines could make the passage through the Narrows to interfere with Ottoman shipping, and 7 of 12 sent (9 British and 3 French) were lost. One, the *E-14*, did get into the Sea of Marmara and sank an Ottoman troopship with 6,000 men aboard, all of whom perished. The *E-11* also blew up an ammunition ship. German submarines were also active. The *U-21* torpedoed and sank the old British battleships *Triumph* and *Majestic*.

The Allies landed two of their new divisions at Suvla Bay, north of Anzac, on the night of August 6–7. Mustafa Kemal, now a corps commander, helped limit the landing to little more than a toehold. The Allied plan called for reinforced units to break out and seize the high ground to the east of Suvla that dominated the landing areas. Although Liman shifted resources north to meet the Suvla Bay threat, Allied commanders wasted this opportunity.

At the end of August the French offered to send a whole army, and the British found two additional divisions for yet another invasion, planned for November. This was postponed when Bulgaria entered the war on the side of the Central Powers. By the middle of September the French government concluded that there was no hope for the campaign. The British government persisted, unwilling to sacrifice a venture in which so much had been invested. Meanwhile, a storm of criticism appeared in the Australian and British press, based on reports by war correspondents about the incompetence of British land commanders.

Gallipoli Campaign 445

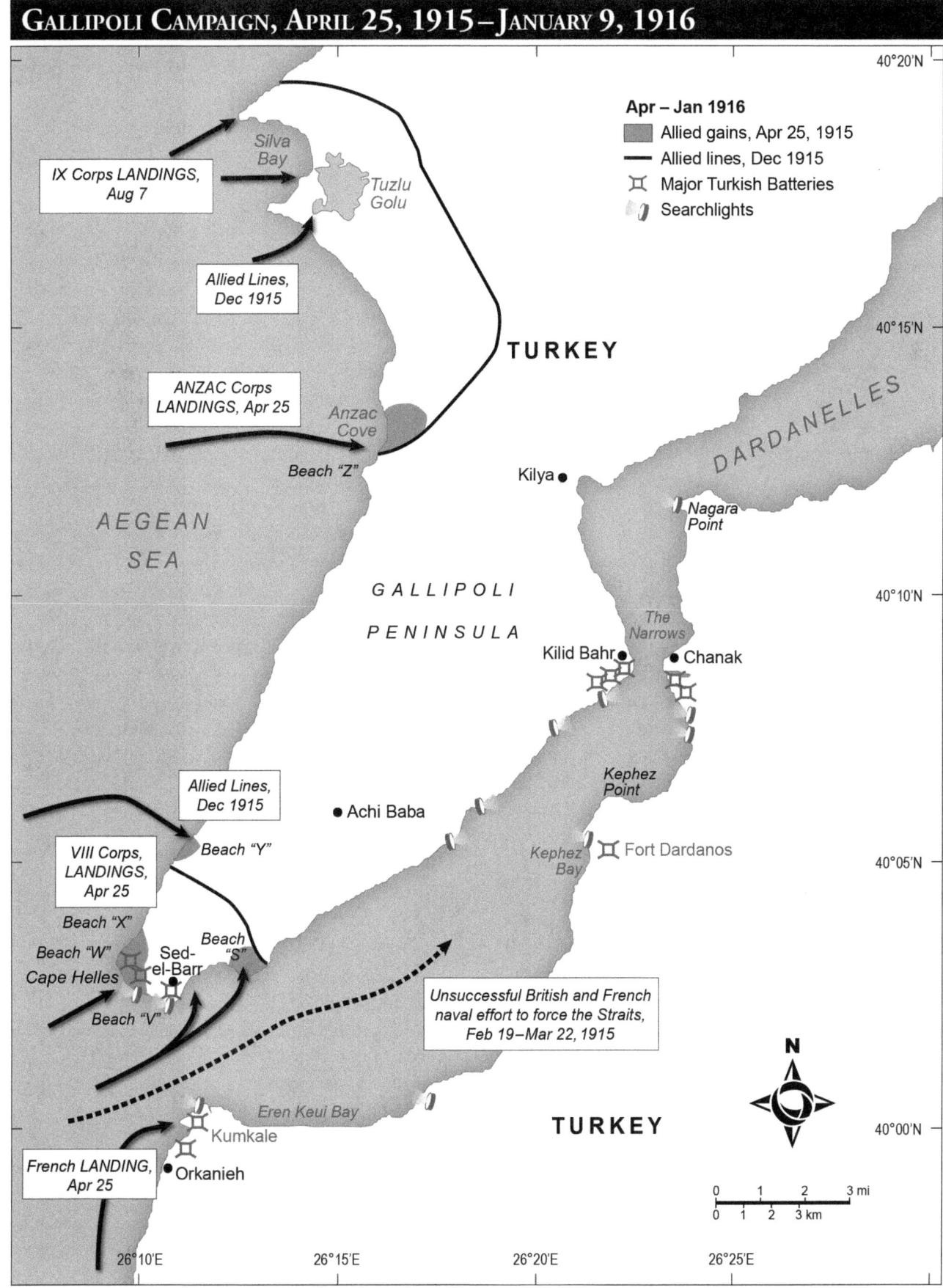

In October 1915 Lieutenant General Sir Charles Monro replaced Hamilton. Pointing out the unsatisfactory nature of the Allied positions ashore and the impending winter, Monro pressed for evacuation. A blizzard at the end of November, the worst in recent memory, resulted in Allied casualties of 10 percent at Gallipoli. Kitchener went out to inspect the situation in person and also argued for evacuation. On December 7 London agreed.

Despite Monro's fears of up to 40 percent losses, Kitchener predicted it would go smoothly. The Allies steadily withdrew supplies by night, and the evacuation was completed during the night of January 8–9, 1916. It was the largest operation of its kind prior to the extraction of the British Expeditionary Force from Dunkerque in 1940. Much to the astonishment of the Allied command, it was carried out with virtually no loss.

Accurate casualty totals for the entire 259-day campaign are not available. The official Ottoman figure of 86,692 killed and 164,617 wounded is undoubtedly too low. A reasonable figure might be 300,000 casualties. Total Allied casualties were about 265,000, of whom some 46,000 died.

The Allied failure meant that the straits remained closed, the Ottoman Empire continued in the war, and easy access to Russia was cut off. The effect of this in bringing about the military collapse of Russia and the Bolshevik Revolution can only be guessed. At the time and for years afterward, Churchill received most of the criticism for the failure. In August 1916 the British appointed a commission to investigate the campaign; at the end of 1917 it concluded that it had been a mistake. The Gallipoli Campaign failed owing to faulty planning with inadequate resources at the onset, poor leadership, and indecision.

Although it had failed, the Gallipoli landing was much studied in the years following the war. The operation utilized considerable experimentation in naval aviation and landing/resupply techniques, which proved influential in the development of U.S. Marine Corps amphibious doctrine in World War II.

Spencer C. Tucker

See also
Dardanelles Campaign

References
Churchill, Winston S. *The World Crisis,* Vol 2. New York: Scribner, 1923.
Great Britain, Dardanelles Commission. *The Final Report of the Dardanelles Commission.* London: HMSO, 1919.
Hamilton, General Sir Ian. *Gallipoli Diary.* New York: George H. Doran, 1920.

James, Robert Rhodes. *Gallipoli: The History of a Noble Blunder.* New York: Macmillan, 1965.
Moorehead, Alan. *Gallipoli.* New York: Harper and Row, 1956.

Gamaat Islamiya

Gamaat Islamiya (al-Gamaa al-Islamiyya) originated as a loosely knit organization of highly militant Sunni Muslim groups based in Egypt. The name was first used to describe a variety of student groups and other militant formations. The militant Gamaat should be distinguished from al-Jihad al-Islami (Egyptian Islamic Jihad), although the groups' ideologies are similar in that they oppose Israel's policies and support armed struggle for Palestine. Within an umbrella of organizations, the Gamaat Islamiya began to be described as a singular and cohesive group by outsiders. It was classified as a terrorist organization by the United State, the United Kingdom, and the European Union.

Formed in the late 1970s, from 1992 to 1998 Gamaat Islamiya, aided by the governments of Iran and Sudan as well as the Islamic terrorist organization Al Qaeda, engaged in an insurgency against the Egyptian government during which some 800 Egyptian policemen and soldiers, Gamaat Islamiya fighters, and civilians (including dozens of tourists) were killed. Gamaat Islamiya is most noted for its involvement in the November 1990 assassination in New York of militant Zionist leader Rabbi Meir Kahane and the February 1993 bombing of New York's World Trade Center. Members of one group within the organization also claimed responsibility for the 1997 massacre of 58 foreign tourists in the southern Egyptian town of Luxor. The group's several hundred followers both in Egypt and in the United States sought the overthrow of the moderate Egyptian government in favor of a purely Islamic regime.

The Gamaat Islamiya's adherents come from southern Egypt, Cairo, and the Nile Delta. Southern villages, including Assiut and Minya, became strongholds because of the vendetta system of family rivalries. The Gamaat Islamiya is believed to be responsible for three attempts on the life of President Hosni Mubarak, including one aborted assassination attempt during one of his visits to the United Nations (UN) in 1993 and a highly organized ambush in Ethiopia in June 1995.

The Egyptian government held the organization accountable for several fatal attacks on security forces, government officials, and tourists and executed several of its members after summary military trials. In February 1994, militants believed to belong to the Gamaat Islamiya issued a public statement warning the 35,000 Americans and Europeans living and working in Egypt to leave the country or face injury or death. In early April 1994, police killed the leader of the group's military wing, Talat Yasin Hammam, and six other militants in a raid on an apartment in an eastern Cairo suburb. Egypt's most wanted Islamic militant, Hammam had received a death sentence in absentia in 1992 on charges of belonging to an illegal organization and attempting to overthrow the government.

The Gamaat Islamiya's spiritual leader, Sheikh Omar Abdel-Rahman, fled Egypt in 1990 and legally entered the United States with a visa specifying him as a religious worker settling in New York. In late April 1994, a Cairo security court sentenced him in absentia to a seven-year prison term on charges of inciting riots and planning a failed assassination of two police officers in 1989. Abdel-Rahman's marriage to an American Muslim convert enabled him to avoid U.S. deportation despite Egypt's calls for his extradition and his status as a prominent figure on an official U.S. terrorist list. He was convicted in the United States in 1996 for his involvement in the 1993 World Trade Center bombing and sentenced to life in prison.

Egyptian security forces scored a number of notable successes in their fight against the Gamaat Islamiya in late 1994 and early 1995. In October 1994 security forces killed the group's regional commando leader, Atif abd al-Ghaffar Shahin, during a skirmish in the Nile River town of Mallawi. Shortly thereafter the overall leader of the organization, Hassan abd al-Jalil, was also hunted down and killed. In January 1995 police shot al-Jalil's successor, Mohammad Sayyid Salim, in the southern city of Sohag and arrested some 40 members of the Gamaat Islamiya, including a regional commander.

In November 1997 Gamaat Islamiya militants opened fire on tourists visiting the popular Temple of Hatshepsut in Luxor, killing more than 60 people, including 58 foreigners. Several days later, members of the Gamaat Islamiya faxed a statement to a foreign news agency claiming responsibility for the attack, saying that it was carried out in order to put pressure on the United States to release Abdel-Rahman. Subsequently, however, Gamaat Islamiya leaders as well as the main group of Jihad Islami announced a unilateral cease-fire and blamed the Luxor attack on an internal faction opposed to the renunciation of violence. The cease-fire went into effect in 1999, and some militants wrote of their misuse of violent tactics.

The Luxor massacre was the last large-scale terrorist attack aimed at Westerners in Egypt, although a violent attack in Kosheh in 2000 left 20 Copts (Christians) and 1 single Muslim dead, and in September 2003 Egyptian police arrested a group of 23 militants, including 19 Egyptians, who intended to join the resistance to the U.S. presence in Iraq. In 2004, bomb attacks on the Sinai Peninsula killed at least 33 people. The Gamaat Islamiya denounced the attacks, calling them "unlawful under Islam" because they resulted in the deaths of Muslims, including women and children. However, the Gamaat Islamiya remains divided, with one faction seeking to uphold the cease-fire and the other unofficial faction advocating a return to violent attacks. The latter is led by Rifa Taha Musa, a signer of Osama bin Laden's February 1998 fatwa (religious decree) ordering attacks against U.S. civilians and also the author of a book that justifies acts of terrorism that cause mass civilian casualties. Musa was imprisoned but released following the uprising that overthrew Egyptian president Hosni Mubarak. Musa eventually fled Egypt for Syria, where he was killed in April 2016 in a U.S. air strike against the Al Qaeda leadership there.

Gamaat Islamiya committed itself to peaceful means following the coup that toppled Mohamed Morsi. It then formed a political party, the Building and Development Party, that secured 13 seats in the 2011–2012 elections to the lower house of the Egyptian parliament.

SPENCER C. TUCKER

See also
Abdel-Rahman, Omar; Al Qaeda; Bin Laden, Osama; Egypt; Morsi, Mohamed; Mubarak, Hosni; Sadat, Anwar

References
Beattie, Kirk J. *Egypt during the Sadat Years.* New York: Palgrave, 2000.
Kepel, Giles. *Jihad: The Rise and Fall of Islamic Extremism.* London: Tauris, 2002.

Ganja, Treaty of (March 10, 1735)

Treaty between Persia and Russia signed on March 10, 1735, near Ganja in modern-day Azerbaijan. Under its terms the two powers allied against the Ottoman Empire and agreed not to enter into separate negotiations with the Porte. Russia pledged to return to Persia the captured territories of Derbent and Baku, while Persia granted Russia the right of free trade in its territory. The treaty also confirmed the provisions of the Treaty of Resht, which obliged Russia to return Gilan to Persia, while Persia agreed to recognize King Vakhtan VI on the throne of Kartli.

ALEXANDER MIKABERIDZE

See also

Nadir Shah; Resht, Treaty of

Reference

Holt, P. M. *The Central Islamic Lands from Pre-Islamic Times to the First World War.* Cambridge: Cambridge University Press, 1994.

Gaugamela, Battle of (October 1, 331 BCE)

Following his successful siege operations against Tyre and Gaza in 332 BCE, King Alexander III of Macedon (Alexander the Great) temporarily turned aside from further conquest to organize his new territories and to solidify his lines of communication. The conquered peoples of Babylon and other places welcomed him as a liberator because of his reputation for leniency to those who surrendered and because he restored the temples that the Persians had destroyed. During December 332 to March 331, Alexander absorbed Egypt and laid plans for its new city of Alexandria.

Alexander then marched back across the empire he had carved out of Asia Minor. This time, however, he moved directly against the distant cities of Persia, crossing the Euphrates on a bridge constructed by a detachment of his men under his general and lover, Hephaestion.

Persian king Darius III had not been idle. Since his defeat at the Battle of Issus in 333, he had assembled a new army. Alexander had a maximum of 47,000 men: 31,000 heavy infantry (Phalangists) and 9,000 light infantry (Peltists), along with 7,000 cavalry. Ancient sources credit Darius with a force of between 200,000 and 1 million men. This is almost certainly an exaggeration, for maintaining a force this large would have been almost impossible given the primitive logistics of the time. Modern estimates place the total size of his army at no more than 100,000 men, of whom up to 40,000 were cavalry. By whatever measurement, Alexander's army was greatly outnumbered.

To Alexander, however, numbers meant little. His force was well trained, well organized, and disciplined, while that of Darius was a polyglot force drawn chiefly from the eastern provinces that included Persians, Medes, Babylonians, Syrians, Armenians, and Hindus.

Darius III and his great host awaited Alexander on the plain at Gaugamela, some 60 miles from the city of Arbela (modern-day Erbil). The clash is sometimes erroneously known as the Battle of Arbela, since that was the nearest settlement. Most probably it took place east of the modern-day city of Mosul in northern Iraq.

Darius chose not to oppose Alexander's approach, trusting in superior numbers. Darius had selected the location so he could make effective use of his superior numbers and

Depiction of the Battle of Gaugamela (Arbela) in 331 BCE, in which forces under King Alexander III the Great of Macedon defeated those of King Darius of Persia. The painting is by Jacques Courtois (1621–1676). (Fine Art Images/Heritage Images/Getty Images)

employ his chariots, which had scythes mounted on their wheel hubs to cut down Alexander's forces. Some sources contend that Darius had the plain cleared of vegetation for ease of maneuver. He was confident that his preparations would bring him victory.

Alexander moved slowly to Gaugamela, hoping to wear down the defenders and exhaust their food stocks. When he finally arrived his chief of staff, Parmenion, urged a night attack in order to offset the numerical disadvantage, but Alexander refused. Apart from the difficulty of maintaining control at night, Alexander opposed any effort to "steal victory like a thief." He would, he said, "defeat his enemies openly and honestly." As it turned out, Darius had feared a night assault and kept his troops awake all night. The next morning the men were exhausted, while Alexander's men were well rested.

Battle was joined on October 1, 331. Alexander, who fought with his Companion cavalry, commanded the right flank of his army, while Parmenion had charge of the left. Macedonian and Greek cavalry protected the two flanks. Alexander arranged the army in oblique formation, refusing his left and moving the army laterally to the right across the Persian front. His plan was to draw the Persians to the flanks, opening a weak point in the center of the Persian line. Everything depended on his flanks holding until Alexander could detect this weakness and strike a decisive blow.

Darius positioned himself in the center of the Persian line with his best infantry. Bessus commanded the cavalry on the Persian left wing with chariots in front, while Mazaeus commanded the right flank of the other cavalry. With their vastly superior numbers of cavalry and much longer line, it appeared that the Persians must inevitably flank Alexander's army.

Darius ordered Bessus to release cavalry to ride around the Macedonian right wing and arrest Alexander's movement. Bessus committed some 11,000 cavalry to the effort, but they were halted by the numerically far inferior force of Macedonian cavalry and Greek mercenary infantry. Clearly Alexander's cavalry was far better disciplined and more closely knit than Persia's local detachments, which had never trained together.

Darius ordered the 100 chariots positioned in front of his left wing to attack Alexander's elite force of Companion cavalry on the Macedonian right. Alexander's infantry screen of javelin throwers, archers, and light infantrymen somewhat blunted the Persian chariot charge before it reached the Companions. The Companions then wheeled aside, allowing the remaining chariots to pass through unopposed and then came up against the lances of Alexander's infantry. The gap then closed, and the Persian charioteers were annihilated in the Macedonian rear.

Darius then ordered a general advance. Mazaeus, who commanded the Persian right wing, advanced against the Macedonian left led by Parmenion. Darius also sent cavalry in an attempt to get around the Macedonian line. At the same time, Bessus sought to push men around the Macedonian right wing to envelop it. These efforts by Bessus and Mazaeus elongated the Persian line as Alexander had hoped, weakening its center. Mazeus's job was especially difficult, as his men had to travel a greater distance to engage Alexander's refused left wing.

Alexander watched for weakness in the Persian line, bringing up his reserves. Once he detected it, he led his Companion cavalry and light infantry in a great wedge-shaped formation into the breach. Twice the Macedonians burst through gaps in the Persian line and drove close to where Darius's chariot stood. Both Persian flanks were now threatened by the great gap that the Macedonians had torn in the center of the line.

The possibility of encirclement led Bessus to retreat, his forces suffering heavy casualties at the hands of the pursuing Macedonians. Darius, now himself in danger of being cut off, panicked and fled. With the Persians in wild retreat, the Macedonians vigorously pressed their advance, scattering the vast Persian host.

Alexander's left wing, heavily engaged with Mazaeus's men, could not keep pace with the rest of the Macedonian advance. Alexander's attempt to encircle Mazaeus failed, however, because his own cavalry drove the Persians back too quickly. The victory was nonetheless sweeping. The Macedonians reported their casualties in the battle at some 500 killed and up to 3,000 wounded while setting Persian losses at close to 50,000.

Bessus and other Persian generals, disgusted with his conduct, murdered Darius. Alexander later caught such regicides as he could and executed them. He did not rest and after the battle advanced rapidly toward the Persian capital of Persepolis so as not to allow the Persian generals time to reorganize their forces.

SPENCER C. TUCKER

See also
Alexander III the Great; Alexander III's Invasion of the Persian Empire; Darius III; Issus, Battle of

References
Arrian [Lucius Flavius Arrianus]. *The Campaigns of Alexander.* Tr. Aubrey de Selincourt. East Rutherford, NJ: Penguin, 1976.

Creasy, Edward S. *Fifteen Decisive Battles of the World.* New York: Harper, 1851.
Fuller, J. F. C. *A Military History of the Western World*, Vol. 1. New York: Funk & Wagnalls, 1954.
Marsden, E. W. *The Campaign of Gaugamela.* Liverpool, UK: Liverpool University Press, 1964.
Tarn, W. W. *Alexander the Great.* Cambridge: Cambridge University Press, 1948.

Gaza, Battle of (November 13, 1239)

Battle fought on November 13, 1239, at Gaza between a contingent of crusaders and Franks of the Kingdom of Jerusalem and the Ayyubid forces of Egypt. The crusaders under Thibaud IV, count of Champagne (since 1234 also king of Navarre), had decided to fortify the city of Ascalon (modern-day Tel Ashqelon, Israel) in order to protect the southern border of the Kingdom of Jerusalem. While they were marching from Acre to Jaffa (November 2–12, 1239), Egyptian troops moved up to Gaza. Several prominent crusaders and local nobles, namely Henry of Bar, Amalric of Montfort, Hugh of Burgundy, Walter of Jaffa, Balian of Sidon, John of Arsuf, Odo of Montbéliard, and Richard of Beaumont, ignored the warnings of Thibaud, Peter of Dreux, and the masters of the Templars, Hospitallers, and Teutonic Knights and decided to lead some 400–600 knights against the enemy. Meanwhile, the main army would continue on to Ascalon.

On November 13 the detached force stopped to rest in a valley surrounded by sand dunes, which its leaders had failed to secure properly and were there surprised by the Muslims. While Hugh of Burgundy and Walter of Jaffa argued in favor of a hasty retreat to Ascalon, Henry of Bar and Amalric of Montfort decided to stay with the infantry and fight. After an initial success of Amalric's crossbowmen, the Christians were lured into pursuing the Muslims, who feigned retreat. The Muslims subsequently managed to surround the Christians. In the ensuing close combat Henry was killed, while Amalric and many others were taken prisoner.

Meanwhile, Hugh and Walter had reached Ascalon, where they convinced the main army to move to the rescue of the Christians trapped at Gaza. This assistance came too late, however. At the sight of the crusading army, the Muslims merely abandoned their pursuit of the remaining Christian knights fleeing the battlefield.

Following the defeat, the Templars and Hospitallers convinced Thibaud of Champagne to retreat to Acre rather than pursue the Egyptians and their prisoners. It fell to Richard of Cornwall, in 1241, to oversee the burial of the casualties from the battle at Ascalon and to negotiate the release of the prisoners taken by the Muslims.

JOCHEN BURGTORF

See also
Crusades in the Holy Land, Christian

References
Jackson, Peter. "The Crusades of 1239–41 and Their Aftermath." *Bulletin of the School of Oriental and African Studies* 50 (1987): 32–60.
Lower, Michael. *The Barons' Crusade: A Call to Arms and Its Consequences.* Philadelphia: University of Pennsylvania Press, 2005.
Painter, Sidney. "The Crusade of Theobald of Champagne and Richard of Cornwall, 1239–1241." In *A History of the Crusades,* Vol. 2, 2nd ed., ed. Kenneth M. Setton et al., 463–485. Philadelphia: University of Pennsylvania Press, 1969.

Gaza, First Battle of (March 26–27, 1917)

World War I Palestine campaign battle. Located along the coastal route from Sinai into southern Palestine, the ancient city of Gaza became a key position for both sides in 1917.

The first British attempt to take the city saw Eastern Force commander Lieutenant General Sir Charles Dobell order Lieutenant General Sir Philip Chetwode's Desert Column to carry out a coup de main. Inaccurate British intelligence suggested that Gaza's garrison consisted of no more than 2,000 men, when in fact it was 4,000.

The battle began in the early hours of March 26, 1917, when Chetwode's two mounted divisions succeeded in establishing a cordon to the north and east of the city, thus preventing the garrison from escaping as well as guarding against any Ottoman relief efforts. Unfortunately for the British, the attack from the south by the infantry of the 53rd (Welsh) Division on Gaza itself was poorly executed. Because of confusion among the division's senior commanders, the attack, originally intended to begin at 8:00 a.m., did not get under way until midday. Unexpectedly vigorous Ottoman resistance coupled with inadequate artillery support hampered progress. Nonetheless, by sunset the 53rd Division had captured all of the high ground in front of Gaza.

Meanwhile Chetwode, increasingly anxious at the lack of progress by the infantry, sent the Australian and New Zealand Mounted Division under Major General Henry Chauvel to attack Gaza from behind. Chauvel's assault began at 4:00

p.m., and by nightfall his horsemen had fought their way into the outlying streets. To the British and Dominion soldiers on the ground, it seemed as if they were on the verge of victory.

Unaware of the true extent of these tactical successes, however, Chetwode and Dobell believed that the overall situation was fraught with danger. Both men agreed that without possession of the wells in Gaza, they could not risk leaving the mounted divisions, whose horses would be facing a second day without water, in position between the undefeated garrison and advancing Ottoman relief forces.

In fact, water had been found for at least some of the British horses, and in any event the Ottoman garrison was near the brink of collapse. A furious Chauvel reluctantly obeyed the order to withdraw that evening after his protests apparently failed to reach either of his senior commanders. A similar breakdown in communications saw the 53rd Division abandon its hard-won gains in the mistaken belief that it had been ordered to fall back to the original positions of the British reserve, the 54th (East Anglia) Division, when the latter unit had actually been ordered forward to link up with the 53rd Division.

Dobell, finally grasping the reality of the situation, tried to recover the lost high ground with both infantry divisions the following morning, but it was then too late. Ottoman relief forces in the form of the 3rd and 16th Divisions and elements of the 53rd Division appeared in strength and quickly forced the British to call off the attack and withdraw to their start lines.

British casualties in the battle totaled 3,967 men, with the 53rd Division accounting for three-quarters of them. Ottoman losses were only 2,447.

DAMIEN FENTON

See also
Gaza, Second Battle of; Gaza, Third Battle of; Murray, Sir Archibald James; Palestine and Syria Campaign, World War I

References
Gullet, Henry S. *Official History of Australia in the War of 1914–18*, Vol. 7, *The Australian Imperial Force in Sinai and Palestine*. Melbourne, Australia: Government Printer, 1923.
MacMunn, George, and Cyril Falls. *Official History of the Great War: Military Operations, Egypt and Palestine, from the Outbreak of the War with Germany to June 1917*. London: HMSO, 1928.
Powles, Charles G. *Official History of New Zealand's Effort in the Great War*, Vol. 3, *The New Zealanders in Sinai and Palestine*. Wellington, New Zealand: Whitcombe and Tombs, 1922.
Wavell, Colonel A. P. *The Palestine Campaigns*. London: Constable, 1928.

Gaza, Second Battle of (April 17–19, 1917)

Battle during the World War I Palestine campaign. Lieutenant General Sir Archibald Murray's optimistic, if not misleading, reports painting the First Battle of Gaza as a British victory led to pressure from London for a renewed assault on the supposedly weakened Ottoman position. With the element of surprise gone, Murray opted for a set-piece frontal assault. Three infantry divisions, the 52nd (Lowland), 53rd (Welsh), and 54th (East Anglia), were to storm the defenses around Gaza and seize the city, while Lieutenant General Sir Philip Chetwode's Desert Column would threaten the Ottoman lines to the south and pin down the Ottoman troops manning the defenses there.

Fire support for the infantry attack was hastily assembled from a number of different sources. Thanks to further extensions of the British railhead, Murray was able to bring forward 16 heavy artillery pieces to add their weight to the field artillery of his three infantry divisions. Murray also managed to obtain 8 tanks and 4,000 gas shells from Britain as well as naval support in the French coastal defense ship *Requin* and two British monitors.

Confronting the British was a formidable Ottoman defensive line that extended 12 miles from Gaza and the coast to Beersheba. In the intervening weeks since the First Battle of Gaza, the Ottoman Eighth Army had constructed a series of mutually supporting strongpoints all along the Gaza-Beersheba axis. Manning these entrenchments were four Ottoman divisions supported by 101 guns (68 of which were within range of the British infantry's proposed approach).

The British attack was divided into two distinct phases. On April 17 the British infantry began the battle by driving in the outlying Ottoman outposts and securing the start lines for the main assault, while the Desert Column began its masking operations to the south. This phase was accomplished with minimal opposition and at the cost of 300 casualties and the loss of one tank. A 24-hour interlude followed, during which the British launched a limited artillery bombardment of the Ottoman positions.

Following this attempt to soften up the Ottoman front line, the main attack occurred the next day. At 5:30 a.m. on April 19, the British guns and the small Anglo-French flotilla offshore erupted into life again.

Unfortunately for the British, the firepower they had assembled for the battle proved hopelessly inadequate. The artillery was spread too thinly to inflict significant damage on the Ottoman trenches. British counterbattery fire was equally ineffective for similar reasons.

Two hours after the barrage began, the three British infantry divisions surged forward, only to be met almost immediately by concentrated Ottoman artillery and machine-gun fire. The accompanying tanks were too few in number to make any real impact and were soon picked off by the Ottoman gunners. The attack bogged down, and although individual battalions of both the 52nd and the 54th Divisions managed to penetrate the Ottoman defenses in several places, fierce Ottoman counterattacks soon drove them back. By nightfall the cost of these valiant but futile efforts had become apparent, and Murray and the other senior British commanders canceled orders to renew the attack the following day.

The Second Battle of Gaza cost the British 6,444 casualties (5,291 of which were suffered by the infantry) and led to Murray's replacement by Lieutenant General Sir Edmund Allenby two months later. Ottoman casualties during the battle totaled only 2,013, most of them wounded.

Damien Fenton

See also

Allenby, Sir Edmund Henry Hynman; Gaza, First Battle of; Gaza, Third Battle of; Murray, Sir Archibald James; Palestine and Syria Campaign, World War I

References

MacMunn, George, and Cyril Falls. *Official History of the Great War: Military Operations, Egypt and Palestine, from the Outbreak of the War with Germany to June 1917.* London: HMSO, 1928.

Wavell, Colonel A. P. *The Palestine Campaigns.* London: Constable, 1928.

Gaza, Third Battle of (October 31–November 7, 1917)

Key battle in the World War I Palestine campaign. With the Sinai Peninsula under complete British control after the Battle of Magruntein (January 8–9, 1917), commander of the Egyptian Expeditionary Force (EEF) Lieutenant General Sir Archibald Murray mounted a limited offensive into Palestine against the heavily defended Ottoman Beersheba-Gaza line. A series of ridges there provided the Turks a natural defensive position.

On March 26–27, 16,000 British and Dominion troops sustained some 4,000 casualties in a failed effort to crack the well-developed Ottoman defenses at Gaza. Murray's after-action report gave the impression that the battle had ended in a British victory, whereupon London ordered him to advance on Jerusalem. This triggered the Second Battle of Gaza (April 17–19). Again the Ottoman forces held. The assaulting British troops suffered 6,444 casualties, the Ottoman side only 2,000. Murray was relieved of command, replaced on June 28 by the former commander of the British Third Army in France, Lieutenant General Edmund Allenby, who had orders to take Jerusalem before Christmas.

Allenby insisted on and received reinforcements. Ultimately, he had 88,000 men in seven infantry divisions and three cavalry divisions, centered on the Australian Light Horse Division. Allenby also transferred the EEF headquarters from Cairo to the front, enabling more efficient and timely staff work. Opposing Allenby, German colonel Friedrich Kress von Kressenstein commanded the Ottoman Fourth Army of nine infantry divisions and a single cavalry division. Supply was a major problem for both sides, with adequate water to sustain operations being the major difficulty for the British; the Ottomans meanwhile were short of virtually all essential supplies, including ammunition, food, and fodder for their horses. Despite their two earlier victories at Gaza, Ottoman morale was low and desertions rife.

Lieutenant General Philip Chetwode, the new commander of the XX Corps under Allenby, developed the British operational plan, which Allenby adopted when he assumed command of the EEF in July. Chetwode rejected yet another frontal assault at Gaza and concluded that the weakest point in the Ottoman defenses was their extreme left flank at Beersheba, 30 miles inland from the Mediterranean. The Ottomans believed that it would be impossible for the British to attack Beersheba because of the shortage of water in the region. As a result, it was held by only one division. If the British could somehow take Beersheba and its water wells, they could then move west behind Gaza and sever its rail and road communications.

Securing adequate water was the key for the plan to succeed. British engineers refilled old Roman cisterns and repaired wells damaged by the Turks. They also worked to improve the flow of others.

At the same time, the British unbent every effort to convince the enemy that they planned yet another frontal assault on Gaza. An intelligence officer allowed false but apparently credible documents outlining an attack on Gaza to fall into Ottoman hands. Lieutenant General Edward Bulfin's XXI Corps of three divisions was assigned the task of carrying out convincing "demonstrations" against Gaza without, however, undertaking a major assault.

Meanwhile, on October 29 Lieutenant General Henry Chauvel's Desert Mounted Corps and Chetwode's XX Corps began their movement toward Beersheba, leaving behind their camps left completely in place. In all, the British force assigned to Beersheba numbered some 40,000 men to attack a position held by only 4,400 Ottoman troops. Although the Ottomans detected the movement, the British deception was so successful that they assumed that it involved only one infantry and one mounted division and that the main EEF attack would still occur at Gaza.

On October 31, the British attacked Beersheba in force. The infantry made a frontal demonstration from the west, while the Desert Mounted Corps swung wide east and attacked from the rear. The all-day engagement finally turned in British favor when a brigade of the Australian Light Horse charged with drawn bayonets, leaping over barbed wire and trenches and entering Beersheba itself. The Ottomans were completely surprised at this unorthodox tactic, and their resistance collapsed. The Australians secured the vast majority of the vital water wells intact. An effort the next day by the British 7th Mounted Brigade, strengthened by the Australian 8th Light Horse Regiment, to seize the Ottoman strongpoint at Khuweilfe that commanded the road leading east to Hebron was unsuccessful, as the Ottomans managed to strengthen it just in time. Subsequent British, Australian, and New Zealand successive mounted assaults during the next four days to take Khuweilfe were all unsuccessful.

By November 4, British engineers had succeeded in raising the water production at Beersheba to a point sufficient to support the British mounted forces. The Ottomans still controlled water supplies to the north, however, and the British mounted brigades could thus operate for only a day at a time away from Beersheba. Still, the British planned to maximize military operations here to draw off resources from Gaza. Meanwhile, on the advice of Chetwode and Chauvel, Allenby delayed the main assault on Gaza until November 6. A limited effort by the 54th (East Anglian) Division on November 2 enjoyed some success, driving back the defenders and holding the captured ground against repeated Ottoman counterattacks. Attempts to break through the Ottoman lines were unsuccessful, however.

The main British attack came at dawn on November 6 and involved all three of Chetwode's divisions. Within an hour, two of the divisions had broken through. The next morning the XXI Corps assaulted Gaza itself, and all objectives were quickly taken. The last portion of the former Ottoman defensive line was secured on November 8. The Ottoman Eighth Army now withdrew northward, up the coast, and the EEF occupied Jerusalem on December 9.

SPENCER C. TUCKER

See also
Allenby, Sir Edmund Henry Hynman; Beersheba, Battle of; Gaza, First Battle of; Gaza, Second Battle of; Kress von Kressenstein, Friedrich Sigismund Georg; Murray, Sir Archibald James

References
Bullock, David L. *Allenby's War: The Palestine-Arabian Campaigns, 1916–1918*. New York: Blandford, 1988.
Gardner, Brian. *Allenby of Arabia: Lawrence's General*. New York: Coward-McCann, 1966.
Great Britain, War Office. *Brief Record of the Egyptian Force under the Command of General Sir Edmund H. H. Allenby: July 1917 to October 1918, Egyptian Expeditionary Force*. 2nd ed. London: HMSO, 1919.
Hughes, Matthew. *Allenby and British Strategy in the Middle East, 1917–1919*. London: Cass, 1999.

Gaza Raid (February 28, 1955)

Israeli military raid of an Egyptian Army outpost in Gaza on February 28, 1955. The raid was undertaken by approximately 50 paratroopers of the Israel Defense Forces (IDF) and came as a complete surprise to the Egyptians. The Gaza Raid resulted in the deaths of 39 Egyptian soldiers and the wounding of another 30.

The attack was supposedly in retaliation for continuing fedayeen attacks on Israel, but Gaza appeared to be a strange target in that it had historically been the most quiet of the Israeli frontier borders. Yet there is more to the story than mere retaliation. Israeli prime minister David Ben-Gurion had come under increasing pressure from the political Right both in and out of the government to take a more proactive stance against fedayeen attacks. Thus, he somewhat reluctantly agreed to sanction the raid.

In retrospect, the Gaza Raid was a major Israeli miscalculation. In fact, before the February raid, the Egyptians—first under King Farouk I and then under President Gamal Abdel Nasser—had discouraged (or at the least had not officially blessed) raids on Israel from Egyptian soil, particularly raids by Palestinian fedayeen forces. Outraged by the audacity of the Israeli Gaza attack, Nasser now began to sanction commando and fedayeen raids against Israel. The Jordanians also began to encourage raids against the Israelis from their territory following the February attack. This marked the beginning of a trend of escalating violence among fedayeen forces, Israel's Arab neighbors, and Israel that would result in many hundreds of deaths.

The Gaza Raid proved to be a political hot potato for Nasser, who now believed that he had to take extraordinary measures to counter the growing threat of Israeli incursions into Egyptian territory. The raid also convinced Nasser and his military advisers that Israel was gaining strength militarily and that this buildup had to be counteracted by a commensurate Egyptian rearmament effort. Shortly thereafter, Nasser approached several Western nations, including the United States, about arms purchases. The Americans and British rebuffed the inquiry, citing the 1950 Tripartite Declaration that pledged no arms sales to Middle Eastern nations. In addition, Nasser's embrace of the Non-Aligned Movement did not sit well in Washington or London. For their part, the French would not sell arms to Nasser's government because of Egypt's support of Algerian rebels in the Algerian War (1954–1962), a colonial conflict in which the French were now deeply involved.

Having been turned down by the major Western powers, Nasser naturally looked to the East, toward the Soviet Union, for his arms needs. Before the year was out, he had consummated a major arms deal with the Soviets. The 1955 arms deal delivered to the Egyptians some 200 tanks and other weapons and amounted to about $325 million (in 1955 dollars). This marked the start of a major Soviet effort to insert its influence in the Middle East. It was also the beginning of an Egyptian-Soviet alliance that would last until the mid-1970s and paved the way for similar Soviet arms deals with Syria and Iraq.

Clearly, the 1955 Gaza Raid set off a chain reaction of events that nobody might have imagined. The Egyptian-Soviet arms deal compelled the United States and Great Britain to pull their financial underwriting of Egypt's Aswan High Dam project. This in turn forced Nasser to nationalize the Suez Canal in 1956, which in turn precipitated the Suez Crisis of October–November 1956.

Paul G. Pierpaoli Jr.

See also
Ben-Gurion, David; Egypt; Egyptian-Soviet Arms Deal; Fedayeen; Nasser, Gamal Abdel; Tripartite Declaration

References
Jabber, Paul. *Not by War Alone: Security and Arms Control in the Middle East.* Berkeley: University of California Press, 1981.
Leng, Russell J. *Bargaining and Learning in Recurrent Crises: The Soviet-American, Egyptian-Israeli, and Indo-Pakistani Rivalries.* Ann Arbor: University of Michigan Press, 2000.
Louis, William R., and Roger Owen, eds. *Suez, 1956: The Crisis and Its Consequences.* New York: Oxford University Press, 1989.

Gaza Strip

A 7-mile-wide, 25-mile-long, heavily populated strip of land along the Mediterranean Sea, adjacent to Egypt's Sinai Peninsula. The Gaza Strip takes its name from its principal city of Gaza. In biblical times the area that is today the Gaza Strip was the home of the Philistines, and the name "Palestine" is derived from "Philistine."

The Gaza Strip has a border of approximately 31 miles with Israel on the northeast and east and 6.6 miles with Egypt on the southwest. It has been one of the main focal points of the Arab-Israeli conflict since 1967, when it became one of Israel's occupied territories. Although much of the strip is now under Palestinian Authority (PA) jurisdiction, borders and main roads are still controlled by Israel, and the entire area remains disputed. At the end of 2007 it had a population of some 1.5 million people.

According to a 1947 United Nations (UN) plan, which never took effect, the Gaza Strip and the West Bank were to form an independent Arab state following the dismantling of the British Mandate for Palestine. Arab leaders, however, rejected the plan and instead waged war. During the Israeli War of Independence (1948–1949), many of the Palestinian people who had lived in what had become Israel either fled or were forced into areas surrounding the new Jewish state, including Gaza. Although a Palestinian government began operation in the Gaza Strip, the 1949 armistice between Israel and Egypt that ended the war gave control of the area to Egypt, which suspended the government in 1959.

Despite the 1949 armistice, significant portions of the Israeli population believed that the Gaza Strip (along with the West Bank and parts of Lebanon and Syria) was part of biblical Eretz Israel (Land of Israel) and therefore should be part of the modern Jewish state. After a failed attempt to gain the strip in the 1956 Sinai Campaign, Israel launched the Six-Day War in 1967. In spite of fighting a war against Egypt, Syria, and Jordan, the Jewish state was nevertheless able to take control of Gaza from Egypt. UN Security Council Resolution 242 called for Israel to withdraw from territories captured in the war, but Israel instead began constructing Jewish settlements in the Gaza Strip.

At the beginning of the 21st century, there were 25 Israeli settlements in Gaza, although in 2005 the Gaza Strip's population of some 1.4 million included only 8,000 Israelis. In May 1994 the historic Declaration of Principles on Interim Self-Government Arrangements (also known as the Oslo Accords) transferred some governmental services of the strip to the PA, but its status remained in dispute.

A high birthrate has contributed to the Gaza Strip's ongoing poverty, unemployment, and low standard of living. Although control of the strip's finances was also transferred to the PA in 1994, government corruption and Israeli border closures severely hindered the economy until 1998, when Israel began taking measures to ensure that border closures resulting from terrorism threats would not so adversely affect cross-border trade. However, with the outbreak of the Second (al-Aqsa) Intifada in 2000, many of these measures were reversed, and the area witnessed another economic downturn.

In 2005, Israeli prime minister Ariel Sharon's government voted to begin disengagement from the Gaza Strip, a plan that met with mixed reactions in the international community. Although the European Union (EU) and the United States supported Sharon's plan to dismantle Israeli settlements in the area and withdraw Israeli forces from many areas, the EU said that the plan did not go far enough in establishing pre-1967 borders. Many Israelis opposed the plan and supported the settlers. Palestinians, while in favor of any move that increased PA jurisdiction, complained that the plan was not comprehensive. Nonetheless, it was hoped that disengagement would mark a step in implementing the so-called Road Map to Peace in the Middle East, a peace plan brokered by the United States, the EU, Russia, and the UN.

As planned, the Israeli government began dismantling the settlements on August 15, 2005. Although the process was contested by the nationalist Right within Israel, by some Jews abroad, and in some confrontational events in Gaza, the Israel Defense Forces (IDF) completed the process on September 12, 2005. Israel has, however, retained offshore maritime control and control of airspace over the Gaza Strip. At the same time, Israel withdrew from the Philadelphi Route adjacent to the strip's border with Egypt following a pledge by Egypt that it would secure its side of the border.

The optimistic attitude prevailing in Gaza when Israel withdrew its troops along with 9,000 Jewish settlers were dashed by fighting among criminal gangs and clashes between Hamas and Fatah that soon escalated and ultimately killed an estimated 160 people and wounded 800 more.

Palestinian militants have used the Gaza Strip to fire Qassam rockets into Israeli border settlements, and Israel carried out several military operations in Gaza in 2006, including the 2006 Gaza War (June 28–November 16), known in Israel as Operation SUMMER RAINS (June 28–July 30), and Operation AUTUMN CLOUDS (November 1–26). The cease-fire broke down completely amid escalating conflict between Hamas and Fatah in 2007.

On June 14, 2007, Hamas took over Gaza entirely, ousting all Fatah officials. This ended the Palestinian unity government and also brought the declaration of a state of emergency by Palestinian president Mahmoud Abbas. The resulting emergency Palestinian government excluded Hamas and was limited to the West Bank.

On June 19, 2007, Abbas cut off all ties and dialogue with Hamas, pending the return of Gaza. This left Fatah, backed by the United States, the EU, and Israel, scrambling to consolidate its control in the West Bank, while Hamas tightened its own control of Gaza and increasingly imposed its brand of religious conservatism, especially as far as women were concerned.

With aid from the West largely cut off, Hamas soon found itself under siege along with the people of Gaza. Few of Gaza's 1.5 million people could leave Gaza for any reason. With the Egyptian border also closed, the economy was in a state of near collapse, with Gazans unable to export products and thus incapable of paying for imports. Gaza was more isolated than ever.

Meanwhile, Hamas continued smuggling in quantities of explosives and arms from Egypt through tunnels. Egyptian security forces uncovered 60 tunnels in 2007 alone. Hamas and other militant groups continued to fire Qassam rockets across the border into Israel. According to Israel, between the Hamas takeover and the end of January 2008, 697 rockets and 822 mortar shells landed in Israel. In response, Israel targeted Qassam launchers and military targets and declared the Gaza Strip a hostile entity. In January 2008, seeking to employ economic means to secure its ends, the Israeli government curtailed travel from Gaza and the entry of goods. It also cut fuel supplies, bringing power shortages, and ordered Israeli banks to cut economic ties with Gaza. These actions resulted in some international condemnation of Israel.

The intensification of the Israel-Gaza confrontation led Israeli prime minister Ehud Olmert to remark in November 2008 that a major confrontation was inevitable. That occurred in the December 27, 2008–January 18, 2009, Gaza War. Israeli claimed its attacks on Gaza were justified owing to some 3,000 rocket attacks on its territory in 2008. Israeli targets included a number of police stations, schools, hospitals, UN warehouses, mosques, and other structures that it claimed were being used to store weapons. An IDF ground invasion of Gaza began on January 3, 2009. Before IDF operations ceased two weeks later, the death toll had reached some 1,100–1,400 Palestinians (295–926 of them civilians) and 13 Israelis, 4 by friendly fire.

Physical destruction in Gaza was immense. The conflict destroyed or damaged thousands of homes as well as many hospitals, farms, and business enterprises. Some 50,000 people were homeless. As many as half a million people were without running water, and 1 million had no electricity. Food and other necessities were in very short supply.

On June 5, 2014, Fatah and Hamas concluded a unity agreement that soon fell apart. Warfare with Israeli resumed that same year, however, in what the Israelis called Operation PROTECTIVE EDGE but what is usually known as the 2014 Gaza War. After the kidnapping and murder of three Israeli teenagers by Hamas members, the IDF carried out Operation BROTHER'S KEEPER, arresting militant Palestinian leaders. Hamas then fired rockets into Israel, and this in turn led to a seven-week conflict during July 28–August 8 in which Israeli ground forces again invaded Gaza. Depending on the source, the fighting claimed between 93 and 936 militants and 761 to 1,617 civilians dead. Israel lost 67 military personnel killed and 468 wounded. Again there was extensive damage to Gaza's infrastructure.

Israel and Egypt maintain a blockade of the Gaza Strip that includes the passage of people in and out. Israel has allowed limited quantities of medical humanitarian aid. The Israeli government of Premier Benjamin Netanyahu maintains that the blockade is legal and is necessary to prevent the smuggling of weapons into Gaza and the launching of rockets from Gaza against its cities. As proof of this, Israel cites the boarding by the IDF of a Panamanian-flagged ship claiming to be carrying construction materials to Gaza but found to contain Syrian-produced rockets. Critics claim that the blockade is nothing short of financial war against Gaza, and certainly it has inflicted immense damage on the economy and the people of Gaza. In 2018, Egypt alleged that Islamist insurgents on the Sinai Peninsula were receiving training and support from extremists within the Gaza Strip. In August 2018, Hamas leaders claimed that an end of the Israeli blockade was near, as negotiations brokered by the UN and Egypt continued to yield results, albeit small. Israel, however, showed no outward signs of easing the blockade or engaging in a truce with Hamas.

SPENCER C. TUCKER

See also
Abbas, Mahmoud; AUTUMN CLOUDS, Operation; Fatah, al-; Gaza Strip Disengagement; Gaza War of 2006; Gaza War of 2008–2009; Gaza War of 2014; Hamas; Intifada, Second; Netanyahu, Benjamin; Olmert, Ehud; Oslo Accords; Palestinian National Authority; Sharon, Ariel; Sinai Campaign of 1956; Six-Day War

References
"Israeli Military Operations against Gaza, 2000–2008." *Journal of Palestine Studies* 38, no. 3 (Spring 2009): 122–138.
Oren, Michael B. *Six Days of War: June 1967 and the Making of the Modern Middle East*. Novato, CA: Presidio, 2003.
Said, Edward W. *The End of the Peace Process: Oslo and After*. New York: Vintage Books, 2001.
Smith, Charles D. *Palestine and the Arab-Israeli Conflict: A History with Documents*. 6th ed. New York: Bedford/St. Martin's, 2006.

Gaza Strip Disengagement (August 15–September 12, 2005)

A plan devised by Israeli prime minister Ariel Sharon to remove Israeli interests from the Gaza Strip. The Israeli government accepted and enacted the plan in August 2005. The Gaza Strip is a narrow slice of land on the east bank of the Mediterranean Sea just north of Egypt. The Israeli pullout also encompassed four Jewish settlements in the northern West Bank, on the western edge of the Jordan River.

Israel captured the Gaza Strip in 1967 during the Six-Day War and occupied the area until September 2005. The disengagement officially began on August 15, 2005, and was completed on September 12, 2005. Coupled with the November 2004 election of Palestinian leader Mahmoud Abbas, the Israeli disengagement gave rise to optimism among many in the region concerning the prospect of peace between the Palestinians and the Israelis.

Sharon first announced his plan for withdrawal on December 18, 2003, at the Fourth Herzliya Conference in Israel. The prime minister stated that he hoped to advance the implementation of the so-called Road Map to Peace, first advanced by the United States in June 2002. Sharon declared that the purpose of the pullout plan was "to reduce terror as much as possible, and grant Israeli citizens the maximum level of security." Sharon and supporters of the plan knew that Israel had to initiate the peace process and not rely on cooperation from the Palestinians.

Some analysts have suggested that the withdrawal was a shrewd strategic maneuver on Sharon's part designed to splinter the already fragile Palestinian unity. As they are geographically separated, there has long been a certain degree of friction and distrust between the Palestinians of the West Bank and those of Gaza. Prior to 1967, the former had spent almost 20 years under Jordanian occupation, while the latter spent the same period under Egyptian control. The Israeli withdrawal from Gaza also forced the Palestinian Authority (PA) to demonstrate for the first time that it was capable of governing and providing basic societal and governmental services to its people. In the year following the Israeli withdrawal, the PA generally failed that test. A different Arab and

Palestinian perspective is that the withdrawal was meant to be the preface for an Israeli offensive on the West Bank.

Despite opposition from Sharon's own Likud Party, which believed that Sharon had betrayed his previous policies supporting the Gaza settlements, he continued to press forward. On June 6, 2004, the Israeli cabinet approved the disengagement. Sharon's insistence on the plan upset many of his closest supporters, including former Israeli prime minister Benjamin Netanyahu, who resigned his post as finance minister, accusing the Israeli government of destroying Jewish towns and villages while receiving nothing in return. However, Sharon garnered support from the leftist Labor Party and international policy makers such as the leaders of the European Union, United Nations (UN) secretary-general Kofi Annan, and U.S. president George W. Bush.

Many Palestinians opposed the plan, as it did not call for Israel to withdraw militarily from the Gaza Strip and did not address any of the nearly intolerable conditions in the West Bank. Others simply did not trust Sharon to keep his word and believed that his support for the plan was nothing more than lip service. Despite opposition from many Palestinians, on August 8, 2005, Sheikh Jamal al-Bawatna, a senior Palestinian religious leader, issued an edict banning shooting attacks against Israeli security forces and settlements out of concern that such incidents would lead to a postponement of the pullout from the Gaza Strip. Prior to the pullout, demonstrators occupied allegedly empty buildings and attacked some Palestinian homes. Skepticism turned to joy when Israel pulled out of Gaza in August and September 2005. The militant Palestinian group Hamas, which had vociferously opposed Israel's presence in Palestine since the group's founding in 1987, claimed victory and celebrated along with thousands of Palestinian supporters worldwide.

Israelis who opposed the plan joined together in nonviolent protests, such as the July 25, 2004, demonstration in which tens of thousands of Israelis formed a human chain 50 miles long from the Nissanit settlement in Gaza to the Western Wall in Jerusalem. Other protests throughout the country occurred, including a symbolic war of flags (orange for those who opposed withdrawal and blue for those who favored withdrawal), until the disengagement was complete. Despite the protests, by July 2005 polls showed that a majority of Israelis supported Sharon and the withdrawal plan.

On August 15, 2005, the Gaza Strip was officially closed for Israeli entrance. On August 17, the forced evacuation of those Israelis who refused to leave on their own began.

Israeli civilians were removed from their homes, and their residences were demolished. While there was much less violence than expected, there were some scenes that witnessed Israeli troops dragging screaming Jews from their homes and synagogues in Gaza. In all, it took the Israel Defense Forces (IDF) and the Israeli police only four and a half days to forcibly evict some 5,000 settlers. Despite the stress on both the soldiers and the civilians, the process of removal was completed on September 12, 2005, when the last soldier left the Gaza Strip and the Kissufim Gate was closed.

Following the Israeli pullout, debate continued on all sides as to what role the disengagement would play in the Arab-Israeli peace process, particularly as Israeli forces bombed and shelled Gaza in the spring of 2006 and then reentered the Gaza Strip in the summer of 2006 in response to the kidnapping of an Israeli soldier.

Gregory Wayne Morgan

See also
Abbas, Mahmoud; Gaza Strip; Hamas; Sharon, Ariel

References
Efrat, Elisha. *The West Bank and Gaza Strip: A Geography of Occupation and Disengagement.* New York: Routledge, 2006.
Makovsky, David. *Making Peace with the PLO: The Rabin Government's Road to the Oslo Accord.* Boulder, CO: Westview, 1996.

Gaza War of 2006 (June 27–November 26, 2006)

Large-scale Israeli-launched incursion into the Gaza Strip during June 27–November 26, 2006, in response to attacks allegedly by Hamas that killed two Israeli soldiers and captured Israel Defense Forces (IDF) corporal Gilad Shalit. The operation is known to Israelis as Operation SUMMER RAINS. The stated Israeli intention was to secure the release of the captive soldier and to stop the firing of Qassam rockets from the Gaza Strip into Israeli territory. Israel carried out strikes against militant Palestinian groups, destroyed infrastructure that the groups used to support their actions, and applied political pressure on the Hamas-led government.

SUMMER RAINS began on June 27 with the Israeli bombing of three bridges and a power plant as Israeli ground troops moved into the Gaza Strip. Also, Israeli fighter jets flew over the summer residence of Syrian president Bashar al-Assad as a warning against his continued support of Hamas and Hezbollah. The following day, Israeli troops entered the Gaza Strip with the aim of securing and destroying Qassam rocket sites. Israeli warships also shelled suspected rocket sites from offshore. Israeli air strikes mainly targeted Hamas training camps and arms caches. Israeli aircraft also dropped thousands of leaflets warning Palestinian civilians to leave their homes in areas of northern Gaza from which it claimed Qassam rockets were being fired.

During the operation, Israeli forces arrested a number of members of the Hamas leadership as well as members of the Palestinian Legislative Council. Unsurprisingly, this led to charges by many Palestinians, and especially those in Hamas, that Israel was trying to oust the Hamas leadership of the Palestinian Authority (PA) that had been democratically elected in January 2006. The operation also destroyed the only power plant in the Gaza Strip, leaving most of the territory without electricity during the brutally hot days of summer. Most Palestinians were also left with no running potable water and no facilities for sanitation and waste processing. This made it difficult for businesses, hospitals, and basic services to function. In addition to the economic consequences of the operation, a building humanitarian crisis in Gaza caught the attention of various international organizations, including the United Nations (UN). Indeed, UN officials decried the toll that the conflict was taking on civilians and urged both sides to resolve their differences peacefully.

Precise casualty figures are difficult to determine. Unverified figures list 7 Israelis killed (2 of them civilians) 42 wounded, and 1 soldier captured. Reportedly 402 Palestinians died, including 117 civilians. Some 1,000 others were wounded, and 65 officials were taken prisoner. There was never a conclusive settlement, and Gilad Shalit was not returned to Israel. (He was released in October 2011 as part of a prisoner exchange.) SUMMER RAINS was slowed through a truce agreement between Israel and militant Palestinian organizations on November 26, 2006, although rockets continued to be launched from Gaza to Israel through December.

DANIEL W. KUTHY

See also
Gaza Strip; Hamas; Palestinian National Authority

References
Efrat, Elisha. *The West Bank and Gaza Strip: A Geography of Occupation and Disengagement.* New York: Routledge, 2006.

Gelvin, James L. *The Israel-Palestine Conflict: One Hundred Years of War.* New York: Cambridge University Press, 2005.

Hroub, Khaled. *Hamas: A Beginner's Guide.* Ann Arbor, MI: Pluto, 2006.

"Israeli Military Operations against Gaza, 2000–2008." *Journal of Palestine Studies* 38, no. 3 (Spring 2009): pp. 122–138.

Gaza War of 2008–2009 (December 27, 2008–January 18, 2009)

The Gaza War of 2008–2009 was yet another round in the fighting between the Israelis and Palestinians. Also known as the Israeli-Gaza War of 2008–2009, to the Israelis as Operation CAST LEAD, and to Hamas as the Gaza Massacre and the Battle of al-Furqan, it was a three-week armed conflict between the Palestinian Hamas organization in the Gaza Strip and Israel. It began on December 27, 2008, and ended on January 18, 2009, in a unilateral Israeli cease-fire.

The Israeli operation was the response to escalating violence following the expiration of a six-months truce in August. In late December there had been a sharp increase in rockets and mortar fire from Gaza against Israeli border towns. The Israeli government claimed that Hamas had fired some 300 rockets and mortar shells into Israel in the course of the previous week, or 10 times the number of the past year. With the support of President Hosni Mubarak's Egyptian government, Israel had largely isolated the 1.5 million people living in the Gaza Strip from the outside world after the radical Hamas organization had seized power there.

The Israeli offensive began with air attacks on targets in the Gaza Strip. These were directed against known militant training camps, rocket-manufacturing facilities, arms caches, and government offices, including the Palestinian Authority legislative building. Most of the early casualties were among Hamas security forces. Among those killed were Major General Tawfeeq al-Jaber, a senior commander of the Hamas police forces, and Ismail Jabari, who headed the special police forces in Gaza. With Prime Minister Ehud Olmert's government calling up reservists and preparing for a possible ground invasion, Hamas leaders vowed to defend Gaza and its people. Indeed, a defiant Hamas responded by launching several hundred additional rockets. Some of these reached 30 miles into Israel, as far as Beersheba.

Early on December 28 the United Nations Security Council called on both sides immediately to halt all military action, but the appeal fell on deaf ears. Israel insisted that the rocket attacks first end, while Hamas demanded termination of the economic blockade of Gaza.

As the fighting continued, the situation in Gaza became increasingly desperate, with hospitals unable to treat the wounded and with food in short supply. Although the Israeli air strikes brought widespread condemnation of Israel from around the Arab world, the U.S. government blamed Hamas for having forced the Israeli action.

Palestinians search for bodies in the rubble of the destroyed home of Hamas senior leader Nizar Rayan after an Israeli missile strike on the refugee camp of Jabaliyaon in Gaza on January 1, 2009, during the Gaza War of December 27, 2008–January 18, 2009. (Abid Katib/Getty Images)

Israel then targeted the homes of Hamas leaders. A 1,000-pound bomb demolished the home of Nizar Rayan, one of the founders of Hamas and its commander in northern Gaza, killing him, his 4 wives, and 10 of his 11 children. Israeli aircraft also attacked a mosque that the Israel Defense Forces (IDF) claims had been used to store missiles, rockets, and other weapons.

On the night of January 3, 2009, as Israeli aircraft and ships offshore continued to shell targets, Israeli ground forces entered the Gaza Strip, proceeding in an east-west direction to slice off the northern part of the territory including Gaza City. However, they did not yet enter the city itself, where armed Hamas militants promised a fight to the death.

The situation in the Gaza Strip was now desperate. In a humanitarian gesture the Israeli government did allow some international aid convoys through, but distribution of supplies proved difficult at best. By January 5 the fighting had claimed more than 500 Palestinian lives, with a reported additional 2,600 wounded. Four Israelis—1 soldier and 3 civilians—had died in the rocket attacks, and 1 soldier was slain in the ground offensive. Hamas meanwhile continued to fire rockets into Israel, 30 of them on January 4. Many Israeli citizens in the border area sought refuge in air raid shelters.

On January 6, Israeli tank shells struck a United Nations (UN) school in the Jabaliya refugee camp crowded with some 1,600 Palestinians seeking refuge. Some 40 people died, many of them children. A subsequent Israeli investigation claimed that the shelling had been in error. By January 8, the UN estimated that two-thirds of the Gaza Strip's 1.5 million people were then without electricity and that half did not have running water.

On January 8, four rockets struck northern Israel, injuring two people. Israel replied with artillery fire on the location from which the rockets were believed to have been launched. With many militant Palestinian groups operating in Lebanon, most observers saw these rockets as an effort to open a new front in the fighting now under way in Gaza and not the work of the militant Hezbollah organization, which had thus far kept tight control of its forces and refrained from intervening in the Israeli-Hamas conflict.

On January 8, a UN Security Council resolution called for an immediate cease-fire in Gaza leading to an Israeli pullout.

The resolution also called for the intensification of efforts to halt illegal shipments of arms and ammunition into Gaza to Hamas. The resolution passed unanimously, with the United States abstaining.

On January 11, IDF troops moved into the heavily populated suburbs of Gaza as Israeli gunboats offshore lobbed several dozen shells into Hamas installations in Gaza City. The Gaza suburbs were now rigged with booby traps and crude homemade explosive devises. Hamas meanwhile continued launching rockets into southern Israel. Hamas leader Ismail Radwan rejected any cease-fire arrangement until Israel removed its troops and halted all air attacks against Gaza. He also demanded full opening of all border crossings, emphasizing the Rafah crossing into Egypt. Israel on its part demanded that Hamas halt rocket attacks against its territory, that smuggling of rocket components via tunnels from Egypt be halted, and that international inspectors monitor the border, which Egypt rejected. Meanwhile, demonstrations on behalf of the Palestinians turned violent in London, New York, and Paris, with hundred of protestors arrested.

On January 15, Israeli forces shelled the UN headquarters in Gaza. The shells set fire to a warehouse, destroying tons of desperately needed food supplies intended for the local population, which greatly increased tensions between Israel and much of the international community and brought an angry protest from UN secretary-general Ban Ki-moon, in Israel to try to arrange a cease-fire. Israeli defense minister Ehud Barak called the attack a "grave error," but Prime Minister Olmert said that Israeli troops had been fired on from the compound. The director of the UN Relief and Works Agency operations in Gaza characterized this as "total nonsense."

On January 16, the UN General Assembly voted 142 to 4 (Israel and the United States voted no) to call on Israel to abide by the January 8 Security Council resolution demanding an immediate cease-fire by both sides in the Gaza Strip. Hamas continued launching rockets, and Israel continued its attacks.

On January 18, Israel announced a unilateral cease-fire in Gaza. Hamas, however, said that it would not enter into any cease-fire agreement until Israeli forces were completely withdrawn from Gaza. Indeed, Hamas launched six rockets into the town of Siderot in southern Israel hours after the proclamation of the cease-fire, although no one was hurt, and Israeli aircraft soon destroyed the rocket launcher.

On January 19, Hamas stood down its fighters as the IDF withdrew from the Gaza Strip. With the cease-fire largely holding (seven rockets were fired into southern Israeli from Gaza since the Israeli unilateral cease-fire), the Israeli government began removing its troops, with all of them withdrawn by January 20. Tel Aviv announced, however, that Israel would not hesitate to retaliate if rockets were again fired into southern Israel.

The more than three weeks of fighting killed an estimated 1,300 Palestinians (159 of them children) and wounded another 5,400. Reportedly 22,000 buildings were destroyed or damaged, most of them in Gaza City. A Palestinian Authority spokesperson put the physical damage alone at $1.9 billion. The Israelis claim that they had destroyed the tunnels used to bring rocket parts from Egypt into the Gaza strip. Thirteen Israelis also died, 10 of them soldiers.

Despite the great physical damage inflicted there, Hamas retained its full control of the Gaza Strip. The Israeli military action brought considerable criticism of Israel from within the Arab world and other states, strengthened the confrontational governments of Syria and Iran, and weakened the more moderate Fatah faction governing the Palestinian territory on the West Bank. The terrorist organization Islamic Jihad, which also operates in the Gaza Strip, announced that it would not be bound by any case-fire until Israel ended its blockade of Gaza and opened all border crossings.

SPENCER C. TUCKER

See also
Barak, Ehud; Gaza Strip; Hamas; Hezbollah; Jihad; Mubarak, Hosni; Olmert, Ehud

References
Bonner, Ethan. "Hamas Shifts from Rockets to Culture War." *New York Times*, July 24, 2009.

Castle, Stephen, and Katrin Bennhold. "Europe Sends Two Missions to Promote a Cease-Fire." *New York Times*, January 5, 2009.

Esposito, Michele K. "The Israeli Arsenal Deployed against Gaza during Operation Cast Lead." *Journal of Palestine Studies* 38, no. 3 (Spring 2009): 75–191.

Sengupta, Kim, and Donald MacIntyre. "Victorious, but Vilified: Israel Has 'Destroyed Its Image and Its Soul.'" *The Independent*, January 18, 2009.

Spyer, Jonathan. "Hamas Seeks New Doctrine after Gaza War Failures." *Jerusalem Post*, September 10, 2009.

Gaza War of 2012 (November 14–22, 2012)

Rockets launched by Hamas militants in Gaza into Israeli territory led Israel to retaliate in Operation PILLAR OF DEFENSE, a series of air strikes against rocket-launching sites and munition-storage facilities but also one precision missile strike that targeted and killed Ahmed al-Jabart, head of the militant wing of the Palestinian Hamas movement, and five other individuals riding in a car. This latter action unleashed a wave of rockets from Gaza into Israel.

Some of the rockets reached as far as Tel Aviv, a worrisome development for Israel and evidently the result of a transfer of missile technology from Iran. Israel responded by calling up some 16,000 Israel Defense Forces (IDF) reservists (the Israeli cabinet authorized a recall of up to 75,000 personnel) and moving up armor toward the Gaza border. Israeli prime minister Benjamin Netanyahu pledged to take "whatever action is necessary."

In the meantime, the IDF launched a series of air strikes on Hamas government buildings. Israeli officials estimated that Hamas possessed some 12,000 rockets. Both Egyptian and Turkish leaders were critical of Israel's role in the violence, while U.S. president Barack Obama said that Israel had the right to take steps to defend itself.

The IDF claimed to have targeted more than 1,500 "terror sites," including command centers and Hamas senior headquarters, smuggling and "terror" tunnels, weapons manufacturing sites, and rocket launchers and launch sites. The Israelis also claimed that 21,506 rockets had been fired from Gaza during the period, with the newly installed Iron Dome antimissile missile defense system paid for by the United States having intercepted and destroyed 421 of them, representing 90 percent of those identified as a threat to populated areas.

After eight days a truce went into effect on November 22, brokered by Egyptian president Mohammad Morsi and U.S. secretary of state Hilary Clinton. The fighting claimed 5 Israelis killed and 240 injured. A total of 162 were killed in Gaza, including 11 women and 42 children; there were also 1,225 wounded. During the fighting, Hamas had also publicly executed 7 Palestinian men alleged to having collaborated with Israel.

Both sides claimed that they had accomplished their objectives. A spokesman for the Israeli military said that the IDF has caused severe damage to the Hamas military capabilities, degrading its capability of some 12,000 rockets and destroying tunnels used to smuggle in weapons. Hamas also claimed victory, with loudspeakers in the Gaza Strip blaring out victory pronouncements and claiming that the people of Gaza had "broken the arrogance of the Jews."

Hamas, however, appeared to be the major winner, having demonstrated to the Arab world its willingness to employ force against Israel, calling attention to the lack of progress in the moribund Arab-Israeli peace talks, and strengthening itself vis-à-vis the Palestinian Authority, which Washington considered the only viable Palestinian partner for negotiations with Israel. Hamas also appeared to have the strong support of Egypt, Turkey, and Qatar. While Israel was certainly stronger militarily, it also appeared to be in a weaker political position than before. Some also questioned the value to Israel of the death of al-Jabari because he had tightly controlled the extremist groups in Gaza, and they might now be more prone to take independent action.

Spencer C. Tucker

See also
Gaza Strip; Hamas; Israel; Morsi, Mohamed

References
Bronner, Ethan. "With Longer Reach, Rockets Bolster Hamas Arsenal." *New York Times,* November 17, 2012.
Londoño, Ernesto, and Michael Birnbaum. "After Israel, Hamas Reach Gaza Cease-Fire, Both Sides Claim Victory." *Washington Post,* November 21, 2012.
Rudoren, Jodi, and Akram Fares. "Mistaken Lull, Simple Errand, Death in Gaza." *New York Times,* November 17, 2012.

Gaza War of 2014 (July 8–August 26, 2014)

Major conflict, also known as the Israeli-Gaza War of 2014 and Operation PROTECTIVE EDGE, involving the Israel Defense Forces (IDF) and Hamas in Gaza. On June 12, 2014, three Israeli teenage boys disappeared while trying to hitchhike home from the southern West Bank. Although presenting no evidence to this effect at the time, Israeli security forces claimed that they had been kidnapped by Hamas and, withholding evidence in their possession until July 1 that suggested the teens had been killed, Israeli security forces immediately launched Operation BROTHER'S KEEPER, in which they arrested numerous militant leaders in the West Bank and demolished the homes of two Palestinians suspected in the abduction.

On June 20 the bodies of the three teenagers were discovered in a field not far from Hebron. Hamas responded to the Israeli actions in the West Bank with the launching of 128 rockets into Israel from the Gaza Strip. Israel then carried out more than 40 air strikes against an announced 34 targets in Gaza on the night of June 30–July 1. These actions were followed by the kidnapping and murder of a Palestinian teenager by Jewish settlers, who were subsequently arrested, the boy having apparently been burned alive. This news brought widespread rioting by Palestinians in Jerusalem and Israeli Arab towns, more rockets fired from Gaza, and increased Israeli air strikes in what becomes known as Operation PROTECTIVE EDGE.

During July 6–7, some 80 rockets were launched into Israel from Gaza, some reaching farther than ever before, even to Tel Aviv. Hamas was believed to then have as many as 10,000 rockets of varying types and ranges. By July 7, the Israeli Air Force had struck some 50 targets in Gaza, including homes belonging to militant leaders, military compounds, and missile-launch sites. This was the worst flare-up along the border since the eight-day Gaza War of 2012.

On July 8, the first official day of Operation PROTECTIVE EDGE, Israeli aircraft struck more than 200 sites in Gaza. That same day the Israeli cabinet authorized the call-up of as many as 40,000 troops, 10,000 more than were called up during the 2012 fighting. Also on July 8, the Israelis thwarted a militant incursion from the sea. On July 13, Israeli forces briefly entered Gaza, raiding a missile launch site. Two days later, Israel accepted an Egyptian proposal for a cease-fire. The plan called for a halt in hostilities, the opening of border crossings once the security situation was stable, and high-level talks among those involved. Hamas's military wing of the Qassam Brigades dismissed any talk of a cease-fire. While Israel halted its operations for six hours, Hamas continued launching rockets. Hamas leaders claimed that they had not been consulted regarding the talks, and in any case the cease-fire did not address their demands for greater freedom of access for Gaza's 1.8 million residents.

On July 17, a United Nations (UN) five-hour cease-fire went into effect, to which both sides agreed, in order to permit humanitarian assistance into Gaza. Shortly before its start, the Israeli military foiled an attempt by 13 Hamas militants trying to enter the southern Israeli community of Sufa through a tunnel.

Despite the Israeli death toll having been kept to a handful because of the rockets' relative inaccuracy, a network of air raid sirens and shelters in Israel, and the Iron Dome rocket interceptor's 90 percent success rate, Prime Minister Benjamin Netanyahu was under increasing pressure to do something about the unrelenting rocket fire from Gaza, with more than 1,500 rockets having been launched into Israel since the beginning of fighting and with 10 days of air strikes and artillery fire having failed to end. Diplomatic efforts to secure a cease-fire involving, among others, Egypt, Qatar, France and the UN, all had failed. Hamas claimed that any deal had to include an end to a blockade of the coastal area and a commitment to the cease-fire reached after the 2012 Gaza War.

Therefore, at 10:00 p.m. on July 17, Israeli forces began a ground offensive in Gaza. The Israeli goal was to destroy both Hamas's rocket-firing abilities and the tunnels used by the militants to infiltrate Israel. This was undertaken with the realization that it would no doubt produce heavier civilian casualties in Gaza as well as Israeli military losses and would also bring international criticism of Israel. Although the Israeli forces called on Gaza residents to evacuate targeted areas, with both the Israeli and Egyptian borders sealed off, there was really no place for the 1.8 million Gaza residents to go.

On July 24, more than 10,000 Palestinians in the West Bank demonstrated against the Israeli operation in Gaza; 2 Palestinian protesters died. On July 25, an Israeli air strike killed Salah Abu Hassanein, leader of Islamic Jihad's military wing. On July 26 the Israeli cabinet agreed to a UN request to extend a cease-fire begun at 8:00 a.m. local time, for 12 hours, on condition that its military could keep dismantling and destroying Hamas's tunnels. Hamas rejected this idea, saying it would not tolerate the presence of Israeli troops on its territory. Gaza militants then fired mortars and launched rockets into Israel late on July 26 and early on July 27. By this date the death toll in Gaza had exceeded 1,000.

On August 1, the latest attempt at a cease-fire, brokered by the UN and scheduled to last 72 hours, collapsed shortly after it was to begin amid accusations that Palestinian militants had killed two Israeli soldiers in a group working to destroy a tunnel at Rafah. The Israeli military resumed shelling of what have been described as militant strongholds in Gaza. The cease-fire had lasted only about 90 minutes.

On August 3, Israel pulled most of its forces from Gaza after having destroyed 32 tunnels into Israel. Two days later, Israel announced that all its forces had been withdrawn, and a 72-hour humanitarian cease-fire began, with negotiations for a longer-lasting cease-fire to take place in Cairo, Egypt. Hamas demanded the opening of border crossings into Egypt and Israel, while Israel wanted Gaza completely demilitarized.

On August 7, fighting resumed after the expiration of the three-day cease-fire and deadlock in talks brokered by Egypt. Hamas then launched 21 rockets into Israel, and after a three-hour delay, Israel resumed air strikes. Hamas, which had seen its popularity rise in Gaza for confronting Israel, nonetheless entered the Cairo talks from a point of military weakness after having lost hundreds of fighters and 2,300 of its estimated arsenal of 3,000 rockets and its attack tunnels into Israel having been destroyed.

On August 11 a new cease-fire went into effect, to last for three days in order to allow humanitarian assistance into

Gaza and permit another round of indirect negotiations in Cairo between Israeli and Palestinian officials. It also collapsed, with Hamas launching dozens of rockets and Israel responding with air strikes.

On August 20 Saleh al-Arouri, a Hamas official in exile in Turkey, claimed responsibility for the kidnapping and murder of the Israeli teenagers. He said that the goal was to begin an intifada in the West Bank and Jerusalem. Hamas leaders claimed that they did not know of this in advance but claimed that the killings were justified as a legitimate action against Israelis on "occupied lands."

Finally, on August 26 after more than seven weeks of fighting, Israel and Hamas announced a cease-fire agreement brokered by Egypt. Unlike previous cease-fires in the conflict, this one has no expiration date. While the cease-fire does not deal with core long-term issues, Israel agreed to ease the blockade on Gaza, open border crossings for more aid to pass through, and extend the fishing limit off the coast to six miles. Both sides agreed to return to Cairo for further talks. Hamas, as it has after every battle with Israel, declared victory. But Israeli officials say that the deal was one that Hamas had repeatedly rejected earlier.

The fighting had claimed the most civilian deaths in the Israeli-Palestinian conflict since the 1967 Six-Day War. Some 2,200 Gazans were killed (a reported 70 percent of them civilians, including 513 children), and as many as 11,100 were wounded. A total of 66 Israeli soldiers and 6 civilians in Israel were also killed, while 469 Israeli military personnel and 261 civilians were injured. Perhaps half a million Gaza citizens were displaced, with some 17,200 homes in Gaza totally destroyed or severely damaged and 37,650 suffering damage. Officials in Gaza estimated that reconstruction would cost some $7.8 billion, with Gaza's gross domestic product only $2.4 billion in 2011. Peace between Israel and the Palestinians appeared more elusive than ever.

SPENCER C. TUCKER

See also
Gaza Strip; Gaza War of 2012; Hamas; Israel

References
Al-Mughrabi, Nidal, and Ari Rabinovitch. "Gaza Ceasefire Takes Hold as Focus Turns to Longer Term." *Reuters*, August 25, 2014.
Culzac, Natasha. "Israel-Gaza Crisis: Reconstruction of Flattened Gaza Will Cost £5 Billion, Palestinian Officials Say." *The Independent*, September 5, 2014.
Kershner, Isabel, and Fares Akram. "Israeli Strike Destroys Apartment Tower in Gaza." *New York Times*, August 23, 2014.
Raghavan, Sudarsan, and William Booth. "Airstrikes, Rocket Launches Continue after Gaza Truce Crumbles." *Washington Post*, August 9, 2014.
Yourish, Karen, and Josh Keller. "The Toll in Gaza and Israel, Day by Day." *New Times*, August 15, 2014.

General Treaty of Peace (1820)

First major diplomatic agreement, also known as the General Maritime Treaty, between the tribal states of what Europeans called the Pirate Coast (southwestern Persian Gulf) and Great Britain. The British authorities were concerned about warfare and piracy in the southern Persian Gulf region (modern-day day Abu Dhabi, Sharjah, Ajman, Umm al-Quwain, and Bahrain) that disrupted maritime trade and pearling. In 1819, Captain T. Perronet Thompson arrived at Ra's al-Khayman with a mission of negotiating with local Arab tribes. On January 8 and March 15, 1820, he negotiated and signed an accord that outlawed piracy on land and sea and required tribesmen to end the slave trade.

The signing of this treaty laid the foundation for more active British involvement in affairs of the southern Persian Gulf. New accords were negotiated in 1835 and 1843, while in 1853 Britain's political resident in the Persian Gulf Colonel A. B. Kemball concluded the Treaty of Perpetual Maritime Peace with the five ruling sheikhs of Abu Dhabi, Dubai, Ajman, Sharjah and Ra's al-Khayman, and Umm al-Qaywayn, who agreed to abide by a total maritime truce in perpetuity; thereafter the area of the Persian Gulf states became known as the Trucial Coast.

ALEXANDER MIKABERIDZE

See also
United Arab Emirates

References
'Anani, Ahmad, and Ken Whittingham. *The Early History of the Gulf Arabs*. New York: Longman, 1986.
Zahlan, Rosemarie Said. *The Making of the Modern Gulf States: Kuwait, Bahrain, Qatar, the United Arab Emirates and Oman*. London: Unwin Hyman, 1988.

Geneva Accord (December 1, 2003)

Peace agreement negotiated extragovernmentally between the Israelis and Palestinians and designed to jump-start the ongoing Middle East peace process and address long-standing roadblocks to an Israeli-Palestinian rapprochement. The Geneva Accord was formally signed on December

1, 2003. It is considered an informal agreement because the negotiations that gave birth to it were not conducted through the official channels of the Israeli government or the Palestinian Authority (PA). While negotiators on both sides had held high-level posts in their respective governments, they were not acting at the specific behest of those governments.

On the Israeli side, the prime mover and negotiator of the Geneva Accord was Yossi Beilin, a leftist politician, former justice minister, and Labor Party member. Beilin had been one of the chief negotiators of the 1993 Oslo Accords and at the time had the backing of Israeli foreign minister Shimon Peres. Beilin had been involved in the Palestinian-Israeli peace process for a number of years, although he had been recently defeated in elections. For the Palestinians, the principal architect of the agreement was Yasser Abed Rabbo, a member of the Palestine National Union and a minister in several PA cabinets. Most recently, he had served as minister of information. Seen as a moderate, propeace Palestinian, Rabbo took part in the failed Camp David Summit in 2000 and is thought to have had Chairman Yasser Arafat's implicit backing as he negotiated the Geneva Accord.

The accord agreed to the creation of a completely independent Palestinian nation to be located largely in the West Bank and the Gaza Strip. In return, the Palestinians were to officially recognize the State of Israel and Jewish claims to the lands that they would subsequently inhabit. All other land claims would be abandoned. The Palestinians would also have to agree to cease and desist from all forms of violence against Israel, including terrorist attacks. Furthermore, all armed groups with ties to the Palestinians that were not officially recognized would have to be disarmed and disbanded. Israel would be expected to submit to an International Commission that would oversee the settlement of Palestinian refugees within its boundaries. The commission would also establish a formula that would govern the number of refugees to be settled in Israel. Beyond that, Palestinians would waive the right of return for others of their refugees. On the perennially thorny issue of the disposition of Jerusalem, the accord called for the city to be divided, with much of East Jerusalem going to the Palestinians.

Under the terms of the Geneva Accord, the Palestinians would receive most of the territory captured by Israel in the 1967 Six-Day War. Israel would annex several areas, including Gush Etzion and Maale Adumim. Jewish settlers in Hebron and Ariel would be obliged to move into officially recognized Israeli territory.

The agreement was not particularly well received in Israel. The Israeli government, led by the Likud Party, refused to support any part of it. The Labor Party did not reject it but also would not support it. Indeed, Labor has remained officially silent on the issue, which is hardly a ringing endorsement. The accord received much play in the Israeli press, but it is believed that public support for it has never exceeded much more than 30 percent.

A number of Palestinian politicians and professionals embraced the basic tenets of the pact, for it went a considerable way in addressing long-standing Palestinian demands. However, the fact that it was informal and nonimplementable and was opposed in Israel limited any broad discussion or enthusiasm for the Geneva Accord among other Palestinians.

PAUL G. PIERPAOLI JR.

See also
Arafat, Yasser; Expellees and Refugees, Palestinian; Gaza Strip; Oslo Accords; Palestinian National Authority; West Bank

References
Lerner, Michael. *The Geneva Accord and Other Strategies for Healing the Israeli-Palestinian Conflict.* Berkeley, CA: North Atlantic Books, 2004.
Tilley, Virginia Q. *The One-State Solution: A Breakthrough for Peace in the Israeli-Palestinian Deadlock.* Ann Arbor: University of Michigan Press, 2005.
Watson, Geoffrey R. *The Oslo Accords: International Law and the Israeli-Palestinian Peace Agreements.* New York: Oxford University Press, 2000.

Geneva Peace Conference (December 21, 1973–January 9, 1974)

Meeting held in Geneva, Switzerland, from December 21, 1973, to January 9, 1974, that was designed to foster peace negotiations between Israel and its Arab neighbors. Occurring in the immediate aftermath of the October 1973 Yom Kippur War, the Geneva Conference was officially sanctioned by the United Nations (UN) and was presided over by UN secretary-general Kurt Waldheim. More specifically, the Geneva Conference was designed to help implement UN Resolution 338 (passed in October 1973) and UN Resolution 242 (passed in November 1967). Indeed, in a closed-door session on December 15, 1973, UN Security Council members met to officially sanction the Geneva Conference, passing Resolution 344 that formally pledged UN support of the peace talks.

Participants included the foreign ministers of Egypt, Jordan, Israel, the United States, and the Soviet Union. Syria had been asked to join the conference but declined because the Palestine Liberation Organization (PLO) had not been invited. At the time the PLO's official position was the destruction of Israel, and therefore neither the Israelis nor the Americans would contemplate meeting with anyone representing the PLO. From the start the conference was rife with tension, and without any official representation from the Palestinians, the likelihood of reaching an agreement was dim indeed.

Throughout the talks the Israeli and Arab ministers would not address one another directly, leaving Waldheim, the Americans, and the Soviets in the awkward position of playing brokers among them. Be that as it may, it was the first time that high-level officials from the Soviet Union, the United States, Arab states, and Israel had gathered around the same table. Almost no progress was made on any issue, and by early January the conferees were ready to depart. Interestingly, the 1973 Geneva Conference did produce the foundation of ongoing talks between the Egyptians and Americans, which culminated in the Camp David Accords of 1978 and the Israel-Egypt Peace Treaty of 1979.

PAUL G. PIERPAOLI JR.

See also
Camp David Accords; Israel-Egypt Peace Treaty; Palestine Liberation Organization; Yom Kippur War

References
Allen, Peter. *The Kom Kippur War*. New York: Scribner, 1982.
Herzog, Chaim. *The Arab-Israeli Wars: War and Peace in the Middle East from the War of Independence to Lebanon*. Westminster, MD: Random House, 1984.

Geography of the Middle East

Although some scholars identify the Middle East in cultural terms to include those countries embracing Islam, the Middle East is generally delineated by geography and consists of those countries of Southwest Asia east of the Mediterranean and Red Seas and west of Afghanistan and Pakistan. In the past, Europeans had often designated the region between the eastern Mediterranean and the Persian Gulf as Asia Minor, the Orient, and the Levant. The first usage of the term "Middle East" can be traced to British maps of the 1850s for the purposes of differentiating the region from the Far East, which is defined as the areas east of India. In 1902, American naval strategist Alfred Thayer Mahan brought the term "Middle East" into prominence in his discussion of the geopolitical challenges of the early 20th century. After World War I, the British designated their forces in the regions of Mesopotamia and Egypt as the Middle Eastern Command, and during World War II the British General Headquarters in the Middle East included Egypt and North Africa. The generalization "Middle East and North Africa" has since been accepted in many works on geography.

There are no standard generalizations of what countries constitute the Middle East. The countries most associated with the Middle East are Bahrain, Egypt, Iran, Iraq, Israel (and the areas constituting the Palestinian Authority), Jordan, Kuwait, Lebanon, Oman, Qatar, Saudi Arabia, Syria, Turkey, Cyprus, the United Arab Emirates, and Yemen.

However, the Maghreb nations of Morocco, Algeria, and Tunisia as well as Libya, Sudan, and Somalia on the Horn of Africa, Afghanistan in Central Asia, and Pakistan in South Asia are sometimes included because of historical and cultural connections. While much of the Middle East is Arabic in language and ethnicity, Cyprus, Israel, Iran, and Turkey are not. Similarly, Cyprus and Israel are not Islamic. With the dissolution of the Soviet Union in 1991, the emergence of Armenia, Georgia, and Azerbaijan in the Caucasus and Kazakhstan, Kyrgyzstan, Tajikistan, Turkmenistan, and Uzbekistan in Central Asia has renewed the challenge of defining the Middle East. For the purposes herein required, the bulk of the discussion will focus on the first grouping of nations.

Contrary to popular belief, the Middle East and North Africa have a great deal of geographic diversity. The Middle East can be classified into two distinct geographical areas: a mountainous northern zone running through Turkey, Iran, and Afghanistan and a southern zone that consists of plains, dissected plateaus, and deserts.

It is mostly in the northern zone of the Middle East where the largest mountain ranges can be found. As a result of the convergence of the Turkish, African, Arabian, Iranian, and African plates, there are high mountain ranges in Turkey, Iran, and the Maghreb. The Taurus Mountains in southern Turkey rise to more than 13,000 feet. The Elburz Mountains stretch along northern Iran, and their highest peak, Mount Damavand, is nearly 18,400 feet high. The Zagros range stretches along western Iran and reaches a height of 13,000 feet.

The southern zone consists of the area along the Tigris-Euphrates River Valley, the Arabian Peninsula, the Red Sea, and the Nile River Valley. This area is marked by deserts such as the Rub-al-Khali in the Arabian Peninsula, the Libyan Desert in North Africa, and the Negev Desert in Israel. Yet it contains very fertile areas along the Nile and the Tigris-Euphrates River Valley. This area can be divided further into an east-west axis along the Red Sea and the Suez Canal. These plateaus are also surrounded by elevated areas, such as the Red Sea Hills in eastern Egypt, the Asir Mountains in the southwestern corner of the Arabian Peninsula, and the uplands along the coast of the eastern Mediterranean Sea. The Yemen Highlands in the southern Arabian Peninsula average about 12,000 feet in height, while Mount Hermon in Syria is more than 9,800 feet in height. In North Africa, the Atlas Mountains rise to about 13,000 feet. This range straddles Morocco and Algeria.

Because much of the climate is arid, obtaining water is crucial to the survival of the Middle East. There are two types of rivers that provide water to the Middle East. One type of river that is common, particularly in Arabia and North Africa, is the wadi, a ravine that contains a watercourse. The wadi is dry for much of the year but fills with water during the rainy season. The more familiar rivers are the permanent ones that provide water on a continual basis. The major river systems such as the Nile, Tigris, and Euphrates provide irrigation and drinking water to many people in the Middle East. The rivers of the Middle East are fed by the snow that falls in the mountains during the winter months. The rivers of the Middle East are at their highest levels between November and February and at their lowest during the hot summer months. The Nile, however, is the only exception, as it floods during the late summer and early autumn after the heavy summer monsoon rains and again during the spring.

The first of the great rivers in the Middle East is the Nile. It is thus no understatement that the Greek historian Herodotus referred to Egypt as the "Gift of the Nile." The Nile stretches 4,132 miles from two sources, the White Nile in Burundi and the Blue Nile in Ethiopia, and flows out to the Mediterranean Sea. The Nile has made possible the flourishing of Egyptian civilization for millennia through its annual flooding, which serves to fertilize the soil with its alluvial deposits.

The Tigris and the Euphrates are other great rivers of the Middle East, and they too have figured prominently in the rise of civilization. Both rivers originate in Asia Minor. The Tigris flows for 1,150 miles, while the Euphrates is 1,700 miles long. Both rivers wind along an easterly course on the Anatolian Peninsula. The Euphrates heads southward through Syria and the Kurdish areas of northern Iraq before flowing on a southeasterly course toward the Persian Gulf and is fed by two tributaries, the Balikh and the Khabur, that flow southward from Turkey to Syria. The Tigris flows along the Zagros Mountains before moving southward toward the Persian Gulf. It is also fed by many lesser tributaries, such as the Great and Lesser Zab, the Diyala, and the Karun. Unlike the Nile's steady and predictable rate of flooding, the Tigris and the Euphrates are subject to fast-moving and destructive floods.

There are other smaller rivers across the Middle East that are no less crucial in providing water to the region. The Jordan River, for example, has several sources, such as the Yarmuk and the Zarqa, in southern Lebanon and Syria. The Jordan flows about 200 miles from north to south into Lake Tiberias, also known as the Sea of Galilee and Lake Kinneret. The Jordan descends about 65 miles into the Ghor Valley and then descends several thousand feet in elevation before ultimately flowing into the Dead Sea.

The Middle East has played a pivotal role in the events of the 20th and early 21st centuries. Key to the significance of the modern Middle East in world politics has been the role of oil. This development began in 1901 when William Knox D'Arcy gained a concession from Persia (Iran) to drill for oil. Throughout the 20th century, the Middle East has figured prominently in international diplomacy as the source of about 40 percent of the petroleum produced for the United States, Europe, and Japan, which account for about 70 percent of its consumers. As of 2002, Saudi Arabia leads the Middle East in producing approximately 9 million barrels of oil per day. Iran comes in second, producing nearly 4 million barrels of oil per day. The United Arab Emirates produces 2.5 million barrels of oil per day, while Kuwait comes close at 2.2 million barrels of oil per day. Algeria, Iran, Iraq, Kuwait, Libya, Qatar, Saudi Arabia, and the United Arab Emirates make up the majority of countries in the Organization of Petroleum Exporting Countries (OPEC).

It is hardly surprising that oil would be used as a political weapon by Middle Eastern countries. In 1973, OPEC imposed an embargo on the United States, the Netherlands, Portugal, South Africa, and Rhodesia because of their support for Israel during the Yom Kippur War. This embargo altered the economic arrangements of the post–World War II period. Indeed, it signaled the end of American independence over its energy policies, reminded the industrial world of its dependence on Middle Eastern oil, and triggered a drastic increase in oil prices. In 1979, the Islamic Revolution in Iran toppled the pro-Western Mohammad Reza Shah Pahlavi, who was a key ally in the Middle East. The resultant anti-American regime in Iran deprived the United States of the world's second-largest oil reserve.

When Iraq invaded Kuwait in August 1990, the United States and its European and Japanese allies forged an international coalition to prevent both Kuwait and Saudi Arabia from falling into the hands of Iraqi dictator Saddam Hussein. In the aftermath of the terrorist attacks on the United

States on September 11, 2001, and the 2003 Iraq War, oil refineries in the Middle East have become vulnerable to sabotage, which would disrupt the regular flow of oil to the United States and Europe.

As with any region, the Middle East has a unique ecosystem that has been altered by the presence of humans. Throughout the 20th century, several species of large mammals, such as lions and tigers, have become extinct. In 1900 the crocodile became extinct, as did the ostrich in the 1930s. Only the ruggedness of the mountains in the northern Middle East and the aridity of the southern Middle East have protected species of gazelle, deer, mountain sheep and goats, wild boar, and the oryx. In the aftermath of the 1991 Persian Gulf War, the diverse plants and animals along the Persian Gulf were severely threatened because of the destruction of Kuwaiti oil fields by the retreating armies of Hussein. The Middle East in previous times had been subject to locust plagues, and only recently has the problem abated.

Water has also been an issue of national security for the nations of the Middle East. Nations that fall along large river systems such as the Nile, the Tigris, and the Euphrates have serious disputes over the allocation of water for irrigation and the pressures of exploding populations. For example, Egypt's Aswan High Dam, completed in 1971, provides hydroelectric power and generates 1.8 million kilowatts for Egypt. This output of energy, however, comes at a high price. As a result of the construction of the dam, the rich alluvial sediment that floods the Nile River Valley annually is trapped behind it, leaving the banks of the lower Nile less fertile than before. Additionally, Sudan and Ethiopia have plans for the development of dams farther upstream. This has raised tensions among the three countries because new dams would drastically threaten the flow of water to Egypt, the strongest power in the basin. The construction of dams along the Tigris and the Euphrates has caused tensions among Turkey, Syria, and Iraq for much the same reasons.

Even within the nations of the Middle East, the need for water has created stresses for the expanding needs of the people. Aside from rivers, aquifers are another source of drinking water. There are seven major groundwater basins in the Middle East. Three of them are found in the Arabian Peninsula, and four are in North Africa, including minor basins in Sinai and Jordan.

An exploding population and increasing water usage have exacerbated the general scarcity of water in the region, particularly in Egypt, Cyprus, Jordan, Palestine, Israel, and the Arabian Peninsula. As a whole, the Middle East devotes 70 percent of its water to agricultural production. In addition to human consumption, climactic changes have accelerated the evaporation rate of water in the region. For centuries, the peoples of the Middle East have improvised in devising methods to extract water through channels or wells. In recent times, water conservation and improved agricultural techniques have become important in addressing the balance between a growing population and a sustainable supply of water.

The geography and topography of the region in which the various Arab-Israeli wars have unfolded have clearly played a role in war strategy. The wide-open deserts, plains, and plateaus have left ground troops and equipment vulnerable to fire from the air and from high ground. By the same token, the level ground has also facilitated tank warfare and has given the advantage to the army with the best mobility (usually Israel's). The heat and aridity of the deserts have also shaped the way in which wars have been fought.

Dino E. Buenviaje

See also
Climate of the Middle East

References
Anderson, Ewan W. *The Middle East: Geography and Geopolitics.* London: Routledge, 2000.
Beck, John A. *The Land of Milk and Honey: An Introduction to the Geography of Israel.* St. Louis: Concordia, 2006.
Drysdale, Alasdair, and Gerald H. Blake. *The Middle East and North Africa: A Political Geography.* New York: Oxford University Press, 1985.
Fisher, W. B. *The Middle East: A Physical, Social, and Regional Geography.* 6th ed. London: Methuen, 1978.
Held, Colbert C. *Middle East Patterns: Places, Peoples, and Politics.* Boulder, CO: Westview, 1994.
Kemp, Geoffrey, and Robert E. Harkavy. *Strategic Geography and the Changing Middle East.* Washington, DC: Brookings Institution Press, 1997.
Melamid, Alexander. *Oil and the Economic Geography of the Middle East and North Africa.* Princeton, NJ: Darwin, 1991.
Orni, Ephraim. *Geography of Israel.* Philadelphia: Jewish Publication Society of America, 1977.

Georgian-Seljuk Wars (11th–13th centuries)

In 1064, Sultan Alp Arslan led the first successful Seljuk invasion of southern regions of Georgia, capturing the fortress of Akhalkalaki. In response, in 1067 the Georgians raided Arran. This provoked Seljuk sultan Alp Arslan's second invasion of Georgia in 1068. During the course of a six-week campaign, Alp Aralan successfully campaigned in central and central western Georgia, capturing a series of fortresses. With Georgian king Bagrat having rejected his demand for tribute, the sultan left Georgia in the fall of 1068. Following his departure, Bagrat raided Ganja, whose ruler recognized the Seljuk sovereignty, thereby recovering some territories lost previously to Alp Arslan.

The great Seljuk victory over the Byzantines in the crucial Battle of Manzikert in 1071 opened the way for their systematic invasion of southern Caucasia. Georgian king Giorgi II gained an important victory over the Seljuks, led by Sarang of Ganja, at Partskhisi in 1074 and even captured the strategic Seljuk fortress of Kars, triggering a Seljuk punitive expedition under Amir Ahmad, who defeated the Georgians at Kvelistsikhe.

The so-called Great Turkish Onslaught (*didi turkoba*) began in Georgia in 1080, when Seljuk tribes arrived in large numbers to settle on Georgian lands and turned the occupied territory into pastures. King Giorgi was forced to recognize Seljuk supremacy and pay tribute to the sultan.

Seljuk domination of Georgia continued unchecked for almost a decade during which the country was devastated by invasions, internal dissent, and natural disasters. In 1089, a bloodless coup d'état forced King Giorgi to abdicate in favor of his 16-year-old son David IV (r. 1089–1125), who began an active campaign against the Seljuks. In 1092 following the death of Malik Shah, King David ceased the payment of annual tribute to the Seljuks and during the next decade gradually liberated most of eastern Georgia, defeating Seljuk invasions in 1105, 1110, and 1116. To strengthen his army, King David launched a major military reform in 1118–1120 and resettled some 40,000 Qipchak families of approximately 200,000 people from the northern Caucasus steppes to Georgia. Recruiting 1 soldier per each family, David raised a 45,000-man strong standing Qipchak army to supplement the regular Georgian feudal troops.

Beginning in 1120, King David began a more aggressive policy of expansion. He established contact with the Christian crusaders in the Holy Land, and there is evidence that the two sides sought to coordinate their military action against the Muslims. In 1121, King David achieved his greatest military victory when the Georgian army routed a massive Muslim coalition in the Didgori Valley, near Tbilisi. The battle, widely known in Georgia as the *dzlevai sakvirveli* (incredible victory), is considered an apogee of Georgian military history. Following this triumph, in 1122 King David captured Tbilisi, the last Muslim enclave remaining from the Arab occupation, and declared it the capital of the Kingdom of Georgia. In 1123–1124, Georgian armies were victorious in neighboring territories of Armenia, Shirwan, and northern Caucasus, greatly expanding the Georgian sphere of influence. By the time of King David IV's death in 1125, Georgia had become one of the most powerful states in all of the Near East.

King Giorgi III (r. 1156–1184) initiated a new wave of Georgian expansion as Georgian armies seized the former Armenian capital of Ani in 1161 and conquered Shirwan in 1167. His daughter, Queen Tamar, continued his successful foreign policy. In 1195 a large Muslim coalition was crushed in the battle at Shamkhor, and another one was crushed at Basian in 1203. The Georgians annexed Arran and Duin in 1203, and in 1209 their armies captured the Emirate of Kars, while the powerful Armen-Shahs, the emirs of Erzurum and Erzinjan, and the north Caucasian tribes became the vassals. Georgian influence also extended to the southern coastline of the Black Sea, where the Empire of Trebizond, a Georgian vassal state, was established in 1204.

Georgia invaded Azerbaijan and northern Persia in 1208–1210, marking the summit of Georgian power. Georgia now controlled a vast territory stretching from the Black Sea to the Caspian Sea and from the Caucasus Mountains to Lake Van.

ALEXANDER MIKABERIDZE

See also
Alp Arslan; Basian, Battle of; Manzikert, Battle of

References
Melikishvili, Giorgi, ed. *Sakartvelos istoriis narkvevebi,* Vol. 3. Tbilisi: Sabchota Sakartvelo, 1970.
Suny, Ronald Grigor. *The Making of the Georgian Nation.* Bloomington: Indiana University Press, 1994.

Ghazi

Term derived from the Arabic word *ghazw* (*razzia*), which means a raid or expedition to gain plunder. The pre-Islamic Arabs conducted raids against one another mainly, but not exclusively, to secure camels. During the lifetime of Prophet Muhammad, the expeditions that he led against his polytheist enemies were called *ghazawat* (sing. *ghazwa*). After Islam spread beyond Arabia, the *ghazi* ideology and concept became an integral part of the concept of holy war (jihad). Thus, *ghazis* became those warriors who operated along the frontiers of the Muslim world and carried out raids against infidels. For example, there were bands of *ghazi* warriors who operated in Transoxania and Khurasan during the Samanid period, and over 20,000 *ghazis* joined Mahmud of Ghazna's army that invaded India.

This ideal was enthusiastically embraced by nomadic converts to Islam, such as the different Turkic tribes that slowly entered the Middle East from Central Asia. Hence, the Ottoman state, one of the greatest Islamic empires, was established through the *ghazi* ideal. Osman's West Anatolian principality began as a small frontier *ghazi* state and grew in both size and wealth through raiding and battling the Byzantines. Therefore, one of the attributes of the Ottoman sultan was that he was a *ghazi* warrior. Thus, it should come as no surprise that several distinguished rulers and generals of Muslim principalities and empires took *ghazi* as a title of honor and prestige.

The *ghazi* concept espoused the ideal of holy war against the nonbelievers and expanded the territories ruled by Islam. It was also a means to defend the Muslims from outside threats by maintaining the offensive against them. Finally, it also aimed at maintaining unity among Muslims and the control of the rulers (whether they were Rashidun caliphs, Samanid princes, or Ottoman sultans) over their warlike subjects.

ADAM ALI

See also
Jihad; Sharia

References
Kennedy, Hugh. *The Prophet and the Age of the Caliphates: The Islamic Near East from the Sixth to the Eleventh Century*. 2nd ed. Harlow: Longman, 2004.
Lapidus, Ira M. "Sultanates and Gunpowder Empires." In *The Oxford History of Islam*, ed. John Esposito. New York: Oxford University Press, 1999.

Ghulams

Arabic word meaning "servant," "boy," or "youth" and also refers to slave-soldiers. Islamic civilization had a different attitude toward slavery than that in Western Europe. Slaves were better treated and often had honorable status, slavery itself being based on an entirely different principle than in the Roman Empire, Byzantium, and Western Europe. Slaves played a minor role in agriculture and industry but became important as personal servants, administrative functionaries, and above all soldiers.

The slave-recruited soldier known as a *ghulam* or mamluk, who was to become so characteristic of medieval Islamic armies, first made a significant impact on Muslim military recruitment in the Abbasid Caliphate during the ninth century. Thereafter a slave could also reach the highest level in Islamic society, eventually including ruler. The military slave was normally freed either when his training was complete or when his first owner or commander died. Furthermore, such military slaves were an elite group from the earliest days, the Turkic people being considered the best. Some were captured in raids, but a greater number probably resulted from a tribal chief selling his own people or when oversized families sold their own children. Indeed, the career opportunities open to a skillful mamluk or *ghulam* and the higher standards of living in the medieval Middle East meant that there was often little resistance to being taken as a mamluk among the Turks of Central Asia.

During the 9th and 10th centuries, those who entered the service of the Abbasid caliphs themselves were generally supplied with Turkic wives, usually of slave origin, and were theoretically forbidden to interbreed with other ethnic groups in an effort ensure the continuation of Turkic fighting capabilities. The mamluk system continued throughout the medieval period. In its fully developed form, a *khawajah* (slave merchant) was the potential recruit's first master within the Islamic world. He assessed an individual's potential and brought suitable candidates to a military slave market such as that in the Citadel of Cairo. The price of these recruits varied considerably, but by the 15th century it averaged around 50 to 70 dinar gold coins. By comparison, a good warhorse cost from 15 to 17 dinars during a similar period.

Mamluks of slave origin were now not only the military elite but also the ruling elite. The best career opportunities were again open to those young slaves purchased by a ruler. These *kuttubs* were sent to a *tabaqah* school for religious, literary, and military education. Discipline was strict, but at the end of his training each *kuttub* received his *itaqah* (certificate of freedom), a uniform, a horse, bows, arrows, quivers, armor, and several swords.

Evidence suggests that at least during the late 13th century when the system reached its peak in Egypt and Syria, the existing systems of training led to attitudes of leadership and loyalty comparable to those expected of a graduate from a modern military academy. For example, the losses suffered by professional Muslim troops during the final siege of crusader-held Acre in 1291 reveal a proportion of 2 officers killed for every 13 men, a considerably higher ratio than the overall proportion of officers to men. Even during the decline of the 15th century, most mamluks in Egypt and Syria still went through these military schools, though their training was now perfunctory.

The army of Safavid Iran was initially composed of tribal units or paid volunteers. However, during the late 16th and early 17th centuries, the most powerful of Safavid rulers, Shah Abbas I, increased the numbers of troops of largely Christian origin, captured or enslaved in various parts of the Caucasus. Having converted to Islam they served as *ghulaman-i khassa,* otherwise called *qullar.* These men, and in many cases their sons, played a significant role in the Safavid state as soldiers, occasionally as senior commanders, and as administrators.

The system survived well into the 19th century. From the 12th century onward other variations on the basic mamluk system evolved in Islamic northern India, Muslim Spain, and Portugal.

DAVID NICOLLE

See also
Abbas I the Great; Abbasid Caliphate; *Devshirme* System; Janissaries; Kapikulu Corps

References
Ayalon, D. "Aspects of the Mamluk Phoneomonon: The Importance of the Mamluk Institution." *Der Islam* 53 (1976): 196–225.
Bianquis, T. *Damas et la Syrie sous la Domination Fatimide (359–468/969–1076).* Damascus: Institut Français de Damas, 1986–1989.
Crone, P. *Slaves on Horses.* Cambridge: Cambridge University Press, 1980.
Lockhart, Laurence. *The Fall of the Safavī Dynasty and the Afghan Occupation of Persia.* Cambridge: Cambridge University Press, 1958.
Pipes, D. *Slave Soldiers and Islam: The Genesis of a Military System.* New Haven, CT: Yale University Press, 1981.

Giddi Pass

Strategic pass in the west-central Sinai Peninsula of Egypt. The Giddi (Jiddi) Pass lies approximately 25 miles east of the Suez Canal near the Little Bitter Lake. The Sinai features very rugged terrain. The southern portion is quite mountainous, confining most vehicle traffic to the coast. In the north, extensive sand dunes that extend in an arc from the Gulf of Suez to southwestern Israel also restrict travel. Transportation routes are somewhat better in central Sinai, which is dominated by the Tih Plateau. The plateau is separated from the sand dunes by several limestone massifs including Giddi Mountain (Jabal al-Jiddi). This north-south–oriented mountain, with peaks rising to 2,750 feet, poses a significant obstacle to east-west travel to and from the southern Suez Canal. Giddi Pass, which is located about 4.5 miles northwest of the highest peak, is one of the few routes between the Tih Plateau and the Suez Canal. The pass is about 18 miles long.

For centuries, people traveling east and west across the central Sinai Peninsula typically used the Darb al-Hajj (pilgrimage route) through Mitla Pass. During the 1956 Suez Crisis and the Sinai Campaign, Israeli forces ignored the Giddi Pass in favor of Mitla Pass to the south and Bir Gifgafah to the north. In the 1960s, however, the Egyptian government embarked on a Sinai road-building program that included the construction of a paved road through the Giddi Pass. Consequently, it became a strategic objective during the 1967 Six-Day War and the 1973 Yom Kippur War.

On June 8, 1967, the fourth day of the Six-Day War, Israeli armored units defeated a force of some 30 Egyptian tanks and seized control of the Giddi Pass. By that time, Egyptian forces were withdrawing in disarray. Aside from one failed Egyptian counterattack, fighting ended at the Giddi Pass.

On October 6, 1973, Egyptian and Syria forces launched attacks against Israel to initiate the Yom Kippur War. Following a meticulous plan, Egyptian forces conducted a successful crossing of the Suez Canal and overran Israel's Bar-Lev Line. On October 14, however, the Egyptians launched a hastily planned offensive against Israeli forces near Giddi Mountain in hopes of diverting Israeli pressure from Syria. The Egyptian Third Army sent a blocking force against Israeli units at the Giddi Pass but made Mitla Pass its primary objective. The Egyptian offensive, one of history's largest tank battles, was a failure, and the Israelis seized the opportunity to launch successful counterattacks that continued until the cease-fire on October 28, 1973.

The Giddi Pass figured prominently in subsequent Egyptian-Israeli peace negotiations. The January 18, 1974, Sinai I agreement involved the withdrawal of Israeli forces from the Suez Canal east to a defensive line that included the Giddi Pass. Israeli forces withdrew from the Giddi Pass as part of the September 4, 1975, Sinai II agreement. That agreement stipulated that electronic sensors as well as human monitors would provide Israel with early warning of Egyptian military movements in the region. Successful international monitoring of the Giddi Pass contributed to the signing of an Egyptian-Israeli peace treaty on March 26, 1979.

CHUCK FAHRER

See also
Bar-Lev Line; Israel-Egypt Peace Treaty; Mitla Pass; Sinai Campaign of 1956; Sinai I and Sinai II Agreements; Sinai Peninsula; Six-Day War; Yom Kippur War

References
Greenwood, Ned H. *The Sinai: A Physical Geography.* Austin: University of Texas Press, 1997.

Herzog, Chaim. *The Arab-Israeli Wars: War and Peace in the Middle East from the War of Independence to Lebanon.* Westminster, MD: Random House, 1984.

Pollack, Kenneth M. *Arabs at War: Military Effectiveness, 1948–1991.* Lincoln: University of Nebraska Press, 2002.

Glubb, Sir John Bagot (1897–1986)

British Army officer and commander of the Arab Legion in Transjordan (present-day Jordan) during 1939–1956. Born on April 16, 1897, in Preston, Lancashire, England, John Glubb was the son of a British Army officer. Glubb was educated at Cheltenham College and the Royal Military Academy at Woolwich. In 1915 he entered the army as a second lieutenant in the Royal Engineers.

During World War I, Glubb served with the British Expeditionary Force (BEF) on the Western Front in France and was wounded three times, leaving him with a crooked jaw. He continued in British military service after the war and in 1920 was posted to Iraq, where he lived among Arab Bedouins and studied their culture. In the process, Glubb gained a strong command of the Arabic language and earned the respect and friendship of many Arabs. He also studied Ottoman political and military strategy. The knowledge he acquired proved to be of great benefit to his military operations in the Middle East.

The native police force that Glubb organized in the early 1920s played a large part in bringing order to Iraq. In 1926 he was seconded to Transjordan and became the administrative inspector for the Iraqi government. In 1930 he went to Transjordan as second-in-command of the Arab Legion. Organized in 1920, the Arab Legion was initially a small police force led by British officer Frederick Peake, a major general in the Jordanian Army known to Jordanians as Peake Pasha.

As second-in-command of the Arab Legion and a brigadier general in the Jordanian Army, Glubb became a close personal friend and trusted political adviser of Jordan's King Abdullah. Glubb organized an effective Bedouin desert patrol consisting of mobile detachments based at strategic desert forts and equipped with communications facilities. Within a few years he had managed to get the Bedouins to abandon their habit of raiding neighboring tribes.

When Peake retired in 1939, Glubb took command of the Arab Legion and made it the best-trained military force in the Arab world. During World War II he led attacks on pro-German leaders in Iraq as well as on the French Vichy regime in control of Lebanon and Syria. The Arab Legion's Mechanized Regiment provided notable service alongside British forces in the 1941 overthrow of Iraq's pro-Nazi Rashid Ali al-Gaylani regime. The British continued to subsidize the Arab Legion. Through World War II most of its officers were drawn from serving British officers.

For the duration of the war, the Arab Legion provided trained guards for the railways from Damascus to Cairo. By 1945 the Arab Legion numbered more than 8,000 men, including 37 British officers. At the conclusion of the war the Arab Legion was downsized to 4,500 men, however.

During the 1948–1949 Israeli War of Independence, Lieutenant General Glubb commanded the Arab Legion against Israel. Although the Arab Legion was the best-equipped and best-trained Arab army, it was relatively small compared to the Israeli forces. The Israeli government, which had been engaged in secret negotiations with King Abdullah, hoped that the Arab Legion would stay out of the war completely. Abdullah, however, ultimately decided that not joining the other Arab states would render untenable his position in the Arab world. After Israeli independence was declared on May 14, 1948, the armies of Egypt, Syria, Iraq, Lebanon, and Jordan invaded Israel. Israeli forces eventually prevailed, and Jordan signed an armistice with Israel on April 3, 1949.

On March 2, 1956, Jordan's King Hussein, bowing to pressure from Arab nationalists, dismissed Glubb as commander of the Arab Legion, which had then grown to a force of 20,000 men. Although Hussein maintained a cordial relationship with Glubb during and after his dismissal, the Jordanian king sought to placate Arab nationalists who claimed that he was under British control.

Returning to Britain, Glubb was knighted. He retired as a British Army lieutenant general. In retirement he wrote numerous books, including *A Soldier with the Arabs* (1957), *Britain and the Arabs* (1959), and *A Short History of the Arab Peoples* (1969). Known as Glubb Pasha, he lectured widely on Arab affairs. Glubb died on March 17, 1986, in Mayfield, East Sussex.

MICHAEL R. HALL

See also
Abdullah I; Arab Legion; Hussein ibn Talal, King of Jordan; Israeli War of Independence; Latrun, Battles of

References
Glubb, John Bagot. *Into Battle: A Soldier's Diary of the Great War.* London: Cassell, 1978.

Glubb, John Bagot. *The Middle East Crisis: A Personal Interpretation.* London: Hodder and Stoughton, 1969.

Glubb, John Bagot. *The Story of the Arab Legion.* London: Hodder and Stoughton, 1950.

Lunt, James D. *Glubb Pasha, a Biography: Lieutenant-General Sir John Bagot Glubb, Commander of the Arab Legion, 1939–1956.* London: W. Collins, 1984.
Royle, Trevor. *Glubb Pasha: The Life and Times of Sir John Bagot Glubb, Commander of the Arab Legion.* New York: Time-Warner Books, 1992.
Young, Peter. *The Arab Legion.* London: Osprey, 2002.

Godfrey of Bouillon (ca. 1060–1100)

One of the leaders of the First Crusade (1096–1099) and subsequently the first Frankish ruler of Jerusalem (1099–1100) following its capture from the Fatimids of Egypt.

Godfrey was born around 1060, the second son of Eustace II, count of Boulogne, and Ida of Bouillon. Since his elder brother Eustace III was intended to receive the paternal inheritance, Godfrey was groomed as heir to his childless maternal uncle, Godfrey III, duke of Lower Lotharingia, on whose death in 1076 he inherited the county of Verdun, the territory of Bouillon, other domains in the Ardennes region, Brabant, and the valley of the middle Meuse. However, the office of duke of Lower Lotharingia, which had been held by several of his ancestors, was withheld from him by Holy Roman emperor Henry IV (r. 1056–1106), who compensated him with the largely powerless office of margrave of Antwerp.

From the outset Godfrey's possession of his hereditary domains was disputed by rival claimants and other enemies. For most of the two decades following his accession, Godfrey was engaged in a relentless struggle to defend his inheritance, and although he was finally made duke of Lower Lotharingia by Henry IV in 1087, he was never able to exercise effective ducal authority.

Godfrey's decision to take part in the First Crusade was the occasion for the dissolution of his inheritance, since the disposal of his landed territories offered the most effective means of raising funds for the forthcoming expedition as well as presenting an opportunity to resolve outstanding disputes with his enemies. By the summer of 1096, he had sold his rights in the county of Verdun to the bishop of Verdun and mortgaged the territory of Bouillon to the bishop of Liège, while smaller domains were sold off or donated to the church.

Godfrey was accepted as leader by a large number of crusaders from Lower and Upper Lotharingia and northeastern France, including his younger brother Baldwin and many other kinsmen and allies. This army left Lotharingia in the middle of August 1096, marching up the Rhine and along the Danube, then through Hungary and the Balkans, arriving at Constantinople (modern-day Istanbul) in December 1096. There, like most of the other crusade leaders, Godfrey took an oath to Emperor Alexios I Komnenos in which he promised to restore to him any former Byzantine territories recaptured by the crusade. He received in return an imperial cash subsidy in the spring of 1097.

After crossing to Asia Minor, Godfrey's largely Lotharingian army was joined by many crusaders who had come east with other contingents, such as his elder brother, Count Eustace III of Boulogne, and numerous French and German crusaders from the "People's Crusades" defeated by the Turks in the autumn of 1096. In the course of the march from Nicaea (modern-day Iznik, Turkey) to northern Syria, Godfrey was recognized as an active commander who had generally good relations with the other leaders. During the winter of 1097–1098, he provided his brother Baldwin with troops and resources for the conquest of the territories of Edessa (modern-day Sanliurfa, Turkey) and Turbessel (modern-day Tellbasar Kalesi, Turkey); he was repaid by Baldwin in the form of money and supplies, and the duke's financial and logistic strength enabled him to maintain and attract the service of numerous crusaders in the course of the march to Palestine.

During the six-week siege of Jerusalem by the crusaders in June–July 1099, Godfrey and his men undertook the investment of the northeastern section of the walls but took up new positions facing the northwestern walls for the assault beginning on July 13. On July 15 he fought in a siege tower that the crusaders dragged up to the walls, and it was troops under his command who achieved the first breakthrough into the city the same day.

On July 27 Godfrey was chosen as ruler of Jerusalem by the leading members of the crusade in preference to Raymond of Saint-Gilles, count of Toulouse. To forestall objections by Raymond and others that it was sacrilegious for a king to be crowned in the city where Christ had worn a crown of thorns, Godfrey declined to adopt a royal title, taking that of prince (*princeps*) and defender of the Holy Sepulchre (*advocatus Sancti Sepulchri*). The territory under his control consisted of Jerusalem, Bethlehem, Hebron, and environs and the coast between Jaffa (modern-day Tel Aviv–Yafo, Israel) and Lydda (modern-day Lod, Israel).

The crusade armies successfully repulsed a Fatimid invasion at the Battle of Ascalon (August 12, 1099), but the subsequent return of the majority of crusaders to the West left

Jerusalem and Jaffa and defied Daibert and his ally Tancred until Baldwin I arrived from Edessa to take up his brother's inheritance.

Godfrey was buried in the Church of the Holy Sepulchre in Jerusalem. His distinction as first Frankish ruler of the liberated Holy Land, his death at a relatively early age, and his reputation for valor and personal piety combined to ensure that subsequent generations regarded Godfrey as the principal hero of the First Crusade. He was celebrated in literature, notably as the central figure of a whole series of epic poems in the Old French Crusade Cycle, with the legendary Swan Knight as his ancestor. He was also generally regarded as one of the three Christian members of the configuration of chivalric heroes known as the Nine Worthies. In Jewish folklore, by contrast, Godfrey acquired a largely undeserved reputation as a notorious persecutor of the Jews.

ALAN V. MURRAY

See also
Ascalon, Battle of; Alexios I Komnenos; Baldwin I of Jerusalem; Crusades in the Holy Land, Christian; Edessa, County of; Eustace III of Boulogne; Jerusalem, Crusader Siege of

References
Andressohn, John C. *The Ancestry and Life of Godfrey of Bouillon* Bloomington: Indiana University Publications, 1947.
Aubé, Pierre. *Godefroy de Bouillon.* Paris: Fayard, 1985.
Murray, Alan V. "The Army of Godfrey of Bouillon, 1096–1099: Structure and Dynamics of a Contingent on the First Crusade." *Revue Belge de Philologie et d'Histoire* 70 (1992): 301–329.
Murray, Alan V. *The Crusader Kingdom of Jerusalem: A Dynastic History, 1099–1125.* Oxford, UK: Prosopographica et Genealogica, 2000.
Murray, Alan V. "The Title of Godfrey of Bouillon as Ruler of Jerusalem." *Collegium Medievale* 3 (1990): 163–178.
Waeger, Gerhart. *Gottfried von Bouillon in der Historiographie.* Zürich, Switzerland: Fretz und Wasmuth, 1969.

Detail of a historiated initial "S" depicts Godfrey of Bouillon being installed as Lord of the city, from *Histoire d'Outremer* by William of Tyre, 15th century. During his short reign as ruler of Jerusalem (1099–1100), Godfrey defeated the Fatimids of Egypt in the Battle of Ascalon. (The British Library)

Godfrey with only around 300 knights and 2,000 foot soldiers to defend and expand the Christian-held territory. Looking to conquer the Fatimid cities of the coast, Godfrey came to an agreement with papal representative Daibert, archbishop of Pisa, who had arrived with a fleet in the autumn of 1099. In order to secure the services of the Pisan ships, Godfrey was obliged to accept Daibert as patriarch of Jerusalem in place of patriarch-elect Arnulf of Chocques (Christmas 1099).

The next year Daibert demanded sole possession of the cities of Jerusalem and Jaffa, a concession that would have reduced Godfrey to impotence, but the departure of the Pisan fleet in the spring of 1100 deprived Daibert of his principal bargaining counter. The relationship between the ecclesiastical and secular powers was still unresolved when Godfrey fell gravely ill in June 1100. On his death on July 18, Godfrey's household knights, led by Warner of Grez, seized control of

Gog and Magog

Apocalyptic term appearing in both the Hebrew Bible and the Christian New Testament as well as the Quran. Gog and Magog also appear in folklore. They are variously identified as supernatural beings, national groups, or even lands.

The first reference to Magog appears in the "Table of Nations" in Genesis 10:2, with Magog given as one of the sons of Japheth. The first reference to Gog and Magog together is in Ezekiel 38:2–3, where Yahweh (God) warns the prophet, "Son of man, set thy face against Gog the land of Magog, the chief prince of Meshech and Tubal, and prophesy against him.... Behold, I come against thee, O Gog, the chief prince of Meshech and Tubel." The same command is repeated at the beginning of Chapter 39, but there is no clear identification of either the ruler or his country. In Chapter 39:5–6, Gog is identified as being accompanied in his invasion of Israel by the nations of Persia, Ethiopia, Libya, and Gomer and the House of Thogorma.

Because of the sheer number of peoples identified by Ezekiel as taking part in the invasion of Israel, some have asserted that Gog is simply a generic figure for all of the enemies of Israel and that reference to it in the Apocalypse denotes the enemies of the church. The book of Revelation (20:7–8) reads "And when the thousand years are expired, Satan shall be loosed out of his prison, and shall go out to deceive the nations that are in the four quarters of the earth, Gog and Magog, to gather them to battle: the number of whom is as the sand of the sea." The Quran (21:96–97) makes reference to Gog and Magog being "let loose" and that at that time "the True Promise shall draw near."

Scholars have also endeavored to identify Gog historically. One possible source is the Lydian king known to the Greeks as Gyges and in Assyrian inscriptions as Gu-gu. Others say that Gog and Magog are two tribes and refer to the Khazar kingdom in the northern Caucasus and the Mongols. Apparently, Gog may also have been used in ancient Israel to identify any northern population. Throughout history there have been repeated claims that Gog and Magog represent particular peoples, including the Goths.

The phrase "Gog and Magog" has been used by some extremists in the Arab-Israeli conflict to justify the unjustifiable. Some have claimed that Ezekiel's prophesy of the invasion of Israel by a vast number of enemies refers to the present conflict in the Middle East in which the Islamic nations will all invade Israel and that this great conflict will see the rise of the Antichrist and end with the destruction of Israel's enemies by God himself. At the outbreak of World War II Avraham Stern, founder of the terrorist group Lehi, declared that the war was a struggle between Gog and Magog and that this justified increased violent action against the British Mandate for Palestine.

SPENCER C. TUCKER

See also
Bible; Quran

References
Berner, Douglas. *The Silence Is Broken: God Hooks Ezekiel's Gog and Magog.* London: Lulu, 2006.
The Catholic Encyclopedia, Vol. 6. New York: Robert Appleton, 1909.

Golan Heights

Strategically located plateau on the border between Israel, Lebanon, and Syria. Israel captured the Golan Heights from Syria during the 1967 Six-Day War and retook it during the 1973 Yom Kippur War. The Golan Heights is an area of great strategic importance for Israel, for it dominates the entire eastern Galilee. Any military force occupying the Golan Heights is well positioned to cut Israel in two. The Golan Heights is also within operational striking distance of Damascus, the Syrian capital, that lies directly to the northeast. Control of the Golan Heights also gives Israeli forces a geographic advantage over Hezbollah forces operating in southern Lebanon.

The Golan Heights forms part of the Holocene volcanic field that reaches almost to Damascus. The heights covers an area of some 775 square miles. To the west are steep rocky cliffs that fall 1,700 feet to the Jordan River and the Sea of Galilee. To the south is the Yarmouk River, to the north lies Lebanon, and to the east is a plain known as the Hawran. In addition to its strategic location, the Golan Heights is important as a water source.

The Syrian government continues to insist on the return of the Golan Heights as a precondition for normalizing relations with Israel, and bilateral peace talks on the highly volatile issue have been unsuccessful. Lebanon claims a small portion of the Golan Heights, known as the Shaba Farms, as part of its territory, a claim that Syria acknowledges.

Following World War I, the Golan Heights was included in the French Mandate for Syria, although in 1924 a small portion of the Golan Heights was designated as part of the British Mandate for Palestine. When Syria became independent in 1944 it secured control of the Golan Heights, which was known within that country as the Syrian Heights. A plateau and part of an ancient volcanic field, it was strategically important to Syria in part because of its water resources, a valuable and often rare commodity in the Middle East.

During 1944–1967, Syria maintained control of the Golan Heights. Following the Israeli War of Independence (1948–1949), Syria used the area as a staging base for attacks against Israeli farming settlements. These actions, along with Israel's retaliatory strikes, were in violation of the Israel-Syria Armistice Agreement that ended the war. Tensions between the two sides increased, and during the 1967 Six-Day War Israel successfully captured the Golan Heights on June 9–10. At the time, approximately 90 percent of the population (mostly Druze Syrians and Circassians) fled the area. They have not been permitted to return. Israel immediately began building Jewish settlements in the area, with the first settlement town of Merom established in July 1967.

Syria refused to make peace with Israel unless the Golan Heights was returned, and Israel continued building settlements in the area, with 12 towns already established there by 1970. Tensions escalated sharply with the surprise attack on Israel by Egypt and Syria that began the Yom Kippur War in 1973. Israel found itself having to fight on two fronts (the Sinai Peninsula and the Golan Heights) but decided to assume the operational defensive against Egypt while taking the offensive against the more serious threat to Israel itself posed by the Syrians in the north. Despite being severely outnumbered by Syrian armor (170 Israeli tanks faced 1,500 Syrian tanks), Israel was able to turn the tide of the war on the northern front on October 8. After Israeli forces pushed the Syrians back to the 1967 border, they continued to drive into Syria proper, reaching to within 25 miles of Damascus before they halted and shifted priority to the southern front against Egypt.

After the war, more than 1,000 United Nations (UN) peacekeeping troops were stationed on the Golan Heights to monitor the cease-fire. The Golan Heights remained under Israeli military administration until 1981, when legislation was passed subjecting the area to Israeli law and granting citizenship privileges to people living there. Although Israel did not use the word "annexation" in the legislation, much of the international community saw the move as such. The UN responded with Security Council Resolution 497, which held that "the Israeli decision to impose its laws, jurisdiction and administration in the occupied Syrian Golan Heights is null and void and without international legal effect." However, the UN also avoided calling the move an annexation.

Possession of the Golan Heights remains central to the ongoing crisis in the Middle East, and Syria has repeatedly refused to normalize relations with the Jewish state until the Golan Heights is returned to Syria. Syria demands a withdrawal of Israel to the 1948 armistice line, which extends Syrian territory to the shores of the Sea of Galilee. Syria claims that its demands are in keeping with UN Security Council Resolution 242 and Resolution 338, which call for Israel to withdraw from the territories it occupied during the 1967 war. During the 1999–2000 peace negotiations, Israel proposed returning most of the Golan Heights to Syria. However, Syria refused the offer on the grounds that this would be less than a complete fulfillment of UN resolutions.

Some 41,000 people lived in the Golan Heights in 2018. The population includes approximately 19,000 Druzes, 20,000 Jews (in 34 settlements), and 2,000 Muslims. Israel maintains that the Golan Heights is a strategically important buffer between Israel and Syria and that it is essential for Israeli security. The Israeli government has refused to enter into direct peace negotiations with Syria (previous talks were brokered by the United States) unless Syria agrees to end Hezbollah attacks launched against Israel from Lebanon.

Spencer C. Tucker

See also
Druzes; Hezbollah; Israel; Israeli War of Independence; Six-Day War; Syria; Yom Kippur War

References
Asher, Jerry, and Eric Hammel. *Duel for the Golan: The 100-Hour Battle That Saved Israel.* Pacifica, CA: Pacifica Press, 1987.
Dunstan, Simon. *Campaign 118: The Yom Kippur War, 1973; The Golan Heights.* Oxford, UK: Osprey, 2003.
Lerman, Hallie. *Crying for Imma: Battling for the Soul on the Golan Heights.* San Francisco: Night Vision, 1998.
Maar'i, Tayseer, and Usama Halabi. "Life under Occupation in the Golan Heights." *Journal of Palestine Studies* 22 (1992): 78–93.
Moaz, Moshe. *Syria and Israel: From War to Peacemaking.* Oxford: Oxford University Press, 1995.

Golden Horde–Ilkhanid Wars (1261–1323)

Following the Great Mongol Conquests and the death of Chinggis Khan, the Mongol Empire was divided among his sons. Juchi received the northwestern provinces where the Golden Horde was formed; this dominion was eventually divided among his sons, including Batu and Berke.

In the 1250s Hulegu, the son of Tolui (one of Chinggis Khan's sons), successfully campaigned in Persia and Iraq, where he established the Ilkhanate; the term "ilkhan" means "subordinate khan," highlighting the Ilkhan's deference to great khans. The relations between the Jochid rulers of the Golden Horde and the Ilkhans proved to be tense, particularly because of Berke's conversion to Islam. Hulegu's campaigns, which resulted in the destruction of the Abbasid Caliphate and considerable devastation in the Islamic realm, caused much resentment in Berke. Also, the Great Khan Mongke granted Hulegu lands in Azerbaijan that had previously been promised to Juchi by Chinggis Khan. This action naturally embittered Berke and eventually led to a rupture with Hulegu; some accounts indicate that those Jochid princes and their forces that supported Hulegu's invasion of Persia were later slaughtered on his orders. Berke sought an alliance with the Mamluk sultan Baybars, who had defeated Hulegu's troops at Ayn Jalut in 1260.

In 1261 as he was preparing to campaign against the Mamluks, Hulegu faced a series of raids by Berke Khan, which marked the first open confrontation among the Mongols. Hulegu's forces marched north and initially scored a victory over Berke's troops before suffering a major defeat on the Terek River in the Caucasus mountains. Despite leading eight major invasions across the Caucasus (in 1265, 1266–1267, 1279–1280, 1288, 1290, 1301, 1319, and 1335–1336), the Golden Horde was unable to defeat the Ilkhans or advance beyond the Caucasus. Yet this prolonged conflict also sapped resources of both states and, most importantly, diverted Ilkhanate attention from further expanding to defending its territory.

The threat of joint actions by the Golden Horde and the Egyptian Mamluks remained strong until the early 14th century and was resolved only in a peace treaty signed between the Mamluks and the Ilkhans in 1323. The rivalry between the Golden Horde and the Ilkhans all but ended with the former's collapse in the 1340s. In the 1380s, it was briefly revived following the rise of Khan Tokhtamish (Toqtamiš) of the Golden Horde, who challenged his former benefactor Timur over the control of southeastern Caucasia. The khan's invasion of Azerbaijan (1386) failed, and Timur's punitive expedition into the Golden Horde greatly contributed to the eventual fragmentation of this state.

ALEXANDER MIKABERIDZE

See also
Hulegu; Mamluk Sultanate

Reference
Jackson, Peter. "The Dissolution of the Mongol Empire." *Central Asiatic Journal* 22 (1978): 186–244.

Goltz, Wilhelm Leopold Colmar von der (1843–1916)

German (Prussian) and Ottoman field marshal. Born in Bielkenfeld, East Prussia (now Ivanovka, Poland), on August 12, 1843, Wilhelm Leopold Colmar von der Goltz was the second son of an impoverished former Prussian Army officer. Educated in a cadet school, Goltz joined the Prussian Army and was commissioned a lieutenant in 1861. He entered the Kriegsakademie in Berlin in 1864 and fought and was wounded in the Austro-Prussian War of 1866. In 1867 he was assigned to the Topographical Section of the Great General Staff in Berlin. During the Franco-Prussian War (1870–1871) he served on the Second Army staff but saw action in several battles.

Following assignment as a staff officer in an infantry division, Goltz was promoted to major in 1878, and during 1878–1883 he was an instructor in military history at the Kriegsakademie, where he wrote a number of studies that influenced a generation of Prussian officers. Goltz became the herald of modern peoples' war and the strategy of preemptive attack, resulting in a conflict with the Prussian military bureaucracy. Consequently, Goltz was doomed to remain second choice to anyone else. Realizing this, he applied for a transfer to the Ottoman Army, which the German Army was then training. Promoted to lieutenant colonel in 1883, he was ordered to Istanbul (Constantinople) as military adviser to the Ottoman Empire.

In Istanbul, the energetic Goltz helped reorganize, modernize, and train an army exhausted by mismanagement and the consequences of the 1877–1878 war against Russia. He remained in the Ottoman Empire from 1883 to 1895 and was promoted to colonel in 1887, to major general in 1891, and to lieutenant general in 1895.

In 1896 Goltz assumed command of the 5th Infantry Division at Frankfurt an der Oder. During 1898–1902 he was head of the Engineer Corps and inspector general of fortresses. Promoted to general of infantry in 1899, he angered some in Berlin by warning of an impending war with Great Britain. This helped bring his assignment to East Prussia as commander of the I Army Corps at Königsberg during 1902–1907. He had been touted as a possible successor to Field Marshal Alfred von Schlieffen as chief of staff of the army but instead remained in East Prussia. In 1908, Goltz was promoted to colonel general and appointed inspector general of the Sixth Army. He was promoted to field marshal in 1911 and retired in 1913.

When the Great War began in early August 1914, Goltz immediately pushed for his reactivation, and on August 23 he was appointed governor-general of occupied Belgium. When the Ottoman Empire entered the war on the German side that November, a month later Goltz returned to the empire as military adviser to the sultan. In April 1915 Goltz assumed command of the Ottoman First Army. In October Goltz, now 72 years old, was appointed commander of the Ottoman Sixth Army in Mesopotamia and proceeded to lay siege at the British garrison at Kut. After defeating relieving British forces, "Goltz-Pasha" died of spotted fever in Baghdad on April 16, 1916. The British surrendered Kut on April 22.

MARKUS PÖHLMANN AND SPENCER C. TUCKER

See also
Kut al-Amara, Siege of; Mesopotamian Theater, World War I; Ottoman Empire

References

Barker, A. J. *The Bastard War: The Mesopotamian Campaign of 1914–1918.* New York: Dial, 1967.

Herwig, Holger H. *The First World War: Germany and Austria-Hungary, 1914–1918.* New York: St. Martin's, 1997.

Teske, H. *Colmar Freiherr von der Goltz: Ein Kämpfer für den militärischen Fortschritt.* Göttingen: Musterschmidt, 1957.

Gordian III, Emperor (225–244)

Roman emperor (r. 238–244) and the grandson of Gordian I, Marcus Antonius Gordianus. Born on January 20, 225, Gordian was thus only 13 when he became emperor in 238. In 241 Gordian III married Furia Tranquillina, the daughter of his praetorian prefect Timesitheus. The following year Gordian III and Timesitheus embarked on a campaign against Sassanid Empire forces led by King Shapur I, who had invaded the Roman province of Mesopotamia. The Romans were victorious in the Battle of Resaena (Resaina) near present-day Ceylanpinar, Turkey, in 243. However, Gordian's father-in-law Timesitheus died in unclear circumstances, and without him the campaign floundered. The Roman forces were then defeated by Shapur in battle in early 244.

On February 11, 244, Gordian either died in battle or was murdered by his own soldiers or his new praetorian prefect, Philip Arabus, who became emperor Philip (r. 244–249). Gordian III was buried at Zaitha. The short reign of Gordian III is illustrative of the precarious position of boy emperors in the later Roman Empire, when emperors needed to be competent military leaders and were surrounded by ambitious generals.

Caillan Davenport and Spencer C. Tucker

See also

Roman-Sassanid Wars

References

Haegemans, K. *Imperial Authority and Dissent: The Roman Empire in AD 235–238.* Leuven: Peeters, 2010.

Potter, David S. *The Roman Empire at Bay: AD 180–395.* New York: Routledge, 2004.

Gouraud, Henri Joseph Eugène (1867–1946)

French Army general and high commissioner for Syria and commander of the French Army of the Levant (1919–1923). Born in Paris on November 17, 1867, Henri Joseph Eugène Gouraud was educated at home and at the Collège Stanislas de Paris. He graduated from L'École Spéciale Militaire de Saint-Cyr in 1890 and was commissioned in the Troupes de marine. Seeking an overseas posting, in 1894 he was assigned to the Sudan and took part in the French penetration to the mouth of the Niger. Promoted to captain in 1897, the next year he commanded the unit that captured West African nationalist leader Samory Touré, who opposed French rule. Promoted to commandant, at age 32 Gouraud was asked to organize the territory situated between Niger and Chad, and in 1900 he established the French post at Niamey.

In 1903 Gouraud was given charge of organizing the Chad, which then connected several French African territories. In 1907 he was named commissioner of Mauritania and promoted to colonel. There he led a campaign against Bedouin tribes who were threatening communication between Morocco and French West Africa. In 1910 Gouraud was assigned to Morocco, where he served under General of Division Louis Lyautey and commanded French forces in the Fez region. Promoted to general of brigade in June 1912, Gouraud commanded all French forces in western Morocco.

With the start of World War I, Gouraud returned to France in the winter of 1914–1915 as commander of the 10th Infantry Division in the Argonne. Promoted general of division in February 1915, he was wounded. In July he took command of the French expeditionary force at Gallipoli, where he was again wounded, this time severely, by an exploding shell, suffering two broken legs and losing his right arm to amputation.

Gouraud returned to active duty in December 1915 as commander of the Fourth Army in Champagne. In December 1916, he replaced Lyautey as resident general in Morocco until June 1917. Gouraud then returned to France to command the Fourth Army.

Gouraud played a key role in the Second Battle of the Marne (July 15–18, 1918). His successful defense against the German offensive here earned him the nickname "The Lion of Champagne."

The French and Americans then went on the offensive, and by the end of the war in November the Fourth Army had driven to the Meuse and retaken the historic city of Sedan. In December, Gouraud assumed charge of the French occupation of Alsace.

In 1916 the French and British governments had concluded the Sykes-Picot Agreement whereby they would, in the event of an Allied victory, partition much of the Ottoman Empire between their two countries. Under this arrangement, France received a mandate over Syria and Lebanon. Dispatched to Syria in November 1919 as commander of the French Army of the Levant, Gouraud encountered strong anti-French resistance led by Emir Faisal, leader of the Arab Revolt (1916–1918) against Ottoman rule, who had been promised an independent Arab kingdom by the British in return for his military assistance and was now king of Syria.

In early 1920 Gouraud's troops moved north to support French forces engaged in the Franco-Turkish War that were forced to withdraw by Turkish National Forces following the Battle of Marash (January 21–February 13, 1920), the opening battle of the Turkish War of Independence.

With French forces withdrawn to Syria, Gouraud was soon locked in combat with the forces of Faisal's short-lived kingdom of Syria. Gouraud decisively defeated Faisal in the Battle of Maysalun (July 24, 1920). The French then occupied Damascus and established firm control of Syria and Lebanon. Gouraud then reorganized these territories administratively and on September 1, 1920, announced creation of the State of Greater Lebanon. Gouraud was the French high commissioner in Syria and Lebanon, in effect the head of government.

Gouraud's administration in Syria borrowed much from his experience in Morocco under Lyautey. French control was secured by manipulating the various groups that made up the Syrian population. Thus, Gouraud created separate autonomous states for the Druze and Alawite communities, with the aim of dividing their interests from those of the Sunni majority. On June 23, 1921, Syrian nationalist Adham Khanjar carried out an unsuccessful effort to assassinate Gouraud. Gouraud also clashed with Druze leader Sultan al-Atrash who was, however, a staunch Syrian nationalist.

Returning to France, Gouraud was appointed military governor of Paris in 1924. He was also a member of the Conseil supérieur de la guerre until 1937. Guraud spent much of the remainder of his life editing his memoirs and died in Paris on September 16, 1946.

SPENCER C. TUCKER

See also
al-Atrash, Sultan; Alawites; Druzes; Mandates, League of Nations; Maysalun, Battle of; Sunni Islam; Sykes-Picot Agreement; Syria; Turkish-Armenian War

References
Gouraud, Henri. *Souvenirs d'un Africain.* 4 vols. Paris: Plon, 1939–1949.
Gouraud, Philippe. *Le General Henri Gouraud au Liban et en Syrie (1919–1923).* Paris: L'Harmattan, 1993.
Paluel-Marmont, Albert. *Le Général Gouraud.* Paris: Plon, 1937.

Granicus, Battle of the (May 334 BCE)

In 336 BCE the aristocrat Pausanias, a member of the king's bodyguard and reportedly also his former lover, assassinated Philip II, king of Macedon. Pausanias was almost immediately slain, and Philip's 20-year-old son Alexander III (356–323) succeeded to the throne.

Two years before, Philip had defeated the principal Greek city-states in the Battle of Chaeronea in 338 and made himself master of all Greece through the Hellenic League, an essential step prior to his planned great enterprise of invading and conquering the Persian Empire. On ascending the throne, Alexander quickly crushed a rebellion of the southern Greek city-states and mounted a short, successful operation against Macedon's northern neighbors. He then took up his father's plan to conquer the Persian Empire.

Leaving his trusted general Antipater and an army of 10,000 men to hold Macedonia and Greece, in the spring of 334 Alexander set out from Pella and marched by way of Thrace for the Hellespont (Dardanelles) at the head of an army of some 30,000 infantry and 5,000 cavalry. Among his forces were men from the Greek city-states. His army reached the Hellespont in just three weeks and crossed without Persian opposition. His fleet numbered only about 160 ships supplied by the allied Greeks. The Persian fleet included perhaps 400 Phoenician triremes, and its crews were far better trained, yet not a single Persian ship appeared.

Alexander instructed his men that there was to be no looting in what was now, he said, their land. The invaders soon received the submission of a number of Greek towns in Asia Minor. King Darius III was, however, gathering forces to oppose Alexander. Memnon, a Greek mercenary general in the Great King's employ, knew that Alexander was short of supplies and cash; he therefore favored a scorched-earth policy that would force Alexander to withdraw. At the same time, Darius should use his fleet to transport the army and invade Macedonia. Memnon also advised that the Persians should avoid a pitched battle at all costs. This wounded Persian pride and influenced Darius to reject the proffered advice.

The two armies met in May. The Persian force was approximately the same size as that of Alexander. It took up position on the east bank of the swift Granicus River in western Asia Minor. The Persians were strong in cavalry but weak in infantry, with perhaps as many as 6,000 Greek hoplite mercenaries. Memnon and the Greek mercenaries were in front, forming a solid spear-wall and supported by men with javelins. The Persian cavalry was on the flanks, to be employed as mounted infantry.

When Alexander's army arrived, Parmenio and the other Macedonian generals recognized the strength of the Persian position and counseled against an attack. The Greek infantry would have to cross the Granicus in column and would be vulnerable while they were struggling to re-form. The generals urged that as it was already late afternoon, they camp for the night. Alexander was determined to attack but eventually followed their advice.

That night, however, probably keeping his campfires burning to deceive the Persians, Alexander located a ford downstream and led his army across the river. The Persians discovered Alexander's deception the next morning. The bulk of the Macedonian army was already across the river and easily deflected a Persian assault. The rest of the army then crossed.

With Alexander having turned their position, the Persians and their Greek mercenaries were forced to fight in open country. Their left was on the river, their right anchored by foothills. The Persian cavalry was now in front, with the Greek mercenary infantry to the rear. Alexander placed the bulk of his Greek cavalry on the left flank, the heavy Macedonian infantry in the center, and the light Macedonian infantry, Paeonian light cavalry, and his own heavy cavalry (the Companions) on the right flank. Alexander was conspicuous in magnificent armor and shield with an extraordinary helmet with two white plumes. He stationed himself on the right wing, and the Persians therefore assumed that the attack would come from that quarter.

Alexander initiated the battle. Trumpets blared, and Alexander set off with the Companions in a great wedge formation aimed at the far left of the Persian line. This drew Persian cavalry off from the center, whereupon Alexander wheeled and led the Companions diagonally to his left, against the weakened Persian center. Although the Companions had to charge uphill, they pushed their way through a hole in the center of the Persian line. Alexander was in the thick of the fight as the Companions drove back the Persian cavalry, which finally broke.

Surrounded, the Greek mercenaries were mostly slaughtered. Alexander sent the 2,000 who surrendered to Macedonia in chains, probably to work in the mines. It would have made sense to have incorporated them into his own army, but Alexander intended to make an example of them for having fought against fellow Greeks.

Spencer C. Tucker

See also
Alexander III the Great; Alexander III's Invasion of the Persian Empire; Darius III

References
Green, Peter. *Alexander of Macedon, 356–323 B.C.: A Historical Biography.* Berkeley: University of California Press, 1991.
Hammond, N. G. L. *Alexander the Great: King, Commander, and Statesman.* 3rd ed. London: Bristol Classical, 1996.
Sekunda, Nick, and John Warry. *Alexander the Great: His Armies and Campaigns, 332–323 B.C.* London: Osprey, 1988.

Greco-Persian Wars (499–479 BCE)

Often simply called the Persian Wars, the Greco-Persian Wars of 499–479 BCE constitute one of the most important conflicts in all recorded history. They were fought between the Persian Achaemenid Empire and the Greek city-states and were the result of the expansion of Persian power. Then the world's mightiest empire, Persia was expanding westward and came into contact with the Greeks. The stage was set when in 547 BCE Persian king Cyrus II (Cyrus the Great, r. 559–530) conquered the Greek city-states that had been established in Ionia (the central coast of Anatolia in present-day Turkey). Cyrus then set up tyrants (rulers) over these.

In 499 the city-state of Hellenic Asia Minor rose in revolt against Persia. This Ionian Revolt of 499–493 is often given as the starting date of the Greco-Persian Wars, although other sources date the wars as starting in 492. During the Ionian Revolt, the mainland Greek city-states of Athens and Eretria provided support and even participated in the Greek capture and destruction of the Persian regional capital of Sardis in western Anatolia in 498.

Persian king Darius I (Darius the Great, r. 522–486) dispatched armies and secured Phoenician naval assistance and crushed the revolt in 493. Determined to protect his empire from further Greek revolts and from the interference of the mainland Greeks and also vowing to have revenge on Athens and Eretria, Darius now embarked on an effort to conquer all of Greece.

In 492 Darius dispatched his son-in-law Mardonius across the Hellespont (Dardanelles) at the head of a large fleet and army. The Persians subdued Thrace but suffered a check on the Macedonian border from a Thracian tribe. Meanwhile, the Persian fleet encountered a storm while rounding Mount Athos, and many of its ships were driven ashore and wrecked. Mardonius wisely returned to Persia, where Darius relieved him of command.

The next year, 491, as his shipyards turned out new vessels, Darius sent envoys to the Greek city-states demanding earth and water as symbols of vassalage. A number of the

Persian Empire, ca. 500 BCE

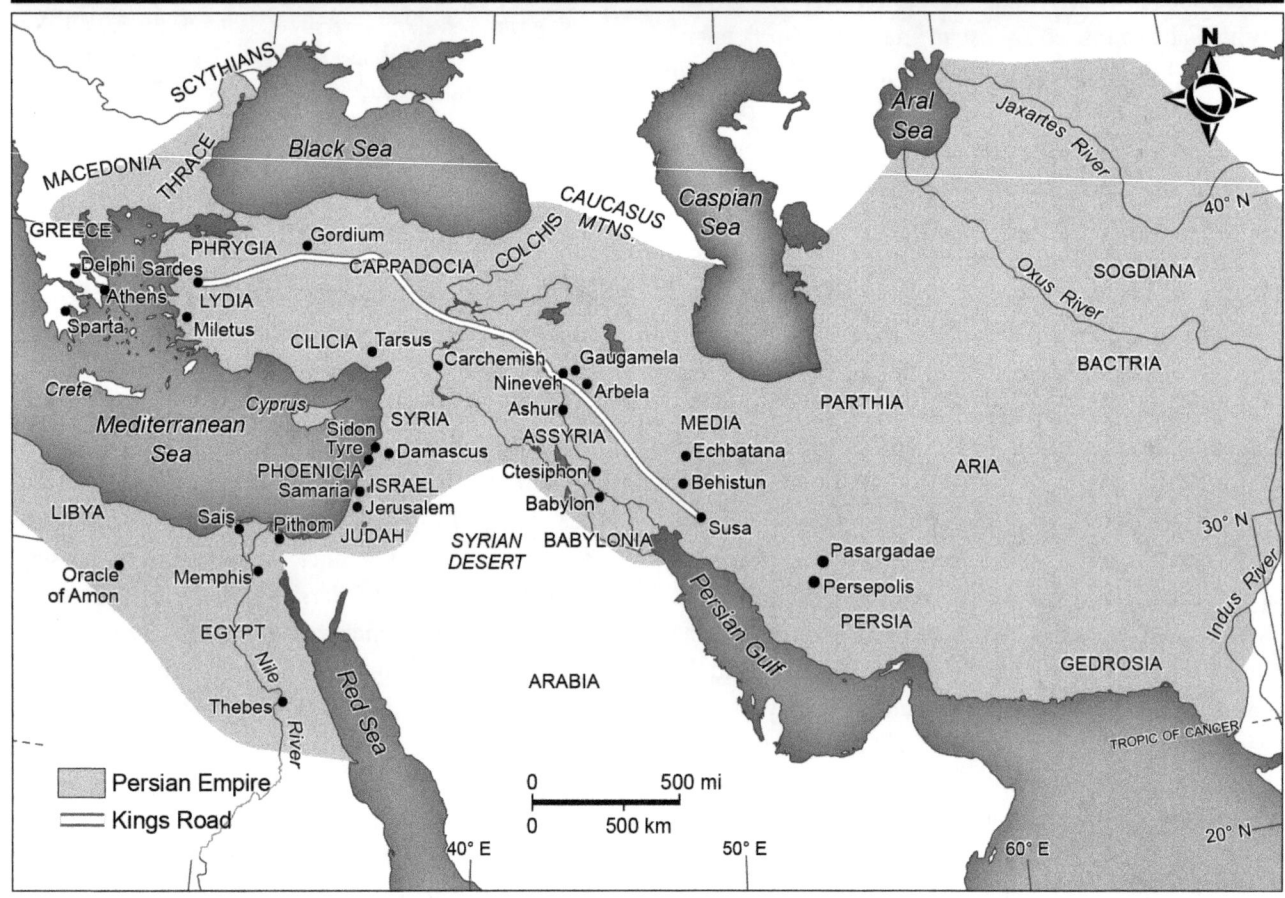

mainland cities, including most of those in northern Greece, submitted to the Persians, but not Athens or Sparta.

Darius launched his second invasion of Greece in 490. Command of the Persian forces went to his nephew, Artaphernes, and a Median noble, Datis. At Tarsus on the Cilician coast, the invasion fleet of some 200 triremes and 400 transports took on board perhaps as many as 25,000 infantry and 1,000 cavalry. The ships then proceeded to Ionia and west through the Cyclades islands.

The Persians captured and sacked Naxos, which had resisted capture a decade earlier. Then the fleet proceeded westward across the Aegean Sea from island to island, picking up conscripts and taking children as hostages. By the time they had landed on Euboea, the invaders numbered perhaps 80,000 men.

When Eretria on Euboea refused to surrender, the Persians destroyed the countryside and laid siege to the city. Eretria held out for a week until the defenders were betrayed from within the walls. In reprisal for Sardis, the Persians burned all the city's temples. The fleet then sailed westward and made landfall on the Greek mainland in the Bay of Marathon, some 26 miles northeast of Athens. The Persians selected this site because Hippias, who had been deposed as the tyrant of Athens in 510 and had fled to Persia and expected on a Persian victory to be installed as governor of all of Greece, told them that the plain there would allow them to employ their cavalry, in which they were overwhelmingly superior to the Greeks.

The Persians hoped by landing at Marathon to draw the Athenian Army away from Athens and destroy it or else hold the smaller Athenian force at Marathon while sending part of their army south to Athens by ship. Athens sent an appeal to Sparta. While the Spartan leaders agreed to assist, they refused to suspend a religious festival that would delay their army's march north until a week hence.

News of the fall of Eretria brought fierce debate in Athens. Some wanted simply to prepare for a siege, but others, including Miltiades, urged that the army be sent out to fight, and this view prevailed. Although the Greek force that reached Marathon numbered only some 11,000 hoplites (infantrymen), 10,000 from Athens and 1,000 from Little Plataea, the Greeks won the ensuing Battle of Marathon (August 12, 490 BCE).

Greece During the Persian Wars

Persian Campaigns Against Greece
- Route of fleet under Mardonius 492 BCE
- ---- Route of fleet under Datis 490 BCE
- .... Route of army under Xerxes 480 BCE
- —— Route of fleet under Xerxes 480 BCE

Legend: Ionian rebels, Greek allies, Neutral states, Persia

The Athenians could not pause to celebrate, for the Persian force dispatched to Athens by sea was then nearing the city. Leaving a small force to guard both prisoners and booty, the remainder of the Athenian Army marched to Athens and arrived just as the Persian fleet was approaching shore for a landing. Realizing they were too late, the Persians withdrew. The Spartans arrived several days later, praised the victors, and returned home.

The Greeks had won one of the important battles of history. The victory was not conclusive, but it did hold the Persians at bay for a decade. Marathon at least allowed the Greeks to imagine that they might triumph a second time.

The next year, 489, Athens sent Miltiades and 70 ships against islands that had assisted the Persians. Miltiades attacked Pardos in the Cyclades islands, but a monthlong siege was unsuccessful. This failure brought his ruin and imprisonment and the ascendancy of Themistocles, which would have wide repercussions for the second Persian invasion.

Following the defeat of his forces in Greece, during 486–485 Darius I began raising a new and far larger force. To pay for it he raised taxes, which brought a revolt in Persian-controlled Egypt in the winter of 486–485 that disrupted grain deliveries and diverted Persian military resources to restore order in that important province. Darius died in late 486. His son and successor, Xerxes, was temporarily distracted by the Egyptian revolt, but once it had been crushed he returned to the plans to invade Greece. Well aware of the Persian preparations, Athenian leader Themistocles took steps to meet the invasion, securing approval to increase the size of the Athenian Navy from 50 to 200 triremes.

When at last he set out on his planned expedition to Greece in 481, Xerxes commanded a considerable invasion force. Its exact size has been the subject of considerable debate. Modern reckoning puts it at perhaps 600 ships and perhaps 180,000 men. This was thus a Persian advantage of at least three to one on land and two to one at sea.

In the spring of 480 BCE, the Persian host reached the Hellespont. There Egyptian and Phoenician engineers had constructed a bridge across the straits that was among the most admired mechanical achievements of antiquity. The Persian forces then passed over the bridge and entered Europe.

The invaders soon occupied Thrace and Macedonia. The northern Greek states were completely intimidated. Surrendering to fear or bribery, they allowed their own troops to be added to those of Xerxes. Only Plataea and Thespiae in the north prepared to fight.

For once, Athens and Sparta worked together. Athens provided the principal naval force, while Sparta furnished the main contingent of land forces sent north against the Persians. The land force was commanded by Leonidas, one of the kings of Sparta. The Greek plan was for the land forces to hold the Persians just long enough for the Greek fleet to be victorious and force a Persian withdrawal.

Themistocles now led the Athenian fleet northward. Joined by other Greek vessels, it numbered 271 frontline ships. The Persian fleet had more than 650 ships. A severe storm reduced the Persian numbers to around 500 serviceable warships, but this was still a comfortable advantage. In August the Greeks met the Persians in a naval battle off the northern coast of Euboea at Artemisium (ca. August 30). The battle was inconclusive, although the Greeks did manage to capture some 30 Persian vessels.

While the Greek fleet was sailing northward to Artemisium, the allied Greek land force of about 4,000 men under Leonidas had marched northward and taken up position at the Pass of Thermopylae. Some 135 miles north of Athens, the pass was selected because there a small force would be able to hold off a much larger one. Three hundred Spartan men-at-arms formed the nucleus of Leonidas's force, accompanied by perhaps 900 helots.

The same day that the ships from the two sides clashed at Artemisium, Xerxes launched his first attack at Thermopylae. For several days the defenders held off the Persian attacks, only to have a traitor betray the secret of an indirect route over the mountains and then lead a Persian force by that approach and turn the Greek position. Learning that the defenders at Thermopylae were about to be cut off, Leonidas permitted the allied Greeks to withdraw. Seven hundred Thespians and 300 Thebans refused and remained with the Spartans. Virtually all were slain.

The Battle of Thermopylae, which is also said to have claimed two of Xerxes's younger brothers, had far more psychological than military importance. While some Greeks saw it as an excuse to ally with the Persians, others admired the Spartan example and redoubled their efforts to resist the invaders.

With news of the defeat at Thermopylae, Themistocles sailed southward with the remaining Greek triremes to Salamis in order to provide security for Athens. With no land barrier now remaining between that city and the Persian land force, the citizens fled, and when Xerxes arrived the Persians easily captured Athens after only symbolic resistance.

Xerxes now had to contend with the remaining Greek ships. He would either have to destroy them or leave behind a sufficiently large force to contain the Greek ships before he could invade the Peloponnese and bring an end to the Greek campaign. Everything suggested the former, for if he left the Greek force behind, his own ships would remain vulnerable to a Greek flanking attack. At the end of August the Persian fleet of something less than 500 ships arrived east of the Salamis Channel. Themistocles now added to his fleet the reserve ships from Salamis and triremes from other states, altogether about 100 additional ships. The combined Greek fleet that assembled at Salamis totaled about 310 ships.

Xerxes and his admirals did not want to engage the Greek fleet in the narrow waters of the Salamis Channel. Accounts differ, but some have the Persians attempting, for about two weeks in early September, to construct causeways across the channel at its narrowest point so that they might take Salamis without having to engage the Greek ships. As the island now contained most of the remaining Athenian population and government officials, the Persians reasoned logically that their capture would bring the fleet's surrender. Massed Greek archers, however, gave those attempting to build the causeways so much trouble that the Persians abandoned this plan.

The causeway effort having failed, Xerxes put part of his vast army in motion toward the Peloponnese, hoping to draw off the Greek ships of that region, enabling him to destroy what remained at his leisure. Failing that, Xerxes sought to do battle with the Greek ships in the open waters of the Saronic Gulf, where his superior numbers would be at advantage. If he had but waited, he might simply have starved Salamis into submission.

With the Greek captains then in an uproar and with every possibility that the Peloponnesian ships would leave the coalition, Themistocles sent a trusted slave to the Persians with a letter for Xerxes informing him that Themistocles had decided to change sides, that the Greeks were bitterly divided and would offer little resistance, and that elements of the fleet were intending to use the cover of darkness to sail away the next night in order to link up with Greek land forces defending the Peloponnese. The Persians could prevent this only by not letting the Greeks escape.

Xerxes took the bait and decided to attack, moving his ships into position that very night. The ensuing Battle of Salamis (ca. September 20) resulted in an overwhelming Greek victory. The remaining Persian ships withdrew that night, Xerxes having ordered them to protect the bridge at the Hellespont.

The Battle of Salamis marked the end of the year's campaign. Xerxes left two-thirds of his forces in garrison in central and northern Greece and marched the remainder back to Sardis. A large number of Persians died of pestilence and dysentery on the way.

A year after the Battle of Salamis, the remaining Persian forces in northern Greece again invaded Attica. Commanded by Mardonius, brother-in-law of Xerxes, they advanced from central Greece and again occupied Athens, burning most of its buildings and razing the rest. Sparta and some other Greek states, however, answered the Athenian appeal for assistance.

The Persian ground force numbered about 50,000 men, including 15,000 Greeks from northern and central Greece. The opposing Greek army, led by King Pausanias of Sparta, totaled about 40,000 men, including Athenians. The Persians also possessed more cavalry and archers.

The Greeks won the ensuing Battle of Plataea, fought near that city in Boeotia (ca. August 27, 479 BCE). Mardonius and his personal guard were among those slain in the wild Persian retreat. For all practical purposes, the Persian field army now ceased to exist.

In the Battle of Mycale (which according to Greek tradition also occurred on August 27, 479 BCE), the Greeks engaged the Persians near Samos. Informed that the Persians had detached their powerful Phoenician naval contingent, King Leotychidas of Sparta led a combined Greek fleet of some 250 triremes against about 100 Persian ships, which were drawn up on land behind a stockade and had significant Persian land force support. Despite being heavily outnumbered, Leotychidas decided to attack the Persians on land. Decoying the Persians from their prepared defenses, the Greeks won the hard-fought Battle of Mycale and burned the Persian ships. This brought to a close the Persian threat to conquer Greece.

The victory of little Greece in the Greco-Persian Wars was momentous for Western civilization, for it made Europe possible and victory allowed the continuation of Greek independence and the dissemination and flowering of Greek literature and the arts. The Greeks were now able to continue their great experiment in liberty, and their control of the sea enabled them to export ideas of freedom and democracy as well as goods throughout the Mediterranean world. Greece entered upon its golden age. There were also those Greeks who believed that one day Greece might actually conquer the Persian Empire. Unfortunately for Greece in the long run, however, the Greeks were never able to unify themselves. The city-states were fiercely independent, which was the seed of their fall. Soon they were dominated by Macedonia, then the Romans, and after them the Ottoman Turks. Greece did not win its independence from the Ottomans until the 1830s.

Spencer C. Tucker

See also
Cyrus II the Great; Darius I; Ionian Revolt; Xerxes I

References
Boardman, John, N. H. L. Hammond, D. M. Lewis, and M. Ostwald, eds. *The Cambridge Ancient History*, Vol. 4, P*ersia, Greece and the Western Mediterranean, c. 525 to 479 BC*. 2nd ed. Cambridge: Cambridge University Press, 1988.
Burn, A. R. *Persia and the Greeks: The Defense of the West, c. 546–478 BC*. Stanford, CA: Stanford University Press, 1984.
Green, Peter. *The Greco-Persian Wars*. Berkeley: University of California Press, 1996.
Herodotus. *The History of Herodotus*. Ed. Manuel Komroff. Translated by George Rawlinson. New York: Tudor Publishing, 1956.
Hignett, G. *Xerxes' Invasion of Greece*. Oxford, UK: Clarendon, 1963.
Holland, Tom. *Persian Fire: The First World Empire and the Battle for the West*. Preston, Lancashire, UK: Abacus, 2006.
Lazenby, J. F. *The Defence of Greece*. Oxford, UK: Aris and Phillips, 1993.
Sealey, Raphael. *A History of the Greek City States, ca. 700–338 B.C.* Berkeley: University of California Press, 1976.

Greco-Turkish War (1919–1922)

The Greco-Turkish War of 1919–1922 is known in Turkey as the Western Front of the Turkish War of Independence (fighting in the east was largely between Turks and Armenians and was known to the Turks as the Eastern Front). The Greeks know the war as the Asia Minor Campaign and the Asia Minor Catastrophe. The Greco-Turkish War was fought largely in Anatolia and was a direct result of the Ottoman Empire's participation and defeat in that war. When World War I began in 1914, there were perhaps 2.5 million Greek-speaking Orthodox Christians living in the Ottoman Empire.

In November 1914 the Ottoman Empire joined the Central Powers in World War I. Meanwhile, King Constantine of Greece, who favored the Central Powers, declared his country's neutrality. Greek premier Eleuthérios Venizélos strongly opposed the king's position and sought intervention on the Allied side in hopes of obtaining Greek-inhabited eastern Thrace, the islands of Imbros and Tenedos, and a good bit of western Anatolia around Smyrna (present-day Izmir).

When Venizélos began negotiations with the Allied side, Constantine dismissed him. Venizélos, however, set up an alternate Greek government under Allied protection, and well into the war in May 1917, British and French forces obliged Constantine to abdicate. Venizélos then secured a Greek declaration of war against the Ottoman Empire.

Defeated in the Middle East by British Empire and Arab forces, the Ottoman Empire left the war in the Armistice of Moudros (October 30, 1918). On November 15, 1918, Ottoman sultan Mehmed VI, who had succeeded to the throne only the month before on the death of Mehmed V, established a new government in Istanbul under the control of British and Greek forces. The British, French, and Italians set up a tripartite administration in Istanbul, placed troops along the Alexandretta-Smyrna-Constantinople railway, and encouraged the establishment of separate Greek and Armenian military forces.

Turkish nationalist resistance quickly developed opposing these Allied moves. This was headed by General Mustafa Kemal in Samsun and General Kazim Karabekir in Erzurum. With no other source of support available, the nationalists secured military aid from the new Bolshevik government of Russia, which also proved to be of diplomatic advantage in subsequent negotiations with the anti-Bolshevik British government.

On May 15, 1919, some 20,000 Greek troops occupied Smyrna. The Greek population there greeted the arriving troops as liberators, and Ottoman Empire forces put up little opposition to the Greek landings. However, a subsequent incident on May 19 led to major clashes between the Greeks and Turks and can be said to mark the beginning of the war. The fighting claimed the lives of 300–400 Turks and 100 Greeks. During late June 1920, 60,000 Greek Army troops began offensive operations to extend Greek control eastward, giving them control over much of western Anatolia as well as Adrianople in Thrace.

Meanwhile, on March 16, 1920, British troops had seized control of government offices in Istanbul and proceeded to set up a pro-Allied government, forcing it to sign on August 10 the harsh Treaty of Sèvres. Among other provisions, the treaty restricted Ottoman authority largely to Anatolia and gave the Allies control over the economy. The treaty also

Greek soldiers in August 1922 preparing to take the offensive during the Greco-Turkish War (1919–1922). (Topical Press Agency/Getty Images)

made the Kingdom of the Hejaz independent and allocated Smyrna and many Aegean islands to Greece. The Ottoman Empire was now on its last leg, with Turkish nationalists calling for the creation of a Turkish republic. The sultanate was abolished on November 1, 1922; the Republic of Turkey was established on October 29, 1923; and the Caliphate officially came to an end on March 3, 1924.

In October 1920, the Greek army renewed its advance eastward in Anatolia to pressure Kemal and the other Turkish nationalist leaders to sign the Treaty of Sèvres. The advancing Greeks were unable to administer a decisive defeat on the Turks, who withdrew in an orderly fashion. In early 1921, the Greek army resumed its advance but met stiff resistance from the entrenched Turks. On January 11, 1921, the Turkish forces halted the Greek advance in the First Battle of Inönü. On March 31, 1921, the Greeks began a new military offensive toward Ankara. The Turks halted this in the Second Battle of Inönü on March 30. In the east, Turkish nationalist forces also defeated the Armenians, reducing Armenia to the province of Erivan. The Turkish nationalists also concluded a treaty with the Bolsheviks of Russia delineating the border between their two countries and providing for additional military assistance to the nationalists. These developments certainly impacted Allied decision making and led to their meeting in London to consider amending the Treaty of Sèvres.

In early July 1921, the reinforced Greeks launched another major offensive against Turkish troops along the Afyon Karahisar–Kutahya–Eskişehir line. The Greeks broke through the Turkish defenses and occupied these strategically important cities but halted for a month to regroup and resupply. Kemal used this delay to retreat to the east of the Sakarya River and organize a 120-mile defensive line there, about 62 miles from Ankara. At this point, the French agreed to withdraw from Anatolia in return for economic concessions.

In early August 1921, the Greek Army advanced on the Turkish defenses. From August 23 to September 13, fighting seesawed back and forth. Then, the Greeks attempted to take Haymana, 25 miles south of Ankara, but the Turks held there. Exhausted and demoralized, the Greeks then withdraw to their lines of June before retreating to Smyrna.

In March 1922, the British allies tried to negotiate a ceasefire between the Greeks and Turks, but Kemal insisted on a Greek withdrawal from Anatolia. The Turks then went on the offensive on August 18, defeating the Greeks in the Battle of Dumlupinar near Afyon on August 30. On September 9 Turkish troops occupied Smyrna, and the remaining Greek forces withdrew to the coast and evacuated Anatolia. Turkish forces took control of Smyrna, and during September a great fire destroyed the Greek and Armenian portions of the city, resulting in the deaths of between 10,000 and 100,000 Greeks and Armenians, many of them refugees who had crowded into the city. Eyewitnesses blamed the Turks for deliberately setting the fires, but the Turks claimed that the Armenians and Greeks had lit the fires themselves in order to discredit the Turks.

In response to the Turkish advance toward Istanbul, British forces landed to protect the straits. Negotiations then commenced, with the Greeks agreeing to the Armistice of Mudanya on October 11, 1922. The opposing sides then opened negotiations in November. The Treaty of Lausanne was signed on July 24, 1923. It superceded the Treaty of Sèvres. Although the Turks agreed to cede all prewar non-Turkish territory in the Middle East and lost almost all the offshore islands in the Aegean and the Mediterranean, the Greeks departed Anatolia, and the Turks avoided any reparations as well as legal restrictions on their government.

The war had seen widespread atrocities committed by Greeks against Turks and by Turks against Greeks and Armenians. Tensions were such that a population exchange seemed to be the only practical solution. A treaty concluded by the two governments saw Greek orthodox citizens of Turkey and Turkish and Greek Muslim citizens residing in Greece subjected to a forced exchange. Some 1.5 million Orthodox Christians from Turkey and 500,000 Turks and Greek Muslims from Greece were uprooted from their homes.

The last British troops evacuated Istanbul on October 2, and the Republic of Turkey was formally established under the presidency of Kemal on October 29, 1923.

ROBERT B. KANE AND SPENCER C. TUCKER

See also
Ataturk, Mustafa Kemal; Lausanne, Second Treaty of; Sèvres, Treaty of; Turkey

References
Clogg, Richard. *A Short History of Modern Greece*. 2nd ed. Cambridge: Cambridge University Press, 1986.
Howard, Douglas A. *The History of Turkey*. Westport, CT: Greenwood, 2001.
Lewis, Bernard. *The Emergence of Modern Turkey*. London: Oxford University Press, 1961.
Shaw, Stanford J., and Ezul Kural Shaw. *History of the Ottoman Empire and Modern Turkey,* Vol. 2, *Reform, Reaction and Republic: The Rise of Modern Turkey, 1808–1975*. Cambridge: Cambridge University Press, 1977.

Green Line

The border of Israel prior to the June 1967 Six-Day War delineated as a result of the truce agreements that followed the 1948–1949 Israeli War of Independence. The Green Line, so named because it was drawn with green marker on the maps at the time, designated the area under Jewish control in Palestine.

The Green Line encompassed about 78 percent of Palestinian territory in 1947 before the Israeli War of Independence. Although it delineated a military boundary only, in effect the Green Line actually defined the de facto state borders between Israel and Egypt, Jordan, Syria, and Lebanon. The sole exception was the municipality of Jerusalem. Israel claimed as sovereign territory the parts of the city administered by Jordan until 1967.

Drawing of the Green Line was based almost exclusively on military considerations. As such, it wreaked havoc on a number of communities, dividing towns and villages and separating farmers from their fields. Jerusalem was especially impacted, being divided into West and East Jerusalem. The Jordanian city of Qalqilyah became virtually an enclave within Israel, while Kibbutz Ramat Rachel was left almost entirely outside of Israeli territory.

During the Six-Day War, Israel occupied sizable territories beyond the Green Line inhabited by perhaps 3 million Palestinians, including many displaced by the 1948–1949 war. The Green Line remains the administrative border for the West Bank territory acquired in the Six-Day War with the exception of East Jerusalem, which was annexed by Israel. In 1981 the Israeli government extended Israeli law to the Golan Heights, which had been taken from Syria in the 1967 war.

Spencer C. Tucker

See also
Israeli War of Independence; Israeli War of Independence, Truce Agreements; Six-Day War

References
Bornstein, Avram. *Crossing the Green Line between the West Bank and Israel.* Philadelphia: University of Pennsylvania Press, 2002.
Cottrell, Robert Charles, et al. *The Green Line: The Division of Palestine.* New York: Chelsea House, 2004.

Green Zone, Iraq

Highly fortified walled-off section of central Baghdad (Iraq), also know as the International Zone, that is the location of many of Iraq's government buildings. The Green Zone was established soon after the invasion of Iraq by U.S. and coalition forces in March 2003. It became the area in which most U.S. and coalition occupation authorities worked and lived. The Green Zone is approximately four square miles in land area.

The Green Zone is entirely surrounded by reinforced concrete walls capable of absorbing explosions from car and truck bombs, improvised explosive devices (IEDs), and suicide bombers. The walls are topped by barbed and concertina wire to foil anyone attempting to scale them. In areas where the likelihood of insurgent infiltration is high, the blast walls are supplemented by thick earthen berms. There are less than half a dozen entry and exit points into and out of the zone, all of which are manned around the clock by well-trained and well-armed civilian guards and military police. Beginning in 2006, Iraqi forces assumed the largest burden of protecting the Green Zone.

The Green Zone is home to many of Iraq's most important government buildings and ministries, including the Military Industry Ministry. The zone encompasses several presidential palaces and villas used by former president Saddam Hussein, his sons Uday and Qusay, and other Baath Party loyalists. The Republican Palace, the largest of Hussein's residences, is located there. Considered Hussein's principal base of power, it was akin to the White House for the U.S. president. For that reason, it was a key target for coalition forces as they moved into Iraq in 2003.

The zone includes several large markets, stores, shops, restaurants, several large hotels, and a convention center. Also found in the Green Zone are the former Baath Party headquarters, a military museum, and the Tomb of the Unknown Soldier. There is also an elaborate underground bunker constructed to shield key government officials during times of war.

Since the coalition invasion, the Green Zone has housed all the occupation officials' offices and residences. It is currently home to the Iraqi government. The vast majority of civilian contractors and independent security firm personnel are also located there. The American, British, Australian, and other international embassies and legations are located within the Green Zone.

Despite the elaborate security measures within the Green Zone, the area has been targeted on numerous occasions for attacks by truck bombs, suicide bombers with explosives-laden backpacks, and rockets and mortars. After measures were taken to further limit egress into the Green Zone, such incidents declined, although they were not entirely eliminated. Nevertheless, there were other attacks on the Green

Zone, including by rocket-propelled grenades (RPGs), IEDs, and even Katyusha rockets.

Some Iraqis and those in the international community have criticized the existence of the Green Zone because it entirely isolates occupation officials and Iraqi government officials from the grim and perilous realities of life in Iraq. Outside the Green Zone lies what has come to be called the Red Zone, an area into which occupation authorities rarely venture and lawlessness and chaos abound. Although occupation forces have been criticized for having established an artificial oasis in a worn-torn nation, the Green Zone will likely remain for some time, walled off from the remainder of Iraq unless or until violence perpetrated by insurgents and terrorists comes to an end.

PAUL G. PIERPAOLI JR.

See also
Hussein, Saddam; Iraq Insurgency

References
Chandrasekaran, Rajiv. *Imperial Life in the Emerald City: Inside Iraq's Green Zone.* New York: Viking Books, 2007.

Mowle, Thomas S., ed. *Hope Is Not a Plan: The War in Iraq from Inside the Green Zone.* Westport, CT: Praeger Publishers, 2007.

Grivas, Georgios (1898–1974)

Cypriot freedom fighter and Greek Army general. Born in Trikomo, Cyprus, on May 23, 1898, Georgios Grivas enrolled in the Royal Hellenic Military Academy in Athens in 1916 and participated in the Greco-Turkish War (1919–1922) following World War I. In 1925 he won a scholarship to the École de Tir and École d'Infanterie at Versailles, France.

Prior to World War II, Grivas served in various Greek Army units and lectured on tactics at the War School. He fought in the defense of Greece following the 1940 Italian invasion and during the German occupation established his own guerrilla group ("X"). After the end of the occupation in 1944 the group was disbanded, and Grivas rejoined the regular army, seeing duty during the civil war against the communists from 1946 to 1949.

Following the victory over the communists in the civil war, Grivas had several meetings with Greek Orthodox archbishop Makarios III on Cyprus to advance the cause of enosis, the union of Cyprus and Greece. In November 1954 Grivas moved back to Cyprus and fomented a violent campaign against the British occupation of the island. He also took the name "Dighenis," a legendary Byzantine hero, and organized the National Organization of Cypriot Fighters (EOKA), which had direct military support from Greece. The EOKA terrorist campaign commenced on April 1, 1955, and reached its climax during Makarios's exile in 1956. Grivas eluded capture on several occasions between December 1955 and May 1956. During the EOKA campaign 504 people died, including 142 Britons and 84 Turks. After the February 8, 1959, Greco-Turkish agreement on Cypriot independence, Grivas ordered a cease-fire. But his dream of enosis had yet to be realized.

Grivas returned to Greece in March 1959, welcomed as a national hero and decorated with the highest honors. Shortly thereafter he formed a political party, the Movement of National Regeneration. In 1964 he went to Cyprus as commander of the Greek Cypriot National Guard. He was recalled to Athens in November 1967. In 1971 he created the armed underground movement EOKA B to operate against the ruling Greek military junta but also his former ally, Makarios III, who now opposed a Greco-Cypriot union. Grivas was forced underground as he waged yet another guerrilla campaign, but he died on January 27, 1974, in Limassol, Cyprus. His supporters continued his efforts, staging a coup against Makarios in 1974. However, this brought not enosis but instead a Turkish invasion and partition of the island.

LUCIAN N. LEUSTEAN

See also
Cyprus; Cyprus, Ottoman Conquest of; Makarios III, Archbishop

References
Dodd, Clement Henry. *The Cyprus Imbroglio.* Huntington, Cambridgeshire, UK: Eothen, 1998.

Gibbons, Harry Scott. *The Genocide Files.* London: Charles Bravos, 1997.

Grivas, Georgios. *The Memoirs of General Grivas,* ed. Charley Foley. London: Longmans, 1964.

Gulf Cooperation Council

The Gulf Cooperation Council (GCC) was formed by Arab states on May 25, 1981, mainly as a counter to the threat posed from the Islamic Republic of Iran. At the time, Iran was in the early stages of its fundamentalist Islamic revolution and was involved in fighting Iraq in the Iran-Iraq War of 1980–1988. In general, the region's Arab nations eyed Iran with great suspicion and hoped to contain Islamic fundamentalism to that state.

The GCC is currently made up of six member states: Bahrain, Kuwait, Oman, Qatar, Saudi Arabia, and the United Arab Emirates (UAE). Among these countries the political systems, socioeconomic forces, and overall culture are quite similar, making cooperation among them relatively easy to achieve. Led by Saudi Arabia, together these states possess roughly half of the world's known oil reserves. The GCC's power therefore is principally economic, and its main goal is to boost the economic might of its members.

On the military side, the GCC established a collective defense force in 1984 (effective since 1986), sometimes called the Peninsula Shield, based in Saudi Arabia near King Khalid Military City at Hafar al-Batin and commanded by a Saudi military officer. Even before the mutual security pact was established, joint military maneuvers had been carried out since 1983. The Peninsula Shield comprises one infantry brigade and is currently estimated to be maintained at 7,000 troops. Oman's proposal to extend the force to 100,000 troops in 1991 was turned down. The force did not participate in the 1991 Persian Gulf War as a distinct unit. Through the GCC, military assistance has been extended to Bahrain and Oman, funded mostly by Kuwait and Saudi Arabia. Plans to integrate naval and ground radar systems and to create a combined air control and warning system based on Saudi AWACS aircraft have been repeatedly delayed until just recently.

While all GCC members agree in their desire to become more independent from U.S. security arrangements, they have yet to find consensus as to how this could best be achieved. This became a contentious issue during the conflict with Iraq in 1991, with some states, foremost Kuwait and Saudi Arabia, forming parts of the international coalition against Iraq, while others remained opposed to the action. Notably, in March 1991 just weeks after the Persian Gulf War ended, the GCC agreed—together with Egypt and Syria—to form a security alliance to protect Kuwait against renewed aggression.

Deep divisions also exist as to whether or how Iran, Iraq, and Yemen could be brought into the GCC. The same is true on the issue of political reforms. Militant Islam is seen as a significant threat by Saudi Arabia, while some other members would like to speed up liberalization of the political process, including the admittance of Islamic parties. Since 2004, the GCC countries also share intelligence in the fight against terror but to a limited extent. In November 2006 Saudi Arabia proposed expanding the GCC's military force, and by 2011 its military arm numbered about 40,000 troops.

The GCC's structure includes a Supreme Council, the highest decision-making body, composed of the heads of the six member states. Meetings are held annually; the presidency of the council rotates in alphabetical order. Decisions by the Supreme Council on substantive issues require unanimous approval. The council also appoints a secretary-general for a three-year term, renewable once. The secretary-general supervises the day-to-day affairs of the GCC. Since April 1, 2011 Abdullatif bin Rashid Al Zayani, a retired lieutenant general from Bahrain, has served as secretary-general. The Ministerial Council convenes every three months, proposes policies, and manages the implementation of GCC decisions. It is usually made up of the member states' foreign ministers. Should problems among member states arise, the Commission for the Settlement of Disputes meets on an ad hoc basis to seek a peaceful solution to disagreements. The Defense Planning Council also advises the GCC on military matters relating to its joint armed forces.

Following the uprising in Bahrain that began in February 2011, Saudi Arabia and the UAE sent ground troops into Bahrain. Kuwait and Oman refrained from participation with troops, although Kuwait did dispatch a naval unit. In 2011 the GCC also began the process of admitting Jordan and Morocco, and in 2013 the GCC also began to contemplate the admission of Yemen. In early 2014 Saudi Arabia, Bahrain, and the UAE all protested Qatar's support for the Muslim Brotherhood, and all three countries withdrew their ambassadors from Qatar in protest.

In September 2014, the GCC agreed to participate in a U.S.-led coalition designed to eradicate the Islamic State of Iraq and Syria (ISIS), which was threatening both of those nations. The GCC began air strikes that same month and pledged to aid anti-ISIS rebels within Syria and also agreed to permit the use of members' air bases by foreign air assets.

In a surprise move, on June 5, 2017, Saudi Arabia, Egypt, the United Arab Emirates, and Bahrain announced that they were severing ties with Qatar. This move dramatically escalated the sharp disagreement over Qatar's support of the Muslim Brotherhood. At the same time, however, the other four Arab states accused Doha of supporting regional archrival Iran by broadcasting radical Islamic propaganda over the Qatari state-run satellite television network Al Jazeera and encouraging Iranian-backed militants in Saudi Arabia's restive and largely Shiite Muslim-populated eastern region of Qatif and in Bahrain. The four states also cut off all transport ties with Qatar and gave its citizens within their countries two weeks to leave. Qatar was also expelled from the Saudi-led coalition fighting in Yemen.

The announcements came only 10 days after U.S. president Donald Trump visited Riyadh and called on Muslim countries to stand united against Islamist extremists. It seemed clear to many analysts that the Saudis and Emiratis felt emboldened by the alignment of their regional interests toward Iran and Islamic extremism with the Trump administration.

Oil prices rose after this news. Qatar is the biggest supplier of liquefied natural gas (LNG) and a major seller of condensate, a low-density liquid fuel and refining product derived from natural gas.

Then on June 23, 2017, Saudi Arabia, the United Arab Emirates, Bahrain, and Egypt sent Qatar a list of demands with a 10-day time frame to comply that sharply escalated what was already the worst crisis among the Persian Gulf states in years. The list includes a demand that Qatar shut down the Al Jazeera news network and affiliates, halt development of a Turkish military base in the country, reduce its diplomatic ties with Iran, cut all ties to extremist organizations, cease interfering in the four countries' affairs, and end the practice of extending Qatari nationality to citizens of the four countries.

THOMAS J. WEILER AND SPENCER C. TUCKER

See also
Bahrain; Iraq; Islamic State of Iraq and Syria; Kuwait; Muslim Brotherhood; Qatar; Saudi Arabia; United Arab Emirates

References
Dietl, Gulshan. *Through Two Wars and Beyond: A Study of the Gulf Cooperation Council.* New Delhi: Lancer Books, 1991.
Ramazani, Rouhollah K. *The Gulf Cooperation Council: Record and Analysis.* Charlottesville: University Press of Virginia, 1988.

Gulistan, Treaty of (October 24, 1813)

Treaty concluded between Persia and Russia in the village of Gulistan (modern-day Goranboy Rayon in Azerbaijan) on October 24, 1813, that ended the first full-scale Russo-Persian war of 1804–1813. Negotiations for the treaty were precipitated by the fall of Lankaran to Russian forces under General Pyotr Kotlyarevsky on January 1, 1813. British diplomat Sir Gore Ouseley, who was influential at the Persian court, acted as mediator. The treaty was signed by Nikolai Rtischev for Russia and Mirza Abolhassan Khan Ilchi for Persia.

The treaty served to confirm the Russian victory in the war and forced Persia to relinquish its claims to southern Caucasia. Persia lost all its territories north of the Aras River. This included Dagestan, all of Georgia, and parts of Armenia and Azerbaijan (Karabagh, Ganja, Shirvan, Baku, etc.). Persia also gave up its rights to navigate the Caspian Sea and granted Russia exclusive rights to maintain naval forces in that body of water as well as capitulatory rights in trade to Russia with Persia.

Russia in return promised to support Crown Prince Abbas Mirza as heir to the Persian throne after the death of Fath Ali Shah. The treaty served to establish a firm Russian presence in the southern Caucasus, which was further consolidated by the Treaty of Turkmanchai (1828) following another Russo-Iranian war during 1826–1828.

ALEXANDER MIKABERIDZE AND SPENCER C. TUCKER

See also
Russo-Persian Wars

Reference
Kazemzadeh, F. "Iranian Relations with Russia and the Soviet Union, to 1921." In *The Cambridge History of Iran.* Vol. 7. *From Nadir Shah to the Islamic Republic,* ed. Peter Avery et al., 314–350. Cambridge: Cambridge University Press, 1991.

Gulnabad, Battle of (March 8, 1772)

A decisive military engagement between Afghan forces and the Safavid Persian Army. By 1700, the Safavids had lost much of their sway in Afghanistan. In 1704 Safavid shah Sultan Husayn dispatched a Georgian-Persian army, led by Georgian king Giorgi XI (Gorgin Khan), to subdue the rebellious Afghani tribes. Gorgin Khan defeated and forced them to accept Safavid rule. However, his heavy-handed oppressive governorship in Afghanistan prompted an Afghani revolt in the spring of 1709, led by Ghilzai tribe chief Mir Vays (Mir Ways). The Afghans defeated the Georgian contingents and expelled the Persians from Afghanistan. The loss of many capable generals and elite troops left Persia exposed to future attacks that eventually culminated in the Afghan Invasion of 1722.

After the death of Mir Vays, his son Mahmud assumed the leadership of a loose coalition of Afghani tribes, and in 1722 he invaded Persia and faced the Safavid Army near Gulnabad on March 8, 1772. Accurate numbers are unknown for the two sides, but it is unlikely that Mahmud had more than 18,000 men, while the Persian forces were substantially larger: about 40,000 men with some two dozen artillery pieces, commanded by Frenchman Philippe Colombe. The Persians, however, failed to exploit their superiority and suffered from lack of unified command, as the army had been divided into several major components to avoid arousing jealousy among its proud commanders.

The battle began with a charge by the Persian right wing, commanded by the experienced Georgian general Rustam

Khan, head of the Safavid royal troops (*qullars*). He secured considerable success against the Ghilzai left wing and reduced Mahmud to a state of panic. But the Persians failed to coordinate their attacks. First, some 12,000 Arab cavalry that followed Rustam's charge stopped to sack the enemy camp instead of pressing the attack. Had the Persian center, under Vizier Muhamad Quli Khan, attacked at this time, the Afghans would have certainly lost the day. The vizier held back, however, allowing Mahmud to drive back Rustam Khan. When the Persian left wing, led by Ali Mardan Khan, finally attacked, the Afghans feigned flight and lured it onto their masked camel guns (*zanburaks*) that opened fire at point-blank range and devastated the Persian ranks. An Afghan cavalry charge then broke through them and wheeled on the rear of the Persian artillery, the crews of which were slaughtered. The rest of the Persian army, deployed in the center under the vizier's command, fled from the battlefield without even making contact with the enemy.

The decisive defeat at Gulnabad effectively marked the end of the Safavid Empire. The Afghans captured Isfahan after a six-months siege but proved unable to hold on to their Persian conquests. Their withdrawal created a political vacuum in Persia, prompting a long conflict among various pretenders to the throne.

ALEXANDER MIKABERIDZE

See also
Isfahan, Siege of; Persia, 18th-Century Wars of Succession

References
Lockhart, Laurence. *The Fall of the Safavi Dynasty and the Afghan Occupation of Persia*. Cambridge: Cambridge University Press, 1958.
Roemer, H. R. "The Safavid Period." In *The Cambridge History of Iran*, ed. W. Fisher, P. Jackson, and L. Lockhart, 189–351. Cambridge: Cambridge University Press, 2001.

Guy of Lusignan (ca. 1150–1194)

King of Jerusalem as consort to Queen Sibyl (1186–1192) and subsequently lord of Cyprus (1192–1194) after its conquest in the course of the Third Christian Crusade in the Holy Land (1189–1192).

Born around 1150, Guy was a son of Hugh VIII of Lusignan, a nobleman from Poitou in southern France. In 1180 Guy's brother Aimery, who had gone to the Holy Land in 1174, proposed Guy as a suitable husband for Sibyl, elder sister of Baldwin IV, king of Jerusalem. Baldwin wanted an ally in case Raymond III of Tripoli, Bohemund III of Antioch, and the Ibelin clan grew too powerful in Outremer. On his marriage Guy was made count of Jaffa (modern-day Tel Aviv–Yafo, Israel) and Ascalon (modern-day Tel Ashqelon, Israel). As a protégé of the king and the king's mother, Agnes of Courtenay, he became an enemy of the opposing faction (the side favored by the chronicler William of Tyre).

In 1183 Baldwin named Guy as his regent and handed over all Crown lands except Jerusalem. However, the two men very quickly quarreled over these lands and over Guy's battlefield performance. When Saladin invaded Galilee in October, Guy led forces out to meet him at Saforie but avoided battle. Baldwin IV then acted to prevent Guy from ruling, designating as heir his young nephew Baldwin V (Sibyl's son by her first husband, William of Montferrat). The king also tried to have his sister divorced in 1184 so that Guy could not serve as regent. Although this attempt failed, it deepened the breach between the king and his sister's family to the point that Guy and Sibyl refused to let Baldwin enter Ascalon. When Guy failed to appear at court that same year, Baldwin IV confiscated Jaffa. He then convened the High Court of the kingdom to make further arrangements for the regency of Baldwin V so that Guy could not even act as his stepson's guardian. Baldwin IV had effectively closed off all of Guy's avenues to power except failing to separate his sister from her husband.

After the deaths of Baldwin IV in 1185 and Baldwin V in 1186, the barons of Jerusalem turned to the king's sisters. Sibyl seized power with the help of Reynald of Châtillon, lord of Transjordan, and Eraclius, patriarch of Jerusalem. She agreed to a divorce from Guy and was crowned by the patriarch, who then called on her to select a suitable husband. Sibyl chose Guy, negating the divorce and reopening all the quarrels that had divided the kingdom during her brother's lifetime.

A significant number of powerful lords, including Reynald, refused to accept the situation. Raymond III urged Isabella's husband, Humphrey IV of Toron, to press his wife's claims, but Humphrey recognized Guy and Sibyl as his sovereigns. Although civil war had been averted, the new king and queen had angered several magnates. Balian of Ibelin, Isabella's stepfather, and his brother Baldwin, who had once planned to marry Sibyl, never reconciled.

Reynald showed his independence by refusing to honor the king's truce with Saladin. When Saladin invaded Galilee in 1187, the largest Frankish army ever assembled advanced to the relief of Tiberias (modern-day Teverya, Israel), where Eschiva, Raymond III's wife, was under siege. Guy and the

Detail of a miniature depicting the defeat of Guy of Lusignan and the loss of the Holy Cross, from *Histoire d'Outremer* by William of Tyre, 15th century. (The British Library)

Templars decided to attack, despite Raymond's strenuous objections against leaving their position. Historians have long discounted chivalry as the reason behind this strategy. It seems much more likely that Guy felt that he had to act either because his refusal to move in 1183 had cost him the regency or because he and the Templars needed a victory to justify spending funds sent by King Henry II of England for the defense of the kingdom. The Franks were trapped at Hattin and virtually wiped out on July 4, 1187.

Guy was captured, and most of Outremer's barons suffered a similar fate or died that day. Saladin took Jerusalem later that summer, marking the end of the First Kingdom of Jerusalem though not of Guy's bids for power.

When Guy was released in 1188, he returned to a desperate situation for himself and for the kingdom. The Franks had retained control of Tyre (modern-day Soûr, Lebanon) with the help of Conrad of Montferrat, a brother of Sibyl's first husband, who had joined the Ibelin clan in opposing Guy. In 1189 Conrad refused to allow Guy entry into Tyre, so Guy laid siege to the city. Here he gained the assistance of men who had arrived from Europe on the Third Crusade (1189–1192). However, the deaths of Sibyl and her two daughters in 1190 further weakened Guy's claim to the throne. The Ibelins proclaimed Isabella queen, divorced her from Humphrey IV of Toron, and married her to Conrad. Guy refused to acknowledge Conrad and attacked the Muslim-held city of Acre (modern-day Akko, Israel).

At this point Philippe II Augustus, king of France, arrived in Outremer. He supported Conrad; together the two joined the siege of Acre in 1191. Guy then left for Cyprus, where he helped Richard I of England conquer the island. Because Richard backed Guy's claim, his problems with Philip grew. Finally, the two kings agreed that Guy would reign and that Conrad would be his heir. In July 1191 Acre fell to the crusaders, and Philip returned to France. Conrad then moved to exclude Guy from power. By this point, Richard's support for Guy's kingship had worn thin. Richard then sold the island of Cyprus to Guy, hoping this would ease the tension.

In April 1192 Conrad was assassinated. His widow, Queen Isabella I, retained the throne, and the barons quickly married her off to Henry of Champagne. Guy then took part in an unsuccessful scheme to wrest Tyre from Henry's grasp. Richard withdrew all aid for Guy and left Outremer later that year. Realizing that he could not secure the throne, Guy relocated to Cyprus with his remaining supporters. There he encouraged magnates from the mainland to relocate, offering land and money fiefs as an incentive. Great families of Outremer built up estates on the island as well as on the mainland; their interests in both places shaped politics over the next century.

Guy died on July 18, 1194. His brother Aimery became lord and later king of Cyprus. The kingdom remained in the hands of the Lusignan family until 1489.

Deborah Gerish

See also

Baldwin IV of Jerusalem; Crusades in the Holy Land, Christian; Hattin, Battle of; Philippe II, King; Richard I, King; Saladin

References

Arrignon, Jean-Pierre. *Les Lusignans et l'Outre-mer: Actes du colloque Poitiers-Lusignan, 20–24 octobre 1993*. Poitiers: Université de Poitiers, 1994.

Edbury, Peter W. *The Kingdom of Cyprus and the Crusades, 1191–1374*. Cambridge: Cambridge University Press, 1991.

Edbury, Peter W. "Propaganda and Faction in the Kingdom of Jerusalem: The Background to Hattin." In *Crusaders and Muslims in Twelfth-Century Syria*, ed. Maya Shatzmiller, 173–189. Leiden: Brill, 1993.

Hamilton, Bernard. *The Leper King and His Heirs: Baldwin IV and the Crusader Kingdom of Jerusalem.* Cambridge: Cambridge University Press, 2000.

Lyons, Malcolm C., and D. E. P. Jackson. *Saladin: The Politics of Holy War.* Cambridge: Cambridge University Press, 1982.

Richard, Jean. "Les révoltes chypriotes de 1191–1192 et les inféodations de Guy de Lusignan." In *Montjoie: Studies in Crusade History in Honour of Hans Eberhard Mayer,* ed. Benjamin Z. Kedar, Jonathan Riley-Smith, and Rudolf Hiestand, 123–128. Aldershot, UK: Variorum, 1997.

H

Haditha, Battle of (August 1–4, 2005)

Military engagement during the Iraq War (2003–2011). The battle occurred during August 1–4, 2005, and was between U.S. marines and Iraqi insurgents belonging to Ansar al-Sunnah, a militant Salafi group operating in and around Haditha, Iraq. Haditha is a city of some 100,000 people located in Anbar Province in western Iraq about 150 miles to the northwest of Baghdad. The city's population is mainly Sunni Muslim.

The battle was precipitated when a large force of insurgents ambushed a 6-man marine sniper unit on August 1; all 6 marines died in the ensuing fight. The rebels videotaped part of the attack, which included footage allegedly showing a badly injured marine being killed. On August 3 the marines, along with a small contingent of Iraqi security forces, decided to launch a retaliatory strike against Ansar al-Sunnah, dubbed Operation QUICK STRIKE. Those involved included about 1,000 personnel from Regimental Combat Team 2.

The operation commenced with a ground assault against insurgent positions southwest of Haditha; this was augmented by four AH-1 Super Cobra attack helicopters. U.S. officials reported at least 40 insurgents killed during this engagement. The next day, August 4, insurgents destroyed a marine amphibious vehicle using a large roadside bomb; 15 of the 16 marines inside it were killed, along with a civilian interpreter. Meanwhile, the marines had conducted a raid on a house suspected of harboring insurgents outside Haditha. In so doing, they discovered a large weapons cache containing small arms and improvised explosive devices (IEDs) and detained 7 insurgents for questioning. Later, 6 of the men admitted to having ambushed and killed the 6 marines on August 1.

After the roadside bombing, coalition forces decided to regroup for a more concerted attack on Haditha itself, which would come in early September. In total, the marines suffered 21 killed; insurgent losses were estimated at some 400.

On September 5, 2005, the 3rd Battalion, 1st Marines, launched a full-scale assault against Haditha, expecting heavy resistance. The resistance did not materialize, however, and the marines took the entire city in four days with very minimal insurgent activity. The operation uncovered more than 1,000 weapons caches and resulted in the detention of an additional 400 militants. Four marines were casualties. In early 2006, 8 Iraqis suspected of involvement in the initial attack on the marine snipers were tried by an Iraqi court, found guilty, and executed.

PAUL G. PIERPAOLI JR.

See also
Iraq Insurgency; Iraq War

References
Hashim, Ammed S. *Insurgency and Counter-Insurgency in Iraq.* Ithaca, NY: Cornell University Press, 2006.

Tracy, Patrick. *Street Fight in Iraq: What It's Really Like over There.* Tucson: University of Arizona Press, 2006.

Hadrian, Emperor (76–138)

Roman emperor. Born on January 24, 76 CE, in Italica (Santiponce, near Seville), Iberia (Spain), Publius Aelius Trainus Hadrianus (Hadrian) was the son of Publius Aelius Hadrianus Afer, cousin of Marcus Ulpius Nerva Traianus, the future emperor Trajan (98–117), and Domitia Paulina of Gades. On the death of his father around 85, Hadrian became the ward of Trajan. Hadrian began his military career early and rose steadily in rank and responsibility to become tribune of three legions in succession in Lower Pannonia, Lower Moesia, and Upper Germany during 95–97. A member of Trajan's staff, Hadrian married Sabina, grandniece of the emperor.

Hadrian distinguished himself in the First and Second Dacian Wars (101–102 and 105–106) and was rewarded by appointment as praetor in 106, then governor of Lower Pannonia (Hungary) in 107. Hadrian served as Trajan's chief of staff during the Parthian War (113–117), and when Trajan became ill, he appointed Hadrian as governor of Syria and commander of the Roman troops there. Just before his death on August 8, 117, Trajan adopted Hadrian as his son and named him as his successor, although there is some question whether the adoption papers were falsified. This mattered little, as Hadrian enjoyed the support of the legions in Syria and secured Senate ratification.

Quickly concluding peace with the Parthians, Hadrian placed his former guardian, Attanius, in charge in Rome. Attanius soon "discovered" a plot that led to the hunting down and execution of four of Trajan's key supporters, ending any possible opposition to Hadrian. Meanwhile, Hadrian crushed a revolt of the Jews, pacified the Danube region, and then returned to Rome in 118.

Hadrian remained in Rome for a year, then left to campaign against the Sarmatians and the Dacians. He was constantly on the move inspecting the empire. He traveled to Gaul and then on to Britain in 121. A major rebellion in Britain had occurred just prior to his arrival, and to protect Roman settlements from the Caledonians, he ordered construction of the great frontier wall there that bears his name. Hadrian also caused the construction of additional forts along the Danube and the Rhine. To ensure that his armies remained in fighting trim and readiness, he established regular drill routines for the troops and conducted personal inspections.

From Britain, Hadrian traveled to Mauretania, where he conducted a brief campaign against rebels in 123. Learning that the Parthians were again preparing for war, he hurried there and concluded a negotiated settlement with the Parthian ruler. Hadrian spent the winter in Bithynia before traveling through Anatolia and then visiting Greece during 124–125 before returning to Italy by way of Sicily. In Rome he inspected the completed Parthenon, then toured Italy in 127 and Africa in 128.

Hadrian waged an unusually harsh war against the Jews, who were constantly in revolt against Rome. He visited the ruins of Jerusalem in 130, but his decision to build the new city of Aelia Capitolina on the site of Jerusalem and populate it with Romans led to a new savage revolt during 132–135 led by Bar Kokhba, who declared himself the Messiah. By the end of the revolt more than half a million Jews had been slain, and many others had died of sickness and hunger. Hadrian ordered Roman temples to be built in Jerusalem on Jewish holy sites and decreed that Jews could enter the city only one day a year, on the anniversary of the destruction of the city.

One of the so-called Good Emperors and a patron of the arts, Hadrian was a humanist who greatly admired Greek culture. An amateur architect, he was also widely known for his relationship with the Greek boy Antinous, who accompanied him on his travels. Following Antinous's mysterious death in the Nile in 130, Hadrian took the entire empire into mourning and deified him. Hadrian himself died on July 10, 138, at his villa at Baiae, near Naples. His remains were later transferred to Rome. His mausoleum on the west bank of the Tiber later became the papal fortress Castel Sant'Angelo.

Spencer C. Tucker

See also
Bar Kochba Revolt; Parthian Empire

References
Birley, Anthony R. *Hadrian: The Restless Emperor.* New York: Routledge, 1997.

Lambert, Royston. *Beloved and God: The Story of Hadrian and Antinous.* London: Phoenix Giants, 1997.

Perowne, Stewart. *Hadrian.* Reprint ed. Westport, CT: Greenwood, 1976.

Haganah

Haganah, Hebrew for "defense," was a Jewish underground self-defense and military organization during 1920–1948 that succeeded the Guild of Watchman (Hashomer) and was the precursor of the Israel Defense Forces (IDF). Hashomer was a small group of no more than 100 Jewish immigrants who began guarding Jewish settlements and kibbutzim in 1909. Haganah was organized to protect the Jewish community (Yishuv) following the Arab riots of 1920 and 1921.

After the demise of the Ottoman Empire in World War I, the League of Nations granted Britain temporary mandatory control of Palestine on July 24, 1922, to act on behalf of both the Jewish and non-Jewish populations. Although the British mandatory government (1922–1948) did not recognize Haganah, it did provide sufficient stability and security for the kibbutzim and the Yishuv to flourish. Nonetheless, the need for Jewish self-defense persisted and grew, as did Haganah.

During 1920–1929 Haganah was composed of localized and poorly armed units of Jewish farmers who took turns guarding one another's farms and kibbutzim. Haganah's structure and role changed radically after the Arab riots and ethnic cleansings of 1929. Haganah began to organize the rural and urban Jewish adult and youth populations throughout Palestine into a much larger, better-equipped, and better-trained but still primarily self-defense force. Although Haganah was able to acquire some foreign weapons, the British mandatory government's effective blockade of weapons to the Jews led Haganah to construct weapons fabrication workshops for ammunition, some small arms, and grenades.

Even as the British mandatory government slowly shifted its support to the Arab population of Palestine, the leadership of the Jewish Agency for Palestine continued to attempt to work closely with the British to promote the interests of the Jewish population in Palestine. Haganah supported this position through its self-defense and military strategy *havlaga* (self-restraint), but not all of Haganah's members agreed with a restrained response to what they perceived as the British mandatory government's pro-Arab bias. This political and policy disagreement and Haganah's prevailing socialist ideology led in 1931 to the formation of a minority splinter group headed by Avraham Tehomi known as Irgun Tsvai Leumi (National Military Organization). Irgun advocated harsh retaliation for Arab attacks and an active military campaign to end British mandatory governance of Palestine.

By 1936, the year that the Palestinian revolt known as the Great Uprising or Arab Revolt (1936–1939) began, Haganah had grown to 10,000 mobilized men and 40,000 reservists. Although the British mandatory government still failed to recognize Haganah, the strategy of *havlaga* seemed to bear fruit when the British Security Forces (BSF) cooperated in the establishment of the Jewish Settlement Police, Jewish Auxiliary Forces, and Special Night Squads as Jewish civilian militia. Additionally, the BSF and Haganah worked together to suppress the Arab Revolt and to protect British as well as Jewish interests.

Despite these perceived gains, in 1937 Haganah again split into right-wing and left-wing factions. The right-wing faction joined Irgun, and some of the members of Irgun, including Tehomi, rejoined Haganah. Irgun had been nothing more than a small and ineffective irritant until this transition changed Irgun into an effective guerrilla force branded as terrorists by the British and some in Haganah.

The Great Uprising matured Haganah and taught it many lessons. Haganah improved its underground arms-production capability, increased the acquisition of light arms from Europe, and established centralized arms depots and 50 strategically placed kibbutzim. Haganah also enhanced the training of its soldiers and officer corps and expanded its clandestine training of the general population.

The British white paper of 1939 openly shifted British support away from the Jews to the Arabs. Jewish immigration, settlement, and land purchases in Palestine were severely restricted, and the British effectively retreated from any support for an independent Jewish homeland. This attempt on the threshold of World War II to appease the Arab world following the Great Uprising failed. Even with this betrayal, David Ben-Gurion asserted that the Zionists should stand against the change in policy while supporting the British during World War II. Haganah responded by organizing demonstrations against the British and by further facilitating illegal immigration through bases in Turkey and Switzerland under the auspices of Aliya Bet, the Organization for Illegal Immigration, created in 1938. Irgun's response was to begin bombing British installations and attacking British interests.

As World War II progressed, on May 19, 1941, Haganah created Palmach to train young people in leadership and military skills and to help defend Palestine if the Germans invaded. Palmach cooperated with the British during 1941–1943, fought behind the lines in Vichy-dominated Lebanon and Syria, worked with Irgun during 1945–1946 against British mandatory rule, and helped facilitate illegal Jewish immigration during 1946–1947 prior to being folded in 1948 into the IDF.

Fearing that the Germans would overrun all of North Africa, Britain negotiated a reciprocal support agreement with Haganah that provided intelligence and even commando assistance. The British retreated from the agreement following their victory at El Alamein (al-Alamayn) in November 1942, although in 1943 they did form the Jewish Brigade and deployed its 5,000 men in Italy in September 1944 before disbanding it in 1946. Although Palestinian Jews were not allowed to enlist in the British Army until

1940, more than 30,000 served in various units of the army during the war.

Haganah focused its operations after the war on the British mandatory government, attacking rail lines, bridges, and deportation ships and even freeing immigrants from the Atlit internment camp. Haganah also worked on preparations for partition. These clashes grew as Haganah facilitated illegal immigration from Jewish displaced person camps in Europe and secured its anticipated partitioned borders. Immediately after partition in 1947, Haganah concentrated on defending the Yishuv against attacks by Palestinian Arabs and the neighboring Arab states.

Haganah took the offensive in the Israeli War of Independence in April 1948. Haganah and Irgun captured Tiberias, Haifa, and the Arab cities of Acre and Jaffa. In Operation NACHSHON they went on to open a road to West Jerusalem. On May 28, 1948, the provisional government of the newly declared State of Israel transformed Haganah into its national military, the IDF, and outlawed all other armed forces. In September 1948 the military activities of Irgun were folded into the IDF.

RICHARD M. EDWARDS

See also
Ben-Gurion, David; El Alamein, Second Battle of; Irgun Tsvai Leumi; Israeli War of Independence; NACHSHON, Operation

References
Bauer, Yehuda. *From Diplomacy to Resistance: A History of Jewish Palestine, 1930–1945.* Translated by Alton M. Winters. Philadelphia: Jewish Publication Society of America, 1970.

Farris, Karl. *Growth and Change in the Israeli Defense Forces through Six Wars.* Carlisle Barracks, PA: U.S. Army War College, 1987.

Mardor, Munya M. *Haganah*, ed. D. R. Elston. Translated by H. A. G. Schmuckler. New York: New American Library, 1966.

Pentland, Pat Allen. *Zionist Military Preparations for Statehood: The Evolution of Haganah Organizations, Programs, and Strategies, 1920–1948.* Ann Arbor, MI: University Microfilms International, 1981.

Haifa Street, Battle of (January 6–9, 2007)

A two-stage combined-arms action by American and Iraqi troops against Sunni insurgents in central Baghdad during January 6–9, 2007. In the Battle of Haifa Street, U.S. Army infantry and cavalry units fought alongside Iraqi soldiers to successfully dislodge enemy insurgents from key urban areas. The engagement pitted about 1,000 U.S. and Iraqi troops against an undetermined number of insurgent fighters.

Haifa Street, a broad boulevard located in central Baghdad, runs northwest from the Green Zone, the home of the Coalition Provisional Authority (CPA), for two miles along the west bank of the Tigris River. Many of the buildings along the street, including the former residences of wealthy Sunni government officials, are 20-story high-rise apartments. Amid increasing sectarian violence in 2006, Sunni and Al Qaeda in Iraq insurgents had taken control of the street and its surrounding neighborhood. They also made use of the high-rise apartment buildings from which they were able to fire down into the streets, posing a serious hazard to civilians and coalition troops. Throughout 2006 insurgents sporadically engaged American and Iraqi forces with sniper fire and grenades lobbed from the residential and office buildings.

The catalyst for the Battle of Haifa Street occurred on January 6, 2007, when Iraqi troops killed 30 Sunni insurgents after discovering a fake checkpoint manned by insurgents. In retaliation, the insurgents executed 27 Shias and distributed leaflets threatening to kill anyone who entered the area. Following an unsuccessful attempt by Iraqi soldiers to clear the neighborhood on January 8, American troops prepared a full-scale offensive to assist the Iraqis.

The first stage of the battle involved approximately 1,000 American and Iraqi troops. On January 9 a reinforced U.S. Army battalion from the 2nd Infantry Division joined the Iraqi 6th Infantry Division to engage in pitched street-by-street combat to clear buildings from north to south along Haifa Street. During the intense one-day operation, the Americans employed snipers and Stryker combat vehicles to methodically clear insurgent strongholds. Ground troops were supported by AH-64 Apache attack helicopters and precision-guided munitions. The U.S. and Iraqi forces mounted a successful retaliation effort against the strong insurgent resistance that included machine-gun fire, rocket-propelled grenades, and coordinated mortar fire. In the course of the battle approximately 70 insurgents were killed or captured, including several foreign fighters. Some 25 others were captured.

U.S. troops subsequently withdrew, leaving Iraqi forces to patrol the area. However, insurgents reinfiltrated the area during the next two weeks. Before dawn on January 24, 2007, Iraqi troops joined a larger American force composed of two reinforced battalions from the 2nd Infantry and 1st Cavalry

Divisions to clear the street again. This second stage of the battle, named Operation TOMAHAWK STRIKE 11, lasted less than one day. U.S. Army units used both Bradley and Stryker combat vehicles to control the street, supported by Iraqi and American troops who cleared apartments while taking sniper and mortar fire. By evening the street and surrounding buildings had been cleared, and a large weapons cache had been seized. Approximately 65 insurgents, including numerous foreign fighters, were killed or captured on January 24. Iraqi forces suffered 20 killed during both engagements. Although a substantial American presence remained for several days following the second battle, control and responsibility for the sector had been relinquished to the Iraqi Army by February 1, 2007.

WILLIAM E. FORK

See also
Al Qaeda in Iraq; Iraq Insurgency

References
Cave, Damien, and James Glanz. "In a New Joint U.S.-Iraqi Patrol, the Americans Go First." *New York Times,* January 25, 2007.
Kagan, Kimberly. "The Iraq Report; From 'New Way Forward' to New Commander." *Weekly Standard,* January 10, 2007–February 10, 2007, 7–10.
Zavis, Alexandra. "The Conflict in Iraq: Military Offensive in Baghdad; U.S.-Iraqi Forces Strike 'Sniper Alley.'" *Los Angeles Times,* January 25, 2007.

Hama Massacre (February 3–28, 1982)

The Hama Massacre or Hama Uprising occurred during February 3–28, 1982, when Hafez al-Assad, Syrian president and strongman since 1971, ordered the Syrian armed forces into Hama to crush an uprising there against his rule.

In the late 1970s and early 1980s, Syrian Sunni Muslim fundamentalists began challenging the Baath Party's secular outlook. The Baath Party stood for Arab nationalism and socialism, while the Muslim Brotherhood saw nationalism as un-Islamic and held that religion should not be separated from government. Urban areas across Syria became centers of political unrest as the majority Sunni Muslims agitated against rule by the minority Alawite Muslim–dominated government.

Hama had long been a conservative stronghold and supporter of the Muslim Brotherhood. Indeed, in April 1964 rioting broke out there, the year after the Baath Party had secured power in a coup d'état. The government dispatched tanks, and the revolt was put down. Some 70 members of the Muslim Brotherhood died in the uprising. Many others were wounded or captured and imprisoned.

Following the Syrian invasion of Lebanon in 1976, Sunni Islamists began a long effort against the government of Syria, leading to guerrilla activities against government officials and the military in a number of cities. The government responded to the Muslim Brotherhood actions with arrests, imprisonment, torture, and killings. After an unsuccessful attempt to assassinate President Assad, the government promptly executed a large number of imprisoned Islamists. In July membership in the Muslim Brotherhood was made a capital offense.

The uprising in Hama began at 2:00 a.m. on February 3, 1982, when a Syrian Army unit operating in the old city came upon the hideout of a guerrilla commander, Omar Jawwad (aka Abu Bakr), and was ambushed. Informed of what had transpired, insurgents on the rooftops then shot and killed a number of the soldiers. As the army rushed in reinforcements, Abu Bakr ordered a "general uprising." Mosque loudspeakers that normally issued calls to prayer now called for jihad against the Baathists. Hundreds of insurgents then attacked police posts and the homes of government officials. By daybreak of the morning of February 3, the insurgents had killed some 70 Baathists, and activists proclaimed Hama a "liberated city."

Neither side was prepared to compromise. Those on the government side certainly understood the need to crush their opponents. Toward that end, President Assad dispatched some 12,000 Syrian soldiers, including a number of elite units, all under the command of his brother Rifaat al-Assad, to restore order. The government employed tanks, artillery, and aircraft, and there was considerable destruction particularly in the insurgent stronghold of the old city. The fighting went on for three weeks, the first week spent by the government in securing control of Hama and the next weeks taken up with ferreting out those held to be insurgents. The government side employed both torture and mass executions of suspected rebel sympathizers.

Estimates of the dead in the fighting vary widely, depending on source. Including some 1,000 soldiers, the uprising claimed from 10,000 to 40,000 killed, with 20,000 being the most likely figure. Most of those perishing were civilians.

Demoralizing to the insurgents was the fact that there were no other city uprisings in support of that at Hama. With it having been crushed, the Islamist insurrection against the government was broken, and the Muslim Brotherhood then operated largely from exile, mostly from Jordan and Iraq.

Assad now increasingly relied on repression to crush any opposition or dissent. Hama would also be the site of violence during the Syrian Civil War (2011 to date).

Spencer C. Tucker

See also
Assad, Hafez al-; Muslim Brotherhood; Syria; Syrian Civil War

References
Benjamin, Daniel, and Steven Simon. *The Age of Sacred Terror.* New York: Random House, 2002.
Fisk, Robert. *Pity the Nation.* London: Touchstone, 1990.
Friedman, Thomas. *From Beirut to Jerusalem.* London: HarperCollins, 1998.
Seale, Patrick. *Asad of Syria: The Struggle for the Middle East.* Berkeley: University of California Press, 1989.

Hamas

Islamist Palestinian organization formally founded in 1987. The stated mission for Hamas (Harakat al-Muqawama al-Islamiyya, or Movement of Islamic Resistance) is the creation of an Islamic way of life and the liberation of Palestine through Islamic resistance. Essentially, Hamas combines Islamic fundamentalism with Palestinian nationalism. Hamas gained about 30–40 percent support in the Palestinian population within five years because of its mobilization successes and the general desperation experienced by the Palestinian population during the First Intifada (1987). In January 2006 Hamas won a majority in the Palestinian Authority's (PA) general legislative elections, which brought condemnation from Israel and a power struggle with PA president Mahmoud Abbas and his Fatah Party.

Hamas is an Islamist movement, as are larger and longer-established groups such as the Muslim Brotherhood and the Palestinian Islamic Jihad. The growth of Islamist movements was delayed among Palestinians because of their status as a people without a state and the tight security controls imposed by Israel.

The Muslim Brotherhood, established in Egypt in 1928, had set up branches in Syria, Sudan, Libya, the Persian Gulf states, Jordan (which influenced the West Bank), and Gaza. However, for two decades the Muslim Brotherhood focused on its religious, educational, and social missions and was quiescent politically. That changed with the First Intifada. The Muslim Brotherhood advocated for the re-Islamization of society and thought, social justice, and an emphasis on *hakmiyya* (the sovereignty of God, as opposed to temporal rule). The Muslim Brotherhood turned to activism against Israel after Islamic Jihad had accelerated its operations during 1986 and 1987. Eventually Islamic Jihad split into three rival organizations. The new movement coming out of the Jordanian and Egyptian Muslim Brotherhood groups, unlike Islamic Jihad, retained its major programmatic emphasis on the Islamization or re-Islamization of society. As the new organization of Hamas emerged out of the Muslim Brotherhood, it was able to draw strength from the social work of Sheikh Ahmed Yassin, who had led the Islamic Assembly (al-Mujamma al-Islami), an organization influential in many mosques and at the Islamic University of Gaza.

In December 1987 Abd al-Aziz Rantisi, who was a physician at Islamic University, and former student leaders Salah Shihada and Yahya al-Sinuwwar, who had been in charge of security for the Muslim Brotherhood, formed the first unit of Hamas. Yassin gave his approval to the new organization but was not directly connected with it.

In February 1988 as a result of a meeting in Amman involving Sheikh Abd al-Rahman al-Khalifa (the spiritual guide of the Jordanian Muslim Brotherhood), Ibrahim Ghawsha (the Hamas spokesperson and Jordanian representative), Mahmud Zahar (a surgeon), Rantisi (acting as a West Bank representative), Jordanian parliament members, and the hospital director, the Muslim Brotherhood granted formal recognition to Hamas. In 1988 Hamas issued its charter, which condemns world Zionism and the efforts to isolate Palestine and defines the mission of the organization. The charter does not condemn the West or non-Muslims but does condemn aggression against the Palestinian people, arguing for a defensive jihad, and also calls for fraternal relations with the other Palestinian nationalist groups.

Hamas is headed by its Political Bureau with representatives for military affairs, foreign affairs, finance, propaganda, and internal security. The Advisory Council, or Majlis al-Shura, is linked to the Political Bureau, which is also connected with all Palestinian communities; Hamas's social and charitable groups, elected members, and district committees; and the leadership in Israeli prisons.

Major attacks against Israel have been carried out by the Izz ad-Din al-Qassam Brigades of Hamas. They also developed the Qassam rocket used to attack Israeli civilian settlements in the Negev Desert. However, much of Hamas's activity during the First Intifada consisted of its participation within more broadly based popular demonstrations and locally coordinated efforts at resistance.

Hamas greatly expanded by 1993 but decried the autonomy agreement between the Israelis and the PLO in Jericho and the Gaza Strip as too limited. By the time of the first elections for the PA's Council in 1996, Hamas was caught

Hamas supporters in the West Bank city of Ramallah celebrate the organization's victory in the Palestinian legislative elections on January 25, 2006. Hamas triggered a political earthquake with its sweeping election victory over the ruling Fatah party. (Pedro Ugarte/AFP/Getty Images)

in a dilemma. It had gained popularity as a resistance organization, but Oslo 1 and Oslo 2 (the Taba Accord of September 28, 1995) were meant to end the intifada. The elections would further strengthen the PLO, but if Hamas boycotted the elections, then it would be even more isolated. Finally, Hamas's leadership rejected participation but without ruling it out in the future, and this gave the organization the ability to continue protesting Oslo. When suicide attacks were launched to protest Israeli violence against Palestinians, however, Hamas was blamed whether or not its operatives were involved.

Hamas funds an extensive array of social services aimed at ameliorating the plight of the Palestinians. It provides funding for hospitals, schools, mosques, orphanages, food distribution, and aid to the families of Palestinian prisoners. Given the PA's frequent inability to provide for such needs, Hamas stepped into the breach and in so doing endeared itself to a large number of Palestinians.

Until its PA electoral triumph in January 2006, Hamas received funding from a number of sources. Palestinians living abroad provided money, as did a number of private donors in the oil-rich Persian Gulf states and other states in the West. Iran has been a significant donor to Hamas. Much aid was directed to renovation of the Palestinian territories, but unfortunately much of that rebuilding was destroyed in the Israeli campaign in the West Bank in 2002, which was intended to combat suicide bombings. The Israel Defense Forces (IDF) has carried out numerous eliminations of Hamas leaders. These include most notably Shihada (2002), Dr. Ibrahim al-Makadma (2003), Ismail Abu Shanab (2003), Yassin (2004), and Rantisi (2004).

Hamas had two sets of leaders, those inside the West Bank and Gaza and those outside. The West Bank leadership is divided along the general structure into political, charitable, student, and military activities. The political leadership is usually targeted for arrests because its members can be located, unlike the secret military units. That leadership has organized very effectively before and since PLO leader Yasser Arafat's 2004 death and has become more popular than the PLO in the West Bank, an unexpected development. Although Arafat was quickly succeeded by Abbas, a sizable number of Palestinians had already begun to identify with

Hamas, mainly because it was better able to provide for the everyday needs of the people.

Hamas unexpectedly won the legislative elections in January 2006. Locals had expected a victory in Gaza but not in the West Bank. Nonetheless, both Israel and the United States steadfastly refused to recognize the Palestinian government now under the control of Hamas. The United States cut off $420 million and the European Union (EU) cut off $600 million in aid to the PA's Hamas-led government, which created difficulties for ordinary Palestinians. The loss of this aid halted the delivery of supplies to hospitals and ended other services in addition to stopping the payment of salaries. To prevent total collapse, the United States and the EU promised relief funds, but these were not allowed to go through the PA. The cutoff in funds was designed to discourage Palestinian support for Hamas.

On March 17, 2007, Abbas brokered a Palestinian unity government that included members of both Hamas and Fatah in which Hamas leader Ismail Haniyeh became prime minister. Yet in May armed clashes between Hamas and Fatah escalated, and on June 14 Hamas seized control of Gaza. Abbas promptly dissolved the unity government and declared a state of emergency. On June 18, having been assured of EU support, he dissolved the National Security Council and swore in an emergency Palestinian government. That same day, the United States ended its 15-month embargo on the PA and resumed aid in an effort to strengthen Abbas's government, now limited to the West Bank. On June 19 Abbas cut off all ties and dialogue with Hamas pending the return of Gaza. In a move to strengthen Abbas's position, on July 1, 2007, Israel restored financial ties to the PA. At the same time Israel imposed an economic blockade against Gaza, which continues into 2019.

In early 2008, Hamas escalated rocket attacks on Israel launched from the Gaza Strip. Although a subsequent six-month cease-fire agreement brought relative calm, the agreement's expiration on December 19 saw the immediate renewal of hostilities. Citing Israel's continued blockade of the Gaza Strip, Hamas commenced launching rockets the next day. As a result, on December 27, 2008, the IDF launched a full-scale assault, code-named Operation CAST LEAD, into Gaza. After the deaths of some 1,300 Palestinians and intense international pressure, the Israelis halted their campaign on January 18.

In November 2012, violence flared anew between Israel and Hamas when the Israelis launched Operation PILLAR OF DEFENSE, designed to punish Hamas for some 100 rocket attacks against Israeli civilians and other acts of provocation on Israeli territory. The operation, consisting chiefly of air strikes against Hamas's weapons depots and Hamas military leaders, resulted in the death of Ahmed Jabari, head of Hamas's military establishment. Hamas claimed that it suffered 79 militant deaths, 53 civilian deaths, and 1 police officer killed.

The Fatah-Hamas break was not substantially mended until early June 2014, when Abbas announced the formation of another unity government. However, unlike the 2007 government, this one did not include any Hamas members in the cabinet. Hamas agreed to support the government without direct participation in it. The United States and most of its allies cautiously backed the new setup, but Israel denounced it because of its ties to Hamas. A renewed conflict between Israel and Hamas in July and August 2014, which resulted in substantial bloodshed, unraveled Abbas's unity government, however. On July 17, Israel escalated the conflict. In Operation PROTECTIVE EDGE Israel sent ground forces into the Gaza Strip while warplanes hammered Hamas targets. On August 26, Hamas and Israel agreed to an open-ended cease-fire. It is estimated that as many as 2,200 Palestinian Gazans died during the 50-day conflict. Israel reported 66 soldiers and 8 civilians killed.

Since late 2014, efforts to achieve a full reconciliation between Hamas and Fatah have waxed and waned, and the "unity" government created in 2014 remained unified in name only. Talks between Hamas and Fatah have continued but have yielded no concrete results, as Fatah leaders have insisted that Hamas turn over control of the Gaza Strip to Fatah and the PA. Meanwhile, in May 2015 Amnesty International issued a report asserting that Hamas was guilty of carrying out extrajudicial arrests, kidnappings, and murders against Palestinians suspected of aiding Israel during the 2014 Israeli-Hamas conflict. The same report also accused Hamas of torturing Palestinians; many of the victims were members of the rival Fatah political party.

More recently Egypt, once a supporter of Hamas, disavowed the Palestinian group. Qatar has since stepped in to fulfill the support role once held by Egypt. Iran meanwhile has recently demonstrated inconsistent support for Hamas. The Turkish government has also sought to aid Hamas, much to the consternation of Israel and the United States. The situation in Gaza has remained dire, however. The Israeli blockade hamstrung Hamas's efforts to provide for the basic needs for Palestinians under its control. Poverty, inadequate health care, and substandard schools remain endemic.

No doubt influenced by the dire conditions in Gaza, where 2 million Palestinians remained trapped in what amounts to an open-air prison, on October 12, 2017, in Cairo, representatives of Hamas met under the watchful eyes of Egyptian intelligence officials with representatives of the PA to sign an agreement that would establish a unity government to treat with Israel. Difficulties lay ahead, however, for while Hamas agreed to give the PA governing authority in Gaza, there remained the issue of control of its rockets and mortars targeting Israel, one of the key PA conditions. The Israeli government also announced that it objected to any agreement that did not recognize Israel and disarm Hamas.

In 2018, tensions between Hamas and Israel were heightened when Hamas operatives began flying incendiary balloons and kites into Israeli airspace. The Israelis responded by tightening their blockade against Gaza. By early August 2018, talks being mediated by Egypt were under way to ease the latest tensions between Hamas and Israel. Nevertheless, on August 9, 2018, Israeli warplanes hammered Hamas targets in the Gaza Strip in retaliation for a series of rocket attacks against southern Israel. On August 21, Hamas leaders asserted that talks involving the blockade were about to yield an end to the impasse, but observers cautioned that a complete end to the blockade was probably not imminent. It was reported that Israel and Hamas had recently discussed an easing of the blockade.

Meanwhile, despite the October 2017 unity agreement, Hamas and the PA/Fatah remained effectively apart as of August 2018. Indeed, Hamas leaders contend that Mahmoud Abbas and the PA continue to impose harsh sanctions against the Gaza Strip that are hurting its residents and preventing a full reconciliation between the two rival governments. Egypt continues to act as a broker in the ongoing dispute between Fatah and Hamas.

Harry Raymond Hueston II, Paul G. Pierpaoli Jr., Spencer C. Tucker, and Sherifa Zuhur

See also
Abbas, Mahmoud; Arafat, Yasser; Fatah, al-; Intifada, First; Intifada, Second; Israel; Muslim Brotherhood; Palestinian Islamic Jihad; Palestine Liberation Organization; Terrorism

References
Legrain, Jean-François. "Hamas: Legitimate Heir of Palestinian Nationalism?" In *Political Islam: Revolution, Radicalism, or Reform*, ed. John Esposito, 159–178. Boulder, CO: Lynne Rienner, 1997.
Mishal, Shaul, and Avraham Sela. *The Palestinian Hamas: Vision, Violence, and Coexistence*. New York: Columbia University Press, 2000.
Tamimi, Azzam. *Hamas: A History from Within*. 2nd rev. ed. Northampton, MA: Olive Branch, 2011.

Hammurabi (ca. 1810–1750 BCE)

King of Babylon. Born around 1810 BCE in Babylon, Hammurabi was the sixth king of the First Babylonian dynasty. He came to the throne in 1792 on the abdication of his father, King Sin-Muballit, for health reasons. On Hammurabi's accession Babylon was one of a number of city-states in central and southern Mesopotamia that warred against one another for control of the Fertile Crescent. Founded in 1894, the city of Babylon was built on both banks of the Euphrates River (present-day Hillah, about 62 miles south of Baghdad in the Babil Governorate of Iraq). Before the reign of Sin-Muballit, Babylon was restricted territorially largely to the city itself. It was overshadowed by a number of more powerful kingdoms, including Elam, Assyria, Isin, Eshnunna, and Larsa. Sin-Muballit brought some additional territory in south-central Mesopotamia under Babylonian hegemony, including the small city-states of Borsippa, Kish, and Sippar.

Babylon was not a major power in the region, and there were numerous threats to it. The kingdom of Eshnunna controlled the upper Tigris River, while Larsa controlled the river delta. The kingdom of Elam to the east had regularly invaded and forced tribute upon the small states of southern Mesopotamia, and in 1801 Elam had sought to secure permanent control of much of the region. To the north King Shamshi-Adad had expanded Assyrian territory from Asia Minor into the Levant and central Mesopotamia.

The first few decades of Hammurabi's reign were peaceful, and he was able to concentrate on a number of public works projects, including strengthening the city defenses by heightening its walls. He also assured himself of priestly support through the expansion of temples. However, Elam became a threat when its ruler attempted to instigate war between Babylon and Larsa. Made aware of Elam's duplicity, Hammurabi concluded an alliance with Larsa, and together they defeated Elam. Larsa, however, contributed little to what was to have been a joint military effort, and angered by this, Hammurabi turned on his ally. Aided by Yamhad and Mari to the north, Babylon defeated Larsa and secured control of all of the lower Mesopotamian plain around 1763.

The absence of their militaries in the war against Larsa, however, brought revolts in both Yamhad and Mari, and Hammurabi then marched north and crushed these and added these kingdoms and others to his own, so that Babylon now also controlled northern Mesopotamia. Within a short span of time, Hammurabi had secured control of all of Mesopotamia. Only Aleppo and Qatna to the west in the Levant remained independent.

Hammurabi then waged a protracted war with King Ishme-Dagan I of Assyria for control of Mesopotamia. Eventually Hammurabi prevailed, ousting Ishme-Dagan I just before his own death. Although not ruled by Babylon, Assyria was obliged to pay tribute.

Hammurabi is no doubt chiefly remembered today for his law code. Inscribed on a stele, it was placed in a public location so that all citizens would become familiar with it. The stele was later taken as a trophy by the Elamites and removed to their capital of Susa, where it was rediscovered in 1901 and is now in the Louvre.

The Code of Hammurabi consisted of 282 laws on 12 tablets written in Akkadian, the language of the people, and was thus accessible to any literate person. The law code provides very specific punishments for stated offenses, with these varying according to the station of the individuals involved. The code is probably best known for its principle of equivalent retaliation for an offense, as in "an eye for an eye and a tooth for a tooth." The code is also one of the first to present the presumption of innocence and to suggest that both sides have the opportunity to provide evidence. However, there is no provision for extenuating circumstances that might alter the prescribed punishments.

Hammurabi died circa 1750 BCE. His successors proved largely inept. Indeed, during the rule of his son Samsu-iluna, the Babylonian Empire soon came apart. The final act came in 1595 when Babylon was sacked and conquered by the powerful Hittite Empire.

Spencer C. Tucker

See also
Assyrian Empire; Babylonian Empire, Old

References
Charpin, Dominique. *Hammurabi of Babylon.* London: Tauris, 2012.
Kriwaczek, Paul. *Babylon: Mesopotamia and the Birth of Civilization.* New York: St. Martin's Griffin, 2012.
Oakes, Joan. *Babylon.* New York: Thames and Hudson, 2008.
Saggs, H. W. F. *The Greatness That Was Babylon: A Survey of the Ancient Civilization of the Tigris-Euphrates Valley.* London: Sidgwick & Jackson, 1988.
Van de Mieroop, Marc. *A History of the Ancient Near East, ca. 3000–323 BC.* Hoboken, NJ: Wiley-Blackwell, 2015.

Hanit, Attack on the (July 21, 2006)

Hezbollah cruise missile attack on an Israeli Navy corvette off the coast of Lebanon. The missile attack occurred on July 21, 2006, during Operation CHANGE OF DIRECTION, the Israeli military operation against Hezbollah in Lebanon. The *Hanit*, an Israeli Navy corvette of some 1,275 tons built in the United States, was commissioned in 1995 as the last of three INS Saar V–class missile corvettes. On July 21 it was on duty about 10 miles off Beirut as part of an Israeli blockade designed to prevent Hezbollah from importing additional weapons by sea from neighboring Syria.

On the evening of July 21, two Chinese-manufactured C-802 (known in the west as Saccade) cruise missiles were fired from shore in the direction of the *Hanit*, probably from truck launchers. Indications suggest that the first missile was intentionally fired high to distract the *Hanit*'s defensive systems, while the second was sent low against the corvette. The first missile struck and sank a merchant ship steaming about 35 miles off the coast, a Cambodian flag vessel with an Egyptian crew. Twelve members of its crew were subsequently rescued. The second struck the *Hanit* at 8:45 p.m., heavily damaging it, starting a fire, and killing 4 of the 64-man crew.

The *Hanit* was able to return to port under its own steam. Repaired, it returned to duty three weeks later. Photographs of the ship after the attack show only a relatively small entrance hole and burn area under the helicopter platform at the stern of the ship, indicating that perhaps the C-802's warhead might not have exploded.

The radar-guided C-802 is a subsonic (0.9 Mach) missile powered by a turbojet engine. The missile weighs some 1,640 pounds and has a 363-pound warhead. Its range is roughly 740 miles. With only very small radar reflectivity, the missile flies at only about 15–20 feet above the surface of the water, making it difficult to detect and intercept. Hit probability is estimated at as high as 98 percent. Along with the U.S. Harpoon, the Saccade is considered to be among the best antiship missiles in the world.

The Israelis were well aware of the importance of massive decoys and jamming. Using such techniques, during the 1973 Yom Kippur War the Israelis had defeated 50 incoming Syrian and Egyptian antiship missiles while sinking eight of their ships for only one Israeli missile boat damaged. The Hanit-class ships mount impressive antimissile defensive systems: 64 Barak point-defense missiles, a 20mm Phalanx rapid-fire cannon, and 20mm and 7.62mm machine guns as well as considerable chaff and decoy expendables and jamming equipment.

The attack succeeded for two reasons. First, unknown to Israeli intelligence, Hezbollah had acquired the C-802 cruise missiles, undoubtedly from Iran via Syria. Second, because of intense Israeli air activity in the area, the commander of the *Hanit* had turned off some of his ship's automated warning and defense systems. Also, the Israel Defense Forces (IDF) remains convinced that Iranian advisers assisted with the missile firings.

SPENCER C. TUCKER

See also
Hezbollah; Lebanon, Israeli Operations against; Yom Kippur War

Reference
Polmar, Norman. "Hezbollah Attack: Lessons for the LCS?" *Naval Institute Proceedings* (September 2006): 88–89.

HARD SURFACE, Operation (June 12, 1963–January 1964)

U.S. military support to Saudi Arabia and the only John F. Kennedy administration projection of military power in the region. On June 12, 1963, President Kennedy authorized Operation HARD SURFACE as part of his effort to deter Egyptian leader Gamal Abdel Nasser from expanding his nation's military participation in the North Yemen Civil War (1962–1970) to Saudi Arabia. Kennedy sought to protect long-standing U.S. strategic interests in the oil-rich kingdom, although the United States had formally recognized the newly declared Yemen Arab Republic on December 19, 1962.

The North Yemen Civil War broke out after republican Yemeni forces overthrew the newly crowned Mutawakkilite king of Yemen, Sayf al-Islam Mohammed al-Badr, actually the heir of the Zaydi imam. They then established the Yemen Arab Republic under Abdullah al-Sallal. The Mutawakkilite regime in northern Yemen had been created after the collapse of the Ottoman Empire at the end of World War I. Egypt provided troops and substantial military support to the Yemen Arab Republic, while Saudi Arabia financed the Imam's "royalist" side with guerrilla forces trained by the British.

Kennedy sought to press Crown Prince Faisal of Saudi Arabia, King Hussein of Jordan, President al-Sallal, and Nasser to bring about the removal of Egyptian troops through a pledge from Saudi Arabia and Jordan to halt their aid to Imam al-Badr. Nasser, however, responded that he would remove his forces only after Jordan and Saudi Arabia halted all military operations, while Faisal and Hussein rejected the U.S. president's plan outright because they claimed that it would mean U.S. recognition of the "rebels" who had ousted the imam and established the Yemen Arab Republic. Faisal also claimed that Nasser wanted to secure Saudi Arabia's oil and use Yemen as a staging area for revolt in the rest of the Arabian Peninsula. The situation was even more complicated, as Great Britain, a staunch ally of the Saudis, had its own designs in southern Arabia, which conflicted with various nationalist groups there. At the same time, United Nations diplomat Ralph Bunche was actively seeking to bring an end to the civil war.

Faisal was determined to secure U.S. military support, and Kennedy responded by assuring him in writing on October 25, 1962, of "full U.S. support for the maintenance of Saudi Arabian integrity." Twice U.S. aircraft staged brief shows of force over Saudi Arabia. In the first instance in November, six F-100 Super Sabre interceptors flew over the cities of Riyadh and Jeddah. On the second occasion, two bombers and a transport flew over Riyadh on a return flight to Paris from Karachi.

Following an Egyptian Air Force strike against the Saudi city of Najran close to the Yemeni border in early January 1963, where Yemeni royalist base camps were located, Faisal again expressed his concerns to Washington, whereupon the United States again sent aircraft over Jeddah in a show of force on January 15. Washington also discussed the possibility of sending antiaircraft batteries to Najran.

Robert Komer, a senior staffer on the National Security Council (NSC), informed Kennedy that Faisal very much wanted the dispatch of U.S. aircraft to the desert kingdom. Officials at the Pentagon were unconvinced and noted that while the U.S. squadron might deter any Egyptian attack, it clearly lacked the military capability to defend Saudi Arabia. U.S. Air Force chief of staff General Curtis LeMay is said to have been especially opposed, claiming that the fighters would be sitting ducks and in any case were needed elsewhere.

Regardless, Komer and Secretary of State Dean Rusk urged that the squadron be sent, and on June 12 Kennedy signed off on Operation HARD SURFACE. Although it involved only a single squadron of 8 F-100s, it also included 560 support personnel and 861.3 tons of equipment.

The Pentagon claimed that Kennedy's only military commitment to the Middle East was simply a token force. The rules of engagement called for the fighters to intercept any Egyptian aircraft violating Saudi airspace and try to escort them out of Saudi airspace or to a convenient runway. If the intruding aircraft were to bomb Saudi targets or attempt to engage the American aircraft, then the F-100 pilots were to shoot them down. The Pentagon insisted that the F-100s be fully prepared for combat and armed with Sidewinder missiles.

Plans hit a snag with the Saudi insistence that the U.S. personnel have passports and visas. This ran afoul of the long-running Saudi ban on Jews entering their kingdom. Word of this soon got out and caused a minor flap in Congress and in the press. The Egyptian press picked it up, noting that the willingness of the Saudis to let Jews into Islam's holiest places was a sure sign of the weakness of the desert kingdom and its reliance on foreign support. On June 27, this impasse was broken by the adoption of a "don't ask, don't tell" policy. The Saudis would not ask if the American airmen were Jews, and the Americans would not tell.

On July 2, the NSC asked for permission to send the F-100s to Saudi Arabia, and Kennedy approved. The 8 F-100s did not entirely halt Egyptian attacks, leaving LeMay to grouse about the ineffectiveness of the operation, but Kennedy and the State Department downplayed these raids and styled the operation an effective deterrent at slight cost.

The U.S. aircraft never did engage Egyptian forces, and President Lyndon B. Johnson allowed the operation to end in January 1964. Nasser indeed increased Egyptian troop strength in Yemen, and the civil war there continued until 1970.

SPENCER C. TUCKER

See also
Nasser, Gamal Abdel; Saudi Arabia; Yemen Civil War

References
Bass, Warren. *Support Any Friend: Kennedy's Middle East and the Making of the U.S.-Israeli Alliance.* New York: Oxford University Press, 2003.
Patterson, Thomas G. *Kennedy's Quest for Victory: American Foreign Policy, 1961–1963.* New York: Oxford University Press, 1989.
United States Department of State. *Foreign Relations, 1961–1963,.* Vol. 17, *Near East, 1961–1962.* Washington, DC: United States Department of State, 1991.

Haredim

Jews commonly referred to as Ultra-Orthodox Jews or, more colloquially, as black hat orthodox. Within Orthodox Jewish communities, the name "Haredim," meaning "those who tremble" (i.e., before the Almighty), is preferred. Non-Haredi Israelis refer to the Haredim as the religious. The Haredim represent the most strictly religious and traditionalist wing of Judaism. Haredi Judaism is best distinguished from other forms of Judaism by its adherents' rejection of secular education and culture in favor of a lifestyle stringently devoted to the Tanakh (the Jewish Bible). The Haredim are easily recognized because of their distinctive dress (black suits and hats for men and ankle- and wrist-length attire for women), the high value they place on child rearing and extended family, and the prestige accorded to men in the Haredi community who dedicate their lives to religious study in yeshivas (religious schools).

Outsiders typically confuse Haredi Judaism with Hasidic Judaism. Hasidism is a pietistic or revivalist movement that emerged in traditional Jewish communities in Eastern and Central Europe during the 18th century. Initially there was hostility between traditionalists and Hasidim, but today nearly all Hasidic groups are best classified as Ultra-Orthodox, although not all Ultra-Orthodox are Hasidic.

The Haredim are distinguished from modern orthodox religious Jews by a number of differences in outlook and practice, not least of which are their perspectives on Zionism and the State of Israel. The modern orthodox, or Dati (meaning "the faithful"), eagerly support the Jewish state with great enthusiasm and generally identify with the ideology currents of religious Zionism, which tend to see the emergence and survival of the modern State of Israel in redemptive terms. The Haredim, by contrast, remain to a great extent antipathetic to Zionism.

Religious Jews have long associated the return of Jewish exiles to Israel with the coming of the biblically foretold Messiah. This anointed one, an heir to King David, it is believed, will rule in Jerusalem over a restored Jewish state. In Orthodox Judaism, the idea of a personal Messiah who leads by divine mandate remains prevalent. As such, the emergence of a secular Jewish state represented a challenge to the traditionalists' worldview. They believed that the return of Jews to Zion was contingent upon Jews' strict Torah observance. In contrast, modern ideologies such as nationalism, socialism, liberalism, and democracy guided the secular Jews who founded Israel. For the Ultra-Orthodox, then, the State of Israel was the product of a heretical movement. As a result, during the early decades of the 20th century, few orthodox rabbis were willing to lend support to Zionist efforts to create a Jewish state in Palestine. Today, while a few Haredi communities continue to reject the State of Israel entirely, most have come to an accommodationist position and indeed receive certain privileges in Israel. This was in large part due to concessions and considerations of the secular Zionists.

Led by David Ben-Gurion, the secular Zionists extended an exemption from military service to yeshiva students during the Israeli War of Independence (1948–1949), an exemption that has remained formal policy ever since. Ben-Gurion's motives for adopting this policy were in part political (to defuse religious opposition to the Zionist state) but also humanitarian, intended to allow for the survival of the traditional yeshiva culture.

Of all Jewish communities, the orthodox communities in Eastern Europe had been the most decimated by Stalinism, the Holocaust, and post–World War II pogroms. In contemporary Israeli politics, the military exemption is highly controversial. Many believe that it serves to marginalize the Ultra-Orthodox because military service often serves as an avenue of professional and political advancement. Separate religious military units have been formed to accommodate Ultra-Orthodox strictures in matters of social interaction between men and women, dietary rules, and maintaining an atmosphere of support for religious study and ritual observance.

The June 1967 Six-Day War had a transformative effect on the relationship between Orthodox Judaism and Zionism. In the initial phases of the war, it appeared that the very survival of the Jewish community in Israel might be at stake, but ultimately Israel's forces triumphed and gained control over areas of deep spiritual significance to religious Jews, most notably the Temple Mount and the adjoining Western Wall. The sole remaining physical structure connected to the temples, the Western Wall, was built circa 19 BCE during King Herod the Great's complete reconstruction of the Second Temple. Within the orthodox communities, the outcome of the war strengthened the position of those who supported Zionism and enhanced the movement toward religious Zionism.

Haredi communities in Israel were typically established by refugees from Central and Eastern Europe during the 1930s and 1940s and from Muslim countries after 1948. There are two significant Haredi political parties represented in the Knesset: United Torah Judaism and Shas. The latter has a constituency among secular Sephardic (Mediterranean and Middle Eastern) Jews, but its ideological orientation is Ultra-Orthodox. These parties primarily focus on legislation of concern to the religious community such as state support for religious schools, maintenance of orthodox rabbinical control of Jewish marriage and divorce in Israel, and opposition to any recognition of nonorthodox Judaism. As to Israeli-Palestinian relations, however, the Haredi parties have expressed willingness to make territorial concessions for the sake of the peace and security of the Jewish people and have supported or participated in centrist or center-left governments that have pursued land for peace. Those religious Zionists who oppose territorial concessions over the biblical boundaries of the land of Israel, by contrast, are represented by the National Religious Party, which typically allies with the secular rightists, most notably the Likud Party.

DANIEL SKIDMORE-HESS AND CATHY SKIDMORE-HESS

See also
Ashkenazic Judaism; Ben-Gurion, David; Hasidic Judaism; Israel; Mizrahi Judaism; Sephardic Judaism; Zionism

References
Efron, Noah J. *Real Jews: Secular vs. Ultra-Orthodox and the Struggle for Jewish Identity in Israel.* New York: Basic Books, 2003.
Fishkoff, Susan J. *The Rebbe's Army: Inside the World of Chabad-Lubavitch.* New York: Schocken, 2005.

Harim, Battle of (August 12, 1164)

Battle fought between a Christian army consisting of forces from the Byzantine Empire, Armenia, the principality of Antioch, and the county of Tripoli, and Muslim forces under Nur al-Din. The Battle of Harim (Harenc) was fought on August 12, 1164, near the town and castle of Artah, some 25 miles east-northeast of Antioch on the road from Antioch to Aleppo.

In 1163 King Amalric I of Jerusalem prepared to mount an invasion of Egypt. This would, however, expose the crusader states to an attack from the east, and Nur al-Din, *atabeg* of Aleppo, who ruled the Syrian province of the Seljuk Empire during 1146–1174, sought to take advantage of the opportunity to invade Lebanon. King Amalric then proceeded northward to support his northern vassals, Bohemund III of Antioch and Raymond III of Tripoli. It happened that a large number of French pilgrims led by Hugh VIII of Lusignan and Geoffrey Martel, the brother of William IV of Angoulême, joined Amalric. In addition, Konstantinos Kalamanos, Byzantine governor of Cilicia, arrived with troops to assist the crusaders. The Christians then met and defeated Nur al-Din in the Battle of al-Buqaia. Amalric then moved against Egypt.

Nur al-Din was determined to secure revenge. Securing assistance from his brother Qutb ad-Din in Mosul, vassals from Aleppo and Damascus, and the Ortoqids of the Jazira, Nur al-Din besieged the fortress of Harim (Harenc) in 1164.

Reginald of Saint Valery, lord of Harim, appealed for assistance, and Raymond III of Tripoli, Bohemund III of Antioch, and Joscelin III of Edessa arrived to relieve the siege and were joined there by Kalamanos, Thoros and Mleh of Armenia, Hugh VIII of Lusignan, and Geoffrey Martel, brother of William IV of Angoulême.

Nur al-Din prepared to give up the siege when they arrived, but the crusaders, remembering their victory at al-Buqaia, eschewed military discipline and attacked. Nur al-Din's troops may have feinted a retreat, but in any case they turned back the crusader charge, then counterattacked, driving their enemies into a swamp, where they were massacred. Kalamanos, Hugh, Raymond, Bohemund, and Joscelin were all taken prisoner and imprisoned in Aleppo. According to one Muslim source, the crusaders lost 10,000 killed.

Nur al-Din now resumed the siege of Harim, which surrendered a few days after the battle. With Amalric absent in Egypt, all three crusader states were now without their rulers, but Nur al-Din did not want to attack Antioch itself for fear of provoking a Byzantine response, as the principality was technically a fief of the emperor. Nur al-Din went on to besiege and capture Banias.

Amalric meanwhile abandoned Egypt and marched north with Thierry of Alsace to relieve Nur al-Din's pressure on Antioch. Bohemund was released from captivity in 1165, but Raymond remained a prisoner until 1173.

SPENCER C. TUCKER

See also
Amalric of Jerusalem; Antioch, Principality of; Crusades in the Holy Land, Christian; Nur al-Din; Tripoli, County of

References
Oldenbourg, Zoé. *The Crusades.* New York: Pantheon Books, 1966.

Runciman, Steven. *A History of the Crusades,* Vol. 2, *The Kingdom of Jerusalem.* Cambridge: Cambridge University Press, 1952.

Smail, R. C. *Crusading Warfare, 1097–1193.* Cambridge: Cambridge University Press, 1956.

William of Tyre. *A History of Deeds Done beyond the Sea.* Translated by E. A. Babcock and A. C. Krey. New York: Columbia University Press, 1943.

Hariri, Rafik (1944–2005)

Lebanese businessman, politician, and premier of Lebanon (1992–1998, 2000–2004). Rafik Baha al-Din Hariri was born in Sidon, Lebanon, on November 1, 1944, the son of a Sunni Muslim farmer. Hariri studied business administration at Beirut Arab University during 1965–1966, then went to Saudi Arabia, where he became an auditor for an engineering firm.

In 1969 Hariri set up his own construction company, CICONEST, which benefited greatly from the Saudi oil boom of the 1970s. He was involved in major construction projects, including offices, hotels, hospitals, and palaces in Lebanon and Saudi Arabia. His reasonable bids on construction work won him the respect of his clients, and he quickly built up businesses and amassed a fortune that made him one of the richest people in the world. In 1978 the Saudi Arabian royal family granted him Saudi citizenship, and he became Saudi Arabia's leading entrepreneur.

Hariri acquired control of the French construction company Oger in 1979 and established Oger International in Paris. His business interests included construction, banking, real estate, telecommunications, and oil.

Already known as a philanthropist, in 1979 Hariri founded the Hariri Foundation for Culture and Higher Education. In 1982 he donated $12 million to Lebanese victims of Israel's invasion of Lebanon, and in 1983 he built a hospital, school, and university in Kafr Falus, Lebanon. He also created a foundation that paid the university fees of at least 12,000 Lebanese students in Lebanon, Europe, and the United States. He reportedly donated about $90 million to charity every year.

In 1983 Hariri played a significant role in the talks that led to a cease-fire in the Lebanese civil war. He then worked

Rafik Hariri (1944–2005), prominent Lebanese businessman and politician who was premier of Lebanon during 1992–1998 and 2000–2004. (European Community)

with U.S. special envoy Philip Habib to produce the Taif Accord of 1989 that ended the Lebanese Civil War. In 1992 Hariri was appointed prime minister of Lebanon in a move designed to attract foreign investors to help fund the massive rebuilding process required after years of civil war and to restore the confidence of the nation's own investors. He was closely involved in the project that rebuilt the historic downtown government district of Beirut, faithfully reproducing the French mandate architecture. In these years Hariri, who owned property in Damascus, had excellent relations with the Syrian government, and Syrian president Hafez al-Assad consulted with him on occasion.

Considered the mastermind of Lebanon's postwar reconstruction program, Hariri was widely expected to retain his post after the extension of President Émile Lahoud's term of office, which occurred in November 1998 as a result of Syrian pressure. Hariri abruptly declined Lahoud's offer to form a new government, accusing the new president of acting unconstitutionally in his negotiations with the National Assembly. Hariri was replaced by former premier and veteran politician Salim al-Huss. In 2000 after less than two years in office, during which his administration was unable to stem economic and political crisis in the country, al-Huss resigned. Less than a week later, Hariri accepted Lahoud's offer to lead a new government as prime minister. On October 20, 2004, Hariri again resigned from the post.

Hariri became unpopular with some Syrian elements and pro-Syria factions in Lebanon when he called for a Syrian withdrawal from Lebanon and utilized his excellent relations with France to exert pressure in this regard. On February 14, 2005, Hariri, 6 of his bodyguards, and 15 other people died in a massive car bomb blast as his motorcade was passing the St. George Hotel in Beirut. An unknown Islamist terrorist group was blamed for the incident. The assassination brought an outpouring of anger from within Lebanon, the formation of an anti-Syrian Lebanese coalition and then a new government, Syria's military withdrawal from Lebanon under international pressure, and a call by the United Nations (UN) Security Council for a special international court to try suspects in the assassination.

Many Lebanese and international observers blamed Syrian officials for the assassination, suggesting that the plan must have been approved at a very high level of the Syrian government. Indeed, there was an eyewitness account that President Bashar al-Assad had threatened Hariri in August 2004. Although the Syrian government denied any knowledge of the deed, the UN investigation implicated Syrian officials along with members of the Lebanese security services. Hariri's violent end was not the last. The years after his death saw the assassination of other anti-Syrian Lebanese politicians.

SPENCER C. TUCKER

See also
Assad, Bashar al-; Hrawi, Elias; Lebanon; Lebanon Civil War; Syria

References
Fisk, Robert. *Pity the Nation: The Abduction of Lebanon.* 4th ed. New York: Nation Books, 2002.
Iskandar, Marwan. *Rafiq Hariri and the Fate of Lebanon.* London: Saqi, 2006.

Harran, Battle of (May 7, 1104)

Battle fought between forces of the Christian crusader states of Antioch and Edessa and the Seljuk forces of Mosul and Mardin. In 1104, Seljuk forces attacked the county of Edessa. Baldwin II, count of Edessa, asked for help from the principality of Antioch and its ruler, Bohemund I. The combined Christian forces of some 12,000 men arrived and laid siege to the city of Harran.

Seljuk forces from Mosul, commanded by Jerkermish, and those from Mardin, led by Sukman, marched to the relief of Harran, although their size is unknown. The two forces met on the plain near Harran. For two days the two sides skirmished. On the third day, May 7, the Islamic forces feigned a retreat across the Balikh River, encouraging the Christian forces to pursue. The Edessans rushed forward to engage their enemy and were then surrounded by Seljuk cavalry and nearly wiped out. Baldwin was among those taken prisoner.

Seeing the defeat of his ally, Bohemund did not press his attack and was able to escape to Edessa. The Seljuks had thus defeated the Christian forces in pitched battle for the first time since the onset of the First Crusade. Edessa never fully recovered, and Antioch was forced to seek Byzantine support.

RALPH MARTIN BAKER

See also
Crusades in the Holy Land, Christian; Seljuk Dynasty

References
Jorgensen, C. *Battles of the Crusades, 1097–1444.* Stroud, UK: Spellmount Publishing, 2007.
Runciman, S. A *History of the Crusades: The Kingdom of Jerusalem and the Frankish East, 1100–1187,* Vol. 2. Cambridge: Cambridge University Press, 1987.

Harun al-Rashid (763–809)

Fifth Abbasid caliph (r. 786–809). The reign of Harun al-Rashid, born on March 17, 763, at Rey, Jibal (in present-day Tehran Province, Iran), is viewed as being a golden age for the caliphate, a period marked by scientific, artistic, and religious accomplishments. Harun established the Bayt al-Hikma (House of Wisdom) library in Baghdad. In 796, he moved his court and government to Ar-Raqqah in present-day Syria.

Nonetheless, Harun's reign was plagued by internal rebellions and costly external wars. The caliphate faced several internal problems. Fragmentation was already occurring in the westernmost reaches of the caliphate. In Spain, a rival caliphate was established by the surviving Umayyads in 755. After a series of revolts and disorders in North Africa, the Idrisid dynasty established itself in the Maghrib in 788, and the Aghlabids emerged as the autonomous rulers of Ifriqiya.

There were also two major uprisings in Egypt, in 788 and 794, prompted by heavy taxation and inept governorship. Both rebellions were put down, however. Syria was also in a state of disorder owing to fighting between the tribal factions of the Yemenis and the Mudaris. These tribes also fought the Abbasid army and the governors who became embroiled in their conflicts. Harun sent an army to Syria that successfully pacified it in 796.

In Persia and Khurasan there was unrest among the local populations who were disillusioned by the failure of the Abbasids to fulfill their pledge to improve the quality of life. These regions had also been only superficially Islamized, and their peoples were still attached to their local religions and traditions. Thus, their uprisings took on Shiite and Kharijite religious forms, which were closer to their pre-Islamic traditions and beliefs. Harun's forces put down a series of Alid revolts in Khurasan and the South Caspian region and also engaged in combat with the Kharijites in Sistan, Fars, and Kirman.

Harun personally led expeditions and raids against Byzantium. In 781 an Abbasid army of 95,000 men reached the Sea of Marmara. In 797 Harun led an attack that yielded some significant territorial gains, but he was forced to conclude an early peace with Empress Irene because of the threat of a Khazar attack. The caliph led some 100,000 men against Byzantium again in 803 and returned with significant booty. Harun's largest effort occurred in 806, however, when the caliph led 135,000 men in attacking and taking Heraclea and Tyana. The success of this expedition and the threat of a concurrent Bulgarian attack forced Byzantine emperor Nicephorus to accept a humiliating treaty that forced him to pay tribute and a personal poll tax for himself and his son. Harun also launched successful naval assaults against Cyprus in 805 and Rhodes in 807, although no permanent gains were accomplished here. On the other hand, the Khazars launched a number of raids into the caliphate, bent on securing booty, and a massive Khazar attack on Armenia in 800 devastated that region.

Harun al-Rashid died on March 24, 809, at Tus, Khorasan (in present-day Razavi Khorasan Province, Iran). The succession resulted in a division of the caliphate and civil war between his sons that eroded the central power and brought the rise of several autonomous local dynasties.

Adam Ali

See also
Abbasid Caliphate; Byzantine-Muslim Wars

References
Glubb, John Baggot. *Haroon al Rasheed and the Great Abbasids.* London: Hodder and Stoughton, 1976.
Kennedy, Hugh. *The Armies of the Caliphs: Military and Society in the Early Islamic State.* New York: Routledge, 2001.

Hashemites

"Hashemite" is the Western name given to a modern dynasty based on the descendants of the Banu Hashim, or Clan of Hashim, within the larger Quraysh tribe. The Hashemites became the rulers of the Hejaz in the western portions of today's Saudi Arabia, Jordan, and Iraq. The Banu Hashim were descendants of the Arab chieftain Quraysh, in turn a descendant of the prophet Ismail, himself the son of the prophet Ibrahim (Abraham). Quraysh first came to the holy city of Mecca during the second century CE. The first generation of Quraysh to rule the city came six generations later in the year 480.

The modern Hashemites trace their direct lineage from Hashim (died ca. 510), the great-grandfather of the Muslim prophet Muhammad. In the same clan line were the Abbasid caliphs who defeated the first imperial caliphal family, the Umayyads. The term "sharif" refers to descendants of Prophet Muhammad who can be found all over the Muslim world because of the spread of the Banu Hashim through the Islamic conquests.

The holy cities of Mecca and Medina were traditionally protected by a leading sharif family. Hussein ibn Ali of the Hashemite Dhau-Awn clan was also a traditional leader in the western Arabian province of Hejaz. The Ottoman sultan Abdulhamid II kept him under house arrest in Constantinople until 1908. The sultan's enemies, the so-called Young

Turks of the Committee of Union and Progress (CUP), at first allied with some of the Arab nationalist groups who, like Hussein, wanted self-rule or a new type of dual Arab-Turkish monarchy. The Young Turks had the sultan appoint Hussein as emir and sharif of Mecca in 1908, and he then returned to the Hejaz. His son, Abdullah, made discreet inquiries of the British about raising a rebellion against the Ottoman-CUP government, and when the CUP turned against the Arab nationalists, the stage was set for the Arab Revolt. Sharif Hussein's aim was to establish an Arab kingdom from the Hejaz to Syria and Iraq and including Palestine. Toward this end, he corresponded with British high commissioner for Egypt Sir A. Henry McMahon.

Hussein led the Great Arab Revolt beginning in 1916 to liberate the Arab lands. Between 1917 and 1924 with the collapse of the Ottoman Empire in World War I, Hussein and his son Ali ruled an independent Hejaz. However, the Arab kingdom they had sought was not realized, for the British had concluded the secret Sykes-Picot Agreement with the French during the war to secure much of the Middle East for themselves. In the postwar Treaty of Lausanne and Treaty of Sèvres with Turkey, the British and French secured as mandates under the League of Nations roughly the same areas spelled out in the Sykes-Picot Agreement. The territory conquered by Sharif Hussein's son Faisal, roughly comprising Syria and Lebanon, was to be returned to the French. Palestine, Iraq, and Transjordan went to the British.

Tribal leader Lord Abd al-Aziz ibn-Saud (known as Ibn Saud), who ruled most of central Arabia, aimed to take back the Hejaz. In 1924 his forces took Mecca, making it a part of the Kingdom of Saudi Arabia. Ibn Saud then annexed the Hejaz and set up his own son Faisal as governor.

These actions effectively ended the Hashemite claim to the Hejaz, but Hussein's two politically active sons, Abdullah and Faisal, became the kings of Transjordan and Iraq, respectively. The Hashemite Kingdom of Iraq lasted from 1921 to 1958, and a line of Hashemite kings has ruled Transjordan, now Jordan, since 1921.

JAMES H. WILLBANKS AND SHERIFA ZUHUR

See also
Abbasid Caliphate; Abdullah I; Faisal I, King of Iraq; Hussein ibn Talal, King of Jordan; Ibn Saud, King; Palestine, Pre-1918 History of; Shia Islam; Sunni Islam; Sykes-Picot Agreement; Umayyad Caliphate; Wahhabism; World War I, Impact on the Middle East

References
Hourani, Albert. *A History of the Arab Peoples.* Cambridge, MA: Harvard University Press, 1991.
Howarth, David A. *The Desert King: The Life of Ibn Saud.* Northampton, MA: Interlink, 1964.
Karsh, Efraim, and P. P. Kumaraswamy. *Israel, the Hashemites, and the Palestinians: The Fateful Triangle.* London: Frank Cass, 2003.
Milton-Edwards, Beverly, and Peter Hinchcliffe. *Jordan: A Hashemite Legacy.* London: Routledge, 2001.
Sabini, John. *Armies in the Sand: The Struggle for Mecca.* London: Thames and Hudson, 1981.
Teitelbaum, Joshua. *The Rise and Fall of the Hashemite Kingdom of Hejaz.* New York: New York University Press, 2001.

Hashomer

Jewish defense organization in Palestine regarded as the forerunner of the Israel Defense Forces (IDF). Hashomer (Hebrew for "guard") was first organized in 1909 by members of the Second Aliya (1904–1914) to provide security for the Jewish settlements in Palestine, especially the largely isolated kibbutzim. Hashomer was formed by members of Poalei Zion, a socialist Zionist group. Its founders were recent immigrants from Russia who had settled in Lower Galilee, and a number of them had participated in a self-defense organization of 1904–1906 known as Bar Giora. Among Hashomer founders were Yitzhak Ben-Zvi, Israel Giladi, Rachel Yanait, Israel Shochat, and Manya Shochat.

Hashomer's stated aims were to protect Jewish lives and property, secure respect for the Jews from among the Arabs, and improve relations with the Arabs while learning their language and customs. Hashomer concluded agreements with a number of Jewish settlements in Lower Galilee in which its members would provide security services in return for a fixed fee. Hashomer achieved considerable success, and in 1911 it expanded its operations beyond Galilee. Hashomer did away with the need to employ Arab watchmen to warn against raids and provided security as well as prevented thefts.

Hashomer clashed with Arabs on a number of occasions and incurred casualties, but its activities also won the admiration of many Jews in Palestine and in the diaspora. Members of Hashomer regarded themselves as the forerunners of a future Jewish national army. They refused to accept the authority of the Yishuv (Jewish community in Palestine) but nonetheless claimed the exclusive right to protect the Jewish settlements.

Shortly after the start of World War I, Hashomer proposed to Turkish authorities the establishment of a Jewish legion in the Ottoman Army, an offer that was refused.

Hashomer's pro-Ottoman Empire position, however, brought it into conflict with the pro-British Jewish intelligence network known as Nili.

In 1920 on the formation of the Jewish self-defense organization Haganah, members of Hashomer were asked to turn over their arms to Haganah and merge with it. This led to a considerable debate among Hashomer members, a number of whom claimed that their organization had the sole right to defend the Jews of Palestine. Not until the Arab riots of 1929 did the last Hashomer holdouts agree to turn over their arms to Haganah, which itself gave way to the IDF during the Israeli War of Independence (1948–1949).

SPENCER C. TUCKER

See also
Haganah

References
Mardor, Munya M. *Haganah*. Edited D. R. Elston. Foreword by David Ben-Gurion. Translated by H. A. G. Schmuckler. New York: New American Library, 1966.

Pappe, Ilan. *A History of Modern Palestine: One Land, Two Peoples*. Cambridge: Cambridge University Press, 2003.

Hasidic Judaism

Hasidic (Chasidic) Judaism is a branch of Judaism that originated in Eastern Europe (Belarus, Poland, and Ukraine) in the 18th century at a time when European Jews were being persecuted. The word "Hasidic" comes from the Hebrew word *chasidut*, meaning "pious," which is derived from the Hebrew root word *chesed*, meaning "loving kindness." Hasidic Judaism is also known as Hasidism (Pietism).

Religious persecution in Eastern Europe drove nearly half of European Jewry to emphasize an inner personal spirituality derived from intensive Talmudic study rather than academic and ethnic beliefs. This inner spirituality, or joy, is expressed outwardly in distinctive religious traditions and practices that allow the Hasidim to grow closer to God through everyday living as well as Torah study. This brings the Hasidim in constant communion (*Devekut*) with God.

Hasidism's founder, Rabbi Israel Baal Shem Tov (1699–1760), also known by the title "master of the good name" (*a'al Shem Tov*, abbreviated as *Besht*), was a scholar, mystic, and healer who taught that the Torah communicated God and the truths of God outwardly through revelation, the outer aspect of the Torah, and inwardly through devotion and piety, the hidden or inner aspect of the Torah. Hasidism asserts that Baal Shem Tov was a miracle worker and was infallible in his teaching and that these same defining attributes continue to be passed through a series of dynastic leaders known as rebbes (rebbis, rabbees), generally meaning "master" and "teacher" and less commonly "mentor."

This great elevation of Hasidic rebbes was one of the main reasons that European Jewry divided into Hasidic Judaism and Orthodox Judaism, called Mitnagdim (opponents) by the Hasidim. Another point of division is the Hasidic assertion that God permeates all that exists. The Mitnagdim understood this belief to be pantheism. But what the Hasidic philosophy actually asserts is the belief that although God does permeate all that exists, God is more than that. Hasidism also expands Judaism's traditional teaching that God implanted a divine spark in all humans by teaching that although the divine spark exists only in the souls of humans, there is a divinely infused spark of goodness in all creation that can be redeemed to perfect the world. It is God's animation of all that exists that allows pious humans to commune with God. This belief in an interactive relationship between God and pious humans, allowing God to influence the actions of pious humans and allowing pious humans to correlatively influence the will of God, derived from the 16th-century rabbi Isaac Ben Solomon Luria's *Kabbalah* (Cabala).

The most common Hasidic prayer style (Nusach Sepharad) is based on Rabbi Luria's integration of Ashkenazic and Sephardic liturgies and is accompanied by melodies called *nigunim* (*nigguns*) that are in themselves descriptive of the mood of the prayer. The *amidah* (standing), the central prayer in all Jewish worship services, is generally recited while standing, and some particularly pious Hasidim concentrate for seven seconds on each of its words. Most Hasidim pray in a Yiddish-influenced, heavily accented Ashkenazic Hebrew and oppose the daily use of oral Hebrew. They believe Ashkenazic Hebrew to be a holy language intended for prayer only, and they also believe that it is debased by common use.

The daily attire for Hasidic men is generally black trousers and coats with a white shirt and a black hat. A long black robe called a *bekishe* with a prayer belt called a *gartel* and a fur headdress are worn for Shabbat (Sabbath). Most Hasidic men wear long sideburns called *payoth*, following the biblical prohibition (Leviticus 19:27) not to shave the sides of one's face. White threads or fringes (*tzitzit* or *tsitsits*) are worn about the waist, either over or under the shirt, as directed by Numbers 15:38. Hasidic boys have their first haircut and are given their first fringed garment on their third birthday. Hasidic women generally wear long black skirts and sleeves past the elbow.

Immersion in a ritual pool of water (*mikvah*) is practiced as an outward manifestation of an inner or spiritual cleansing. Hasidic men generally practice this ritual cleansing prior to Jewish holidays, and many ritually wash daily prior to morning prayers. Female Hasidim generally immerse in a *mikvah* seven days after the end of their menstrual cycle.

The largest Hasidic fellowship, the Lubavitch (some 100,000 adherents), is based in Brooklyn, New York. There are also large populations residing in Israel along with other Hasidim such as the Gor (Gerer), Vizhnitz, and Bealz (Belzer) groups. The Belzer, Bobov, Bostoner, Breslov, Gerer, Munkacz, Puppa, Rimnitz, Satmar, and Vizhnitz Hasidim are the largest of the remaining Hasidic groups.

RICHARD M. EDWARDS

See also
Ashkenazic Judaism; Mizrahi Judaism; Sephardic Judaism

References
Biale, David. *Cultures of the Jews: A New History*. New York: Schocken, 2002.
Dimont, Max. *Jews, God and History*. New York: Simon and Schuster, 1962.
Harris, Lis. *Holy Days: The World of the Hasidic Family*. New York: Touchstone, 1995.
Haumann, Heiko. *A History of East European Jews*. Budapest, Hungary: Central European University Press, 2001.
Robinson, George. *Essential Judaism: A Complete Guide to Beliefs, Customs & Rituals*. New York: Pocket Books/Simon and Schuster, 2001.
Seltzer, Robert. *Jewish People, Jewish Thought*. New York: Macmillan, 1980.
Shalomi, Zalman Schachter, and Nathaniel Miles-Yepez, eds. *Wrapped in a Holy Flame: Teachings and Tales of the Hasidic Masters*. San Francisco: Wiley, 2003.

Hasmonean Tunnel Incident (September 23–28, 1996)

Armed clash between Palestinians and Israeli border police and Israel Defense Forces (IDF) soldiers that began on September 23, 1996, in the Old City of Jerusalem on the Temple Mount (Haram al-Sharif). The Hasmonean Tunnel Incident is sometimes referred to as the Kotel Tunnel Incident.

The Temple Mount is a holy site for Christians, Jews, and Muslims. For Jews, it is the site of the first and second Jewish Temples and is said to be the site of the third and final Temple to be rebuilt upon the coming of the Messiah. For Muslims, it is the site of two very important religious shrines: the Dome of the Rock and the al-Aqsa Mosque.

Located in the Old City of eastern Jerusalem, the Temple Mount area remained under Jordanian control from 1948 to 1967, at which point the Israelis seized control of it as a result of the Six-Day War. A series of tunnels dating back to antiquity run beneath the site. After 1967, Israeli historians and archaeologists began excavations at the site. In an attempt to find and reconstruct lost portions of the Western Wall, the Israelis uncovered the Hasmonean Tunnel, which is along the northern edge of the wall, in 1987. It is actually a large aqueduct dating to the second century BCE.

The Hasmonean Tunnel Incident was sparked when the Israeli government allowed archaeologists doing excavations near the Western Wall to open a new exit to the tunnel in the area. On the night of September 23, 1996, between 11:30 p.m. and 12:00 a.m. and under heavy police guard, a new exit was opened off the Hasmonean Tunnel. When the Palestinians realized what had happened, they were outraged because of the proximity of the tunnel to the Temple Mount, particularly the al-Aqsa Mosque. Some Muslim leaders in Jerusalem also claimed that the tunnel exit had damaged the al-Aqsa Mosque, under which part of the aqueduct ran.

Palestinian Authority (PA) president Yasser Arafat immediately denounced the tunnel as an act of Israeli aggression against the Islamic religion. He called for a general strike and for demonstrations to be staged throughout the Palestinian territories. Even before Arafat's official condemnation of the Israeli move, protesters began to clash with Israeli forces, throwing rocks and bottles. Israeli worshippers at the Western Wall were also subjected to mob attacks.

What began as protests on September 24 quickly turned into fierce fighting between Palestinian militants and Israeli security forces. Indeed, many claim that this incident nearly turned into a full-fledged intifada against Israel. Although the worst of the fighting had died down by September 28, it was days after that before the riots in the Palestinian territories were entirely quelled. In the four days of heavy fighting, as many as 100 Palestinians and 15 Israeli soldiers and border policemen were killed.

The Hasmonean Tunnel Incident helped convince right-wing Israeli prime minister Benjamin Netanyahu to sign the January 1997 Hebron Protocol with the PA under which Israel would withdraw from the West Bank city of Hebron as agreed to in the 1993 Oslo Accords. While the majority of the Israeli population supported the signing of this agreement, some hard-liners viewed it as an outrageous act of capitulation. Palestinians tended to see the Hasmonean Tunnel Incident as a victory for their side.

DANIEL W. KUTHY AND PAUL G. PIERPAOLI JR.

See also

Al-Aqsa Mosque Massacre; Arafat, Yasser; Netanyahu, Benjamin; Oslo Accords; Palestinian National Authority

References

Bickerton, Ian J., and Carla L. Klausner. *A Concise History of the Arab-Israeli Conflict.* 4th ed. Upper Saddle River, NJ: Prentice Hall, 2004.

Gorenberg, Gershom. *The End of Days: Fundamentalism and the Struggle for the Temple Mount.* New York: Oxford University Press, 2000.

Hattin, Battle of (July 3–4, 1187)

The Battle of Hattin, fought in the Holy Land during the Second Crusade of 1147–1149, resulted in a major Muslim victory over the Christian forces. Hattin is located in Galilee seven miles west of Tiberius and the Sea of Galilee.

Crusader Reynald of Châtillon, lord of the castle at Kerak on the road between Damascus and Mecca, had carried out a series of attacks on Muslim caravans and towns along the Red Sea. When King Guy de Lusignan of the Latin Kingdom of Jerusalem failed to punish Reynald for these actions, the brilliant Muslim military leader Egyptian sultan Saladin (Salah ad-Din) vowed to do so. In June 1187 Saladin mounted an invasion of Palestine.

On June 26, 1187, Saladin crossed the Jordan River at the head of a force of some 20,000 men and laid siege to the crusader stronghold of Tiberius. King Guy's advisers called for an immediate effort to raise the siege. Count Raymond of Tripoli, the ablest of the crusader generals, whose wife was then in Tiberius, urged Guy to wait. Raymond knew that Tiberius was well supplied and believed it best to delay any relief effort until Saladin's forces experienced supply problems in the countryside. Also, the extreme heat of summer would make campaigning difficult then. Guy ignored this wise counsel. He ordered Christian castles and strongpoints to provide much of their garrisons and in late June led a relieving Christian army of approximately 1,200 knights and 18,000 infantry toward Tiberius.

On July 2 the Christian force reached Sephoria, about equidistant between Acre and Tiberius. Again Raymond urged caution, and again he was rebuffed. Although Raymond had warned Guy that there was only one spring accessible to the army along its planned route, the army continued east.

Informed of the crusader approach, Saladin was pleased. He knew the effects that lack of water would have on the heavily armored crusader force. Saladin immediately sent light cavalry to attack the Christians, bringing them to a halt on July 3 in the middle of the parched and barren land. The Muslim attackers and the heat of the day forced the

Illustration depicting Muslim forces under Saladin capturing the Holy Cross during the Battle of Hattin on July 4, 1187, from *Chronica maiora* by Matthew Paris, 13th century. (Fine Art Images/Heritage Images/Getty Images)

Christians to take up position near the village of Hattin and next to two mounds known as the Horns.

Saladin's men surrounded the crusaders and kept constant arrow fire on their camp during the night of July 3–4. What little water the Christians had was consumed. Saladin also had his men set fire to nearby brush upwind of the crusader camp, blowing smoke into it and making it even more difficult for the men and horses.

The next morning, July 4, Saladin still refused to close with the heavily armored Christians. Bringing up fresh stocks of arrows, he ordered his bowmen to continue their harassing fire. In an effort to end this the Christian cavalry charged the Muslims, but this separated the infantry from the cavalry and enabled the Muslims to destroy the latter piecemeal. At the very end of the battle Raymond and a small force of cavalry cut their way through the Muslim lines, but they were the only ones to escape. The rest of the crusaders, out of water, their horses dying of thirst, and under constant harassing fire from the Muslim archers, were forced to surrender. Guy was among the prisoners.

Exact casualty totals are unknown, but certainly the majority of the Christians were either taken prisoner or killed. While Saladin ordered Reynald executed, he treated Guy well and subsequently released him on the latter's promise that he would not fight again. Raymond later died of wounds sustained in the battle.

Saladin's victory at Hattin had tremendous consequences. This worst crusader defeat ever led to the Muslim conquest of most of Palestine, the Christian garrisons of which had been too badly depleted to put together the force taken in the battle. During the next months Saladin captured Tiberius, Acre, and Ascalon, although crusaders arriving by sea managed to hold off the Muslims at Tyre. Saladin laid siege to Jerusalem on September 20, and that city surrendered on October 2, 1187. Unlike the behavior of the Christians in the First Crusade, Saladin treated the defeated well.

Most of the Latin Kingdom of Jerusalem had now been lost to the Christians, not to be regained, but the Europeans controlled the Mediterranean Sea, and the Christian states soon mounted a new series of crusades in the Holy Land. These crusades, however, were increasingly motivated by secular rather than religious reasons.

SPENCER C. TUCKER

See also
Crusades in the Holy Land, Christian; Guy of Lusignan; Saladin

References
France, John. *Western Warfare in the Age of the Crusades, 1000–1300.* Ithaca, NY: Cornell University Press, 1999.

Gore, Terry L. *Neglected Heroes: Leadership and War in the Early Medieval Period.* Westport, CT: Praeger, 1995.
Tyerman, Christopher. *Fighting for Christendom: Holy War and the Crusades.* New York: Oxford University Press, 2005.

Havlaga

Term meaning "self-restraint" in Hebrew and referring to a policy of passive defense against Arab attacks in Palestine and later Israel. *Havlaga* was the official policy of the Yishuv (Jews in Palestine) until the Arab Revolt of 1936–1939. That conflict sparked a sharp debate among the Yishuv in terms of its response to Arab violence. Since the founding of the secret Jewish self-defense organization Haganah in 1920, Arab attacks were nearly always met not by retaliatory violence but rather by measured responses utilizing British law enforcement authorities. The official position was to prevent and repel Arab raids and, when possible, pursue the perpetrators and hand them over to British mandate officials.

Jewish leaders in Palestine adopted *havlaga* as a way to influence public perception of Arabs and Jews. First, they feared that retaliation against the Arabs would compel the British to see the violence as a Jewish-Arab civil conflict instead of a one-sided Arab-inspired affair. Second, many feared that retribution would raise the ire of the British public and diminish any chances of British support for a Jewish homeland. Also, some Yishuv leaders feared that retaliation against Arabs would only serve to radicalize moderate Arabs and embolden the extremists.

When the Arab Revolt began in 1936, the policy of *havlaga* came under great scrutiny. At first trying to maintain the policy as the violence became widespread, Jewish leaders including David Ben-Gurion, Vladimir Jabotinsky, and Chaim Weizmann urged calm and the continuation of self-restraint. Believing that the uprising would be short-lived, they figured to outlast the attacks. But the Arab Revolt endured, taking more and more Jewish lives and destroying much of their property. By mid-1937, many Jews in Palestine began to call for a more proactive response to Arab attacks. More and more Jews had come to the conclusion that *havlaga* was actually encouraging Arab violence and adversely affecting Jewish public opinion in the Yishuv and other parts of the world. Some made the argument that *havlaga* was undermining the morale of Jewish security forces and Haganah.

Soon, Haganah commanders began to carry out sporadic retaliatory strikes. When the radical Jewish paramilitary group Irgun Tsvai Leumi (National Military Organization) organized in 1937, its members were not about to adhere to the *havlaga* policy. Instead, Irgun pressed for a firm policy of retribution and engaged in bombings against Arab interests in Jerusalem and Haifa. By 1939, even Haganah had deviated from *havlaga* in response to raids emanating from the Arab-Palestinian village of Baldat al-Shaykh, which it attacked in the summer of 1939. Then, on July 2, 1939, Haganah issued a statement declaring that while it would refrain from launching wholesale or random retaliatory actions against the Arabs, it reserved the right to pursue individuals responsible for violence against the Yishuv into their own villages. After the Arab Revolt ended, *havlaga* again became the official policy of Palestinian Jews, although there were certainly exceptions. By the mid-1940s, the policy once more came under great scrutiny. In Israel today there are still those who adhere to *havlaga,* and the old debates about its effectiveness continue to reverberate throughout the nation.

PAUL G. PIERPAOLI JR.

See also
Arab Revolt in Palestine; Ben-Gurion, David; Haganah; Irgun Tsvai Leumi; Jabotinsky, Vladimir Yevgenyevich

References
Bickerton, Ian J., and Carla L. Klausner. *A Concise History of the Arab-Israeli Conflict.* 4th ed. Upper Saddle River, NJ: Prentice Hall, 2004.

Levine, David. *The Birth of the Irgun Zvai Leumi: The Jewish Resistance Movement.* Jerusalem: Gefen, 1996.

Hayreddin Barbarossa (ca. 1483–1546)

Greco-Turkish corsair and Ottoman Empire admiral. Born Khizr (Khidr) in Greece around 1483, Khair ad-Din (in Turkish Hayreddin), but better known as Barbarossa for his fiery red beard, followed his four older brothers into a livelihood of piracy, becoming involved in the struggle for control of the coast of the Maghrib (Northwest Africa). Hayreddin and one of his brothers captured a number of towns along the Algerian coast. Accepting the suzerainty of Ottoman sultan Selim I in 1517 in return for material assistance, Hayreddin captured Algiers in 1519 and set it up as his naval base. There he built up his naval force and employed larger galleys to raid Malta in 1532.

In 1533 Sultan Suleiman I the Magnificent (1520–1566) awarded Hayreddin the title kapitan pasha (admiral). Hayreddin secured Ottoman control of the eastern Mediterranean. Later in 1533, he took Koroni and Patras in Greece from Venice. In 1534 he captured Tunis, although Charles V retook it the next year. In 1537 Hayreddin attacked the southeastern coast of Italy, then assisted in Suleiman's siege of Corfu until forced to retire by a fleet under Genoese admiral Andrea Doria. During 1537–1538 Hayreddin captured several Venetian fortresses on the Greek mainland as well as a number of Greek islands.

In the Battle of Préveza off western Greece (September 27, 1538), Hayreddin, with about 90 galleys and 50 small galiots, managed to outmaneuver Andrea Doria's superior force of 130 full-size Venetian, Papal, Spanish, and Genoese galleys, making himself master of the eastern Mediterranean. Taking advantage of fighting between the Habsburgs and France in 1542, Hayreddin joined with French naval forces to raid the coast of Catalonia in Spain in 1543. Sacking Nice that same year, he spent the winter of 1543–1544 at Toulon.

Hayreddin was then at court in Istanbul until his death on July 4, 1546. For generations Turkish ships passing his tomb at Besiktas in Istanbul would fire a salute. A bold and resourceful commander, he was also a highly efficient and capable administrator. Hayreddin showed special skill in attacking land targets from the sea.

SPENCER C. TUCKER

See also
Suleiman I

References
Bradford, Ernle D. S. *The Sultan's Admiral: The Life of Barbarossa.* New York: Harcourt, Brace & World, 1968.

Goffman, Daniel. *The Ottoman Empire and Early Modern Europe.* Cambridge: Cambridge University Press, 2002.

Guilmartin, John Francis, Jr. *Gunpowder and Galleys: Changing Technology and Mediterranean Warfare at Sea in the Sixteenth Century.* Cambridge: Cambridge University Press, 1974.

Hebron Massacre (August 23–24, 1929)

The West Bank town of Hebron (al-Khalil in Arabic) is one of the most important geographic sites for Christians, Jews, and Muslims. Located in the town is the Tomb of the Patriarchs, the traditional burial place of Abraham, the biblical prophet from whom all three religions trace their origins, Hebron has also been one of the major flash points between Arabs and Israelis in the past 100 years. Today, half of the building containing the Tomb of the Patriarchs is a mosque, while the other half is a synagogue.

For hundreds of years a Sephardic Jewish community lived in Hebron in relatively peaceful coexistence with the

Arab majority. By the middle of the 1920s the Jewish community in Hebron numbered about 800 people, with only a small percentage of that number being relatively recent Ashkenazic arrivals.

In September 1928, tensions between Muslims and Jews flared in Jerusalem when Haj Amin al-Husseini, the mufti of Jerusalem, accused the Jews of carrying out unauthorized construction at the Western Wall. The following year in early August, Muslims and Jews again clashed over Jewish demands for access to the Western Wall and Muslim concerns about encroachment of the al-Aqsa Mosque. A series of inflammatory sermons delivered by al-Husseini preceded a wave of disturbances that built in intensity.

Concerned about Jewish security there, leaders of Haganah, the secret Jewish self-defense force, went to Hebron on August 20 and proposed a defensive plan for the Jews in the town. The leaders of the Sephardic community, who were largely anti-Zionist, refused the offer and insisted that Haganah leave immediately. They were convinced that the local Arab leaders would shield them from whatever violence might sweep the rest of the country.

On August 23, false reports began reaching Hebron of Jews desecrating Muslim holy places in Jerusalem. As tensions rose in Hebron, an angry mob killed a student at the Ashkenazic Yeshiva. At the time, the entire Hebron police force consisted of 34 men: a single British officer, Raymond Cafferata, with 18 mounted policemen and 15 on foot. One member of Cafferata's force was a Jew, but all others were Arabs.

Although Cafferata managed to calm things temporarily on August 23, the next morning things got out of hand. Arabs in Hebron went on a rampage of murder and rape, with the police powerless to stop the carnage. Almost all of the Arab constables joined the mob. Cafferata later testified that he came upon one Arab in the act of beheading a child and another Arab nearby butchering a woman with a dagger. Cafferata shot both of the attackers, one of whom was one of his own constables.

Overwhelmed, Cafferata called for reinforcements, which arrived only five hours later. The lack of a timely response led to bitter recriminations against the British mandate government. The British at the time, however, had only 292 policemen and fewer than 100 soldiers in all of Palestine.

By the time it was over, the Hebron Massacre had resulted in the deaths of 68 Jews and the wounding of another 58. Hebron's Arabs, however, did manage to shield some 435 Jews from the carnage. At least 28 Arab families risked their lives to hide their Jewish neighbors. Elsewhere in Palestine another 65 Jews were killed, including 18 in Safed. British police and soldiers killed 116 Arabs during the widespread violence.

Hebron's surviving Jews were evacuated to Jerusalem. In 1931 a handful of families returned to Hebron, but they again were evacuated by the British during the Arab Revolt of 1936. After that, no Jews lived in Hebron until the entire West Bank was captured by Israel during the Six-Day War in 1967. A few of the remaining massacre survivors attempted to reclaim their property, but they never did succeed.

The large Jewish community in Hebron today is made up of settlers who live on occupied or disputed land, although they claim to be the representatives of the Jews murdered and evicted from Hebron in 1929. The Tomb of the Patriarchs remains one of the flash points between Muslims and Jews, heavily guarded by the Israel Defense Forces.

DAVID T. ZABECKI

See also
Arab Revolt in Palestine; Ashkenazic Judaism; Haganah; Husseini, Haj Amin al-; Palestine, British Mandate for; Sephardic Judaism; Six-Day War; Zionism

References
Dershowitz, Alan M. *The Case for Israel.* New York: Wiley, 2004.
Morris, Benny. *Righteous Victims: A History of the Zionist-Arab Conflict, 1881–2001.* New York: Vintage Books, 2001.
Segev, Tom. *One Palestine, Complete: Jews and Arabs under the British Mandate.* New York: Owl Books, 2001.

Hebron Mosque Massacre (February 25, 1994)

Also known as the Cave of the Patriarchs Massacre, this was the killing of 29 Palestinian Muslims by a lone militant Israeli gunman at the Mosque of Abraham (Ibrahim) in Hebron, in the West Bank, on February 25, 1994. Also known as the Cave of the Patriarchs and the Tomb of the Patriarchs, the mosque site is held holy by Christians, Jews, and Muslims. The attack occurred during a period of religious holidays that saw both Jews and Muslims using the site for their observances. For Muslims, the event was Ramadan, the monthlong period of prayer, fasting, charity, and self-introspection. The Jews were observing Purim, a remembrance of Jews in Persia who had escaped a scheme to murder them en masse as told in the book of Esther.

Divided into two sections—one Muslim and one Jewish—the Cave of the Patriarchs includes Isaac Hall, which is reserved for Muslims, and Jacob and Abraham Halls, utilized by Jews. On February 25, 1994, at 5:00 a.m., a group of some 750 Palestinian Muslims entered the complex to pray. Israeli security forces guarding the mosque that morning were significantly understaffed. Shortly after the early-morning prayers commenced, a lone gunman, Baruch Goldstein, dressed in an Israeli Army uniform and carrying an assault rifle, got past the security detail and entered Isaac Hall. Placing himself in front of the lone exit and immediately behind the Muslim worshippers, he began firing randomly into the crowd. Pandemonium ensued, and before the gunfire stopped, 29 Palestinians had died, many of gunshot wounds but some trampled to death as the worshippers tried to escape. An additional 125 Palestinians were injured.

Goldstein, who was wrestled to the floor and then killed by his would-be victims, was an American-born Orthodox Jew who had immigrated to Israel in the mid-1980s. He was also a member of the radical Jewish Defense League and was a follower of Rabbi Meir David Kahane, an extremist American-born Jew who advocated open warfare against all Arabs and vehemently opposed the Israeli-Palestinian peace process.

The Hebron Mosque Massacre shocked Israelis and the world and cast a dark shadow over the emergent Israeli-Palestinian peace process, which had gained momentum only during the previous year via the Oslo Accords. The massacre sparked protests in many Arab nations, and major rioting claimed the lives of another 26 Palestinians as well as 9 Jews in the West Bank and other occupied territories. Protests in Jordan turned particularly violent, and a British tourist in Amman died at the hands of an unruly mob.

The Israeli government and all mainstream political parties roundly condemned the massacre. The Israelis offered compensation to the victims and stepped up efforts to disarm and detain would-be Jewish terrorists. Israeli prime minister Yitzhak Shamir convened a formal inquiry into the massacre chaired by Judge Meir Shagmar, then head of the Israeli Supreme Court. The inquiry determined that Goldstein had acted alone and had not shared his plans with anyone else and also concluded that security forces had not appropriately interacted with other local officials or Israeli national forces such as the Israel Defense Forces (IDF).

PAUL G. PIERPAOLI JR.

See also
Oslo Accords; Religious Sites in the Middle East, Muslim

Reference
Peri, Yoram. *The Assassination of Yitzhak Rabin.* Stanford, CA: Stanford University Press, 2000.

Hejaz Railroad, Attacks on (1916–1918)

Arab raids on the Hejaz rail line that in effect ended Ottoman control of Arabia. In 1900, Sultan Abdul Hamid had ordered the construction of the Hejaz railway, running from Damascus to Mecca. Partly financed by Muslim donations, the railway was intended to carry religious pilgrims to Mecca for hajj. The sultan also recognized that the railway could easily be extended to the coast of Yemen and used to move troops against the Wahhabi, a puritanical sect controlled by Abdul Aziz Ibn Saud in Arabia.

The railway's roadbed followed the so-called Frankincense Road on the east side of the Hejaz escarpment away from the Red Sea. Construction began in 1901 but was halted in 1908 with the revolt by the Young Turks. The rail line reached from Damascus to Medina (in present-day Saudi Arabia), a length of 820 miles; the last 280-mile section to Mecca was never completed.

In 1916 the Arab Revolt began with attacks on the rail station at Medina. During 1917, Arab raiders kept more than 25,000 Ottoman troops busy protecting the line. At first the Ottomans kept up with the destruction, but as 1917 progressed the unrepaired damage mounted. More significant was the destruction of rolling stock. On December 22, Arab raiders captured an entire Ottoman troop train.

Arab forces intensified their attacks in 1918, striking both trains and stations. By April, attacks had moved northward to Ma'an. In June the British began air attacks on Amman, Qatrana, and other places. By September, the Ottomans were in retreat toward Damascus, and on September 23 the Arabs took Ma'an. On October 1, 1918, Arab forces occupied Damascus. Medina's Ottoman governor nonetheless resisted until 1919.

Extensively damaged, the Saudi Arabian section of the line was never rebuilt. Indeed, rusting wreckage from Arab attacks led by Lieutenant Colonel T. E. Lawrence still litters the roadbed to this day. The Syrian and Jordanian sections of the line provide local transportation.

ANDREW J. WASKEY

See also
Arab Revolt of World War I; Ibn Saud, King; Lawrence, Thomas Edward

References
Lawrence, T. E. *Revolt in the Desert.* San Diego: Wordsworth Editions, 1998.
Ochsenwald, William. *The Hijaz Railroad.* Charlottesville: University of Virginia Press, 1980.

Schneider, James. *Guerilla Leader: T. E. Lawrence and the Arab Revolt*. New York: Bantam, 2011.
Tauber, Eliezer. *The Arab Movements in World War I*. London: Frank Cass, 1993.

Hellespont

The Hellespont (modern-day Dardanelles) was the narrow strait between the Thracian Chersonese (modern-day Gallipoli Peninsula) on the north and the Troad to the south. Since the time of the ancient Greeks, the Hellespont has been regarded as part of the boundary between Europe (the Chersonese) and Asia (Troad). The Hellespont led from the Aegean Sea to the Propontis (modern-day Sea of Marmara), thus forming part of the only maritime route between the Aegean and the Black Sea. The Hellespont had considerable importance as a trade route, especially after Greek cities such as Athens came to depend on grain and other commodities from the Black Sea. The straits are only three-quarters of a mile wide at their narrowest point.

This narrow crossing made the passage between Abydus (on the Asian side) and Sestos (in the Chersonese) the major crossing point between the continents in antiquity. In Roman times, major roads led to Sestos and Abydus so that travelers and armies could cross the straits by boat. Centuries earlier Xerxes, in about 482 BCE, did not expect his army to use boats (or to swim) but instead built two bridges of over 300 ships lashed together so they could march across; Herodotus gives a detailed description of the method of construction. When a storm broke up the first bridges, Xerxes had the men who built them beheaded and the straits themselves lashed and branded; a second set of bridges allowed the army to cross. In 335 Alexander the Great's army crossed at the same point though without a bridge, as Alexander invaded Asia partly, he said, as revenge for Xerxes's invasion of Greece in 480. Alexander himself sacrificed a bull to Poseidon and the Nereids at the mouth of the Hellespont and poured a libation from a golden goblet, seeking success as he was about to set foot on Asia.

But it is the importance of the Hellespont as a passage between the Aegean and the Black Sea that has most led to conflict in the area. As recently as 1915 during World War I, control of the straits was the objective of the Gallipoli Campaign. In antiquity it was in many periods equally important, and cities such as Sestos will also have benefited by taxing cargoes. The great Bronze Age site identified as Troy was in a strategic position on the Asian side of the entrance to the strait. As early as the sixth century Athens took an interest in the area, seizing nearby Sigeum from the Mytileneans and colonizing Elaious at the tip of the Chersonese. In the latter stages of the Second Peloponnesian War, the area saw much fighting as Sparta competed with Athens for control of this all important area. Sestos was the key Athenian naval base, and the final battle of the war occurred when Lysander, based at Lampsacus on the Asian side, surprised and destroyed the Athenian fleet on the European shore of the Hellespont at Aegospotami.

In the Hellenistic period, the Hellespont was at various times controlled by the Seleucids, the Ptolemies, Macedonia, and Pergamum. Under the Romans, the Hellespont was no longer of such vital importance until Constantinople became the seat of empire and the Hellespont once again became critical as a route for seaborne trade and communication with the Mediterranean.

Peter Londey

See also
Aegospotami, Battle of; Alexander III the Great; Greco-Persian Wars; Xerxes I

References
Allen, Susan Heuck. 2001. "The Hellespont as a 'Contested Periphery,'" *American Journal of Archaeology* 105 (2001): 265.
Herodotus. *The Histories*. Translated and edited by Robin Waterfield and Carolyn Dewald. New York: Oxford University Press, 2008.
Tsetskhladze, Gocha R., Sümer Atasoy, Alexandru Avram, Şevket Dönmez, and James Hargrave, eds. *The Bosporus: Gateway between the Ancient West and East (1st Millennium BC-5th Century AD). Proceedings of the Fourth International Congress on Black Sea Antiquities, Istanbul, 14th-18th September 2009*. BAR international series, S2517. Oxford: Archaeopress. 2013.

Hellespont Campaign (411–410 BCE)

A campaign early in the Decelean War (413–404 BCE)—the resumption of full hostilities in the Second Peloponnesian War (431–404)—fought to control the vital sea-lane through the Hellespont. Without securing grain passing through the straits, Athens would not be able to feed its citizenry and would have to surrender. Although the Hellespont Campaign ended with Athenian victory, it saw the beginnings of Persian support to Sparta. which formed an important part of the latter's ultimate victory in the Peloponnesian War.

The campaign was conducted against the backdrop of the huge Athenian losses in Sicily and political turmoil in

Athens. In 411 BCE, influenced by an offer from prominent Athenian statesman Alcibiades to secure Persian help, an oligarchic coup overthrew the government. The fleet and troops at Samos remained loyal to the democracy, and the Hellespont campaign was conducted by them, not the oligarchy in Athens.

In any case, Alcibiades failed to deliver, and in April 411, when Sparta recognized Persian sovereignty in Asia Minor (abandoning the Greek cities there), the satrap Tissaphernes agreed to fund the Peloponnesian fleet. This laid the foundations for ultimate Spartan naval dominance in the region.

Early that summer the Spartan Dercyllidas, supported by Pharnabazus, the Persian satrap for the Hellespont, occupied Abydus. In September Mindarus, the new Spartan admiral, tired of Tissaphernes's games regarding funding, transferred his fleet north to work with Pharnabazus. Mindarus reached the Hellespont undetected and disrupted the shipping route.

In response, the Athenians under Thrasybulus and Thrasyllus moved northward and won a close-run naval battle off Cynossema and cleared the route through the Hellespont. In April–May 410 at Cyzicus in Ionia, the Athenians under Alcibiades won another major victory. Alcibiades drove ashore and captured the 60 ships of the Peloponnesian fleet (Mindarus was killed), defeated the Peloponnesian and Persian land forces, and recaptured Cyzicus.

This campaign removed a serious Peloponnesian threat and led to the restoration of democracy at Athens and the formal return of Alcibiades. It boosted Athenian confidence so much that Athenian leaders (with hindsight, foolishly) rejected peace overtures from Sparta.

Iain Spence

See also
Hellespont

References
Kagan, Donald. *The Fall of the Athenian Empire*. Ithaca, NY: Cornell University Press, 1987.
Tritle, Lawrence. *A New History of the Peloponnesian War*. Malden, MA: Wiley-Blackwell, 2010.

Henry of Constantinople (ca. 1178–1216)

Second (and most successful) Latin emperor of Constantinople (1206–1216). Sometimes referred to as Henry of Flanders and Henry of Hainaut, Emperor Henry was probably born at Valenciennes around 1178, the third son of Baldwin V, count of Hainaut, and Margaret, countess of Flanders.

Henry took the cross in 1200 and followed his brother Count Baldwin IX of Flanders (VI of Hainaut) on the Fourth Crusade (1202–1204). He is mentioned only rarely in the early stages of the crusade. Once the crusaders had arrived at Constantinople (modern-day Istanbul, Turkey), he was put in charge of the second squadron and accompanied his brother, who commanded the vanguard when the crusading army confronted the army of Alexius III Angelos outside the walls of the city (July 17, 1203). In 1204 Henry led a successful foraging raid against the Greek city of Philea. On the return to Constantinople, he defeated an ambush prepared by Alexios V Doukas Mourtzouphlos, capturing a holy icon of the virgin Mary that Alexios V had brought to assure himself of victory.

After the election of Baldwin as Latin emperor (May 1204), Henry was one of the leaders in the conquest of Greek lands, participating in the occupation of Thrace and then crossing the Dardanelles to capture Adramyttium (modern-day Edremit, Turkey). There he was supported by the local Armenians, who followed him with their families across the straits when Baldwin, faced by a Greek rebellion in Thrace, hastily recalled Henry. The Armenians were unable to keep pace and were subsequently massacred by the Greeks. Henry was too late to bring any aid to his brother, who was captured by the Bulgarians at Adrianople (modern-day Edirne, Turkey), but he encountered the survivors under the command of Geoffrey of Villehardouin at Rodosto.

Henry was recognized as regent of the empire and fought to hold his brother's empire together during his absence. In July 1205 he unsuccessfully laid siege to Adrianople and Demotika, and in October he renewed the treaty of partition with the Venetians. A new Bulgarian invasion (January 1206) forced the Greeks to appeal to Henry, who advanced to Adrianople and then pursued the retreating Bulgarians far into their own territory.

With confirmation of the death of Baldwin in 1206, Henry was chosen as the second Latin emperor and crowned on August 20, 1206. Henry drove off a new invasion by Kalojan, then rescued some 20,000 prisoners while ravaging Kalojan's territory. Henry also sent troops across the straits to occupy Cyzicus (near modern-day Erdek, Turkey) and Nikomedia (modern-day Izmit, Turkey), and a reconciliation with Boniface of Montferrat was sealed by Henry's marriage to Agnes of Montferrat (February 4, 1207). However, attempts to attack Kalojan were thwarted by the need to rescue the Franks in Asia Minor, so to secure his rear, Henry negotiated a two-year truce with Theodore I Laskaris, Greek emperor of Nicaea. Henry then reoccupied Thrace and raided deep into Bulgaria. Before he could combine forces with Boniface, the latter was killed in a skirmish on September 4, 1207. Henry then had to rescue his Greek ally, David Komnenos, ruler of Paphlagonia, from the attacks of Theodore Laskaris before facing one of the greatest crises of his reign, the revolt of the Lombards of Thessalonica against the regency of Boniface's widow, Margaret (Mary) of Hungary, for her infant son Demetrius. During the winter of 1206–1207, Henry outmaneuvered the plotters and in a brilliant campaign smashed Lombard resistance and secured Thessaly.

In May 1209 Henry held an assembly at Ravennika at which he secured the homage of the rulers of the Morea and Athens. He crushed Lombard resistance at the siege of Thebes and in June 1209 entered Athens. The year 1211, however, saw the emergence of four threats. From the west, Michael Komnenos Doukas, ruler of Epiros, attacked Thessalonica in alliance with Henry's former ally, the Vlach prince Strez. No sooner had Henry driven them back and invaded their lands than he was recalled to Constantinople by the threat of an attack on the city by Theodore I Laskaris. Henry's army was then threatened on the march through Thrace by Boril of Bulgaria.

Having disposed of this threat, Henry carried the war to Theodore by crossing the straits and defeating him in a battle near the Luparchos River. He then recaptured Adramyttium and advanced south to the frontier with the Seljuk sultanate of Rum. The outcome of these campaigns was a peace with Nicaea that left the Franks in possession of the southern coast of the Dardanelles and the Sea of Marmara. Boril of Bulgaria sought peace, offering his daughter as a bride to the now widowed emperor. With some reluctance, Henry married the Bulgarian princess and together with his son-in-law advanced to Niš against the Serbs with whom Strez had sought shelter. A disagreement between the allies forced Henry to withdraw. A second expedition against Niš, this time in conjunction with the king of Hungary, also had to withdraw when the king made a separate peace with the Serbs.

Henry died suddenly on June 11, 1216. Although there were some rumors that his Bulgarian empress had poisoned him, there is no evidence that his death was due to anything other than marsh fever. By far the most successful of the Latin emperors of Constantinople, Henry was an energetic and talented soldier. He defeated both internal and external enemies and proved to be a shrewd diplomat.

PETER S. NOBLE

See also
Alexios III Angelos; Baldwin I of Constantinople; Boniface I of Montferrat; Constantinople, Latin Empire of; Crusades in the Holy Land, Christian; Theodore I Laskaris

References
Longnon, Jean. *Les compagnons de Villehardouin.* Genève: Droz, 1978.
Van Tricht, Filip. "De jongelingenjaren van een keizer van Konstantinopel: Hendrik van Vlaanderen en Henegouwen (1177–1202)." *Tijdschrift voor Geschiedenis* 111 (1998): 187–219.
Van Tricht, Filip. "La gloire de l'empire: L'idée impériale de Henri de Flandre-Hainaut, deuxième empereur latin de Constantinople (1206–1216)." *Byzantion* 70 (2000): 211–241.
Van Tricht, Filip. "La politique étrangère de l'empire de Constantinople de 1210 à 1216." *Le Moyen Age* 107 (2001): 219–238, 409–438.
Verlinden, Charles. *Les Empereurs belges de Constantinople.* Bruxelles: Charles Dessart, 1945.
Wolff, Robert Lee. "The Latin Empire of Constantinople, 1204–1261." In *A History of the Crusades,* Vol. 2, ed. Kenneth M. Setton et al. 187–233. 2nd ed. Philadelphia: University of Pennsylvania Press, 1969.

Henry VI of Germany (1165–1197)

King of Germany (1169–1197) and Sicily (1194–1197), Holy Roman emperor (1191–1197), and organizer of a crusade to the Holy Land (1197–1198). Henry was born into the Staufen dynasty in Nijmegen in 1165, the second son of Holy Roman emperor Frederick I, known as Barbarossa (r. 1155–1190), and his second wife, Beatrix of Burgundy. The death of his elder brother Frederick left Henry as heir to the German monarchy. At the age of four Henry was elected king by the German princes at the Diet of Bamberg (June 1169) and crowned at Aachen in August.

When Henry came of age in 1178, he began to take on political responsibilities. At Mainz in 1184 he was knighted along with his younger brother Frederick, duke of Swabia (originally named Conrad). Later that same year Henry was betrothed to Constance, daughter of King Roger II of Sicily and aunt of the ruling King William II of Sicily. William's marriage was childless and the line of succession uncertain; by allying himself to the mighty Staufen dynasty, he hoped to secure the position of the Hauteville family in Sicily. For Frederick Barbarossa the Sicilian alliance brought a powerful ally in the Italian peninsula but also offered at least a prospect that Henry might eventually succeed to the Sicilian kingdom.

At the end of 1185 Henry joined his father in Italy, where Barbarossa was again attempting to assert imperial control. The next year Henry's marriage to Constance of Sicily was celebrated in Milan. About this time he seems to have received the title of caesar, probably as a signal of

Holy Roman Emperor Henry VI (1165–1197), from the Codex Manesse, between 1305 and 1340. (Library of the Ruprecht Karl University, Heidelberg, Germany/Fine Art Images/Heritage Images/Getty Images)

Frederick I's intention to have him recognized as coemperor, a desire that was opposed by the papacy.

Henry remained in Italy until 1187. In the autumn, news arrived of the great crusader defeat in the Battle of Hattin and the subsequent fall of Jerusalem to Saladin. Frederick Barbarossa and Frederick of Swabia took the cross at the so-called Court of Jesus Christ (Curia Iesu Christi) at Mainz on March 27, 1188, in the presence of Henry VI, who was to take over government in the absence of his father.

During the Third Crusade (1189–1192), Frederick Barbarossa was in frequent contact with Henry, among other things admonishing him to have the Italian cities equip a fleet and send it to the East to persuade the Byzantine emperor to support the crusade. William II of Sicily died childless on November 18, 1190, and was succeeded by an illegitimate half brother, Tancred of Lecce. Henry now made peace with enemies in Germany, with the intention of pursuing his wife's claims to the throne of Sicily. However, these plans received a setback upon news of the death of Frederick Barbarossa during the crusade (June 10, 1190) that reached Germany in the autumn of that year. A German army went to Italy, and Henry followed across the Alps in early 1191. He was crowned Holy Roman emperor on April 14 in Rome by new pope Celestine III.

Emperor Henry now launched a campaign to secure his claims to Sicily. However, he met with defeat outside Naples, and Constance was taken captive. Yet Henry still had strongholds in southern Italy, and he managed to secure his position in Germany. The pope tried to negotiate peace between Henry and Tancred to little avail, although Constance was released in 1192. Then events turned to Henry's advantage. At Milan he met with French king Philippe II Augustus, returning from the Third Crusade. Henry and Philip concluded an alliance directed against King Richard I Lionheart of England, who was the principal ally of both King Tancred of Sicily and Henry's enemies in Germany. The turning point came when Richard was taken captive in 1192 by Duke Leopold V of Austria while returning from the Third Crusade, and Leopold handed him over to Henry. As a condition of his release, Richard was to pay a vast ransom and also to supply 50 ships for the campaign against Sicily. Deprived of a powerful ally, the German opposition collapsed; its leader, Henry the Lion, sought an accommodation with the emperor (March 1194).

In May 1194 Emperor Henry marched south with perhaps 20,000 men supported by Genoese and Pisan fleets. In August these forces attacked the Sicilian kingdom, and after the capture and sack of Salerno in September the other cities surrendered one by one. In November Henry entered Palermo in triumph. On December 25, 1194, he was crowned king of Sicily; the next day Constance gave birth to a son, Frederick Roger.

Henry's chief political aims from this point were to assert the authority of the Holy Roman Empire throughout Christendom and to secure the succession for his son in both the empire and Sicily. Diplomatic successes in these areas greatly enhanced Henry's prestige and authority throughout the eastern Mediterranean. In 1195 he proposed organizing a crusade to the Holy Land, hoping that this would help him gain the agreement of the papacy to his plans for hereditary rule of the Staufen dynasty in the empire and Sicily. Yet Henry was unable to reach an accommodation with Pope Celestine III, although the German princes were prepared to recognize his son Frederick (II) as king of Germany. The emperor returned to the kingdom of Sicily in April 1197, but his preparations for the crusade were delayed by a rebellion in May. It is uncertain whether Henry intended to lead the crusade himself, although he does appear to have taken the cross in March 1195. In any event, he appointed Conrad of Querfurt, bishop of Hildesheim, and the imperial marshal Henry of Kalden as leaders of the expedition. During the summer Henry fell ill with malaria, succumbing to it on September 28. He was buried in the cathedral of Palermo.

As with his father, Henry did not live to see the completion of the crusade he had launched. He was widely regarded by contemporaries as the most powerful ruler in Christendom, and his death at 31 years old plunged the empire into crisis. In Sicily he was succeeded by the infant Frederick, who had also been intended for the German throne. However, with the prospect of a rival Welf candidate emerging there, it was Henry's younger brother Philip of Swabia who was crowned king of Germany by the supporters of the Staufen family.

JANUS MØLLER JENSEN

See also
Crusades in the Holy Land, Christian; Frederick I or Frederick Barbarossa; Hattin, Battle of; Philippe II, King; Richard I, King

References
Csendes, Peter. *Heinrich VI*. Darmstadt: Wissenschaftliche Buchgesellschaft, 1993.
Freed, John B. *Frederick Barbarossa: The Prince and the Myth*. New Haven, CT: Yale University Press, 2016.
Görich, Knut. "Verletzte Ehre: König Richard Löwenherz als Gefangener Kaiser Heinrichs." *Historisches Jahrbuch* 123 (2003): 65–91.
Naumann, Claudia. *Der Kreuzzug Kaiser Heinrichs VI*. Frankfurt am Main: Lang, 1994.
Opll, Ferdinand. *Friedrich Barbarossa*. Darmstadt: Wissenschaftliche Buchgesellschaft, 1990.

Heraclius (ca. 575–641)

Byzantine emperor (610–641). Born around 575 in North Africa, possibly in Cappadocia, the son of the military governor of Carthage, Heraclius led his father's fleet to Constantinople against the tyrant Phocas in 610. Phocas had killed Emperor Maurice and seized the crown eight years before. Heraclius overthrew Phocas and became emperor himself on October 5, 610.

When Heraclius took power, Byzantium was under heavy pressure from the West in the form of Avars and Slavs in Europe and in the East from the Persians. Phocas had provoked a savage war with Persia (602–628), which had opened the way for the Avars and Slavs to infiltrate western Byzantine holdings in Southeastern Europe. Byzantine power was also in disarray, thanks to the inept rule of Phocas.

In 611 Persian forces under Shah Khosrow II had moved into Syria, taking Antioch and other places. Two years later the Persians captured Damascus, and in 614 Jerusalem fell. Taking advantage of this, the Slavs moved in large numbers into Greece and Albania, while the Avars pressed into Thrace and Bulgaria. The Byzantine Empire appeared caught in a vice. In 618 the Persians moved south against Egypt, finally taking Alexandria in 619 following a great siege.

Heraclius meanwhile concentrated on rebuilding the Byzantine army. Pronouncing his forces ready to take the offensive, he landed an army by sea in Cilicia in southern Anatolia in April 622, defeating the Persians in the Battle of Issus (October). He then marched north into Pontus on the south shore of the Black Sea and was victorious over the Persians at Halys (spring of 623). He next invaded Media (today central Iran), laying waste to much of it, then moved across Mesopotamia into Cilicia, defeating a Persian army at the Sarus River in the autumn of 625. Heraclius hoped to force the Persians to shift their attention north to defend the city of Ctesiphon.

Shah Khosrow II, however, sought to turn the tables by ordering an all-out offensive against Constantinople. Persian agents were able to work out an alliance with the Avars to move against the city from the west. The Persians and Avars then laid siege to Constantinople (June–August 626). Heraclius, trusting that the city's powerful land defenses and Byzantine naval strength would be able to hold, refused to return from Armenia. His strategy worked, with his opponents dissipating their forces in a futile effort to take the Byzantine capital. The Avars and Persians withdrew their greatly weakened forces from before Constantinople that fall. Avar strength was further sapped by a revolt of the Slavs.

With Persian military strength now greatly reduced, Heraclius pursued the war in Anatolia. Moving southwest into Mesopotamia, he defeated the Persians in the great Battle of Nineveh (December 12, 627). The next year, Heraclius took Dastagard and raided in the vicinity of Ctesiphon. Meanwhile, a coup d'état ousted Shah Khosrow II, beginning a bloody civil war. The Persian general Shahrvaraz then struck a bargain with Heraclius in which he agreed to return Egypt, Palestine, Syria, and the other conquered territories to Byzantium in return for permission to march on Ctesiphon and take power. By 630 Heraclius had recovered all of Egypt and western Asia Minor, and the Byzantine Empire was at peace.

The long struggle had exhausted both the Persians and the Byzantines, however, making both susceptible to pressure from the new threat posed by Islam. Arab armies raided into Palestine in 633, and three years later as a consequence of the defeat of a large Byzantine force in the Battle of the Yarmouk River (August 636), they took Palestine. Heraclius then abandoned Syria altogether. Arab forces then began to raid into Egypt in 639. The Arabs then defeated a relief expedition and took Alexandria in 640, going on to seize all of Egypt. By the time of Heraclius's death on February 11, 641, in Constantinople from a painful illness, the Muslims had taken the entire Middle East, which they held from that point forward.

An extraordinarily capable and daring strategist characterized by great patience and determination, Heraclius was also a talented administrator but fell victim to circumstances beyond his control.

SPENCER C. TUCKER

See also
Byzantine-Sassanid War; Nineveh, Battle of; Yarmouk River, Battle of

References
Haldon, J. F. *Byzantium in the Seventh Century.* Cambridge: Cambridge University Press, 1990.
Kaegi, Walter Emil. *Byzantium and the Early Islamic Conquests.* Cambridge: Cambridge, University Press, 1992.
Kaegi, Walter Emil. *Heraclius, Emperor of Byzantium.* Cambridge: Cambridge University Press, 2003.
Treadgold, Warren. *A History of the Byzantine State and Society.* Stanford, CA: Stanford University Press, 1997.

Herzl, Theodor (1860–1904)

Founder of the Zionist movement who had a tremendous impact on the modern Middle East. Theodor Herzl was born in Budapest, Hungary, on May 2, 1860. In 1878 his assimilated German-speaking Jewish family moved to Vienna, where he obtained a doctorate in law from the University of Vienna in 1884. He practiced law only briefly, drawn instead to a literary calling. He published numerous unremarkable dramas and established a reputation as a fashionable cosmopolitan journalist, notably as a Parisian correspondent for the Viennese Neue Freie Presse (New Free Press) during 1881–1895 and thereafter as its literary editor.

Herzl's influential book *Der Judenstaat: Versuch einer modernen Lšsung der Judenfrage* (The Jewish State: An Attempt at a Modern Solution of the Jewish Question), published in 1896, was not, as customarily thought, a simple reaction to the anti-Semitism of the Dreyfus Affair in France in which a Jewish French Army officer was falsely accused of treason. Rather, it was the culmination of evolving reflections. Herzl did not invent Zionism and claimed only to state the facts more clearly. Indeed, he believed that anti-Semitism persisted even in the face of emancipation because the so-called Jewish question was national rather than social. The normalization of the Jewish condition therefore required a Jewish state in any territory made available for mass migration.

The insistence on sovereignty distinguished Herzl's stance from the predominant practical or philanthropic Zionism, which was aimed at small-scale settlement in Palestine. Herzl's contribution was thus to view the Jewish question in Europe as a unitary thing requiring a unitary solution, both of which he redefined as political and international. By the force of his persona and above all through his leadership of the Zionist Congress, which he founded in Basel in 1897, he turned an idea into a driving force.

Herzl devoted the ensuing years to sustaining the movement and seeking the international support he considered essential to success. After failing to win assistance from Germany and Turkey, he increasingly placed his hopes on Great Britain, although his willingness to accept Uganda even as a provisional substitute for Palestine nearly split the movement in 1903 on the eve of his death.

Herzl's character and policies abound in paradoxes and blend the realistic and the naive, accounting for his brilliant successes as well as his shortcomings. The combination of intellectual oversimplification and attention to minute but symbolic detail allowed the essentially aristocratic Westerner to cast himself in the role of a charismatic leader whose dream of a reborn nation inspired the Eastern masses and bridged factional differences regarding its precise character. His ultimate vision of the new commonwealth was Eurocentric but not chauvinistic (or even particularly Jewish). What he envisioned was a nonmilitarized technologically advanced society dedicated to social justice in which Jews and Arabs lived together in prosperity. He declared that his next dream was to assist in the liberation of the Africans.

Herzl died at age 44 in Edlach near Vienna, Austria, on July 3, 1904.

JAMES WALD

See also
Zionism

References
Elon, Amos. *Herzl.* New York: Holt, Rinehart and Winston, 1975.
Herzl, Theodor. *The Jewish State.* Mineola, NY: Dover, 1989.
Laqueur, Walter. *A History of Zionism: From the French Revolution to the Establishment of the State of Israel.* Reprint ed. New York: Schocken, 2003.

Pawel, Ernst. *The Labyrinth of Exile: A Life of Theodor Herzl.* New York: Farrar, Straus and Giroux, 1989.

Robertson, Ritchie, and Edward Timms, eds. *Theodor Herzl and the Origins of Zionism.* Edinburgh, UK: Edinburgh University Press, 1997.

Hezbollah

Lebanese radical Shia Islamist organization. Founded in Lebanon in 1984, Hezbollah is a major political force in Lebanon and, along with the Amal movement, the principal political party representing the Shia community in Lebanon. Hezbollah also operates a number of social service programs, schools, hospitals, clinics, and housing assistance programs for Lebanese Shiites.

One of the core founding groups of Hezbollah, meaning "Party of God," fled from Iraq when President Saddam Hussein cracked down on the Shia Islamic movement in the shrine cities. Lebanese as well as Iranians and Iraqis studied in Najaf and Karbala, and some 100 of these students returned to Beirut and became disciples of Sayyid Muhammad Husayn Fadlallah, a Lebanese cleric who was also educated in Najaf. Meanwhile, in the midst of the ongoing civil war in Lebanon (1975–1990), a Shia resistance movement developed in response to Israel's invasion of Lebanon in 1982, which resulted in huge numbers of casualties, prisoners taken, and displaced people.

The earliest Lebanese Shia political movement was established under the cleric Musa al-Sadr and known as the Movement of the Dispossessed. The Shias were the largest but poorest sect in Lebanon and suffered from discrimination, political underrepresentation, and a dearth of government programs and services that persists to this day. After al-Sadr's disappearance, his nonmilitaristic movement was subsumed by the Amal Party, which fought in the civil war. However, a wing of Amal, Islamic Amal led by Husayn al-Musawi, split off after it accused Amal of not resisting the Israeli invasion.

On the grounds of resistance to Israel, Islamic Amal made contact with Iran's ambassador to Syria, who had once found refuge as an Iranian dissident in the Palestinian camps in Lebanon. Iran sent between 1,000 and 1,200 Revolutionary Guards to the Bekaa Valley to aid an Islamic resistance to Israel. At a Lebanese Army barracks near Baalbek, the Revolutionary Guards began training Shia fighters identifying with the resistance, or Islamic Amal.

Fadlallah's followers now included displaced Beiruti Shias and displaced southerners, and some coordination between his group and the others began to emerge in 1984. The other strand of Hezbollah came from the Islamic Resistance in southern Lebanon led by Sheikh Raghib Harb, who was killed by the Israelis in 1984. In February 1985 Harb's supporters announced the formation of Hezbollah, led by Sheikh Subhi Tufayli.

Another Shia militant group was the Organization of the Islamic Jihad, led by Imad Mughniya. It was responsible for the 1983 bombings of the U.S. and French peacekeeping forces' barracks and the U.S. embassy and its annex in Beirut. Hezbollah, however, is to this day accused of bombings committed by Mughniya's group. Hezbollah stated officially that it did not commit the bombing of U.S. and French forces but also did not condemn those who did. Regardless, Hezbollah's continuing resistance in the south earned it great popularity with the Lebanese, whose army had split and had failed to defend the country against the Israelis.

With the 1989 Taif Agreement the Lebanese Civil War should have ended, but in 1990 fighting broke out, and the next year Syria mounted a major campaign in Lebanon. The Taif Agreement did not end sectarianism or solve the problem of Muslim underrepresentation in government. Militias other than Hezbollah disbanded, but because the Lebanese government did not assent to the Israeli occupation of southern Lebanon, Hezbollah's militia remained in being.

The leadership of Hezbollah changed over time and adapted to Lebanon's realities. The multiplicity of sects in Lebanon meant that an Islamic republic there was impractical, and as a result Hezbollah ceased trying to impose the strictest Islamic rules and focused more on gaining the trust of the Lebanese community. The party's Shura Council was made up of 7 clerics until 1989; from 1989 to 1991 it included 3 laypersons and 4 clerics, but since 2001 it has been entirely composed of clerics. An advisory politburo has from 11 to 14 members. Secretary-General Abbas Musawi took over from Tufayli in 1991. Soon after the Israelis assassinated Musawi, Hassan Nasrallah, who had studied in Najaf and briefly in Qum, took over as secretary-general.

In 1985 as a consequence of armed resistance in southern Lebanon, Israel withdrew into the so-called security zone. Just as resistance from Hezbollah provided Israel with the ready excuse to attack Lebanon, Israel's continued presence in the south funded Lebanese resentment of Israel and support for Hezbollah's armed actions. In 1996 the Israelis mounted Operation GRAPES OF WRATH against Hezbollah in southern Lebanon, pounding the entire region from the air for a two-week period.

Subhi Tufayli, the former Hezbollah secretary-general, opposed the party's decision to participate in the elections of 1992 and 1996. He was soon expelled from Hezbollah and began armed resistance. The Lebanese Army was then called in to defeat his faction.

In May 2000 after suffering repeated attacks, Israel withdrew its forces from southern Lebanon, a move that was widely interpreted as a victory for Hezbollah. Hezbollah disarmed in some areas of the country but refused to do so in the border area because it contests the Jewish state's control of the Shaba Farms region.

Sheikh Fadlallah, who died in 2010 of natural causes, survived an assassination attempt in 1985 allegedly arranged by the United States. He illustrates the Lebanonization of the Shia Islamist movement. Fadlallah had moved away from Iranian Ayatollah Khomeini's doctrine of government by clerics, believing that it is not suitable in the Lebanese context, and called for dialogue with Christians. Fadlallah, like some of the Iraqi clerics, called for the restoration of Friday communal prayer for the Shias. He also issued numerous reforming views, such as decrying the abuse of women by men. Fadlallah was not, however, closely associated with Hezbollah's day-to-day policies.

Some Israeli and American sources charge that Iran directly conducts the affairs of Hezbollah and provides it with essential funding. While at one time Iranian support was crucial to Hezbollah, the Revolutionary Guards were withdrawn from Lebanon some time ago. The party's social and charitable services claimed independence in the late 1990s. They are supported by a volunteer service and by local and external donations. Iran has certainly provided weapons to Hezbollah. Some found their way into Lebanon, and Syria has also provided freedom of movement across its common border with Lebanon as well as supply routes for weapons.

After 2000, Hezbollah disputed Israeli control over the Shaba Farms area. Meanwhile, pressure began to build against Syrian influence in Lebanon with the constitutional amendment to allow President Émile Lahoud (a Christian and pro-Syrian) an additional term. Assassinations of anti-Syrian, mainly Christian, figures also periodically occurred. The turning point was the 2005 assassination of Prime Minister Rafik Hariri. This led to significant international pressure on Syria to withdraw from Lebanon, although pro-Syrian elements remained throughout the country.

Hezbollah now found itself threatened by a new coalition of Christians and Hariri-supporting Sunnis who sought to deny its aim of greater Shia power in government. The two sides in this struggle were known as the March 14th Alliance, for the date of a large anti-Syrian rally, and the March 8th Alliance, for a prior and even larger rally consisting of Hezbollah and anti-Syrian Christian general Michel Aoun. These factions have been sparring since 2005.

Demanding a response to the Israeli campaign against Gaza in the early summer of 2006, Hezbollah forces killed three Israeli soldiers and kidnapped two others, planning to hold them for a prisoner exchange. The Israel Defense Forces (IDF) responded with a massive campaign of air strikes throughout Lebanon, and not just on Hezbollah positions. Hezbollah responded by launching missiles into Israel, forcing much of that country's northern population into shelters. In this conflict, the United States backed Israel. At conflict's end, Sheikh Nasrallah's popularity surged in Lebanon and in the Arab world, and even members of the March 14th Alliance were furious over the destruction of the fragile peace in post–civil war Lebanon.

In September 2006 Hezbollah and its ally Aoun began calling for a new national unity government. The existing government, dominated by the March 14th Alliance forces, refused to budge, however. Five Shia members and one Christian member of the Lebanese cabinet also resigned in response to disagreements regarding the proposed tribunal to investigate Syrian culpability in the Hariri assassination. At the same time, Hezbollah and Aoun argued for the ability of a sizable opposition group in the cabinet to veto government decisions. Hezbollah and Aoun called for public protests, which began in downtown Beirut in December 2006. There was one violent clash in December and another in January of 2007 between the supporters of the two March alliances. Meanwhile, the United Nations Interim Force in Lebanon (UNIFIL) took up positions in southern Lebanon. Its mission, however, is not to disarm Hezbollah but only to prevent armed clashes between it and Israel.

In 2008 when a unity government took hold in Lebanon, Hezbollah and its allies captured 11 of 30 cabinet seats, giving the coalition the power to veto. Beginning in 2012 amid the ongoing Syrian Civil War, Hezbollah decided to aid Bashar al-Assad's government in its fight against antigovernment rebels. This resulted in several Israeli air strikes against Hezbollah convoys allegedly bound for Syrian fighters; the convoys included antiaircraft missiles. Hezbollah's involvement in the Syrian Civil War has raised concerns that the conflict might further destabilize Lebanon. Meanwhile, Hezbollah and its affiliates have been blamed for several terror attacks, including a 2012 bus bombing in Bulgaria that left six people dead. In 2009, Egypt uncovered and foiled a Hezbollah plot that would have attacked Egyptian and Israeli targets in the Sinai Peninsula. In 2011, Hezbollah brought down the 2008 government; similarly, it also brought down the replacement government in 2013 following a disagreement over the makeup of Lebanese security forces. In the summer of 2014, the group strongly supported Hamas in its conflict with Israel in the Gaza Strip.

In January 2015, Hezbollah militants attacked an Israeli military convoy at Shebaa Farms. The attack, which Hezbollah claimed was retaliation for an Israeli assault on a Hezbollah convoy in southern Syria, killed two Israeli soldiers and wounded seven others. Meanwhile, Hezbollah's support of Assad's government continued unabated; beginning in 2015, the group has also been involved fighting elements of the Islamic State of Iraq and Syria (ISIS), which had seized large swaths of Syrian territory beginning in 2014. Hezbollah has also been working closely with Iran, which has significantly increased its involvement in the Syrian Civil War. There have also been reports that Hezbollah sent fighters into Iraq beginning in 2014 as part of Iran's intervention in that country. On May 10, 2016, a top-level Hezbollah military commander, Mustafa Badreddine, was killed in an air strike near the Damascus airport. Although the media in Lebanon blamed his death on an Israeli air strike, Hezbollah insisted that anti-Assad rebels had killed Badreddine.

As part of its ramped-up effort to arrest the growing influence of Hezbollah's ally Iran in the region, on November 19, 2017, the Saudi government secured the support of most of the 22 members of the Arab League at its meeting in Cairo in condemning the actions of Hezbollah and branding it a terrorist organization. Meanwhile, in October 2017 the Donald Trump administration announced a plan that would reinvigorate the U.S. campaign against Hezbollah and its leadership. This was to include targeting its financial arrangements and placing sanctions on individuals and organizations that are known to aid the organization internationally.

In the May 2018 Lebanese parliamentary elections, Hezbollah and its allied political parties picked up a substantial number of new seats, bringing the Hezbollah coalition's total strength to 67 seats out of a total of 128. Israel and much of the West viewed this as a major setback that could potentially threaten the Lebanese government. Iran, on the other hand, saw the election results as a major victory. With U.S.-Iranian relations plummeting by the summer of 2018, the U.S. government is expected to redouble its efforts to blunt Hezbollah's activities in Lebanon and the wider Middle East.

HARRY RAYMOND HUESTON II, SPENCER C. TUCKER, AND SHERIFA ZUHUR

See also
Aoun, Michel; Assad, Bashar al-; Hariri, Rafik; Iran; Islamic State of Iraq and Syria; Khomeini, Ruhollah; Lahoud, Emile Jamil; Lebanon; Lebanon, Israeli Operations against; Lebanon Civil War; Lebanon-Israeli War; Shia Islam; Suicide Bombings; Syria; Syrian Civil War; Taif Accords; Terrorism

References
Hajjar, Sami G. *Hezbollah: Terrorism, National Liberation, or Menace?* Carlise Barracks, PA: Strategic Studies Institute, U.S. Army War College. 2002.
Harik, Judith Palmer. *Hezbollah: The Changing Face of Terrorism.* London: Tauris, 2005.
Norton, Augustus Richard. *Hezbollah: A Short History.* Princeton, NJ: Princeton University Press, 2014.

Holocaust (1941–1945)

The purposeful and systematic murder of some 6 million European Jews by the Nazi German regime during World War II. The Holocaust, also known by the Nazis as the Final Solution (Endlösung) and in Hebrew as Shoah, represented German dictator Adolf Hitler's efforts to exterminate the Jews of Europe, which, he bizarrely claimed, would solve many of the problems of European societies. Hitler came close to succeeding in this grisly endeavor and also targeted for extermination Roma peoples (also referred to as Gypsies), persons with mental and physical limitations, homosexuals, and political and religious dissenters. The mass killings occurred in numerous concentration camps in Eastern Europe. Initially, the world viewed the situation with indifference. Indeed, many nations, including the United States, turned away Jewish refugees. Partially in response to such indifference and once the war was over, Jewish leaders—with backing from key world politicians—were determined to establish a Jewish state to provide a haven for Jews and defend them against any future persecution.

The Holocaust was once thought to have begun with the Wannsee Conference held at a villa of that name outside of Berlin on January 1942, but most scholars now see it as having begun with the German invasion of the Soviet Union in the summer of 1941. The Wannsee meeting instead formalized a process that was in effect already under way. The very nature of the Holocaust also remains open to debate. Scholars have disagreed about whether the circumstances of the war merely permitted the evolution of the Final Solution as a crime of opportunity or whether the Nazi regime had planned the horrific extermination from the beginning. Finally, in the 1980s and 1990s a small but vociferous group of so-called historians on the fringe of popular culture asserted that the Holocaust had never occurred or had at the very least not been the work of Hitler. Among these was British historian David Irving. Such an assertion is utterly preposterous, of course, as the historical record is replete with thousands of photographs and many thousands of documents detailing the Holocaust and those responsible for its execution. Having had both their day in court and exposure to criticism by the academic community, the complete falsehood of these claims has been clearly established.

Coming to power in 1933, the Hitler regime initiated during the next six years a number of actions and policies, most notably the Nuremberg Laws, designed to force Jews to leave Germany. Boycotts, expulsions from government positions, laws criminalizing Jewish-Gentile intermarriage, prohibitions against Jews owning land, nullification of citizenship, restrictions on professional activity, registration regulations, and the wearing of yellow stars and public identification all were aimed at encouraging Germany's 600,000 Jews to leave. Almost half did flee, largely bereft of their possessions, but few countries welcomed them. Many chose to leave for Austria because of existing cultural affinities with Germany. Thus, after the German annexation of Austria (Anschluss) in 1938, Germany's Jewish population exceeded that of 1933, owing to the return of the refugees and the native Austrian Jews.

The Nazis resorted to violence against the Jews in November 1938 in what has come to be known as Kristallnacht (Crystal Night) for the numerable panes of glass shattered in Jewish shops. More than 7,000 Jewish businesses were destroyed along with more than 500 synagogues. Some 100 Jews were killed, and 30,000 were seized and sent to concentration camps. The closing of borders when the war began in September 1939 halted any further Jewish exodus, however.

The acquisition of western Poland opened a new phase in the persecution of Jews. Those areas of Poland that had belonged to Germany centuries earlier were annexed, while much of eastern Poland was taken by the Soviet Union. But the Germans made the remainder of Poland, centered on Warsaw, the destination for dispossessed Jews. Deportations were carried out with extreme brutality. Jews were usually transported east in railroad boxcars, under appalling conditions, to ghettos in Warsaw, Lodz, Kraków, and Lublin. That many died en route was a welcome by-product of the process for the Nazis rather than a cause for concern. Little or no advance warning was provided, and Jews went away carrying but one suitcase of clothing. Within the ghettos, conditions were dreadful. The Nazis moved the Jews first from Germany, then the western countries, and then Eastern Europe, and for the most part deportations continued throughout the war. When the Nazis began to exterminate the Jews, deportations bypassed the ghetto cities, and Jews went straight to the death camps.

Following the German armies into Poland in 1939 was a Schutzstaffel (SS) unit known as the Einsatzgruppe (Special Task Force), charged with eliminating likely resistance to military occupation. Polish government officials, professionals, teachers, professors, and business executives, among them many Jews, perished. When German forces invaded the Soviet Union in 1941 on three fronts, behind each was an Einsatzgruppe. SS leader Reinhard Tristan Eugen Heydrich charged these groups with eliminating the same categories of so-called undesirables in addition to Bolshevik (communist) functionaries. A fourth Einsatzgruppe was committed where needed. The scope and ferocity of the fighting in the east, to say nothing of the fact that it soon became apparent that the campaign would not be short, ruled out moving Russian Jews to city ghettos. The Einsatzgruppen simply killed large numbers of Jews rather than attempt to move them, and in some areas, particularly the Baltic region, locals participated in settling old scores and securing Jewish property. As the Germans moved east and acquired control over more and more Jews, it became clear that deportation to Poland would not be sufficient, for the ghettos were full, and transportation was not available.

An exasperated Hermann Göring, arguably second-in-command under Hitler, told Heydrich at the end of July 1941 to provide some plan for the Final Solution of the Jewish question. Heydrich complied, presenting a plan in the January 20, 1942, meeting of senior SS and government officials at the Wannsee villa in a Berlin suburb. The plan was twofold. First, Jews in the Soviet Union would be worked to death or killed on the spot, because sending them west would be a poor use of transportation. Second, Jews remaining in Germany and elsewhere would be transported to new killing camps. These were termed annihilation camps (*Vernichtungslager*). Auschwitz, Treblinka, Sobibor, Majdanek, and Chelmno were the principal death camps, and all were located in Poland. The existing ghettos in Poland would be emptied, and the inhabitants would be moved to the killing camps for eventual extermination.

Upon arrival in the railroad freight cars (some Jews from Western Europe were sent east in passenger cars), selection took place at the railhead. SS medical personnel—among the most notorious, Josef Mengele at Auschwitz—made a hasty but final determination of who initially survived and

Entrance gate to Auschwitz, Nazi Germany's largest concentration camp during World War II. Auschwitz in Poland played a central role in the "Final Solution," the systematic extermination of millions of Jews, which was a major factor in bringing about the creation of the state of Israel in 1948. (Corel Corporation)

who did not. Guidelines called for eliminating any persons who seemed unfit for the brutal labor that awaited. Thus, the elderly, the unhealthy or disabled, and very young children went straight to the gas chambers. Realizing that mothers would not easily be separated from their children, they too were gassed. Those selected went into the annihilation camps to be worked to death. Almost none would ever come out. Food rations were less than 900 calories per day, a level that leads to a slow and sure death from malnutrition and exhaustion.

Theresienstadt (Terczin), located in Czechoslovakia, was the model concentration camp, the showplace where Jews who had international reputations were sent so that friends and colleagues in the West could ascertain that they were alive. In late 1943 the Nazis tired of this charade, however, and sent the Terczin inmates to Auschwitz as well.

Much has been made of the lack of Jewish resistance, although there was some both in Warsaw and in a few of the camps. At first, deportations did not seem terribly sinister. In the Nazi racial hierarchy, Poles were barely ahead of Jews, and thus sending the Jews to Poland seemed to fit with Nazi logic. Once moved east, those who wanted to resist faced even greater obstacles. Means of resistance, such as weapons, were not available. And the Polish Underground Army was not about to help the Jews. Anti-Semitism was certainly one reason. Another reason was the fact that the Poles refused to hand over any weapons to what they perceived as a lost cause. Escape was almost as hopeless. Where could one go? Poland itself had seen considerable anti-Semitism, and most local inhabitants near the camps were in any case terrified of the Nazis and would not risk harboring escapees. The nearest neutral nations were hundreds of miles distant, and the Nazis punished with death anyone who assisted escapees.

The Nazi destruction of the killing camps as the war ended, the fact that most summary executions took place on the spot with imperfect record keeping, the postwar realignments of political and administrative boundaries, and the trauma of the heavy fighting in and around the massacre sites in the east all conspire to make any tally of Holocaust victims at best an estimate. Most scholars accept a figure of at least 6 million for the number of Jewish victims. This figure does not include perhaps millions of Roma, up to 2 million non-Jewish Poles, political prisoners, opponents of the regime, and homosexuals, let alone Red Army prisoners of war, many of whom were simply starved to death. Jews tend to define the Holocaust as an event unique to them because their religion/race was the source of persecution. Non-Jews include all the victims, for indeed the Nazi persecutions had the same end.

After the Allies liberated the camps in 1945, there were two questions: Who was responsible for the incredible massacre, and how could the rest of society have allowed it? Blame fell initially on the SS personnel who had run the camps, but the Waffen-SS (Fighting SS) brazenly denied its role, instead blaming the specialized Death's Head-SS (Totenkopfverbaende). To a certain extent, members of the Waffen-SS succeeded in deflecting blame, claiming that they were merely soldiers like all of the others, and in truth both soldiers and policemen did participate in the process. German Army (Wehrmacht) veterans denied complicity in the extermination of the Jews, asserting that it was purely the work of the SS, but the army was well aware of what was transpiring. When the Hamburg Institute for Social Research organized a photographic exhibit in 1995 that revealed the Wehrmacht participating in atrocities, a firestorm of controversy followed. Tarnishing the Wehrmacht's good-soldier image amounted to iconoclasm of the first instance, and the sensation was enormous. The issue is controversial to this day, for it countered half a century of effective self-denial on the part of rank-and-file Germans.

The churches shared the blame as well, but especially troublesome were the accusations concerning the role of the pope. What the pope knew and why he did not condemn the killings became the framing issues in the debate. Eugenio Pacelli, who became pope as Pius XII, was a Germanophile, known as the "German Pope." In 1959 Swiss playwright Rolf Hochhuth wrote *The Deputy: A Christian Tragedy,* accusing Pius XII of being Hitler's accessory. A more recent biography of Pius titled *Hitler's Pope* (1999) draws the same conclusion. Papal defenders make a pragmatic argument: by speaking out against the killings, Pius would not have saved a single Jew, but his actions might have turned the wrath of Hitler on Catholics as well, and millions more innocent victims might have perished. The German Evangelical-Lutheran Church also stood accused of failing to repudiate the killings. It too had its heroes, but overall its record in acting against the Holocaust does not appear to be a proud one.

Even the Allies came under fire for failing to aid the Jews before and during the war. The Nazis made no attempt to hide their treatment of the Jews prior to 1939. Jewish organizations in the United States entreated President Franklin D. Roosevelt to admit more Jews, but indifference and anti-Semitism triumphed. As increasing evidence of the Holocaust came to light during the war, Jewish agencies again urged the United States to do more, even to bomb the death camps and the rail lines leading to them. Two Czech Jews (Rudolf Virba and Alfred Weztler) escaped to Switzerland, described in detail the killing camps, and gave the U.S. embassy a map of the sprawling Birkenau subcamp of Auschwitz, but it was hand-drawn and rejected as insufficient. At first the U.S. military could argue that the camps lay beyond the range of its bombers, but this changed by the summer of 1944. Then it was a matter that military targets had priority, although Auschwitz inmates worked the Buna plant, the world's largest synthetic rubber plant. And in August 1944 the Eighth Air Force did strike the plant, but the official line was that winning the war, best done by hitting military targets, would simultaneously end the persecution.

In the early 1970s, a number of self-professed historians at the fringes of popular culture began to question the very existence of the Holocaust as a historical event. Not denying that large numbers of Jews died or that Nazis treated Jews brutally and that large numbers perished miserably, they deny instead the existence of a coherent plan and set of tools and processes used to exterminate the Jewish race. Called Holocaust Revisionists, they argue that the Germans moved Jews to the east for labor reasons, that the camps existed to provide labor pools, that the Nazis were brutal, and that the number who died in these camps was very high. This argument has made little headway, and courts as well as prominent academics and historians have rejected it out of hand.

A more intriguing debate that emerged in the 1990s was the question of intention: whether Hitler had planned all along (Intentionalists) to kill the Jews or whether through the war he and his fellow Nazis simply encountered an irresistible opportunity and the functional means (hence the moniker Functionalists) to carry out the extermination. The debate has sparked strong emotions. The guilt of the Germans appears to some to be mitigated to some extent if Hitler was merely a functionalist who took advantage of contingencies and circumstances, while the burden of guilt is much greater if Hitler had planned from the start to kill the Jews and if the German population acted in complicity to this desire. The debate was reignited in 1996 when American Daniel Goldhagen published a book provocatively titled *Hitler's Willing Executioners*. There was nothing new to be found among the charges, but the book punctured some 40 years of denial and reawakened the question of who in Germany had known what and when.

In the end, the Nazi-inspired Holocaust stands as one of the largest mass exterminations of human beings in modern history. It was at its core a genocide perpetrated across a large swath of Europe. There can be no doubt that the world's Jews, after having suffered through or witnessed such horrific persecutions, were determined to establish a Jewish state at the end of World War II. Indeed, the Holocaust gave new meaning and new urgency to Zionism. And many world leaders, perhaps out of guilt, perhaps out of outrage, helped to bring the Zionist vision to reality in 1948.

MICHAEL B. BARRETT

See also
Israel; Zionism

References
Bartov, Omer. *The Eastern Front 1941–45: German Troops and the Barbarization of Warfare*. 2nd ed. Palgrave/St. Martin's, 2001.
Browning, Christopher R. *The Origins of the Final Solution: The Evolution of Nazi Jewish Policy, September 1939–March 1942*. Lincoln: University of Nebraska Press, 2004.
Dawidowicz, Lucy S. *The War against the Jews, 1933–1945*. New York: Holt, Rinehart, and Winston, 1975.
Gilbert, Martin. *The Holocaust: The History of Jews of Europe during the Second World War*. New York: Henry Holt, 1987.
Goldhagen, Daniel Jonah. *Hitler's Willing Executioners: Ordinary Germans and the Holocaust*. New York: Knopf, 1996.

Holy League (1571)
See Lepanto, Battle of

Homs, First Battle of (December 11, 1260)

The First Battle of Homs (or Hims) was fought on December 11 between the Syrian Arabs and the Mongols who had invaded Syria. After sacking Baghdad, invading Syria, and capturing Aleppo, Mongol leader Hulegu Khan left in Syria part of his army, about 12,000 men, under Ketbugha, one of his most trusted generals, while he himself marched to northwestern Persia. Historians have traditionally explained Hulegu's sudden departure as a response to the news of the death of the Great Khan Mongke and the subsequent power struggle over succession.

In leaving Ketbugha in Syria, Hulegu certainly underestimated his opponents in Egypt, for on September 3, 1260, the Mamluks defeated Ketbugha's Mongol force at Ayn Jalut (Goliath's Well), marking the first important defeat suffered by the Mongols. Hulegu was infuriated by this unprecedented setback and organized a punitive expedition under Baydar (some sources say Ilge Noyan or Koke-Ilge), who had been one of Ketbugha's officers and had escaped death at Ayn Jalut. The Mongols recaptured Aleppo and then advanced into southern Syria.

On December 10, 1260, the Mongols encountered the Muslim coalition of the lords of Aleppo, Hama and Homs, under the overall command of al-Ashraf, near the tomb of the famous Arab commander Khalid ibn al-Walid at Homs. The battle, which pitted some 6,000 Mongols against about 1,400 Muslims, took place on the outskirts of Homs, with the Mongols deployed into eight formations (*atlab*), the first of 1,000 men and the rest arranged behind it. The Muslim forces were divided into center (under al-Ashraf), right wing (al-Mansur of Hama), and left wing (led by the emirs of Aleppo) units.

Little is known about how the battle unfolded, although historian al-Yunini writes that the Mongols were discomforted by the fog and the sun. In the end the Muslims, despite their numerical inferiority, emerged victorious. Scholars suggest that the decisive role in the battle was played by the arrival of Zamil ibn Ali, a Bedouin leader in northern Syria, whose troops suddenly appeared in the Mongol rear during the battle. Most of the Mongol army was either killed or captured, including a young Mongol named Ketbugha who joined the Mamluk Army and 34 years later became a Mamluk sultan. The victory at Homs reinforced the Muslim feeling of superiority over the Mongols. Some Mamluk chronicles consider it more important than the Battle of Ayn Jalut, since the Muslims had numerical superiority at the latter.

ALEXANDER MIKABERIDZE

See also
Mamluk-Ilkhanid Wars; Mongol Invasion of the Middle East

References
Amitai-Preiss, Reuven. *Mongols and Mamluks: The Mamluk-Ilkhanid War, 1260–1281*. Cambridge: Cambridge University Press, 1995.
Boyle, J. A. *The Mongol World Empire 1206–1370*. London: Variorum, 1977.

Morgan, D. O. "The Mongols in Syria 1260–1300." In *Crusade and Settlement*, ed. Peter Edbury. Cardiff: University College of Cardiff Press, 1985.

Nicolle, David. *The Mongol Warlords*. London: Brockhampton Press, 1990.

Homs, Second Battle of (October 29, 1281)

For a variety of reasons, following the First Battle of Homs of December 11, 1260, neither Hulegu nor his successor made any serious attempts to exact revenge on the Mamluks and their allies or reconquer Syria for the next 21 years. The Mamluks used this period to reform their forces and establish political alliances with the crusader states and the Golden Horde in order to be better prepared for future fighting with the Ilkhan Mongols. Between 1261 and 1277 the Mamluks and the Mongols were engaged in a prolonged border skirmishing, with neither side willing or able to undertake a major attack. In 1277, however, Mamluk leader Baybars became concerned by Mongol expansion into the Sultanate of Rum and launched a preemptive invasion into Asia Minor, where he defeated the Mongols at Abulustayn that April.

Baybars did not have long to enjoy the glory of his victory, as he died suddenly on July 1, 1277. His successor as Mamluk sultan, Baraka Khan (al-Malik al-Said Berke Khan), proved to be incapable of living up to his father's legacy, and his reign was cut short in 1279 by a group of senior officers led by Qalawun, Baybars's close associate, who faced domestic challenges to his rule. Informed of developments in Egypt and Syria, Abaka Khan was keenly interested in exploiting the infighting among the Mamluks, and in the summer of 1281 he dispatched a large army under his brother Mengu Temur into Syria.

The two sides met once again at Homs. The Mongol army of some 40,000–50,000 men included large contingents from Georgia (led by King Demetre), Armenia (led by King Leon), and Rum. Qalawun was well informed about the enemy's battle plan through his spies and had carefully selected positions at Homs. The Mongol left flank was commanded by Mazuq Agha and Hinduqur; the right wing included the Rumi, Georgian and Armenian forces; the center was under Mengu Temur himself. Qalawun divided his forces into six parts, with five of them forming the front line while he personally commanded the reserve of the elite royal mamluks. The Mamluk forces was probably equal in size to the Mongols and represented virtually all troops the sultanate could muster.

The two armies met early on the morning of October 29, 1281, between Homs and Rastan. The Mongol army was exhausted from a daylong march and was still stretched out over some 15 miles when it encountered the Mamluks. The Mongol right wing was first to attack—it routed the Mamluk left wing and pursued it beyond Homs, where the Mongols halted to rest, expecting the rest of the Mongol army to complete what seemed to be a decisive victory. But the tide of battle soon changed. The Mamluk right wing held firm against early Mongol attacks, and its counterattack, supported by the sultan's royal mamluks, routed the Mongol left wing, which then spread confusion into the Mongol center, where unnerved Mengu Temur called a retreat. Once the Mongol right wing and center began to withdraw, Qalawun sent most of his army in pursuit. The Mongol retreat soon turned into a rout as the Mamluks pursued their enemy to the Euphrates River, killing or capturing thousands in the process.

Meanwhile, the Mongol right wing returned to the battlefield. Qalawun, with fewer than 2,000 men, was largely defenseless, but his quick senses saved the situation. He concealed his men and ordered his banners to be furled and the drums to remain silent. The Mongols thus passed by without noticing the small Mamluk force and, upon learning the fate of the rest of the army, departed the battlefield.

Thus, by nightfall in the Second Battle of Homs, the Mamluks scored a major victory over the Mongols. Abaka was furious at the Mongol defeat and immediately began planning another campaign to Syria, but he died in 1282 before it could be realized.

ALEXANDER MIKABERIDZE

See also

Abulustayn, Battle of; Baybars I; Mamluk-Ilkhanid Wars; Mongol Invasion of the Middle East; Qalawun

References

Amitai-Preiss, Reuven. *Mongols and Mamluks: The Mamluk-Ilkhanid War, 1260–1281*. Cambridge: Cambridge University Press, 1995.

Boyle, J. A. *The Mongol World Empire, 1206–1370*. London: Variorum, 1977.

Morgan, D. O. "The Mongols in Syria 1260–1300." In *Crusade and Settlement*, ed. Peter Edbury. Cardiff: University College of Cardiff Press, 1985.

Nicolle, David. *The Mongol Warlords*. London: Brockhampton, 1990.

Homs, Third Battle of (December 23, 1299)

Almost 20 years passed after the Mongols' 1281 attempt before another Ilkhan Mongol ruler attempted to invade Syria. By then, the formidable Mamluk Army that Sultan Baybars I had forged had become but a shadow of its former self, with disunity of command and overconfidence plaguing the army.

In 1299 Ilkhan Ghazan organized a third Ilkhan invasion of Syria, crossing the Euphrates River and capturing Aleppo before proceeding south; as on previous occasions, the Mongol army featured contingents from Armenia and Georgia. Young sultan al-Malik al-Nasir Muhammad mobilized the Mamluk forces in southern Palestine, but floods there swept away the Mamluk supply trains, depriving the army of food and causing a decline in morale. In early December, the sultan marched north of Damascus to the plains of Homs. During this three-day march the Mamluks wore full battle gear, exhausting themselves and their mounts.

The two sides met at Wadi al-Khaznadar on December 1299. This engagement, also known as the Third Battle of Homes, saw the Mongols suffer an initial setback as the Mamluk attack caught them unprepared. Many Mongol archers actually fought dismounted, hiding behind their horses. The Mamluk attack was led by some 500 *naft* (Greek fire) throwers.

Ghazan, however, was able to regroup his men and counterattack, breaking the Mamluk flank and causing the Mamluk army to flee from the battlefield. After the battle, Ghazan pushed southward to Damascus before withdrawing home. The subsequent attempt by the Mongols to return to Syria resulted in their defeat at Marj al-Saffar (April 20–22, 1303), bringing an end to Mongol incursions into Syria.

ALEXANDER MIKABERIDZE

See also
Homs, Second Battle of; Mamluk-Ilkhanid Wars; Mongol Invasion of the Middle East

References
Amitai-Preiss, Reuven. *Mongols and Mamluks: The Mamluk-Ilkhanid War, 1260–1281.* Cambridge: Cambridge University Press, 1995.
Boyle, J. A. *The Mongol World Empire, 1206–1370.* London: Variorum, 1977.
Morgan, D. O. "The Mongols in Syria 1260–1300." In *Crusade and Settlement,* ed. Peter Edbury. Cardiff: University College of Cardiff Press, 1985.
Nicolle, David. *The Mongol Warlords.* London: Brockhampton Press, 1990.

Hormuz, Strait of

Narrow body of water that connects the Persian Gulf to the Gulf of Oman and the Indian Ocean. The Strait of Hormuz is bounded in the north by Iran and on its south by the United Arab Emirates (UAE) and the Sultanate of Oman. The waters of the Strait of Hormuz are predominately within the claimed territorial waters of these three nations because the United Nations Convention on the Law of the Sea defines territorial waters as 12 nautical miles from shore. At its narrowest point the strait is 21 nautical miles wide, but there are islands throughout its length, most of which belong to Iran. The strait is designated as an international shipping lane. As such, ships are allowed to transit it under the rules of "innocent" or "transit" passage, which permit maritime traffic in key straits that separate international bodies of water.

Because of its location, the Strait of Hormuz is considered a strategic choke point. Some 20 percent of world oil shipments transit the strait on any given day aboard commercial tankers. The key nation in this regard is Iran, whose largest port and naval base, Bandar Abbas, is located at the northernmost tip of the strait.

Iran has fortified several islands—the Tunb Islands and Abu Musa—that dominate the strait. Abu Musa in particular has long been a source of conflict between Iran and the UAE, especially since Iran's occupation of it in the early 1970s.

The Strait of Hormuz has always been a significant factor in modern wars. During World War II, it was the key conduit for American Lend-Lease aid through Iraq and Iran to the Soviet Union. Since then, the strait has been the chief avenue for U.S. seaborne trade into the Persian Gulf region and oil out of it. The strait became even more an issue after the 1979 Islamic Revolution in Iran, which deposed pro-U.S. shah Reza Pahlavi. After that, the United States began to station a number of warships in the Persian Gulf to protect U.S. interests in the region.

Near the end of the Iraq-Iran war (1980–1988), Iran attempted to close the strait by mining it to deprive Iraq and other Persian Gulf states of their oil revenues. The United States responded by reflagging oil tankers and forcibly reopening the strait in Operation EARNEST WILL. Not long after, the United States used the strait as the main conduit for sea-supplied military matériel in support of Operations DESERT SHIELD (1990) and DESERT STORM (the Persian Gulf War, 1991). Thereafter, the United States maintained a strong naval presence in the region, to include at least one aircraft carrier battle group and often several such groups. Most recently, the strait was critical to the maritime power projection of the 2003 Anglo-American–led invasion of Iraq (Operation IRAQI FREEDOM).

Without access to the Strait of Hormuz, the United States and other Western powers would be severely limited in influencing events in the Middle East. U.S. policy makers in particular continue to keep a wary eye on the Strait of Hormuz, especially given Iran's alleged nuclear ambitions and the often harsh rhetoric coming from its rightist leaders.

JOHN T. KUEHN

See also
EARNEST WILL, Operation; Iran; Iran, Islamic Revolution in; Iran-Iraq War; Iraq War; Persian Gulf War, Overview; United Arab Emirates

References
Bowden, Mark. *Guests of the Ayatollah: The First Battle in America's War with Militant Islam.* New York: Atlantic Monthly Press, 2006.

Marolda, Edward J., and Robert J. Schneller Jr. *Shield and Sword: The Untold Story of the United States Navy and the Persian Gulf War.* Annapolis, MD: Naval Institute Press, 2001.

Houthi, Hussein Badr al-Din al- (?–2004)

Yemeni political and religious leader. The place and date of Sheikh Badr al-Din al-Houthi's birth are unknown, and there is not much information on his early life. He was the charismatic leader of the Zaydi Shia sect constituting 45–50 percent of Yemen's population; followers of the al-Houthi movement, as it came to be called, are estimated at 30 percent of the Yemeni population.

Between 1993 and 1999, al-Houthi was a member of parliament representing the Al-Haqq Party. In 1992 a movement known as the Shabab Mu'minin (Believing Youth) developed, apparently to counter growing Salafist influence and to assert a new Zaydi identity. Al-Houthi led this movement until 1997, when it split.

Following the U.S. invasion of Iraq in 2003, some members of the Zaydi community protested against the U.S. occupation of Iraq and the Yemeni government's close ties with the United States. Al-Houthi was identified as a leader of these protests. Since the attack on the U.S. Navy destroyer *Cole* in Aden in October 2000, the United States had become concerned about the growth of Al Qaeda in Yemen, and the Yemeni government took great strides to downplay the al-Houthi movement, characterizing it as a deviant and terrorist group and claiming that it had links to Iran and Libya, which were never firmly established.

Al-Houthi portrayed his movement as primarily seeking social justice and basic human, political, and religious rights. His movement did not call for an end to the Saleh government but did oppose its alliances with the United States and the manipulation of Salafi or Wahhabist elements among the Zaydis. Al-Houthi's movement represented a challenge from within the Shia elite, for al-Houthi was a sayyid, a descendant of Prophet Muhammad with roots in the Zaydi imamate that had dominated northern Yemen until the establishment of a Yemeni republic in 1962.

The al-Houthi rebellion was also known as the al-Sa'dah conflict. It took place in northern Yemen about 150 miles from Sana'a. In 2004, fighting involving al-Houthi's followers broke out against the Yemeni government there. The Yemeni government employed force to crush the movement.

Following 82 days of fighting in 2004 and after some 1,500 troops and civilians were killed and thousands had fled their villages, Yemeni government forces killed al-Houthi in Jarf Salman, a village in the Marraan mountains in Sa'dah, on September 10, 2004. Fighting broke out again in March 2005. Some 400 persons were killed within two weeks, hundreds of locals were detained, hundreds of religious schools and religious summer camps were closed, and the government ordered that 1,400 charities be closed.

After al-Houthi's death the movement came under the leadership of Abd al-Malik al-Houthi; his brother, Yusuf Madani; his son-in-law, Abdullah Ayedh al-Razami; and the spiritual leadership of Badr al-Din al-Houthi, his father. Intermittent fighting continued thereafter, leading to the Yemeni Civil War beginning in 2015 that saw the Saudi Arabian government supporting the Yemeni government against al-Houthi's followers, now known simply as Houthis.

SHERIFA ZUHUR

See also
Al Qaeda in the Arabian Peninsula; *Cole*, USS, Attack on; Yemen; Yemen Civil War

References
Carapico, Sheila. *Civil Society in Yemen: The Political Economy of Activism in Modern Arabia.* Cambridge: Cambridge University Press, 2007.

Dresch, Paul. *A History of Modern Yemen.* Cambridge: Cambridge University Press, 2008.

Hill, Ginny. "Yemen: Fear of Failure." Chatham House Briefing Paper. London: Royal Institute of International Affairs, 2008.

Knickmeyer, Ellen. "In Yemen, a Mostly Concealed Sectarian Fight Endures." *Washington Post,* Saturday June 7, 2008, A09.

Houthis

Zaidi Shia-led cultural and political movement active in Yemen and founded by Hussein Badreddin al-Houthi in 1994. The official name of the group is Ansar Allah (Supporters of God), but since al-Houthi's death in 2004, its adherents have become popularly known simply as Houthis. Since 2004, the Houthis have been led by Badreddin al-Houthi's brother, Abdul-Malik al-Houthi.

The Zaidi people are composed of numerous tribes that have historically resided in northern Yemen; they make up about one-third of Yemen's total population. In 2004 the Houthis commenced an insurgency against the Yemeni government, which they claimed ignored or discriminated against the Zaidi people. The Houthi insurgency is ongoing, and by late 2016 Houthi rebels controlled much of northwestern Yemen.

Initially, Ansar Allah embraced a relatively moderate vision of Shia Islam and was rather tolerant and inclusive in its worldview. Over the years, however, the group became less inclusive and more intent on overthrowing the existing sociopolitical order in Yemen, which it claimed was corrupt and unresponsive to the needs of rank-and-file Yemenis. Since Hussein Badreddin al-Houthi's 2004 death at the hands of Yemeni government forces, the Houthis have allied themselves with numerous organizations and states, including Hezbollah, Syria, North Korea, Russia, and Iran, the latter of which has provided Houthi fighters with major logistical and military support.

The Houthis took part in the 2011 Yemeni Revolution, part of the larger Arab Spring movement, but ultimately rejected a compromise solution to the unrest, claiming that it did not offer sufficient meaningful change on the part of Yemen's government. They also rejected the new regime now led by Abd Rabbuh Mansur Hadi, which it had vowed to unseat when he came to power in 2012. Hadi has received strong support from Saudi Arabia.

Between 2012 and 2015 the Houthis made major territorial gains, with the size of the group's armed personnel swelling to nearly 100,000. When the group captured Yemen's capital city, Sana'a, in January 2015, President Hadi moved his government to Aden. At the same time, Saudi Arabia commenced a military campaign against the Houthis, which soon included a host of other countries including the United States. That intervention is ongoing. By 2015, Al Qaeda in the Arabian Peninsula (AQAP) and the Islamic State of Iraq and Syrian (ISIS), both Sunni organizations, were engaged in their own conflict against Yemen's beleaguered government as well as Houthi rebels.

Since seizing Sana'a and establishing a de facto rump government in Yemen, the Houthis have managed to appeal to a fairly broad section of Yemen's population by pledging to rid the country of corruption, cronyism, and opaque governance. They have also promised to increase job opportunities and deliver reliable utilities to many urban Yemenis. Some Yemenis, however, particularly city dwellers, tend to view the Houthis as rough-hewn bumpkins who have no understanding of modern governance. Yemen's Sunni population also distrusts the Houthis.

As of August 2018, the Houthis firmly controlled about one quarter of western Yemen, including Sana'a. Meanwhile, the Saudi-led military campaign against the Houthis continued. In May, October, and December 2017, Houthi rebels fired missiles into Saudi territory. The December attack had targeted the Saudi royal palace. Although the missiles failed to inflict damage, the Saudi government and its allies were outraged by the attacks. In January 2018, the Organization of Islamic Cooperation publicly condemned the December Houthi missile attack. More Houthi missile launches against Saudi targets occurred in 2018, including one in August 2018 against the Jizan Industrial City. In that attack, 1 Saudi civilian was killed and 11 more were wounded. Also in August 2018, Houthi leaders suggested that they were open to a comprehensive peace settlement in Yemen but that any such deal must include provisions for a new transitional presidency and the timely selection of a new permanent president.

Paul G. Pierpaoli Jr.

See also
Al Qaeda in the Arabian Peninsula; Iran; Islamic State of Iraq and Syria; Saudi Arabia; Yemen; Yemen Civil War

References
Day, Stephen W. *Regionalism and Rebellion in Yemen: A Troubled National Union*. New York: Cambridge University Press, 2012.

Fraihat, Ibrahim. *Unfinished Revolutions: Yemen, Libya, and Tunisia after the Arab Spring*. New Haven, CT: Yale University Press, 2016.

Hrawi, Elias (1925–2006)

Lebanese political leader and president of Lebanon (1989–1998). Elias (Ilyas) Hrawi was born on September 4, 1925, in Hawsj Al-Umara near the town of Zahla in the Bekaa Valley. The son of a wealthy landowner and a Maronite Christian, Hrawi graduated with a degree in business from Saint Joseph University in Beirut. He became wealthy from a vegetable export business and food processing factory in the Bekaa Valley and from heading agricultural cooperatives. When the export business was halted by the civil war in Lebanon during 1975–1990, he began oil importation and operated a gas station chain in Beirut.

Hrawi followed his two brothers into politics and was elected to the Lebanese National Assembly in 1972. In the 1980s, he began to play an increasing role in the nation's political life. A member of the National Assembly from 1972 until 1989 and a member of the chamber's independent Maronite bloc, he worked to maintain good relations with both Christian and Muslim groups, partly due to the growing Muslim population in his constituency.

On November 24, 1989, two days after the assassination of President René Mouawad, Hrawi was elected president of Lebanon during an emergency National Assembly session. He was the first Lebanese president to come from outside the Maronite area of Mount Lebanon. The election occurred amid an ongoing civil war between Syrian-supported Muslim militias and Christian army forces. Hrawi formed a civilian government rival to the military government headed by General Michel Aoun, former Christian commander in chief of the Lebanese Army, whose aim was to expel all Syrian forces from Lebanon. Hrawi's task was to implement the Taif Agreement, a national charter of reconciliation designed to transfer executive power from the presidency to a cabinet composed equally of Christian and Muslim ministers and to expand the legislature to allow for equal representation there as well. Aoun rejected the agreement, however, because it allowed Syria to participate in the implementation of the plan over a two-year period. Indeed, Hrawi's critics claimed that he too closely supported Syrian interests in Lebanon.

Backed by the Syrian Army, Hrawi campaigned to remove Aoun but soon withdrew the effort out of concern that he would alienate the Christian community, which had divided into factions supporting and opposing the Taif Agreement. In May 1990, battling Christian forces signed a truce, paving the way for the approval of constitutional changes to implement the agreement, which Hrawi signed into law on September 21, 1990. Hrawi continued his efforts to oust Aoun, and forces loyal to Hrawi attacked Aoun's headquarters on October 13, 1990, forcing him to flee. Hrawi then moved to restore national government control to the whole of Lebanon. In October 1995, under Syrian pressure, the National Assembly amended the constitution to allow Hrawi to remain in office for an additional three years without benefit of election. His critics charged that this action subverted democracy and undermined the delicate political balance in Lebanon.

During almost a decade as president, Hrawi came to be seen as an old-school leader who had been manipulated by the Syrian government. He was often overshadowed by the far more dynamic Lebanese political leader, Prime Minister Rafik Hariri, with whom Hrawi often differed on political and economic reform issues. Émile Lahoud succeeded Hrawi in November 1998. Hrawi died of cancer at the American University Hospital in Beirut on July 7, 2006.

Spencer C. Tucker

See also
Aoun, Michel; Hariri, Rafik; Lebanon; Lebanon Civil War; Syria

Reference
Fisk, Robert. *Pity the Nation: The Abduction of Lebanon.* 4th ed. New York: Nation Books, 2002.

Hulegu (1218–1265)

Mongol prince and founder of the Ilkhanate, the Mongol state in Persia. Hulegu (Hulagu) was born on October 15, 1218, the son of Chinggis Khan's (Genghis Khan) youngest son Tolui. In 1253 Hulegu's elder brother, the Great Khan Mongke, dispatched him westward with an army to assume overall command of the Mongol forces operating in Persia and the Caucasus. Having largely annihilated the Ismaili Assassins (1256) and destroyed the Abbasid caliphate in Baghdad (1258), Hulegu entered Syria and captured Aleppo in January 1260. But in the spring he withdrew into Azerbaijan with the bulk of his army, and a smaller force left in Palestine under his general Kitbuqa was overwhelmed by the Egyptian Mamluks in the Battle of Ayn Jalut on September 3, 1260. Syria and Palestine were lost.

Hulegu was unable to avenge this defeat, owing to the disintegration of the empire following Mongke's death (1259) and the outbreak in 1261 of war with his cousin Berke, khan of the Mongols of the Golden Horde. It was probably at this juncture that Hulegu established himself as virtually an autonomous ruler in Persia and Iraq, recognized by his brother, the new *qaghan* Qubilai (Kublai) in the Far East.

In 1262 Hulegu inaugurated a series of Ilkhanid overtures to the Latin West by writing to King Louis IX of France, urging concerted action against the Mamluks. Hulegu's envoy to Pope Urban IV reported his desire for baptism (ca. 1263). Hulegu's mother, Sorqaqtani, had been a Nestorian Christian, as was his principal wife, Doquz Khatûn. Nevertheless, he also manifested a marked interest in Tibetan Buddhism and remained attached to the shamanistic practices of his forebears until his death on February 8, 1265. His son Abaqa Khan succeeded him.

Peter Jackson

See also
Ayn Jalut, Battle of; Golden Horde–Ilkhanid Wars; Homs, First Battle of; Mamluk-Ilkhanid Wars

References
Boyle, John Andrew. "Dynastic and Political History of the Ilkhans." In *The Cambridge History of Iran,* Vol. 5, *The Saljuq and Mongol Periods,* ed. J. A. Boyle, 340–355. Cambridge: Cambridge University Press, 1968.
Jackson, Peter. "The Crisis in the Holy Land in 1260." *English Historical Review* 95 (1980): 481–513.
Meyvaert, Paul. "An Unknown Letter of Hulagu, Ilkhan of Persia, to King Louis IX of France." *Viator* 11 (1980): 242–258.

Hunkar Iskelesi, Treaty of (July 8, 1833)

Defensive alliance between the Ottoman Empire and the Russian Empire. In 1830–1832, the Ottoman Empire struggled to restrain its ambitious vassal Mehmet Ali of Egypt, whose armies occupied Palestine and Syria and threatened to reach Istanbul (Constantinople) itself. In late 1832, the Egyptians scored a decisive victory at Konya that removed the last significant Ottoman force between them and the imperial capital.

In this situation, early in 1833 Sultan Mahmud II turned to the traditional Ottoman foe of Russia for assistance. Russian emperor Nicholas I, although eager to bring about the partition of the Ottoman Empire, was unwilling to allow the strengthening of Mehmet Ali's Egypt and in February 1833 dispatched an expeditionary force to protect Istanbul. Faced with Russian intervention, Mehmet Ali negotiated the Convention of Kutahya that gave him provinces in Syria.

Meanwhile, on July 8, 1833, Nicholas and Mahmud negotiated the Treaty of Hunkar Iskelesi to strengthen their newly established relationship. Both rulers pledged to guarantee the territorial integrity of the other's domains. Secret provisions of the treaty exempted Ottoman from providing military help to Russia in exchange to closing the straits to non-Russian warships.

Upon learning about the treaty, Britain and France became suspicious of its secret provisions, fearing that these had given Russia freedom of action in the Ottoman Empire. During the eight years it was in force, the Treaty of Hunkar Iskelesi was a point of major concern for the leaders of the Great Powers, who ultimately insisted on replacing it with the London Straits Convention of 1840.

Alexander Mikaberidze

See also
Egyptian-Ottoman Wars; Mahmud II, Sultan; Mehmed Ali; Russo-Ottoman Wars

References
Hale, William. *Turkish Foreign Policy, 1774–2000.* London: Frank Cass, 2000.
Karsh, Efraim, and Inari Karsh. *Empires of the Sand: The Struggle for Mastery in the Middle East 1789–1923.* Cambridge, MA: Harvard University Press, 1999.
MacKenzie, David. *Imperial Dreams, Harsh Realities: Tsarist Russian Foreign Policy, 1815–1917.* Fort Worth, TX: Harcourt Brace College, 1994.

Husaybah, Battle of (April 17, 2004)

Battle near the Iraqi town of Husaybah, close to the Syrian border, on April 17, 2004, that pitted U.S. marines from the First Marine Expeditionary Force against Iraqi insurgents. The 14-hour battle occurred concurrently with Operation VIGILANT RESOLVE, also known as the First Battle of Fallujah (April 4–May 1, 2004), the U.S. effort to capture the city of Fallujah.

From Husaybah the insurgents had been attempting to attack U.S. forces in order to divert resources from the operation against Fallujah. The insurgent force numbered about 300 and was operating from positions in the vicinity of the former Baath Party headquarters in Husaybah. U.S. forces there numbered 150.

On April 17, the insurgents drew the Americans from their base on the outskirts of Husaybah with a roadside bombing, followed by a mortar assault. When the marines retaliated, they encountered an ambush during which they were hit with small-arms and machine-gun fire. The marines then called in reinforcements.

The resulting fighting lasted the entire day and late into the night, with the marines advancing building by building to clear the insurgents. During the night, AH-1 Cobra helicopter gunships also attacked insurgent positions in the city.

Although the marines were victorious, 5 marines were killed and 9 others were wounded. The insurgents suffered an estimated 150 killed in action, an unknown number of wounded, and 20 captured.

Richard B. Verrone

See also
Fallujah, First Battle of; Iraq Insurgency

References

Murray, Williamson, and Robert H. Scales Jr. *The Iraq War: A Military History.* Cambridge, MA: Belknap, 2005.

Ricks, Thomas E. *Fiasco: The American Military Adventure in Iraq, 2003 to 2005.* New York: Penguin, 2007.

West, Bing. *No True Glory: A Frontline Account of the Battle for Fallujah.* New York: Bantam, 2006.

Hussein, Saddam (1937–2006)

Iraqi politician, leading figure in the Baath Party, and president of Iraq (1979–2003). Born on April 28, 1937, in the village of Awja, near Tikrit, to a family of sheep herders, Saddam Hussein attended a secular school in Baghdad and in 1957 joined the Baath Party, a socialist and Arab nationalist party. Iraqi Baathists supported General Abd al-Karim Qassim's ouster of the Iraqi monarchy in 1958 but were not favored by President Qassim.

Wounded in an unsuccessful attempt to assassinate Qassim in 1959, Hussein subsequently fled the country but returned after the 1963 Baathist coup and began his rise in the party, although he was again imprisoned in 1964. Escaping in 1966, Hussein continued to ascend the Baathist ranks, becoming second in authority when the party took full and uncontested control of Iraq in 1968 under the leadership of General Ahmad Hassan al-Bakr, a relative of Hussein. The elderly Bakr gradually relinquished power to him so that Hussein eventually controlled most of the government.

Hussein became president when Bakr resigned, allegedly because of illness, in July 1979. A week after taking power, Hussein led a meeting of Baath leaders during which the names of his potential challengers were read aloud. They were then escorted from the room and shot. Because Iraq was rent by ethnic and religious divisions, Hussein ruled through a tight web of relatives and associates from Tikrit, backed by the Sunni Muslim minority. He promoted economic development through Iraqi oil production, which accounted for 10 percent of known world reserves. Hussein's modernization was along Western lines, with expanded roles for women and a secular legal system based in part on sharia and Ottoman law. He also promoted the idea of Iraqi nationalism and emphasized Iraq's ancient past, glorifying such figures as the kings Hammurabi and Nebuchadnezzar.

Before assuming the presidency, Hussein had courted both the West and the Soviet Union, resulting in arms deals with the Soviets and close relations with the Soviet Union and France. He was also instrumental in convincing Mohammad Reza Shah Pahlavi of Iran to curb his support of Iraqi Kurds. Hussein's efforts to take advantage of the superpowers' Cold War rivalry, including rapprochement with Iran, fell apart with the overthrow of the shah in the 1979 Iranian Revolution. The shah's successor, Ayatollah Ruhollah Khomeini, a radical fundamentalist Muslim, bitterly opposed Hussein because of his Sunni background and secularism.

After a period of repeated border skirmishes, Iraq declared war on Iran in September 1980. Hussein's ostensible dispute concerned a contested border, but he also feared Iran's fundamentalism and its support for the Iraqi Shia Muslim majority. Initial success gave way to Iraqi defeats in the face of human-wave attacks and ultimately a stalemate. By 1982 Hussein was ready to end the war, but Iranian leaders desired that the fighting continue. In 1988 the United Nations (UN) finally brokered a cease-fire but not before the war had devastated both nations. The war left Iraq heavily in debt, and Hussein requested relief from his major creditors, including the United States, Kuwait, and Saudi Arabia. He also sought to maintain high oil prices. His efforts were in vain; creditors refused to write off their debts, and Kuwait maintained a high oil output, forcing other oil-producing nations to follow suit.

Hussein was also enraged by Kuwaiti slant drilling into Iraqi oil fields. His demands became more strident, and he declared Kuwait a "rogue province" of Iraq. After securing what he believed to be U.S. acquiescence, he ordered Iraqi forces to attack and occupy Kuwait on August 2, 1990. Hussein miscalculated the U.S. reaction. President George H. W. Bush assembled an international military coalition, built up forces in Saudi Arabia (Operation DESERT SHIELD), and then commenced a relentless bombing campaign against Iraq in January 1991. The ground war of February 24–28, 1991, resulted in a crushing defeat of Iraqi forces. Although Hussein withdrew from Kuwait, coalition forces did not seek his overthrow, and he remained in power, ruling a nation devastated by two recent wars.

Hussein retained control of Iraq for another decade, during which he brutally suppressed Kurdish and Shia revolts, relinquished limited autonomy to the Kurds, acquiesced to the destruction of stockpiles of chemical weapons, and pursued a dilatory response to UN efforts to monitor his weapons programs. Convinced—wrongly as it turned out—that Hussein had been building and stockpiling weapons of mass destruction, President George W. Bush asked for and received authorization from Congress to wage war against Iraq. U.S. and coalition forces invaded Iraq in March 2003.

Saddam Hussein, shown here in October 1999, was the president and dictator of Iraq from 1979 until he was overthrown by a U.S.-led coalition in the Iraq War of 2003. Subsequently brought to trial and convicted by the new Iraqi government, he was executed in 2006. (AFP/Getty Images)

Coalition forces took Baghdad on April 10, 2003, and captured Hussein on December 14, 2003, to be brought to trial on charges of war crimes and crimes against humanity.

On November 5, 2006, the Iraqi Special Tribunal found Hussein guilty in the deaths of 148 Shiite Muslims in 1982 whose murders he had ordered. That same day, he was sentenced to hang. Earlier on August 21, 2006, a second trial had begun on charges that Hussein had committed genocide and other atrocities by ordering the systematic extermination of northern Iraqi Kurds during 1987–1988, resulting in as many as 180,000 deaths. Before the second trial moved into high gear, however, Hussein filed an appeal, which was rejected by the Iraqi court on December 26, 2006. Four days later on December 30, 2006, the Muslim holiday of Id al-Adha, Hussein was executed by hanging in Baghdad. Before his death, he told U.S. Federal Bureau of Investigation interrogators that he had misled the world to give the impression that Iraq had weapons of mass destruction in order to make the country appear stronger in the face of its enemy, Iran.

Daniel E. Spector

See also
Baath Party; Bush Doctrine; Iran-Iraq War; Iraq; Iraq War; Khomeini, Ruhollah; Kurds; Kuwait, Iraqi Invasion of; Persian Gulf War, Overview; Qasim, Abdul Karim

References
Bengio, Ofra. *Saddam's Word: Political Discourse in Iraq.* New York: Oxford University Press, 1998.

Karsh, Efraim. *Saddam Hussein: A Political Biography.* New York: Grove/Atlantic, 2002.

Miller, Judith, and Laurie Mylroie. *Saddam Hussein and the Crisis in the Gulf.* New York: Times Books, 1990.

Wingate, Brian. *Saddam Hussein: The Rise and Fall of a Dictator.* New York: Rosen, 2004.

Husseini, Haj Amin al- (1895–1974)

Palestinian Arab nationalist, Muslim religious leader and scholar, and mufti of Jerusalem during 1921–1948 who vehemently opposed the creation of an Israeli state in Palestine. Haj Mohammad Amin al-Husseini was born in Jerusalem to an aristocratic family, probably in 1895. He studied religious law for a year at the al-Azhar University in Cairo, and in 1913 he made the requisite pilgrimage to Mecca, earning the honorific title *haj*. In 1919 he attended the Pan-Syrian Congress in Damascus, where he supported Emir Faisal's bid to be king of Greater Syria, which was to include Syria, Lebanon, Jordan, and Palestine.

The 1916 Sykes-Picot Agreement, however, precluded establishment of a Greater Syria. Thus, Husseini abandoned Pan-Arabism centered around Damascus. Instead, he adhered to an ideology centered on creation of a Palestinian entity revolving around Jerusalem.

In 1920, Husseini instigated an Arab attack against Jews in Jerusalem and was jailed by the British authorities in the mandate. In 1921 when the existing mufti (a Muslim scholar who interprets Islamic holy law, or sharia) died, Sir Herbert Samuel, Britain's first high commissioner in Palestine, pardoned Husseini and appointed him the new mufti. Husseini also became president of the newly created Supreme Muslim Council, making him the most important religious and political leader of the Palestinian Arabs.

In 1937 Husseini expressed his solidarity with Nazi Germany, asking Berlin to oppose the establishment of a Jewish state, help stop Jewish immigration to Palestine, and provide arms to the Arabs. That same year, German SS officer Adolf Eichmann visited Husseini in Jerusalem. In response, the British government removed Husseini from his position and sent him into exile in Syria.

Just before the start of World War II Husseini went to Iraq, where in 1941 he supported the anti-British regime of Rashid Ali al-Gaylani. After the British removed al-Gaylani from power, Husseini fled to Germany disguised as a woman, a violation of Islamic law. He spent the remainder of the war organizing and recruiting Muslims in the Balkans, especially through radio broadcasts.

In 1946 Husseini escaped house arrest in Paris and fled to Egypt, where he lived until the 1960s. In 1948, Jordan's King Abdullah gave the title of mufti of Jerusalem to Hussam al-Din Jarallah. In 1948 Husseini was proclaimed president of the All Palestine Government in Gaza. Recognized only by Egypt, Syria, Iraq, Lebanon, Saudi Arabia, and Lebanon, his government was entirely dependent on Egyptian support, which was eventually withdrawn in 1959. Husseini retired from public life after serving as president of the 1962 World Islamic Congress, which he had founded in 1931. He died in Lebanon on July 4, 1974.

MICHAEL R. HALL

See also

Iraq; Israel; Palestine, British Mandate for; Sykes-Picot Agreement

References

Jbara, Taysir. *Palestinian Leader Hajj Amin Al-Husayni, Mufti of Jerusalem.* New York: Kingston Press, 1985.

Mattar, Philip. *The Mufti of Jerusalem.* New York: Columbia University Press, 1988.

Hussein ibn Ali ibn Mohammed (1856–1931)

Sharif of Mecca and king of the Hejaz. Born in Istanbul (Constantinople) sometime around 1856 into the family of Hashem, traditionally held as descendants of Prophet Muhammad and therefore holders of the title sharif (sherif, emir), Hussein ibn Ali ibn Mohammed studied in Mecca from age eight. In 1893 Sultan Abdul Hamid II caused Hussein to be brought to Istanbul and, although making him a member of the Council of State, held him in virtual captivity until 1908, when Hussein was appointed sharif of Mecca on the death of his uncle Abdullah.

Hussein maintained a loyalty to the sultan but resented the Hejaz railroad as an encroachment on Arab autonomy and feared the Young Turks who came to control the Ottoman government. Hussein had also long hoped for an independent Arab kingdom under his own rule. World War I provided that opportunity.

As early as February 1914, Hussein was in communication through his son Abdullah with British authorities in Cairo. Abdullah met with British high commissioner in Egypt Lord Herbert Kitchener and told him that the Arabs were prepared to revolt against Istanbul if the British would pledge their support for such a move. The British remained skeptical until the Ottoman Empire's entrance into the war in October 1914. Kitchener was then secretary of state for war in London, and on his advice Sir Harold Wingate, British governor-general of the Sudan, and Sir Henry McMahon, British high commissioner in Egypt, kept in touch with Hussein.

Meanwhile, in the spring of 1915 Hussein sent his third son, Emir Faisal, to Damascus to reassure Ottoman authorities there of his loyalty but also to sound out Arab opinion. Faisal was originally pro-Ottoman, but the visit to Damascus and the profound discontent of the Arab population there completely changed his views.

Hussein then entered into active negotiations with McMahon. Hussein promised to declare war on the Ottoman Empire and raise an Arab army to assist the British in return for British support for him as king of a postwar Pan-Arab state. On June 5, 1916, Hussein initiated the Arab Revolt, and on November 2 he proclaimed himself "king of the Arab countries," which caused the British government some embarrassment with the French. Finally, the Allies worked out a compromise by which they addressed Hussein as "king of the Hejaz."

Hussein left the military leadership of the revolt to his four sons. Throughout the revolt, Hussein worried about the ambitions of Ibn Saud. McMahon's pledge to Hussein preceded by just six months the Sykes-Picot Agreement (1916) between the British and French governments, which represented a breach of the promises made to the Arabs by laying claims to lands controlled by the Ottoman Empire. Hussein was profoundly upset when he learned of the Sykes-Picot Agreement in December 1917, published by the new Bolshevik government of Russia. He refused to sign the peace agreements at the end of the war in protest against the mandate system created by the 1919 Paris Peace Conference.

Hussein's son Faisal received Syria but was deposed and became king of Iraq under British protection. Son Abdullah became king of the newly created Transjordan. Hussein declared himself caliph of Islam in March 1924, but he was forced to abdicate as king of the Hejaz to his son Ali when Ibn Saud conquered most of the Hejaz. Hussein went into exile in Cyprus and died in Amman, Transjordan, on June 4, 1931.

SPENCER C. TUCKER

See also
Abdullah I; Arab Revolt of World War I; Faisal I, King of Iraq; Hejaz Railroad, Attacks on; Ibn Saud, King; McMahon-Hussein Correspondence; Ottoman Empire; Ottoman Empire, Post–World War I Revolution in; Sykes-Picot Agreement

References
Adelson, Roger. *London and the Invention of the Middle East: Money, Power, and War, 1902–1922.* New Haven, CT: Yale University Press, 1995.
Fromkin, David. *A Peace to End All Peace: The Fall of the Ottoman Empire and the Creation of the Modern Middle East.* New York: Avon, 1989.
Hourani, Albert. *A History of the Arab Peoples.* Cambridge, MA: Harvard University Press, 1991.
Kedourie, Elie. *In the Anglo-Arab Labyrinth: The McMahon-Husayn Correspondence and Its Interpretations.* Cambridge: Cambridge University Press, 1976.

Nevakivi, Jukka. *Britain, France and the Arab Middle East, 1914–1920.* London: Athlone, 1969.
Tauber, Eliezer. *The Arab Movements in World War I.* London: Frank Cass, 1995.

Hussein ibn Talal, King of Jordan (1935–1999)

King of Jordan (1953–1999). Born in Amman on November 14, 1935, into the Hashemite family that claims direct descent from Prophet Muhammad's clan, Hussein ibn Talal was the son of Prince Talal ibn Abdullah. Hussein was educated in Jordan and then at Victoria College in Alexandria, Egypt, before transferring to the prestigious Harrow School in Britain. He was with his grandfather, King Abdullah, when the king was assassinated in 1951.

Hussein's father was crowned king but was forced to abdicate the throne on August 11, 1952, because of mental illness. Hussein was proclaimed king as Hussein I and returned from Britain to take up his the throne at age 17. He formally ascended the throne on May 2, 1953.

Hussein's policies tended to be contradictory but also realistic, a useful combination that got him through the early years of his reign. The nation's stability was threatened by a large influx of Palestinian refugees on the West Bank, which had been recently annexed by Jordan in a move that was not popular with the Israelis, the Palestinians, or other Arab states. In addition, Jordan still enjoyed considerable financial and military support from Britain, which also displeased Arab leaders who were working to build Arab nationalism and alliances. Hussein continued the close ties with Britain until 1956. At that time, he was pressured to dismiss General John Bagot Glubb, the British head of the Arab Legion that had been formed in 1939 to fight in World War II.

The dismissal of Glubb was a popular move among Jordanians, but Hussein delayed another year before terminating the Anglo-Jordanian Treaty and signing the Arab Solidarity Agreement that pledged Egypt, Syria, and Saudi Arabia to provide Jordan with an annual subsidy of $36 million. When Hussein accepted U.S. aid in 1958, however, Egyptian and Syrian leaders began to campaign against him.

By the mid-1960s, Hussein was making attempts to alleviate the increasing isolation that separated Jordan from neighboring Arab states. After some hesitation, he linked his country with Egypt and Jordan in war against Israel, permitting Jordanian long-range artillery fire against Jewish areas of Jerusalem and the suburbs of Tel Aviv in the 1967 Six-Day

War. The Israelis had hoped that Jordan would remain neutral, but Hussein's steps brought retaliatory Israeli air strikes. Hussein later said that he made the decision because he feared that Israel was about to invade. The war was a disaster for Jordan, which lost the entire West Bank and its air force and suffered some 15,000 casualties. After the war Hussein helped draft United Nations (UN) Resolution 242, which urged Israel to give up its occupied territories in exchange for peace.

In the early 1970s, Hussein was forced to challenge the presence of the Palestine Liberation Organization (PLO) in his country because the PLO had turned the region into a war zone and challenged Hussein's authority over his own territory. After an assassination attempt on Hussein and the hijacking of four British airliners by the Popular Front for the Liberation of Palestine and their destruction in Jordan, the king decided that Palestinian militants were threatening the very survival of Jordan and that he must take action. In 1970 in what became known as Black September, Hussein began a controversial military campaign against the PLO, forcing it from Jordanian territory. Although he achieved his goal and the PLO moved its headquarters to Lebanon, the unrest lasted until July 1971, and his action undermined his position as the principal spokesperson for the Palestinian people.

Hussein regained favor in the Arab world when he rejected the 1979 Israel-Egypt Peace Treaty. He received considerable international criticism for his neutrality regarding Iraqi leader Saddam Hussein's invasion of Kuwait and for not joining the coalition against Iraq in the 1991 Persian Gulf War. Jordan had to remain faithful to its own policy toward Iraq, which had resulted from their initial emergence as Hashemite kingdoms and was reflected in their close economic ties. King Hussein nonetheless continued to play a significant role in the ongoing Middle East peace talks. In July 1994 he signed a peace agreement with Israeli prime minister Yitzhak Rabin.

On the domestic front, Hussein was a popular but autocratic leader who guided his nation to relative prosperity. He saw to it that more Jordanians had access to running water, proper sanitation, and electricity. He also actively promoted education and dramatically increased the literacy rate. In the late 1960s he oversaw construction of a modern highway system in the kingdom.

In 1992 Hussein began to take some steps toward the liberalization of the political system and the development of a multiparty system. That same year he was diagnosed with pancreatic cancer. He underwent treatment several times in the United States, each time designating his brother Hasan as regent during his absence. Less than two weeks before his death in 1999, Hussein surprised the world by naming his eldest son Abdullah as crown prince and designated heir, publicly denouncing Hasan's performance as regent and ensuring his own immediate family's control of the throne. Abdullah became King Abdullah II upon Hussein's death in Amman on February 7, 1999. Beloved by Jordanians for his attention to their welfare, Hussein had strengthened Jordan's position in the Arab world and contributed to the foundations of peace in the region.

Jessica Britt

See also
Camp David Accords; Jordan; Palestine Liberation Organization; Rabin, Yitzhak

References
Dallas, Roland. *King Hussein: A Life on the Edge.* New York: Fromm International, 1999.
Dann, Uriel. *King Hussein and the Challenge of Arab Radicalism: Jordan, 1955–1967.* Oxford: Oxford University Press, 1997.
Hussein, King of Jordan. *Uneasy Lies the Head: The Autobiography of His Majesty King Hussein I of the Hashemite Kingdom of Jordan.* New York: B. Geis, 1962.
Matusky, Gregory, and John P. Hayes. *King Hussein.* New York: Chelsea House, 1987.
Satloff, Robert B. *From Abdullah to Hussein: Jordan in Transition.* New York: Oxford University Press, 1993.

Hyksos

People of mixed origin from Western Asia who ended the Thirteenth Dynasty and came to control much of northern Egypt in the Second Intermediate Period (ca. 1640–1550 BCE), reigning as kings of Egypt in the Fourteenth to Sixteenth Dynasties. The name Hyksos is derived from the Egyptian term *heka-heswt,* meaning "rulers of foreign lands." Apparently the first-century CE Jewish historian Josephus mistranslated this as "shepherd kings." The Hyksos were also called Aamu (Asiatics) because they were primarily of Near Eastern origin.

Evidently a dispute between rival claimants for the throne allowed the invading Hyksos to take control circa 1680. They destroyed much of Egypt at the time, including its art, and they squandered its accumulated wealth.

We know much more about the Hyksos now thanks to the systematic excavation of their capital, Avaris (Tell el-Dab'a), by the Austrian Archaeological Institute. It used to be thought that they had invaded from Syria-Palestine and conquered the Delta, but the archaeological record suggests that the reverse is true. With the breakdown of international trade and the fragmentation of political power at the end of the Egyptian Middle Kingdom (ca. 2050–1800 BCE), traders from Cyprus and the Levant began to move into the delta and settle there. Eventually a wealthy state emerged and expanded up into Syria-Palestine.

Tell el-Dab'a and its surroundings became the capital of this kingdom. The town itself, its houses, and particularly its burials were unlike those of the Egyptians and followed Levantine traditions instead. On the southwestern edge of the town a palatial compound was built along the eastern edge of the Pelusiac branch of the Nile. Archaeologists have discovered the remains of a massive fortification wall running along the banks of the Nile branch. Evidence of the palace gardens was indicated by tree pits and a series of flowerpots sunk into the ground at regular intervals. The palace itself was a monumental building on a low-level platform. Although it was entirely razed by the Egyptians after their reconquest, many fragments of the mural decoration of the building have been recovered. They have Minoan scenes in a Minoan fresco technique. A large water-supply system made of limestone blocks has also been found. More recently, a massive stone defensive wall made of stone blocks measuring more than 1,500 feet long has been discovered at the site.

The Hyksos spread their influence throughout Lower Egypt at sites such as Farasha, Bubastis, and Tell el-Yahudiya. Some of these cities were fortified with a large sloping mound, or glacis, built around them. Although the Hyksos dominated the country as far south as Middle Egypt, there is scant archaeological evidence of their presence. The Hyksos apparently adopted Egyptian styles of art and writing and even worshipped some Egyptian gods, notably Seth, who became assimilated with some of their own deities.

Hyksos conquest of northern Egypt was facilitated by the weakening of the central government at the end of the Middle Kingdom and their employment of superior weapons technology, including the horse-drawn chariot and the composite bow, both of which they introduced into Egypt. Although the rulers of Avaris claimed to be kings of Upper and Lower Egypt, Hermopolis seems to have marked their southern boundary. A message to the Nubian king at Kerma suggesting they make an alliance and split Egypt between them was the final straw that spurred the Egyptian rulers of the Theban area into action.

The Hyksos transformed Egypt not only by introducing many technological advances but also by doing away with the country's isolationist tradition and spurring the Egyptians to create a great empire to safeguard the country's borders.

Seqenenre Tao (r. 1560–1552 BCE) built a campaign palace at Deir el-Ballas just north of Thebes. Seqenenre was killed in battle with the Hyksos, but his sons led the war that defeated Khamudi, their last king, and drove the Hyksos into Syria-Palestine. By about 1580 BCE Egypt was again united under a line of native rulers.

PETER LACOVARA AND SPENCER C. TUCKER

See also
Egypt, Ancient

References
Bietak, Manfred. *Avaris: The Capital of the Hyksos, Recent Excavations at Tell el-Dab'a*. London: British Museum Press, 1996.

Quirke, Stephen. "The Hyksos in Egypt 1600 BCE: New Rulers without an Administration." In *Regime Change in the Ancient Near East and Egypt: From Sargon of Agade to Saddam Hussein*, ed. Harriet Crawford, 123–139. Oxford: Oxford University Press, 2007.

Roberts, R. Gareth. "Hyksos Self-Presentation and 'Culture.'" In *Decorum and Experience: Essays in Ancient Culture for John Baine*, ed. Elizabeth Frood and Angela McDonald, 285–290. Oxford, UK: Griffith Institute, 2013.

Ibelin, Battle of (May 29, 1123)

The Battle of Ibelin, also known as the Battle of Yibneh, was fought between an invading Egyptian army and Franks of the Kingdom of Jerusalem on the plain near Ibelin (modern-day Yavne, Israel). In May 1123 Vizier al-Mamun, Fatimid ruler of Egypt, sent a joint naval and land expedition to the Egyptian forward base at the coastal city of Ascalon (modern-day Tel Ashqelon, Israel) in southern Palestine. Al-Mamun hoped to capitalize on the absence of King Baldwin II of Jerusalem, who had been captured by the Turks of northern Syria. The Egyptian land force consisted of Sudanese archers on foot supported by dense formations of Arab and Berber light cavalry.

When the Fatimid naval forces laid siege to Jaffa, regent of Jerusalem Eustace I Granarius sent an appeal for assistance to a Venetian fleet en route to the Holy Land and assembled the kingdom's land forces at Caco, southeast of Caesarea (modern-day Har Qesari, Israel). The Frankish force consisted of knights and men-at-arms on horseback and spearmen and bowmen on foot. The Frankish land force marched south, bypassing Jaffa, and met the Egyptian army near Ibelin on May 29, 1123.

Unfortunately for the Fatimids, their relatively immobile array provided the Frankish heavy cavalry with an ideal target. The Franks attacked, but the battle lasted only a short time because the Egyptians were unable to withstand the shock of the crusader cavalry charges. The Egyptian cavalry then fled, resulting in both a major rout and Frankish massacre of the Egyptian infantry. The Venetian ships then subsequently dispersed the Egyptian naval force. This turned out to be the last great Fatimid invasion of the Latin Kingdom of Jerusalem.

ALAN V. MURRAY AND SPENCER C. TUCKER

See also
Baldwin II of Jerusalem; Crusades in the Holy Land, Christian; Fatimid Dynasty; Jerusalem, Latin Kingdom of

References
Röhricht, Reinhold. *Geschichte des Königreichs Jerusalem (1100–1291)*. Innsbruck: Wagner, 1898.
Smail, R. C. *Crusading Warfare, 1097–1193*. New York: Barnes & Noble Books, 1995.

Ibn Saud, King (1875–1953)

Founder and first king of the present-day Kingdom of Saudi Arabia (1932–1953). Abd al-Aziz ibn Abd al-Rahman al-Saud, more commonly known as Ibn Saud, was born in Riyadh, capital of the central Saudi Arabian emirate of Nejd, probably on January 15, 1875, although birth dates given vary widely from 1875 to 1880. He was the son of Abd al-Rahman ibn Faisal al-Saud (1850–1928) and Sara bint Ahmad al-Sudairi, the daughter of a powerful clan leader from central Arabia. Ibn Saud received a traditional religious Islamic education and was trained in martial arts and traditional skills such as riding, tracking, shooting, and fencing.

The al-Saud family was ousted from power in 1891 by the al-Rashid clan of the northern emirate of Hail. Between 1891 and 1902 the deposed Emir Abd al-Rahman and his family lived in exile in Kuwait. Leading a daring expedition, young Ibn Saud succeeded in recapturing Riyadh in January 1902. When his father Abd al-Rahman declined to reassume the position of emir, Ibn Saud became the dynasty's new ruler.

The first decade of Ibn Saud's reign required that he reestablish authority over Nejd, which had come under the control of the rival al-Rashid clan during the al-Saud family's years in exile. Ibn Saud accomplished this through a mixed policy of armed force, negotiations, and forging marriage alliances with important nomadic Bedouin tribes and settled clans. By 1913 he was in a position to shift his attention to the Persian Gulf coast, which was then controlled by the Ottoman Empire. He succeeded in ousting the Ottomans from Al-Hasa Province and established regular contacts with the British. For their part, the British maintained permanent diplomatic representations in Kuwait and other Persian Gulf emirates.

In the run-up to the fighting and during World War I, Ibn Saud sought to establish himself as the leading ally of the British on the Arabian Peninsula. The British wanted this also in order to secure the neutrality of the leader of the Nejd during their own military operations in Mesopotamia. In the subsequent friendship treaty of December 26, 1915, the British recognized Ibn Saud as ruler of the Nejd and its dependencies, agreed to protect him against his external enemies, and granted him an annual subsidy. In return, Ibn Saud agreed to maintain friendly relations with Britain, not alienate any part of his kingdom to a foreign power, and refrain from attacking British-supported gulf coast sheikhdoms.

Although Ibn Saud did not take arms against the Turks, he also did not respond to the sultan's call for a jihad (holy war). As a consequence, the Turks were not able to receive supplies by sea from the Persian Gulf coast. He was also free to fight his archenemies, the pro-Ottoman al-Rashid clan.

By the end of World War I, Ibn Saud's policies had yielded considerable dividends. He consolidated his control over the tribes and settlements in central Arabia and ousted the Ottomans from their positions along the Persian Gulf. He also outmaneuvered the al-Rashid clan, reducing their authority to their northern capital of Hail. When this last stronghold of the al-Rashid clan fell in 1921, Ibn Saud turned against the newly established Hashemite Kingdom of Hejaz. After taking the holy cities of Mecca and Medina, he

Abd al-Aziz Ibn Saud (1875–1953), founder and first king during 1932–1953 of the present-day kingdom of Saudi Arabia. (Library of Congress)

was proclaimed king of the Hejaz in 1926. By the 1930s the new king had also extended his authority over the Asir and Najran regions adjacent to Yemen.

During 1928–1930 the king's authority was challenged by revolting Bedouin irregulars known as the Ikhwans. They had been instrumental to Saudi conquests but were effectively disbanded to secure peaceful relations with neighboring countries. Following the capture or execution of the Bedouin ringleaders, Ibn Saud became the unchallenged king of the unified Kingdom of Saudi Arabia in 1932.

Oil was discovered in the country's Eastern Province in 1938, but the full exploitation of this new resource was interrupted by World War II. In the course of the war, Ibn Saud joined the Allied cause for pragmatic rather than principled reasons, because Britain and since the start of oil exploration the United States as well had been bankrolling him for decades. As a result of his rapidly declining health and inexperience with the growing complexities of international relations and state finances, Ibn Saud became an increasingly passive ruler while also not passing the necessary authority to others.

On February 14, 1945, Ibn Saud met with President Franklin D. Roosevelt on board the heavy cruiser USS *Quincy*, and this marked the symbolic beginning of the postwar strategic partnership between the United States and Saudi Arabia. With respect to its alleged immediate purpose of obtaining Ibn Saud's agreement to a huge increase in the settlement of Jewish refugees in Palestine, the meeting was a failure.

Ibn Saud consistently held to the position that the Palestinians should not be made to pay the price for the sufferings inflicted on the Jews by others. Although he withdrew more and more from daily politics in the last decade of his reign, his position did not waver from the unreserved support given to Arab interests. With the aging king withdrawing further into the background, it was Prince Faisal (1906–1975) who became the architect of Saudi foreign policy. While the Saudis were upset by the American endorsement of the State of Israel, which in their view was a violation of Roosevelt's pledge not to act contrary to Arab interests, they took care to preserve their relationship with the United States. With oil production mainly conducted by American companies, the United States took over Britain's position as the paymaster of Saudi Arabia's treasury.

Ibn Saud died in Taif on November 9, 1953, leaving 48 sons and an unknown number of daughters. His oldest surviving son, Saud, succeeded him.

CAROOL KERSTEN

See also
Ottoman Empire; Saudi Arabia; Saudi-Hashemite War; Saudi-Kuwaiti War; Saudi-Ottoman War; Saudi-Rashidi Wars; Saudi-Yemeni War

References
Al-Sa'ud, Abdul Aziz al-Saud. *The Holy Quran and the Sword: Selected Addresses, Speeches, Memoranda and Interviews*. 4th ed. Edited by Mohydin al-Qabesi. Riyadh: Saudi Desert House for Publications and Distribution, 2002.
Armstrong, H. C. *Lord of Arabia*. London: Arthur Barker, 1934.
De Gaury, Gerald. *Arabia Felix*. London: George Harrap, 1947.
Lacey, Robert. *The Kingdom*. London: Hutchinson, 1981.
Philby, H. St. J. B. *Arabian Jubilee*. London: Robert Hale, 1952.
Van der Meulen, Daniel. *The Wells of Ibn Saud*. New York: Praeger, 1957.
Vassiliev, Alexei. *The History of Saudi Arabia*. London: Saqi, 1998.

Ibrahim Pasha (1789–1848)

Egyptian military commander and administrator. Ibrahim ibn Mehmed Ali was born in 1789 in Kavalla, Rumelia (in present-day Greece), part of the Ottoman Empire. Ibrahim was the son of Mehmed Ali, an Albanian officer in the Ottoman Army. In 1798, French forces led by General Napoleon Bonaparte invaded the Ottoman province of Egypt. After the defeat of the French in Egypt by the British and Ottomans, Mehmed Ali maneuvered to become khedive of Egypt, a position similar to viceroy of the Ottoman sultan.

In 1805 Mehmed Ali brought Ibrahim and his brother Tusun to Egypt, and during the next several years Ibrahim served in his father's government in a variety of positions, including governor of Upper Egypt. During the following years Mehmed Ali consolidated his position as unchallenged ruler of Egypt, power he relinquished to Ibrahim in 1848.

Although Mehmed Ali theoretically ruled Egypt as a representative of the sultan, he devoted his energies to expanding his influence beyond Egypt's borders and winning recognition of Egyptian independence. Ibrahim was instrumental in helping his father to achieve these goals, leading the army in several campaigns. In 1816, the sultan asked Mehmed Ali to send Egyptian troops to quell a rebellion against his authority organized by the Wahhabis, who had seized control of the Hejaz region in western Arabia. It was on this expedition that Ibrahim gained his first military experience. After a victorious campaign, he returned to Egypt.

In 1823, Ibrahim commanded forces seeking to expand Egyptian control up the Nile into Sudan. After his return from Sudan, Ibrahim helped modernize the Egyptian. Then in 1824 Sultan Mahmud II again asked for Egyptian assistance, this time to subdue a revolt against Ottoman rule in Greece. Ibrahim led Egyptian forces in Greece and took the Peloponnesus and Athens. In 1827, however, the British, French, and Russian fleets cooperated to destroy the Ottoman and Egyptian navies in the Battle of Navarino Bay. Ibrahim was then forced to withdraw Egyptian forces and return to Egypt.

By the 1830s, Mehmed Ali was challenging Ottoman power rather than pretending to act as an Ottoman agent. In 1831, a dispute between Mehmed Ali and the Ottoman government led to an Egyptian invasion of Syria. Ibrahim commanded the Egyptian armies sent through Palestine to conquer the cities of Acre, Aleppo, Homs, and Damascus and then defeated an Ottoman army at Alexandretta. In the wake of this victory, Ibrahim conquered much of Anatolia, then forced the Bailan Pass and crossed the Taurus Mountains in preparation for an attack on the Ottoman capital of Istanbul (Constantinople).

With the western Great Powers committed to the stability of the Ottoman Empire and opposed to any operation against the Ottoman capital, Ibrahim was forced to sign the Convention of Kutahya on May 4, 1833. In exchange for sparing Istanbul, the agreement recognized Egyptian claims to Syria and the southern Anatolian city of Adana. Ibrahim then became governor of the new Egyptian provinces. He proved to be a capable administrator and sought to expand irrigation and encouraged modern industries. However, his heavy-handed administrative methods antagonized the Syrians and encouraged anti-Egyptian sentiment.

Sultan Mahmud II was unwilling to accept the loss of his territory. Ibrahim was able to turn back an Ottoman invasion of Syria in 1838. The following year, however, the British joined forces with the Ottomans. Although Ibrahim won a great victory against the Ottomans at Nizip on June 24, 1839, the British ultimately forced Mehmed Ali to cede Syria back to the Ottomans. As compensation, Mehmed Ali's position as khedive was made hereditary, ensuring that his family would continue to rule Egypt after his death. This agreement was recognized in the Treaty of London in 1840.

In his later life Mehmed Ali became mentally unstable, and in 1848 he relinquished control of the state to Ibrahim. Ibrahim's position as khedive was confirmed by the Ottoman sultan, with Ibrahim traveling to Istanbul to receive his investiture. He became ill in Istanbul, however, and died shortly after his return to Cairo on November 10, 1848.

JAMES M. BURNS

See also
Egyptian-Ottoman Wars; Konya, Battle of; Mehmed Ali

References
Durand-Viel, Georges. *Les campagnes navales de Mohammed Aly et d'Ibrahim*. Paris: Imp. Nationale, 1935.

Fahmy, Khaled. *All the Pasha's Men: Mehmed Ali, His Army and the Making of Modern Egypt*. Cambridge: Cambridge University Press, 1997.

Ikhwan

The religious and political Islamic revival movement, emphasizing Wahhabi tenets, that occurred among the badu (Bedouins) of Arabia. By the early 20th century, Ibn Saud achieved considerable success in efforts to secure supreme authority in the Nejd (central Arabia), but he lacked stable and broadly based support. Toward this end he welcomed the preaching of Abdallah ibn Muhammad ibn Abd al-Latif (the *qadi* of Riyadh) and Shaikh Isa (the *qadi* of al-Hasa), who emphasized strict observance of fundamental tenets of Islam, loyalty to the brethren, obedience to leaders, and rejection of contacts with the West. The early followers of this movement established their first settlement (*hijra*) in the area of al-Artawiya in early 1913.

By 1920 there were more than 50 Ikhwan *hijras* in Arabia, and their numbers quickly grew, exceeding 120 by 1929. Ibn Saud supported and encouraged such sedentarization in order to bring the badu more closely under his control. The Ikhwans were supposed to give up the habits and duties of the tribal way of life. Ibn Saud gave the Ikhwans money, seed, equipment, and materials to establish their settlements and cultivate lands.

The Ikhwans practiced an austere form of egalitarianism, shying away from wealth and corruption. They banned all kinds of music (except military drums), coffee, tobacco, alcohol, lavish clothing, and gambling. They only answered greetings from fellow Ikhwans, while upon meeting a European or Arabs from other regions they buried their faces in their hands so as to avoid being "tarnished." They believed that anyone who did not join them was polytheist and subject to death, which explains their fanaticism in "purifying" Islam, which produced many atrocities.

Each member of the Ikhwan *hijra* was subject to conscription. Conscripts were divided into three categories. The first included men who were permanently ready for action. The second comprised reservists, while conscripts of the third category usually stayed behind in the settlements and were called to action only in times of emergency. When called on a campaign, each Ikhwan had to provide his own camel, arms, and food.

The Ikhwan movement thus provided Ibn Saud with an extremely mobile, tough, and dedicated striking force. The military skills of the Ikhwans and the fear that their fanatical zeal inspired in their opponents were important elements in Ibn Saud's campaigns against Asir in 1920, Hail in 1921, al-Jawf in 1922, and Hejaz in 1924–1925. Ibn Saud himself never fully shared the Ikhwan beliefs and was suspicious of their egalitarian trends, but he also used the Ikhwans for his own ends. Thus, although Ikhwans shied away from contacts with the West, Ibn Saud cultivated relations with Britain and even received regular British subsidies, which he claimed to be part of tribute that Muslim rulers collected from the Christians.

Yet, their religious fervor also made the Ikhwans difficult to control, and the Saudi leadership was compelled to grant certain freedom of action to Ikhwan leaders Faisal al-Dawish and Ibn Bijad. An unauthorized Ikhwan raid into Kuwait and Iraq in 1927–1928 and resultant British anger compelled Ibn Saud to move against his subordinates. Mobilizing Nejdi fighters, he defeated the Ikhwan army in the Battle of Sibilah (March 31, 1929) and destroyed the movement by early 1930.

ALEXANDER MIKABERIDZE

See also
Ibn Saud, King; Saudi-Hashemite War; Saudi-Kuwaiti War; Saudi-Rashidi Wars

References
Glubb, John. *War in the Desert: An RAF Frontier Campaign.* London: Hodder & Stoughton, 1960.
Vassiliev, Alexei. *The History of Saudi Arabia.* London: Saqi Books, 1998.

Ilghazi ibn Artuq, Najm al-Din (ca. 1062–1122)

Ilghazi ibn Artuq was founder of the Mardin-Mayyafarikin branch of the Turkoman Artuqid dynasty. He contributed significantly to the check of the Frankish advance to the north and east of Outremer before the time of Zangi and Saladin, although personal vice (drunkenness) and self-interested aspirations (consolidation of his Mardin possessions) prevented him from effecting a decisive victory against the principality of Antioch.

Ilghazi was born around 1062, the son of Artuq, Turkoman leader and founder of the Artuqid dynasty. Ilghazi was initially in the service of the Seljuks, but in 1108–1109 he seized the town of Mardin. He fell out with the Seljuks because of his reluctance to join the Muslim coalition against the Franks in 1111–1115 and also because of his part in a Turkoman alliance against the Seljuk emir of Mosul. It was only after 1118 that he reestablished good relations with Seljuk sultan Muhammad I's successor, Mamud I. In 1117–1118 Ilghazi seized power in Aleppo in response to its inhabitants' plea to save the city from the power of Roger of Salerno, regent of Antioch, thus ending the short-lived rule of the Seljuk dynasty there.

Around 1118 Ilghazi became master of Diyar Bakr and subsequently took possession of Martyropolis (Mayyafarikin), which had experienced successive Seljuk and Danishmendid rule. In the summer of 1119 he mounted an invasion of the principality of Antioch, inflicting a major defeat on the forces of Prince Roger in the Battle of Ager Sanguinis (Field of Blood) yet wasted this great victory, which he won without the support of the Seljuk sultan by failing to capture the city of Antioch (modern-day Antakya, Turkey). This victory over Roger was nonetheless the crowning achievement of Ilghazi's career, earning him renown in the Muslim world, while the caliph bestowed on him the honorific title Najm al-Din (Star of Religion).

In 1120 and 1122 Ilghazi launched further attacks against Frankish northern Syria, while in 1121 he participated in an abortive Seljuk campaign in Georgia. He died at Mayyafarikin in late 1122, and his inheritance was divided among his sons and nephews.

ALEXIOS G. C. SAVVIDES

See also
Ager Sanguinis, Battle of; Artuqid Dynasty; Danishmendid Dynasty; Saladin; Seljuk Dynasty; Zangi, Imad ad-Din

References
Hillenbrand, Carole. "The Career of Najm al-Din Il-Ghazi." *Der Islam* 58 (1981): 250–292.
Hillenbrand, Carole. "The Establishment of Artūqid power in Diyar Bakr in the Twelfth Century." *Studia Islamica* 54 (1981): 129–153.
Hillenbrand, Carole. *A Muslim Principality in Crusader Times.* Leiden: Nederlands Historisch-Archaeologisch Instituut te Istanbul, 1990.

Ilkhan Dynasty (ca. 1261–1353)

Dynasty of Mongol rulers in Persia (ca. 1261–1353) founded by Chinggis Khan's grandson Hulegu and viewed as possible allies of the Christian West in the war against the Mamluk Sultanate of Egypt. The term "ilkhan" appears to mean "subordinate khan." Some uncertainty surrounds the creation of the Ilkhanate around the year 1261 as the Mongol Empire dissolved in civil war. Mamluk sources allege that Hulegu, hitherto merely lieutenant on behalf of his brother, the Great Khan Mongke, usurped control over Persia and established himself as a khan on a level with the other regional Mongol rulers. But according to Ilkhanid minister and historian Rashid al-Din, Mongke had privately intended Hulegu and his descendants to rule the country in perpetuity.

The Ilkhans were repeatedly called upon to repel invasions from north of the Caucasus by their relatives, the khans of the Golden Horde, who claimed the pasturelands of Azerbaijan and northwestern Persia. Hulegu and his successors, prevented from devoting their full attention to the war against the Mamluks, negotiated with the pope and Western monarchs for concerted action against Egypt.

Such exchanges became more frequent in the reign of Hulegu's son and successor Abaka, who was in touch with the crusade of Edward of England (1270–1272) and whose envoys attended the Second Council of Lyons (1274). Renewed after a brief hiatus in the reign of the Muslim

Amad Tegüder, relations peaked under Arghun (r. 1284–1291). Ilkhan ambassadors to the West were often Christians, either Nestorians such as Rabban Sawma (1287) or expatriate Italians such as Buscarello di' Ghisolfi (1289), and they emphasized their master's readiness to embrace the Christian faith. Yet no Ilkhan became a Christian, and no synchronized campaign ever occurred. Some Hospitallers from Margat joined an invading army sent by Abaka into northern Syria in 1281, and King Henry II of Cyprus and the Templars endeavored to collaborate with the Ilkhan Ghazan when his forces drove the Mamluks temporarily from Syria and Palestine in 1299–1300, an episode greeted with widespread and unrealistic enthusiasm in Western Europe. Ghazan's successor Öljeitü (r. 1304–1316), the last Ilkhan to launch an invasion of Syria or to make overtures to the West, was followed by Abu Sa'id (r. 1316–1335), who in 1323 made peace with the Mamluks.

Ilkhanid efforts to secure Western cooperation failed for various reasons, including logistical difficulties and residual Latin distrust of Mongol rulers who were as yet unbaptized. That Ghazan and Öljeitü were Muslims was apparently unknown in the West, perhaps in part because it did not affect their foreign policy.

Peter Jackson

See also
Golden Horde–Ilkhanid Wars; Homs, First Battle of; Homs, Second Battle of; Homs, Third Battle of; Hulegu; Mamluk-Ilkhanid Wars; Mongol Invasion of the Middle East

References
Boyle, John Andrew. "Dynastic and Political History of the Ilkhans." In *The Cambridge History of Iran*, Vol. 5, *The Saljuq and Mongol Periods*, ed. J. A. Boyle, 340–417. Cambridge: Cambridge University Press, 1968.
Jackson, Peter. *The Mongols and the West, 1221–1410*. London: Routledge, 2005.
Morgan, David. *The Mongols*. Oxford, UK: Blackwell, 1986.

IMMINENT THUNDER, Operation (November 15–21, 1990)

Joint exercise during November 15–21, 1990, by U.S. amphibious units and the Saudi military on the eve of the 1991 Persian Gulf War. Operation IMMINENT THUNDER was undertaken as part of a broader deception campaign.

On August 2, 1990, Iraqi forces invaded and quickly overran Kuwait. An international coalition led by the United States then formed to expel Iraqi forces from Kuwait. Coalition commander U.S. General H. Norman Schwarzkopf, concerned about the strength of Iraqi forces now dug in along the Kuwaiti–Saudi Arabian border in the so-called Saddam Line, ordered deceptive measures to cause the dispersal of Iraqi forces. Among these was the effort to convince Iraqi leaders that the coalition planned to carry out a large amphibious assault against Kuwait. Operation IMMINENT THUNDER was central to this plan.

Coalition leaders hoped that the deception would cause the Iraqis to deploy additional forces to the Kuwaiti coast, thereby weakening their lines along the Saudi border. To accomplish this end, U.S. Marine Corps and naval units carried out a series of exercises, ostensibly in preparation for an assault on Kuwait. The first of these consisted of two small amphibious training missions on the Omani Coast. Intelligence reports confirmed that the Iraqis were paying close attention to the exercises and enhancing their coastal defenses.

The culmination of the amphibious deception plan was Operation IMMINENT THUNDER, the largest landing exercise of the Persian Gulf crisis. A U.S. naval amphibious task force centered on the aircraft carrier *Midway* assembled in the Gulf of Oman under the command of U.S. Rear Admiral Daniel P. March, coalition naval forces commander. The task force included 10,000 sailors as well as some 8,000 marines from the 4th Marine Expeditionary Brigade and the 13th Marine Expeditionary Unit. The marines were supported by air units, including helicopter strike groups. The exercise was publicly announced as the final preparation before a campaign to liberate Kuwait.

IMMINENT THUNDER commenced on November 15, 1990, and continued through November 21. It involved 16 ships, 1,100 aircraft, and approximately 1,000 marines. A small number of Saudi and other Arab air and ground forces also participated. U.S. Navy, Marine Corps, and Air Force personnel and assets all took part. The task force conducted landings and other exercises along the northeast coast of Saudi Arabia, in an area about 80 miles south of Kuwait. The exercise had originally been planned for Ras Al Mishab, only 20 miles from the Kuwaiti border. As this was well within Iraqi missile range, IMMINENT THUNDER was transferred southward. Air units from the United States and Saudi Arabia conducted practice missions, while Saudi and other Arab amphibious forces participated in landings with the U.S. marines. On the first day, coalition aircraft flew 115 sorties under the direction of air controllers on the battleship *Missouri* who simulated coordination of air and naval strikes on land targets.

While the maneuvers were mainly to deceive the Iraqis, coalition planners did gain valuable information and

Operation IMMINENT THUNDER (November 15–21, 1990) was an amphibious landing exercise and successful deception prior to the 1991 Persian Gulf War. It served to convince Saddam Hussein that the Allied coalition would be carrying out an amphibious operation as part of the effort to drive Iraqi forces from Kuwait. (U.S. Department of Defense)

experience from IMMINENT THUNDER. The exercise tested systems developed to coordinate air, land, and sea elements. Especially important to U.S. planners was practicing an operation that would allow amphibious forces to link with conventional ground forces. The inclusion of Saudi forces also provided a test of coalition joint warfare capabilities and interoperability in communications, logistics, and transport. The operation also provided a means for U.S. personnel to become acclimated to the region and to test equipment for potential performance problems in a desert environment. The U.S. Navy also tested its Aegis Combat System, which allowed air controllers to coordinate multiple aircraft during the practice landings and reinforced the utility of the system for amphibious assaults. Tests of communications equipment and procedures were also successful, as were helicopter refueling exercises. IMMINENT THUNDER also included tests of remote-controlled surveillance aircraft.

Problems were discovered in the coalition's weather satellite and forecasting systems, and steps were taken to address this prior to the actual invasion of Kuwait. The navy had planned to use hovercraft during the exercises to highlight U.S. technological advantages; however, high seas and rough weather forced the abandonment of the effort after two attempts. This forced the navy to reconsider the conditions under which the vehicles could be utilized.

To maximize the deception, U.S. military planners launched a broad media campaign to highlight the exercises. Reporters and journalists from around the world were invited to observe the maneuvers, and the U.S. military provided transport for television crews to fly to the region and broadcast images of the practice landings. At the conclusion of IMMINENT THUNDER, U.S. president George H. W. Bush traveled to Saudi Arabia and attended a Thanksgiving service with the marines on November 23.

The deception worked well. The Iraqis deployed six divisions numbering some 80,000 troops along the Kuwaiti coast prior to the invasion.

After IMMINENT THUNDER was concluded, coalition military planners finalized their planning. While these plans called for the task force to serve in a diversionary capacity, plans were developed for an amphibious assault near Ash Shuaybah in Kuwait, depending on the rate of the ground advance. If coalition forces met heavy resistance, the landings would serve as a second front. Meanwhile, and concurrent with Operation IMMINENT THUNDER, the coalition air campaign, the U.S. naval amphibious task force participated in the continuing blockade of Iraq.

The amphibious task force subsequently conducted a smaller training mission, Operation SEA SOLDIER III in Oman, a rehearsal for a brigade-size landing, in order to continue the deception and to refine combined and joint communications and coordination capabilities and address problems encountered during IMMINENT THUNDER. SEA SOLDIER III included more than 3,500 marines and 1,000 vehicles.

Coalition forces commenced the air campaign on January 17, 1991, and the ground invasion followed on February 24. The speed of the latter eliminated any need for an amphibious second front, and the war was over by February 28.

TOM LANSFORD

See also
Persian Gulf War, Naval Operations; Saddam Line, Persian Gulf War; Schwarzkopf, H. Norman, Jr.

References
Brown, Ronald J. *U.S. Marines in the Persian Gulf, 1990–1991: With Marine Forces Afloat in Desert Shield and Desert Storm.* Washington, DC: History and Museums Division, U.S. Marine Corps, 1998.

Hoskins, Andrew. *Televising War: From Vietnam to Iraq.* London: Continuum, 2004.

MacArthur, John R. *Second Front: Censorship and Propaganda in the 1991 Gulf War.* Berkeley: University of California, 2004.

Marolda, Edward, and Robert Schneller. *Shield and Sword: The United States Navy and the Persian Gulf War.* Annapolis, MD: U.S. Naval Institute Press, 2001.

Pokrant, Marvin. *Desert Shield at Sea: What the Navy Really Did.* Westport, CT: Greenwood, 1999.

Improvised Explosive Devices

Improvised explosive devices (IEDs) have been employed in warfare almost since the introduction of gunpowder. They remain the weapon of choice for insurgent and resistance groups that lack the numerical strength and firepower to conduct conventional operations against an opponent. IEDs are the contemporary form of booby traps employed in World War II and the Vietnam War. Traditionally, IEDs are used primarily against enemy armor and thin-skinned vehicles.

A water cart filled with explosives was employed in a futile effort to assassinate Napoleon Bonaparte in Paris as he traveled to the opera on Christmas Eve 1800. The emperor escaped injury, but the blast killed the little girl the conspirators paid to hold the horse's bridle and killed or maimed a dozen other people. In more recent times, IEDs have been employed against civilian targets by Basque separatists and the Irish Republican Army. Molotov cocktails, or gasoline bombs, are one form of IED. The largest, most deadly IEDs in history were the U.S. jetliners hijacked by members of the Al Qaeda terrorist organization on September 11, 2001, and used to attack the World Trade Center in New York City and the Pentagon in Arlington, Virginia.

IEDs became one of the chief weapons employed by insurgents and terrorists against Israel as well as the chief weapon used by insurgents during the Iraq War (2003) and the ensuing Iraqi insurgency to attack U.S. forces and Iraqi police to carry out sectarian violence. The simplest type of IED is a hand grenade, rigged artillery shell, or bomb triggered by a trip wire or simple movement. It might be as simple as a grenade with its pin pulled and handle held down by the weight of a corpse. When the corpse is raised, the grenade explodes. Bombs and artillery shells are also used as IEDs. Such weapons can be exploded remotely by wireless detonators in the form of garage door openers and two-way radios or infrared motion sensors. More powerful explosives and even shaped charges can be used to attack armored vehicles. Casualty totals are one way to judge the effectiveness of a military operation, and growing casualties from IEDs in the 1980s and 1990s induced the Israeli Army to withdraw from southern Lebanon.

SPENCER C. TUCKER

See also
Iraq Insurgency; Iraq War; Lebanon-Israeli War

References
Crippen, James B. *Improvised Explosive Devices (IED).* New York: CRC Press, 2007.

DeForest, M. J. *Principles of Improvised Explosive Devices.* Boulder, CO: Paladin, 1984.

Tucker, Stephen. *Terrorist Explosive Sourcebook: Countering Terrorist Use of Improvised Explosive Devices.* Boulder, CO: Paladin, 2005.

Inab, Battle of (June 29, 1149)

A major battle fought during the Second Christian Crusade in the Holy Land (1147–1149). The Battle of Inab, also known as the Battle of Ard al-Hâtim and the Battle of Fons

Muratus, was fought at the fortress of Inab in the Seljuk Sultanate (modern-day Syria).

In 1146 crusader leader Raymond of Poitiers, prince of Antioch, had invaded the province of Aleppo belonging to the Seljuk Empire. Although Raymond registered several victories, his forces failed in their effort to capture Damascus in 1148. Nur al-Din intensified his attacks on the southern part of the principality of Antioch. Then in the summer of 1149, he assembled a force of some 6,000 cavalry from his own troops and those of Unur, ruler of Damascus, and moved to besiege Inab, one of the main strongholds of the principality of Antioch east of the Orontes. Raymond, confident of victory as he had twice before defeated Nur al-Din, marched to the relief of Inab with a small force of some 400 knights and 1,000 foot soldiers, including men under Kurd Ali ibn-Wafa, leader of the Hasshashin (Assassins) and an avowed enemy of Nur al-Din. The Muslims fell back, having initially overestimated their opponents' numbers. While Ali counseled a withdrawal, Raymond's chief lieutenants pressed for an advance. On June 28 Raymond's troops camped on low ground in the plain between Inab and the marshes east of the Orontes, and during the night Nur al-Din, now apprised of Frankish strength, surrounded their positions.

The next day, June 29, the Franks tried in vain to fight their way out of encirclement; almost all were captured or killed, including Prince Raymond, whose skull Nur al-Din had mounted as a trophy of victory. Antioch was now left without a ruler, as Raymond's son Bohemund III was still a minor. In the course of the summer Nur al-Din was able to capture all of the remaining Antioch strongholds east of the Orontes, including Artah, Harim, Imm, and Afamiyah, Syria. He then went on to besiege Antioch itself, which was now virtually defenseless, but was bought off with a large quantity of treasure. Harim was only recovered in 1157 and then permanently lost to the crusaders in 1164. Now a hero in the Islamic world, Nur al-Din was determined to destroy the crusader states through a holy war, or jihad.

ALAN V. MURRAY AND SPENCER C. TUCKER

See also
Crusades in the Holy Land, Christian; Jihad; Nur al-Din

References
Cahen, Claude. *Le Syrie du Nord à l'époque des croisades et la principalité franque de Antioche.* Paris: Geuthner, 1940.
Mallet, Alex. "The Battle of Inab." *Journal of Medieval History* 39, no. 1 (2013): 48–60.
Runciman, Steven. *A History of the Crusades.* 3 vols. Cambridge: Cambridge University Press, 1952–1954.
Smail, R. C. *Crusading Warfare, 1097–1193.* New York: Barnes & Noble, 1995.

INHERENT RESOLVE, Operation (August 8, 2014–)

INHERENT RESOLVE is the name for U.S. and coalition military operations against the Islamic State of Iraq and Syria (ISIS). These commenced against ISIS in Iraq on August 8, 2014, and against ISIS in Syria on September 22, 2014. Since August 21, 2016, the U.S. Army's XVIII Airborne Corps has been responsible for Combined Joint Task Force–Operation INHERENT RESOLVE (CJTF-OIR).

In early June 2014, ISIS launched a major offensive in Iraq. Having already made major inroads in Syria and Iraq, by June 22 ISIS had expanded its holdings to include virtually all of Anbar Province of western Iraq and much of northern Iraq; the group was also only some 60 miles from Baghdad and threatening an advance on the capital. Half a million Iraqis were displaced from their homes, and in two weeks of steady retreat before the far smaller ISIS forces, Iraqi soldiers simply abandoned their posts and weapons and fled. The Iraqi military was revealed as suffering from both appallingly poor leadership and rampant corruption. Prime Minister Nuri al-Maliki had largely excluded the minority Sunnis and Kurds from power and treated the army as a political prize, ignoring U.S. calls for inclusiveness. Indeed, the well-trained Kurdish security forces known as the Peshmerga were the only effective fighters against ISIS but lacked ammunition and heavy weapons, which al-Maliki's Shiite-dominated government was reluctant to provide.

U.S. president Barack Obama responded to the crisis by sending some 300 U.S. military personnel to beef up security at the U.S. embassy in Baghdad and commencing flights by a handful of Predator drones armed with Hellfire missiles over the city in addition to the manned and unmanned aircraft flying daily reconnaissance missions. These flights began on June 15. Meanwhile ISIS continued to acquire territory, and some 200,000 Iraqis, many of them Christians, fled into the Kurdish region.

On August 7, Obama authorized two military operations in Iraq. The first was to be "targeted air strikes" to protect American personnel and help Iraqi forces battling ISIS fighters then threatening Irbil, the largest city in Iraq's Kurdish region. The second was to deal with a humanitarian crisis that Obama characterized as a "potential act of genocide" by aiding religious minority groups facing possible slaughter by ISIS. ISIS had occupied the largest Iraqi Christian city, Qaraqosh, and ordered residents to convert to Islam or be slain. Thousands of families from the Yazidi minority of Kurdish descent, whose religion is considered a pre-Islamic

A U.S. Army CH-47 Chinook helicopter being refueled at Qayyarah West Airfield, Iraq, on May 29, 2017, part of Operation INHERENT RESOLVE, the coalition effort to defeat the Islamic State of Iraq and Syria (ISIS). (U.S. Army)

sect that draws from Christianity, Judaism, and Zoroastrianism, were under siege by ISIS in the Sinjar Mountains in intense summer heat without food or water. While offering air and logistical support, Obama pledged that U.S. ground troops would not be returning because, as he explained, "there is no American military solution to the larger crisis in Iraq."

U.S. military cargo planes flying at low altitude dropped food and water supplies to the Yazidis, and on August 8 in the first U.S. air strikes in Iraq following the U.S. withdrawal from that country at the end of 2011, two U.S. fighter aircraft attacked ISIS artillery positions, while Iraqi aircraft struck other ISIS targets. At the same time, however, ISIS fighters captured Mosul Dam, Iraq's largest hydroelectric facility, just north of that city.

In an unprecedented development prompted by the gravity of the situation, the Iraqi government authorized ammunition and small arms for Peshmerga fighters battling ISIS. On August 19, Kurdish forces aided by U.S. aircraft recaptured Mosul Dam. That same day ISIS executed American journalist James Foley, who had gone missing in Syria in November 2012. The execution by beheading was videotaped and put on the Internet, causing widespread international outrage.

On August 25, the United States commenced surveillance flights over Syria to identify ISIS targets there for possible future air strikes. Five days later, aircraft from the United States, Australia, France, and Britain dropped food and water to the beleaguered Iraqi town of Amirli, besieged by ISIS, 105 miles north of Baghdad. U.S. air strikes supported the humanitarian mission. The Shiite Turkmen of Amirli had chosen to remain and had fortified their town of 15,000 people with trenches and armed positions. While Amirli had fought off the initial attack in June, it had been surrounded by the militants since mid-July.

The siege of Amirli was lifted on August 31, which was held to be an important victory for the Iraqi Army, Kurdish fighters, and Shiite militiamen. On September 2 ISIS beheaded a second American journalist, Steven J. Sotloff, saying that this was retaliation for the U.S. bombing of ISIS positions in northern Iraq. Again, the execution was videotaped and distributed via the Internet.

At the NATO summit in Wales on September 5, 2014, Obama announced establishment of a "core coalition" to battle ISIS. It consisted of 10 nations, including France, Germany, and Britain. U.S. secretary of state John Kerry made clear that the countries involved would not be sending troops to Iraq or Syria. The coalition members proclaimed a multipronged strategy of a military effort accompanied by halting financial transfers to ISIS, coordinating intelligence gathering, and preventing their own citizens from joining ISIS.

On September 10 in a nationally televised address, Obama informed the American people that the United State would launch air strikes against ISIS targets in Iraq. This decision had the potential to embroil the nation in another Middle East conflict, and his goal to "dismantle and ultimately destroy" the Sunni jihadists represented a considerable turnaround from the president's previous policies in the region. After previously rejecting advice from top advisers that the United States arm and train the Syrian rebels fighting President Bashar al-Assad and ISIS, Obama now called for specific congressional approval to do so.

This was a major expansion of a campaign previously limited to protecting U.S. advisers working with Iraqi forces and preventing the slaughter of minority groups in northern Iraq. In addition, 475 more U.S. military advisers were to be sent to Iraq, raising the total of American forces there to some 1,700. At the same time, Obama made clear that this effort would not involve "American combat troops fighting on foreign soil."

Secretary of State Kerry had already departed for the Middle East in an effort to add such Sunni states as Jordan and Saudi Arabia to the anti-ISIS coalition. At the same time the Obama administration shifted $25 million in military aid to Iraqi forces, including the Kurdish fighters.

Obama insisted that he had the authority to ratchet up air strikes against ISIS under war powers granted more than a decade earlier to fight Al Qaeda, but in asking Congress for additional authority to arm and train the moderate Syrian rebels to fight the ISIS extremists, he effectively shifted a covert operation by the Central Intelligence Agency (CIA) to a mission led by the Defense Department. Approval also would allow the United States to accept money from other countries to support Syrian opposition forces.

On September 19, the U.S. Senate added its stamp to the House of Representatives' approval of Obama's request to arm and train certain Syrian rebel groups. This vote in effect allowed the Obama administration to commence hostilities against an enemy in Syria, relying on the war declarations passed with the authorizations to use military force in 2001 and 2002 that targeted Al Qaeda and Saddam Hussein.

Meanwhile on September 15, two days after the ISIS beheading of British hostage David Haines, an international conference convened in Paris to deal with the ISIS threat. Some 40 nations agreed to contribute to the fight, although the countries involved and their roles were not then specified. Securing the support of influential Middle Eastern countries such as Egypt and Saudi Arabia was considered critical in countering the notion that this was simply a crusade by Western nations against Islam. Also on September 15, U.S. aircraft for the first time went to the aid of Iraqi security forces near Baghdad who had come under attack by ISIS fighters.

On September 22, cruise missiles and aircraft from the United States and allied Arab nations struck ISIS targets in Syria in the first U.S. military offensive in that war-torn country. The strikes were centered on the city of Raqqa, the declared capital of ISIS's self-proclaimed Islamic State. The goal was to take out command-and-control and training facilities. Bahrain, Saudi Arabia, the United Arab Emirates, Jordan, and Qatar all participated, and some 20 targets were struck, among them the presumed headquarters of the Khorasan group, an affiliate of the Al Qaeda umbrella terrorist organization now working with Al Qaeda's Syrian affiliate, the al-Nusra Front.

U.S. and coalition air strikes during the next few days targeted ISIS positions in eastern Syria, including mobile oil refineries used by ISIS to help finance its operations. These strikes were aimed at cutting off up to $2 million a day to ISIS from oil produced by the mobile refineries. Saudi Arabian and United Arab Emirates (UAE) aircraft outnumbered those of the United States in this operation targeting a dozen locations. The UAE aircraft were led by Major Mariam Al Mansouri, the first female UAE fighter pilot. Air strikes also occurred against ISIS military targets in Iraq. Meanwhile the anti-ISIS coalition continued to grow, with the Australian, Dutch, Belgian, and British governments agreeing to join the fight.

On September 24 Obama addressed the United Nations General Assembly and declared U.S. leadership in the effort to destroy ISIS. In a strongly worded statement, he also called on the Arab world to end Islamic extremism.

On September 30 Turkish soldiers and tanks took up positions along the border with Syria as the Turkish government debated whether to deploy troops to battle ISIS. An estimated 150,000 people had entered Turkey during the past few days alone in order to escape ISIS, whose self-proclaimed capital of Raqqa was only 60 miles from the Turkish border and whose fighters in mid-September had opened an operation to secure control of Kobanî, a largely Kurdish town just across the Turkish border in Syria. By the end of the month, ISIS had taken some 350 Kurdish villagers and displaced 150,000 people. U.S. air strikes meanwhile targeted ISIS positions near Kobanî.

On October 2 the Turkish parliament voted 298 to 98 to authorize military force against ISIS in Syria and Iraq, although what action the government planned to take was unclear. Turkish president Recep Tayyip Erdoğan had been outspoken in his demands that Syrian president al-Assad be removed from power and had urged establishment of a no-fly zone over portions of Syria, but Turkey was also reluctant to go it alone.

With Turkish tanks and troops remaining in place, on October 8 ISIS fighters commenced the siege of Kobanî. Turkey's failure to act brought rioting by Turkish Kurds in which at least nine demonstrators died. Protests, organized in part by the pro-Kurdish Peoples' Democratic Party, occurred across Turkey and in several foreign cities. The rioting revealed the dilemma for Turkish leaders. Since 1984 some 40,000 people had been killed in clashes between Turkish government forces and its Kurdish minority, led by the Kurdistan Workers' Party (PKK), which seeks greater rights for the Kurds. In March 2013, PKK jailed leader Abdullah Ocalan had called for a cease-fire. As PKK militants withdrew to the Iraqi mountains and the beginnings of a peace process emerged, the conflict seemed to have reached a turning point, but the failure of the Turkish government to aid Kobanî and indeed in turning back Turkish Kurds wanting to fight for the city caused Kurdish anger to explode anew.

On October 12, however, Ankara announced that it would permit U.S. and other coalition forces battling militants in Syria and Iraq to use some of its bases, which would make it easier for coalition air forces attacking ISIS positions. The next day, however, in another sign of the often conflicting goals of coalition members aligned against ISIS, Turkish warplanes attacked not Kobanî but rather positions held by the PKK in southeastern Turkey. Meanwhile, the battle for Kobanî raged on and intensified as U.S. and other coalition forces continued their air strikes in support of the Kurds. Were ISIS to capture Kobanî, it would control three official border crossings between Turkey and Syria and some 60 miles of their common frontier.

At the same time, Iraqi government forces abandoned to ISIS a key military base in Sunni-dominated Anbar Province. ISIS fighters had also encircled Haditha, Anbar's last large town not yet under its control. Iraqi government forces still controlled the Ayn al-Asad military base, defending Iraq's second-largest dam and the provincial capital of Ramadi, but some 80 percent of Anbar Province was under ISIS control.

On October 19 Iraqi lawmakers approved new prime minister Haider al-Abadi's remaining cabinet nominees, completing formation of a more inclusive government better able to confront the ISIS challenge. Khaled al-Obeidi, a Sunni lawmaker from Mosul, became minister of defense; Mohammed Salem al-Ghabban, a Shiite lawmaker, was the minister of interior; and Hoshyar Zebari, a Kurdish politician and Iraq's long-serving foreign minister, was approved as minister of finance.

On October 19 for the first time in the war against ISIS, U.S. military aircraft air-dropped to Kurdish fighters in Kobanî weapons provided by Kurdish authorities in Iraq as well as ammunition and medical supplies. A major turning point in the battle occurred the next day when the Turkish government agreed to let some Kurds cross the Turkish border into Syria to join the fight for Kobanî, but Ankara specified that these had to be Kurds from Kurdistan and not Kurds from Turkey itself. This decision opened a corridor to Syria for the Peshmerga fighters. The semiautonomous northern region of Iraqi Kurdistan is one of Turkey's major security allies and a principal exporter of oil to that nation. Indeed, in June Turkey signed a 50-year energy pact with the Kurdistan Regional Government. Iraqi Kurdistan had also been at odds with the PKK and its affiliates in Syria.

Meanwhile, it appeared that al-Abadi was determined to root out corruption and inept leadership in the Iraqi military. On November 12 he announced the removal of 36 military commanders and the installation of 18 others. On December 1, he informed parliament that he had learned of 50,000 "ghost soldiers" in only four Iraqi divisions. These were Iraqis supposedly in the military but paying a fee to corrupt commanders to escape duty. Al-Abadi vowed to punish those responsible.

Meanwhile, in late November heavy fighting occurred for the city of Ramadi, the capital of Anbar Province. If Ramadi were to fall, ISIS would have a large swath of territory from the western outskirts of Baghdad north through Syria to the Turkish border.

While they were losing ground in Anbar Province, Iraqi forces, assisted by coalition air strikes, were making gains in Diyala Province. There Peshmerga forces, along with the Iraqi military and police, retook the strategic towns of Jalawla and Saadiya as well as Baiji refinery, the country's largest, which had been lost to ISIS in June. There were also reports of Iranian cooperation with the coalition, with its warplanes having attacked ISIS targets in Iraq on December 1, although Tehran formally denied this. On December 8, U.S. officials announced commitments of 1,500 troops from other nations to join the 3,000 U.S. troops advising and training Iraqi and Kurdish forces in the fight against ISIS.

On December 20, Peshmerga fighters recaptured the northern Iraqi town of Sinjar. Its capture in August and ISIS's wide-scale atrocities there had helped bring about the international coalition. At the same time Kurdish fighters, who included women, were reportedly gaining ground in the fight for Kobanî. On December 24, however, the coalition suffered its first aircraft loss when a Jordanian F-16 went down and its pilot was captured in ISIS-controlled eastern Raqqa Province in Syria. ISIS claimed that it had shot down the jet, but U.S. officials denied this. Although the situation was still in some flux, by the end of 2014 it was apparent not only that the push by ISIS into Iraq had run out of steam but also that the coalition forces were gaining ground in the fight against it.

During 2015 and 2016 coalition forces attached to INHERENT RESOLVE, along with allied indigenous troops in Iraq and Syria, made much headway against ISIS. During this time President Obama increased troop deployments to both nations, as did a number of other coalition nations. This was particularly the case in Syria. This resolve began to pay handsome dividends by late 2017, at which time ISIS's stranglehold had been largely broken in both Iraq and Syria. Republican presidential candidate Donald J. Trump promised a renewed effort to defeat ISIS if he became president, a pledge he appeared to keep after taking office in January 2017. At the same time, the increased effectiveness of Iraqi forces and anti-ISIS forces in Syria no doubt played a sizable role in the gradual demise of ISIS power.

The Trump administration granted greater leeway to the military, and in the spring of 2017 conventional forces from the 11th Marine Expeditionary Unit as well as special operations forces in the form of the 75th Ranger Regiment deployed to Syria to support U.S.-backed forces in liberating Raqqa from ISIS occupation. The deployment marked a new escalation in the U.S. war in Syria.

In early May 2017, Trump approved a plan to arm the Kurdish People's Protection Units (YPG). This had been proposed by the American military to allow the YPG to take part in the liberation of Raqqa. This move, however, drew immediate strong condemnation from Turkey, which was waging military operations against radical Kurdish groups in Turkey and opposed any plans to arm the Kurds, wherever they might be.

On June 18, 2017, two U.S. Navy F/A-18E aircraft shot down a Syrian Su-22 fighter just south of Tabaqh, Syria, in the first U.S. shoot-down of a Syrian piloted aircraft since the United States commenced air operations in Syria in 2014. The incident occurred after the aircraft ignored warnings and attacked the U.S.-backed anti-ISIS Syrian Democratic Forces (SDF). Moscow responded to the shoot-down several days later by threatening to target as hostile all aircraft flown by the United States and its allies in the anti-ISIS coalition. The Russians also said that they had suspended use of the hotline with the United States created in 2015 to prevent collisions of Russian aircraft supporting the Syrian government in that country's airspace. By late 2017, however, the hotline had been reestablished.

Operation INHERENT RESOLVE aircraft played a key role in supporting Iraqi ground forces in the retaking from ISIS of the Iraqi cities of Ramadi (November 25, 2015–February 9, 2016) and Mosul (October 17, 2016–July 9, 2017) as well as the capture of Raqqa, the ISIS capital in Syria (June 6–October 17, 2017). Civilian casualties from the air strikes were substantial, however.

Meanwhile, in July 2017 shortly after talks in Hamburg with Russian president Vladimir Putin, Trump reversed Obama's policy and ended the secret U.S. program of arming the Syrian rebels. Critics called this a victory for Putin but also for Syrian president Assad.

By January 2018 both the Iraqi and Syrian governments had declared victory over ISIS, although the ongoing Syrian Civil War continued unabated in the late summer of 2018. Syrian strongman Bashar al-Assad had substantially solidified his grip on power by that point, and the likelihood that he would step down or be removed from office appeared increasingly remote. In the spring of 2018, Trump announced that he planned to draw down U.S. troop deployments in Syria. That announcement, however, drew much criticism by both Republicans and Democrats, so he later opted to keep deployments there steady. In Iraq meanwhile, the U.S. and Iraqi governments agreed to a gradual drawdown of U.S. troops there beginning in March 2018. U.S. military officials hoped to have just 4,000 U.S. troops in Iraq by the end of 2018, a sharp reduction from the peak deployment of some 8,900 just a year earlier. The remaining troops would be used primarily for training purposes.

As of August 1, 2018, coalition forces had carried out a total of some 27,500 air strikes against ISIS and al-Nusra targets in Iraq and Syria. Approximately 80 percent of the sorties were by U.S. aircraft, with the remainder by other members of the coalition such as the United Kingdom, France, and Australia.

SPENCER C. TUCKER

See also
Abadi, Haider al-; Al Qaeda; Assad, Bashar al-; Erdoğan, Recep Tayyip; Iraq; Islamic State of Iraq and Syria; Kobanî, Siege of; Kurds; Maliki, Nuri Muhammed Kamil al-; Mosul, Second Battle of; Peshmerga; Ramadi, Recapture of; Syria; Syrian Civil War

References
Abdulrahim, Raja. "Islamic State, Rival Al Nusra Front Each Strengthen Grip on Syria." *Los Angeles Times,* November 28, 2014.
Cloud, David, and Brian Bennetan. "U.S., Allies Rush Heavy Weapons to Kurds to Fight Militants in Iraq." *Los Angeles Times,* August 11, 2014.
Khalilzad, Zalmay. "To Fight the Islamic State, Kurdish and Iraqi Forces Need Expedited Aid." *Washington Post,* August 13, 2014.
"La France renforce son dispositif militaire en Irak avec trois Rafale." *Le Monde,* October 8, 2014.
Rush, James. "ISIS Air Strikes: US Brings in Apache Helicopters as British Jets Target Militants In Iraq." *The Independent,* October 8, 2014.

İnönü, İsmet (1884–1973)

Turkish general and statesman. Born on September 24, 1884, in Izmir, Aidin Vilayet, in the Ottoman Empire, İsmet İnönü was the son of Hacı Reşid Bey, a member of the Ottoman bureaucracy. İsmet graduated from the Military School in 1903 and became an artillery officer. He then graduated from the War Academy in 1906. After serving in various posts in the Ottoman military, he joined the Nationalist Forces in Ankara in 1920 during the Greco-Turkish War of 1919–1922. İsmet was appointed the commanding general of the Western Front Command of the Ankara government in August 1921 after he distinguished himself as a military commander when he checked Greek forces in two battles in January and March 1921 around the small town of İnönü near Eskişehir in central Anatolia. His name was so much associated with these two battles that he adopted İnönü as his surname in 1934. İsmet Pasha represented the Ankara government in negotiations culminating in the Mudanya Armistice in October 1922. He then became the chief negotiator for the Ankara government in Lausanne, Switzerland, in November 1922–July 1923, culminating in the Treaty of Lausanne (July 24, 1923).

After the peace, İsmet Pasha became one of the most prominent figures in the civilian politics of modern-day Turkey as well. He served as prime minister in 1923–1937 and became the second president of the Turkish Republic in 1938 after Mustafa Kemal Ataturk died in November of the same year. İsmet İnönü's presidency lasted until 1950, when Celal Bayar (1883–1986) replaced him. İsmet İnönü's political career was far from over, and he was elected as prime minister again in November 1961 after the military coup of 1960 and remained in that post until February 1965. İsmet İnönü was one of the most prominent military and civilian figures in early republican history and was labeled aptly as the "Second Man" by many after Mustafa Kemal Ataturk, the founder of the modern Turkish republic.

BESTAMI S. BILGIÇ

See also
Ataturk, Mustafa Kemal; Greco-Turkish War; Lausanne, Second Treaty of; World War I, Impact on the Middle East

References
Akşin, Sina. *Turkey from Empire to Revolutionary Republic: The Emergence of the Turkish Nation from 1789 to the Present.* New York: New York University Press, 2007.
Heper, Metin. *İsmet İnönü: The Making of a Turkish Statesman.* Leiden: Brill, 1998.

Intifada, First (1987–1993)

A spontaneous protest movement by Palestinians against Israeli rule and an effort to establish a Palestinian homeland through a series of demonstrations, improvised attacks, and riots. The First Intifada (literally meaning "shaking off") began in December 1987 and ended in September 1993 with the signing of the Oslo Accords and the creation of the Palestinian Authority (PA).

The founding of Israel in 1948 created a situation in which Palestinians and citizens of the new Israeli state suddenly found themselves occupying a single body of land but under Israeli control. This basic reality would remain the most contentious issue in the region for decades to come. It also led to an emerging Palestinian national consciousness calling for Israel's destruction. Such anti-Israeli sentiment was generally shared by other Arab nations and by the Arab world at large, and material and military support often followed suit. While the Palestinians had not resisted under the repressive measures of the 1950s and 1960s, their treatment became even worse later, especially with the ascendance of the Likud Party in Israel. Many Palestinians, and especially the young, became more convinced of the need for resistance from 1968 to the early 1970s, then just as Palestinians experienced even poorer treatment, more property encroachment, and more difficulties, their leadership moved toward negotiation as a strategy. By the time of the intifada, most Palestinians had experienced or knew those who had experienced Israel's de jure or de facto draconian civil and criminal enforcement practices including torture, summary executions, mass detentions, and the destruction of property and homes.

In 1987 strained relations between Palestinians and Israelis were pushed to the limit on October 1 when Israeli soldiers ambushed and killed seven Palestinian men from Gaza alleged to have been members of the Palestinian terrorist organization Islamic Jihad. Days later, an Israeli settler shot a Palestinian schoolgirl in the back. With violence against Israelis by Palestinians also on the increase, a wider conflict may have been inevitable.

The tension only mounted as the year drew to a close. On December 4, an Israeli salesman was found murdered in Gaza. On December 6, a truck driven by the Israel Defense Forces (IDF) struck a van, killing its four Palestinian occupants. That same day, sustained and heavy violence involving several hundred Palestinians took place in the Jabalya refugee camp, where the four Palestinians who died in the traffic accident had lived. The unrest spread quickly and eventually involved other refugee camps. By the end of December, the violence had made its way to Jerusalem. The Israelis reacted with a heavy hand, which did nothing but fan the fires of Palestinian outrage. On December 22, 1987, the United Nations (UN) Security Council officially denounced the Israeli reaction to the unrest, which had taken the lives of scores of Palestinians.

The result of the escalating spiral of violence was the intifada, a series of Palestinian protests, demonstrations, and ad hoc attacks whose manifestations ranged from youths throwing rocks at Israeli troops to demonstrations by women's organizations. While quite spontaneous at first, a shadowy organization, the Unified Leadership of the Intifada, emerged, issuing directives via numbered statements. Along with a series of general strikes and boycotts, the demonstrations caused such disruption to the Israeli state that the government responded with military force. Heated tensions proved to be a hotbed for further violence, which led to increasingly violent reprisals on both sides. While the Palestinians had begun by relying on rocks and superior numbers under the auspices of the Unified Leadership, they were soon throwing Molotov cocktails and grenades as well as simply burning tires and using spray paint to write graffiti of the intifada. Israeli rules were such that the Palestinian flag and its colors were banned, so these were displayed by the demonstrators. In the meantime, Israeli defense minister Yitzhak Rabin exhorted the IDF to "break the bones" of demonstrators. Rabin's tactics resulted in more international condemnation and a worsening relationship with Washington, which had already been on the skids. Moshe Arens, who succeeded Rabin in the Ministry of Defense in 1990, seemed better able to understand both the root of the uprising and the best ways of subduing it. Indeed, the number of Palestinians and Israelis killed declined during the years 1990 to 1993. However, the intifada itself seemed to be running out of steam after 1990, perhaps because so many Palestinian men were in prison by then.

Despite continued violence on the part of Hamas (Islamic Resistance Movement), on September 13, 1993, Rabin, now prime minister, and Palestine Liberation Organization (PLO) chairman Yasser Arafat signed the historic Oslo Accords on the White House lawn. The accords, which brought both Rabin and Arafat the Nobel Peace Prize, called for a five-year transition period during which the Gaza Strip and the West Bank would be jointly controlled by Israel and the PA, with power eventually meant to be turned over to the Palestinian people.

The First Intifada caused both civil destruction and humanitarian suffering, but it also produced gains for the Palestinian people before it was brought to an end. First, it solidified and brought into focus a clear national consciousness for the Palestinian people and made statehood a clear national objective. Second, it cast Israeli policy toward Palestine in a very negative light on the world stage, especially the killing of Palestinian children. Third, it was seen by some Israelis to indicate that their primary struggle was with Palestinians and not all Arabs. Thus, it rekindled public and political dialogue on the Arab-Israeli conflict across Europe, in the United States, and in other Middle Eastern states. Fourth, the First Intifada threatened the leadership role of the PLO in Tunis, illustrating the self-mobilization of the population in the territories, leading eventually to friction between the Tunis old guard and younger leadership. Finally, it cost Israel hundreds of millions of dollars in lost imports and tourism.

At the time the Oslo Accords were signed in September 1993, the six-year-long intifada had resulted in well over 1,000 deaths, most of them Palestinian. It is believed that approximately 1,160 Palestinians died in the uprising, of which 241 were children. On the Israeli side, 160 died, 5 of whom were children. Clearly, the IDF's inexperience in widespread riot control had contributed to the high death toll, for in the first 13 months of the intifada alone more than 330 Palestinians were killed. Indeed, the policies and performance of the IDF split Israeli public opinion on the handling of the intifada and also invited international scrutiny.

In more recent years, continued terrorist attacks by pro-Palestinian interests and Israeli control of the Palestinian territories long beyond the timeline set by the Oslo Accords and the failure of the accords to proceed have caused unrest both in the international community and in Palestinian-Israeli relations. In 2000, a new wave of violent Palestinian protest broke out and would eventually become known as the al-Aqsa (Second) Intifada.

PAUL G. PIERPAOLI JR.

See also
Arafat, Yasser; Hamas; Intifada, Second; Palestine Liberation Organization; Palestinian Islamic Jihad; Rabin, Yitzhak

References
Brynen, Rex, ed. *Echoes of the Intifada: Regional Repercussions of the Palestinian-Israeli Conflict.* Boulder, CO: Westview, 1991.

Farsoum, Samih K., and Naseer H. Aruri. *Palestine and the Palestinians: A Social and Political History.* 2nd ed. Jackson, TN: Westview, 2006.

Hunter, F. Robert. *The Palestinian Uprising: A War by Other Means.* Berkeley: University of California Press, 1991.

Peretz, Don. *Intifada: The Palestinian Uprising.* Boulder, CO: Westview, 1990.

Said, W. Edward. *Intifada: The Palestinian Uprising against Israeli Occupation.* Boston: South End, 1989.

Schiff, Ze'ev, and Ehud Ya'ari. *Intifada: The Palestinian Uprising—Israel's Third Front.* New York: Simon and Schuster, 1990.

Intifada, Second (2000–2004)

A popular Palestinian uprising and period of enhanced Israeli-Palestinian hostilities that began on September 28, 2000, following the collapse of the Camp David peace talks that summer, and came to an unofficial end in 2004. The al-Aqsa Intifada is so named because it began at the al-Aqsa Mosque in the Old City of Jerusalem. On September 28, 2000, Israel's Likud Party leader Ariel Sharon, accompanied by a Likud Party delegation and 1,500 police and security forces, entered and moved through the Haram al-Sharif complex, the area of Jerusalem's Old City also called the Temple Mount. There the al-Aqsa Mosque and the Dome of the Rock are located. The enclave is one of Islam's three most holy sites and is sacred to Jews as well. Many observant Jews will not walk on the Temple Mount for fear of desecrating the remnants of the Temple underneath it. Some Jewish and Christian organizations have called for the destruction of the Dome of the Rock or its transferal to an Arab country so that Jews can reclaim the site.

Sharon said that he was investigating Israeli complaints that Muslims were damaging archaeological remains below the surface of the Temple Mount. By agreement, at that time the area was then supervised by Palestinian rather than Israeli security, with Israeli tour guides handing over their charges to their Arab counterparts during times when the area was open to non-Muslims.

Palestinians believed that Sharon's actions demonstrated Israeli contempt for limited Palestinian sovereignty and for Muslims in general. Anger began to build as a result, and soon riots and demonstrations erupted. Israeli troops launched attacks in Gaza, and on September 30, 2000, television footage showed the shooting of an unarmed 12-year-old boy, Muhammad Durrah, hiding behind his father as Israeli forces attacked. Protests then grew more violent, involving Israeli Arabs as well as Palestinians. For the first time also, stores and banks were burned in Arab communities. Thousands of Israelis also attacked Arabs and destroyed Arab property in Tel Aviv and Nazareth during the Jewish holiday of Yom Kippur. On October 12, two Israeli reservists were lynched by a mob at the Ramallah police station, further inflaming Israeli public opinion. In retaliation, Israel launched a series of air strikes against the Palestinians.

On October 17 Israeli and Palestinian officials signed the Sharm El Sheikh Agreement to end the violence, but it continued nevertheless. Sharon's election as prime minister in February 2001 heightened Israel's hard-line tactics toward the Palestinians, such as the use of U.S.-manufactured F-16 aircraft for the first time. Both Palestinians and Israelis admitted that the Oslo period was now over. Some Palestinians characterized their response as the warranted resistance of an embittered population that had received no positive assurances of sovereignty from years of negotiations. Others began or encouraged suicide attacks, also new to the situation, as in the June 1, 2001, attack on Israelis waiting to enter a Tel Aviv discotheque and another attack on a Jerusalem restaurant on August 9, 2001. While some attacks were claimed by various Palestinian organizations, the degree of organizational control over the bombers and issues such as payments made to the so-called martyrs' families remain disputed.

These attacks in public places terrified Israelis. Those of modest economic means had to use public transportation, but most malls, movie theaters, stores, and day care

Palestinian protesters throwing stones at Israeli troops during clashes in the Gaza Strip on October 2, 2000, part of the Second Intifada (al-Aqsa Intifada) of 2000–2005. (Andre Durand/AFP/Getty Images)

centers hired security guards. Israeli authorities soon began a heightened campaign of targeted killings, or assassinations, of Palestinian leaders. Some political figures began to call for complete segregation of Arabs and Israelis, even within the Green Line (the 1967 border). This would be enforced by a security wall and even population transfers, which would involve evicting Arab villagers and urban residents from Israel in some areas and forcing them to move to the West Bank.

A virulent campaign against Palestine Liberation Organization (PLO) chairman and Palestinian Authority (PA) president Yasser Arafat's leadership began in Israel with American assent, complicating any negotiations between the two sides. Arafat was charged with corruption and with supporting the intifada. Israelis argued that he had actually planned it, a less than credible idea to most professional observers. However, when the Israel Defense Forces (IDF) captured the ship *Santorini* filled with weapons purchased by Ahmad Jibril, head of the Popular Front for the Liberation of Palestine (PFLP) General Command (a PLO faction that did not accept the Oslo Accords) in May 2001 and with the January 2002 capture of the *Karine-A*, a vessel carrying weapons allegedly from Iran, the anti-Arafat campaign increased.

The regional response to the al-Aqsa Intifada consisted of cautious condemnation by Egypt and Jordan, which had concluded peace agreements with Israel and calls of outrage from other more hard-line states such as Syria. In February 2002, Crown Prince Abdullah called for Arabs to fully normalize relations with Israel in return for Israeli withdrawal from the occupied territories. This plan was formally endorsed at an Arab League summit in Beirut in March, although Israeli authorities prohibited Arafat from attending the summit. The proposal was never acknowledged by Israel.

Instead, in response to a suicide bomber's attack on the Netanya Hotel on March 28, 2002, in which 30 Israeli civilians died, the Israeli military began a major military assault on the West Bank. The PA headquarters were targeted, and international negotiations became necessary when militants took refuge in the Church of the Nativity in Bethlehem. Charges of a massacre in the IDF's onslaught on Jenin were investigated, showing a smaller death count of 55.

The Israeli military response to the intifada did not successfully convince Palestinians to relinquish their aims of sovereignty and seemed to spark more suicide attacks rather than discouraging them. In contrast, political measures and diplomacy produced some short interruptions in the violence, which gradually lengthened on the part of some Palestinian organizations and actors. In March 2003 Mahmoud Abbas, under pressure from Israel and the United States, became the first Palestinian prime minister of the PA because the United States refused to recognize or deal with Arafat. On April 30, 2003, the European Union, the United States, Russia, and the United Nations (UN) announced the so-called Road Map to Peace that was to culminate in an independent Palestinian state.

The plan did not unfold as designed, however, and in response to an Israeli air strike intended to kill Abd al-Aziz Rantisi, the leader of Hamas, militants launched a bus bombing in Jerusalem. At the end of June 2003, Palestinian militants agreed to a *hudna* (truce), which lasted for seven weeks and longer on the part of certain groups. There was no formal declaration that the intifada had ceased, and additional Israeli assassinations of Palestinian leaders as well as suicide attacks continued. Arafat's November 2004 death, Palestinian elections, and the Israeli response to their outcome took the spotlight in late 2004 and throughout 2005.

Casualty numbers for the al-Aqsa Intifada are disputed. Approximately 1,000 Israelis had died, and 6,700 more were wounded by September 2004. By 2003 the Israelis reported that 2,124 Palestinians had been killed, but a U.S. source reported 4,099 Palestinians killed and 30,527 wounded by 2005. Israel's tourism sector has suffered a considerable decline at a time in which inflation and unemployment were already problematic.

An outcome of the al-Aqsa Intifada in the global context of the September 11, 2001, terror attacks on the United States was that Israeli officials have tended to brand all Palestinian resistance, indeed all activity on behalf of Palestinians, as being terrorism. This discourse and the heightened violence have lent credence to those who call for separation rather than integration of Israelis with Arabs. Therefore, the building of the security barrier known as the Israeli Security Fence, which effectively cuts thousands of Palestinians off from their daily routes to work or school, was widely supported by Israelis. Similarly, Sharon's idea of withdrawal from Gaza was essentially funded by this idea, but his government had to confront those who were unwilling to relinquish settlements in that area.

The intifada resulted in crisis and despair among some Israeli peace activists and discouraged many independent efforts by Israelis and Palestinians to engage the other. A 2004 survey showed that the number of Israelis in general who believed that the 1993 Oslo Peace Accords would lead to settlements declined during the intifada, and greater numbers believed that Israel should impose a military solution on the Palestinians. Such opinions may well have shifted, however, following Israeli attacks on Lebanon in the summer of 2006.

The intifada also had deleterious effects on Palestinians who had hoped for the blossoming of normalcy in the West Bank, particularly as 85 percent of those in Gaza and 58 percent in the West Bank live in poverty. Since the outbreak of the intifada, the IDF has demolished 628 housing units in which 3,983 people had lived. Less than 10 percent of these individuals were implicated in any violence or illegal activity.

Another outcome of the intifada was its highlighting of intra-Palestinian conflict. This included that between the Tunis PLO elements of the PA and the younger leaders who emerged within the occupied territories, between Fatah and Hamas, and between Fatah and the al-Aqsa Martyrs Brigades. Also evident were the difficulties of responding to Israeli demands for security when security for Palestinian citizens was not in force. Some Palestinian Israeli citizens have asserted their Palestinian identity for the very first time as a result of the intifada. The conflict most certainly caused discord in the Arab world as well.

Sherifa Zuhur

See also

Al-Aqsa Mosque Massacre; Arafat, Yasser; Fatah, al-; Hamas; Intifada, First; Oslo Accords; Palestine Liberation Organization; Popular Front for the Liberation of Palestine; Sharon, Ariel; Terrorism

References

Baroud, Ramzy, et al. *The Second Palestinian Intifada: A Chronicle of a People's Struggle.* London: Pluto, 2006.

Khalidi, Walid. "The Prospects of Peace in the Middle East." *Journal of Palestine Studies* 32 (Winter 2003): 50–63.

Reinhart, Tanya. *The Road Map to Nowhere: Israel/Palestine since 2003.* London: Verso, 2006.

Shulz, Helena Lindholm. "The al-Aqsa Intifada as a Result of Politics of Transition." *Arab Studies Quarterly* 24 (Fall 2002): 21–47.

Stork, Joe. "Erased in a Moment: Suicide Bombing Attacks against Israeli Civilians." *Human Rights Watch* (2002): 1–160.

Ionian Revolt (499–493 BCE)

In 547 BCE Persian king Cyrus II (Cyrus the Great, r. 559–530 BCE) conquered the Greek city-states that had been established in Ionia (the central coast of Anatolia in present-day Turkey). Cyrus then set up tyrants (rulers) over these.

In 499 Aristagoras, tyrant of the Ionian city-state Miletus, with Persian support, mounted an expedition to conquer the Greek island of Naxos, the largest island in the Cyclades island group in the Aegean Sea. This military effort was rebuffed. Fearing that this failure would bring his dismissal, Aristagoras then initiated a revolt of all Hellenic Asia Minor against Persian rule.

King Darius I (Darius the Great, r. 522–486) demanded earth and water, symbols of submission from the Greeks. While some Greek city-states including Aegina submitted, others refused, and the Greco-Persian Wars began.

During the ensuing Ionian Revolt (499–493), Aristagoras traveled to the city-states of mainland Greece to solicit aid. Athens agreed to contribute 20 ships, and Eretria committed 5, but Sparta's leaders were reluctant to campaign so far from home and refused assistance to their fellow Greeks in Ionia. The mainland Greeks also assisted the Ionian Greeks in capturing the Persian regional capital of Sardis in western Anatolia in 498. The Greeks wanted to sack Sardis, but a great fire destroyed the city.

The Ionian Revolt continued for some time, with both sides essentially deadlocked throughout 497–495. In 496 the island of Cyprus revolted against Persia, as did Caria on the coast of Asia Minor. Persian forces transported there by the Phoenicians retook Cyprus, while a Phoenician fleet suppressed Caria. In 494 the Persians sent a large force against Miletus, the center of the Ionian Revolt. The Persians crushed an Ionian fleet of 333 triremes in a great sea battle off Lade in the gulf opposite Miletus, then captured and sacked Miletus itself. They destroyed much of the city, killed most of its men, and enslaved the women and children. The Persians then took all Ionian cities on the eastern shore of the Hellespont (Dardanelles) as well as Byzantium on the European side of the Bosporus and Chalcedon on the Asian side. In addition, they secured and sacked the islands of Chios, Lesbos, and Tenedos, in effect bringing large-scale fighting to a close. The last Greek resistance ended with the Persian capture of the port city of Soli in Cilicia in 493.

Seeking to secure the western frontier of his empire from further revolts and from the interference of the mainland Greeks and also vowing to have revenge on Athens and Eretria, Darius now embarked on an effort to conquer all Greece. The ensuing Greco-Persian Wars of 499–479 BCE are one of the most important conflicts in all recorded history.

Spencer C. Tucker

See also

Cyrus II the Great; Greco-Persian Wars

References

Burn, A. R. *Persia and the Greeks: The Defense of the West, c. 546–478 BC*. Stanford, CA: Stanford University Press, 1984.

Green, Peter. *The Greco-Persian Wars*. Berkeley: University of California Press, 1996.

Herodotus. *The History of Herodotus*. Edited by Manuel Komroff. Translated by George Rawlinson. New York: Tudor Publishing, 1956.

Hignett, G. *Xerxes' Invasion of Greece*. Oxford, UK: Clarendon, 1963.

Holland, Tom. *Persian Fire: The First World Empire and the Battle for the West*. Preston, Lancashire, UK: Abacus, 2006.

Lazenby, J. F. *The Defence of Greece*. Oxford, UK: Aris and Phillips, 1993.

Murray, Oswyn. 1988. "The Ionian Revolt." In *The Cambridge Ancient History*, Vol. 4, *Persia, Greece and the Western Mediterranean, c. 525 to 479 BC*, ed. John Boardman, N. H. L. Hammond, D. M. Lewis, and M. Ostwald, 461–490. 2nd ed. Cambridge: Cambridge University Press, 1988.

Sealey, Raphael. *A History of the Greek City States, ca. 700–338 B.C.* Berkeley: University of California Press, 1976.

Ipsus, Battle of (Spring, 301 BCE)

The Battle of Ipsus was fought in 301 BCE between the successors of Macedonian king Alexander III (the Great) to see who would control his vast empire. Legend has it that when Alexander lay dying in Babylon in 323, he was asked to whom he left his vast empire. He is said to have replied "Kratisto" (to the strongest). Predictably, a struggle soon ensued among a considerable number of Alexander's chief lieutenants, known as the Diadochi (Successors). The so-called Diadochi Wars began in 323 and extended to 275. Fighting began in earnest in 316. It was a shifting struggle, marked by guile and bribery.

By 301 there were six remaining Diadochi: Seleucus I Nicator, Lysimachus, Cassander, Ptolemy I, Antigonus I Monophthalmus, and Antigonus's son Demetrius I. Seleucus ruled Mesopotamia, Lysimachus was in Thrace, Cassander held Macadeon, Ptolemy held Egypt, Antigonus ruled Asia Minor, and Antigonus's son Demetrius controlled Greece. Demetrius had previously attacked Rhodes. Supported by Ptolemy, however, Rhodes had successfully withstood a siege, and Demetrius had then returned to Greece, ousting

Cassander there and reinstating the Corinthian League. Locked in combat with Demetrius, Cassander appealed for assistance from Lysimachus, Seleucus, and Ptolemy.

Supported by some forces from Cassander, Lysimachus crossed the Hellespont (Dardanelles) and invaded Antigonus's stronghold of Asia Minor. Demetrius, who had been engaging Cassander, then sailed from Greece to assist his father in Asia Minor in the hope that they could dispatch Lysimachus before Seleucus could arrive with his substantial forces. Ptolemy meanwhile had begun an invasion of Syria but retired on false reports that Antigonus had been victorious.

The two sides came together in battle in the spring of 301 BCE at the village of Ipsus (present-day Sipsin, Turkey) in Phrygia. Antigonus and Demetrius had some 70,000 infantry, 10,000 heavy Macedonian cavalry, and perhaps 75 war elephants. Seleucus and Lysimachus fielded 64,000 infantry and 15,000 light cavalry, but Seleucus had secured 500 elephants in return for a pledge not to invade India, and he had 400 of these with him.

Accounts of the battle are sketchy, but apparently both armies deployed their infantry in phalanx formation, facing one another, with the cavalry on the flanks and war elephants as a screen in front. Seleucus, however, committed only about 100 of his war elephants in front, holding the other 300 in reserve. Antigonus attacked, with Demetrius commanding the heavy cavalry to break the opposing cavalry and wheel in behind his enemy.

The battle initially unfolded as Antigonus intended, but Demetrius was so successful that he drove the opposing cavalry from the field and took himself out of the battle. Seleucus then deployed his reserve elephants as a screen to block Demetrius from returning. Accounts differ as to whether these events were by design on the part of Seleucus or were mere happenstance.

Meanwhile, the Seleucid light cavalry on the other flank advanced against Antigonus's phalanx and broke it with arrows. Antigonus, then 81 years old, was determined to stand and fight, awaiting the return of his son. Antigonus was killed, and Demetrius never did attempt to return. Informed of the results of the fighting, Demetrius escaped with some 9,000 men back to Ephesus.

The Battle of Ipsus marked the definitive end to Alexander's empire. Had Antigonus won, no doubt that empire would have been largely reconstituted. Only Ptolemy, ruling in Egypt, would have remained of Antigonus's opponents, and he could have soon been defeated. Such an empire would have presented a serious obstacle to Roman expansion. As it worked out, the eastern empire now broke into a series of smaller states, none of which could stand alone against Rome.

Spencer C. Tucker

See also
Diadochi, Wars of the; Seleucus I Nicator

References
Billows, Richard A. *Antigonos the One-Eyed and the Creation of the Hellenistic State.* Berkeley: University Of California Press, 1990.
Cary, M. *The History of the Greek World, from 323 to 146 B.C.* London: Methuen, 1932.
Plutarch. *The Lives of the Nobles Grecians and Romans.* Translated by John Dryden, revised by Arthur Hugh Clough. New York: Modern Library, 1979.

Iran

The Islamic Republic of Iran is situated in Southwest Asia. The name "Persia" was, however, the name primarily used by the international community to describe Iran during most of its history. The name "Iran" did not come into wide use until after the mid-1930s. Occupying 636,293 square miles, Iran is slightly larger than the U.S. state of Alaska. Iran is the second-largest nation in the Middle East and the world's 18th largest. Iran is bordered by the Persian Gulf and the Gulf of Oman to the south; Turkey, Azerbaijan, the Caspian Sea, and Armenia to the north; Afghanistan and Pakistan to the east; and Iraq to the west. Iran has long been important because of its strategic location at the geographic nexus of the Middle East, Europe, and Southwest Asia. Iran's population in 2018 was some 82 million. Its capital and largest city is Tehran.

Iran's considerable influence in world affairs is due to its location and its considerable reserves of fossil fuels. Iran possesses both the world's fourth-largest oil reserves and the largest natural gas supply. Iran is a member of the United Nations (UN), the Economic Cooperation Organization, the Non-Aligned Movement, the Organization of Islamic Cooperation, and the Organization of Petroleum Exporting Countries. Iran's governmental system is based on the 1979 Iranian Constitution that combines elements of parliamentary democracy with a theocracy governed by Islamic jurists, all headed by a supreme leader.

Iran has numerous ethnic and linguistic groups, but its official language is Persian. Some 90–95 percent of the population adheres to Shia Islam, which is the state religion. Because Sunni Muslims comprise the great majority of Muslims in the Middle East and the world, Shia Iranians

IRAN

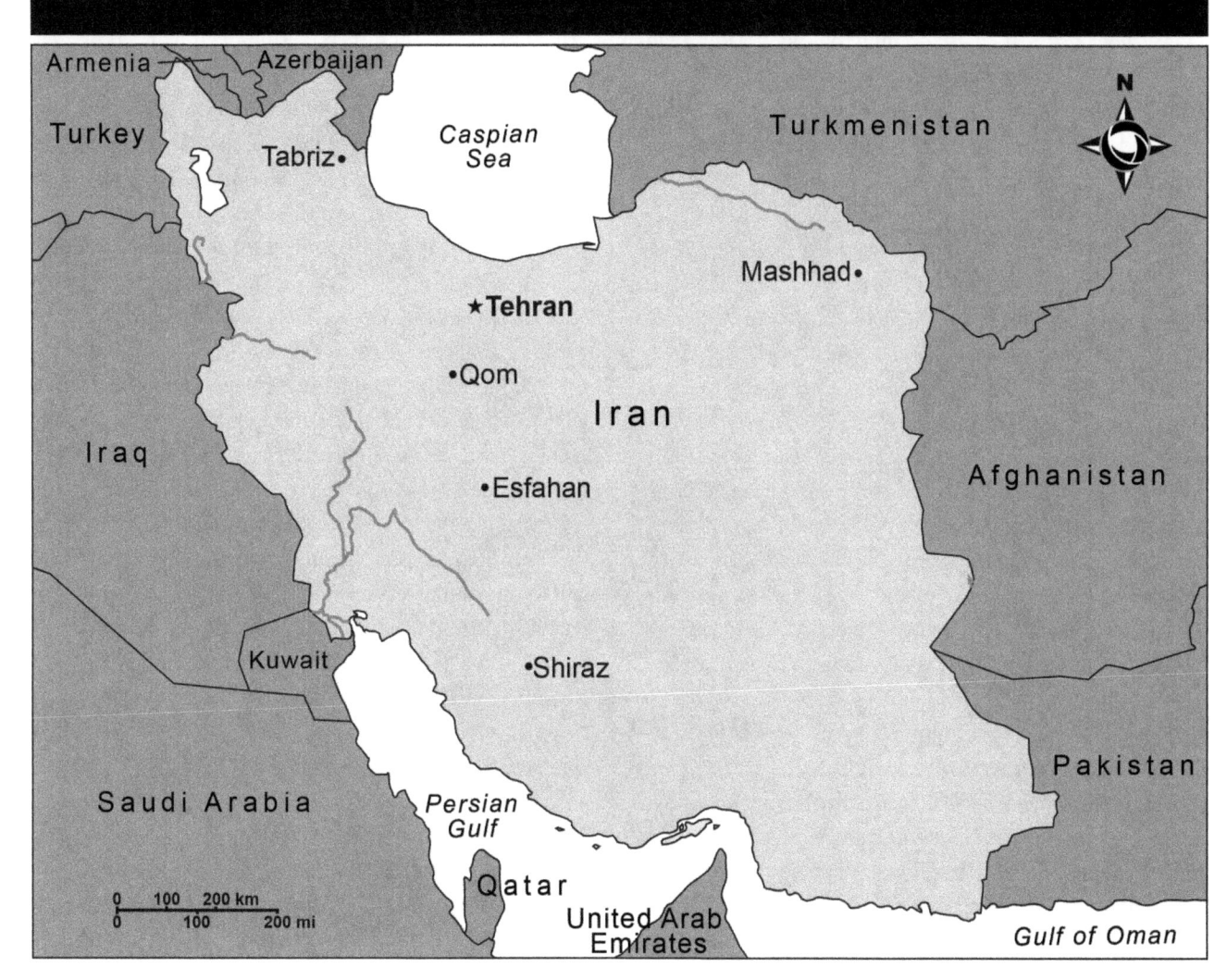

have tended to view the actions of Sunni-dominated governments as a direct threat. Sunni Muslims, principally Kurds and Balochs, constitute some 4 percent of the population. The remaining 2 percent are non-Muslim religious minorities, including more than a quarter million Christians (most of Armenian background) as well as Jews, Bahais, Mandeans, Yazidis, Yarsanis, and Zoroastrians. Despite the attitude of the current Iranian government toward the State of Israel, Judaism has a long history in Iran dating back to the Persian conquest of the Kingdom of Judah and the so-called Babylonian Captivity of the Jews in the sixth century BCE. As many as 10,000 Jews live in Iran. Although this seems to be a small number, it is the largest Jewish population in the Middle East outside of Israel.

Dating from the Proto-Elamite and Elamite Kingdoms in 3200–2800 BCE, Persia was one of the world's oldest civilizations and came to be one of the most important empires of the ancient world and, for a time, its largest and most powerful. The first Persian Empire appeared in 625 BCE and reached the height of its influence in the Achaemenid Empire established by Cyrus the Great in 550 BCE. At its greatest extent, the empire extended from significant parts of the Balkans in Europe eastward to the Indus Valley of present-day India. Alexander III (the Great) of Macedon conquered Persia in 330 BCE, but his own vast empire was divided following his early death in 323. The Parthian Empire, one of the successor states, lasted only from 247 BCE to 224 AD. Its successor, the Sassanid Empire, survived until 651. One of the leading world powers, it fought numerous wars with the rival Roman-Byzantine Empire.

Rashidun Arabs conquered Persia by 651 and converted it to Islam. Arabic also replaced Persian as the official language, although Persian remained the language of the common people. During the Safavid dynasty (1501–1736), the Twelver school of Shia Islam became the official religion. Under its great ruler and military leader Nadir Shah (1736–1747), Persia was arguably the world's most powerful empire, including all of modern-day Iran, Azerbaijan, Bahrain, and Armenia; most of Georgia, the northern Caucasus, Iraq, Kuwait, and Afghanistan; and parts of Turkey, Syria, Pakistan, Turkmenistan, and Uzbekistan.

Persia's strategic geographical location bordering Russia, India, and the Persian Gulf made it a natural target in the struggle between the Great Powers, primarily Russia and Britain. This was especially true during the weak Qajar dynasty (1795–1925), when Persia was quite unable to resist pressure from outside powers and lost territory in the Caucasus. During the Constitutional Revolution of 1905–1907, Mozzafar-al-Din Shah (r. 1896–1907) was forced to issue a decree in 1906 that created a limited constitutional monarchy. The first Persian parliament, the Majlis, convened in October 1906. Then in 1907 the Anglo-Russian Convention divided Persia into spheres of influence: Russian in the north and center, British in the southeast, and a neutral zone between the two.

Persia declared its neutrality during World War I (1914–1918) but nonetheless became a battleground for German, Ottoman, Russian, and British forces. In March 1915 Russia agreed to British control over the neutral zone, where oil had been discovered in 1908, leading the next year to the establishment of the Anglo-Persian Oil Company.

The Germans and allied Ottomans sought to destroy the British-controlled oil facilities in Khuzestan and secure access to Afghanistan via Persia. The Ottomans also sought to acquire Transcaucasia. Many in Persia favored an Ottoman-German alliance because the Ottomans were Muslims fighting against the much-distrusted Russians and British and also because the Ottoman sultan had proclaimed jihad (holy war) against the Allies. Kaiser Wilhelm II of Germany had also posed as a protector of Islam.

The Ottomans invaded Azerbaijan in the fall of 1914; by May 1916, however, Russian forces had defeated the Ottoman invasion, although the Ottomans were able to arrest the Russian advance and also achieve success in southern Persia against the British. In addition, German agents in southern Persia were able to instigate revolts among the Bakhtiari, Qashqai, and Tangistani tribes. The most famous of those emissaries was Wilhelm Wassmuss, a former consul in Bushire who became known as "the German Lawrence." The British area of influence soon fell under German control, cutting the British off from Tehran and forcing them to divert troops from Mesopotamia to protect the Khuzestan oil fields.

Early in 1916, however, the British formed a new local armed force, the South Persia Rifles, commanded by General Sir Percy Sykes. By the fall of 1916 the South Persia Rifles had recaptured the most important cities from the Germans and linked up with the Russian forces in Isfahan. In late 1917 British forces regained control of the south from the Germans and their tribal allies.

In Tehran in August 1915 Mustawfi al-Mamalik, a nationalist pro-German leader, became prime minister and initiated secret talks with the Germans. The third Majlis was also predominantly pro-German and anti-Russian. The Germans were supported by nationalist members of the Democratic Party, Shia clerics, tribal leaders, and the Swedish-officered Gendarmerie. In November 1915 Russian forces marched from Qazvin toward Tehran. The Majlis was dissolved, but a provisional government was formed first in Qom. It then moved to Hamadan and finally to Kermanshah. The British and Russian ministers persuaded young Ahmad Shah Qajar (r. 1909–1925) and his cabinet to remain in the capital. By March 1917 as a result of Russian and British military successes, the dissident government was forced to withdraw to Ottoman territory. By late 1917, the Russians and the British again controlled most of Persia.

With the Bolshevik Revolution in Russia of November 1917, most Russian military formations in Persia disintegrated, but the British were able to move into that territory in northern Persia. The British also sent expeditions to Transcaucasia, eastern Persia, and Turkistan. Despite the end of the war in November 1918, the British did not withdraw from Persia until 1921.

Persia had suffered greatly from the war. The foreign occupation, the corrupt and ineffective Persian government, tribal rebellions, separatist nationalist movements, and a famine in 1918–1919 all led to a major economic and political crisis. In late 1920 in the midst of growing unrest throughout Persia, some 1,500 men of the so-called Persian Soviet Socialist Republic, reinforced by elements of the Russian Bolshevik Red Army, prepared to march from Rasht on Tehran. Ahmad Shah Qajar was both weak and inept. The British, who now had a major economic stake in Iran, were greatly concerned.

On January 14, 1921, British general Edmund Ironside, then commanding the Allied force in Persia, chose Reza Khan, commander of the Tabriz Battalion, to lead the major Persian military formation, the 3,000–4,000-man Cossack Brigade, as a brigadier general and the first Persian so selected. The next month with British support, Reza Khan marched on Tehran, and on February 21 he seized control in a largely bloodless coup d'état.

Although military actions extended well into 1922, Reza Khan was able to pacify the entire country. On October 28, 1923, he became prime minister, serving until November 1, 1925. On December 15, 1925, he established the Pahlavi dynasty, with himself as Reza Shah Pahlavi I.

Reza Shah laid the foundations of the modern Iranian state. He instituted agricultural, economic, and educational reforms and began the modernization of the country's transportation system. He also built up the military. These and other reforms threatened the status of the Shia clerics in Iran, who began to oppose the shah and policies that were seen as impinging on their areas of authority. Desiring to stress the country's pre-Islamic traditions and to include Iranians who were not from Fars (the central province), Reza Shah in 1935 changed the country's name from Persia to Iran.

Germany had a significant economic influence and presence in Iran prior to the outbreak of World War II (1939–1945), for in the 1930s Reza Shah had turned to it for economic assistance. His admiration of Germany, which had no tradition of imperial intervention in Iran or in the Middle East, was well known, as was his distrust of Britain and the Soviet Union.

Reza Shah declared Iran neutral in the war. However, after the Germans attacked the Soviet Union in June 1941, Iranian involvement became inevitable. The Soviet Union was now allied with Britain, and as German forces drove farther eastward and threatened the Caucasus, the strategic significance of Iran grew. The Allies sought to protect the British-controlled oil fields in Khuzestan and to use Iran and, in particular, its newly built Trans-Iranian railroad to transport military supplies to the Soviet Union. The British and Soviet representatives in Iran demanded that the government expel German nationals and allow the Allies to utilize the railroad to transport war materials. When Reza Shah refused on the grounds of Iranian neutrality, the Allies invaded and occupied the country.

On August 25, 1941, Soviet forces entered Iran from the northwest, while the British entered from Iraq. The Allies suppressed Iranian military and naval resistance in just three days. Reza Shah was forced to abdicate on September 16, 1941. Sent into exile, he died in South Africa in 1944. He was succeeded as shah by his 22-year-old son, Mohammad Reza.

The Soviet and British zones of occupation closely mirrored the spheres of influence into which Iran had been divided by the Anglo-Russia Convention of 1907. The Soviets occupied the north, the British took control in the south, and Tehran and other central areas were placed under joint Anglo-Soviet protection. In January 1942 Iran, the Soviet Union, and Great Britain signed the Tripartite Treaty of Alliance. The Great Powers promised to respect Iranian territorial integrity, sovereignty, and political independence; safeguard the Iranian economy from the effects of the war; and withdraw from Iranian territory within six months of the end of hostilities.

By the spring of 1942, Iran had severed diplomatic relations with Germany, Italy, and Japan and expelled their nationals, and on September 9, 1943, Iran declared war on Germany. Two months later, U.S. president Franklin D. Roosevelt, British prime minister Winston L. S. Churchill, and Soviet leader Joseph Stalin met in Tehran in one of the most important conferences of the war. The three Allied leaders promised during the meeting to provide economic assistance to Iran and address its problems after the war.

During the war, much of the central government strength built up by Reza Shah was lost. The war years saw political instability, social disintegration, the rise of separatist movements, and economic hardship brought on by inflation and a poor harvest in 1942 with widespread famine. The Soviet Union and Britain also revived their long-standing rivalry for influence in Iran. The Soviets closed their occupation zone to free entry and supported left-wing trade unions and the Communist Party (banned in 1937, it was revived in 1941 under the new name Tudeh [Masses]). The Soviets also supported separatist leftist movements in Iranian Kurdistan and Azerbaijan. Indeed, Soviet activities led to the establishment of an autonomous state of Azerbaijan in December 1945. Meanwhile, the British in the south supported conservative elements, including the tribes, Muslim clerics, and the proponents of monarchy. The British sponsored the right-wing, pro-Western, anticommunist National Will Party.

The U.S. government was aware of the strategic importance of Iran, and after the United States entered the war in December 1941, American troops arrived in Iran. The Persian Gulf Command, which eventually numbered 30,000 men, helped orchestrate the movement through Iran of Lend-Lease supplies to the Soviet Union. American financial and military advisers also arrived at the request of the Iranian government. One U.S. mission worked on reorganizing Iran's finances, while another took charge of the reorganization of the Iranian Gendarmerie (rural police).

In the first half of 1944, two American oil companies and then the Soviet government attempted to secure oil concessions from the Iranian government in order to undermine the monopoly of the Anglo-Iranian Oil Company (AIOC), which during the war had artificially deflated the price of oil in order to minimize the cost of the war to the British economy. The Majlis, however, passed a bill, authored mainly by Mohammad Mossadegh, leader of the National Front Party, that prohibited oil-concession agreements with any foreign company until after the end of the war. Certainly, the popularity of the shah suffered because of his ties to the West.

Mossadegh became prime minister on April 28, 1951, and soon became the shah's most prominent critic. Mossadegh secured the nationalization by the Majlis of the AIOC on May 1. Washington chose to regard this as a clear example of Mossadegh's communist tendencies. Britain responded by imposing an embargo on Iranian oil and blocking the export of products from the formerly British properties. Because Britain was Iran's primary oil consumer, this had great impact on the Iranian economy. On July 16, 1952, Mossadegh insisted on the right of the prime minister to name the minister of war and the chief of staff of the army, something that had been vested in the shah. The shah's refusal precipitated a political crisis.

Aware of his great popularity with the Iranian people, Mossadegh promptly resigned. This led to widespread protests and demands that he be returned to power. Unnerved, on July 21 the shah reappointed Mossadegh, who then took steps to consolidate his power. These included the implementation of land reforms and other measures, which to many in Britain and the United States seemed socialist. Although Mossadegh had not had any direct contact with the Soviets, the events in Iran were nevertheless of great concern to U.S. policy makers who, based on Soviet efforts to annex northern Iran at the end of World War II, feared a communist takeover.

Washington refused Mossadegh's repeated requests for financial aid because he refused to reverse the AIOC nationalization. By the summer of 1953, Mossadegh's intransigence and his legalization of the leftist Tudeh Party led the United States to join Britain and the temporarily exiled shah in a covert plot in August to overthrow him. Known as Operation TPAJAX (the "TP" referring to the Tudeh Party), the coup was successful on August 19, and the shah returned to power from Rome on August 22. The overthrow of Mossadegh would be a rallying point in anti-U.S. protests during the 1979 Iranian Revolution.

The decade that followed saw the creation in 1957 of the Sazeman-e Ettelaat va Amniyat-e Keshvar (National Information and Security Organization, SAVAK), the shah's dreaded secret police. It also brought a number of failed or overly ambitious economic reforms. Iranian economic policy gave preference to large state projects rather than a true free market economy, and the largely state-run economy failed to perform as promised. This and pressure by the United States finally led the shah to propose the White Revolution. This ambitious undertaking included land reform, privatization of government-owned firms, electoral reform, women's suffrage, the nationalization of forests, rural literacy programs, and profit sharing for industrial workers. The White Revolution proved far less than revolutionary, however. It was also accompanied by a brutal crackdown on Iranian dissidents and fundamentalist clerics, which did nothing to endear the shah to his own people.

By the early 1960s Ayatollah Ruhollah Khomeini, a conservative Muslim cleric, was the shah's most prominent opponent. Khomeini attacked the regime for its secular focus and the shah for his elaborate and regal Western lifestyle. A staunch foe of Israel, Khomeini was also critical of Iran's close relationships with the United States, which was the chief supporter of Israel, and with Israel, which was helping to train SAVAK. Thus, when SAVAK arrested, tortured, and killed activists opposed to the regime, the United States and Israel were blamed along with the shah. Khomeini's considerable popularity prevented the shah from eliminating him but not from exiling him. Forced to leave Iran in 1964, Khomeini continued to denounce the shah, Zionism, and the United States.

When the White Revolution failed to achieve the desired results, leftist groups such as the Mujahideen-e Khalq and Fidiyann-e Islami Khalq joined the National Front Party and religious conservatives in opposing the regime. During the 1970s, opposition to the regime saw overt acts of defiance such as the wearing of the *hijab* by Iranian women; attendance at mosques, the imams of which openly criticized the shah; performance of religious plays on holidays; and demonstrations to memorialize slain protesters.

When an article critical of Khomeini ran in a Tehran newspaper in January 1978, the city's streets filled with Khomeini supporters and regime opponents. The shah's failure to quell the riots that followed emboldened his opponents, and each demonstration led to another riot and a new set of martyrs and then memorial demonstrations.

Following massive general strikes in the autumn of 1978, the shah lost control. Announcing that he was going abroad for a short holiday, he left Iran on January 16, 1979, never to return (he died of cancer in Cairo, Egypt, where he was granted asylum, on July 27, 1980). Meanwhile, a transitional government composed of the various opposition groups took power in Iran.

Khomeini made a triumphant return to Iran from exile on February 1, 1979, and immediately set about resurrecting the country's Islamic heritage. It was clear that he was no liberal, but Iranian secular and leftist politicians gave him their full support in the false assumption that he was merely a figurehead who would eventually cede power to the secular groups.

Within two weeks of Khomeini's return, the military announced its intention to remain neutral, thereby avoiding prosecution by local Islamic Revolutionary Committees, or Komitehs, composed of armed militant Shiites organized around local mosques who functioned as vigilantes enforcing Islamic values and laws. Meanwhile, senior officials of the former regime were arrested, tried by a revolutionary court, and executed.

In March 1979, a 97 percent vote in a national referendum ratified Khomeini's decision to establish an Islamic republic. He went on to create a separate paramilitary force, the Revolutionary Guard Corps, which served as a secret police. On April 1, 1979, the Islamic Republic of Iran came into being.

During the summer of 1979, Khomeini loyalists crafted a new constitution and a government that was nominally democratic with an elected parliament, elected municipal councils, and an elected president but also had a Council of Guardians composed of 12 clerics and jurists. The Council of Guardians held real power, as it approved candidates seeking elected office and also approved or vetoed legislation passed by the parliament. The council was tasked with ensuring that legislation and politics remained strictly Islamic. The constitution also confirmed Khomeini and his successors as the supreme leaders of the government, with the right to appoint the heads of the armed forces, the head of the Revolutionary Guard Corps, and half of the members of the Council of Guardians. The Communist Party, liberal organizations, and even moderate groups that had initially supported the revolution and now opposed Khomeini's theocratic state were marginalized and excluded from the new government, and some of their members were executed for allegedly being anti-Islamic.

Relative moderates such as Mehdi Bazargan and Abolhasan Bani-Sadr, the first prime minister and president, respectively, after the shah's departure, were soon forced from power by Khomeini, the supreme *faqih* (expert in Islamic law) and de facto national leader.

Angered by U.S. president Jimmy Carter's decision to allow the shah to undergo cancer treatments in the United States, on November 4, 1979, Iranian students stormed the U.S. embassy in Tehran and seized 53 American diplomatic personnel as hostages. Khomeini had supported the students and their demands that the United States turn over the shah for trial in exchange for releasing the hostages. The ensuing diplomatic crisis, which lasted for 444 days (November 4, 1979–January 20, 1981), paralyzed the Carter administration; brought an aborted U.S. military rescue mission, Operation EAGLE CLAW, on April 24, 1980, that nonetheless claimed through accident the lives of eight Americans and the injuring of five other; and may well have cost Carter reelection as president.

The incoming administration of President Ronald Reagan (1981–1989) viewed the new Iranian regime as a threat to American interests in the Middle East and to its closest ally, Israel. This led the United States to support Iraq in the Iran-Iraq War of 1980–1988.

The war was in many ways a continuation of the ancient Persian-Arab rivalry fueled by 20th-century border disputes and competition for hegemony in the Persian Gulf and the Middle East. The long-standing rivalry between these two nations was abetted by a collision between the Pan-Islamism and revolutionary Shia Islamism of Iran and the Pan-Arab nationalism of Iraq.

The border between the two states had been contested for some time, and in 1969 Iran had abrogated its treaty with Iraq on the navigation of the Shatt al-Arab waterway, Iraq's only outlet to the Persian Gulf. Iran had seized islands in the Persian Gulf in 1971, and there had been border clashes between the two states in middecade. Minorities issues also intruded. Both states, especially Iraq, have large Kurdish populations in their northern regions, while an Arab minority inhabits the oil-rich Iranian province of Khuzestan, and a majority Shia Muslim population in Iraq is concentrated in the south of that country.

Given circumstances, it was natural that the leaders of both states would seek to exploit any perceived weakness in the other. Thus, Iraqi president Saddam Hussein sought to take advantage of the upheaval following the fall of the shah and the establishment of Khomeini's Islamic fundamentalist regime. This had brought an end to U.S. military assistance to Iran, which meant a shortage of spare parts. Hussein saw an opportunity to punish Iran for its support of Kurdish and Shia opposition to Sunni Muslim domination in Iraq. More important, it was a chance for Iraq to secure both banks of the Shatt al-Arab as well as Khuzestan, acquire the islands of Abu Musa and the Greater and Lesser Tunbs on behalf of the United Arab Emirates, and overthrow the militant Islamic regime in Iran.

On the eve of the war Iraq enjoyed an advantage in ground forces, while Iran had the edge in the air. Iraq had a regular army of some 300,000 men, 1,000 artillery pieces, 2,700 tanks, 332 fighter aircraft, and 40 helicopters. Iran had a regular army of 200,000 men, somewhat more than 1,000 artillery pieces, 1,740 tanks, 445 fighter aircraft, and 500 helicopters.

The Iraqi invasion on September 22, 1988, came as a complete surprise. Hussein justified it as a response to an alleged assassination attempt sponsored by Iran on Iraqi foreign minister Tariq Aziz. Striking on a 300-mile front, Iraqi troops were initially successful against the disorganized Iranian defenders. The Iraqis drove into southwestern Iran and secured the far side of the Shatt al-Arab. In November they captured Khorramshahr in Khuzestan Province and in places penetrated as much as 30 miles into Iran. But the Iraqis threw away the opportunity for a quick and decisive victory by their overly cautious advance. Another factor was certainly the rapid Iranian mobilization of resources, especially the largely untrained but fanatical Pasdaran (Revolutionary Guard Corps) militia.

Recovering from the initial shock of the invasion, the Iranians soon established strong defensive positions. Their navy also carried out an effective blockade of Iraq. Although on the first day of the war Iraqi aircraft destroyed much of the Iranian Air Force infrastructure, most of the Iranian aircraft survived, and Iraq lacked the long-range bombers to achieve strategic effectiveness against such a large country. Indeed, Iranian pilots flying U.S.-manufactured aircraft soon secured air superiority over the Iraqi Soviet-built aircraft, enabling the Iranians to carry out ground support missions with both airplanes and helicopters.

Far from breaking Iranian morale as Hussein hoped, the Iraqi invasion rallied public opinion behind the Islamic regime. Ideologically committed Iranians flocked to join the army and Pasdaran. By March 1981 the war had settled into a protracted stalemate, with much of the ground combat resembling the trench warfare of World War I. During March 22–30, however, the Iranians launched a highly successful counteroffensive, driving the Iraqis back as much as 24 miles in places. The Iranians resumed their offensive during April 30–May 20, again pushing the Iraqis back, and on May 24 recaptured the city of Khorramshahr, securing there large quantities of Soviet-manufactured weapons. Flush with victory, the Iranians proclaimed as their war aim the overthrow of Hussein.

With the war now going badly, Hussein proposed a truce and the withdrawal of all Iraqi troops from Iranian soil. He also declared a unilateral cease-fire. Sensing victory, Iran rejected the proposal and reiterated its demand for Hussein's ouster.

With the Iranian rebuff, Hussein withdrew his forces back into well-prepared static defenses within Iraq, reasoning that Iraqis would rally to his regime in defense of their homeland. For political reasons, Hussein announced that the purpose of the withdrawal was so Iraqi forces might assist Lebanon, which had been invaded by Israeli forces in June 1982.

Iranian leaders also rejected a Saudi Arabian–brokered deal that would have secured it $70 billion in war reparations by the Arab states to Iran and complete Iraqi withdrawal from Iranian territory in return for peace. Iranian leaders continued to insist on Hussein's removal and also insisted that some 100,000 Shiites expelled from Iraq before the war be permitted to return home and that the reparations figure be $150 billion. There is some suggestion that Iran did not expect these terms to be accepted and hoped to be able to continue the war with an invasion of Iraq. Indeed, Khomeini announced his intention to see the establishment of an Islamic republic in Iraq, presumably with the Iraqi Shiite majority in charge.

The Iranians sought to utilize their numerical advantage in a new offensive, although Hussein had managed to substantially increase the number of Iraqis under arms. Launched on July 20, 1982, the offensive was directed against Shiite-dominated southern Iraq, with the goal of capturing Basra, Iraq's second-largest city. Iranian human-wave assaults, prompted by a shortage of ammunition, encountered well-prepared Iraqi static defenses, supported by artillery. The Iraqis also employed poison gas. Hussein had managed, however, to substantially increase the number of Iraqis under arms.

Although the Iranians registered modest gains, these were at heavy human cost. Particularly hard hit were the untrained and poorly armed units of boy-soldiers who volunteered to march into Iraqi minefields to clear them with their bodies for the trained Iranian soldiers to follow. On July 21, Iranian aircraft struck Baghdad. Iraq retaliated in August with attacks on the Iranian oil-shipping facilities at Khargh Island and also sank several ships.

During September–November the Iranians launched new offensives in the northern part of the front, securing some territory inside Iraq before Iraqi counterattacks drove the Iranians back into their own territory. In the southern part of the front in November, the Iranians advanced to within artillery range of the vital Baghdad-Basra highway.

Between February and August 1983, Iran launched five major offensives against Iraq. Before the first of these, however, beginning in early February the Iraqi Air Force carried out large-scale air attacks against Iranian coastal oil-production facilities, producing the largest oil spill in the history of the Persian Gulf region. In their first ground offensive of February, the Iranians hoped to take advantage of their greater troop strength to isolate Basra by cutting the Baghdad-Basra road at Kut al-Amara. Their drive was halted and then thrown back, with the Iraqis claiming to have destroyed upwards of 1,000 Iranian tanks. The later Iranian 1983 offensives included a drive into northern Iraq. These, however, registered scant gains, and both sides suffered heavy casualties.

Determined to prevent the spread of Islamic fundamentalism regimes in the Middle East, the Reagan administration in the United States made a firm commitment to support Iraq. Washington supplied Baghdad with intelligence information in the form of satellite photography and also provided economic aid and weapons.

Believing that more aggressive tactics were necessary to induce Iran to talk peace, Hussein announced that unless Iran agreed to halt offensive action against Iraq by February 7, 1984, he would order major attacks against 11 Iranian cities. Iran's answer was a ground attack in the northern part of the front, and Hussein then ordered the air and missile attacks against the cities to proceed. Iran then retaliated in what became known as the War of the Cities. There were five such air campaigns during the course of the war.

In February 1984 the Iranians launched the first in a series of ground offensives, in the central part of the front. It saw a quarter million men engaged on each side, with the Iranians attempting to take Kut al-Amara to cut the vital Baghdad-Basra road there. The Iranians came within 15 miles of the city but were then halted.

The Iranians enjoyed more success in a February–March drive against Basra, which almost broke through. The Iranians did capture part of the Majnun (Majnoon) Islands with their undeveloped oil fields, then held them against an Iraqi counterattack supported by poison gas. The Iranians occupied the islands until near the end of the war.

With his forces having benefited from substantial arms purchases financed by the oil-rich Persian Gulf states, in January 1985 Hussein launched the first Iraqi ground offensive since 1980. It failed to register significant gains, and the Iranians responded with an offensive of their own in March. Now possessing better-trained troops, the Iranians eschewed the costly human-wave tactics of the past, and their more effective tactics brought the capture of a portion of the Baghdad-Basra road. Hussein responded to this emergency with chemical weapons and renewed air and missile strikes against 20 Iranian cities, including Tehran.

On February 17, 1986, in a surprise offensive employing commandos, Iranian forces captured the strategically important Iraqi port of al-Faw, southeast of Basra at the southeast end of the al-Faw Peninsula on the Shatt al-Arab waterway. In January 1987 Iran launched Operation KARBALA-5, a renewed effort to capture the city of Basra in southern Iraq. When it ground to a halt in mid-February, the Iranians launched Operation NASR-4 in northern Iraq, which threatened the Iraqi city of Kirkuk (May–June).

On July 24, 1987, the United States initiated Operation EARNEST WILL to protect oil tankers and shipping lanes in the Persian Gulf. The so-called Tanker War had begun in March 1984 with the Iraqi air attack on Kharg Island and nearby oil installations. Iran then retaliated with attacks, including the use of mines, against tankers carrying Iraqi oil from Kuwait as well as those of the Persian Gulf states supporting Iraq. On November 1, 1986, Kuwait petitioned the international community to protect its tankers, whereupon the United States announced that it would provide protection for any U.S.-flagged tankers, with other tankers free to accompany them. These steps protected neutral tankers proceeding to or from Iraqi ports and ensured that Iraq would have the economic means to continue the war.

On the night of May 17, 1987, an Iraqi Mirage F-1 fighter on antiship patrol fired two Exocet antiship missiles at a radar contact, apparently not knowing that it was the U.S. Navy frigate *Stark*. Although only one of the missiles detonated, both struck home and badly crippled the frigate, killing 37 crewmen and injuring another 50. The crew managed to save the ship, which made port under its own power.

During February 1988, the Iraqis launched a renewed wave of attacks against Iranian population centers, and the Iranians reciprocated. The attacks included not only aircraft but also surface-to-surface missiles, principally the Soviet-built Scud type. Iraq fired many more missiles than did Iran (some 520 as opposed to 177). Also during February and extending into September, the Iraqi Army carried out a massacre of Kurds in northern Iraq. Known as the al-Anfal (Spoils of War) Campaign, it claimed as many as 300,000 civilian lives and destroyed some 4,000 villages.

Meanwhile, on April 14, 1988, the U.S. Navy frigate *Samuel B. Roberts*, taking part in Operation EARNEST WILL, struck an Iranian mine in the Persian Gulf. No one was killed, but the ship nearly sank. On April 18, the U.S. Navy responded with Operation PRAYING MANTIS, its largest battle involving surface warships since World War II and the first surface-to-surface missile engagement in the navy's history. U.S. forces damaged two Iranian offshore oil platforms, sank one Iranian frigate and a gunboat, damaged another frigate, and sank three Iranian speedboats. The U.S. lost one helicopter.

By the spring of 1988, Iraqi forces were sufficiently regrouped to enable them to launch major operations. By contrast, Iran was now desperately short of spare parts, especially for its largely U.S.-built aircraft. The Iranians had also lost a large number of aircraft in combat. As a result, by late 1987 Iran was less able to mount an effective defense against the resupplied Iraqi Air Force, let alone carry out aerial counterattacks against a ground attack.

The Iraqis mounted four separate offensives. In the process they were able to recapture the strategically important al-Faw Peninsula lost in 1986, drive the Iranians away from Basra, and make progress in the northern part of the front. The Iraqis' victories came at little cost to themselves, while the Iranians suffered heavy personnel and equipment losses. These setbacks were the chief factor behind Khomeini's decision to agree to a cease-fire in 1988.

On July 3, 1988, the crew of the U.S. Navy cruiser *Vincennes*, patrolling in the Persian Gulf and believing that they were under attack by an Iranian jet fighter, shot down Iran Air Flight 655, a civilian airliner carrying 290 passengers and crew. There were no survivors. The U.S. government subsequently agreed to pay $131.8 million in compensation for the incident. It expressed regret only for the loss of innocent life and did not apologize to the Iranian government. This incident may have helped to convince Khomeini of the dangers of the United States actively entering the war, thus making him more amenable to ending it.

War weariness and pressure from other governments induced both sides to accept a cease-fire agreement on August 20, 1988, bringing the eight-year war to a close. Iran announced a death toll of nearly 300,000 of its citizens, but some analysts place this figure as high as 1 million or more.

The war ended with none of the outstanding issues resolved, as the UN-arranged cease-fire merely ended the fighting, leaving these two isolated states to pursue an arms race with each other and with the other states in the region. Negotiations between Iraq and Iran remained deadlocked for two years after the cease-fire. In 1990 Iraq, concerned with securing its forcible annexation of Kuwait, reestablished diplomatic relations with Iran and agreed to withdraw its troops from occupied Iranian territory, divide sovereignty over the Shatt al-Arab, and exchange prisoners of war. The war, while very costly to Iran, did serve to consolidate popular support behind the Islamic Revolution.

Khomeini died on June 3, 1989. His Islamic Religious Party continued to dominate the government bureaucracy and the policy-making apparatus. It also eliminated many political or religious rivals. Iranian president Akbar Hashemi Rafsanjani, who assumed office that August, pursued a pragmatic probusiness policy in an effort to rebuild the national economy without effecting any dramatic break in revolutionary ideology. In August 1997, moderate reformist Mohammad Khatami succeeded Rafsanjani as president. Khatami attempted, without success, to introduce democratic reforms.

According to the U.S. government, Iran in the 1980s was the single most important state sponsor of terrorism. Certainly Iran strongly supported the Palestinian struggle against Israel and criticized the United States for its blind support of the Jewish state. Iran also supported both Hamas in Gaza and Hezbollah in Lebanon. Hezbollah was founded by Shia clerics trained in Iraq, and Iran has provided it financial support, military training, and arms, greatly aiding Hezbollah in its efforts to confront Israel and gain political control in Lebanon.

The leaders of Iran have routinely stated that Israel must be destroyed. With Israel possessing nuclear weapons and having the most powerful military in the Middle East, any direct Iranian strike against the Jewish state would be suicidal, however. For their part, Israeli leaders have regularly argued that Israel might need to mount a preemptive strike against Iran's nuclear facilities in order to prevent it from acquiring nuclear weapons.

During the 1990s, U.S. president Bill Clinton attempted without success to pursue détente with Iran and sought to restore economic relations with that country. More recently, however, the United States accused Iran of being a key supporter of the insurgency in Iraq following the Anglo-American invasion of that nation in 2003.

In 2007 Washington grudgingly agreed to talks with Iranian officials, the first of their kind since the 1979 Iranian Revolution, this in an attempt to discuss key issues, including Iranian pilgrim traffic into Iraq and the alleged Iranian aid to anti-American elements in that country. A chief concern not only for Israel but also for its strongest ally, the United States, remains the threat of Iran acquiring nuclear weapons and the long-range missile technology needed to deliver them against Israel and Europe.

The 2005 presidential election brought conservative populist candidate Mahmoud Ahmadinejad to power. Reelected twice, he served from August 2005 to August 2013. Ahmadinejad took a hard-line stance toward Israel and the United States and was an outspoken Holocaust denier. During the George W. Bush administration (2001–2009), Secretary of State Condoleezza Rice announced that the U.S. government would try to spur regime change in Iran through "soft approaches" and dedicated $74 million to that project. This, together with threats against Iran regarding its nuclear development program, tended to galvanize Iranian sentiment against external interference.

When Barack Obama became president of the United States in January 2009, he signaled a willingness to engage Iran diplomatically. At the same time, his government came under intense pressure from Israel and conservatives in the United States to force the Iranians' hands vis-à-vis their suspected nuclear weapons program. Between 2009 and 2013, the Obama administration worked diligently with the international community, including China and Russia, to impose tougher sanctions on Iran, which it was hoped would result in a softening of Iran's position regarding its nuclear program. The sanctions indeed hurt the Iranian economy and made Ahmadinejad, Iran's hard-line and controversial president, increasingly unpopular among many Iranians.

In June 2013, Hassan Rouhani was elected as Ahmadinejad's successor. Rouhani, who is considerably more moderate than his predecessor, vowed to improve relations with the West and signaled his determination to enter into serious multilateral talks in order to resolve the issue of his nation's nuclear program. On September 13, 2013, Rouhani spoke directly with Obama via telephone, making it the highest-level exchange between Iranian and American leaders since the 1979 Iranian Revolution. Meanwhile, nuclear talks continued, and by year's end a preliminary framework for an eventual agreement had been reached.

Finally, after 2 additional years of grueling negotiations between Iran and leading Western powers, including Russia, a historic accord was achieved on July 14, 2015. The agreement, which was widely criticized in Israel and among Republican politicians in the United States, placed stringent controls on Iran's nuclear activities, which were designed to keep the country at least 1 year away from producing a nuclear bomb. It did so by cutting the number of Iranian centrifuges by two-thirds and by placing strict caps on uranium enrichment and uranium stockpiles for at least 15 years. The agreement also subjected Iran's nuclear facilities to regular inspections and verification by UN weapons inspectors. Iran, in turn, saw significant frozen funds freed and economic sanctions lifted after compliance with the deal was verified.

The development of long-range missiles by Iran that would be capable of striking Israel and even Europe continues to be a concern. In April 2016, Iran announced that the Russian government had begun shipping to Iran SD-300 surface-to-air missiles. This came in spite of strong objections from the United States, Israel, and Saudi Arabia. The $800 million contract, signed in 2007, had been frozen by Russia in 2010 because of the international sanctions but was unfrozen by Russian president Vladimir Putin in 2015 even before sanctions were lifted. Israel and the United States fear that the missiles could be used to protect Iranian nuclear sites from air strikes. Reportedly the S-300 has a speed of five times that of sound and a range of some 150 miles and can shoot down any medium-range missile in the world today.

Iran would seem to be at a crossroads. As the West had hoped, Iranian moderates backing President Rouhani made substantial gains in the spring 2016 parliamentary elections but failed to achieve a majority. The apparent yearning of younger well-educated Iranians for a more open, tolerant, and democratic society, with closer ties with the West, has not weakened the hold of the clerics on the instruments of state power. Iran also continues to be, along with Russia, the chief support of the regime of President Bashar al-Assad in Syria and also supplies weapons and financial assistance to Hezbollah in Syria and actively supports the Shiite Houthi rebels in Yemen. Iran is also very much involved in seeking to influence policies of the Shiite-dominated Iraqi government. Indeed, the Sunni-Shiite confrontation between Iran and Saudi Arabia has, if anything, intensified in the last few years. An attack by Iranians on the Saudi embassy in Tehran that followed the execution by Saudi Arabia of a prominent Shiite cleric accused by the Saudi government of treason in January 2016 led Saudi Arabia to break diplomatic ties with Iran.

On May 20, 2017, thanks to a strong turnout from Iran's urban middle classes, President Rouhani won reelection with 57 percent of the 41 million votes cast. The significant margin of victory was considered a mandate to continue his efforts to expand personal freedoms and revive the economy. His victory was also seen as strengthening the hands of moderates and reformists as Iran prepared for the end of rule by 78-year-old supreme leader Ayatollah Ali Khamenei. Still, Rouhani had his work cut out for him, especially in the financial sphere.

On June 7, 2017, Islamic State of Iraq and Syria (ISIS) assailants, including some disguised as women, stunned Iran with two brazen attacks in Tehran itself, attacking both the parliament building and the tomb of Iran's revolutionary founder Khomeini. Seventeen people were killed and 52 wounded in the near-simultaneous assaults that occurred over several hours. Six attackers also were killed, with 5 suspects detained. The attacks were the first by ISIS in Iran, with Iran subsequently identifying five of the perpetrators as Iranian Kurds recruited by ISIS. Despite the ISIS claim, Iran blamed Saudi Arabia and the United States as having been behind the attacks.

Iran struck back on June 18. In a major escalation of its war in Syria and the first time it had fired missiles at another country in three decades, the Islamic Revolutionary Guard Corps announced that it had fired several ground-to-ground midrange missiles from bases in Kermanshah Province, western Iran, against ISIS forces in the Deir Ezzor region in Eastern Syria.

At the end of December 2017 major rioting occurred in various Iranian cities, with injuries and some deaths reported. These resulted from widespread frustration regarding the Iranian economy. With the securing of the Iranian nuclear deal and the lifting of economic sanctions, the Iranian people assumed that there would be attendant substantial improvement in the laggard economy; instead, there was major economic mismanagement leading to higher unemployment and inflation, while rampant corruption went unchecked. There was also a push for equal rights for women, who were more involved in the workplace than in any other country in the region. Many Iranians were also frustrated by what they saw as an undue concentration of national resources and energy on foreign affairs to include substantial support for the Houthi rebels in Yemen, Hezbollah in Lebanon, and the Assad regime in Syria.

During 2018, Iran's domestic and foreign policies faced substantial challenges. On May 8, 2018, President Donald Trump formally withdrew the United States from the 2015 Iran Nuclear Deal, which he repeatedly termed "the worst deal ever." The U.S. withdrawal from the deal threatened to unravel the entire agreement. Rouhani's government decried the move, which it viewed as a major betrayal. The other parties to the agreement, including U.S. allies such as France and Great Britain, were determined to keep the deal intact, but Iran warned that it might well renege on its commitments if the remaining parties did not mitigate the effects of the U.S. withdrawal. The Trump administration had bitterly denounced the agreement because of its so-called sunset provisions and because it had done nothing to curb Iran's aggressive military and foreign policy actions in such places as Yemen, Syria, and Iraq. Trump immediately moved to reimpose crippling sanctions on Tehran, including a ban on Iranian oil exports. At the same time, the U.S. government began to demand that other nations, including those still committed to the 2015 deal, comply with the renewed sanctions or face potential economic conflict with Washington. In June 2018, Iran warned that it would walk away from the deal entirely if other countries bowed to American pressure.

At the same time, Iran's economy continued to lag, and by the late summer of 2018 it seemed perched on the precipice of virtual collapse. In large measure, its economy had already begun to suffer the ill effects of the American withdrawal from the nuclear deal. Unemployment remained stubbornly high, inflation was gaining momentum, Iranian markets were marked by increasing instability, and Iran's currency was in a virtual free fall. Rouhani's government seemed unable to stanch the economic hemorrhaging, and the president was under building pressure to counter the downturn and respond more aggressively to U.S. actions. In June and July 2018, numerous Iranian cities were rocked by large demonstrations, some of which turned violent. Ayatollah Khamenei meanwhile urged calm and ordered the arrests of individuals thought to be responsible for the unrest.

By August 2018, U.S.-Iranian relations had plummeted to new lows. Rouhani and Trump engaged in a war of words, leading the Iranian president to warn Washington that "a war with Iran would be the mother of all wars." In Iran, there was growing concern that the United States was preparing for direct military action against the Iranian regime, although such a scenario was quite unlikely. Meanwhile, by August 2018, there were signs that Russian efforts to reduce Iran's involvement in the Syrian Civil War were being substantially limited, a development that Moscow blamed on U.S. actions vis-à-vis Iran and Israel's unrealistic demands that Iran be excluded from the Syrian peace process altogether.

Elena Andreeva, Louis A. DiMarco, Adam B. Lowther, Paul G. Pierpaoli Jr., Spencer C. Tucker, and Sherifa Zuhur

See also

Achaemenid Empire; Alexander III the Great; Anglo-Persian War; Assad, Bashar al-; Earnest Will, Operation; Hamas; Hezbollah; Hussein, Saddam; Iran, Islamic Revolution in; Iran Air Flight 655, Downing of; Iran Hostage Crisis; Iran Hostage Rescue Mission; Iran-Iraq War; Iran Nuclear Deal; Khomeini,

Ruhollah; Nadir Shah; Parthian Empire; Persian Front, World War I; PRAYING MANTIS, Operation; Reza Shah Pahlavi; Safavid Dynasty; Sassanid Empire; Shia Islam; *Stark* Incident; Syrian Civil War; Yemen Civil War

References

Abrahamian, Ervand. *A History of Modern Iran.* Cambridge: Cambridge University Press, 2008.

Ahmad, Ishtiag. *Anglo-Iranian Relations, 1905–1919.* New York: Asia Publishing House, 1974.

Ansari, Ali. *A History of Modern Iran since 1921: The Pahlavis and After.* Boston: Longman, 2003.

Cordesman, Anthony H., and Abraham R. Wagner. *The Lessons of Modern War: The Iran-Iraq War,* Vol. 2. Boulder, CO: Westview, 1990.

Draper, Theodore. *A Very Thin Line: The Iran-Contra Affairs.* New York: Hill and Wang, 1991.

Jordan, Hamilton. *Crisis: The Last Year of the Carter Presidency.* New York: Putnam, 1982.

Karsh, Ifraim. *The Iran-Iraq War, 1980–1988.* Oxford, UK: Osprey, 2002.

Katouzian, Homa. *The Persians: Ancient, Medieval, and Modern Iran.* New Haven, CT: Yale University Press, 2010.

Lenczowski, George. *Russia and the West in Iran, 1918–1948: A Study in Big-Power Rivalry.* Ithaca, NY: Cornell University Press, 1949.

Majd, Mohammad Gholi. *Persia in World War I and Its Conquest by Great Britain.* Lanham, MD: University Press of America, 2003.

Marr, Phebe. *The Modern History of Iraq.* 2nd ed. Boulder, CO: Westview, 2004.

Olson, William J. *Anglo-Iranian Relations during World War I.* London: Cass, 1984.

Palmer, Michael A. *Guardians of the Gulf: A History of America's Expanding Role in the Persian Gulf, 1833–1992.* New York: Free Press, 1992.

Rajaee, Farhang. *The Iran-Iraq War: The Politics of Aggression.* Gainesville: University Press of Florida, 1993.

Ramazani, Rouhollah K. *The Foreign Policy of Iran: A Developing Nation in World Affairs, 1500–1941.* Charlottesville: University Press of Virginia, 1966.

Ramazani, Rouhollah K. *Iran's Foreign Policy, 1941–1973: A Study of Foreign Policy in Modernizing Nations.* Charlottesville: University Press of Virginia, 1975.

Ryan, Paul. *The Iranian Rescue Mission.* Annapolis, MD: Naval Institute Press, 1985.

Saikal, Amin. *The Rise and Fall of the Shah.* Princeton, NJ: Princeton University Press, 1980.

Wilber, Donald N. *Iran: Past and Present.* Princeton, NJ: Princeton University Press, 1955.

Willet, Edward C. *The Iran-Iraq War.* New York: Rosen Publishing Group, 2004.

Wise, Harold L. *Inside the Danger Zone: The U.S. Military in the Persian Gulf, 1987–1988.* Annapolis, MD: Naval Institute Press, 2007.

Wright, Robin. *In the Name of God: The Khomeini Decade.* New York: Simon and Schuster, 1989.

Iran, Islamic Revolution in (1978–1979)

Iran's Islamic Revolution of 1978–1979 began as an uprising against Shah Mohammad Reza Pahlavi, whose autocratic rule and ties to the West were extremely unpopular in his country. The shah's most determined opposition was organized by the Shiite religious leaders, known as the ulema. After the fall of the shah's government in February 1979, a referendum held in March revealed near unanimous support for an Islamic republic. The revolution in Iran became an inspiration for Islamic revivalists everywhere and caused a complete overhaul of the U.S. government's Middle East policy.

The Pahlavi dynasty had ruled since 1925, but the shah had gone into temporary exile in 1953, part of a successful U.S. Central Intelligence Agency effort to oust Premier Mohammad Mossadegh. After that, he appeared to many Iranians to be controlled by his U.S. advisers. His efforts to use Iran's oil wealth to rapidly modernize the country also created wide divisions between those who benefited from his Westernizing measures and those who did not. His campaign to clamp down on rural landlords, bazaar merchants, and the ulema created a potentially powerful opposition. One fierce critic was Ayatollah Ruhollah Khomeini in the sacred city of Qom who was exiled by the shah.

In 1978 sit-ins by religious students in Qom were fired on by police, which led to a series of riots. Demanding the return of Khomeini from exile in Iraq, the students threatened to continue the riots, but the shah forced Iraq to expel Khomeini, who then moved to Paris. From there, he was able to organize many other dissidents in exile and influence events in Iran through Western news outlets. Rallies, riots, and strikes continued until the shah was forced to cede the government to his vice president, Shapur Bakhtiar, on January 6, 1979.

Khomeini called for the overthrow of Bakhtiar and set up the Revolutionary Islamic Council. Bakhtiar gave in to popular pressure and allowed Khomeini to return to Iran. Shortly thereafter, the Iranian Army ended its support of the government as many soldiers joined the demonstrators. On February 11, the government fell.

As the founder of the Islamic Republic of Iran and its supreme religious leader until his death in 1989, Khomeini implemented far-reaching government and religious mandates, seeking to erase all trace of the shah's Westernization programs. Ironically, Khomeini's government became fully as repressive as that of the shah.

ALEXANDER MIKABERIDZE

See also
Iran; Khomeini, Ruhollah

References

Amir, Arjomand Said. *The Turban for the Crown: The Islamic Revolution in Iran.* Oxford: Oxford University Press, 1988.

Wright, Robin. *The Last Great Revolution: Turmoil and Transformation In Iran.* New York: Knopf, 2000.

Iran Air Flight 655, Downing of (July 3, 1988)

Iran Air Flight 655 (IR655) was an Iranian passenger jetliner mistakenly shot down by a U.S. naval warship in the Persian Gulf on July 3, 1988. The event occurred during the highly destructive Iran-Iraq War of 1980–1988 and came on the heels of incidents in 1987 and 1988 that had seen engagements of both Iranian and Iraqi forces with U.S. warships operating in the Persian Gulf. They had occurred after the Ronald Reagan administration had vowed to keep vital shipping lanes open by providing U.S. Navy warship escorts for neutral ships through the perilous waters of the Persian Gulf in Operation EARNEST WILL (1987–1988). At the time, both Iranian and Iraqi forces were targeting civilian cargo and tanker ships in the region in an effort to deprive the other of commerce and supplies.

At the time of the tragedy of Flight 655, tensions were running very high in the Persian Gulf. On March 17, 1987, an Iraqi Mirage F-1 jet fighter mistakenly fired two air-to-surface missiles at USS *Stark,* a Perry-class guided-missile frigate on routine duty in the Persian Gulf. The attack resulted in the deaths of 37 crew men and heavy damage to the ship. Little more than a year later, in April 1988 another U.S. guided-missile frigate, the Oliver Hazard Perry–class USS *Samuel P. Roberts,* hit an Iranian-laid mine in the Persian Gulf, which almost sank the ship. No lives were lost, but the ship underwent almost $90 million in repairs. This incident prompted American retaliation against Iranian assets via Operation PRAYING MANTIS on April 18, 1988. With tensions running dangerously high in the Persian Gulf by the summer of 1988, other violent incidents were almost inevitable.

At 10:17 a.m. (local time) on July 3, 1988, Iran Air Flight 655 (IR655) took off from Bandar Abbas, Iran, bound for Dubai, United Arab Emirates. There were 290 people, including the crew, on board the Airbus A300, a medium-range wide-body passenger jetliner. It began to fly over the Strait of Hormuz shortly after takeoff during the short 30-minute flight. At the same time, the *Vincennes* was steaming through the straits returning from escort duty in the Persian Gulf. Earlier that morning, a helicopter from the *Vincennes* had received warning fire from several Iranian patrol boats. The *Vincennes* subsequently exchanged fire with the Iranian vessels, which then promptly withdrew.

Only minutes later, radar on board the *Vincennes* picked up IR655, and radar operators mistook it for an American-made Grumman F-14 Tomcat fighter. The Airbus's profile closely resembled that of the F-14. Also, the *Vincennes* crew members knew that the plane had taken off from Bandar Abbas, from which Iran operated both commercial aircraft as well as F-14 fighters and other military aircraft. Crew members also believed that the plane was descending as it was approaching the ship, which was later discounted as inaccurate. In fact, the aircraft was turning away from the ship as it was fired on.

The *Vincennes* attempted seven times (three times on the civilian military frequency and four times on the military emergency frequency) to contact the crew of IR655, which did not respond. However, the U.S. warship failed to use air traffic control frequencies, so it is likely that the Airbus's crew members did not receive the radio messages or did not know that the messages were directed at them.

Now believing that the ship was under attack, when the airplane was about 11 nautical miles from the *Vincennes* its crew fired two SM-2MR medium-range surface-to-air missiles at 10:24 a.m. Both missiles hit their target, sending the airliner plunging into the Straits of Hormuz. There were no survivors; all 290 people on board were killed.

The downing of the aircraft caused international consternation and greatly embarrassed the Ronald Reagan administration. The events surrounding the tragedy were immediately contested by the Iranian government, which claimed that Flight 655 was doing nothing wrong or illegal. It also voiced great skepticism that experienced radar operators could mistake a passenger jetliner for an F-14 fighter. Furthermore, Tehran asserted that even if the aircraft had been a military fighter, the *Vincennes* had no reason to shoot it down because it was still technically in Iranian airspace, had not followed an attack pattern, and indeed had not taken any hostile actions at all. Iran concluded that the *Vincennes* crew had acted impetuously and improperly and was quick to point out that when Iraq attacked the *Stark* the year before, Washington concluded that the Iraqi pilot realized—or should have realized—that his target was an American warship. The very same thing, Tehran argued, could be said of the *Vincennes* crew.

U.S. Navy officials found no wrongdoing on the part of the *Vincennes* crew, who were in fact awarded combat-action ribbons. Although the U.S. government issued a "note of regret" about the loss of innocent lives, it neither admitted responsibility nor apologized for the incident. The affair plunged Iranian-American relations further into the deep freeze, although some assert that it may have convinced Iran's leader, Ayatollah Ruhollah Khomeini, to finally end the Iran-Iraq War, realizing that it could not prevail so long as the United States was working against him. Indeed, the war ended little more than a month later. In 1989 Iran took its case to the International Court of Justice, but not until 1996 did the American government agree on a payment settlement, which was $131.8 million. About half that amount went to the families of those killed in the crash; the remainder went to the Iranian government in reimbursement for the lost jetliner.

PAUL G. PIERPAOLI JR.

See also
EARNEST WILL, Operation; Iran; Iran-Iraq War; Iraq; PRAYING MANTIS, Operation; *Stark* Incident

References
Hiro, Dilip. *The Longest War: The Iran-Iraq Military Conflict.* New York: Routledge, 1991.
Karsh, Efraim. *The Iran-Iraq War 1980–1988.* London: Osprey, 2002.
Rogers, Will, Sharon Rogers, and Gene Gregston. *Storm Center: The USS Vincennes and Iran Flight 655: A Personal Account of Tragedy and Heroism.* Annapolis, MD: Naval Institute Press, 1992.

Iran Hostage Crisis (November 4, 1979–January 20, 1981)

Diplomatic confrontation between Iran and the United States that lasted 444 days (November 4, 1979–January 20, 1981) and involved the seizure and captivity of U.S. embassy personnel in Tehran by radical Iranian students. The standoff crippled President Jimmy Carter's administration, led to a second energy crisis, and contributed to the election of Ronald Reagan as U.S. president in November 1980. The genesis of the crisis was internal turmoil in Iran and a backlash against the regime of Mohammad Reza Shah Pahlavi (ca. 1941–1979), which began in earnest in 1978. By January 1979, mass protests and violence threatened to plunge Iran into chaos.

In 1953 Shah Pahlavi, a staunch ally of the United States, had been returned to power in a bloodless coup engineered by the U.S. Central Intelligence Agency (CIA) against nationalist Prime Minister Mohammed Mossadegh. The United States sold the shah's government billions of dollars of weaponry in return for an Iranian pledge to keep its oil flowing and work to prevent destabilization in the region. But the shah's regime was riddled with cronyism and corruption, and his efforts at reform, while genuine, were largely failures. The shah's secular regime was also bent on Westernizing Iran. Such efforts did not sit well with conservative Islamic opponents.

In early January 1979, nationwide protests against the shah forced him to flee the country on January 16, never to return. A new interim government was established, but it failed to win the support of rightist Islamic leaders who sought to establish an Islamic regime. The most important of the Islamic fundamentalists was Ayatollah Ruhollah Khomeini, who had spent many years in exile.

In February 1979, Khomeini returned to Iran. He refused to cooperate with the interim government and stirred up popular resentment against the United States. The situation in Iran continued to deteriorate as anti-Western demonstrations—encouraged by Khomeini and his supporters—rendered the interim government impotent. Khomeini's supporters began to act as the de facto government, giving him the power to engage in major policy decisions.

In October 1979, the Carter administration permitted the gravely ill shah to enter the United States for medical treatment. Carter's decision, while certainly justified on humanitarian grounds, sparked renewed anti-American protests in Iran. Declaring the United States as the "Great Satan," Khomeini incited his followers and other protesters to demonstrate their antipathy toward American interests.

On November 4, 1979, a mob of angry protesters, many of them young college students, stormed the U.S. embassy in Tehran, took control of it, and held some 70 embassy personnel hostage. These acts were a gross violation of international law, as it is understood that a nation's foreign embassies are extensions of its national sovereignty.

Although Khomeini probably did not order the taking of the embassy, he clearly supported the action as it unfolded and refused to negotiate in good faith with the United States. Thirteen women and nonwhite hostages were released during November 19–20, and one more was released in July 1980 for health reasons. In return for the release of the remaining hostages, the Iranians demanded that the shah be returned to Iran for trial, that the assets he took with him be immediately returned, and that the United States apologize for its meddling in Iranian affairs.

The Carter administration refused the conditions, and a long stalemate ensued. Carter incited more anti-American protests in Iran when he froze several billion dollars of

This photo of November 4, 1979, the first day of the occupation of the U.S. Embassy in Tehran, shows the American hostages being paraded by their militant Iranian captors. (Bettmann/Getty Images)

Iranian assets and halted the importation of Iranian oil to the United States. The moratorium on Iranian oil precipitated a full-blown oil crisis in the United States that drove gasoline and fuel oil prices to historic highs and wrecked an economy that was already teetering on the edge of a meltdown. When Carter left office in January 1981, inflation was at least 13 percent, and interest rates on certain consumer loans had skyrocketed to 18 percent or more. Further complicating the Iran hostage crisis was the Soviets' December 1979 invasion of Afghanistan, which put U.S.-Soviet relations in the deep freeze and upped the ante in superpower control over the Middle East.

Many Americans were deeply frustrated with the hostage crisis, which seemed to showcase American weakness despite its mighty military resources. They were also chagrined at the resultant energy crisis and deep economic recession. Carter spent much of his time trying to defuse and resolve the crisis but to no avail. Given the tense world situation and the worsening relations with the Soviet Union, the United States could ill afford to provoke a war in the Middle East. Indeed, to do so might have resulted in a direct confrontation with the Soviet Union. In April 1980, a secret operation to free the American hostages ended in disaster when a helicopter developed engine problems in the Iranian desert and two military planes collided in the ensuing chaos, killing eight servicemen.

The aborted mission was made public and served only to deepen U.S. pessimism toward the Carter administration and the ongoing crisis. Republican presidential nominee Ronald Reagan lambasted Carter's handling of the crisis and his foreign and domestic policies in general. Many Americans, fed up with the long hostage crisis, saw in Reagan an answer to the nation's emasculation. To his considerable credit, Carter chose to greatly limit his campaign appearances to give his undivided attention to the unfolding crisis. Reagan went on to win a relatively narrow victory in November 1980, owing in no small measure to the Iran Hostage Crisis.

By early January 1981, Carter had finally reached an agreement whereby the U.S. hostages would be freed. The United States promised to return some $8 billion in frozen

Iranian assets and lift trade sanctions against the country. Approximately 20 minutes after Reagan was sworn in as president on January 20, he announced that the hostages had been freed. Although the long affair was over, its impact on American and international politics continues to play out to the present.

Paul G. Pierpaoli Jr.

See also

Anglo-Iranian Oil Crisis; Carter Doctrine; Iran; Iran Hostage Rescue Mission; Khomeini, Ruhollah; Reza Shah Pahlavi

References

Carter, Jimmy. *Keeping Faith: Memoirs of a President.* Fayetteville: University of Arkansas Press, 1995.

Christopher, Warren. *American Hostages in Iran: The Conduct of a Crisis.* New Haven, CT: Yale University Press, 1985.

Iran Hostage Rescue Mission (Operation EAGLE CLAW, April 25, 1980)

Failed U.S. mission to rescue American hostages being held in Iran on April 25, 1980, code-named Operation EAGLE CLAW. On November 4, 1979, during the Iranian Revolution, radical Iranian students seized the U.S. embassy in Tehran, taking 52 Americans captive. The ensuing hostage crisis created a division within the Jimmy Carter administration. National Security Advisor Zbigniew Brzezinski urged the president to take a hard stance and was an ardent proponent of a rescue operation. Secretary of State Cyrus Vance opposed military action and believed that persistent and carefully constructed negotiations could resolve the crisis. He maintained that a rescue attempt would in fact place the captives in greater danger. Vance considered the Iranian threats against their lives to be purely rhetorical, as dead hostages would be of no value to the Iranians. He argued that if the captives were rescued, the terrorists would simply take more hostages. The secretary of state also asserted that military action against Iran could turn the entire Muslim world against the United States.

Initially President Carter, like Vance, feared that any military action would result in the execution of the hostages. The president did allow for tentative mission planning and preparation to begin, however.

On April 11, 1980, after the Iranian students publicly threatened the hostages, Carter gave his approval for a rescue attempt. He dismissed Vance's warnings about reprisals from other Middle Eastern countries, believing that Islamic fundamentalist Iran enjoyed little support from its Arab neighbors. The president determined that not taking action would be more costly than taking action. Indeed, he was especially concerned that the United States not appear soft on terrorism and weak in the eyes of leaders of the Soviet Union, with which relations had already rapidly deteriorated. Vance then resigned, having protested against the proposed rescue operation for nearly six months.

Carter and Brzezinski ordered the operation to proceed in accordance with four constraints. These were planning secrecy, protecting the lives of the hostages, keeping Iranian casualties to a minimum, and maintaining a small task force. The element of surprise was also encouraged. Carter met with the task force planners personally on April 16. The U.S. Army's Delta Force, commanded by Colonel Charles Beckwith, was charged with executing the raid, while Colonel James Kyle commanded the mission's air force elements. Meanwhile, White House chief of staff Hamilton Jordan met with representatives from Iran on April 18 in a final attempt to reach a diplomatic solution to the hostage crisis. He was informed that the Iranian government would not be able to address the issue until after parliamentary elections in mid-May. With his efforts to achieve an immediate diplomatic resolution frustrated and being under increasing pressure from the American public and media to take action, Carter authorized Operation EAGLE CLAW on April 23. He also made a fateful pledge to the task force commanders that he would accept full responsibility for the mission.

The ill-fated rescue mission never reached Tehran. The plan failed because of weather conditions over the Iranian desert and an unfortunate set of circumstances that occurred at the mission's forward refueling point, code-named Desert One. On April 24 when the mission began, sandstorms caused the operation to fall an hour behind schedule. Mechanical failures reduced the eight U.S. Navy RH-53D Sea Stallion helicopters in the mission to only five. Meanwhile, civilians in automobiles threatened operational secrecy by stumbling upon the forward refueling point. The decision to abort the mission because of the lack of serviceable helicopters had already been made when an accident occurred at Desert One around 2:00 a.m. on April 25. A helicopter rotor struck a grounded MC-130 transport aircraft, causing a massive explosion. The task force, including five wounded, was evacuated immediately. Eight dead American servicemen and the four remaining Sea Stallions were abandoned in the desert.

The failed operation was a dark episode in Carter's presidency. In August 1980, an investigative body led by Admiral James L. Holloway analyzed Operation EAGLE CLAW and concluded that the accident at the forward refueling point was the result of human error brought on by the dark, dusty, and cluttered conditions at Desert One. The government examined the state of U.S. special operations forces after the catastrophe at Desert One. The Senate Armed Services Committee consulted with Colonel Beckwith and drew several conclusions from the failed mission, including the importance of standardized training for all special operations forces and the need to create a permanent joint command. The committee also recommended the establishment of forward staging areas around the globe. These would allow special operations forces to be deployed faster and more efficiently. Based on these findings and those of the Holloway Committee, the Joint Special Operations Command was formed on December 15, 1980. In 1987, Congress created the position of assistant secretary of defense for special operations and low-intensity conflict and the United States Special Operations Command. Passage of this legislation guaranteed regular funding, standardized training, and specialized weapons and equipment for special operations forces in all branches of the U.S. military.

The American hostages were not released until January 20, 1981. The failure to secure their freedom earlier undoubtedly helped Republican Ronald Reagan win the presidency in the November 1980 elections.

Jeffrey LaMonica

See also
Iran, Islamic Revolution in

References
Beckwith, Charlie, and Donald Knox. *Delta Force: The Army's Elite Counterterrorist Unit.* New York: Avon Books, 1983.
Carter, Jimmy. *Keeping Faith: Memoirs of a President.* Fayetteville: University of Arkansas Press, 1982.
Cogan, Charles. "Desert One and Its Disorders." *Journal of Military History* 67 (2003): 273–296.
Jordan, Hamilton. *Crisis: The Last Year of the Carter Presidency.* New York: Putnam, 1982.
Kyle, James, and John Eidson. *The Guts to Try: The Untold Story of the Iran Hostage Rescue Mission by the On-Scene Desert Commander.* New York: Orion Books, 1990.
Ryan, Paul. *The Iranian Rescue Mission.* Annapolis, MA: Naval Institute Press, 1985.

Iran-Iraq War (1980–1988)

The war between Iran and Iraq during September 22, 1980–August 20, 1988, marked a continuation of the ancient Persian-Arab rivalry fueled by 20th-century border disputes and competition for hegemony in the Persian Gulf and Middle East regions. In the late 1970s the long-standing rivalry between these two nations was abetted by a collision between the Pan-Islamism and revolutionary Shia Islamism of Iran and the Pan-Arab nationalism of Iraq.

The border between the two states had been contested for some time, and in 1969 Iran had abrogated its treaty with Iraq on the navigation of the Shatt al-Arab waterway, Iraq's only outlet to the Persian Gulf. In 1971 Iran had seized islands in the Persian Gulf, and there had been border clashes between the two states in middecade. The rivalry between the two states was also complicated by minorities issues. Both states, especially Iraq, have large Kurdish populations in their northern regions, while an Arab minority inhabits the oil-rich Iranian province of Khuzestan.

Given their long-standing rivalry and ambitions, it was natural that the leaders of both states would seek to exploit any perceived weakness in the other. Thus, Iraqi president Saddam Hussein sought to take advantage of the upheaval following the fall of Mohammad Reza Shah Pahlavi and the establishment of Ayatollah Ruhollah Khomeini's Islamic Republic after the Iranian Revolution (Islamic Revolution) of 1978–1979. This event had been precipitated by the disbandment of the shah's military establishment and an end to U.S. military assistance to Iran, which meant a shortage of spare parts. Hussein saw in this situation an opportunity to punish Iran for its support of Kurdish and Shia opposition to Sunni Muslim domination in Iraq. More important, it was a chance for Iraq to reclaim both banks of the Shatt al-Arab as well as Khuzestan; acquire the islands of Abu Musa, Greater Tunb, and Lesser Tunb on behalf of the United Arab Emirates; and overthrow the militant Islamic regime in Iran.

On the eve of the war, Iraq enjoyed an advantage in ground forces, while Iran had the edge in the air. Iraq had a regular army of some 300,000 men, 1,000 artillery pieces, 2,700 tanks, 332 fighter aircraft, and 40 helicopters. Iran had a regular army of 200,000 men, somewhat more than 1,000 artillery pieces, 1,740 tanks, 445 fighter aircraft, and 500 helicopters.

The war began on September 22, 1980, when Iraqi forces invaded western Iran along their common border. The Iraqi attack came as a complete surprise to Iran. Hussein justified it as a response to an alleged assassination attempt sponsored by Iran on Iraqi foreign minister Tariq Aziz. Striking on a 300-mile front, Iraqi troops were initially successful against the disorganized Iranian defenders. The Iraqis drove into southwestern Iran, securing the far side of the Shatt al-Arab. In November they captured Khorramshahr

Iraqi soldiers on the front lines in March 1982 during the Iran-Iraq War (1980–1988). (Peter Jordan/Time Life Pictures/Getty Images)

in Khuzestan Province. In places, the Iraqis penetrated as much as 30 miles into Iran. But Iran is a large country, and the Iraqi forces moved too cautiously, throwing away the opportunity for a quick and decisive victory. Another factor in their stalled offensive was certainly the rapid Iranian mobilization of resources, especially the largely untrained but fanatical Pasdaran (Revolutionary Guard Corps) militia.

Recovering from the initial shock of the Iraqi invasion, the Iranians soon established strong defensive positions. Iran's navy also carried out an effective blockade of Iraq. On the first day of the war, Iraqi air strikes destroyed much of the Iranian Air Force infrastructure, but most of the Iranian aircraft survived, and Iraq lacked the long-range bomber aircraft to be truly effective strategically against a country as large as Iran. Indeed, Iranian pilots flying U.S.-manufactured aircraft soon secured air superiority over the Iraqi Air Force's Soviet-built airplanes. The Iranians were then able to carry out ground support missions utilizing both airplanes and helicopters that played an important role in checking the Iraqi advance.

Far from breaking Iranian morale as Hussein had hoped, the Iraqi attack served to rally public opinion around the Islamic regime. Ideologically committed Iranians flocked to join the Pasdaran and the army. By March 1981, the war had settled into a protracted stalemate. With both sides having constructed extensive defensive positions, much of the combat came to resemble the trench warfare of World War I.

In January 1982, Jordanian volunteers began arriving to assist the Iraqis, but this addition had little impact on the fighting. Then on March 22, the Iranians launched a major counteroffensive. Their forces included large numbers of ill-trained but fanatical Pasdaran fighters. Lasting until March 30, the offensive enjoyed considerable success, driving the Iraqis back as far as 24 miles in places.

During April 30–May 20 the Iranians renewed their attacks, again pushing the Iraqis back. Then on the night of May 22–23, the Iranians encircled the city of Khorramshahr, which the Iraqis had captured at the beginning of the war, forcing its surrender on May 24. There the Iranians captured large quantities of Soviet-manufactured weapons. Flush with victory, the Iranians now proclaimed as their war aim the overthrow of Saddam Hussein.

With the war now going badly for his country, Hussein proposed a truce and the withdrawal of all Iraqi troops from Iranian soil within two weeks of a truce agreement. Iraq also declared a unilateral cease-fire. Sensing victory, Iran rejected the proposal and reiterated its demand for the ouster of Hussein.

Given the Iranian rebuff and realizing that he had no legitimate hope of retaining his forces in Iran, Hussein now withdrew them back into well-prepared static defenses in Iraq, reasoning that Iraqis would rally to his regime in a fight to defend their homeland. For political reasons, Hussein announced that the purpose of the withdrawal was to allow Iraqi forces to assist Lebanon, which had been invaded by Israeli forces on June 6, 1982.

Meanwhile, Iranian leaders rejected a Saudi Arabian–brokered deal that would have witnessed the payment of $70 billion in war reparations by the Arab states to Iran and complete Iraqi withdrawal from Iranian territory in return for a peace agreement. Iranian leaders insisted that Hussein be removed from power, that some 100,000 Shiites expelled from Iraq before the war be permitted to return home, and that the reparations figure be set at $150 billion. There is some suggestion that Iran did not expect these terms to be accepted and hoped to use the failure of negotiations as justification to continue the war with an invasion of Iraq. Indeed, Iranian leader Ayatollah Khomeini announced his intention to install an Islamic republic in Iraq.

The Iranians now sought to utilize their numerical advantage in a new offensive, which was launched on July 20, 1982. It was directed against Shiite-dominated southern Iraq, with the objective being the capture of Iraq's second-largest city, Basra. Iranian human-wave assaults, occasioned by a shortage of ammunition, encountered well-prepared Iraqi static defenses, supported by artillery. Hussein had also managed to increase substantially the number of Iraqis under arms.

Although the Iranians did manage to register some modest gains, these came at heavy human cost. In the five human-wave assaults of their Basra offensive (Operation RAMADAN), the Iranians sustained tens of thousands of casualties. Particularly hard hit were the untrained and poorly armed units of boy-soldiers who volunteered to march into Iraqi minefields to clear them with their bodies for the trained Iranian soldiers, who would follow. The Iraqis also employed poison gas against the Iranians, inflicting many casualties. On July 21, Iranian aircraft struck Baghdad. Iraq retaliated in August with attacks on the vital Iranian oil-shipping facilities at Khargh Island, which also sank several ships.

During September–November, the Iranians launched new offensives in the northern part of the front, securing some territory near the border town of Samar, which Iraq had taken at the beginning of the war. The Iranians also struck west of Dezful and, in early November, drove several miles into Iraq near Mandali. Iraqi counterattacks forced the Iranians back into their own territory. In the southern part of the front on November 17, the Iranians advanced to within artillery range of the vital Baghdad-Basra Highway.

Iran was now receiving supplies from such nations as the People's Republic of China, the Democratic People's Republic of Korea (North Korea), and Albania. Iraq was securing supplies from the Soviet Union and other Warsaw Pact states as well as from France, Great Britain, Spain, Egypt, Saudi Arabia, and the United States. Iraq's chief financial backers were Saudi Arabia, Kuwait, and the United Arab Emirates.

In the course of 1983, Iran launched five major offensives against Iraq. Before the first of these, however, during February 2–March 9 the Iraqi Air Force carried out large-scale air attacks against Iranian coastal oil-production facilities, producing the largest oil spill in the history of the Persian Gulf region. Again seeking to utilize their advantage in troop strength, during February 7–16 Iranian leaders launched a ground attack hoping to isolate Basra by cutting the Baghdad-Basra Highway at Kut. They drove to within 30 miles of their objective but were then halted and thrown back. In the fighting, the Iraqis claimed to have destroyed upward of 1,000 Iranian tanks.

During April 11–14, the Iranians attacked west of Dezful but failed to make meaningful gains. On July 20, Iraqi aircraft again struck Iranian oil-production facilities. Three days later, the Iranians attacked in northern Iraq but again registered few gains. The Iranians mounted a major offensive west of Dezful on July 30 but failed to break through. In the second week in August, however, the Iranians blunted an Iraqi counterattack. Both sides suffered heavy casualties.

In late October the Iranians launched yet another attack in the north to close a salient there opened by Iranian Kurdish rebels. Iraqi leader Hussein was disappointed in his hope that the failed Iranian ground offensives and ensuing heavy casualties would make that regime more amenable to peace talks. Indeed, Iranian leader Ayatollah Khomeini restated his determination to overthrow the Iraqi regime.

Determined to prevent the spread of militant Islamism in the Middle East, the Ronald Reagan administration in the United States made a firm commitment to support Iraq. Washington supplied Baghdad with intelligence information in the form of satellite photography and also furnished economic aid and weapons. In a National Security decision directive of June 1982, Reagan determined that the United

States must do whatever necessary to prevent Iraq from losing the war.

Believing that more aggressive tactics were necessary to induce Iran to talk peace, Hussein announced that unless Iran agreed to halt offensive action against Iraq by February 7, 1984, he would order major attacks against 11 Iranian cities. Iran then mounted a ground attack in the northern part of the front, and Hussein ordered air and missile attacks against the cities to proceed. These lasted until February 22. Iran retaliated in what became known as the War of the Cities. There were five such air campaigns in the course of the war.

On February 15, 1984, the Iranians launched the first in a series of ground offensives. It fell in the central part of the front and pitted 250,000 Iranian troops against an equal number of Iraqi defenders. During February 15–22 in Operation DAWN 5 and during February 22–24 in Operation DAWN 6, the Iranians attempted to take the city of Kut to cut the vital Baghdad-Basra Highway there. The Iranians came within 15 miles of the city but were then halted.

The Iranians enjoyed more success in Operation KHANIBAR during February 24–March 19. This renewed drive against Basra came close to breaking through the stretched Iraqi defenders. The Iranians did capture part of the Majnoon Islands, with their undeveloped oil fields, then held them against an Iraqi counterattack supported by poison gas. The Iranians occupied these islands until near the end of the war.

With his forces having benefited from substantial arms purchases financed by the oil-rich Persian Gulf states, on January 18, 1985, Hussein launched the first Iraqi ground offensive since late 1980. It failed to register significant gains, and the Iranians responded with their own offensive, Operation BADR, beginning on March 11. Now better trained, the Iranian Army eschewed the costly human-wave tactics of the past, and its more effective tactics brought the capture of a portion of the Baghdad-Basra Highway. Hussein responded to this considerable strategic emergency with chemical weapons attacks and renewed air and missile strikes against 20 Iranian cities, including Tehran.

In February 17, 1986, in a surprise offensive employing commandos, Iranian forces captured the strategically important Iraqi port of Faw, southeast of Basra at the southeast end of the Faw Peninsula on the Shatt al-Arab waterway. In January 1987, Iran launched Operation KARBALA-5, a renewed effort to capture Basra. When the operation ground to a halt in mid-February, the Iranians launched NASR-4 in northern Iraq, which threatened the Iraqi city of Kirkuk during May–June.

The so-called Tanker War had begun in March 1984 with the Iraqi air attack on strategic Kharg Island and nearby oil installations. Iran had then retaliated with attacks, including the use of mines, against tankers carrying Iraqi oil from Kuwait and on any tankers of the Persian Gulf states supporting Iraq. On November 1, 1986, the Kuwaiti government petitioned the international community to protect its tankers. The Soviet Union agreed to charter tankers, and on March 7, 1987, the United States announced that it would provide protection for any U.S.-flagged tankers. This would protect neutral tankers proceeding to or from Iraqi ports, ensuring that Iraq would have the economic means to continue the war.

On the night of May 17, 1987, an Iraqi French-manufactured Mirage F-1 fighter aircraft on antiship patrol fired two AM-39 Exocet antiship cruise missiles at a radar contact, apparently not knowing that it was the U.S. Navy frigate *Stark* (FFG-31). Although only one of the missiles detonated, both struck home and crippled the frigate, killing 37 crewmen and injuring another 50. The crew managed to save their ship, which then made port under its own power.

On July 20, 1987, the United Nations (UN) Security Council passed unanimously U.S.-sponsored Resolution 598. The resolution deplored attacks on neutral shipping and called for an immediate cease-fire and withdrawal of armed forces to internationally recognized boundaries. On July 24, 1987, the United States initiated Operation EARNEST WILL to protect oil tankers and shipping lanes in the Persian Gulf.

Acting in retaliation for Iranian ground offensives, during February 1988 the Iraqis launched a renewed wave of attacks against Iranian population centers, and the Iranians reciprocated. These attacks included not only aircraft but also surface-to-surface missiles, principally the Soviet-built Scud type. Iraq fired many more missiles than did Iran (reportedly some 520 as opposed to 177). Also, during February and extending into September, the Iraqi Army carried out a massacre of Kurds in northern Iraq, known as the al-Anfal (Spoils of War) Campaign. It claimed as many as 300,000 civilian lives and the destruction of some 4,000 villages.

Meanwhile, on April 14, 1988, the U.S. Navy frigate *Samuel B. Roberts,* involved in Operation EARNEST WILL, was badly damaged when it struck an Iranian mine in the Persian Gulf. No one was killed, but the ship nearly sank. Four days later, the navy responded with Operation PRAYING MANTIS, the navy's largest battle involving surface warships since World War II. This one-sided battle also saw the first surface-to-surface missile engagement in U.S. naval history. U.S.

forces damaged two Iranian offshore oil platforms, sank one Iranian frigate and a gunboat, damaged another frigate, and sank three Iranian speedboats. The United States lost one helicopter.

By the spring of 1988, Iraqi forces had been sufficiently reorganized to enable them to launch major operations. By contrast, Iran was now desperately short of spare parts, especially for its largely U.S.-built aircraft. The Iranians had also lost a large number of aircraft in combat operations. As a result, by late 1987 Iran was less able to mount an effective defense against the resupplied Iraqi Air Force, let alone carry out aerial counterattacks against a ground attack.

The Iraqis mounted four separate offensives in the spring of 1988. In the process they were able to recapture the strategically important Faw Peninsula, which had been lost in 1986; drive the Iranians away from Basra; and make progress in the northern part of the front. The Iraqi victories came at little cost to themselves, while the Iranians suffered heavy personnel and equipment losses. These Iranian setbacks were the chief factor behind Khomeini's decision to agree to a cease-fire as called for in UN Security Council Resolution 598.

On July 3, 1988, the crew of the U.S. Navy cruiser *Vincennes*, patrolling in the Persian Gulf and believing that they were under attack by an Iranian jet fighter, shot down Iran Air Flight 655, a civilian airliner carrying 290 passengers and crew. There were no survivors. The U.S. government subsequently agreed to pay $131.8 million in compensation for the incident. It expressed regret only for the loss of innocent life and did not apologize to the Iranian government. The incident may have served to convince Iranian leader Ayatollah Khomeini of the dangers of the United States actively entering the conflict against Iran and thus made him more amenable to ending the war.

War weariness and pressure from other governments induced both sides to accept a cease-fire agreement on August 20, 1988, bringing the eight-year war to a close. Total Iraqi casualties, including 60,000 men taken prisoner by Iran, numbered about 375,000 (perhaps 200,000 of these killed). This figure does not include those killed in the Iraqi government campaign against its own Kurdish population. Iran announced a death toll of nearly 300,000 people, but some estimates place the figure as high as 1 million or more. The war ended with a status quo ante bellum, with none of the outstanding issues resolved. The UN-arranged cease-fire merely ended the fighting, leaving these two isolated states to pursue an arms race with each other and with the other states in the region.

Negotiations between Iraq and Iran remained deadlocked for two years after the cease-fire. In 1990 Iraq, concerned with securing its forcible annexation of Kuwait, reestablished diplomatic relations with Iran and agreed to the withdrawal of Iraqi troops from occupied Iranian territory, the division of sovereignty over the Shatt al-Arab, and a prisoner-of-war exchange.

Hussein, despite having led his nation into a disastrous war, emerged from it with the strongest military in the Middle East, second only to Israel. His power unchallenged in Iraq, he trumpeted a great national victory. The war, however, put Iraq deeply in debt to its Persian Gulf Arab neighbors, and this played a strong role in the coming of the Persian Gulf War. Indeed, the $14 billion debt owed to Kuwait was a key factor in Iraq's decision to invade that nation in 1990. In Iran, the war helped consolidate popular support behind the Islamic Revolution.

SPENCER C. TUCKER

See also
EARNEST WILL, Operation; Hussein, Saddam; Iran; Iraq; Khomeini, Ruhollah; Kurds, Massacres of; PRAYING MANTIS, Operation; *Stark* Incident

References
Cooper, Tom. *Iran-Iraq War in the Air: 1980–1988.* Atglen, PA: Schiffer Publishing, 2004.
Farrokh, Kaveh. *Iran at War: 1500–1988.* Oxford, UK: Osprey, 2011.
Hiro, Dilip. *The Longest War: The Iran-Iraq Military Conflict.* London: Routledge, 1990.
Johnson, Rob. *The Iran-Iraq War.* Houndmills, Basingstoke, Hampshire, UK: Palgrave Macmillan, 2010.
Karsh, Efraim. *The Iran-Iraq War: 1980–1988.* Oxford, UK: Osprey, 2002.
Murray, Williamson, and Kevin Murray. *The Iran-Iraq War: A Military and Strategic History.* New York: Cambridge University Press, 2014.
Pollack, Kenneth M. *Arabs at War: Military Effectiveness, 1948–1991.* Lincoln: University of Nebraska Press, 2004.
Rajaee, Farhang. *The Iran-Iraq War: The Politics of Aggression.* Gainesville: University Press of Florida, 1993.
Razoux, Pierre. *The Iran-Iraq War.* Translated by Nicholas Elliott. Cambridge, MA: Belknap Press of Harvard University Press, 2015.
Willet, Edward C. *The Iran-Iraq War.* New York: Rosen, 2004.

Iran Nuclear Deal (July 14, 2015)

Western leaders had long held that the Islamic Republic of Iran was seeking to build a nuclear weapon, while Tehran repeated insisted that its nuclear program was solely for peaceful purposes. Following years of informal talks and missed deadlines, agreement was finally reached on July 14, 2015. What became known as the Joint Comprehensive Plan of Action (JCPOA) was formally adopted on October 18, 2015, and implemented on January 16, 2016.

The Islamic Republic of Iran had long been a fierce enemy of Israel, committed in its public utterances at least to the destruction of the Jewish state. Israeli prime minister Benjamin Netanyahu, whose government had on several occasions actively considered a military strike against Iran in an effort to destroy or at least set back its nuclear research, claimed that Iran would find ways to violate any agreement. On March 3, 2015, in an unprecedented step, Netanyahu, who was then two weeks away from a national election, addressed a joint session of the U.S. Congress, invited to do so by the Republican party leadership in the House of Representatives without consulting with President Barack Obama. Netanyahu offered no new plan but warned Obama against accepting a nuclear deal with Iran that would, he believed, be a "countdown to a potential nuclear nightmare" by a country that "is as radical as ever," cannot be trusted, and "will always be an enemy of America."

Iran was eager to see sanctions imposed on it by the Western powers lifted in order to help jump-start its moribund economy. Both sides then agreed to open formal talks. The negotiations involved the Republic of Iran on the one side and a group of world powers, known as the P5+1 (the permanent members of the United Nations Security Council, consisting of the United States, the United Kingdom, Russia, France, and China plus Germany) and the European Union. (These negotiators were alternately known as the EU3+3 for the three members of the European Union and three other powers.)

Negotiations for a framework deal took placed in Lausanne, Switzerland, during a series of meetings between March 26 and April 2, 2015. Agreement on a framework deal was announced in a press conference on April 2.

Then on July 14, negotiators concluded the final agreement in Vienna, Austria. It provided for a rolling back of Iran's nuclear work in exchange for the easing of the economic sanctions that had been imposed on Iran. The agreement called for Iran to reduce the number of centrifuges enriching uranium by two-thirds, from about 19,000 to 5,060. This restriction would last for 10 years. The centrifuges taken out of operation would be stored in a site monitored by the International Atomic Energy Agency (IAEA). Iran also pledged not to enrich uranium beyond 3.67 percent and to reduce its total stockpile of uranium by some 98 percent from 10,000 kilograms to 300 kilograms. These constraints would be in place for 15 years. Provision was made for the excess stockpile to be sold overseas or downgraded to a lower level of enrichment.

Iran was permitted to maintain one nuclear enrichment site, Natanz. Its underground Fordo site would be converted into a "nuclear, physics and technology center." Iran also agreed to rebuild its heavy water reactor at Arak so that it was unable to produce weapons-grade plutonium.

International experts held that these measures would increase the amount of time it would take Iran to produce one nuclear bomb, referred to as "breakout time," to one year. Analysts then currently estimated Iran's breakout time to be only two to three months.

Under the deal, IAEA inspectors were to have increased access to Iran's uranium enrichment sites for 25 years. Iran's supreme leader Ali Khamenei had rejected allowing inspectors into military facilities and giving them interviews with nuclear scientists, both of which the United States had insisted were vital. Under a compromise, the final deal outlined a dispute-resolution mechanism if Iran turns down IAEA requests for access.

Once the IAEA verified that Iran has complied with the restrictions on its nuclear program, the United Nations, the European Union, and the United States were to lift nuclear-related sanctions on the country. The agreement included a "snap-back" provision, which called for the quick reimposition of sanctions if the agreement were to be violated. Possible violations would be investigated and UN sanctions reintroduced within 65 days.

The international arms embargo on Iran—a key sticking point in the final weeks of the negotiations—was to be gradually lifted. The UN ban on Iran trading in conventional weapons would end after five years, followed by the ban on ballistic missile technology after eight years. Both of those timelines could be moved up if the IAEA concludes that Iran's nuclear program is entirely peaceful.

The deal met with public celebrations in Iran but came under immediate harsh criticism from the Israeli government and from a number of Republicans in the U.S. Congress. Particularly concerning was a required review by the U.S. Congress that could hold up the easing of some U.S. sanctions relief for 60 days but was unlikely to upend the deal in its entirety. President Barack Obama, who presented the agreement to the American public in televised remarks, stressed the safeguards involved and said that the only alternative to it is a military option, which he said would cost trillions of dollars and countless lives. In August 2015, the British government heralded what it called a new atmosphere in Tehran and reopened its embassy in Tehran almost four years after it had been closed after protesters had attacked the building.

The Joint Comprehensive Plan of Action was implemented on January 16, 2016. On that date Iran released 4 imprisoned Iranian Americans. Another American left Iran in a separate arrangement. In exchange, the United States released 7 Iranian Americans it was holding and dismissed outstanding charges against 14 Iranians outside the United States. At the same time, the U.S. government flew to Iran pallets of currency totaling $400 million, part of $1.7 billion in Iranian assets frozen by the U.S. government. Although Iran was legally entitled to the funds, this drew considerable criticism as the timing looked as if it was an arms for hostage swap, prohibited by U.S. law. Republican Party presidential candidate Donald J. Trump was especially critical and condemned the JCPOA outright.

After implementation of the JCPOA, relations between Iran and the West remained mixed at best, Iran having been actively involved in providing direct military support to the Bashar al-Assad regime in the Syrian Civil War (2011–present) and to the Houthi rebels in the Yemen Civil War (2015–present). The United States imposed several new nonnuclear sanctions against Iran, some of which were condemned by Iran as a possible violation of the deal. Then in early March 2016 Iran carried out ballistic missile tests, with one of the Qadr H missiles carrying the inscription "Israel should be wiped off the Earth." Israel called on Western powers to punish Iran for the tests, which Washington said did not violate the nuclear deal but may well have violated United Nations Security Council Resolution 2231, which the Iranians rejected out of hand. On March 17, however, the U.S. Treasury Department sanctioned Iranian and British companies for involvement in the Iranian ballistic missile program.

Meanwhile, Trump had vowed during the 2016 presidential campaign to scuttle the agreement, which he deemed "the worst deal ever." On May 8, 2018, he dealt the agreement a potentially fatal blow when he formally withdrew the United States from the nuclear deal. His administration cited the deal's so-called sunset provisions and Iran's continuing destabilizing actions in the Middle East as justifications for the withdrawal. His administration held out faint hope that a new deal might be reached with Tehran in the future, but Iran had already stated that it would not engage in any more negotiations concerning its nuclear program. The other parties to the nuclear agreement vowed to continue its provisions and remained committed to the deal. Iran has asserted, however, that it might renege on its commitments if the remaining parties are unable to blunt the effects of the U.S. withdrawal, including renewed U.S. sanctions against Tehran. By August 2018, the U.S. and Iranian governments were engaged in a bitter war of words and mutual recriminations. Meanwhile, Iran's flagging economy was fueling large demonstrations and mounting unrest within Iran.

Spencer C. Tucker

See also
Assad, Bashar al-; Iran; Netanyahu, Benjamin; Syrian Civil War; Yemen Civil War

References
Solomon, Jay, and Carol E. Lee. "Iran Agrees to Outline of Deal." *Wall Street Journal,* April 3, 2015.
U.S. Department of State. "Joint Comprehensive Plan of Action." https://www.state.gov/e/eb/tfs/spi/iran/jcpoa/.
Weisman, Jonathan, and Julie Hirschfeld Davis. "Republican Lawmakers Vow Fight to Derail Nuclear Deal." *New York Times,* July 14, 2015.

Iraq

The Republic of Iraq encompasses 169,234 square miles. Slightly smaller in size than the U.S. state of California, Iraq is the third-largest state in the Middle East behind only Saudi Arabia and Iran. Iraq is bordered by Saudi Arabia to the west and south, Kuwait and the Persian Gulf (for 36 miles) to the south, Iran to the east, and Syria and Turkey to the north. Because of its size, oil wealth, and strategic location, Iraq has played a key regional role.

Iraq's 2018 population was some 39.3 million. Baghdad is the country's capital and largest city. Arabs constitute 75–80 percent of the population, while 15 percent are Kurds. Assyrians, Turkmen, and much smaller minorities such as Mandeans, Armenians, Circassians, Iranians, Shabakis, Yazidis, and Kawliyas constitute 5–10 percent. Around 95 percent of the population is Muslim. Although Sunnis dominated the Iraqi power structure in the second half of the 20th century, Shiites, concentrated in southern Iraq, constitute as much as 65 percent of Iraqi Muslims today. Christianity, Yarsanism, Yezidism, and Mandeanism are also present.

Known as the "Cradle of Civilization," Iraq occupies Mesopotamia, the historic fertile "land between the rivers," referring to the Tigris and Euphrates Rivers, that saw the world's oldest civilization, the Sumerian, about 4,000 BCE. Sumeria introduced the first writing system and thus recorded history. The Babylonian and Assyrian Empires that followed projected their power as far as the Caucasus, Persia, Egypt, and Arabia. In the sixth century BCE, King

IRAQ

Cyrus II the Great of Persia defeated the forces of the Neo-Babylonian Empire. In the fourth century BCE, it was the turn of Alexander III the Great of Macedon. The Parthians conquered the region in the third century BCE. The Romans then took control. The Sassanid Persians absorbed the region in 224 CE, and for the next four centuries today's Iraq was a Persian province.

The Arabs conquered Mesopotamia during 633–644 and established Islam as the predominant religion. The move of the Abbasid Empire's capital in 750 from Damascus to Baghdad gave Iraq renewed prominence. By the ninth century, Baghdad was an economic and cultural center for the entire Muslim world.

Iraq fell under Black Sheep Turkmen rule in the 14th and 15th centuries, but in 1466 the White Sheep Turkmen defeated their rivals and assumed control. In 1533 Iraq came under rule by the Ottoman Turks, although there were periods of Persian hegemony, and in 1747 Iraq was ruled by the Mamluks. In 1831, however, the Ottomans overthrew the Mamluks and assumed direct rule.

During World War I the Ottoman Empire declared for the Central Powers. The Allied victory in the war saw Britain as master of the former Ottoman provinces of Mosul, Baghdad, and Basra, which form modern-day Iraq, and on April 28, 1920, the San Remo Agreement awarded Iraq to Britain as a League of Nations mandate.

British ally Faisal bin Hussein bin Ali al-Hashimi of the Hashemite dynasty had led the Arab Revolt against the Ottomans in World War I and was proclaimed king of Syria by the Syrian National Congress in Damascus in March 1920. Syria had been assigned to the French, however, and a French army drove him out in July. The British then promised Faisal Iraq as a new kingdom. During May–October 1920, however, the British were obliged to put down a revolt in Iraq against their rule, which they accomplished largely through airpower in the form of Royal Air Force bombers.

On August 23, 1921, the British formally installed Faisal as king of Iraq. The Anglo-Iraqi Treaty of October 10, 1922, granted Iraq independence but left Britain in control of foreign and military affairs. Faisal was king until his death, probably through poisoning, on September 8, 1933.

Iraq's strategic importance was greatly enhanced by the discovery of oil in 1925. Although the British formally granted Iraq its independence on October 3, 1932, they retained considerable influence. The treaty protected British oil interests and granted Britain military bases. Faisal attempted to build a unified nation, but Iraq, like so much else of the Middle East, was an arbitrary creation and was badly fractured between Sunnis and Shias; among Arabs, Kurds, and Turkman; and between urban and rural attitudes.

In December 1938, pro-British general Nuri al-Said became prime minister. Instability increased when King Ghazi I died in an accident on April 4, 1939. With the new king Faisal II being only four years old, his uncle Abdul Illah became regent. Nuri put down an attempted army coup in March 1939 and another in February 1940. He wanted to declare war on Germany but encountered opposition from Iraqi nationalists, who insisted on concessions from Britain first. In consequence, Nuri declared Iraq's neutrality, severing relations with Germany but not those with Italy.

Axis successes in the Mediterranean beginning in the fall of 1940 encouraged Iraqi nationalists, who saw circumstances favorable to ending remaining British control. In March 1940 Rashid Ali Rashid Ali al-Gaylani replaced Nuri and came under the influence of four nationalist pro-Axis generals who called themselves the Golden Square. In May 1941, however, the regent forced Gaylani to resign because of the latter's pro-Axis connections. Taha al-Hashimi became prime minister.

Axis military successes and hints of aid emboldened the Golden Square, who staged a coup on April 2 and restored Gaylani to power. He immediately formed a cabinet with men of Axis inclinations. The regent and Nuri both fled.

Iraq was now a major oil producer (2.5 million metric tons in 1940), and had it sided with the Axis, its location on the Persian Gulf would also have enabled Germany to threaten the British lifeline to India. Encouraged by hints of Axis aid, on May 2, 1941, Iraqi troops opened artillery fire on the British air base at Habbaniya. The Royal Air Force immediately went into action, and Britain also dispatched some 5,800 troops, including the 1,500-man Arab Legion from Transjordan. It was clear that without immediate Axis assistance the British would triumph.

The German government brought pressure to bear on Vichy France, which allowed Axis aid to transit through Syria to Mosul, albeit in insufficient quantities to affect the outcome. British forces broke the siege at Habbaniya, occupied Fallujah, and surrounded Baghdad by the end of May. Gaylani and some supporters then fled to Iran. In deference to Nuri and Regent Abdul Illah, the British did not enter Baghdad, a decision that allowed the remnants of the Golden Square to attack Baghdad's Jewish community and kill some 150 Jews.

Again prime minister Nuri set up a pro-British administration, and Iraq became an important supply center for Allied assistance to the Soviet Union. Iraq declared war on the Axis on January 16, 1943.

Israel's declaration of independence on May 14, 1948, brought declarations of war from the Arab states. Iraq provided some 18,000 troops in the Israeli War of Independence (1948–1949). Arab military failure in the war brought persecution of Iraqi Jews, whose loyalty was suspect, a process repeated during subsequent Arab-Israeli wars.

In 1955 Iraq joined the pro-Western Baghdad Pact, allying itself with Turkey, Iran, and Pakistan in a mutual defense agreement sponsored by the United States, which, however, was not a member. The pact was a direct affront to the long-simmering nationalist sentiments within the Iraqi Army. Indeed, the pact became the catalyst that ignited revolution in 1958, the first in a string of coups and countercoups plaguing Iraq until the Baathists finally consolidated power in 1968.

On July 14, 1958, members of the secret nationalist organization known as the Free Officers Movement, led by Colonel Abd al-Karim Qasim, seized control of Baghdad and executed both Faisal II and Nuri. The revolutionaries then abolished the monarchy, proclaimed Iraq a republic, and sought closer ties to the Soviet Union. Qasim became prime minister, but his policies ultimately brought internal conflict. In the Ramadan Revolution of February 9, 1963, a coalition of anticommunist military officers and secular Arab nationalists and Baathists in Baghdad overthrew Qasim, who was slain.

Colonel Abdul Salam Arif became president, with Hasan al-Bakr as prime minister. But members of the National Council of the Revolutionary Command who had taken the reins of power soon turned against one another. The military and the Baath Party were fundamentally at odds regarding policy. President Arif died in a helicopter crash on April 13, 1966, perhaps the result of sabotage by Baathist elements in the military. His more pliable brother, Abdul Rahman Arif, took over and was president until 1968.

Iraq's failure to support fellow Arab states in the Six-Day War (June 5–10, 1967) led to widespread rioting in Baghdad. Then on July 17, 1968, members of the Baath Party seized key locations in Baghdad. Ahmed Hasan al-Bakr became president, prime minister, and secretary-general of the Revolutionary Command Council. His cousin Saddam Hussein worked to eliminate opponents of the new regime. Hussein proved to be an adroit though ruthless operator, and his patronage system broke down the historic bonds in Iraqi society.

The new Baathist regime did institute numerous needed reforms. These included agricultural investment, land reform, the renegotiation of oil contracts, and hospital and school construction. All were designed to bring all of the country into the regime's broader network of patronage. With corruption widespread, most economic reforms were unsuccessful. From 1973 onward Iraq was largely dependent on oil revenues. Iraq played only a minor role in the Yom Kippur War (Ramadan War) of October 1973, with an armored division assisting the Syrians on the Golan Heights front. On July 16, 1979, al-Bakr left office, ostensibly for reasons of health. Hussein was now president, ruler of Iraq in name and fact.

Early in 1979 Iran underwent a revolution that led to an Islamic Republic under Ayatollah Ruhollah Khomeini. The long-standing rivalry between Iran and Iraq for regional hegemony was abetted by border disputes and a collision between the Pan-Islamism of Iran and the Pan-Arab nationalism of Iraq. In many ways, however, the ensuing clash was a continuation of the ancient Persian-Arab rivalry, fueled by 20th-century border disputes and competition for hegemony in the Persian Gulf region and the Middle East.

The border had been contested for some time, and in 1969 Iran had abrogated its treaty with Iraq on the navigation of the Shatt al-Arab waterway, Iraq's only outlet to the Persian Gulf. Iran had seized Persian Gulf islands in 1971, and there were border clashes between the two states in middecade. Minorities' issues also intruded. Both states, especially Iraq, have large Kurdish populations in their northern regions, while an Arab minority inhabits the oil-rich Iranian province of Khuzestan, and the Shia Muslim majority population of Iraq is concentrated in the south of that country.

Hussein sought to take advantage of the upheaval following the establishment of Khomeini's Islamic fundamentalist regime, which had ended U.S. military assistance to Iran, meaning a shortage of spare parts. In deciding to go to war with Iran, Hussein sought to secure both banks of the Shatt al-Arab and Khuzestan Province, acquire islands on behalf of the United Arab Emirates, and overthrow Iran's Islamic regime. On the eve of war Iraq enjoyed an advantage in ground forces, while Iran had the edge in the air.

The Iraqi invasion on September 22, 1980, caught Iran by surprise. Hussein justified it as a response to an alleged assassination attempt sponsored by Iran on Iraqi foreign minister Tariq Aziz. Striking on a broad front, the Iraqis enjoyed initial success. They secured the far side of the Shatt al-Arab and in November captured Khorramshahr in Khuzestan. But Hussein threw away the chance for a quick, decisive victory by an overly cautious advance, while Iran rapidly mobilized its resources.

The Iranians soon established a strong defense, while their navy also carried out an effective blockade of Iraq. Far from breaking Iranian morale, the invasion rallied public opinion behind the Islamic regime, and by March 1981 the war had become a protracted stalemate greatly resembling the trench warfare of World War I.

An Iranian offensive in March 1981 drove the Iraqis back, and on May 24 they recaptured Khorramshahr. Hussein then proposed a truce and an Iraqi withdrawal from Iranian territory. He also declared a unilateral cease-fire. Sensing victory, Iran rejected the proposal and demanded Hussein's ouster.

Hussein then withdrew his forces into well-prepared static defenses within Iraq. Iranian leaders meanwhile rejected as insufficient a Saudi Arabian–brokered deal that would have given Iran $70 billion in reparations by the Arab states and a complete Iraqi withdrawal from Iranian territory. Khomeini apparently now hoped to establish an Islamic republic in Iraq, presumably with its Shiite majority in charge.

In July 1982 the Iranians launched a new offensive, this time against Shiite-dominated southern Iraq with the goal of capturing Basra, Iraq's second-largest city. Iraqi resistance included the use of poison gas, and Iran secured only modest gains at heavy human cost. Each side also employed aircraft and missiles against the other's cities, with five separate such campaigns during the war. Iraq attacked Iranian oil-shipping facilities and later production facilities, which produced the largest oil spill in the history of the Persian Gulf region.

New Iranian offensives that autumn in the northern part of the front secured some territory inside Iraq before being driven out. In the southern part of the front, Iranian forces secured gains in a drive on the vital Baghdad-Basra highway. Between February and August 1983 Iran launched five major offensives, first against Basra and then in the north, but had only slight gains for heavy casualties. Determined to prevent the spread of Islamic fundamentalism regimes in the Middle East, U.S. president Ronald Reagan supported Iraq, providing it with satellite photography as well as economic aid and weapons.

In February 1984, the Iranians launched the first in a series of ground offensives in the central part of the front to take Kut al-Amara and there cut the vital Baghdad-Basra highway. The Iranians came within 15 miles of the city before being halted. An Iranian drive against Basra also almost broke through.

With his forces having benefited from substantial arms purchases financed by the Persian Gulf states, in January 1985 Hussein launched his first ground offensive since 1980 but scored only scant gains. The Iranians responded with an offensive of their own in March, capturing a portion of the Baghdad-Basra road. Hussein responded to this emergency with chemical weapons and renewed air and missile strikes against Iranian cities, including Tehran.

On February 17, 1986, Iranian forces captured the strategically important Iraqi port of al-Faw, southeast of Basra on the Shatt al-Arab waterway. During January–February 1987, Iran again tried but failed to take Basra. During May–June the Iranians tried to capture Kirkuk in northern Iraq.

On July 24, 1987, the United States initiated Operation EARNEST WILL, an effort to protect oil tankers and shipping lanes in the Persian Gulf. Iran had responded to the March 1984 Iraqi air attack on Kharg Island and nearby oil installations by employing sea mines against tankers carrying Iraqi oil from Kuwait as well as those of the Persian Gulf states supporting Iraq. Responding to a Kuwaiti appeal, Washington agreed to provide protection for any U.S.-flagged tankers and other tankers accompanying these to and from Iraqi ports. This action ensured that Iraq would have the economic means to continue the war.

On the night of May 17, 1987, an Iraqi Mirage F-1 fighter on antiship patrol fired two Exocet antiship missiles at a radar contact, its pilot apparently not knowing that his target was the U.S. Navy frigate *Stark*. Although only one detonated, both missiles struck home and badly crippled the frigate, killing 37 crewmen and injuring another 50. The crew managed to save the ship, however.

Air and missile attacks by both sides against the cities of the other continued. Also during February and extending into September, the Iraqi Army carried out a massacre of its own Kurdish population in northern Iraq. Known as the al-Anfal (Spoils of War) Campaign, it claimed as many as 300,000 Kurdish lives and the destruction of some 4,000 villages.

In the spring of 1988, with Iran now desperately short of spare parts especially for its largely U.S.-built aircraft, Iraq launched four major offensives, recapturing the strategically important al-Faw Peninsula lost in 1986, driving the Iranians away from Basra, and making progress in the northern part of the front. These Iraqi victories came at little cost to themselves, while the Iranians suffered heavy personnel and equipment losses. These setbacks were the chief factor behind Khomeini's decision to agree to a cease-fire in 1988.

On July 3, 1988, the crew of the U.S. Navy cruiser *Vincennes*, patrolling in the Persian Gulf and believing that they were under attack by an Iranian jet fighter, shot down Iran Air Flight 655, a civilian airliner carrying 290 passengers and crew. There were no survivors. The U.S. government subsequently agreed to pay $131.8 million in compensation. This incident may have helped to convince Khomeini of the dangers of the United States actively entering the war, thus making him more amenable to ending it.

Both sides accepted a cease-fire agreement, arranged by the United Nations (UN), on August 20, 1988. There are no reliable casualty totals, but each side probably suffered at least 300,000 dead. Negotiations between Iraq and Iran remained deadlocked for two years after the cease-fire, but in 1990, concerned with securing its forcible annexation of Kuwait, Iraq reestablished diplomatic relations with Iran and agreed to withdraw its troops from occupied Iranian territory, divide sovereignty over the Shatt al-Arab, and exchange prisoners of war.

With Iraq having sustained war costs of some $561 billion, Hussein turned to Saudi Arabia and Kuwait for financial relief, only to meet rebuff. During Ottoman rule, Kuwait had been part of Basra Province; it had only become an independent emirate during the British mandate, and this provided Hussein with the claim that Kuwait was an Iraqi province. Hussein also accused the Kuwaitis of overdrilling that had forced down the price of oil, much to the detriment of the Iraqi economy. He also asserted that Kuwait was illegally slant-drilling into Iraqi oil fields along their common border.

On August 2, 1990, Iraqi troops invaded their small neighbor of Kuwait and quickly occupied it. Hussein then proclaimed its annexation. Much of the international community condemned the action and demanded an Iraqi withdrawal. UN Security Council Resolution 661 imposed wide-ranging sanctions on Iraq. These included a trade embargo that excluded only medical supplies, food, and other essential items. The UN also authorized a naval blockade of Iraq.

The U.S. government was deeply concerned about the occupation of Kuwait and a possible Iraqi military incursion into Saudi Arabia or at least pressure on that country and the threat to world oil supplies. It also worried about Iraqi programs to produce chemical, biological, and nuclear weapons, the so-called weapons of mass destruction (WMD). U.S. officials also feared that the balance of power in the region would be upset and would imperil Israel.

On paper, Iraq appeared formidable. Its army numbered more than 950,000 men, and it had some 5,500 main battle tanks, 6,000 armored personnel carriers (APCs), and about 3,500 artillery pieces. Hussein ultimately deployed 43 divisions to Kuwait, positioning most of them along the border with Saudi Arabia.

In Operation DESERT SHIELD, designed to protect Saudi Arabia and prepare for the liberation of Kuwait, U.S. president George H. W. Bush put together an impressive coalition that included Syria, Egypt, and Saudi Arabia as well as Britain, France, and many other states. Altogether 34 nations participated, and coalition assets grew to 665,000 troops and substantial air and naval assets.

Hussein remained intransigent but also quiescent, allowing the coalition buildup to proceed unimpeded. When the deadline to withdraw from Kuwait passed without Iraqi action, coalition commander U.S. Army general H. Norman Schwarzkopf unleashed Operation DESERT STORM on January 17, 1991. It began with a massive air offensive against targets in Kuwait and throughout Iraq, including Baghdad. Although Iraq possessed nearly 800 combat aircraft and an integrated air defense system controlling 3,000 antiaircraft missiles, coalition aircraft soon had destroyed the bulk of the Iraqi Air Force. Complete air superiority ensured success on the ground.

Night after night B-52s dropped massive bomb loads in classic attrition warfare; many Iraqi defenders were simply buried alive. Schwarzkopf also mounted an elaborate deception to convince the Iraqis that the coalition was planning an amphibious assault against Kuwait, thereby pinning down there a number of Iraqi divisions. In reality, Schwarzkopf planned a return to large-scale maneuver warfare.

The coalition campaign involved three thrusts. On the far left, 200 miles from the coast, highly mobile U.S. and French forces were to swing wide and cut off the Iraqis on the Euphrates River, preventing resupply or retreat. The center assault of the VII Corps would occur some 100 miles inland and consisted of the heavily armored mailed fist of U.S. and British divisions. Its mission was to thrust deep and destroy the elite Iraqi Republican Guard divisions. The third and final thrust would be on the coast. Consisting of the U.S. 1st Marine Expeditionary force, one U.S. armored division, and allied Arab units, it would drive on Kuwait City.

On February 24 Allied forces executed simultaneous drives, while the 101st Airborne Division established a position 50 miles behind the border. As they moved up the coast toward Kuwait City, the U.S. marines were hit in the flank by Iraqi armor. In the largest tank battle in their history, the marines, supported by coalition airpower, easily defeated the Iraqis in a surrealist day-into-night atmosphere caused by the smoke of burning oil wells set afire by the retreating Iraqis.

As the marines, preceded by a light Arab force, prepared to enter Kuwait City, the Iraqis fled north with whatever they could loot. Thousands of civilian vehicles and personnel were caught in the open on the highway from Kuwait City and were there pummeled by air and artillery on what became known as the "Highway of Death."

On February 27 the Allies came up against an Iraqi rear guard of 300 tanks and APCs covering the withdrawal of four Republican Guard divisions northward toward Basra. In perhaps the most lopsided tank battle in history, in the Battle of Medina Ridge units of the U.S. 1st Armored Division easily defeated the Iraqis at scant cost to themselves. The afternoon of February 27 also saw the VII Corps engaged in intense combat. An armored brigade of the Medina Republican Guard Division was in defensive positions hoping to delay the coalition. The advancing 2nd Brigade of the U.S. 1st Armored Division spotted the Iraqis and took them under fire. The ensuing Battle of Norfolk was the largest single engagement of the war. In only 45 minutes, 69 Iraqi tanks and 38 APCs were destroyed. As the VII Corps closed to the sea, such as I Corps to its left, with a much larger distance to travel, raced to reach the fleeing Republican Guard divisions before they could escape to Baghdad.

In only 100 hours of ground combat coalition forces had liberated Kuwait, but on February 28 Bush stopped the war. He feared both the wisdom and cost of an assault on Baghdad with the possibility that Iraq might break up into a Kurdish north, a Sunni Muslim center, and a Shiite Muslim south. Bush wanted to see Iraq intact to counter a resurgent Iran.

The war was among the most lopsided in history. Iraq lost 3,700 tanks, more than 1,000 other armored vehicles, and 3,000 artillery pieces. The coalition lost 4 tanks, 9 other combat vehicles, and 1 artillery piece. The coalition sustained 500 casualties (150 dead), many from accidents and friendly fire. Iraq sustained perhaps 60,000 deaths and some 80,000 taken prisoner. Perhaps an equal number simply deserted.

It did not take long for Saddam Hussein to reestablish his authority. Bush had called for the Iraqi people to force Hussein to resign. Shiite Muslims in southern Iraq and Kurds in northern Iraq, both of which had been persecuted by Hussein, rebelled against the government. The refusal of the coalition to support the insurgents, however, allowed Hussein to suppress the uprisings with brutal force. The cease-fire agreement ending the war negotiated by Schwarzkopf permitted the Iraqi government to continue to fly helicopters, and these were employed with devastating effectiveness. Both the Kurds and the Shiites underwent persecution during the rest of Hussein's presidency. Hussein also defied UN inspection teams by refusing to account for all of his biological and chemical weapons, the so-called WMD.

To protect the Kurds and the Shias, the United States, Britain, and France belatedly established two no-fly zones (NFZs) in Iraq. The NFZ in northern Iraq, Operation NORTHERN WATCH, was established on March 3, 1991, and ran from the 36th parallel northward. Not until August 2, 1992, however, did the Bush administration establish an NFZ in the south to the 32nd parallel. In 1996 it was expanded to the 33rd parallel. The northern NFZ was initially part of PROVIDE COMFORT, the relief operation aiding the Kurds. The southern NFZ was maintained by Operation SOUTHERN WATCH. After the French withdrew in 1998, U.S. and British aircraft continued to enforce the NFZs until the Iraq War that began in March 2003.

Continuing UN sanctions devastated the already-reeling Iraqi economy. The sanctions had called for 30 percent of Iraqi oil exports to be set aside for war reparations, but the Iraqi economy had grown to depend on its oil exports at the expense of other industries, especially agriculture. With the diminishment in oil revenues, many Iraqis experienced malnourishment and grinding poverty, while hyperinflation nearly wiped out the middle class. Food rationing did little to improve the situation. Power shortages caused widespread problems, and many manufacturing facilities had to be shut down.

In 1991, the Iraqi government had rejected UN proposals to trade its oil for food and other humanitarian supplies. On May 20, 1996, however, a memorandum of understanding was reached between the Iraqi government and the UN by which Iraq could sell oil to purchase food and other humanitarian supplies. This program suffered from deliberate illegal diversion of funds and did little to alleviate the plight of average Iraqis. By 2000, as many as 16 million Iraqis depended on some form of government assistance merely to survive.

The United States, Britain, and France (until 1998) continued to limit Hussein's power through punitive military operations. These aircraft and missile strikes damaged infrastructure and put even more of a strain on the Iraqi economy. Operation VIGILANT WARRIOR of October 8, 1994, was a U.S. response to the deployment of Iraqi troops toward the Kuwaiti border. After some 170 U.S. aircraft and 6,500 military personnel were deployed to southern Iraq, Hussein recalled his troops. Operation DESERT STRIKE of September 3, 1996, was in response to the movement of 40,000 Iraqi troops into northern Iraq, which threatened the Kurds. More than two years later on December 16, 1998, the United States and Great Britain began Operation DESERT FOX, a four-day bombing campaign, after Iraq's refusal to comply with UN Security Council resolutions that called for the dismantling of certain weapons and the Iraqi government's interference with UN weapons inspectors charged with ensuring Iraqi compliance with UN resolutions. DESERT FOX targeted research and developmental facilities in order to destroy any hidden WMD and the Iraqi government's ability to produce them. Then on February 16, 2001, U.S. and British aircraft launched missiles to damage Iraq's command and control facilities.

All the bombing to force Iraqi compliance with UN mandates did little to weaken Hussein's hold on power. The secular Baath government embarked on a so-called faith campaign, depicting the struggle as a jihad (holy war). Meanwhile, Hussein insisted on absolute loyalty.

Following the Al Qaeda terrorist attacks on the United States on September 11, 2001, that killed nearly 3,000 people, the George W. Bush administration took a more assertive stance with Iraq. Bush and his closest advisers saw Iraq as a threat. Many Bush advisers mistakenly insisted that Iraq possessed WMD or was attempting to acquire such, and they claimed that an invasion of Iraq would easily remove Hussein, secure the alleged WMD, and serve as a warning to other rogue states. Beyond that, they saw a democratic Iraq as a force for change in the entire region. Some even held that Iraqi oil would pay for the invasion.

As invasion plans proceeded, Bush hoped to secure UN approval. On September 12, 2002, he addressed the UN Security Council and made his case for an invasion. Much of the international community was skeptical and did not believe that Iraq posed a threat or had links to such terrorist organizations as Al Qaeda, which the Bush administration also alleged. On October 10 and 11, however, the U.S. Congress passed the Authorization for Use of Military Force against Iraq Resolution of 2002 (Iraq War Resolution), which Bush signed into law on October 16. On November 8, 2002, the UN Security Council passed Resolution 1441, which offered Iraq a final chance to comply with its disarmament agreements. This required that Iraq destroy all WMD and the means to deliver them and also provide complete documentation of such.

On February 5, 2003, U.S. secretary of state Colin Powell addressed the UN General Assembly and presented evidence, some of which was later proven to be false, that Iraqi officials were impeding the work of the weapons inspectors, continuing to develop WMD, and directly supporting Al Qaeda. The United States and Great Britain, among others, then proposed a UN resolution calling for the use of force against Iraq. Other countries, including U.S. allies Canada, France, and Germany, urged continued diplomacy. Bush then decided to pursue an invasion without UN authorization.

On March 20, 2003, a U.S.- and British-led coalition invaded Iraq. The operation was mounted solely from Kuwait. It was also hastily reworked, for after lengthy negotiations Turkey refused to allow the 4th Infantry Division to stage from that country. Nonetheless, coalition forces advanced north quickly and on April 5–10 fought the Battle of Baghdad. After the fall of the capital and the official end to the Iraqi government, Hussein went into hiding. Coalition forces entered Kirkuk on April 10 and Hussein's hometown of Tikrit on April 15.

On May 1, 2003, Bush declared that major combat operations in Iraq had ended and that the postinvasion reconstruction phase had begun. However, the war was far from over; indeed, the postinvasion period would prove very difficult for coalition forces. With insufficient numbers of coalition forces to keep order, Iraq soon fell into chaos with the looting of palaces, museums, and even arms depots.

On April 20, 2003, the United States had established the Coalition Provisional Authority (CPA), and on May 11 Bush selected diplomat Lewis Paul Bremer III as its head. Bremer made two most unfortunate decisions. On June 3, he ordered the de-Baathification of Iraq. Some 30,000 Baath Party officials were removed from their positions and banned from future employment in the public sector. The next day, Bremer dissolved Iraq's 500,000-member army. This order left Iraq without a military or police force to stop the continuing chaos. These moves also produced a large number of opponents to the coalition presence. Violence against the occupation forces steadily increased. Individuals, largely Sunnis, employed ambush tactics, improvised explosive devices and suicide bombings against coalition forces, who now faced a long battle with Iraqi insurgents in their attempt to bring peace to Iraq. This led to a number of costly battles, including two for the city of Fallujah (April 4–May 1 and November 7–December 23, 2004).

Sectarian strife also increased, and by mid-2004 Iraq appeared perched on the edge of full-blown civil war. Sunni extremists, rightly fearful of dominance by the Shiite majority, employed car bombs and suicide bombings against Shiites, while Shiite members of the new Iraqi Army used extralegal means against Sunni civilians. Shiite death squads killed many Iraqi civilians and sought to cleanse neighborhoods of Sunni residents.

With the ongoing violence, on June 28, 2004, governing authority was transferred to the Iraqi Interim Government, led by Prime Minister Ayad Allawi. The generally pro-Western Allawi launched a campaign to weaken the rebel forces of Shiite cleric Muqtada al-Sadr. On September 1 Allawi pulled out of peace negotiations with Sadr, and fighting ensued in what became known as the Battle of Sadr City. Sadr eventually agreed to a cease-fire and took part in the legislative elections on January 30, 2005.

In the elections, the Iraqi people chose representatives for the 275-member National Assembly. Some 8.4 million people cast their ballots. Two Shiite parties won a majority of the seats, with 85 women among those elected. Many Sunnis boycotted the elections, however. The assembly was immediately charged with writing a constitution and approved the Iraqi Transitional Government on April 28, 2005, which went into operation on May 3. The constitution was approved on October 15, 2005, and described Iraq as a democratic, federal, representative republic.

On December 15, 2005, a second general election was held to elect a permanent Iraqi Council of Representatives. Following approval by the National Assembly, a permanent

Iraqi government was established on May 16, 2006. Turnout for this election was high, at 79.4 percent, and the level of violence was lower than during the previous election. The United Iraqi Alliance, a coalition of Arab Shiite parties, won the most votes, at 41.2 percent. Nuri al-Maliki, a member of the Islamic Dawa Party, a conservative Shiite group, became prime minister. Maliki negotiated a peace treaty with Sadr's rebel forces in August 2007.

U.S. forces had captured Saddam Hussein on December 13, 2003, in Dawr, a small town north of Baghdad. He was eventually tried by an Iraqi Special Tribunal for crimes committed against the inhabitants of the town of Dujail, which had been the site of an unsuccessful assassination attempt against Hussein in 1982. Hussein was charged with the murder of 148 people and with having ordered the torture of women and children and illegally arresting 399 others. Found guilty on November 5, 2006, he was sentenced to death by hanging and was executed on December 30.

In January 2007 President Bush presented a new U.S. military strategy, the stated goal of which was to reduce the sectarian violence and secure both Baghdad and Anbar Province. In what became known as a troop surge, five additional U.S. Army brigades totaling some 20,000 troops were deployed to Iraq between January and May 2007. Other troops had their tours extended. The success of the surge has been debated. Certainly another key factor in the reduction of violence was the decision of many Sunnis to work with the coalition forces.

On December 4, 2008, the U.S. and Iraqi governments concluded a status of forces agreement, which stipulated that U.S. troops would depart from all Iraqi cities by June 30, 2009, and leave Iraq entirely by December 31, 2011. U.S. forces were no longer allowed to hold Iraqi citizens without charges for more than 24 hours. Also, U.S. contractors were to lose immunity from prosecution in Iraqi courts. It was widely assumed that a new status of forces agreement plan would be negotiated after expiration of the 2008 version, but new U.S. president Barack Obama had run on a pledge of ending the Iraq War, and he announced soon after taking office in January 2009 that U.S. combat operations would cease in 2010. About 200 marines were to remain to help train the Iraqi Army and provide security for U.S. diplomatic personnel.

When it came time to renegotiate a new agreement, however, there was no consensus. U.S. military leaders wanted as many as 24,000 troops. But the Obama administration rejected this in favor of perhaps 10,000 troops in strategic locations after the exit. A figure of 3,500 was also bandied about, but even that low figure ran up against opposition from within the Iraqi parliament and Washington's insistence that any troops be immune to Iraqi—although not American—criminal prosecution. Thus, no agreement was ever reached, for which U.S. Republican Party leaders chose to blame Obama. The last U.S. troops left Iraq on December 18, 2011, two weeks ahead of the schedule provided by the existing status of forces agreement.

Iraq meanwhile continued to experience major problems. Although the economy had improved somewhat, corruption was endemic, and unemployment remained astronomically high (60–70 percent in 2008). At the same time, the Iraqi foreign debt rose. Since the withdrawal of coalition troops, the Iraqi economy has failed to make any major gains, and in many sectors it has steadily deteriorated. Much of this was due to a growing insurgency and ongoing sectarian violence, combined with the ineffective and graft-ridden Maliki government. Although unemployment had dropped to 30 percent by the end of 2013, most Iraqis were employed in the public sector (60 percent), and per capita gross domestic product was only about $4,000 per year.

In the last several years, Iraq has witnessed an alarming reemergence of the antigovernment insurgency. This has included sectarian violence and the rise to prominence of Islamic extremist groups, including most notably Al Qaeda in Iraq and the Islamic State of Iraq and Syria (ISIS). By early 2014, ISIS had seized control of virtually all of Iraq's vast Anbar Province. Maliki's government was unable to stem the rising tide of deadly violence. Indeed, Mailiki's policies saw the Shiites run roughshod over the Sunnis and Kurds, setting the stage for a renewal of deadly violence in the form of sectarian car bombings and suicide bombings. May 2013 was the deadliest month in Iraq since the height of the Iraqi insurgency in 2006–2007.

In May 2014, the U.S. government announced an arms deal with Iraq that promised at least $1 billion in new aircraft, armored vehicles, and surveillance technology. Meanwhile, the Iraqis also engaged in a major arms deal with the Russians, who agreed to sell them aircraft and bunker-busting rockets, among other items.

By midsummer 2014 the Iraqi situation appeared dire, with ISIS having secured both Fallujah (December 30, 2013–January 4, 2014) and Iraq's second-largest city of Mosul (June 4–10) and having advanced to within 90 miles of Baghdad. Until then, the Iraqi Army had performed abysmally in its fight against ISIS; indeed, many soldiers simply deserted or fled in the face of ISIS military operations. In August, Maliki was now under great domestic and international pressure to step down. Even those in his own party believed that he must go. In the meantime, the United States began dispatching growing but relatively small numbers of military advisers to Iraq even as U.S. and allied aircraft began bombing raids against ISIS targets in northern and western Iraq. As the renewed insurgency in Iraq continued to gain momentum, the U.S. government assembled a multinational military coalition, Operation INHERENT RESOLVE, to blunt the ISIS campaigns in Iraq and Syria. The coalition included numerous Arab and Muslim nations and involved tens of thousands of air strikes and, increasingly, deployments of ground troops to the region.

Maliki finally agreed to relinquish his office on September 8, 2014. He was succeeded by Haider al-Abadi, also of the Dawa Party. The Shiite Abadi vowed to reinvigorate Iraq's army and work closely with the new international coalition formed to stop and eventually eradicate ISIS. He also pledged more governmental transparency and efforts to bridge the gaping chasm between the majority Shiite and minority Sunni and Kurdish populations.

Throughout 2015 Iraqi forces battled ISIS, achieving modest success in winning back some territory claimed by the extremist group. Worrisome to Washington, Iran had also begun providing direct military support to the Iraqi government. The collapse of oil prices during the second half of 2015 had a chilling effect on Iraq's economy, still highly dependent on oil exports. Indeed, by early 2016 the Abadi government announced that the greatly reduced oil revenues were beginning to affect its ability to continue the fight against ISIS.

Violence continued, with bombings a frequent occurrence. A UN report of January 2016 stated that between January 2014 and November 2015, nearly 19,000 Iraqi civilians had died owing to violence in Iraq, while at least 40,000 others had been injured. An additional 3 million Iraqis had been displaced from their homes. In May 2016 the government began a long-anticipated offensive to retake Fallujah, the essential prelude to moving against the ISIS stronghold of Mosul. Fallujah fell to the government forces on June 26. The government claimed that more than 1,800 ISIS militants had been killed during the battle to retake Fallujah and the villages surrounding it. Meanwhile, largely Sunni civilians who had fled the fighting were in dire straits, living in hastily prepared refugee camps without even basic amenities. The Sunnis were, of course, the very group the Shia-dominated government is trying to win over.

On October 16, 2016, the Iraqi armed forces, assisted by the United States and other coalition forces (largely in the form of airpower) and Iranian-supported militia, as well as Kurdish troops, opened Operation QADIMUN YA NAYNAWA (WE ARE COMING NINEVEH), the offensive to retake Mosul from ISIS. This largest ever deployment of Iraqi forces since the 2003 Iraq War, saw ISIS fighters heavily outnumbered. ISIS, however, had also had a long time to prepare for the offensive and construct elaborate defenses, strongpoints, and tunnels. Fighting was fierce, with the Iraqi government finally announcing on July 20, 2017, that Mosul had been secured. Reconstruction was expected to take as long as five years and cost as much as $50 billion.

On October 4, Iraqi Army forces and Iranian-backed militia supported by coalition air strikes secured control of a key border crossing after taking from ISIS most of the Iraqi town of Qaim. The next day the Iraqi government announced the capture by its forces of the town of Hawija, the last ISIS stronghold near Kurdish-held Kirkuk in northern Iraq. This left only a stretch of territory along the western border with Syria remaining under the control of the Islamic state. Then on December 9, 2017, Iraqi premier al-Abadi officially announced the end of the costly Iraqi campaign to clear ISIS forces from his country.

With ISIS in Iraq effectively defeated, the Iraqi government turned its attention to crushing Kurdish efforts to secure independence, for on September 25, 2017, the Iraqi Kurds celebrated in their regional capital of Erbil and in other Kurdish areas of northern Iraq the results of a referendum on independence held on September 22. The announced vote was 92 percent in favor of independence. This immediately encountered strong opposition from the Shiite-dominated Iraqi central government and from neighboring Turkey, Syria, and Iran, all of which had strong Kurdish minorities and opposed creation of a Kurdish state and its ensuing irredentist claims. Indeed, Turkish strongman president Recep Erdoğan called the vote a threat to his country's national security and held out the strong possibility of Turkish economic action and even military intervention.

The Iraqi government itself immediately vowed to send troops into the Kurdish areas to secure control of the oil fields there. It also demanded that the Kurds surrender control of Erbil International Airport. With the Kurds having few heavy weapons and lacking any allies, the result was a foregone conclusion. Al-Abadi sent federal forces into the region, and on October 6, they took direct control of the strategic city of Kirkuk (the region accounts for some 6 percent of world oil production), which had been under Kurdish control since 2014. Some violence occurred, with several dozen Kurdish fighters reportedly killed and others wounded. All of this posed a dilemma for the United States, which had relied on the Kurds and provided small arms and ammunition to their highly effective Peshmerga fighters against ISIS.

Given the Iraqi central government's overwhelming military advantage, the government of the autonomous Kurdish region offered to "freeze" its independence efforts and open talks with Baghdad, which demanded that the referendum result be annulled before talks could occur. Faced with overwhelming force, on October 17 the Kurdish separatists surrendered to central government control all disputed oil fields in northern Iraq.

With the Kurds now all but certain to lose their autonomy as well, Marsoud Barzani, leader of the Kurdistan Democratic Party (KDP) since 1979 and president of the Iraqi Kurdistan Region since 2005, resigned the presidency on November 1, 2017. Barzani blamed the United States for failing to stand by its Kurdish allies.

What the future held for Iraq was still uncertain, but at the end of 2017 Iran appeared to have gained considerable influence in Baghdad over the course of the last several years, while the United States and other Western powers did not seem to have garnered much if anything for their important military support of the central government in recovering its national territory that had been lost to ISIS.

In March 2018, much to the consternation of Washington, Turkey launched a military campaign to eradicate Kurdish separatist fighters in northern Iraq. This caused U.S.-Turkish relations to plummet. At the same time, with insurgency activities on the decline in Iraq, Prime Minister al-Abadi's government was anxious to implement a drawdown of U.S. and coalition forces in Iraq. In February 2018, his government reached an agreement with Washington that would see a major reduction in U.S. ground troops in Iraq by year's end. Nevertheless, as of August 2018, there were still some 5,000 U.S. troops in Iraq, whose principal role was one of assistance to and training of Iraqi government forces. Although Baghdad had declared victory over the ISIS insurgency, Iraq remained an unpredictable and violent place in late 2018. Indeed, while insurgents' military activities may have dropped off, the country witnessed a series of deadly terror attacks against Iraq civilians throughout the year, signaling that Iraq will likely face substantial internal threats for the foreseeable future.

Meanwhile, the May 2018 Iraqi parliamentary elections augured a troubling future. Muqtada al-Sadr's alliance won 54 seats in the Iraqi parliament. Al-Sadr has been a consistent and loud critic of the United States, and in the aftermath of the election he asserted that it should play no role in Iraqi affairs. Al-Sadr has been eyed suspiciously by his opponents, including the U.S. government, for his alleged ties to the Iranian regime.

Louis A. DiMarco, Jack Vahram Kalpakian,
Adam B. Lowther, Gregory Wayne Morgan,
Paul G. Pierpaoli Jr., and Spencer C. Tucker

See also

Abadi, Haider al-; Abbasid Caliphate; Alexander III the Great; Allawi, Ayad; Al Qaeda in Iraq; Anglo-Iraqi Treaties of 1922 and 1930; Arif, Abd al-Salam; Assyrian Empire; Babylonian Empire, Old; Babylonian Empire, Neo-; Baghdad, 2003 Battle of; Baghdad Pact; Bakr, Ahmad Hassan al-; Bremer, Lewis Paul, III; Chemical Weapons and Warfare; Cyrus II the Great; Desert Fox, Operation; Earnest Will, Operation; Faisal I, King of Iraq; Faisal II, King of Iraq; Fallujah, First Battle of; Fallujah, Second Battle of; Fallujah, Third Battle of; Hussein, Saddam; Iran; Iran, Islamic Revolution in; Iran Air Flight 655, Downing of; Iran-Iraq War; Iraq Insurgency; Iraq War; Islamic State of Iraq and Syria; Israeli War of Independence; Khomeini, Ruhollah; Kuwait; Kuwait, Iraqi Invasion of; Kuwait, Iraqi Occupation of; Kuwait, Liberation of; Maliki, Nuri Muhammed Kamil al-; Mamluk Sultanate; Mandates, League of Nations; Mosul, Second Battle of; Northern Watch Operation; Nuri al-Said; Ottoman Empire; Persian Gulf War, Overview; Provide Comfort, Operation; Qasim, Abdul Karim; Schwarzkopf, H. Norman, Jr.; September 11, 2001, Attacks on the United States; Shatt al-Arab Waterway; Six-Day War; Southern Watch, Operation; *Stark* Incident; Sumer; Tigris and Euphrates Valley; Vigilant Warrior, Operation

References

Abdullah, Thabit. *A Short History of Iraq*. London: Pearson, 2003.

Allawi, Ali A. *The Occupation of Iraq: Winning the War, Losing the Peace*. New Haven, CT: Yale University Press, 2007.

Butt, Gerald. *The Lion in the Sand: The British in the Middle East*. London: Bloomsbury, 1995.

Dodge, Toby. *Inventing Iraq: The Failure of Nation-Building and a History Denied*. New York: Columbia University Press, 2003.

Hamdi, Walid M. *Rashid al-Gailani and the Nationalist Movement in Iraq, 1939–1941: A Political and Military Study of the British Campaign in Iraq and the National Revolution of May 1941*. London: Darf, 1987.

Hopwood, Derek, Habib Ishow, and Thomas Koszinowski, eds. *Iraq: Power and Society*. Reading, UK: Ithaca Press, 1993.

Inati, Shams Constantine. *Iraq: Its History, People, and Politics*. Amherst, MA: Humanity Books, 2003.

Karsh, Efraim. *Islamic Imperialism*. New Haven, CT: Yale University Press, 2006.

Makiya, Kanan. *Republic of Fear: The Politics of Modern Iraq*. Berkeley: University of California Press, 1998.

Marr, Phebe. *The Modern History of Iraq*. 2nd ed. Boulder, CO: Westview, 2003.

Murray, Williamson, and Robert H. Scales Jr. *The Iraq War: A Military History*. Cambridge, MA: Harvard University Press, 2003.

Oren, Michael B. *Six Days of War: June 1967 and the Making of the Modern Middle East.* Novato, CA: Presidio, 2003.
Pelletiere, Stephen. *The Iran-Iraq War: Chaos in a Vacuum.* New York: Praeger, 1992.
Polk, William R. *Understanding Iraq: The Whole Sweep of Iraqi History, from Genghis Khan's Mongols to the Ottoman Turks to the British Mandate to the American Occupation.* New York: Harper Perennial, 2006.
Tripp, Charles. *A History of Iraq.* Cambridge: Cambridge University Press, 2007.

Iraq, Sanctions on

The international community imposed sanctions on Iraq beginning on August 6, 1990, four days after Iraqi forces invaded Kuwait. Various sanctions remained in place until May 22, 2003, at which time the Saddam Hussein government had been overthrown by the Anglo-American–led invasion of Iraq in March 2003. This was one of the longest and hardest sanction regimes ever imposed by the international community and the United Nations (UN) on one of its member states.

On August 2, 1990, Iraq's armed forces occupied Kuwait. Four days later UN Security Council Resolution 661 imposed comprehensive trade sanctions on Iraq. The sanctions prohibited the importation of any Iraqi commodities or products into all UN member states as well as the sale or supply of any products to Iraq. The resolution excluded the sale of medical supplies to Iraq as well as foodstuffs for humanitarian purposes.

Although the Persian Gulf War officially ended on February 28, 1991, the Security Council continued to employ sanctions against Iraq. Security Council Resolution 687 of April 3, 1991, instructed the government of Iraq to destroy, remove, and render harmless all its weapons of mass destruction (WMD) and medium-range missiles. The UN also decided to send to Iraq a team of international inspectors to supervise the implementation of the resolution. Continuing economic sanctions were supposed to maintain international pressure on Iraq to cooperate with the inspectors.

Because the 1991 war caused major damage to Iraq's infrastructure, including power plants, oil refineries, pumping stations, and water treatment facilities, the sanctions crippled Iraqi efforts to revive the economy and created a humanitarian crisis. In response to the plight of Iraqi civilians, UN secretary-general Javier Pérez de Cuéllar submitted a report to the Security Council on March 20, 1991, describing in detail the humanitarian crisis existing in Iraq after the war. In its conclusions, the report recommended that the international community work rapidly to reconstruct Iraq to improve the humanitarian situation there.

As a means of improving the humanitarian situation in Iraq, the Security Council passed Resolutions 706 and 712 in August and September 1991, respectively. These resolutions allowed for the limited sale of Iraqi crude oil for the strict purpose of purchasing basic humanitarian goods for the Iraqi population. The government of Iraq rejected the offer, however, and demanded that all sanctions be immediately abolished.

The sanctions inflicted much more damage on Iraqi society during the 1990s. United Nations Children's Fund (UNICEF) surveys revealed that in the southern and central regions of Iraq, home to approximately 85 percent of the country's population, the mortality rate of children under the age of five had nearly tripled, from 56 deaths per 1,000 live births during 1984–1989 to 131 deaths per 1,000 live births during 1994–1999. Infant mortality (defined as children in their first year) increased from 47 per 1,000 live births to 108 per 1,000 live births within the same time frame.

The harsh conditions in Iraq soon caused a rift among the Security Council's permanent members. The United States and the United Kingdom advocated continuing the sanctions until the Iraqi government fulfilled all its obligations in compliance with Security Council Resolution 687. Their stance, however, was challenged by China, France, and Russia, which claimed that the sanctions only enhanced the suffering of the Iraqi people without influencing the Iraqi government to comply with Resolution 687.

On April 14, 1995, the UN Security Council suggested in Resolution 986 that the Iraqi government accept international supervision of the sale of Iraq's crude oil in return for humanitarian aid and basic needs such as food, medicine, and other essential civilian supplies. This diplomatic initiative finally bore fruit in May 1996 when the UN and Iraq signed a memorandum of understanding (MOU). Iraq began exporting crude oil under UN supervision in December 1996.

The MOU began the Oil-for-Food Programme, which operated until the invasion of Iraq by American- and British-led forces on March 20, 2003. The program was officially terminated on November 21, 2003, when authority was handed to the Coalition Provisional Authority, the entity that assumed the governance of Iraq headed by an American. On May 22, 2003, the Security Council abolished all sanctions against Iraq.

When the Oil-for-Food Programme began, Iraq was permitted to sell $2 billion of oil every six months. Two-thirds of the profits were channeled to humanitarian needs. In 1999 the Security Council decided to abolish the ceiling.

Under the program, the government of Iraq sold oil worth $64.2 billion. Of that amount, $38.7 billion was spent on humanitarian aid. Another $18 billion was given as compensation for lawsuits stemming from the occupation of Kuwait by Iraq. Finally, $1.2 billion was used to fund the program itself.

A total of $31 billion in humanitarian aid and equipment was transferred to Iraq under the program. Additional supplies and equipment totaling $8.2 billion were planned to be delivered to Iraq when the war broke out in March 2003. The program also helped to minimize the damage wrought by severe droughts in Iraq during 1999–2001.

During its seven years of operation, the program had a positive impact on civilian nutrition and health. It raised the average daily caloric intake for every Iraqi from 1,200 calories to 2,200 calories per day. The spread of contagious diseases such as cholera was also contained. The sewage system improved slowly during the 1990s, as did the delivery of medicine, particularly after the Oil-for-Food Programme was launched.

While the Oil-for-Food Programme succeeded in improving humanitarian conditions in Iraq, the diet quality was still poor. This caused malnutrition because of deficiencies in vitamins and minerals, which led to the spread of anemia, diarrhea, and respiratory infections, especially among young children. Furthermore, the program was criticized for restricting aid to food rather than also allowing the repair of infrastructure and the generation of employment. Because the aid was distributed through the government of Iraq, it actually helped the government maintain its hold over the people.

The full deficiencies of the aid plan became known after the occupation of Iraq began in 2003. In 2004 following complaints from U.S. senators and congressional representatives regarding irregularities in the UN-managed Oil-for-Food Programme, the UN created an independent inquiry committee (IIC) led by American banker Paul A. Volcker. The IIC completed its work at the end of 2005. The committee report pointed to mismanagement by the UN, corruption and bribery by top UN officials, and manipulation of the aid scheme by the government of Iraq, which received $1.8 billion in illegal aid. Also, IIC experts estimated that the government of Iraq was able to illicitly smuggle approximately $11 billion of oil outside Iraq, thereby circumventing the Oil-for-Food Programme.

CHEN KERTCHER

See also
Iraq; Iraq War; Persian Gulf War, Overview

References
Alexander, Kern. *Economic Sanctions: Law and Public Policy.* London: Palgrave Macmillan, 2009.
Arnove, Anthony. *Iraq under Siege: The Deadly Impact of Sanctions and War.* London: Pluto, 2000.
Lopez George A., and David Cortright. "Containing Iraq: The Sanctions Worked." *Foreign Affairs* 83, no. 4 (2004): 90–103.
Malone, David M. *The International Struggle over Iraq: Politics in the UN Security Council, 1980–2005.* Oxford: Oxford University Press, 2006.

Iraqi Invasion of Kuwait (1990)

See Kuwait, Iraqi Invasion of

Iraq Insurgency (2003–)

On March 19, 2003, an international coalition led by the United States and Great Britain invaded Iraq from Kuwait with the aim of toppling the regime of Iraqi president Saddam Hussein. Some 200,000 U.S., British, and other allied troops, supported by air and naval forces, overwhelmed the Iraqi defenders, and major combat operations were declared at an end on May 1. An Iraqi insurgency then occurred, at first targeting coalition forces and then spiraling into sectarian violence between Sunni, Shia, and Kurdish populations inflamed by the terrorist organization of Al Qaeda in Iraq. U.S. forces formally withdrew from Iraq in December 2011, but the sectarian violence continues.

In what is now regarded as a mistaken decision, U.S. administrator in Iraq Lewis Paul Bremer disbanded the Iraqi military and much of the institutional structure of the Hussein regime. Those associated with Hussein's Baath party were dismissed from their posts. A disproportion of these were Sunnis, who had been favored by Hussein, while Shiites had been persecuted. The Sunnis now rightly feared the majority Shiites would exact revenge. This was accompanied by massive looting, the loss of public services, the lack of humanitarian assistance, and the failure to adequately plan for postconflict operations that all worked against national stability, fueled the opposition, and laid the foundation for an insurgency.

Former Baathists and the Fedayeen Saddam (Saddam's Men of Sacrifice), paramilitary fighters loyal to Hussein, sparked the initial insurgency under the group al-Awda (The Return), personally led by Hussein until his capture by U.S. forces in Operation IRON HAMMER on December 13, 2003.

Iraqi Sunnis were the chief source of opposition to the occupiers, and many former members of the Iraqi Army turned to irregular warfare against the occupiers. A favored tactic was the employment of more powerful improvised explosive devices (IEDs) in the form of roadside bombs targeting coalition patrols. Although guerrilla attacks in the early days of the war were not particularly sophisticated, they heightened tensions between Iraqis and coalition forces. The latter's reaction to the attacks, including detentions and destruction of some structures and crops to reduce cover for ambushes, as well as the employment of artillery fire that inflicted civilian casualties garnered further support for the insurgents.

Beginning in late 2003, foreign fighters and those supported by Iran and Syria aggressively infiltrated the Sunni, Baathist, and Fedayeen resistance groups. Additionally, at this stage Al Qaeda elements and Islamists merged with the indigenous insurgency, as was shown in the introduction of suicide bombings. Attacks against a hotel housing United Nations officials, the employment of car bombs against personnel of the International Red Cross, and other such international targets indicated an enemy willing to conduct terrorist-style attacks as opposed to waging strictly guerrilla warfare. This stage was known as the Ramadan Offensive and was led by Abu Musab al-Zarqawi, leader of Tawhid wal-Jihad.

By the spring of 2004, fighting in the Sunni areas of the cities of Tikrit, Ramadi, and Fallujah was paralleled by a distinct and separate insurgency in majority Shia areas such as Najaf and Basra as well as predominantly Shia neighborhoods in Baghdad. This was in part fueled by discontent over the occupation and growing sectarian violence fomented by elements of the embryonic Al Qaeda in Iraq organization. The principal leader of the Shia insurgency was Muqtada al-Sadr, who established the Shia militia known as the Mahdi Army. Additionally, al-Sadr's camp fought a rival Shia and political group vying for power. Only after the deaths of several thousand Mahdi militiamen and civilians did al-Sadr negotiate settlements with the provisional Iraqi government.

Meanwhile, the Sunni insurgency intensified, forcing Operation VIGILANT RESOLVE, a U.S. Marine Corps–led operation in April 2004 to clear the entire Sunni-dominated city of Fallujah. In what became known as the First Battle of Fallujah, the insurgents massed more than 2,000 fighters, divided in small-size units and employing urban guerrilla tactics. At the same time, other insurgents attacked coalition positions in Ramadi. The First Battle of Fallujah lasted from April 4 to May 1 and cleared most of the city, although it remained a sanctuary for Sunni insurgents as well as Zarqawi's fighters. The insurgents also established safe havens in the Sunni-predominant cities of Baquba, Samarra, and Ramadi.

The transfer of power from the Coalition Provisional Authority to the Iraqis in 2004 did not end the insurgency. Al-Sadr's Mahdi Army reengaged coalition forces in the Shiite holy city of Najaf, and a prolonged battle for the holy shrine of Imam Ali lasted several weeks. Only after several coalition operations and negotiations between the Iraqi interim government and Mahdi leadership was another truce arranged in Sadr City. Critically, in October 2004 Zarqawi's militia pledged allegiance to Al Qaeda leader Osama bin Laden and declared itself Al Qaeda in Iraq. It became the deadliest element of the Iraqi Sunni insurgency, tapping into international Al Qaeda networks to secure fighters, weapons, and financial support.

Coalition forces responded to violence in key Sunni areas by multibattalion operations in such locations as Samarra, Fallujah, and Babil. The Second Battle for Fallujah, Operation PHANTOM FURY pitted some 5,000 U.S., 2,000 Iraqi, and 850 British troops against 5,000–10,000 insurgents during November 7–December 23, 2004. Coalition forces telegraphed their intentions in advance, encouraging civilians to flee in anticipation of the battle, which allowed the coalition to employ air strikes and artillery fire prior to the ground penetration of the city. The insurgents employed guerrilla-style tactics as well as IEDs placed on corpses and in homes. Snipers, mortars, car bombs, and individual suicide bombers were also commonly employed. These claimed U.S. losses of 95 killed and 560 wounded, Iraqi Army casualties of 8 killed and 43 wounded, and British casualties of 4 killed and 10 wounded. Some 1,200–1,500 insurgents were killed and 1,500 captured. Eight hundred civilians also died.

The Iraqi elections of 2005 brought Kurdish and Shiite control of the Iraqi government. The Sunnis, many of whom had boycotted the election, believed themselves further disenfranchised. The insurgency took a particularly nasty turn by actively targeting civilians in roadside bombs, suicide bombings, and indirect fire attacks, directly correlating with the rise of Al Qaeda in Iraq. Sectarian violence heightened, with the majority of the insurgents drawn from Sunni areas of the country and the Iraqi government dominated by Shia and Kurds.

Even with the death of Zarqawi in 2006, violence soared. There was also an influx of foreign fighters from Egypt, Syria, and other Arab states. Attacks, such as the bombing by Al Qaeda in Iraq against the holy Shia al-Askari Mosque, fueled the sectarian divide and resulted in thousands of Sunni and Shia civilian deaths.

Meanwhile, Al Qaeda in Iraq had taken control of the Sunni insurgency in Anbar Province in western Iraq, pushing aside tribal leaders and former Baathists and eventually causing a rift between the extremist Salafi fighters and Iraqi Sunnis. The accompanying civilian violence and aggressiveness of the Al Qaeda and foreign insurgents backfired, however, bringing the Sunni Awakening movement in 2006.

Led by influential Anbar Province tribal leaders and strongly supported by Lieutenant General David H. Petraeus, now commander of the Multi-National Force–Iraq, the Subi Awakening movement turned the tide against Al Qaeda in Iraq and is credited with ending the insurgency in many Sunni areas.

Despite a reduction in violence since 2008, increased participation of all Iraqi sects in the national government, and the formal departure of U.S. forces in December 2011, hostilities continued. Some elements of Al Qaeda in Iraq remained active, and concerns abounded regarding the demonstrated Shia determination to control the government at the expense of Sunnis and Kurds, Iranian influence, Muqtada al-Sadr's Mahdi Army, the Sons of Iraq, and Shia and other militias.

Unfortunately for Iraq, sectarian violence and radical Sunni Islamic extremism in Iraq increased. By January 2014, rebels associated with the Islamic State of Iraq and Syria (ISIS) had seized control of virtually all of Anbar Province, including Fallujah, where U.S. forces had fought two bloody battles to save the city. Within days the Sunni rebels had also captured the city of Ramadi, also in Anbar Province. The situation underscored the inability of Shiite Nuri al-Maliki, prime minister of Iraq from 2006 to 2014, to govern his country effectively and demonstrates the pitfalls of his governing style, which excluded Iraq's Sunni minority from any true decision making.

During 2013, more than 8,000 Iraqis died in sectarian violence and other strife. January 2014 proved to be the deadliest month in Iraq in six years, with more than 1,000 Iraqis killed in car bombings, suicide bombings, and other violence. Among the dead were 795 civilians. The mounting violence in Iraq was deeply troubling to the West, particularly the United States, not the least because numerous anti-Western and radical Islamist groups, including Al Qaeda and ISIS, had put down roots there. Indeed, ISIS was largely responsible for the seizure of virtually all of Anbar Province during 2013. Although the United States initially ruled out any new significant troop deployments to Iraq, the Barack Obama administration began selling and shipping armaments to the Iraqi government, including Hellfire missiles and Scan Eagle surveillance drones.

By midsummer 2014, Obama began dispatching military "advisers" to Iraq to assist in the fight against ISIS, serving as part of Operation INHERENT RESOLVE, an international coalition effort to stamp out the Islamist group. By the end of year that deployment had reached some 3,000 advisory personnel, most of them associated with U.S. air support being provided to the Iraqi government. The first U.S. air strikes against ISIS began in early August 2014. The air campaign soon accelerated, and in September it was widened to include ISIS targets in neighboring Syria.

Sectarian violence continued, however, with the Kurds having established an autonomous area in northern Iraq. Meanwhile, the Iraqi government was severely handicapped by plunging oil prices in the second half of 2015 that had a chilling effect on Iraq's economy, which is highly dependent on oil exports. Indeed, by early 2016 Premier Haider al-Abadi's government announced that greatly reduced oil revenues were beginning to affect its ability to continue the fight against ISIS. On a more positive note, by early 2016 Abadi's efforts to reform Iraqi politics and rid the nation of corruption and cronyism had begun to bear some fruit.

Throughout 2016 violence against civilians in Iraq continued to accelerate, with car and suicide bombs claiming the lives of at least 368 people between March and July alone. Most of the attacks were sponsored by ISIS, but other Sunni extremist groups had also been involved in the attacks. In June 2016, Iraqi forces retook Fallujah in the third battle for that city (May 23–June 28), which had been under ISIS control since early 2014. Although Fallujah was very heavily damaged, in the fighting the Iraqi government hailed its success there as a major turning point in the fight against ISIS.

Meanwhile, reacting to the mounting violence in Iraq and the continuing fight against ISIS, by July 2016 the United States had some 4,500 military personnel in Iraq, mainly in an advisory and support capacity. At the same time, U.S. and allied warplanes continued to hit ISIS targets in both Iraq and Syria. In October 2016, Iraqi and allied Kurdish forces began the much anticipated battle for Mosul, earlier Iraq's second-largest city and at this time the last major urban stronghold of ISIS control in Iraq.

During 2017, Iraqi and coalition forces routed ISIS insurgents throughout Iraq. On July 10, Iraqi forces retook Mosul from ISIS control. On November 17, Iraqi troops captured the last two ISIS strongholds in Iraq. This prompted al-Abadi to declare victory over ISIS on December 9. Nevertheless, the ISIS threat in Iraq had not been entirely vanquished. Small contingents of its fighters remained hidden in the Iraqi hinterlands, and the group perpetrated a series of deadly terrorist attacks against Iraqi civilians during 2018. In 2019, perhaps several hundred ISIS insurgents remained holed up in Iraq's Anbar desert. Although the intense military aspects of the Iraqi insurgency had slackened rather dramatically as of the summer of 2018, Iraq remains an unstable and dangerous place. It seemed likely that the insurgency would morph into a sustained hit-and-run guerrilla conflict, replete with attacks against Iraqi civilian targets.

LARISSA MIHALISKO, PAUL G. PIERPAOLI JR., SPENCER C. TUCKER

See also
Abadi, Haider al-; Al Qaeda in Iraq; Bremer, Lewis Paul, III; Fallujah, First Battle of; Fallujah, Second Battle of; Fallujah, Third Battle of; Improvised Explosive Devices; Iraq War; Islamic State of Iraq and Syria; Maliki, Nuri Muhammed Kamil al-; Mosul, Second Battle of; Petraeus, David Howell; Sadr, Muqtada al-; Troop Surge, U.S., Iraq War; Zarqawi, Abu Musab al-

References
Gordon, Michael R., and Bernard E. Trainor. *The Endgame: The Inside Story of the Struggle for Iraq, from George W. Bush to Barack Obama.* New York: Pantheon, 2012.

Hashim, Ahmed. *Insurgency and Counter-Insurgency in Iraq.* Ithaca, NY: Cornell University Press, 2006.

Kilcullen, David. *The Accidental Guerrilla: Fighting Small Wars in the Midst of a Big One.* New York: Oxford University Press, 2009.

Montgomery, Gary W., and Timothy S. McWilliams. *Al Anbar Awakening: Iraqi Perspectives*, Vol. 2. Quantico, VA: Marine Corps University Press, 2009.

Iraq No-Fly Zones

Restrictions imposed on the flight of Iraqi military aircraft following the 1991 Persian Gulf War. As part of the March 3, 1991, cease-fire agreement ending the conflict, coalition forces insisted on a no-fly zone in the northern part of Iraq. Extending north from 36 degrees north latitude, it was designed to protect the Kurds from Iraqi government aircraft. In discussions with the Iraqis regarding the cease-fire agreement, coalition military commander General H. Norman Schwarzkopf allowed the Iraqis to continue to fly armed helicopters. Not until April 10 did the United States order Iraq to cease all military action in the northern zone.

No prohibition was imposed on the flight of military aviation in the southern part of the country. During the Persian Gulf War the Shiites in the south had answered the call of the George H. W. Bush administration to rebel, but after the conflict they had been abandoned by the United States. Iraqi dictator Saddam Hussein ordered a bloody repression in which as many as 50,000 Shiites died. Not until a year and a half later, on August 2, 1992, did the Bush administration proclaim a no-fly zone in the south that covered Iraqi territory south of the 32nd parallel. On September 3, 1993, the William J. Clinton administration extended the southern no-fly zone north to reach to the 33rd parallel and the suburbs of Baghdad.

The northern and southern no-fly zones were designed to protect civilians in these areas from air attack and to demonstrate to the Iraqi people that their government would not have full sovereignty over these regions until Hussein was driven from power. In effect, the no-fly zones led to a continuation of warfare, albeit at a low level, between the United States and Britain on the one hand and Iraq on the other extending from the Persian Gulf War to the March 2003 invasion of Iraq that began the Iraq War.

Initially American, British, and French pilots conducted the no-fly patrols, but the French withdrew from participation in 1996. Most patrols were fairly routine, but on December 29, 1992, a U.S. plane shot down an Iraqi MiG-25 when it entered the southern no-fly zone. To circumvent the southern no-fly ban, the Iraqi government used its ground forces to begin a program of draining the Euphrates River marshes inhabited by the rebellious Shiite Marsh Arabs.

The air patrols and air strikes against ground targets were controversial. The United States and Britain alone among Security Council members justified the no-fly zones as being in accordance with UN Security Council Resolution 688. This resolution of April 5, 1991, condemned the repression of the civilian population in many parts of Iraq, but it made no mention of no-fly zones. Other Security Council members, most notably the People's Republic of China and Russia, sharply criticized the British and U.S. air actions.

In the last weeks of the Bush administration, Iraqi air defenses fired on British and U.S. aircraft patrolling the no-fly zones. In response, on January 13, 1993, the Bush administration ordered air attacks against Iraqi air defense sites. More than 100 sorties were flown against Iraqi radar and missile air defense sites near Nasiriyah, Samawa, Najaf, and Al Amara. Then, in response to Hussein's noncompliance with UN inspectors searching for weapons of mass destruction (WMD), on January 17, 1993, the Americans attacked the Zafraniyah nuclear weapons program factory on the outskirts of Baghdad. Fearful of the possible loss of pilots in the downing of aircraft, the Bush administration decided to carry out this attack with 42 Tomahawk cruise missiles alone.

President Clinton continued the retaliatory air strikes of his predecessor. These met increasing opposition from the governments of France, Russia, and Turkey. Tragedy struck in the northern no-fly zone in April 1994 when two U.S. F-15Cs mistakenly shot down two U.S. Army helicopters carrying allied officers to meet with Kurdish officials in northern Iraq.

The undeclared air war continued. Iraqi forces employed their radar sites to target British and U.S. aircraft and occasionally to fire missiles at them. Under the rules of engagement, pilots were authorized to attack ground targets in the event of a radar lock-on, which would be preparatory to a missile launch. In December 1998 in Operation DESERT FOX, U.S. and British aircraft carried out an extensive bombing campaign to destroy suspected Iraqi WMD programs. By 1999 the United States maintained at considerable expense some 200 aircraft, 19 naval ships, and 22,000 American military personnel to enforce the no-fly zones.

The no-fly zones and the low-level warfare that ensued there reflected, at least as far as the United States and Great Britain were concerned, the lack of a satisfactory end to the Persian Gulf War in 1991. At the time, Bush administration officials assumed that Hussein would soon be driven from power, but that proved incorrect. At least the northern no-fly zone provided de facto autonomy for a large portion of the Kurdish population. The no-fly zones ceased to exist with the beginning of the Iraq War (Operation IRAQI FREEDOM) on March 19, 2003.

SPENCER C. TUCKER

See also
DESERT FOX, Operation; Hussein, Saddam; Marsh Arabs; Persian Gulf War, Cease-Fire Agreement; Schwarzkopf, H. Norman, Jr.

References
Byman, Daniel L., and Matthew C. Waxman. *Confronting Iraq: U.S. Policy and the Use of Force since the Gulf War.* Santa Monica, CA: Rand Corporation, 2000.

Gordon, Michael R., and Bernard E. Trainor. *The Generals' War: The Inside Story of the Conflict in the Gulf.* Boston: Little, Brown, 1995.

U.S., Congress, House of Representatives, Committee on Armed Services. *United States Policy Toward Iraq.* Hearing, 106th Congress, 1st Session. Washington: Government Printing Office, 1999.

Iraq War (March 19, 2003– December 15, 2011)

The Iraq War, also known as Operation IRAQI FREEDOM until September 2010, when it was renamed Operation NEW DAWN, occurred in two phases: the first was the invasion and rapid conquest of Iraq by coalition forces led by the United States; the second saw a lengthy insurgency against the occupying coalition forces and the new Iraqi government. Dates for the war are usually given as March 20, 2003, to December 15, 2011, when the last U.S. troops departed, but this end date is misleading, as sectarian violence continued after the U.S. departure, and it and outright warfare in Iraq are ongoing.

The historic roots of the violence in Iraq go back at least as far as the peace settlement following World War I that broke up the old Ottoman Empire and created new states in the Middle East in Palestine, Lebanon, Syria, and Iraq and placed them under European control in a mandate system. The arbitrary borders of these states ignored religious rivalries, such as between Shia and Sunni Muslims, and ethnic divisions. Thus, the Kurds were denied a state and found themselves a minority in Iraq, Syria, Turkey, and Persia (Iran). By 1990 Iraq had a Shia majority (60 percent of the population) concentrated in the south of the country and a Kurdish minority (17 percent) in the north but was ruled with an iron fist by Saddam Hussein, a Sunni. The Sunnis (20 percent) were concentrated in western Iraq and completely dominated the government and military.

Following a long, sanguinary, and financially costly war with Iran (1980–1988), which he had originated, Iraqi dictator Hussein sent his forces into oil-rich Kuwait on August 2, 1990, and then annexed it. International diplomatic efforts to remove the Iraqis from Kuwait proving futile, a coalition of 34 states led by the United States attacked Iraq and liberated Kuwait in the Persian Gulf War (Operation DESERT STORM, January 17–February 28, 1991). With Kuwait free of the Iraqi Army, U.S. president George H. W. Bush, who had assembled the impressive international coalition, ordered a halt to the fighting, allowing the elite Republican Guard divisions, the Iraqi Army's most effective units, to largely escape intact, ensuring Hussein's continued hold on power. Coalition forces commander U.S. general H. Norman

Explosion of a second car bomb aimed at U.S. and Iraqi forces arriving to inspect the site of another car bomb detonated an hour earlier, south Baghdad, April 14, 2005. (U.S. Department of Defense)

Schwarzkopf also erred in a cease-fire agreement of March 3, 1991, that permitted the Iraqis to fly helicopters.

Hussein quickly reestablished his authority, employing the Republican Guard units and helicopters to put down rebellions by both the Shias in the south and the Kurds in the north. The United States had encouraged both groups to rebel against the central government during the war but took no action while as many as 50,000 Shias perished in the subsequent repression. Hussein also began a program of draining the swamps populated by the southern so-called Marsh Arabs to better control that restive group.

Hussein further defied United Nations (UN) inspection teams by failing to account for and destroy all his biological and chemical weapons, the so-called weapons of mass destruction (WMD). Stymied, the UN withdrew its inspectors. In order to help protect the Kurds and Shias, the United States and Britain continued to enforce the no-fly zone set by the cease-fire north of the 36th parallel and then a southern zone set in 1992 at the 32nd parallel and in 1993 extended to the 33rd parallel, from which Iraqi fixed-wing aircraft were prohibited. U.S. and British aircraft struck Iraqi ground radars and antiaircraft positions that on occasion fired on their aircraft, and larger strikes also took place.

Increasingly, though, the administration of U.S. president George W. Bush, elected in November 2000, adopted a tough attitude toward Iraq. This followed and was closely tied to the worst terrorist attack in U.S. history by the Islamist Al Qaeda terrorist organization on September 11, 2001, against the World Trade Center in New York and the Pentagon in Washington, D.C., resulting in the deaths of nearly 3,000 people. After the Taliban government of Afghanistan refused Washington's demands to hand over members of Al Qaeda and especially its leader Osama bin Laden, U.S. forces invaded Afghanistan. They and opposition Northern Alliance (Afghan) forces easily overthrew the Taliban. However, they failed to capture bin Laden or, more importantly, to completely eliminate Taliban and Al Qaeda fighters who subsequently mounted a years-long insurgency that continues today.

Encouraged by what appeared to be a quick victory in Afghanistan with a relatively modest commitment of U.S. ground troops, the Bush administration then shifted its attention to Iraq. In a speech to the U.S. Congress, Bush asserted his intention to root out international terrorism and to confront those states that supported it. He singled out an "Axis of Evil" of Iraq, Iran, and the Democratic People's Republic of Korea (North Korea). Under U.S. and British pressure, the UN Security Council unanimously passed Resolution 1141 calling on Iraq to reveal information regarding WMD and for UN inspectors to report progress to the Security Council. It also threatened force unless Iraq fully complied.

Iraq claimed that it had nothing to hide and no WMD, but the UN inspections went slowly and met many Iraqi-imposed obstacles. A frustrated President Bush and the so-called neocons (neoconservatives) in his administration now demanded military action. The neocons saw such a war as a chance to not only overthrow Hussein but also produce a democratic, pro-U.S. Iraq and opportunity to reshape the entire Middle East. Some held that given Iraq's oil, the war could be won at little cost in treasure to the United States.

A coalition of countries that had vested financial interests in the status quo in Iraq—France, Germany, and Russia—blocked U.S. and British efforts to secure a UN Security Council resolution supporting an invasion. Bush and British prime minister Tony Blair then decided to proceed against Iraq without a UN resolution. Bush sought and won on October 11, 2002, a congressional mandate authorizing the use of force against Iraq if he deemed it necessary. Public opinion was very much divided, although a slight majority of the U.S. population supported such action, while Blair's government took its decision in the face of British popular opposition.

Despite the fact that since 1990 U.S. and British air and naval power had kept Hussein contained, Bush defended a ground invasion as necessary to locate and destroy Iraqi WMD, to end Hussein's alleged effort to acquire nuclear weapons, and to terminate a claimed link between the Iraqi government and Al Qaeda. Misgivings voiced by lower-level analysts at the State Department and the Central Intelligence Agency (CIA), who had a far better understanding of Iraqi realities, never reached the president or were brushed aside. Certainly there was a rush to war from his influential advisers, especially Vice President Dick Cheney, Secretary of Defense Donald Rumsfeld, and Deputy Secretary of Defense Paul Wolfowitz. No serious consideration was given to the risks involved, particularly the bitter rivalries among the religious/ethnic factions within Iraq. Both Cheney and Rumsfeld asserted that U.S. forces would be welcomed as liberators. Moreover, the seemingly quick and cheap victory in Afghanistan led Rumsfeld and others to publicly belittle and ignore assessments by military advisers, notably U.S. Army chief of staff General Eric Shinseki, that occupying and effectively controlling Iraq would require many hundreds of thousands of American ground troops.

Meanwhile, a military buildup had been under way for some time in Kuwait. More than 300,000 American military men and women were deployed under coalition commander U.S. Army general Tommy Franks, head of Central Command. Unlike DESERT STORM, however, there was no broad grouping of powers arrayed with the United States, and Saudi Arabia refused use of its bases for air strikes against Iraq. Although some Persian Gulf states, notably Kuwait and Qatar, did cooperate, members of this so-called Coalition of the Willing ultimately included some 75 nations, but the military forces were drawn chiefly from the United States, Britain, and Australia. Notably absent were key U.S. European allies France and Germany.

Washington experienced a major setback when the Turkish parliament, despite promises of up to $30 billion in financial assistance, refused to allow U.S. forces to use Turkish territory to open up a northern front, a key component of the U.S. strategic plan. Three dozen ships laden with equipment for the 30,000-man U.S. 4th Infantry Division lay off Turkish ports but never were permitted to unload. Only after the war began were they redirected through the Suez Canal to Kuwait. In consequence, the 4th Infantry Division became part of the follow-on force. A disinformation campaign to the effect that the Turkish military would pressure Ankara to allow the forces of its NATO ally the United States to operate from Turkey apparently proved successful, as Hussein retained two regular Iraqi divisions north of Baghdad, and these troops took no part in combating the coalition offensive.

The Iraq War—dubbed Operation IRAQI FREEDOM—actually began on the night of March 19, 2003, just hours after the expiration of President Bush's ultimatum to Hussein. It commenced with a cruise missile strike against a purported meeting of the Iraqi leadership in Baghdad. This strike failed to decapitate the Iraqi government as intended, however. On succeeding nights, Baghdad was repeatedly hit from the air with cruise missile attacks and air strikes by B-1, B-2, and B-52 bombers against key headquarters and command and control targets. This shock-and-awe air campaign employed 70 percent precision-guided (smart) aerial weapons and 30 percent unguided (dumb) munitions, as opposed to only 10 percent smart weapons during the 1991 Persian Gulf War. Also in contrast to 1991, a good many of the air strikes occurred away from the capital. As in the Persian

Gulf War, coalition forces early on established complete air superiority.

Even before March 19, though, U.S., British, and Australian special forces had deployed into Iraq for both reconnaissance and strike roles. One of their missions was to destroy Iraqi watch posts on the southern border. Special forces also secured key bridge and crossing points across the Tigris and Euphrates Rivers.

On March 20, the 100,000-man coalition invasion ground force moved into southern Iraq from Kuwait. The few Iraqi missiles launched at coalition staging areas in general and Kuwait City in particular were almost all downed by improved Patriot antimissile missiles. Coalition ground forces moved north on three axes: the U.S. Army's V Corps to the west, the U.S. Marine Corps 1st Expeditionary Force in the center, and British forces to the east. The Iraqi capital of Baghdad, a city of 5 million people, lay 300 miles to the northwest.

In the west the offensive was led by UH-60 Black Hawk and Boeing AH-64 Apache helicopters, with the 7th Armored Cavalry Regiment the leading ground element, followed by the 3rd Infantry Division and follow-on units of the V Corps. The western offensive made the most rapid progress, largely because it swung westward and moved through sparsely populated areas. In the center part of the front, the 1st Marine Expeditionary Force skirted to the west of the Euphrates River, through the cities of Nasiriyah and on to Najaf and Karbala. On the eastern part of the front, the British had the task of securing the port of Umm Qasr and Iraq's second-largest city of Basra with its largely Shia population of 500,000. It was not clear how the Shias would react, following their abandonment by the United States in 1991. After clearing the channel for mines, a British ship docked at Umm Qasr with relief supplies.

Airpower played a key role in the coalition advance. In northern Iraq, aircraft ferried men and supplies into the Kurdish-controlled zone, opening a front there against the Iraqi Army but also against Ansar al-Islam, a militant Islamic group with a base camp and training facilities at Kalak on the Iranian border. Coalition airpower dominated the skies, with Iraqi aircraft and helicopters rarely even getting off the ground. Helicopter gunships and the A-10 Thunderbolt II (Warthog) tank-buster proved highly effective. Another important factor was the technical and tactical ability of coalition troops to fight at night, whereas the Iraqis lacked the equipment and training to do so effectively.

U.S. marines were successful in seizing the oil fields north of Basra—some 60 percent of the nation's total production—and the key refineries. A few wellheads were set afire and some equipment was damaged, but overall damage was slight.

Meanwhile, the British were at Basra. Wishing to spare the civilian population and hoping for an internal uprising, they did not move into the city proper until the night of April 2. In the meantime they imposed a loose blockade and, to demoralize the defenders, carried out a series of raids into the city to destroy symbols of the regime, such as Baath Party headquarters and images of Hussein. At the same time, they distributed relief supplies to win over the civilian population.

As U.S. special forces secured airfields in western Iraq, on the night of March 26 1,000 members of the 173rd Airborne Brigade dropped into Kurdish-held territory in northern Iraq to operate in conjunction with lightly armed Kurdish forces, open a northern front, and threaten the key oil production center of Mosul. Hussein loyalist Baath Party terror cells carried out attacks on civilians, including in Basra, while the so-called Saddam Fedayeen, or "technicals," irregulars often wearing civilian clothes, carried out attacks employing civilian vehicles mounting machine guns and rocket-propelled grenades against coalition supply convoys plying the lines of communication north from Kuwait. Near Najaf, Iraqi missiles destroyed two M1 Abrams tanks, the first time this had been accomplished, but the 7th Cavalry Regiment secured bridges south of the town, completing its encirclement.

A week into the war, the coalition advance north stalled in an operational pause because of a *shamal* (strong sandstorm) on March 26; fierce U.S. Army and Marine Corps firefights for Nasiriyah, Najaf, and other places; and the need to protect lengthy logistical lines now under increasing Iraqi attack. Friendly fire incidents remained a nagging problem. There were more casualties from these (including two aircraft—one British and one U.S.—shot down by Patriot missiles and a Patriot battery engaged by a U.S. aircraft) than during the Persian Gulf War.

The Iraqi leadership now repositioned the six "elite" Republican Guard divisions around the city of Baghdad to defend the capital. Reportedly Hussein had drawn a red line beyond which the coalition would not be allowed to cross and within which he would employ WMD. This seemed increasingly possible with coalition discoveries of caches of gas masks and the nerve gas antidote, atropine, and when some Iraqi Republican Guard troops with gas masks were taken prisoner. As the Baghdad and Medina Republican Guard divisions moved to take up new positions south of Baghdad, they came under heavy coalition air attack, seriously degrading their fighting ability.

The coalition advance quickened again during April 1–2. U.S. troops were within 50 miles of Baghdad, and U.S. secretary of state Colin Powell (who had been chairman of the Joint Chiefs of Staff during the Persian Gulf War) traveled to Ankara and secured Turkish government approval for coalition equipment to be moved through Turkey to troops on the northern front. On April 3 U.S. forces reached the outskirts of Baghdad and during the next two days secured Saddam International Airport, some 12 miles from the city center. Because of the speed of the advance, the airport was taken with minimal damage to its facilities. When the surrounding territory was secured, the airport became a major coalition staging area. The general Iraqi population seemed to sense the shift of momentum and an imminent coalition victory. Advancing troops reported receiving friendly receptions from civilians and increasing surrenders of Iraqi troops.

By April 5 the 3rd Infantry Division was closing on Baghdad from the southwest, the marines were closing from the southeast, and the 101st Airborne Division was repositioning to move in from the north. Baghdad in effect came under a loose blockade in which civilians were allowed to depart and sanctuaries were created for civilians and surrendering Iraqi forces. On that day also, the 2nd Brigade of the 3rd Infantry Division pushed through downtown Baghdad in a three-hour-long operation (nicknamed "Thunder Run"), inflicting an estimated 1,000 Iraqi casualties. This was a powerful psychological blow to Hussein's regime, which had claimed that U.S. forces were nowhere near the city and that it still controlled the international airport. The operation showed that allied forces could move at will and led to an exodus of Baath Party officials and Iraqi Army personnel, who now joined ordinary citizens trying to escape.

The U.S. raid into Baghdad was repeated on April 6 and 7. In a fierce firefight on the 6th, U.S. forces killed an estimated 2,000–3,000 Iraqi soldiers for 1 killed of their own. U.S. forces also toppled a large statue of Hussein and occupied one of his presidential palaces. Also on April 6 the first C-130 aircraft landed at the renamed Baghdad International Airport, and the coalition announced that it was providing 24-hour air cover over Baghdad to protect U.S. forces there.

On April 7 three 3rd Infantry Division battalions remained in the city, while the next day marine elements moved into southeastern Baghdad, securing a military airfield. With the 101st Airborne coming in from the west and then fanning out to the north and the 3rd Infantry Division moving in from the southeast, the ring around the capital was closed. By that day there was at least a brigade in the city.

On April 9 resistance in Baghdad collapsed as civilians, assisted by U.S. marines, toppled another large statute of Hussein. Sporadic fighting continued in parts of the city, however, as diehard Baath loyalists sniped at U.S. troops, but Iraqi government central command and control had ended.

The next day, April 10, a small number of Kurdish fighters, U.S. special forces, and 173rd Airborne Brigade troops liberated Kirkuk. They quickly took control of the northern oil fields from the Kurds to prevent any possibility of Turkish intervention. The next day, Iraq's third-largest city, Mosul, fell when Iraq's V Corps commander surrendered some 30,000 men. Apart from some sporadic shooting in Baghdad and massive looting there and in other cities, the one remaining center of resistance was Hussein's ancestral home of Tikrit.

On April 12 the 101st Airborne relieved the marines and the 3rd Infantry Division in Baghdad, allowing them to deploy northwest to Tikrit. The battle for Tikrit, however, failed to materialize. Hussein's stronghold collapsed, and on April 14 coalition forces entered the city. That same day the Pentagon announced that major military operations in Iraq were at an end; all that remained was mopping up. President Bush officially proclaimed victory on May 1 aboard the aircraft carrier *Abraham Lincoln* against a large banner with the words "Mission Accomplished."

With no WMD discovered and no link with Al Qaeda proven, the Bush administration now modified its justifications for war. Although presidential candidate Bush had steadfastly denounced the Democrats for military interventions around the world and "nation building," he now claimed that the war was necessary to remove Hussein and his family from power and to democratize Iraq. Hussein, who was not taken prisoner until December 13, 2003, was tried by the interim Iraqi government and executed on December 30, 2006.

As of May 1, 2003, the United States had suffered 138 deaths: 114 from combat and 24 from other causes. The British sustained 42 dead, 19 of them from accidents. Estimates of Iraqi casualties vary widely, from 7,600 to 10,800 dead. Civilian dead may have topped 10,000.

Victory would have been even swifter had U.S. forces been able to operate from Turkey. It was also clear that had the additional American ground forces of up to 500,000 sought initially by U.S. military planners but rejected by Rumsfeld been made available, this would have prevented some of the extensive looting in the wake of the coalition victories that did much to embolden the opposition. Additional forces would also have been able to secure Hussein's massive munitions and weapons stockpiles, which for months thereafter supplied resistance fighters with the stockpiles with which they could make the improvised explosive devices (IEDs) that would plague the occupation forces for years to come and produce the vast majority of U.S. and coalition casualties during the ensuring counterinsurgency operations.

Among major errors by the United States in Iraq following the overthrow of Hussein's regime were two disastrous decisions by Paul Bremer, administrator of the Coalition Provisional Authority (CPA): Bremer ordered the Iraqi Army disbanded and ordered a purge of members of Hussein's Baath Party, who constituted the majority of experienced Iraqi governmental employees as well as a number of teachers. On Bremer's order these skilled and mostly apolitical individuals were banned from holding any positions in Iraq's new government and public service. This decision created a formidable opposition to the new Shia-dominated government, which sought to impose Shia hegemony over the entire country. De-Baathification certainly fueled the insurgency that now swept Iraq. Disbanding the Iraqi Army destroyed security and let that burden fall solely on the occupying forces, most of whom could not speak Arabic and understood little of Iraq and its customs.

The insurgency appeared in the form of kidnappings, political assassinations, suicide bombings, car and truck bombs, IEDs, and other terrorist activities. The violence was carried out primarily by, but not limited to, Sunni Arabs—many of them former members of the armed forces—who now found themselves bereft of power and influence and under the thumb of the majority Shiites. Their attacks were directed against both the foreign troops now occupying Iraq, seen as propping up the new Shia-dominated government, and the Shias themselves. The insurgents came to include foreign fighters—jihadists who came to Iraq to establish an Islamic state and to wage war against the West. Also present was Al Qaeda in Iraq, a branch of the international terrorist organization determined to strike at the United States.

Soon a virtual civil war had engulfed Iraq, waged by a large number of disparate groups against coalition military forces and the Iraqi government. Foreign governments, chiefly Syria and Iran, were not above supporting the insurgency, despite being coreligionists of the Iraqi Shias, because it served to weaken their longtime rival of Iraq and lengthened the odds against establishment of a strong pro-Western government there. Some former Baathists, including the acknowledged leader of the resistance, Ibrahim al-Duri, were in Syria. They also strongly opposed the establishment of U.S. bases and a permanent American presence in Iraq.

It would take considerable time to establish intelligence networks to deal with the insurgents, and initial U.S. and Iraqi government tactics were haphazard and ineffective. These consisted chiefly of indiscriminate and sometimes culturally insensitive night searches, interrogations, and blanket incarcerations. Such actions angered many formerly friendly or neutral Iraqis. Moreover, the revelations in late 2003 of widespread and systematic abuse of detainees perpetrated by U.S. military personnel and civilian contractor interrogators at Abu Ghraib prison generated a massive international outcry and condemnation of the American-led occupation.

As the insurgency spread, full-scale military operations against insurgent-controlled areas ensued. They included Operations DESERT THRUST carried out by the 1st Brigade of the 1st Infantry Division, PHANTOM FURY (also known as the Second Battle of Fallujah, carried out in the Sunni city by U.S., British, and Iraqi troops during November 7–December 23, 2004), and TOGETHER FORWARD (an unsuccessful effort by U.S. and Iraqi Army forces during June 14–October 24, 2006, to improve security in the capital of Baghdad). These large-scale operations had only a temporary and limited effect, however. As soon as security was reestablished and troops were withdrawn, the insurgents returned.

The most notable counterinsurgency effort was mounted during 2007. The so-called troop surge saw an additional 21,500 U.S. military personnel sent to Iraq. Critics, however, pointed out that violence had receded in some areas only because of "ethnic cleansing" in neighborhoods, whereby Shias were driven out of predominantly Sunni areas and vice versa. In the spring of 2009, moreover, there was an upsurge in bombings in both Shia and Sunni areas of Baghdad. Most insurgent activity involved only Sunni-Shia confrontations, but there was also armed resistance against the Iraqi government by members of Muqtada al-Sadr's Mahdi Army.

Perhaps the key reason for the decrease in violence was the bargain struck beginning in 2005 by the U.S. military with Sunni tribal sheikhs that led to the creation of the National Council for the Salvation of Iraq, known also as the Sunni Salvation Movement, National Council for the Awakening of Iraq, Sunni Awakening movement, and Sons of Iraq. It was a series of agreements between tribal Sunni sheikhs, especially in heavily Sunni Anbar Province, whereby local defense forces would be paid to maintain security in their communities.

The violence again increased when Shiite prime minister Nuri al-Maliki refused to integrate the Sons of Iraq into the Iraqi security services. By 2013 they had virtually ceased to exist. Many former members of the Sons of Iraq joined the radical Islamic State of Iraq and Syria (ISIS).

The steady withdrawal of coalition partners put pressure on the United States to do the same. U.S. president Barack Obama had planned to leave a residual U.S. force in Iraq that would have as its chief mission training the Iraqi Army, but the refusal of Maliki, who took office in May 2006, to agree to a status of forces agreement that would provide immunity from Iraqi prosecution for U.S. armed forces led Obama to withdraw all remaining U.S. forces according to the timetable previously set by the Bush administration. The U.S. military withdrawal was completed on December 15, 2011.

The second phase of the Iraq War had claimed 4,487 U.S. military personnel killed. The United Kingdom lost 179 and other coalition forces 139. Wounded amounted to 32,226 for the United States, 315 for Britain, and more than 212 for other coalition partners. Even larger numbers of personnel had received medical treatment for noncombat injuries, illnesses, or diseases. The Iraqi Awakening Councils lost more than 1,000 killed and 500 wounded. By that date also Iraqi insurgent dead numbered some 26,500, while the number of documented Iraqi civilians killed in the violence easily topped 100,000.

Unfortunately, after the U.S. withdrawal from the country, Iraq has experienced steadily increasing sectarian violence and actual armed conflict leading to mounting civilian casualties. In April 2014 alone, some 750 Iraqis died in bombings and other insurgency-related unrest. Those contributing to the violence included Sunni extremists, Shiite militia groups, and a number of radical Islamist groups, including those with ties to Al Qaeda. A new threat emerged, however, in the form of the Islamic State of Iraq and Syria, or ISIS. By mid-2014, it had seized control of virtually all of Anbar Province and was actually threatening Baghdad.

The Iraq War clearly resulted in increased Sunni-Shia tensions throughout the Middle East. The war also significantly advanced Iranian influence in the region. Iran has increased its military assistance to its coreligionists in Lebanon, to Hamas against Israel, to Iraq, and to the regime of President Bashar al-Assad in Syria, where civil war began in March 2011.

This is certainly not what the Bush administration had sought or anticipated when it plunged the United States into a war to topple Saddam Hussein from power. Hussein was indeed a cruel dictator and mass murderer who ruled by terror, but he also had held Iraq together. A more inclusive post-Hussein Iraqi government might have carried off this difficult task as well, but Maliki and his Shiite colleagues rejected this course. As of this writing, the long-term consequences of the Iraq War remain quite unclear, but certainly it has brought greater instability to the region. The long war may well result in the redrawing of state borders in the Middle East, to include Syria and Iraq, this time not by peacemakers in Paris but instead by fighting on the ground between rival religious sects.

Spencer C. Tucker

See also
Al Qaeda; Ansar al-Islam; Baath Party; Basra, Battle for; Fallujah, First Battle of; Fallujah, Second Battle of; Fallujah, Third Battle of; Hussein, Saddam; Improvised Explosive Devices; Iran-Iraq War; Iraq; Iraq Insurgency; Iraq No-Fly Zones; Islamic State of Iraq and Syria; Kuwait, Iraqi Invasion of; Maliki, Nuri Muhammed Kamil al-; Marsh Arabs; Persian Gulf War, Overview; Sadr, Muqtada al-; Shia Islam; Sunni Islam

References
Atkinson, Rick. *In the Company of Soldiers: A Chronicle of Combat.* New York: Little, Brown, 2004.
Cavaleri, David. *Easier Said Than Done: Making the Transition between Combat Operations and Stability Operations.* Ft. Leavenworth, KS: Combat Studies Institute Press, 2005.
Cordesman, Anthony H. *The Iraq War: Strategy, Tactics, and Military Lessons.* Washington, DC: Center for Strategic and International Studies, 2003.
DiMarco, Louis A. *Traditions, Changes and Challenges: Military Operations and the Middle Eastern City.* Ft. Leavenworth, KS: Combat Studies Institute Press, 2004.
Franks, Tommy R. *American Soldier.* New York: HarperCollins, 2004.
Gaddis, John Lewis. *Surprise, Security and the American Experience.* Cambridge, MA: Harvard University Press, 2005.
Gordon, Michael R., and Bernard E. Trainor. *Cobra II: The Inside Story of the Invasion and Occupation of Iraq.* New York: Pantheon, 2006.
Murray, Williamson, and Robert H. Scales Jr. *The Iraq War: A Military History.* Cambridge, MA: Belknap, 2005.
Pirnie, Bruce R., and Edward O'Connell. *Counterinsurgency in Iraq (2003–2006).* Santa Monica, CA: Rand Corporation, 2008.
Ricks, Thomas E. *Fiasco: The American Military Adventure in Iraq.* New York: Penguin, 2006.
Trainor, Bernard E., and Michael R. Gordon. *Cobra II: The Inside Story of the Invasion and Occupation of Iraq.* New York: Pantheon, 2006.
Woodward, Bob. *Bush at War.* New York: Simon and Schuster, 2002.
Woodward, Bob. *Plan of Attack.* New York: Simon and Schuster, 2004.
Woodward, Bob. *State of Denial: Bush at War, Vol. III.* New York, Simon and Schuster, 2007.

Zinmeister, Karl. *Boots on the Ground: A Month with the 82d Airborne Division in the Battle for Iraq.* New York: St. Martin's, 2004.

Zinmeister, Karl. *Dawn over Baghdad: How the U. S. Military Is Using Bullets and Ballots to Remake Iraq.* New York: Encounter Books, 2004.

Irgun Tsvai Leumi

Right-wing paramilitary Zionist underground movement in Palestine from 1931 to 1948. Better known later as Etzel for its contracted Hebrew initials, the Irgun Tsvai Leumi (National Military Organization) became renowned for launching immediate and harsh retaliatory attacks on persons or organizations that had initiated violence against the Jewish community in Palestine (Yishuv). It was also known for its advocacy of military action against the British, who held a mandate over Palestine until May 1948. The British categorized Irgun as a terrorist organization, and the Jewish Agency for Palestine, Haganah, and Histadrut declared many of its operations to be acts of terrorism.

Even as the British slowly shifted their support to Palestine's Arab population in the 1930s, the leadership of the Jewish Agency for Palestine, in particular David Ben-Gurion, continued to work closely with the British to promote the interests of the Jewish population in Palestine. Haganah supported this position through its self-defense and military strategy of *havlaga,* or self-restraint. But not all of the Haganah membership agreed with a restrained response to the perceived British pro-Arab bias. This political and policy disagreement coupled with Haganah's prevailing socialist ideology caused a minority of its members, led by Avraham Tehomi, to leave Haganah in 1931 and form Irgun. Irgun was based on premises formulated by Vladimir Jabotinsky, who had led the Jewish Legion when it fought with the British to remove the Ottoman Turks from Palestine in World War I. He believed strongly that swift retaliatory action would forestall Arab attacks on the Yishuv.

By 1936 Irgun was little more than a pawn of the extreme nationalist Revisionist Zionists (Revisionist Party), led by Jabotinsky. The Revisionists had seceded from the World Zionist Organization (WZO) and were advocating the creation by force of a Jewish homeland, spanning both banks of the Jordan River. In 1937 Haganah again split into right-wing and left-wing factions. The right-wing faction joined Irgun, and some of the members of Irgun, including Tehomi, rejoined Haganah. Until this time, Irgun had been little more than a small and ineffective irritant in the region.

When Arab attacks during the Arab Revolt of 1936–1939 killed some 400 Jews, Irgun began launching retaliatory attacks against Arabs, utilizing car bombs in areas of high Arab congregation. These endured until the beginning of World War II and killed as many as 250 Arab civilians. Irgun, which considered the British mandatory government to be illegal under international law, also directed acts of terrorism and assassination against the British. When the British white paper of 1939 openly shifted British support away from the Jews to the Arabs by severely restricting Jewish immigration, settlement, and land purchases in Palestine, Irgun focused on attacking British military installations and interests. Irgun's rationale for the attacks was that the new and more severe British restrictions on Jewish immigration from Europe were contributing to Nazi Germany's genocide against Jews that soon became known as the Holocaust. Indeed, Irgun demonstrated that immigration to Palestine had saved approximately 18,000 European Jews prior to the shift in British policy, which began in earnest in early 1940.

During 1941–1943, Irgun suspended its attacks on British interests and supported the Allies against Germany and its Arab allies in the Middle East. However, a small group of men known as the Stern Gang, the Fighters for the Freedom of Israel, or Lehi and led by Avraham Stern separated from Irgun in 1941 and continued to attack the British in Palestine during this period. When Irgun was under the command of Menachem Begin (1943–1948), the organization declared war against the British in February 1944 and resumed attacks on Arab villages and British interests.

On November 6, 1944, in Cairo, Lehi assassinated Walter Edward Guinness, Lord Moyne, heir to the Guinness beer fortune and the British minister resident in the Middle East. The murder was allegedly in retaliation for the 1939 white paper's restrictions on Jewish immigration that were contributing to the deaths of Jews in the Holocaust. At that point, Haganah and the Jewish Agency for Palestine launched a campaign against Irgun and Lehi named Sezon (Hunting Season), which turned over to the British a number of the members and leaders of Irgun. The British, with more than 100,000 soldiers in Palestine alone, ultimately arrested and jailed about 1,000 Irgun and Lehi members.

In an attempt to fight more effectively against the continuing British restrictions on Jewish immigration, Irgun, Lehi, and Haganah allied during October 1944–July 1945 as the Jewish Resistance Movement. This alliance ended in August 1945 after Irgun killed 91 soldiers and British, Arab, and Jewish civilians on July 22, 1946, when it bombed the British military, police, and civil headquarters at the King

David Hotel in Jerusalem. Begin and Irgun claimed to have issued three warnings in an attempt to limit casualties. Nevertheless, the British arrested, tried, convicted, and hanged several members of Irgun. When Irgun responded by hanging 2 British sergeants, the executions stopped, although British arrests of Irgun members continued. On May 5, 1947, Haganah and Irgun combined forces to breach the wall of the supposedly secure British prison at Akko (Acre), thereby freeing 251 prisoners.

In anticipation of and following the United Nations (UN) partition of Palestine in 1947, from July 1947 to June 1948 Irgun and Haganah increasingly coordinated their forces. Irgun's greatest victory and largest operation was the capture of the Arab city of Jaffa. On May 28, 1948, the provisional government of the newly declared State of Israel transformed Haganah into its national military, the Israel Defense Forces (IDF). In doing so, Israel outlawed all other armed forces. In September 1948 the military activities of Irgun were folded into the IDF. Begin meanwhile adapted what remained of the movement into a political party that was the precursor of the Herut (Freedom) Party, which merged in 1965 with the Liberal Party to form the Gahal Party. Gahal served as the foundation for the present-day Likud Party.

RICHARD M. EDWARDS

See also
Begin, Menachem; Ben-Gurion, David; Haganah; Holocaust; Palestine, British Mandate for

References
Begin, Menachem. *The Revolt*. Los Angeles: Nash Publishing, 1972.
Bell, J. Bowyer. *Terror out of Zion: Irgun Zvai Leumi, Lehi and the Palestine Underground, 1929–1949*. New York: St. Martin's, 1979.
Ben Ami, Yitshaq. *Years of Wrath, Days of Glory: Memoirs from the Irgun*. New York: R. Speller, 1982.
Levine, David. *The Birth of the Irgun Zvai Leumi: The Jewish Resistance Movement*. Jerusalem: Gefen, 1996.

Isfahan, Siege of (March– October 23, 1722)

By 1700, the Safavids had lost much of their sway in Afghanistan. As a consequence, in 1704 Safavid shah Sultan Husayn dispatched a Georgian-Iranian army, led by Georgian king Giorgi XI (Gorgin Khan), to subdue the rebellious Afghani tribes. Gorgin Khan defeated the Afghans and forced them to accept Safavid rule. However, his heavy-handed and oppressive governorship in Afghanistan prompted an Afghani revolt in the spring of 1709, led by Ghilzai tribe chief Mir Vays (Mir Ways). The Afghans defeated the Georgian contingents and expelled the Persians from Afghanistan. The loss of capable generals and elite troops left Persia exposed to attack. After the death of Mir Vays, his son Mahmud assumed the leadership of a loose coalition of Afghani tribes and in 1722 invaded Iran and routed the Safavid army near Gulnabad on March 8, 1722.

The destruction of the Safavid army took the Ghilzai leader by surprise, and he did not immediately realize the full extent of his victory. Concerned about ambushes, he spent three days on the battlefield before cautiously advancing to Isfahan, which he could have easily captured had he pursued the Persians immediately after his victory. Mahmud captured Farahabad, Sultan Husayn's favorite castle, without a fight, and then plundered Julfa, Isfahan's suburb populated by Armenian merchants.

The Afghans then laid siege to the city itself, while the Safavid leadership continued to show indecision and lack of resolve. The shah retained counselors whose advice had contributed to the Persian defeats and dismissed those who could have helped him. Persian attempts to negotiate revealed to the Afghans the full gravity of the situation facing the Safavids.

Sultan Husayn failed to evacuate the civilian population of Isfahan and instead imposed a general ban on leaving it. Most importantly, he decided to remain inside the capital instead of escaping to provinces to raise fresh troops. Meanwhile, the Georgians, who had played such a prominent role in the Safavid state and could probably have defeated the Afghans on their own, refused to come to Sultan Husayn's help because of his earlier mistreatment of them.

In April, the Ghilzai captured a bridge in the Abbasabad quarter and established a bridgehead into Isfahan. While the Afghans could not completely surround the city owing to the size of their army, Mahmud skillfully deployed his men at crucial points, making it virtually impossible to get in or out of it. Life inside the city quickly deteriorated as supplies ran out and desperate residents turned against each other; within weeks, cannibalism became rife. By August hundreds of people were dying each day from starvation and diseases, their corpses piling up in the city streets. After six months of siege Sultan Husayn realized that further resistance was futile, and he surrendered the city to Mahmud on October 23. At a meeting in the castle of Farahabad, the shah announced his abdication in favor of Mahmud, presenting him with the bejewelled tuft of heron's feathers (*jiqa*), the symbol of monarchy. Two days later Mahmud entered Isfahan in triumphant procession.

The fall of Isfahan marked the twilight of the Safavid dynasty. In 1726 most Safavid princes were massacred, and Shah Sultan Husayn was executed. The Ghilzai supremacy in Iran lasted seven years, but this period was full of domestic turmoil and foreign threats. In the 1730s, Nadir Khan expelled the Afghans and briefly restored the Safavid dynasty to the throne before claiming it for himself.

The city of Isfahan itself, once the crown jewel of Iran, suffered greatly during the siege, its infrastructure damaged or destroyed and its population decimated. The city never recovered from this destruction and was later eclipsed by Shiraz, Mashhad, and finally Tehran.

ALEXANDER MIKABERIDZE

See also
Gulnabad, Battle of; Persia, 18th-Century Wars of Succession

References
Floor, Willem, ed. *The Afghan Occupation of Safavid Persia 1721–1729*. Paris: Association pour l'avancement des études iraniennes, 1998.
Lockhart, Laurence. *The Fall of the Safavi Dynasty and the Afghan Occupation of Persia*. Cambridge: Cambridge University Press, 1958.

Islamic Army of Aden

An Al Qaeda regional affiliate in southern Yemen. The group's name, Islamic Army of Aden (IAA), references the alleged revelation of Prophet Muhammad that "twelve thousand will appear from Aden Abyan who will aid God and His Messenger." The IAA emerged in the mid-1990s as one of several loosely connected organizations established by Afghan-Soviet War veterans and various local and international Islamic jihadists. The battlefield experience of the former Afghan mujahideen, combined with the extraordinarily large number of weapons available in Yemen (estimated at three firearms to each resident), facilitated the creation of a formidable movement.

The IAA emerged under the leadership of Zein al-Abidin al-Mihdar (aka Abu al-Hassan) against the backdrop of civil unrest following the shaky unification of North and South Yemen in 1990. The group called for the overthrow of the government in Sana'a and the removal of all U.S. and British ambassadors from the country. Despite this dual-track agenda, the IAA targeted only foreigners, never the Yemeni government itself.

The IAA gained notoriety through statements applauding the 1998 U.S. embassy attacks in Kenya and Tanzania and the group's subsequent kidnapping of 16 Western tourists, who were seized in the name of Al Qaeda leader Osama bin Laden. Yemeni forces captured Abu al-Hassan in an operation to free the hostages, 4 of whom were killed. He was executed and succeeded by Hatem bi Fareed.

The IAA established a training camp in the mountains of Abyan and adjusted its strategy to focus on high-visibility targets. In coordination with local Al Qaeda members, the organization carried out a failed attack on USS *The Sullivans* and took credit for the bombings of USS *Cole* (October 12, 2000) and the tanker *M/V Limburg* (October 6, 2002), although primary responsibility for these strikes has always lain with Al Qaeda. The day after the *Cole* incident, another IAA member was charged with throwing a hand grenade into the British embassy.

The IAA issued most threats and statements through Abu Hamza al-Masri, a British-Egyptian dual-national cleric known for preaching a violent and politicized interpretation of Islam. The George W. Bush administration froze his assets in 2002 on the grounds that he was a primary financier for the IAA, and the UK government revoked his citizenship a year later after he was determined to be a threat to national security. Al-Masri was arrested in London in May 2004.

The IAA itself has suffered from a number of setbacks as a result of heightened counterterrorist efforts since September 11, 2001. In 2002 a missile from a U.S. Predator aircraft struck a car carrying four suspected IAA members along with an Al Qaeda regional commander and a Yemeni American recruiter. The next year Yemeni forces stormed one of its main compounds, killing several senior members. Following the raid Abd al-Nabi accepted President Ali Abdullah Saleh's offer of a full pardon for all insurgents who surrendered to the government. Deprived of its leader, the IAA effectively collapsed, and there is little evidence that the group has been active since 2003. That said, there have been periodic reports of ex-IAA militants joining jihadist extremists in Yemen, Iraq, and elsewhere.

JULIE MANNING

See also
Al Qaeda; Al Qaeda in the Arabian Peninsula; Bin Laden, Osama; *Cole*, USS, Attack on

References
Cook, David. *Paradigmatic Jihadi Movements*. West Point, NY: Combating Terrorism Center, 2006.
"Yemen: Coping with Terrorism and Violence in a Fragile State." *ICG Middle East Report* 8 (2003): 1–32.

Islamic Civil War, First (656–661)

The Muslim civil war, or *fitna*, lasted from the murder of the caliph Uthman (Osman) in 656 to the assassination of the last of the Rashidun caliphs, Ali, in 661. Ali was chosen as caliph after Uthman's murder. Zubayr and Talha, two prominent companions of Prophet Muhammad, advised him to keep Uthman's governors in place for the time being and to unify Muslims by punishing the mutineers who had taken part in the siege of Uthman's house and his murder. However, Ali did not heed their council and took no action due to either indecisiveness, inability, or refusal. In fact, he alienated himself from many by trying to replace the governors of the provinces with his own candidates.

Because of his failure to punish Uthman's murderers, Ali lost standing and support among many Muslims in the empire. Furthermore, as a result of these actions Zubayr, Talha, and Aisha raised the banners of rebellion and marched to Basra. In the ensuing Battle of Bassorah (Battle of the Camel) on November 7, 656, Ali crushed the rebels and then turned his attention to Syria, where Muawiyah, Uthman's cousin, was governor and had refused to acknowledge Ali's caliphate or the governor he appointed to replace him. The subsequent Battle of Siffin was inconclusive, and both sides agreed to resolve their differences through arbitration. Ali's acceptance of this caused a rift among his supporters, and a number of them abandoned his cause and became known as the Kharijites.

Ali lost the arbitration that decided that Uthman's death was unjust. He refused to acknowledge the outcome of the arbitration and withdrew to Kufa, while Muawiyah was proclaimed caliph by his followers in Damascus. Before Ali could again march against Syria, he had to deal with the dissidents who had left his army at Siffin. He met this group of Kharijites near Nahrawan and tried to convince them to rejoin his army. No agreement could be reached, however, and some 3,000 Kharijites were massacred.

The two caliphs ruled their domains from Damascus and Kufa until 661, when Ali was assassinated by a Kharijite. Muawiyah was then able to consolidate the caliphate and establish the Umayyad dynasty.

Adam Ali

See also
Ali ibn Abi Talib; Bassorah, Battle of; Muawiyah I; Siffin, Battle of; Umayyad Caliphate

References
Glubb, John Baggot. *The Great Arab Conquests*. London: Hodder and Stoughton, 1963.
Hodgson, Marshall G. S. *The Venture of Islam: Conscience and History in a World Civilization*. Chicago: University of Chicago Press, 1977.
Madelung, Wilferd. *The Succession to Muhammad: A Study of the Early Caliphate*. Cambridge: Cambridge University Press, 1997.

Islamic Civil War, Second (680–692)

The second Muslim civil war, or *fitna*, began in 680 when Yazid succeeded his father Muawiyah as caliph. Many people were opposed to this succession because they felt that the Umayyads were establishing an Arab dynastic monarchy, which was viewed as despotic and un-Islamic. The civil war lasted for 12 years into the reigns of Marwan and his son Abd al-Malik.

Several different groups opposed the Umayyads. In 680 Husayn ibn Ali, grandson of Prophet Muhammad and the son of Ali ibn Abi Talib, the fourth Rashid caliph and Fatima the daughter of Muhammad, gathered supporters in Mecca and marched toward Kufa in an attempt to raise an army there. His small party of 72 men was cut off and massacred at Karbala on October 10 by Umayyad forces. The Kufans attempted to avenge Husayn's death but were also defeated by the Umayyads. Another Alid revolt in Kufa, led by Mukhtar ibn Abi Ubayd, sought to raise another son of Ali, Ibn al-Hanafiyya, to the caliphate, but this uprising was put down in 687 by the Zubayrid governor of Basra.

The other major opponent of the Umayyads was Abd Allah ibn al-Zubayr. Between 681 and 692, he managed to assert his control over most of the Islamic empire. However, the new Umayyad caliph, Marwan, and the Kalb, his tribal supporters, defeated the Zubayrids and the tribes of Qays in the Battle of Marj Rahit on August 18, 684. This victory secured Umayyad control of Syria, while Egypt also fell to the Umayyads soon afterward. In Iraq, Musab ibn al-Zubayr, the governor of Basra, had to contend with Kharijite rebels as well as Mukhtar's revolt in Kufa.

These struggles wore down the Zubayrids, and the Syrians were able to defeat Musab and take Iraq in 691. Abd Allah ibn al-Zubayr was thus largely confined to Mecca, where he was killed in 692 while fighting a Syrian army led by Hajjaj. While the Kharijites also rebelled in Nejd, Iraq, and Iran, their revolts were localized and thus not a major threat to the caliphate.

Adam Ali

See also
Muawiyah I; Umayyad Caliphate

References

Glubb, John Baggot. *The Great Arab Conquests.* London: Hodder and Stoughton, 1963.

Hodgson, Marshall G. S. *The Venture of Islam: Conscience and History in a World Civilization.* Chicago: University of Chicago Press, 1977.

Kennedy, Hugh. *The Prophet and the Age of the Caliphates: The Islamic Near East from the Sixth to the Eleventh Century.* 2nd ed. Harlow, UK: Longman, 2004.

Islamic Radicalism in the 20th and 21st Centuries

Radical Islam can be defined as a militant form of Islamic thought that claims religious validation for a variety of political, military, and paramilitary activities, frequently directed against Israel and the West. A common view in the West, supported to some extent by the popular media, suggests that contemporary terrorism and insurgency proceed from the Islamic notion of jihad, or holy war, articulated in the Quran.

It is certainly true that contemporary Muslim extremists tie their attacks explicitly to jihad and its basis in Islamic tradition. However, such ideas do not represent a continuous, dominant strain in Islamic or Arab thought over the past 1,400 years. While the idea of holy war clearly played a role in the initial Arab conquests of the early Middle Ages, in later medieval conflicts, and in some anticolonial movements of the late 19th century, it does not act as the dominant ideological justification for modern Arab unity or for political and military conflict in the period after World War II.

On the contrary, in the 20th century Arab nationalism in the guise of Baathism or Nasserist Arab socialism served as the primary ideological basis for conflict in the Middle East. Arab political leaders of the mid-20th century did not employ the idea of jihad to a great extent, even in their opposition to Israel. The notion of holy war, as it is currently embraced by extremist groups, grew largely in response to a number of late 20th-century factors: the failure of secular Arab political and military initiatives, the 1979 revolution in Iran, the Soviet invasion of Afghanistan, the Israeli invasion of Lebanon, the end of Soviet support for Arab regimes in the Middle East, the Palestinian Intifada, the Persian Gulf War (1991), and the Iraq War (2003–2011).

Radical Islam is sometimes referred to as Islamic fundamentalism or Islamic extremism. Some Muslim writers refer to it as a variant of Islamic revivalism. Radical Islamic beliefs combine an anti-Western political agenda with a set of theological principles. In the mid-20th century, radical Islam grew in the Middle East in response to Western imperialism and the spread of Western values in the region. In 1929 Hassan al-Banna, an Egyptian opposed to the growing secularism in the Muslim world, founded the Ikhwan Islamiyya (Muslim Brotherhood). His goal was to transform Egypt into an Islamic state modeled after the ideal days of Prophet Muhammad and his companions. The organization began as an Islamic charity but evolved into a more radical group, and in the 1940s it assassinated several prominent Egyptian officials. However, in 1949 al-Banna was killed by one of the Egyptian intelligence services.

At the time of al-Banna's death another Egyptian, Sayyid Qutb, was working toward an education degree at the University of Northern Colorado. He had been sent to the United States in 1948 by the Egyptian government to study the U.S. educational system. However, the more he saw of Western society, the more alienated he became. He returned to Egypt in 1950 and joined the Muslim Brotherhood. Qutb wrote several influential works, including *Social Justice in Islam,* a lengthy commentary on the Quran, and a shorter book, *Ma'alim fi-l-Tariq* (Milestones, or Signposts on the Road). In these he argued that before the coming of Prophet Muhammad, the world was in *jahiliyah* (spiritual darkness), a condition dominated by opposition to Allah. For a brief time Prophet Muhammad and his companions lived in a pure Islamic society ruled by submission (Islam) to the will of Allah.

According to Qutb, modernity was a time of great danger, as Islam faced a new kind of *jahiliyah*. The new *jahili* societies included the atheistic communists, the corrupted Christian and Jewish societies, Arab nationalist states, and Muslim states that cooperated with the West. All of these opponents had to be defeated through jihad for Islam to prevail. Qutb was hanged by Gamal Abdel Nasser's government in 1966, and his fate illustrates the opposition of secular Arab authorities toward Islamic radicalism for much of the 20th century.

The Muslim Brotherhood and the views of Qutb influenced many radical organizations: the Egyptian Islamic Liberation Movement, the Islamic Group Movement, and ultimately the Palestinian group Hamas. It is important to point out that Arab governments largely opposed the growth of Islamic radicalism during the period from World War II to the 1980s. Arab regimes in the mid-20th century based their identity and their warfare with Israel primarily in terms of Arab nationalism rather than Islamic unity. Indeed, such regimes, supported by the Soviet Union, often viewed activist Islam as a threat. Even the Palestine Liberation Organization (PLO) framed its foundational documents in terms of nationalism, Arab socialism, and anti-Zionism. However, this pattern changed in the closing decades of the 20th century.

In 1979, a theocratic Shiite regime headed by Ayatollah Ruhollah Khomeini took power in Iran and confronted the United States by seizing the U.S. embassy in Tehran and holding its staff hostage. That same year, the Soviet Union invaded the nation of Afghanistan and installed a puppet regime there. Both events would fuel the growth of radical Islamic political activity. The Iranian regime sponsored Islamic fundamentalist political and paramilitary activity against Israel and the West, most particularly the Shiite group Hezbollah, active in Lebanon and Israel.

In Afghanistan, Soviet occupation produced native opposition, creating a generation of mujahideen motivated primarily by radical Islamic ideas and encouraged and supplied by the United States as a counter to Soviet influence. While the Afghani resistance resulted in the withdrawal of the Soviets from the country after nine years of warfare, it also resulted in the establishment of Afghanistan as a haven for radical Islamic activity. Indeed, during the 1980s thousands of recruits from Arab nations went to Afghanistan to fight the Soviets. Already immersed in Wahhabism, the strict version of Islam prominent in Saudi Arabia, they developed an anti-Western agenda based on the writings of Qutb, among others. One of the Saudi Arabian citizens fighting in Afghanistan, Osama bin Laden, ultimately went on to found the Al Qaeda organization in 1989.

In the closing decades of the 20th century as conventional warfare against Israel fueled by Arab nationalism failed, as receding Soviet power freed former Middle Eastern client states of communist influence and deprived them of military and financial aid, and as the Iranian and Afghani crises produced a generation of anti-Western fighters motivated largely by radical Islam, anti-Israeli and anti-Western activity in the Muslim world adopted a religious character. Such feeling inspired the first Palestinian uprising against Israeli occupation of the West Bank and Gaza, the First Intifada, in 1987. Groups such as Hamas played a leading role in the intifada, as radical Islam came to rival Arab nationalism as the defining ideology behind the struggle against Israel. Such ideas appealed particularly to the powerless and the disenfranchised in Palestinian society. The rhetoric of the PLO is indicative of this change. Whereas once its agenda centered on secular Arab socialism and nationalism, the PLO adopted language of martyrdom and holy war and gave rise to its own radical group, the al-Aqsa Martyrs' Brigade.

The U.S. military presence in Saudi Arabia in preparation for the Persian Gulf War in 1991 led bin Laden to establish Al Qaeda with the goal of overthrowing what it regarded as corrupt Islamic regimes and ending Western influence in the Middle East. The U.S.-led invasion of Iraq in 2003 gave rise to the Islamist fundamentalist Islamic State of Iraq and Syria (ISIS). Other radical Islamist organizations today include Al-Shabaab in Somalia, Boko Haram in northeastern Nigeria, and Ansar Dine in Mali.

Fundamentalist Islam continues to be a potent force in Middle Eastern politics to the present day.

Andrew J. Waskey and Robert S. Kiely

See also

al-Aqsa Martyrs Brigades; Al Qaeda; Bin Laden, Osama; Hamas; Intifada, First; Intifada, Second; Islamic State of Iraq and Syria; Khomeini, Ruhollah; Nasser, Gamal Abdel; Palestine Liberation Organization; Suicide Bombings; Terrorism; Wahhabism

References

Dekmejian, R. Hrair. *Islam in Revolution: Fundamentalism in the Arab World.* Syracuse, NY: Syracuse University Press, 1996.

Mitchell, Richard P. *The Society of the Muslim Brotherhood.* New York: Oxford University Press, 1993.

Nasr, Seyyed Vali Reza. *Mawdudi & the Making of Islamic Revivalism.* New York: Oxford University Press, 1996.

Sivan, Emmanuel. *Radical Islam: Medieval Theology and Modern Politics.* New Haven, CT: Yale University Press, 1985.

Islamic State of Iraq and Syria

Radical Sunni jihadist organization variously known as the Islamic State of Iraq and Syria (ISIS), the Islamic State of Iraq and The Levant (ISIL), the Islamic State (IS), and Daesh that is currently active chiefly in Iraq and Syria, although it has carried out terrorist actions in Europe and as far distant as the Philippines in Asia. ISIS is a successor organization of Al Qaeda in Iraq and was formally established in 2006, at which time it became known as the Islamic State of Iraq (ISI). ISIS is currently led by Abu Bakr al-Baghdadi, an Iraqi born in Samara in 1971 who took part in the post-2003 Iraqi insurgency following the Anglo-American–led invasion of Iraq in March 2003; he was also a member of Al Qaeda in Iraq. Al-Baghdadi has been the acknowledged leader of ISIS since 2010.

As with Al Qaeda in Iraq, ISIS sought to expel all foreign troops and personnel from Iraq and wage war against the Shia-dominated secular government of Iraq. These organizations have not only battled coalition and Iraqi armed forces but have also engaged in myriad acts of terrorism and war crimes that have frequently involved civilians. ISIS, however, had ambitions beyond these activities. It sought to establish an Islamic regime, based on strict sharia law, within Iraq and Syria. ISIS even hoped eventually to extend its reach into the Levant, which encompasses Lebanon, Palestine, and Jordan.

By 2010, Baghdadi had emerged as a top leader of Al Qaeda in Iraq. However, his vision of founding an Islamic emirate clashed with the more modest goals of that group, so he began to assemble his own rebel group. Thereafter he co-opted several other jihadist organizations, most notably the Mujahideen Shura Council (MSC), and began recruiting followers who shared his more expansive vision. Observers believed that Baghdadi enjoyed success in recruiting fighters (many are foreigners, and some even hailed from Western Europe and the United States) because he was a charismatic military strategist and battlefield commander rather than a theologian.

By the spring of 2013, ISIS had become a potent force in both Iraq and Syria. In Syria, ISIS has taken full advantage of the bloody civil war there that had been raging since early 2011. ISIS rebels have been battling Syrian government forces defending the regime of President Bashar al-Assad as well as other antigovernment rebel groups. Many Syrians have come to despise ISIS because of its violence toward civilians, attacks on other rebel groups, and uncompromising positions, which include the subjugation and enslavement of women. In early 2014, Western-backed Syrian rebels and even other Islamist groups launched a major campaign to expel ISIS from Syria. The campaign met with only modest success, however, and after that time ISIS extended its reach within Syria to include areas populated by the Kurds.

ISIS had an even greater impact in Iraq, however, and by the summer of 2014 was threatening the very existence of the Iraqi government of Prime Minister Nuri al-Maliki. Throughout 2013, ISIS made major advances in northern and western Iraq. By late January 2014, ISIS and affiliated groups had managed to seize control of virtually all of Anbar Province. In early June 2014 the group enjoyed even bigger gains, taking Mosul (Iraq's second-largest city) as well as Tikrit. ISIS forces reached to only some 60 miles north of Baghdad and were attempting to drive farther south.

The fall of Mosul stunned the Iraqi government and much of the international community. By mid-June, the United States and other Western nations were involved in urgent negotiations to determine how they should aid Maliki's government and prevent all of Iraq from falling into the hands of ISIS. Unfortunately, the corrupt, ineffectual, and anti-Sunni Maliki regime proved virtually incapable of halting ISIS's advance, and many components of the Iraqi Army simply bolted and fled in the face of ISIS offensives.

During the summer of 2014, the Barack Obama administration began formulating a comprehensive strategy to reverse ISIS's advances. This would come to involve cobbling together a multinational coalition, including a number of Arab states, to participate in air strikes against ISIS targets, arming moderate Syrian rebel groups combating ISIS fighters, sending more military hardware to the Iraqi government, dispatching some 3,000 military "advisers" to Iraq, and commencing air strikes against ISIS. The air strikes began on August 8, 2014, and the U.S.-coalition air campaign against ISIS in Syria commenced on September 23. The operation began on June 15, 2014, and continued into 2019. At the same time that the Obama administration had announced its intent to defeat ISIS it was also lobbying for Maliki to be replaced as Iraqi prime minister. Under great internal and international pressure, he finally resigned on September 8 and was succeeded by Haider al-Abadi, who pledged to pursue conciliatory policies in Iraq and to work cooperatively with the United States and its coalition partners in order to subdue the ISIS insurgency. The rise of ISIS was certainly the worst crisis to hit Iraq since the beginning of the postinvasion insurgency during 2003–2004 and greatly complicated the internecine civil war in neighboring Syria.

By early 2015, there were numerous signs that the anti-ISIS effort was beginning to show some incipient signs of progress. Syrian officials reported that ISIS had killed 1,878 people (the vast majority of them civilians) between June 2014 and January 2015, and Kurdish Peshmerga fighters recaptured the Syrian border town of Kobanî on January 26, 2015. They also pushed ISIS out of the Iraqi city of Sinjar, a development that was hailed as a turning point in the war against ISIS.

The threat from ISIS was considerably larger than its military operations in Iraq and Syria might suggest. Indeed, the group routinely violated basic international law and human rights by kidnapping innocent foreign civilians, beheading them, and then releasing videos of the executions on the Internet. And in addition to targeting innocent civilians, ISIS also engaged in the severe repression of women in areas under its control, including the kidnapping, sexual exploitation, and enslavement of women and even young girls.

On April 1, 2015, the Iraqi government declared a major victory over ISIS forces after having driven the group from Tikrit. Throughout the spring of 2015 Iraqi forces, aided by air support from the United States and other coalition governments, aggressively pursued ISIS. Meanwhile, since the summer of 2014 Iran has been launching air strikes against ISIS targets within Iraq and Syria. Iran has also sent special militia forces, known as the Quds Force, to Iraq to engage ISIS on the ground. The United States and Iran, although fighting on the same side in this instance, repeatedly declared that the two nations were not coordinating their military operations. Iranian militia units played a major role in the retaking of Tikrit.

Throughout the remainder of 2015 and into 2016, ISIS continued its activities, recruiting members from across the globe including Europe and even the United States. The group also increased its presence in Libya, which resulted in Egyptian air strikes against ISIS targets in that war-torn nation. By June 2015, ISIS had established "official" provinces in Libya, Egypt (Sinai Peninsula), Saudi Arabia, Yemen, Algeria, Afghanistan, Pakistan, Nigeria, and the northern Caucasus. Since that time it has claimed ties to Islamist extremist groups in Somalia, Bangladesh, and the Philippines.

In Iraq meanwhile, Iraqi forces continued to reduce the amount of territory controlled by ISIS. By mid-2015, U.S. officials claimed that some 10,000 ISIS fighters had been killed in air strikes by American and allied warplanes since late 2014. In Syria, ISIS continued to wreak havoc against the regime of President Bashar al-Assad. With the opposition apparently gaining ground, Russia intervened directly in the civil war there in September 2015, ostensibly to help defeat ISIS but for the most part to prop up its longtime ally, Assad. That intervention took the form of air strikes, but the United States and international organizations claimed that many of these were mounted not against ISIS but instead against the non-ISIS moderate opposition groups supported by the United States and other nations also battling the Assad government.

On October 31, 2015, an ISIS group operating in Egypt's Sinai Peninsula brought down a Russian civilian jetliner, killing all 224 people on board. That tragedy led to more Russian air strikes in Syria. Russian involvement in Syria, however, only complicated the situation on the ground. In November 2015, Turkish forces shot down a Russian warplane that had allegedly violated Turkish air space. Late in the year Russia, the United States, and other powers sponsored a series of peace talks that, however, made little progress toward ending Syria's long civil war.

By early 2016, the Obama administration had dispatched a small contingent of special operations troops to Syria in recognition that air strikes alone were not doing enough to eradicate ISIS in that country. Meanwhile, a cease-fire in Syria, brokered by Russia and the United States, went into effect on February 27, 2016. This was to be followed by talks aimed at imposing a lasting peace settlement on the war-torn country. On March 14, Russia announced that it was withdrawing many of its aircraft and personnel from Syria in a bid to jump-start peace talks. Nevertheless, Russian involvement in the Syrian Civil War continued, mainly in a support capacity to Syrian government forces. By late March ISIS in Syria was on the defensive and had lost territory, including the ancient city of Palmyra, where it had carried out the deliberate destruction of priceless ancient monuments.

The Iraqi city of Mosul had been occupied by ISIS for more than two years when an international coalition, led by Iraqi, Kurdish, and U.S. forces, launched a major offensive in October 2016 to regain control from the terrorist group. The massive-scale operation to remove up to 5,000 ISIS fighters from the city was complicated by the 1.5 million civilians reported to still be inside the city. Thousands of refugees fled to Syria within the first week of the offensive, and thousands more were expected to join them on a constant basis until Mosul was back under Iraqi control, which was expected to take weeks or months and could lead to major civilian loss of life. The United Nations warned that the flood of refugees could become a catastrophic humanitarian crisis because camps along the Syrian border were ill-equipped to handle such a massive influx of people. As people continued to flee, ISIS put up strong resistance and set fire to oil wells to reduce the tactical abilities of coalition forces. Abu Bakr al-Baghdadi was believed to be trapped within the city as the offensive was ongoing but then escaped, possibly injured. Mosul was finally recaptured in July 2017.

Meanwhile, ISIS continued to recruit followers from throughout the world, both to join it as fighters in the Middle East but also to act as lone wolves in carrying out terrorist attacks against innocent civilians in their own countries. ISIS claimed responsibility for attacks against civilians in Tunisia, Kuwait, Lebanon, and Paris in the second half of the year. ISIS was also responsible for terrorist bombings in Brussels, Belgium, in March 2016. And in California in late November 2015, a husband and wife team perpetrated a mass shooting that killed 14 and wounded 24. The wife had reportedly pledged allegiance to ISIS online in the months leading up to the attack.

ISIS also was behind two attacks on April 9, 2017, against Coptic Christians in Egypt. At least 27 people died and 78 others were injured in a blast outside a church in the northern city of Tanta. In Alexandria, 18 civilians and 4 police officers were killed when a suicide bomber blew himself up outside St. Mark's Coptic Cathedral in Alexandria, the largest Christian church in Egypt, Northeast Africa, and the Middle East.

ISIS also claimed responsibility for a lone wolf suicide bombing in Manchester, England, in May 2017 that killed 25 people and wounded many more. On June 3 in central London, a van plowed into a crowd of pedestrians on London Bridge. Three men then exited the van and began stabbing people at nearby Borough Market. Before police shot them to death, the attackers had killed 7 innocent civilians, while 48 others had been hospitalized, some in critical condition. ISIS claimed responsibility. These terrorist acts in Britain were by British citizens who had been born there and radicalized.

In late May 2017 the United States began arming members of the People's Protection Units (YPG), a Kurdish military organization in Syria. The weaponry included heavy machine guns and antitank weapons. Approved by President Donald J. Trump in early May, the plan had been proposed by the American military to allow the YPG to take part in the liberation of the ISIS capital of Raqqa. This move, however, drew immediate strong condemnation from Turkey, which is waging its own military operations against radical Kurdish groups in Turkey and opposes any plans to arm Kurds, wherever they might be, and raised the possibility that Turkey, which was supporting INHERENT RESOLVE military operations against ISIS, might withdraw that assistance.

ISIS also extended its reach to the southern Philippines. In late May 2017 the Philippine government placed the heavily Muslim southern island of Mindanao under marshal law after ISIS-linked Islamic militants seized control of Marawi City. The Abu Sayad group mounted the attack in retaliation for a botched government attempt to capture its leader, Isnilon Hapilon. Assisted by another ISIS affiliate, Maute, the militants stormed Marawi, putting to flight tens of thousands of its residents. Philippine troops were rushed to Marawi, with reports of widespread destruction and many deaths in the ensuing fighting and the militants reportedly holding hostage a priest and some 200 members of his congregation.

On June 7, 2017, six ISIS assailants, including some disguised as women, stunned Iran with two brazen near-simultaneous attacks in Tehran against both the parliament building and the tomb of Iran's revolutionary founder, Khomeini. Seventeen people were killed and 52 others were wounded in the assaults that occurred over several hours. The 6 attackers, at least 5 of whom were apparently recruited by ISIS from among Iranian Kurds, were killed, with 5 suspects detained. The attacks were the first by ISIS in Iran. Despite the ISIS claim, Iran blamed Saudi Arabia and the United States as having been behind the attacks.

Iran struck back on June 18. In a major escalation of its war in Syria and the first time it had launched missiles at another country in three decades, the Islamic Revolutionary Guard Corps announced that it had launched several ground-to-ground midrange missiles from bases in Kermenshah Province in western Iran against ISIS forces in the Deir ez-Zor region in eastern Syria.

On October 4, 2017, Syrian government forces, supported by intense Russian air strikes and Iranian-backed militia on the ground, took control of the remainder of the Syrian provincial capital city of Deir ez-Zor. At the same time, Iraqi Army forces and Iranian-backed militia supported by coalition air strikes secured control of a key border crossing after taking from ISIS most of the Iraqi town of Qa'im.

On October 5 the Iraqi government announced the capture by its forces of the town of Hawija, the last ISIS stronghold near Kurdish-held Kirkuk in northern Iraq. This left only a stretch of territory along the western border with Syria remaining under the control of the Islamic state. Then on December 9, 2017, Iraqi premier al-Abadi officially announced the end of the costly Iraqi campaign to clear ISIS forces from his country. By the summer of 2018 only a token number of ISIS fighters were believed to be situated in Iraq, likely in the Anbar Desert region.

Despite the end of the campaign in Iraq, ISIS continued its presence in Syria, where it remained under pressure from U.S. and Russian air strikes as well as those of the Syrian Air Force and troops on the ground. An important milestone there was reached on October 17, 2017, when U.S.-backed troops concluded major military operations in taking Raqqa, which ISIS had captured in late 2013 and proclaimed as the capital of its self-proclaimed caliphate. On November 7, 2017, Syrian president Bashar al-Assad declared victory over ISIS in his country, although the larger civil war there continued unabated. Small pockets of resistance continued, but the last ISIS-held village in Syria was eliminated in late March 1919.

No doubt ISIS will continue to exist in both Iraq and Syria, especially in areas along the Euphrates River where it is known to have many sympathizers and where the elusive and possibly injured ISIS leader al-Baghdadi is thought to be hiding.

As noted, ISIS remained active in countries and parts of the world other than the Middle East. Expectations of ISIS attacks in other countries were especially apparent in Egypt. A devastating attack against a Sufi Muslim mosque in the Sinai Peninsula on November 24, 2017, claimed more than 300 lives, with many others wounded. On July 13, 2018, ISIS claimed responsibility for two bombings in Pakistan near the Afghan border that claimed the lives of 154 people. Jihadists will certainly continue to be a threat to the West, whether as suicide bombers attacking crowds of innocent civilians or driving vehicles into gatherings of civilians, but there is no longer a geographical location from which ISIS can publicly proclaim credit for such attacks, and that is a considerable achievement.

PAUL G. PIERPAOLI JR. AND SPENCER C. TUCKER

See also
Abadi, Haider al-; Al Qaeda; Assad, Bashar al-; Baghdadi, Abu Bakr al-; INHERENT RESOLVE, Operation; Iraq; Kobanî, Siege of; Maliki, Nuri Muhammed Kamil al-; Peshmerga; Syrian Civil War

References
Barrett, Richard. *The Islamic State*. New York: Soufan Group, 2014.
Dhiman, S. C. *Islamic state of Iraq and Syria (ISIS): Reconciliation, Democracy, and Terror*. Delhi: Neha, 2015.
Dreyfuss, Robert. *Devil's Game: How the United States Helped Unleash Fundamentalist Islam*. New York: Macmillan, 2006.
Malik, S. K. *The Quranic Concept of War*. Himalayan Books, 1986.
Micallef, Joseph V. *Islamic State: Its History, Ideology and Challenge*. Portland, OR: Antioch Downs Press, 2015.
Roy, Olivier. *The Failure of Political Islam*. Cambridge, MA: Harvard University Press, 1994.

Ismail, Khedive (1830–1895)

Egyptian ruler. Europeans called Ismail "the Magnificent," while Egyptians more guardedly described their ruler as "the Builder." Ismail was a controversial member of the Mehmed Ali dynasty. His qualities, or lack of such, are still debated by historians to this day. He dominated much of Northeast Africa from 1863 to 1879, spent vast sums of money, initiated several wars, and had a decided impact on the history of Egypt and the Sudan.

Ismail was born on December 31, 1830, in Cairo. His father, Ibrahim Pasha, had a keen interest in things military. Ismail supposedly witnessed Ibrahim's 1839 victory at Nezib and was a graduate of the French military academy of St. Cyr and the École Supérieur de Guerre. On becoming *wali* (governor) of Egypt in 1863, Ismail immediately set about expanding the Egyptian armed forces. Within a decade his large army had state-of-the-art small-arms and artillery plus a significant cadre of foreign mercenaries to provide technical instruction.

Ismail also borrowed heavily from European banking syndicates and issued long runs of Egyptian bonds. While Ismail's continual need for money was not exclusively related to military spending—he constructed the Middle East's first opera house and helped complete the Suez Canal—the armed forces consumed a considerable portion of these revenues. With the army having expanded from 3,000 men in 1863 to nearly 100,000 in 1875, salaries alone were a considerable economic drain.

Ismail employed his army to crush Greek rebels in Crete (1866–1867), maintain the Hajj ports in Arabia, and secure territory in the Horn of Africa. Encouraged by mercenary hires such as Samuel Baker, Charles Gordon, and Charles Stone, Ismail supported Egyptian imperial expansion into Darfur, Somalia, and Abyssinia (Ethiopia).

On paper, Egypt had a potent military machine, and in small campaigns against poorly organized Sudanese resistors it proved capable. When facing more serious opposition, as in the Second Russo-Turkish War (1876–1877) and the Egyptian-Ethiopian War (1875–1884), however, Egyptian arms fared poorly.

Deposed by his nominal overlord the Ottoman sultan, who did so with the blessing of the European powers in 1879, Ismail sailed off into a gilded exile. Unlike his father and grandfather, he was incapable of creating or leading a powerful military machine. Indeed, it could be argued that Ismail's military and financial policies sowed the seeds of the revolution led by Colonel Ahmed Arabi that nearly overthrew the Mehmed Ali dynasty in 1882.

JOHN P. DUNN

See also
Arabi, Ahmed; Egypt, Athenian Intervention in; Egyptian-Ottoman Wars; Ibrahim Pasha; Mehmed Ali

References
Crabites, Pierre. *Ismail, the Maligned Khedive*. London: G. Routledge and Sons, 1933.
Dunn, John P. *Khedive Ismail's Army*. London: Routledge, 2005.

Ismail Ali, Ahmad (1917–1974)

Egyptian military officer. Ahmad Ismail Ali was born on October 14, 1917, in Cairo, Egypt, and graduated from the Cairo Military Academy in 1938. During World War II he saw action in the Western Desert. In the Israeli War of Independence (1948–1949) he fought as a brigade commander in the Egyptian Army. From 1950 to 1953 he taught at the Cairo Military Academy. He also fought with Egyptian forces in the Sinai, opposing the Franco-British-Israeli intervention to secure the Suez Canal in 1956. He served as commander of forces at Port Said from 1957 to 1960.

After a brief tour in the Congo on a peacekeeping operation, Ismail served from 1961 to 1967 as a military adviser to the Egyptian government. During the 1967 Six-Day War, he was a divisional commander. In March 1969 Egyptian president Gamal Abdel Nasser appointed Ismail chief of military operations, but he was later fired after a successful Israeli raid into Egypt caused embarrassment. He then served as head of the Egyptian Intelligence Service.

In 1972 Ismail was appointed commander in chief of the Egyptian Army. On January 21, 1973, he assumed the post of commander in chief of the Combined Armed Forces of Egypt, Libya, and Syria, and a week later, on January 28, he assumed the title of commander in chief of the Arab Fronts.

During the 1973 Yom Kippur War, Ismail was serving as the Egyptian minister of defense. Prior to the conflict, he had been actively involved in preparations for a preemptive attack on Israel. In February 1972 in his capacity as defense minister, he traveled to Moscow to secure both aircraft and missiles for offensive and defensive purposes. The goal was to build a missile defense system capable of providing protection during the planned crossing of the Suez Canal from the Israeli Air Force, which had all but destroyed the Egyptian Air Force on the ground in the 1967 Six-Day War.

Ismail spearheaded an Egyptian disinformation campaign to confuse Israeli intelligence about the forthcoming Egyptian and Syrian attacks. While visiting Romania, he let it slip that the Egyptians were inept at handling their Soviet military hardware, including the missiles. Before the 1973 war, he prepared war plans with General Saad el-Shazly, Egyptian chief of staff, that called for a massive surprise attack against Israel.

El-Shazly was opposed to Ismail's plans and refused to obey his orders. On October 14, 1973, el-Shazly reluctantly obeyed a direct order from President Anwar Sadat to advance against Israel. In a great tank battle designed to relieve pressure on the Syrians on the Golan Heights, the Egyptians were defeated. On October 16 Ismail was still at odds with el-Shazly, who wanted to withdraw west of Suez. By the morning of October 20, el-Shazly had been relieved of command. General Abd al-Ghani Gamasi (Jamasi) replaced him.

In November 1973, Ismail was promoted to field marshal. He died of cancer in London on December 25, 1974.

Andrew J. Waskey

See also
Egypt; Six-Day War; Yom Kippur War

References
el Badri, Hassan. *The Ramadan War, 1973.* Fairfax, VA: T. N. Dupuy Associates Books, 1979.
Herzog, Chaim. *The War of Atonement: The Inside Story of the Yom Kippur War.* London: Greenhill Books, 2003.
Rabinovich, Abraham. *The Yom Kippur War: The Epic Encounter That Transformed the Middle East.* New York: Schocken, 2005.
Shazly, Saad el. *The Crossing of the Suez.* Rev. ed. San Francisco, CA: American Mideast Research, 2003.

Ismail I, Shah (1487–1524)

Founder of the Safavid Empire of Persia. Shah Ismail I consolidated a Persian Empire for the first time in more than 800 years and effected the historic conversion of the country to Twelver Shiism, a minority Islamic sect.

Ismail was born on July 17, 1487, into a family centered in Ardabil, Azerbaijan, that had long been connected to both the political and religious leadership of the Turkmen tribes of the region. An ancestor, Sheikh Safi al-Din, was the spiritual leader of a local Sufi order (the Safaviyeh tariqah) that later aligned itself with Shiism. The disciples of this religious order became known as Safavids. The family, in addition to inheriting the leadership of the Safavid movement, also claimed to be related to the line of imams. Imams were the early spiritual leaders of Islam who in Shiite tradition possessed a right to secular rulership through direct descent from Ali, the son-in-law and cousin of Prophet Muhammad. Thus, Ismail's claim to legitimacy was founded on the notion of a hereditary divine right.

Both Ismail's grandfather, Sheikh Junayd, and father, Sheikh Haydar, died in battle. Their legacy was the fusion of Safavid religious zeal with the warrior traditions of *ghaza,* or combat in the name of the faith, among the tribesmen who supported the Safavids, called Qizilbash (meaning "red heads") for their distinctive red turbans. Ismail would eventually ride into battle at their head, but he was only an infant when his father died, and he spent much of his childhood hiding in exile awaiting his moment.

In 1499 when he was 12, Ismail came forward as the nominal leader of a reinvigorated Safavid movement. His Qizilbash army overcame the massed forces of the dominant Ak Koyunlu (White Sheep) Turkmen at Sharur in 1501. After the Battle of Tabriz, the Safavids took possession of Tabriz, the traditional Turkmen capital. In the seven years that followed, further military success to the south and west enlarged the boundaries of Ismail's growing empire to include most of the area of modern western Iran, eastern Turkey, and much of Iraq. In the process, Ismail's government began to integrate ethnic Turkish and Persian leaders into the imperial administration.

Although he took the title of shah (emperor), to his followers Ismail seemed semidivine: a holy child-emperor who literally represented the return of the prophesied hidden 12th imam to establish a Shiite kingdom on Earth. As Safavid forces spread across the country, they imposed Shiism as the official religion, actively suppressed the institutions of the Sunni majority, and coerced conversions on pain of death. Ismail recruited Arab Shia *ulema* (religious scholars) to administer the new state religion and funded the creation of new sufi shrines.

The general triumph of Ismail and the Safavid-Qizilbash coalition represented the conjuncture of many different social developments of the time. Ismail was an avatar of the perpetual aspiration for religious renewal, but the ground for his holy war against Sunni enemies was prepared by other contexts. The weakening of regional powers in the late 15th century by the rise of the Ottomans and the Uzbeks created the political opportunity, and efforts by the Ottoman Empire and the Ak Koyunlu state to introduce tax reform in the midst of economic decline fomented a backlash against Sunni legalism.

As it grew into a regional military power, the new Safavid Empire encountered hostility from ever larger opponents. To the east, Ismail expanded Safavid control to the Oxus River by campaigning against Sunni Uzbek tribes. In a decisive battle near the city of Marv (in what is now Uzbekistan), the Safavids ambushed and defeated a larger army in 1510. Ismail reputedly had the skull of the enemy leader, Muhammad Shaybani, refashioned as an ornamented drinking cup; he then sent the cup to another rival, the Ottoman sultan.

To the west, the powerful Ottoman Empire was antagonized by support for the Safavids among its own population in eastern Anatolia and Ismail's imposition of Shiism on recalcitrant Sunni subjects. Official persecution of religious minorities on both sides and an exchange of intemperate diplomatic messages prepared the way for war. At one point, Ismail responded to a bellicose message from Sultan Selim I by sending the sultan's secretary a box of opium. It was a pointed sign of disrespect for the sultan, with the insinuation that he was addled by drug use.

In 1514, an Ottoman army equipped with muskets and artillery invaded Safavid territory under the command of the sultan. Ismail's troops, outnumbered and without guns, were defeated at Chaldiran after a bitter struggle. Yet while the city of Tabriz fell to the Ottomans, a mutiny in the Ottoman ranks forced the sultan's withdrawal. In 1517, Safavid forces rebounded by extending their conquests in the northwest over Sunni tribes in modern Georgia.

An unsteady recognition of a balance of power between Ottomans and Safavids followed, despite border clashes and intermittent warfare during the next 100 years. Ismail I died on May 23, 1524, at only age 36. The Safavid dynasty would rule for two more centuries and establish the basis for the modern nation-state of Iran.

Brad Brown

See also
Abbas I the Great; Chaldiran, Battle of; Ottoman-Safavid Wars; Shia Islam; Tahmasp I, Shah

References
Jackson, Peter, and L. Lockhart, eds. *Cambridge History of Iran*, Vol. 6. Cambridge: Cambridge University Press, 1986.
Morgan, David. *Medieval Persia, 1040–1797*. New York: Longman, 1988.

Ismailis

An important Shiite Muslim community that has subdivided into a number of major branches and minor groups in the course of a complex history dating back to the middle of the eighth century. Today the Ismailis number several millions, belong to a variety of ethnic groups, and are scattered as religious minorities in many countries of Asia, the Middle East, Africa, Europe, and North America.

The Ismailis have recognized a line of imams or spiritual leaders in the progeny of Ismail, son of Imam Ja'far al-Sadiq (d. 765), a direct descendant of Ali ibn Abi Talib, Prophet Muhammad's cousin, son-in-law, and the first Shia imam, hence their designation as Ismaili. By the 870s, the Ismailis had organized a revolutionary movement against the established Sunni-Abbasid order, aiming to install the Ismaili imam to a new Shiite caliphate ruling over the entire Muslim community. The religio-political message of the movement, known as the *da'wa* (mission), was disseminated by a network of *da'is* (missionaries) in many regions from North Africa to Central Asia and the Indian subcontinent.

The early success of the Ismaili movement culminated in the foundation of the Fatimid caliphate in North Africa in 909. The Ismaili imam now ruled as Fatimid caliph over an important state that soon evolved into a major empire stretching from North Africa to Egypt, Palestine, and Syria. The Fatimid period (909–1171) represented the golden age of Ismailism when Ismaili thought and literature attained their summit and Ismailis made important contributions to Islamic civilization, especially after the seat of the Fatimid caliphate was transferred to Cairo, itself founded by the Fatimids in 969. The early Ismailis elaborated an esoteric system of religious thought as well as distinctive institutions of learning.

The early Ismailis split into two rival communities in 899, when a dissident faction, the Qarmatians, refused to recognize continuity in the Ismaili imamate, awaiting the return of their seventh imam, Muhammad ibn Ismail ibn al-Sadiq, as the messianic Mahdi and restorer of true Islam. The loyal Fatimid Ismailis themselves, those who recognized the Fatimid caliphs as their imams, experienced a major schism in 1094 revolving around a succession dispute. As a result, the Ismaili community was permanently subdivided into the rival Musta'lian and Nizari factions, named after two sons of the Fatimid caliph/imam al-Mustansir (1036–1094), who had both claimed their father's heritage. Al-Musta'li (1094–1101) and the later Fatimid caliphs were recognized as imams by the (Musta'lian) Ismailis of Egypt, Yemen, and western India. On the other hand, the (Nizari) Ismailis of Iran, Syria, Central Asia, and parts of India upheld the rights of Nizar (d. 1095), the original heir-designate of al-Mustansir, and his progeny to the Ismaili imamate.

The Musta'lian Ismailis themselves split into a number of major and minor groupings. From the time of the demise of the Fatimid dynasty in 1171, the Musta'lian Ismailis were represented solely by the Tayyibi branch, which found its stronghold in Yemen. The Tayyibi Ismailis, whose imams have remained in concealment since the 1130s, have been led by *da'is* with absolute authority. By the end of the 16th century, the Tayyibis split into Daudi and Sulaymani factions. By that time, the Tayyibis of South Asia, known as Bohras and belonging mainly to the Daudi branch, outnumbered their Sulaymani coreligionists in Yemen. The Daudi and Sulaymani Tayyibis have followed different lines of *da'is*, but both communities have remained rather traditional in their outlook.

The Nizari Ismailis acquired political prominence under the initial leadership of Hasan Sabbah (d. 1124), who founded the Nizari state of Persia with a subsidiary in Syria. The Nizari state, centered at the fortress of Alamut, comprised a network of mountain strongholds and towns in several regions in the midst of the Seljuk Empire. The Seljuk Turks launched numerous unsuccessful military campaigns against the Nizari strongholds of Persia, while the Nizaris failed to uproot the Seljuks. Hasan and his seven successors at Alamut ruled as *da'is* and then after 1164 as Nizari imams until their state was eventually destroyed by the Mongols in 1256. The Nizaris of Syria, who had numerous military and diplomatic encounters with the Christian crusaders in the Holy Land, were made famous in medieval Europe as the Assassins, the followers of a mysterious "Old Man of the Mountain."

The Nizari Ismailis survived the Mongol debacle in the 13th century. Many of the Persian Nizaris, who had escaped from the Mongol massacres, adopted Sufi and other external guises to protect themselves against further persecution. By the middle of the 15th century, the Nizari imams emerged in central Persia and initiated a revival in the missionary and literary activities of their community. They were particularly successful in Central Asia and South Asia, where large numbers of Hindus were converted and became known locally as Khojas. In the 1840s the Nizari imam of the time, who had received the honorary title "Aga Khan" (lord and master) from the Iranian monarch, emigrated to India, initiating the modern period in the history of the community. Under the leadership of their last two imams, Sultan Muhammad Shah Aga Khan III (1885–1957) and Prince Karim Aga Khan IV, who in 1957 succeeded his grandfather, the Nizari Ismailis have entered the modern age as a progressive community with high standards of education and gender equality.

The Nizari Khojas, together with the Tayyibi Bohras, were also among the earliest Asian communities to have settled in East Africa. In the 1970s and subsequently, most East African Ismailis immigrated to the West due to the anti-Asian politics of certain African governments.

FARHAD DAFTARY

See also

Ali ibn Abi Talib; Assassins; Fatimid Dynasty; Qarmatians

References

Daftary, Farhad. *The Ismailis: Their History and Doctrines*. 2nd ed. Cambridge: Cambridge University Press, 2007.

Daftary, Farhad. *A Short History of the Ismailis*. Edinburgh, UK: Edinburgh University Press, 1998.

Walker, Paul E. *Fatimid History and Ismaili Doctrine*. Aldershot, UK: Ashgate, 2008.

Israel

The State of Israel, the only Jewish nation in the world, has an area of some 8,019 square miles and is thus slightly larger than the U.S. state of Massachusetts. Israel's population in 2018 was some 8.45 million. Its modern capital has been Tel Aviv, although by 2018 there was a major domestic and international push to relocate it to Jerusalem. Israel is bordered to the west by the eastern Mediterranean, to the north by Lebanon, to the east by Jordan and Syria, and to the southwest by Egypt. Israel's government is a parliamentary democracy, and the country boasts an advanced Western-style economy. Israel also possesses nuclear weapons.

According to the Jewish bible, the Torah (or the Christian Old Testament), Jews trace their origins to some 4,000 years ago to the prophet Abraham and his son Isaac. A series of Jewish kingdoms and states intermittently ruled Palestine for more than a millennium thereafter. For many centuries Jews were the majority population of Palestine or, as the Jews called it, Israel (meaning "land of God"), but they were forced to endure diaspora, or dispersion from their homeland. The first of these exiles came under Tiglath-Pileser III of Assyria in 733 BCE and was completed by Sargon II with the destruction of the Kingdom of Israel in 722. In 587 BCE King Nebuchadnezzar II of Babylon conquered the Kingdom of Judah and, according to the Bible, destroyed the Temple and exiled part of the Jewish population to Babylon. This exile ended after 70 years on the declaration of King Cyrus I of Persia, with the Jews allowed to return home and construct the Second Temple. Alexander III the Great of Macedon conquered the region in 334 BCE. After his death it was part of the Ptolemaic Empire and then the Seleucid Empire.

In 63 BCE Roman armies invaded and established a protectorate, with a vassal Judaean kingdom under Herod the Great. In 6 CE the kingdom was organized as the Roman province of Judaea. Following a revolt by the Jews in 66, the Romans laid siege to and destroyed the Second Temple and most of Jerusalem. This event marked the beginning of the Roman Exile (Edom Exile), with many Jews killed or sold into slavery.

Another Jewish revolt, this time under Bar Kokhba during 132–135, brought another defeat. Emperor Hadrian changed the name of Jerusalem to Aelia Capitolina and turned it into a pagan city and prevented Jews from living there. Much of the population then became Greco-Roman. After a period of Byzantine rule, in 634–641 the Arabs, having adopted Islam, conquered the region, which then remained under Muslim control for the next 1,300 years.

Securing Jerusalem was a primary goal of the Christian crusades (1096–1291). In 1099 the crusaders laid siege to and captured the city, after which they massacred some 60,000 people, including 6,000 Jews seeking refuge in a synagogue. In 1260 control passed to the Mamluk sultans of Egypt, but in 1527, with their victory over the Mamluk Sultanate, the Ottoman Turks took charge.

In the 19th century, nationalism became a primary force in European affairs. The large Jewish population of the Russian Empire was then undergoing periodic savage persecutions (pogroms), but anti-Semitism was also rife in many countries including France, as in the Dreyfus Affair. Jews came to the conclusion that the only way they could secure protection was to establish their own state. The result at the end of the 19th century was Zionism, whereby Jews sought a national homeland. Under Austrian Jew Theodor Herzl, the first World Zionist Congress (WZC) met in Basel, Switzerland, in 1897. Subsequent WZCs affirmed that the Jewish national homeland had to be Palestine.

In 1914 the Ottoman Empire entered World War I on the side of the Central Powers. During the conflict French diplomat François-Georges Picot and British diplomat Sir Mark Sykes negotiated an agreement regarding the disposition of the Middle East territory belonging to the Ottoman Empire. Signed on May 16, 1916, it assigned what would be postwar Iraq, Transjordan, and Palestine to Britain, while France was to receive control of what would be Syria and Lebanon. At the same time, however, British authorities in Egypt negotiated with the Arabs and promised the establishment of an Arab kingdom if they would rise up against the Ottomans. This occurred in the Arab Revolt (1916–1918). In another major demarché, in order to secure Jewish support for the Allied war effort, British foreign secretary Arthur James Balfour, on November 2, 1917, issued what became known as the Balfour Declaration. It announced British support for the "establishment in Palestine of a national home for the Jewish people."

Following the Allied victory in World War I, at the San Remo Conference in Italy in April 1920 Britain and France secured approval of the other major Allied Powers for the establishment of the former Ottoman Middle East as League of Nations mandates along the lines of the Sykes-Picot Agreement. In April 1921, however, Britain split Palestine into the Emirate of Transjordan, comprising territory east of the Jordan River, and Palestine to the west.

Already a growing number of Jews had arrived in Palestine and settled there. Many of them, financed by wealthy West European Jews, had purchased land from the Arabs.

Israel

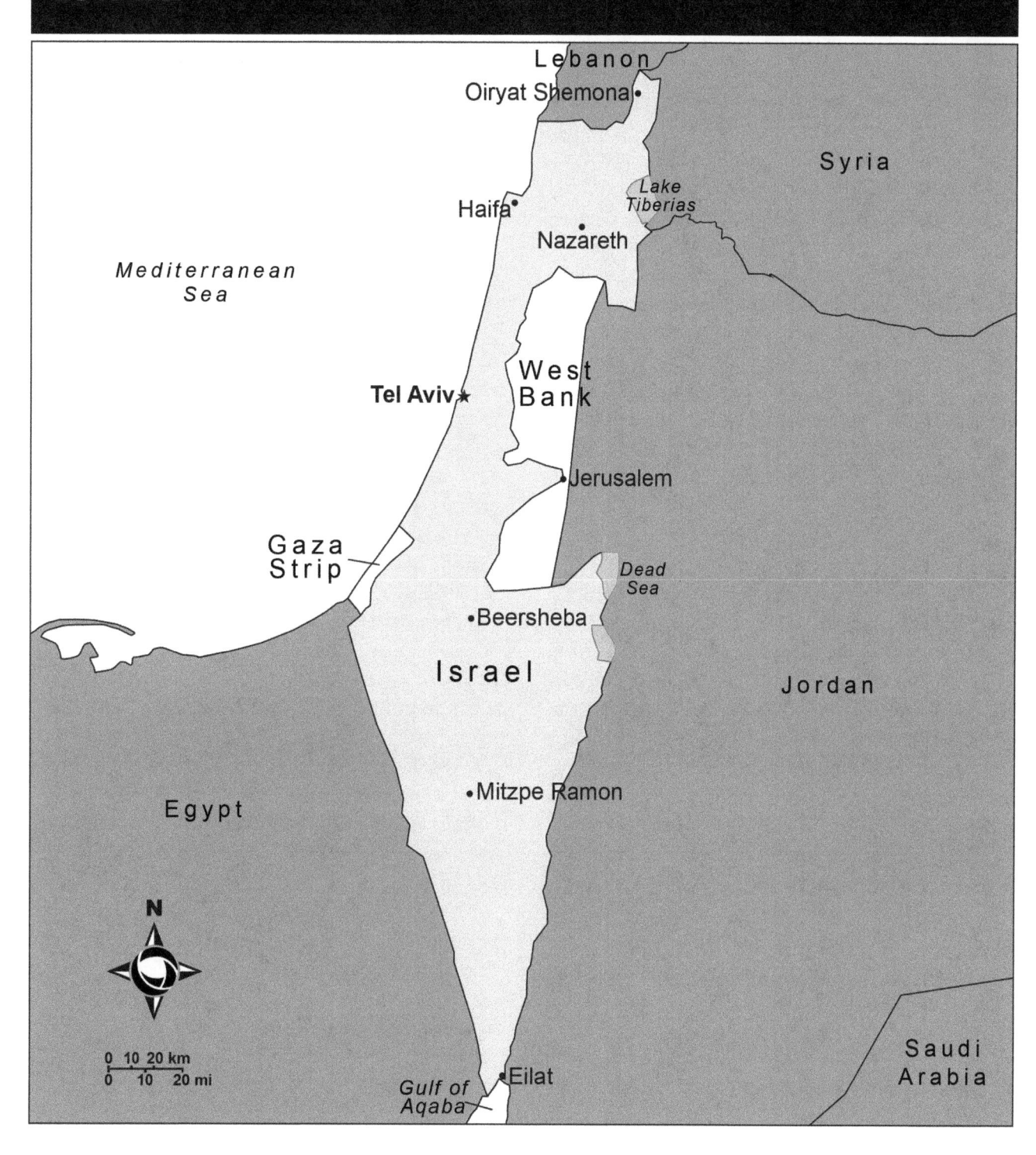

These numbers increased after the war, which the Palestinian Arabs came to view with growing alarm, seeing themselves becoming marginalized in their own land. In response to continuing Jewish immigration, sporadic Arab attacks occurred against Jews as well as British officials in Palestine.

The escalating violence was the result of the impossible British policy of permitting Jewish immigration while at the same time attempting to safeguard Arab rights. Continued immigration brought more Jewish land purchases and in turn more violence.

In 1920 Arabs began sporadically attacking Jewish settlements, and in response Jews formed Haganah, a clandestine defense organization. Heightened violence by 1929 led the British to halt all Jewish settlement in Palestine, but Jewish outcries caused the British to reverse this policy. Militant Jewish groups also began to take action against what they saw as restrictive British immigration policies. A three-way struggle thus ensued between the British and militant Arabs and Jews. In 1936, a full-fledged Arab revolt began. Lasting until 1939, it forced the British to dispatch to Palestine 20,000 additional troops and resulted in the deaths of some 5,000 Arabs and many more injured. It also brought a temporary alliance between the British and the Jews.

In 1937 the British government considered partitioning Palestine into separate Arab and Jewish states but then a year later rejected this as not feasible. In 1939 London announced that Palestine would become an independent state within 10 years. The British also sharply curtailed Jewish immigration and restricted the sale of Arab land to Jews. This policy of attempting to favor the Arabs continued during World War II, when the British even diverted warships to intercept and turn back ships carrying Jews attempting to escape the Holocaust, the Nazi scheme to exterminate all the Jews within their grasp.

Realization of the full extent of the Holocaust, which had brought the deaths of more than 6 million Jews, dramatically changed attitudes throughout most of the world in favor of Jewish settlement in Palestine and even the creation of a Jewish state there. Probably most Jews now believed that the only way to prevent a new Holocaust was the creation of a Jewish nation-state. Armed Zionist terrorist organizations, such as Lohamei Herut Yisrael (Lehi) and Irgun, were increasingly at war with the British Palestine administration, which was refusing to allow the resettlement in Israel from Europe of more than 250,000 Jewish Holocaust survivors. For their part, the Arabs failed to understand why they should be made victims for something not of their doing in the Holocaust.

On February 14, 1947, exasperated by its inability to solve the Palestinian problem, the British government turned matters over to the new United Nations (UN). That August the United Nations Special Commission on Palestine (UNSCOP) recommended that the British mandate be terminated and that Palestine be granted its independence on the basis of separate Arab and Jewish states. Although the Arabs numbered 1.2 million and the Jews just 600,000, the Jews would have had some 56 percent of the land. Jews supported the plan; understandably, the Arabs did not. Now desperate to quit Palestine, the British government announced acceptance of the UNSCOP recommendation and declared in September 1947 that its mandate of Palestine would terminate on May 14, 1948.

On November 29, 1947, the UN General Assembly officially approved the partition of Palestine. The Council of the Arab League announced that it was prepared to prevent the creation of a Jewish state by force if necessary, and immediately following the UN vote, militant Palestinian Arabs and foreign Arab fighters attacked Jewish communities in Palestine, beginning the Arab-Jewish Communal War (November 30, 1947–May 14, 1948). The United States, with the world's largest Jewish population, became the chief champion and most reliable ally of a Jewish state, a position that cost it dearly in its relations with the Arab world and greatly impacted subsequent geopolitics in the Middle East and throughout the world.

The British completed their pullout on May 14, 1948, and that same day David Ben-Gurion, the executive chairman and defense minister of the Jewish Agency, immediately declared the independence of the Jewish State of Israel. Leader of the Mapai (Workers' Party), Ben-Gurion became the new state's first prime minister.

At first, the interests of the United States and those of the Soviet Union regarding the Jewish state converged. U.S. recognition of Israel came only shortly before that of the Soviet Union. Moscow found common ground with Jewish suffering at the hands of the Nazis in World War II and also identified with the socialism espoused by the early Jewish settlers in Palestine and their anti-British stance. The Cold War, the reemergence of official anti-Semitism in the Soviet Union, and Moscow's desire to court the Arab states soon changed that, however.

Immediately following Ben-Gurion's declaration of independence, Egypt, Lebanon, Jordan, Syria, and Iraq invaded Palestine, beginning the Israeli War of Independence (May 14, 1948–January 7, 1949). In the war, the Jews successfully defended their new state and defeated the Arab armies. A series of armistices with neighboring states ended the fighting, with Israel left in control of an additional 26 percent of the land of mandate Palestine west of the Jordan River. Jordan, however, controlled large portions of Judaea and Samaria, later known as the West Bank.

The establishment of Israel and the subsequent war created some 600,000–700,000 Palestinian Arab refugees. Why these refugees fled their homes is much disputed, but clearly a great many were forced to flee by the Israelis. In any case, Israel refused to allow their return after the war. The matter of the right of return has been a major stumbling block to any peace settlement ever since.

Meanwhile, the Israelis set up the machinery of state. Mapai and its successor parties would govern Israel for the next 30 years. These were social democratic parties with strong roots in Zionism. As such, they were hawkish on defense but inclined toward moderate socialism in the socioeconomic sphere. The provisional government governed until February 14, 1949, following democratic elections on January 25, 1949, that established a unicameral parliament—later known as the Knesset—of 120 members. The executive (cabinet) was selected by the Knesset and was subject to it. Israel also adopted a system of proportional representation in which Knesset seats were based on the percentage of votes received. Even parties receiving relatively few votes had representation. Such parties included those representing the Arab population, those espousing various degrees of Jewish orthodoxy, the communists, and Revisionist Zionist groups.

On May 11, 1949, meanwhile, Israel was admitted to the UN. The Mapai Party remained the dominant political party after the second Knesset elections on July 30, 1951, which saw the formation of a coalition government with the religious parties.

Legislation of July 1950 established the Law of Return, granting any Jew the right to settle in Israel. In 1951 alone 687,000 Jews arrived, some 300,000 of these from Arab states. Ben-Gurion remained prime minister until 1953. He returned to that position in October 1955 and remained in office until 1963.

Israel's early years were dominated by the great challenge of absorbing and integrating into society hundreds of thousands of Jewish immigrants, including those from Eastern and Central Europe (Ashkenazi Jews), West European Jews (Sephardim Jews), and Middle Eastern or Oriental Jews (Mizrahi Jews). The differences in terms of cultural background and socioeconomic status among the various groups of Jews initially proved to be a challenge for the Israeli government.

In addition to money raised from Jewish communities overseas, especially in the United States, and the U.S. government, financial assistance came from an unlikely source. Chancellor Konrad Adenauer of the Federal Republic of Germany (West Germany) secured passage of legislation to provide billions of dollars in assistance to Israel during a 12-year period with payments to individual victims of the Holocaust. Israel's formative years also witnessed the creation of a mixed socialist-capitalist economy. Included in the expansion and maturation of the economy were agricultural incentives for the cultivation of additional land.

The 1949 cease-fires that ended the 1948–1949 war were not followed by peace agreements. The Arab states not only refused to recognize the existence of Israel but also refused to concede defeat in the war. They soon had imposed an economic and political boycott on Israel. Also, throughout most of the 1950s Israel suffered from repeated attacks and raids from the neighboring Arab states as well as from Palestinian Arab paramilitary and terrorist groups. Aggressive Israeli retaliation failed to stop the attacks and raids. Tension increased with the 1952 coup and revolution in Egypt led by Gamal Abdel Nasser. Indeed, Nasser proved to be an outspoken opponent of Israel and the West and a champion of Arab nationalism and unity. He supported cross-border raids into Israeli territory by so-called fedayeen (guerrilla fighters) from the Gaza Strip and formed alliances with other Arab states. He also cultivated close ties with the Soviet Union.

In 1956 Nasser nationalized the Suez Canal, which provided the pretext for the French, British, and Israeli governments to secretly plan war against Egypt. The British sought to retake control of the canal, while the French wanted to end Nasser's support of the Algerian independence movement. Israel saw the Suez Crisis as an opportunity to cooperate with Britain and France to check Nasser's power and influence, if not overthrow him.

On October 29, 1956, Israeli forces invaded the Sinai and headed for the Suez Canal. This provided the excuse for the British and the French to intervene. The U.S. government applied considerable pressure, and all three states soon agreed to withdraw. Israel, however, secured the right to free navigation through the Suez Canal and on the waterways through the Strait of Tiran and the Gulf of Aqaba. On November 7, the UN deployed a United Nations Emergency Force (UNEF) as a buffer between Egypt and Israel.

During 1957–1967, Israel was primarily preoccupied with domestic politics, including continued agricultural and industrial development. Its border with Egypt generally remained calm, although incidents with Syria in particular increased, especially over water rights as Israel diverted water from the Jordan River for irrigation purposes. This led Syria and Lebanon to divert water upstream from the Jordan. In response to this so-called water war, Israel destroyed Lebanese and Syrian projects designed to reduce water flow downstream.

Ben-Gurion resigned as prime minister in 1963 and two years later defected from the Mapai Party to create a new political organization, the Rafi Party (Israeli Labor List).

Upon Ben-Gurion's resignation, Levi Eshkol of Mapai was prime minister until his death in 1969, when Foreign Minister Golda Meir replaced him as Israel's fourth prime minister.

On May 23, 1960, in Buenos Aires, Argentina, Israeli agents captured fugitive Nazi official Adolf Eichmann, who had charge of the deportation of Jews to the death camps during World War II. Spiriting him out of Argentina, Eichmann was brought to Israel, where he was placed on trial for crimes against humanity and the Jewish people. Convicted, he was hanged on May 31, 1962, the only time the death penalty was imposed according to Israeli law. In 1965 after much internal debate and controversy, Israel established formal diplomatic relations with West Germany.

On February 22, 1966, a coup brought a military government to power in Syria. It was committed to the Palestinian cause and the liberation of Palestine, and incidents along Israel's border with Syria increased significantly. Throughout the spring of 1967, Israel faced increasing attacks from Syria and from the Palestine Liberation Organization (PLO), a quasi-terrorist organization created in 1964 to represent the Palestinians Arabs and coordinate efforts with Arabs states to liberate Palestine. The PLO also mounted raids from Jordan.

On May 13, 1967, the Soviet Union provided Egypt with false information that Israel was mobilizing troops on the Syrian border, and on May 16 Nasser declared a state of emergency. Egypt, Syria, and Jordan then all mobilized their forces.

Buoyed by strong support in the Arab world for his belligerent stance, Nasser on May 16 demanded that the UNEF quit the Sinai immediately. The UNEF complied on May 19. Syrian and Egyptian forces were now on maximum alert.

Nasser then announced Egypt's intention to close the Strait of Tiran to Israeli shipping. This was the principal route for Israeli trade with Asia and the transit point for 90 percent of its oil imports. Israel had already let it be known that it would consider such a step a cause for war.

Nasser's announcement regarding the Strait of Tiran was largely a bluff, for he assumed that the threat of closing the strait would force Israel to withdraw its supposed increased forces along the Syrian border. On May 22, however, Egyptian minister of defense Field Marshal Abdel Hakim Amer ordered Egyptian forces to close the strait the next day. A countermanding order would have signaled weakness, and Nasser now ordered the Egyptian military to prepare for war. On May 30 Jordanian king Hussein arrived in Cairo and there concluded a mutual security pact with Egypt.

On paper, the balance of forces heavily favored the Arab states. The Israel Defense Forces (IDF) had 230,000 troops, 1,100 tanks, 200 artillery pieces, 260 combat aircraft, and 22 naval vessels. Egypt and Syria together had 263,000 men, 1,950 tanks, 915 artillery pieces, 521 combat aircraft, and 75 naval vessels. Counting Iraqi and Jordanian forces, the Arab advantage swelled to 409,000 men, 2,437 tanks, 1,487 artillery pieces, 649 combat aircraft, and 90 naval vessels.

Now certain of war and unwilling to allow the Arab forces time to fully mobilize their much larger resources, on June 4, despite strong U.S. opposition, Israeli prime minister Levi Eshkol authorized a preemptive strike against Egypt.

The Arab-Israeli war of 1967, known to history as the Six-Day War, began on the morning of June 5 and for all practical purposes was over by noon. The Israeli Air Force (IAF) offensive of that day remains one of the most stunning successes in modern warfare. Destruction of the Egyptian Air Force was essential if the Israeli Army was to enjoy success, yet Israel was outnumbered by Egypt and Syria two to one in combat aircraft. It would also be difficult for the Israeli Army to defend against Egyptian and Syrian air attacks coming from two different directions, and Israel was too small in area for early warning systems to provide sufficient time for Israeli fighters to scramble.

The IAF achieved a brilliant success not only against the Egyptians but also against Syria and Jordan. And following an Iraqi air strike on Israel, the IAF also attacked Iraqi air bases in the Mosul area. The IAF could now turn to close air support of Israeli mechanized ground forces, which had begun operations in the Sinai simultaneous with the initial air attacks.

The Egyptians, it should be noted, were handicapped by the fact that 50,000 of their best troops were tied down in the civil war in Yemen. Gaza surrendered on June 6. As the Israelis drove forward in the Sinai, Egyptian Army commander Field Marshal Amer ordered a general withdrawal. Meanwhile, Israeli air and amphibious forces secured Sharm El Sheikh.

On June 8 Israeli units reached the Suez Canal, and by the end of the day the Sinai east of the Suez Canal was firmly under Israeli control. A cease-fire went into effect on June 10. Egypt had lost 80 percent of its military equipment and had some 11,500 troops killed, 20,000 wounded, and 5,500 taken prisoner. The IDF sustained 338 killed. On June 9, meanwhile, Nasser had offered his resignation, but large supportive Egyptian public demonstrations caused him to remain.

Israeli leaders had urged King Hussein of Jordan to stay out of the war, informing him at the onset of fighting that their dispute was with Egypt. Hussein wanted to avoid participation but came under heavy public pressure to act, in one of the most fateful decisions of the modern Middle East. He was also deceived by false early Cairo broadcasts claiming major Egyptian military successes. Hussein hoped to satisfy his allies with minimum military action short of all-out war. Jordanian 155mm guns went into action against Tel Aviv, and Jordanian aircraft attempted to strafe a small Israeli airfield. These steps, however, led Israel to declare war on Jordan.

The Israelis quickly surrounded the Old City of Jerusalem. Although Jordanian forces there put up a stiff fight, the Israelis were able to prevent them from relieving. The Israelis also captured Latrun, opening the road between Tel Aviv and Jerusalem to Jewish traffic for the first time since 1947. On June 7 the Israelis stormed the Old City, forcing a Jordanian withdrawal. That same day the Israelis captured Bethlehem, Hebron, and Etzion. Despite Jordanian counterattacks, the Israelis also advanced on and seized Nablus. Jordanian forces then withdrew across the Jordan River, and both Israel and Jordan agreed to a cease-fire.

The Syrian front at first saw only artillery duels, with the Syrians not wishing to initiate offensive action. On June 9, with resources released from other fronts, the Israelis began major offensive action and broke through Syrian defenses in the northern Golan, resisting calls from the United States not to occupy the Golan Heights. Instead, the Israelis advanced on and captured Quneitra. Only when the Golan Heights was firmly in their hands did they agree to a cease-fire of June 10.

There also was some fighting at sea. On June 8 the *Liberty*, a U.S. electronic intelligence-gathering ship, was in international waters some 13 miles off El Arish when it came under attack by Israeli air and naval units. Thirty-four Americans died in the attack, and another 172 were wounded, many seriously. Although the ship was badly damaged, its crew managed to keep it afloat and make Malta, escorted by ships of the U.S. Sixth Fleet. The Israeli government later apologized for the attack and paid nearly $13 million in compensation. Official inquiries concluded that it was a matter of mistaken identity.

In the Six-Day War, Israel suffered some 800 dead, 2,440 wounded, and 16 missing or taken prisoner. Arab losses, chiefly Egyptian, were some 14,300 dead, 23,800 wounded, and 10,500 missing or taken prisoner. Israel lost 100 tanks and 40 aircraft, while the Arabs lost 950 tanks and 368 aircraft.

The Six-Day War vastly increased the amount of territory controlled by Israel. Israel gained from Egypt all of the Sinai east of the Suez Canal, including the Gaza Strip; from Jordan, it secured the entire east bank of the Jordan River and the Old City of Jerusalem; and from Syria, it added the Golan Heights.

These Israeli territorial acquisitions would make securing a Middle East peace settlement much more difficult. Although Israel returned the Sinai to Egypt in 1978 and withdrew from the Gaza Strip in 2005, it has showed a marked reluctance to yield the Golan Heights, the West Bank, and Old Jerusalem. Politically conservative Israelis and Ultra-Orthodox Jews consider the West Bank part of the ancient Jewish state never to be given up.

Humiliated by their defeat, the Arab states refused to negotiate with, recognize, or make peace with Israel. This was spelled out in the Khartoum Arab Summit Communiqué of September 1, 1967. The war united much of Israeli society and muted, if not silenced, most political disputes for several years. On January 21, 1968, the Mapai Party merged with two other socialist political parties to form the Labor Party.

In 1967, the so-called War of Attrition began with Egyptian forces shelling Israeli targets in the Sinai along the Suez Canal and with Israel responding with retaliatory raids and air strikes. Israel also constructed the Bar-Lev Line, an elaborate series of defensive fortifications to shield Israeli forces from Egyptian artillery fire. Nasser sought Soviet military aid and support, including surface-to-air missiles (SAMs). By 1969, the euphoria from Israel's decisive 1967 victory had turned into disillusionment with rising Israeli casualties and the fact that peace was still elusive.

Israel also experienced increasing incidents along its border with Jordan in PLO raids. These triggered retaliatory Israeli attacks that ultimately provoked a civil war between the PLO and the Jordanian government in 1970, which culminated in the so-called Black September that saw heavy fighting between the Jordanian Army and the PLO, which was expelled from Jordan to Lebanon. During Black September, Syria sought to intervene on the side of the PLO but was deterred from doing so by Israel.

On August 7, 1970, with American support, UN-brokered peace talks between Egypt and Israel brought a cease-fire and a temporary end to the War of Attrition. But no settlement was reached regarding Israel's 1967 occupation of Arab territories.

Egyptian president Gamal Abdel Nasser died in September 1970. His successor, Anwar Sadat, was determined to change the status quo regarding Israel. Sadat sought a peace process that would lead to Israeli withdrawal from the Sinai but without a formal general peace agreement. Toward that end, he resumed negotiations that Nasser had ended in 1955.

The failure of his diplomatic efforts in 1971, however, led Sadat to begin planning a military operation to break the political stalemate. Sadat believed that even a minor Egyptian military success would change the military equilibrium and force a political settlement. Israel's strength was in its air force and armored divisions in maneuver warfare. Egyptian strengths were the ability to build a strong defense line and new Soviet-supplied SAMs deployed in batteries along the canal and deep within Egypt. Sadat hoped to paralyze the IAF with the SAMs and counter the Israelis' advantage in maneuver warfare by forcing them to attack well-fortified and well-defended Egyptian strongholds.

In an attempt to dilute the Israeli military forces on the Sinai front and place maximum stress on his opponent, Sadat brought in Syria for a coordinated surprise attack. The key to success was secrecy. Were Israel to suspect that an attack was imminent, it would undoubtedly launch a preventive attack, as in 1967. That part of Sadat's plan, at least, was successful. A combination of effective Egyptian deceptive measures and Israeli arrogance contributed to Israel's failure to comprehend the threat.

On the Israeli-Egyptian front, Egypt amassed nearly 800,000 soldiers, 2,200 tanks, 2,300 artillery pieces, 150 SAM batteries, and 550 aircraft. Along the canal, Egypt deployed five infantry divisions with accompanying armored elements, supported by additional infantry and armored independent brigades. This force was backed by three mechanized divisions and two armored divisions. Israel had only a single division supported by 280 tanks.

Not until the early morning hours of October 6 did Israeli military intelligence conclude that an Egyptian attack was imminent. Brigadier General Eli Zeira, Israeli director of intelligence, warned Lieutenant General David Elazar, IDF chief of staff, but Prime Minister Golda Meir decided against a preemptive strike.

The Yom Kippur War of October 6–25, 1973, also known as the Ramadan War, the October War, and the 1973 Arab-Israeli War, commenced at 2:00 p.m. on October 6 on Yom Kippur, the holiest day for Jews, when Egypt launched a massive air strike against Israeli artillery and command positions. At the same time, Egyptian artillery shelled the Bar-Lev Line fortifications. Egyptian commandos crossed the canal followed by engineers, who quickly constructed bridges, allowing the Egyptians to pass across sizable numbers of infantry and armor. By October 8, Egyptian infantry and some 500 tanks had pushed three to five miles east of the canal, which was defended by the SAM batteries.

The Israelis meanwhile mobilized two armored divisions and on October 8 launched a quick counteroffensive to repel the Egyptians. These encountered the far larger and more well-equipped Egyptian force protected by handheld antitank missiles. The Egyptians crushed the Israeli counteroffensive. Israeli ground support aircraft also suffered heavy losses against Egyptian antiaircraft defenses, especially from SAMs. Following this setback, the Israeli General Staff decided to halt offensive actions on the Suez front and give priority to the Syria front.

Sadat now overruled his ground commander, Field Marshal Ahmed Ismail Ali, and, following Syrian pleas for assistance, ordered a resumption of the offensive on October 11. This, however, took Egyptian forces out of their prepared defensive positions and removed them from the effective SAM cover on the other side of the canal. On October 14 the Israelis threw back the Egyptians and inflicted heavy losses.

On October 15–16 the Israelis located a gap, unknown to the Egyptian high command, between the two Egyptian divisions. One Israeli division drove through that gap, and part of it crossed the canal. An Israeli paratroop brigade then established a bridgehead on the west bank. The Israeli high command now sought to establish a SAM-free zone over which Israeli aircraft could maneuver and cut off Egyptian troops east of the canal.

With the Egyptians threatening the Israelis west of the canal, heavy fighting occurred in the so-called Battle of the Chinese Farm during October 14–18. The Egyptians suffered heavy losses, and a second Israeli armored division crossed the canal and drove westward, rolling up Egyptian base camps and capturing antiaircraft positions and SAM sites. An Israeli effort to capture Ismailia failed, however. The Egyptians also turned back an Israeli effort to take Suez during October 23–24, and a cease-fire went into effect on October 25.

On the Syrian front, President Hafez al-Assad sought to regain the Golan Heights, captured by Israel in 1967, thereby gaining security for its northern settlements from sporadic Syrian bombardment. Unlike Sadat, Assad had no intention of using the war as leverage for a settlement with Israel.

On October 6, simultaneous with the Egyptian air strikes to the south, Syria launched a massive air strike accompanied by heavy artillery fire against Israeli positions on the Golan Heights. Syrian ground forces then advanced. They counted some 60,000 men in two armored divisions (600 tanks) and two infantry divisions (another 300 tanks). The

Syrians also had some 140 artillery batteries. Opposing them, the Israelis had some 12,000 troops, 177 tanks, and 11 artillery batteries.

With the exception of one important outpost, Israeli forces were not taken by surprise. Israeli tanks were in hull-down positions behind earthen barricades, with infantry in their fighting positions. The one exception was Mount Herman. Syrian helicopters carried commandos to the back of the fortified Israeli observation post on Mount Hermon, which provided an excellent view of the Golan Heights and the Damascus Plateau. The two-platoon Israeli garrison was taken completely by surprise, and all were slain, including those who surrendered.

The main Syrian attack by the four divisions occurred against two Israeli brigades, but Israeli mobilization was rapid, with reservists soon in place. Within a day the Israelis halted the northern Syrian thrusts. The two southern Syrian thrusts, however, nearly entered the Jordan River Valley. Had they been able to push beyond the escarpment, the Syrians could have cut Israel in two.

The IAF went into action, and although many of the Israeli jets fell prey to Syrian SAMs and mobile antiaircraft guns, a great many Syrian tanks were knocked out. Israeli close air support, the rapid arrival of reserves, and unimaginative Syrian attacks prevented the Syrians from retaking the southern Golan.

During October 8–9 the Israelis counterattacked in the south, and on October 10 they mounted a major counteroffensive north of the Quneitra-Damascus road, pushing the Syrians back to and beyond the prewar Israeli-Syrian border.

Beginning on October 9 also, Israel launched an air campaign deep within Syria, striking the Ministry of Defense in Damascus as well as seaports, industrial sites, and fuel-storage areas. Profoundly impacting the Syrian economy, these attacks continued until October 21.

On October 12 the Israelis began to withdraw some units south to fight on the Sinai front. Nonetheless, by October 14 they had opened up a salient inside Syria some 10 miles deep, 30 miles wide, and only 25 miles from Damascus. The Israelis held it during October 15–19, despite fierce Syrian and Iraqi counterattacks, with Iraq having now entered the war. On October 15 the Israelis repulsed an Iraqi armored division, and on October 19 they halted another counterattack against the salient, this one spearheaded by Jordanian units. The Israelis maintained these positions until the cease-fire of October 24. On October 22 following two failed assaults on October 8 and 21, Israeli helicopter-borne forces retook Mount Hermon.

In the fighting for the Golan Heights, Israel lost nearly 800 dead and 250 tanks put out of action, along with a number of ground support aircraft shot down. Certainly a key factor was the ability of the Israelis to quickly return disabled tanks to battle. Syrian losses were perhaps 8,000 men killed, 1,150 tanks destroyed, and 118 aircraft lost.

There was also fighting at sea, with the Egyptians imposing a naval blockade of Israel's Mediterranean coast while also halting seaborne traffic to Eilat. On the first night of the war, Israeli missile boats attacked the chief Syrian Mediterranean port of Latakia (Ladhaqiyya). Syrian missile boats engaged them, and in the first naval battle in history between missile-firing ships, the Israelis defeated the incoming Syrian fire-and-forget Styx missiles while using their own radar-guided Gabriel ship-to-ship missiles to destroy three Syrian missile boats and a minesweeper. The Syrian Navy then remained in port for the rest of the war. The Battle of Latakia brought new prestige for the Israeli Navy, previously regarded as only a poor relation of its highly regarded army and air force.

Among other naval engagements, on October 8–9 off the Egyptian port of Damietta, Egyptian missile boats sortied to engage an Israeli missile boat task force, which sank four of them for no losses of its own. In an action the next night off Port Said in Egypt, another Egyptian missile boat was sunk. The remaining Egyptian missile boats then withdrew to Damietta and Alexandria.

Both the United States, supporting Israel, and the Soviet Union, supporting the Arab states, were caught off guard by the war, although the Soviets probably learned of the Egyptian and Syrian plans several days in advance of the actual attacks. Both the Soviets and the Americans sent supplies to their sides during the war. Between October 14 and 21 the United States airlifted some 20,000 tons of supplies to Israeli, as opposed to some 15,000 tons by the Soviet Union to the Arab states.

A Soviet announcement on October 24 that it was placing seven airborne divisions on alert brought a U.S. announcement the next day that its armed forces were on precautionary alert. Any possibility of a Soviet-U.S. armed clash ended with a UN Security Council resolution, with both the Soviet and U.S. representatives voting in the affirmative, that established a 7,000-man force to enforce the cease-fires in the Sinai Peninsula and the Golan Heights. The cease-fires went into effect on October 25.

Casualty figures for the Yom Kippur War (Ramadan War) vary. Israel suffered 2,521–2,800 killed in action, 7,250–8,800 wounded, and 293 taken prisoner. Some 400 Israeli tanks were destroyed; another 600 were disabled but returned to service. The IAF lost 102 airplanes and 2 helicopters. There were no navy losses.

Arab losses were some 5,000–15,000 Egyptians and 3,000–3,500 Syrians killed; the number of wounded is unknown. Iraq lost 278 killed and 898 wounded, while Jordan suffered 23 killed and 77 wounded. A total of 8,372 Egyptians, 392 Syrians, 13 Iraqis, and 6 Moroccans were taken prisoner. The Arab states lost 2,250–2,300 tanks, 400 of which were taken by the Israelis in good working order and added to their inventory. Arab aircraft losses were 450–512. Nineteen Arab naval vessels, including 10 missile boats, were sunk.

Although the outcome secured Israel's borders, the war shocked the Israeli people. An investigatory agency, the Agranat Commission, led to the removal of several high-ranking officers. The commission did not assess civilian leadership responsibility. The Yom Kippur War shook Israel's confidence and morale. In the December 1973 Knesset elections the Labor Party lost seats, and the newly formed right-wing Likud Party gained strength. Political fallout from the war led Prime Minister Golda Meir to resign on April 10, 1974. Minister of Defense Moshe Dayan followed her in June. Meir was succeeded by Yitzhak Rabin, also of the Labor Party.

Although the Arab states lost the war, Egyptian president Anwar Sadat achieved his aim of erasing the trauma of their rapid defeat in the Six-Day War of 1967. The Yom Kippur War also allowed him to negotiate as an equal with Israel. On January 18, 1974, Israel and Egypt signed a disengagement agreement by which Israel agreed to pull back its forces from west of the Suez Canal and from the length of the front to create security zones. Another agreement, known as Sinai II, of September 4, 1975, saw Israel withdraw another 12–24 miles, with UN observer forces taking over that area. Still, Israel held more than two-thirds of Sinai.

During this period, Arab states along with the PLO proved much more effective in publicizing the plight of the Palestinians. Increasing acts of terrorism by the PLO also focused world attention on the Arab-Israeli conflict and the Palestinian cause. On October 14, 1974, the UN General Assembly authorized the PLO to participate in a series of debates. Included was PLO chairman Yasser Arafat, considered a terrorist in Israel and the West. He addressed the body, and on November 10, 1975, in Resolution 3379 the General Assembly declared Zionism racist. (Resolution 3379 was revoked in 1991 by General Assembly Resolution 4686.) Israeli prime minister Rabin refused to negotiate with the PLO because it refused to recognize Israel and proclaimed as its goal the destruction of the Jewish state.

With little loss of life, on July 4, 1976, in a daring raid, Israeli commandos rescued 94 Israeli passengers and 12 crew members of an Air France plane taken by Palestinian hijackers to Entebbe, Uganda, under the protection of Ugandan dictator Idi Amin. The hijackers threatened to kill the passengers unless 40 Palestinian terrorists in Israeli and Western European prisons were released. The successful operation proved to be a major morale boost for Israel and its military.

In May 1977 Likud ended Labor's 29-year political reign, and Menachem Begin became prime minister. Now seeking to jump-start the peace process, Egyptian president Sadat shocked the world by announcing on November 9, 1977, his willingness to go to Jerusalem for a face-to-face meeting with the Israelis to negotiate peace. Accepting an invitation by Begin, Sadat arrived in Israel on November 19, the first Arab head of state to do so, effectively recognizing Israel's right to exist. Sadat both met with Begin and addressed the Knesset. Although every other Arab state refused to negotiate with Israel, after two years of negotiations mediated by U.S. president Jimmy Carter, Egypt and Israel made peace on September 17, 1978. In these Camp David Accords, Israel withdrew from the Sinai in exchange for Egypt recognizing Israel. Discussions about the status of the Palestinians took place but never achieved common ground. Sadat's assassination on October 6, 1981, effectively ended the process. Meanwhile, most Arab leaders condemned the peace treaty, and Egypt was suspended from the Arab League.

On July 7, 1981, the IAF bombed the Osiraq nuclear reactor in Iraq, thwarting possible Iraqi efforts to acquire nuclear weapons. Then on June 6, 1982, Israeli forces invaded Lebanon, which had been experiencing a civil war since 1975, ostensibly to defend its northern border from increasing terrorist attacks from Lebanon but also to expel both the PLO and Syrian forces from Lebanon, which it did by laying siege to Beirut and forcing the PLO to relocate to Tunisia. The 1982 Lebanon War came at terrible human cost and material destruction in Lebanon, and Israel failed to achieve its broad policy objectives of creating a stable pro-Israeli government in Lebanon. In 1983, Begin resigned and was replaced by fellow Likud member Yitzhak Shamir. Israel withdrew from most of Lebanon in June 1985 but maintained a buffer zone there in southern Lebanon until May 24, 2000, when it surrendered that territory as well.

A major Palestinian uprising, the First Intifada, erupted in 1987 in the Israeli-occupied territories of the West Bank and the Gaza Strip and demanded significant Israeli military resources. The images of armed Israeli soldiers battling Palestinian youths, mostly throwing stones, led to considerable international criticism of Israel. In 1991 following Iraq's August 1990 invasion of Kuwait, Iraq targeted Israel with Scud missiles in an ultimately unsuccessful attempt to provoke Israel into attacking Iraq and cause the Arab states to withdraw from the multinational U.S.-led coalition force.

The collapse of the Soviet Union in December 1991 and the end of the Cold War brought into Israel hundreds of thousands of Jews from the Soviet Union. This also left many Arab states, previously allied with Moscow, isolated and gave the United States much more influence and leverage in the region. Accordingly, peace talks were held in 1991 and 1992 among Israel, Syria, Lebanon, Jordan, and the Palestinians. Those talks paved the way for the 1993 Oslo Accords between Israel and the PLO, stipulating the beginning of Palestinian self-rule in the West Bank and the Gaza Strip and peace between Israel and Jordan on October 26, 1994.

Initial Israeli support for the Oslo Accords waned following a series of terrorist attacks by Hamas—a Palestinian terrorist group founded in 1987 at the beginning of the First Intifada—which opposed peace with Israel. On November 4, 1995, a right-wing Jewish nationalist assassinated Prime Minister Rabin for his peace efforts with the Palestinians and willingness to cede occupied territory in the West Bank. Many observers believe that Rabin's death effectively ended Israeli willingness to make meaningful territorial concession for peace.

Continued Hamas terrorism led to the election as prime minister of hard-liner Benjamin Netanyahu of Likud. Netanyahu refused to pursue the "land for peace" dialogue with the Palestinians, and the peace process stalled. In 1999 Labor's Ehud Barak defeated Netanyahu, and in 2000 talks between Barak and Yasser Arafat, mediated by U.S. president Bill Clinton, came very close but failed to produce agreement on a Palestinian state owing to Arafat's intransigence.

Collapse of the peace talks and a provocative visit on September 28, 2000, by Likud's Ariel Sharon to the contested religious site known to Jews as the Temple Mount and to Muslims as the Dome of the Rock sparked the Second or Al-Aqsa Intifada, which lasted until February 8, 2005. Sharon was elected prime minister in March 2001 and was reelected in 2003.

Under Sharon, the Israeli government began constructing a series of solid wall barriers to separate Israel proper from most of the West Bank. The stated purpose of the barrier was the prevention of terrorist attacks. The barrier itself, known in Hebrew as the Separation Wall and to the Arabs as the Apartheid Wall, runs only partly along the 1949 Jordanian-Israeli armistice line (the Green Line) and partly through the West Bank, diverging eastward from the armistice line by up to 12 miles in order to include on the western (Israeli) side concentrations of highly populated Jewish settlements, such as East Jerusalem. The barrier has been widely condemned as a violation of international law and a major impediment to the establishment of a viable independent Palestinian state.

In the face of the Second Intifada and stalled peace talks with the Palestinians, in September 2005 Israel withdrew from the Gaza Strip, although it controlled its borders, coast, and airspace. Hamas soon came to dominate Gaza. After Sharon suffered a massive stroke on January 4, 2006, Ehud Olmert became acting prime minister. Olmert was formally elected to the post following the victory of his Kadima Party in the legislative elections of April 14, 2006.

On January 25, 2006, elections were held for the second Palestinian Legislative Council, the legislature of the Palestinian National Authority. To the surprise of many, these were won by the more militant Hamas, which campaigned on a platform of change and reform, winning 74 of the 132 seats, while the ruling Fatah won only 45 seats. The Hamas victory was regarded as a major setback for the peace process.

On June 25, 2006, after a Hamas raid killed two Israeli soldiers and captured another, Israel launched Operation SUMMER RAINS, a series of attacks into the Gaza Strip and arrests of Hamas leaders in the West Bank. The next month, the Olmert government became involved in a monthlong conflict in Lebanon following an attack by Hezbollah on Israel that killed three Israeli soldiers and captured two. Hezbollah is an Iranian- and Syrian-backed Shia Islamic extremist group and a major political entity in Lebanon. To the surprise of many, Hezbollah, which was well armed and had established strong defensive positions in southern Lebanon, fought very well indeed. This July 12–August 14, 2006, Lebanon War (also called the 2006 Israel-Hezbollah War and known in Lebanon as the July War and in Israel as the Second Lebanon War), devastated much of southern Lebanon. Israel failed to achieve its broad policy objectives, and Hezbollah appeared strengthened.

Meanwhile, Israeli voters remained keenly interested in such issues as the role of the Orthodox minority, the rights of Israeli Arabs, the fate of Israeli settlements in the West

Bank, and the ups and downs of the economy. The two nearest and most direct threats to Israel remained Hamas and Hezbollah, although the Israeli government expressed great concern regarding threats by Iran and what it asserted was Iran's desire to acquire nuclear weapons. Iranian president Mahmoud Ahmadinejad, a Holocaust denier, repeatedly called for the destruction of Israel.

After midnight on September 6, 2007, the IAF carried out Operation ORCHARD, a surprise raid on a suspected nuclear development facility in the Deir ez-Zor region of Syria. Yet in early 2008, Syrian president Bashar al-Assad revealed that Israel and Syria had been engaged in secret peace discussions, with Turkey as a mediator.

In December 2008, the shaky Hamas-Israeli cease-fire ended when Hamas fighters began launching rockets on Israel from Hamas-controlled Gaza. Israel responded with heavy air strikes, and on January 3, 2009, the government sent troops into Gaza. This First Gaza War (Israeli Operation CAST LEAD) of December 27, 2008–January 18, 2009, wrought considerable physical destruction in Gaza and killed perhaps 1,300 Palestinians, while Israel lost 13 dead (10 of them military personnel). Tensions remained high thereafter.

In February 2009 after Olmert declared his intention to resign the premiership, parliamentary elections occurred but resulted in an unclear mandate. Israeli president Shimon Peres then asked Netanyahu to form a coalition government, which by necessity would include members from the Likud, Kadima, and other parties. During his second premiership, Netanyahu showed very little inclination to try to resolve the Israeli-Palestinian conflict through meaningful negotiation, all the while increasing the number of Jewish housing settlements on the West Bank. Netanyahu repeatedly warned of the dangers of Iran's suspected nuclear weapons ambitions, and his hard-line approach resulted in badly strained relations with the Barack Obama administration in Washington. Netanyahu's political coalition won a majority of seats in the 2013 elections, which saw him continue as prime minister. While he continued his policies toward economic liberalization, renewed peace talks with the Palestinians that commenced in the summer of 2013 yielded no tangible results.

After the kidnapping of 3 Israeli teenagers in the West Bank on June 12, 2014, the IDF initiated Operation BROTHER'S KEEPER to find the teens. Israeli authorities arrested some 350 Palestinians, including nearly all Hamas leaders in the West Bank. Five Palestinians were also killed. The bodies of the 3 teenagers were subsequently discovered, and Netanyahu blamed Hamas. Palestinian president Mahmoud Abbas maintained that there was no evidence that Hamas was behind the kidnappings, and others were also skeptical. In response, however, Hamas in Gaza began launching rockets that targeted Israeli cities. Netanyahu responded with overwhelming force.

During July 8–August 26, 2014, Israeli forces again invaded Gaza, in Operation PROTECTIVE EDGE. In this 2014 Gaza conflict, Israel lost 66 soldiers and 6 civilians killed, while Palestinian dead numbered about 2,300. Many more were wounded on each side, and physical damage in Gaza was immense.

Angered by the April 2014 agreement between the Fatah-dominated Palestinian National Authority and Hamas to hold national elections in late 2014 and form a compromise unity government, Netanyahu increased Jewish housing construction in Arab areas. This brought sharp condemnation internationally, including from the European Community and the Obama administration.

On December 2, 2014, Netanyahu fired his cabinet and called for new elections to be held in March 2015, in advance of the date mandated by law. This occurred amid rising criticism of Israel from the United States and Western Europe, with many believing that Netanyahu had rejected the two-state solution in favor of outright Israeli annexation of the West Bank. In a stunning development, on December 23, 2014, Foreign Minister Avigdor Lieberman denounced Netanyahu's Palestinian policy, accusing him of not doing anything to advance the peace process.

On March 3, 2015, in an unprecedented interjection in U.S. politics, Netanyahu was invited by the majority Republican Party members in the U.S. Congress to address a joint session to voice his adamant opposition to a pending diplomatic agreement with Iran regarding that country's nuclear weapons program. The speech greatly angered the Obama administration and brought U.S.-Israeli relations to a historic low. On March 16, the day before Israeli national elections, in order to attract right-wing votes, Netanyahu announced his opposition to a two-state solution. His coalition narrowly won, whereupon he publicly reversed his position on a two-state solution.

On August 22 only weeks after the nuclear deal with Iran was concluded, U.S. and Israeli media outlets revealed that in 2009 and 2010 Israeli leaders, including Netanyahu, had drawn up plans to attack Iran but shelved the scheme when it encountered stiff resistance from some Israeli cabinet members. In October 2015 Netanyahu created an international stir when he stated that Haj Amin al-Husseini, Jerusalem's grand mufti during World War II, had helped convince Nazi leaders to implement the Holocaust. This claim, which has long been debunked by scholars, created even more antipathy between Muslims and Israelis.

By March 2016, Netanyahu's coalition government showed considerable signs of strain as a number of Ultra-Orthodox members threatened to revolt over the government's plans to create non-Orthodox prayer space at the Western Wall. On May 20 Israeli defense minister Moshe Yaalon resigned, claiming that the nation was being taken over by "extremist and dangerous elements" after Netanyahu moved to replace him with longtime Netanyahu rival and far-right politician Avigdor Lieberman to strengthen the governing coalition. As the Defense Ministry also runs civil affairs in the occupied West Bank, this did not bode well for the Palestinians there. A former chief of Israel's armed forces, Yaalon had shored up relations with the Pentagon that provided a counterweight to Netanyahu's policy feuds with President Obama regarding peace talks with the Palestinians and Iran's nuclear program. By contrast, Lieberman was inexperienced militarily and known for his past hawkish talk against Palestinians, Israel's Arab minority, and Egypt, an important Israeli regional security partner.

Meanwhile, ongoing construction of new Israeli settlements in the West Bank, undertaken in defiance of public opinion, makes a two-state solution far more difficult. By the summer of 2018, peace between Israel, the Palestinians, and Israeli's Arab neighbors remained as elusive as ever. Nonetheless, the election of Donald Trump as U.S. president allowed Netanyahu to reset relations with the United States as Trump had talked during the presidential campaign about the need to improve relations with Israel and had expressed his support for making Jerusalem the capital of the Jewish state.

In September 2017, the Israeli Supreme Court ruling struck down an arrangement that allowed Ultra-Orthodox Jews exemption from compulsory military service, calling this both discriminatory and unconstitutional. The issue has long divided Israelis in a nation where all men and women are liable for military service at age 18. Exemption from military service for Orthodox Jews involved in full-time Torah study is regarded as a major issue in the struggle to shape the future character of the Israeli state.

On October 12, 2017, representatives of Hamas in Gaza and the Palestinian Authority in the West Bank met in Cairo to sign an agreement that would end their decade-long break and create a unity government that could treat with Israel. Problems remained, however, for while Hamas agreed to hand over the government of Gaza to the PA, it was refusing to give up control of its rockets and mortars aimed at Israeli, which was one of the key PA conditions. The Netanyahu government also announced that it would oppose any agreement that did not recognize Israel and disarm Hamas. As of August 2018, however, the unity government had yet to come to fruition, and Israel had begun to carry out targeted air strikes against select Hamas targets after that group began sending incendiary balloons and rockets into Israeli territory.

President Trump handed Israeli prime minister Netanyahu a tremendous gift in December 2017 when, without extracting any concessions from the Israeli government in return, he delivered on a campaign promise and simply announced that the U.S. government was recognizing Jerusalem as the capital of Israel and that the American embassy would be moved there as quickly as possible. This reversed long-standing U.S. policy in the region, and although many Jews in Israel received the move jubilantly, the decision was condemned by the vast majority of the international community including prominent Israeli allies, and it led to considerable Palestinian demonstrations and some violence and deaths. Most analysts concluded that the U.S. policy change marked the end of the two-state solution, while the Palestinian Authority issued a statement that the United States had forfeited its position as an honest broker and that it would no longer work with the United States in attempting to reach a peace agreement with Israel.

The United Nations General Assembly voted overwhelmingly to condemn the U.S. decision in a vote of 128 to 9 (most of them small states dependent on U.S. aid) with 35 abstentions. This vote came after U.S. ambassador to the UN Nikki Haley issued a direct threat to the organization, saying that the United States would think twice about funding the world body if it voted to condemn Trump's decision.

In April 2018, Netanyahu accused Iran of having violated the 2015 Iran Nuclear Deal, although the evidence his government offered to support this was already well known and did not involve recent Iranian activities. Less than a month later, On May 8, much to Netanyahu's delight, Trump formally withdrew U.S. support from the Iran Nuclear Deal and announced that his government would reimpose punishing economic sanctions on Iran. Meanwhile, by the summer of 2018 the Israeli government was upping its ante vis-à-vis the Syrian Civil War, demanding that Iran be excluded from any negotiations that might conclude a lasting peace in Syria. In July 2018, the Israeli Knesset enacted a so-called Basic Law, or Nation-State Law, which formally declared Israel a "Jewish state," a measure that Netanyahu wholeheartedly supported. The legislation was met with much criticism—inside Israel and beyond—because it potentially jeopardized the future of Arab, Muslim, and other non-Jewish citizens, particularly the Palestinians. The law would make brokering an Israeli-Palestinian peace settlement all the more daunting. Nevertheless, it fit into Netanyahu's far-right agenda, which he has been steadily implementing for several years. Meanwhile, in February 2018, Israeli police recommended that Netanyahu be charged with corruption, a development that the premier termed "baseless."

Stefan Brooks, Paul G. Pierpaoli Jr., Daniel E. Spector, and Spencer C. Tucker

See also

Alexander III the Great; Ali, Ahmad Ismail; Amer, Abdel Hakim; Aqaba, Gulf of; Arab Revolt in Palestine; Arafat, Yasser; Assad, Hafez al-; Balfour Declaration; Barak, Ehud; Bar Kochba Revolt; Bar-Lev Line; Begin, Menachem; Ben-Gurion, David; Black September; Camp David Accords; Crusades in the Holy Land, Christian; Cyrus the Younger; Dayan, Moshe; Egypt; Eshkol, Levi; Gaza War of 2006; Gaza War of 2008–2009; Gaza War of 2014; Hadrian, Emperor; Haganah; Hamas; Herzl, Theodor; Holocaust; Hussein ibn Talal, King of Jordan; Intifada, First; Intifada, Second; Irgun Tsvai Leumi; Israeli War of Independence; Jerusalem, Capture of; Jerusalem, Crusader Siege of; Jerusalem, Latin Kingdom of; Jerusalem, Roman Siege of; Jewish Brigade; Jewish Legion; Jewish-Roman War, First; Jordan; Judaea; Latakia, Battle of; Lebanon-Israeli War; *Liberty* Incident; Lohamei Herut Israel; Maccabean Revolt; Mamluk Sultanate; Meir, Golda Mabovitch; Nasser, Gamal Abdel; Nebuchadnezzar II; Netanyahu, Benjamin; Osiraq Raid; Oslo Accords; Ottoman Empire; Palestine, British Mandate for; Palestine Liberation Organization; Palestinian National Authority; Palmach; Rabin, Yitzhak; Sadat, Anwar; San Remo Conference; Sargon of Akkad; Shamir, Yitzhak; Sharon, Ariel; Sinai I and Sinai II Agreements; Six-Day War; Strait of Tiran Crisis; Suez Crisis; Sykes-Picot Agreement; Syria; Tiglath-Pileser III; War of Attrition; World War I, Impact on the Middle East; Yom Kippur War; Zionism

References

Bickerton, Ian J. *A Concise History of the Arab-Israeli Conflict*. Upper Saddle River, NJ: Prentice Hall, 2005.

Bowen, Jeremy. *Six Days: How the 1967 War Shaped the Middle East*. London: Simon and Schuster, 2003.

Bregman, Ahron. *Israel's Wars: A History since 1947*. London: Routledge, 2002.

Dunstan, Simon. *The Yom Kippur War, 1973*. Oxford, UK: Osprey, 2007.

Flapan, Simha. *The Birth of Israel: Myths and Realities*. New York: Pantheon Books, 1987.

Fromkin, David. *A Peace to End All Peace: The Fall of the Ottoman Empire and the Creation of the Modern Middle East*. New York: Owl, 1989.

Gilbert, Martin. *Israel: A History*. New York: RosettaBooks, 2014.

Hammel, Eric. *Six Days in June: How Israel Won the 1967 Arab-Israeli War*. New York: Simon and Schuster, 1992.

Herzog, Chaim. *The Arab-Israeli Wars: War and Peace in the Middle East*. New York: Random House, 1982.

Morris, Benny. *1948: The First Arab-Israeli War*. New Haven, CT: Yale University Press, 2008.

Oren, Michael B. *Six Days of War: June 1967 and the Making of the Modern Middle East*. New York: Presidio, 2003.

Rabinovich, Abraham. *The Yom Kippur War: An Epic Encounter That Transformed the Middle East*. New York: Schocken Books, 2004.

Rosenberg, Joel C. *Israel at War*. Carol Stream, IL: Tyndale House Publishers, 2012.

Ross, Dennis. *Doomed to Succeed: The U.S.-Israel Relationship from Truman to Obama*. New York: Farrar, Straus and Giroux, 2015.

Sachar, Abram L. *The Redemption of the Unwanted: From the Liberation of the Death Camps to the Founding of Israel*. New York: St. Martin's, 1983.

Sachar, Howard M. *A History of Israel: From the Rise of Zionism to Our Time*. New York: Knopf, 1976.

Shapira, Anita. *Israel: A History*. Lebanon, NH: Brandeis University Press of New England University Press, 2012.

Shepherd, Naomi. *Ploughing Sand: British Rule in Palestine, 1917–1948*. New Brunswick, NJ: Rutgers University Press, 1999.

Israel-Egypt Peace Treaty (March 26, 1979)

Peace accord between Egypt and the State of Israel signed on March 26, 1979, in Washington, D.C. The Israel-Egypt Peace Treaty was the culmination of an ongoing peace process between the Israelis and Egyptians that dated to November 1977. It was also the result of the Camp David Accords, signed by Egyptian president Anwar Sadat and Israeli prime minister Menachem Begin on September 17, 1978.

The peace treaty stipulated that the two nations would officially recognize the sovereignty of the other and end the state of war that had existed between them since 1948. It also stipulated that Israel would withdraw from the Sinai Peninsula. Finally, it guaranteed Israel the right of passage through the Suez Canal and recognized that both the Strait of Tiran and the Gulf of Aqaba were international waterways subject to international law and maritime guidelines. The Israel-Egypt Peace Treaty was the first such treaty between an Arab state and Israel.

The Camp David Accords of 1978 had emerged from 13 days of intensive negotiations at the U.S. presidential retreat at Camp David. President Jimmy Carter had mediated the talks between Sadat and Begin. But it was Sadat's unprecedented move in November 1977 that had made the historic Israeli-Egyptian peace process possible. On November 19, 1977, Sadat became the first Arab leader in history to visit Israel in an official capacity. He went at the invitation of Begin and addressed the Knesset (Israeli parliament). Sadat's speech offered conciliatory words and a genuine desire to end the conflict between Israel and Egypt and laid out specific steps that might be taken to broker an enduring peace. Specifically, he called for the implementation of United Nations (UN) Resolutions 242 and 338, which among other things called for the withdrawal of Israeli forces from land captured in the 1967 Six-Day War. Sadat's visit stunned many Israelis as well as much of the world.

Most Arab nations, however, were outraged that Sadat would choose to negotiate with the Israelis. Not only did this go against the prevailing Arab philosophy that viewed Israel as a threat and a tool of Western hegemony, but it also meant that Sadat was essentially recognizing the legitimacy of the State of Israel, something that no Arab state had been willing to do. Equally troubling to Arab states was that this peace overture was coming from Egypt, at the time the most powerful Arab state in the region and the birthplace of modern Arab nationalism under Gamal Abdel Nasser.

When the Camp David Accords were signed, there was no clear consensus or binding agreement that a formal, comprehensive peace treaty would be signed. Indeed, between September 1978 and March 1979, both parties to the accords had considerable hesitations about signing a formal treaty. Sadat had come under intense pressure from other Arab leaders not to sign a peace agreement. He also encountered resistance within his own country. For his part, Begin was under enormous pressure not to allow the issue of Palestinian independence to enter into any formal discussions or accords with the Egyptians. Indeed, Begin's refusal to do so nearly torpedoed the peace settlement.

Although Sadat lost the support of most Arab leaders and Egypt was expelled from the Arab League after the treaty was signed, his government did gain the support of the United States, both diplomatically and economically. In fact, the United States gave Egypt and Israel subsidies worth billions of dollars as a result of the rapprochement. These subsidies continue to the present day. From the Israeli perspective, the peace treaty was a coup because Egypt had now been separated from its Arab neighbors. Yet from a geopolitical perspective, the Israeli-Egyptian peace process led to the breakdown of the united Arab front against Israel, creating a power vacuum of sorts once Egypt fell out of that orbit. This allowed nations such as Iran and Iraq to fill in the gap, with disastrous consequences. Only months after the Israel-Egypt Peace Treaty was signed, the Iran-Iraq War (1980–1988) broke out, which demonstrated Iraqi president Saddam Hussein's ambitions to become the undisputed Arab leader of the Middle East.

On the other hand, the Camp David process and the resultant peace treaty demonstrated that fruitful negotiations between Arabs and Israelis are indeed possible. Furthermore, they showed that progress toward peace can come only with meaningful dialogue, mutual cooperation, and strong leadership. Nevertheless, it would take another 15 years for a second Arab-Israeli peace treaty to come about, this time between the Jordanians and Israelis. Currently, only Egypt and Jordan have concluded such agreements.

PAUL G. PIERPAOLI JR.

See also
Aqaba, Gulf of; Arab League; Arab Nationalism; Begin, Menachem; Camp David Accords; Egypt; Israel; Israel-Jordan Peace Treaty; Nasser, Gamal Abdel; Sadat, Anwar; Strait of Tiran Crisis; Suez Crisis

References
Carter, James E. *Keeping Faith: Memoirs of the President.* New York: Bantam, 1982.
Kamel, Mohamed Ibrahim. *The Camp David Accords: A Testimony.* London: Kegan Paul International, 1986.
Lenczowski, George. *The Middle East in World Affairs.* 4th ed. Ithaca, NY: Cornell University Press, 1980.
Quandt, William. *Camp David: Peacemaking and Politics.* Washington, DC: Brookings Institution, 1986.

Israeli Air Strikes Beginning the Six-Day War (June 5, 1967)

The Six-Day War began on the morning of June 5, 1967, and was, for all intents and purposes, over by noon on the first day, the result of the preemptive attack by the Israeli Air Force (IAF). This aerial offensive remains one of the most stunning successes in modern warfare. In a mere three hours, the Israelis achieved air supremacy by destroying much of the Egyptian Air Force on the ground. Attacks against Egypt were followed by sorties against targets in Syria, Jordan, and western Iraq, thus ensuring that Israeli ground operations could go forward unimpeded.

The Israel Defense Forces (IDF) was heavily outnumbered in terms of men and equipment. Figures vary widely, but one estimate is as follows: manpower, mobilized strength of 230,000 for Israel versus 409,000 for Egypt,

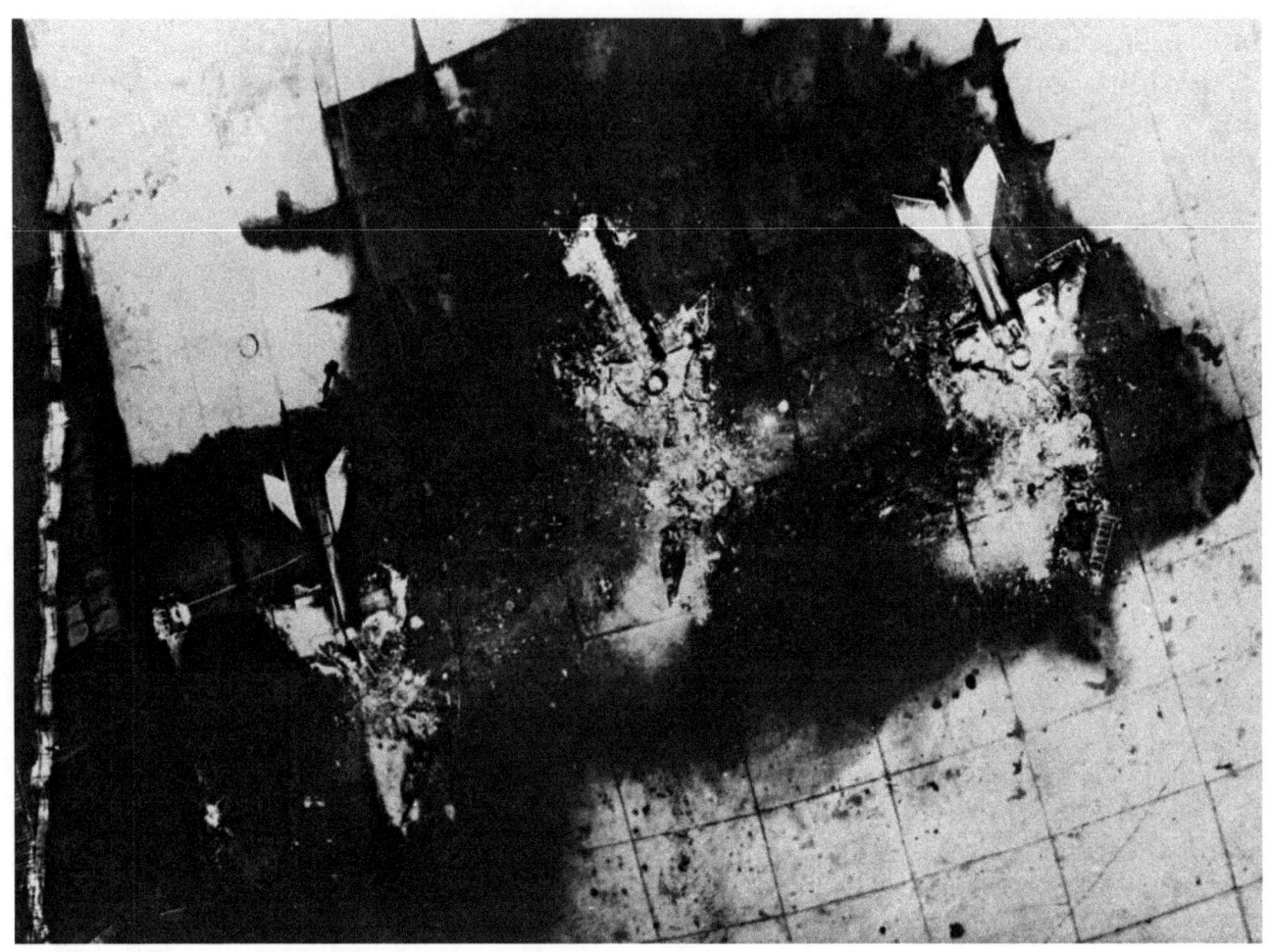

Three Egyptian MiG-21 jet fighter/interceptor aircraft destroyed by the Israeli Air Force during the attacks on Egyptian airfields that began the Six-Day War on June 5, 1967. (Israeli Government Press Office)

Syria, Jordan, and Iraq; tanks, 1,100 versus 2,437; artillery, 260 versus 649; naval vessels, 22 versus 90; and aircraft, all types, 354 versus 969.

Minister of Defense Moshe Dayan, chief of staff of the IDF Lieutenant General Yitzhak Rabin, and Premier Levi Eshkol determined that war was inevitable and decided that Israel should launch a preemptive attack. Defense against an Arab air attack would be difficult because Israel was too small for early warning systems to provide sufficient time for Israeli fighters to scramble. Tel Aviv was 25 minutes' flying time from Cairo but only 4.5 minutes from the nearest Egyptian air base at El Arish. For whatever reason, Egyptian leader Gamal Abdel Nasser did not believe that the Israelis would strike first, despite his own announced eagerness for battle.

The Israeli air attack relied on accurate, timely, and precise intelligence information. The plan called for a first strike against Egypt, the most formidable of Israel's opponents. IDF fighters would take off from airfields all over Israel, fly under radio silence and at low altitude west over the Mediterranean to avoid radar, and then turn south to strike Egyptian airfields as simultaneously as possible. Rather than attacking at dawn, the IAF strikes were timed to coincide with the return of Egyptian pilots to base from their morning patrols, when most Egyptian pilots would be having breakfast.

One of the best-trained air forces in the world, the IAF was well prepared for its mission. Air crews had been thoroughly briefed as to objectives and procedures. Ground crews were also highly trained and able to reduce turnaround time between missions to a minimum. The operation was quite daring in that it would employ almost all Israeli fighter and fighter-bomber aircraft, leaving only a dozen fighters behind to fly combat air patrols in defense of Israel.

The IAF achieved complete tactical surprise. It went into action at 7:45 a.m. (8:45 a.m. Cairo time). One unexpected development was that Field Marshal Abdel Hakim Amer, the United Arab Republic (UAR) commander in chief, and his deputy, General Mahmud Sidqi, were in the air flying from

Cairo to inspect units in the Sinai when the attacks occurred. Unable to land in the Sinai, they returned to Cairo. Thus, for 90 minutes two key UAR commanders were out of touch with their units and unable to give orders.

The first Israeli wave struck 10 Egyptian airfields, hitting all of them within 15 minutes of the scheduled time. On the final approach to the targets, Israeli aircraft climbed to make themselves suddenly visible on radar in order to induce Egyptian pilots to attempt to scramble in the hopes of catching the pilots in their aircraft on the ground. Only 4 Egyptian aircraft, all trainers, were in the air at the time of the first strikes, and all were shot down. Subsequent waves of Israeli attacking aircraft, about 40 per flight, arrived at 10-minute intervals. These met increased Egyptian opposition, mostly antiaircraft fire. Only 8 Egyptian MiGs managed to take off during the strikes, and all were shot down.

In all, the IAF struck 17 major Egyptian airfields with some 500 sorties in just under three hours, destroying half of the Egyptian Air Force's strength. Most of the Egyptian aircraft were destroyed by accurate Israeli cannon fire, but the Israelis also dropped 250-, 500-, and 1,000-pound bombs. Special bombs with 365-pound warheads, developed to crack the concrete runways, were dropped on Egyptian airfields west of the Suez Canal, but none of these were employed against the Sinai airfields, which the Israelis planned for subsequent use by their own aircraft. During the war, Egypt lost a total of 286 aircraft: 30 Tu-16 heavy bombers, 27 Ilyushin medium bombers, 12 Su-7 fighter-bombers, 90 MiG-21 fighters, 20 MiG-19 fighters, 75 MiG-17/15 fighters, and 32 transport planes and helicopters.

Later that same day, June 5, Israeli aircraft struck Syria and Jordan. Israeli leaders urged King Hussein of Jordan to stay out of the war. He desired to do so but was under heavy pressure to act and hoped to satisfy his allies with minimum military action short of all-out war. Jordanian 155mm Long Tom guns went into action against Tel Aviv, and Jordanian aircraft attempted to strafe a small airfield near Kfar Sirkin. The Israeli government then declared war on Jordan. Following an Iraqi air strike on Israel, IAF aircraft also struck Iraqi air units based in the Mosul area. In all during the war, the Arabs lost 390 aircraft of their prewar strength of 969 aircraft of all types (Egypt, 286 of 580; Jordan, 28 of 56; Syria, 54 of 172; Iraq, 21 of 149; and Lebanon, 1 of 12). Israeli losses numbered 32 aircraft shot down of 354 before the war, only 2 of these to aerial combat.

With its opposing air forces largely neutralized, the IAF could turn to close air support and other missions in support of Israeli mechanized ground forces, which had begun operations in the Sinai simultaneous with the initial air attacks.

Spencer C. Tucker

See also
Amer, Abdel Hakim; Dayan, Moshe; Eshkol, Levi; Hussein ibn Talal, King of Jordan; Nasser, Gamal Abdel; Rabin, Yitzhak; Six-Day War

References
Hammel, Eric. *Six Days in June: How Israel Won the 1967 Arab-Israeli War.* New York: Scribner, 1992.
Oren, Michael B. *Six Days of War: June 1967 and the Making of the Modern Middle East.* Novato, CA: Presidio, 2003.
Rubenstein, Murray, and Richard Goldman. *Shield of David: An Illustrated History of the Israeli Air Force.* Englewood Cliffs, NJ: Prentice Hall, 1978.
Van Creveld, Martin. *The Sword and the Olive: A Critical History of the Israeli Defense Force.* New York: PublicAffairs, 2002.
Weizman, Ezer. *On Eagles' Wings: The Personal Story of the Leading Command of the Israeli Air Force.* New York: Macmillan, 1977.

Israeli Air Strike on Presumed Syrian Nuclear Facility (September 6, 2007)

Israeli air attack on September 6, 2007, against an unidentified facility in Syria, believed by Israeli and U.S. intelligence sources to be a partially constructed nuclear reactor. Reportedly the attack was carried out by four Israeli F-16 aircraft dropping six 1,000-pound precision-guided bombs. Apparently the facility was identified by satellite photography as closely resembling the Yongbyon nuclear facility in North Korea used to reprocess nuclear fuel into bomb-grade material. The attack was roundly condemned by both Syria and North Korea, which had been known to be providing assistance to the Syrian ballistic missile program.

Unlike criticism by U.S. president Ronald Reagan's administration of the Israeli strike on Iraq's Osiraq nuclear reactor in 1981, there was no such negative reaction from President George W. Bush's administration, strongly suggesting that Bush administration officials were briefed by the government of Prime Minister Ehud Olmert ahead of time and gave tacit approval to the strike. Unlike the Osiraq facility, which was believed to be close to operational status, the Syrian facility was apparently only in the early stages of development and was presumed to be years away from being able to produce weapons-grade plutonium. Although Syria is a signatory of the Nuclear Non-Proliferation Treaty, this does not bind it to report a nuclear reactor in the early stages of construction as long as its purpose is the generation of electricity. In his only comment on the strike, Syrian president Bashar al-Assad acknowledged only that Israeli aircraft had struck a military building, which was not in use.

Some analysts interpreted the strike as a clear warning by Israel and, for that matter, by the United States to Iran not to proceed with its own nuclear ambitions. Although Israel is itself widely believed to possess a stockpile of nuclear weapons, it has long said that it will not permit hostile powers on its borders to have nuclear weapons or even develop them. Given the small size of Israel, one atomic bomb could for all practical purposes wipe out the Jewish state. Interestingly, no other Arab government apart from Syria criticized the Israeli raid, suggesting that there was general opposition among Middle East governments to a nuclear-armed Syria.

SPENCER C. TUCKER

See also
Assad, Bashar al-; Olmert, Ehud; Osiraq Raid

References
Erlanger, Stephen. "Israel Silent on Reports of Bombing within Syria." *New York Times,* October 15, 2007.
Kessler, Glenn, and Robin Wright. "Israel, US Shared Data on Suspected Nuclear Site." *Washington Post,* September 21, 2007.

Israeli-Hezbollah War

See Lebanon, Israeli Operations against

Israeli-Lebanon War (2006)

See Lebanon-Israeli War

Israeli Security Fence

A combined barrier wall and fortified fence separating Israel from the Palestinian-controlled West Bank. The Security Fence is also the largest infrastructure project in Israeli history. When completed, the barrier (also known as the separation fence or the segregation wall) will be approximately 415 miles in length as it meanders along a rather circuitous route in and around the West Bank. The Israelis insist that the construction of the security fence was an absolute necessity, given the number of terrorist attacks unleashed on Israel by militant Palestinians particularly after the beginning of the Second (al-Aqsa) Intifada, which began in September 2000 and ended in 2005. The barrier is meant to foil would-be car and truck bombers as well as individual suicide bombers.

As early as 1992, Israeli politicians had begun to talk about pursuing a separation policy with the Palestinians: separating Israelis from Palestinians by way of imposing physical barriers between the two populations. Indeed, in 1994 Israeli prime minister Yitzhak Rabin approved the erection of a barrier separating Israel from the Gaza Strip after militants had unleashed a number of violent attacks against Israel from that area.

In 2000 even prior to his failed summit with Palestine Liberation Organization (PLO) chairman Yasser Arafat, Israeli prime minister Ehud Barak spoke of building a more comprehensive barrier between Israelis and Palestinians. Barriers erected along the border between South Korea and North Korea and along parts of India's border with Pakistan have been widely recognized as effective means of preventing unwanted infiltration.

It was not until mid-2001, however, after the start of the Second Intifada and after the bombing of a Tel Aviv discotheque that killed 21 people that the Israeli public began clamoring for the erection of a security fence along the West Bank. In July 2001 the Israeli Defense Cabinet approved the building of the fence. The first phase of the barrier began in late 2002, under the government of Ariel Sharon, and was completed in late July 2003. When the fence is finally completed, the cost of construction alone will have topped $2 billion, and an estimated 400,000 Palestinians could be separated from the remaining Palestinian population on the West Bank.

The security fence along the border of the West Bank is not a wall per se, at least not along much of the route. Some 90 percent of it will be a high-tech fence outfitted with surveillance cameras at regular intervals. For much of its length, a (usually) gravel road will run parallel to the fence for the purposes of patrol, interdiction, and maintenance. In some spots where infiltration has been especially troublesome, the fence will be augmented by trenches and even armored vehicles. Underground sensors, land mines, and unmanned aerial vehicles will also help secure the chain-link–type fence. On average, the barrier is roughly 160 feet wide. The 10 percent nonfence portion of the barrier will consist of concrete walls—some as high as 30 feet—built to enclose areas that have been hotbeds of past terrorist activities.

The initial route proposed for the barrier was projected to be at least three and a half times longer than Israel's internationally recognized border with the West Bank and would annex large areas of Palestinian farmland, scores of Palestinian villages, and sections of several Palestinian urban areas. For example, the wall cuts right through the middle of the Palestinian towns of Abu Dis and al-Izariyyah (Bethany), just east of Jerusalem. This separates thousands of residents from their relatives, jobs, schools, churches, mosques, and health care facilities.

Critics of this strategy raised concerns that depending on the final route chosen for the incomplete sections, the wall would reduce Palestinian areas of the West Bank by as much as one-third. These remaining Palestinian areas would be subdivided into a series of noncontiguous cantons, each of which would be surrounded by the barrier and by land that would be unilaterally annexed by Israel. For example, by 2004 the Palestinian city of Qalqilya was surrounded on all sides by the security fence, making it impossible for anyone to come into or go out of the city without permission from Israeli occupation authorities.

While the Israeli government claims that the security fence is the only reasonable way to protect its citizens from terrorist attacks, others—including some Israelis and most Palestinians, who deplore the fence—argue that there are ulterior motives for the barrier. The wall's detractors claim that Israel is illegally annexing Palestinian territory by gerrymandering the course of the fence. They also claim that Israel is able to force Palestinians to sell their land near the fence in the name of defense and national security. The barrier, of course, also makes it more burdensome for Palestinians to access jobs and resources on the other side of the wall, translating into economic dislocation. And in addition to preventing terrorist attacks, Israeli security personnel can and do use the fence as a way to screen all those who enter Israel from the West Bank. In this way, they can keep out anyone they consider undesirable.

The security wall has created unintended consequences, however. In Jerusalem, for example, Palestinians who had been living beyond where the barrier was erected have been compelled to move back into the city. The result has been serious housing shortages as well as higher rents and real estate values. And recently, Palestinians have begun to move into traditionally Jewish parts of the city to find housing.

For Palestinian subsistence farmers, the security fence has proven to be a heavy burden. Because the barrier's route includes some of the most fertile land in the region, farming there has always been a mainstay. But the presence of the barrier has made it difficult for farmers to reach their fields and bring their produce to market. The results of this have been devastating to a group that was already economically disadvantaged.

Not surprisingly, the Israeli decision to build this mammoth barrier—many times longer than the infamous Berlin Wall of the Cold War—has been highly controversial. The Palestinians, who refer to the barrier as the "racist segregation law," argue that Israel is doing nothing more than creating an apartheid-like system in Palestine that separates people based on ethnicity and religion. Palestinians have repeatedly challenged the construction of the wall and its proposed path, and on two separate occasions the Israeli Supreme Court has forced the government to change the path of the project to better protect Palestinian rights.

Both the United Nations (UN) and the International Court of Justice (ICJ) have issued nonbinding resolutions calling for the dismantlement of the barrier wall. The ICJ has deemed the wall to be a violation of international law, while the UN General Assembly adopted a resolution that condemned the barrier by a vote of 150 to 6, with 10 abstentions. The George W. Bush administration waffled on the building of the wall, but all in all Israel has enjoyed U.S. government approval. Indeed, Israel publicly rejected the ICJ's judgment on the wall's construction. In 2004 the International Committee of the Red Cross claimed that the security fence posed "serious humanitarian and legal problems." The World Council of Churches meanwhile deemed the barrier a violation of basic human rights.

Despite the difficulties, border disputes, and negative international reaction that the security fence has engendered, many Israelis insist that the barrier is the only way to prevent attacks on Israeli civilians without resorting to a permanent wartime situation in which both Israeli and Palestinian civilians would be targeted. The Israelis continue to cite impressive statistics showing that the security fence has had the desired effect. Indeed, since construction commenced, the number of terrorist attacks on Israeli citizens is down by more than 90 percent. The number of Israelis killed in such attacks has declined by better than 70 percent, while the number of those wounded has dropped by more than 85 percent.

Not all Israelis agree with the decision to erect the fence, however. Some have argued that constructing the barrier inside occupied territory actually increases the risks to Israeli security. Such critics include a number of prominent military and security officers who formed groups such as the Council for Peace and Security, which challenged the barrier's route. Avraham Shalom, former head of Israel's security service Shin Bet, has said that the wall "creates hatred, . . .

expropriates land, and annexes hundreds of thousands of Palestinians to the state of Israel. The result is that the fence achieves the exact opposite of what was intended."

Projected to run some 440 miles, the security fence was not yet complete, with some 125 miles left undone. Numerous international organizations continue to voice their opposition, and the Palestinians have mounted numerous legal challenges to the fence. In February 2016, Israeli prime minister Benjamin Netanyahu announced a plan to erect a security fence around all of Israel in a bid to secure the country from terror attacks. The proposal was met with much derision, particularly because Netanyahu referred to Palestinians and people from other neighboring countries as "wild beasts." At the same time, an uptick in attacks by militant Palestinians against Israelis prompted the Israeli government to close remaining gaps in the existing fence, especially in Jerusalem.

PAUL G. PIERPAOLI JR. AND STEPHEN ZUNES

See also
Arab Economic Boycott of Israel; Barak, Ehud; Gaza Strip; Intifada, Second; Israel; Palestinian National Authority; Settlements, Israeli; Sharon, Ariel; Suicide Bombings; West Bank

References
Ahronheim, Anna. "Israel Completes 10km Stretch of West Bank Security Barrier near Hebron." *Jerusalem Post*, February 5, 2017.
Bickerton, Ian J., and Carla L. Klausner. *A Concise History of the Arab-Israeli Conflict*. 4th ed. Upper Saddle River, NJ: Prentice Hall, 2004.
Dowty, Alan. *Israel/Palestine*. Malden, MA: Polity, 2005.
Hall, John G. *Palestinian Authority: Creation of the Modern Middle East*. Langhorne, PA: Chelsea House, 2002.
Lagerquist, Peter. "Fencing the Last Sky: Excavating Palestine after Israel's 'Separation Wall.'" *Journal of Palestine Studies* 33, no. 2 (Winter 2004): 5–15.
Zunes, Stephen. "Implications of the U.S. Reaction to the World Court Ruling against Israel's 'Separation Barrier.'" *Middle East Policy* 11, no. 4 (Winter 2004): 72–85.

Israeli Settlements
See Settlements, Israeli

Israeli War of Independence (1948–1949)

The causes of the Israeli War of Independence, also known as the First Arab-Israeli War, are deep-rooted. Nineteenth-century nationalism in Europe also impacted Jews. Persecutions of Jewish populations in Europe late in that century, especially in Russia and Poland but also to a lesser extent in Central and Western Europe (e.g., the Dreyfus Affair in France), led to the establishment of the Zionist movement, or desire among many Jews for a national state. Palestine, the historic homeland of the Jews before the diaspora, was the favored and most likely location for such a state, and Jews throughout Europe contributed to the purchase of land there. Mostly East European Jews emigrated and settled in Palestine.

In order to secure the support of world Jewry for the Allied cause in World War I, in 1917 the British government issued the Balfour Declaration, which expressed support for the formation of a Jewish national homeland in Palestine. Increased Jewish immigration and continued loss of Arab lands through purchase by Jews, however, inflamed the Arab population of Palestine, which as a consequence of World War I became a British mandate. Violence flared in Palestine in what became a triangular struggle among the British authorities, the Arabs, and the Jews.

There was thus already considerable violence in Palestine by the time of World War II, when the Holocaust, the Nazi effort to eradicate the Jewish people, which resulted in the deaths of about 6 million Jews, heightened sympathy worldwide for the survivors. The Holocaust also greatly increased the determination of Jews to establish a nation-state as the only effective means to guarantee their future security. Sympathy for this was especially strong in the United States, which had the largest population of Jews in the world and where Jews were an important political pressure group.

After World War II and with Britain determined to quit an increasingly divided and violent Palestine, efforts were made to partition Palestine into Jewish and Arab states. These plans failed—largely on Arab intransigence—and the neighboring Arab states mobilized their forces for the anticipated military showdown and, in their minds, victory over the Jews.

Violence between Arabs and Jews was already under way when, with the expiration of the British mandate on May 14, 1948, Jewish Palestinian leader David Ben-Gurion announced the independence of the State of Israel. The United States, closely followed by the Soviet Union, recognized the new Jewish state. The Jewish declaration, however, touched off the Israeli War of Independence (May 14, 1948–January 7, 1949).

Arab forces ranged against Israel included regulars from Egypt, Iraq, Lebanon, Syria, and Transjordan, supplemented by volunteers from Libya, Saudi Arabia, and Yemen.

Israeli War of Independence, 1948–1949

Officially, the Arab forces operated under the auspices of the Arab League, formed in 1945. King Abdullah of Transjordan was named commander in chief of the Arab armies, although cooperation among the Arab forces was almost nonexistent and a chief cause of their military failure throughout the course of the war.

The Arab states anticipated an easy military victory, and on paper the odds certainly favored them. The Arab armies not only heavily outnumbered Jewish forces but also retained a wide edge in heavy weaponry.

On May 15, the Arab League announced its intention to create a unified Palestinian state to include the Jewish and Arab regions of the United Nations (UN) partition plan. On May 26 the Israeli government created the Israel Defense Forces (IDF), incorporating the irregular Jewish militias that had existed under the British mandate, to include Haganah, led by Israel Galili, and the Palmach, commanded by Yigal Allon. The IDF initially numbered fewer than 30,000 troops but by mid-July had more than doubled in size. The IDF continued to grow exponentially, and by the end of 1948 it numbered more than 100,000 troops. At least initially, these forces had virtually no heavy weapons in the form of artillery, armored vehicles, or aircraft.

The combined Arab armies, which began the conflict with some 30,000 troops, increased in size to only 40,000 men in July 1948 and 55,000 by October. Most independent observers expected the Arabs to score a quick military victory largely because they enjoyed a crushing superiority in heavy weapons at the beginning of the conflict.

As the fighting continued, the Israeli government was able to secure some arms from abroad, beginning with a shipment of 25 aircraft from Czechoslovakia in late May. That nation continued to provide weapons to the IDF for the remainder of the war, even during UN-mandated cease-fires that prohibited arms sales to any belligerent.

During the first phase of the war, May 14–June 1, in the central part of the front, Arab armies from Transjordan and Iraq advanced on Jerusalem with the aim of driving all Jews from the city. The best Arab fighting force in the war, the Transjordan Arab Legion, secured the eastern and southern portions of the new part of the city. The legion also occupied most of Old Jerusalem and laid siege to the remainder. Although Jewish forces, ably led by American volunteer Colonel David Marcus, failed to break through the Arab roadblock on the Tel Aviv–Jerusalem road, they managed to construct a new access road to Jerusalem through the mountains just before a UN-sponsored truce went into effect on June 11.

Meanwhile, Lebanese and Syrian forces invaded Palestine from the north. The Lebanese were stopped at Malkya. The Syrian invasion, which was both larger and supported by tanks and artillery, was defeated by Jewish settlers at Degania, the oldest kibbutz in Palestine, although they possessed only light weapons. The Israelis also blunted an ineffective Iraqi invasion that crossed the Jordan River south of the Sea of Galilee. Soon the Iraqi Army shifted to a defensive posture in the regions of Jenin and Nablus.

Only in the south did Arab forces register significant territorial gains. Here two Egyptian brigades commanded by Major General Ahmed Ali el-Mawawi advanced into Palestine. The principal Egyptian force moved up the coastal road to take Gaza and threaten Tel Aviv. A smaller force moved inland from Abu Ageila by way of Beersheba toward Jerusalem. Although the Egyptian coastal force secured Ashdod, only 25 miles from Tel Aviv, it bogged down shortly thereafter. The inland column succeeded in making contact with the Arab Legion at Bethlehem on May 22.

The first phase of the war ended with a UN-declared truce that went into effect on June 11. Although the truce included an arms embargo for all belligerents, both sides in the war saw this as an opportunity to rest, resupply, and reequip their forces, and the Israelis were able to smuggle in arms and ammunition from Czechoslovakia during the monthlong truce.

During the cease-fire, UN mediator Folke Bernadotte advanced a new partition plan, but both sides immediately rejected it. On July 9 the cease-fire collapsed, and the IDF assumed the offensive. The second phase of the war occurred during July 9–18.

In the renewed fighting, the primary IDF objective was to regain control of the vital Tel Aviv–Jerusalem corridor in the central sector. In heavy fighting, the IDF secured the corridor after a massive assault on Lod (Lydda) that included the first Israeli use of bomber aircraft. Defended by Transjordian troops and supplemented by Palestinian irregulars and units of the Arab Liberation Army, Lod surrendered on July 11. The next day the IDF captured Ramle, another key location in the vital corridor.

In the north the IDF launched Operation DEKEL, a major push against Syrian and Lebanese troops in the lower Galilee region. The IDF captured Nazareth on July 16. Only against Egyptian forces in the southern sector did the IDF fail to make any significant progress in the July fighting. Here the IDF goals were to sever Egyptian supply lines and reopen communications with the Negev. The second phase of the

Israeli soldiers employing a captured Egyptian antitank gun at Abu Agela during Operation HOREV, December 15, 1948. (Israeli Government Press Office)

war (July 9–18) ended with another UN-brokered truce, which went into effect on July 18.

Bernadotte presented yet another partition plan, this time calling for Transjordan to annex the Arab regions. The plan also called for the creation of an independent Jewish state and the establishment of Jerusalem as an international city. All belligerents again rejected the plan, and on September 17, the day after Bernadotte had presented his latest solution to the conflict, he was assassinated by Israeli members of Lehi, a Zionist militia.

The truce remained in effect until October 15, when the third phase of the war (October 15–November 5, 1948) began. The IDF ended the cease-fire with a series of offensives designed to drive Arab armies completely from Israeli territory. The first strike was against Egyptian Army troops in the Negev. Operation YOAV, commanded by Yigal Allon, sought to cut off the Egyptian troops along the coast from those to the interior in the Negev. The success of this operation forced the Egyptian Army to abandon the northern Negev.

The IDF also enjoyed success in the northern sector. On October 24 Operation HIRAM commenced in the upper Galilee region, with the IDF destroying remnants of the Arab Liberation Army, driving Lebanese forces completely out of Palestine, and pushing several miles into Lebanon. Shaky cease-fires were arranged in the north between Israeli forces and Syrian and Lebanese forces on November 30.

The fourth and final phase of the war occurred between November 19, 1948, and January 7, 1949, beginning with an Egyptian Army offensive on November 19. Although they failed in their design of relieving the Fallujah pocket, the Egyptians were able to expand their coastal holdings around Gaza.

With cease-fires holding elsewhere, beginning on December 20, 1948, the IDF launched a major offensive designed to drive Egypt from the war. The IDF isolated Rafah on December 22 and secured both Asluj and Auja on December 27. Halted by Egyptian forces in their effort to take El Arish, the Israelis turned to the northeast. With the IDF about to launch a major attack on Rafah, Egypt requested an immediate armistice, which the UN Security Council granted. The cease-fire went into effect on January 7, 1949.

With the cease-fire, UN mediator Dr. Ralph Bunche began armistice discussions between Israel and the Arab belligerent states. Armistice agreements, but no peace treaties, were ultimately concluded between Israel and all the Arab belligerents except Iraq. The arrangement with Egypt, which went into effect on February 24, left Egyptian troops in occupation of the Gaza Strip. In the March 23 agreement with Lebanon, Israel agreed to withdraw from territory it had captured in southern Lebanon. The Israeli-Transjordanian armistice of April 3 allowed Transjordanian troops to remain in control of the West Bank and East Jerusalem. The Israeli-Syrian armistice of July 20 resulted in the creation of a demilitarized zone along the Israeli-Syrian border.

The war ended with the new Jewish state occupying about three-fourths of the former British Mandate for Palestine, or about 50 percent more land than offered in Bernadotte's original partition proposal. The war claimed about 6,000 Israeli lives, one-third of them civilians. Arab losses were much higher, about 10,000 killed.

Although the figure is in dispute, as many as 1 million Arab Palestinians may have either voluntarily left or were driven from their homes and lands, forced to live in makeshift refugee camps in the adjacent Arab states, which insisted on keeping them in refugee camps until they were allowed to return. Refugee status has been passed on to their descendants, who have also denied citizenship in their host countries on the insistence of the Arab League in order to preserve their Palestinian identity "and protect their right of return to their homeland." More than 1.5 million Palestinians still live in 58 recognized refugee camps, while more than 5 million Palestinians live outside Israel and the Palestinian Territories.

Some 10,000 Jews were displaced by the war. After the war, many Jews either voluntarily left or were expelled by the Arab states, and a number of them and other Jews living elsewhere in the world moved to Israel to help build the new Jewish state. From May 1948 to the end of 1951 some 700,000 Jews settled in Israel, in effect doubling its Jewish population.

This relative small and short war had immense consequences. The surprising Israeli victory humiliated the Arab states and fueled demand for revenge, which continues in some quarters today. Indeed, this dynamic resulted in two major wars—the 1967 Six-Day War and the 1973 Yom Kippur War (Ramadan War)—as well as many smaller conflicts, incursions, and terror attacks. Failure to reach a comprehensive peace settlement would see vast sums spent on armaments (in both Israel and the Arab states) rather than on infrastructure and social programs. The lack of a peace settlement also embroiled the major world powers in a series of crises, many of which revolved around securing the area's vast oil supplies, and would become a constant source of unrest in the Middle East. In the early 21st century, this perennially unstable environment has produced a major war in Iraq and significant rebellions in Yemen, Egypt, Libya, and Syria. It has also led to the rise of extremist, fundamentalist Islamic groups such as the Islamic State of Iraq and Syria (ISIS), which now imperils Iraq as well as Syria.

Spencer C. Tucker

See also
Abdullah I; Allon, Yigal; Balfour Declaration; Ben-Gurion, David; Haganah; Holocaust; Marcus, David; Palestine, British Mandate for; Palmach; Zionism

References
Bowyer Bell, John. *Terror Out of Zion: The Fight for Israeli Independence.* New Brunswick, NJ: Transaction Publishers, 1996.
Bregman, Ahron. *Israel's Wars: A History since 1947.* London: Routledge, 2002.
Heller, Joseph. *The Birth of Israel, 1945–1949: Ben-Gurion and His Critics.* Gainesville: University Press of Florida, 2001.
Herzog, Chaim. *The Arab-Israeli Wars: War and Peace in the Middle East.* New York: Random House, 1982.
Joseph, Dov. *The Faithful City: The Siege of Jerusalem, 1948.* New York: Simon and Schuster, 1960.
Karsh, Efraim. *The Arab-Israeli Conflict: The Palestine War, 1948.* New York: Osprey, 2002.
Kurzman, Dan. *Genesis 1948: The First Arab-Israeli War.* New York: World Publishing, 1970.
Morris, Benny. *1948: The First Arab-Israeli War.* New Haven, CT: Yale University Press, 2008.
Pollack, Kenneth M. *Arabs at War: Military Effectiveness, 1948–1991.* Lincoln: University of Nebraska Press, 2002.
Rogan, Eugene L., and Avi Shlaim, eds. *The War for Palestine: Rewriting the History of 1948.* 2nd ed. Cambridge: Cambridge University Press, 2007.
Sachar, Howard M. *A History of Israel.* New York: Knopf, 1979.

Israeli War of Independence, Truce Agreements (February 24, 1949–July 20, 1949)

The truce agreements, or General Armistice Agreements, ended the Israeli War of Independence (1948–1949) and secured Israel's independence. Israel signed four separate pacts, with Egypt (February 24, 1949, at Rhodes), Lebanon (March 23, 1949, at Ras en Naquora), Jordan (April 3, 1949, at Rhodes), and Syria (July 20, 1949, at Hill 232 near Mahanayim). The other major Arab participant in the conflict, Iraq, and those states that provided token help, Saudi Arabia and Yemen, refused to meet with the Israeli officials and did not sign truce agreements. The American diplomat Ralph Bunche, as a representative of the United Nations (UN), mediated the agreements.

The UN played a central role in bringing the parties together, particularly after the September 17, 1948, assassination of the original mediator, Count Folke Bernadotte. The November 16, 1948, UN Security Council Resolution S-1080 even threatened military intervention to encourage an armistice.

All of these agreements created armistice demarcation lines. The lines set provisional boundaries that military forces and civilians were forbidden to cross. They also ensured the exchange of prisoners of war and made a preexisting unarmed observer peacekeeping mission, the UN Truce Supervision Organization (UNTSO), overseer of the armistices. Each agreement established Mixed Armistice Commissions, and UNTSO reported armistice violations directly to the Security Council.

The first armistice negotiations began on January 12, 1949, when Egyptian and Israeli representatives met under UN auspices on the Greek island of Rhodes. Throughout the talks, Egyptian forces remained besieged around Fallujah in the Negev Desert. While negotiations were carried out on the basis of equality and none of the Arab states had been decisively defeated, they all undertook armistice negotiations because of Israel's military success. The Israelis withdrew from land they captured in the Sinai Peninsula, but Egypt retained control of a thin coastal area of Palestine, which became known as the Gaza Strip.

Of the agreements, that between Israel and Lebanon functioned most smoothly, becoming the model for the Jordan and Syria agreements. Under this arrangement, Israel withdrew from villages it occupied near the Litani River, and the demarcation line conformed to the prewar international frontier.

The Israeli and Jordanian agreement encompassed the most change. Jordan's British-commanded Arab Legion occupied the West Bank, including East Jerusalem and the Old City. The Jordanians withdrew some of their forces in the Sharon Plain area, and the final agreement respected all earlier Jerusalem accords between the two sides.

Syria, the state most reluctant to meet with Israeli representatives, signed its agreement under Western pressure during the brief rule of Husni al-Zaim. To better correspond with the prewar international frontier, the Syrians withdrew from territory they occupied, creating three contentious demilitarized zones.

As a result of its military gains, largely enshrined in these accords, Israel controlled nearly 75 percent of mandatory Palestine, a much larger area than the Arab-rejected 1947 UN partition plan had granted the Jewish state. This territory denotes what is often referred to as Israel's pre-1967 borders.

The Arab states considered all of the truce talks to be purely military discussions, while the Israelis sought to establish more far-reaching political settlements. The Arab signatories were all military officers, while the Israelis included both soldiers and civilians among their representatives. During the negotiations, much to the frustration of the Israelis, the sides did not always meet face to face, often transmitting statements through UN officials. Most importantly, the Arab governments did not consider the agreements to have granted official recognition to Israel. Indeed, the Arab states deemed the truce agreements as temporary cessations of hostilities and continued to carry out belligerent acts against Israel, including economic boycotts. They also pledged to present a common front against Israel, believing that their opponent had benefited from negotiating with each country individually.

Significantly, until the 1970s Arab peace offers were based on the UN partition plan or the 1948 Bernadotte proposals, not the 1949 truce agreements. In contrast, Israeli peace offers usually took the armistice agreements as their starting point. Deliberately vague in order to foster compromise and because both the UN and Israel considered them a first step toward peace, the 1949 truce agreements survived longer than anyone expected. Indeed, they still officially govern Syria's relations with Israel. All parties regularly violated the agreements throughout the 1950s and beyond, however, and the initial transition from armistice to peace came only after three additional wars and the signing of the 1979 Israel-Egypt Peace Treaty.

ANDREW THEOBALD

See also
Bernadotte, Folke; Israeli War of Independence

References
Bailey, Sydney D. *How Wars End,* Vol. 2, *The United Nations and the Termination of Armed Conflict, 1946–1964.* Oxford, UK: Clarendon, 1982.

Caplan, Neil. *Futile Diplomacy,* Vol. 3, *The United Nations, the Great Powers, and Middle East Peacemaking, 1948–1954.* London: Frank Cass, 1997.

Herzog, Chaim. *The Arab-Israeli Wars: War and Peace in the Middle East from the War of Independence to Lebanon.* Westminster, MD: Random House, 1984.

Institute for Palestinian Studies. *Arab-Israeli Armistice Agreements, February–July 1949: U.N. Texts.* Beirut: Institute for Palestinian Studies, 1967.

Rosenne, Shabtai. *Israel's Armistice Agreements with the Arab States: A Juridical Interpretation.* Tel Aviv: International Law Association, Israel Branch, 1951.

Israel-Jordan Peace Treaty (October 26, 1994)

Comprehensive peace accord between Israel and Jordan signed on October 26, 1994, at the border settlement of Wadi Arabah. Officially titled the Treaty of Peace between the State of Israel and the Hashemite Kingdom of Jordan, the agreement settled long-standing territorial conflicts and fully normalized diplomatic and economic relations between the two states. It was intended as part of the larger Arab-Israeli peace process that had begun in 1991 at the Madrid Conference and had continued in the Oslo Accords, agreed to and signed by the Israelis and Palestinians the previous summer. The treaty was only the second one of its kind signed between the Israelis and an Arab nation, the first one having been that negotiated with Egypt in 1979.

Relations between Jordan and Israel had been complex and sometimes hostile. Be that as it may, Israel's relations with Jordan were generally not as difficult as those with the other Arab states. Jordan's King Hussein, while cleaving to anti-Israeli stances alongside his Arab neighbors because a large proportion of Jordan's population was Palestinian, was also a pragmatist. Thus, his actions did not always match his anti-Zionist rhetoric. He was also reliably pro-Western in orientation, which surely tempered his anti-Israeli policies. Also, his relatively modest territorial demands and Jordan's proximity to Israel worked as a moderating force in the Israeli-Jordanian relationship.

This does not mean, however, that Jordanian-Israeli relations were not without serious tensions. Indeed, in the run-up to the 1967 Six-Day War, Israeli leaders implored King Hussein not to join the Egyptian-led coalition arrayed against Israel. King Hussein ignored the forewarning, and Jordan suffered the consequences. By war's end, the Israelis had seized control of East Jerusalem and the strategically and economically crucial West Bank, which had been an economic lifeline to the Kingdom of Jordan. The Israeli occupation of the West Bank would also significantly complicate future peace negotiations with the Palestinians, who believe that the West Bank must be at the heart of any future Palestinian state. Indeed, the Jordanians conferred their claim to the West Bank to the Palestine Liberation Organization (PLO) in 1988.

In 1970 as the Jordanians prepared to expel the PLO from their country in what came to be called Black September, Israel tacitly aided them in the struggle by dispatching fighter jets to menace Syrian forces that had begun to intervene in Jordan on the side of the PLO.

In 1973 although caught off guard by the Egyptian and Syrian attack on Israel in the Yom Kippur War (Ramadan War), King Hussein was soon under pressure from these two Arab states to join the conflict. Although he tried to keep out of it, nonetheless he was drawn in, ironically to stave off a crushing Syrian defeat. He did not commit his air force, realizing that this would bring a crushing Israeli retaliation as in 1967, but did send an armored brigade into Syria, ironically to save the Syrians from the threat posed by the Israeli counteroffensive that threatened to carry to Damascus.

In 1987 Israeli foreign minister Shimon Peres undertook a tentative attempt to arrive at a Jordanian-Israeli peace settlement. In secret deliberations, he and King Hussein agreed that the West Bank would be ceded back to Jordan in exchange for mutual peace and security guarantees. The deal was never consummated because internal Israeli politics prevented such a sweeping move. Be that as it may, the peace attempt did strengthen relations between the two nations, and a year later Jordan abandoned its claim to the West Bank and agreed to help settle the Palestinian-Israeli impasse without violence.

It was really the 1993 Oslo Accords that set the stage for the Israel-Jordan Peace Treaty. In light of what appeared at the time to be a historic period in Arab-Israeli peacemaking, King Hussein was more receptive to a peace deal with Israel. U.S. president Bill Clinton and Secretary of State Warren Christopher had also begun to nudge King Hussein toward a peace agreement, even promising to reduce or eliminate Jordan's foreign aid debts to the United States. Perhaps what clinched the deal for the king was Egyptian president Hosni Mubarak's support of an Israeli-Jordanian peace accord, although Syrian president Hafez al-Assad opposed the agreement. The diplomacy worked, and King Hussein, ever the pragmatist, agreed to a nonbelligerency treaty with the Israelis. The Washington Declaration, signed in Washington, D.C., on July 25, 1994, ultimately led to the signing of the formal peace treaty on October 26, 1994.

The provisions of the treaty included the establishment of the Jordan River as the boundary between the two nations, the full normalization of diplomatic and economic relations, cooperation in antiterrorism, respect for each other's territory, a more equitable distribution of Jordan River water and other joint water supplies, and a joint effort at alleviating the

Palestinian refugee problem. Soon thereafter the Israeli-Jordanian border became an open one, and Israelis and Jordanians embarked on tourist and business excursions in each other's countries. Unfortunately, the Israeli-Jordanian peace settlement did not lead to a wider peace in the region.

PAUL G. PIERPAOLI JR.

See also
Assad, Hafez al-; Black September; Hussein ibn Talal, King of Jordan; Israel; Israel-Egypt Peace Treaty; Jordan; Jordan River; Mubarak, Hosni; Oslo Accords; Palestine Liberation Organization; Six-Day War; West Bank; Yom Kippur War

References
Freedman, Robert Owen, ed. *The Middle East and the Peace Process: The Impact of the Oslo Accords.* Gainesville: University Press of Florida, 1998.
Majali, Abdul Salam, et al. *Peacemaking: An Inside Story of the 1994 Jordanian-Israeli Treaty.* Norman: University of Oklahoma Press, 2006.
Peres, Shimon. *The New Middle East.* New York: Henry Holt, 1993.
Weinberger, Peter. *Co-opting the PLO: A Critical Reconstruction of the Oslo Accords, 1993–1995.* New York: Rowman and Littlefield, 2006.

Issus, Battle of (November 333 BCE)

Following his victory in the May 334 Battle of the Granicus River, Macedonian king Alexander III (the Great) marched south, continuing the liberation of the Greek coastal cities of Asia Minor. He met real opposition only at Miletus, which he captured following a brief siege.

Alexander then took the momentous decision of disbanding his fleet of some 160 triremes. He kept only the Athenian detachment, to serve as transports and provide hostages, and a squadron in the Hellespont (Dardanelles). With the Persian fleet of more than 400 triremes dominating the eastern Mediterranean, Alexander could not hope to win a sea battle, and maintaining the fleet was expensive. His commanders opposed this decision, as the Persians might now easily cut off the army in Asia Minor and prevent both its resupply and its return to Macedonia and Greece. They could also raid Greece and stir up revolts against Alexander there. Alexander, however, believed that his men would fight harder knowing that retreat was not possible. He also seems to have profoundly distrusted his Greek allies, so much so that he was prepared to risk his entire campaign rather than entrust its safety to a Greek fleet.

Alexander told his generals that he intended to move against the Persian fleet from the land instead, taking the Persian and Phoenician naval bases along the eastern Mediterranean coast. During 334–333 he conquered much of the coast of Asia Minor. Alexander's early military successes owed much to his reputation for mercy, justice, and toleration. It certainly helped his cause that his rule brought improved administration, lower taxes, and public works projects. The only difficult operation occurred at Halicarnassus, where the defenders were led by the Greek mercenary Memnon. Alexander took the city after a siege.

While Alexander secured the remaining coastal cities, Persian king Darius III now loosed Memnon, his only first-class general, against Alexander's lines of communication. Memnon soon took sick and died, however.

Darius was gathering yet another army for another military test with the invader when he learned that Alexander had moved south into Syria. Darius therefore moved before he was fully ready. Crossing the Amarnus Mountains, he positioned his forces behind Alexander, cutting off his line of communications. With the potentially hostile cities of Phoenicia to the south, Alexander had no choice but to turn and fight.

The two armies came together at Issus in early November 333 (possibly November 5). The numbers are in dispute. Darius probably had more men—perhaps as many as 100,000 (Macedonian reports of 600,000 are complete propaganda). Alexander had only 30,000. Darius positioned his army on the narrow coastal plain on the north side of the steep-banked Pinarus River, a front of about three miles. This meant that only part of his force could engage at any one time. Largely untrained troops held the Persian left and right; Darius placed archers to their fronts to buttress them. In the center of the Persian line were the 2,000 Royal Bodyguards, the elite force in the army. Darius was with them in a great ornamental chariot. As many as 30,000 Greek mercenaries were on either side of the bodyguards, while Persian cavalry anchored the far right flank on the Gulf of Issus. If the Persians could but hold, Alexander's days would be numbered.

Alexander arrived before the Persian line in late afternoon. The Persian cavalry screen that had been south of the Pinarus masking Darius's dispositions and intent now withdrew across the river. Alexander halted to reorganize his line. Seeing Darius massing his cavalry on his right flank near the seashore against the Macedonian left wing under Parmenio, Alexander shifted his Thessalonian cavalry there behind the phalanx so as to conceal their movement. He also dispatched a mixed force of light-armed troops to deal with a Persian detachment in the hills that had worked its way behind his right wing. He also detached cavalry from the center to strengthen his right wing, but the Persians on his far right made no attempt to attack and were soon routed. Alexander then recalled most of his troops sent against them, leaving only 300 cavalry to protect his far right flank.

Having completed his dispositions, Alexander resumed the advance. His forces were also on a three-mile front. He halted just out of bowshot, hoping that the Persians would attack. As he occupied a strong, prepared defensive position, Darius understandably refused. Alexander then ordered his own men forward. Determining that the infantry on the Persian left was the weak part of the enemy line, Alexander had his Macedonian heavy cavalry (the Companions) on the right of his line.

Battle was joined when the Persian archers let loose a volley of arrows said to be so thick that they collided with one another in air. The archers then withdrew back into the mass of infantry, as Alexander led the Companions in an assault against the light infantry on the Persian left, which almost immediately broke.

The Macedonian attack in the center did not go as well. The men had difficulty getting across the river and then encountered a steep bank and stake-palisades placed by the Persians. Desperate hand-to-hand fighting ensued, pitting the Macedonian infantrymen against equally tough Greek mercenaries. Alexander meanwhile rolled up the Persian left.

Alexander then shifted his cavalry to strike the rear of the Greek mercenaries and the Royal Bodyguard in an effort to kill or capture Darius. Alexander was wounded in the thigh during the fighting, some reports say by Darius himself. The horses pulling Darius's chariot were wounded and suddenly reared and bolted. Darius managed to control them but, in danger of capture, shifted to a smaller chariot and fled the field.

Things were not going well for Alexander elsewhere, however. The Macedonian center was hard-pressed, as were the Thessalonians on the left, by the Persian heavy casualty. Alexander therefore had to break off his pursuit of the Great King. He swung his right wing into the Persian army's Greek mercenaries from the flank, rolling them up. When the men of the Persian heavy cavalry saw this and learned of the flight of Darius, they too decamped. Retreat became rout. Alexander pursued but was forced to break this off with the arrival of darkness.

Persian losses may have been as high as half of the force, or 50,000 men, while Alexander reported some 450 dead. Among the captives were Darius's wife, mother, and two daughters. The loot included some 3,000 talents in gold. Alexander also recovered Darius's royal mantle and insignia, which he had stripped off in flight.

Issus was a glorious victory, but it was not decisive. More than 10,000 Greek mercenaries escaped and would form the nucleus of yet another Persian army. Darius still lived, and as long as this was the case, the fight would continue.

Spencer C. Tucker

See also

Alexander III the Great; Alexander III's Invasion of the Persian Empire; Darius III; Granicus, Battle of the

References

Green, Peter. *Alexander of Macedon, 356–323 B.C.: A Historical Biography.* Berkeley: University of California Press, 1991.

Hammond, N. G. L. *Alexander the Great: King, Commander, and Statesman.* 3rd ed. London: Bristol Classical, 1996.

Sekunda, Nick, and John Warry. *Alexander the Great: His Armies and Campaigns, 332–323 B.C.* London: Osprey, 1988.

Italo-Ottoman War (1911–1912)

The Italian conquest of the Ottoman Empire's Libyan provinces in 1911–1912 helped set the stage for the outbreak of World War I in 1914. Italy's victory in Libya, aided by its occupation of the Dodecanese Islands in the southern Aegean Sea, convinced the Balkan League (Bulgaria, Greece, Montenegro, and Serbia) that the Ottoman Empire was too weak to stop them from liberating the rest of Southeastern Europe from Ottoman rule. The ensuing First and Second Balkan Wars, which saw the Ottomans evicted from most of the Balkan peninsula largely to the benefit of Serbia, rang alarm bells in Vienna and set in motion the events that would lead to the July Crisis of 1914 and the descent into a general European war a month later.

Italian designs on Libya hark back to the early 1800s, although serious planning for conquest of the region dates from November 1884, when Italian government leaders concluded that the French, who had just acquired a protectorate over Tunisia, were about to seize Morocco as well. This would have brought all of North Africa under French control except for Egypt and Libya. Italian leaders saw this as a threat to their country's maritime security and to its future as an imperial power, a future already put in jeopardy by France's takeover of Tunisia, the economy of which Italy had dominated for decades. Some Italians also coveted what they believed, quite mistakenly as it turned out, was a lucrative caravan trade across the desert from sub-Saharan Africa to the Libyan port of Tripoli.

Italians chose to portray their attempt to seize Libya as the reconquest of a lost colony, for the region had been part of the Roman Empire in ancient times. Also, the Italian government saw Libya—as well as Eritrea and Ethiopia—as places in which to settle the country's surplus population. The loss of so many of its citizens to the New World was a sensitive issue in Italian politics in the early 20th century. This led some Italian politicians and journalists to make exaggerated claims about the agricultural and commercial potential of Libya. Other Italian politicians and statesmen coveted Libya for strategic reasons, to secure needed ports and naval bases in North Africa in order to maintain control over the central Mediterranean.

A successful diplomatic campaign secured approval of the venture from the major European powers. France, the only power that might have opposed the Italian scheme, was won over by Italian support for its position in the Moroccan Crises of 1905–1906 and 1911. The pretext employed by the government of Prime Minister Giovanni Giolitti to justify the invasion of Libya was alleged Ottoman bias against Italian businesses in the colony and the presumed inability of Ottoman authorities there to guarantee the security of expatriates. An ultimatum presented to the Sublime Porte on September 28, 1911, gave the Ottoman government 24 hours to agree to Italian military occupation of Libya. Although the Porte's response was conciliatory, Rome declared it unsatisfactory and ordered its fleet into action. The army was mobilized, but since Italy used regular army conscripts to fight its wars in Africa—the only European nation to do so—precious time had to be spent assembling the some 45,000 men of the invasion force and outfitting them for tropical warfare.

The first Italian soldiers landed at Tripoli, Libya's largest city, on October 9, by which time it had already been occupied, following a short bombardment, by some 7,000 Italian sailors. They had set up a defensive arc around the city, well within range of naval gunfire. In the meantime, the small Ottoman garrisons in the main cities of Libya, a force totaling fewer than 5,000 men, had withdrawn into the interior, where they joined Arab and Berber militia and tribal levies to mount a resistance to the invaders. This was heightened by the Italian government having eschewed a protectorate over Libya, much like the French in Tunisia and the British in Egypt, which would have allowed the Turks to retain a fictive sovereignty while ceding the actual running of the country to the occupying power. But on November 5, 1911, the Italian government issued a decree formally annexing Libya. It soon became clear that this was unwise.

The Italians had also concluded that the Arab and Berber populations of Libya, who viewed the Ottomans as corrupt and repressive, would greet the Italians as liberators. This supposition proved false, for the shared faith of ruler and subject outweighed all other considerations. This and the Ottomans' unexpectedly firm military commitment made the conflict in Libya very rough going for Italy.

On October 23, 1911, some 500 Italian soldiers were killed in a surprise attack, with civilian participation, on a weakly defended sector of the defense cordon around Tripoli. This so-called Massacre of Sciara Sciat led to severe reprisals by the Italian army, including summary executions and the opening of concentration camps in Libya and Italy. This in turn stirred up considerable anti-Italian sentiment in Europe, particularly in Britain.

From October 1911 well into 1912, Italian forces remained pretty much confined to their coastal beachheads, despite receiving reinforcements in November 1911 and a considerable advantage in weaponry, including aircraft and dirigibles used to bomb Ottoman positions. This was in fact the first time that aircraft were used in a combat role rather than simply for reconnaissance. The Italian army in Libya also pioneered the use of armored cars and, with the help of Guglielmo Marconi, developed a system of battlefield wireless communication.

Lack of progress in the war stemmed in part from the difficult terrain and climate and the low morale of the largely conscript force but also was a product of the army's lingering fear of being caught in "another Adowa." This Italian defeat at the hands of the Ethiopians in 1896, the bloodiest encounter in the whole of the European colonial wars, had brought down a government in Rome, and fears of a repetition were only heightened by the Sciara Sciat massacre. Many of the Italian generals who served in Libya, including the commander, General Carlo Caneva, were veterans of the East African fighting.

Ottoman Army leadership proved somewhat more inspired, although even with mass Arab and Berber support, the Ottoman regulars, denied reinforcements by a tight Italian naval blockade, were consistently outnumbered in the field and seldom able to take the offensive. Ottoman officers who served in Libya included Mustafa Kemal, founder and first president of the new Turkish republic in 1923, and Ismail Enver, who as Enver Pasha served as Ottoman minister of war from 1913 to 1918.

Enver played a particularly important role in effectively liaising with the Senussi, the powerful Sufi brotherhood who served as the spiritual and to some extent political leaders of the Bedouins of the desert interior. The orthodox Senussi traditionally had kept the Ottomans, not considered very good Muslims, at arm's length, and this had been seen by Italian officials as an indication that they might rally to Italy or at least remain neutral. As it turned out, after a brief period on the fence the Senussi, on the urging of Enver, assumed the leadership of Bedouin reinforcements for the Ottoman regulars in Cyrenaica, with the result that Italians troops were unable to penetrate into the interior of that province for the duration of the conflict.

The fighting between Italy and the Ottoman Empire could only be brought to an end when the Italians decided to expand the war to the eastern Mediterranean, something they earlier had promised anxious European powers they would not do. There were fears that such action might set alight the "Balkan tinderbox" by encouraging Balkan states such as Serbia and Bulgaria to try to drive the Ottomans from the rest of Southeastern Europe. There had been Italian raids along the Red Sea coast of the empire, and some aid had been given to anti-Ottoman rebels in Yemen and the nearby emirate of Asir. Italian military hawks, however, wanted a free hand in the eastern Mediterranean, where they could operate against the Ottoman islands in the Aegean and blockade or perhaps even attack Istanbul (Constantinople).

Rome had resisted this pressure, but the continuing stalemate in the Libyan desert forced its hand. A naval raid on the Dardanelles was followed by Italian occupation of Rhodes and other islands in the Dodecanese chain in the Aegean Sea. This plus looming conflict in the Balkans brought the Porte to the negotiating table.

On October 18, 1912, a settlement was reached at Lausanne in Switzerland granting Italy sovereignty over Libya. The Italians also agreed to evacuate the Dodecanese Islands as soon as the Turks left Libya, but Ottoman failure to fully draw down its Libyan garrison followed by participation in World War I on the side of the Central Powers allowed Italy to occupy the islands into World War II.

The Italo-Ottoman War (also known as the Italo-Turkish War) was the only war between European powers from 1878 to World War I but had far-reaching consequences. The war was costly for Italy, if more in treasure than in blood. Disease killed 1,948 Italian soldiers, while only 1,432 died as a result of combat. But what many of them were calling a "war for a desert" by the end of the fighting cost Italy some 527 million lire and had drawn off more than 100,000 of its soldiers and much of its military equipment. Worse, the fighting in Libya did not end with the Peace of Lausanne. An Arab and Berber insurrection festered on until 1932, when Benito Mussolini's army employed scorched-earth tactics to finally stamp it out. In 1916 when the Italian army entered its second year of heavy fighting in the Alps against the Austrians during World War I, more than 40,000 of its soldiers were still battling guerrillas in Libya.

The indigenous struggle against the Italians in Libya, which gained support, largely moral, from Muslim peoples around the world, has been called the first Pan-Islamic resistance movement against Western colonialism. Its long battle against Italian colonialism has been credited with providing modern-day Libya with the necessary credentials to declare itself an independent nation-state.

By liberating the Dodecanese Islands from the Ottomans, quite without intending to, the Italians gave a fillip to enosis, the movement to bring all Greek-speaking peoples in the Mediterranean region under the Greek flag. Italian refusal to honor the islanders' demands for union with Greece would lead to a rift with Athens on the eve of World War I. This split only worsened afterward, when the two countries fell out over the spoils from the assumed breakup of the Ottoman Empire after its defeat in the war.

Yet the most significant outcome of the 1911–1912 war was its contribution to the heightening of tensions in Southeastern Europe that would lead to the outbreak of world war in 1914. Libya itself in fact became a peripheral theater of World War I, as Ottoman soldiers and Senussi-led irregulars opened a front in western Egypt and Chad, forcing Britain and France to commit troops to the region.

BRUCE VANDERVORT

See also
Ataturk, Mustafa Kemal; Balkan Wars; Enver Pasha; Ottoman Empire

References
Askew, W. C. *Europe and Italy's Acquisition of Libya, 1911–1912.* Durham, NC: Duke University Press, 1942.

Bosworth, R. J. B. *Italy, the Least of the Great Powers: Italian Foreign Policy before the First World War.* Cambridge: Cambridge University Press, 1979.

Labanca, Nicola. *Libia: Una Guerra coloniale italiana.* Rovereto: Museo storico italiano della guerra, 2011.

Vandervort, B. *To the Fourth Shore: Italy's War for Libya, 1911–1912.* Rome: Stato Maggiore dell'Esercito, Ufficio Storico, 2012.

IVORY JUSTICE, Operation (July 24–August 1990)

U.S. military exercise begun on July 24, 1990, to demonstrate to Iraq the U.S. ability to protect the United Arab Emirates (UAE) and other American allies in the Persian Gulf region. The operation failed to dissuade Iraqi president Saddam

Hussein from invading Kuwait on August 2, 1990, possibly because of its small scale.

During the first half of 1990, however, the relationship of the Western powers with Hussein soured when he began to agitate for war against Israel and revived long-standing Iraqi territorial claims to Kuwait. Hussein was angry with Kuwait and the UAE for driving down the price of oil through overproduction, which significantly reduced Iraqi national income from oil exports. Both Kuwait and the UAE could prosper with declining oil prices, because they controlled oil distribution points and refining. Iraq, in contrast, depended almost solely on the sale of crude oil and, with oil prices low, was unable to service its huge debt from the 1980–1988 Iran-Iraq War.

On July 16, 1990, Iraqi foreign minister Tariq Aziz delivered a memorandum to the secretary-general of the Arab League laying out Iraq's charges against Kuwait and the UAE. It accused them of driving down the price of oil and depriving Iraq of $89 billion of potential income. It also accused Kuwait of slant-drilling into Iraq's Rumaila oil field and charged Kuwait with having moved some of its military posts and other installations into territory claimed by Iraq along their common border.

The Kuwaiti government regarded the memorandum as a bluff by Iraq to secure financial concessions. Although Kuwait put its armed forces on alert, it also offered to negotiate a settlement. At the same time, however, U.S. analysts reported that Iraqi Republican Guard divisions were moving toward the Kuwaiti border; indeed, by July 19, three Republican Guard divisions totaling some 35,000 men were within 30 miles of the border.

Although the Kuwaiti government was not overly concerned about an invasion, leaders of the UAE believed that they had reason to fear a military attack. During the Iran-Iraq War, Hussein had accused the UAE of a lack of support, and in 1986 Iraqi aircraft had attacked two UAE oil rigs. Although the Iraqi Foreign Ministry later claimed that this had been a mistake, most observers believed that it had been a deliberate effort to intimidate the UAE. To protect its oil rigs and other facilities, the UAE instituted a standing patrol of Dassault Mirage 2000 fighters and on July 22, 1990, requested assistance from the United States.

Two days later on July 24, the U.S. government launched Operation IVORY JUSTICE. Two Boeing KC-135 Stratotankers, along with a Lockheed C-141 Starlifter and support equipment and personnel, arrived in the Persian Gulf that same day. The tankers were to refuel UAE fighters in flight, allowing them to loiter above UAE airspace and intercept any incoming Iraqi aircraft. The emirates also requested a ground link to the U.S. Airborne Warning and Control System (AWACS) and Northrop Grumman E-2C Hawkeye radar aircraft flying in the Persian Gulf region. Such a link would allow the emirates to monitor air traffic and receive advance warning of any Iraqi air attack. The U.S. Navy's Central Command was also involved. Rear Admiral William Fogarty, commanding Joint Task Force–Middle East, ordered two frigates into the northern Persian Gulf. Their radars would provide additional warning of any Iraqi air attack on the UAE.

IVORY JUSTICE did not go smoothly, however. Refueling probes on the Mirage 2000 were incompatible with the KC-135's drogues, rendering aerial refueling impossible. In any case, the UAE fighter pilots had not been trained in aerial refueling.

The operation would have been more impressive had additional available forces been committed. The *Independence* carrier battle group was nearby and could have been ordered to the Strait of Hormuz, but the U.S. Navy believed that the shallow, restricted waters of the Persian Gulf were unsuitable for effective carrier operations.

Even though the U.S. force in IVORY JUSTICE was small, it did raise concerns in Baghdad. Word of the increased U.S. military presence led to some Arab government protests, but the UAE claimed that it was nothing more than routine training. Iraqi leaders complained to U.S. ambassador to Iraq April Glaspie, who reassured them that the United States wanted improved relations with their country. During her one meeting with Hussein, Glaspie sought to strike a conciliatory tone, in line with official policy.

In the final analysis, the very limited show of force of IVORY JUSTICE may have led Hussein to believe that the United States would not challenge an Iraqi invasion of Kuwait, which occurred on August 2. IVORY JUSTICE was then subsumed by Operation DESERT SHIELD, the buildup of U.S. and then coalition forces in Saudi Arabia.

TIM J. WATTS

See also
Arab League; Hussein, Saddam; Iraq; Kuwait, Iraqi Invasion of; United Arab Emirates

References
Freedman, Lawrence, and Efraim Karsh. *The Gulf Conflict, 1990–1991: Diplomacy and War in the New World Order.* Princeton, NJ: Princeton University Press, 1993.

Gordon, Michael R., and General Bernard E. Trainor. *The Generals' War: The Inside Story of the Conflict in the Gulf.* New York: Little, Brown, 1995.

Izz ad-Din al-Qassam Brigades

Armed paramilitary wing of the Palestinian group Hamas. The al-Qassam Brigades were formally established in 1991 by Yahya Ayyash, the key military strategist for Hamas. The al-Qassam Brigades, named for Izz ad-Din al-Qassam, the militant Palestinian leader of the Black Hand organization in the 1920s, have mounted attacks and terror campaigns against Israelis. Ayyash claims to have established the brigades to facilitate Hamas's political goals, which in the early 1990s were meant to stymie any Palestinian compromise or accommodation with Israel. Specifically, Hamas was vehemently opposed to the 1993 Oslo Accords and competed with Fatah, its main rival within the Palestinian nationalist movement.

The al-Qassam Brigades operate amid much secrecy and are not organized along typical military lines. Rather, they are small, largely independent cells directed by the head of the organization. It is not uncommon for the various cells to be completely unaware of other cells' goals or activities. Hamas and the brigades have been the strongest in the Gaza Strip, although they tried to maintain a significant presence in the West Bank as well. During 2004, however, retaliatory strikes by Israel Defense Forces (IDF) against brigade cells in the West Bank decimated those there.

From 1992 to 2000, al-Qassam Brigades fought an on-again, off-again guerrilla campaign against the IDF as well as Israeli civilians. Palestinian Authority (PA) president Yasser Arafat was unable to rein in the brigades. When the Second (al-Aqsa) Intifada began in September 2000, the brigades played a role in fomenting unrest and in arming and training militants to carry out terrorist attacks against Israel, but other attacks were organized by Islamic Jihad or carried out by individuals.

By 2003 the al-Qassam Brigades had developed in a different manner, not only focusing on terrorist attacks but also, with intra-Palestinian conflict on the rise, acting as a security force. Although multiple IDF attacks took a toll on the brigades' foot soldiers and leadership alike, the group continued to maintain its cohesion and attract many new recruits. Hamas accepted a truce in 2004 as part of an overall truce between the PA and Israel. Hamas then took advantage of the time to reconstitute and rearm itself.

After the Israelis pulled out of the Gaza Strip in August 2005, the al-Qassam Brigades sought to dominate the area in the ongoing effort by Hamas to supplant Fatah. Nevertheless, the brigades decreased their activity against the Israelis by generally honoring the truce that had begun in 2004 and was reiterated in 2005. Meanwhile, the PA was under heavy pressure to disarm Hamas. That attempt failed, however, when Hamas won the 2006 legislative elections.

Emboldened by their electoral success, Hamas leaders sought to assert control in Gaza. Indeed, the brigades formed a potent security source there beginning in May 2006, soon clashing with militias supported by Fatah. In June 2006, the al-Qassam Brigades allegedly supported Hezbollah's capture of an IDF soldier, Gilad Shalit, that precipitated the Israel-Gaza War, lasting for nearly a month. Brigade soldiers were heavily involved in the fighting. On July 12, 2006, Mohammed Dayf (Deif), leader of the al-Qassam Brigades, narrowly escaped an Israeli attack on a house in Gaza in which a Hamas official and his entire family were killed. The al-Qassam Brigades retain a strong presence in the Gaza Strip.

Paul G. Pierpaoli Jr.

See also

Arafat, Yasser; Fatah, al-; Gaza Strip; Hamas; Hezbollah; Intifada, Second; Oslo Accords; Palestine Liberation Organization; Palestinian National Authority; West Bank

References

La Guardia, Anton. *War without End: Israelis, Palestinians, and the Struggle for a Promised Land.* New York: Thomas Dunne, 2002.

Mishal, Shaul, and Avraham Sela. *The Palestinian Hamas: Vision, Violence, and Coexistence.* New York: Columbia University Press, 2000.

Pappe, Ilan. *A History of Modern Palestine: One Land, Two Peoples.* Cambridge: Cambridge University Press, 2003.

Rubin, Barry. *Revolution until Victory? The Politics and History of the PLO.* Reprint ed. Cambridge, MA: Harvard University Press, 2003.

J

Jabotinsky, Vladimir Yevgenyevich (1880–1940)

Zionist leader, author, soldier, and founder of the Jewish Legion of World War I. Vladimir Yevgenyevich (Ze'ev Yina) Jabotinsky was born into a middle-class Jewish family in Odessa in Ukraine, Russia, on October 18, 1880. He left Russia in 1898 to study law in Italy and Switzerland and then became a highly acclaimed foreign correspondent for several Russian newspapers.

In 1903 with a pogrom seemingly imminent in Odessa, Jabotinsky helped form the first Zionist self-defense group. As a consequence of a pogrom in Kishniev, Russia, that same year, he became active in Zionist work. He helped organize self-defense units within the Jewish communities of Russia but also became an outspoken advocate of full civil rights for Russian Jews. As a delegate to the Sixth Zionist Congress in Basel in 1903, he opposed the scheme to establish a Jewish homeland in East Africa. Soon the most important Zionist speaker and journalist in Russia, he worked to promote Jewish culture in Russia and helped establish the Hebrew University in Jerusalem.

With the beginning of World War I, Jabotinsky became a war correspondent. He and Joseph Trumpeldor worked to establish Jewish military units as part of the British Army. Jabotinsky believed that the Ottoman Empire was doomed and that Jewish support for the Allies in the war would help bring about creation of a Jewish state in Palestine. Their efforts began with the Zion Mule Corps of several hundred Jewish men that served with distinction in the Gallipoli Campaign. From the beginning, Jabotinsky wanted the Jewish units to be frontline forces rather than auxiliaries. Later, the Jewish Legion (also known as the Jewish Battalions) served with distinction in other campaigns against the Ottomans. Enlisting in the 38th Battalion of Royal Fusiliers as a private, Jabotinsky was soon a lieutenant and participated in the British crossing of the Jordan River and the liberation of Palestine from Ottoman rule. He was both decorated for bravery and mentioned in dispatches.

After the war, Jabotinsky joined the Zionist Committee and for a while headed its Political Department. British authorities in Palestine denied his requests to arm a small number of Jews for self-defense purposes. Nonetheless, he was able to arm perhaps 600 men in secret self-defense groups.

The early April 1920 rioting by Arabs in Jerusalem led to the deaths of 6 people, the wounding of several hundred, and the destruction of Jewish property and torching of several synagogues. Jabotinsky had sought to create a legal Jewish police force for Jerusalem that would help to balance the Arab police there. During the riots he secured permission from the British to introduce 100 armed Jews into the city, but when he tried to do this he was promptly arrested along with 19 other Jews. The British then searched his residence and discovered arms there. Jabotinsky was tried and sentenced to 15 years at hard labor for weapons possession. Following a public outcry regarding the British conclusion

Zionist leader Vladimir Jabotinsky (1880–1940), founder of the Jewish Legion of World War I. (Library of Congress)

that Jews were responsible for the riots and the outrageous verdicts handed out against the Jews, Jabotinsky served only a few months in Akko Prison before he was amnestied in July 1920. The April 1920 Arab riots meanwhile led to the establishment in Palestine of the Jewish self-defense organization Haganah.

In March 1921 Jabotinsky joined the Executive of the World Zionist Organization (WZO), headed by Chaim Weizmann. Disagreeing sharply with British policies in Palestine and with what he considered the lack of Jewish resistance to them, Jabotinsky resigned in January 1923. That same year he helped found and headed the youth movement Betar (Hebrew acronym for B'rit Trumpeldor, the League of Joseph Trumpeldor).

In 1925 Jabotinsky founded in Paris his own organization, the Union of Zionist Revisionists (B'rit Herut-Hatzohar), and became its president. It called for the immediate establishment in Palestine of a Jewish state. Jabotinsky argued that this state should occupy both sides of the Jordan River and seek continued immigration until Jews were a majority there and should also establish a military organization to defend the new creation. He much admired the British form of government and wanted the future Jewish state to be similar to it as a liberal democracy.

From 1925 Jabotinsky made his home in Paris except during 1928–1929, when he lived in Jerusalem and was director of the Judea Insurance Company and edited the Hebrew daily newspaper *Doar Hayom.* In 1929 he left Palestine to attend the Sixteenth Zionist Congress, after which the British denied him reentry. For the rest of his life, he lived abroad.

When the Seventeenth Zionist Congress of 1931 rejected Jabotinsky's demand that it announce that the aim of Zionism was the creation of a Jewish state, he resigned from the WZO and founded his own New Zionist Organization (NZO) in Vienna in 1935. The NZO demanded free immigration of Jews into Palestine and establishment of a Jewish state. Supplementing the NZO were its military arm, the Irgun Tsvai Leumi (National Military Organization), established in 1937 and commanded by Jabotinsky, and the Betar youth movement. Jabotinsky hoped that Betar might train the young Jews of the diaspora so that they could return to Palestine and fight for the establishment of a Jewish state. These organizations cooperated in abetting illegal immigration by ship to Palestine.

Fluent in a number of languages, Jabotinsky also continued to write. Deeply concerned in the 1930s about rampant anti-Semitism in Poland, he called for the evacuation of its entire Jewish population and relocation to Palestine. During 1939–1940 he traveled in Britain and the United States. He advocated establishment of a Jewish army that would fight on the Allied side against Nazi Germany. Jabotinsky suffered a massive heart attack while visiting the Betar camp near Hunter, New York, and died on August 4, 1940. In 1964 his remains and those of his wife were reinterred in Israel. The State of Israel also created in his honor a medal that is awarded for distinguished accomplishment.

SPENCER C. TUCKER

See also
Arab Revolt of World War I; Haganah; Irgun Tsvai Leumi; Jewish Legion; Palestine, British Mandate for; Zionism

References
Jabotinsky, Vladimir. *The Story of the Jewish Legion.* New York: Bernard Akerman, 1945.
Katz, Shmel. *Lone Wolf: A Biography of Vladimir Ze'ev Jabotinsky.* 2 vols. Fort Lee, NJ: Barricade Books, 1996.
Sachar, Howard M. *A History of Israel: From the Rise of Zionism to Our Time.* 3rd ed. New York: Knopf, 2007.
Shavit, Yaacov. *Jabotinsky and the Revisionist Movement, 1925–1948.* New York: Routledge, 1988.
Shepherd, Naomi. *Ploughing Sand: British Rule in Palestine, 1917–1948.* New Brunswick, NJ: Rutgers University Press, 1999.

Jadid, Salah al- (1926–1993)

Syrian military officer, prominent figure within the Syrian Baath Party, and de facto Syrian leader during 1966–1970. Salah al-Jadid was born in 1926 in a small village near Latakia (Ladhakiyya), Syria, a member of the minority Alawite community. He joined the military at a young age and ultimately rose to the rank of general.

Al-Jadid actively participated in the March 8, 1963, coup that brought the Baath Party to power in Syria. As a consequence of this event, he became Syrian Army chief of staff. During the course of the next three years he used his position as chief of staff to consolidate Baathist and sectarian control of the armed forces. In 1965 he assumed the position of deputy secretary-general of the Baath Party, a position with less power than he previously had.

In 1966, however, al-Jadid chose to wield his still considerable influence in another coup that installed a more hard-line, neo-Baathist regime. This made him virtual ruler of Syria. Lacking widespread popular support, damaged by Syria's defeat in the Six-Day War (1967), and badly weakened by internal divisions, al-Jadid's government fell to another military coup only four years later. The coup de grâce for al-Jadid's reign had been his ill-fated decision to send Syrian-backed Palestinian troops into Jordan during what came to be known as Black September. The pragmatists in the Baath Party, especially Minister of Defense Hafez al-Assad, decried al-Jadid's moves and launched the so-called Corrective Revolution on November 13, 1970. This coup ousted al-Jadid from power, and he was replaced by al-Assad. Al-Jadid spent the next 23 years in al-Mazzah Prison in Damascus, where he died on August 19, 1993.

Jonas Kauffeldt

See also
Alawites; Assad, Hafez al-; Baath Party; Black September; Syria

References
Ma'oz, Moshe. *Syria and Israel: From War to Peacemaking.* Oxford, UK: Clarendon, 1995.
Van Dam, Nikolaos. *The Struggle for Power in Syria: Politics and Society under Asad and the Ba'th Party.* London: Croom Helm, 1996.

Jaffa, Battle of (August 5, 1192)

Important battle during the Third Christian Crusade in the Holy Land (1189–1192). Although combat for Jaffa began on July 27, 1192, the date for the battle is usually given as August 5, when the major combat took place. It was fought between the crusader forces of English king Richard I (Richard the Lionheart) and Egyptian sultan Salah-al din Yusuf ibn Ayyub (Saladin) at the Palestinian port city of Jaffa (modern-day Tel Aviv–Yafo, Israel).

Following their victory in the Battle of Arsuf (September 7, 1191), Richard's crusader forces moved on Jaffa, an important step in the goal of retaking Jerusalem. Realizing that he could not hold the city, Saladin evacuated it and demolished most of his fortresses in southern Palestine, including Ascalon (modern-day Tel Ashqelon, Israel), Gaza, Blanche-Garde (Tell es-Safi), Lydda, and Ramla (Ramleh). Richard went on to capture the fortress of Darum (modern-day Deir al-Balah in the Gaza Strip), the sole fortress that Saladin had garrisoned. With Christian control of the seacoast threatening his hold on Jerusalem, Saladin rebuilt his forces, and Richard settled for negotiations with the Muslim leader. Meanwhile, Richard planned to use Jaffa, the closest port to Jerusalem, as his base of operations against the holy city.

In late November the crusaders advanced inland from Jaffa with the goal of retaking Jerusalem. They got close to the city, and it appeared that Jerusalem might then be easily taken, but the onset of very poor weather with heavy rain and hailstorms in addition to fears that a prolonged siege might see the army cut off in the interior by a Muslim relief force led to a withdrawal. During the winter the crusaders rebuilt the defenses of Ascalon, and the spring of 1192 saw not only further negotiations between Richard and Saladin but also a second crusader advance on Jerusalem that got to within sight of the city before another withdrawal, forced by dissension among the crusader leadership.

Meanwhile, Richard grew concerned regarding the machinations of French king Philippe II Augustus and his own brother John, who was ruling in England in his absence. This information caused Richard to begin a withdrawal from Muslim-held territory with the plan of quitting the Holy Land altogether and returning home.

Still smarting from his defeat at Arsuf, Saladin sought to take advantage of the situation, and on July 27 he laid siege to Jaffa. Its Christian garrison put up a stout defense and held out for three days until the Muslims stormed the city walls; the remaining defenders were forced to withdrew to the citadel. The defenders had, however, purchased just enough time for news to reach Richard, then at Acre (modern-day Akko, Israel), who quickly mounted a relief expedition, and set sail for Jaffa.

On August 1 with Muslim banners flying from Jaffa's walls, Richard leapt overboard and personally led his men ashore to attack the city from the sea. Caught by surprise and believing that the arriving ships might be part of a far larger force, Saladin's men fled inland in disorder just as they were on the brink of a complete victory.

Richard had too few men to defend Jaffa's broken walls and so set up his camp outside them. He had some 2,300 knights and infantry as well as an unknown number of sailors and members of the Jaffa garrison. Saladin meanwhile reassembled his scattered forces and sought to take advantage of his numerical superiority. Saladin's strength has been given at 7,000–10,000 men. Following a night march, he attacked at dawn on August 5.

Fortunately for Richard, the attackers had been discovered before they could launch their assault, and the king managed to organize a stout defense. He ordered his spearmen to kneel and drive their shields and the butt of their spears or lances into the ground with the tips facing outward against the Muslim horsemen. His Genoese and Pisan crossbowmen then formed up behind the wall of shields and spears, operating in pairs with one loading while the other fired.

Saladin's lightly armored Egyptian, Turkish, and Bedouin cavalry came up against Richard's defenses time and again but each time were met by clouds of crossbow bolts and driven back without penetrating, their horses being especially vulnerable. Richard then led in person a charge by his knights, and Saladin's men withdrew. The crusaders would claim that the Muslims had lost some 700 men killed, along with 1,500 horses, while they gave their own losses as only 2 dead, although many more were wounded.

The Battle of Jaffa proved pivotal, for it led to the Treaty of Jaffa of September 2 between Richard and Saladin. This three-year truce enabled the crusaders to keep most of the gains they had made during the Third Crusade just when it appeared that they were about to lose them.

SPENCER C. TUCKER

See also
Arsuf, Battle of; Jaffa, Treaty of; Richard I, King; Saladin

References
Gillingham, John. *Richard I.* New Haven, CT: Yale University Press, 1999.
Röhricht, Reinhold. *Geschichte des Königreichs Jerusalem (1100–1291).* Innsbruck, Austria: Wagner, 1898.
Runciman, S. *A History of the Crusades,* Vol. 3, *The Kingdom of Acre and the Later Crusades.* Cambridge: Cambridge University Press, 1987.
Verbruggen, Jan Evans. *The Art of Warfare in Western Europe during the Middle Ages.* Woodbridge, UK: Boydell, 1997.

Jaffa, Treaty of (September 2, 1192)

Treaty that effectively ended the Third Christian Crusade in the Holy Land (1189–1192). The victory of Christian forces under King Richard I (Richard the Lionheart) in the Battle of Jaffa (August 5, 1192) enabled Richard to conclude a treaty with Egyptian sultan Salah-al din Yusuf ibn Ayyub (Saladin) that was satisfactory to the Christian side.

Signed on September 2, 1192, in the Palestinian port city of Jaffa between Richard and Saladin, the treaty established a three-year truce between the two warring sides. It also protected recent Christian gains in Palestine. Although the crusaders did not achieve their goal of retaking Jerusalem, the treaty provided for free passage of Muslims and Christians across each others' lands. Christians were guaranteed access to the Holy Sepulchre in Jerusalem without having to pay tolls.

Saladin secured the return of the important strongholds of Ascalon (modern-day Tel Ashqelon, Israel), Gaza, and Darum (modern-day Deir al-Balah in the Gaza Strip), but their fortifications were to be demolished. The Franks retained Jaffa. The treaty also provided for free trade. In effect the treaty recognized the existence of the Kingdom of Jerusalem.

With the conclusion of the treaty the Third Crusade came to an end. Many Christian pilgrims now visited Jerusalem to see the holy sites there. Richard was not among them. He sent Hubert Walter, bishop of Salisbury, as his representative while he himself sailed from Acre for Europe on October 9, 1192. Many other crusaders also departed.

SPENCER C. TUCKER

See also
Crusades in the Holy Land, Christian; Jaffa, Battle of; Richard I, King; Saladin

References
Asbridge, Thomas. *The Crusades: The Authoritative History of the War for the Holy Land.* New York: HarperCollins, 2001.
Lyons, Malcolm C., and D. E. P. Jackson, *Saladin: The Politics of the Holy War.* Cambridge: Cambridge University Press, 1982.
Mayer, Hans Eberhard, *The Crusades.* 2d ed. Translated by John Gillingham. Oxford: Oxford University Press, 1988.
Riley-Smith, Jonathan. *The Crusades: A History.* New York: Blomsbury, 2014.

Jam, Battle of (September 24, 1528)

Major victory of Safavid shah Tahmasp of Persia against the Uzbeks. Following the death of Shah Ismail in 1524, Iran went through a civil war that critically weakened the state. Such political strife was exploited by the Ottomans in the west and the Uzbeks in the east, both of whom attacked Safavid territory. New Safavid shah Tahmasp I (r. 1524–1576) struggled to contain Ottoman expansion but was more successful against the Uzbeks, who under the leadership of Ubayd Allah Khan launched several invasions of Khurasan. They raided Herat in 1524 and Mashhad in 1526, returning again to Herat in 1528.

Hastening to relieve the siege of Herat, Tahmasp intercepted the Uzbeks on September 24, 1528, at Jam, where he scored a decisive victory. The battle is notable for the Safavid use of new tactics that they adopted from their neighbors. Like the Ottomans at Chaldiran in 1514 and the Mughals at Panipat in 1526, Tahmasp's men used firearms and artillery (small culverins and swivel guns mounted on wagons) to deadly result. The shah deployed artillery in the center protected with wagons and seasoned troops under his personal command; the Baburnama succinctly states that this battle formation was "in the Anatolian fashion."

Although the Uzbeks managed to turn the Persian flanks and plunder their camp, Tahmasp's center stood firm, and artillery inflicted heavy losses on the Uzbek cavalry. Tahmasp then ordered his men to cease fire, rallied them around his royal standard, and launched a decisive counterattack that shattered the Uzbek cavalry.

The Battle of Jam helped Tahmasp to consolidate his authority in northeastern Iran, but he was unable to fully exploit its consequences because of the Ottoman threat from the west. The Uzbeks, despite suffering a heavy defeat at Jam, were not destroyed. They soon regrouped and continued to invade Iran until the death of Ubayd Allah Khan in 1540.

ALEXANDER MIKABERIDZE

See also
Chaldiran, Battle of; Ismail I, Shah; Tahmasp I, Shah

References
Babur. *The Baburnama: Memoirs of Babur, Prince and Emperor.* Translated by W. M. Thackston. New York: Random House, 2002.

Jackson, Peter, and Lawrence Lockhart, eds. *The Cambridge History of Iran: The Timurid and Safavid Periods,* Vol. 6. Cambridge: Cambridge University Press, 1986.

Mathee, Rudi. "Unwalled Cities and Restless Nomads: Firearms and Artillery in Safavid Iran." In *Safavid Persia: The History and Politics of an Islamic Society,* ed. Charles Melville, 389–416. London: I. B. Tauris, 1996.

Janissaries

Turkish for "new soldier" (*yenicari*), the men of the infantry units forming the Ottoman sultan's household troops and bodyguards. Traditional accounts credit Sultan Orhan (r. 1326–1362) as the founder of the Janissary Corps. Modern historians attribute its creation to Orhan's son, Murad I (r. 1362–1389), around 1365. The Janissaries became the first Ottoman standing army and the first standing army in Europe since the Roman Empire. They replaced the forces, composed mostly of tribal warriors (*ghazis*), whose loyalty and morale were sometimes suspect.

The first Janissaries were prisoners of war and slaves. After the 1380s, their ranks were filled under the *devşirme* system. The "recruits" were mostly Christian boys, preferably of the ages of 14 to 18; however, those ages 8–20 could be taken. Initially the recruiters favored Greeks and Albanians, but as the Ottoman Empire expanded into Southeastern Europe and northward, the devşirme came to include Albanians, Bulgarians, Georgians, Armenians, Croats, Bosnians, and Serbs and later Romanians, Poles, Ukrainians, and southern Russians.

During the reign of Sultan Murad III (r. 1574–1595), the Janissaries began enrolling outside the devşirme system. In 1683, Sultan Mehmet IV (r. 1648–1687) abolished the devşirme because increasing of numbers Muslim Turkish families had enrolled their sons into the force. From then on, volunteers for the Janissary Corps were mostly of Muslim origin.

Janissaries trained under strict discipline in monastic-like conditions in "cadet" schools, where they were expected to remain celibate and single until after they retired. The

Table 1. Increase in the Size of the Janissary Corps

Year	Number of Janissaries
1389	~2,000
1514	10,156
1567–68	12,798
1609	37,627
1661	54,222
1665	49,556
1670	49,868
1680	54,222

Gábor Ágoston, "The Ottoman Warfare in Europe, 1453–1812," in Jeremy Black ed., *European Warfare, 1453–1815* (New York: Palgrave Macmillan, 1999), 135.

Portrait of an early-18th-century Janissary commander, or *aga*, by the workshop of Flemish-French painter Jean Baptiste Vanmour, who died in Istanbul in 1737. (Rijksmuseum, Amsterdam)

young recruits were also expected to convert to Islam. Unlike other Muslims, they could not have beards, only a moustache. Janissaries also learned to follow the beliefs of the dervish saint Hajji Bektash Wali, disciples of whom had blessed the first troops.

For all practical purposes, Janissaries belonged to the sultan and carried the title "door slave," indicating their collective bond with the sultan. Janissaries were taught to consider the corps as their home and family and the sultan as their father. They lived in their own barracks and during peacetime served as policemen and firefighters. They were forbidden from participation in any outside economic activity or trade. Only those who proved sufficiently strong earned the rank of true Janissary at the age of 24 or 25. The corps inherited the property of dead Janissaries, amassing wealth like some religious orders and foundations.

In return for their loyalty and their fervor in war, Janissaries gained special privileges and benefits. They received a quarterly cash salary during peacetime as well as war, a significant difference from the contemporary practice of paying troops only during wartime. They also received booty during wartime and enjoyed a high standard of living and respected social status.

The Janissaries had a full complement of support units. There were units to prepare the roads the Janissaries would travel on, set up the tents, and bake bread. The Janissaries had a quartermaster corps that carried and distributed weapons and ammunition and its own internal medical auxiliaries, Muslim and Jewish surgeons who traveled with the corps during campaigns and had organized methods to move the wounded and the sick to mobile hospitals behind the lines. The Janissaries were also skilled combat engineers, as demonstrated during the siege of Vienna in 1529.

During the early centuries, in peacetime the Janissaries carried clubs or cutlasses unless they served as border troops. On campaign, they were archers and used axes and sabers for close-in fighting. In the 1440s they began adopting firearms and by the early 16th century were equipped with muskets. Janissaries also made extensive use of early grenades and hand cannon and, after the late 1600s, employed pistols.

The Janissaries fought in every major campaign of the Ottoman Empire, including the 1453 capture of Constantinople, the defeat of the Egyptian Mamluks, and the wars against Hungary and Austria. The sultan himself always led Janissary troops into battle.

With the passage of time, the Janissaries became aware of their military prowess and importance. In 1449 they revolted for the first time, demanding higher wages, which they received. After 1451, every new sultan paid each Janissary an accession reward and raised his pay rank. In 1566, Selim II (1566–1574) gave Janissaries permission to marry.

In 1618 the teenage Osman II became sultan, determined to curb Janissary excesses. In 1622 the Janissaries, hearing rumors that he was preparing to move against them, revolted, took the sultan captive, imprisoned him, and murdered him shortly afterward.

As with the Praetorian Guard of the Roman Empire, the Janissaries became very much a law unto themselves and a serious threat to the empire's stability. Yet over the 1600s and into the 1700s, they were also increasingly ineffective militarily at a time when the militaries of the European armies were growing in size and undergoing vast improvements. The results were seen in lost wars with Austria and Russia and commensurate losses in Ottoman territory after 1683.

By the mid-18th century, many Janissaries had taken up trades and crafts outside of their military service, gained the right to marry and enroll their children in the corps, and lived away from the barracks. Many had become landholders, administrators, and scholars, and retired or discharged Janissaries received pensions. This evolution away from their original military vocation was the essence of the system's demise.

In 1807 when Selim III (r. 1789–1807) tried to modernize the army along West European lines, the Janissaries revolted again and deposed him in favor of Mustafa IV. Mustafa had Selim III killed, and a second rebellion deposed Mustafa and saw Mahmud II become sultan in 1808. Mahmud II (r. 1808–1839) had the captured Mustafa executed and eventually came to a compromise with the Janissaries. Ever mindful of the Janissary threat, the sultan spent the next years discreetly securing his position. The Janissaries' abuse of power, military ineffectiveness, and resistance to reform and the high cost of salaries to men, many of whom were not actually serving soldiers, became increasingly intolerable.

In 1826 Mahmud II informed the Janissaries that he was forming a new army, organized and trained along modern European lines. The Janissaries again mutinied and advanced on the sultan's palace. In the ensuing fight, artillery fire set their barracks on fire, killing some 4,000 Janissaries. The sultan had the survivors either exiled or executed and confiscated their possessions. The event is now known as the Auspicious Incident.

Robert B. Kane

See also
Devshirme System; *Ghulams;* Ikhwan; Kapikulu Corps

References
Askan, Virginia H. *Ottoman Wars: An Empire Besieged*. Harlow, UK: Pearson Longman, 2007.
Howard, Douglas A. *The History of Turkey*. Westport, CT: Greenwood, 2001.
Shaw, Stanford J. *History of the Ottoman Empire and Modern Turkey*. Cambridge: Cambridge University Press, 1987.

Jarring Mission (December 9, 1967–October 1973)

Diplomatic mission named for Swedish diplomat Dr. Gunnar Jarring that sought to implement a United Nations (UN) resolution calling for peace in the Middle East in the aftermath of the Six-Day War in June 1967. Jarring commenced the mission in December 1967, and sporadic negotiations continued until October 1973.

On November 22, 1967, the UN Security Council unanimously passed Resolution 242, which called for a lasting and comprehensive peace settlement in the Middle East. UN secretary-general U Thant duly appointed Jarring as his special representative to implement the resolution. Jarring had considerable diplomatic experience as ambassador to the UN, the United States, and the Soviet Union. He was serving as Sweden's ambassador to the Soviet Union when he took up the Middle East assignment.

Given the complexity of regional circumstances and tensions, Jarring had a very difficult job. Resolution 242 had called for the withdrawal of Israeli troops from the occupied territories (the West Bank, East Jerusalem, the Gaza Strip, the Sinai Peninsula, and the Golan Heights) in return for an end to the conflict. It also called for an end to the state of war that existed between Israel and Egypt, Jordan, and Syria. In addition, the resolution emphasized the sovereignty and territorial inviolability of all the countries of the Middle East and affirmed freedom of navigation in international waterways.

Jarring's mission became significantly more difficult because of the various interpretations of the resolution. The formula of land for peace, or the vacating of occupied territory in return for a peace guarantee, became immediately controversial. The definite article "the" was absent from the English version before the word "territories," which rendered a very wide meaning. The definite article was present in the French version, which suggested that the territories were those annexed by Israel. The omission of the word "Palestinians" before the word "refugees" also generated controversy.

Beginning in early 1968, Jarring shuttled among the capitals of the Middle East. Israel, Egypt, Jordan, and Lebanon recognized his role as peacemaker. Syria rejected the Jarring Mission, however, arguing that only a total Israeli withdrawal from occupied territories would suffice before peace negotiations could begin. Most Arabs as well as the Soviet Union took the position that there could be no direct talks with Israel without troop withdrawals.

Jarring did not make a lot of progress throughout much of 1968, and hostilities between warring parties continued in spite of a cease-fire. Indeed, the fighting became known as the War of Attrition. Toward the latter part of 1968, Palestinian and Israeli commandos became involved in attacks on each other, and the Israeli Air Force was striking targets in both Egypt and Jordan. Although Jarring's efforts seemed futile in the face of continued violence, peace efforts continued. Both the United States and the Soviet Union put forth their own peace proposals, and Jarring continued his shuttle diplomacy.

In his report, Jarring noted that the parties concerned had initially seemingly accepted Resolution 242, but a second round of discussions beginning in August 1968 had revealed obvious differences. Israel regarded the resolution as a "statement of principles," while Egypt considered it as an already acceptable plan that was the basis for an agreement. By this time, it was generally agreed that the ambiguous withdrawal clause applied to all the territories occupied by Israel since June 5, 1967. Israel, however, argued that it was applicable only when an agreement had been reached on a "secure and recognized" border.

Differences in interpretations of the resolution continued, however, and meetings between the parties did not occur. Jarring was also made aware of discussions in April 1969 among the United States, the Soviet Union, Britain, and France. From June 1970 to January 1971, he tried to hold discussions that would bring together the governments of Israel, Egypt, and Jordan as per an American proposal of June 1970. Negotiations continued under Jarring's supervision until the October 1973 Yom Kippur War. Despite his considerable efforts, he had been unable to forge anything close to a peace agreement.

PATIT MISHRA

See also
Six-Day War; War of Attrition; Yom Kippur War

References
Bailey, Sydney D. *Four Arab-Israeli Wars and the Peace Process.* New York: St. Martin's, 1982.
Dupuy, Trevor N. *Elusive Victory: The Arab-Israeli Wars, 1947–1974.* Garden City, NY: Military Book Club, 2002.
Herzog, Chaim. *The Arab-Israeli Wars: War and Peace in the Middle East from the War of Independence to Lebanon.* Westminster, MD: Random House, 1984.
Pimlott, John. *The Middle East Conflicts from 1945 to the Present.* New York: Crescent, 1983.

Jassy, Treaty of (January 9, 1792)

Peace treaty concluded between Russia and the Ottoman Empire on January 9, 1792, at Jassy (Iasi, Romania) that ended the Russo-Ottoman War of 1787–1792 and established the Dniester River as the Russian-Ottoman border. Russia retained territories it occupied east of the river (including the port of Ochakov) but ceded Moldavia and Bessarabia to the Porte. Sultan Selim III recognized the Russian presence in the Crimea and the northern Black Sea coast, while Russian empress Catherine II acknowledged Ottoman authority in the Balkans.

ALEXANDER MIKABERIDZE

See also
Russo-Ottoman Wars

Reference
Shaw, Stanford. *History of the Ottoman Empire and Modern Turkey.* Cambridge: Cambridge University Press, 1977.

Jawhar (?–992)

One of the greatest Fatimid generals of Egypt, Jawhar, whose full name was Abu al-Hasan Jawhar ibn Abd Allah, was a Christian from Dalmatia (not a Greek or Sicilian as some writers previously suggested). He was kidnapped by Muslim pirates operating in the Adriatic and brought as a slave to Kairouan. After serving several masters, he was gifted to Caliph al-Mansur, whose son and successor granted him his freedom.

Extremely capable, Jawhar quickly advanced through the ranks, becoming vizier and commander in chief of the Fatimid Army. His first major campaign was directed against northwestern Africa in 958. Departing from al-Nasuriyya, in two years of fighting he succeeded in extending Fatimid caliph al-Mu'izz's authority westward to Tahart, Tlemcen, Sijilmasa Fez, Tangier, and Ceuta.

Beginning in 966, Jawhar began preparing to accomplish the long-standing Fatimid ambition of conquering Egypt. He made a tax-collecting tour throughout the Fatimid realm, inspecting wells and frontier towns that could be used for invasion. In 967 the Fatimid caliph signed a peace with the Byzantine emperor, freeing additional resources for the Egyptian expedition. By the time Jawhar returned from his inspection tour in late 968 the Fatimid Army had been assembled, and in February 969 Jawhar departed with some 100,000 men from Kairouan.

After two months of marching, Jawhar reached Alexandria in May 969. There he faced only limited resistance, as the reigning Ilkhshidid regime had disintegrated from years of internecine warfare and famine. Effective power was in the hands of feuding factions. At Alexandria, Jawhar was met by an embassy of Egyptian notables offering him the submission of the country. Jawhar accepted the offer and granted the envoys a general letter of safety, which remained the most important document of this era. The letter explained the reasons for the Fatimid campaign in Egypt and outlined the future political, economic, and religious policies of the new regime. More importantly, the letter provides a fascinating look into a wide range of issues affecting contemporary Egypt, such as internal security, illegal taxation, and quality of coinage.

Nevertheless, Jawhar also faced isolated resistance from Ilkhshidi and Tuluni regiments, whom he decisively defeated in early July. In mid-July, Jawhar took possession of Fustat, where he began constructing a new city with a royal palace that came to be known as al-Qahira (Cairo), meaning "Victorious." He then subdued an uprising in Lower Egypt and dispatched part of his army under Jafar ibn Fallah to Syria, where the Fatimid troops captured Damascus.

The Fatimid expansion into Syria, however, provoked a counterattack by the Qarmatians, whose forces invaded Egypt in 971. Jawhar won a complete victory over them near Cairo on December 24, 971, and spent the next two years pacifying the country. In 973, Jawhar invited Caliph al-Mu'izz into his new capital at Cairo, transferring the political center of the Fatimid state from Tunisia to Egypt. But the caliph's arrival proved to be unfortunate for the warrior. Suspicious of his popularity and authority, the caliph stripped him of all honors, which, however, were restored to Jawhar by al-Mu'izz's successor in 976.

Jawhar's last campaign was in Syria. Initially he failed to capture Damascus and was besieged in Ascalon, but Caliph al-Aziz arrived with a relief army, enabling Jawhar to undertake a successful campaign. Jawhar spent the remainder of his life in retirement before dying at an advanced age in January 992.

ALEXANDER MIKABERIDZE

See also
Fatimid Dynasty

References
Hrbek, I. "Die Slawen im Dienste der Fatimiden." *Archiv Orientalni* 21 (1953): 543–581.
Lev, Yaacov. *State and Society in Fatimid Egypt*. Leiden: Brill, 1991.

Jeddah, Siege of (February 10–December 17, 1925)

During World War I, Sharif Hussein ibn Ali proclaimed Arabian independence and claimed the title of the first king of the Hejaz. His action provoked great resistance among the Wahhabis, who had long challenged his authority. In 1924 Abdul Aziz Ibn Saud, the Wahhabi leader who had consolidated his authority over the Nejd and the Asir and sought to unite the peninsula under his own control, attacked the Hejaz, defeating Hussein, who abdicated his throne to his son Ali ibn Hussein.

After occupying Mecca, Ibn Saud invested the last Hejaz stronghold of Jeddah (Jidda), which resisted for nearly a year, from February 10 to December 17, 1925. With Ali ibn Hussein giving up the crown, the victorious Ibn Saud proclaimed himself king of the Hejaz and Nejd in January 1926. The capture of Jeddah gave Ibn Saud control of the entire Arabian Peninsula and contributed to the establishment of Saudi Arabia.

ALEXANDER MIKABERIDZE

See also
Hussein ibn Ali ibn Mohammed; Ibn Saud, King; Saudi-Hashemite War

Reference
Vassiliev, Alexei. *The History of Saudi Arabia*. London: Saqi, 1998.

Jenin, Battle of (April 3–11, 2002)

The town of Jenin, located in the northern West Bank with a present population of approximately 34,000 people, was the site of a fierce battle during April 3–11, 2002, between the Israel Defense Forces (IDF) and Palestinian terrorists. The Battle of Jenin gave rise to widespread but unfounded charges of a massacre by the IDF.

At the beginning of April 2002 in response to a wave of attacks on Israeli civilians, the IDF launched Operation DEFENSIVE SHIELD against what it called a terrorist infrastructure. In so doing, it reoccupied towns turned over to Palestinian control including Jenin (which had reverted to Palestinian control in 1996), from which nearly half of the 28 suicide bombers of the preceding three months had originated. The operation was just one among several Israeli military moves during the Second (al-Aqsa) Intifada, which began in earnest in 2000.

The Palestinian refugee camp at Jenin, in existence since 1953, was a formidable IDF objective. It was defended by 150–250 well-entrenched Islamic Jihad, Hamas, al-Aqsa, and Tanzim fighters whose arsenal included a large number of mines and booby traps. Fortunately, most of the camp's 14,000 or so inhabitants had already fled. Rather than destroying Jenin with air strikes and artillery, in order to minimize civilian casualties the IDF chose to commit some 1,000 ground troops, although this increased the risk of Israeli casualties. Thirteen infantry reservists died in a single ambush on April 9. Thereafter, the IDF made more extensive use of armored bulldozers and helicopter fire to demolish houses from which attacks emanated. The tactic speeded completion of the assault but fed growing rumors of atrocities.

Early in the battle, Palestinian officials accused the IDF of massacring up to 3,000 civilians (later a figure of 500 became more common). Authoritative Western (mainly European) newspapers adopted the discourse, noting with outrage alleged monstrous crimes in a devastated camp that were comparable to the September 11 terrorist attacks on the United States and the genocides of Cambodia and Bosnia.

The Israeli government vehemently denied atrocity charges. International nongovernmental organizations agreed that there had been no massacre or mass executions. They concluded, however, that some IDF actions needlessly endangered civilians or caused loss of life through excessive or disproportionate use of force, thus constituting war crimes. They also noted that Palestinian forces had deliberately violated the laws of war by fighting amid the civilian population.

The generally accepted death toll in the fighting at Jenin during April 3–11 is 23 Israeli soldiers and 52–56 Palestinians, including perhaps 22 civilians. The fighting leveled an area of perhaps one and a half acres within a combat zone of six acres, or 6 percent of the camp.

The Israeli closure of the area during hostilities fueled the suspicions of journalists, who lacked experience in covering close combat, that something amiss was transpiring. Many were predisposed to believe Palestinian charges, recalling the Sabra and Shatila Massacre of Palestinians by Christian militia during the Israeli invasion of Lebanon in 1982. Because of the polarizing news coverage, subsequent literature on the battle remains largely partisan, and a definitive account is lacking. Among film treatments, Muhammad Bakri's *Jenin, Jenin* upholds the initial atrocity narrative, whereas Pierre Rehov's *The Road to Jenin* challenges it. Gil Mezuman's *Jenin Diary* documents the experiences of his IDF reserve unit.

Jenin proved to be an object lesson in the practical and moral dilemmas of modern urban warfare, when irregular troops take refuge among noncombatants, regular forces are tasked with dislodging them, and journalists have to cover the struggle. It was a military victory for Israel, a propaganda victory for the Palestinians, and an unqualified defeat for the press.

JAMES WALD

See also
al-Aqsa Martyrs Brigades; DEFENSIVE SHIELD, Operation; Expellees and Refugees, Palestinian; Fatah, al-; Hamas; Intifada, Second; Lebanon-Israeli War; Palestinian Islamic Jihad; Palestinian National Authority; Suicide Bombings; West Bank

References
Baroud, Ramzy, ed. *Searching Jenin: Eyewitness Accounts of the Israeli Invasion.* Seattle, WA: Cune, 2003.
Goldberg, Brett. *A Psalm in Jenin.* Tel Aviv: Modan, 2003.
Reporters without Borders, eds. *Israel/Palestine: The Black Book.* Sterling, VA: Pluto, 2003.

Jericho Conference (December 1, 1948)

Meeting of Palestinian Arab leaders convened on December 1, 1948, in Jericho on the West Bank to settle Arab land claims as a result of the 1948–1949 Israeli War of Independence. The government of Palestine ceded control of Arab Palestinian territories (the West Bank and East Jerusalem)—apart from Gaza—to the Hashemite Kingdom of Jordan at the Jericho Conference. This was an attempt to ensure Arab control over those territories not already lost to Israel in the fighting that followed the partition of Palestine by the United Nations (UN) on May 15, 1948. The common government of Palestine was formed in a meeting called by the High Arab Board and presided over by Ahmad Hilmi Pasha on September 30, 1948, following the perceived failure of the Arab forces in the war.

The failure of the Arab coalition to prevent the formation of the State of Israel in 1948 and the expansion of Israel's borders beyond those granted in the UN partition plan led to the dispersion of more than 1 million Palestinians who either fled of their own accord or were forced to flee by the Israelis throughout the Arab states. The upheaval threw both the Palestinian and Arab leadership into chaos. In an attempt to bring order, King Abdullah I of Jordan was authorized to represent and speak for the dispersed and displaced Palestinian people at an October 1, 1948, conference of refugee Palestinian leaders in Amman.

The Jericho Conference, also known as the Palestine Congress and the Jericho Congress, was a much larger conference of 2,000 to 3,000 prominent Palestinian Arabs primarily from west of the Jordan River. It was held on December 1, 1948, at the suggestion of King Abdullah and with the approval of British foreign secretary Ernest Bevin, who was concerned that Israel would take control of all of the territory partitioned to the Palestinians. Sheikh Muhammed Ali al-Ja'bari, the mayor of Hebron from 1948 to 1976, headed the conference. At the meeting, al-Ja'bari's proposal for the immediate annexation by Jordan of what remained of Arab Palestine land—roughly 80 percent—apart from Gaza was accepted. The Jericho Conference reconfirmed Abdullah as the official representative of the interests of the Palestinians until such time as the Palestinians could themselves regain and maintain control over the majority of the land of Arab Palestine. Abdullah was then crowned the king of Palestine, but his desire to have the West Bank, East Jerusalem, and the al-Aqsa environs named the Kingdom of Palestine never came to fruition.

Israel almost immediately recognized King Abdullah's leadership of Arab Palestine apart from Gaza. Yet the Jericho Conference was not met by universal acceptance in the Arab world. On December 10, 1948, King Farouk I of Egypt, who had favored the so-called All Palestine Government alternative, responded to the meeting's outcome by stigmatizing the Palestinians who had attended the Jericho Conference.

RICHARD M. EDWARDS

See also
Abdullah I; Farouk I, King of Egypt; Israeli War of Independence; Jordan; Palestine, British Mandate for; West Bank

References
Nowar, Ma'an A., and Maon Abeu Neuwear. *The History of the Hashemite Kingdom of Jordan: The Creation & Development of Transjordan.* Reading, UK: Ithaca Press, 1989.
Robbins, Philip. *A History of Jordan.* Cambridge: Cambridge University Press, 2004.
Salibi, Kamal S. *The Modern History of Jordan.* London: Tauris, 1998.

Jerusalem, Capture of (December 9, 1917)

Symbolic turning point in the Palestine Campaign. Jerusalem was not only an important administrative center, transportation hub, and headquarters of the German-Ottoman Yildirim (Thunderbolt) Army Group but was also a city of enormous symbolic value. When Lieutenant General Sir Edmund Allenby assumed command of the British forces in Palestine in June 1917, he pledged to be in Jerusalem by Christmas.

After the British broke through the Gaza-Beersheba Line in November 1917, General der Infanterie Erich von Falkenhayn's Yildirim Army Group retired to a new defensive line from just beyond Jaffa to Bethlehem. In late November the British XXI Corps wheeled right into the Judaean Hills, directly threatening Jerusalem. Between November 27 and December 3, General Mustafa Fevzi Pasha's Ottoman Seventh Army conducted a vigorous counteroffensive just west of the Holy City but failed to make much headway against the Allied forces.

Both sides were determined to avoid making Jerusalem a battlefield. Falkenhayn had no desire to waste forces to defend the city in an operation that had every chance of becoming a siege and trapping large numbers of his forces. Allenby was anxious to avoid damage to a location sacred to Jews, Christians, and Muslims alike. Consequently, the plans for the final British assault on the Ottoman Jerusalem position called for an encirclement operation: two divisions facing the Ottoman earthworks west of Jerusalem would wheel north, leaving the city to their right, while one division would advance northward from Hebron, passing east of Jerusalem.

Direction of the operation fell to Lieutenant General Philip Chetwode, commander of the British XX Corps. Early on December 8, without benefit of preliminary bombardment, its 60th and 74th Divisions advanced on the Ottoman positions west of Jerusalem on a 4.5-mile-wide front from Nabi Samwil to Ain Karim. By 7:00 a.m. the first Ottoman line had been captured, but then resistance stiffened.

Meanwhile, the advance of the southern flanking detachment led by Major General S. F. Mott and consisting of the 53rd Division and XX Corps cavalry had been delayed, as Mott was hesitant to engage Ottoman artillery around Bethlehem without express orders for fear of doing damage to the city, something he had been told to avoid at all costs. Only when explicitly ordered forward by Chetwode did Mott resume his advance in the afternoon. This lack of progress by the flanking column caused the 60th Division to halt for the remainder of the day. That pause gave the defenders a chance to escape, and that night the battered Ottoman XX Corps, consisting of the 26th and 53rd Divisions, withdrew from Jerusalem. In the late morning of December 9, British patrols found the Ottoman defensive works abandoned. Total casualties for the Yildirim Army Group from October through December 1917 were 25,337 killed, wounded, captured, or missing, a rate well in excess of 50 percent, as opposed to 18,000 total casualties for Allenby's forces, which moreover enjoyed a two-to-one superiority in men and far better artillery.

Allenby himself entered Jerusalem at noon on December 11, 1917, walking in through the Jaffa Gate in a well-considered gesture aimed at favorably setting him apart from the arrogance of German emperor Wilhelm II, who had entered the Holy City in 1898 on horseback by a gap made in the wall specifically for that occasion. The gesture by Allenby was part of a carefully prepared propaganda effort, capitalizing on the symbolic value of Jerusalem and aimed at catching the imagination of the world.

The Allied capture of Jerusalem was a great blow to Ottoman prestige in the region, while for the Allies it helped offset the bad news from Russia and Italy.

DIERK WALTER

See also
Allenby, Sir Edmund Henry Hynman; Palestine and Syria Campaign, World War I

References
Bruce, A. P. C. *The Last Crusade: The Palestine Campaign in the First World War.* London: Murray, 2002.
Erickson, Edward J. *Ordered to Die: A History of the Ottoman Army in the First World War.* Westport, CT: Greenwood, 2000.
Falls, Cyril. *Military Operations: Egypt and Palestine, from June 1917 to the End of the War.* London: HMSO, 1930.
Newell, Jonathan. "Allenby and the Palestine Campaign." In *The First World War and British Military History,* ed. Brian Bond, 189–226. Oxford, UK: Clarendon, 1991.
Wavell, Colonel A. P. *The Palestine Campaigns.* London: Constable, 1928.

Jerusalem, Crusader Siege of (June 7–July 15, 1099)

The siege of Jerusalem occurred during the First Crusade (1096–1099). Perhaps 60,000 crusaders had gathered at Nicaea (modern-day Iznik, Turkey) in June 1097, but there had been heavy losses in the fighting, and many crusaders had remained behind at the coast. There were thus probably only some 1,200–1,300 knights and 12,000 crusaders on foot when they reached Jerusalem. Jaffa (modern-day Tel Aviv–Yafo, Israel), the port for Jerusalem, had been largely demolished. In addition, a powerful Fatimid fleet was based at Ascalon (modern-day Tel Ashqelon, Israel), while Jerusalem itself was held by some 400 Fatimid cavalrymen, supported by a sizable garrison. The crusaders knew that they had to move quickly, for large Fatimid forces would soon gather at Ascalon.

On the approach of the crusaders, the Fatimid garrison expelled native Christians from Jerusalem and rendered the springs outside the walls unusable. Little wood was available in the vicinity for the construction of siege engines, and Muslim raiders from Ascalon harassed the army.

The crusaders arrived at Jerusalem on June 7, 1099. During the siege Duke Godfrey of Bouillon commanded some 13,000 men, including 1,300 knights. Fatimid governor of Jerusalem Emir Iftikhar ad-Dawla could count on as many as 20,000 men. The defenders had poisoned nearby wells and cisterns, and the heat was oppressive. The crusaders knew that they would have to work quickly. As early as June 12 they attempted an assault but, lacking sufficient scaling ladders and war machines, were easily repulsed. This material arrived on June 17 when six supply ships sailed into the port of Jaffa, which had been abandoned by the Egyptians. Within several weeks the crusaders had constructed a large number of mangonels and scaling ladders and two large wooden siege towers.

On the night of July 13–14, the crusaders braved defensive Muslim fire to push the towers against the city walls. On the morning of July 15, Duke Godfrey led attackers in one of the towers over a wooden drawbridge; other crusaders employed scaling ladders in a well-coordinated attack that ended with the crusaders inside the city.

Many of the Muslims sought refuge in the al-Aqsa Mosque; Tancred, one of the crusader leaders, promised that their lives would be spared and gave them his banner as proof. Once the Christian forces had taken the city, however, they embarked on an orgy of destruction, slaughtering all Muslims who could be found regardless of location, including those within the al-Aqsa Mosque. The victims included women and children. Some Muslims were beheaded, others were slain with arrows or forced to jump from the towers, and still others were tortured or burned to death. Atrocities of this kind were part and parcel of medieval warfare when a city had refused to surrender, but what happened at Jerusalem was certainly excessive. Estimates of the number slain reach as high as 70,000 people.

Jews fared no better; the Christians herded them into a synagogue and burned them alive. Their bloodlust at last spent, the victors proceeded to the Church of the Holy Sepulchre, the grotto of which they believed had once held the body of the crucified Christ, and there gave thanks to the God of Mercies for their victory.

On August 2, 1099, in the Battle of Ascalon (Askelon), Duke Godfrey led 10,000 crusaders against a relief force of 50,000 Egyptians under Emir al-Afdal. Unlike the Seljuk Turks, who relied primarily on mounted archers, the Egyptian Fatimids counted on fanaticism and shock action. They were thus at great disadvantage against the heavily armored and well-armed crusaders. A cavalry charge gave the Christians an overwhelming victory. The

Latin Kingdom of Jerusalem lasted only 50 years, however, from 1099 to 1148.

SPENCER C. TUCKER

See also
Ascalon, Battle of; Crusades in the Holy Land, Christian; Godfrey of Bouillon

References
Asbridge, Thomas. *The First Crusade: A New History.* New York: Oxford University Press, 2005.
Baldwin, Marshall W., ed. *A History of the Crusades,* Vol. 1, *The First Hundred Years,* ed. Kenneth M. Setton. Madison: University of Wisconsin Press, 1969.
Tyerman, Christopher. *Fighting for Christendom: Holy War and the Crusades.* New York: Oxford University Press, 2005.

Jerusalem, Latin Kingdom of

The Latin Kingdom of Jerusalem was the largest of the Frankish principalities or states in the Near East established by the First Crusade (1096–1099). It took its name from its capital city of Jerusalem. The kingdom was ruled and dominated by a minority of Christian settlers who originated in Western Europe; they belonged to the Latin (Roman) Church, in contrast to the majority of the subject population, and were known to contemporaries as Franks or Latins (hence the name "Latin kingdom").

At its widest extent, attained by the third quarter of the 12th century, the kingdom occupied most of historical Palestine. In the north it bordered on the county of Tripoli a few miles north of Beirut; in the south, Frankish rule extended as far as the port of Aila on the Gulf of Aqaba. The kingdom thus covered an area corresponding to all of modern Israel, the West Bank, and the Gaza Strip, together with some adjacent parts of modern Jordan, Syria, and Lebanon.

In 1187 Muslim leader Saladin defeated the kingdom's army at the Battle of Hattin and proceeded to reduce its territory to a coastal enclave around the city of Tyre (modern-day Soûr, Lebanon). The military assistance brought to Outremer by the Third Crusade (1189–1192) recovered most of the Palestinian coast, and some parts of the interior were also subsequently recovered. However, in the later 13th century this reduced kingdom, with its capital at Acre (modern-day Akko, Israel), was gradually worn down by the Mamluk Sultanate of Egypt and Syria, which finally captured its last surviving stronghold in 1291.

On July 15, 1099, the army of the First Crusade captured the city of Jerusalem from the Fatimid dynasty of Egypt, which had managed to seize it the previous year from its Seljuk governor. The crusaders had already captured the port of Jaffa (modern-day Tel Aviv–Yafo, Israel); the nearby town of Lydda (modern-day Lod, Israel), and Bethlehem.

The crusade leaders seem to have accepted that Palestine formed a kingdom, although there was no agreement about its precise form of government or its future ruler. Some crusaders regarded this kingdom as belonging to Christ and thought it would be sacrilegious to appoint a king to rule it, but on July 17 it was decided to proceed with the election of a secular ruler, to be chosen by the leading men of the army. Raymond of Saint-Gilles, count of Toulouse, clearly hoped to be made ruler, having previously been thwarted in his designs to establish a principality in northern Syria. However, Raymond had antagonized large sections of the army, and on July 22 the leaders elected Godfrey of Bouillon, duke of Lower Lotharingia. Godfrey took the titles of prince and defender of the Holy Sepulchre, thus sidestepping objections to a royal title in the city of Christ. On August 1 Arnulf of Chocques was elected as Latin patriarch.

On August 12, the nascent Latin principality survived its first major threat when the crusaders defeated a major Fatimid invasion near Ascalon (modern-day Tel Ashqelon, Israel). However, the subsequent departure of the majority of the crusaders to return to their homes exposed the weakness of the Franks of Palestine. Godfrey had only some 300 knights and 2,000 foot soldiers available to control Jerusalem and southern Judaea, including Bethlehem and Hebron, and a coastal strip around Jaffa, Lydda, and Ramla. Jaffa, the only Christian-held port, did not have a good deepwater harbor, while the Muslims still controlled the rest of the coast, including the major ports of Acre and Tyre, as well as Beirut, Sidon (modern-day Saïda, Lebanon), Haifa (modern-day Hefa, Israel), Caesarea (modern-day Har Qesari, Israel), Arsuf (near modern-day Herzliyya, Israel), and Ascalon. Communication between Godfrey's two blocs of territory was tenuous and could easily be disrupted by Fatimid forces operating from their base at Ascalon. A third bloc of Christian-held territory was found in Galilee, where the crusader Tancred and his predominantly Norman followers clearly intended to found an independent principality and were not necessarily disposed to defer to Godfrey of Bouillon.

If Frankish rule in the Holy Land was to survive, it would be essential to control all of Palestine and above all to capture the major ports necessary to secure communications with the West. The requisite naval assistance arrived in a fleet under the command of Daibert, archbishop of Pisa. As the price of this support, Godfrey was obliged to accept Daibert as patriarch of Jerusalem in place of Arnulf of Chocques. Daibert received a quarter of the city of Jerusalem as a patriarchal lordship, but he soon began to make further territorial claims, producing a breach with Godfrey, who died unexpectedly of illness on July 18, 1100. Fearing the ambitions of Daibert and Tancred, the knights of Godfrey's household, led by the Lotharingian nobleman Warner of Grez, seized the citadel of Jerusalem. Determined that the rulership of Palestine should be subject to hereditary succession, they summoned Godfrey's younger brother, Count Baldwin I of Edessa, to take up his inheritance. Daibert was then forced to agree to crown Baldwin king in order to retain the patriarchate.

The coronation of King Baldwin I (r. 1100–1118) occurred in the Church of the Nativity in Bethlehem on Christmas Day 1100. His assumption of the royal title was a clear signal that he was determined to tolerate no ambiguities as to the limits of his power. He was able to have Daibert deposed in 1102, and thereafter Baldwin was able to appoint candidates of his own choice. He was also able to force Tancred to accept that Galilee was part of the kingdom.

Baldwin I was determined to extend Frankish control over all of Palestine. He defeated Fatimid invasions in 1101, 1102, and 1105. He also secured naval support by agreements with Genoa and Venice, necessarily conceding to them property, trading privileges, and ultimately autonomous quarters in various cities of the kingdom, which nonetheless give the republics a stake in the kingdom's survival. Genoese and Venetian (and later Pisan) fleets were also important in bringing large numbers of Christian pilgrims, keen to visit the newly liberated holy places, who could also be enlisted during their stays to fight alongside the king's meager forces. With the help of these external forces, Baldwin I was able to capture the ports of Arsuf and Caesarea (1101), Acre (1104), and Beirut and Sidon (1110). By the end of the reign, only Tyre and Ascalon remained in Muslim hands. Baldwin had also begun to penetrate the region south and east of the Dead Sea, and he mounted an invasion of Egypt in the course of which he died (1118).

The childless Baldwin I had designated his surviving elder brother, Count Eustace III of Boulogne, as his successor. However, Eustace's partisans among the magnates were outmaneuvered by a more powerful group, which chose the late king's distant cousin Baldwin (II) of Bourcq, then count of Edessa. The reign of Baldwin II (1118–1131) saw the defeat of the Franks of Antioch by the Turks of northern Syria in the Battle of Ager Sanguinis (June 28, 1119), which meant that Baldwin had to spend most of the next four years in the north, acting as regent of Antioch and defending the Frankish territories. Captured by the Turks in 1123, he remained a captive for more than a year. During his captivity an unsuccessful attempt was made to depose him. More importantly, the barons and prelates concluded an alliance with the Venetians that defeated a Fatimid invasion and captured the port of Tyre (1124).

The kingdom was now secure from major Muslim invasions until the 1160s. In 1126 Baldwin II invaded the Hauran, east of Lake Tiberias, and in 1129 he enlisted crusaders from the West to mount an unsuccessful attack on Damascus itself. Baldwin II also established military religious orders, which came about through establishment of the Order of the Templars and the militarization of the existing charitable Order of the Hospital. They would play an increasingly important part in defense of the kingdom.

The succession to Baldwin II was secured through the marriage of his eldest daughter, Melisende, to Fulk V, count of Anjou. The joint reigns of Melisende (1131–1162) and Fulk (1131–1143) were disrupted by a revolt in 1133–1134 staged by Melisende's kinsman Hugh of Jaffa, who feared that Fulk intended to set aside arrangements that vested joint rule in the royal couple and their young son Baldwin III. Although the revolt was put down, Fulk was forced to abide by the existing constitutional settlement. The king was also obliged to devote considerable time to affairs in the north, where he exercised the regency of Antioch (1131–1136). However, Fulk put considerable efforts into improving the security of his own kingdom by constructing castles around Fatimid-held Ascalon in Galilee and also in Transjordan. On Fulk's death, sole rule passed to Melisende, as Baldwin III was still a minor.

By this time a new Muslim leader had arisen to fill the power vacuum in northern Syria: Imad al-Din Zangi, ruler of Mosul and Aleppo. In 1144 Zangi captured the Christian city of Edessa (modern-day Sanliurfa, Turkey). After Zangi was murdered in 1146, his lands were divided between his two sons. The elder son, Saif al-Din Gazi, succeeded him in Mosul; the younger, Nur al-Din, took over Aleppo and concentrated on expanding his power in Syria. Since 1139 the Franks of Jerusalem had maintained an alliance with Damascus, which was the most important Muslim state in the Near East still independent of Zangi and his successors.

The Second Crusade (1147–1149) was launched in response to the victories of Zangi and Nur al-Din, but only much-reduced Western forces reached Outremer following their difficult passage through Anatolia. Neither King Conrad III of Germany nor Louis VII could be persuaded to attack Aleppo, as urged by Prince Raymond of Antioch. In June 1148 Baldwin III (r. 1143–1163), Queen Melisende, the magnates of the kingdom, and the crusade leaders decided on an attempt to capture Damascus. As a strategic decision, this was by no means as senseless as scholars once believed. The regime of Unur, *atabeg* of Damascus, was increasingly unstable, and in 1147 he had concluded an alliance with Nur al-Din. A combined Frankish-crusader attack may well have been the last opportunity to secure Damascus and parts of its territory before it passed under Nur al-Din. However, in the event, the campaign was executed incompetently and the siege failed; in 1154 the people of Damascus expelled their ruler and welcomed Nur al-Din as lord of the city.

In the years following the Second Crusade, young King Baldwin III became increasingly impatient at having to share power with his mother. In a short civil war in 1152, he succeeded in excluding his mother from government. The following year Baldwin besieged and captured Ascalon, the last Muslim-held city in Palestine. In 1158 he married Theodora, a niece of Byzantine emperor Manuel I Komnenos. Relations between Byzantium and the kingdom were generally cordial during this period.

The childless Baldwin III was succeeded by his younger brother Amalric (r. 1163–1174), who was obliged to divorce his wife, Agnes of Courtenay, as their marriage was regarded as bigamous by the Latin Church and leading magnates. As king, Amalric concentrated on attempts to invade and conquer Egypt. The increasing instability of the unpopular Shiite Fatimid caliphate, in contrast to the majority Sunni population, meant that a Frankish intervention was becoming increasingly necessary to prevent Egypt from falling under the control of Nur al-Din. Amalric mounted invasions of Egypt in 1163, 1164, and 1167, forcing Egyptian vizier Shawar to abandon his alliance with Nur al-Din and pay considerable tribute to Amalric.

Still hoping to control Egypt, Amalric concluded a treaty with Byzantine emperor Manuel I Komnenos, whose niece Maria he married in 1168. At the end of that year Amalric launched another major invasion of Egypt but without coordinating it with the Byzantine Navy. Nur al-Din sent an army under his general Shirkuh, who seized control in Egypt. Shirkuh was succeeded as vizier of Egypt by his nephew Saladin, who repulsed a final invasion led by Amalric in 1169. Saladin dissolved the Egyptian Army and abolished the Fatimid caliphate.

On Nur al-Din's death in 1174, Saladin, already de facto ruler of Egypt, seized Damascus, Homs, and Hama from Nur al-Din's heirs. Amalric died later that same year, his inheritance now surrounded by territories controlled by Saladin.

The reigns of Amalric's son Baldwin IV (r. 1174–1185) and his heirs were characterized by the increasing threat posed by Saladin, who was determined to liberate Jerusalem for Islam and recover Palestine from the Franks. His forces invaded the kingdom in 1177, 1179, 1182, 1183, 1184, and 1187. Invasions were interspersed with periods of truce, during which Saladin attempted to extend his control over Muslim Syria, seizing Aleppo and its territory in 1183. Individual crusaders and their retinues came to the Holy Land during this time, but there was no major crusading effort from the West on the scale of the Second Crusade, despite appeals from the Kingdom of Jerusalem.

Baldwin IV suffered from leprosy and could not be expected to marry and produce an heir. A regent was thus required to rule when Baldwin was incapacitated by illness. A suitable husband also had to be found for his next heir, his sister Sibyl. Repeated disputes concerning these two issues added to political rivalries, greatly hampering efforts to resist Saladin.

Baldwin IV died in 1185. His successor, Baldwin V (r. 1185–1186), the son of Sibyl and her first husband, William Longsword, had been crowned as coruler during the reign of his predecessor. As Baldwin was a minor, the regency had been entrusted to Count Raymond III of Tripoli, who was opposed by a significant party around Sibyl and her second husband, Guy of Lusignan. This faction seized power when Baldwin V died, and Sibyl and Guy were crowned rulers. The kingdom was thus politically divided when Saladin led a great invasion into Galilee. Against the advice of Raymond of Tripoli and others, King Guy gave battle at a site known as the Horns of Hattin, where the Franks of Jerusalem suffered their greatest military defeat (July 3–4, 1187). Guy himself was taken prisoner, while most of the kingdom's leaders and fighters were killed or captured. In the aftermath of the battle Saladin's troops were able to overrun the entire kingdom, with the exception of the port of Tyre.

The crusader defeat at Hattin, and above all the surrender of Jerusalem in October 1187, sent shock waves around the West, and Pope Gregory VIII proclaimed a new crusade. Some military and naval assistance reached Outremer quickly, but it was a considerable time before major armies arrived in the course of the Third Crusade (1189–1192). A land army from Germany under Holy Roman emperor Frederick I Barbarossa broke up after his death in Cilicia (1190). However, seaborne expeditions led by King Richard I (the Lionheart) of England and King Philippe II Augustus of

France succeeded in recovering most of the coast from Tyre to Ascalon, although it proved impossible to retake Jerusalem itself. The kingdom's capital was now the port city of Acre. Additional territory to the north of Tyre was later secured by the German crusade sent by Barbarossa's son, Emperor Henry VI during 1197–1198.

The Christian recovery was hampered by disputes over the throne of Jerusalem. Guy of Lusignan (released from captivity in 1188) was supported by Richard of England, whereas Philippe and others favored Conrad of Montferrat, an Italian nobleman who had won distinction while leading the defense of Tyre. The death of Sibyl and her daughters left Guy without any legitimate rights to the throne. A compromise in 1192 awarded the throne to Conrad (I), who was married to Sibyl's younger sister and heir, Isabella I. Guy was compensated with Cyprus, which Richard had conquered before arriving in Outremer. Conrad was assassinated before he could be crowned, and so the kingdom passed, along with the hand of Queen Isabella, first to Henry of Champagne (r. 1192–1197) and then to Aimery of Lusignan, king of Cyprus (r. 1198–1205).

From the death of Saladin in 1193 until 1260, the Muslim powers that surrounded the kingdom were divided. Damascus, Aleppo, Kerak, and Egypt were ruled by different members of Saladin's family (the Ayyubids), who were constantly at war with each other, a circumstance the Franks were able to exploit. In 1250 there was a change of government in Egypt when Turkish Mamluks (slave-soldiers) seized power and established a regime known as the Mamluk Sultanate. Yet as Aleppo and Damascus were still ruled by the Ayyubids, the Franks could still play the rival powers. So, between 1193 and 1260 there were repeated truces, alternating with crusading expeditions seeking to recover new territory.

Richard the Lionheart had planned to attack Egypt in 1192 but was unable to persuade the whole crusade army to accompany him. Nevertheless, many of the later crusades saw Egypt as the key to the Holy Land, believing that if Egypt could be conquered, then the Holy Land would be secure; even if Egypt proved impossible to hold permanently, a strike against the major center of Muslim power might be sufficient to force the Ayyubids and later the Mamluks to surrender sufficient territory in Palestine to enable the Franks to hold a restored Kingdom of Jerusalem (including Jerusalem itself) with defensible frontiers. This is why Egypt was chosen as the original goal of the Fourth Crusade (1202–1204), although it was eventually diverted to Constantinople (modern-day Istanbul, Turkey). The Fifth Crusade (1218–1221) was initially successful in capturing the Egyptian port of Damietta, but its chances of success were destroyed by quarrels between the papal legate and the secular princes.

The lack of a strong central authority in the kingdom, which was already apparent after 1174, became even more serious during the 13th century. Up to 1268 several of the monarchs were either underaged (Maria la Marquise and Isabella II) or absentees (Conrad II and Conradin), requiring regents to govern for them. There were frequent disputes about the choice of regent as well as resistance to the policies of both regents and monarchs. Effective power passed to a number of different groups and institutions that struggled to defend their interests and to control the kingdom. There were also the military orders—the Templars, Hospitallers, and Teutonic Knights—that now had much greater political weight than in the period before Hattin. They acquired large areas of land and castles, which they often bought from impecunious nobles. They also sometimes followed opposing policies and became embroiled in factional disputes rather than fighting the Muslims. Third, there were the communities from the Italian trading cities of Genoa, Venice, and Pisa, which had their own quarters in the major ports, such as Acre and Tyre, where they enjoyed considerable autonomy. Rivals in Europe, they also brought their disputes and wars to the Holy Land. Fourth, there were burgess confraternities, groups of freemen who formed associations to defend local rights. Finally, various monarchs and other powerful figures who arrived from the West on crusade expeditions often overruled or ignored local institutions.

In 1228 Frederick II, the Holy Roman emperor and king of Sicily, came to the East, having previously married the heiress to the throne, Isabella II, granddaughter of Isabella I. Frederick recovered the city of Jerusalem as part of a 10-year truce concluded with al-Kamil, Ayyubid sultan of Egypt, rather than by fighting. As Jerusalem technically belonged to Damascus, not to Egypt, and as the Franks were not allowed to fortify the city, many considered this truce as being more for Frederick's interests than theirs. It seemed that Frederick was more interested in making a treaty to protect the commercial interests of his kingdom of Sicily than in protecting Outremer. Supported by the Teutonic Knights, the Genoese, and Pisans, Frederick staged a crowning ceremony in the Church of the Holy Sepulchre. However, he was opposed by the secular church, the other military orders, and the majority of the nobility. As Isabella II had died in 1228, this party refused to recognize Frederick's rights to the throne, accepting only that he was regent for his infant son Conrad II (IV of Germany).

Frederick's return to the West in 1229 was followed by an intermittent civil war between his supporters and mercenaries (known as Lombards) and the majority of the Franks, led by the powerful Ibelin family. More crusaders from the West arrived in 1239–1240, led by Thibaud IV of Champagne and Richard of Cornwall, to coincide with the expiry of Frederick II's truce. They refortified Ascalon and gained territory in Galilee. However, in 1244 the city of Jerusalem was captured by the Khwarazmians, nomadic mercenaries in the service of Ayyubid Egypt, and on October 17 that same year the Egyptians destroyed a Frankish army in the Battle of La Forbie near Gaza. Most of the recent territorial gains were lost again soon after. The kingdom's territory now consisted of the area between Beirut and Caesarea from the coast to the line of the Jordan, with a much narrower coastal strip extending south as far as Jaffa.

The marriage of Frederick II to Isabella II brought the Staufen dynasty to the throne. Yet neither of their two successors, Conrad II (r. 1228–1254) or his son Conrad III, better known as Conradin (r. 1254–1268), ever visited their kingdom. Government was by a series of regents. The death of Conrad III without heirs saw the succession pass to King Hugh III of Cyprus (Hugh I of Jerusalem), who was descended from Isabella I and her third husband, Henry of Champagne. Hugh I (r. 1268–1284) was succeeded, in turn, by his son Henry II (r. 1285–1324), who was to be the last reigning king of Jerusalem.

To the mid-13th century the Franks were still in a relatively strong position, and the kingdom was still rich from the trade that passed through its ports. But from that time the economy began to decline. From 1256 trade with the West was disrupted by wars between the Italian merchant cities of Genoa, Venice, and Pisa and by the conquests of the Mongols in Central Asia. Advancing into the Middle East, the Mongols captured Aleppo and Damascus in 1260. The leaders of the Kingdom of Jerusalem decided to remain neutral, assisting neither the Mongols nor the Mamluks of Egypt. However, on September 3, 1260, Mamluk sultan Qutuz defeated the Mongols in the Battle of Ayn Jalut in Galilee.

This decisive Mamluk victory saved the Kingdom of Jerusalem and Egypt from the Mongols, but it also enabled the Mamluks to take over Aleppo and Damascus, which had previously opposed them. The kingdom was again surrounded, and during the next three decades the Mamluk generals captured fortress after fortress and city after city until the kingdom was reduced to a few fortified cities along the coastline. Repeated Mamluk campaigns and their scorched-earth tactics in Palestine destroyed the agriculture and infrastructure of the kingdom so that the Franks could not regroup and recover. Unlike Saladin, who used to allow the Christian defenders of a castle or town to go in peace if they surrendered, the Mamluks routinely slew the defenders of the castles and towns they captured. Saladin's policy had been intended to encourage quick surrenders. The Mamluks relied on their superior siege machinery to capture fortresses quickly and aimed at destroying their enemy completely.

In May 1291 the last Frankish-held stronghold, the city of Acre, fell to the forces of Mamluk sultan Khalil. Some inhabitants managed to escape by sea to Cyprus, but the rest were either killed or taken prisoner. Many plans were drawn up to recover the Holy Land, but these all came to nothing. The Lusignan kings of Cyprus continued to call themselves "king of Jerusalem" after 1291, though the title was also claimed by the kings of Naples and Sicily and by the kings of Aragon. The ecclesiastical institutions of the kingdom, such as the patriarch of Jerusalem, also continued in name.

ALAN V. MURRAY AND HELEN J. NICHOLSON

See also

Ager Sanguinis, Battle of; Amalric of Jerusalem; Ayn Jalut, Battle of; Ayyubid Dynasty; Baldwin I of Jerusalem; Baldwin II of Jerusalem; Baldwin III of Jerusalem; Baldwin IV of Jerusalem; Conrad III, King of Germany; Crusades in the Holy Land, Christian; Fatimid Dynasty; Frederick I or Frederick Barbarossa; Frederick II, Holy Roman Emperor; Godfrey of Bouillon; Guy of Lusignan; Hattin, Battle of; Henry VI of Germany; Louis VII, King of France; Mamluk Sultanate; Manuel I Komnenos, Emperor; Nur al-Din; Philippe II, King; Richard I, King; Saladin; Zangi, Imad ad-Din

References

Boas, Adrian. *Jerusalem in the Time of the Crusades: Society, Landscape and Art in the Holy City under Frankish Rule.* London: Routledge, 2001.

Edbury, Peter W. *Crusader Institutions.* Oxford, UK: Clarendon, 1980.

Edbury, Peter W. *The Latin Kingdom of Jerusalem: European Colonialism in the Middle Ages.* London: Weidenfeld & Nicolson, 1972.

Hamilton, Bernard. *The Leper King and His Heirs: Baldwin IV and the Crusader Kingdom of Jerusalem.* Cambridge: Cambridge University Press, 2000.

Murray, Alan V. *The Crusader Kingdom of Jerusalem: A Dynastic History, 1099–1125.* Oxford: Prosopographica & Genealogica, 2000.

Phillips, Jonathan. *Defenders of the Holy Land: Relations between the Latin East and the West, 1119–1187.* Oxford, UK: Clarendon, 1996.

Richard, Jean. *The Latin Kingdom of Jerusalem.* 2 vols. Amsterdam: North-Holland, 1979.

Riley-Smith, Jonathan. *The Feudal Nobility and the Kingdom of Jerusalem, 1174–1277.* London: Macmillan, 1972.

Tibble, Steven. *Monarchy and Lordships in the Latin Kingdom of Jerusalem, 1099–1291.* Oxford, UK: Clarendon, 1989.

Jerusalem, Roman Siege of (70 CE)

The siege of the city of Jerusalem began in the spring of 70 CE and ended that September, effectively ending the First Jewish-Roman War of 66–73 CE. Following his victory in the War of Four emperors in 69, Vespasian ordered his son Titus, Roman commander in Judaea, to take Jerusalem, providing the Flavian dynasty with the victory against foreign enemies needed for legitimacy. Jerusalem was held by three competing factions led by Eleazar Ben Simon, John of Gischala, and Simon bar Giora.

Titus surrounded Jerusalem with four legions in the spring of 70. The defenders of the city were divided among the three factions, which were sometimes able to cooperate against the Romans. Food was a major problem for the defenders, however. By the beginning of the summer, the Romans had breached the third and second city walls. The Romans then turned to take the Antonia Fortress that overlooked the Jerusalem Temple and the Temple Mount. In surprise sallies, however, the Jews were able to hinder the Romans and destroy their siege equipment. Tightened security and a wooden wall placed around Jerusalem stopped these assaults.

By summer, the Jews were running very low on food. By August, the Romans had captured the Antonia Fortress and broken into the Temple, burning it down on the ninth day of Av, the Jewish day of mourning for the destruction of the First Temple. From there, the Romans moved into the rest of the city. In a month of fighting they secured it in September, destroying all resistance.

The Romans either killed or enslaved most of the surviving inhabitants of Jerusalem. Titus returned to Rome in 71 for a triumph, bringing with him large numbers of slaves and considerable treasure.

NATHAN SCHUMER

See also
Jewish-Roman War, First

References
Furneaux, Rupert. *The Roman Siege of Jerusalem.* New York: D. Mackay, 1972.

Price, Jonathan J. *Jerusalem under Siege: The Collapse of the Jewish State, 66–70 CE.* Leiden: Brill, 1992.

Jewish Brigade

Jewish unit within the British Army during World War II. With the beginning of World War II in September 1939, Chaim Weizmann, head of the World Zionist Organization (WZO), offered the British government the full support of the Jewish community in Palestine and requested the right to form a Jewish military unit that would fight under a Jewish flag within the British Army. The government of Prime Minister Neville Chamberlain rejected the request. Many individual Jews joined the British forces, however, and a number fought in Greece in 1941.

In May 1940 the Chamberlain government fell and was replaced by one headed by Winston Churchill. The new prime minister did not share Chamberlain's misgivings about a Jewish military unit, if only because such a formation would release some British troops for service elsewhere. Churchill broached the matter with U.S. president Franklin Roosevelt, who said that he had no objection. On September 6, 1940, during the height of the Battle of Britain, Churchill arranged a meeting with Weizmann and assured him of his full support for a Jewish military unit.

Churchill requested that a memorandum be drafted. It had three main points. First, it called for the recruitment of the largest possible number of Jews in Palestine, who would then be formed into battalions or larger formations. Second, it noted that the Colonial Office had insisted that equal numbers of Arabs and Jews be recruited, but because it was most likely that the number of Jews would be significantly higher than Arabs, any excess beyond an equal number must be trained in Egypt or some other Middle Eastern location. Third, officer cadres sufficient to staff a Jewish division were to be immediately selected in Palestine and trained in Egypt.

Within a week, Foreign Secretary Anthony Eden informed Weizmann of the approval of the draft memorandum and that plans were under way to form a Jewish army along the lines of the Czechoslovak and Polish forces in exile. The British initially planned for a force of about 10,000 men, 4,000 of whom were to come from Palestine. The force would be trained in Britain and then shipped back to the Middle East. Weizmann was ecstatic at the prospects, and in February 1941 he was introduced to Major General Leonard A. Hawes, designated as the new unit's commander. At this point, however, Colonial Secretary Lord Lloyd suddenly died. His replacement, Lord Moyne, strongly opposed the plans, pointing out to Churchill that the delicate political balance in the Middle East might be upset by such a step and also stressing supply shortages and logistical shortcomings. Churchill reluctantly concurred and informed Weizmann that the matter was being deferred for six months because of "supply problems." At the end of the period, however, Moyne continued to delay.

In the meantime, smaller Palestinian units were created consisting entirely of Jews and with Jewish officers. The British conceived of this procedure as one to produce mixed Arab-Jewish companies of so-called Pioneers who would serve as truck drivers, maintenance personnel, and the like. But because few Arabs signed up, the parity rule soon disappeared. In early 1940, some 500 Palestinian Jews were involved in maintenance work with the British Army in France. The defeat of France in July brought their temporary return to Palestine. They then became ground personnel with the Royal Air Force in North Africa. When Italy entered the war, another 400 Palestinian Jews were allowed to enlist to fill air force crew openings, and some were accepted for pilot training.

By early 1942, some 11,000 Jews were serving with the British forces in the Middle East. While their units were nominally of mixed Arab-Jewish composition, in reality they were almost all Jewish. The Zionists demanded that the scattered companies be organized into battalions. London gave way, and on August 6, 1942, some 18,000 Palestinian Jews were incorporated into purely Jewish battalions. By then, fully a quarter of them were in frontline assignments. Palestinian Jews distinguished themselves in fighting alongside the Free French in the Battle of Bir Hacheim (May 26–June 11, 1942). Only some 45 of 1,000 who fought in that battle survived.

Following the Allied invasion of Italy and with the widespread revelations of the Holocaust, Churchill revived the matter of creating a Jewish army. It was an easier sell to the Arabs that Jewish forces would be fighting in Europe and not stationed in the Middle East. On July 12, 1944, Churchill drafted a memorandum calling for the establishment of a Jewish army group. In subsequent weeks, plans were coordinated with the Jewish Agency.

In October 1944 British brigadier Ernest Benjamin took command of the Jewish Brigade, which had its own colors. The unit's shoulder patch consisted of a Star of David on a background of one white vertical stripe between two blue vertical stripes. In February 1945, 3,400 members of the Jewish Brigade arrived in Italy to join the British Eighth Army fighting there.

The Jewish Brigade was in many respects a triumph for Zionist diplomacy during the war. The officers and the noncommissioned officers of the brigade were able for the first time to learn larger-unit tactics and organization. The lessons learned would stand them, Haganah, and Israel in good stead during the Israeli War of Independence (1948–1949).

Spencer C. Tucker

See also
Haganah; Holocaust; Israeli War of Independence

References
Laqueur, Walter. *A History of Zionism: From the French Revolution to the Establishment of the State of Israel.* Reprint ed. New York: Schocken, 2003.
Reinharz, Jehuda. *Chaim Weizmann: The Making of a Statesman.* New York: Oxford University Press, 1993.
Sachar, Howard M. *A History of Israel: From the Rise of Zionism to Our Time.* 3rd ed. New York: Knopf, 2007.
Weizmann, Chaim. *Trial and Error: The Autobiography of Chaim Weizmann.* New York: Harper, 1949.

Jewish Legion

Formation of Jewish volunteers, also known as the Jewish Battalions, raised by the British and who fought in World War I. Expelled by the Ottoman Empire following its entrance into the war on the side of the Central Powers, Palestinian Jews who retained citizenship with Entente countries gathered in Egypt in December 1914. Many of them, led by Vladimir Jabotinsky and Joseph Trumpeldor, petitioned to join the British Army. London initially rejected their offer but later formed the 650-man Zion Mule Corps under Colonel John H. Patterson, with Trumpeldor as his second-in-command. The Mule Corps served with distinction in the Gallipoli Campaign of 1915, carrying supplies to the front lines until disbanded at the campaign's conclusion.

Jabotinsky and others continued to lobby for the creation of Jewish combat units, believing that these would further the Zionist cause. In August 1917 shortly after issuance of the Balfour Declaration, British prime minister David Lloyd George and Foreign Secretary Arthur Balfour approved the formation of a Jewish regiment. Patterson, assisted by Jabotinksy, who became his aide-de-camp, recruited a battalion from Jewish refugees and Mule Corps veterans. This battalion, the 38th Royal Fusiliers (City of London Regiment), completed training in February 1918 and arrived in Alexandria, Egypt, in March. In April Britain formed the 39th Battalion, primarily from U.S. and Canadian Jewish volunteers, and in June recruited the 40th Battalion from Jews who had remained in Palestine. Grouped together and attached to the Australian and New Zealand Mounted Division, the Jewish battalions forced a crossing of the Jordan River, paving the way for Lieutenant General Sir Edmund Allenby's successful autumn offensive and the capture of Damascus.

Britain also formed the 41st and 42nd Reserve Battalions from Jewish volunteers. These remained in Britain and supplied replacements for the three combat battalions. In all, some 6,500 Jews served in these five battalions, including David Ben-Gurion, Israel's future first prime minister. Most of these veterans settled in Palestine after the war.

STEPHEN K. STEIN

See also
Allenby, Sir Edmund Henry Hynman; Balfour Declaration; Ben-Gurion, David; Jabotinsky, Vladimir Yevgenyevich; Zionism

References
Jabotinsky, Vladimir. *The Story of the Jewish Legion.* New York: Bernard Akerman, 1945.

Patterson, John Henry. *With the Judeans in the Palestine Campaign.* New York: Macmillan, 1922.

Patterson, John Henry. *With the Zionists in Gallipoli.* New York: George H. Doran, 1916.

Sachar, Howard M. *A History of Israel: From the Rise of Zionism to Our Time.* 3rd ed. New York: Knopf, 2007.

Jewish-Roman War, First (66–73 CE)

The First Jewish-Roman War occurred between 66 and 73 CE in Roman Judaea. Though nominally under Roman rule from 63 BCE, Judaea was integrated into the empire under the rule of the client monarch Herod the Great. Herod had allied with Marcus Antonius and Octavian and was declared king of the Jews in 40/39 BCE. Herod conquered Judaea in 37 BCE, repressed dissent, and established a kingdom that lasted in various manifestations to the early second century CE. Herod's son Archelaus was deposed in 6 CE and a Roman governor put in place. He was at first called the prefect of the Jews, later procurator.

The Roman governor had a small military force at his disposal: five cohorts of infantry and one of cavalry recruited from Greek cities in the province. The governor was based in the capital city of Caesarea and was responsible for taxation, building projects, and maintaining order. He inherited the machinery of government from the Herodian state and coexisted with the Jewish Herodian kings, who had managerial power over the Temple in Jerusalem. The Roman governor of Syria, however, had authority over the local Roman governor and the Herodian client-king.

The province of Judaea was managed on a day-to-day level through the Jewish priestly elites of Jerusalem. The high priest managed the Temple; he was appointed at first by the governor but eventually by the Herodian king. Following Herod's renovation of the Temple and creation of larger ports, Jerusalem had been enriched by a pilgrimage economy. This benefited the Jewish elites, making Temple service quite lucrative and bringing competition for positions in the Temple. These overlapping areas of jurisdiction had much to do with the revolt's outbreak.

Economic anxieties may also have been an important cause of the rebellion. Archaeological evidence suggests that the population increased in this period, as did the urbanization of Palestine. Increased population pressure strained the system. Cities were home to urban elites who owned estates in the countryside and acquired the lands of traditional farmers.

The cultural clash between Rome and Jerusalem was also an important cause of the rebellion. Jewish culture was focused on the Temple and allegiance to an aniconic, singular, exclusive God. Still, it is difficult to convey how bizarre Judaism was to the rest of the ancient world. Romans regularly ridiculed the Jews, joining their contempt to a longstanding Greek tradition of anti-Judaism. Jews, because of their monotheistic religion, were unable to take part in the traditional governing systems of the Roman world. They could not acknowledge the divinity of the emperor, nor could they display loyalty to the symbols of Rome, because their religion preached a strict aniconism. They also misconstrued the traditional Roman practices of euergetism and patronage. Roman governors were also caught by surprise when Jews reacted to Roman benevolence with riots, as during the 26–36 CE governorship of Pontius Pilate when he sought to build an aqueduct using money from the Temple.

Tensions increased during the procuratorship of Gessius Florus (64–66 CE), who had scant respect for the Jewish elites and favored the Greeks of Caesarea in their struggles with the Jews. This led to an incident in Caesarea that is considered the cause of the war.

In Caesarea, a Greek sacrificed a bird outside a synagogue, setting off a riot and inciting Jerusalem. When Florus entered the city, a group of young priests paraded around asking for money to give the governor as if he were a beggar. Enraged, Florus ordered out troops. However, the Jews drove him and his soldiers from the city. Then, Eleazar ben Anaias suspended the sacrificial service for the emperor, openly declaring rebellion.

At this point there were two anti-Roman parties in Jerusalem: the Zealots, led by Eleazar ben Simon, and the Sicarii, led by Menahem ben Yair. After the Romans had been disposed of, the Zealots turned on the Sicarii, slaying Menahem and driving his followers from the city. Throughout Syria,

Jews attacked Greeks. In response, Greeks in many Greek cities killed their Jewish inhabitants.

All of this disorder impelled Roman governor of Syria Cestius Gallus to march on Jerusalem. He reached the city but for an unknown reason turned back and was then ambushed by the Jewish forces. His army was routed at the Battle of Beth-Horon in October 66. Emperor Nero then directed Vespasian to suppress the revolt.

Ananus ben Ananus, leader of the faction that had come to power following the defeat of Cestius Gallus, now controlled Jerusalem. Ananus and his allies dispatched military leaders to various regions of Palestine. One led a failed attack on the port city of Ashcalon (modern-day Ashkelon, Israel). Another, the historian Josephus, attempted to organize Galilee to resist the Romans. Josephus ran afoul of a local magnate, John of Gischala. Thus, when the Romans arrived in force in 67, Galilee was divided between Josephus, John, and Roman loyalists (such as the city of Sepphoris).

In the spring of 67, Vespasian landed at Ptolemais and led his army into Galilee. Many Jewish cities capitulated on his arrival; he besieged others, putting the inhabitants to the sword. In the siege of Jotapata, a minor fortified town, Josephus went over to the Romans. Josephus's rival, John of Gischala, fled with a band of followers to Jerusalem. By 68, Vespasian and Titus had subdued northern Judaea and moved down the coast, setting up a base in Caesarea.

In Jerusalem, John of Gischala joined Eleazar ben Simon's faction. They then butchered Ananus ben Ananus and his allies. John of Gischala emerged as a faction leader after defecting from Eleazar. While this civil war in Jerusalem was occurring during 68–69, Vespasian conquered all of Judaea except Jerusalem, forcing Simon bar Giora and his army to seek refuge in the city. Jerusalem was now divided among Eleazar ben Simon and the Zealots, John of Gischala, and Simon bar Giora.

Meanwhile, the Roman Empire was in chaos. In 68, Nero was deposed. Galba, Otho, and Vitellius then held power successively during 68–69. In the spring of 69 CE, the Danube legions, followed by those of Egypt and Syria, declared Vespasian emperor. In the winter of 69, Vespasian's forces defeated and killed Vitellius. Vespasian departed for Rome in the summer of 70, but he instructed his son Titus to end the Jewish Revolt and destroy Jerusalem.

Detail of a relief depicting sacred Jewish objects such as the menorah and silver trumpets being taken from the Temple in Jerusalem and carried in a Roman triumph (*triumphus*) in 71 CE. The relief is on the inside of the Arch of Titus in Rome. (Allan T. Kohl/Art Images for College Teaching)

Titus arrived at Jerusalem in March 70. The defenders of the city, weakened by internal strife, had some initial success in hindering the Roman siege equipment. In response, the Romans encircled Jerusalem with parapets. Food ran out in the city, bringing starvation. In August after many attempts, the Romans captured the Antonia fortress above the Temple. By mid-August they had broken into the Temple and burned it. In September they took control of the entire city, killing thousands of Jews and effectively ended the war. Roman casualties had been heavy, because Titus was under pressure to capture the city as soon as possible in order to shore up the legitimacy of his father's reign by triumphing over a foreign enemy.

Mopping-up operations continued in 71. The last pocket of Jewish resistance was crushed in the siege of Masada in 73, marking the end of the First Jewish-Roman War.

The outcome of the war was never in doubt. The Flavians, however, magnified the level of Jewish resistance in order to enhance their hold on power. The Flavians imposed a tax on the Jews in place of the tax that was traditionally paid to the Jerusalem Temple. The Roman tax went to the Capitoline Temple of Jupiter Optimus Maximus, which had been damaged during the Flavian capture of Rome and symbolized the subjugation of the Jewish people. The Flavians also rebuilt Rome, using the spoils of the Jewish War to erect monuments such as the Arch of Titus and the new Coliseum.

The First Jewish-Roman War also had important consequences for the nascent Christian community in Judaea. By 70, Christians were spread throughout the Mediterranean. It is in this period after 70 that Christianity seems to have separated from Judaism. Christians believed that the war validated their theology, as they considered the destruction of the Temple punishment for the rejection of Jesus.

The province of Judaea also changed in fundamental ways. In 70, Judaea was annexed directly to the Roman Empire. This meant that it was governed by Roman law, with traditional Jewish laws no longer enforced and much of the province choosing to practice Greco-Roman civic paganism. The destruction of the Temple marked the beginning of the rabbinic movement, the form of Judaism that is practiced today.

NATHAN SCHUMER

See also
Beth-Horon, Battle of; Jerusalem, Roman Siege of; Judaea; Masada; Titus, Emperor; Vespasian, Emperor

References
Gambash, Gil. *Rome and Provincial Resistance*. New York: Routledge, 2015.

Goodman, Martin. *Rome and Jerusalem*. New York: Knopf, 2007.
Goodman, Martin. *Ruling Class of Judaea*. Cambridge: Cambridge University Press, 1987.
Schürer, E. *The History of the Jewish People in the Age of Jesus Christ*. 3 vols., rev. ed. Edinburgh, UK: T. & T. Clark, 1973–1987.
Schwartz, Seth. *Imperialism and Jewish Society, 200 B.C.E. to 640 C.E.* Princeton, NJ: Princeton University Press, 2001.

Jihad

The term "jihad" (*jehad*) is often translated as "holy war." It means "striving" or "to exert the utmost effort" and refers both to a religious duty to spread and defend Islam by waging war (lesser jihad) and an inward spiritual struggle to attain perfect faith (greater jihad). The distinction between lesser and greater jihad is not accepted by all Muslims in all circumstances. Many distinguish between jihad as an individual versus a collective duty, as when Muslims face invasion or cannot practice their faith, and jihad in its defensive or offensive forms. In general, the broad spectrum of modern Islam emphasizes the inner spiritual jihad.

Within the spectrum of Islamic belief, definitions of jihad have also rested on historical circumstances. Indian reformer Sayyid Ahmad Khan argued for a more limited interpretation of jihad whereby believers could perform charitable acts in place of armed struggle, which was only incumbent if Muslims could not practice their faith. The reform movement of Muhammad ibn abd al-Wahhab in 18th-century Arabia, in contrast, reasserted the incumbency of jihad as armed struggle for all believers. As the Quran contains verses that promote mercy and urge peacemaking but also verses (referred to as the Sword Verses) that more ardently require jihad of believers, there is a scriptural basis for both sides of this argument.

Quranic thought on the nature of jihad began to evolve when Muhammad moved from Mecca to Medina in 622 and created an Islamic state. The initial Quranic jihadic sanction (22:39) was for fighting in self-defense only, "those who stay at home," that could be taken as condemnation of those who abstained from an early key battle of the Muslims against the Meccan forces. Many Muslim scholars held that the admonition to pursue an aggressive jihad "with their wealth and their persons" (Quran 4:95) overrode verses revealed earlier on. Fighting and warfare (*qital*) are, however, differentiated from jihad, which is always accompanied by the phrase *'ala sabil Allah* (on the path of God) in the same way that just war is differentiated from other forms of conflict.

Some scholars differentiate the fulfilling of jihad by the heart, the tongue, or the sword as a means of discouraging Muslims from seeing armed struggle as a commandment, but such teachings have by and large been contradicted by the revival of activist jihad, first in response to colonialism and then again in the 20th century.

The broad spectrum of Islam considers foreign military intervention, foreign occupation, economic oppression, non-Islamic cultural realignment, colonialism, and the oppression of a domestic government, either secular or Islamic, of an Islamic people or country to be a sufficient reason, if not a Quranic mandate, to participate in a defensive jihad. The more militant and fundamental end of the Islamic spectrum asserts that a social, economic, and military defensive jihad is justifiable and necessary. However, a widespread discussion of jihad is ongoing in the Muslim world today in response to the rise of militancy, and there is a concerted effort to separate the concepts of jihad and martyrdom from each other when they are the rallying call of irresponsible extremists such as Osama bin Laden and his ilk.

Notable defensive jihads in the more recent history of Islam include the resistance of the Afghan (1979) and Chechnya mujahideen against their respective Soviet and Russian occupations and the Algerian War of Independence against France. Some Islamic religious scholars, such as Dr. Abdullah Yusuf Azzam, a former teacher of bin Laden, argued for jihad against the West. Numerous clerics and scholars have held, along with the views of their communities, that the Palestinian struggle against Israel is a defensive jihad because of the infringements on life and liberty, the use of collective punishment, and the seizure by Israel of *waqf* (endowment) lands.

Offensive jihad was essentially adopted by the early Muslim community, as no defensive action would have sufficed to protect them against the allied tribal forces determined to exterminate them. In such a jihad, the Peoples of the Book (*dhimma*), meaning other monotheistic traditions including Judaism and Christianity, must be treated differently than enemies who are unbelievers (*kuffar*). However, the Peoples of the Book must submit to Islamic rule, including the paying of poll and land taxes. Rules of engagement, truces, and treatment of prisoners and non-Muslims were all specified in medieval texts concerned with *siyar,* or Islamic international law.

Classical Islamic law and tradition asserts that a jihad that is a collective duty (simplified in Western texts as an offensive jihad) can only be declared by the caliph, the successor to Prophet Muhammad and the lawful temporal and spiritual authority for the entire Islamic community. On the other hand, no authority other than conscience or the awareness of an oppression targeting Islam or Islamic peoples is necessary to participate in an individually incumbent jihad.

When the Mongols attacked Baghdad in 1258, the caliphate, long since a divided patchwork of sultanates and emirates, ceased to exist. It was the only legal, governmental, and clerical structure recognized by the classical interpretation of Islamic doctrine as being capable of declaring jihad. This did not prevent the Ottoman sultans from declaring themselves caliphs and calling for jihad, but the Muslim world did not recognize them as such. Other jihads were declared in the early modern period, such as those by the Mahdiyya of the Sudan, the Wahhabi movement in Arabia, and the Sanusiyya in today's Libya.

Leaders of such movements, like contemporary jihadists such as the Islamic State of Iraq and Syria (ISIS), have sometimes proclaimed jihads by issuing a fatwa or statement. Although a fatwa is supposed to be a legal response issued by a qualified jurist, self-proclaimed leaders and clerics sometimes say that the traditional *ulema*, crushed by modern state governments, have failed in their duty and therefore claim the right to speak in their stead.

Although many Muslims recognize their respective governments and political leaders as worthy of defining and declaring defensive jihads, there are many others who perceive their governments as illegitimate Islamic states or illegitimate Islamic political leaders. Turkey, Egypt, and Pakistan, for example, are quasi-democratic states that grant secular political parties and politicians the same rights as Islamic political parties and politicians. Islamic militant groups in all three countries see these governments and their leaders as heretical and illegitimate under Islamic law (sharia). In a similar vein, some Muslims, most notably the *takfirists,* declare jihad against Muslim governments perceived as oppressive, anti-Islamic, or corrupt (being non-Muslim in their eyes). Additionally, many of the Islamic theocratic monarchies (e.g., Saudi Arabia) are deemed illegitimate by fundamentalist Muslims. This perception is due in part to the willingness of some of these monarchies and democracies to cooperate and form alliances with non-Islamic nations or with nations that wage economic, cultural, or military war against Islam and Muslims. Additionally, some of these monarchies and democracies limit the power of the clerics within their countries.

Various Islamic movements, most notably Al Qaeda, have stepped into the void created by the disappearance of the caliphate and the resultant fractured Islamic political and religious world. These groups have interpreted Islam as they wish and declare jihad as they desire, although often with the assistance and support of some clerics and of leaders with a degree of religious knowledge. Because early Muslims killed in jihad were considered martyrs, there is an extensive tradition that exalts martyrdom. This adds to the modern jihadists' appeal, particularly to younger or more desperate followers. Defensive jihad, inclusive of martyrdom, is deemed appropriate in order to end Israel's occupation of the perceived Islamic territories of the West Bank, East Jerusalem, and Gaza, if not all of Palestine.

A martyr secures a place in Paradise and may intercede for other Muslims. Antiterrorist campaigns in the Muslim world have argued, against the weight of literature and popular belief, that modern jihadists are not martyrs if they set out to martyr themselves because suicide is not allowed in Islam. Noncombatant Muslims who perish in a jihad are also considered martyrs. Jihadists thus excuse the deaths of innocents caught in their cross fire with targets or authorities. They explain the deaths of non-Muslim civilians as being deserved for their failure to submit to Islam or for their open oppression of Islam or Islamic peoples. In the case of Israeli civilians, the fact that all provide military service to their country means that they are not really considered civilians by the jihadists.

The term "jihad" is incorporated into the organizational names of numerous militant groups, including the Egyptian Islamic Jihad, the Egyptian Tawhid wal-Jihad, and the Palestinian Islamic Jihad.

The struggle in contemporary Islam to redefine jihad and detach its meaning from adventurism, martyrdom, and attacks on Muslim governments as well as Westerners is one of the most significant challenges at this time in history.

RICHARD M. EDWARDS AND SHERIFA ZUHUR

See also
Baghdad, 1258 Siege of; Bin Laden, Osama; Fatwa; Hamas; Islamic State of Iraq and Syria; Palestinian Islamic Jihad

References
Bostrom, Andrew G., ed. *The Legacy of Jihad: Islamic Holy War and the Fate of Non-Muslims.* Amherst, NY: Prometheus, 2005.
Delong-Bas, Natana. *Wahhabi Islam: From Revival and Reform to Global Jihad.* Oxford: Oxford University Press, 2004.
Esposito, John L. *Unholy War: Terror in the Name of Islam.* New York: Oxford University Press, 2002.
Fregosi, Paul. *Jihad in the West: Muslim Conquests from the 7th to the 21st Centuries.* Amherst, NY: Prometheus, 1998.
Kepel, Gilles. *Jihad: The Trail of Political Islam.* Cambridge, MA: Belknap, 2003.

John of Brienne (ca. 1170–1237)

King of Jerusalem (1210–1212) as consort to Maria of Montferrat, queen of Jerusalem, and subsequently regent (1212–1225) for their daughter, Isabella II. John was then Latin emperor of Constantinople (1231–1237).

Born around 1170, John was the fourth son of Erard II, count of Brienne in Champagne. In 1208 John was selected to marry the heiress to the Latin Kingdom of Jerusalem, Maria (la Marquise) of Montferrat. He has often been regarded as a poor choice, as he was without the resources to support the kingdom, and some considered him too old, though on his marriage he was probably only in his 30s. He had military prowess, a family with a crusading pedigree, and the support of Philippe II Augustus of France, Pope Innocent III, and his fellow Champenois lords, together with Walter of Montbéliard, a kinsman already prominent in the East, to recommend him.

John reached Acre with 300 knights on September 13, 1210, and married Maria the next day. They were crowned in Tyre on October 3, 1210. John soon led his force on a raid into the hinterland but achieved little. In May 1211 he secured a six-year truce with the Muslims. In 1211 or 1212 a daughter, Isabella (II), was born to the couple, and Maria died. John was no longer king but regent for his daughter. However, he continued to style himself "king" and was recognized as such by the church, although he may have encountered opposition from the Frankish barons.

In 1214 John formed an alliance with the kingdom of Cilicia through marriage to Stephanie, the eldest daughter of King Leon I. John took a prominent part in the Egyptian campaign of the Fifth Crusade (1218–1221) but clashed with Pelagius, the papal legate, regarding its direction. When Leon died in 1219, John withdrew from the crusade army to pursue a claim to the Cilician throne, but he rejoined the crusaders when both Stephanie and their son died.

In March 1223 John attended a conference at Ferentino, Italy, with Pope Honorius III, Holy Roman emperor Frederick II, and other representatives from Outremer. It was agreed that Frederick would marry John's daughter Isabella. John then toured Europe seeking assistance for the Franks in Outremer and in 1224 married Berengaria, sister of Ferdinand III of Castile. In November 1225 Isabella was married to Frederick II, who then demanded that John surrender the Kingdom of Jerusalem to him, to which he was forced to accede. In 1228–1229 Frederick, who was also king of Sicily, had to curtail an expedition to the Holy Land when John led a papal army against his territories.

In 1228 Robert, the Latin emperor of Constantinople, died, leaving an 11-year-old heir, Baldwin II. The regency council needed a military leader to defend the empire at a crucial juncture, and in April 1229 it was agreed that John's daughter by Berengaria, Mary, should marry the young emperor, while John would become coemperor for life. In 1231, John was crowned in Constantinople. The empire was impoverished and suffered constant attack and, despite some minor victories, was still in danger at the time of John's death. In 1237 John took holy orders with the Franciscans, whom he had patronized. John died on March 23, 1237, at Constantinople.

Linda Goldsmith

See also
Baldwin II of Constantinople; Constantinople, Latin Empire of; Frederick II, Holy Roman Emperor; Jerusalem, Latin Kingdom of

References
Buckley, J. M. "The Problematical Octogenarianism of John of Brienne." *Speculum* 32 (1957): 315–322.
Hamilton, Bernard. "King Consorts of Jerusalem and Their Entourages from the West from 1186 to 1250." In *Die Kreuzfahrerstaaten als multikulturelle Gesellschaft*, ed. Hans Eberhard Mayer, 13–24. München: Oldenbourg, 1997.
Lock, Peter. *The Franks in the Aegean, 1204–1500.* London: Longman, 1995.

Joint Comprehensive Plan of Action
See Iran Nuclear Deal

Jordan

The Arab state of Jordan occupies 35,637 square miles (making it about the size of the U.S. state of Indiana) on the east bank of the Jordan River. Officially known as the Hashemite Kingdom of Jordan, it borders Israel and the West Bank to the west, Syria and the Golan Heights to the north, Iraq to the east, and Saudi Arabia to the east and south. Its 2018 population was some 9.5 million. Jordan's capital city is Amman.

Arabs constitute some 98 percent of the population, while Circassians and Armenians each number about 1 percent. Islam is the dominant religion. Muslims make up about 92 percent of the country's population, with 93 percent of these adhering to Sunni Islam. Christians constitute some 6 percent, but this percentage is down sharply from some 30 percent in 1950, owing to substantial Muslim immigration into Jordan and high Muslim birthrates. Traditionally Christians hold 2 cabinet positions in the government and they are reserved 9 seats out of the 130 in Parliament. Other smaller religious minorities include Druzes and Baha'is.

Jordan is a constitutional monarchy, but the king wields considerable power. Among many international organizations to which it belongs, Jordan is a founding member of both the Arab League and the Organization of Islamic Cooperation. The kingdom's relatively small size, semiarid climate, and paucity of natural resources (especially in oil and water) have contributed to it having one of the smallest economies in the region and heavy government debt, unemployment, and poverty, which in turn have brought dependence on foreign aid from both Western and Persian Gulf allies.

Jordan saw human habitation early in prehistory. Later a succession of tribal kingdoms appeared and were in near constant warfare with the Hebrew Kingdom of Israel and the Kingdom of Judah west of the Jordan River. The region then became part of the Akkadian Empire, followed by the Egyptian, Hittite, Assyrian, Neo-Babylonian, and Achaemenid Empires. Macedonian king Alexander III (the Great) conquered the Achaemenid Empire in 332 BCE. Following his death in 323, Jordan was fought over between the Ptolemies in Egypt and the Seleucids in Syria. The Romans arrived in 63 BCE. When in 324 CE the Roman Empire split into the Western and Eastern (Byzantine) Empires, Jordan became part of the Byzantine Empire, with Christianity as the state religion. For some of this time, the Sassanian Empire controlled parts of the region, however.

In 636 the Arabs defeated the Byzantines in the decisive Battle of Yarmouk and secured control of the Levant. Rule by the Rashidun, Ummayad, and Abbasid caliphates followed. Twelfth-century Fatimid rule was interrupted by the Christian crusades, but Saladin defeated the crusaders and founded the Ayyubid dynasty (1171–1260). Mamluk rule followed, but in 1516 the Ottomans defeated the Mamluks, and the Levant became part of the Ottoman Empire.

Ottoman control over Transjordan and much else of the region came to an end during World War I (1914–1918). In 1915 the British opened secret negotiations with Hussein bin Ali, sharif and emir of Mecca, promising the creation of an independent Arab state in the Hejaz and Levant in return for military assistance against the Ottomans. Beginning in 1916, Jordanians took part in what became known as the Arab Revolt in alliance with the British. The war ended with

Jordan

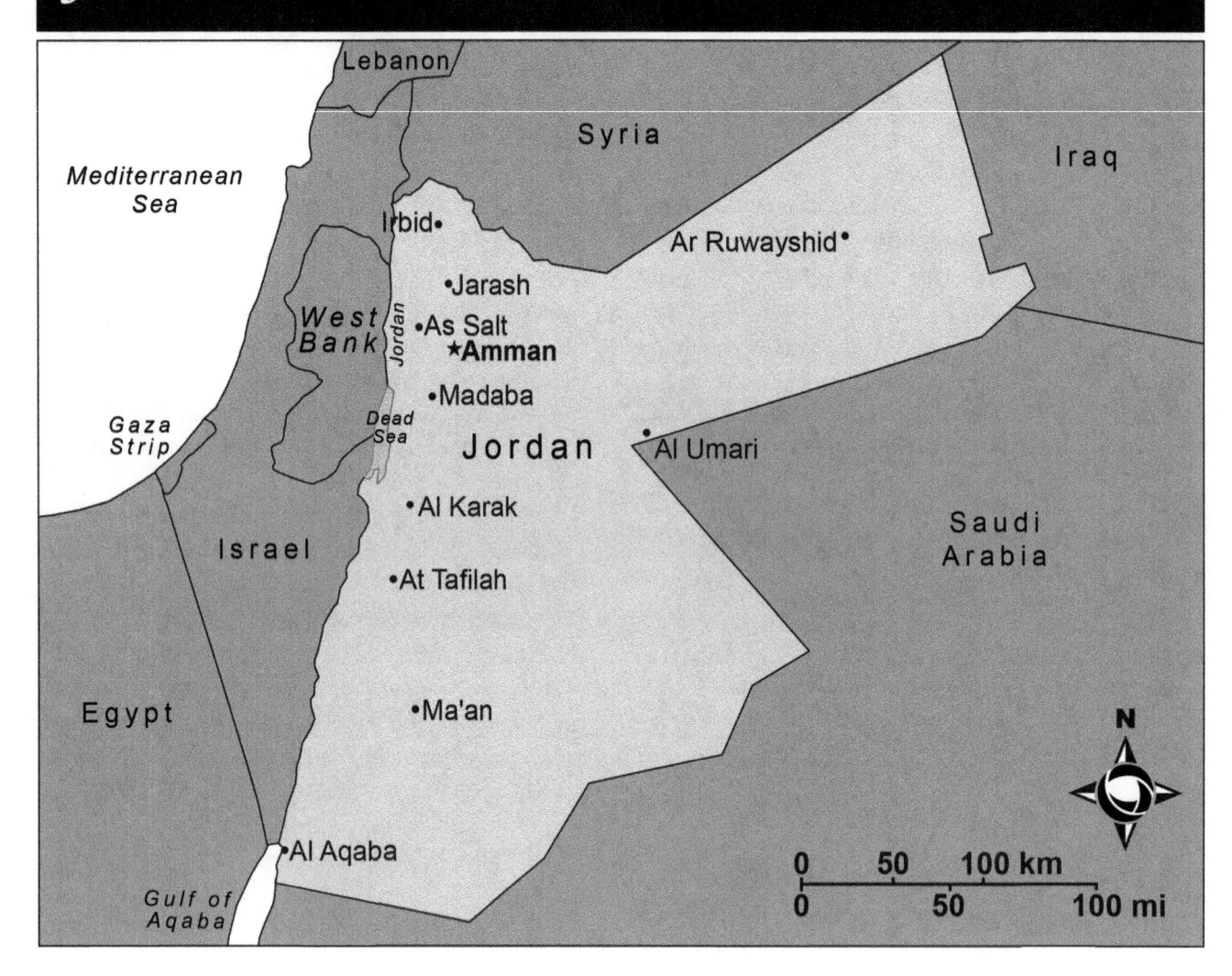

most of the territory of the Hejaz and Levant, including land east of the Jordan River, liberated from Ottoman control.

At the same time the British had been promising the Arabs an independent state, they had also been secretly negotiating with the French, and the ensuing Sykes-Picot Agreement of 1916 divided much of the Levant into British and French spheres of influence. The Balfour Declaration of November 2, 1917, was another blow to the Arabs, for in it the British government promised its support for a Jewish "homeland" in Palestine. Arab nationalists certainly regarded this as a betrayal of their wartime agreement with the British.

With the end of the war the region was divided, and the borders of five new states were arbitrarily drawn for Iraq, Syria, Lebanon, Transjordan, and Palestine. The French secured mandates for Syria and Lebanon; the British mandates were Palestine, Iraq, and Transjordan. On October 22, 1920, after taking over Transjordan, the United Kingdom formed what was known as the Mobile Force, a military unit of 150 men commanded by British Army captain (later major general) Frederick Gerard Peake, known as Peake Pasha. It was to defend the territory from tribal warfare or invasion and protect the important Jerusalem-Amman road. Soon the Mobile Force had grown to some 1,000 men. On October 22, 1922, it merged with the Reserve Mobile Force, with Peake now an employee of the Emirate of Transjordan. The new force, paid for by the British and with British officers, was officially named Al Jeish al-Arabi (the Arab Army) but was better known as the Arab Legion.

The territory known as Transjordan was from April 1, 1921, ruled by Emir Abdullah ibn Hussein, the second of three sons of Hussein, sharif of Mecca. On July 24, 1922, the League of Nations recognized Transjordan as a state under the British Mandate for Palestine.

In 1930 captain (later lieutenant general) John Bagot Glubb became second-in-command of the Arab Legion. A close personal friend and trusted adviser of Abdullah, Glubb was widely known to Jordanians as Glubb Pasha. He took command of the Arab Legion on Peake's retirement in 1939 and made it into the best-trained military force in the Arab world. Certainly, the Arab Legion rendered effective service during World War II in the British-led Iraq and Syria campaigns of 1941.

World War II marked the effective end of the colonial era, and on May 25, 1946, Transjordan received its independence, now officially known as the Hashemite Kingdom of Jordan. Abdullah I ruled as king. The ground force of the Arab Legion, which now numbered some 8,000 men, became the Jordanian Arab Army.

Britain was unable to resolve the matter of Palestinian governance, and a three-way war developed there between Arab nationalists, Jews, and the British Army. With the Arab rejection of a partition agreement, the British simply terminated their Palestine mandate, and on May 14, 1948, the Jews in Palestine proclaimed the independence of the State of Israel. As with most other Arab leaders, Abdullah flatly rejected this, and a day later the Arab Legion joined the armies of other nations in an invasion that became the War of Israeli Independence (May 15, 1948–March 10, 1949). Officially, the Arab forces were under the auspices of the Arab League, which had been formed in 1945. Abdullah held nominal command of the Arab armies, but cooperation among these forces was almost nonexistent and a chief cause of their ensuing military failure.

At the beginning of the war in the central part of the front, Arab forces from Transjordan and Iraq advanced on Jerusalem with the aim of driving the Jews from the city. The Arab Legion, which was certainly the best Arab fighting force in the war, secured the eastern and southern portions of the new part of the city and occupied most of Old Jerusalem.

The Israeli-Transjordan armistice at the end of the war on April 3, 1949, saw Transjordan retain control of the West Bank of the Jordan River and East Jerusalem. To reflect this territorial change, on December 1, 1948, Abdullah officially changed his country's name to the Hashemite Kingdom of Jordan. During the war, a great many Palestinian Arabs were displaced by the fighting and fled into Transjordan territory. Jordan, unlike other Arab states, allowed Palestinians to take Jordanian citizenship.

On July 20, 1951, a Palestinian assassinated Abdullah while he was in the Al-Aqsa Mosque in Jerusalem, purportedly because of the belief that he was secretly negotiating with Israel. Abdullah was succeeded by his son Talal; as Talal was mentally ill, his son Prince Hussein became the effective ruler as king Hussein I on August 11, 1952, at age 17. He would rule Jordan for the next 47 years.

A series of anti-Western demonstrations in Jordan, combined with the October 1956 Suez Crisis, compelled Hussein to sever military ties to Britain. He also dismissed Glubb Pasha in order to show political independence from the United Kingdom and to Arabize the Jordanian officer corps.

In February 1958, Hussein formed the Arab Federation with Iraq. The king viewed this as a needed countermeasure to the newly established United Arab Republic (UAR), formed between Egypt and Syria and dominated by Egypt's Pan-Arab president Gamal Abdel Nasser. The Arab Federation fell apart by the autumn, however, after the Iraqi king was overthrown and slain in a coup. Later that same year, leaders of the UAR called for the overthrow of the Lebanese and Jordanian governments. Hussein then requested aid from the British, who sent troops to Jordan to quell antigovernment protests. The Americans simultaneously sent forces to Lebanon to bolster its besieged Christian-led government.

Jordan's relations with the UAR remained tense. Indeed, in 1963 when a rival Jordanian "government-in-exile" was set up in Damascus, Hussein declared a state of emergency. The crisis subsided when the Americans and British publicly endorsed Hussein's rule. For good measure, Washington placed on alert the U.S. Navy's Sixth Fleet in the Mediterranean.

After the mid-1960s and more than a decade of crises and regional conflicts, Hussein turned his attention to domestic issues. Determined to improve the welfare of his people, he launched major programs to increase literacy, enhance educational opportunities, bolster public health initiatives, and lower infant mortality. Hussein achieved considerable success. By the late 1980s literacy rates approached 100 percent, and infant deaths were down dramatically. Jordan's economy also began to expand as the nation engaged in more international trade, while relations with Egypt improved. Hussein also began to build a modern and reliable transportation system and moved to modernize the country's infrastructure. Notably, he accomplished this without resorting to overly repressive tactics. Indeed, throughout the period, Jordanians enjoyed a level of freedom virtually unrivaled in the Middle East.

By the spring of 1967, however, the Middle East was poised on the brink of a new war. Considerable low-key fighting had been occurring in the form of Palestinian raids against Israel mounted from Syria and Jordan. Israel met this undeclared war on its territory by retaliatory strikes against guerrilla camps and villages in the Golan Heights of Syria and in Jordan. The year 1965 saw an Arab attempt to divert the flow of the Jordan River, and this brought Israel Defense Forces (IDF) attacks against the diversion sites in Syria. This in turn led to a mutual defense pact between Egypt and Syria against Israel on November 4, 1966. On November 13, 1966, the IDF also mounted a large-scale attack on the Es Samu Palestinian refugee camp in Jordan, said to be a terrorist base. Jordan dispatched troops and aircraft, and in the ensuing clash with the IDF they suffered 16 killed, 51 wounded, a number of vehicles destroyed, and one plane shot down. The Israelis lost 1 soldier killed and 10 wounded. Three civilians died, and 96 were wounded.

After Egypt blockaded Israeli shipping in the Gulf of Aqaba on May 22, 1967, Egyptian minister of defense Field Marshal Abdel Hakim Amer ordered Egyptian forces to close the straits the next day. A countermanding order by Nasser would have signaled weakness, and he now issued orders to the Egyptian military to prepare for war.

With both sides mobilizing, on May 30 King Hussein, normally a moderating force, arrived in Cairo and concluded with Egypt a mutual security pact. The 1967 Arab-Israeli War, known as the Six-Day War for its duration of June 5–10, began with a preemptive Israeli air strike on Egypt. As Israel was locked in combat with both Egypt and Syria, Israeli leaders employed diplomatic channels to urge Hussein to stay out of the war. Hussein wanted to avoid participation but came under heavy pressure to act, and he was deceived by early Cairo broadcasts claiming major Egyptian military successes. Hussein hoped to satisfy his allies with minimum military action short of all-out war. Jordanian 155mm "Long Tom" artillery went into action against Tel Aviv, and Jordanian aircraft attempted to strafe a small Israeli airfield near Kfar Sirkin. These steps, however, led Israel to declare war on Jordan.

Hussein's decision had great consequences for the Middle East, as the IDF captured all Jerusalem and the entire West Bank. Also, as many as 300,000 Palestinians fled to Jordan from the West Bank, swelling the Palestinian refugee population there to almost 1 million. This massive influx severely taxed Jordanian infrastructure, schools, health care, and other resources and engendered considerable resentment among some Jordanians.

The large number of Palestinians in Jordan by 1968 also brought greatly increased influence for Palestinian militants—especially militants such as the fedayeen. These groups were well armed (receiving significant assistance from Syria and Egypt) and posed a serious threat to Hussein's rule. By 1970, it appeared as if the Palestinian resistance fighters were in the process of creating a Palestinian state within a state, much as they would do in Lebanon.

By early 1970 Palestinian guerrilla groups and the Palestine Liberation Organization (PLO) were skirmishing with Jordanian troops. Open warfare erupted in June. On June 9, Hussein escaped death when would-be assassins opened fire on his motorcade. In particularly bloody fighting during September 1970, the Jordanian Army triumphed, and thousands of Palestinians, including the leadership of the PLO, fled Jordan for Syria and Lebanon. From the Palestinian perspective, the fighting and forced expulsion of the PLO leadership was a great betrayal. Indeed, they referred to the events of September 1970 as Black September.

The early 1970s saw continued unrest. In 1972 King Hussein tried to create a new Arab federation, which would have included the West Bank. Israel as well as most of the Arab states flatly rejected the idea. In 1973, although King Hussein was caught off guard by the Egyptian and Syrian attack on Israel in the Yom Kippur War, he was soon under pressure from these two Arab states to join the conflict. He tried to keep out of the conflict but was nevertheless drawn in, ironically to stave off a crushing Syrian defeat. He did not commit his air force, realizing that this would bring a crushing Israeli retaliation as in 1967, but on October 13 he sent the crack 40th Armored Brigade, equipped with British-made Centurion tanks, into Syria, ironically to save that nation from the threat posed by the Israeli invasion to Damascus and the survival of the Syrian Army. The 40th Brigade came into battle with the Israelis on October 16 and fought bravely, holding until the Syrians were told by their Soviet advisers to withdraw.

Hussein strengthened relations with neighboring Syria beginning in the late 1970s, and he vigorously opposed the 1979 Israeli-Egyptian peace treaty. Hussein supported Iraq in the long Iran-Iraq War (1980–1988).

The 1980s were difficult years economically for Jordan, as job creation failed to keep pace with population growth, resulting in high unemployment. Inflation became a major problem, foreign investment fell off, and exports declined. In 1989, riots occurred in southern Jordan regarding the lack of jobs and a government-mandated increase in basic commodities, including electricity and water. This situation led Hussein to seek U.S. financial aid in the late 1980s when the nation's foreign debt burden grew substantially.

Hussein miscalculated when he chose to back Iraqi president Saddam Hussein in his August 1990 seizure of Kuwait, for U.S. and much European aid to Jordan was sharply curtailed. Saudi Arabia and (later) Kuwait also withheld financial assistance, and the economy went from bad to worse. When some 700,000 Jordanians returned to Jordan because they were now unwelcome in Saudi Arabia and in Kuwait following its liberation in the 1991 Persian Gulf War, the economic situation became truly dire. Jordan's tourism declined precipitously, oil prices were high, and exports suffered. By 1995 the government put unemployment at 14 percent, but other sources claimed that it was perhaps twice that figure. Not until 2001 did the economy begin to regain its footing. Hussein's decision to back Iraq also put Jordanian-U.S. relations in a holding pattern, and relations with other major Western powers were little better.

By 1993–1994, however, Jordanian-U.S. relations were on an upswing. Jordan became an active partner in the Arab-Israeli peace process, and Hussein supported United Nations–imposed sanctions on Iraq. On July 25, 1994, Hussein signed a historic nonbelligerent agreement with the Israelis in the Washington Declaration. This was followed by the October 26, 1994, signing of the Israel-Jordan Peace Treaty.

King Hussein died of cancer on February 7, 1999. He had named his eldest son as crown prince and successor, who now ruled as King Abdullah II. Abdullah has tried to continue Jordan's role as the force of moderation in the Middle East. He has attempted to keep dialogue open between the Israelis and the Palestinians and continues to counsel both sides that discussions and agreements are preferable to conflict and war.

Although Abdullah publicly criticized the Anglo-American war in Iraq that began in March 2003, he quietly provided assistance to the United States and Britain during the invasion and its aftermath and partnered with the coalition forces in an attempt to bring a semblance of order to that war-torn country.

Jordan itself has been surprisingly free of terrorist activity. A notable exception was the November 2005 terrorist bombing of three hotels in Amman by Al Qaeda in Iraq, an organization led by a native Jordanian. The blasts killed 57 people and wounded at least 100 others.

On February 1, 2011, in an effort to preempt the opposition and avoid the events that had swept Tunisia and then Egypt and became known as the Arab Spring, Abdullah ordered his entire cabinet to resign, brought back a reformist prime minister, and pledged to embark on democratic reform. He also met with the leaders of the Muslim Brotherhood for the first time in nearly a decade. Abdullah's efforts to reform Jordan's political system and provide more freedoms for his people continued into 2018.

Jordan firmly supported efforts to combat the Islamist State of Iraq and Syria (ISIS) when it seized large stretches of Syria and Iraq following the start of the Syrian Civil War in 2011. By 2013 it was serving as a conduit for the shipment of small arms to rebel groups fighting both ISIS and the Syrian government of president Bashar al-Assad. In June 2013 Jordan was host to EAGER LION, a military exercise involving some 15,000 military personnel from 18 different nations that saw the United States deploy to Jordan both F-16 fighter aircraft and Patriot missiles. In mid-June the Pentagon announced that the aircraft and Patriot missiles would remain in Jordan after the end of the exercise on June 23.

On September 23, 2014, Jordanian aircraft joined other Arab nations and the United States in attacking ISIS targets in Syria. This coalition was soon dubbed Operation INHERENT RESOLVE and has been led by the United States. The operation was continuing as of 2019. On December 24, 2014, however, one of the anti-ISIS coalition aircraft, a Jordanian F-16, was downed in Syria's eastern Raqqa Province in territory controlled by ISIS, and its pilot, Lieutenant Muath al-Kaseasbeh, was captured. On February 3, 2014, ISIS released a video showing his murder. Placed in a cage, al-Kaseasbeh was doused with flammable fluid, then set on fire and burned to death. As recently as a few days before, ISIS had been negotiating for an exchange involving female suicide bomber Sajida al-Rishawi, whose explosive vest had failed to detonate during the 2005 Amman hotel bombing and who was on death row in Jordan. King Abdullah, then in Washington for talks with U.S. president Barack Obama, immediately returned home and addressed the nation amid widespread anti-ISIS demonstrations. The Jordanian government promptly executed al-Rishawi and Ziad al-Karbouly, another terrorist, and launched a series of bombing raids against ISIS targets. ISIS leaders apparently hoped the video would put pressure on Jordan to leave the coalition, as air attacks on fellow Sunni Muslims in ISIS by the U.S.-led coalition had not been popular in Jordan, but the deed served to unite Jordanian public opinion against ISIS.

On March 26, 2015, Jordanian aircraft joined Saudi Arabia and its Persian Gulf region allies in launching air strikes in Yemen in an effort to counter Iran-allied Houthi rebel forces besieging the city of Aden. Then in December, Jordan joined a coalition of 34 predominantly Muslim nations formed under Saudi leadership that pledged to fight terrorism.

Islamic extremists view Jordan with contempt because of its peace treaty with Israel and strong orientation toward the West, and on November 9, 2015, Al Qaeda carried out a terrorist attack in Amman. In this deadliest such attack in the kingdom's history, the terrorists struck three hotels, killing 60 people and wounding 115. Jordan then tightened its internal security.

By 2018 the Jordanian political situation appeared stable, despite the addition of more than 1.4 million Syrian refugees from the long-running Syrian Civil War, added to the 2 million Palestinians. Jordan also welcomed thousands of Christians fleeing ISIS. All of this placed a considerable strain on Jordanian resources and infrastructure, however. Tourism has been a major boon to the economy and helped to offset Jordan's lack of natural resources.

Since President Donald Trump took office in early 2017, Abdullah has personally met with Trump or spoken to him over the phone on numerous occasions. In their first face-to-face meeting in Washington in January 2017, Abdullah was successful in convincing the president not to support the continued building of Israeli settlements in disputed occupied territories. Abdullah tried—unsuccessfully—to urge Trump not to move the U.S. embassy in Israel to Jerusalem, stating that such a move could be "catastrophic" to the Israeli-Palestinian peace process. Abdullah and Trump met again in June 2018 to discuss peace talks in Syria and Trump's plans for a comprehensive Israeli-Palestinian peace deal. Abdullah reportedly encouraged Trump to support a two-state solution to the Israeli-Palestinian dilemma, but the president remained largely silent on the issue.

Paul G. Pierpaoli Jr. and Spencer C. Tucker

See also
Abdullah I; Alexander III the Great; Arab Legion; Arab Revolt in Palestine; Assad, Bashar al-; Balfour Declaration; Black September; Fedayeen; Glubb, Sir John Bagot; Hussein, Saddam; Hussein ibn Talal, King of Jordan; Iran-Iraq War; Islamic State of Iraq and Syria; Israeli War of Independence; Israel-Jordan Peace Treaty; Kuwait, Iraqi Invasion of; Mandates, League of Nations; Nasser, Gamal Abdel; Palestine Liberation Organization; Persian Gulf War, Overview; Saladin; Six-Day War; Sykes-Picot Agreement; Transjordan Campaign; United Arab Republic; Yarmouk River, Battle of; Yom Kippur War

References
Abdullah ibn al-Husayn, King. *King Abdallah of Jordan: My Memoirs Completed (al-Takmilah)*. Trans. Harold W. Glidden. Washington, DC: American Council of Learned Societies, 1954.

Cordesman, Anthony H. *The Military Balance in the Middle East*. Westport, CT: Praeger, 2004.

El Edross, Syed Ali. *The Hashemite Arab Army, 1908–1979*. Amman, Jordan: Central Publishing House, 1986.

Lunt, James D. *Hussein of Jordan: Searching for a Just and Lasting Peace*. New York: William Morrow, 1989.

Mutawi, Samir A. *Jordan in the 1967 War*. Cambridge: Cambridge University Press, 2002.

Nevo, Joseph, and Illan Pappe, eds. *Jordan in the Middle East: The Making of a Pivotal State*. London: Frank Cass, 1994.

Salibi, Kamal S. *The History of Modern Jordan*. New York: William Morrow, 1993.

Satloff, Robert B. *From Abdullah to Hussein: Jordan in Transition*. New York: Oxford University Press, 1993.

Wilson, Mary C. *King Abdullah, Britain and the Making of Jordan*. Cambridge: Cambridge University Press, 1988.

Jordan River

Key Middle East waterway that flows through the Great Rift Valley and empties into the Dead Sea. The Great Rift Valley, with its freshwater resources, was also important for the passage of early hominids from Africa into Asia and Europe between 1 million and 2 million years ago. The Jordan River provides much-needed water in a dry desert region and has remained a contentious issue among Israel, Syria, Lebanon, Jordan, and the Palestinians.

The Jordan River rises in the western and southern Anti-Lebanon Mountains, where springs and snowmelt give rise to the Barayghit and Hasbani Rivers of Lebanon and the Laddan and Baniyas Rivers from Syria. These then coalesce. The river occupies the Jordan trough, part of the Great Rift Valley, and has a straight length of just 70 miles but a meandering length of about 200 miles. The river is about 60 feet at its widest and has a steep gradient, falling some 2,380 feet from its source at Mount Hermon to the Dead Sea. This is why it is called Jordan, a Hebrew term meaning "descender." At its source the Jordan River is 1,000 feet above sea level. At its end it is 1,300 feet below sea level, earning it the status as the world's lowest river. The river is not navigable. It can be waded across in many locations and is not very wide at some points. The main crossing is at the Allenby Bridge on the road from Jerusalem to Damascus.

The Jordan River can be divided into three constituent parts. The first is the section from its source to Lake Hula. The second is a roughly 10-mile stretch from Lake Hula to the Sea of Galilee (Lake Kinneret). The third part, about 65 miles in length, covers the area from the Sea of Galilee to its terminus in the Dead Sea. The latter section is also known as the Ghor, which in the north forms the border between Israel and Jordan and in the south the border between Israel and the West Bank. The Yarouk River, which is the Jordan's largest tributary, enters 5 miles south of the Sea of Galilee. The Jabbok River also joins the Jordan River in this section. The Jordan Valley is home to rich fishing grounds and diverse bird populations.

The Jordan River is an important source of water for Syria, Israel, and Jordan. Together with the Sea of Galilee, the river provides most of the water for agriculture, hydroelectric power, and domestic consumption. Water scarcity and the control of water resources are contentious issues in this arid region. The flow of water in the Jordan River has been reduced by as much as 90 percent because of draws for water supplies, and its diminished flow into the Dead Sea is responsible for the great contraction of the latter.

Israel's National Water Carrier Project focuses on the Sea of Galilee as a reservoir, while Jordan's East Ghor Project captures water from the Yarouk River for irrigation before it reaches the Jordan River. Similar projects in Syria and Lebanon also harness waters from the headstreams.

The Jordan River is prominently featured in the Bible. This reflects its significance as a key source of water, a barrier, and a tribal or national boundary. There are numerous references to the Jordan River in both the Old and New Testaments, especially in relation to Jericho. According to the New Testament, John the Baptist baptized Jesus in the Jordan River, an act of great significance to Christians.

ANTOINETTE MANNION

See also
Israel; Jordan; Syria

References
Allan, John A. *The Middle East Water Question: Hydropolitics and the Global Economy.* London: Tauris, 2002.
Lowi, Miriam R., et al., eds. *Water and Power: The Politics of a Scarce Resource in the Jordan River Basin.* Cambridge: Cambridge University Press, 1993.

Joscelin I of Edessa (?–1131)

A leading Frankish lord of Outremer, Joscelin I of Courtenay was sequentially lord of Turbessel (1101–1113), lord of Tiberias (1113–1119), and count of Edessa (1119–1131).

Little is known of his youth except that his family ruled the lordship of Courtenay in the Gâtinais in central France. Joscelin came to Syria in 1101. There he joined his cousin Baldwin, count of Edessa (subsequently Baldwin II of the Kingdom of Jerusalem), who endowed him with substantial lands around Turbessel (modern-day Tellbasar Kalesi, Turkey).

Suddenly one of the most powerful men in northern Syria, Joscelin became his cousin's main supporter. He was captured along with Baldwin at the Battle of Harran (May 7, 1104) and held for ransom by Artuqid ruler Suqman ibn Artuq in Hisn Kayfa. Following Suqman's death, Joscelin fell into the hands of Suqman's brother Ilghazi. In 1106 or early 1107, Joscelin obtained his release and went to Edessa (modern-day Sanliurfa, Turkey) to gather the ransom for Baldwin. He returned to captivity as a condition of Baldwin's release in 1108 but was freed shortly thereafter. However, on their return to Edessa, the two cousins found that Tancred, who had acted as regent during their captivity, was unwilling to relinquish control of the county. Both sides called upon Turkish allies, and fighting ended only when King Baldwin I of Jerusalem pressured Tancred to return Edessa to Baldwin of Bourcq.

In 1110 Mawdud, *atabeg* of Mosul, launched an attempt to expel the Franks from northern Syria, returning annually until his assassination in 1113. He attacked Turbessel in 1111. Most of his attacks, however, targeted the more accessible Frankish lands east of the Euphrates, especially Edessa and its environs. In 1113 Baldwin seized all of Joscelin's lands, outraged by the prosperity he enjoyed while Baldwin himself suffered raid after raid. Joscelin fled to Jerusalem, where King Baldwin I gave him the lordship of Tiberias. Despite the confiscation of his Edessan lands, Joscelin supported Baldwin of Bourcq for the throne of Jerusalem following Baldwin I's death in 1118. Baldwin II rewarded him the following year with the county of Edessa.

As count of Edessa, Joscelin was a vigorous military leader. His attacks on Aleppo led to a treaty in 1121, gaining for Edessa the northern part of Aleppo's territories as well as a portion of its suburbs. However, Joscelin's domination of northern Syria did not last long. On September 13, 1122, he and his cousin Waleran of Le Puiset were captured by forces of Nur al-Dawla Balak, ruler of Aleppo, and imprisoned in Harput, a fortress northeast of Melitene (modern-day Malatya, Turkey). Baldwin II came north to act as regent of Edessa and Antioch, but in April 1123 he fell captive himself, joining Joscelin and Waleran in Harput. A group of Armenian soldiers from Besni mounted an operation to rescue Baldwin and Joscelin in May 1123. In disguise, the soldiers seized control of the citadel and took Balak's family captive, but before they could free the captives and escape, Balak returned with his troops and besieged the fortress. Joscelin and three Armenian companions slipped out under the cover of night, and Balak recaptured Harput on September 16, 1123, massacring many of the Franks and Armenians.

In the absence of the king, the defense of Antioch as well as Edessa fell to Joscelin. He launched attacks on Balak's territories and allied with his Muslim enemies. Meanwhile, Joscelin and Queen Morphia of Jerusalem gained Baldwin's release on June 24, 1124, in exchange for a large ransom, the fortress of Azaz, and 17 Frankish hostages, who included Joscelin's young son, Joscelin II. Waleran remained in Turkish custody and was subsequently executed.

With the aid of Baldwin II, Joscelin once again dominated northern Syria, defeating Aq Sunqur, *atabeg* of Mosul, in the Battle of Azaz on June 11, 1125.

The arrival in 1127 of the young heir to Antioch, Bohemund II, spurred Joscelin to attack the principality. Joscelin had grown accustomed to exercising considerable influence in Antioch since Baldwin II's return to Jerusalem in 1125. Again, Baldwin II's intervention reestablished peace. Following Bohemund II's death in battle in February 1130, Joscelin regained influence over Antioch, being made regent by Baldwin II as a check against Bohemund's ambitious widow, Alice.

Joscelin married twice. His first wife was the daughter of Rupen of Cilicia and the mother of his son, Joscelin II. Sometime before 1119, Joscelin I married Maria, sister of Roger of Antioch, who was the mother of his daughter Stephanie. Testaments to Joscelin I's courage and martial prowess appear in Latin, Arabic, Armenian, and Syriac chronicles.

Joscelin was seriously injured while besieging a castle near Aleppo in 1131. Shortly thereafter, he learned that Emir Ghazi II Danishmend was marching against the fortress town of Kesoun (modern-day Keysun, Turkey). When Joscelin's own son, the future Joscelin II, refused to aid the town because of the size of the Muslim force, Joscelin I ordered that his own army decamp, while he was borne on a litter before the army. When Ghazi heard of Joscelin's approach, the latter's military reputation was such that he withdrew. Thus, Joscelin won a final battle before dying shortly thereafter.

Christopher MacEvitt

See also
Artuqid Dynasty; Baldwin II of Jerusalem; Edessa, County of; Harran, Battle of; Ilghazi ibn Artuq, Najm al-Din

References
Amouroux-Mourad, Monique. *Le Comté d'Edesse, 1098–1150*. Paris: Bibliothèque de l'Institut français de Beyrouth, 1988.
Cahen, Claude. *La Syrie du Nord à l'époque des croisades et la principauté franque d'Antioche*. Paris: Geuthner, 1940.
Nicholson, Robert L. *Joscelyn I, Prince of Edessa*. Urbana: University of Illinois Press, 1954.

Rheinheimer, Martin. *Das Kreuzfahrerfürstentum Galiläa*. Frankfurt am Main: Lang, 1990.
Riley-Smith, Jonathan. *The First Crusaders, 1095–1131*. Cambridge: Cambridge University Press 1997.

Jovian (331–364)

Jovian was a Roman emperor who ruled during 363–364. Born in 331 at Singidunum (modern-day Belgrade, Serbia) in 331, Jovian was the son of the senior imperial commander Varronianus. Prior to his accession, Jovian served as commander of the palace guard. When Julian died during the Persian campaign without nominating a successor, Jovian was proclaimed emperor by the army on June 27, 363. Jovian was either forced upon the army by a small group of officers or was a compromise candidate acceptable to both the eastern and western factions of the army and imperial hierarchy. Jovian subsequently negotiated a humiliating peace treaty with Sassanid Persia before returning to Roman territory. The treaty ceded to the Persians the areas west of the Tigris River that had been won by the emperor Galerius.

Jovian died in his sleep at Dadastana on February 17, 364, without having named an heir. The causes of his death are unknown; he may have died of natural causes or suffocated from the fumes of a charcoal brazier. He was succeeded by Valentinian I (364–375), also the choice of the officers' council.

Mark Hebblewhite

See also
Julian, Emperor

References
Heather, Peter. 1999. "Ammianus on Jovian." In *The Late Roman World and Its Historian: Interpreting Ammianus Marcellinus*, ed. J. W. Drijvers and D. Hunt, 105–116. London: Routledge.
Lenski, Noel. "The Election of Jovian and the Role of the Late Imperial Guards." *Klio* 82, no. 2 (2000): 492–515.
Potter, David S. 2004. *The Roman Empire at Bay, AD 180–395*. New York: Routledge, 2004.

Judaea

The term "Judaea" signifies two distinct geographic regions. Judaea primarily indicates the district surrounding the city of Jerusalem, now east-central Israel and a large part of the West Bank. The geographical designation "Judaea" also came to signify the Roman province that consisted of most of present-day Israel, the West Bank, and the east bank of the Jordan River. This Roman province was formed from the domains of the Jewish client-king Herod, who ruled during 39–4 BCE. In 6 CE after the banishment of Herod's heir, Archelaus, the kingdom became a Roman province with an equestrian governor. Judaea, however, retained its association with the region around Jerusalem.

The ancient boundaries of the district of Judaea are described by the historian Josephus as stretching from the Jordan River to the port city of Jaffa on the Mediterranean coast. The northwestern boundary was the port of Akko and the southern boundary was the Negev Desert. Much of Judaea is in the hill country. It has little rainfall, and the land is relatively arid.

In the biblical period, the district of Judaea was the home of the Israelite tribe of Judah, who presumably settled there during the Israelite conquest. A consistent Israelite presence was maintained until 586 BCE, when the Babylonian Empire overran the province and deported the inhabitants. In the Persian period, a renewed Jewish presence was established around the temple-city of Jerusalem.

The Hellenistic period of Judaean history began with the conquest of Alexander the Great. In 301 BCE, Judaea was incorporated into the Ptolemaic province of Coele-Syria. Then in 200 BCE, the Seleucids conquered Coele-Syria. An internal Jewish civil war of 167 drew in the Seleucid king Antiochus IV. A local priestly family named the Hasmoneans came to power. Following the implosion of the Seleucid Empire, Judaea emerged as a regional power and an ally of the Romans. The Hasmonean dynasty conquered the neighboring peoples, especially during the reigns of John Hyrcanus (134–104) and Alexander Yannai (103–76). They ruled modern-day Israel and its territories as well as the east bank of the Jordan River.

Civil war occurred in 67 BCE between Aristobolus and Hyrcanus, the two heirs to the Hasmonean throne. Hyrcanus was supported by the Idumean Antipater, father of the future king Herod. The arrival of Pompey Magnus in Judaea in 63 BCE led to resolution of the civil war in Hyrcanus's favor, but the Mediterranean coast was detached from the kingdom of Judaea.

Hyrcanus and Antipater supported the Caesarians during the Caesarian-Pompeian civil war. After the murder of Caesar in 44 BCE, they first supported the Liberators, then Mark Antony. In 40 the Parthians invaded, restoring Aristobolus's son Antigonus to the throne. At the same time the Roman Senate, at the recommendation of Mark Antony and Octavian, made Herod, the son of Antipater, king of Judaea. During 39–37, Herod fought Antigonus and the Parthians, driving them out of Judaea. After the Battle of Actium (31), Octavian again confirmed Herod as king of Judaea. After Octavian became emperor, he attached the mountainous regions of southern Syria, Trachonitis, Batanea, and Auranitis to Herod's kingdom. Herod settled veteran soldiers and mercenaries in these areas to repress banditry and stabilize the regions.

Herod ruled both Greek and Jewish subjects, maintaining peace and stability in a multiethnic kingdom. He rebuilt the Second Temple, making it into an important pilgrimage center for the Jewish diaspora. He also sponsored building projects in Greek cities throughout the Mediterranean and created the city of Caesarea, which became the new capital of Judaea.

Herod's rule lasted from 39 to 4 BCE. After his death, the peace he had imposed unraveled as rebellions spread throughout the province. These were crushed by the governor of Syria, Publius Quinctilius Varus. Herod's son Archelaus was made ethnarch of a reduced kingdom, while two of Herod's other sons ruled in Galilee and southern Syria. Augustus stripped Archelaus of his throne in 6 CE, and Judaea became a Roman province, governed by an equestrian prefect and under the jurisdiction of the proconsular governor in Syria. The prefect was supported by a small military force recruited from the surrounding Greek cities.

Judaea briefly returned to Herodian rule at the beginning of the reign of Emperor Claudius in 41. The grandson of Herod, Agrippa I, ruled southern Syria. A close friend of Claudius, he helped raise Claudius to the throne in the aftermath of Gaius's assassination. In recompense, Claudius added Judaea to Agrippa's kingdom. Upon Agrippa's death in 44, Judaea reverted to Roman rule. During Roman imperial rule from 6 to 66, Judaea had an anomalous provincial status, since much of the ruling machinery of the Herodian state was left in place. The governor was based in Caesarea, the old Herodian capital, and the military force at his disposal was originally the nucleus of the Herodian army.

After the Jewish revolt and the First Jewish-Roman War of 66–73, Judaea was annexed as an imperial province. Its governor was an ex-praetor, and the X Legion was stationed at Jerusalem. In the 130s another legion, the VI Ferrata, was settled in Palestine in southern Galilee at Legio. The outbreak of the Bar Kochba revolt in 132 and its quelling in 135 led to the effective extinction of the Jewish inhabitants of Judaea. In 136 Emperor Hadrian renamed the province of Judaea as Syria Palaestina after its ancient Philistine inhabitants. "Palestine" has been the term employed for the region until the founding of the modern-day State of Israel in 1948.

NATHAN SCHUMER

See also
Bar Kochba Revolt; Jewish-Roman War, First

References
Goodman, Martin. *Rome and Jerusalem: The Clash of Ancient Civilizations.* New York: Knopf, 2007.
Schäfer, Peter. *The History of the Jews in the Greco-Roman World: The Jews of Palestine from Alexander the Great to the Arab Conquest.* New York: Routledge, 2003.
Schwartz, Seth. *Imperialism and Jewish Society: 200 B.C.E. to 640 C.E.* Princeton, NJ: Princeton University Press, 2001.

Judaism
See Ashkenazic Judaism; Hasidic Judaism; Mizrahi Judaism; Saphardic Judaism

Judas Maccabeus (ca. 190–130 BCE)

Leader of a revolt by the Jews against Rome. Judas Maccabeus (Judah Maccabee) was born around 190 BCE, one of five sons of Mattathias the Hasmonean, a Jewish priest from the village of Mod'lin in Judaea. In 167 BCE Seleucid ruler Antiochus IV arrived in Jerusalem following a military defeat in Egypt. Opposed to Judaism, he desecrated the Temple and ordered Jews to honor a Greek god. These actions led to a confrontation in Mod'lin when Mattathias refused to make sacrifice to a Greek god, and he and his sons Judas, Eleazar, Simon, John, and Jonathan slew a Seleucid general and some soldiers. This event triggered the protracted Maccabean Revolt (167–160 BCE). When Mattathias died in 166, Judas assumed leadership of the revolt, which came to be named for him. The surname of Maccabeus (Maccabee) given Judas may mean "hammer," for his leadership in battle, although other scholars claim that it means "the one designated by Yahweh (God)."

A natural leader and military commander of considerable ability, Judas Maccabeus at first avoided major engagements with the well-armed Seleucids and employed guerrilla tactics to defeat a succession of their generals sent to Judaea. In 167 BCE at the Ascent of Lebonah (167), he wiped out an entire Seleucid unit. In 166 he defeated a small Seleucid force under Apollonius, governor of Samaria, at Nahal el-Haramiah. Apollonius was among the dead. This victory led to many Jews joining the cause.

Shortly thereafter in 166 BCE, Judas defeated a larger Seleucid force under Seron near Beth-Horon. He was then victorious at Emmaus, defeating Seleucid generals Micanor and Gorgias. His defeat of the Seleucids at Beth Zur (Bethsura) near Hebron in 164 BCE allowed him to take much of Jerusalem, including the Temple, although some Seleucids continued to hold out in the Acra (citadel). Continuing the siege of the Acra, Judas expanded his control over the whole of Judaea.

With Antioches campaigning to the east, Seleucid regent Lysias invaded Judaea and defeated Judas at Beth Zachariah (162 BCE) but then was forced to return to Syria to suppress a revolt there. That same year, however, Bacchides, commander of Seleucid forces in Judaea, defeated Judas at Jerusalem, driving him from the city.

Judas rallied, however, and in 161 BCE he defeated Syrian general Nicanor at Adasa, Nicanor among those killed. That same year, however, Judas was defeated and slain by a far more numerous Seleucid force, said to number 20,000 men, under Bacchides in the Battle of Elasa.

While most scholars date the revolt as ending in 160 BCE, armed resistance against the Seleucids continued under Jonathan, who enjoyed considerable success with the guerrilla tactics first employed by his brother. Establishing his headquarters at Jerusalem in 152, Jonathan was recognized as de facto ruler of Judaea until 143 BCE, when he was captured in an ambush at Ptolemais (Acre, Akko) and killed by dissident Jews.

Judas is widely praised in the First Book of Maccabees, and he is acclaimed by Jews as one of the greatest military leaders in their history. The Festival of Lights, Chanukah (Hanukkah, meaning "Dedication") in the month of December commemorates the cleansing and rededication of the Temple following the removal of its pagan statuary by Judas in 164 BCE.

Spencer C. Tucker

See also
Antiochus IV Epiphanes; Maccabean Revolt; Seleucid Empire

References
Robinson, Theodore H., and W. O. E. Oesterley. *A History of Israel.* Oxford, UK: Clarendon, 1932.
Schäfer, Peter. *The History of the Jews in the Greco-Roman World.* New York: Routledge, 2003.

Julian, Emperor (331–363)

Roman emperor during 361–363. Flavius Claudius Julianus was born in Constantinople (modern-day Istanbul) in 331, the son of Julius Constantius, half brother of Constantine I, and Basilina. Julian would become the last male descendant of the dynasty of Constantine. His grandfather was Constantius I. Julian had an older half brother, Gallus, and his several cousins included Constantius II. When Constantine died in 337 and Constantius II became coaugustus in the east, he ordered the purge of Julian's family. All of Julian's direct relatives except Gallus were murdered. Julian and Gallus became Constantius's prisoners and lived a secluded life for many years. Julian was raised an Arian Christian, and during his exile in Cappadocia he was introduced to the Greek classics. A bright student, he would write works on panegyrics, philosophy, satires, and religious discourses. In 351, Julian began his study of Neoplatonism and soon after secretly converted to paganism. His brother Gallus became caesar in 351, only to be executed in 354.

In November 355 Constantius named Julian his caesar, married him to his sister, and sent him to face the growing Germanic threat in Gaul. Julian's campaigns in Gaul proved highly successful and made him a popular general. He retook Cologne in 356 and crushed the German confederation under King Chnodomarius in the Battle of Strasbourg in 357. After the battle Julian's soldiers attempted to acclaim him augustus, which Julian immediately refused. Julian spent the next few years reestablishing Roman control of the Rhine frontier.

In 359, king of the Sassanian Persian Empire Shapur II (the Great) renewed war against Rome in the east. In February 360, Constantius ordered a large portion of Julian's Gallic army to move east in support of his campaign. The soldiers rebelled and at Paris proclaimed Julian augustus; this time he did not refuse. Once he had settled matters in the west, Julian marched east against Constantius in early 361. The empire was spared another civil war when on November 3 Constantius died of illness in Cilicia.

Julian openly declared his paganism (hence the name Julian the Apostate). As emperor, he sought to advance Hellenism and followed a policy of pagan activism but met little success in his efforts to reestablish traditional Greco-Roman polytheism. Although he did not persecute Christians, he removed many of the church's privileges and subsidies while heavily favoring pagan interests. He attempted to restore and rebuild the ancestral cults and temples of the traditional Roman religion. The brevity of his reign meant that nearly all his religious measures were short-lived.

Julian soon turned his thoughts to a campaign against the Sassanid Persian Empire. After a tumultuous stay in Antioch, Julian clashed with the city's Christian population, and moved his army against Shapur in March 363. With 65,000 Roman troops plus additional auxiliaries and a fleet of some 1,100 ships, Julian's campaign experienced initial success. By May, the Romans had reached the Sassanian capital of Ctesiphon and defeated a Sassanian army. However, Shapur's arrival with a sizable force made a siege of the city impractical. In a fateful decision, Julian burned his fleet. The Romans soon found themselves isolated and outmaneuvered. The Persians then harassed the Roman withdrawal. In one of the engagements Julian was fatally wounded in the liver with a spear thrust; he died on June 26, 363.

NIKOLAUS LEO OVERTOOM

See also
Constantius II, Emperor; Ctesiphon, 363 Battle of; Roman-Sassanid Wars; Sassanid Empire; Shapur II the Great

References
Bowder, Diana. *The Age of Constantine and Julian.* New York: Barnes & Noble, 1978.
Bowersock, G. W. *Julian the Apostate.* Cambridge, MA: Harvard University Press, 1978.
Browning, Robert. *The Emperor Julian.* Berkeley: University of California Press, 1976.
Murdoch, Adrian. *The Last Pagan: Julian the Apostate and the Death of the Ancient World.* Rochester, VT: Inner Traditions, 2008.
Ricciotti, Giuseppe. *Julian the Apostate.* Translated by M. Joseph Costelloe. Milwaukee, WI: Bruce, 1960.

Justinian I the Great, Emperor (483–565)

Byzantine emperor. Born near Skopje in Illyria of Latin-speaking peasant parents in 483, Flavius Petrus Sabbatius Justinianus (Justinian) had an uncle who became Emperor Justin I in 518. His uncle, then a general, arranged for Justinian to come to Constantinople in 505 and be educated. Justin, who was childless, adopted his nephew and gave him command of some of his troops. Shortly before his death on August 1, 527, Justin named Justinian as coemperor (augustus) and his heir.

As emperor, Justinian had to deal with crumbling Byzantine power and pressure from without the empire from Persians to the east and Barbarians from the north and west. To rebuild the army, Justinian relied in large part on mercenary troops, while soldier-settlers helped protect the frontiers. Justinian proved astute in his selection of military commanders and other officials. The most important of these was his general, Belisarius. Justinian's consort, Empress Theodora, also proved extraordinarily useful.

Belisarius soon led a military campaign against the Persians, defeating them in the Battle of Dara (530). Although he was subsequently beaten at Callinicum (531), Belisarius concluded with the Persians the Perpetual Peace in September 532. Justinian survived the Nika Revolt (532) in Constantinople largely because of the courage of Theodora and loyalty of Belisarius and another general, Narses.

Peace with the Persians enabled Justinian to order Belisarius to conquer Vandal North Africa in 533–534. Success in that endeavor encouraged Justinian in an attempt to reestablish personal control of Italy, then a semi-independent Gothic kingdom, and he ordered Belisarius to invade Sicily in 535. That island taken, Belisarius crossed the Straits of Messina to southern Italy in 536. Although Belisarius occupied Rome, he was unable to bring the campaign to an end because of stubborn resistance and Justinian's failure to supply needed reinforcements. In consequence, fighting in Italy continued for 17 years.

With the renewal of war with Persia in 539, Justinian transferred Belisarius to that front during 542–544. Belisarius subsequently returned to Italy during 544–548. Justinian was jealous of Belisarius and, following the death of Theodora in 548, replaced him as his principal military commander with Narses, who brought Belisarius's work in Italy to a successful conclusion during 551–554. The war with Persia continued. Following a truce during 545–549, it ended in 562.

Meanwhile, Justinian expanded Byzantine control over North Africa and even briefly expanded Byzantine power into Spain following a campaign there in 554 by Belisarius, whom he dismissed afterward. Justinian also ordered construction of fortifications in the Balkans along the Danube and at Thessalonika and Thermopylae to stop inroads by the Bulgars and Slavs. He was also a great builder and caused the construction of a number of new structures in Constantinople, including the great Cathedral of St. Sophia (Hagia Sophia). An important lawgiver, he oversaw the codification of Roman civil law, which ultimately became the basis of much of continental European law.

Justinian called Belisarius out of retirement in 559 to defeat a major incursion by the Bulgars, then jailed him on a charge of treason in 562 before rehabilitating him in 563. Justinian died in Constantinople on November 14, 565. His nephew followed him as emperor as Justin II.

Diligent (he was known as "the emperor who never sleeps"), ambitious, and highly intelligent, Justinian proved to be a capable administrator, but his efforts to restore the empire to its former greatness proved elusive.

SPENCER C. TUCKER

See also
Belisarius; Byzantine Empire; Nika Uprising

References
Barker, John W. *Justinian and the Later Roman Empire*. Madison: University of Wisconsin Press, 1966.
Evans, James Allan. *The Empress Theodora: Partner of Justinian*. Austin: University of Texas Press, 2003.
Moorhead, John. *Justinian*. London: Longman, 1994.

K

Kabakchi Incident (May 25, 1807)

A revolt in Istanbul (Constantinople) that brought the deposition of Sultan Selim III. During his reign of 1789–1807, Selim III sought rapid modernization of his armed forces. Among his reforms was the creation of the Nizam-i Cedid troops, who received European training and weaponry. These reforms, however, threatened the power of traditional groups, particularly the ulema and the Janissaries, who, together with conservative political circles, propagated the idea that military innovation modeled after Europe would eventually threaten Islamic values and engender an infidel state.

When Selim III sought to introduce the Nizam-i Cedid troops in the Balkans in 1806, these opposing forces refused to admit the troops into Edirne in what is known as the Second Edirne Incident. The sultan's political opponents used this incident to breath life into a political conspiracy against him, and on May 25, 1807, several newly recruited units in the fortresses along the Bosporus were incited to revolt against the government and refused to wear the European-style uniforms of the Nizam-i Cedid army.

Led by Sergeant Kabakchi Mustafa, these units marched to Istanbul and forced the demoralized sultan to accept their demands. The Nizam-i Cedid army was disbanded, and reformist officials were handed over and murdered. Despite his concessions, Selim could not save his throne and was deposed on May 29, 1807, in favor of Mustafa IV. Selim was assassinated the following year in an attempted counter-coup orchestrated by his supporters.

ALEXANDER MIKABERIDZE

See also
Ottoman Empire; Selim III, Sultan

References
Aksan, Virginia. *Ottoman Wars 1700–1870: An Empire Besieged.* Harlow, UK: Longman/Pearson, 2007.
Shaw, Stanford J. "The Transition from Traditionalistic to Modern Reform in the Ottoman Empire: The Reigns of Sultan Selim III (1789–1807) and Sultan Mahmud II (1808–1839)." In *The Turks,* Vol. 4, ed, Hasan Celal Guzel, C. Cem Oguz, and Osman Karatay, 130–149. Ankara: Yeni Turkiye Yayınları, 2002.

Kadesh, Battle of (1274 BCE)

Fought near Kadesh (believed to be Carchemish on the Euphrates River in northwestern Syria) in 1274 BCE, the battle was waged between Egyptian forces led by Pharaoh Ramesses II and a Hittite army led by King Muwatallish.

Almost everything about this battle is in dispute, including the exact date, the location, the strength of the forces involved, and the performance of the Egyptian troops. It is, however, mentioned in both Egyptian and biblical accounts, so its occurrence is fairly certain. Ramesses II was campaigning in Syria with the plan of taking the important city of Kadesh. His army was in four separate divisions and advancing against Hittite forces that he believed to be to the north. Ramses was with the Amon division and decided to camp northwest of Kadesh, which he had bypassed on the report of spies who had been captured and tortured. Actually sent by the Hittites, they had given spurious information as to the location of the main Hittite army, claiming that it was far distant when it was in fact close by and largely secreted behind Kadesh. No sooner had the Egyptians begun to set up camp than Hittite king Muwartallish appeared from the south, sending a reported 2,500 chariots (some across the Euphrates, probably by means of a dam) to attack the Re division, which was unprepared for battle. The Egyptians fled to the north away from their supply bases.

Meanwhile, Ramesses and the Amon division came under attack in their camp from another Hittite force from south of Kadesh. Ramesses sent messengers by a side route to the west to speed the arrival from the south of the two other Egyptian divisions, the Ptah and Sutekh.

Deserted by many if not most of his troops, who fled northward, Ramesses was saved by his own personal bravery in standing his ground but also by the timely arrival of elite auxiliary forces—probably mercenaries from Judah, not part of the four Egyptian divisions—who cut through the Hittites surrounding the pharaoh. This saved Ramesses from death or captivity and brought him out to the Ptah and Sutekh divisions, which had not participated in the battle. His generals urged Ramesses to return to Egypt with his remaining forces, which he did.

Ramesses claimed a great victory, but it was in fact a draw, with the Hittites still controlling Kadesh and Syria. Nonetheless, they found themselves under continued pressure from both the Egyptians and the Assyrians and ultimately sought a peace agreement with Egypt, regarded by some scholars as the world's first signed treaty.

Spencer C. Tucker

See also
Egypt, Ancient; Ramesses II the Great

References
Goedicke, Hans, ed. *Perspectives on the Battle of Kadesh.* Baltimore: Halgo, 1985.

Kitchen, Kenneth. *Pharaoh Triumphant: The Life and Times of Ramesses II, King of Egypt.* London: Aris & Phillips. 1983.

Murnane, William J. *The Road to Kadesh.* Chicago: Oriental Institute, 1990.

Velikovsky, Immanuel. *Ramses II and His Time.* New York: Doubleday, 1978.

Kafr Qasim Massacre (October 29, 1956)

Massacre of Arab civilians by members of the Israeli Border Police and Israeli Army in the town of Kafr Qasim on October 29, 1956. The mass killings that claimed 49 lives (including 23 children and an unborn child) coincided with the opening of hostilities in the Suez Crisis, when Israeli forces invaded Egypt's Sinai Peninsula. Kafr Qasim was close to Tel Aviv and part of the Small Triangle area of villages populated by Arabs, located not too far from the Green Line, then the recognized border between Israel and Jordan. Believing that Jordan would enter the war on the side of Egypt, Israeli officials dispatched border police under the command of Israel Defense Forces (IDF) brigadier general Issachar Shadmi to the area of Kafr Qasim in order to ensure calm in the border area and prevent Israeli Arabs from joining Jordanian forces. Living in the Arab villages in the vicinity were some 40,000 Arab Israelis.

Shadmi's first action was to move back the curfew for Arabs from 10:00 p.m. to 5:00 p.m. He is also said to have issued shoot-on-sight orders for any Arab seen violating the new curfew. Major Shmuel Malinki, who headed the border patrol in Kafr Qasim, asked for clarification of the orders. Specifically, he was concerned about workers returning from the fields or jobs outside the village. If they had not known about the curfew, surely they could not be shot for violating it. Although Shadmi denied ever having had the discussion with Malinki, Malinki claimed that he reaffirmed the order and that there would be no arrests.

At 4:30 p.m. on October 29, word went out concerning the new curfew to go into effect only a half hour later. Most villagers returned when they heard the news. Some did not, and it is hard to determine if they had indeed been warned. Slavishly following Shadmi's orders, a platoon commanded by Lieutenant Gabriel Dahan shot 49 Arabs between 5:00 and 6:30 p.m. as they tried to return home. Border patrol soldiers in the nearby villages did not follow suit, as Shadmi's orders had been overridden by local unit commanders. The victims at Kafr Qasim were hastily buried in a mass grave.

News of the massacre traveled quickly, despite the Israeli government's attempts to conceal it. Amid much outrage, Prime Minister David Ben-Gurion lifted the press blackout in early January 1953, and the full details of the massacre were made known. Meanwhile, the government launched an investigation into the events that, however, was kept from the media. After international pressure and frequent street protests in Israel, 11 soldiers and border police were charged with murder. In October 1958, 8 were found guilty and sent to prison. Malinki and Dahan were given lengthy prison terms, but Shadmi was exonerated on murder charges and was given a token reprimand for having illegally changed the curfew. When Dahan complained that he had no choice but to follow orders, the judge retorted that none of the other platoons had followed the order, so he clearly had a choice. By 1959 all of the convicted parties were out of jail, the result of several postconviction appeals and commutations by Israeli military leaders and the Israeli president.

The Kafr Qasim case was instructive in that the Israeli court made it clear that while disobeying military orders on a purely subjective basis is prohibited, one has an obligation to disobey orders that are obviously illegal and morally reprehensible. Certainly, the killing of 49 innocent people for no apparent reason met both criteria. In 1957, the Israeli government tried to make amends for the tragedy by offering survivors of the massacre cash and land grants. The Kafr Qasim Massacre also led to significant reforms in the way Israel interacted with Arabs living within its borders.

PAUL G. PIERPAOLI JR.

See also
Ben-Gurion, David; Sinai Campaign of 1956; Suez Crisis

Reference
Lustick, Ian. *Arabs in the Jewish State: Israel's Control of a National Minority.* Austin: University of Texas Press, 1980.

Kafur, Abu al-Misk (905–968)

Black eunuch ruler of Egypt, the only black man from sub-Saharan Africa to rise from humblest origins to one of the highest position in the Islamic world. Little is known about Abu al-Misk Kafur's early life. He was born either in Nubia or Ethiopia probably in 905. In his youth, he was captured and sold into slavery in Cairo.

Kafur's presentation in literature is rather contradictory, mixing admiration for superb talent with ridicule for his race and physical unsightliness. He was said to be deformed and clumsy, but his ugliness concealed brilliant intelligence and political acumen. As a slave he had the good fortune of being sold to ruler of Egypt Muhammad al-Ilkshid, who quickly appreciated his talents. Kafur must certainly have had great merit, since al-Ilkshid entrusted him with tutoring his sons and later gave him command of his household troops. When al-Ilkshid died in 946, Kafur became the guardian to Unujur (Anujir), who inherited his father's realm. Kafur administered the state with great ability. Overshadowed by a powerful vizier, Unujur tried unsuccessfully to escape, prompting Kafur to recruit black soldiers (*al-kafuriyya*) to consolidate his authority.

Kafur ruled over Egypt for two decades and showed himself to be a skillful statesman. He was ready to compromise and willing to abandon a peripheral province rather than maintain the country on permanent war footing. In the 940s, Kafur capably protected al-Ikhshidid interests in Palestine, which Saif al-Dawla, the Hamdanid lord of Syria, sought to conquer. In 946, Kafur defeated Saif near Nasira and captured Damascus. After regrouping, Saif returned to Damascus in the spring of 947 but again suffered defeat at Marj Rahit. Kafur retained Palestine and southern Syria but allowed Saif to keep Aleppo, thus relieving the Ilkhshid state of the need to counter the Byzantine expansion into northern Syria.

Exploiting the absence of the Ilkhshidid army in Syria, Ghabun, governor of Middle Egypt, revolted and tried to capture Fustat before Kafur routed him in 947. In 957 in response to Nubian incursions into southern Egypt, Kafur organized a major expedition to Nubia, briefly capturing Qasr Ibrim. Nonetheless, the conflict with the Nubians continued for years.

When Unujur died in 960, Kafur arranged the accession of his brother Abu'l-Hasan Ali but retained real power in his own hands. Kafur avoided direct confrontation with the Byzantine Empire until the Byzantines attacked Cyprus in 960s. Kafur then dispatched the Egyptian fleet to Cyprus, but the Byzantines destroyed it between 960 and 963, which allowed them to raid the Egyptian and Syrian coasts. After Ali died in 966, Kafur sidelined his heir and assumed the supreme authority under the title *al-ustadh* (master), which was conferred upon him by a complaisant Abbasid caliph. Kafur ruled over Egypt, Palestine, and southern Syria until his death.

Domestically, the last years of Kafur's life proved to be challenging for him, since a series of low Nile floods in 963–969 resulted in a devastating famine in Egypt. Internationally, Kafur enjoyed such a high reputation that in 966 when Bedouins raided the great pilgrim caravan from Damascus, some 200 camel loads of booty were handed over to Kafur as a goodwill gesture.

Kafur pursued scholarly endeavors and was a generous patron of scholars and the arts. In his famous *Muqaddimah,* great Muslim historian Ibn Khaldun used Kafur as an example of the way in which rulers could be eclipsed by more competent ministers. Kafur died in April 968 and was buried in Jerusalem.

ALEXANDER MIKABERIDZE

See also
Fatimid Dynasty; Jawhar; Saif al-Dawla

References
Boanquis, Thierry. "Autonomous Egypt from Ibn Tulun to Kafur." In *The Cambridge History of Egypt*, ed. Carl F. Petry, 86–120. Cambridge: Cambridge University Press, 1998.

Brett, Michael. *The Rise of the Fatimids: The World of the Mediterranean and the Middle East in the Fourth Century of the Hijra.* Leiden: Brill, 2001.

Kapikulu Corps

Ottoman military formation. Legend has it that the Kapikulu Corps was established by Kara Halil Candarli, brother-in-law of Sheikh Edebali, a Muslim mystic in western Anatolia in the early 14th century. Its infantry units, the Yeni Ceri (Janissaries), whose name means "new troops," were supposedly founded in 1326 when the recruits were also blessed by Hacci Bektas, from whose broad upraised sleeve the Janissaries adopted the flap that fell behind their traditional white felt caps. In reality this Muslim mystic had died many years before, while the first Janissaries actually seem to have been prisoners of war following the Ottoman invasion of eastern Thrace in the 1360s. Nevertheless, the Bektasi sect of dervishes, followers of Hacci Bektas, did maintain close links with the Janissary Corps, some living in its barracks, serving as chaplains, and participating in parades.

Prisoners captured during raids provided the expanding Ottoman state with substantial military manpower during the 14th century, so it was not until the early 15th century that the *devshirme* system was formalized. Thereafter this human levy, though strictly against Islamic law, provided the bulk of recruits for the various elements of the Kapikulu Corps. Those deemed the most intelligent were selected for training as *ic oglani,* pages in the sultan's Topkapi Palace, while the rest went to work on farms, where they learned Turkish and the Muslim faith before becoming qualified Janissaries. Meanwhile, the *ic oglani* were trained for up to seven years with the focus on character building, leadership, military and athletic prowess, languages, religion, science, and a creative art of the pupil's own choosing. Three further examinations selected men for the Kapikulu cavalry or to be Kapikulu officers, while the best became military or administrative leaders. All remained bachelors until their training ended, whereupon most married women who had been through a parallel schooling system in the palace harem.

The Kapikulu Corps grew steadily from the 14th to 18th centuries, with rulers regarding it as a counterbalance to turbulent provincial military forces. Sultan Mehmet II (r. 1444–1446 and 1451–1481) placed them under the command of men who had themselves risen through the *devshirme* system, by which time the Janissaries numbered about 12,000. Sultan Suleiman I (r. 1520–1566 CE) raised the Kapikulu to 48,000 men, including 20,000 Janissaries.

The Kapikulu cavalry was militarily more important and had higher prestige than the Janissary infantry. By the late 16th century the Kapikulu cavalry numbered some 6,000 men and included the sons of *suvarileri* (troopers); Arab, Persian, and Kurdish Muslims; and ex-Janissaries who had distinguished themselves in battle. The Kapikulu Corps also included smaller artillery and engineer units.

DAVID NICOLLE

See also
Devshirme System; Janissaries

References
Goodwin, G. *The Janissaries.* London: Saqi, 1997.

Gross, M. L. *The Origins and Role of the Janissaries in Early Ottoman History.* Amsterdam: Middle East Research Association, 1969–1970.

Miller, B. *The Palace School of Mohammed the Conqueror.* Cambridge MA: Harvard University Press, 1941.

Weissmann, N. *Les Janissaires: Etude de l'Organisation Militaire des Ottomans.* Paris: Librairie Orient, 1964.

Karameh, Battle of (March 21, 1968)

Military engagement involving Palestine Liberation Organization (PLO) fighters and Jordanian Army forces against the Israel Defense Forces (IDF) on March 21, 1968. Karameh is a Jordanian village located near the Israeli border. At the time of the battle the PLO, headed by Chairman Yasser Arafat, had its headquarters in Jordan. The town of Karameh served as the military and political control center of Fatah, the largest and most powerful of the PLO factions. It too was headed by Arafat.

Following the June 1967 Six-Day War, PLO and Fatah forces began stepping up their guerrilla attacks against Israel from Jordanian territory as part of the War of Attrition mounted by Egyptian forces. However, since late February 1968, IDF forces had been hitting back with escalating retaliatory strikes. Determined to stop the attacks and destroy the PLO and Fatah leadership, Israeli officials began planning a major ground offensive into Jordan, focused on Karameh.

On March 21, 1968, IDF armored forces, totaling some 15,000 men, stormed the makeshift Allenby Bridge (the original one had been destroyed in the Six-Day War) and moved against Palestinian fighters in and around Karameh, who erected a number of defensive positions there. Although hopelessly outnumbered and outgunned by Israeli forces, the PLO fighters fought valiantly. Jordan's King Hussein was highly ambivalent about sending his forces to reinforce the Palestinians. However, Jordanian Army tanks and artillery were finally sent in, and the combined Jordanian-Palestinian force inflicted considerable losses on the IDF, which then withdraw by day's end back into Israeli territory.

Several Israeli tanks were destroyed in the fighting, as were a number of other armored vehicles. The IDF had suffered 28 deaths and 69 wounded. The Jordanian Army lost 40 soldiers killed, while the PLO lost more than 200. Both sides claimed victory, but the battle was certainly a public relations bonanza for Fatah and the PLO, who used it to garner popular support. Within two days of the battle, Fatah claimed 5,000 new recruits. For many, the Battle of Karameh enhanced PLO claims for an autonomous Palestinian state. The Soviet Union, for instance, after 1968 backed the PLO and Fatah, something that heretofore it had refused to do.

Yet there were also negative repercussions for the PLO. Karameh effectively ended Fatah's strategy of launching raids against Israel from the border areas, making PLO raiding against Israel much more difficult. Karameh also set the PLO and Fatah on a collision course with King Hussein of Jordan. Emboldened by the battle, the PLO continued to raid into Israel, albeit from greater distances. Yet the Jordanian government did not want to see Jordan drawn into war with Israel. Ultimately Jordanian-PLO clashes resulted in the so-called Black September in 1970 that saw major fighting between the Jordanian Army and the PLO, resulting in the expulsion of the PLO from Jordan.

PAUL G. PIERPAOLI JR.

See also
Arafat, Yasser; Black September; Fatah, al-; Hussein ibn Talal, King of Jordan; Jordan; Palestine Liberation Organization; Six-Day War; War of Attrition

References
Dobson, Christopher. *Black September: Its Short, Violent History.* New York: Macmillan, 1974.
Golan, Galia. *The Soviet Union and the Palestine Liberation Organization: An Uneasy Alliance.* New York: Praeger, 1980.
Nassar, Jamal R. *The Palestine Liberation Organization: From Armed Struggle to the Declaration of Independence.* New York: Praeger, 1991.
Reische, Diana. *Arafat and the Palestine Liberation Organization.* New York: Franklin Watts, 1991.

Karbala, Battle of (October 10, 680)

Key battle between the forces of the Umayyad caliph Yazid and Husayn ibn Ali, Prophet Muhammad's grandson, that had a profound impact on the Islamic community. Many Muslims were displeased with Yazid's succession to the caliphate, and some prominent figures openly defied the new caliph. Husayn, the son of Caliph Ali, was among those who refused to swear allegiance to Yazid. Husayn fled to Mecca. After sending his cousin to assess the situation in Kufa and receiving word that the inhabitants of the city were ready to support him, Husayn set out to join them with his family and close supporters.

However, things changed when Yazid appointed Ubayd Allah ibn Ziyad as the new governor of Kufa and ordered him to restore order in the rebellious city. Despite warnings from friends, companions, and Bedouins he met along the way, Husayn refused to veer from his objective. At Karbala, Husayn and his 72 followers were intercepted and surrounded by a much larger number of Umayyad troops from Kufa. After a standoff in which the small party suffered greatly from thirst and heat, Husayn and his male supporters were all killed in battle on Muharram 10 (October 10, 680). Husayn's head was severed and sent to the caliph.

Husayn was survived by his sickly son, Ali, whose line provided the future imams of the Shias. The events at Karbala were central to the development of Shiism as a religious sect, and the battle is commemorated each year by Shia Muslims in the Remembrance of Muharram.

ADAM ALI

See also
Ali ibn Abi Talib; Umayyad Caliphate

References
Madelung, Wilferd. *The Succession to Muhammad: A Study of the Early Caliphate.* Cambridge; New York: Cambridge University Press, 1997.
Rogerson, Barnaby. *The Heirs of the Prophet Muhammad and the Roots of the Sunni-Shia Schism.* London: Little, Brown, 2006.

Karbala, First Battle of (March 31–April 6, 2003)

The city of Karbala is located in central Iraq some 60 miles southwest of Baghdad and is regarded as one of the holiest sites in Shia Islam. Three notable battles have occurred there: one in October 680, one during the Iraq War in 2003, and one between Iraqi factions in 2007.

The 2003 Battle of Karbala occurred during March 31–April 6, when U.S. troops attempted to evict Iraqi forces from the city. Divisional units involved in the fight included those from the U.S. 3rd Infantry, 1st Armored Division, and the 101st Airborne Division; Iraqi forces consisted of members of the Fedayeen Saddam and Syrian mercenaries.

During the initial phase of the 2003 invasion of Iraq, advance units of the U.S. 3rd Infantry pushed their way through Republican Guard forces southeast of Karbala and arrived in the area on March 31. While some troops kept a watchful eye on the Iraqis in Karbala, the main body bypassed the city and attacked Baghdad through the Karbala Gap. This meant that U.S. forces would have to clear the Iraqis from Karbala later.

This task fell principally to the 101st Airborne Division, supported by the 2nd Battalion, 70th Armored Regiment, 1st Armored Division. On April 2, 2003, a U.S. Army UH-60 Blackhawk helicopter was shot down near Karbala, killing seven soldiers and wounding four others. This event appeared to indicate a significant Iraqi military presence in the city.

In the operation to take control of Karbala, three battalions of the 101st Airborne Division were to be inserted via helicopter at three landing zones (LZs) on the outskirts of the city—designated LZs Sparrow, Finch, and Robin. M-1 Abrams tanks and M-2 Bradley Fighting Vehicles of the 2nd Battalion, 70th Armored Regiment, were assigned to support the troopers.

On the morning of April 5, 23 UH-60 Blackhawks escorted 5 CH-47 Boeing Chinook helicopters ferrying three battalions of the 502nd Infantry to their LZs. At LZ Sparrow, the 3rd Battalion met heavy but uncoordinated resistance. The 2nd Battalion inserted to the south at LZ Robin found numerous arms caches in schools as well as a suspected terrorist training camp. As night fell, the battalion had cleared 13 of its 30 assigned sectors. The 1st Battalion, landed at LZ Finch to the southeast, captured a large store of weapons. Meanwhile, the armor support arrived and reinforced the ground advance.

The operation continued until 5:00 p.m. on April 6, when all sectors were declared secured. The Americans suffered 8 men killed. One UH-60 helicopter was also lost, and an M-1 Abrams tank was disabled. Iraqi casualties were estimated at as many as 260.

WILLIAM P. HEAD

See also
Iraq War; Karbala, Battle of; Karbala, Second Battle of; Karbala Gap

References
Atkinson, Rick. *In the Company of Soldiers: A Chronicle of Combat*. New York: Henry Holt, 2005.
NBC Enterprises. *Operation Iraqi Freedom: The Insider Story*. Kansas City, MO: Andrews McMeel Publishing, 2003.

Karbala, Second Battle of (August 27–29, 2007)

Karbala is located in central Iraq some 60 miles southwest of Baghdad and is one of the holiest cities in Shia Islam. Notable battles have been fought there: one in October 680 CE among Islamic factions, one during the coalition invasion of Iraq in 2003, and one between Iraqi factions in 2007.

The August 27–29, 2007, Battle of Karbala began as thousands of Shia pilgrims gathered in the city for the annual festival of Mid-Sha'ban. The fighting occurred between members of the Mahdi Army, charged with providing security for the pilgrims, and the Iraqi Security Forces (police), most of whom belonged to the Badr Organization.

By August 27, 2007, a large security force was present in Karbala because pilgrims had been killed there during previous pilgrimages. Early that evening, an exchange of small-arms fire occurred between the Mahdi Army and local police. The number of forces on each side is unknown. The Mahdi Army was a militia force loyal to Iraqi Shia cleric Muqtada al-Sadr. Senior members of Iraq's Interior Ministry soon accused the Mahdi Army of attacking government forces guarding two shrines under the control of the Supreme Islamic Iraqi Council.

On August 28, the Iraqi government deployed more troops to the city. On August 29, Prime Minister Nuri al-Maliki imposed a curfew that directed pilgrims to end their devotions early. Although he claimed that the situation was under control, sporadic shooting continued. Only after additional Iraqi security forces had arrived and most of the pilgrims had departed did the violence end. Casualties in this factional struggle were estimated at 30–40 killed and more than 100 wounded. Perhaps 10 Iraqi policemen died in the confrontation.

In the aftermath of this fighting, Ali Sharia, head of the Mahdi Army in Karbala, was arrested and brought to trial for inciting the violence at Karbala. In August 2008, he was convicted and sentenced to death.

WILLIAM P. HEAD

See also
Karbala, Battle of; Karbala, First Battle of; Maliki, Nuri Muhammed Kamil al-; Sadr, Muqtada al-

References
Craig, Charles. "Iraq Militia Fighting for Supremacy." *Time*, August 29, 2007, http://www.time.com/time/world/article/0,8599,1657449,00.html.
"Iraqi PM Orders Curfew in Karbala." BBC News, August 29, 2007, http://news.bbc.co.uk/2/hi/middle_east/6968236.stm.
"Toll Rises in Karbala Fighting." Al Jazeera, August 28, 2007, http://english.aljazeera.net/news/middleeast/2007/08/2008525141014347965.html.

Karbala Gap

A sandy 20-mile wide plain located in central Iraq's Karbala Province, some 55 miles south-southwest of the Iraqi capital of Baghdad. Situated between Lake Buhayrat al-Razzazah to the west and the Euphrates River to the east, the Karbala Gap is an area of marshes and rich farmland; it is also the location of the city of Karbala, with a population of some 500,000 people. Given its location, geographical constraints, and the proximity to Baghdad, the Karbala Gap is a major choke point and last natural obstacle for an invading force moving from the south against Baghdad. A major battle had been fought here in 680 CE.

The importance of the Karbala Gap was well known and had been the object of pre-2003 Iraq War U.S. war-gaming exercises. During the Iraq War, both U.S. Army 3rd Infantry Division commander Major General Buford Blount and Iraqi Army corps commander Lieutenant General Ra'ad al-Hamdani, who had charge of defending the area, recognized that passage by the gap was the only way for mechanized forces to quickly reach Baghdad.

Blount's major concerns were the possible Iraqi employment of chemical weapons and destruction of the bridges crossing the Euphrates. Al-Hamdani's major worry was the lack of manpower to block the U.S. drive northward. The Iraqi high command had committed the Medina and Nebuchadnezzar Republican Guard divisions to block the Karbala Gap, but al-Hamdani argued for reinforcements. The Iraqi leadership rejected this, however, because it feared going against President Saddam Hussein's orders and having troops cut off from the defense of Baghdad.

On April 1, 2003, following delay imposed by a massive *shamal* (sandstorm), units of the 3rd Infantry Division attacked through the Karbala Gap. That day, strongly supported by the divisional artillery and helicopters, the 3rd Brigade secured control of the eastern outskirts of Karbala, while its 1st Brigade attacked from the other side. On April 2, U.S. forces moved against the al-Qa'id Bridge over the Euphrates River (Objective Peach), east of Karbala and near Hindiyah. The bridge had been marked for demolition, but this had not yet been carried out when that afternoon three U.S. tanks got across the span. Although Iraqi engineers then detonated some charges, the bridge survived, and the Americans quickly cut other detonation lines and rooted out the Iraqi engineers to prevent further damage. U.S. engineers then used the bridging trains following the 3rd Infantry Division to throw several other spans across the river.

Iraqi counterattacks on April 2, including what was for all intents and purposes a suicide attempt to explode charges on the main bridge, were turned back by American armor and highly effective close air support. Two divisions of the Iraqi Republican Guard had been effectively destroyed in the battle, and the way to Baghdad was now open.

SHAWN LIVINGSTON AND SPENCER C. TUCKER

See also
Iraq War; Karbala, Battle of; Karbala, Second Battle of; Republican Guard, Iraq

References
Brown, Todd S. *Battleground Iraq: Journal of Company Commander.* Washington, DC: Department of the Army, 2007.

Hodierne, Robert, and Riad Kahwaji. "History Explains Stiff Iraqi Resistance at Karbala Gap." *Navy Times* 52, no. 28 (2003): 21.

Zimmerman, Dwight. *Beyond Hell and Back: How America's Special Operations Forces Became the World's Greatest Fighting Unit.* New York: St. Martin's, 2007.

Karbugha (d. 1102)

Karbugha (Karbuqa, Kerbogha, Kerbogah) was a leading Seljuk military commander under Seljuk sultan Barkiyaruq (r. 1094–1105). Karbugha was also lord of Mosul in northern Iraq during 1095–1102. No information about his early life is available.

In 1094 Barkiyaruq ordered Karbugha and his brother Tuntash to aid Aq Sungur of Aleppo against Tutush I, king of Syria, during the civil war for the sultanate. In May 1094 Tutush defeated the Aleppo army, and Karbugha and his brother were held captive at Homs until Tutush was killed in February 1095, when Barkiyaruq obtained their release from the new king of Aleppo, his cousin Riwan. With a force of Turkoman mercenaries, Karbugha captured the city of Mosul after a nine-months siege. He became the first Seljuk lord of the city, ending a century of Arab domination by the Banu 'Uqayl family, and was so recognized by the sultan.

In late 1097 the Christian armies of the First Crusade (1096–1099) entered Syria and laid siege to the city of Antioch (modern-day Antakya, Turkey). Karbugha marched against the crusaders with a large force from Mosul and Mesopotamia. He was joined by numerous Seljuk and Turkoman allies, including Duqaq of Damascus, Balduk of Samosata, and many others; only Riwan of Aleppo, whose troops had been defeated by the crusaders on February 9, 1098, did not join. It seems that Karbugha acted on his own initiative in order to expand his influence in Syria. Karbugha and his allies unsuccessfully besieged Edessa (modern-day Sanliurfa, Turkey), held by the forces under crusader Baldwin of Boulogne and his Armenian allies. They then moved on to

Antioch, arriving there on June 5, 1098, only to find that the crusaders had captured the city two days earlier following a prolonged siege. The Muslims then besieged the city themselves, but on June 28 the crusaders sortied and defeated Karbugha's army. Many of the Turkoman leaders resented Karbugha's treatment of them and conspired to retreat when the fighting began, while Riwan of Aleppo sent messages to the Turkoman commanders, resulting in friction between them and the Arab commanders and the desertion of considerable forces from the army.

Karbugha did not interfere in Syrian affairs again and was occupied in the civil war between Barkiyaruq and his brother Muhammad Tapar in Persia until his death in Azerbaijan in September 1102.

TAEF EL-AZHARI

See also
Antioch, Sieges of; Seljuk Dynasty

References
El-Azhari, Taef. *The Saljūqs of Syria during the Crusades, 463–459 A.H./1070–1154 A.D.* Berlin: Schwarz, 1997.
France, John. *Victory in the East: A Military History of the First Crusade.* Cambridge: Cambridge University Press, 1994.
Hillenbrand, Carole. *The Crusades: Islamic Perspectives.* Edinburgh, UK: Edinburgh University Press, 1999.

Karim Khan Zand, Muhammad (ca. 1705–1779)

Persian military commander and founder of the Zand dynasty who ended civil strife in the wake of the collapse of the Safavid dynasty. Born around 1705, Muhammad Karim Khan was a member of the Lur tribe. He rose from obscurity while serving under Nadir Shah.

After the shah's assassination in 1747, Karim Khan entered into an alliance with Ali Mardan Khan, head of the Bakhtiari tribe, who controlled central Persia. The two men seized Isfahan in 1757 and restored Shah Ismail III, the grandson of the last Safavid shah, to the throne but retained real power in their hands. However, after Ali Mardan broke the alliance, Karim Khan had him killed and took control of southern and central Persia.

Karim Khan gradually took control of western Persia, defeating rival Azad Khan near Qazvin and extending his authority to Azerbaijan. In the early 1750s Karim Khan defeated the Qajar tribesmen and limited their authority to Mazanderan. By the early 1770s he controlled all of Persia except Khurasan (where he tolerated the rule of the blind Shah Rukh, Nadir Shah's grandson).

Karim Khan then switched his attention to Iraq, capturing Basra in 1775. He never claimed the title of shah, instead maintaining the powerless Shah Ismail III on the throne and ruling as a *vakil* (deputy, regent). Karim Khan's pragmatic and commonsense policies restored peace in the realm. He reorganized the fiscal system, promoted agriculture and commerce, and presided over a construction boom, particularly in his capital of Shiraz. He also pursued active cooperation with the British East India Company in the Persian Gulf.

Although illiterate himself, Karim Khan earned a reputation as a patron of the arts, attracting scholars to his court. He died on March 13, 1779, in the Zand Palace in Shiraz. His passing marked the beginning of yet another period of anarchy in Persia, which ended only with the rise of the Qajar dynasty.

ALEXANDER MIKABERIDZE

See also
Agha Muhammad Khan Qajar; Nadir Shah; Persia, 18th-Century Wars of Succession

References
Axworthy, Michael. *A History of Iran: Empire of the Mind.* New York: Basic Books, 2008.
Perry, John R. *Karim Khan Zand.* Oxford, UK: Oneworld, 2006.

Karlowitz, Treaty of (January 26, 1699)

Treaty signed on January 26, 1699, at Sremski Karlovci (Karlowitz), a town in modern-day northern Serbia, that ended the Austro-Ottoman War of 1683–1697.

In 1683, Ottoman sultan Mustafa II initiated a second siege of Vienna. It failed, and the Ottoman Empire and the Holy League, consisting of the Habsburg Monarchy, the Polish-Lithuanian Commonwealth, and the Republic of Venice and Russia, became embroiled in a series of conflicts that lasted 16 years. The war essentially ended after the Battle of Zenta, in which the Habsburgs, for the loss of 500 men, defeated the Ottomans, who lost 30,000 men. The Habsburgs also captured the sultan's harem, 87 cannon, the royal treasure chest, and the Ottoman state seal.

In early November 1698, delegates of both sides began peace negotiations at Sremski Karlovci. They were seated at a round table, the first time one was used, and met in a tent with four entrances so that none of the delegates had precedence when entering.

According to the treaty signed there on January 26, 1699, the Ottomans ceded most of Hungary, Transylvania, and Slavonia to the Habsburgs; returned Podolia to Poland; and ceded most of Dalmatia and the Peloponnesus peninsula to Venice. In 1715 the Ottomans reconquered the Peloponnesus, regaining control of it officially in the 1718 Treaty of Passarowitz.

The Treaty of Karlowitz marked the beginning of the Ottoman decline and made the Habsburg Empire the dominant power in Central Europe.

Robert B. Kane

See also
Ottoman-Habsburg Wars; Passarowitz, Treaty of

References
Asken, Virginia H. *Ottoman Wars 1700–1870: An Empire Besieged*. Harlow, UK: Pearson Longman, 2007.
Coles, Paul. *The Ottoman Impact on Europe*. London: Harcourt, Brace & World, 1968.
Finkel, Caroline. *Osman's Dream: The Story of the Ottoman Empire 1300–1923*. New York: Basic Books, 2005.

Kars, Battle of (August 9–19, 1745)

The last major battle of the Ottoman-Persian War of 1742–1746. The Battle of Kars on August 9–19, 1745, was fought near that city in eastern Anatolia between the army of Persian ruler Nadir Shah and Ottoman Empire forces under Yegen Mehmet Pasha.

The Treaty of Constantinople that ended the Ottoman-Persian War of 1730–1736 did not last, for the Persians insisted that a small Shiite sect, the Jafari, be declared orthodox. This religious dispute led the Ottomans to declare war on April 30, 1742. Ottoman sultan Mahmud I (r. 1730–1754) then made preparations to invade the Caucasus and western Persia, while Persian ruler Nadir Shah (r. 1736–1747) raided Baghdad and unsuccessfully besieged Mosul (September 1743).

Nadir Shah resumed offensive operations early in 1744. The Persians moved west from Hamadan, besieging Kars in July 1744. Nadir then turned to quell a revolt in Dagestan incited by the Ottomans, razing portions of Dagestan and killing thousands of inhabitants. In June 1745 he returned to Derbent. He then proceeded southward but in poor health, transported by litter. The army halted at Yerevan, where Nadir recovered his health and was informed that two large Ottoman armies were proceeding eastward, one apparently headed for the city of Kars and the other making for Mosul.

Nadir Shah divided his army, sending part of it under command of his son Nassarollah Mirza to engage the Ottomans headed toward Mosul while he proceeded with the other part of the army to meet the Ottomans at Kars. Moving westward, Nadir camped with his army on a hill near Yeghevārd, where some 10 years before he had defeated another Ottoman army. Yegen Mehmet Pasha's Ottoman army approached, then camped about six miles from the Persians, where they entrenched. Nadir Shah commanded some 80,000 men; the Ottoman force was much larger, perhaps numbering 140,000. The Persian army, however, was much better organized and well led.

Fighting commenced on August 9, 1745, and lasted for 11 days. The initial combat was heavy but indecisive. With the Persians having suffered heavy casualties in their attacks on the Ottoman encampment (indeed, most of the Persian casualties were incurred on the first day of fighting), Nadir Shah decided to surround the Ottoman encampment, cutting it off from resupply and starving the Ottomans into surrender. Seeking to prevent this, the Ottomans employed artillery fire, but Persian counterbattery fire proved much more effective. Demoralization spread in the Ottoman camp, and a number of soldiers deserted.

With the siege of the Ottoman encampment proceeding, on August 19 Nadir Shah received news that his son's army had defeated the Ottoman army before Mosul. Given this, Nassarollah Mirza requested permission from his father to invade Ottoman Mesopotamia. Nadir immediately ordered the letter conveyed to the Ottoman commander in a bid to convince him of the futility of further resistance. On entering the Ottoman encampment, however, Nadir Shah's emissaries learned that some of the Ottoman soldiers had risen up in mutiny and that Yegen Mehmet Pasha was dead, either a suicide or killed by the mutinous troops. The Ottoman troops then broke out of the encampment in an effort to escape but a large number were cut down by pursuing Persian cavalry. The battle claimed somewhat fewer than 8,000 Persian casualties. Estimates of Ottoman casualties are on the order of 35,000 to 50,000.

The last great victory of Nadir Shah, the Battle of Kars dashed any hopes that Mahmud I might have had of victory in the war and forced him to accept peace. A treaty was signed in September 1746 in Kordan, northwest of Tehran. The sultan again recognized Nadir Shah as the ruler of Persia, and Persia's frontiers were restored to those of the 1639 Treaty of Zuhab (Qasr-e-Shirin). The treaty recognized present-day Iraq (including Baghdad and the Shatt al-Arab), western Caucasia, and Kurdish territories as part of the Ottoman Empire, while Persia secured southwestern Caucasia.

Spencer C. Tucker

See also
Nadir Shah; Ottoman-Persian Wars of the 18th and 19th Centuries; Zuhab, Treaty of

References
Aksan, Virginia. *Ottoman Wars: An Empire Besieged, 1700–1870.* London: Longman, 2007.
Avery, Peter, Gavin Hambly, and Charles Melville, eds. *The Cambridge History of Iran: From Nadir Shah to the Islamic Republic,* Vol. 7. Cambridge: Cambridge University Press, 1991.
Axworthy, Michael. *Nader Shah: From Tribal Warrior to Conquering Tyrant.* New York: I. B. Tauris, 2006.
Faroqhi, Suraiya, ed. *The Cambridge History of Turkey: The Later Ottoman Empire, 1603–1839,* Vol. 3. Cambridge: Cambridge University Press, 2006.
Shaw, Stanford J. *History of the Ottoman Empire and Modern Turkey.* 2 vols. Cambridge: Cambridge University Press, 1976–1977.
Ward, Steven. *Immortal: A Military History of Iran and Its Armed Forces.* Washington, DC: Georgetown University Press, 2009.

Kars, Treaty of (October 13, 1921)

A treaty between Turkey and Soviet Russia and representatives of the newly established Soviet authorities in Georgia, Armenia, and Azerbaijan. The treaty was signed at Kars in northeastern Turkey on October 13, 1921. Based on the earlier Treaty of Moscow, the Treaty of Kars determined the borders between the various states. The contracting states agreed not to recognize any peace treaty or other international act imposed on any one of them by another power.

Under the treaty terms, the northeastern border of Turkey was determined by a line that began at the village of Sarpi on the Black Sea, passed by Mount Khedis Mta, and followed the former northern administrative borders of the sanjaks of Ardahan and Kars. As a result, Turkey took control of territory that had belonged to Georgia and Armenia. In return, Turkey agreed to cede to Georgia suzerainty over Batumi and the territory to the north of the frontier but under special conditions. The local population was to enjoy administrative autonomy, and Turkey was to be assured free transit through Batumi for commodities and all materials destined for or originating in Turkey without customs duties and charges. Turkey and Georgia also agreed to facilitate the crossing of the border by the inhabitants of the bordering zones on the condition that they would observe the customs, police, and sanitary regulations.

The treaty greatly affected the future of the Republic of Armenia, the territory of which was also partitioned. Most of Kars Province of the Russian empire was given to Turkey, while Armenia gained parts of the former Elizavetpol governorate. Turkey, Azerbaijan, and Armenia also agreed that the region of Nakhichevan constituted an autonomous territory under the protection of Azerbaijan.

ALEXANDER MIKABERIDZE

See also
Alexandropol, Treaty of

References
Hovannisian, Richard G. *The Armenian People from Ancient to Modern Times: Foreign Dominion to Statehood; The Fifteenth Century to the Twentieth Century.* New York: Palgrave Macmillan, 2004.
Sakwa, Richard. *The Rise and Fall of the Soviet Union, 1917–1991.* London: Routledge, 1999.

Kassites

A people of the ancient Near East who controlled Babylonia during some four centuries from the end of the Old Babylonian Empire around 1595 BCE until about 1155 BCE. The period of their rule is also known as the Second, or Middle, Babylonian dynasty.

Records on the Kassites are scanty. The Kassites probably originated in the Zagros Mountain area (now the Lorestan Province of present-day Iran). Apparently they first appeared in Mesopotamia and were repulsed by Babylonian king Samsu-iluna (r. 1749/1750–1712 BCE), the son of Hammurabi. They persisted and subsequently secured territory within the Tigris-Euphrates Valley on the northern reaches of Babylonia. They then took over the whole of Babylonia, establishing the Second Babylonian dynasty.

The first Kassite kings probably ruled jointly with the last Babylonian kings of the First Babylonian dynasty. The Kassite capital city was Dur-Kurigalzu, located in southern Mesopotamia near the confluence of the Tigris and Diyala Rivers and some 19 miles west of the center of present-day Baghdad. The horse, which was sacred to the Kassites, was probably first introduced into Babylonia during the period of their rule.

The Kassites proved generally adept rulers. Operating through a system of provincial governors, they controlled Babylon longer than any other dynasty. They also brought southern Mesopotamia firmly under Babylonian rule rather than it being an allied territory. This made Babylon a major power, although on occasion it was overshadowed by Assyria to the north and Elam to the east. Under Kassite rule merchants from Babylon traded with Egypt, Assyria, and even Armenia.

Nonetheless, Babylonia came under attack from Assyria and was dominated by that kingdom for much of the period after the accession in Assyria of Ashur-uballit I (r. 1365–1330), who made his nation the major power in the Near East. In the 1360s Ashur-uballit invaded and ravaged Babylon to avenge the murder of its Kassite king, who happened to be married to Ashur-uballit's daughter. Ashur-uballit then installed another Kassite, Kurigalzu II, as king. Assyrian king Enlil-nirari (r. 1330–1319) also invaded Babylonia, and Adad-nirari I (r. 1307–1275) annexed Babylonian territory. Assyrian king Tukulti-Ninurta I (r. 1244–1208) conquered Babylonia, deposing the Kassite ruler Kashtiliash IV, and ruled there himself during 1235–1227.

Finally, in the 12th century, with Kassite rule weakened by a number of local insurrections, the kingdom of Elam (located in present-day western and southwestern Iran) brought to an end their rule in Babylonia. The last Kassite king, Enlil-nadin-ahi, was deposed and taken to Susa, where he died. The Kassites briefly regained control over Babylonia during Dynasty V (1025 BC-1004 BCE) but were then deposed for a final time by an Aramean dynasty.

The Kassites survived as a distinct ethnic group in the mountains of Lorestan, long after the end of their rule in Babylon. In 702 BCE Assyrian king Sennacherib is reported as having defeated the Kassites in battle near Hulwan in Persia. During the later period of the Achaemenid Empire (first Persian Empire), Kassites ware reported as living in the mountains to the east of Media and were one of several tribute-seeking mountain tribes that on occasion mounted raids that resulted in regular payments from the imperial court. Kassites are, however, recorded as having fought on the Persian side against Alexander III the Great in 331 BCE. Alexander later attacked the Kassites in their own territory, after which they halted their raiding activity.

SPENCER C. TUCKER

See also
Alexander III the Great; Alexander III's Invasion of the Persian Empire; Assyrian Empire; Babylonian Empire, Neo-; Babylonian Empire, Old; Sennacherib

References
Boardman, J., et al., eds. *The Cambridge Ancient History*, Vol. 3, *The Prehistory of the Balkans, the Middle East and the Aegean World, Tenth to Eighth Centuries BC.* New Work: Cambridge University Press, 1982.

Bryce, Trevor. *The Routledge Handbook of the Peoples and Places of Ancient Western Asia: The Near East from the Early Bronze Age to the Fall of the Persian Empire.* London: Routledge, 2009.

Healy, Mark. *The Ancient Assyrians.* London: Osprey, 2003.

Oppenheim, A. Leo. *Ancient Mesopotamia: Portrait of a Dead Civilization.* Chicago: University of Chicago Press, 2013.

Khadairi Bend, Battle of (December 13, 1916–January 29, 1917)

First battle in the British offensive that captured Baghdad. During this engagement, the British used their significant advantages in men and artillery to systematically root Ottoman forces from their defenses covering Kut.

For the Ottomans, 1916 was their most successful year in Mesopotamia. On April 29 a British-Indian Army force under Major General Charles Townshend had surrendered at Kut al-Amara following a five-month siege. The defeat was a powerful blow to British prestige in the Middle East. To add insult to injury, several efforts to break through and relieve Townshend's force had failed, with heavy British casualties.

In August, Lieutenant General Sir Frederick Maude received command of British forces in Mesopotamia. Maude was determined to strengthen his logistical base before undertaking any offensive action. He thus improved Basra as a port and supply center, and he also gathered a fleet of motor vehicles to transport supplies. Because the major lines of communication in Mesopotamia were the Tigris and Euphrates Rivers, Maude also built a river flotilla, securing vessels to carry supplies as well as gunboats to support operations. Troop reinforcements also arrived, and by the end of the year Maude had more than 166,000 men in five divisions.

Maude disguised his intentions as to which river he planned to use, forcing the Ottomans to divide their numerically smaller force. Kazim Bey's Ottoman XVIII Corps manned the defenses along the Tigris River, but Kazim had fewer than half the soldiers Maude would deploy against him. Maude's forward movement was hampered more by restrictions imposed by the British government in London than by the Ottoman forces opposing him. Until November, London insisted that he make no move toward Baghdad; after the restriction was lifted, Maude was still under pressure not to incur heavy casualties.

On December 13, 1916, Maude finally began his offensive. His immediate objective was to clear the formidable Ottoman defenses from the Khadairi Bend of the Tigris River north of Kut, with the intention of recapturing Kut. To accomplish this, he hoped to maneuver the Ottomans from their defenses. In a night march, Maude advanced one corps along the right bank of the Tigris. The British and Indian formations outflanked the Ottomans by moving across the desert; they first moved north and then turned back east toward the Tigris, threatening to sever Ottoman communications north.

On December 20 the British forces reached the Tigris. They could have moved faster, but Maude continued to be wary of casualties. Having cut off the Khadairi Bend position, the British then began to systematically reduce it. On the night of December 22, British engineers began to saps forward from their own trenches. After a few yards, these saps were joined to form a new line of trenches. By January 7, 1917, the British had advanced their lines in such fashion some 2,000 yards. British artillery now regularly shelled the Ottomans to prevent them from interfering with this process.

On January 9 following a heavy bombardment, British and Indian Army troops launched a frontal assault and quickly secured the first Ottoman trench. Continuing the assault, by the evening of January 10 the British had nearly driven the Ottoman defenders into the Tigris. A heavy Ottoman counterattack the next day nearly broke through the British line, but reserves were able to contain it. After that, the battle dissolved into small cleanup operations.

Operations were completed on January 29. Ottoman losses were about 3,000 men, while those of the British were approximately 2,000. Maude could now begin his attack on Kut.

TIM J. WATTS

See also
Kut al-Amara, Siege of; Mesopotamian Theater, World War I; Townshend, Sir Charles Vere Ferrers

References
Barker, A. J. *The Bastard War: The Mesopotamian Campaign of 1914–1918.* New York: Dial, 1967.

Erickson, Edward. *Ordered to Die: A History of the Ottoman Army in the First World War.* Westport, CT: Greenwood, 2000.

Moberly, F. J. *The Campaign in Mesopotamia, 1914–1918.* 3 vols. Nashville: Battery Press, 1997–1998.

Townshend, Charles. *Desert Hell: The British Invasion of Mesopotamia.* Cambridge, MA: Belknap Press of Harvard University Press, 2011.

Khafji, Battle of (January 29–February 1, 1991)

First major land battle of the Persian Gulf War (Operation DESERT STORM) that occurred from January 29 to February 1, 1991. The fight unfolded after units of the Iraqi Army crossed the border from Kuwait into Saudi Arabia and occupied the town of R'as al-Khafji. The Iraqis were forced out of Khafji after heavy fighting with American, Saudi Arabian, and Qatari forces.

The Iraqi army occupying Kuwait had been bombarded relentlessly by coalition aircraft since the commencement of the air campaign on January 17, 1991. With casualties and material losses mounting and morale plummeting, the Iraqi high command decided on a bold plan to regain the initiative in the war. Three Iraqi divisions would launch a ground attack into Saudi Arabian territory, inflict a humiliating defeat on the Saudis, and provoke a coalition counterattack. The Iraqis hoped that they could inflict such heavy casualties on the counterattacking Americans that public opinion in the United States would turn against the war.

In order to carry out the plan, the Iraqi 5th Mechanized Division pushed down the coastal highway from Kuwait toward Khafji. The 5th Division attack was supported by several hundred Iraqi commandos who sailed along the coast in small boats, landed behind Saudi lines, and raided communication links. To the right of the 5th Division, the Iraqi 3rd Armored Division was to overwhelm the border posts held by the Saudis and U.S. marines before swinging left to attack the port city of Al Mish'ab, south of Khafji. Farther inland the Iraqi 1st Mechanized Division would cover the flank of the other two attacking divisions.

The attacks of the Iraqi 1st and 3rd Divisions were stalled on the evening of January 31, however, by determined U.S. marine resistance at the frontier border posts, followed by devastating American air attacks that caught Iraqi vehicles out in the open. The coastal commando raids were intercepted and destroyed by U.S. and British Royal Navy warships. However, elements of the Iraqi 5th Division succeeded in scattering Saudi frontier defenses and storming into Khafji.

The civilian population of Khafji, which normally numbered about 10,000, had been evacuated at the start of the war. A 12-man U.S. marine reconnaissance detachment was left stranded behind Iraqi lines in Khafji, from where they began calling in air strikes.

Frantic to liberate Khafji from the invaders, the Saudi government ordered immediate counterattacks. Two poorly coordinated Saudi attacks, backed up by a detachment of Qatari tanks, failed on the evening of January 30 and the next morning. The Saudis were fortunate to escape with light casualties, thanks largely to the wild inaccuracy of Iraqi fire. However, massive American air strikes ensured that the Iraqis would be unable to reinforce their troops in Khafji. The Iraqi defenders in the town were also worn down by the nonstop air attacks. A third Saudi attack on February 1 finally succeeded in overwhelming the demoralized Iraqis in Khafji, who had been abandoned to their fate by the Iraqi high command.

Estimated Saudi and Qatari losses in the fighting for Khafji numbered 18 dead and 50 wounded. Seven to 10 Saudi V-150 armored personnel carriers and 2 Qatari AMX tanks were destroyed. The Iraqis lost anywhere from 60 to 100 killed, 400 taken prisoner, and at least 50 tanks destroyed in Khafji itself. But further heavy losses to coalition air strikes among Iraqi units to the north of Khafji may have resulted in more than 2,000 Iraqi casualties plus the loss of 300 vehicles.

The success of American airpower at the Battle of Khafji led some theorists to claim that airpower was now the decisive factor in modern warfare, although that claim has not been widely accepted. The battle also revealed the serious shortcomings in the Saudi armed forces and in the command and control capabilities of the Iraqi Army.

PAUL WILLIAM DOERR

See also
Kuwait, Iraqi Invasion of; Persian Gulf War, Overview; Qatar; Saudi Arabia

References
Gordon, Michael R., and General Bernard E. Trainor. *The General's War: The Inside Story of the Conflict in the Gulf.* New York: Little, Brown, 1995.

Pollack, Kenneth. *Arabs at War.* Lincoln: University of Nebraska Press, 2002.

Warden, John. "Employing Air Power in the Twenty-first Century." In *The Future of Air Power in the Aftermath of the Gulf War,* ed. Robert L. Pfalzgraff Jr. and Richard H. Schultz, 125–157. Maxwell Air Force Base, AL: Air University Press, 1992.

Khalid bin Sultan, Prince (1949–)

Saudi prince, military officer, assistant minister of defense and aviation, and inspector general for military affairs for the Kingdom of Saudi Arabia. He also served as a lieutenant general and commander of Joint Forces and theater of operations during the 1991 Persian Gulf War.

Prince Khalid bin Sultan ibn Abd al-Aziz al-Saud was born on September 23, 1949, in Makkah, Saud Arabia; he is the eldest son of the first crown prince and minister of defense, Prince Sultan, and the grandson of the kingdom's modern founder, King Abd al-Aziz, known as Ibn Saud. Khalid studied at the Princes' School in Riyadh and attended the British Royal Military Academy at Sandhurst, graduating in 1967. He continued his advanced military training in the United States at the U.S. Army Command General Staff College and the U.S. Naval Postgraduate School, and he obtained Air War Certification at the U.S. Air War College at Maxwell Air Force Base. He also earned a master's degree in political science at Auburn University.

With a reputation as an air defense expert, Khalid moved up rapidly in the military, holding the positions of air squadron chief, training officer and assistant staff officer for operations, army inspectorate chief, director of the administration of air defense projects, deputy chief of the air force, chief of air defense, and chief of the strategic missiles force.

Saudi air and air defense forces have played a special role in the kingdom's defense planning. One reason for this is the kingdom's vast open spaces, most of which are inaccessible except by air. Another reason is that with the deliberate decision to keep the military establishment quite small (an idea that Khalid later challenged), air defense became more crucial, and the kingdom traditionally relied on the West—first on Great Britain and later the United States—for military support. Saudi Arabia has spent billions on the acquisition of advanced weaponry, aircraft, and missiles.

Khalid was involved in numerous arms deals, certainly with the purchase of the medium-range surface-to-surface CSS-2 East Wind missiles from China. He wrote that he and his half brother, Bandar, formerly ambassador to the United States, negotiated the acquisition of these missiles for an estimated $3.5 billion.

On the eve of the Persian Gulf War in 1991, Khalid was named commander of the Joint Forces and theater of operations at the rank of lieutenant general. The Joint Force Command allowed countries, in particular Arab and Muslim nations, to place their troops under Saudi leadership rather than that of the United States. In all, the Joint Forces Command included personnel from 24 nations. Saudi Arabia provided up to 100,000 personnel for the conflict. Prince Khalid's position in the war demonstrated Saudi Arabia's political leadership, not to mention its military capabilities. However, at the same time, the large wave of opposition within Saudi Arabia to military participation with the United States and the presence of Western troops in the kingdom unleashed strong reactions in the form of religiously based protests against the al-Saud family and the government as a whole.

Following the Persian Gulf War, Khalid was promoted to the rank of field marshal. He left government service in 1991. He remained out of government service until 2001, when he was called back to become the assistant minister of defense and inspector general for military affairs. In the interceding years he was involved in private business during, and he published his account of DESERT STORM and Saudi Arabia's history in *Desert Warrior: A Personal View of the Gulf War* (1995), written with Patrick Seale. In the book, Khalid disagreed with certain statements and assessments made by coalition commander General H. Norman Schwarzkopf in his 1992 book *It Doesn't Take a Hero.*

In November 2009 Khalid led a Saudi military intervention in Yemen, attacking Houthi opponents of the Yemeni regime. The campaign was largely a failure and resulted in considerable criticism of Khalid. Widely expected to be named Saudi minister of defense, he was instead appointed deputy minister of defense in November 2011, a post he held until April 2013.

An avid scuba diver, Prince Khalid has involved himself in marine ecology, which he supports in the Living Oceans Foundation, and he funded a multinational team of scientists called Scientists without Borders to assess the health of coral reefs and marine life in the Caribbean. Khalid has also created a chair for environmental research at King Saud University.

SHERIFA ZUHUR

See also
Houthis; Persian Gulf War, Overview; Saudi Arabia; Schwarzkopf, H. Norman, Jr.

References
Gause F. Gregory III. *Oil Monarchies: Domestic and Security Challenges in the Arab Gulf States.* Washington, DC: Council on Foreign Relations, 1994.

Khalid bin Sultan, Prince, with Patrick Seale. *Desert Warrior: A Personal View of the Gulf War by the Joint Forces Commander.* New York: HarperCollins, 1995.

Munro, Alan. *Arabian Affair: The Gulf War from Saudi Arabia.* Washington, DC: Potomac Books, 1996.

Khalid ibn al-Walid (ca. 592–642)

One of greatest of Arab generals in the period of the Muslim conquests during the seventh century. Khalid ibn al-Walid (later known as Sayf-'ullah al-Maslul, the Sword of Allah) was born in Mecca, around 592, the son of a chief of the Quraysh clan. In traditional practice, he was removed from his family soon after birth and raised in a Bedouin tribe in the desert until age five or six, when he returned to Mecca. His father, reportedly a warrior of some renown, trained him in horsemanship and martial arts.

Although Khalid did not take part in the Battle of Uhud (615), the first engagement between the new Muslim community at Medina and the confederacy of the Quraysh of Mecca, he did participate in the Quraysh campaign against the Muslims in 627 that led to the Battle of the Trench. After the Treaty of Hudaybiyyah in 628, Khalid converted to Islam and fought for Muhammad from that point forward.

Khalid distinguished himself in the Battle of Mu'tah (629) against the Ghassanids. When the three leading Medinan commanders were killed in the fight, Khalid was selected to command and was able to extract his small force of some 3,000 men against far larger Ghassanid and Byzantine forces. Reportedly Khalid broke a number of swords during the battle, and it was from this point that he was known as Sayf-'ullah al-Maslul. He commanded one of the four Muslim armies that captured the city of Mecca (630). Later that year he commanded the cavalry in the Battle of Hunayn, and he participated in the Siege of Ta'if.

Following the death of Prophet Muhammad in 632 and during the reign of the first caliph, Abu Bekr, Khalid helped put down revolts by several prophets, the last being Musaylima in the Battle of Akraba (633). That same year, Abu Bekr decided to conquer Persian-held Mesopotamia, entrusting this task to Khalid with an army of 18,000 men. Khalid won a series of battles over the Persians in 633 including Walaja and Ullais, both in May. Invading Syria in June 634, in the Battle of Ajnadain in Palestine (July) he defeated a Byzantine army under Theodore.

Abu Bakr died in August 634. His successor as caliph, Umar, removed Khalid from his command, probably because he feared that Khalid might attempt to take power. The new military commander, Abu Ubaidah ibn al-Jarrah, continued Khalid in command of the cavalry and relied heavily throughout subsequent campaigns on his operational advice. In October 634, Khalid defeated a Byzantine force that had trapped a Muslim army at Abu-al-Quds.

Khalid served under Ubaidah in the victory over the Byzantines in the Battle of Fihl (Pella or Gilead) near Baisan (January 635). Continuing north, the Arab forces were again victorious over the Byzantines in the Battle of Marjal-Saffar near Damascus and went on to capture Emesa (Homs) and Damascus but abandoned these places when threatened by a larger Byzantine force in 636. Retiring to the Yarmouk River and heavily outnumbered, Khalid was again victorious over the Byzantine armies commanded by Mahan of Armeniad in the important Battle of the Yarmouk River (August 636), after which the Arab forces recaptured both Damascus and Emesa. In 638 Caliph Umar dismissed Khalid from his posts. Khalid died in Emesa, Syria, in 642, apparently upset that it was his lot to die in bed rather than in battle.

Said to be physically strong, the resourceful Khalid enjoyed the distinction of never having been defeated in more than 50 battles and as many small engagements. Pakistan's principal main battle tank, the *Khalid,* is named for him.

SPENCER C. TUCKER

See also
Yarmouk River, Battle of

References
Akram, A. I. *The Sword of Allah: Khalid bin al-Waleed: His Life and Campaigns.* Rawalpindi, Pakistan: National Publishing House, 1970.
Nicolle, David. *Yarmuk 636 A.D.: The Muslim Conquest of Syria.* Osprey Campaign Series #31. London: Osprey, 1994.
Tabari, Muhammad ibn Jarir. *The Victory of Islam.* Translated by Michael Fishbein. Ithaca, NY: SUNY Press, 1997.

Khanaqin, Battle of (June 3, 1916)

Ottoman Army victory that halted a Russian Army drive into Mesopotamia. The offensive that ended at Khanaqin marked the only Russian attempt at a coordinated effort with its British ally.

Before World War I, the Russian and British governments had agreed to divide Persia into two spheres of influence, separated by a neutral zone. When war began in 1914, the Persian government declared its neutrality. Although many Persians were sympathetic toward the Ottoman Empire on religious grounds, the Persian government had neither the forces nor the will to fight. German agents took advantage of Persia's neutrality to wage a vigorous propaganda campaign, resulting in a number of public demonstrations against the Entente.

The Ottomans took advantage of Persia's neutrality to occupy the city of Kotur in December 1914. Meanwhile, the Russian government had sent troops to occupy Oiyadin in northern Persia in November 1914. These moves easily pushed the lightly armed Ottoman forces out of Kotur and back into Ottoman territory. In November 1915 Russian troops under General N. N. Baratov marched on and secured control of the Persian capital of Tehran in response to reports of a possible German coup.

The situation along the Persian border with Mesopotamia remained stable through much of 1915. In September, British troops under Major General Charles Townshend moved up the Tigris River toward Baghdad. Defeated during November 22–25 at Ctesiphon, only 20 miles south of Baghdad, Townshend retreated to Kut al-Amara, where his force was promptly besieged by the Ottomans. British relief efforts in December 1915 and January 1916 failed, and in desperation the British appealed to their Russian allies in Persia for assistance.

In response, Baratov moved into western Persia to threaten Baghdad. On February 26, 1916, he secured Kermanshah. The Russians moved next to Kharind, only 125 miles from Baghdad. The British hoped that Baratov would then push on to Baghdad, forcing the Ottomans to raise the siege at Kut. The Ottoman Army had few resources available to prevent his advance, but unfortunately for the British, Baratov remained at Kharind for three months. The Russians were at the end of a long supply line, and Baratov was anxious to resupply and consolidate before advancing farther.

After the fall of Kut on April 29, 1916, Ottoman forces there were available for other assignments. Other seasoned Ottoman divisions were also available, thanks to the Allied evacuation of the Gallipoli Peninsula by January 1916, and these slowly made their way to Mesopotamia. Ottoman Sixth Army commander Halil Pasha then agreed to send his XIII Corps to attack Baratov at Kharind.

Ali Insan Pasha commanded the XIII Corps, which centered on three fresh divisions. Insan massed his forces near the border with Persia and then advanced toward Baratov's positions. When the Russians learned of the Ottoman move, Baratov undertook a preemptive strike, crossing the border and, on June 3, attacking the Ottoman 6th Infantry Division of the XIII Corps at the border town of Khanaqin.

In the Battle of Khanaqin, Baratov employed his infantry to pin the Ottomans in place, while his cavalry tried to encircle them. Insan's corps outnumbered the Russians, however, and the confident Insan fended off the infantry assault and used his reserves to crush the Russian cavalry. Ottoman losses were only around 400 men. Russian casualties were much greater.

Following his victory, Insan pushed into Persia. Baratov conducted a skillful fighting retreat, but Insan defeated the Russians in a series of small-scale actions and eventually reached Hamadan, while Baratov withdrew to the north and awaited reinforcements.

Insan was disappointed that few Persians joined his army. As no Ottoman reinforcements were forthcoming and his extended supply line left his force short of virtually everything, Insan had no choice but to withdraw back into Ottoman territory. He had succeeded, however, in preventing a major Russian invasion of Mesopotamia.

TIM J. WATTS

See also

Ctesiphon, 1915 Battle of; Gallipoli Campaign; Kut al-Amara, Siege of; Mesopotamian Theater, World War I; Persian Front, World War I; Townshend, Sir Charles Vere Ferrers

References

Barker, A. J. *The Bastard War: The Mesopotamian Campaign of 1914–1918*. New York: Dial, 1967.

Butler, Daniel Allen. *Shadow of the Sultan's Realm: The Destruction of the Ottoman Empire and the Creation of the Modern Middle East*. Dulles, VA: Potomac Books, 2011.

Erickson, Edward J. *Ordered to Die: A History of the Ottoman Army in the First World War*. Westport, CT: Greenwood, 2000.

Moberly, F. J. *The Campaign in Mesopotamia, 1914–1918*. 3 vols. Nashville: Battery Press, 1997–1998.

Nicolle, David. *The Ottoman Army, 1914–1918*. London: Reed International, 1999.

Khandaq, Battle of the (January–February 627)

Important early Islamic battle known as the Battle of the Trench and the Battle of the Confederates, it was a 27-day-long siege during January and February 627 of Prophet Muhammad's city of Yathrib (modern-day Medina, Saudi Arabia) by Arab and Jewish tribes organized by the leaders of Medina's rival Mecca. Abu Sufayn had command of what was both the largest and last offensive against the forces loyal to Prophet Muhammad in Yathrib. Mobilizing their Bedouin allies and also the Jews of Yathrib, Banu Qurayza, to attack the city from the south, Abu Safayn had some 10,000 men with 600 horses and camels.

Yathrib could muster only some 3,000 defenders, but three sides of the city were protected by lava formations, and the prophet caused a trench (*khandaq*) to be dug across the unprotected northern approaches to the city. These defenses enabled the prophet's followers to neutralize their opponents' cavalry and superior numbers.

A combination of factors led to the lifting of the siege and the withdrawal of the besieging forces after 27 days. A series of small raids by the prophet's followers along the trench defenses helped sap the morale of the besiegers, and the prophet's agents successfully sowed seeds of mistrust between the different tribes of the coalition, helping to break it up. The timing of the attack was also fortuitous for the defenders, as it occurred after the harvest, with an attendant shortage of supplies needed to sustain large numbers of men and animals. Poor weather was also a contributing factor.

Their defeat was a great blow both to Meccan prestige. It also resulted in financial loss, as it ended much of their trade with Syria. Finally, it cemented Muhammad's position im Yathrib.

Adam Ali and Spencer C. Tucker

See also

Badr, Battle of; Muhammad, Campaigns of the Prophet

References

Gabrielli, Fransesco. *Muhammad and the Conquests of Islam*. Translated by Virginia Luling and Rosamund Linell. London: World University Library, 1968.

Hodgson, Marshall G. S. *The Venture of Islam: Conscience and History in a World Civilization*. Chicago: University of Chicago Press, 1977.

Khan Yunis

Palestinian town and refugee camp located in the southern Gaza Strip. The town is the site of two massacres, allegedly by Israelis, that took place during and immediately after the 1956 Sinai Campaign. The first occurred on November 3, 1956, and the second one is thought to have taken place five weeks later on December 11.

The 1956 campaign began on October 28, 1956, with an Israeli attack of the Sinai. Israel claimed self-defense in its attack, reacting both to terrorist attacks mounted from Egypt and to the threat posed by the conclusion of a joint Egyptian-Syrian-Jordanian military command structure. The British and French governments were in collusion with Israel and soon attacked Egypt, supposedly to secure the Suez Canal. Soviet threats to intervene but primarily heavy pressure from the United States led Britain and then France and Israel to agree to withdraw.

Arab sources contend that following the Israeli withdrawal in early 1957, a mass grave was discovered at Khan Yunis. It contained the bodies of Palestinian Arabs who had been bound and killed by gunfire. There were at least 40 bodies in the grave, but some sources put the figure at more than 500. Each body had a bullet wound to the back of the head as if the person had been shot execution-style at close range. The dead might possibly have been killed by members of the Israeli 11th Infantry and 37th Armored Brigades, which had exercised control over the area. The killings were believed to have been in retaliation for attacks into Israel by the Egyptian-backed fedayeen.

As with many events in the region, the true nature of what happened at Khan Yunis is shrouded in mystery. Arab sources claim that the Israelis lined up women and children and executed them for no reason. Israeli military sources report that those killed and buried there were guerrillas who had engaged Israeli forces occupying the area. As irregular soldiers under international law, these fedayeen fighters were not entitled to the protection of The Hague or Geneva Conventions, and most armies accepted the execution of such combatants if caught.

The United Nations (UN) Special Report of November 1 to mid-December 1956 cites 275 civilians killed by gunfire at Khan Yunis on November 3, 1956. The report does not delve into what may have caused the killings but simply states that the Israeli authorities claimed that the dead were insurgents and fedayeen found in possession of arms. However, Arab refugees interviewed by the UN claimed that the killings were unprovoked and random. A later massacre allegedly took place at Khan Yunis on December 11, 1956, in which an additional 275 people were executed.

RODERICK VOSBURGH

See also
Fedayeen; Sinai Campaign of 1956

References
Herzog, Chaim. *The Arab-Israeli Wars: War and Peace in the Middle East from the War of Independence to Lebanon.* Westminster, MD: Random House, 1984.

Turner, Barry. *Suez 1956.* London: Hoddle, Doyle, and Meadows, 2006.

United Nations. *Special Report of the Director of the United Nations Relief and Works Agency for Palestinian Refugees in the Near East: Covering the Period 1 November to Mid-December 1956.* New York: United Nations General Assembly, Eleventh Session, 1957.

Kharijites

The seceders who went out from supporting Ali ibn Abi Talib as fourth caliph. The term "Kharijites" has been applied to a variety of Muslims. Immediately following the death of Prophet Muhammad a dispute arose over who should succeed him. One group supported Ali ibn Abi Talib, the cousin and son-in-law of Muhammad who was married to Muhammad's daughter Fatima. However, the community chose Abu Bakr, the father of Aisha, one of the wives of Muhammad. Umar (Omar) ibn al-Khattab succeeded Abu Bakr when the latter died two years later in 634. Umar was assassinated in 644 by a disgruntled slave and was succeeded by Uthman (Osman) ibn Affan.

Uthman was a member of the same Quraysh (Quraysh) tribe as Muhammad but was from the Umayyad family rather than the Beni Hassan (Hashemite) clan into which Muhammad had been born. As caliph, Uthman was accused of unfair distributions of booty and of nepotism in appointments. A group of disgruntled Muslims from Egypt and the Arab garrison city of Kufa on the Euphrates assassinated him in 656. Their action began the First Civil War (656–661).

Following Uthman's assassination in Medina, Ali ibn Abi Talib was elected fourth caliph by the Median community. Ali was the cousin and son-in-law of Muhammad by marriage to Fatima. Ali's position as caliph was disputed by Muawiyah ibn Abi Sufyan, who was an Umayyad kinsman of Uthman and governor of Damascus. He wanted those responsible for the murder of Uthman to face trial, but he knew that some of Ali's supporters had been the conspirators and so refused to follow Ali.

Forces supporting Muawiyah and Ali fought the Battle of Siffin on the banks of the upper Euphrates River in what is now Ar-Raqqah, Syria, during July 26–28, 657. With the battle inconclusive, the two sides agreed to arbitration. This, however, angered many of Ali's followers, who withdrew their support to become the Kharijites. They argued that the issue should be fought out and that Allah would grant victory to those who were his true followers.

The arbitration did not go well for Ali, because Muawiyah chose a pretended neutral, Amr al-Aas, who was really his strong supporter, and Ali's advocate, Abu Musa al-Ashari, failed to support him. When the arbitrators called for both Ali and Muawiyah to resign, both refused. There were now three groups with claims regarding the succession to Muhammad. Those in support of Ali argued that the caliph should come from the Hashemite family of Muhammad. Those supporting Muawiyah, however, argued that the caliph should be someone from the Quraysh tribe of Muhammad. The Kharijites, however, argued that any Muslim who was pure in heart could become the caliph by being elected by the whole Muslim community.

The battle cry of the Kharijites, as Muslim purists, was "only God has the right to decide." They moved to a village at Harura and began attacking those who did not agree with them, declaring them infidels to be put to death.

Eventually many Kharijites settled in Nahrawan on the Tigris River. Led by Abdullah ibn Wahab, they were defeated by Ali in the Battle of Nahrawan in 658. Those few who survived reorganized. In 661 Kharijites in Mecca conspired to kill the governor of Egypt; Muawiyah, the governor of Syria; and Caliph Ali in a simultaneous attack. This plot, carried out on the 17th of Ramadan (January 20, 661) by three young Kharijites, met with limited success. The governor of Egypt was wounded in the attack by Amr ibn Bakr. Barq ibn

Abdullah failed in his attempt on Muawiyah. However, Abd-al-Rahman ibn Muljam al-Sarimi was successful, mortally wounding Ali with a poison-coated sword as the caliph was at prayer in the mosque at Kufay.

Shortly after the death of Ali, his opponent Muawiyah, the son of Abu Sofian who had been a bitter opponent of Muhammad, was chosen caliph. He was forced at times to suppress small groups of Kharijites who soon splintered into many small groups.

A few Kharijite groups, such as the Ibadis, survive. Their doctrines inspired a number of revolts in Islamic history. The Ibadis were to develop a stronghold in Algeria among the Berbers at Tahert. It was destroyed by the Fatimid caliphs in the 10th century.

ANDREW J. WASKEY

See also
Ali ibn Abi Talib; Muawiyah I

References
Kenney, Jeffrey T. *Muslim Rebels: Kharijites and the Politics of Extremism in Egypt.* Oxford: Oxford University Press, 2006.
Mahmud, S. F. *A Short History of Islam.* New York: Oxford University Press, 1988.
Ruthven, Malise. *Islam in the World.* 2nd ed. New York: Oxford University Press, 2000.

Khartoum Resolution (September 1, 1967)

Joint resolution passed on September 1, 1967, in Khartoum, Sudan, by eight member states of the Arab League: Algeria, Egypt, Jordan, Syria, Lebanon, Iraq, Kuwait, and Sudan. Coming in the immediate wake of the stunning Israeli success of the June 1967 Six-Day War, the heads of eight Arab countries convened in Khartoum during August 29–September 1, 1967, with the express purpose of establishing a united front against Israel. As a result of the recent war, the Israelis had seized the Sinai Peninsula, the West Bank, the Gaza Strip, and the Golan Heights.

The Khartoum Resolution—actually a series of resolutions—not only established official Arab positions vis-à-vis Israel and the Arab-Israeli conflict but also acted as a vehicle by which Arab nations drew closer together and helped them put aside their differences. Perhaps most notable in this regard was Egyptian president Gamal Abdel Nasser's pledge to cease and desist from his ongoing attempts to destabilize the Middle East and topple Arab monarchies in the Persian Gulf. In return, Egypt was promised economic incentives, which were sorely needed at the time. The idea of supranational Arab unity, then, took a backseat to national and regional stability.

The Khartoum Resolution stressed seven principles. First, warfare against Israel would continue. Second, the oil boycott enacted against the West during the Six-Day War was to end. Third, the Yemeni Civil War should be ended. Fourth, economic aid packages for Egypt and Jordan would commence as soon as was practical. Resolutions five through seven, soon to be known as the "three nos," stated unequivocally that there would be no peace with Israel, no recognition of Israel, and no negotiations with the Israelis.

Clearly, the Khartoum Resolution seemed to have closed the door to any potential peace effort between Arabs and Israelis and lent credence to hard-liners in the Israeli government who argued that peace initiatives with the Arabs were pointless. Over the subsequent years, several of the countries involved in the Khartoum Resolution backed away from its positions, beginning with Egypt after the 1973 Yom Kippur War.

PAUL G. PIERPAOLI JR.

See also
Arab League; Nasser, Gamal Abdel; Six-Day War

References
Bickerton, Ian J., and Carla L. Klausner. *A Concise History of the Arab-Israeli Conflict.* 4th ed. Upper Saddle River, NJ: Prentice Hall, 2004.
Parker, Richard B., ed. *The Six-Day War: A Retrospective.* Gainesville: University Press of Florida, 1996.
Schulze, Kirsten E. *The Arab-Israeli Conflict.* New York: Longman, 1999.

Khirokitia, Battle of (July 7, 1426)

A hotly contested battle fought near the village of Khirokitia (modern-day Khoirokoitia) between Nicosia and Limassol on the island of Cyprus. Cypriot, Genoese, and Catalan corsairs had been raiding Egyptian coastal towns, and King Janus of Cyprus had himself attacked the Syrian coast. Mamluk sultan of Egypt Barsbay had retaliated by attacking Cyprus in 1424 and 1425.

On July 1, 1426, a Mamluk force of some 5,000 men invaded Cyprus, capturing the town of Limassol. Janus met them with some 4,500 Cypriot troops on July 7 at Khirokitia but was defeated and taken prisoner. The Mamluks then captured and sacked the Cypriot capital city of Nicosia on July 11, carrying off 6,000 captives. King Janus was taken back to

Egypt but ransomed for 200,000 ducats eight months later and returned to the island in May 1427 after having agreed to become the sultan's vassal and pay an annual tribute of 5,000 ducats.

ALEXIOS G. C. SAVVIDES

See also
Mamluk Sultanate

References
Hill, George. *History of Cyprus,* Vol. 2. Cambridge: Cambridge University Press, 1948.
Housley, Norman. *The Later Crusades.* Oxford: Oxford University Press, 1992.

Khobar Towers Bombing (June 25, 1996)

Major terrorist attack against U.S. and allied military personnel in Saudi Arabia. At approximately 10:20 p.m. (local time) on June 25, 1996, a truck exploded next to Building #131 of the Khobar Towers complex in Dhahran, Saudi Arabia. At the time, the eight-story structure housed U.S. Air Force service members and other foreign military personnel. The blast killed 19 U.S. servicemen and wounded 498 others (of varying nationalities, including Americans). In the immediate aftermath of the attack, the U.S. government named the radical Saudi group known as Hezbollah al-Hejaz as the perpetrator. Ten years later in 2006, the U.S. government formally concluded that Hezbollah al-Hejaz had received aid and support from the Iranian government, an accusation that Iran has unequivocally denied.

The vehicle used in the bombing was a large tanker truck, which had been packed with gasoline and explosives. It is estimated that the explosion was equivalent to at least 20,000 pounds of TNT, and the truck's height amplified the effects of the detonation, giving it the added lethality of an air-burst explosion. The bombing destroyed or badly damaged six high-rise units in the complex, with Building #131 taking the brunt of the explosion. The detonation created a crater 85 feet wide and 35 feet deep.

The Khobar Towers bombing occurred just seven months after a lethal car bombing in Riyadh, Saudi Arabia; the perpetrators of that attack alleged that their mission was to force the U.S. military to leave Saudi Arabia. After the Riyadh bombing, U.S. military commanders placed U.S. forces in Saudi Arabia on higher alert. Although U.S. Air Force personnel had reported suspicious activity just beyond the Khobar Towers complex, Saudi law forbade them from taking any action to stop such activity, and the Saudi government did not investigate the reports seriously.

After-action reports suggest that there had been multiple warnings about the Khobar Towers being a target of terrorists, but neither the U.S. government nor the Saudi government took appropriate countermeasures. The Bill Clinton administration was criticized for its role in the intelligence failures, as was the Central Intelligence Agency (CIA), which was lambasted for underestimating the capabilities of would-be terrorists within Saudi Arabia. Military commanders also faulted the Department of Defense for having failed to cover windows in the facility with protective film, which would have reduced the lethality of the blast. After the bombing, all U.S. forces were withdrawn from the Khobar Towers complex and relocated to Al Kharj's Prince Sultan Air Base.

In June 2001, a U.S. court indicted numerous individuals believed to have been complicit in the bombing. The following month, the Saudis announced that they had 11 of those men in custody but refused to extradite them to the United States; their subsequent whereabouts and disposition are not known. In August 2015 Ahmed Ibrahim al-Mughassil, a high-ranking member of Hezbollah al-Hejaz, was arrested in Beirut, Lebanon, and charged with complicity in the 1996 bombing. He was reportedly extradited to Saudi Arabia. Some weeks later both the Saudi and U.S. governments confirmed the arrest, but there is as yet no word on al-Mughassil's legal disposition. He had been on the Federal Bureau of Investigation's most-wanted terrorists list for almost two decades.

PAUL G. PIERPAOLI JR.

See also
Saudi Arabia

References
Atwan, Abdel Bari. *The Secret History of Al Qaeda.* Berkeley: University of California Press, 2006.
Jehl, Douglas. "Fatal Lapses—A Special Report: How U.S. Missteps and Delay Opened Door to Saudi Blast." *New York Times,* July 7, 2006.
Leonnig, Carol D. "Iran Held Liable in Khobar Attack." *Washington Post,* December 23, 2006.

Khomeini, Ruhollah (1900–1989)

Shiite cleric, leader of the 1979 revolution that overthrew Shah Mohammed Reza Pahlavi, and religious and political head of the Islamic Republic of Iran (1979–1989). Born Ruhollah Mustafa al-Musavi on May 17, 1900, in Khomayn (Khumayn), some 180 miles south of the capital of Tehran, he was the son and grandson of Shiite religious scholars and leaders (*fuqaha*). Musavi was instructed in Islam and the Quran by his elder brother Ayatollah Pasandideh following the death of his mother. His father had been murdered when Musavi was seven months old. Musavi studied Islamic law at Arak and moved with his teacher in the 1920s to Qum, where he was recognized as a *mujtahid* and gave lectures at the Faziye Seminary there. He began to express views on the need to Islamize politics by the 1950s and in response to Shah Mohammad Reza's actions in the 1960s. In the 1950s Musavi was proclaimed an ayatollah (gift of God). At that time he changed his surname to that of his birthplace. In 1962, the last grand ayatollah to be recognized as the ultimate authority, Burujerdi, died, and Khomeini's views were regarded as much more important.

Khomeini was sharply critical of liberalizing foreign influences and governments that he believed were leading Iran away from true Islam. The primary force behind this Westernizing and modernizing trend in Iran was the shah, a staunch ally of the United States. Khomeini, who publicly denounced the regime, was arrested and imprisoned for eight months. On his release, he was exiled from Iran to Turkey in November 1964 after challenging the emancipation of women and the shah's reduction of religious estates through his land reforms.

Khomeini eventually settled in the Shia holy city of Najaf in central Iraq. It was there that he developed the doctrine that an Islamic state should be ruled by the clergy (vilayet-e faqih, or rule of the jurist). When Iraqi president Saddam Hussein forced Khomeini from Najaf, he and his followers moved to France in 1978 and from there urged the ouster of the shah and his U.S. allies. Khomeini also published numerous statements and books, among them *Islamic Government* (*Hukumah Islamiyyah*), a series of lectures delivered at Najaf in 1970. This laid out his principal beliefs in an Islamic state in which the clergy should play a guiding and political role. Making excellent use of the foreign media—not available to him in Iraq—Khomeini was a major influence in the Iranian Revolution and flight of the shah abroad on January 16, 1979. Khomeini returned to Iran from France on February 1, acknowledged by millions of Iranians as the leader of the revolution. Mahdi Bazargan was appointed prime minister of an interim government, but he became critical of Khomeini's Islamic Republican Party (IRP), and the IRP eliminated its civilian rivals and some clerics.

On November 4, 1979, Khomeini's followers, most of them young, zealous Iranian students, stormed the U.S. embassy in Tehran and took 70 Americans hostage in

One of the modern era's most influential revolutionary leaders, Iranian cleric Ayatollah Khomeini used the Islamic Revolution of 1979 to establish a fundamentalist Islamic regime in Iran. (François Lochon/Gamma-Rapho via Getty Images)

blatant defiance of international law. Bazargan resigned. During the next 14 months, the U.S. government attempted without success to secure the release of the hostages through sanctions against Iran and the freezing of Iranian assets. The hostage takers were seemingly encouraged by Khomeini, who refused to intervene and bring an end to the standoff. President Jimmy Carter's failure to resolve the Iranian Hostage Crisis brought with it great frustration and embarrassment. A disastrous aborted hostage rescue attempt in April 1979 only added to American frustration over the situation. The hostage crisis was a major cause of Ronald Reagan's victory over Carter in the U.S. presidential election of November 1980. Only minutes after Reagan took the oath of office on January 20, 1981, the hostages were released.

In December 1980 Khomeini secured his goal of a new constitution in which Iran was officially declared an Islamic republic. Within several years hundreds of Khomeini's opponents had been executed. The clergy in Iran were still committed to their traditional roles in education and law. Part of the task of the Islamic revolution was then to transform Iran's laws and prevailing practice to conform with sharia, or Islamic law. Soon dress codes were imposed that required women to wear the *hejab* in addition to the traditional chador. The legislature imposed a new criminal code based on Islamic law. Alcohol was banned, and for many years Western and Persian music was banned.

Khomeini's Iran remained rather insular on the international stage and became a vociferous opponent of Israel. Although Iran was not itself an active participant in warfare against Israel, it separated itself from the former shah's pro-Israeli positions and sent aid and training to organizations that did so, including Hezbollah in Lebanon.

As Khomeini's revolution progressed, Iraq's Saddam Hussein attempted to take advantage of the turmoil of the revolution and the weakened state of the Iranian military by invading Iran in September 1980. This began the devastating Iraq-Iran War that lasted until 1988, when the two sides accepted a truce brokered by the United Nations (UN). Just as Khomeini had been headstrong about not bringing a quick end to the 1979–1981 hostage crisis, so too was he unwilling to end the war expeditiously. Only after Iran had suffered devastating human losses (some sources estimate more than 1 million dead) and the ground conflict appeared stalemated did Khomeini realize that nothing further could be gained by prolonging the war.

As his own health declined and a clerical power struggle ensued, Khomeini attempted to preserve the revolution and the Islamic state by strengthening the authority of the presidency, the parliament, and other institutions. In so doing he further entrenched the power of religious conservatives, who more often than not pursued counterproductive foreign policies that further isolated their country. The long war with Iraq also severely strained the Iranian economy.

Khomeini died on June 3, 1989, in Tehran. His legacy was a country bound by Islamic rules and practice, a weakened economy, and enmity toward the United State.

Richard M. Edwards

See also
Carter Doctrine; Hezbollah; Hussein, Saddam; Iran; Iran, Islamic Revolution in; Iran Hostage Crisis; Iran Hostage Rescue Mission; Iran-Iraq War; Reza Shah Pahlavi

References
Bill, James A. *The Shah, the Ayatollah, and the United States.* New York: Foreign Policy Association, 1988.
Heikal, Mohamed. *Iran, the Untold Story: An Insider's Account, from the Rise of the Shah to the Reign of the Ayatollah.* New York: Pantheon, 1982.
Hoveyda, Fereydoun. *The Shah and the Ayatollah: Iranian Mythology and Islamic Revolution.* Westport, CT: Praeger, 2003.
Khomeini, Imam. *Islam and Revolution.* Translated by Hamid Algar. Berkeley, CA: Mizan, 1981.
Marschall, Christin. *Iran's Persian Gulf Policy: From Khomeni to Khatami.* Oxford, UK: Routledge/Curzon, 2003.

Khosrow I Anushiravan (496?–579)

King of the Persian Sassanian Empire (224–651) who ruled from 531 to 579. One of the greatest of Persian rulers, Khosrow I reformed the fiscal, administrative, and military institutions of the empire; suppressed the Mazdakite movement that had demanded radical social and economic reforms; defeated the forces of the Roman Empire; and reestablished the Sassanian state as the dominant power in Southwest Asia. In recognition of his many accomplishments, Khosrow I was given the titles of Anushiravan (Immortal Soul) and Dadgar (the Just).

No reliable historical information exists regarding Khosrow's early life. Probably born in 496, he was the son of Sassanian king Kavad I (r. 488–531). The identity of Khosrow's mother is unknown. Khosrow was not his father's eldest son, but he was favored as successor to the throne by the Persian nobility and the Zoroastrian religious hierarchy because of his opposition to the Mazdakite reformist religious movement. Its leader, Mazdak, advocated fundamental social and economic reforms in favor of the lower classes, which the Persian nobility saw as a direct threat to their own status. Apparently Kavad I designated Khosrow as his successor, but on his death his oldest son, Kavus, attempted to succeed his father. The Persian elites, however, saw him as a supporter of Mazdak, while Khosrow was viewed as a defender of the status quo. Supported by the ruling elite, Khosrow defeated his brother and ascended the throne.

The new king inherited an empire bruised and battered by a sharp decline in state revenue, court intrigues, nomadic invasions from north and east, and Roman incursions from the west. With numerous internal challenges to address, Khosrow ended war with the Romans and signed a peace treaty with Emperor Justinian. Under its terms, the Persians agreed to withdraw from Lazica (present-day Georgia) in return for the Romans evacuating those parts of Armenia historically ruled by the Sassanians. The Romans also agreed to pay Khosrow 11,000 pounds of gold in return for his commitment to defend the mountain passes in the Caucasus region.

Khosrow then addressed the internal challenges confronting his empire, particularly the Mazdakite movement, which his father had initially welcomed but that had brought his deposition in 496. Kavad I had escaped imprisonment. After securing refuge with the Hephthalites, in 499 he had raised an army and regained his throne. Kavad now understood that to secure his position he had to accommodate the Persian nobility and the Zoroastrian religious establishment. This lesson was also not lost on Khosrow, who as king ordered Mazdak seized and executed. Thousands of Mazdak's followers were also arrested and imprisoned, and many were executed. Although the movement was forced underground, it did survive and enjoyed a revival of sorts after the fall of the Sassanian dynasty and the introduction of Islam in 651.

At the same time, Khosrow adopted reforms to curtail the power of the Persian nobility and increase that of the central government. He also strengthened the Persian Army, expanded the size of the Sassanian bureaucracy, and restructured the archaic tax system. The reorganized administrative system had a council of ministers (a divan) headed by a prime minister, who presided over a highly efficient bureaucracy. Khosrow also empowered the lower gentry while reducing somewhat that of the great feudal families.

Khosrow reformed and strengthened the Persian military. To centralize the decision-making process under the Sassanian monarch, he replaced the post of the supreme commander in chief by four commanders responsible for the security of the eastern, western, northern, and southern regions of the empire. These reported directly to the king. The same was true of commanders on the frontiers.

Khosrow also improved the quality of army mounts and weapons and strengthened the frontier defenses. One wall erected on the southeastern coast of the Caspian Sea helped defend his northeastern borders from incursions of nomadic tribes from the Central Asian steppes. Another at the town of Darband (Derbent) on the western shores of the Caspian in present-day Shirvan (Republic of Dagestan) was intended to block attacks by the Khazars and Turkic as well as Hunic tribes using the Caucasus as a corridor to penetrate Sassanian-held territory.

His military reorganization completed, Khosrow embarked on a campaign to recover the territories lost by his grandfather, Peroz, and his father, Kavad. Under Emperor Justinian I (r. 527–565), the Byzantine Empire adopted an aggressive policy toward the Sassanian state, building fortifications in Mesopotamia and annexing Armenia. Justinian also tried to persuade the Arab Lakhmid king of Hira, a traditional ally of the Sassanians, to ally with the Byzantines against the Persian king and encouraged the Huns to invade Persian territory.

Khosrow responded by declaring war and marching his army against Syria. In 540 he crossed the Euphrates and attacked and captured Antioch (modern-day Antakya in present-day southern Turkey). The city was plundered, and a large number of its inhabitants were forced to resettle in the Sassanian capital of Ctesiphon. The Romans responded by attacking northern Mesopotamia and Armenia. The conflict between the two empires dragged on for several years before Khosrow and Justinian agreed to a truce. The emperor agreed to pay Khosrow 2,000 pounds of gold, and in return the Persian monarch released the Romans he had taken prisoner. Khosrow also managed to secure control of Lazica on the eastern shores of the Black Sea, whose territory corresponded with the present-day Republic of Georgia and parts of northeastern Turkey.

The truce with the Byzantines proved to be short-lived, and Mesopotamia and Armenia were devastated by the new fighting. The regional Arab kingdoms were forced to take sides, with the Lakhmids remaining loyal to the Sassanian king and the Ghassanids allying with Justinian. The fighting ended in a Sassanian victory, with the Byzantines forced to pay 400 pounds of gold annually. According to a new peace treaty of 562, the Sassanians agreed to guard and protect the Caucasus region from the invading Huns, Alans, and other nomadic groups, who posed a direct threat to the eastern frontiers of the Byzantine Empire, while the emperor promised not to violate the peace agreement by sending his armies against Persian-held possessions in Mesopotamia and the Caucasus.

Though preoccupied for much of his reign with warfare against the Byzantine state in the west, Khosrow also was actively involved in expanding Persian power and influence elsewhere. Sassanian forces conquered Yemen in the southwestern corner of the Arabian Peninsula, giving the Sassanians control of the sea routes linking the Red Sea to the Indian Ocean. In the northeast Khosrow's principal target was the Hephthalite Empire. Hephthalite forces had defeated Sassanian armies in the second half of the fifth century, killing Khosrow's grandfather, Peroz, and holding his father, Kavad, hostage. Khosrow entered into an alliance with the Turks, and with their support during 560–563, Sassanian forces defeated the Hephthalites. The Sassanians thus recovered Tokharestan (formerly Bactria) in northern Afghanistan, Kabulestan in central Afghanistan, Zabolestan in eastern Iran, and Gandhara in northwestern Pakistan.

Khosrow I was also a great patron of the arts and sciences, exhibiting a great interest in philosophical and religious issues. In 529 when Justinian shut down the Academy of Athens, Khosrow recruited members of its faculty to re-create the academy at Ctesiphon, there to translate the works of Plato and his successors into Persian. Khosrow also expanded and strengthened the prestigious medical school at Gondishapur.

Historians of the Islamic era celebrated Khosrow as the greatest of all Persian kings. Among Khorsrow's many building projects was the magnificent palace he caused to be built at Ctesiphon near present-day Baghdad. The palace and its gigantic arch, known as Taq-e Kasra and the Archway of Khosrow, is a monument to the brilliance of Sassanian architecture and engineering. Of baked bricks, it stands 93 feet high and is the largest single-span vault of unreinforced brick in the world.

Although Ctesiphon was taken and sacked and the palace was destroyed by the Arabs in 636, Khosrow I's rule provided a model of benevolent and efficient administration for future dynasties, including the Abbasids, the Ottomans, and the Safavids.

Mehrdad Kia

See also

Justinian I the Great, Emperor; Roman-Sassanid Wars; Sassanid Empire; Zoroastrianism

References

Daryaee, Touraj. *Sasanian Persia: The Rise and Fall of an Empire.* New York: I. B. Tauris, 2013.

Farrokh, Kaveh. *Shadows in the Desert: Ancient Persia at War.* Oxford, UK: Osprey, 2007.

Pourshariati, Parvaneh. *Decline and Fall of the Sasanian Empire: The Sasanian-Parthian Confederacy and the Arab Conquest of Iran.* London: I. B. Tauris, 2008.

Procopius. *History of the Wars Books I–II.* Translated by H. B. Dewing. Cambridge, MA: Harvard University Press, 2006.

Rosen, William. *Justinian's Flea the First Great Plague and the End of the Roman Empire.* London: Penguin Books, 2008.

Kirkuk

The oldest site of continuous human occupation in Iraq, Kirkuk is located approximately 142 miles north of Baghdad and rests on along the Hasa River atop the remains of the 11th-century BCE Assyrian capital city of Arrapha in Iraqi Kurdistan. Kirkuk is a city of some 825,000 people. It is predominantly populated by Iraqi Kurds and Turkomen, which along with the fact that Kirkuk is a critical component of the Iraqi petroleum industry has made it a critically strategic center during all of Iraq's political turmoil since World War I. The city played a significant political and geostrategic role during the run-up to the 2003 Iraq War.

In its early incarnation, Kirkuk was a bloody battleground for at least three empires: the Assyrian, the Babylonian, and the Median, for whom the city on the banks of the Hasa was a strategic stronghold. Under the Babylonians the city was called Kurkura, while under the Greeks it was known as Karkha D-Bet Slokh, which translates as "citadel of the house of Seleucid." By the seventh century CE following the Arab invasion of the Sassanid Empire, Muslim Arabs were calling the city Kirkheni, meaning "citadel."

The discovery of oil in 1927 at Bab Gurgur, near Kirkuk, led to the city becoming the hub of petroleum production in northern Iraq. The oil rush led to the Iraqi annexation of the former Ottoman wilayah of Mosul, of which Kirkuk was a part. From 1963 onward, the Iraqi Arabs attempted to transform the ethnic makeup of the entire region to take power away from the Kurds and ensure that Iraqi Arabs stayed in control of the oil fields. In 1975 the Iraqi Baath Party, under Ahmad Hassan al-Bakr, began to "Arabize" the Kirkuk area by imposing restrictions on Kurds and Turkomen who lived there while trying to replace them with Arabs from central or southern Iraq. As many as 1,400 Kurdish villages were razed, and over half a million Kurds were forcibly relocated. The Arabization process intensified following the failed Kirkuk/Kurdish uprising after the Persian Gulf War in 1991, and it is estimated that between 1991 and 2003 as many as 120,000 Kurds and Turkomen were forcibly relocated out of Kirkuk.

In the lead-up to the Iraq War (2003), Kirkuk, along with Mosul, proved to be sticking points that prevented the United States from being able to launch a prong of its assault into Iraq from bases in Turkey. The Turkish parliament wanted guarantees that Kurdish fighters would not be allowed to capture Kirkuk or Mosul. Because the United States would not or could not make such a promise, Turkey refused to grant the Americans and their allies permission to launch attacks from Turkish soil. The Turks also saw this move as a means of squelching the Iraqi Kurds' nationalism, as many of the Kurds view Kirkuk as the "Kurdish Jerusalem."

On April 11, 2003, after days of heated battles, the U.S.-led coalition forces and Kurdish Peshmerga fighters secured Kirkuk from Saddam Hussein's Baath Party loyalists. Victims of Kirkuk's Arabization attempted to return once the area was free of the Baath Party, yet the new postwar Iraqi government did little to resolve this crisis, leaving most returning Kurds in a refugee limbo.

After the withdrawal of U.S. troops from Iraq in 2011, Kirkuk, now under the de facto control of Iraqi Kurds, witnessed an uptick in violence and terrorist attacks. In June 2014, Kirkuk was overrun and occupied by Islamic State of Iraq and Syria (ISIS) insurgents, who imposed a brutal occupation on the city. After many months of heavy fighting, Iraqi, Kurdish, and allied forces took control of Kirkuk. Then on October 16, 2017, the Iraqi government dispatched Iraqi Army troops to Kirkuk, and they took control of the area's oil fields and Kirkuk as Kurdish Peshmerga fighters, who had held the city since 2014, fled. The Iraqi government action came in response to the September 2017 Kurdish independence vote, which Baghdad strongly opposes. It remains unclear whether the Iraqi government and Iraqi Kurds can arrive at some sort of agreement over the permanent government jurisdiction of Kirkuk.

B. Keith Murphy

See also
Baath Party; Bakr, Ahmad Hassan al-; Kurds; Peshmerga; Turkey

References
Astarjian, Henry D. *The Struggle for Kirkuk: The Rise of Hussein, Oil, and the Death of Tolerance in Iraq.* Westport, CT: Praeger Security International, 2007.

Polk, William Roe. *Understanding Iraq.* New York: HarperCollins, 2005.

Kobanî, Siege of (September 27, 2014– January 26, 2015)

Key battle in the fight against the Islamic State of Iraq and Syria (ISIS). After having already taken much of northern Syria in the ongoing civil war there (2011 to the present) and most of Anbar Province in Iraq (displacing half a million Iraqis), in early June 2014 ISIS launched a major offensive in northern Iraq. ISIS fighters seized Iraq's second-largest city of Mosul and also captured Tikrit, displacing another half million Iraqis, then advanced south toward Baghdad. By June 22 they were only some 60 miles from the Iraqi capital city. These territorial acquisitions accompanied by widespread ISIS atrocities—including the summary execution of non-Muslims refusing to convert to Islam, the raping and enslavement of women, and the beheading of hostages— prompted the formation of a broad-based international coalition headed by the United States to defeat and indeed destroy ISIS.

Then beginning on September 17, ISIS launched a major offensive to capture the important largely Kurdish town of Kobanî (also known as Kobanê or Ayn al-Arab), located in northern Syria on the border with Turkey and one of three major crossing points into that country. The offensive included tanks and artillery. By the beginning of October, ISIS fighters had taken some 350 Kurdish villages and towns in the Kobanî vicinity; displaced some 150,000 Kurds, most of whom sought refuge in Turkey and were attacking Kobanî itself.

This presented the Turkish government with a dilemma, and on September 30 Turkish soldiers and tanks took up position along the border with Syria as the government debated whether to intervene militarily. Meanwhile, on September 27 for the first time, U.S. and coalition air strikes targeted ISIS positions near Kobanî.

On October 2, the Turkish parliament voted 298 to 98 to authorize military force against ISIS. Although Turkish president Recep Tayyip Erdoğan had been outspoken in his insistence that Syrian president Bashar al-Assad must be removed from power and had urged the establishment of a no-fly zone over portions of Syria, he was also reluctant to intervene in Kobanî. With Turkish tanks and troops remaining in place, on October 8 ISIS fighters commenced a siege of Kobanî.

Turkey's failure to act brought rioting by that country's Kurdish minority in which at least nine protests, organized in part by the pro-Kurdish Peoples' Democratic Party, occurred across Turkey and in several foreign cities. Since 1984 some 40,000 people had been killed in clashes between Turkish government forces and its Kurdish minority, led by the Kurdistan Workers' Party (PKK), which sought greater rights for the Kurds. In March 2013, however, imprisoned PKK leader Abdullah Ocalan had called for a cease-fire. PPK fighters had withdrawn to the Iraqi mountains, and the beginnings of a peace process had emerged. The Turkish failure to intervene to aid Kobanî, and indeed its turning back of Turkish Kurds wanting to fight for the city, fueled Kurdish anger anew. Ankara feared the establishment of an independent radical Kurdish state that would seek a larger Kurdistan to include the Kurdish portions of Turkey. Nonetheless, in a statement from prison, Ocalan warned that "the reality of Kobanî and the peace process are not separable." On October 12, however, Ankara announced that it would permit U.S. and other coalition forces battling militants in Syria and Iraq to use some of its bases, which would make it easier for coalition air forces to assist the Kobanî defenders. However, the next day, Turkish warplanes attacked not Kobanî but PKK positions in southeastern Turkey.

Meanwhile, the battle for Kobanî raged on and intensified as U.S. and other coalition forces continued air strikes in support of the Kurds. If ISIS were to capture Kobanî, it

An explosion in the Syrian town of Kobanî, also known as Ain al-Arab, after a U.S.-led coalition airstrike, as seen from the nearby Turkish border village of Mursitpinar, Sanliurfa Province, on October 22, 2014. (NurPhoto via Getty Images)

would control three official border crossings between Turkey and Syria and some 60 miles of their common frontier.

On October 19, for the first time in the coalition campaign against ISIS, U.S. military aircraft air-dropped to the Kurdish fighters in Kobanî weapons provided by Kurdish authorities in Iraq as well as ammunition and medical supplies. Then the next day the Turkish government announced that it would allow some Kurds to cross the Turkish border into Syria to join the fight for Kobanî, but only those from Kurdistan and not those from Turkey itself. This decision opened a corridor to Syria for the Peshmerga fighters. The semiautonomous northern region of Iraqi Kurdistan is one of Turkey's major security allies and a principal exporter of oil to Turkey. Indeed, in June Turkey signed a 50-year energy pact with the Kurdistan Regional Government. Iraqi Kurdistan had also been at odds with the PKK and its affiliates in Syria.

The struggle for control of Kobanî raged on, but by mid-January 2015 the national army of Syrian Kurdistan, known as the People's Protection Units (YPG), supported by the Peshmerga, other Kurdish volunteers, and members of the Free Syrian Army, had turned back a number of ISIS assaults.

Finally, on January 26, 2015, the YPG and its allied fighters drove the last ISIS units from the city. The Battle of Kobanî reportedly resulted in the deaths of more than 1,000 ISIS fighters and 324 YPG troops as well as 12 allied rebels. Reportedly hundreds of other ISIS militants died in the U.S.-led coalition air strikes on the city and surrounding countryside.

For sometime thereafter, however, most of the villages in the Kobanî canton remained under ISIS control. Kurdish forces supported by allied Arab armed groups and aided by coalition air strikes then made rapid advances. By early February ISIS fighters had been driven some 15 miles from the city, and by the end of April almost all of the villages in the canton captured earlier by ISIS had been retaken. The Battle of Kobanî is considered by many analysts to have been a turning point in the fight against the Islamic State.

In late June 2015 ISIS again attacked Kobanî, killing some 233 civilians. Since then, however, the city has remained free from ISIS control, and the slow and arduous task of rebuilding has begun.

Spencer C. Tucker

See also
Assad, Bashar al-; Erdoğan, Recep Tayyip; Iraq; Islamic State of Iraq and Syria; Kobanî Massacre; Kurds; Mosul, Second Battle of; Peshmerga; Syrian Civil War

References
Abdulrahim, Raja. "Islamic State, Rival Al Nusra Front Each Strengthen Grip on Syria." *Los Angeles Times*, November 28, 2014.
Cloud, David, and Brian Bennetan. "U.S., Allies Rush Heavy Weapons to Kurds to Fight Militants in Iraq." *Los Angeles Times*, August 11, 2014.
Khalilzad, Zalmay. "To fight the Islamic State, Kurdish and Iraqi Forces Need Expedited Aid." *Washington Post*, August 13, 2014.
"La France renforce son dispositif militaire en Irak avec trois Rafale." *Le Monde*, October 8, 2014.
"Military Airstrikes Continue against ISIL in Syria and Iraq Supporting Operation Inherent Resolve, U.S. Central Command." U.S. Department of Defense, January 14, 2015, http://www.defense.gov/home/features/2014/0814_iraq/Airstrikes6.html.
Rush, James. "Isis Air Strikes: US Brings in Apache Helicopters as British Jets Target Militants in Iraq." *The Independent*, October 8, 2014.

Kobanî Massacre (June 25–26, 2015)

Mass killing in Kobanî, Syria, perpetrated by the Islamic State of Iraq and Syria (ISIS.) On June 25, 2015, several dozen ISIS militants entered the town of Kobanî and the neighboring village of Brakh Bootan and there massacred as many as 154 civilians. At least another 200 were injured. Kobanî is a strategically located town populated largely by Kurds adjacent to the Turkish border. In the autumn of 2014 ISIS seized control of Kobanî, in the process killing many civilians and forcing thousands of others to flee. In January 2015 a Kurdish counteroffensive, supported by American-led coalition air strikes, liberated Kobanî. Although a number of refugees returned to the town, sporadic fighting continued there.

ISIS fighters penetrated Kobanî on June 25 disguised as members of the People's Protection Units (YPG), a largely Kurdish militia group that had been fighting ISIS for some time and was also charged with protecting Kurdish towns. The attack began with at least three separate suicide car bombings. After the car bombs were detonated, more ISIS fighters moved into Kobanî, shooting civilians and taking hostages, most of whom were later killed. YPG fighters subsequently engaged in running gun battles with ISIS militants in and around Kobanî for several more days. The YPG then besieged Kobanî before ultimately driving the ISIS rebels out.

The ISIS attacks on Kobanî and Brakh Bootan represented a renewed ISIS offensive after it had recently suffered serious military setbacks when Kurdish troops and coalition air assets managed to push the extremist group to within 30 miles of its headquarters in Raqqa, Syria. The Kobanî massacre demonstrated the continued fluidity of the fighting in Syria, even after certain areas were declared to have been liberated from ISIS control. The Kobanî massacre was emblematic of ISIS's terrorist campaign, which included mass killings of noncombatants, sexual enslavement, crucifixions, and beheadings. Fortunately, by 2018 ISIS had been virtually defeated in both Syria and Iraq, although Kobanî remains a dangerous place.

PAUL G. PIERPAOLI JR.

See also
Islamic State of Iraq and Syria; Syrian Civil War

References
Shaheen, Kareem. "Kurdish Forces Besiege ISIS Fighters in Kobani after Massacre of Civilians." *The Guardian*, June 26, 2015, http://www.theguardian.com/world/2015/jun/26/kurdish-forces-have-besieged-isis-fighters-in-kobani-say-activists.
Westall, Sylvia, and Tom Perry. "Islamic State Kills at least 145 Civilians in Syria's Kobani." Reuters, June 26, 2015, http://www.reuters.com/article/2015/06/26/us-mideast-crisis-syria-idUSKBN0P60UY20150626.

Konya, Battle of (December 21, 1832)

Important battle of the First Egyptian-Ottoman War of 1831–1833. After securing Acre (Akko) following their successful siege of December 4, 1831–May 27, 1832, Egyptian forces under Ibrahim Pasha smashed Ottoman forces at Homs (July 8, 1832) and the Syrian Gates (July 29). Although this rapid advance confounded Ottoman strategists, it also forced Ibrahim to leave behind both artillery and garrison troops. He entered Anatolia in December with about 50,000 men.

The principal Ottoman field force, numbering more than 80,000 men, was moving into eastern Anatolia when it collided with Ibrahim's screen outside the city of Konya during December 18–19, 1832. Commanded by Grand Vizier Rescid Mehmed Pasha, the Ottoman field force suffered from several disadvantages. First, a significant portion of these men were irregulars who were incapable of facing Egyptian regulars in a set-piece battle. Equally important, the Ottoman regulars were in the midst of a military reformation and were not as well trained or well led as their Egyptian counterparts.

The battle began on the very foggy morning of December 21. Rescid ordered his army to advance, while the Egyptians held steady, both flanks covered by infantry squares to negate the Ottoman advantage in light cavalry. Poor training, weak leadership, and the heavy fog caused Ottoman units to separate, especially on their left flank. Noting significant gaps in the Ottoman formation, Ibrahim ordered a counterattack. This quickly unhinged the Ottoman left, forcing Rescid to charge with his bodyguards in hopes of restoring order. Instead, the grand vizier was taken prisoner, and the left wing collapsed. A halfhearted effort to continue the fight ended when an Egyptian grand battery blasted the center and right wings.

Ottoman casualties were 10 times that of the Egyptians, and those who escaped the battle dispersed into Anatolia. Ibrahim's victory at Konya removed the last significant Ottoman force between his army and the imperial capital of Istanbul (Constantinople).

JOHN P. DUNN

See also

Egyptian-Ottoman Wars; Ibrahim Pasha; Mehmed Ali

References

Afaf Lufti al-Sayyid-Marsot. *Egypt in the Reign of Muhammad Ali.* Cambridge: Cambridge University Press, 1984.

Khaled Fahmy. *All the Pasha's Men: Mehmed Ali, His Army, and the Making of Modern Egypt.* Cambridge: Cambridge University Press, 1997.

Köprülü Abdullah Pasha (1694–1735)

Ottoman statesman and general in the first half of the 18th century. The son of Grand Vizier Köprülü Fazil Mustafa Pasha and grandson of Köprülü Mehmet Pasha, Köprülü Abdullah Pasha married the daughter of Grand Vizier Fazil Mustafa Pasha and gained a prominent position as the military commander of Constantinople (*qaim-maqamı*). In later years he held various posts as governor of Khania, Khios, and Sivas before being appointed the *vali* of Van (eastern Anatolia) and commander in chief for the Ottoman campaign against Tabriz in 1723.

Köprülü gained considerable success capturing Nahçıvan, Ardamil, and Karabagh in the summer of 1724. In August 1725, he sacked Tabriz in what was the last Ottoman conquest of the city. In 1726 Köprülü became the governor of Raqqa (Syria), and in later years he governed Candia, Egypt, Euboia, and Qaraman.

By the early 1730s the Ottoman Empire faced the growing power of Nadir Shah, who moved to reclaim Iranian influence in the Caucasus and in Iraq. In 1735, Köprülü was appointed commander in chief of Ottoman forces to deal with the Persian threat. He managed to raise the Persian siege of Ganja (January 1735) and in May forced Nadir to retreat from Kars. But in the decisive battle at Baghavard near present-day Kars on June 14, 1745, and despite a considerable Ottoman superiority in manpower, Nadir Shah inflicted a decisive defeat on the Ottoman forces under Köprülü, who was killed in the battle.

ALEXANDER MIKABERIDZE

See also

Baghavard, First Battle of; Köprülü Fazil Ahmed Pasha; Köprülü Mehmed Pasha; Nadir Shah; Ottoman-Safavid Wars

References

Avery, Peter, et al., eds. *The Cambridge History of Iran,* Vol. 7, *From Nadir Shah to the Islamic Republic.* Cambridge: Cambridge University Press, 1991.

Lockhart, Laurence. *The Fall of the Safavi Dynasty and the Afghan Occupation of Persia.* Cambridge: Cambridge University Press, 1958.

Nizri, Michael. *Ottoman High Politics and the Ulema Household.* New York: Palgrave Macmillan, 2014.

Köprülü Fazil Ahmed Pasha (1635–1676)

Ottoman grand vizier, general, and statesman. Born in 1635 in Veles (then named Köprülü and now in Macedonia), Ahmed Köprülü was the second member of the Köprülü family from Albania that furnished three grand viziers to the Ottoman Empire under Sultan Mehmed IV (r. 1648–1687). Ahmed Köprülü's father was Mehmed Köprülü, grand vizier during 1656–1661, who did much to reform and centralize state administration and to strengthen the Ottoman state militarily. Mehmed Köprülü recommended his son as his successor to Mehmed IV, and the sultan's confidence in Mehmed Köprülü's advice was such that he appointed Ahmed, even though he was only 26. Ahmed Köprülü assumed the position of grand vizier in 1665 and held it until his death in 1676.

As with his father, in domestic matters Köprülü was a just and capable administrator. He did not shrink from eliminating those who posed a threat, but he was called "Fazil," meaning "fair-minded," for his reduction of taxes and support of education.

Köprülü was a significant military leader. In 1663 he initiated war with the Austrian Habsburgs over control of Hungary. Whereas his father had shrunk from campaigning on the Danube, Ahmed Köprülü embraced it. In 1663 he led a large Ottoman army in an invasion of Habsburg (Royal) Hungary, with the intention of taking Vienna. In part because there were no defensive preparations but also because many Hungarian peasants saw them as liberators, the Ottomans enjoyed early success with little opposition except from forces under Miklós Zrinyi. Crossing the Danube and catching the Habsburgs by surprise, Köprülü captured the important stronghold of Neuhäusel (now Nové Zámky) in present-day southwestern Slovakia.

After passing the winter in Belgrade, Köprülü renewed the invasion in 1654. Preceding him was a Tartar force that ravaged the countryside and created widespread panic. Köprülü was determined to take all the Habsburg fortresses on the route to Vienna. Planning to cross the Raab River, he encountered a smaller allied Habsburg and Hungarian army led by Raimondo Montecuccoli, which defeated the Ottomans in the Battle of Szentgotthard (Battle of the Raab River or Battle of the Convent of St. Gothard, August 1, 1664).

This important engagement broke the spell of Ottoman victories and revealed Ottoman weaknesses in equipment, training, and tactics. Losses on both sides had been heavy, and Holy Roman emperor Leopold I, alarmed by the designs of French king Louis XIV on the Spanish Netherlands and by unrest in Royal Hungary, seized on the opportunity to make peace. The resulting Treaty of Vasvar on August 10, 1664, favored the Ottomans, who were allowed to retain control of the frontier fortresses they had captured in Nagyvarad (Grosswardein) and Ersekujvar (Neuhäusel). The Habsburgs also recognized Ottoman suzerainty over Transylvania, and there was a 20-year truce.

Shifting his attention to a weaker foe, in 1666 Köprülü sailed with a large force to Crete in an effort to bring to a close fighting there that had been draining the empire's resources for 25 years. In 1669 after a three-year siege, Köprülü finally captured the "impregnable" fortress of Candia (present-day Heraklion). A major reverse for the Venetians who had been holding the city, it gave the Ottomans virtual control of the island. This in effect made the eastern Mediterranean an Ottoman preserve.

In 1672, taking advantage of disunion in Poland, Köprülü assembled a large army for an invasion of that country. Although Ottoman forces secured the southern province of Podolia (in present-day Ukraine), the invasion finally roused the Poles to the Ottoman threat. John Sobieski led a Polish force that defeated the invaders in the Battle of Khotyn (November 11, 1673), and they withdrew.

The Ottomans returned, but Sobieski, now king of Poland as John III Sobieski (r. 1674–1696), and some 6,000 men defeated a force of 20,000 Ottomans in the Battle of Lwów (now Lviv, November 24, 1675) in present-day western Ukraine. Sobieski was again victorious at Đurawno (September 25–October 14, 1676). Although Köprülü signed a treaty at Đurawno, he was not deterred in his designs. However, he died several days later on October 19, 1676, at only age 42, leaving the military effort to Ibrahim Pasha. Köprülü was succeeded as grand vizier by his brother-in-law and adopted member of the family, Kara Mustafa Pasha, the third Köprülü to hold the position during the reign of Mehmed IV.

Despite his near constant warfare, which kept the Janissaries occupied and out of the political arena, Köprülü left the Ottoman state stronger than when he had assumed office. He had also secured additional territory in Europe for the empire. These advances were not without cost, for they raised the specter of conflict with Russia, which was to plague the Ottomans for centuries to come.

SPENCER C. TUCKER

See also
Janissaries; Köprülü Mehmed Pasha; Ottoman-Habsburg Wars; Ottoman-Polish Wars of the 17th Century; Vasvár, Treaty of

References
Barber, Noel. *The Sultans.* New York: Simon and Schuster, 1973.
Kinross, John. *The Ottoman Centuries: The Rise and Fall of the Turkish Empire.* London: J. Cape, 1977.
Shaw, Stanford J. *History of the Ottoman Empire and Modern Turkey.* Cambridge: Cambridge University Press, 1976.

Köprülü Mehmed Pasha (1583?–1661)

Ottoman grand vizier, general, and statesman. The founder of a family of warrior statesmen that produced three grand viziers in the 17th century during the reign of Mehmed IV (r. 1648–1687), Mehmed Köprülü was born of humble origins, probably in 1583, in Rojnik, Berat, Albania. Recruited into the sultan's service, Köprülü was initially a scullion and then a cook in the sultan's household. Given increased responsibility, he eventually rose to the position of pasha and was made governor of a succession of provinces: Eğri in 1647, Karamanid in 1648, and Amadolu in 1650. He served as vizier of the divan briefly in 1652 but had been dismissed following a power struggle and had retired to an estate in northern Anatolia.

In 1656 the Ottoman Empire was in crisis. Its foreign enemies had grown more powerful, and the Ottoman Navy could no longer defend its own coasts. Ottoman forces were faring poorly in the Ottoman-Venetian War (1645–1670), fought over Crete. The Venetians and the Maltese and Barbary corsairs were roaming at will in the eastern Mediterranean. Venetians and Maltese ships, then blockading the Dardanelles, had inflicted a major defeat on the Ottoman Navy in the Battle of the Dardanelles (June 26–27, 1656), sinking most of the Ottoman ships and thus severing the Ottoman lines of communication between Istanbul (Constantinople) and Crete. Food prices soared in Istanbul amid the possibility that the Venetians might mount an attack the city. Power struggles were rife within Istanbul, and there were plots by important viziers to replace Sultan Mehmed IV.

In these circumstances Sultana Turhan Hortice, the mother of Mehmed IV, approached the retired Köprülü, then in his early 70s, about assuming the position of grand vizier. Köprülü demanded extraordinary powers including a pledge that all his decisions be accepted without question, even by the sultan himself. These terms were accepted, and Mehmed IV appointed Köprülü grand vizier on September 15, 1656.

A shrewd and capable administrator, Köprülü knew all of the weaknesses of the Ottoman government and was well acquainted with its leading personalities. He began his government by purging corrupt and inefficient administrators and ruthlessly eliminating all those he perceived to be a threat to the regime and to his authority. He is said during his short tenure to have caused the execution of some 35,000 people.

Köprülü enjoyed success against the Ottoman state's external enemies. Upon becoming grand vizier, he set out to enforce discipline within the army. In January 1657 Köprülü employed Janissary forces to put down a rebellion by the household cavalry Sipahi troops in Istanbul.

Köprülü also strengthened the Ottoman land defenses by erecting new fortresses on the Don and Dnieper Rivers against the Cossacks. He also embarked on an immediate massive shipbuilding program. The latter had swift result, for in another battle in the Dardanelles (July 19, 1657) the Ottomans defeated the Venetians. This victory enabled the Ottomans to regain control that November of some of the Aegean islands, including Tenedos and Lemnos, and to reopen supply lines to their forces in Crete.

At the same time, Köprülü launched a series of military campaigns during 1658–1659 to crush rebellions by a number of pashas in Anatolia. In 1658 he ordered Ottoman forces into Transylvania, where vassal Prince György II Rákóczi had invaded Poland without permission. While an Ottoman army invaded from the south, Köprülü called on his Tartar and Cossack allies to invade from the north. This simultaneous convergence of forces was too much for Rákóczi. Although Rákóczi won an early battle against the Ottomans at Lippa (May 1658), he was soon driven out to his estates in Habsburg Hungary. The three occupying armies devastated Transylvania, bringing to a close Hungary's so-called Second Golden Age. This also marked the end of Transylvania as a European power and protector of Hungarian liberties. In August 1660 Köprülü annexed Yanbova (Jenö) and Várad.

In July 1660 a fire destroyed a large part of Istanbul, leading to food shortages and plague. Köprülü oversaw the city's reconstruction. His honesty and integrity were recognized by all. Köprülü died at the height of his influence in Edirne on October 31, 1661. He was succeeded by his son Ahmed Köprülü.

Mehmed Köprülü's short six-year tenure as grand vizier temporarily halted the decline in Ottoman power. He had strengthened the state both internally and militarily against its external foes, and his victories in Transylvania advanced Ottoman territory and rendered virtually inevitable the subsequent major confrontation with the Habsburgs.

SPENCER C. TUCKER

See also
Köprülü Fazil Ahmed Pasha; Ottoman-Habsburg Wars; Ottoman-Polish Wars of the 17th Century

References
Barber, Noel. *The Sultans.* New York: Simon and Schuster, 1973.
Kinross, John. *The Ottoman Centuries: The Rise and Fall of the Turkish Empire.* London: J. Cape, 1977.
Shaw, Stanford J. *History of the Ottoman Empire and Modern Turkey.* Cambridge: Cambridge University Press, 1976.

Koran
See Quran

Köse Dağ, Battle of (June 26, 1243)
Important battle in the history of the Middle East fought between the force of the Mongol Empire, led by Baiju, and those of the Seljuk Sultanate of Rum, led by Sultan

Kaykhusraw II. The Battle of Köse Dağ (Kosedagh) occurred on June 26, 1243, at Köse Dağ, some 36 miles east of Sivas in northeastern Anatolia (present-day Turkey).

The Mongols were expanding their control reach westward and eager to include Anatolia in their holdings. In the winter of 1242–1243 a Mongol army led by Baiju attacked the Sultanate of Rum and seized the city of Erzurum in eastern Anatolia. Sultan Kaykhusraw immediately moved to meet the invaders. The Empire of Trebizond contributed some men, and there were also some Frankish mercenaries and Georgian auxiliaries. Most Georgians, however, were forced to fight on the Mongol side. Altogether the sultan had some 60,000–80,000 men, of whom perhaps 20,000–25,000 took part in the battle. Including Armenian and Georgian levies, the Mongol force numbered some 30,000–40,000 men.

Baiju downplayed concerns raised by the Georgians regarding the superior numerical strength of the Seljuk forces. Kaykhusraw, however, disregarded wise counsel that he simply await the Mongol advance and threw away his great advantage in numbers by pressing ahead with perhaps a third of his force led by inexperienced commanders.

When the advance Seljuk force encountered the Mongols the latter feigned retreat, then turned suddenly and attacked. The battle was over quickly, with the Seljuk forces panicking and collapsing. Much of the army simply deserted. Kaykhusraw II survived and was permitted to become a vassal ruler in the vast Mongol Empire. The Mongol victory was decisive, for the Battle of Köse Dağ established their control of Anatolia. The Empire of Trebizond became a vassal state of the Mongol Empire, as did the Armenian Kingdom of Cilicia. For a time the Seljuk sultanate continued but as a Mongol province, although the Seljuk dynasty came to an end early in the 13th century.

SPENCER C. TUCKER

See also
Ayn Jalut, Battle of; Rum, Sultanate of; Trebizond, Empire of

References
May, Timothy. *The Mongol Conquests in World History.* London: Reaktion Books, 2011.

Morgan, David. *The Mongols.* 2nd ed. Hoboken, NJ: Wiley-Blackwell, 2007.

Rossabi, Morris. *The Mongols: A Very Short Introduction.* New York: Oxford University Press, 2012.

Saunders, J. J. *The History of the Mongol Conquests.* Philadelphia: University of Pennsylvania Press, 2001.

Turnbull, Stephen. *Genghis Khan and the Mongol Conquests, 1190–1400.* New York: Routledge, 2003.

Kress von Kressenstein, Friedrich Sigismund Georg (1870–1948)

Bavarian Army general. Born in Nürnberg, Bavaria, on April 14, 1870, Friedrich Sigismund Georg Kress von Kressenstein completed gymnasium there and entered the Bavarian Army as an ensign in 1888. Kress attended the Kriegsakademie in Munich. In 1904 he assumed command of an artillery battery. In 1906 he was assigned to the Bavarian General Staff in Munich. In 1907 Kress served on the staff of the Bavarian 4th Infantry Division, and the next year he joined the Great General Staff at Munich. He was promoted to captain in March 1911.

In January 1914 Kress was assigned as a member of the German Military Mission to the Ottoman Empire, headed by Lieutenant General Otto Liman von Sanders. Kress served in the Ottoman War Ministry and at Ottoman Army headquarters before becoming chief of staff of the Ottoman Army's VIII Corps that September. When the Ottoman Empire entered the war in November, Kress was promoted to lieutenant colonel.

In January 1915 Ottoman minister of marine and governor of Syria Ahmed Djemal Pasha, who hoped to spark Egyptians to join in a jihad (holy war) against the British, led 22,000 men on a 10-day march across the Sinai Peninsula from Beersheba. Kress actually commanded the force. The men literally dragged artillery, boats, and bridging equipment across the desert.

Fortunately for the British, aircraft provided warning of the Ottoman approach, enabling British commander in Egypt General Sir John Maxwell to shift resources to meet it. On February 2 Ottoman forces reached the canal and attempted to cross it, only to be driven back at a cost of 2,000 casualties. This Ottoman assault against the Suez Canal caused the British to keep men in Egypt who were badly needed at Gallipoli and also gained Kress considerable recognition.

In July 1915, Kress became chief of staff of the Ottoman Fourth (later Eighth) Army, which made another futile effort to seize the canal in 1916, ending in defeat in the Battle of Romani (August 4–9). He then commanded the Eighth Army opposing the British advance under General Sir Archibald James Murray from Egypt into Gaza and Palestine, for which Kress would be awarded the Pour le Mérite.

Skillfully defending Gaza with few effectives, Kress received much credit for the defeat of attacking British forces in the First and Second Battles of Gaza (March 26–27 and April 17–19, 1917) but was pushed from Jerusalem by British forces under Lieutenant General Edmund Allenby in December 1917. Promoted to colonel in December 1917, Kress remained in command of the Ottoman Eighth Army, stopping Allenby's advance along the Palestine-Lebanese coast, until his transfer to the Caucasus region in June 1918.

Kress next led a German-Ottoman column in occupying Tbilisi in Georgia and then took part in defending Abkhazia from the attacking Red Army. He remained in the Transcaucasus region until February 1919.

After the war Kress continued in the new Reichswehr, serving on its staff in Berlin. He commanded the 7th Infantry Division in Munich during 1923–1929. Kress retired as a general of artillery in 1929 and died in Munich on January 16, 1948.

MICHAEL B. BARRETT AND SPENCER C. TUCKER

See also
Allenby, Sir Edmund Henry Hynman; Djemal Pasha, Ahmed; Gallipoli Campaign; Gaza, First Battle of; Gaza, Second Battle of; Gaza, Third Battle of; Jerusalem, Capture of; Liman von Sanders, Otto; Murray, Sir Archibald James; Palestine and Syria Campaign, World War I; Romani, Battle of; Suez Canal

References
Bruce, Anthony P. C. *The Last Crusade: The Palestine Campaign in the First World War.* London: Murray, 2002.
Falls, Cyril. *Armageddon, 1918: The Final Palestinian Campaign of World War I.* Philadelphia: University of Pennsylvania Press, 2003.
Haupt, W. "Deutsche Truppen im Kaukasus 1918." In *Deutsches Soldatenjahrbuch*, 140–148. Munich: Schild, 1971.
Kress von Kressenstein, Friedrich. *Mit den Türken zum Suezkanal.* Berlin: Vorhut-Verlag Otto Schlegel, 1938.

Kuchuk Kainardji, Treaty of (July 21, 1774)

Peace treaty between the Ottoman Empire and Russia in the wake of the Russo-Ottoman War of 1768–1774. The treaty, signed at the village of Kuchuk Kainardji (in present-day Bulgaria) on July 21, 1774, proved to be rather consequential for the Ottoman Empire and had long-term effects on the history of the Middle East.

The agreement consisted of 28 articles (plus two secret provisions). Under Russian pressure, Sultan Abdulhamid I recognized the independence of the Crimean Khanate, which was annexed by Russia just nine years later, but maintained as a caliph his religious authority over it. This was the first time that a separation into secular and spiritual authority was established in the Ottoman Empire as well as the first time that an Ottoman ruler surrendered a territory largely populated by Muslims.

According to other provisions, the Porte ceded the major fortress of Kilburnu, Kerc, Yenikale, and Azak and the territories of Greater and Lesser Kabarda, allowing Russia to establish a strong presence in the northern Caucasus and the Black Sea. The Ottoman Empire retained Moldavia and Walacia but recognized Russia's special position in the region. Russia agreed to withdraw from the parts of northern Caucasus and the islands in the Aegean Sea. The Ottoman authorities also conceded capitulations that gave Russian merchants commercial privileges throughout the empire. The sultan also agreed to pay a heavy war indemnity of 15,000 purses (4.5 million rubles).

The most consequential articles of the treaty dealt with Russia's role inside the Ottoman Empire. Russia received the right to open consulates in any places within the Ottoman Empire. The sultan agreed to let Russia establish a Russian Orthodox Church for local Russians in the Galata district of Istanbul (Constantinople). Yet Article 7 granted Russia the right to represent (and protect) the church and its personnel. These provisions proved to be highly controversial, as disagreements regarding their interpretation quickly emerged between Moscow and Istanbul. Russia interpreted them as granting it the status of the protector of Ottoman Orthodox Christians, which would allow it to actively interfere in the Ottoman domestic affairs.

The Treaty of Kuchuk Kainardji was crucial in the development of the "Eastern question" and contributed to the outbreak of the Crimean War in 1853.

ALEXANDER MIKABERIDZE

See also
Russo-Ottoman Wars

References
Davison, Roderic H. "Russian Skill and Turkish Imbecility: The Treaty of Kuchuk Kainardji Reconsidered." *Slavic Review* 3, no. 35 (1976): 364–483.
Finkel, Caroline. *Osman's Dream: The Story of the Ottoman Empire, 1300–1923.* London: John Murray, 2005.

Kurdan, Treaty of (September 4, 1746)

The Treaty of Kurdan, signed in Kurdan, Persia, on September 4, 1746, ended more than a decade of hostilities between the Ottoman Empire and Persia. The treaty reaffirmed the boundary arrangement established by the 1639 Treaty of Zuhab.

ALEXANDER MIKABERIDZE

See also
Ottoman-Safavid Wars; Zuhab, Treaty of

Reference
Sicker, Martin. *The Islamic World in Decline: From the Treaty of Karlowitz to the Disintegration of the Ottoman Empire.* Westport, CT: Greenwood, 2000.

Kurds

The Kurdish people or Kurds live in West Asia in the mountainous region known as Kurdistan that encompasses southeastern Turkey, eastern Syria, northern Iraq, and western Iran. Kurdistan includes the oil fields around Kirkuk and is rich in other natural resources. The largest number of Kurds—some 15 million—live in Turkey, while there are an estimated 7 million in Iran, 6 million in Iraq, and some 2 million in Syria. With 30 million to 35 million people, Kurds constitute the world's largest ethnic group without a state, something they have long sought.

The great majority of Kurds are Sunni Muslims, and their language is related to Persian (which is spoken chiefly in Iran, Afghanistan, and Tajikistan). There are numerous dialects of Kurdish Persian, though most Kurds can be divided into two primary dialect groups: Sorani and Kumanji. Just as they have their own language, the Kurds maintain their own unique culture and traditions.

Until the first few decades of the 20th century, most Kurds lived a pastoral, nomadic existence and divided themselves into tribes. For centuries, they led a somewhat isolated lifestyle that clung to tradition that was well ordered by tribal hierarchy and customs. The Kurds' principal avocation was goat and sheep herding, which was migratory in nature. In this sense, they were not unlike the Bedouins to the south.

A Kurdish state appeared on the verge of realization following World War I. With the breakup of the Ottoman Empire, the Kurds began to call for their own nation of Kurdistan. While the British gave some lip service to this idea, the Turks effectively quashed it, with both Iraq and Iran agreeing that they would recognize no Kurdish state encompassing any part of their territory. The Treaty of Sèvres between the victorious Allies and Turkey in 1920 promised the Kurds autonomy leading to statehood following a plebiscite, but a second treaty with Turkey, the Treaty of Lausanne of 1923, recognized Turkish sovereignty over northern Kurdistan, while the remainder of the Kurdish territory fell in Iran and the new states of Iraq and Syria.

The Kurds were circumscribed within newly created states, none of which were interested in allowing them to continue their centuries-old lifestyle and customs. Indeed, the Kurds came under great pressure to abandon their ways and to assimilate into the majority culture. They were also greatly limited in their migratory patterns, which served only to further marginalize them. World War II did not change the situation, although militant Kurds have continued calls for an independent Kurdish state.

The Kurds now found themselves subjected to discrimination and general oppression. Nowhere was the oppression worse than in Turkey. The Turkish government refused to recognize the Kurds as a distinct ethnic group. It also forced the Kurds to abandon their language, banned their traditional garb, and lured them into urban areas to curtail their pastoral life. This, of course, only brought more discrimination and resulted in high unemployment and poverty rates for urbanized Kurds.

Iraq and Iran also saw Kurdish unrest. During 1961–1963 there was an uprising of Kurds in northern Iraq following the Iraqi government's refusal to grant them autonomy. Northern Iraq saw another Kurdish rebellion during 1974–1975. Abetted by Iran, it collapsed when Iran resolved its border dispute with Iraq in March 1975. In late 1979 a Kurdish revolt also occurred in Iran during the Iranian Revolution of that year.

In 1988 in what can only be described as a massacre, Iraqi leader Saddam Hussein ordered Iraq's army and air force into the Kurdish north of the country. Employing both conventional attacks and chemical warfare, the Iraqi military destroyed some 2,000 villages and killed upwards of 180,000 Kurds. The Iraqi Army crushed other Kurdish revolts following the Persian Gulf War of 1991 and in 1995.

Since 1984 Turkey, with half of the world's Kurdish population representing as much as 20–25 percent of its own population (no one knows for sure, as the Turkish government has outlawed ethnic classification), has experienced a Kurdish insurgency, led by the Partiya Karkerên Kurdistan (Kurdistan Workers' Party, PKK). Initially composed largely of students and led by Abdullah Öcalan, the PKK was established on November 27, 1978, in the village of Fis near Lice, Turkey. In addition to Kurdish nationalism, the PKK initially espoused a Marxist ideology.

Almost immediately after its formation, the PKK was locked in combat with right-wing parties in Turkey and with those Kurdish leaders it accused of collaboration with the Turkish government. Since 1984, the PKK has been waging an armed struggle against the Turkish state to secure an autonomous Kurdistan and greater cultural and political rights for Turkish Kurds. This began with attacks and bombings against Turkish government institutions and military installations, all not exclusively in Turkey.

In the mid-1990s the PKK initiated a series of suicide bombings, a majority of which were carried out by women. In March 1995 the Turkish Army carried out Operation STEEL CURTAIN, sending 35,000 troops into the Kurdish zone of northern Iraq in an effort to trap several thousand guerrillas and halt PKK cross-border raids. In the late 1990s, Turkey increased pressure on the PKK when an undeclared war between Turkey and Syria ended open Syrian support. In February 1999 Turkish commandos seized PKK leader Öcalan in Kenya. He was brought before a Turkish court, and his death sentence was subsequently commuted to life imprisonment as part of negotiations for Turkish membership in the European Union. Öcalan remains in prison. That same month the Turkish Army again invaded northern Iraq to wipe out PKK bases there.

Meanwhile, the Turkish government sought to allay international criticism by somewhat relaxing legislation directed against the Kurds, including bans on broadcasting and publishing in the Kurdish language. At the same time, the PKK found itself blacklisted in a number of states. Both the United States and the European Union characterized it as a terrorist organization.

A low-level insurgency continued, with PKK ambushes of Turkish military patrols and retaliatory Turkish military responses. Kurdish hopes for at least autonomy received a boost from the Iraq War that began in 2003 when the Kurds in northern Iraq all but established their own state. The war also led to tensions between the Turkish government and the United States and coalition forces, with Ankara accusing Washington of failing to wipe out PKK bases in northern Iraq, from which it claims raids have been launched into Turkey.

Another congress, held in November 2003, saw the PKK/KADEK rename itself as the People's Congress of Kurdistan, or Kongra-Gel (KGK). It sought to set aside the creation of a national state in favor of working within the existing nation-states. As a consequence of this, some 1,500 militants left the organization along with a number of leading reformers, including Nizamettin Tas and Abdullah Öcalan's younger brother Osman Öcalan.

In June 2004 Kongra-Gel ended a cease-fire with the Turkish government, claiming that Turkish security forces had refused to respect the truce. Ankara claimed that some 2,000 Kurdish fighters had crossed into Turkey from bases in mountainous northern Iraq. Despite the clashes, the PKK and its ancillary organizations continued to enjoy substantial support from Turkish Kurds.

In 2005, the original name of the organization PKK was restored. Increased clashes, with bombings and attempted bombings in resort areas in western Turkey and in Istanbul, occurred tha same year. A radical Kurdish separatist group calling itself the Kurdish Freedom Hawks (TAK), which advocated an independent Kurdish state, claimed responsibility for many of these. The TAK attacks certainly damaged efforts by the PKK leadership to negotiate with the Turkish government and establish a new cease-fire. In October 2006, however, the PKK allegedly declared a unilateral cease-fire. This led to a sharply diminished number of attacks, although these continued in response to Turkish security forces' significant counterinsurgency operations especially in southeastern Turkey, with its significant Kurdish population. Typical of the ongoing insurgency was an attack on April 29, 2009—the deadliest incident in six months—when PKK guerrillas killed eight Turkish soldiers in two attacks along the Iraqi border with Iraq. Guerrillas shot to death one soldier, and seven others were killed in their armored personnel carrier when it was hit by a roadside bomb.

The failure of negotiations between the PKK and the Turkish government led to 2012 being the most violent year between the PKK and the Turkish state since 1999. With the start of the Syrian Civil War in 2011, the Kurds in Syria established control over their home areas, assisted in this by the PKK and the Kurdistan Regional Government in Irbil.

In late 2012 the Turkish government began secret talks for a cease-fire with the imprisoned Abdullah Öcalan, who claimed that the time for violence had passed. Turkish president Recep Tayyip Erdoğan's government enacted significant reforms, and the PKK agreed to a cease-fire on March 21, 2013. On April 25 the PKK announced that it would leave Turkey altogether for the semiautonomous Kurdish region of Iraq. This relocation began on schedule in May. The Iraqi government in Baghdad, however, declared that it would not tolerate the presence of armed nongovernment groups in its territory, holding that they posed a threat to Iraqi security and stability.

In late July 2013, however, the PKK issued an ultimatum demanding that the Turkish government implement reforms. The PKK also accused Ankara of supporting extremist groups in Syria against the Kurds there. In mid-July 2014, the PKK was locked in combat within Syria with the Islamic State of Iraq and Syria (ISIS), and PKK forces played a role in the escape of tens of thousands of Yazidis from ISIS-encircled Mount Sinjar. The United States had begun providing weapons directly to the Kurdish forces fighting Islamic extremists in northern Iraq. Previously the United States had only provided arms to the central Iraqi government in Baghdad, but Kurdish Peshmerga fighters had been losing ground to ISIS. This U.S. aid was important in allowing the Peshmerga to take the initiative.

In September 2014 during the ISIS siege of the Kurdish city of Kobanî in Syria, just across the border from Turkey, the PKK received direct U.S. military support, but the Turkish government of President Erdoğan objected, leading to large protests by Kurds in Turkey against the government that led to clashes between the demonstrators and security forces, the deaths of 31 people, and an end to the cease-fire of more than a year.

The Turkish government restricted the movement of PKK fighters seeking to join the defenders of Kobanî, arresting 260 PPK fighters who were moving back into Turkey in an effort to cross to Kobanî. On October 14 Turkish Air Force planes attacked PKK positions in the vicinity of Daglica in Hakkari Province, claiming that these were in response to PKK attacks on a Turkish military outpost in the area. The PKK, however, said that Turkish forces had been shelling their positions for days beforehand and that the PKK attack on the outpost was in retaliation for the artillery fire.

In July 2015 Turkey finally became involved in the war against ISIS, but the Turkish Air Force not only struck ISIS targets but also bombed PKK targets in northern Iraq, only several days after the PKK was suspected of assassinating 2 Turkish police officers in Ceylanpinar. In the ensuing fighting between late July and September, the Turkish government claimed 150 government personnel and more than 2,000 Kurdish rebels killed. In late March 2016, the PKK helped launch the Peoples' United Revolutionary Movement with nine other Kurdish and Turkish revolutionary leftist, socialist, and communist groups with the avowed aim of overthrowing the Turkish government of Erdoğan and establishing a truly democratic regime.

In July 2016 an abortive coup by junior Turkish Army officers against Erdoğan gave him the opportunity to move to vastly increase his power. He declared a state of emergency and used this to purge more than 100,000 people, supposedly for plotting against the Turkish state. He also declared victory, despite widespread charges of voter fraud, in an April 2017 referendum that gave him near-dictatorial powers.

As he moved to consolidate his power and oversaw the firing and/or arrest of government officials and teachers, Erdoğan also arrested legitimately elected lawmakers and officials of the Kurdish moderate Peoples' Democratic Party (HDP) in southwestern Turkey, where the HDP has an electoral majority, charging them with supporting the PKK despite the fact that the HDP had come out against the coup attempt. This crackdown has gutted what was once touted as a political bloc that could help end the PKK's four-decades-long insurgency.

In early May 2017 U.S. president Donald Trump approved a plan to arm the Kurdish People's Protection Units (YPG). This had been proposed by the American military to allow the YPG to take part in the liberation of the ISIS capital of Raqqa, Syria. This move, however, drew immediate strong condemnation from Turkey, which is waging military operations against radical Kurdish groups in Turkey and opposes any plans to arm the Kurds, wherever they might be.

ISIS also recruited Iranian Kurds. On June 7, 2017, 6 assailants, including some disguised as women, stunned Iran with two brazen attacks in Tehran itself, striking both the parliament building and the tomb of Iran's revolutionary founder, Khomeini. Seventeen people were killed and 52 were wounded in the near-simultaneous assaults that occurred over several hours. The 6 attackers also were killed, with 5 suspects detained.

Fighting the Kurdish insurgency has been a considerable drain on Turkish state finances. It also has had a high human cost. Reliable figures are hard to come by, but the Turkish government puts the death toll from 1984 to August 2015 at 36,345: 6,741 civilians, 7,230 security forces, and 22,374 PKK fighters. According to the Humanitarian Law Project, 2,400 Kurdish villages have been destroyed and 18,000 Kurds have been executed by the Turkish government, while as many as 3 million people (most of them Kurds) have been displaced by the conflict.

On December 9, 2017, in Iraq, Prime Minister Haider al-Abadi officially announced the end of the costly Iraqi campaign to clear ISIS forces from his country. The Iraqi government then turned its attention to the Kurds, for on September 25 the Kurdish administration in their regional capital of Erbil announced the results of a referendum, with 92 percent of the voters in support of independence for their region of northern Iraq. This immediately encountered strong opposition from the Shiite-dominated Iraqi central government and from Turkey, Syria, and Iran, all of which had strong Kurdish minorities and opposed creation of a Kurdish state and what would be its ensuing irrendentist claims. Turkish president Erdoğan called the referendum a threat to his country's national security and threatened economic action and even Turkish military intervention.

The Iraqi government itself promptly vowed to send troops into the Kurdish areas to secure control of the oil fields there, particularly near Kirkuk. It also demanded that the Kurds surrender control of Erbil International Airport by September 29. With the Kurds having few heavy weapons and lacking any allies, the result was a foregone conclusion. Al-Abadi ordered Iraqi forces into the region, and on October 6 they took direct control of the strategic city of Kirkuk (the region producing some 6 percent of the world's oil), which had been under Kurdish control since 2014. Some violence occurred, with several dozen Kurdish fighters killed and others wounded. All of this posed a dilemma for the United States, which had relied heavily on the Kurds and provided small arms and ammunition to their highly effective Peshmerga fighters against ISIS. Nevertheless, the United States refused to back the Kurdish independence declaration, and on November 1, 2017, Masoud Barzani, the president of the Iraqi Kurdistan Region (KRG) who had championed independence, was forced to resign his post.

Given the Iraqi central government's overwhelming military strength, the government of the autonomous Kurdish region offered to "freeze" its independence efforts and open talks with Baghdad, but the Iraqi government demanded that the referendum result be annulled before talks could occur. Faced with overwhelming force, on October 17 the Kurdish separatists surrendered to central government control all disputed oil fields in northern Iraq.

As 2018 progressed, sporadic talks between the KRG and Iraq's government in Baghdad occurred in an attempt to repair the rift between them. However, no agreement has yet been reached, and complete Kurdish autonomy appeared increasingly elusive. Meanwhile, Turkey has upped the ante in its conflict with the Kurds in the border areas of Syria and Iraq. In fact, Erdoğan commenced a sustained military campaign beginning in the winter of 2018 designed to defeat Kurdish rebels in northern Iraq, much to the irritation of U.S. leaders. Indeed, U.S.-Turkish relations remain badly strained partly because of Turkish actions against the Kurds.

Spencer C. Tucker

See also
Erdoğan, Recep Tayyip; Hussein, Saddam; Iran; Iran-Iraq War; Iraq; Kobanî, Siege of; Kurds, Massacres of; Peshmerga; Syria; Syrian Civil War; Turkey; Yazidis

References
Bulloch, John, and Harvey Morris. *No Friends but the Mountains: The Tragic History of the Kurds.* New York: Oxford University Press, 1993.
Ciment, James. *The Kurds: State and Minority in Turkey, Iraq, and Iran.* New York: Facts on File, 1996.
McDowall, David. *Modern History of the Kurds.* London: I. B. Tauris, 1997.
Natali, Denise. *The Kurds and the State.* Syracuse, NY: Syracuse University Press, 2005.
Öcalan, Abdullah. *Prison Writings: The Roots of Civilisation.* Translated by Klaus Happel. London: Pluto, 2007.
Tahiri, Hussein. *The Structure of Kurdish Society and the Struggle for a Kurdish State.* Costa Mesa, CA: Mazda Publications 2007.

Kurds, Massacres of

The Kurdish people are spread across a number of countries in the Middle East, including Turkey, Iraq, Syria, and Iran. Kurds have campaigned for their own homeland for many years and have suffered persecution throughout most of their history. During recent times, Kurds have also been subjected to repeated repressions and massacres.

Following an uprising led by Mustafa Barzani from 1961 to 1963, the Kurds were given some representation in the Iraqi government. However, after the outbreak of the Iran-Iraq War in September 1980, the Kurdish leadership tended to side with Iran, and as a result Iraqi dictator Saddam Hussein began a program of systematic persecution against the Kurds. Iraqi attacks increased dramatically from 1986 on. The lead figure directing these attacks was Ali Hasan al-Majid, a cousin of President Hussein. The use of chemical weapons during the attacks on the Kurds would earn al-Majid the sobriquet "Chemical Ali."

During the campaign as a whole, the Iraqi Army would deploy more than 200,000 troops against the Kurds. The campaign, launched by al-Majid himself, was split into seven phases between February and September 1988. This campaign against the Kurds was to become known as the al-Anfal Campaign, meaning "the spoils of war." In each phase, an area of Kurdish-dominated territory was sealed off and then attacked. Tactics against the Kurds included the employment of aircraft to bomb the Kurdish villages as well as ground forces to secure Kurdish settlements and detain and interrogate all males between the ages of 15 and 70. It was then official Iraqi policy either to execute these men immediately or transport them along with their families to the Topzawa Camp just outside the northern Iraqi town of Kirkuk. Here the men of proscribed age were segregated and summarily shot; the bodies were then bulldozed into shallow burial pits.

This deliberate plan of genocide grew as the campaign progressed. In the first stage (between February 23 and March 19, 1988), there was no official policy calling for the killing of all adult males; however, by the last phase (August 25–September 6, 1988) al-Majid did promulgate such a policy. Within Kirkuk, there was mass deportation of Kurdish families. The Baath Party then built large-scale housing projects and encouraged poor Arabs from the south of Iraq to settle in them. This policy of so-called Arabization allowed Baghdad to better control the oil-rich area around Kirkuk.

Perhaps the most infamous incident during the al-Anfal operation was the chemical attack that took place against the Kurdish town of Halabja. Although there were a total of 40 separate chemical attacks in the entire six-month campaign against the Kurds, the one against Halabja was by far the most significant. Halabja, located 150 miles northeast of Baghdad, had an estimated population of 80,000 people. Eight Iraqi Air Force aircraft struck the town on the evening of March 16, 1988, and the attacks continued throughout the night. Chemical agents employed in the attack included mustard gas and nerve agents such as sarin and tabun. During this one attack, more than 5,000 civilians were killed and many thousands others were injured.

Initially, Baghdad claimed that the attack had been intended to strike Iranian troops, but between 1992 and 1994 the organization Human Rights Watch effectively proved Iraqi culpability in the Halabja massacre. During its duration, the al-Anfal campaign claimed perhaps as many as 50,000 civilian lives and destroyed some 2,000 villages, 1,750 schools, and 2,500 mosques.

Following the outbreak of the 1991 Persian Gulf War, the Kurds in Iraq rose up against the Hussein regime and under the protection of an allied air umbrella were able to establish their own governments in so-called safe havens established by the United Nations. In 2003, the Kurdish leadership supported the American-led invasion of Iraq and has now established effective control over Kirkuk and the surrounding areas. Thus far, it has prevented any further atrocities against the Kurdish people in Iraq. Former Iraqi dictator Saddam Hussein and Ali Hasan al-Majid were both charged for their roles in the al-Anfal campaign. Tried and found guilty by an Iraqi Special Tribunal for crimes against humanity, both men were executed.

Yet Iraq is not the only place where the Kurds have recently suffered. Within Turkey, Turkish security forces have leveled thousands of Kurdish villages and displaced as many as several million Kurds since 1982. In Iran during the revolutionary period from 1979 to 1982, Islamic Revolutionary Guards killed some 10,000 Kurds. Attacks on Kurdish settlements continue. The most recent incidents occurred on July 9, 2005, following the murder of a Kurdish activist.

In Syria too there have been incidents. On March 12, 2004, 180 Kurdish civilians were killed or injured in clashes with Syrian forces in Qamishli, a Kurdish city in the northeastern part of the country, while the Islamic State of Iraq and Syria (ISIS) also moved against the Kurds of Syria and Iraq during 2013–2017.

Ralph Martin Baker

See also
Chemical Weapons and Warfare; Hussein, Saddam; Iran; Iran-Iraq War; Iraq; Islamic State of Iraq and Syria; Kurds; Majid al-Tikriti, Ali Hassan al-; Persian Gulf War, Overview; Syria; Syrian Civil War; Turkey

References
Lawrence, Quil. *Invisible Nation: How the Kurds' Quest for Statehood Is Shaping Iraq and the Middle East.* New York: Walker, 2008.
McDowall David. *The Kurds: A Nation Denied.* Austin, TX: Harry Ransom Humanities Research Center, 1992.
Potter, Lawrence, and Gary Sick. *Iran, Iraq, and the Legacies of War.* New York: Macmillan, 2004.
Rudd, Gordon W. *Humanitarian Intervention: Assisting the Iraqi Kurds in Operation Provide Comfort.* Washington, DC: U.S. Army, 2004.
Yildiz, Kerim, and Tom Blass. *The Kurds in Iraq: The Past, Present and Future.* London: Pluto, 2004.

Kutahya Convention (May 4, 1833)

During the Egyptian-Ottoman War of 1831–1833 when the last Ottoman field force was destroyed by Egyptian commander Ibrahim Pasha at Konya (December 21, 1832), very little remained to block an Egyptian march on Istanbul. The "Eastern question" seemed ready to be definitively answered until a Russian squadron landed troops to protect the Ottoman capital city on February 20, 1833. This led the sultan's rebellious Egyptian vassal Mehmet Ali to take pause and then agree to a truce brokered by the Great Powers.

The Kutahya Convention of May 4, 1833, ended hostilities between Egypt and the Ottoman Empire. It required Ibrahim to pull back from Anatolia but recognized Egyptian control of Greater Syria, Crete, and the Hejaz. It also guaranteed ratification of Hunkar Iskelesi, a defensive treaty between Russia and the Ottoman Empire concluded on July 8, 1833. As one Ottoman diplomat explained this strange connection between two bitter foes, "a drowning man will clutch a serpent."

The combination of the treaties of Kutahya and Hunkar Iskelesi upset the status quo in the Near East. They turned British, Austrian, Russian, and French attention to this region, and the combination brought a new round of fighting in 1839–1840, Great Power intervention, and ultimately the Treaty of London (July 15, 1840).

John P. Dunn

See also

Egyptian-Ottoman Wars; Hunkar Iskelesi, Treaty of; Ibrahim Pasha; London, 1840 Treaty of; Mehmed Ali

References

Durand-Viel, Georges. *Les campagnes navales de Mohammed Aly et d'Ibrahim.* Paris: Imp. Nationale, 1935.

Fahmy, Khaled. *All the Pasha's Men: Mehmed Ali, His Army and the Making of Modern Egypt.* Cambridge: Cambridge University Press, 1997.

Kut al-Amara, Siege of (December 7, 1915–April 29, 1916)

The World War I siege of Kut al-Amara saw the defeat of a large British force in Mesopotamia by the Ottoman Army. The worst reverse for the British Army prior to the surrender of Singapore during World War II, the surrender of the force at Kut raised Ottoman morale and lowered British prestige around the world.

Following his failure to win the Battle of Ctesiphon (November 22–25, 1915) and then take Baghdad, Major General Charles V. F. Townshend led his overextended force back to his base at Kut on December 3. Kut was located in a loop of the Tigris River 120 miles upriver from the British base at Amara. Closely pursued by Ottoman forces, Townshend believed that his men were not able to retreat farther.

Townshend sent his cavalry and wounded away, along with his boats. He also expelled many of the 7,000 inhabitants of Kut and prepared the place for a siege. The British War Office ordered Townshend not to allow himself to be surrounded, but the Ottomans had already invested Kut on December 7. Townshend assured his superiors that he had supplies sufficient for two months, as Kut was a local center for the grain trade. At first, he allowed his soldiers to continue to receive full rations to keep up morale. However, Townshend failed to search private homes and seize the considerable stocks of food available there.

When the siege began, British forces in Kut numbered 12,000 men, 2,000 of whom were sick or wounded. The Ottoman XVIII Corps of about 20,000 men encircled Kut. During December the Ottomans launched several unsuccessful attacks on the British positions, resulting only in heavy casualties on both sides.

Meanwhile, British major general Fenton Aylmer was assembling a relief force at Amara. Known as the Tigris Corps, it eventually consisted of the 3rd Lahore, 7th Meerut, and 13th Western Divisions of the Indian Army. Mesopotamian theater commander General John Nixon pressed Aylmer to move as quickly and directly as possible. Reports that eight Ottoman divisions released by the British withdrawal from Gallipoli were moving toward Kut added urgency to the British relief operation.

Aylmer's first target was the Ottoman camp at Sheikh Sa'ad, 20 miles downstream from Kut. Aylmer did not realize that the force facing him there was larger than his own. Pressured to relieve Townshend, Aylmer ordered frontal assaults on January 6 and 7, 1916. In these the advancing British and Indian troops were decimated by Ottoman small-arms fire, with the loss of more than 4,000 men. Medical facilities were almost nonexistent, and many wounded died needlessly from lack of treatment.

Unexpectedly, Ottoman commander General Nureddin ordered a retreat after dark on January 7. This decision led to him being sacked and replaced by elderly German field marshal Colmar von der Goltz, who proved to be an excellent choice. The Ottomans then established another strong position at the Wadi, six miles upstream from Sheikh Sa'ad. Nixon continued to urge Aylmer on, but the field general now realized that he was outnumbered. The Ottoman position was anchored by the Tigris River on the right and an impassable swamp on the left.

On January 13, Aylmer tried to outflank the Ottomans with his right while pinning them with a frontal assault. Lacking good maps, the British flanking column became lost. The resulting frontal assault failed with heavy casualties, and Aylmer called a halt at the end of the day, depressed by his failure and by Townshend's reports that supplies in Kut were quickly dwindling. Aylmer then ferried most of his troops to the right bank of the Tigris and launched another frontal assault on January 21. Townshend declined to launch a diversionary attack.

Aylmer's second assault was a failure, with the relief force losing another 2,700 killed or wounded. Medical care was still practically nonexistent, and there were freezing temperatures the night following the attack. Many British wounded suffered unnecessarily, and troop morale plummeted.

The garrison in Kut could hear the fighting between the relief force and the Ottomans, and when it remained distant, morale in Kut also declined. Not only did Townshend not mount a diversionary attack, but he also did not order aggressive patrolling. Many of his men sank into apathy.

The Ottoman forces were content to surround Kut and wait for it to fall, and only occasional sniping broke the monotony. Townshend cut rations in January, although he soon discovered that more supplies were available than expected. When Townshend reported that he had supplies sufficient for 84 days, new British commander in Mesopotamia Lieutenant General Percival Lake allowed Aylmer nearly six weeks to build up his strength.

By March 7, the Tigris Corps had 37,000 men and 66 guns. Aylmer then moved his force through the open desert to avoid Ottoman positions along the Tigris. His goal was the Ottoman position at Es Sinn, just across the river from Kut. Although the resulting battle was plainly visible in Kut, Townshend once again did not attempt to assist the relieving force.

Patrols sent out at dawn on March 8 by Aylmer found the Ottoman positions at the Dujaila redoubt, key to their position at Es Sinn, unoccupied. Headquarters would not allow British troops to move in and occupy this area before the scheduled artillery bombardment, and by the time a frontal assault was launched three hours later, the Ottomans were in position and able to cut down the attackers with small-arms fire. A later attack on the Sinn Abtar redoubt also failed when the Ottomans were allowed time to organize their defenses there. The battle at Es Sinn claimed more than 4,000 British casualties.

A last attempt by ground troops to reach Kut, later known as the First Battle of Kut, began on April 5. Lieutenant General George Gorringe had relieved Aylmer and attempted another frontal assault at Hanna on the left bank of the Tigris. Gorringe broke off his attacks on April 22, with the Tigris Corps having sustained just under 10,000 casualties.

On April 15 the British began airdrops of supplies into Kut, the first attempt in history at aerial resupply. With a maximum of nine aircraft participating, over the next two weeks the British dropped 16,800 pounds of supplies in 140 flights. Later estimates held that this extended the garrison's food supply by an additional four days.

The last British effort to resupply Kut came on April 24 when the transport ship *Julnar*, fitted with iron plates for protection and manned by a volunteer crew of 15 men, attempted to run the Ottoman Tigris defenses with 270 tons of supplies. The ship reached a point four miles from Kut on the morning of April 25 but was ensnared by steel cables, strung by the Ottomans across the Tigris, and then captured.

On April 26 Townshend asked for an armistice. He offered the Ottomans £1 million and all the artillery in Kut in exchange for paroling the garrison. Although the offer was considered, the Ottomans insisted on an unconditional surrender. After destroying as much equipment as possible, Townshend surrendered on April 29. More than 8,000 British and Indian troops went into captivity. Through mistreatment and neglect leading to starvation, nearly 5,000 died before the end of the war.

The Siege of Kut was an important Ottoman victory in the war, greatly raising Ottoman morale and prestige in the Middle East. The British government, on the other hand, was forced to pour more resources into Mesopotamia, which from Britain's standpoint was a very troubling development.

Tim J. Watts

See also
Ctesiphon, 1915 Battle of; Goltz, Wilhelm Leopold Colmar von der; Mesopotamian Theater, World War I; Nixon, Sir John Eccles; Persian Front, World War I; Townshend, Sir Charles Vere Ferrers

References
Barker, A. J. *The Bastard War: The Mesopotamian Campaign of 1914–1918.* New York: Dial, 1967.
Davis, Paul K. *Ends and Means: The British Mesopotamian Campaign and Commission.* Toronto: Associated University Presses, 1994.
Erickson, Edward J. *Ordered to Die: A History of the Ottoman Army in the First World War.* Westport, CT: Greenwood, 2000.
Moberly, F. J. *The Campaign in Mesopotamia, 1914–1918.* 3 vols. Nashville: Battery Press, 1997–1998.
Townshend, Charles. *Desert Hell: The British Invasion of Mesopotamia.* Cambridge, MA: Belknap Press of Harvard University Press, 2011.

Kuwait

The State of Kuwait, strategically located at the northern end of the Persian Gulf, is bordered by Saudi Arabia to the south, Iraq to the west and north, and the Persian Gulf to the east. Kuwait occupies some 6,880 square miles, including the Kuwaiti share of the Neutral Zone defined by agreement with Saudi Arabia in 1922 and partitioned by mutual agreement in 1966. Kuwait is thus about the size of the U.S. state of Hawaii. Kuwait's 2018 population was some 4.1 million. More than half of this number are noncitizen workers attracted by job opportunities in the oil-rich Persian Gulf nation.

Kuwait had been part of Ottoman-ruled Basra Province since the 17th century. The Utub tribes that settled in the area early in the 18th century called their central town Kuwait (founded in 1613 and originally primarily a fishing village), the Arabic diminutive for *kut,* meaning a fortress built near water. During 1775–1779 the Persians laid siege

Kuwait

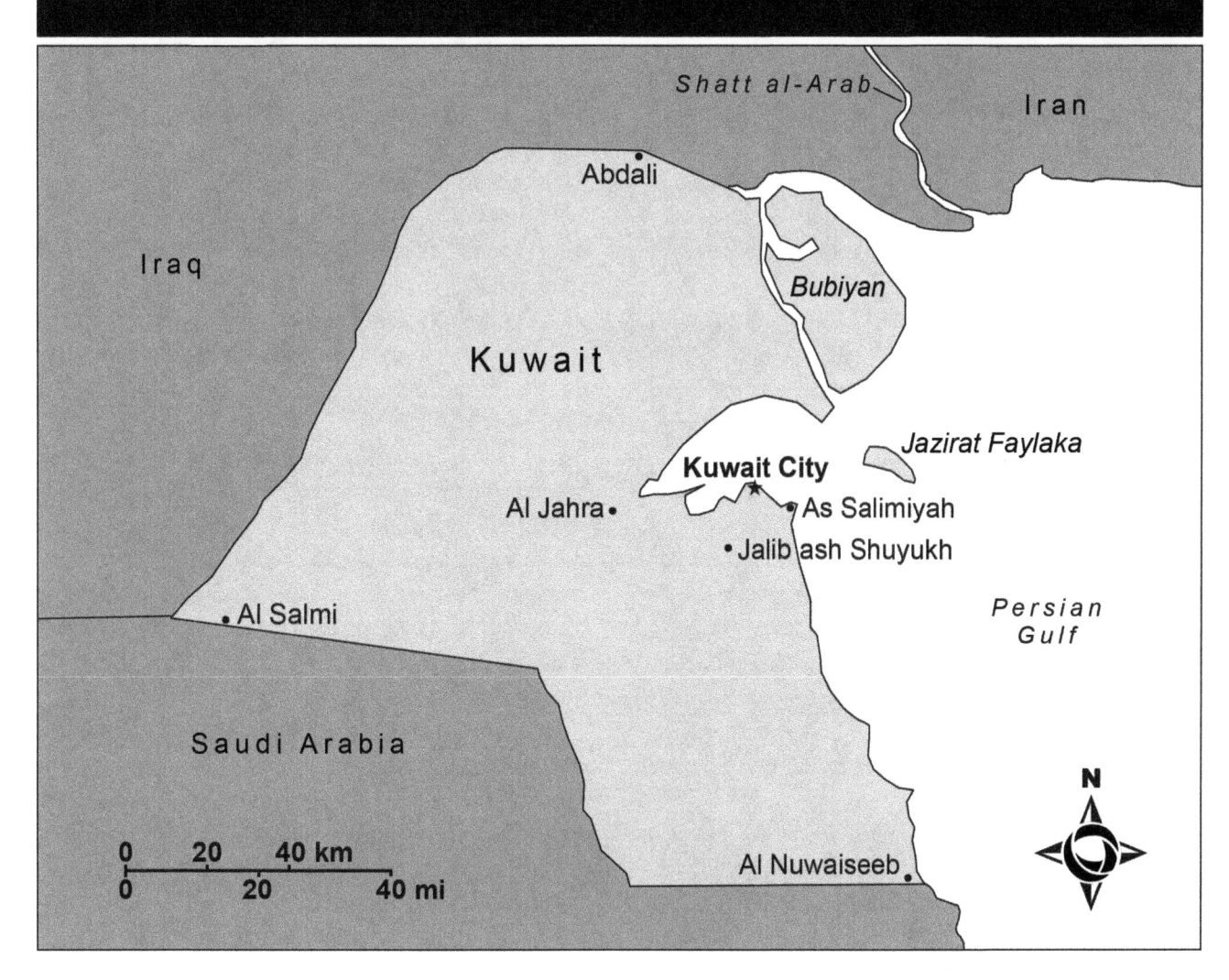

to Basra, at which time a number of Iraqi merchants took refuge in Kuwait and helped expand its trade as well as its boat-building industry. Indeed, in the 18th century Kuwait was the center of the regional boat-building trade. In 1756 the al-Sabah family established an autonomous sheikhdom in Kuwait and focused on developing the local pearl beds and taking advantage of location to promote regional trade. Thereafter the Ottoman Empire exercised only nominal rule.

In 1792 the British East India Company arrived in Kuwait and secured lucrative trading routes. In the late 19th century, the British government grew concerned when Kuwait was touted as the possible terminus of the German-backed Berlin-to-Baghdad railroad project. With Kuwait having now eclipsed Basra, it was by then an important regional training center. The British were worried about possible German domination, as the Persian Gulf controlled access to the Suez Canal, which had become Britain's imperial lifeline to India.

In 1898 the Ottoman government in Istanbul (Constantinople) sought to exert more control over Kuwait. To forestall this and anxious to prevent German influence in the Persian Gulf region, the British concluded an agreement with Kuwait on January 23, 1899, whereby Kuwait became a British protectorate. In return for a financial subsidy, Kuwaiti sheikh Mubarak al-Sabah granted Britain control of Kuwait's foreign affairs and defense and promised not to grant economic concessions or conclude a military alliance with any other power.

In 1904 Kuwait's territory was formally drawn as a 40-mile radius around its center at Kuwait City. In 1913 an Anglo-Ottoman convention defined Kuwait as an "autonomous caza" of the Ottoman Empire. Kuwaiti sheikhs were regarded as Ottoman provincial subgovernors. In the convention Britain recognized Ottoman interests in Kuwait in return for a pledge that Istanbul would not interfere in Kuwaiti internal affairs.

The Ottoman Empire sided with the Central Powers in World War I, but during the war the British maintained a troop presence in Kuwait. Following the war the British had to deal with Wahhabi attacks into Kuwait, which they repulsed in 1919 and 1927–1928. As a consequence of the Allied victory in World War I, Britain also secured a League of Nations mandate over Iraq.

The 1922 Treaty of Ugair set the Kuwaiti southern border with Saudi Arabia and established the Saudi-Kuwaiti Neutral Zone, an area of some 2,000 square miles. In the Treaty of Lausanne of 1923, Turkey renounced all claims to the former Ottoman possessions in the Arabian Peninsula.

In December 1934 Kuwait granted an oil concession to a consortium of the American Gulf Oil Company and the British Anglo-Persian Oil Company. A significant oil find occurred in February 1938, and soon thereafter Kuwait became one of the world's major oil producers.

In October 1960 the rulers of Kuwait and Saudi Arabia met and decided that the Neutral Zone between their two countries should be divided. An agreement to that effect was signed on July 7, 1965, and formally took effect in December 1969.

On June 19, 1961, Britain granted Kuwait full independence, and six days later Iraqi leader Abd al-Karim Qasim claimed that Kuwait was part of Iraq, as parts of Kuwait had been in the province of Basra during the period of Ottoman rule. Qasim also threatened an invasion. The British sent troops to Kuwait, and the crisis passed. As a consequence, however, Kuwait firmly aligned itself with the West—the United States in particular. The 1979 Iranian Revolution served to further strengthen this alliance, with Kuwait—which has a majority Sunni Muslim population—worried about its minority Shiite Muslims. No precise figures are available, but Sunnis are believed to account for 60–70 percent of Kuwait's population, with the Shiites at 30–40 percent.

Kuwait strongly supported Iraq during the 1980–1988 Iran-Iraq War. Assistance included nearly $35 billion in grants, loans, and other aid to the Iraqi government. With the end of the war, Iraq was essentially bankrupt. Having amassed a debt of some $70 billion, it was desperate for cash. Because his country was a major oil producer and oil was the principal Iraqi export, Iraqi leader Saddam Hussein counted on oil revenues to rebuild the Iraqi economy and ensure the stability of his regime.

Casting his war with Iran largely as an effort to protect the Persian Gulf states, especially Kuwait, from Iranian Shiite Islamic fundamentalism, Hussein chose to regard these states as ungrateful for Iraq's wartime sacrifices. He now pressed for forgiveness of the debt, but Kuwait refused.

Finally, there was the long-standing Iraqi government claim of Kuwait as a province dating back to the arbitrary administrative boundaries during the period of the Ottoman Empire. This was a matter of securing not only Kuwaiti oil but also that nation's long coastline. Iraq's sole access to the Persian Gulf was the Shatt al-Arab waterway, sovereignty over which was a point of contention with its enemy, Iran. Securing Kuwait would give Iraq easy access into the Persian Gulf.

The war with Iran had left Iraq with one of the world's largest military establishments, and Hussein was determined to use this to advantage. For some time Washington had been concerned over Iraq's expanding nuclear industry and a chemical and biological capability that Hussein had employed in the war against Iran as well as against some of his own people, the Kurds. Then in mid-July 1990, American intelligence satellites detected Iraqi forces massing near the Kuwait border.

In February 1990 at a summit meeting of the Arab Cooperation Council in Amman, Jordan, Hussein asked King Hussein of Jordan and President Hosni Mubarak of Egypt to inform the Persian Gulf states that Iraq insisted that its debts be forgiven and that it needed an immediate infusion of some $30 billion. Hussein reportedly said that if he was not given the money, he "would know how to get it." This not so veiled threat was accompanied by Iraqi military maneuvers near the Kuwaiti border.

In late May 1990 at an Arab League summit in Baghdad, Hussein claimed that Iraq was being subjected to "economic warfare" and would not long tolerate such treatment. He now demanded $27 billion from Kuwait. The Kuwaitis replied that they did not have such a large sum to give or lend. A month later at an OPEC meeting, Kuwait offered $500 million to Iraq over three years, which Hussein characterized as paltry and insulting.

On July 16, 1990, Iraq publicly accused Kuwait both of violating the OPEC oil-production quotas through excessive production and thus driving down the price of oil and of employing slant drilling to steal Iraqi oil from the Rumaila oil field shared by both countries. That same day, Iraqi foreign minister Tariq Aziz informed an Arab summit meeting in Tunisia that "we are sure some Arab states are involved in a conspiracy against us" and vowed not to "kneel."

On July 17 in a speech to the Iraqi people, Hussein repeated his claim that Kuwait and the United Arab Emirates (UAE) were violating OPEC oil-production quotas and threatened unspecified military action if it continued. Iraq also demanded $2.4 billion from Kuwait for oil allegedly "stolen" in drilling from the Rumaila oil field. The next day, Kuwait canceled all military leaves and placed its small military on alert. It also called for an emergency session of the Gulf Cooperation Council, a defense group of Persian Gulf states, and also of the Arab League. Kuwaiti leaders concluded that Hussein's demands were tantamount to extortion and would only invite more blackmail later. They also refused to believe that Hussein would invade another Arab state.

On July 21 the U.S. Central Intelligence Agency (CIA) reported that Iraq had moved some 30,000 troops and hundreds of tanks to the Kuwaiti border. U.S. policy in this crisis was unclear. Fearful of radical Islam in Iran, both the Soviet Union and the United States had assisted Iraq in its war with Iran. Indeed, Washington had provided valuable satellite intelligence. Washington assumed that Hussein was weary of war and would in any case need a protracted period of peace to rebuild. At the same time, U.S. ambassador to Iraq April Glaspie had followed the George H. W. Bush administration's policy of delivering "mixed messages," which Hussein chose to interpret as allowing him operational freedom in the Persian Gulf region. He probably believed that his moves against Kuwait would not be challenged by the United States. On its part, the U.S. State Department did not believe that Hussein would actually mount a full-scale invasion. If military action occurred, Washington expected only a limited offensive to force the Kuwaitis to accede to Iraqi demands of bringing the cost of oil in line. Clearly Washington underestimated Hussein's ambitions. The intelligence was there, but the administration failed to act on a Pentagon call for a show of force to deter possible Iraqi aggression. Indeed, the Bush administration did not draw a firm line in the sand until Hussein had already crossed it.

Kuwaiti leaders also concluded that Iraq's provocative action was a bluff to increase the price of oil and blackmail Kuwait into acceding to Hussein's demands. On July 22, Aziz repeated his criticism of Kuwait and the UAE after Hussein met in Baghdad with Egyptian president Hosni Mubarak, acting as a mediator between Iraq and Kuwait. Mubarak subsequently claimed to have received assurances from Hussein that Iraq would not attack Kuwait, but Iraqi officials asserted that Hussein had said that nothing would happen to Kuwait so long as negotiations continued.

On July 26 Kuwait agreed to lower its oil production quotas, which would have the effect of increasing the worldwide price of oil, but Hussein had already begun moving additional troops and armor to the Kuwaiti border. Under Saudi Arabian auspices, Kuwaiti and Iraqi representatives met in Jeddah on July 31 in an effort to resolve their differences. The Iraqis claimed that Kuwait was unwilling to negotiate in good faith. The Kuwaitis said that the Iraqis were not interested in negotiations but instead sought to dictate a solution. Iraqi demands now included Kuwait ceding disputed territory along the border, increasing Iraq's oil pumping rights, and providing a $10 billion cash payment to Iraq. On August 1 the meeting adjourned early because one of the Iraqi diplomats was taken ill, but both sides agreed to resume talks in Baghdad in a few days.

At 2:00 a.m. local time on August 2, 1990, Iraq invaded Kuwait. Iraq then reportedly possessed the world's fourth-largest standing army, numbering some 450,000 men. The invading force numbered perhaps 100,000 men and as many as 700 tanks. Iraqi Republican Guards commander Lieutenant General Ayad Futahih al-Rawi had command. Surprisingly, given Hussein's saber rattling in the weeks before the invasion, the small Kuwaiti armed forces were not on alert.

The invasion force consisted of four Republican Guard divisions as well as Iraqi Army special forces units equivalent to a full division. Kuwaiti armored cars had no chance of stopping the massed Iraqi T-72 tanks. Elite Iraqi troops airlifted by helicopter seized Kuwait City, while Iraqi aircraft attacked Kuwaiti air bases and secured air superiority as Iraqi seaborne commandos sealed off the Kuwaiti coast.

Although the Kuwaiti armed forces did what they could, Kuwait was completely occupied in only 48 hours. The Iraqis failed in their effort to seize Kuwaiti emir Sheikh Jabir al-Ahmad al-Jabir al-Sabah. He managed to escape, although Iraqi commandos killed his brother, Sheikh Fahd, who was in the palace. With Kuwait occupied, the Iraqis proceeded to build up their forces along the Saudi-Kuwaiti border.

Saddam Hussein's cousin, Ali Hassan Abd al-Majid al-Tikriti, became the governor of Kuwait and instituted a brutal and repressive regime that included the plundering of Kuwaiti resources and infrastructure and the killing of many Kuwaiti citizens. Iraq's military looted and pillaged Kuwait's consumer economy almost at will. Crimes against the Kuwaiti citizenry, expatriates, and foreign nationals included murder and rape. Torture was rampant.

Washington's reaction to the invasion was surprisingly swift. President Bush was deeply concerned about the impact of the invasion on the supply of oil and oil prices as well as the influence of the invasion on Saudi Arabia, which possessed the world's largest oil reserves and shared a common border with Kuwait. Bush and others of his generation styled Hussein's aggression as a challenge akin to that of Adolf Hitler and made much of a supposed and quite inaccurate contrast between dictatorship (Iraq) and democracy (Kuwait). On August 8 Bush ordered the deployment of forward forces to Saudi Arabia in what became Operation DESERT SHIELD. The troops were to bolster the Saudis and demonstrate resolve in the midst of diplomatic maneuvering. Hussein proved intransigent, and war loomed between Iraq and a growing U.S.-led coalition of nations. Hussein then began building up Iraqi forces along the Kuwaiti-Saudi border.

U.S. president George H. W. Bush led the effort to forge an international coalition, first to defend Saudi Arabia against possible Iraqi attack and then to force Iraq to quit Kuwait. U.S. Army general H. Norman Schwarzkopf Jr., commander of the U.S. Central Command (CENTCOM), oversaw military operations. As the a buildup of international coalition forces went forward, the United Nations Security Council imposed a January 15, 1991, deadline for Iraq's unconditional withdrawal. Ultimately 34 nations were involved in the coalition efforts.

With Iraqi's refusal to leave Kuwait and expiration of an ultimatum, Operation DESERT STORM began on January 17, 1991, in a bombing campaign against targets in Kuwait and Iraq. Coalition forces enjoyed complete air superiority and greatly degraded Iraqi ground force units. Hussein remained defiant, however.

The impending assault to liberate Kuwait as part of Operation DESERT SABRE, the ground component of DESERT STORM, included tying down elite Iraqi Republican Guard divisions by a left-wing flanking maneuver into southern Iraq by the U.S. Army XVIII Airborne and VII Corps. The U.S. Navy and the 5th Marine Expeditionary Brigade, feinting an amphibious landing on the Kuwaiti coast, also tied down as many as 10 of 43 Iraqi divisions there.

At 4:00 a.m. local time on February 24 after preliminary infiltration operations, the U.S. 1st and 2nd Marine Divisions in Marine Central Command, followed by Joint (Arab) Forces Command–North on their left and Joint (Arab) Forces Command–East on the Persian Gulf coast, initiated the ground assault on Kuwait. Of the 14 coalition divisions, 6 (Joint Arab and U.S. marines) were initially devoted to a northerly attack into Kuwait from Saudi Arabia, directly confronting only 5 Iraqi divisions.

The offensive went smoothly, with the marines repulsing repeated Iraqi counterattacks. The Joint Arab troops reached Kuwait City by the evening of February 26. The Joint Arab Forces–North consisted of Saudi, Kuwaiti, and Egyptian forces, with Syrian troops in reserve.

On February 26 Hussein ordered his surviving forces to evacuate Kuwait, emptying fortifications around Kuwait City that may have been more difficult for coalition forces to take. Iraqi units fleeing west and north from Kuwait along the highways linking it with Basra in southern Iraq came under continuous air attack from U.S. Navy and Air Force aircraft.

On February 27 Saudi-commanded units passed through the Marine Central Command sector along with Joint Arab Forces Command–North columns to liberate Kuwait City itself. A cease-fire went into effect at 8:00 a.m. on February 28. Iraq accepted unconditionally all UN Security Council resolutions regarding Iraq's occupation of Kuwait, thereby renouncing for good the annexation of Kuwait. The ground war had lasted 100 hours.

Although Kuwait had been heavily damaged during the Iraqi occupation and subsequent war, the nation's immense oil wealth and small size allowed it to rebuild quickly and efficiently. Thereafter, Kuwait remained a firm ally of the United States, and with Saudi Arabia and Turkey opposed to the plan, Kuwait was the major staging area for the U.S.-led effort to oust Saddam Hussein from power in March 2003. In return the United States has been restrained in any criticism of Kuwaiti internal affairs. In May 2005, however, Kuwait's parliament did grant full political rights to women. The United States maintains a significant military and naval presence in the region that helps protect the al-Sabah ruling family of Kuwait.

Kuwait has not been a major player in the Arab-Israeli conflict. As Kuwait did not obtain independence from Britain until 1961, it did not participate in the 1948 and 1956 wars in and around Israel. After independence Kuwait aligned itself with the Arab side in the Arab-Israeli conflict, sending only small numbers of troops to fight in the 1967 and 1973 wars. These were token forces, and Kuwait focused on internal development of its oil resources. The large proportion of Palestinians in the Kuwaiti workforce has not led to an active support of the Palestinian cause. It may indeed have led to a suspicion of Palestinians as a possible source of problems, as had occurred in Jordan and Lebanon in the 1970s and 1980s. Palestine Liberation Organization (PLO) support for Iraq in the 1990 conflict with Iraq did not enhance Kuwaiti support for anti-Israeli activities. Kuwait did not provide any substantial support for Hezbollah in its 2006 conflict with Israel. The fact that Hezbollah is a Shia group while the ruling family in Kuwait is Sunni likely played a role in this, along with the fact that Kuwait has a substantial Shia minority and remains wary of Shia-dominated Iran.

Kuwaiti emir Jaber died in January 2006. Saad al-Sabah succeeded as emir but was removed nine days later by the Kuwaiti parliament owing to his poor health. Sabah al-Sabah then became emir and continues in that position today.

The Kuwaiti economy is based largely on petroleum, which accounts for some 94 percent of export revenue and perhaps half of the national income. Kuwait has led the Arab world in efforts at economic diversification. Nonpetroleum enterprises include shipping, water desalination, and financial services. Kuwait has some of the Arab world's largest banks, and the Kuwait Stock Exchange is the Arab world's second largest. The Kuwaiti dinar is the highest-valued currency in the world, and Kuwait is the world's fourth-richest nation in terms of per capita income.

When the Arab Spring commenced in 2011, Kuwait experienced street protests calling for reforms. To head off trouble, the parliament was dissolved in December 2011, and the prime minister resigned. New parliamentary elections were held in 2013. Distrust of the government remains, however, amid ample evidence of graft and corruption. Nevertheless, Kuwait's ruling family has managed to stay somewhat aloof from the political instability. During the 2008–2009 Hamas-Israeli conflict some Kuwaiti legislators publicly protested Israeli tactics, but the Kuwaiti government did not take any significant punitive measures against Israel. There were more anti-Israeli protests during the Hamas-Israeli conflict of 2014, which prompted the Kuwaiti government to call for an end to the Israeli blockade of the Gaza Strip.

On June 26, 2015, a suicide bombing occurred at a Shia Muslim mosque in Kuwait. The blast killed 27 people and injured another 227. The Islamic State of Iraq and Syria (ISIS) claimed responsibility. Twenty-nine people were arrested and subsequently tried for the bombing. Fifteen were found guilty, and 7 were sentenced to death (5 in absentia). It remains the largest terror attack in Kuwait's history.

Stefan Brooks, Benedict Edward Dedominicis, Gregory Wayne Morgan, Daniel E. Spector, and Spencer C. Tucker

See also
Hussein, Saddam; Hussein ibn Talal, King of Jordan; Iran-Iraq War; Islamic State of Iraq and Syria; Kuwait, Iraqi Invasion of; Kuwait, Iraqi Occupation of; Kuwait, Liberation of; Mubarak, Hosni; Qasim, Abdul Karim; Sabah, Jabir al-Ahmad al-Jabir al-

References
Abu-Hakima, Ahmad Mustafa. *The Modern History of Kuwait, 1750–1965*. London: Luzac, 1983.

Al Yahya, Mohammad Abdul Rahman. *Kuwait: Fall and Rebirth*. London: Kegan Paul International, 1993.

Assiri, Abdul-Reda. *Kuwait's Foreign Policy: City-State in World Politics*. Boulder, CO: Westview, 1990.

Casey, Michael S., Frank W. Thackeray, and John E. Findling. *The History of Kuwait*. Westport, CT: Greenwood, 2007.

Cordesman, Anthony J. *Kuwait: Recovery and Security after the Gulf War*. Boulder, CO: Westview, 1997.

Crystal, Jill. *Kuwait: The Transformation of an Oil State*. Boulder, CO: Westview, 1992.

Daniels, John. *Kuwait Journey*. Luton, UK: White Crescent, 1971.

Gordon, Michael R., and Bernard E. Trainor. *The Generals' War: The Inside Story of the Conflict in the Gulf*. New York: Little, Brown, 1995.

Jassan, Hamdi A. *The Iraqi Invasion of Kuwait: Religion, Identity, and Otherness in the Analysis of War and Conflict*. Sterling, VA: Pluto, 1999.

Polk, William R. *Understanding Iraq: The Whole Sweep of Iraqi History, from Genghis Khan's Mongols to the Ottoman Turks to the British Mandate to the American Occupation*. New York: HarperCollins, 2005.

Ray, Kurt. *A Historical Atlas of Kuwait*. New York: Rosen, 2003.

Scales, Robert H. *Certain Victory: The U.S. Army in the Gulf War*. Washington, DC: Brassey's, 1994.

Tripp, Charles. *A History of Iraq*. New York: Cambridge University Press, 2002.

Tucker, Spencer C. *Persian Gulf War Encyclopedia: A Political, Social, and Military History*. Santa Barbara, CA: ABC-CLIO, 2014.

United States Army. *Area Handbook Series: Persian Gulf States*. Washington, DC: U.S. Government Printing Office, 1984.

Kuwait, Iraqi Invasion of (August 2, 1990)

At 2:00 a.m. on August 2, 1990, Iraqi forces invaded Kuwait. Two weeks before, on July 17, 1990, Iraqi dictator Saddam Hussein had threatened military action against that small Persian Gulf nation for its overproduction of Organization of Petroleum Exporting Counties (OPEC) oil quotas, which had helped drive down the price of oil.

Relations between the two countries had heretofore been close. In 1979 a radical regime had come to power in Iran, and Kuwait subsequently proved to be a staunch ally during Iraq's protracted war (1980–1988) with Iran. Hundreds of thousands of people died on both sides in the war, and Iraq had accumulated a considerable war debt of some $80 billion. Hussein was thus anxious that oil prices be as high as possible, and Kuwaiti excess production worked against this. Kuwait was also the major creditor for the Iraqi war effort, to the tune of some $35 billion. Hussein demanded that these

Iraqi tanks roll through downtown Kuwait City during the invasion of Kuwait, August 2, 1990. (The LIFE Images Collection/Getty Images)

loans be forgiven, reasoning that Iraq had borne the brunt of the fight in defense of Arab interests and deserved monetary concessions.

Hussein was also angry over Kuwaiti slant drilling into Iraqi oil fields along their common border. Finally, Iraq had long claimed Kuwait as a province dating back to the arbitrary administrative boundaries during the period of the Ottoman Empire. Iraq's desire to gobble up its small neighbor certainly did not begin with Hussein. When Britain granted Kuwait its independence in 1961, Iraqi strongman Abd al-Karim Qasim had immediately asserted Iraq's claim to sovereignty. This was not only a matter of securing Kuwaiti oil but also that nation's long coastline. Iraq's sole access to the gulf was the Shatt al-Arab waterway, the sovereignty over which was a matter of contention with its enemy Iran. Securing Kuwait would mean easy Iraqi access into the Persian Gulf.

The war with Iran had left Iraq with one of the world's largest military establishments, and Hussein was determined to employ it to advantage. For some time Washington had been concerned over Iraq's expanding nuclear industry and a chemical and biological capability that Hussein had used in the war against Iran as well as against some of his own people, the Kurds. Then, in mid-July 1990, American intelligence satellites detected Iraqi forces massing near the Kuwaiti border.

Yet U.S. policy was unclear. Fearful of radical Islam in Iran, both the Soviet Union and the United States had assisted Iraq in its war with Iran. Washington had provided valuable satellite intelligence. Up until the invasion of Kuwait, moreover, Washington assumed that Hussein was weary of war and would in any case need a protracted period of peace to rebuild. At the same time, U.S. ambassador to Iraq April Glaspie had followed the George H. W. Bush administration policy and delivered "mixed messages" that seemed to allow Hussein operational freedom in the Persian Gulf. Hussein probably believed that his moves against Kuwait would not be challenged by the United States. On its part, the State Department did not believe that Hussein would actually mount a full-scale invasion. If military action occurred, Washington expected only a limited offensive to force the Kuwaitis to accede to Iraqi demands to bring the cost of oil in line. Clearly Washington underestimated Hussein's ambitions. The intelligence was there, but the administration had failed to act on a Pentagon call for a show of force to deter possible Iraqi aggression. Indeed, the George H. W. Bush administration did not draw a firm line in the sand until Hussein had already crossed it.

Commander of the Republican Guard Lieutenant General Ayad Futahih al-Rawi had charge of the invasion force. It consisted of the Iraqi Hammurabi Armored Division and Tawakalna Mechanized Division, supported by Iraqi special forces and the Medina Armored Division. The Hammurabi and Tawakalna divisions easily overcame the sole Kuwaiti brigade deployed along the common border, then headed south to al-Jahrad at the head of the Gulf of Kuwait before turning east to Kuwait City. Kuwaiti armored cars had no chance of stopping the massed Iraqi T-72 tanks.

By 5:00 a.m. fighting had begun for Kuwait City. Heliborne elite Iraqi troops were airlifted into the city, preventing any Kuwaiti withdrawal back into it. At the same time, Iraqi seaborne commandos sealed off the Kuwaiti coast. Meanwhile, the Medina Armored Division screened the Iraqi invasion force against the remote possibility of any intervention by the Gulf Cooperation Council's Peninsula Shield Brigade situated in northern Saudi Arabia. By evening it was all but over. Four Iraqi infantry divisions moved in behind the mobile forces to occupy the country and conduct mopping-up operations. The three Iraqi heavy divisions then took up defensive positions along the border with Saudi Arabia to the south. Kuwait was completely occupied in less than 48 hours. In all, the Iraqis lost in the battle two fighter aircraft, six helicopters, and several armored vehicles. Most Kuwaiti Air Force aircraft took refuge in Saudi Arabia.

Once the battle was won, the Iraqis settled in for a brutal occupation that claimed the lives and property of many Kuwaitis. The Iraqis failed in their effort to seize the emir of Kuwait, Sheikh Jaber al-Ahmed al-Sabah. He managed to escape, but Iraqi commandos killed his brother, Sheikh Fahd, who was in the palace. The Iraqis then proceeded to loot much of the public and private wealth of Kuwait. Hussein set up a brief puppet government under Alaa Hussein Ali, before annexing Kuwait outright and installing an Iraqi provincial government.

The U.S. reaction was surprisingly swift. President Bush was deeply concerned over the impact of the invasion on the supply of oil and oil prices as well as on Saudi Arabia, which possessed the world's largest oil reserves and shared a common border with Kuwait. Bush and others of his generation styled Hussein's aggression as a challenge akin to that of Adolf Hitler and made much of a supposed and quite inaccurate contrast between dictatorship (Iraq) and democracy (Kuwait).

On August 8 Bush ordered the deployment of forward forces to Saudi Arabia in Operation DESERT SHIELD. The troops were to bolster the Saudis and demonstrate resolve in the midst of diplomatic maneuvering. Saddam Hussein proved intransigent, and war loomed between Iraq on the one side and a growing coalition headed by the United States that included Arab states.

SPENCER C. TUCKER

See also
Hussein, Saddam; Iran-Iraq War; Iraq; Kuwait

References
Abu-Hakima, Ahmad Mustafa. *The Modern History of Kuwait, 1750–1965.* London: Luzac, 1983.

Al Yahya, Mohammad Abdul Rahman. *Kuwait: Fall and Rebirth.* London: Kegan Paul International, 1993.

Casey, Michael S., Frank W. Thackeray, and John E. Findling. *The History of Kuwait.* Westport, CT: Greenwood, 2007.

Crystal, Jill. *Kuwait: The Transformation of an Oil State.* Boulder, CO: Westview, 1992.

Jassan, Hamdi A. *The Iraqi Invasion of Kuwait: Religion, Identity, and Otherness in the Analysis of War and Conflict.* Sterling, VA: Pluto, 1999.

Kuwait, Iraqi Occupation of (August 2, 1990–February 27, 1991)

The Iraqi occupation of Kuwait began on August 2, 1990, when Iraqi forces stormed across the Kuwait-Iraq border. Kuwaiti forces were caught by surprise and, hopelessly outnumbered, put up such defense as was possible. Emir Jaber III Ahmad al-Jaber al-Sabah escaped. Within the span of only several days, Iraqi forces controlled Kuwait.

Following the invasion, Iraqi president Saddam Hussein moved quickly to consolidate his power over Kuwait, which he held to be a rogue province of Iraq. He thus appointed his first cousin, Ali Hassan Abd al-Majid al-Tikriti, as the governor of Kuwait. With the full support of Hussein, al-Tikriti instituted a brutal and repressive occupation. It included the plundering of Kuwaiti resources and infrastructure and the killing of many Kuwaiti citizens. Iraq's military looted, plundered, and pillaged Kuwait's consumer economy almost at will, sending back to Iraq large quantities of automobiles and luxury goods. Kuwait became a virtual ghost town of looted and burned shops and stores; in many cases, these establishments were stripped of light fixtures and furniture.

The Kuwaiti National Museum was not spared. Its collection of priceless Islamic artifacts was looted, and almost every room in the museum was gutted by fire.

Iraqi troops imposed a brutal regime that did not spare the Kuwaiti people. Crimes against the citizenry included murder, rape, and torture. Nor were these limited to Kuwaitis, for expatriates and foreign nationals equally suffered. In the aftermath of the six-month occupation, the Kuwaiti government reported that 5,733 people had been systematically tortured by Iraqi troops. Iraqi documents captured after the liberation of Kuwait revealed orders from Baghdad for the summary execution of home owners whose buildings bore anti-Iraqi or pro-Kuwaiti slogans. Orders also directed troops to kill on sight any civilian caught on the streets after curfew or anyone suspected of being involved in any resistance activity. Iraqi forces were also accused of engaging in extrajudicial killings of government officials and members of the Kuwaiti military.

Following the liberation of Kuwait, numerous Iraqi torture facilities were discovered. Reports from the few who managed to escape Kuwait following the invasion recounted public executions and bodies left hanging from lampposts or dumped by the side of the street. According to both the United Nations (UN) and Kuwait, some 600 Kuwaiti nationals were abducted to Iraq and disappeared. Iraqi officials also used Westerners captured in Kuwait as hostages, or human shields, until they were released, as an alleged act of goodwill on the part of Iraq, in December 1990.

It is worth pointing out, however, that some allegations by the exiled Kuwaiti government of human rights abuses were later found to be bogus. For example, in the run-up to the Persian Gulf War a young Kuwaiti girl, later determined to be a member of the Kuwaiti royal family, testified before the U.S. Congress that she had witnessed Iraqi troops stealing hospital incubators for newborn infants and leaving the babies to die on the cold floor. Her account was later proven false. Despite such false claims, the wanton brutality of Iraq's occupation of Kuwait cannot be denied.

Food and water supplies meant for the Kuwaiti population were routinely diverted to the Iraqi Army, yet even this proved insufficient to feed the occupying Iraqi troops. As the UN-approved embargo and blockade of Iraq began to strangle its economy, Iraqi troops killed Kuwaiti zoo animals for food. In one final act of defiant revenge, Iraqi forces set fire to hundreds of Kuwaiti oil wells as they withdrew from Kuwait as a consequence of the ground assault by American and coalition forces. This gratuitous destruction not only crippled Kuwait's oil production for many months but also created an environmental disaster.

The Iraqi invasion led to the deployment to Saudi Arabia of an international coalition of forces that ultimately routed Iraq's army during the Persian Gulf War (Operation DESERT STORM) and expelled Iraqi troops from Kuwait. The first Iraqi troop withdrawals from Kuwait began on February 26, 1991. Two days later and following the cease-fire agreement on February 27, the Iraqi occupation of Kuwait ended, restoring Kuwaiti independence.

STEFAN BROOKS

See also
Hussein, Saddam; Iraq; Kuwait; Kuwait, Iraqi Invasion of; Kuwait, Liberation of; Sabah, Jabir al-Ahmad al-Jabir al-

References
Gordon, Michael R., and Bernard E. Trainor. *The Generals' War: The Inside Story of the Conflict in the Gulf.* New York: Little, Brown, 1995.
Khadduri, Majid, and Edmund Ghareeb. *War in the Gulf, 1990–91: The Iraq-Kuwait Conflict and Its Implications.* Oxford: Oxford University Press, 2001.
Long, Jerry. *Saddam's War of Words: Politics, Religion and the Iraqi Invasion of Kuwait.* Austin: University of Texas Press, 2004.
Sifry, Michah, and Christopher Cerf, eds. *The Gulf Reader: History, Documents, Opinions.* New York: Random House, 1991.

Kuwait, Liberation of (February 27, 1991)

The liberation of Kuwait, which marked the culmination of the Persian Gulf War, occurred following the 100-hour February 24–27 ground offensive launched by a U.S.-led coalition that ended in a crushing Iraqi military defeat.

Iraq, which then reportedly possessed the world's fourth-largest standing army, of 450,000 men, invaded Kuwait on August 2, 1990, with 100,000 troops and as many as 700 tanks. The small state of Kuwait was quickly overrun, and Iraqi president Saddam Hussein declared it Iraq's "reunited" 19th province. Hussein then began building up Iraqi forces along the Kuwait-Saudi border.

U.S. president George H. W. Bush led the effort to forge an international coalition, first to defend Saudi Arabia against possible Iraqi attack and then to force Iraq to quit Kuwait. U.S. Army general H. Norman Schwarzkopf Jr., commander of U.S. Central Command (CENTCOM), oversaw military operations. As the buildup of international coalition forces went forward, the UN Security Council imposed a January 15, 1991, deadline for Iraq's unconditional withdrawal.

With Iraq's refusal to leave Kuwait, Operation DESERT STORM began on January 17, 1991, in a bombing campaign against targets in Kuwait and Iraq. Coalition forces enjoyed complete air superiority and greatly degraded Iraqi ground force units. Hussein remained defiant, however.

The impending assault to liberate Kuwait, as part of Operation DESERT SABRE, the ground component of DESERT STORM, included tying down elite Iraqi Republican Guard divisions by a left-wing flanking maneuver into southern Iraq by the U.S. Army XVIII Airborne and VII Corps. The U.S. Navy and the 5th Marine Expeditionary Brigade, feinting an amphibious landing on the Kuwaiti coast, also tied down as many as 10 of 43 Iraqi divisions there.

At 4:00 a.m. local time on February 24 after preliminary infiltration operations, the U.S. 1st and 2nd Marine Divisions in Marine Central Command, followed by Joint (Arab) Forces Command–North on their left and Joint (Arab) Forces Command–East on the Persian Gulf coast, initiated the ground assault with pinning attack operations against Iraqi fortifications in Kuwait. Meanwhile, the XVIII and VII Corps, along with French and British divisions, sought to neutralize reinforcements of the Iraqi Republican Guard, the elite units of the Iraqi armed forces. Of the 14 coalition divisions, 6 (Joint Arab and U.S. marine) were initially devoted to a northerly attack into Kuwait from Saudi Arabia, directly confronting only 5 Iraqi divisions.

After breaching extensive minefields and taking al-Jaber airfield with 1 dead and 12 wounded from Iraqi rocket fire, both U.S. marine divisions repulsed repeated Iraqi counterattacks launched on February 25 from the burning Burgan oil field, part of some 700 Kuwaiti oil wells that would be set afire by Iraqi troops. The marines destroyed or captured nearly 200 Iraqi tanks. Meanwhile, the Joint Arab Forces, both Saudi and Qatari, advanced up the coast on February 24 after heavy shelling by U.S. warships, quickly passing through gaps in the first line of defenses (with 2 Saudis dead and 4 wounded in an air-ground friendly fire incident) to reach the second line, which they overran on February 25. This operation resulted in 6 coalition troops killed and 21 wounded. Iraqi resistance then largely collapsed, and the Joint Arab troops reached Kuwait City by the evening of February 26. Marine forces approaching on the left from al-Jaber continued to advance and destroyed more than 100 additional Iraqi tanks. Employing a combination of U.S. naval gunfire and marine ground units, the coalition eliminated the remnants of the Iraqi armored brigade based at Kuwait International Airport.

Joint Arab Forces–North consisted of Saudi, Kuwaiti, and Egyptian forces, with Syrian troops in reserve. Beginning their northerly advance into western Kuwait on February 24, they encountered only light resistance and took large numbers of Iraqi prisoners before turning east to reach Kuwait City by 5:00 p.m. on February 26.

On February 26 Hussein ordered his surviving forces to evacuate Kuwait, emptying fortifications around Kuwait City that may have been more difficult for coalition forces to take. Iraqi units fleeing west and north from Kuwait along the highways linking it with Basra in southern Iraq had been under continuous air attack from U.S. Navy and Air Force aircraft since the previous night. The planes dropped aerial mines to prevent their advance or retreat on the roads out of Kuwait. The U.S. Army's 1st "Tiger" Brigade of the 2nd Armored Division attacked, cleared, and occupied the 25-foot-high Mutla Ridge outside of the Jahrah suburb of Kuwait next to the juncture of two multilane highways, destroying numerous Iraqi antiaircraft emplacements and adding its firepower to the assault below on what became known as the "Highway of Death."

In the chaotic flight, Iraqi military and commandeered civilian vehicles as well as Kuwaiti hostages, prisoners, and refugees, including Palestinian militiamen, were trapped on the main highway to the north of Jahrah to Basra as well as on the coastal road spur to Basra by the continuous and unhindered U.S. and British attacks and the ensuing turmoil. Many of those who abandoned their vehicles and fled into the desert were also killed. Estimates of the casualties among the total of 1,500–2,000 vehicles destroyed along these two conflated stretches of the Highway of Death remain in dispute, ranging from as low as 200 to as many as 10,000. Officers of the Tiger Brigade, the first American unit to arrive at the Highway of Death, stated that the unit found only about 200 Iraqi corpses among the thousands of destroyed vehicles. The unit also reported the capture of some 2,000 Iraqis who had taken refuge in the desert. Other observers reported that hundreds of bodies, including those of women and children, continued to be buried several days later. Most of the vehicles destroyed on the main northern highway route were commandeered civilian vehicles seized by regular Iraqi Army personnel. Predominantly military vehicles belonging to Republican Guards units were destroyed on the coastal route, with the U.S. Army 3rd Armored Division joining the assault.

On February 27 Saudi-commanded units passed through the Marine Central Command sector, along with Joint Arab Forces Command–North columns, to liberate Kuwait City itself. After making contact with Egyptian Army units, U.S. Army Tiger Brigade troops cleared the major military airfield, the Kuwaiti Royal Summer palace, and bunker complexes.

A cease-fire went into effect at 8:00 a.m., February 28. Iraq accepted unconditionally all UN Security Council resolutions regarding Iraq's occupation of Kuwait, thereby renouncing for good the annexation of Kuwait.

BENEDICT EDWARD DEDOMINICIS

See also

Hussein, Saddam; Iraq; Kuwait; Kuwait, Iraqi Invasion of; Kuwait, Iraqi Occupation of; Persian Gulf War, Cease-Fire Agreement; Persian Gulf War, Overview; Schwarzkopf, H. Norman, Jr.

References

Bin, Alberto, Richard Hill, and Archer Jones. *Desert Storm: A Forgotten War.* Westport, CT: Praeger, 1998.

Human Rights Watch. *Needless Deaths in the Gulf War: Civilian Casualties during the Air Campaign and Violations of the Laws of War.* New York: Human Rights Watch, 1991.

Schubert, Frank N., and Theresa L. Kraus, eds. *The Whirlwind War: The United States Army in Operations Desert Shield and Desert Storm.* Washington, DC: U.S. Government Printing Office, 1995.

Lahoud, Émile Jamil (1936–)

Lebanese Army general and president of Lebanon during 1998–2007. Émile (Imil) Jamil Lahoud (Lahud) was born on January 12, 1936, in Beirut, Lebanon. His father, General Jamil Lahoud, was a Maronite Christian and a founding officer of the Lebanese Army who later served as labor and social affairs minister in 1960 and as a member of the National Assembly in 1960 and 1964. Lahoud's mother was of Armenian descent and was born in Syria.

Continuing the family tradition, the younger Lahoud enrolled in the Lebanese military academy as a cadet in 1956 and was commissioned a sublieutenant in the Lebanese Navy in 1959. During 1958–1960 he studied naval engineering in Britain. He later earned a degree in maritime engineering in Britain and studied at the U.S. Naval War College at Newport, Rhode Island, during 1972–1973 and 1979–1980.

Lahoud rose steadily through the ranks of the Lebanese military throughout the 1970s and 1980s, serving in various military leadership positions and several senior posts at the Defense Ministry. He was promoted to rear admiral in 1985. In November 1989 he was advanced to vice admiral and assumed the post of commander of the Lebanese armed forces. Reportedly this appointment had the blessing of the Syrian government.

As commander of the Lebanese military, Lahoud established a reputation for efficiency and integrity. He worked to rebuild the fragmented forces, which had splintered into feuding Muslim and Christian militias during the country's 15-year civil war. Under his leadership, nearly all of the militias were disarmed and dissolved, and order was restored to the military as the army was reunited and rebuilt.

In late 1998, with Syria largely controlling Lebanese affairs since 1989, Syrian president Hafez al-Assad negotiated with retiring president Elias Hrawi and gave his consent to Lahoud's candidacy for the presidency. With Syrian backing, Lahoud's election by the National Assembly was little more than a formality. Nonetheless, on October 15, 1998, Lahoud was voted in unanimously by all 118 deputies present. He was sworn in on November 24. His ascendancy to the presidency required a last-minute amendment to the Lebanese Constitution (1926), which had banned state officials from serving as president within three years of leaving their state posts.

Although the appointment of a military commander as president prompted criticism from those concerned about an increased military role in politics, many expressed expectations that the former armed forces chief would take on a new challenge to root out sectarianism as iterated in the Taif Agreement (1989) and corruption in the public sector. According to the Lebanese Constitution, the president was limited to one six-year term. In 2004, again under Syrian pressure, the Lebanese parliament voted to extend Lahoud's term for an additional three years, to 2007. (The same situation had occurred with his predecessor, Hrawi.) Opposition leaders in Lebanon cried foul because this had been carried out in violation of the constitution and under foreign pressure. Certainly this was seen as a clear sign of the Syrian control of Lebanese politics. Critics included Maronite cardinal Nasrallah Sfeir and Druze leader Walid Jumblat (Junblat). Another outspoken opponent was Prime Minister Rafik Hariri, who resigned to protest the extension of Lahoud's term of office. Hariri was later assassinated, and the murder was suspected to have been instigated or arranged by Syria.

Lahoud's tenure in office saw continuing unrest in Lebanon, the withdrawal of Syrian forces, the Israeli bombardment of Lebanon in July and August 2006, and the March 8th Alliance (Hezbollah and Michel Aoun's followers) protests against the government. In a 2006 interview, Lahoud voiced strong support for Hezbollah, which he said had "freed our country" and stood up to Israel, and for its leader Hassan Nasrallah.

Following a six-months political deadlock, Lahoud was succeeded as president by former army chief Michel Suleiman.

Spencer C. Tucker

See also
Assad, Hafez al-; Hariri, Rafik; Hrawi, Elias; Lebanon; Lebanon, Israeli Operations against

Reference
Fisk, Robert. *Pity the Nation: The Abduction of Lebanon*. 4th ed. New York: Nation Books, 2002.

Laodicean War (246–241 BCE)
See Syrian-Egyptian Wars

Latakia, Battle of (October 6, 1973)

The Battle of Latakia (Ladhakiyya, Syria) occurred on the night of October 6, 1973, the first day of the Yom Kippur War (Ramadan War). The naval engagement takes its name from Syria's chief seaport on the Mediterranean Sea. It was fought between Israeli and Syrian missile boats, the first battle between missile-firing ships in naval history.

The Egyptian and Syrian attacks that began the war on October 6, 1973, caught Israeli forces by surprise, but Israeli Navy missile boats put to sea that very evening to carry out a long-planned attack against units of the Syrian Navy. It was the first combat test for the missile boats, on which the Israeli Navy had expended much energy over the previous decade. The task would not be easy, as the Israeli Gabriel antiship missile used a joystick tracking system requiring that the operator keep it on target by radar. Also, the missile had never been fired in actual combat. The Soviet SS-N-2 Styx fire-and-forget (meaning that it does not require human tracing once fired) missile employed by the Syrians was combat-proven, with Egyptian missile boats having fired several of them to sink the Israeli destroyer *Eilat* in October 1967 and then in May 1968 to sink the small wooden fishing vessel *Orit*. In addition, Israeli-developed electronic countermeasures (ECM) to defeat the Styx had never been tested in combat. Were these to fail, the Israeli missile boats would be easy prey for the radar-guided Styx missile, which had a range of some 27 miles, more than twice the 12-mile range of the Israeli Gabriel.

Nonetheless, with Israel's army and air force fighting desperately on land and in the air to contain the Egyptian and Syrian offensives, the navy was determined to do its part and remove the possibility of a Syrian naval attack on the Israeli Mediterranean coast. The Israeli plan was to lure the Syrian missile boats out and engage them at the maximum range of their Styx missiles, which the Israelis hoped to defeat through chaff and ECM. Once the Syrians had shot away their missiles, the Israelis planned to close and engage the Syrian boats at the effective range of their own missiles. Come what may, the Israelis were determined to engage the Syrians.

Commander Michael Barkai commanded the Israeli naval flotilla committed to the operation. It consisted of five missile boats (the Saar-class *Ga'ash*, *Hanit*, and *Miznak* and the Reshef-class *Mivtach* and *Reshef*). Barkai took his flotilla wide to the west toward Cyprus to avoid Syrian coastal radar, planning to attack from the north, the direction the Syrians would least expect. The boats proceeded in two parallel columns: Barkai's own *Miznak* (flagship), *Ga'ash*, and *Hanit* to port and the *Mivtach* and *Reshef* to starboard and slightly behind, several miles closer to shore.

Some 35 miles southwest of Latakia the *Miznak*, which was leading, picked up a radar contact four miles to the northwest moving east across the Israeli course and apparently making for Latakia at full speed. Lookouts on the *Miznak*'s bridge reported that the vessel had a low profile and was moving without lights. Fearful that it might be a civilian ship, Barkai ordered 40mm rounds fired. The unknown vessel then opened up with return machine-gun fire. A searchlight on one of the Saar boats enabled the Israelis to identify the vessel as a Syrian torpedo boat, undoubtedly a picket boat to warn against an attack. The three Saar-class missile boats in Barkai's column then opened fire on the torpedo boat but failed to hit it. The torpedo boat was too small a target to warrant a missile, and the *Reshef* in the right-hand column opened fire with its 76mm gun at extreme range of about 10 miles. Soon the wooden torpedo boat was dead in the water.

Syrian naval headquarters meanwhile had received a message from the picket boat of the attack and ordered a minesweeper, also on picket duty and some 10 miles from shore, to immediately seek the protection of Syrian coastal guns at full speed. Headquarters also informed three Syrian missile boats that had just headed from Latakia south of the Israeli presence at sea.

Barkai had to assume that the Syrian torpedo boat had reported the Israeli presence. He abandoned the carefully rehearsed Israeli plan of an attack from the north and fighting at optimum distance in favor of an immediate descent on Latakia from the west. Barkai, however, detached the *Hanit* to sink the Syrian torpedo boat.

As the four remaining Israeli missile boats headed east, the *Reshef* picked up another radar contact some 15 miles to the east. It was the Syrian minesweeper heading at full speed to safety. The *Ga'ash* sent a Gabriel at the target, but this was the extreme length of its range. The Syrian ship was able to increase the range in the two minutes it took the Gabriel to reach the area, and the missile fell short. The *Reshef* in the starboard column then fired another Gabriel at some 12 miles. This missile struck the 560-ton Syrian minesweeper dead on. The *Reshef* then fired a second Gabriel. It too hit home, although the minesweeper remained afloat. The detached *Hanit* subsequently finished it off from close range with another Gabriel and 76mm cannon fire.

As it prepared to fire its second missile and the four Israeli missile boats were continuing their course for Latakia, the *Reshef* picked up three additional radar contacts. These were one Osa-class and two Komar-class Syrian missile boats that had turned to meet the attackers. As the Israeli missile boats continued on course, the Syrians fired their missiles at a range from which the Israelis could not reply. Their targets were the closest Israeli vessels, the *Reshef* and *Mivtach*. On the approach of the Syrian missiles, the Israelis fired off chaff rockets and employed the jamming and deceptor systems to send out false radar signals to the incoming Styx missiles.

The Israeli ECM systems functioned perfectly. The Syrian missiles either flew harmlessly overhead or fell short. Now confident of success, the Israelis pressed their attack. Only one of the Syrian missile boats—the *Osa*—still had missiles left. It turned to face the Israeli flotilla as the two Komar-class missile boats fled for Latakia and as the Israelis sought to close, also at full speed. At this critical juncture, a short circuit on the *Reshef* prevented a missile launch. The *Mivtach* was not equipped with missiles, and this left only the *Ga'ash* and *Miznak* capable of engaging the Syrians. They let loose a salvo of Gabriel missiles while at the same time defeating two more Styx missiles fired against them by the *Osa*. The 330-pound Gabriel warheads were more than sufficient to destroy the two Komar-class Syrian missile boats, which were about a third the size of the minesweeper and loaded with fuel.

The *Osa*, its missiles expended, raced for the shore, where its captain simply ran it up on the shore. Barkai was determined to destroy it with gunfire. He ordered the other three missile boats to keep out of range of the Syrian shore batteries, which had begun to fire, and took the *Miznak* in to a range of about half a mile, firing its three 40mm cannon. Soon the beached *Osa* was ablaze and exploding. The battle was over. Shortly after midnight on October 7, the Israeli missile boats returned to base.

The Syrian Navy remained in port for the rest of the war. The battle also brought new prestige to the Israeli Navy, previously regarded by most observers as only a poor relation of Israel's highly regarded army and air force. Israeli ECM techniques employed in the battle set a new standard for subsequent naval engagements employing missiles.

Spencer C. Tucker

See also
Baltim, Battle of; Yom Kippur War

References
Erell, Shlomo. "Israeli Saar FPBs Pass Combat Test in the Yom Kippur War." *U.S. Naval Institute Proceedings* (September 1974): 115–118.

Rabinovich, Abraham. *The Boats of Cherbourg: The Secret Israeli Operation That Revolutionized Naval Warfare*. New York: Seaver, 1988.

Latrun, Battles of (May 25–July 18, 1948)

A series of engagements fought between Israel Defense Forces (IDF) and the Jordanian Arab Legion during the 1948–1949 Israeli War of Independence (First Arab-Israeli War). The first battle of Latrun was the single bloodiest defeat suffered by a modern Israeli army. The town of Latrun, situated about nine miles west of Jerusalem, sits on the first dominating piece of high ground rising from the coast. During the Crusades the Templars built a stronghold at Latrun, the gateway to the Judaean hills. Following the Arab Revolt of

1936–1939, the British constructed a police fort, called a Taggert Fort, at Latrun to control the main road from Tel Aviv to Jerusalem.

With the Israeli declaration of independence and beginning of the war on May 14, 1948, two battalions of the 4th Brigade of the Transjordan Arab Legion occupied the fort at Latrun and the surrounding positions, including Hill 314. From there they were able to interdict Jewish supply columns into Jerusalem, effectively cutting off the Jewish population in the city. Israeli prime minister David Ben-Gurion was concerned that the Jews would lose all claims to Jerusalem if they could not break the siege before a cease-fire brokered by the United Nations (UN) went into effect on June 11. Despite objections of Yigal Yadin and other Haganah commanders who argued that they simply did not have the military resources to accomplish the mission, Ben-Gurion ordered that the road be opened.

The first Israeli attack was launched early on May 25. Shlomo Shamir commanded a force of some 1,650 soldiers of the 7th Brigade and 450 soldiers of the 32nd Battalion. Many of the Israeli soldiers were newly arrived immigrants, Holocaust survivors from Europe's displaced persons camps. Most had virtually no military training, spoke little Hebrew, and did not even know how to release the safety on their rifles.

As an underground army, the Israeli Haganah defense force had conducted a number of successful operations against irregular Arab elements. As the new IDF (established on May 26, 1948) Jewish Army, however, it had never before fought a conventional battle against a regular force, and the Arab Legion was the best-trained and best-equipped army in the Middle East, with about two-thirds of its officers being British.

Advancing in bright moonlight, Shamir's troops were easy targets for the Arab machine guns and modern 25-pounder field guns. The total Israeli artillery consisted of two 65mm French-manufactured guns dating from 1906. Twelve hours after they started, the remnants of the attacking force staggered back to their lines of departure. Although the casualty figures have long been disputed, the Israeli official figure is 139 dead, almost all on the Jewish side.

After the failure of this first attack, Ben-Gurion appointed Colonel David Marcus, an American volunteer, as overall commander of the Jerusalem front with orders to lift the siege. The Israelis again attacked Latrun on May 30. This second attack was much better planned and executed and was supported by 22 locally fabricated armored cars and 13 half-tracks that Israeli agents had purchased in Antwerp. The battle was thus the first armored attack launched by Israeli forces. However, it was still insufficient to overcome the Arab Legion defenders.

Following failure of the second attack, Marcus concluded that the only solution was to go around the Arab Legion. Sending engineers and construction crews into the wild Judaean hills south of Latrun, he oversaw the extension and improvement of a series of goat trails into a credible military road, which he wryly called the Burma Road. He meanwhile launched a number of holding attacks against Latrun to pin down the Jordanians and prevent them from disrupting his road-building operation. Despite enormous obstacles, the new land bridge was completed on June 9, lifting the siege of Jerusalem. That same day Marcus launched a third attack to take Latrun, this time from the rear. Again, the professional and well-armed Arab Legion could not be budged.

After the breakdown of the first cease-fire on July 9, the Israelis made a fourth attempt during July 14–18 to capture Latrun. They again failed. Even though they had managed to establish a thin land corridor into Jerusalem, Latrun remained a dagger pointed at the vital logistics artery. The Jordanian position was also only a few miles from Israel's only international airport.

The IDF finally took Latrun during the 1967 Six-Day War. Today the Taggert Fort is the official headquarters of the IDF's Armored Corps and the home of its Armor Museum.

David T. Zabecki

See also

Arab Revolt in Palestine; Ben-Gurion, David; Haganah; Marcus, David

References

Berkman, Ted. *Cast a Giant Shadow*. Garden City, NY: Doubleday, 1962.

Collins, Larry, and Dominique Lapierre. *O Jerusalem!* New York: Simon and Schuster, 1972.

Herzog, Chaim. *The Arab-Israeli Wars: War and Peace in the Middle East from the War of Independence to Lebanon*. Westminster, MD: Random House, 1984.

Lausanne, First Treaty of (October 18, 1912)

Treaty concluded in Lausanne, Switzerland, between Italy and the Ottoman Empire on October 18, 1912. The treaty, which ended the Italo-Ottoman War of 1911–1912, compelled the Porte to withdraw its forces from Tripoli and recognize Italy's control of Libya. Italy removed its forces from the Aegean Islands and agreed to the presence of a religious representative of the Ottoman sultan in Tripoli. The war had revealed the great weakness of the Ottoman Empire and thus contributed to the outbreak of the First Balkan War (1912–1913).

ALEXANDER MIKABERIDZE

See also
Balkan Wars; Italo-Ottoman War

References
Ahmida, Ali Abdullatif. *The Making of Modern Libya*. Albany: State University of New York Press, 1994.
McCullagh, Francis. *Italy's War for a Desert*. Chicago: F. G. Browne, 1913.

Lausanne, Second Treaty of (July 24, 1923)

Peace treaty between the Allied Powers and Turkey signed on July 24, 1923, at Lausanne, Switzerland. Unlike the 1920 Treaty of Sèvres, the terms of which the Allies had dictated to the Ottoman government, the Treaty of Lausanne was a negotiated peace. The Treaty of Sèvres had been a humiliation for the Ottomans. Under its terms Greece assumed control over Smyrna and the hinterland as well as all of Ottoman Europe outside of Constantinople. The treaty also removed the Arabic-speaking lands and Armenia from Ottoman control and established an autonomous Kurdistan under League of Nations guidance. The treaty also fixed the size of the Ottoman Army at 50,000 men, left in place the capitulations that gave foreigners the right of extraterritoriality, and established foreign control over many aspects of the Ottoman financial system.

The terms of the treaty set off a wave of nationalism in Turkey, personified in Mustafa Kemal, known as Ataturk. On August 19, 1920, the National Assembly, called into session by the sultan to approve the Treaty of Sèvres, instead rejected it and denounced as traitors those who had supported it. The sultan then dissolved the parliament, which led Kemal to establish a rival government in the interior of Anatolia. He soon concluded an agreement with Russia that proved beneficial to both nations. Turkey recognized Russian incorporation of Azerbaijan, Georgia, and half of Armenia. In return, Turkey received surplus Russian arms and Russia's diplomatic support, including its recognition of Turkish control over the other half of Armenia.

Kemal soon took advantage of the Russian arms to go to war against Greece in Smyrna. Although Greek prime minister Eleuthérios Venizélos sent forces into Anatolia, Kemal carried out a brilliant military campaign in the Greco-Turkish War of 1920–1922, during which he retook Smyrna and its hinterland and then turned north against Constantinople. Italy, which had come to see Greece as a more immediate rival than Turkey, agreed to withdraw its own occupation troops after a defeat at Kemal's hands in central Anatolia. This led the British and French to also depart.

Turkish success on the battlefield produced gains at the bargaining table. In November 1922 a conference to consider revisions to the Treaty of Sèvres opened in the Swiss city of Lausanne. Plenipotentiaries from eight nations negotiated there for seven months. As evidence of their parity at the conference, Turkish diplomats successfully rejected a draft treaty presented in April 1923. The two sides resumed talks until a revision met with the approval of all parties in July.

The Treaty of Lausanne abrogated the terms of the Treaty of Sèvres and included no provisions for the autonomy of Kurdistan, thus recognizing its reincorporation into Turkey. The Capitulations continued in theory, but only a handful of Western legal and medical advisers remained in Turkey after 1923. Eastern Thrace and all of Anatolia returned to Turkish control, settling border disputes with both Greece and Bulgaria. The military terms of the treaty were also favorable to Turkey. Greece agreed not to fortify its Aegean islands and also promised not to fly military aircraft over Turkish airspace.

The treaty also resolved the delicate issue of the Bosporus and the Dardanelles. The International Straits Committee established at Sèvres and composed of Great Britain, France, and Italy remained in place, but Turkey became a member. More importantly, the committee lost the right of intervention granted in the previous treaty. Thereafter, determinations about the security of the straits were the preserve of the League of Nations. In exchange for these concessions, Turkey recognized British control of Cyprus and Italian authority in the Dodecanese Islands.

The Treaty of Lausanne also freed Turkey from reparation payments that the Ottoman government had accepted in the Treaty of Sèvres. In return, Turkey agreed to pay to the other signatories outstanding prewar debts incurred by the Ottomans.

The treaty represented a major triumph for Kemal and the Turkish nationalists. Eleuthérios Venizélos, former prime minister, signed for Greece. He had been one of the most vocal supporters of Greek territorial aims in Turkey, and his signature symbolized the end of Greek designs across the Aegean Sea. The United States and Russia, although not signatories, lent support.

The treaty also led to one of the largest forced movements of populations in history. It took religion as a basis for defining ethnicity and implicitly argued that religious minorities could not exist within the newly created borders. As a result, more than 1.2 million Eastern Orthodox Christians moved from Turkey to Greece; 150,000 of them were from Constantinople (soon to be renamed Istanbul). Similarly, 380,000 Muslims moved from Greece to Turkey. The flood of refugees caused financial and social problems for both nations.

The Treaty of Lausanne must be understood as a monumental triumph for Turkey. It formally ended any chance of the return of the sultanate and established Turkey as a power in the Middle East, Eastern Europe, and Central Asia. The biggest losers under the treaty were the independence-minded Kurds and the Armenians, who now had to live under Turkish and Soviet control. The treaty also significantly reduced tensions in the region among Greece, Italy, and Turkey, thus calming the Balkans considerably.

MICHAEL S. NEIBERG

See also
Ataturk, Mustafa Kemal; Greco-Turkish War; Mandates, League of Nations; Sèvres, Treaty of; Turkey

References
Busch, Briton Cooper. *Mudros to Lausanne: Britain's Frontier in West Asia, 1918–1923.* Albany: State University of New York Press, 1976.
Kinross, John Patrick Balfour. *The Ottoman Centuries: The Rise and Fall of the Turkish Empire.* New York: Morrow, 1977.
McCarthy, Justin. *The Ottoman Peoples and the End of Empire.* London: Hodde Arnold, 2001.

Lavon Affair (July–December 11, 1954)

Part of a secret Israeli plan to have Egyptian Jewish citizens carry out acts of sabotage against American and British interests in Egypt with the aim of alienating the United States and Britain from the regime of Egyptian president Gamal Abdel Nasser. The Lavon Affair of 1954, known to the Israeli secret services as Operation SUZANNAH, involved Israel's military intelligence branch (Aman) organizing, training, and funding a group of Egyptian Jewish saboteurs. The operation was named the Lavon Affair after Israeli defense minister Pinhas Lavon, although he was not responsible for it. Rather, Colonel Benyamin Gibli, chief of Aman, initiated the operation with the intended aim of possibly preventing Egypt from nationalizing the Suez Canal.

Aman had recruited members of a secret Egyptian ring prior to 1954, when Israeli intelligence officer Avram Dar went to Cairo posing as a British businessman named John Darling. There he trained a number of Egyptian Jews for covert operations. Aman also covertly brought the Egyptian Jews to Israel for training in the use of explosives. Aman activated the ring in the spring of 1954. In July of that year the saboteurs bombed post offices, a railway terminal, two U.S. Information Agency libraries, and a British theater. Egyptian authorities arrested ring member Robert Dassa when his bomb prematurely ignited in his pocket. The authorities searched Dassa's home and found incriminating evidence and names of accomplices. On October 5, 1954, the Egyptians announced the arrest of a 13-person spy ring and put its members on trial on December 11.

As a result of a public trial, two of the defendants were acquitted, five received sentences ranging from seven years to life imprisonment, and two were sentenced to death and hanged. Two others had already committed suicide in prison. Because the Israeli government refused to acknowledge the operation during the trial, the Israeli public remained uninformed, and the Jewish press characterized the trial as an outrageous anti-Jewish frame-up.

Subsequent revelations regarding the operation later caused a scandal in the Israeli government, and both Lavon and Gibli were forced to relinquish their positions. The Lavon Affair also damaged Israel's relations with the United States and Great Britain. Not surprisingly, the operation's tactics caused deep-seated suspicion of Israeli intelligence methods both in the Middle East and around the world.

PAUL J. MAGNARELLA

See also
Egypt; Israel; Nasser, Gamal Abdel; Suez Canal

References
Black, Ian, and Benny Morris. *Israel's Secret Wars: A History of Israel's Intelligence Services.* New York: Grove, 1994.
Golan, Aviezer. *Operation Susannah.* New York: Harper and Row, 1978.
Hirst, David. *The Gun and the Olive Branch: The Roots of Violence in the Middle East.* 2nd ed. New York: Nation Books, 2003.

Lawrence, Thomas Edward (1888–1935)

British Army officer and partisan of the Arab cause. Born on August 15, 1888, at Tremadoc, Caernarvonshire, in Wales, Thomas E. Lawrence was the second of five illegitimate sons of Sir Thomas Chapman. Lawrence was about 10 years old when he learned of this, and some believe that it had a permanent imprint on his personality. Educated at

Jesus College, Oxford, he traveled to the Middle East in the five years prior to World War I to prepare material for his university thesis on the architecture of crusader castles. An expedition he accompanied to the Sinai in 1914, ostensibly to explore the area, was in reality designed to gain information for the War Office on military dispositions on the Ottoman Empire's frontier east of Suez.

On the outbreak of World War I, Lawrence failed to meet the height requirement of 5'5" for the army and was posted to the Geographical Section of the War Office. Sent to Cairo, he was attached to the military intelligence staff as an intelligence officer concerned with Arab affairs. In October 1916 he accompanied a mission to the Hejaz, where Hussein ibn Ali, sharif of Mecca, had proclaimed a revolt against the Ottoman Empire. The following month Lawrence, now a captain, was ordered to join as political and liaison officer for Hussein's son, Faisal, commanding an Arab force southwest of Medina. Lawrence was instrumental in acquiring considerable material assistance from the British Army in Cairo for the Arab cause. Recognizing that the key to Ottoman control lay in the Damascus-Medina railway, along which the Ottomans could send reinforcements to crush the Arab Revolt, Lawrence accompanied Faisal and his army in a series of attacks on the railway, earning the name "Emir Dynamite" from the admiring Bedouins.

On July 6, 1917, Lawrence led a force of Huwaitat tribesman in the capture of the port of Aqaba at the northernmost tip of the Red Sea. It became a temporary base for Faisal's army. From there, Lawrence attempted to coordinate Arab movements with the campaign of Lieutenant General Sir Edmund Allenby, who was advancing from Jerusalem in southern Palestine.

In November 1917 Lawrence was captured at Dar'a by Ottoman forces while conducting a reconnaissance of the area in Arab dress. He underwent a short period of humiliating torture but escaped and was present at the Battle of Tafila. For all his flamboyant poses and his adoption of Arab costume, Lawrence was never a leader of Arab forces. Command always remained firmly in the hands of Emir Faisal. Lawrence was, however, an inspirational force behind the Arab Revolt, a superb tactician, and a highly influential theoretician of guerrilla warfare. During the last two years of the war, his advice and influence combined with the Hashemites' own motivations to bind the Arabs to the Allied cause, thereby tying down some 25,000 Ottoman troops who would otherwise have opposed British forces. For his war service Lawrence was awarded the Distinguished Service Order and was promoted to lieutenant colonel. Subsequently he was present at the capture of Damascus on October 1, 1918, and returned the following month to England, where he was demobilized.

Lawrence witnessed the defeat of his aspirations for the Arabs when their hopes for a nation were dashed by the French claim to the mandates of Syria and Lebanon. Upon returning to England, he lobbied vainly against the detachment of Syria and Lebanon from the rest of the Arab countries as a French mandate. He also worked on his war memoir. In 1921 he was wooed back to the Middle East as adviser on Arab affairs to Colonial Minister Winston Churchill. However, after the Cairo political settlements regarding the Middle East, Lawrence rejected offers of further positions and left the government in protest.

In August 1922, Lawrence enlisted (under the name John Hume Ross) in the Royal Air Force but was discharged six months later when his identity was disclosed by a London newspaper. He then enlisted as T. E. Shaw in the Royal Tank Corps and transferred to the Royal Air Force in 1925, remaining with that service until he was discharged in February 1935. He died at Bovington Camp Hospital on May 19, 1935, following a motorcycle accident.

Lawrence became an almost mythic figure in his own lifetime. His reputation was to an extent self-generated through his own literary accounts, including his war memoir *The Seven Pillars of Wisdom* (1922) and lecture tours, assisted by his postwar election to a research fellowship at Oxford University.

James H. Willbanks

See also
Allenby, Sir Edmund Henry Hynman; Arab Revolt of World War I; Faisal I, King of Iraq; Hussein ibn Ali ibn Mohammed; World War I, Impact on the Middle East

References
James, Lawrence. *The Golden Warrior: The Life and Legend of Lawrence of Arabia.* New York: Paragon House, 1993.
Lawrence, T. E. *Seven Pillars of Wisdom.* 1936; reprint, New York: Anchor, 1991.
Wilson, Jeremy. *Lawrence of Arabia: The Authorized Biography of T. E. Lawrence.* New York: Collier, 1992.

League of Nations Covenant Article 22

Provision in the Covenant of the League of Nations, the supranational organization (and predecessor to the United Nations) established by the representatives of the victorious powers at the Paris Peace Conference following World War I on June 28, 1919. Article 22 of the covenant called for the creation of a mandate system, which transferred the former colonies of Germany and the former territories of the Ottoman Empire in the Middle East to the custody of the League of Nations. Nations or regions falling under a mandate would be administered by a third-party nation upon the approval of the League of Nations.

The principles of the mandate system had their legal precedent under the Roman principle of *mandatum,* which placed persons and property under the care of responsible parties. More recent precedents included the 1885 Berlin Conference, which established safeguards for the people of the Congo, and the 1892 Brussels Conference, which banned the import of alcohol and weapons to the Congo. During the Paris Peace Conference, the signatories agreed to commit themselves to the protection and well-being of their colonies.

Under existing international law, colonies were considered to be "wards" under the responsibility of the colonial power. However, the question soon arose as to whom the colonial power was responsible. Through Article 22, the League of Nations was the authority that would oversee the conduct of the colonial powers in question. The former colonies and territories of Germany and the Ottoman Empire were distributed among the victorious allied powers. Britain and France benefited the most by acquiring the majority of these territories as mandates. The British dominions of Australia and New Zealand were given mandates as rewards for their service in the war. In the Middle East proper, Britain gained a mandate over Palestine, while the French administered mandates in Syria and Lebanon.

The mandates were classified as either A, B, or C, according to the political and cultural development of the nations under mandate. The areas formerly controlled by the Ottoman Empire in the Middle East were classified as A mandates because they were on the brink of independence and particularly because they had rebelled against the Turks during the war. The mandate powers in question were supposed to guide their mandates in the final steps toward statehood. The B mandates, consisting of the former German colonies in Central Africa, were considered to be at a lower developmental stage than the A mandates, and so it was the responsibility of the mandate powers to oversee their material needs and to prevent abuses such as slavery, exploitation of labor, and the importation of illicit liquor and drugs. They were also to allow access to other nations for trade purposes. The C mandates were deemed to be at the lowest level of development, for whom independence was not considered in the short term. How the mandate system differed from old-fashioned colonialism was that the mandatory powers were required to make an annual report to the League of Nations. Ironically, Article 22 seemed to fly in the face of President Woodrow Wilson's call for self-determination, but the brainchild of the League of Nations had been forced to compromise to get the organization up and running. Not surprisingly, problems arose from the creation of the mandate system. The question of whether the league or the mandate power held the final authority continued to bedevil officials throughout the existence of the mandate system. In addition, international law did not have a mechanism for temporary sovereignty over a particular area. The League of Nations did not have enforcement powers within the mandates, so mandate commission members could not visit a mandate to investigate problems. Issues of ascendant nationalism soon created tensions in Middle Eastern states, which ironically were supposed to be in the final stages of independence. Despite these problems, however, Article 22 helped change the face of colonialism and may have contributed to its ultimate demise after World War II. From the perspective of those people living in the mandates, however, especially in the Middle East, the situation seemed little different from the colonialism of the old order. In a sense, one might argue that League of Nations mandates in places such as the Middle East solved short-term difficulties but only amplified long-term problems.

DINO E. BUENVIAJE

See also
Arab Nationalism; Palestine, British Mandate for

References
Northedge, F. S. *The League of Nations: Its Life and Times 1920–1946.* Leicester, UK: Leicester University Press, 1986.
Ostrower, Gary B., and George Lankevich, eds. *League of Nations, 1919.* New York: Putnam Publishing Group, 1996.
Scott, George. *The Rise and Fall of the League of Nations.* New York: Macmillan, 1973.

Lebanon

Lebanon (officially the Lebanese Republic) is located on the eastern end of the Mediterranean Sea and is bordered by Israel to the south and Syria to the east and north. Lebanon covers 4,015 square miles, and its 2018 population was some 6.15 million. Because the relative size of the religious groups is a sensitive issue, there has been no national census since 1932. Muslims number perhaps 54 percent (Shias, 27 percent; Sunnis, 27 percent). Druzes constitute 5.6 percent; the Druze sect emerged during the 11th century from a

Lebanon

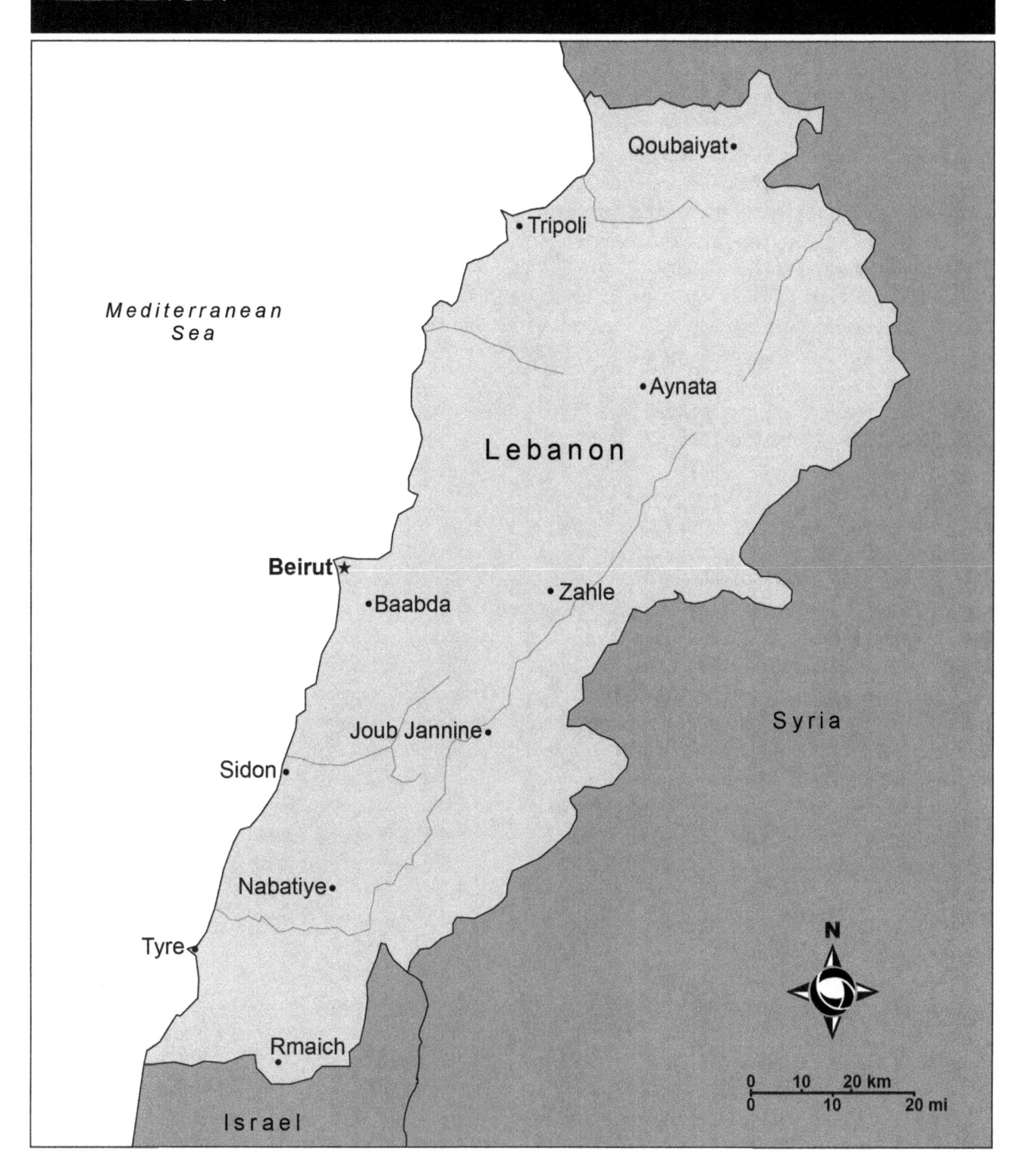

branch of Shia Islam. Christians are some 40.5 percent of the Lebanese population. There are also small numbers of Jews, Baha'is, Buddhists, Hindus, and Mormons.

Lebanon's strategic location led to frequent invasions in ancient times, resulting in a chaotic history and great religious and cultural diversity. Its location fostered a maritime culture under the Canaanites and Phoenicians circa 1550–539 BCE. In 64 BCE, Rome established control. Lebanon became a Christian center under the Maronites, who survived the Arab conquest. The Druzes also established themselves there. During the Christian crusades (1096–1291) the Maronites reestablished ties with the Roman Catholic Church.

Lebanon passed under the rule of the Ottoman Empire in 1516. The Ottoman Empire joined World War I on the side of the Central Powers. The defeat of the latter in 1918 saw the areas of modern-day Lebanon and Syria controlled by France as a League of Nations mandate from October 29, 1923. Britain meanwhile secured mandates over Iraq and Palestine.

During World War II a pro-Axis coup occurred in Iraq, and the Germans applied pressure on the Vichy French government to permit the transport of arms there through Syria. Deeply concerned about the possible loss of Iraqi oil and the threat to British communications with India, British and Free French forces invaded Syria and Lebanon in June–July 1941. Free French high commissioner to the Levant General Georges Catroux announced on November 26 that Lebanon would become independent under the authority of the Free French government. Elections were held in 1943, and on November 8 the new Lebanese government unilaterally abolished the mandate. The French responded by imprisoning the members of the government. Following strong international pressure, Free French authorities released those arrested on November 22, 1943, celebrated by Lebanese as their independence day. Foreign troops withdrew from Lebanon entirely on December 31, 1946.

Lebanon became a charter member of the United Nations (UN) in 1945, the same year it joined the Arab League. Although independence and international status were welcomed by the Lebanese, sectarian tensions have continually threatened internal peace. This along with 60 years as a participant in the Arab-Israeli conflicts has left Lebanon with only a few years absent of internal and external conflict since 1945.

The Lebanese government operated under an unusual political arrangement of confessionalism in which power was shared among the different religious communities. Lebanon's unwritten National Pact of 1943 was based on the 1932 census and awarded the Maronite Christians a privileged place in the government. Generally a Maronite is the president, the prime minister is a Sunni, the Speaker of parliament is a Shiite, and the deputy Speaker of parliament and deputy prime minister is Greek Orthodox.

As demographic developments led to a Muslim majority by the 1960s, Maronite predominance came under increasing pressure from various Muslim groups. The fact that the Muslims were not a monolithic force further complicated matters. The Shias, along with the Druzes and a small number of Alawites, outnumbered the Sunnis, and these groups often had contentious relations. On top of this, the Cold War and the ongoing Arab-Israeli conflict presented Lebanon with major challenges.

As a member of the Arab League, Lebanon was a reluctant participant in the Arab military effort to defeat Israel on the latter's declaration of independence in May 1948. Lebanese forces and Lebanese volunteers in the Arab Liberation Army fought alongside those from Syria in the northern front of the Israeli War of Independence (1948–1949), but the fighting ended with Israel in control of the Jordan River, the lakes of Galilee and Huleh, and a panhandle of territory jutting north and bordering on both Lebanon and Syria. Lebanon's only success of the war was the June 5–6, 1948, capture of Al-Malkiyya. Lebanon was directly impacted by the war, with the flight there of some 100,000 Palestinians from Israeli-occupied areas. Israel then refused to permit their return. Lebanon was not a major player in the subsequent Arab-Israeli wars and thus avoided military losses and potential occupation.

This did not mean that Lebanon remained at peace, however, for sectarian troubles and the evolving Cold War between the United States and the Soviet Union brought their own challenges. Both sides in the Cold War sought to support regimes that they believed would aid them in the worldwide conflict.

In January 1957, President Dwight Eisenhower requested a congressional resolution authorizing use of force in the Middle East to prevent the spread of communism. Known as the Eisenhower Doctrine, it was in response to waning British influence in the region following the 1956 Suez Crisis. Having lost faith in British capabilities, Eisenhower declared his intention to take the lead in keeping the region from Soviet control.

Events in the region during 1957 and 1958 were seen by the United States as a warning of the rise of both communism and radical Arab nationalism. In 1957 King Hussein of Jordan established diplomatic relations with the

Soviet Union. In February 1958 the most radical regimes in the region, Egypt and Syria (both supported by the Soviet Union), merged to form the United Arab Republic (UAR). Then in July 1958, the pro-Western Iraqi monarchy was overthrown by a radical military junta.

Faced with these developments along with relentless propaganda by Arab nationalists against his more pro-Western regime and internal threats to his rule, including an insurrection demanding that Lebanon join the UAR, Lebanese president Camille Chamoun requested direct American intervention to defend his government. Eisenhower invoked his new doctrine and ordered 5,000 U.S. marines to Lebanon. They arrived in Beirut on July 15. Meanwhile, the British sent forces into Jordan.

The main issue at stake in Lebanon became Chamoun's effort to change the constitution to allow him to continue to rule the nation after his term of office expired. Eisenhower instructed his personal representative and experienced international troubleshooter Robert Murphy to pressure Chamoun to yield power to circumvent civil war. Chamoun eventually conceded, and former general Fuad Chehab, a popular figure in Lebanon, replaced him, allowing American forces to be withdrawn.

For the next decade and a half, the Muslim and Christian populations seemed to be working well together. Indeed, during the 1960s Lebanon was often referred to as the "Switzerland of the Middle East," a nation where diverse communities thrived in mutual tolerance. Lebanon enjoyed considerable prosperity owing to tourism, agricultural production, commerce, and extensive banking.

The apparent harmony did not last long, however. Gradually the Muslim population became the clear majority, and Lebanon could not avoid becoming involved in the Arab-Israeli conflict. A number of the Palestinian refugees in Lebanon began carrying out hit-and-run actions across the border in Israel. Lebanese Christians opposed this, fearing that Israeli reprisals would threaten Lebanese independence.

The Six-Day War in 1967 and the 1973 Yom Kippur War (Ramadan War), coupled with the expulsion of radical Palestinians from Jordan in 1970 and 1971, saw more Palestinians relocate to Lebanon, greatly increasing their influence there. The refugees lived in wretched camps that served as breeding grounds for anti-Israeli terrorists. While the Lebanese military tried to maintain order and restrain the Palestinian guerrillas from using Lebanon for attacks against Israel, this was largely unsuccessful. In 1975, clashes between Lebanese Christians and Muslims expanded into full-scale civil war (April 13, 1975–October 13, 1990), pitting Christian groups against the forces of the Palestine Liberation Organization (PLO) and Druze and Muslim militias. In the fighting between March 1975 and November 1976 alone, some 40,000 died and 100,000 more were wounded.

In June 1976 Lebanese president Elias Sarkis requested Syrian Army intervention to help restore peace, and that October the Arab League agreed to establish a predominantly Syrian Arab deterrent force to restore calm.

Attacks by the PLO across the border into northern Israel meanwhile led Israeli prime minister Menachem Begin to send troops into southern Lebanon in March 1975 in Operation LITANI. The operation brought the deaths of 1,100–2,000 Lebanese and Palestinians and 20 Israelis. It also resulted in the internal displacement of 100,000 to 250,000 people in Lebanon. PLO forces retreated north of the Litani River. U.S. pressure forced an Israeli withdrawal and brought creation of the United Nations Interim Force in Lebanon (UNIFIL), charged with providing security in southern Lebanon.

With UNIFIL incapable of fulfilling its mandate, major PLO cross-border strikes resumed in April 1982. While Israel conducted both air strikes and commando raids across the border, it was unable to prevent increasing numbers of PLO personnel from locating there. PLO rocket and mortar attacks regularly forced thousands of Israeli civilians to flee homes and fields in northern Galilee to seek protection in bomb shelters.

The attempted assassination and serious wounding in London on June 3, 1982, of Israeli ambassador to Britain Shlomo Argov led Begin to order the bombing of Palestinian targets in western Beirut and southern Lebanon during June 4–5, 1982. The PLO responded by attacking Galilee with rockets and mortars, triggering the Israeli decision to invade Lebanon.

On June 6, Israeli defense minister Ariel Sharon, acting under instructions from Begin, ordered a massive Israeli military invasion in Operation PEACE FOR GALILEE (the Lebanon War). Ultimately the Israel Defense Forces (IDF) committed some 76,000 troops, 800 tanks, 1,500 armored personnel carriers (APCs), and 364 aircraft. Syria committed perhaps 22,000 men, 352 tanks, 300 APCs, and 96 aircraft, while the PLO had perhaps 15,000 men, 300 tanks, and 150 APCs.

The Israelis sought to destroy the PLO in southern Lebanon, evict the Syrian Army from Lebanon and bring about the removal of its missiles from the Bekaa Valley, and influence Lebanese politics. Israel sought an alliance with the Maronite Christians, specifically Bashir Jumayyil (Gemayel), leader of the Phalange (al-Kata'ib) and head of the unified command of the Lebanese Forces. While the Phalange was mainly a political association, the unified command of the Lebanese Forces was an umbrella organization of Christian militias. Jumayyil opposed growing Muslim power in Lebanon and the Syrian presence, and he sought close ties with the West and Israel.

Within a few days, IDF forces had reached the outskirts of Beirut. Tyre and Sidon, two cities within the 25-mile limit, were both heavily damaged in the Israeli advance. Rather than stand their ground and be overwhelmed by the better-equipped Israelis, the PLO withdrew back on western Beirut.

Fighting also occurred between the Israelis and Syrian forces in the Bekaa Valley. Unable to meet Israel on equal footing and being bereft of allies, Syria rejected an all-out military effort. Most of the battle was in the air. The Israeli Air Force neutralized Syrian surface-to-air missiles in the Bekaa Valley and downed dozens of Syrian jets, perhaps as many as 80. The Israelis also employed helicopter gunships to attack and destroy Syrian tanks and APCs. The Israelis trapped the Syrian forces in the Bekaa Valley and were on the verge of severing the Beirut-Damascus highway on June 11 when Moscow and Washington brokered a cease-fire.

Fighting between the IDF and the PLO continued, however, with the IDF closing a ring around Beirut by June 13. Israeli hopes that the Maronite Christian militias would ferret out the PLO trapped in the city proved illusory. The IDF was not prepared to undertake street-by-street fighting that would entail heavy casualties for its own forces and so for some seven weeks carried out land, sea, and air attacks against Beirut, cutting off its electricity and access to food and water. International observers accused the Israelis of indiscriminate shelling of the city that destroyed some 500 buildings in the first week alone.

Although Sharon secured Begin's support for a large-scale operation to conquer western Beirut, on July 16 the full Israeli cabinet rejected this. On August 10, with American envoy Philip Habib having submitted a draft agreement to Israel, Sharon ordered saturation bombing of Beirut, during which at least 300 people died. U.S. president Ronald Reagan formally lodged a protest with the Israeli government, and on August 12 the Israeli cabinet stripped Sharon of most of his powers.

On August 21 following U.S. mediation, 350 French paratroopers arrived in Beirut, followed by 800 U.S. marines and Italian Bersaglieri plus additional international peacekeepers, for a total multinational force (MNF) of 2,130 men. The MNF supervised the removal of the PLO, first by ship and then overland, to Tunisia, Yemen, Jordan, and Syria. By the end of the operation on September 1, some 8,500 PLO troops had departed for Tunis and 2,500 to other Arab countries.

Following the evacuation of the PLO, the ongoing civil war escalated among various Christian, Muslim, and Druze factions vying for control of Lebanon. Furthermore, Israeli and Syrian forces in Lebanon continued to clash, threatening an all-out war between the two nations. The MNF returned after the assassination on September 14 of Jumayyil, then Lebanese president-elect, and massacres by Lebanese Christian militias in several refugee camps.

As time passed, MNF forces were embroiled in the fighting and came to be viewed as supporters of the Lebanese government. On October 24, 1983, a suicide bomber, believed to be a Shiite, drove a van filled with explosives through a barrier and to the marine barracks at the Beirut airport, killing 241. At the French headquarters, another bomb killed 58 soldiers. Public pressure in the United States and the collapse of the Lebanese Army in February 1984 forced Reagan to withdraw the marines, and the other MNF nations soon followed.

The Lebanese Civil War raged on, and Israel and Syria continued to maintain significant forces in Lebanon. The Lebanese government was not able to assert its authority over large parts of the country, and Israel kept forces in the south to prevent raids and rocket attacks against its territory. Syrian strongman President Hafez al-Assad dispatched additional forces and attempted to control Lebanese policies as well as provide arms and training to militias sympathetic to Syria. Nevertheless, this did bring some stability to Lebanon and some semblance of economic recovery. The relative calm was, however, periodically interrupted by conflict between Israeli forces and Shiite militias, predominantly Hezbollah, which was armed by Syria.

A political impasse continued as the Lebanese parliament deadlocked regarding the election of a successor to Jumayyil as president. In May 1888 the Arab League established a committee to try to resolve the situation, and on September 16, 1989, it secured acceptance of its peace plan. A cease-fire went into effect, and ports and airports were reopened. The Lebanese parliament agreed to the National Reconciliation Accord, also known as the Taif Agreement (it was negotiated at Taif, Saudi Arabia). This specified a timetable for the withdrawal of Syrian forces and established a formula to end the confessionalist political arrangement, although there was no timetable for implementation. The agreement increased the Chamber of Deputies to 128 members, with seats to be shared equally between Christians and Muslims rather than elected by universal suffrage, which would have provided a Muslim majority (excluding the expatriate community, a majority of which is Christian). The cabinet was also to be equally divided between Christians and Muslims.

The agreement was ratified on November 5, 1989. That same day the parliament elected René Mouawad as president. Mouawad was assassinated only 17 days later in a car bombing in Beirut as his motorcade returned from Lebanese Independence Day ceremonies. Elias Hrawi succeeded him.

The Lebanese Civil War formally ended on October 13, 1990. Its toll was 150,000 dead and 200,000 injured as well as the displacement of nearly 1 million civilians. The physical destruction was immense, with major damage to the Lebanese infrastructure.

In May 2000 Israel had withdrawn its forces from southern Lebanon, hoping that this would lead to a stable border. Instead the border became more dangerous, as Hezbollah soon controlled much of southern Lebanon, fortifying positions there with Syrian assistance.

On February 14, 2005, former prime minister Rafik Hariri was assassinated by a car bomb. Many Lebanese blamed Syria, while the Syrian government claimed that Israeli intelligence services were responsible. Other prominent Lebanese were also killed, but Hariri's assassination triggered the Cedar Revolution, a series of demonstrations demanding withdrawal of Syrian troops and an international investigation into the assassination. International pressure did bring a Syrian withdrawal, completed by April 26, 2005. Although a UN investigation into Hariri's death concluded that the assassination was most likely carried out by the Syrian intelligence services, no individuals have ever been brought to justice.

On July 12, 2006, Hezbollah launched rockets into Israel and carried out a cross-border raid, killing three Israeli soldiers and capturing two others. The Israeli reaction was massive and was not anticipated by Hezbollah leader Hassan Nasrallah, who later admitted that the raid would not have been launched if he had known the likely Israeli response.

Israel commenced air attacks and a massive ground invasion of southern Lebanon in what is known as the 2006 Lebanese War: a month of heavy fighting in southern Lebanon until a tenuous UN cease-fire was negotiated on August 14. Hezbollah had about 1,000 fighters well dug into prepared positions in southern Lebanon, backed by other militias and a civilian population that largely supported them, facing up to 30,000 members of the IDF.

Hezbollah claimed 74 dead during the monthlong fighting, while Israel reported 440 confirmed Hezbollah deaths. Militias supporting Hezbollah suffered 31 dead, while the Lebanese Army sustained 41 dead and about 100 wounded.

Israel reported 119 dead, 400 injured, and 2 captured. UN observer forces in the area suffered 7 dead and 12 wounded. The worst toll was among Lebanese civilians, with perhaps 1,200 dead and 3,600 more injured. As many as 250,000 Lebanese were displaced by the fighting. Israel suffered 44 civilian deaths and more than 1,300 injured. Lebanon also suffered extensive damage to its infrastructure from Israeli artillery fire and air strikes.

The robust defense put up by Hezbollah came as a surprise. Hezbollah was able to fire 4,000 rockets into Israeli territory, including not only short-range Katyushas but also middle-range missiles capable of hitting Haifa and other points believed to be safe from the usual Hezbollah rockets. In southern Lebanon, Hezbollah was able to resist Israeli armored attacks, destroying 20 main battle tanks in two engagements. A missile attack against an Israeli warship was also a surprise.

The cease-fire called for a halt in the fighting, an end to the Israeli blockade, the deployment of UN forces to southern Lebanon to maintain peace, and a Lebanese Army takeover of areas previously dominated by Hezbollah.

During May 20–September 7, 2007, fighting occurred between the Lebanese Armed Forces and Fatah al-Islam, an Islamist militant organization. The fighting, centered in Nahr al-Bared, a Palestinian refugee camp near Tripoli, was the most severe internal warfare since the 1975–1990 Lebanese Civil War. Minor clashes also occurred in the Ain al-Hilweh refugee camp in southern Lebanon, and there were several bombings in and around Beirut. At least 169 soldiers, 287 insurgents, and 47 civilians died.

During 2006–2008 there were a series of protests against pro-Western prime minister Fouad Siniora demanding the creation of a national unity government in which mostly Shia opposition groups would have veto power. When Émile Lahoud's presidential term ended in October 2007, the opposition refused to vote for a successor unless a power-sharing deal was reached, leaving Lebanon without a president.

On May 9, 2008, Hezbollah and Amal forces seized control of western Beirut, leading to more fighting in which at least 62 people died. The Doha Agreement of May 21, 2008, ended the fighting, and Michel Suleiman became president, heading a national unity government. This was, however, a victory for the opposition, which secured the veto. In early January 2011, the national unity government collapsed owing to the belief that the Special Tribunal for Lebanon was expected to indict members of Hezbollah for the assassination of Hariri. The parliament elected Najib Mikati as prime minister. He was the candidate of the Hezbollah-led March 8 Alliance.

In 2011, the Arab Spring brought civil war in Syria. This conflict threatened to expand to Lebanon, causing more incidents of sectarian violence and armed clashes between Sunnis and Alawites in Tripoli. By March 2016 there were some 1.069 million Syrian refugees in Lebanon, representing one-fifth of that nation's population and threatening to undermine Lebanon's already fragile political system. Also on March 2, 2016, the Saudi Arabian government, apparently bent on punishing Lebanon for Hezbollah forces having taken an active role in the fighting in support of the Iranian-backed regime of President Bashar al-Assad in the Syrian Civil War, slashed billions of dollars in aid for Lebanon, urged Sunnis not to visit Lebanon as tourists, and identified Hezbollah, Lebanon's most powerful political and armed organization, as a terrorist organization.

In December 2016 a political deal was reached that made Saad Hariri, son of the assassinated former prime minister Rafik Hariri and an ally of Saudi Arabia, the prime minister, while President Michael Aoun, a political ally of Hezbollah, became president and head of state.

Saudi pressure on Lebanon increased in late 2017. To the surprise of all, Saad Hariri, who has a family construction business based in Saudi Arabia, announced from Riyadh on November 4 that he was resigning as Lebanese prime minister, accusing Iran of destabilizing Lebanon and the region. Many believed that the Saudis, furious with Hariri for his 2016 political deal with Hezbollah, had forced him to resign. There were even accusations that he was being held in Saudi Arabia against his will. Then on November 10, Lebanon was plunged into a state of heightened anxiety when Saudi Arabia ordered its citizens to leave that country. However, Hariri returned to Lebanon on November 21 and announced that he had suspended his decision to resign, satisfied that all of Lebanon's political parties, including Hezbollah, had agreed to stay out of the affairs of other countries. Saudi Arabia kept up the pressure on Hezbollah, however. That same month at a meeting in Cairo of the Arab League, Saudi Arabia secured the support of most of the league's 22 member states for a resolution that condemned Hezbollah's actions and branded it a terrorist organization.

A continuing threat to Lebanese stability is the presence in the country of more than 450,000 Palestinian refugees. They remain stateless, and the majority live in difficult conditions, many of them in refugee camps, despite their having been in Lebanon for as long as 70 years. Palestinians are barred from more than 30 professions, including white-collar jobs. They also cannot own property or attend public schools, and they are not protected by labor laws. They view with dismay the decision of U.S. president Donald Trump to recognize Jerusalem as the capital of Israel, seeing in this the end of the two-state solution in the former Palestine. Meanwhile, the presence in Lebanon of several hundred thousand Syrian refugees, who have migrated to that country since 2011, has strained government resources and threatens to disrupt the delicate balance of political power in the country.

In August 2018, high-level talks between Russian and Lebanese leaders yielded promises of increased economic ties and more military ties between Russia and Lebanon. Russia also promised to speed the repatriation of Syrian refugees residing in Lebanon back to Syria.

Brent Geary, Daniel E. Spector, and Spencer C. Tucker

See also
Alawites; Arab Spring; Assad, Bashar al-; Assad, Hafez al-; Chamoun, Camille; Doha Agreement; Druzes; Eisenhower Doctrine; Hariri, Rafik; Hezbollah; Lahoud, Émile Jamil; Lebanon, First U.S. Intervention in; Lebanon, Israeli Operations against; Lebanon, Israeli Security Zone in; Lebanon, Second U.S. Intervention in; Lebanon Civil War; Lebanon-Israeli War; Litani, Operation; Mandates, League of Nations; Maronites; Ottoman Empire; Palestine Liberation Organization; Sharon, Ariel; Syria; Syrian Civil War; Taif Accords

References
Friedman, Thomas. *From Beirut to Jerusalem.* New York: Anchor Books, 1995.
Gendzier, Irene. *Notes from the Minefield: United States Intervention in Lebanon and the Middle East, 1945–1958.* New York: Columbia University Press, 1997.
Harris, William. *Lebanon: A History, 600–2011.* New York: Oxford University Press, 2014.
Herzog, Chaim. *Arab-Israeli Wars: War and Peace in the Middle East from the War of Independence through Lebanon.* New York: Vintage, 1984.
Hurewitz, J. C. *Middle East Politics: The Military Dimension.* New York: Praeger, 1969.
Kaufman, Burton I. *The Arab Middle East and the United States: Inter-Arab Rivalry and Superpower Diplomacy.* New York: Twayne, 1996.
Levitt, Matthew. *Hezbollah.* Washington, DC: Georgetown University Press, 2016.
Mackey, Sandra. *Lebanon: A House Divided.* New York: Norton, 2006.
Rabil, Robert G. *Embattled Neighbors: Syria, Israel and Lebanon.* Boulder, CO: Lynne Rienner, 2003.
Traboulsi, Fawwaz. *A History of Modern Lebanon.* 2nd ed. London: Pluto, 2012.
U.S. Army. *Area Handbook Series: Lebanon.* Washington, DC: U.S. Government Printing Office, 1989.
Warner, Geoffrey. *Iraq and Syria, 1941.* London: Davis-Poynter, 1974.

Wright, Robin. *Sacred Rage: The Wrath of Militant Islam.* New York: Simon and Schuster, 2001.

Zweig, Ronald W. *Britain and Palestine during the Second World War.* Suffolk, UK: Boydell and Brewer, 1986.

Lebanon, First U.S. Intervention in (July 15–October 25, 1958)

In July 1958, the United States intervened militarily in Lebanon. U.S. president Dwight D. Eisenhower sought to ensure that the pro-Western regime of President Camille Chamoun (1952–1958) would not be overthrown and that the nation would not be plunged into a full-blown civil war. Sending troops to Lebanon was also a warning to Soviet leaders and their ally, Egypt's President Gamal Abdel Nasser, not to destabilize the Middle East. Finally, Washington hoped to reassure pro-Western governments in Iran, Pakistan, and Turkey of American resolve in the region. The 1958 intervention, known as Operation BLUE BAT, was officially launched on July 15, 1958, and ended just three months later with the departure of U.S. forces on October 25.

President Eisenhower's decision to dispatch the troops was based in part on his foreign policy stance expressed in a message to Congress on January 5, 1957, which became known as the Eisenhower Doctrine. Asserting that the United States was determined to deny the Soviet Union the opportunity to dominate and control the Middle East, the president pledged to assist both economically and militarily any Middle Eastern nation in the preservation of its independence to include the deployment of U.S. military forces "against armed aggression from any nation controlled by international Communism."

At the time, the United States regarded with alarm the rise of Arab hostility toward the West and the growing influence of the Soviet Union in the Middle East. Particularly worrisome to Washington were the policies of Egypt and Syria, which had developed great antipathy toward the West. After Nasser had nationalized the Suez Canal in 1956, Britain, France, and Israel invaded Egypt. The resulting 1956 Suez Crisis inflamed Arab hostility toward the West and boomeranged in that it enhanced Nasser's prestige in the region and his policies of Pan-Arabism.

Eisenhower viewed the Suez Crisis as having effectively ended British and French influence in the Middle East, creating a power vacuum. To deny the Soviet Union the opportunity to exploit the situation, thwart Nasser's Pan-Arab policies (which enjoyed Soviet support), and protect the supply of oil, Eisenhower was prepared to intervene militarily in the Middle East should that prove necessary.

The first real test of the Eisenhower Doctrine came in Lebanon in 1958. By the spring of that year, a series of international and domestic events had plunged the country into crisis. Relations with Egypt deteriorated when President Chamoun, a Christian, refused to sever diplomatic relations with Britain and France following their invasion of Egypt during the Suez Crisis, which angered Lebanese Muslims who supported Nasser, including Lebanese prime minister Rashid Karami, a Sunni Muslim. Meanwhile, hostile Egyptian propaganda against Chamoun exacerbated Lebanese Muslim resentment toward his regime. Chamoun's refusal to denounce the 1955 Baghdad Pact and his decision to place Lebanon under the umbrella of the Eisenhower Doctrine further angered Nasser and Lebanon's Muslims. Karami regarded the Baghdad Pact as a threat to Arab unity and an attempt to divide the Arab world.

On February 1, 1958, Egypt and Syria formed a unitary state in the United Arab Republic. Many Lebanese Muslims, including Karami, sought to have Lebanon join the union. Chamoun refused, preferring to ostensibly keep Lebanon neutral. Lebanese Muslims viewed Chamoun's decision as proof of his desire to remain aligned with the West. The president's position further alienated his Muslim countrymen.

In terms of domestic politics, the 1958 Lebanese Crisis grew principally from growing Muslim disenchantment with Christian domination of both the government and the military, especially when Muslims held that Christians were no longer in the majority. Lebanon's only official census, in 1932, had served as the basis for distributing political power among Lebanon's Christians and Muslims (both Sunni and Shiite) as well as other religious faiths such as that of the Druzes. Using dubious statistics such as counting Christian Lebanese living abroad, the 1932 census showed a slim majority of Christians living in Lebanon. When Lebanon gained its independence in 1943 from France, an informal agreement, known as the National Pact, served as the basis for reconciling religious rivalries by attempting to create a stable, united, and peaceful country among people of different faiths and sought to ensure that no one religion would dominate the government.

Based on the 1932 census, the National Pact stipulated that the president would be a Christian of the dominant Maronite sect (which accounted for approximately 50 percent of the Christians), the prime minister would be a Sunni

Muslim, the speaker of the parliament would be a Shiite Muslim, and the commander of the Lebanese military would be a Maronite. The National Pact also established, per the 1932 census, that the ratio of seats in the parliament, cabinet offices, and positions in the bureaucracy would be awarded on a ratio of six to five, Christians to Muslims. In sum, the basis of both the government as well as the idea of a Lebanese national identity was principally a function of religious faith, making national unity tenuous at best and Lebanese democracy an illusion. Although never committed to writing or affirmed by the people, the National Pact was nonetheless accepted by the religious-political elite of the country as the basis for establishing a government and preserving national unity. But as the Muslim population increased, the legitimacy of the 1932 pact came into question, and sectarian tensions grew.

Lebanese Muslims generally identified with the Arab world and Nasser's Pan-Arabism, while Lebanese Christians mostly identified with the West and opposed Nasser's policies; meanwhile, Middle Eastern politics aggravated the tensions between the groups, undermining the tenuous unity of this multireligious nation. By the mid-1950s, Muslims had rejected the imbalance of political power established by the National Pact and demanded a new census, believing that its results would show that they were now the largest religious community in the country, thereby giving them majority control of the government. Finally, Chamoun's 1958 decision to amend the constitution that would allow him a second term touched off simmering religious tensions.

In May 1958, violent disturbances broke out throughout Lebanon as Chamoun's opponents called for a general strike against the government. Chamoun ordered the commander of the Lebanese armed forces, General Fuad Shihab, to intervene. Fearing great bloodshed between Christians and Muslims, he refused. He reasoned that suppressing the rebellion would destroy the military's neutrality, not preserve national unity, and would plunge the military into the growing civil war. Indeed, the military was itself composed of both Christians and Muslims, and Shihab knew that any military intervention would dissolve the military into sectarian factions.

Shihab's wise decision to keep the military neutral spared Lebanon a full-scale civil war that summer, and had not international events intruded, Lebanon might have overcome the crisis with another political solution. The urgency and danger of the crisis, however, increased when on July 14, 1958, Pan-Arab nationalists overthrew and killed King Faisal II, the pro-British monarch of Iraq and the key figure behind the Baghdad Pact. Fearing that the coup was part of a concerted effort to take advantage of Lebanon's disorder, overthrow his regime, and turn the country into a solidly Arab-Muslim state with close ties to Nasser and the Soviet Union, Chamoun appealed for American military assistance.

Alarmed at the unexpected coup in Iraq and determined to prevent a friendly regime in Lebanon from suffering the same fate while also seeking to reassure the pro-Western governments of Turkey, Iran, and Pakistan, the American president invoked the Eisenhower Doctrine and dispatched 14,000 U.S. troops to secure Chamoun's regime. Washington made clear to Chamoun, however, that it was not intervening to assist or to endorse his questionable reelection bid.

Of the 14,000 U.S. soldiers who landed in Lebanon on July 15, 1958, about 8,500 were from the army; the remainder were marines. The United States also had 70 warships and support ships in the Mediterranean with an additional 40,000 men at sea, ready to be deployed in short order if necessary.

The presence of U.S. troops as peacekeepers averted other foreign influence in the Lebanon crisis and signaled to all warring factions, including Chamoun, that the United States would not tolerate a civil war in Lebanon. Chamoun's decision to resign, not amend the constitution, and not seek a second term, along with parliament's selections of General Shihab as Chamoun's successor on July 31, averted a civil war and cooled sectarian tensions. That same day a cease-fire was declared in the city of Tripoli, the scene of some of the worst fighting.

The U.S. troops remained in Lebanon for just 103 days, until October 25, and suffered only 1 combat casualty. Meanwhile, a total of between 2,000 and 4,000 Lebanese had died. This time at least, Lebanon had been spared a full-scale civil war.

STEFAN BROOKS

See also

Chamoun, Camille; Egypt; Eisenhower Doctrine; Faisal II, King of Iraq; Lebanon; Lebanon, Second U.S. Intervention in; Nasser, Gamal Abdel; Pan-Arabism and Pan-Arabist Thought; Syria; United Arab Republic

References

El-Khazen, Farid. *The Breakdown of the State in Lebanon, 1967–1976.* Cambridge, MA: Harvard University Press, 2000.

Fisk, Robert. *Pity the Nation: Lebanon at War.* Oxford: Oxford University Press, 2001.

Harris, William. *The New Face of Lebanon: History's Revenge.* Princeton, NJ: Mark Wiener Publishers, 2005.

Mackey, Sandra. *Lebanon: A House Divided.* New York: Norton, 2006.

Lebanon, French Interventions in, 1860
See Mount Lebanon Civil War

Lebanon, Israeli Invasion of, 1978
See LITANI, Operation

Lebanon, Israeli Operations against (July 13–August 14, 2006)

Fighting between the Israeli military and Hezbollah fighters carried out over a 32-day period in southern Lebanon and northern Israel. Known to the Israeli military as Operation CHANGE OF DIRECTION, it began on July 13, 2006, and ended on August 14, 2006.

On July 12, 2006, Hezbollah fighters crossed the Israeli-Lebanese border into northern Israel and killed three Israel Defense Forces (IDF) soldiers and captured two others, evidently with the intent to use them for prisoner exchange purposes. This closely followed a similar operation mounted by Hamas in southern Israel in which one Israeli soldier was captured and two others were killed.

Holding the Lebanese government responsible for not enforcing security in the southern part of its country, Israel on July 13 began implementing an air, land, and sea blockade against Lebanon. The Beirut International Airport was also bombed. There were a number of Israeli objectives in CHANGE OF DIRECTION. The Israelis sought the return of the two kidnapped IDF soldiers but also wanted to remove the Hezbollah threat against Israeli territory by destroying its armaments and outposts and to establish long-term stability along the northern border. They also hoped to strengthen the anti-Syrian and anti-Hezbollah forces within Lebanon.

Israel's operation consisted chiefly of air and naval strikes on Lebanon's infrastructure, which destroyed a total of 42 bridges and damaged 38 roads. This effort also caused extensive damage to telecommunications, electricity distribution, ports, airports, and even private-sector facilities, including a milk factory and food warehouses. Roughly 70 percent of Lebanese civilians living in southern Lebanon fled north during the conflict. For its part, Hezbollah responded by launching an average of more than 100 Katyusha rockets per day into northern Israel, targeting such cities as Haifa and hitting hospitals, chemical factories, military outposts, and residential areas. Although the Israeli Air Force tried to strike at the launchers, they were virtually impossible to find, and many of the rockets were fired from residential areas, even near mosques.

Israeli air strikes against Lebanon and Hezbollah Katyusha rocket launches into Israel continued until July 21, 2006, when a new dimension was added to the conflict. Israel now began massing troops on the border and called up five battalions of army reservists (3,000 men) for a ground invasion. The ground offensive commenced on July 22, 2006, in the village of Marun al-Ras. IDF forces engaged Hezbollah fighters in Bint Jbayl, the largest Lebanese town near the border. One week later, Israel declared that it would occupy a strip inside southern Lebanon with ground troops. Meanwhile, four unarmed UN observers died when an errant Israeli air strike hit their observation post near the border.

U.S. secretary of state Condoleezza Rice visited the region during July 24–25 and again during July 29–31 in an effort to negotiate a cessation of hostilities. However, she opposed a cease-fire that would merely return the status quo. Meanwhile, discussions at the United Nations (UN) centered on how a negotiated solution to the conflict could prevent further violence and how an international—or Lebanese—force might control southern Lebanon and disarm Hezbollah. Talks were also undertaken in Rome among American, European, and Arab leaders in an attempt to reach a satisfactory end to the conflict but to no avail.

On August 5, 2006, Lebanon rejected a draft UN resolution, proposed by the United States and France, that called for a full cessation of hostilities between Israel and Hezbollah. Lebanon claimed that the resolution did not adequately address Lebanese concerns. Nevertheless, the Lebanese government affirmed two days later that it would send 15,000 troops to the south as soon as Israeli troops withdrew from the area. Lebanon's prime minister, Fuad Siniura, repeatedly called for a quick and decisive cease-fire and for the immediate withdrawal of Israeli troops from southern Lebanon. His demands were echoed by thousands of demonstrators in cities around the world.

The IDF's ground offensive into Lebanon and its fierce clashes with Hezbollah fighters continued until August 11, 2006, when the UN Security Council unanimously approved UN Resolution 1701 in an effort to end hostilities. The resolution, which was approved by both the Lebanese and Israeli governments, also called for the disarming of Hezbollah, Israel's withdrawal from Lebanon, and the deployment of the Lebanese Army and an enlarged UN Interim Force in Lebanon (UNIFIL) in southern Lebanon. Nevertheless, the 72 hours that preceded the effective date of the cease-fire on August 14, 2006, witnessed the fiercest fighting of the monthlong conflict.

The Lebanese Army began deploying into southern Lebanon on August 17, 2006. However, Israel's air and sea blockade was not lifted until September 8, 2006. On October 1, 2006, the Israeli Army reported that it had completed its withdrawal from southern Lebanon, although UNIFIL denied these assertions.

The conflict killed an estimated 1,187 Lebanese civilians as well as 44 Israeli civilians, severely damaged Lebanese infrastructure, displaced some 1 million Lebanese and 300,000 Israelis, and disrupted life across all of Lebanon and northern Israel. By September, 60 percent of the towns and villages in the south had no water or electricity. Even after the cease-fire, 256,000 Lebanese remained internally displaced, and much of southern Lebanon remained uninhabitable because of more than 350,000 unexploded cluster bombs in some 250 locations south of the Litani River. Moreover, the Lebanese coasts witnessed a tragic oil spill that resulted from Israel's bombing of fuel tanks. About 40 percent of the coastline was affected. Both Hezbollah and Israel were accused of violating international humanitarian law during the conflict.

Hezbollah launched an estimated 3,970 rockets into Israel during the conflict, and the Israeli Air Force carried out about 15,500 sorties, striking more than 7,000 targets in Lebanon. Between 250 and 600 Hezbollah fighters were killed. Thirteen Hezbollah fighters were captured by the IDF during the conflict. The IDF reported 119 Israeli soldiers killed, more than 400 wounded, and 2 taken prisoner. The Lebanese Army suffered casualties as well: 46 killed and more than 100 injured. Finally, 7 UN personnel were killed, and 12 others were injured.

The parties to the conflict were in fact tangled in asymmetric warfare. On one hand, Hezbollah's munitions included some 14,000 short- to medium-range missiles and rockets in calibers ranging from less than 100mm up to 302mm, some of the warheads of which were loaded with ball bearings to maximize their lethality. In addition, Hezbollah possessed four types of advanced ground-to-ground missiles: Fajr 4 and 5, Iran 130, and Shahin 335mm rockets with ranges of 54 to 90 miles. Hezbollah also possessed Iranian-built Zilzal 2 and 3 launchers, wireless detonators, Ra'ad 1 liquid fuel missiles, radar-guided ship-to-shore missiles, and a large number of optical devices.

Israel, on the other hand, possessed an impressive diversity of munitions, including precision-guided munitions, made in Israel or imported from the United States. It also completely dominated the skies and, in addition to fixed-wing jet aircraft, employed AH-64 Apache and AH-1 Cobra attack helicopters inside Lebanon. At least two unmanned aerial vehicles (UAVs) provided 24-hour coverage over Lebanon, with the Israel Aircraft Industries' Searcher 2 and the Elbit Systems Hermes 450 transmitting real-time targeting data directly into F-15 and F-16 cockpits.

In addition, the Israelis used American GBU-28 bunker-buster bombs on Hezbollah's Beirut headquarters. Multiple Launch Rocket System (MLRS) platforms were heavily used, and phosphorous munitions, which are restricted under the third protocol of the Geneva Conventions, were used as well. Although Israel's operation at first focused mainly on aerial and naval offensives, ground incursions became increasingly necessary. This was because most of Hezbollah's forces were able to make use of an extensive network of underground tunnels. Israeli troops faced fierce resistance and an unexpectedly strong performance by Hezbollah fighters, who multiplied ambushes and surprise attacks. Indeed, Hezbollah fielded an impressively innovative military force well tailored to meet a specific foe on particular terrain. Israeli intelligence, on the other hand, proved inadequate in this operation. For example, during the war Israeli forces launched a commando raid on Baalbek, capturing the Imam Khomeini Hospital where they supposedly found Iranians and a Syrian. No Iranians had been there for years, but a number of civilians were kidnapped and not returned. One may have been the central target of this raid, a grocer named Hasan Dib Nasrallah, unfortunately not the leader of Hezbollah. In fact, none of the objectives that the IDF had set for Operation CHANGE OF DIRECTION were realized. In a significant sense, the conflict was the result of both sides having misjudged the other. Hezbollah has stated that it would not have kidnapped IDF soldiers had it known the severity of Israel's response. Israel meanwhile was taken aback by the effectiveness of the Hezbollah defenses. There was sufficient anger in Israel over the results of the operation that the government was forced to appoint an investigating committee. In January 2007 IDF chief of staff Dan Halutz resigned in the face of increasing criticism of the IDF's performance in the war.

RANA KOBEISSI

See also
Hezbollah; Israel; Lebanon

References
Allen, Lori, Suheir Abu Oksa Daoud, Nubar Hovsepian, Shira Robinson, Rasha Salti, Samer Shehata, Joshua Stacher, and Michelle Woodward. "Life under Siege." In *Middle East Report No. 240*. Washington, DC, Fall 2006.

International Crisis Group. "Israel/Hizbullah/Lebanon: Avoiding Renewed Conflict." In *The International Crisis Group Middle East Report No. 59*. Brussels, Belgium, November 2006.

Schiff, Ze'ev. "The Fallout From Lebanon." *Foreign Affairs Magazine* (November–December 2006): 13–41.

USG Humanitarian Situation Reports #30–#32. August 29–31, 2006.

Lebanon, Israeli Security Zone in

A strip of territory in southern Lebanon that by 2000 encompassed an area of 600 square miles. Israel first created a security zone after its 1978 invasion of Lebanon in Operation GRAPES OF WRATH. The Israelis began a collaboration with Major Saad Haddad, who had broken away from the Lebanese Army in 1976 and had established the Free Lebanon Army. The Israelis intended for Haddad's army to aid them in curtailing Palestinian and Lebanese anti-Israeli attacks in the south. When Haddad announced control over the security zone, he was dismissed from the Lebanese Army, and his own force became the South Lebanon Army (SLA). The SLA fought against the Palestinian Resistance Movement until the much broader Israeli invasion of Lebanon in 1982 in Operation PEACE FOR GALILEE. The devastation of southern Lebanon in the 1982 invasion was accompanied by massive repression and arrests of civilians as well as fighters. After the Israelis retreated to the zone in 1985, the SLA assisted the Israelis and kidnapped and held numerous prisoners without charge for years in the infamous Khiam detention center or transferred them to Israel.

The area became for many years the site of reciprocal rocket and artillery attacks between Hezbollah guerrillas and Israeli forces. Opposition to the maintenance of this zone grew in Israel, however. Six weeks ahead of a planned withdrawal, Israel officially abandoned the zone over a two-day period in May 2000, paving the way for Hezbollah fighters and former residents to reclaim the land, and freed the Khiam prisoners. Because of the SLA's brutal practices and collaboration with Israel, many SLA members and their families fled to Israel. A number subsequently returned to Lebanon. Some 2,700 faced legal charges. Most of those tried received light sentences in an effort to promote reconciliation.

SPENCER C. TUCKER AND SHERIFA ZUHUR

See also
Hezbollah; Israel; Lebanon; Lebanon Civil War; Palestine Liberation Organization

References
Amnesty International. *Israel's Forgotten Hostages and Lebanese Detainees in Israel and the Khiam Detention Centre*. Pamphlet. July 1997.

Ball, George W. *Error and Betrayal in Lebanon: An Analysis of Israel's Invasion of Lebanon and the Implications for U.S.-Israeli Relations*. Washington, DC: Foundation for Middle East Peace, 1984.

Hamizrachi, Beate. *The Emergence of the South Lebanon Security Belt: Major Saad Haddad and the Ties with Israel*. New York: Praeger, 1988.

O'Ballance, Edgar. *Civil War in Lebanon, 1975–1992*. London: Palgrave Macmillan, 1998.

Lebanon, Second U.S. Intervention in (August 24, 1982–February 26, 1984)

The second U.S. military intervention in Lebanon began on August 20, 1982, and was prompted by the Israeli invasion of Lebanon (the Lebanese-Israeli War) on June 6, 1982, during the Lebanese Civil War (1975–1990). In response to continuing raids and attacks on Israeli soil by Palestinian guerrillas—principally those associated with Yasser Arafat's Palestine Liberation Organization (PLO)—from bases in southern Lebanon, the government of Menachem Begin ordered the Israel Defense Forces (IDF) to invade its northern neighbor. Although publicly proclaiming that the goal was only to destroy Palestinian forces in southern Lebanon, Begin and Defense Minister Ariel Sharon expanded the objectives to include eviction of the PLO from all of Lebanon. As a result, Israeli forces then besieged and blockaded the Lebanese capital of Beirut. Despite heavy Israeli bombardment for 70 days, PLO forces refused to surrender. Israel, however, demurred from invading Beirut proper, fearing heavy casualties from a guerrilla war in the city's rubble-strewn streets and alleys.

Meanwhile, mounting civilian casualties in Lebanon and growing international opposition to the Israeli invasion compelled the United States to intervene in Lebanon as part of the international peacekeeping force known as the Multinational Force (MNF) in Lebanon. With no end in sight to the siege of Beirut, Israel, the PLO, and Lebanon's embattled government all looked to the United States for a settlement. During the intervention, 1,200 U.S. marines from the 1st Battalion of the 8th Marine Regiment and the 2nd Marine Division were to supervise, along with British, French, and Italian troops of the MNF, the evacuation from Lebanon of the PLO. They were also charged with supervising the withdrawal of Israeli and Syrian forces from Beirut and its environs and ensuring the safety of Palestinian civilians. The U.S. marines began landing on August 24, 1982, and were based at Beirut International Airport.

The basic terms of the international intervention and PLO evacuation had been negotiated by American envoy Philip Habib. The Habib Agreement stipulated that Israel would end its siege of Beirut and not invade the city or harm Palestinian civilians if PLO fighters withdrew from Beirut and left the country, which they did under the protection of the Multinational Force. By September 1, 1982, U.S. troops had been withdrawn, and the conditions of the Habib Agreement had been fulfilled.

However, the September 14, 1982, assassination of newly selected Lebanese president Bashir Gemayel, leader of the dominant Christian Maronite faction and an Israeli ally, prompted Israel to invade Muslim-dominated West Beirut that month. At the same time, on September 16–18, Israeli forces had allowed Gemayel's Phalange militia to enter two Palestinian refugee camps, Sabra and Shatila, leading to the massacre of as many as 3,500 Palestinians. Many Americans, including President Ronald Reagan, regretted that the U.S. troops had been withdrawn so quickly and called for another multinational force to protect civilians and somehow bring a semblance of peace and stability to Lebanon by separating the warring groups in Lebanon's seven-year-long civil war.

The September massacres at Sabra and Shatila prompted the redeployment of 1,200 U.S. marines to Lebanon later that month to support and stabilize the weak and embattled Lebanese government. The Reagan administration feared that allowing Lebanon's pro-Western government to collapse would turn the entire country into a hostile Arab state. This, they feared, might allow Syria, aided at the time by the Soviet Union, to control all of Lebanon. Alternatively, Lebanon might have become a client state of Iran's radical Shiite government, which was arming and supporting Lebanese Shiite groups at the time. The marines served in an MNF along with France and Italy, arriving in Beirut on September 29 and again setting up headquarters at Beirut airport.

Unfortunately, the U.S. intervention in the civil war and support for Lebanon's government was not welcomed by most of Lebanon's warring factions and, in the wake of Israel's invasion of Lebanon and in light of America's historic ties with Israel, stoked a strong climate of anti-Americanism in the country. Indeed, most Lebanese distrusted the motives behind the American intervention, believing that the Reagan administration had both given its approval of and supported Israel's invasion of Lebanon in June 1982 and its subsequent occupation of Beirut. With such sentiments running high, the United States ran the risk of being dragged into Lebanon's civil war and into conflict with rival neighboring governments, namely Israel and Syria but also Iran. Nevertheless, during the winter of 1982–1983 the MNF was largely successful in limiting the number of attacks by Lebanon's rival groups and the Israeli military.

Not surprisingly, however, with America's military presence in Beirut viewed as not only a tempting target but also an intolerable obstacle to the objectives of the warring groups, the MNF and U.S. marines gradually came under increasing attack from both Druze and other various Muslim militias in the spring of 1983. To make matters worse, because they were garrisoned at Beirut International Airport, the marines were dangerously exposed to attack, occupying flat terrain with minimal protection behind sand bags, surrounded by heavily armed groups occupying both nearby tall buildings and the hills and mountains ringing the airport and the city. The U.S. marines also held a strategic target long coveted by the warring factions.

In April 1983 the American embassy in Beirut was bombed, resulting in the deaths of 63 people. The attack was an ominous sign for U.S. forces in Lebanon. In August after the Israelis had withdrawn from Beirut, U.S. forces engaged in fighting with both Druze and Shiite militias.

In September 1983 the United States interceded on behalf of Lebanese president Amin Gemayel's army, which was battling Druze militias in the village of Souq al-Gharb in the mountains above Beirut. This took the form of naval gunfire from ships of the U.S. Sixth Fleet off the Lebanese coast. This was followed up by French aerial bombardments. In so doing, the United States and France had been drawn into the Lebanese Civil War on the side of the Christian-led government, while Iran supported Lebanese Shiite groups, including the terrorist group Hezbollah, fighting both the Israeli occupation and the Lebanese government. By now, most Lebanese Muslims were outraged by Western intervention in the conflict.

In support of President Gemayel's troops battling Druze fighters, U.S. naval gunfire shelled villages inhabited not only by the Druzes but also by Shiites and some Sunnis, causing significant civilian casualties. To many Lebanese Muslims as well as Muslims throughout the Middle East, America's intervention on behalf of a government they opposed ended any pretense of American neutrality, and in consequence, attacks against the U.S. marines, along with the French and Italian forces, increased. Opposition to the negotiations and to the U.S. support for the Gemayel regime led to a series of terrorist attacks, including the bombing on April 18, 1983, of the U.S. embassy in west Beirut (63 dead) and of the U.S. embassy annex in east Beirut on September 20, 1984 (8 killed).

Then just before 6:30 a.m. on October 23, 1983, a truck with 2 men drove through a Lebanese checkpoint on the Beirut Airport road without stopping. The vehicle then turned into the airport parking lot, increased speed, and proceeded toward the headquarters building. Orders prohibited the marines from having small arms loaded, but reports indicate that this probably would not have made much difference. A sentry did get off some shots with a pistol but without effect. Crashing through several barriers and other obstacles, the truck penetrated the first floor of the building housing the U.S. service personnel, when the suicide bombers detonated the tons of explosives in the truck. The blast claimed the lives of 305 victims (220 U.S. marines, 18 sailors, and 3 soldiers; 58 French paratroopers and 6 civilians were also killed), along with the 2 suicide bombers. Seventy-five others in the building suffered nonfatal injuries. Islamic Jihad (allegedly also known as Hezbollah, or the Party of God), a Shiite terrorist group armed and supported by Iran, claimed responsibility.

On December 3, 1983, two U.S. Navy F-14s flying over Lebanon were fired on by Syrian antiaircraft artillery, and the next day aircraft from the U.S. Navy carriers *Kennedy* and *Independence* were launched against Syrian targets; two were shot down, and one U.S. airman was taken prisoner by the Syrians.

Given this situation and resurgent fighting in Beirut, President Reagan on February 7, 1984, ordered the marines to "redeploy to their ships," which was completed on February 26, 1984.

On May 30, 2003, a U.S. federal judge ruled that the suicide truck bombing of the marine barracks in Beirut had indeed been carried out by Hezbollah with the approval and funding of Iran's government, giving the survivors and families of those killed in the attack the right to sue Iran for damages. Iran, however, continues to deny any responsibility for the bombing and has dismissed the ruling as nonsense.

STEFAN BROOKS AND SPENCER C. TUCKER

See also
Arafat, Yasser; Hezbollah; Lebanon; Lebanon Civil War; Lebanon-Israeli War; Palestine Liberation Organization; Palestinian Islamic Jihad

References
El-Khazen, Farid. *The Breakdown of the State in Lebanon, 1967–1976.* Cambridge, MA: Harvard University Press, 2000.

Fisk, Robert. *Pity the Nation: Lebanon at War.* Oxford: Oxford University Press, 2001.

Harris, William. *The New Face of Lebanon: History's Revenge.* Princeton, NJ: Mark Wiener Publishers, 2005.

Mackey, Sandra. *Lebanon: A House Divided.* New York: Norton, 2006.

Olson, Steven P. *The Attack on U.S. Marines in Lebanon on October 23, 1983.* New York: Rosen, 2003.

Lebanon Civil War (April 13, 1975– August 1990)

The Lebanese Civil War, which lasted from 1975 to 1990, had its origin in the conflicts and political compromises of Lebanon's colonial period. It was exacerbated by the nation's changing demographics, Christian and Muslim interreligious strife, and Lebanon's proximity to both Syria and Israel. Indeed, the Lebanese Civil War was part and parcel of the wider Arab-Israeli conflict and was emblematic of the inherent volatility and instability of the Middle East after World War II.

Lebanon in its present-day borders dates to 1920, when the French administered a mandate over the region. The French added several districts to the historic *mustashafiyya*, Mount Lebanon, a separate administrative district that had called for Western protection in the 19th century, eventually establishing Greater Lebanon. This meant the inclusion of areas whose populations had always been administered from Syria and did not necessarily support separation from that country. These heavily Sunni and Shia Muslim areas diluted the previous Maronite Christian and Druze majority of Mount Lebanon. When Lebanon won its independence from France in 1943, an unwritten power-sharing agreement was forged among the three major ethnic and religious groups. These included Maronite Christians (then in the majority), Sunni Muslims, and Shiite Muslims.

Lebanon's Muslim groups were discontented with the 1943 National Pact, which established a dominant political role for the Christians, especially the Maronites, in the central government. Druzes, Muslims, and leftists joined forces as the National Movement in 1969. The movement called for the taking of a new census, as none had been conducted since 1932, and the subsequent drafting of a new governmental structure that would reflect the census results.

Muslim and Maronite leaders were unable to reconcile their conflicts of interest and instead formed militias, undermining the authority of the central government. The government's ability to maintain order was also handicapped by

Young Christian women, all members of the Phalangist party, during street fighting in Beirut, Lebanon, on November 2, 1975. (Bettmann/Getty Images)

the nature of the Lebanese Army. It was composed of a fixed ratio of religions, and as members defected to militias of their own ethnicity, the army would eventually prove unable to check the power of the militias, the Palestine Liberation Organization (PLO), or other splinter groups.

Maronite militias armed by West Germany and Belgium drew supporters from the larger and poorer Christian population in the north. The most powerful of these was al-Kata'ib, also known as the Phalange, led by Bashir Jumayyil (Gemayel). Others included the Lebanese Forces, led by Samir Jaja (Geagea), and the Guardians of the Cedars.

Shiite militias, such as the Amal militia, fought the Maronites and later fought certain Palestinian groups and occasionally even other Shiite organizations. Some Sunni factions received support from Libya and Iraq. The Soviet Union encouraged Arab socialist movements that spawned leftist Palestinian organizations, such as the Popular Front for the Liberation of Palestine (PLFP) and the Democratic Front for the Liberation of Palestine. Prior to the civil war, the rise of Baathism in Syria and Iraq was paralleled by a surge of Lebanese Baathists. Within the civil war, these were also reflected in groups such as al-Saiqa, a Syrian-aligned and largely anti-Fatah Palestinian fighting force, and the Arab Liberation Front, an Iraqi-aligned Baathist movement.

In 1970 Jordan's King Hussein expelled the PLO from the country after the events of Black September. PLO chairman Yasser Arafat thus regrouped his organization in the Palestinian refugee areas of Beirut and southern Lebanon, where other refugees had survived since 1948. The National Movement attracted support from the PLO Rejection Front faction, prominently including the PFLP, although Arafat and Fatah initially sought to remain neutral in the inter-Lebanese conflict. The National Movement supported the Palestinian resistance movement's struggle for national liberation and activities against Israel, and although Palestinians could not vote in Lebanon and, being outside of the political system, had no voice in its reformation, they nonetheless lent moral support to the movement's desire for political reformation. By the early 1970s, the Palestinian Resistance groups, although disunited, were a large fighting force. Maronites viewed the Resistance and the PLO as disruptive and a destabilizing ally of the Muslim factions.

On the morning of April 13, 1975, unidentified gunmen in a speeding car fired on a church in the Christian East Beirut suburb of Ayn ar Rummanah, killing 4 people, including 2 Maronite-Phalangists. Later that day, Phalangists led by Bashir Jumayyil killed 27 Palestinians returning from a political rally on a bus in Ayn ar Rummanah. Four Christians were killed in East Beirut in December 1975, and in growing reprisals Phalangists and Muslim militias subsequently massacred at least 600 Muslims and Christians at checkpoints, igniting the 1975–1976 stage of the civil war.

The fighting eventually spread to most parts of the country, precipitating President Suleiman Franjieh's call for support from Syrian troops in June 1976, to which Syria responded by ending its prior affiliation with the Rejection Front and supporting the Maronites. This technically put Syria in the Israeli camp, as Israel had already begun to supply the Maronite forces with arms, tanks, and military advisers in May 1976. Meanwhile, Arafat's Fatah joined the war on the side of the National Movement.

Syrian troops subsequently entered Lebanon, occupying Tripoli and the Bekaa Valley, and imposed a cease-fire that ultimately failed to stop the conflict. After the arrival of Syrian troops, Christian forces massacred some 2,000 Palestinians in the Tal al-Za'atar camp in East Beirut. Another massacre by Christian forces saw some 1,000 people killed at Muslim Qarantina.

Some reports charge al-Saiqa, the Syrian-backed Palestinian force, or a combination of al-Saiqa, Fatah, and the Palestine Liberation Army along with some Muslim forces with an attack on the Christian city of Damur, a stronghold of Camille Chamoun and his followers. When the city fell on January 20, the remaining inhabitants were subject to rape, mutilation, and brutal assassinations. The civilian dead numbered at least 300, with one estimate being as high as 582. Graves were desecrated, and a church was used as a garage. Also, former camp dwellers from Tal Za'tar were resettled in Damur and then evicted again after 1982. As a result of the massacre, other Christians came to see the Palestinian presence as a threat to their survival.

The nation was now informally divided, with southern Lebanon and the western half of Beirut becoming bases for the PLO and other Muslim militias and with the Christians in control of East Beirut and the Christian section of Mount Lebanon. The dividing thoroughfare in Beirut between its primarily western Muslim neighborhoods and eastern Christian neighborhoods was known as the Green Line.

In October 1976 an Arab League summit in Riyadh, Saudi Arabia, gave Syria a mandate to garrison 40,000 troops in Lebanon as the bulk of an Arab deterrent force charged with disentangling the combatants and restoring calm. However, in no part of the country had the war actually ended, nor was there a political solution offered by the government.

In the south, PLO combatants returned from central Lebanon under the terms of the Riyadh Accords. Then on March 11, 1978, 8 Fatah militants landed on a beach in northern Israel and proceeded to take control of a passenger bus and head toward Tel Aviv. In the ensuing confrontation with Israeli forces, 34 Israelis and 6 of the militants died. In retaliation, Israel invaded Lebanon four days later in Operation LITANI, in which the Israel Defense Forces (IDF) occupied most of the area south of the Litani River, resulting in approximately 2,000 deaths and the evacuation of at least 100,000 Lebanese. The United Nations (UN) Security Council passed Resolution 425, calling for an immediate Israeli withdrawal, and also created the UN Interim Force in Lebanon, charged with maintaining peace. Under international pressure to do so, Israeli forces withdrew later in 1978.

However, Israel retained de facto control of the border region by turning over positions inside Lebanon to the group later known as the South Lebanon Army (SLA), led by Major Saad Haddad. Israel meanwhile had been supplying Haddad's forces. The SLA occupied Shia villages in the south, informally setting up a 12-mile-wide security zone that protected Israeli territory from cross-border attacks. Violent exchanges quickly resumed among the PLO, Israel, and the SLA, with the PLO attacking SLA positions and firing rockets into northern Israel. Israel conducted air raids against PLO positions, and the SLA continued its efforts to consolidate its power in the border region.

Syria meanwhile clashed with the Phalange. Phalange leader Jumayyil's increasingly aggressive actions (such as his April 1981 attempt to capture the strategic city of Zahla in central Lebanon) were designed to thwart the Syrian goal of brushing him aside and installing Franjieh as president. Consequently, the de facto alliance between Israel and Jumayyil strengthened considerably. In fighting in Zahla in April 1981, for example, Jumayyil called for Israeli assistance, and Prime Minister Menachem Begin responded by sending Israeli fighter jets to the scene. These shot down two Syrian helicopters. This led Syrian president Hafez al-Assad to order surface-to-air missiles to the hilly perimeter of Zahla.

In July 1981 Israeli forces attacked Palestinian positions, provoking retaliatory shelling by the PLO. The Israeli response to this shelling culminated in the aerial bombardment of a West Beirut suburb where Fatah's headquarters were located, killing 200 people and wounding another 600, most of them civilians. The PLO rejoinder was a huge rocket attack on towns and villages in northern Israel, leaving 6 civilians dead and 59 wounded. These violent exchanges prompted diplomatic intervention by the United States. On July 24, 1981, U.S. special Middle East envoy Philip Habib brokered a cease-fire agreement with the PLO and Israel. The two sides now agreed to cease hostilities in Lebanon proper and along the Israeli border with Lebanon. The cease-fire was short-lived.

On June 3, 1982, the Abu Nidal organization attempted to assassinate Israeli ambassador Shlomo Argov in London. Although badly wounded, Argov survived. Israel retaliated with an aerial attack on PLO and PFLP targets in West Beirut that led to more than 100 casualties, a clear violation of the cease-fire. The PLO responded by launching a counterattack from Lebanon with rockets and artillery.

Then on June 6, 1982, Israeli forces began Operation PEACE FOR GALILEE, an invasion of southern Lebanon to destroy PLO bases there. The Israeli plan was subsequently modified to move farther into Lebanon, and by June 15 Israeli units were entrenched outside Beirut. Israel laid siege to Beirut, which contained some 15,000 armed members of the PLO. During a period of several weeks, the PLO and the IDF exchanged artillery fire. On a number of occasions the Palestinians directed their fire into Christian East Beirut, causing an estimated 6,700 deaths of which 80 percent were civilians. On August 12, 1982, Habib again negotiated a truce that called for the withdrawal of both Israeli and PLO elements. Nearly 15,000 Palestinian militants had been evacuated to other countries by September 1. Within six months, Israel withdrew from most of Lebanon but maintained the security zone along the Israeli-Lebanese border.

Bashir Jumayyil was elected Lebanon's president on August 23, 1982, with acknowledged Israeli backing. But on September 14, 1982, he was assassinated. The next day, Israeli troops crossed into West Beirut to secure Muslim militia strongholds and stood back as Lebanese Christian militias massacred as many as 2,000 Palestinian civilians in the Sabra and Shatila refugee camps. This event was protested throughout the Arab world, especially because of the Israeli presence in Beirut.

With U.S. backing, the Lebanese parliament chose Amin Jumayyil to succeed his brother as president and focused anew on securing the withdrawal of Israeli and Syrian forces. On May 17, 1983, Lebanon, Israel, and the United States signed an agreement on Israeli withdrawal that was conditioned on the departure of Syrian troops. Syria opposed the agreement and declined to discuss the withdrawal of its troops. In August 1983, Israel withdrew from the Shuf (a district of Mount Lebanon to the southeast of Beirut), thus removing the buffer between the Druzes and the Christian militias and triggering another round of brutal fighting.

By September the Druzes had gained control over most of the Shuf, and Israeli forces had pulled out from all but the southern security zone. The collapse of the Lebanese Army in February 1984 following the defection of many Muslim and Druze units to militias was a major blow to the government. On March 5, 1984, the Lebanese government canceled the May 17 agreement.

This period of chaos had witnessed the beginning of retaliatory attacks launched against U.S. and Western interests, such as the April 18, 1983, suicide attack at the U.S. embassy in West Beirut that left 63 dead. Then on October 23, 1983, a bombing in the Beirut barracks that hit the headquarters of U.S. military personnel left 241 U.S. marines dead. A total of 58 French servicemen also died in the attack. Months later, American University of Beirut president Malcolm Kerr was murdered inside the university on January 18, 1984. After U.S. forces withdrew in February 1984, anti-Western terrorism as well as that directed against Lebanese enemies continued, including a second bombing of the U.S. embassy annex in East Beirut on September 20, 1984, that left 9 Americans dead, including 2 U.S. servicemen.

Between 1985 and 1989, factional conflict worsened as various efforts at national reconciliation failed. The economy collapsed, and the militias that had participated in crime, car theft, hijackings, and kidnappings for ransom expanded their activities. The larger militias were also involved in profiteering, land investment, and sales, and they rather than the government also collected tariffs and customs.

Heavy fighting took place in the War of the Camps in 1985 and 1986 as the Shia Muslim Amal militia sought to rout the Palestinians from Lebanese strongholds. Many thousands of Palestinians died in the war. Sabra, Shatila, and Burj al-Barajnah were reduced to ashes. Combat returned to Beirut in 1987, with Palestinians, leftists, and Druze fighters allied against Amal, eventually drawing further Syrian intervention. Violent confrontation flared up again in Beirut in 1988 between Amal and Hezbollah.

Meanwhile, Lebanese prime minister Rashid Karameh, head of a government of national unity set up after the failed peace efforts of 1984, was assassinated on June 1, 1987. President Jumayyil's term of office expired in September 1988. Before stepping down, he appointed another Maronite

Christian, Lebanese Armed Forces commanding general Michel Aoun, as acting prime minister, contravening the National Pact. Muslim groups rejected the violation of the National Pact and pledged support to Selim al-Hoss, a Sunni who had succeeded Karameh. Lebanon was thus divided between a Christian government in East Beirut and a Muslim government in West Beirut with two presidents.

In February 1989 Aoun attacked the rival Lebanese Forces militia. By March he turned his attention to other militias, launching what he termed a "War of Liberation" against the Syrians and their allied Lebanese militias. In the months that followed, Aoun rejected both the Taif Agreement that ultimately ended the civil war and the election of another Christian leader as president. A Lebanese-Syrian military operation in October 1990 forced him to take cover in the French embassy in Beirut. He later went into exile in Paris.

The Taif Agreement of 1989 marked the beginning of the end of the fighting. In January 1989 a committee appointed by the Arab League, chaired by a representative from Kuwait and including Saudi Arabia, Algeria, and Morocco, had begun to formulate solutions to the conflict. This led to a meeting of Lebanese parliamentarians in Taif, Saudi Arabia. There in October they agreed to the national reconciliation accord. Returning to Lebanon, they ratified the agreement on November 4 and elected René Moawad as president the following day.

Moawad was assassinated 18 days later on November 22 in a car bombing in Beirut as his motorcade returned from Lebanese Independence Day ceremonies. He was succeeded by Elias Hrawi, who remained in office until 1998. In August 1990 the Lebanese parliament and the new president agreed on constitutional amendments. The National Assembly expanded to 108 seats and was divided equally between Christians and Muslims. Because the Muslim sects together now outnumbered the Christians, this decision did not represent a one-vote–one-man solution but was nonetheless an improvement on the previous situation. In March 1991 the parliament passed an amnesty law that pardoned all political crimes prior to its enactment. In May 1991 the militias were dissolved, and the Lebanese Armed Forces began to slowly rebuild as Lebanon's only major nonsectarian institution.

MOSHE TERDIMAN

See also
Arab League; Arafat, Yasser; Assad, Hafez al-; Begin, Menachem; Black September; Chamoun, Camille; Hezbollah; Hrawi, Elias; Hussein ibn Talal, King of Jordan; Israel; Lebanon; Lebanon-Israeli War; LITANI, Operation; Palestine Liberation Organization; Popular Front for the Liberation of Palestine; Shia Islam; Suicide Bombings; Sunni Islam; Syria

References
Barakat, Halim, ed. *Toward a Viable Lebanon.* London: Croom Helm, 1988.
Collings, Deirdre. *Peace for Lebanon? From War to Reconstruction.* Boulder, CO: Lynne Rienner, 1994.
El-Khazen, Farid. *The Breakdown of the State in Lebanon, 1967–1976.* Cambridge, MA: Harvard University Press, 2000.
Fisk, Robert. *Pity the Nation: Lebanon at War.* Oxford: Oxford University Press, 2001.
Hanf, Theodor. *Coexistence in Wartime Lebanon: Decline of a State and Rise of a Nation.* London: Centre for Lebanese Studies and Tauris, 1993.
Petran, Tabitha. *The Struggle over Lebanon.* New York: Monthly Review Press, 1987.
Picard, Elizabeth. "The Political Economy of Civil War in Lebanon." In *War, Institutions, and Social Change in the Middle East,* ed. Steven Heydemann, 292–322. Berkeley: University of California Press, 2000.
Rabinovich, Itamar. *The War for Lebanon, 1970–1985.* Rev. ed. Ithaca, NY: Cornell University Press, 1986.
Salibi, Kamal S. *Lebanon and the Middle Eastern Question.* Oxford, UK: Center for Lebanese Studies, 1988.

Lebanon-Israeli War (June 6–September 1982)

The Lebanon-Israeli War, also known as the Israeli Invasion of Lebanon and Operation PEACE FOR GALILEE, began on June 6, 1982, when Israeli defense minister Ariel Sharon, acting in full agreement with instructions from Prime Minister Menachem Begin, ordered Israel Defense Forces (IDF) troops into southern Lebanon to destroy the Palestine Liberation Organization (PLO) there.

In 1977 Begin had become the first Israeli prime minister from the right-wing Likud Party. He sought to maintain Israeli hold over the West Bank and Gaza but also had a deep commitment to Eretz Israel, the ancestral homeland of the Jews that embraced territory beyond Israel's borders into Lebanon and across the Jordan River.

Sharon, also a prominent member of Likud, shared Begin's ideological commitment to Eretz Israel. Indeed, Sharon played an important role in expanding Jewish settlements in the West Bank and Gaza. He took a hard-line approach toward the Palestinians, endeavoring to undermine PLO influence in the West Bank and Gaza, and was also influential in the formation of Israeli foreign policy.

In June 1978 under heavy U.S. pressure, Begin withdrew Israeli forces that had been sent into southern Lebanon in the Litani River operation. The United Nations Interim Force in Lebanon (UNIFIL) then took over in southern

Lebanon. It was charged with confirming the Israeli withdrawal, restoring peace and security, and helping the Lebanese government reestablish its authority in the area. The Israeli failure to remove PLO bases in southern Lebanon was a major embarrassment for the Begin government.

UNIFIL, however, proved incapable of preventing PLO forces from operating in southern Lebanon and striking Israel, which led to Israeli reprisals. Attacks back and forth across the Lebanese-Israeli border killed civilians on both sides as well as some UNIFIL troops. Israel meanwhile provided weapons to the force later known as the South Lebanon Army, a pro-Israeli Christian militia in southern Lebanon led by Major Saad Haddad, and the force used them against the PLO and local villagers.

In July 1981 U.S. president Ronald Reagan sent Lebanese-American diplomat Philip Habib to the area in an effort to broker a truce during the Lebanese Civil War. On July 24 Habib announced agreement on a cease-fire, but it was in name only. The PLO repeatedly violated the agreement, and major cross-border strikes resumed in April 1982 following the death of an Israeli officer from a land mine. While Israel conducted both air strikes and commando raids across the border, it was unable to prevent a growing number of PLO personnel from locating there. Their numbers increased to perhaps 6,000 men in a number of encampments, as PLO rocket and mortar attacks regularly forced thousands of Israeli civilians to flee their homes and fields in northern Galilee and seek protection in bomb shelters.

On June 3, 1982, three members of a Palestinian terrorist organization connected to Abu Nidal attempted to assassinate in London Israeli ambassador to Britain Shlomo Argov. Although Argov survived the attack, he remained paralyzed until his death in 2003. Abu Nidal's organization had been linked to Yasser Arafat's Fatah faction within the PLO in the past, and the Israelis used this as the excuse to bomb Palestinian targets in West Beirut and other targets in southern Lebanon during June 4–5, 1982. The PLO responded by attacking Israeli settlements in Galilee with rockets and mortars. It was this PLO shelling of the settlements rather than the attempted assassination of Argov that provoked the Israeli decision to invade Lebanon.

Operation PEACE FOR GALILEE began on June 6, 1982. It took its name from the Israeli intention to protect its vulnerable northern region of Israel from the PLO rocket and mortar attacks launched from southern Lebanon. Ultimately, Israel committed to the operation some 76,000 men, 800 tanks, 1,500 armored personnel carriers (APCs), and 364 aircraft. Syria committed perhaps 22,000 men, 352 tanks, 300 APCs, and 96 aircraft, while the PLO had about 15,000 men, 300 tanks, and 150 APCs.

The Israeli operation had three principal objectives. First, Israeli forces sought to destroy the PLO in southern Lebanon. Second, Israel wanted to evict the Syrian Army from Lebanon and bring about the removal of its missiles from the Bekaa Valley. Although Sharon perceived Syrian forces in Lebanon as a major security threat to Israel, he maintained that the IDF would not attack them unless it was first fired upon. Third, Israel hoped to influence Lebanese politics. Israel sought to ally itself with the Maronite Christians, led by Bashir Jumayyil (Gemayel), the leader of the Phalange (al-Kata'ib) and head of the unified command of the Lebanese Forces.

While the Phalange was mainly a political association, the Lebanese Forces was an umbrella military organization composed of several Christian militias. Jumayyil had carried out a series of brutal operations to destroy the autonomy of the other Christian militias and had incorporated them into his Lebanese Forces. He was opposed to relinquishing the power held by the Maronites in traditionally Christian-dominated Lebanon to the Sunni and Shia Muslims of Lebanon. Many in the Phalange maintained that their heritage was Phoenician and not Arab, and they sought to maintain their historic linkages with France and the West. To this end, Jumayyil maintained a close relationship with Israel. As with the Israelis, he harbored intense opposition to a Syrian presence in Lebanon.

Palestinian militias were not only entrenched in the southern part of the country but were also well established in West Beirut. Understandably, the Israeli cabinet was loath to place its troops into an urban combat situation that was bound to bring heavy civilian casualties and incur opposition from Washington and Western Europe. Begin and Sharon informed the cabinet that the goal was merely to break up PLO bases in southern Lebanon and push back PLO and Syrian forces some 25 miles, beyond rocket range of Galilee.

Once the operation began, however, Sharon quickly changed the original plan by expanding the mission to incorporate Beirut, which was well beyond the 25-mile mark. Many in the cabinet now believed that Begin and Sharon had deliberately misled them. The IDF advanced to the outskirts of Beirut within days. Tyre and Sidon, two cities within the 25-mile limit, were both heavily damaged in the Israeli advance. The entire population was rounded up, and most of the men were taken into custody. Rather than standing their ground and being overwhelmed by the better-equipped Israelis, the Palestinian fighters and PLO leadership withdrew back on West Beirut. Sharon now argued in favor of a broader operation that would force the PLO from Beirut, and for some 10 weeks Israeli guns shelled West Beirut, killing both PLO forces and civilians.

Fighting also occurred with Syrian forces in the Bekaa Valley. Unable to meet Israel on equal footing and bereft of allies, Syria did not engage in an all-out effort. Rather, much of the battle was waged in the air. By June 10, the Israeli Air Force had neutralized Syrian surface-to-air missiles and had shot down dozens of Syrian jets. (Some sources say that the ultimate toll was as many as 80 Syrian aircraft.) The Israelis employed AH-1 Cobra helicopter gunships to attack and destroy dozens of Syrian armored vehicles, including Soviet-built T-72 tanks. The Israelis also trapped Syrian forces in the Bekaa Valley. Israel was on the verge of severing the Beirut-Damascus highway on June 11 when Moscow and Washington brokered a cease-fire.

In Beirut, meanwhile, Sharon hoped to join up with Jumayyil's Lebanese Forces. Sharon hoped that the Lebanese Forces might bear the brunt of the fighting in West Beirut, but Jumayyil was reluctant to do this, fearing that such a move would harm his chances to become the president of Lebanon.

Begin's cabinet was unwilling to approve an Israeli assault on West Beirut because of the probability of high casualties. Meanwhile, the United States had been conveying ambiguous signals regarding its position in the conflict. This only encouraged Arafat to entrench himself and the PLO in West Beirut.

Sharon disregarded cabinet opposition and placed the western (predominantly Muslim) part of the city under a siege from air, land, and sea. He hoped that this might convince the citizens to turn against the PLO. The bombing and shelling resulted in mostly civilian casualties, however, provoking denunciations of Israel in the international press. The PLO believed that it could hold out longer under siege than the Israelis could under international pressure, leading Israel to intensify its attack on Beirut in early August. Believing that there was an impending full-scale assault, the PLO then consented to a UN-brokered arrangement whereby American, French, and Italian peacekeeping forces, known as the Multinational Force in Lebanon, would escort the PLO fighters out of Lebanon by the end of the month. (The PLO relocated to Tunis.) Habib assured the PLO that the many refugees in camps in Lebanon would not be harmed.

On August 23, 1982, Jumayyil was elected president of Lebanon. He was dead within two weeks, the victim of assassination on September 14, 1982, by a member of the pro-Damascus National Syrian Socialist Party. Jumayyil had indeed paid for his connection to the Israelis. While the National Syrian Socialist Party took responsibility for the murder of Jumayyil, some suspected an Israeli conspiracy to kill him owing to his more recent attempts to disassociate himself from Israel.

Following the assassination of Jumayyil, Israeli forces occupied West Beirut. This was in direct violation of the UN agreement calling for the evacuation of the PLO and protection of the Palestinian refugees who remained behind. With the PLO removed, the refugees had virtually no defense against the Israelis or their Christian allies.

Once Israel had control of the Palestinian refugee camps, in September 1982 Sharon invited members of the Phalange to enter the camps at Sabra and Shatila to "clean out the terrorists." The Phalange militia, led by Elie Hobeika, then slaughtered more than 1,000 refugees in what he claimed to be retaliation for Jumayyil's assassination. Estimates of casualties in the Israeli invasion and subsequent occupation vary widely, although the numbers may have been as high as 17,826 Lebanese and approximately 675 Israelis killed.

Israel had achieved a number of goals. It had accomplished its immediate aim of expelling the PLO from Lebanon and temporarily destroying its infrastructure. Israel had also weakened the Syrian military, especially as far as air assets were concerned. The Israelis had also strengthened the South Lebanon Army, which would help control a buffer, or security zone, in the south.

However, the invasion had negative repercussions as well. Much of Beirut lay in ruins, with damage estimated as high as $2 billion, and the tourist industry was a long time in recovering. Operation PEACE FOR GALILEE also became an occupation. In May 1983 with assistance from the United States and France, Israel and Lebanon reached an agreement calling for the staged withdrawal of Israeli forces, although the instruments of this agreement were never officially exchanged. In March 1984 under Syrian pressure, the Lebanese government repudiated it. In January 1985, Israel began a unilateral withdrawal to a security zone in southern Lebanon, which was completed in June 1985. Not until June 2000 did Israel finally withdraw all its forces from southern Lebanon.

Rather than producing a stable, pro-Israeli government in Beirut, the occupation led to contentious new resistance groups that kept Lebanon in perpetual turmoil. There was also considerable unrest in Israel. A protest demonstration in Tel Aviv that followed the Sabra and Shatila massacres drew a reported 300,000 people. Responding to the furor within Israel over the war, the Israeli government appointed the Kahan Commission to investigate the massacres at Sabra and Shatila. The commission found that Israeli officials were indirectly responsible, and Sharon was forced to resign as minister of defense. Begin's political career also suffered greatly. Disillusioned by the invasion and the high Israeli casualties, he resigned as prime minister in 1983, withdrawing entirely from public life.

Brian Parkinson and Spencer C. Tucker

See also
Begin, Menachem; Israel; Lebanon; litani, Operation; Palestine Liberation Organization; Sharon, Ariel

References
Friedman, Thomas. *From Beirut to Jerusalem.* New York: Anchor Books, 1995.
Rabil, Robert G. *Embattled Neighbors: Syria, Israel and Lebanon.* Boulder, CO: Lynne Rienner, 2003.
Rabinovich, Itamar. *The War for Lebanon, 1970–1985.* Rev. ed. Ithaca, NY: Cornell University Press, 1986.

Leilan, Battle of (November 9, 1733)

The Battle of Leilan, also identified as the Battle of Kirkuk and the Battle of Agh-Darband, was fought at Leilan near Kirkuk in present-day Iraq (then in the Mosul Vilayet of the Ottoman Empire) on November 9, 1733. It was waged between the forces of the Safavid Empire, led by Nadir Shah, and Ottoman Empire forces under Topal Osman Pasha and was the last battle of Nadir Shah's Mesopotamia campaign.

Invading Mesopotamia in 1733, Nadir Shah defeated one Ottoman army, then laid siege to Baghdad. But he turned with part of his force to do battle with a larger Ottoman relief force under Topal Osman and suffered his first military defeat in the Battle of Kirkuk or Battle of Samarra (July 19), whereupon the Ottoman garrison at Baghdad sortied and defeated the Persian troops there. Despite these disasters, Nadir rallied his remaining forces and held off Topal.

Topal Osman's army was then weakened by the Ottoman government. Although he maintained a numerical advantage over his foe, many of his experienced troops were transferred and replaced by low-quality levies. Topal Osman's request that he be replaced by a younger general (he was then 70) was denied. Although informed of a rebellion in southern Persia under the leadership of Mohammad Khan Baluch against his rule, Nadir was determined to defeat Topal Osman first and only then return to Persia to crush the rebellion. Now with the arrival of reinforcements from Persia, Nadir again took the offensive.

Informed of the approach by the Agh-Darband Valley of a 12,000-man Ottoman advance force under Memish Pasha, Nadir laid an ambush, dispatching troops under Haji Beg Khan to lure the Ottomans into the main body of the Persian army. Memish Pasha took the bait, and Nadir destroyed the Ottoman advance force, with some 30,000 of his own men attacking it from two sides. Memish Pasha was among those slain.

Nadir then moved rapidly against the main body of Ottoman troops, who were only about three miles distant. Topal Osman deployed, and heavy fighting soon commenced. After several hours of unrelieved musketry, Nadir Shah ordered the Persian infantry to charge the Ottoman ranks. Nadir also sent two bodies of cavalry, each about 15,000 strong, against the Ottoman flanks. He accompanied one of these. With his own men now faltering, Topal Osman mounted a horse and desperately tried to rally his men or die in the process. The old Ottoman general was shot twice before he fell from his horse, whereupon a Persian cavalryman cut off his head and took it to Nadir Shah who, now victorious, ordered it reunited with the rest of his body and sent to the Ottomans with full military honors.

The battle ended with some 20,000 Ottoman casualties in addition to the loss of all their artillery and most of their baggage. Nadir was unable to exploit the victory. His hopes of renewing the siege of Baghdad and taking that city fell victim to the need to put down Mohammad Khan's revolt in Fars. Nadir Shah then concluded the Treaty of Baghdad with Ahmed Pasha and departed with his army for Persia. Although Nadir Shah had avenged his only military defeat, in a very real sense Topal Osman's earlier victory over him was definitive in saving Baghdad from Persian rule.

Spencer C. Tucker

See also
Baghdad, 1733 Battle of; Nadir Shah; Ottoman-Persian Wars of the 18th and 19th Centuries

References
Axworthy, Michael. *The Sword of Persia: Nader Shah, from Tribal Warrior to Conquering Tyrant.* New York: Palgrave Macmillan, 2006.
Lockhart, Laurence. *Nadir Shah: A Critical Study Based Mainly upon Contemporary Sources.* New York: AMS Press, 1973.
Maynard, John Sr. *Nadir Shah.* Oxford, UK: B. H. Blackwell, 1885.

Leo III the Isaurian (ca. 680–741)

Byzantine emperor. Leo III, whose original name was Konon, is popularly known as Leo the Isaurian. He was born possibly in 685 in Germanikeia, a city in the ancient country of Commagene in the Roman province of Syria (present-day Maraş in southeastern Turkey). It is not clear when, but he entered the service of Byzantine emperor Justinian II (r. 685–695) and was sent by him on a diplomatic mission and then was appointed general (*strategus*) by Emperor Anastasius II (r. 713–715). When Anastasius was deposed, Leo joined with another general, Artabasdus, to overthrow the usurper and the new emperor Theodosius III (r. 715–717), who had done little to prepare the empire for an impending Muslim assault on Constantinople. Leo entered Constantinople on March 25, 717, and then forced the abdication of Theodosius and assumed the throne, taking the name Leo III.

As emperor, Leo immediately set to work preparing Constantinople for attack, strengthening its defenses and laying in stocks of food to meet a large Muslim force sent by Caliph Suleiman ibn Abd al-Malik and commanded by his general Muslama. The Muslims hoped to take advantage of the chaos in the Byzantine Empire to capture the great city of Constantinople. Their siege of the Byzantine capital began in August 717 and lasted a full year, with the Muslims withdrawing in August 718. The final Byzantine victory was largely due to Leo's efforts: his preparations for the siege, his generalship during it, and his diplomatic skills that secured the support of the Bulgars.

Having preserved his empire from Muslim overlordship, Leo turned his attention to administrative reform. In 718 he suppressed a rebellion in Sicily, and the next year he crushed an attempt to restore deposed emperor Anastasius II. Leo also reorganized the army, helped restore depopulated areas of the empire by inviting Slavic settlers to live there, and formed alliances with the Khazars and the Georgians. Leo's reforms were so successful that when the Muslims again invaded the empire in both 726 and 739, they were decisively defeated.

Leo also introduced important legal reforms in the empire that changed taxes and raised the status of serfs to free tenants. He rewrote the law codes, and in 726 he published a collection of his legal reforms, the *Eclogia*.

Leo's most striking reforms were probably in the area of religion, where he insisted on the baptism of all Jews and Montanists in the empire in 722 and then embarked on iconoclasm, issuing a series of edicts that prohibited the worship of images. Although many people supported his iconoclasm, a number of others, especially in the western part of the empire, did not. In 727 the imperial fleet crushed a revolt in Greece that had been prompted chiefly by religious reasons. Leo replaced the patriarch of Constantinople, who disagreed with him on the matter of icons. Leo also clashed with Popes Gregory II and Gregory III in Italy on this issue. In 727 Leo sent a large fleet to Italy to crush a revolt in Ravenna, but a great storm largely destroyed the fleet, and southern Italy successfully defied him, with the Exarchate (Byzantine province) of Ravenna in effect becoming free of Byzantine control. Leo continued as emperor until his death on June 18, 741. He was succeeded by his son, Constantine V.

A resourceful, energetic, and bold general, Leo saved the Byzantine Empire and, not incidentally, Western civilization from Muslim control. He also won time for the Byzantine Empire to recover from its early political chaos and survive.

SPENCER C. TUCKER

See also
Constantinople, Muslim Siege of

References
Bury, J. B. *A History of the Later Roman Empire from Arcadius to Irene*. 2 vols. Amsterdam: Hakkert, 1966.
Gero, Stephen. *Byzantine Iconoclasm during the Reign of Leo III, with Particular Attention to the Oriental Sources*. Louvain: Secrétariat du Corpus SCO, 1973.
Guilland, Rodolphe. "L'expédition de Maslama contre Constantinople (717–718)." In *Études Byzantines*. Paris: Presses universitaires de France, 1959.
Ladner, Gerhart. "Origin and Significance of the Byzantine Iconoclastic Controversy." *Mediaeval Studies* 2 (1940): 127–149.
Ostragorsky, George. *A History of the Byzantine State*. Trans. John Hussey. New Brunswick, NJ: Rutgers University Press, 1969.
Treadgold, Warren. *A History of the Byzantine State and Society*. Stanford, CA: University of Stanford Press, 1997.

Leopold V of Austria (1157–1194)

Duke of Austria (1177–1194) and Styria (1192–1194) and participant in the Third Crusade (1189–1192) who is notorious for his imprisonment of his fellow crusader Richard I the Lionheart, king of England. Born in 1157, Leopold was the son of Henry II of Babenberg, duke of Austria, and Theodora Komnene. Leopold succeeded his father as duke on February 24, 1177. In 1182 Leopold made a pilgrimage to the Holy Land, and he subsequently gifted a supposed relic of the True Cross to the Cistercian monastery of Heiligenkreuz. In 1186 Leopold laid the foundations for a vast increase in Babenberg power when he secured recognition as heir to the childless Ottokar IV, duke of Styria, in the Treaty of Georgenberg, which was confirmed a year later by Frederick I Barbarossa, the Holy Roman emperor.

During the Third Crusade, Leopold did not join the emperor's army but instead traveled independently to the

Holy Land with a large number of Austrian knights, arriving at Acre (modern-day Akko, Israel) in the spring of 1191. There he came to be regarded as the leader of the much-depleted German crusader contingent, which had been left leaderless after the deaths of the emperor and his son Frederick V, duke of Swabia. However, Leopold and the other German leaders found themselves increasingly sidelined in the direction of the crusade by the two Western kings, Richard I of England and Philippe II Augustus of France. After the capture of Acre from Saladin's forces (July 12, 1191), Richard cast down Leopold's banner from the battlements of the city as a sign that he and Philip were unwilling to concede Leopold any share in the spoils. Shortly afterward Leopold returned to Austria.

Leopold took possession of the duchy of Styria after the death of Ottokar IV (May 8, 1192). Later that year Leopold had the opportunity to exact revenge on Richard, when the English king, returning from crusade with only a few companions, was recognized and arrested by one of Leopold's men in the village of Erdberg (now in Vienna) in December. Clearly opportunism and revenge played their part in the duke's actions. An additional factor, however, was the enmity toward Richard of Emperor Henry VI, who had ordered his vassals to apprehend the English king if the opportunity presented itself. Richard was imprisoned in the castle of Dürnstein on the Danube while Leopold negotiated with the emperor. The duke handed over his prisoner to Henry VI on March 23, 1193, in exchange for half the expected ransom of 100,000 marks. A renegotiation of the ransom terms brought more favorable terms, including a further payment and the prospect of the marriage of Richard's niece Eleanor to one of Leopold's sons.

Despite its financial benefits, Leopold's detention of Richard, a returning crusader whose person should have been inviolable, brought him considerable opprobrium, and in 1194 Pope Celestine III excommunicated him. At the end of that year Leopold suffered a crushed leg after falling from his horse and died, still excommunicate, after a botched amputation of his gangrenous foot (December 31, 1194). The duke's horrendous death was widely regarded as divine retribution for his imprisonment of the English crusader king. Leopold was succeeded by his two sons Frederick I (in Austria) and Leopold VI (in Styria).

ALAN V. MURRAY

See also
Crusades in the Holy Land, Christian; Frederick I or Frederick Barbarossa; Frederick V, Duke of Swabia; Henry VI of Germany; Philippe II, King; Richard I, King; Saladin

References
Ashcroft, Jeffrey R. "Der Minnesänger und die Freude des Hofes. Zu Reinmars Kreuzliedern und Witwenklage." In *Poesie und Gebrauchsliteratur im deutschen Mittelalter: Würzburger Colloquium 1978*, ed. Volker Honemann, Kurt Ruh, Bernhard Schnell, and Werner Wegstein, 219–238. Tübingen: Niemeyer, 1979.
Gillingham, John. *Richard I*. New Haven, CT: Yale University Press, 1999.
Graz, Othmar Pickl. *800 Jahre Steiermark und Österreich 1192–1992: Der Beitrag der Steiermark zu Österreichs Größe*. Austria: Historische Landeskommission für Steiermark, 1992.
Lechner, Karl. *Die Babenberger: Markgrafen und Herzöge in Österreich, 976–1246*. Wien: Böhlaus, 1976.

Lepanto, Battle of (October 7, 1571)

The naval Battle of Lepanto pitted an Ottoman fleet against the Holy League of Spain, Venice, and the Papacy. It was the largest galley engagement of the gunpowder era and also the first great fleet action decided by artillery.

Early in 1570 Venice rejected an Ottoman demand that it surrender Cyprus. The Venetians decided to fight and appealed to Pope Pius V for aid. When the Ottomans invaded Cyprus, Pius persuaded King Philip II of Spain to join with the papacy and Venice in the Holy League, ratified in May 1571.

The galley remained the principal ship type in the Mediterranean in the late 16th century. The galley of 1571 was little changed from that of the Battle of Salamis in 480 BCE. Motive power was provided by lateen-rigged sails on two masts when wind permitted or by oars when the wind did not and in battle. The graceful, long, shallow-draft galley was well suited to the more sheltered Mediterranean waters. Its striking power remained the ram, although cannon were also mounted in the bow and trained by turning the vessel. Captains attempted to destroy their opponents with the ram and, should that not prove successful, by boarding and hand-to-hand combat.

A new ship type had also appeared in the galleass. Introduced by the Venetians, it resembled the galley in appearance but was larger and more seaworthy and carried more men. An attempt at compromise between the galley and the sailing ships of Northern Europe, the galleass had three masts, with the fore and main square rigged. The vessel combined the freedom of movement of the galley with the seaworthiness and fighting power of the sailing warship but, as with most compromises, was not a successful type, being sluggish and slow. Another ship type, smaller than the

Depiction of the Battle of Lepanto, October 7, 1571. The largest rowed galley engagement of the gunpowder era, it marked the beginning of the decline in Ottoman naval power in the Mediterranean. (Photos.com)

galley, was the Ottoman gaillot. Based on an older Byzantine design, it had 18–24 oars and shipped only about 100 men.

In the summer of 1570 Philip II assembled squadrons of galleys from Naples and Sicily, in addition to contracted Genoese galleys under Genoese admiral Giovanni Andrea Doria. These joined with Venetian and papal ships to relieve Cyprus. Philip II hoped that Doria might also recover Tunis, where the Ottomans had ousted the ruler friendly to Spain. In mid-September the allied fleet, commanded by papal admiral Marcantonio Colonna, reached the Ottoman coast opposite Cyprus. Doria, however, believed the season too late to continue operations and withdrew his squadrons over the protests of his allies, bringing the campaign to an end.

The next September the allies assembled at Messina an armada of 207 galleys, 6 galleasses, and two dozen great ships. In addition to their crews and rowers, the fleet shipped some 20,000 marine infantry. In early October the fleet learned of the surrender of Famagusta on August 1, 1571. This last Venetian stronghold on Cyprus had succumbed following a 10.5-month siege that cost the Ottomans perhaps 50,000 dead. Don Juan of Austria, Philip II's half brother and supreme commander of the allied fleet, now decided to seek out and destroy the Ottoman fleet. At Corfu, Don Juan sent out reconnaissance vessels under Gil de Andrtade, who located the Ottoman fleet at Lepanto in the Gulf of Patras in the Ionian Sea.

Ali Pasha commanded the Ottoman fleet of nearly 300 galleys and smaller galliots. Including 16,000 soldiers, the Ottoman fleet carried perhaps 88,000 men. Ali Pasha's fleet had screened Ottoman operations on Cyprus all summer, ravaging Venetian possessions in the Aegean and Ionian Seas in late August and September and then raiding the Adriatic before returning to Lepanto (Navpaktos), where the Gulf of Corinth meets the Gulf of Patras.

Don Juan now brought his armada to the Gulf of Patras. The Ottomans decided to fight and on Sunday, October 7, 1571, emerged from their anchorage and formed an extended crescent-shaped line of three squadrons. The 40 smaller galliots backed the center of the Ottoman line. Although Ali's 300 ships were more than the Holy League could muster, they were also lighter and not as well protected, and they had nothing that could match the Venetian galleasses.

The allied armada rowed to close with the Ottomans. There were sharp divisions of loyalties within the fleet, and before sailing Don Juan had mixed his squadrons so that each ally had galleys. He also arrayed his armada into left, center, and right squadrons, backed by a rear guard of 30 galleys under Álvaro de Bazán, 1st Marquis of Santa Cruz. The center included most of his bigger galleys. Don Juan assigned the heavier and more powerful galleasses a more aggressive role in the battle, positioning them in pairs well in advance of each squadron. Another innovation was to remove the beaks from the galleys to allow their bow guns greater traverse. In taking these steps, Don Juan assigned the primary role to the artillery, as opposed to muskets, pikes, slings, and swords. He also announced before the battle that all Christian slave oarsmen in the fleet would be pardoned and freed if the Ottomans were defeated.

The battle commenced near noon. The galleasses, which mounted more cannon (each had 10 heavy guns, 12 lighter guns, and small man-killers on the rail), used their heavier guns to engage the Ottoman ships and disrupt their advance. At first the Ottomans did not attempt to board and unleashed volleys of arrows. Once these were exhausted the battle degenerated into the customary melee, with attempts to board and hand-to-hand combat.

The disorganized Ottoman right under Mehmet Sirocco failed to turn the Holy League's in-shore wing, commanded by Venetian Agostino Barbarigo. The latter's line then swung shoreward to trap the Ottomans against the beach. The bigger guns of Don Juan's center battered the Ottoman center as its ships closed to board. Don Juan personally led an attack on Ali Pasha's flagship, but before the two vessels could close, Ali Pasha was shot and killed. Later his head was cut off and raised to the masthead for all to see.

The 90 galleys of the Ottoman left under Uluj Ali did not close with the Holy League's right wing of 57 galleys under Doria but sailed wide in an effort to turn its flank. When Doria keep pace, Uluj Ali turned his wing abruptly and raced for the gap between Doria and the allied center under Don Juan. The two Venetian galleasses assigned to Doria were unable to reach their assigned station but did bombard the rear of the Ottoman center. The Ottomans then overwhelmed 3 galleys belonging to the knights of Malta and savaged 7 galleys of the Holy League vanguard under Juan de Cardona, who trailed Doria. But the Marquis of Santa Cruz detected Uluj Ali's maneuver in time and checked the Ottoman rush with his rear guard until Don Juan and Doria could close to complete the allies' triumph. The battle was over by 4:00 p.m. Although both sides had invoked God, the battle proved that God tends to favor the side with larger and more guns.

Uluj Ali escaped with only 35 galleys, mostly Algerian, and many of these had to be destroyed later as unseaworthy. The Ottomans lost more than 200 galleys (117 were captured intact) and 20,000 people dead. Some 15,000 Christian galley slaves on the Ottoman ships were freed; most were Greeks who returned to Greece. The allies lost 10–15 ships sunk and perhaps 7,500 dead. Among the 15,000 allied wounded was Miguel de Cervantes, author of *Don Quixote*.

The battle was psychologically crucial for the Holy League, whom the Ottomans had often defeated. Lepanto settled nothing in the short run, though, as the Christian alliance soon broke up. The Ottomans kept Cyprus and Tunis, but their navy never regained the same quality or prestige. Unhappy with Philip II's desire to use the Holy League against Tunis and Algiers, Venice made a separate peace with the Ottomans in 1573. Philip II then found himself under pressure to do the same. With revolt in the Low Countries and trouble with France and England, in 1578 he concluded a truce with Ottoman sultan Murad III.

SPENCER C. TUCKER

See also
Ottoman Empire

References
Beeching, Jack. *The Galleys at Lepanto*. New York: Scribner, 1983.
Braudel, Fernand. *The Mediterranean and the Mediterranean World in the Age of Philip II*. 2 vols. New York: Harper & Row, 1972.
Guilmartin, J. F. *Gunpowder and Galleys*. New York: Cambridge University Press, 1974.
Pierson, Peter. "Lepanto." *MHQ: Quarterly Journal of Military History* 9, no. 2 (1997): 6–19.
Rodgers, William Ledyard. *Naval Warfare under Oars, 4th to 16th Centuries: A Study of Strategy, Tactics and Ship Design*. Annapolis, MD: Naval Institute Press, 1967.

Liberty Incident (June 8, 1967)

On June 8, 1967, the electronic intelligence gathering ship USS *Liberty* was attacked by Israeli Air Force and naval units while it was some 13 nautical miles off El Arish on Egypt's Sinai Peninsula. The reasons for the attack and charges of a cover-up have been the topics of conspiracy theories, but numerous inquiries in both the United States and Israel have concluded that the attack resulted from mistaken identity.

The U.S. Navy acquired the 7,725-ton civilian cargo ship *Simmons Victory* and converted it into an auxiliary technical research ship (AGTR). The conversion was completed in 1965, and the ship was renamed the *Liberty* (AGTR-5). Initially it operated off the west coast of Africa. With the Six-Day War in June 1967, the *Liberty* was directed to collect electronic intelligence on Israeli and Arab military activities from the eastern Mediterranean. Commander William L. McGonagle had command.

The attack occurred on the fourth day of the war. On June 4, the day before the start of the war, the Israeli government had asked the United States if it had any ships in the area.

Washington responded that it did not because the *Liberty* was only then entering the Mediterranean.

By June 8 the Israelis had routed Egyptian forces in the Sinai Desert and Jordanian forces on the West Bank and were preparing to move aggressively against Syria. The Israelis, aware that their coastlines were vulnerable to naval attack, had warned the United States to keep its ships at a safe distance.

On June 8 the *Liberty* was off the coast monitoring communications. Responding to the Israeli warning, Washington had sent several messages to the *Liberty* not to close within 100 miles of the coast, but these messages were rerouted because of an overloaded U.S. Navy communications system and did not reach the ship before the Israeli attack.

A series of explosions in El Arish, which had been recently captured by the Israelis, led the Israelis to conclude that the town was being shelled by an Egyptian ship. It was later determined that the explosions had occurred accidentally in an abandoned ammunition dump. Israeli aircraft patrolling off the coast nonetheless mistakenly identified the *Liberty* as an Egyptian vessel. There was no wind, and a large U.S. flag flying from the *Liberty* was drooping and not identifiable. Identification markings on the side and stern of the ship were apparently not visible to the Israeli pilots, who attacked the ship head-on.

The Israeli attack began at 1:57 p.m. local time on June 8. Two or three Israeli air force planes, probably Dassault Mirage IIIs, strafed the ship with 30mm cannon fire. The first Israeli pilot to reach the ship was Yiftav Spector, one of Israel's leading aces. This attack was followed by a comparable number of Dassault Mystères, which dropped napalm. More than 800 bullet holes were later counted in the ship's hull. Some 20 minutes later three Israeli torpedo boats arrived on the scene, and members of the *Liberty*'s crew opened fire on them with two .50-caliber machine guns in the mistaken belief that the ship was under Egyptian attack.

McGonagle could not signal the Israeli vessels, as all the ship's searchlights had been destroyed. The Israeli torpedo boats fired a number of torpedoes at the *Liberty*, one of which struck the ship on its starboard side and opened a large hole. The torpedo boats then approached to closer range and commenced machine-gun fire against the American sailors, some of whom were attempting to launch life rafts. The torpedo boats then left the area.

The Israelis claimed that they did not know the *Liberty* was a U.S. ship until a life raft with U.S. Navy markings was found drifting in the water. Three hours after the attack, the Israeli government informed the U.S. embassy in Tel Aviv of events. Although the *Liberty* had been badly damaged, its crew managed to keep the ship afloat, and it was able to proceed to Malta under its own power, escorted by ships of the U.S. Sixth Fleet.

Thirty-four American personnel died in the attack, and another 172 were wounded, many seriously. For his heroism and leadership, Commander McGonagle, who was wounded early in the attack, was subsequently awarded the Medal of Honor. His ship received the Presidential Unit Citation. Following stopgap repairs, the *Liberty* returned to the United States and was decommissioned in 1968. It was scrapped in 1970.

The Israeli government subsequently apologized and paid nearly $13 million in compensation. Those dissatisfied with the official inquiries in the United States and Israel have speculated that the Israelis knew that they were attacking a U.S. ship and did so because they feared that intercepts by the *Liberty* would reveal that Israel was about to attack Syria. But such a theory fails to explain why Israel would risk the anger of its only superpower supporter. Knowledge of the imminent Israeli attack on Syria was also widespread and hardly a secret by June 8.

PAUL WILLIAM DOERR AND SPENCER C. TUCKER

See also
Six-Day War

References
Bamford, James. *Body of Secrets*. New York: Doubleday, 2001.
Cristol, A. Jay. *The Liberty Incident: The 1967 Israeli Attack on the US Navy Spy Ship*. Washington, DC: Brassey's, 2002.
Ennis, James M., Jr. *Assault on the Liberty: The True Story of the Israeli Attack on an American Intelligence Ship*. New York: Random House, 1979.
Oren, Michael B. *Six Days of War: June 1967 and the Making of the Modern Middle East*. Novato, CA: Presidio, 2003.
Rabin, Yitzhak. *The Rabin Memoirs*. Boston: Little, Brown, 1979.

Libyan-Egyptian War (July 21–24, 1977)

A brief border war fought between Libya and Egypt in July 1977. In early summer, massive demonstrations were organized by the Libyan government to protest the rapprochement between Egypt and Israel. Libyan leader Muammar Gaddafi accused Egyptian president Anwar Sadat of provoking tensions inside his country so that Egypt might seize the Libyan oil fields. Despite the Egyptian government's denial, Gaddafi ordered tens of thousands of Egyptians working and living in Libya to leave the country by July 1 or face arrest.

As tensions between the two countries escalated, a brief skirmish between border guards on July 21, 1977, caused the start of the war. The four-day war (July 21–24) saw both sides utilize tanks, artillery, and aircraft. Libyan forces suffered greatly at the hands of the Egyptians, however, and much of the Libyan Air Force was destroyed on the ground by an Egyptian attack on the base at al-Adam. By July 24, mediation by President Houari Boumedienne of Algeria and Yasser Arafat of the Palestine Liberation Organization led to a cease-fire and armistice.

Overall, the war claimed some 100 Egyptian casualties, while Libya lost perhaps 400 men, 60 tanks, and more than 20 aircraft. Although the two sides reverted to a status quo ante bellum, Egypt was the clear winner, having secured and held throughout air superiority and with this control of ground combat as well.

ALEXANDER MIKABERIDZE

See also
Arafat, Yasser; Sadat, Anwar

References
Cleveland, William L. *A History of the Modern Middle East*. Boulder CO: Westview, 2004.
Pollack, Kenneth M. *Arabs at War: Military Effectiveness, 1948–1991*. Lincoln: University of Nebraska Press, 2002.

Liman von Sanders, Otto (1855–1929)

German Army general and Ottoman field marshal. Born on February 17, 1855, at Stolp, Pomerania (now Stupsk, Poland), Otto Liman entered the army in 1874 as an officer candidate in the 115th Infantry Regiment at Darmstadt. He attended the Kriegsakademie in Berlin during 1878–1881. In 1887 he was assigned to the Great General Staff in Berlin. Promoted to captain in 1889, he was assigned to the staff of the 28th Infantry Division at Karlsruhe. He returned to the Great General Staff in 1893 and was promoted to major in 1894. Assigned to the staff of the XI Corps the next year, he served on the staff of the 14th Uhlan Regiment at Avold and then commanded the 6th Husars Regiment at Leobschütz in 1901. He was promoted to lieutenant colonel in 1901 and to colonel in 1904.

In 1906 Liman took command of the 15th Cavalry Brigade. Promoted to generalmajor in 1908, in 1911 he became inspector general of cavalry at Saarbrücken, then assumed command of the 22nd Infantry Division at Kassel and was promoted to generalleutnant. Ennobled in 1913, Liman then added the name of his deceased Scottish wife, Sanders, to his own.

Field Marshal Otto Liman von Sanders helped bring order to the Ottoman army after that country's entry on the side of the Central Powers. He commanded its Fifth Army against the Allies at Gallipoli in 1915 and then headed Ottoman forces in Palestine and Syria. (Library of Congress)

In June 1913 Kaiser Wilhelm II sent Liman to the Ottoman Empire to lead German military advisers dispatched at the request of the Young Turks, who sought to modernize their military establishment. Initially Liman was to command a corps of the Ottoman army at Istanbul (Constantinople). Russian protests over this appointment led to a diplomatic confrontation that ended with his appointment in January 1915 as inspector general of all Ottoman forces with the ranks of Turkish field marshal and German general der kavallerie (U.S. equiv. lieutenant general). The Ottoman Army was in near complete disarray following the First and Second Balkan Wars of 1912–1913 and lacking in such essentials as clothing and medical facilities. Liman worked to train and equip the army along German lines while attempting to further German interests.

When the Ottoman Empire entered the war on the side of the Central Powers in November 1914, Liman recommended an attack on Ukraine, but Minister of War Enver Pasha decided instead on a winter expedition into the

Caucasus that ended disastrously for the Ottoman Empire. Liman held a field command in this campaign.

Liman gained world attention in the Gallipoli Campaign (April 25, 1915–January 9, 1916), when he commanded the Ottoman Fifth Army on the Gallipoli Peninsula against an amphibious assault by British Empire and French forces attempting to force the Dardanelles. Although the Allies gained lodgments ashore, they were unable to advance inland, and the ensuing bloody stalemate brought an Allied evacuation in early January 1916. For his efforts, Liman was acclaimed a hero in Germany and awarded the Pour le Mérite.

In February 1916 Liman was assigned command of armies in eastern Anatolia. The Ottomans were then carrying out a forced deportation and genocide of the Armenians, a policy that Liman strongly opposed. He saw his forces reduced to near starvation as many of the local farmers were killed or ejected from their lands. He also strongly opposed an October 1917 German-Ottoman convention that was to take effect after the war in which the Ottomans would have exercised control over all German officers in that country.

On March 1, 1918, Liman took command from General der Infanterie Erich von Falkenhayn of Army Group F (Yildirim, or "Thunderbolt") consisting of the Ottoman Fourth, Seventh, and Eighth Armies with the impossible task of shoring up defenses in Palestine and Syria. From his headquarters in Nazareth, he worked to organize his poorly equipped forces, continually drained by Enver siphoning off men for the Caucasian front. Deceived into believing that British forces under Lieutenant General Edmund Allenby would attack east of the Jordan River, Liman was caught by surprise when on September 18, 1918, the Allies struck to the north at the village of Megiddo, and he only narrowly escaped capture. He then attempted to rally his remaining troops and make a stand at Aleppo. Following the October Armistice of Mudros, Liman returned to Istanbul to supervise the repatriation of German troops.

When Liman attempted to return to Germany in February 1919, British forces arrested him and held him at Malta for six months as a suspected war criminal. He retired from the army in October 1919 and died in Munich on August 22, 1929. A capable and resourceful commander, Liman was constantly hamstrung by the mistaken decisions of his superiors, but he nonetheless emerged from the war with a far better reputation than most German Western Front commanders.

HAROLD WISE AND SPENCER C. TUCKER

See also
Allenby, Sir Edmund Henry Hynman; Enver Pasha; Gallipoli Campaign; Megiddo, Battle of; Palestine and Syria Campaign, World War I

References
Liman von Sanders, Otto. *Five Years in Turkey*. Translated by Carl Reichmann. Annapolis, MD: United States Naval Institute, 1927.

Moorehead, Alan. *Gallipoli*. New York: Harper, 1956.

Trumpener, Ulrich. *Germany and the Ottoman Empire, 1914–1918*. Princeton, NJ: Princeton University Press, 1968.

Weber, Frank G. *Eagles on the Crescent: Germany, Austria, and the Diplomacy of the Turkish Alliance, 1914–1918*. Ithaca, NY: Cornell University Press, 1970.

LITANI, Operation (March 14–21, 1978)

Official name given to the Israel Defense Forces (IDF) invasion of southern Lebanon up to the Litani River that occurred during March 14–21, 1978. On March 11, 1978, 9 Palestinian terrorists landed on an Israeli beach, murdered an American tourist, captured 2 buses, and headed for Tel Aviv where, in a firefight with Israeli security forces, they were killed along with 28 Israeli passengers. Seventy-eight other Israelis were wounded in the assault. This was the culmination of a long series of Palestinian attacks originating from southern Lebanon.

At the time of the March 11 attack, Israel's new Likud Party government had just recently ended three decades of Labor Party dominance. The new government was headed by Prime Minister Menachem Begin, who was anxious to appear tough on the issue of terrorist attacks. Begin thus decided on a swift response to the Palestinian attack.

On the night of March 14, some 7,000 Israeli troops, accompanied by armor, artillery, and close air support, entered southern Lebanon with the stated goal of pushing the Palestine Liberation Organization (PLO) away from the Israeli border. The Israelis also hoped to bolster a splinter group within Lebanon, the South Lebanon Army (SLA), an Israeli ally. The resulting operation lasted for seven days and was the largest military operation the IDF had undertaken since the 1973 Yom Kippur War. Eventually some 25,000 IDF troops were involved in the operation, which indeed saw the IDF reach the Litani River. The operation was a success for the Israelis, as PLO fighters retreated north of the river line. Lebanese deaths and casualties were extraordinarily high, however. Estimates of Lebanese dead range from as low as 300 to as high as 2,000. Worse, the Israeli incursion created perhaps as many as 250,000 refugees. The IDF suffered 20 dead.

In response to the invasion, on March 19 the United Nations (UN) Security Council adopted Resolution 425 (by a vote of 12 to 0) calling for the withdrawal of Israeli forces from Lebanon. On March 20 the Security Council adopted Resolution 426, entrusting the UN Interim Force in Lebanon (UNIFIL) to enforce this mandate and monitor the activities of the PLO guerrillas. On March 21 the IDF ceased offensive operations. UNIFIL arrived in Lebanon on March 23, 1978. Not until June 1978 did Israel agree to pull its forces out of Lebanon, exempting its security zone. At the same time, it turned over positions inside Lebanon to the SLA. In the years that followed, the SLA and the PLO periodically harassed UNIFIL forces.

Ultimately, UNIFIL failed to bring the Lebanese government's authority to the southern part of the nation where, despite UNIFIL efforts, the PLO reestablished itself. Southern Lebanon as a result remained a highly volatile and unstable area, a characteristic that has endured to the present day. Incidents in which the PLO and the Israelis exchanged fire were numerous. For the Israelis, the success of Operation LITANI, particularly the fact that Israeli troops managed to operate without clashing with the Syrians, made the operation a dress rehearsal for the 1982 invasion of Lebanon, known as Operation PEACE FOR GALILEE. That operation, however, was considered only marginally successful. In 2000 the UN Security Council concluded that as of June 16, 2000, Israel had met the conditions of Resolution 425 by withdrawing all its forces from Lebanon. Southern Lebanon would once again become an issue in July and August 2006 when a short but bloody war occurred between Israeli forces and Hezbollah guerrillas located in southern Lebanon and Israel.

MICHAEL DOIDGE

See also
Hezbollah; Lebanon; Lebanon-Israeli War; Palestine Liberation Organization

References
Bregman, Ahron. *Israel's Wars: A History since 1947.* 2nd ed. New York: Routledge, 2002.
Cobban, Helena. *The Palestinian Liberation Organization: People, Power and Politics.* New York: Cambridge University Press, 1984.
Fisk, Robert. *Pity the Nation: The Abduction of Lebanon.* 4th ed. New York: Nation Books, 2002.
Shlaim, Avi. *The Iron Wall: Israel and the Arab World.* New York: Norton, 2001.

Lod Airport Massacre (May 30, 1972)

Mass shooting on May 30, 1972, at Lod Airport in Tel Aviv, Israel. The Lod Airport attack was carried out by three Japanese men associated with the Japanese Red Army, an extreme left-wing militant group known for its terrorist activities. The Japanese Red Army had as its goals the overthrow of the Japanese government and the fomenting of a worldwide communist revolution. The group had historic ties to the Popular Front for the Liberation of Palestine (PFLP), having received both monetary funding and arms from the militant Palestinian organization. The three men responsible for the Lod Airport attack—Tsuyoshi Okudaira, Kozo Okamoto, and Yasuyuki Yasuda—had been sponsored and trained by the PFLP but were also acting at the behest of the Popular Front for the Liberation of Palestine-General Command (PFLP-GC). The PFLP-GC recruited the Japanese terrorists because they knew that airport security was vigilant of would-be Palestinian terrorists but not those of Japanese descent.

To aid their anonymity, the three terrorists inconspicuously boarded Air France flight 132 in Paris, bound for Tel Aviv. They showed no signs of trouble during the flight and were dressed in conservative business attire to further conceal themselves. They carried with them only long, thin cases that resembled an attaché case or draftsman's bag. They casually deplaned in Tel Aviv on May 30, produced assault guns from their cases, and began to fire randomly into the waiting room lounge, which was full of people. When their ammunition had run out, the men produced grenades and began throwing them into the panicked crowd, producing even more mayhem. Yasuda died from bullet wounds inflicted either by one of his compatriots or by airport security personnel, and Okudaira died when he threw himself on top of a grenade and detonated it. Only Okamoto survived the massacre. By the time airport security had gained control over the situation, 26 had died and another 78 had been wounded. Included among the dead were 16 Puerto Rican Americans on their way to a pilgrimage in the Holy Land. Okamoto, who was also badly hurt in the attack, was tried, convicted, and sentenced to life imprisonment in Israel.

In the immediate aftermath of the massacre, the PFLP-GC and PFLP claimed responsibility, stating that it was retribution for the 1948 Deir Yassin Massacre of Palestinians perpetrated by the Irgun Tsvai Leumi (National Military Organization). Okamoto left his Israeli prison cell in 1983 during a prisoner exchange between the Israeli government and the Palestinians. In 1997 he was again arrested in the occupied territories but was allowed to return to Lebanon, where he secured political refugee status.

PAUL G. PIERPAOLI JR.

See also

Deir Yassin Massacre; Irgun Tsvai Leumi; Popular Front for the Liberation of Palestine; Popular Front for the Liberation of Palestine–General Command; Terrorism

References

Hoffman, Bruce. *Inside Terrorism.* New York: Columbia University Press, 1999.

Shoham, Shlomo G., ed. *Terrorism and the International Community.* Oshawa, Ontario: De Sitter, 2005.

Lohamei Herut Israel

Radical armed Zionist organization active in Palestine during the 1940s. The last years of the British Mandate over Palestine were ones of great instability and even intense conflict. One organization, Lohamei Herut Israel (Fighters for the Freedom of Israel), also known as Lehi and the Stern Gang, contributed to the volatile situation by launching attacks against British authorities and the Arab population in Palestine.

Founded in September 1940 as a splinter group from the Irgun Tsvai Leumi (National Military Organization), Lehi was an intensely nationalist Jewish organization. It demanded an immediate end to British rule and rejected any notion of compromise or cooperation with the mandate government. The group, which never numbered more than a few hundred fighters, was disbanded by 1949.

Zionism and the Jewish drive for statehood in Palestine gave rise to a constellation of armed groups that struggled to speed the reestablishment of an independent Israel. Avraham Stern (also known as Yair), a radical Irgun member who denounced any plans to limit the borders of a Jewish Palestine, formed Lehi in response to a commitment by other Jewish militias to suspend attacks against the British after the outbreak of World War II. Stern failed to see that a defeat of Nazi Germany would necessarily strengthen Jewish interests and instead approved efforts in 1940 to approach Britain's foes and offer them an alliance.

Such ties never materialized, but Lehi's leadership was hardly dissuaded by the setback and initiated an independent terror campaign against the British. The first significant attack in this offensive was the December 1940 bombing of the immigration offices in Haifa, a symbolic strike against British-imposed restrictions on the flow of Jews into Palestine. In response, the British condemned Lehi and dismissed it as a criminal organization whose members had to be neutralized. However, even Stern's death at the hands of the British security forces failed to curtail the threat posed by the organization.

Under new leaders, the most prominent of whom was Yitzhak "Michael" Shamir, a future Israeli prime minister, Lehi continued its attacks, including the infamous killing of Lord Moyne, the British minister resident in Cairo, on November 6, 1944. The murder shocked the British and prompted the Jewish community in Palestine to crack down on the terrorists carrying out such attacks.

At the conclusion of World War II, a broad alliance and unified command emerged among Jewish armed groups in the mandate. Intent on driving out the British and speeding the establishment of an independent Israel, the militias, known collectively as the Hebrew Resistance Movement, renewed their joint operations against the security forces and Arab interests. Lehi fighters played a prominent role in the revived campaign, including participation in some of the most heinous terrorist acts committed during the last years of the mandate.

On January 4, 1948, Lehi operatives detonated a truck bomb outside the Arab National Committee offices at city hall in Jaffa, killing 26 people and wounding scores more. Members of Lehi also joined the April 9, 1948, attack on the Arab village of Deir Yassin near Jerusalem. In a matter of hours, Jewish fighters massacred more than 100 civilians and underscored their determination to drive Arabs out of lands claimed for the State of Israel. Immediate and later efforts, be they Arab, British, or Jewish, to publicize the incident ensured that it gained notoriety and became an action symbolic of the intense emotions that dominated the conflict over control of Palestine.

However, a terrorist attack of perhaps even greater significance was the assassination in Jerusalem of Count Folke Bernadotte, a Swedish nobleman and the United Nations (UN) mediator, on September 17, 1948. Carried out by fighters from Hazit HaMoledet (Homeland Front), a subgroup of Lehi, the killing revealed the level of radicalism that existed in the region, at least among a minority of activists, within the Zionist movement.

In the wake of the Bernadotte murder, the new Israeli government took steps to dismantle Lehi and imprison its leaders. Natan Yellin-Mor, one of the organization's most prominent figures, was soon convicted of involvement in the Bernadotte plot. However, within a year the authorities approved his early release and allowed him to occupy a seat in the Knesset (Israeli parliament). From armed outlaw activism to its establishment as a political party, Lehi assumed a position as a recognized and legitimate body within the ideological spectrum of Israel, and many of its former fighters found a home in the Israel Defense Forces (IDF).

JONAS KAUFFELDT AND SERGIO CATIGNANI

See also
Arab-Jewish Communal War; Bernadotte, Folke; Irgun Tsvai Leumi; Palestine, British Mandate for; Terrorism

References
Bell, J. Bowyer. *Terror out of Zion: Irgun Zvai Leumi, Lehi and the Palestine Underground, 1929–1949*. New York: St. Martin's, 1979.
Goldberg, Giora. "Haganah, Irgun and 'Stern': Who Did What." *Jerusalem Quarterly* 25 (Fall 1982): 116–120.
Heller, Joseph. *The Stern Gang: Ideology, Politics, and Terror, 1940–1949*. London: Frank Cass, 1995.
Marton, Kati. *A Death in Jerusalem*. New York: Arcade, 1996.
Morris, Benny. *Righteous Victims: A History of the Zionist-Arab Conflict, 1881–2001*. New York: Vintage Books, 2001.

London, 1840 Treaty of (July 15, 1840)

A treaty formally known as the Convention for the Pacification of the Levant signed on July 15, 1840, between the governments of Britain, Austria, Prussia, and Russia on the one hand and the Ottoman Empire on the other. The treaty was to end the fighting between the de facto ruler of Egypt, Mehmed Ali, and the Ottoman Empire; limit Mehmed's territorial gains from the Ottoman Empire; and preserve the territorial integrity of the Ottoman Empire.

In 1831, Mehmed Ali invaded Syria with the Egyptian Army in an attempt to establish an independent Egypt after Sultan Abdulmecid I refused to give him Syria and the Morea (Peloponnesus) in return for his assistance against the Greeks in the late 1820s. On December 21, 1832, the Egyptian Army, led by Ibrahim Pasha, soundly defeated the Ottoman Army in the Battle of Konya. With nothing standing between the Egyptians and the Ottoman capital of Istanbul (Constantinople), the European powers intervened and negotiated the Convention of Kutahya in May 1833.

Dissatisfied with the terms of the convention, Mehmed Ali launched another offensive against the Ottoman Empire and again destroyed the Ottoman Army in the Battle of Nezib on June 24, 1839. Adding to the disaster was the defection of the Ottoman fleet to Mehmed Ali.

At this point, Sultan Mahmud II died. He was succeeded by 16-year-old Abdulmecid I. Britain preferred a weakened but intact Ottoman Empire that would grant Britain concessions to maintain its influence in the Middle East and brought heavy pressure to bear for a settlement that would maintain the Ottoman Empire.

As a result, in July 1840 Britain, France, Austria, Russia, and Prussia intervened on the side of Abdulmecid to drive Egyptian forces from Syria. A British fleet bombarded Beirut on September 11, 1840, and an Anglo-Ottoman force captured Acre on November 3. The arrival of these forces caused local uprisings against the Egyptians in Syria. Meanwhile, a British naval force anchored off Alexandria, and the Egyptian Army withdrew back to Egypt.

Mehmed Ali now had to accede to British demands. According to the Treaty of 1841, he surrendered all conquered territory except Sudan and the province of Acre (roughly present-day Israel, which nonetheless would remain part of the Ottoman Empire) but received the hereditary governorship of Egypt for life, with the succession going to the eldest male in his family. Mehmed Ali also had to return the Ottoman fleet, which had defected to Alexandria. Finally, the Egyptian ruler was forced to accept the Anglo-Ottoman Convention of 1838, which established "free trade" in Egypt, forcing him to establish new tariffs that were favorable to imports. As a result, cheap manufactured imports flooded Egypt and decimated local industries.

ROBERT B. KANE

See also
Egyptian-Ottoman Wars; Kutahya Convention; Mehmed Ali

References
Askan, Virginia. *Ottoman Wars 1700–1870: An Empire Besieged*. Harlow, UK: Pearson Longman, 2007.
Palmer, Alan. *The Decline and Fall of the Ottoman Empire*. New York: M. Evan, 1972.

London, 1913 Treaty of (May 30, 1913)

Treaty resolving territorial adjustments after the end of the First Balkan War of 1912 between the Balkan League (Bulgaria, Greece, Montenegro, and Serbia) and the Ottoman Empire. Following the end of hostilities on December 12, 1912, the principal belligerents met in London along with representatives of Britain, Austria-Hungary, Germany, Italy, and Russia to hammer out a peace settlement. The treaty was signed on May 30, 1913.

The main points of contention at the conference were the status of Albania, which had declared its independence on November 28, 1912; the Sanjak of Novi Pazar, which had been under Austro-Hungarian protection since 1878; and the status of Kosovo, Macedonia, and Thrace. All the territorial settlements were at the expense of the Ottoman Empire, which had lost the war.

Most of the Balkan states would have preferred a division of Albania among themselves, but both Austria-Hungary and Italy strongly supported the creation of an independent Albania. Austria-Hungary favored a buffer state as a check against Serbian expansion, while Italy wanted to increase its influence in the Balkans through an Albanian state. The treaty confirmed Albania's independence and obliged Greece, Montenegro, and Serbia to evacuate their troops from its territory.

Despite this limitation on their expected gains, the Balkan powers secured other territory. Kosovo was divided among Albania, Montenegro, and Serbia. Greece received most of Thrace. However, no decision was made regarding Macedonian territory under dispute. The Ottoman Empire also ceded the island of Crete, while the Great Powers were to determine the disposition of the other Aegean islands.

With division of the territories ceded to the Balkan League not addressed in the treaty, Serbia refused to abide by the division of Macedonia agreed to with Bulgaria in March 1912. As a result, the tenuous peace between the Balkan states did not last and led to the outbreak of the Second Balkan War in June 1913, when Bulgaria attacked Serbia and Greece.

ABRAHAM O. MENDOZA

See also
Balkan Wars

Reference
Fromkin, David. *A Peace to End All Peace: The Fall of the Ottoman Empire and the Creation of the Modern Middle East.* New York: Holt, 1989.

London Round Table Conference (February 7–March 17, 1939)

A conference called by the British government that sought to mollify mounting Arab anger over increasing Jewish immigration into Palestine and plans for partition. Following the 1917 Balfour Declaration, the British government had issued position papers stating that the declaration was not an endorsement of a Jewish state in Palestine. In 1936, however, the Peel Commission had recommended partition of Palestine into Jewish and Arab states. In January 1938 the government established the Woodhead Commission to implement the Peel Commission by reporting back specific recommendations on boundaries. The British government hoped that the Woodhead Report might mollify the Arabs.

The Woodhead Report, published on November 9, 1938, rejected the Peel Commission's findings. Its members were sharply divided and held that no partition plan would satisfy both Arabs and Jews. It recommended several possible alternatives, all of which involved a smaller Jewish state, restricted largely to the coastal plain.

The British government held that some sort of accommodation might yet be possible between Arabs and Jews in Palestine and in February 1939 opened the London Round Table Conference (also known as the St. James Palace Conference) on Palestine. Already the British were seeking to restrict Jewish immigration. In December 1938 the mandatory government in Palestine had rejected Jewish calls for the rescue of 10,000 Jewish children from Eastern Europe.

Among attendees at the London talks were Emir Abdullah of Transjordan, Foreign Minister Nuri al-Said of Iraq, Prince Faisal of Saudi Arabia, and ranking officials from Egypt. The British also released Arab Higher Committee members interned in the Seychelles and accepted them as representatives of the Palestinian Arab delegation. The Jewish side was led by Chaim Weizmann, David Ben-Gurion, and Yitzhak Ben-Zvi. The Jewish delegation also included non-Palestinians such as Rabbi Stephen Wise, the leading spokesman of the Zionist cause in the United States, and Lord Reading, Britain's most distinguished Jew and a former viceroy of India.

The conference was held at St. James Palace in London during February 7–March 17, 1939. The Arab side refused to meet in the same room with the Jewish delegates, and as a result both delegations entered and left by separate entrances and met in different rooms. Thus, there were in reality two parallel conferences.

Weizmann sought to mollify Arab fears and implored the British not to cut off immigration in "this blackest hour of Jewish history." Jamil al-Husseini, the chief Arab spokesman, was uncompromising. He called for an immediate end to the mandate and to Jewish immigration in return for a treaty that would protect legitimate British interests in Palestine.

The Arabs also demanded that the British government make public the pledges it had made to Sharif Hussein during World War I. The Colonial Office reluctantly agreed, and on February 15 it released the letters between British high commissioner for Egypt Sir A. Henry McMahon and Hussein. The British meanwhile pressed the Jewish delegation to accept a ceiling on immigration for several years, after which immigration totals were to be based on Arab consent. When the Jewish side rejected this, chief British spokesman Colonial Secretary Malcolm MacDonald threatened them with the possibility of a British withdrawal from Palestine that would leave the Jews vulnerable to superior Arab power.

During the last two weeks of the conference, the British government proposed a number of possible solutions. These included a federation of cantons, a bicameral governmental structure with a lower house based on proportional representation and an upper house based on parity between Jews and Arabs, and other even more exotic formulations. None of these were acceptable to either side. On March 11, MacDonald bluntly told the Jewish delegation that Jewish immigration was at the heart of Arab anger and of a reviving anti-Semitism in Britain itself.

With no hope of agreement, on March 15 at the end of the conference MacDonald proposed that Jewish immigration be limited to 75,000 people over the next five years, with immigration thereafter dependent on Arab agreement. He also stated the British government's desire to curtail land sales to Jews. His sole concession to the Jewish side was that the British government would not seek to impose an independent Palestinian state with a majority Arab government. This policy was in fact made official in the white paper of March 17, 1939.

SPENCER C. TUCKER

See also
Abdullah I; Balfour Declaration; McMahon-Hussein Correspondence; Nuri al-Said; Peel Commission; White Paper of 1939

References
Bethell, Nicholas. *The Palestine Triangle: The Struggle for the Holy Land, 1935–48*. New York: Putnam, 1979.
Hurewitz, J. C. *The Struggle for Palestine*. New York: Schocken, 1976.
Sachar, Howard M. *A History of Israel: From the Rise of Zionism to Our Time*. 3rd ed. New York: Knopf, 2007.

London Straits Convention (July 13, 1841)

Agreement concluded on July 13, 1841, between the governments of Russia, Britain, France, Austria, and Prussia that closed the straits—the Bosporus, the Sea of Marmara, and the Dardanelles linking the Black Sea to the Mediterranean—to all warships during wartime.

In 1831 Mehmed Ali, de facto ruler of Egypt, revolted against the Ottoman Empire. The Egyptian Army drove into Syria and then Anatolia, defeating Ottoman forces and threatening the Ottoman capital of Istanbul (Constantinople). Believing that an Ottoman defeat could bring a general war among the major European states, Russian tsar Nicholas I intervened to support the Ottomans. In 1833 Russia, joined by Austria and Prussia, agreed to take all necessary steps to preserve the Ottoman Empire. The ensuing Treaty of Hünkâr Iskelesi between the Ottoman Empire and Russia promised mutual assistance should either be attacked by a foreign power, while a secret provision closed the straits to all warships except those of the Ottoman Empire and Russia in case of war.

In 1839, Egypt and the Ottoman Empire again went to war. The Russian government worked with those of Austria and Prussia to convince the French, who had sided with Egypt, to accept a multilateral agreement. These new negotiations produced the Straits Convention of 1841, with guarantees similar to those of the earlier treaty but with no secret provisions benefiting Russia. Indeed, it benefited Britain by denying the Russian Black Sea Fleet direct access to the Mediterranean.

It is believed that Tsar Nicholas I was motivated to agree to closure of the straits because he feared that unease of the other Great Powers regarding the close relationship between Russia and the Ottoman Empire established by the Treaty of Hünkâr Iskelesi might bring war against Russia. Nonetheless, Anglo-Russian tensions remained, leading to the Crimean War (1853–1856).

The Montreux Convention Regarding the Regime of the Turkish Straits, negotiated in 1936 and technically still in force, closes the strategic straits to all warships in times of war.

ROBERT B. KANE

See also
Egyptian-Ottoman Wars

References
Askan, Virginia. *Ottoman Wars, 1700–1870: An Empire Besieged*. Harlow, UK: Pearson Longman, 2007.
Palmer, Alan. *The Decline and Fall of the Ottoman Empire*. New York: M. Evan, 1972.
Shaw, Stanford J., and Ezul Kural Shaw. *Reform, Reaction and Republic: The Rise of Modern Turkey, 1808–1975*, Vol. 2, *History of the Ottoman Empire and Modern Turkey*. Cambridge: Cambridge University Press, 1977.
Zuercher, Erik J. *Turkey: A Modern History*. London: I. B. Tauris, 1993.

Long Campaign in Hungary (1443–1444)

A multinational military effort on the part of a number of European states to thwart a potential Ottoman advance into Hungary led by prominent Hungarian general John Hunyadi and Polish king Władysław III (crowned Ulászló I of Hungary in 1440) through the Balkans. Extending from July 22, 1443, to January 25, 1444, the multinational Christian forces, which included Hungarian, Bohemian, Polish, and German cavalry and infantry, along with Lithuanian auxiliaries and smaller Walacian and Serbian contingents, fought Ottoman forces in the Balkans. Ulászló and Hundayi led the Long Campaign into the Ottoman-held territories. While this campaign saw a number of victories for the European forces, these failed to remove the Ottomans from the Balkans. Hunyadi was able to defeat the Ottomans in three major engagements (Nis, Sofia, and Snaim) during the Long Campaign, but the Ottomans were nonetheless able to regroup and retain possession of their territory despite the military reserves and rebellions against their authority. Indeed, the Ottomans went on to strengthen hold on the Balkans, eventually taking the last bastion of Byzantium, the city of Constantinople, in 1453, and Belgrade in 1521, as well as Hungary in the 17th century.

ABRAHAM O. MENDOZA

See also
Long War in Hungary; Ottoman-Hungarian Wars

References
Held, Joseph. *Hunyadi: Legend and Reality*. New York: Columbia University Press, 1985.
Kinross, John Patrick Balfour. *The Ottoman Centuries: The Rise and Fall of the Turkish Empire*. New York: Morrow, 1977.

Long War in Hungary (1593–1606)

A conflict between the Habsburgs and the Ottomans during 1593–1606. The Long War was part of a greater intra-European effort to drive the Ottomans from Ottoman-held Hungary. While fought using the rhetoric of crusade, it was essentially a geostrategic objective on the part of the Habsburgs to expand into Hungary.

In 1595, Pope Clement VIII arranged an alliance between Christian states to fight together against the Ottomans. While the ultimate Ottoman goal was to take Vienna, the Habsburgs and their allies merely sought to remove the Ottomans from Hungary. Habsburg-led forces included contingents from Austria, Hungary, and Bohemia as well as smaller forces from Walacia, Moldavia, Transylvania, and Spain. Most of the engagements during this conflict took place in western Hungary and in Ottoman-held regions in the Balkans.

Habsburg forces successfully captured the strategic fortresses of Gyor, Visegrad, and Esztergom along the Danube but were hesitant to take the city of Buda. Walacian forces were able to capture a series of Ottoman strongholds along the Lower Danube. Moreover, Moldavians defeated the Ottomans in Moldova. Walacian forces were able to defeat the Ottomans in the Battle of Calugareni in 1595 but were unable to make good on securing territory from them. Regardless of the advances made against Ottoman forces by the European forces, the entrenched Ottomans were able to defend their holdings.

The Ottomans defeated the Habsburgs and their Transylvanian allies in the Battle of Mezokeresztes in Hungary in October 1596, despite Habsburg superiority in weaponry. Indeed, the Ottomans held the Habsburg-led forces in check for much of the remainder of the conflict. Moreover, Transylvanian uprisings against both the Ottomans and the Habsburgs hampered any sort of resolution of the conflict.

The Long War ultimately ended with the Peace of Zsitvatorok on November 11, 1606. While the treaty stabilized the Habsburg-Ottoman borderlands, it also allowed the Ottomans to maintain their control over Hungary, which would become the strategic object of future conflict for the Habsburgs.

ABRAHAM O. MENDOZA

See also
Ottoman-Habsburg Wars; Ottoman-Hungarian Wars; Zsitvatorok, Peace of

References
Dunn, Richard S. *The Age of Religious Wars, 1559–1715*. 2nd ed. New York: Norton, 1970.
Kinross, John Patrick Balfour. *The Ottoman Centuries: The Rise and Fall of the Turkish Empire*. New York: Morrow, 1977.

Louis VII, King of France (1120–1180)

King of France (1137–1180) and one of the leaders of the Second Crusade (1147–1149). Born in 1120 in Paris, Louis VII succeeded his father, Louis VI, on August 1, 1137, within days of his marriage to Eleanor, duchess of Aquitaine. Louis VII's marriage to Eleanor brought him the vast territory of Aquitaine, but the marriage was annulled in 1152 because of the failure to produce a male heir.

The early part of Louis VII's reign proved unstable. Louis maintained his father's hostility toward their leading vassal, Thibaud IV, count of Blois, brother of King Stephen of England, and campaigned against him in 1142–1143. Further instability arose out of disputed ecclesiastical elections in which Louis consistently resisted papal wishes, determined to prevent the erosion of his royal prerogatives by Pope Innocent II.

Louis announced his desire to undertake a pilgrimage on Christmas Day 1145, at Bourges, to little enthusiasm, but this changed when Queen Melisende of Jerusalem wrote to Pope Eugenius III asking for help following the fall of the city of Edessa (modern-day Sanliurfa, Turkey) to Nur al-Din in 1144. Louis responded to Eugenius's appeal by summoning an assembly at Vézelay for Easter 1146, where the Cistercian abbot Bernard of Clairvaux preached the crusade with great success.

The underfinanced and ill-organized Second Crusade eventually began in 1147 in two main parties led by King Conrad III of Germany and Louis, who was accompanied by Eleanor. The hostility of Byzantine emperor Manuel I Komnenos to the enterprise heightened the difficulties of the journey, as did the failure of the German and French armies to cooperate. After a difficult journey during which the French suffered defeat at Laodikeia in Phrygia, Louis reached Antioch (modern-day Antakya, Turkey), where he was soon at loggerheads over strategy with Prince Raymond, his wife's uncle. Eleanor took Raymond's part, provoking a lasting breach with Louis. The subsequent crusader campaign against Damascus proved to be a debacle that saw heavy French casualties. Louis stayed on as a pilgrim before returning home via a visit to Eugenius III at Rome in October 1149.

A new threat was the rising power of Henry Plantagenet, count of Anjou, which was consolidated when he married Eleanor in 1154, two years after the annulment of her marriage to Louis. Lacking the necessary resources or the military skill to challenge Henry, Louis was circumscribed in his response, though he would eventually use marriage alliances with Champagne as a means of defense against this mighty vassal. Louis's prestige increased dramatically when he supported first Alexander III against Frederick I Barbarossa and the antipope Victor IV and then Thomas Becket, Henry's exiled and eventually (1170) martyred archbishop. During the 1170s Louis successfully incited the sons of Henry II to revolt against their father, but he was unable to take full advantage of the situation. Louis VII died at Saint-Pont, Allier, in central France on September 18, 1180, and was succeeded by his son Philip II.

Katharine Keats-Rohan

See also
Manuel I Komnenos, Emperor; Nur al-Din

References
Evergates, Theodore. "Louis VII and the Counts of Champagne." In *The Second Crusade and the Cistercians*, ed. Michael Gervers, 109–117. New York: St. Martin's, 1992.
Graboïs, Aryeh. "The Crusade of Louis VII, King of France: A Reconsideration." In *Crusade and Settlement*, ed. Peter W. Edbury, 94–104. Cardiff, UK: University of Cardiff Press, 1985.
Pacaut, Marcel. *Louis VII et son royaume.* Paris: Sevpen, 1964.
Graboïs, Aryeh. "Louis VII pèlerin." *Revue d'histoire de l'église de France* 74 (1988): 5–22.
Rowe, John G. "The Origins of the Second Crusade: Pope Eugenius III, Bernard of Clairvaux and Louis VII of France." In *The Second Crusade and the Cistercians*, ed. Michael Gervers, 79–89. New York: St. Martin's, 1992.
Saissier, Yves. *Louis VII.* Paris: Fayard, 1991.

Louis IX, King of France (1214–1270)

King of France (1226–1270) and leader of Christian crusades in the Holy Land during 1248–1254 and 1270. Commonly known as Saint Louis, he was born in Poissy France, on April 25, 1214, the son of King Louis VIII of France and Blanche of Castile. Louis IX came to the throne on his father's premature death in 1226, his mother acting as regent. Louis had reached his majority by the time he first decided to take the cross in 1244. Some chroniclers report that while the king was seriously ill, he vowed to go on crusade to the Holy Land if God cured him. Others state that it was the king's mother, Blanche, who made the oath on her son's behalf and that Louis then took the vow as his own.

The decision to undertake a crusade was in part a response to a steady deterioration in the position of the Frankish states in Outremer, but Louis was also motivated by more personal reasons. He had been brought up in an atmosphere of religious devotion and was himself a pious man. He heard mass daily, frequently listened to sermons and lessons, and developed close relations with the mendicant orders. He endowed many religious foundations, was generous in the distribution of alms, and venerated relics. In 1239 he purchased the relics of the Passion, including the Crown of Thorns, from Baldwin II, Latin emperor of Constantinople, and had the Sainte-Chapelle constructed in Paris in order to house them.

Four years elapsed between Louis's assumption of the cross in 1244 and his departure for the East in 1248. This delay was not the result of any hesitation on Louis's part but rather of his concern to create the conditions in which the crusade would succeed. He endeavored to achieve peace in the West and unite Christendom in the interests of the expedition and sought to gain spiritual support by righting injustices, soliciting the prayers of the religious orders, and prohibiting those activities that might inspire the wrath of

Depiction of the embarkation of French king Louis IX (St. Louis) on the Seventh Crusade in 1248. Louis sought to conquer Egypt, then use its wealth to fund a campaign to take Jerusalem. The crusade was a failure and Louis was taken prisoner. Ransomed, he returned to France in 1254. (The British Library)

God. He also made meticulous logistical preparations, which included raising money, stockpiling food and arms, and engaging ships to transport the army.

The crusade attacked Egypt and in May 1249 captured the city of Damietta. In April 1250, however, the expedition ended in defeat, and the king and much of his army were captured. After a month of imprisonment, Louis was released and made his way to the Holy Land, where he spent four years rebuilding and refortifying its defenses. Recognizing the Franks' lack of manpower, he left behind a contingent of knights and crossbowmen led by a trusted lieutenant, Geoffrey of Sergines. Louis continued to fund this force at a cost of approximately 4,000 livres per year to the royal treasury until his death in 1270.

It is unclear to what extent Louis was affected by his experiences of defeat and imprisonment at the hands of the Muslims. Some historians have argued that he was preoccupied by the failure of the expedition and the need to redeem it and that he was convinced that it was his own sins or those of his soldiers that had provoked God's displeasure and thus led to defeat. There is no indication that Louis immediately turned to the organization of a new crusade on his return, but he did adopt a more austere lifestyle and was still concerned by the plight of the holy places. He wore plainer dress, ate simply, and increased his personal devotions. He founded, endowed, or made grants to the religious orders and hospitals that looked after the poor and sick, and he fostered the presence of Dominicans and Franciscans in his entourage. Louis even considered giving up the crown and entering a monastery. In a wider context, the king sought to eliminate sin from within his realm by legislating against blasphemy and usury, reformed the administration of the kingdom, and strengthened royal justice. On the international stage, Louis tried to secure peace by reaching territorial settlements with Aragon and England and by acting as an arbiter in the disputes of others. His actions enhanced his personal prestige and that of the French Crown, and both France and Europe as a whole benefited from his efforts.

From the early 1260s the consolidation of Mamluk power under Sultan Baybars I (d. 1277) posed a new threat to Outremer, though only relatively small contingents left the West to assist the Franks. In 1267 Louis decided to again take up the cross, recognizing that many would follow his example. The crusade did not attract the same numbers as his first crusade, but again, Louis made meticulous spiritual and practical preparations to ensure that the army would be both morally and physically prepared and therefore have every possibility of success.

The crusade was intended to relieve the Holy Land, but it was diverted to the Muslim city of Tunis in July 1270. Disease soon broke out in the Christian army, and Louis himself was struck down. He died on August 25, 1270, having failed to restore the holy places or to secure the Holy Land.

Louis was revered for his political achievements, his personal virtues, and his unparalleled attempts to assist the Holy Land. His life and crusades are well known from the biographical account written by his contemporary, John of Joinville. Louis was canonized in 1297.

LINDA GOLDSMITH

See also
Baldwin II of Constantinople; Baybars I; Crusades in the Holy Land, Christian

References
Hallam, Elizabeth M. *Capetian France: 987–1328.* London: Longman, 1980.
Jordan William C. *The Crusades c. 1071–c. 1291.* Cambridge: Cambridge University Press, 1999.
Jordan, William C. *Ideology and Royal Power in Medieval France: Kingship, Crusades and the Jews.* Aldershot, UK: Variorum, 2001.
Jordan, William C. *Louis IX and the Challenge of the Crusade: A Study in Rulership.* Princeton, NJ: Princeton University Press, 1979.
Le Goff, Jacques. "Saint Louis and the Mediterranean." *Mediterranean Historical Review* 5 (1990): 21–43.
Mercuri, Chiara. "San Luigi e la crociata." *Mélanges de l'Ecole Française de Rome: Moyen Age* 108 (1996): 221–241.
Richard, Jean. *Saint Louis: Crusader King of France.* Cambridge: Cambridge University Press, 1992.
Strayer, Joseph R. "The Crusades of Louis IX." In *A History of the Crusades,* Vol. 2, ed. Kenneth M. Setton, 487–518. Philadelphia: University of Pennsylvania Press, 1969.

Lucius Verus (130–169)

Roman coemperor (r. 161–169) with his adopted brother Marcus Aurelius (r. 161–180). Lucius Verus was born in 130, the son of Emperor Hadrian's heir Lucius Aelius Caesar, who died prematurely in 138. Lucius Verus was then adopted by Hadrian's second heir and eventual successor, Antoninus Pius, along with Marcus Aurelius. Verus and Marcus were brought up in the imperial household, tutored by the famous orator Cornelius Fronto. When Antoninus Pius died in 161, Marcus Aurelius and Lucius Verus succeeded to the throne, although only Marcus held the office of *pontifex maximus* (chief priest) and the title *pater patriae* (father of the fatherland). Verus married Marcus's daughter, Lucilla, in 164.

The most pressing concern for the new emperors was the situation on the Roman eastern frontier. War had begun with the Parthian (Arsacid) Persian Empire over the client kingdom of Armenia, and Lucius set out for the east in 162. He preferred to remain in Antioch, so most of the actual fighting with the Persians was directed by his officers, who reclaimed Armenia in 163. In 165–166, the general Avidius Cassius captured Seleucia and Ctesiphon, bringing the war to a successful conclusion. Lucius and Marcus celebrated a joint triumph upon Lucius's return to Rome in 166.

The coemperors embarked on a second campaign against the northern tribes in 168 and spent the following winter at Aquileia. However, the camp was assailed by plague brought back by the soldiers from Persia. As the imperial retinue returned to Rome, Lucius suffered a stroke and died.

CAILLAN DAVENPORT

See also
Marcus Aurelius, Emperor; Parthian Empire; Roman-Parthian Wars

Reference
Birley, Anthony R. *Marcus Aurelius: A Biography.* Rev. ed. New York: Routledge, 2001.

Lydia

A kingdom in western Anatolia (modern-day Turkey) that grew to prominence during the seventh and sixth centuries BCE, frequently clashing with the Greek city-states of Ionia. The most famous of the historically attested kings of Lydia was Croesus (ca. 595–547), who was the last king of the Lydians, as the kingdom was defeated and absorbed into the Persian (Achaemenid) Empire.

There is little archaeological or historical evidence for the Lydians prior to the eighth century BCE. The Greek historian Herodotus preserved a spurious list of kings and dynasties from early Lydian history, but it is not until the reign of Gyges (ca. 680–644) that a Lydian king is corroborated in other historical material. Beset by invasion, Gyges's petition for assistance from Assurbanipal, the king of Assyria, is preserved in the archives of Assyria and dated to circa 664. Later, around 660, Gyges is said to have sent mercenaries to Egypt to assist Pharaoh Psammetichus I.

Lydia clearly had well-developed cultural ties and trade relationships with the other great kingdoms of the Near East. Indeed, trade routes between the Greek cities of the west and the powers of the Near East, fostered by cultural bonds, were as integral to the famed wealth of the Lydian kings as were the electrum refineries and coin mints of the capital city Sardis.

Under Gyges, Lydia began encroaching on the Ionian Greek cities of the Aegean coast, attacking both Smyrna and Miletus. Gyges's successor Ardys (ca. 644–late seventh century BCE) even captured Priene, although the Lydians never managed to establish a permanent foothold on the Aegean coast. Despite frequent conflict, the Lydian royal family maintained close ties with the Greek world, including intermarriage with prominent Greek families such as that of Melas, the tyrant of Ephesus. The Lydians also gave offerings to and worshipped at Greek temples and sanctuaries, such as at Delphi, Assesus (a sanctuary in the territory of Miletus), and the great temple to Artemis at Ephesus. But ultimately Croesus, according to Herodotus, fatally misunderstanding a message from the oracle at Delphi, invaded the territory of the Persian (Achaemenid) Empire. When he was defeated by Cyrus, both the Lydian kingdom and the Lydian capital of Sardis swiftly fell to the Persians circa 547.

RUSSELL BUZBY

See also
Achaemenid Empire; Ashurbanipal

References
Cahill, Nicholas D. *Lidyalilar ve Dunyalari: The Lydians and Their World.* Istanbul: Yapi Kredi Kultur Sanat Yayincilik, 2010.
Dedeoglu, Hasan. *The Lydians and Sardis.* Istanbul: A Turizm Yayinlari, 2003.
Roosevelt, Christopher. *The Archaeology of Lydia, from Gyges to Alexander.* New York: Cambridge University Press, 2009.

Lysimachus (ca. 355–281 BCE)

Macedonian general of Alexander III the Great and one of the Diadochi (successor) generals who fought to control the empire after Alexander's death in 323 BCE. Lysimachus was born circa 355 BCE in Crannon or Pellaan to a family of Thessalian Greek heritage. His father was a high-ranking nobleman and intimate of King Philip II of Macedon. Lysimachus grew up as a Macedonian and was educated at the Macedonian court in Pella. He proved to be an able officer and rose to the prestigious rank of *somatophylax* (bodyguard) during the reign of Philip II (r. 359–336).

Lysimachus performed well in Alexander's invasion of the Persian Empire and won recognition for his actions during the invasion of India. In the division of the empire after the death of Alexander, Lysimachus received the underdeveloped region of Thrace. Hard fighting against the Thracian tribes brought him control of the hinterland, over which Lysimachus set out to impose the same tight control as over the Greek cities on the coast.

Lysimachus prudently stayed out of the wars among Alexander's successors but did follow others in taking the title of king in 306, thus formally opposing any attempt at restoring Alexander's empire. The main threat of this kind came from Antigonus I Monophthalmus in the western part of Alexander's Asiatic empire. In 302 in collaboration with Seleucus I in Babylon and the other kings, Lysimachus invaded Asia Minor and, in a brilliant defensive campaign, pinned down Antigonus until he and Seleucus were able to defeat and kill Antigonus in the Battle of Ipsus (301).

As his reward, Lysimachus secured the rich territory of Asia Minor. Now with wider ambitions, he extended his kingdom northward across the Danube until a defeat by the Getae forced him to make the Danube his frontier in 297. He joined with Pyrrhus of Epirus in stopping the attempt by Antigonus's son Demetrius I Poliorcetes to take the kingdom of Macedonia. The two divided the kingdom, but two years later Lysimachus took over all of it (287–285).

Lysimachus was now at the height of his power, ruling a territory extending from the Adriatic to the Black Sea. His personal life had so far been sedate, but infatuation with a new wife, Arsinoe (the daughter of Ptolemy I), led him to believe her allegations that his son and heir, the highly popular Agathocles, was plotting against him. Lysimachus's murder of Agathocles alienated the nobility, who called in Seleucus. In the Battle of Corupedium in Asia Minor in February 281, Seleucus defeated and killed Lysimachus. Tough in combat and a highly capable administrator, Lysimachus was a dour individual lacking in charisma.

DOUGLAS KELLY

See also
Alexander III the Great; Antigonus I Monophthalmus; Demetrius I Poliorcetes; Diadochi, Wars of the; Seleucus I Nicator

Reference
Lund, Helen S. 1992. *Lysimachus: A Study in Early Hellenistic Kingship.* New York: Routledge, 1992.

Ma'an, Siege of (April 17–September 28, 1918)

Mesopotamian theater battle in World War I. The town of Ma'an, located on the rail line between Jerusalem and Aqaba, had been used as a base for Ottoman operations against forces of the Arab Revolt. In early April 1918 following a halt in the British advance into Transjordan and to the Dead Sea at Amman, Arab Northern Army commander Prince Faisal ibn Hussein planned an attack on Ma'an. His goals were to secure future Allied advances in the area from attacks from the rear and to cut off Amman from reinforcement along the Hejaz railway from the south. All available Ottoman troops, including most of the garrison of Ma'an, then had been relocated to Amman in an attempt to halt the British advance there.

The attack on Ma'an began on April 17, 1918, with Arab forces cutting the Hejaz railroad both north and south of the town. Arab Army regulars under Jafaar Pasha, supported by British armored cars and camel units, then attacked the town from the north, south, and west. Although the attacking Arab forces held a numerical advantage over the Ottoman defenders, operations were suspended when Jafaar's small French artillery detachment ran short of ammunition. The majority of the Arab forces then fell back on Senna, which had been taken on April 13. Following this stalemate, a siege began.

Ottoman negotiations to surrender were broken off by the arrival of 3,000 men of the Ottoman Army II Corps from Amman. These additional troops strengthened the Ottoman defenses in Ma'an as well as their resolve and thus prolonged the siege. Jafaar then cut off Ottoman resupply into Ma'an from Ottoman-controlled Medina along the Hejaz railway to the south.

Ma'an was now effectively isolated from the outside. The combined forces of Prince Faisal and Major General Sir Edward Chaytor's Australian and New Zealand Mounted Division then pursued the survivors up the Hejaz railway. On September 28, Chaytor's forces cut the Ottomans off and secured the surrender of 4,500 of them.

ALEX CORRELL

See also
Amman Campaign; Faisal I, King of Iraq; Hejaz Railroad, Attacks on; Mesopotamian Theater, World War I; Transjordan Campaign

References
Barker, A. J. *The Bastard War: The Mesopotamian Campaign of 1914–1918.* New York: Dial, 1967.

Buchanan, George. *Tragedy of Mesopotamia.* New York: AMS Press, 1974.

Lawrence, T. E. *Revolt in the Desert.* Herefordshire, UK: Wordsworth Editions, 1997.

Moberly, F. J. *The Campaign in Mesopotamia, 1914–1918.* 3 vols. Nashville: Battery Press, 1997–1998.

Townshend, Charles. *Desert Hell: The British Invasion of Mesopotamia.* Cambridge, MA: Belknap Press of Harvard University Press, 2011.

Maccabean Revolt (167–160 BCE)

Following a Roman victory over the Seleucid Empire in 192 BCE, the Seleucids struggled to pay the heavy annual tribute demanded by Rome. These taxes were paid in the temples of the Seleucid territories and were much resented in Judaea. In 167 BCE Seleucid ruler Antiochus IV arrived in Jerusalem following a military defeat in Egypt. Eager to raise funds and in any case opposed to Judaism, he sold the office of high priest to an individual not qualified to hold the position under Jewish law. He also outlawed Judaism and ordered the establishment in its place of an imperial cult. Antiochus desecrated the Temple by ordering raised in it a statue of himself as Zeus. These actions and his insistence on the Hellenization of the Jews brought on a Jewish revolt.

Mattathias the Hasmonean, a Jewish priest from the village of Mod'lin in Judaea, refused to make sacrifice to a Greek god, and he and his sons Judas, Eleazar, Simon, John, and Jonathan killed a Seleucid general and some soldiers, triggering the protracted Maccabean Revolt (167–160 BCE). When Mattathias died in 166, his eldest son Judas assumed leadership of the revolt, which came to be named for him. The surname of Maccabeus (Maccabee) given Judas may mean "hammer," signifying his leadership in battle, although other scholars claim that it means "the one designated by Yahweh (God)."

A natural leader and military commander of considerable ability, Judas Maccabeus at first avoided major engagements with the well-armed Seleucids and employed guerrilla tactics to defeat a succession of their generals sent to Judaea, although his military efforts were first directed against Hellenized Jews, of whom there were a great number. In 167 at the Ascent of Lebonah, his men annihilated an entire Seleucid unit; in 166 at Nahal el-Haramiah, he defeated a small Seleucid force under Apollonius, the governor of Samaria. Apollonius was among the dead. This victory led to many Jews joining the cause.

Shortly thereafter in 166 BCE, Judas defeated a larger Seleucid force under Seron near Beth-Horon. Judas was then victorious at Emmaus, defeating Seleucid generals Micanor and Gorgias. Judas's defeat of the Seleucids at Beth Zur (Bethsura) near Hebron in 164 allowed him to take much of Jerusalem, including the Temple, although some Seleucids continued to hold out in the Acra (citadel). While continuing the siege of the Acra, Judas expanded his control over the whole of Judaea.

With Antiochus campaigning to the east, Seleucid regent Lysias invaded Judaea and defeated Judas at Beth Zachariah (162 BCE), but Lysias was then forced to return to Syria to suppress a revolt there. That same year Bacchides, commander of Seleucid forces in Judaea, defeated Judas at Jerusalem, driving him from the city.

Judas rallied, however, and in 161 he defeated Syrian general Nicanor at Adasa; Nicanor was among those killed. That same year Judas was defeated and slain in the Battle of Elasa by a far more numerous Seleucid force, said to number 20,000 men, commanded by Bacchides.

Judas is widely praised in the First Book of Maccabees, and he is acclaimed by Jews as one of the greatest military leaders in their history. The Festival of Lights, or Chanukah (Hanukkah, meaning "Dedication") in the month of December commemorates the cleansing and rededication of the Temple following the removal of its pagan statuary by Judas in 164.

While many scholars date the revolt as ending in 160 BCE, armed resistance against the Seleucids continued under Jonathan, who enjoyed considerable success with the guerrilla tactics first employed by his brother. Establishing his headquarters at Jerusalem in 152, Jonathan was recognized as de facto ruler of Judaea until 143, when he was captured in an ambush at Ptolemais (Acre, Akko) and killed by dissident Jews. In 142, however, Jonathan's brother Simon, who had been elected to succeed Jonathan, secured recognition of Judaea's independence, with himself as king.

SPENCER C. TUCKER

See also
Antiochus IV Epiphanes; Judas Maccabeus; Seleucid Empire

References
de Lange, Nicholas, ed. *The Illustrated History of the Jewish People*. London: Aurum, 1997.
Robinson, Theodore H., and W. O. E. Oesterley. *A History of Israel*. Oxford, UK: Clarendon, 1932.
Schäfer, Peter. *The History of the Jews in the Greco-Roman World*. New York: Routledge, 2003.
Skolnik, Fred, and Michael Berenbaum. *Encyclopaedia Judaica*, Vol. 9. Detroit: Macmillan Reference USA in association with the Keter Publishing House, 2007.

MacMichael, Sir Harold (1882–1969)

British career civil servant and high commissioner for the British Mandate for Palestine (1938–1944). Harold MacMichael was born in 1882. He graduated from Magdalene College, Cambridge, and after passing the civil service examination in 1904 was assigned to the Sudan. He had a lengthy tenure there and also served as British governor of Tanganyika.

In March 1938 MacMichael assumed the post of high commissioner for the British Mandate for Palestine, succeeding Sir Arthur Grenfell Wauchope. MacMichael's arrival in Palestine heralded a shift in British policy toward the mandate, occasioned by the Arab Revolt of 1936–1939. Wauchope had interpreted immigration policies liberally. With the Arab Revolt and the approach of World War II, however, British leaders greatly feared a possible Axis move against Egypt and Britain's imperial lifeline of the Suez Canal. London believed that Arab unrest might facilitate this and possibly even result in Britain's expulsion from the Middle East.

With the release of the British government white paper in 1939, MacMichael retreated from the liberal policies of his predecessor regarding Jewish immigration, choosing instead to interpret regulations quite rigidly. This occurred in the midst of persecutions of Jews in Germany and in Poland and continued even with evidence of the Holocaust, the Nazi effort to exterminate the Jews in Europe. British authorities took into custody all Jews immigrating to Palestine illegally and sent them on to the Indian Ocean island of Mauritius. Land transfer regulations of 1940 sought to prohibit the further sale of Arab property to Jews.

In March 1943, MacMichael broadcast a message outlining the British government's plans for the postwar economic development program. Largely based on the 1939 white paper, the message created widespread Jewish anger. Mounting Jewish opposition to this and to the British immigration policy in the midst of the Holocaust led to the onset of Jewish terrorism, principally by the Irgun Tsvai Leumi (National Military Organization) and Lohamei Herut Israel (Lehi), against the British authorities in Palestine. Militant Zionists in Palestine held MacMichael responsible for much of British policy in Palestine. Indeed, MacMichael narrowly escaped an attempt on August 8, 1944, on his life that wounded his wife.

Upon leaving Palestine MacMichael was assigned to Malaya, where he wrote its constitution. He then served in Malta. MacMichael died in Folkstone, England, in 1969.

SPENCER C. TUCKER

See also
Arab Revolt in Palestine; Holocaust; Irgun Tsvai Leumi; Lohamei Herut Israel; Palestine, British Mandate for; Wauchope, Sir Arthur Grenfell; White Paper of 1939

References
Sachar, Howard M. *A History of Israel: From the Rise of Zionism to Our Time.* 3rd ed. New York: Knopf, 2007.
Shepherd, Naomi. *Ploughing Sand: British Rule in Palestine, 1917–1948.* New Brunswick, NJ: Rutgers University Press, 1999.

Madrid Conference (October 30–November 1, 1991)

Conference held in Madrid, Spain, during October 30–November 1, 1991, that brought together for the first time Syrian, Lebanese, Jordanian, Palestinian, and Israeli officials with the aim of beginning the process of securing a comprehensive Middle East peace settlement. The United States and the Soviet Union cosponsored the meeting. Also in attendance were officials from Egypt, the European Union, and the Gulf Cooperation Council. The Madrid Conference convened on October 30 and lasted three days. No formal declarations or accommodations resulted from the meeting, as it was designed principally to bring together the warring parties and serve as a springboard for future bilateral and multilateral conferences between Arabs and Israelis.

The Madrid Conference came in the immediate aftermath of the 1991 Persian Gulf War and the waning days of the Cold War. President George H. W. Bush's administration, in its attempt to construct a so-called new world order, set a goal of bringing lasting peace to the Middle East. In this the administration was aided—at least symbolically—by Soviet leader Mikhail Gorbachev. The Soviet Union would be officially dissolved only eight weeks after the Madrid Conference ended, but it was nonetheless important for Bush to engage the Soviets in the peace process, because Russia and other post-Soviet successor states had vested interests in the Middle East. In addition, a number of Arab nations had enjoyed close ties to the Soviets.

It was understood by the parties attending the meeting that the resultant peace process should be guided by the land-for-peace formula first promulgated by the United Nations (UN) in November 1967 in UN Security Council Resolution 242 and later reiterated in UN Resolutions 338 and 425. The talks were designed to provide the proper dialogue between Israel and the Arab states of Lebanon, Syria, and Jordan so that bilateral peace treaties could soon be realized. In approaching the Palestinian-Israeli dilemma the congress was to begin a two-stage process, which included the establishment of interim self-government for the Palestinians followed by the creation of a permanent Palestinian government that would ultimately lead to an autonomous Palestinian state. These guidelines were also the basic framework for the Oslo peace process and the Oslo Accords, which were finalized in August 1993. Indeed, the Oslo process began almost immediately after the Madrid Conference ended. The Oslo process was, however, opposed by a number of those involved in the Madrid Conference because of the purely bilateral nature of the accords as well as their design and substance.

Multilateral talks began in Moscow in January 1992 and focused on five major concerns: water allocation, environmental preservation, refugee issues, economic development, and regional arms control. Israel initially balked at discussing refugee and economic problems, and Syria and Jordan refused to join in multilateral talks because no real progress had been made in bilateral negotiations. In October 1994, however, Jordan and Israel signed a historic peace treaty. Several attempts were made to negotiate an Israeli-Syrian peace treaty, but last-minute complications torpedoed the effort. As a result of the Madrid Conference and the Oslo Accords that followed, the Palestinians were allowed to set up their own governing entity, the Palestinian Authority (PA).

The peace process stalled in the latter half of the 1990s as violence flared anew in the region and Israeli politics forced a retrenchment from wide-ranging peace initiatives. Formal bilateral talks would not resume until January 2000, and they made little headway thereafter. The dramatic September 13, 1993, signing of the Declaration of Principles between Israel and the Palestine Liberation Organization (PLO) on the White House lawn with a beaming President Bill Clinton looking on was a direct result of the Madrid Conference. Indeed, the stipulations contained in the declaration were the same basic guidelines as those propounded in Madrid. Perhaps the biggest winner in all of this was Israel, as the process that had begun in Madrid resulted in several key nations finally recognizing that state. These included India and the People's Republic of China as well as Tunisia, Morocco, Qatar, and Oman. The Arab economic boycott of Israel also began to loosen.

PAUL G. PIERPAOLI JR.

See also
Oslo Accords; Palestine Liberation Organization; Palestinian National Authority

References
Brown, Nathan J. *Palestinian Politics after the Oslo Accords: Resuming Arab Palestine.* Berkeley: University of California Press, 2003.
Freedman, Robert Owen, ed. *The Middle East and the Peace Process: The Impact of the Oslo Accords.* Gainesville: University Press of Florida, 1998.
Watson, Geoffrey R. *The Oslo Accords: International Law and the Israeli-Palestinian Peace Agreements.* New York: Oxford University Press, 2000.
Weinberger, Peter. *Co-opting the PLO: A Critical Reconstruction of the Oslo Accords, 1993–1995.* New York: Rowman and Littlefield, 2006.

Magnesia, Battle of (December 190 BCE)

Fought in December 190 BCE, the Battle of Magnesia was the concluding battle of the Roman-Seleucid War. The battle occurred near Magnesia ad Sipylum on the plains of Lydia in Asia Minor and was fought between a Roman army, led by the consul Lucius Cornelius Scipio and the Roman ally Eumenes II of Pergamum, and the army of Antiochus III the Great of the Seleucid Empire.

Following the defeat of Macedon in the Battle of Cynoscephalae (197), the only Hellenistic power strong enough to threaten Roman control of Greece was the Seleucid Empire. Its king, Antiochus III the Great, invaded Greece on assurances that the Greeks would join him to throw off the Roman yoke. However, this did not occur, and after being defeated by the Romans at Thermopylae (191), Antiochus fled to Asia Minor. After the Seleucid Navy was beaten in the Battles of Eurymedon and Myonessus (190), a large Roman army, with forces from Rhodes and Pergamum, crossed the Hellespont. The army was led by the consul Lucius Cornelius Scipio, accompanied by his elder brother Publius Cornelius Scipio Africanus, the conqueror of Hannibal at Zama in 202 in the Third Punic War.

The Romans had 25,000 infantry, 3,000 cavalry, and 16 elephants. Antiochus had 60,000 infantry, more than 12,000 cavalry, and 16 elephants. More specifically, he had 16,000 *sarissa* phalangites in the center; on the right wing were 1,500 Galatian heavy infantry, 4,000 heavy cavalry, 1,200 horse archers, 10,000 light infantry, and 54 elephants. On the left wing were 3,500 Galatian and Cappadocian heavy infantry, 2,700 auxiliaries, 4,000 heavy cavalry, scythed chariots and camels, 2,500 light cavalry, and 24,000 assorted light infantry.

Antiochus had fortified a position across a river, and after a few days of inaction the Romans moved nearer, securing their left flank with the river while lacking sufficient cavalry to protect both flanks. The battle saw victories on the right wing of each army. Antiochus might have won the battle except for Eumenes II of Pergamum's cavalry support to the Romans. Despite being outnumbered almost three to one, Eumenes crushed Antiochus's left wing through his aggression, first using light troops to nullify the chariots and camels and then in the disorder charging with his 3,000 heavy cavalry to rout the rest down to the phalanx. In the center the Seleucid phalanx was able to hold off the Roman infantry until forced by Eumenes's cavalry to edge behind their fortifications.

On the other flank Antiochus personally led a decisive heavy cavalry charge to rout the Roman infantry on the left wing, resting on the river. Unfortunately, rather than turn and attack the exposed Roman flank and relieve his phalanx in the center, Antiochus pursued too far. The Roman camp guard of 2,000 infantry rallied the retreating men and, aided by 200 cavalry brought by Eumenes's brother from the other wing, counterattacked Antiochus. The enthusiasm of this small force and the defeat of most of his left wing prompted Antiochus to flee. The rout spread to the rest of the army, including the victorious phalanx in the center. Antiochus reportedly lost 50,000 infantry and 3,000 cavalry in the battle, while Romans losses were reported at only 350 men.

Antiochus's defeat at Magnesia did not win any real territory for Rome but did pave the way for later eastward expansion and forced Antiochus to submit to Rome.

GRAHAM WRIGHTSON

See also
Antiochus III Megas; Eumenes II of Pergamum; Pergamum; Seleucid Empire

References
Derow, Peter. "The Arrival of Rome: From the Illyrian Wars to the Fall of Macedon." In *A Companion to the Hellenistic World*, ed. Andrew Erskine, 51–70. Oxford, UK: Blackwell, 2003.
Grainger, John D. *The Roman War of Antiochus the Great*. Leiden: Brill, 2002.
Pietrykowski, Joseph. *Great Battles of the Hellenistic World*. Barnsley: Pen and Sword, 2009.

Mahmud, Muhammad Sidqi (1923–)

Egyptian military officer and chief of the Egyptian Air Force (1953–1967). Muhammad Sidqi Mahmud was born in Egypt, probably in 1923. He attended the Egyptian Military Academy and then joined the air force. In the early 1950s he joined the Free Officers Movement that advocated land reform, modernization, and Arab nationalism. The Free Officers Movement seized control of Egypt in 1952, and Mahmud became commander of the Egyptian Air Force the next year. This appointment was part of a larger program of military appointments designed to give Gamal Abdel Nasser control of the armed forces in his power struggle with President Mohammad Naguib. Nasser ousted Naguib from power in October 1954.

Given the tensions between Nasser's Egypt and the West, the Egyptian Air Force relied heavily on the Soviet Union for training and matériel, and Mahmud presided over this process. As with many of the other Free Officers, he tended to take a parochial view of his service as a personal power base, which hindered the formation of a coordinated defense policy. In 1956 during the Sinai Campaign, French and British air forces wrought considerable destruction on Egyptian air assets on the ground. Nevertheless, Nasser chose not to fire Mahmud for this debacle.

In 1967 in the run-up to the Six-Day War, Mahmud warned the Egyptian leadership about the inability of his forces to undertake the air operations necessary to support a successful Egyptian ground offensive. Mahmud, now a lieutenant general, protested to Nasser that the Egyptian Air Force would sustain heavy losses in the event of an Israeli first strike. Both Nasser and Field Marshal Abdel Hakim Amer chastised Mahmud for this position. Perhaps because of this, Mahmud predicted Egyptian Air Force losses of around 20 percent in the event of an Israeli preemptive strike.

On June 5, 1967, the first day of hostilities in the Six-Day War, the Israelis destroyed the majority of the Egyptian Air Force on the ground. The Israeli pilots were far better trained, but they were also familiar with the weaknesses of the MiG-21 fighter, thanks to an Iraqi defector who had flown one to Israel in 1966. They also struck when the vast majority of the Egyptian crews were having breakfast and few planes were in the air and when Amer and Mahmud were in the air on their way to inspect troops in the Sinai. By the afternoon of June 5, Egypt had lost the entirety of its bombers and the vast majority of its fighters. This left the army at a serious disadvantage and ultimately resulted in a disorganized Egyptian ground retreat.

The Six-Day War was an abject failure for Egypt. Mahmud and others were blamed and imprisoned. Amer appears to have committed or was forced to commit suicide on September 14, 1967. Mahmud was tried before a military tribunal in February 1968 and was sentenced to 15 years in prison for dereliction of duty. Nasser had him retried, however, because of popular protests that erupted over what was perceived to be a lenient sentence. On August 29, 1968, Mahmud was again found guilty and sentenced to life imprisonment at hard labor. Pardoned on January 27, 1974, by Egyptian president Anwar Sadat, Mahmud assiduously avoided politics thereafter. While he must bear blame for the poor air force training before the Six-Day War, he cannot be blamed for the leadership's decision that Egypt could absorb an Israeli first strike, for he plainly warned of the likely consequences.

MICHAEL K. BEAUCHAMP

See also
Amer, Abdel Hakim; Egypt; Nasser, Gamal Abdel; Six-Day War

References

Bowen, Jeremy. *Six Days: How the 1967 War Shaped the Middle East.* New York: Thomas Dunne, 2005.

Oren, Michael B. *Six Days of War: June 1967 and the Making of the Modern Middle East.* Novato, CA: Presidio, 2003.

Mahmud II, Sultan (1785–1839)

Ottoman sultan. Mahmud II was born at Topkapi Palace in Istanbul (Constantinople), on July 20, 1785. The posthumous son of Sultan Abdul Hamid I, Mahmud, often referred to as "Peter the Great of Turkey," would carry out important and much-needed military, administrative, and financial reforms.

In 1808 Mahmud's predecessor, his half brother Mustafa IV, ordered Mahmud and deposed Sultan Selim III executed in order to secure his position during a rebellion. Selim was slain, but Mahmud escaped death, having been hidden by his mother. The rebellion was a success. Mustafa IV was deposed, and Mahmud became sultan on July 28, 1808.

Early in Mahmud's reign, Ottoman governor of Egypt Mehmed Ali recaptured the holy cities of Medina (1812) and Mecca (1813) from Abdullah bin Saud, executing the latter and restoring Ottoman control. This success was more than counterbalanced by numerous reverses elsewhere, however. Russia sought to take advantage of perceived Ottoman weakness in two Russo-Turkish wars during 1808–1812 and 1828–1829. Greece was another matter, for in 1821 the Greeks began a war of independence from the Ottoman Empire that saw them successful in 1832. The Ottomans also suffered a major military reverse in the Battle of Erzurum (1821) during the Ottoman-Persian War of 1821–1823, when, thanks to their recent military reforms, 30,000 Persians led by Crown Prince Abbas Mirza defeated a much larger force of 50,000 Ottomans. The crushing defeat of the Ottoman Navy in the Battle of Navarino Bay (1827) during the Greek War of Independence was yet another wake-up call regarding Ottoman military backwardness. Another military reverse for the Ottomans came in 1830 when French forces secured Algiers and then gradually expanded their control outward. In 1831–1833 and again in 1839–1841 Mahmud's vassal Mehmed Ali revolted, seeking to end Ottoman control of Egypt.

All of the above revealed a pressing need for reform, and not just that of the military. The latter would, however, encounter strong opposition from the reactionary yet politically powerful Janissary Corps, which had often interfered in affairs of state, even to overthrowing sultans. Well aware that the Janissaries would never allow meaningful reform, Mahmud ordered the 135,000-man Janissary Corps dissolved in what became known as the Auspicious Incident of June 15, 1826, and replaced with a new force under modern Western lines. Most of the Janissaries revolted, but Mahmud was prepared for this and put down the revolt. A number of the Janissaries were slain and others were killed or imprisoned. After the defeat at Navarino, Mahmud also gave attention to rebuilding the Ottoman Navy along modern lines, with the first steam warships acquired in 1828.

In 1839 Mahmud introduced the Council of Ministers to advise the sultan. Accompanying this were modernization in dress and architecture. More importantly, Mahmud II carried out an extensive administrative reorganization in the empire as well as major legal, educational, and land reforms. All this reached culmination in the Decree of Tanzimat (reorganization) by his son and successor Sultan Abdul Hamid I. Mahmud II died in Istanbul on July 1, 1839.

SPENCER C. TUCKER

See also

Auspicious Incident; Constantinople, 1832 Treaty of; Egyptian-Ottoman Wars; Erzurum, First Treaty of; Janissaries; Ottoman-Persian Wars of the 18th and 19th Centuries; Russo-Ottoman Wars

References

Levy, Avigdor. "The Ottoman Ulema and the Military Reforms of Sultan Mahmud II." *Asian and African Studies* 7 (1971): 13–39.

Lewis, Bernard. *The Emergence of Modern Turkey.* 2nd ed. New York: Oxford University Press, 1968.

Palmer, Alan. *The Decline and Fall of the Ottoman Empire.* New York: M. Evans, 1992.

Majid al-Tikriti, Ali Hassan al- (1941–2010)

High-ranking Iraqi government official, minister of defense (1993–1995), and cousin of Baath Party leader and Iraqi dictator Saddam Hussein. Because of his role in the use of chemical weapons to suppress ethnic uprisings by the Kurds and Shiites, he earned the sobriquet "Chemical Ali." Ali Hassan Abd al-Majid al-Tikriti was born sometime in 1941 in Tikrit into a family of relatively modest means.

Majid, along with many others from Tikrit, joined the Baath Party in 1958 and enlisted in the Iraqi Army that same year. He was arrested during the 1963 coup when Colonel Abd al-Salm Arif seized power and moved against the Baathists. After the Baath Party seized power in 1968, Majid rose steadily within the party ranks along with his cousin Saddam Hussein and many other men from Tikrit, a number of them interrelated. This cadre formed the base of Hussein's power, as all were family members or members of the same tribe, people whom he could trust. By 1978, Majid headed the Regional Secretariat Office of the Baath Party. That same year after graduating from the National Defense Academy, he was appointed to the Military Bureau.

When Hussein became president of Iraq in 1979, replacing Ahmad al-Hassan Bakr, Majid's star continued to rise. In 1982 he became a member of the Regional Command. After an assassination attempt on Hussein in 1983, Majid was charged with punishing those connected—even tangentially—with the attempt. During 1984–1987 he was the director-general of (internal) security, making him a key part of Hussein's security apparatus that ensured the survival and continuation of the regime.

In 1987 Hussein appointed Majid governor of the northern bureau, which included Kurdistan in northern Iraq. By 1987 during the Iraq-Iran War, the security situation in northern Iraq was seen as precarious, with a growing Kurdish resistance movement distracting the government from the war effort against Iran. To bring an end to the Kurdish insurgency, Majid ordered attacks against civilian Kurds, using chemical weapons including mustard gas and sarin. One attack on Halabja resulted in more 5,000 deaths, leading to Majid's sobriquet "Chemical Ali." Following the Halabja massacre, Majid oversaw an Arabization campaign in Anfal that involved the forced transfer of Kurdish populations and the continued use of chemical weapons to break the Kurdish resistance.

In 1989 Majid became minister of local administration, a position designed to oversee the repopulation with Arabs of the areas that he had depopulated in Kurdistan in his last posting. After the invasion of Kuwait in August 1990 Majid was made governor of Kuwait, in which position he oversaw the organized Iraqi looting and sacking of the nation and the elimination of opposition to Iraqi rule.

With the 1991 Persian Gulf War and the Shiite rebellion centered in Basra against the regime, Hussein placed Majid in charge of the southern forces to put down the insurgency, which he did with brute force. In 1991 Majid became a member of the Revolutionary Command Council. He served as minister of the interior during 1991–1993, and from 1993 to 1995 he headed the Ministry of Defense. The constant shifts in assignments also revealed Hussein's paranoid nature. No official served in any key military or security post for long, lest he come to pose a threat to the regime. Rotation in office was a key element of Hussein's modus operandi, even if the rotation occurred among a limited elite.

In 1995 Majid was removed from office for allegedly having traded with Iran, but in 1998 he reemerged as governor of the southern portion of Iraq where government power was limited because of the no-fly zone established by the coalition after the Persian Gulf War. Shortly before the Iraq War began in March 2003, Hussein divided the nation into four administrative areas, and Majid had charge of the southern portion. Majid was arrested on August 17, 2003, and subsequently handed over to Iraqi authorities. Placed on trial on charges of crimes against humanity and genocide arising from his campaign against the Kurds, Majid was unapologetic, arguing that his actions had been approved by the legitimate Iraqi government and that he was simply carrying out orders. On June 24, 2007, an Iraqi court found Majid guilty. The court gave him five death sentences, to be carried out by hanging. A series of judicial and political hurdles delayed the sentence, but it was finally carried out in Baghdad on January 25, 2010.

MICHAEL K. BEAUCHAMP

See also
Arif, Abd al-Salam; Baath Party; Chemical Weapons and Warfare; Hussein, Saddam; Iran-Iraq War; Iraq; Kurds; Kurds, Massacres of

References
Aburish, Said K. *Saddam Hussein: The Politics of Revenge*. New York: Bloomsbury, 2000.
al-Khalil, Samir. *Republic of Fear: The Politics of Modern Iraq*. Berkeley: University of California Press, 1989.
Cleveland, William L. *A History of the Modern Middle East*. Boulder, CO: Westview, 2004.

Makarios III, Archbishop (1913–1977)

Archbishop of the Orthodox Church of Cyprus and first president of Cyprus (1959–1977). Mikhail Khristodolou Mouskos, the son of a shepherd, was born in Pano Panayia, Cyprus, on August 13, 1913. As a novice monk in the Kykkos Greek Orthodox monastery, he adopted the name Makarios. He subsequently studied theology at the University of Athens and Boston University. Ordained in 1946, he was elected bishop of Kition in 1948.

In 1950 Makarios organized a plebiscite among Greek Cypriots, who represented 80 percent of the island's population. This indicated strong support for union with Greece (enosis). Makarios was elected archbishop of Cyprus on

October 18, 1950, as Makarios III and became known as a champion of enosis.

In February 1954 Makarios III met with Greek prime minister Alexander Papagos, who tacitly supported enosis. In April 1955 Makarios lent his support to General Georgios Grivas, leader of the terrorist National Organization of Cypriot Fighters, to begin an armed campaign against British forces, which still controlled the island. Makarios III's support of terrorism led British authorities to exile him in 1956 to the Seychelles Islands. In 1957 he left the Seychelles and took up residence in Athens, where he kept up his enosis campaign.

In 1958, however, Makarios seemed to change his attitude toward enosis and suggested in an interview that he was prepared to accept Cypriot independence. After the Greeks and Turks decided to move forward with Cypriot independence in February 1959, he was elected president on December 13, 1959, with a Turkish Cypriot as vice president. Makarios initially tried to unite the Greek and Turkish communities, but his efforts were stymied by deep-seated ethnic hostilities and individuals who still wished to proceed with enosis. In November 1963 Makarios sought amendments to the constitution, a request that led to violent clashes between Greeks and Turks on the island. In December 1967 he was forced to accede to the Turkish Cypriot Provisional Administration in charge of Turkish affairs.

In February 1968 Makarios won reelection to the presidency of Cyprus, but in 1973 the three other Cypriot bishops asked him to resign. Makarios refused, standing successfully for a third term in 1973. His time in office was marked by repeated assassination attempts by those supporting enosis, who claimed that he had betrayed their cause.

In July 1974 a Greek-sponsored coup deposed Makarios, and he was forced to flee the country, first to Malta and then to London. The Turkish government used the coup as a pretext to invade the northern third of Cyprus, proclaiming a separate state there. Makarios returned to Cyprus as president of the Greek part of the island in December 1974. He died on August 3, 1977, in Nicosia.

LUCIAN N. LEUSTEAN

See also
Cyprus; Cyprus, Ottoman Conquest of; Grivas, Georgios; Turkey

References
Clogg, Richard. *A Concise History of Greece*. 2nd ed. Cambridge: Cambridge University Press, 2002.
Mayes, Stanley. *Makarios: A Biography*. London: Macmillan, 1981.
Vanezis, Procopius Nichola. *Makarios: Life and Leadership*. London: Abelard-Schuman, 1979.

Maliki, Nuri Muhammed Kamil al- (1950–)

Iraqi political leader, prime minister (May 20, 2006–September 8, 2014), and vice president of Iraq (September 9, 2014–present). For many years, Nuri Muhammed Kamil Hasan al-Maliki was a leader of the Islamic Dawa Party, an Islamist organization that was ruthlessly suppressed by former Iraqi president Saddam Hussein.

Maliki was born in Abi Gharq, Iraq, near Karbala, on June 20, 1950. He received a bachelor's degree at the Usul al-Din College in Baghdad and a master's degree in Arabic literature at Salahaddin University in Sulamaniyah. It was during his college years that he became politically active, joining the Islamic Dawa Party in 1968 and steadily rising in its hierarchy. Maliki was of the jihadist faction within the party.

When Iraqi president Hussein cracked down on the Dawa Party in the 1970s, its members were sentenced to death, even in absentia. Maliki fled Iraq in October 1979 through Jordan to Syria, where he remained until 1982. He then relocated to Iran. In September 1989 he returned to Damascus, remaining in Syria until the fall of Hussein's government in April 2003.

While in Syria, Maliki had supervised the Dawa Party's publication *Al-Mawqif* and became the head of the organization in Damascus and in Lebanon, participating in the Iraqi opposition coalition known as the Joint Action Committee in 1990. He toured the Middle East and Europe to solicit support for the Iraqi opposition and convened in Beirut in 1991 an important conference of the various Iraqi opposition groups.

On his return to Iraq in 2003, Maliki served in various positions in the new Iraqi interim government; he was named to the National Council, headed the security committee of the transitional Iraqi National Assembly, and was elected to the new National Assembly, where he served on the National Sovereignty Committee. He also became the chief spokesperson and negotiator for the alliance of the various Shia parties and groups known as the United Islamic Alliance during the drafting of the new Iraqi Constitution.

When Prime Minister Ibrahim al-Jafari was unable to obtain support from the United States and certain Iraqi groups, Maliki was nominated as his successor. Maliki took office on May 20, 2006; he also served as the acting minister of the interior until June 2006.

Maliki has been described as a pragmatist who represented the Arab-Iraqi–centered orientation of the Dawa Party and was not overly influenced by Iran. However, it remained difficult for Iraqi officials to avoid U.S. pressure and deal with sectarian and party loyalties in the context of

Iraqi prime minister Nuri al-Maliki at a press conference in Berlin on July 22, 2008. Leader of the Islamic Dawa party, al-Maliki was prime minister from May 20, 2006 to September 8, 2014. He was then elected as one of three Iraqi vice presidents, a position he still holds despite attempts to abolish it. (Mark Waters/Dreamstime.com)

intersectarian fighting, which further delayed reestablishing stability in Iraq. Maliki's initial generally good working relationships with various opposition parties were strained later, in part because of the tension between Washington and Baghdad regarding differing goals and priorities.

Under the Maliki government, the U.S. military forged new alliances with Sunni tribal elements to defeat Al Qaeda in Iraq and other Sunni insurgency groups and urged measures to reverse de-Baathification, causing concerns among Iraqi Shiites. A point of controversy was legislation regarding the sharing of oil revenues, resisted by Sunni and Kurdish leaders. A major Maliki triumph, however, was passage of the status of forces agreement of December 2008. U.S. forces, the last contingent of the international military coalition to leave Iraq, were withdrawn in December 2011 upon the failure to reach a new agreement.

In the 2010 parliamentary elections, the Dawa Party was part of the larger State Law of Coalition, established by Maliki. It won 89 seats, giving it just 2 fewer seats than the Iraqi National Movement. Maliki nevertheless remained prime minister. His coalition secured 3 additional seats in the April 2014 parliamentary elections, giving it the largest voting bloc of any coalition or party.

With the departure of coalition forces in 2011, the political and security situation in Iraq steadily worsened, and Maliki became involved in an increasingly vitriolic and bloody crackdown against Iraq's minority Sunni population. When he secured reelection in 2010, he promised a broadly representative government that would involve Sunnis. Instead, once coalition forces vacated Iraq, he reversed course and purged his government of Sunnis and ordered the arrests of thousands of political dissidents, most of them Sunnis. Iraq's Sunnis were now effectively shut out of the governing process.

Such policies emboldened antigovernment militants and extremists and alienated many rank-and-file Iraqis. As time went on Maliki became more dictatorial, while his regime fostered cronyism, endemic corruption, and political- and religious-based repression.

Maliki's regime fanned the flames of a potent, radical Sunni insurgency and permitted other extremist groups, such as Al Qaeda in Iraq and the Islamic State of Iraq and Syria (ISIS), to gain significant footholds in Iraq. At the same time, Maliki had permitted the Iraqi Army to languish; morale was low, training was subpar, and leadership was weak and preferential toward Shiites. By early 2014 much of Anbar Province, including Fallujah and Ramadi, had been taken over by these extremist groups, and the Iraqi Army was ill-prepared to counter the growing threat. In January 2014, the Barack Obama administration announced an emergency sale of Hellfire missiles to Iraq to help Maliki fend off ISIS gains. In May 2014, the U.S. government announced a $1 billion sale of warplanes, armored vehicles, and surveillance equipment to the Iraqi government. Meanwhile, civilian casualties sharply escalated, and in April 2014 alone at least 750 Iraqis had died in sectarian- and insurgency-based attacks.

In the summer of 2014 ISIS made major gains in Iraq, seizing Iraq's second-largest city, Mosul, and threatening to unleash a genocide against Iraq's Yazidi and Christian populations. The radical group also threatened to kill en masse any Muslims who did not subscribe to its extremist Islamic tenets. In June 2014 with ISIS units less than 100 miles from Baghdad, pressure on Maliki to step down increased substantially. By then, the Obama administration had publicly rebuked the prime minister and suggested that he resign. Even Iran, a heretofore strong supporter of the Maliki government, had lost confidence in him. Despite growing calls for him to step aside, even from many of his allies and those in his own party, Maliki resisted as long as he could. Finally, on August 16 he announced that he would resign, allowing Haider al-Abadi, also of the Dawa Party, to assume the premiership. Maliki formally stepped down on September 8, 2014, at which time he became Iraq's vice president, a largely ceremonial post. He also remained secretary-general of the Islamic Dawa Party. The change in leadership was welcome news to U.S. policy makers, who vowed more aid in the fight against ISIS.

SHERIFA ZUHUR

See also
Abadi, Haider al-; Al Qaeda; Hussein, Saddam; Iraq; Iraq Insurgency; Islamic State of Iraq and Syria; Sadr, Muqtada al-; Yazidis

References
Raghvan, Sudarsan. "Maliki's Impact Blunted by Own Party's Fears: Hussein-Era Secrecy Persists, Analysts Say." *Washington Post*, August 3, 2007, A-01.
Shanahan, Rodger. "The Islamic Da'wa Party: Past Development and Future Prospects." *Middle East Review of International Affairs* 8(2) (June 2004): 112–125.
Woodward, Bob. *The War Within: A Secret White House History, 2006–2008.* New York: Simon and Schuster, 2008.

Malik Shah I (1055–1092)

Jalal al-Dawla Mu'izz al-Din Abu'l-Fath Malik Shah I was the third sultan (1072–1092) of the Great Seljuk Empire, under whom the power of the sultanate reached its greatest extent. (He is not to be confused with Malik Shah I of the Sultanate of Rum [r. 1110-1116]). Born on August 8, 1055, Malik Shah was a son of Sultan Alp Arslan. Malik Shah was named his father's heir in 1066. After his father's death on December 15, 1072, Malik Shah was proclaimed sultan but had to defeat his paternal uncle Qawurd, who had challenged him for supreme authority. Malik Shah also had to put down two rebellions by his brother Tekish in 1081 and 1084, but thereafter his rule was secure.

Malik Shah's power was founded on two principal pillars: the central administration headed by his father's Persian vizier, Niam al-Mulk, and his large standing army of slave-soldiers. Many of the more far-flung parts of the empire were granted to members of the Seljuk family as princes or governors. In the east of the empire, Malik Shah carried on wars against the Ghaznawids and Qarakhanids; in the west, he fought against Georgia, Byzantium, and the Fatimid caliphate. He appointed his brother Tutush I as ruler of southern Syria and Palestine (1078), but as the conquest of northern Syria proceeded, Malik Shah later installed governors of his own choosing in Aleppo, Antioch, and elsewhere.

The first signs of instability in Seljuk rule began to appear when Niam al-Mulk was assassinated (October 1092). Malik Shah's relationship with the Abbasid caliph in Baghdad, who had originally legitimized Seljuk rule, deteriorated toward the end of his reign. It is possible that the sultan intended to depose the caliph, but he died at Baghdad while hunting on November 19, 1092, at only 37 years of age in circumstances that are still disputed among historians.

Whether or not the sultan was murdered as was his vizier, the deaths of its two most powerful men within such a short period plunged the Seljuk Empire into disarray. Malik Shah's widow Terken Khatun had her young son Mamud proclaimed sultan by the caliph, but this move was contested by another son, Barkiyaruq, and by Tutush in Syria. The ensuing civil wars, which continued into the 12th century, greatly limited the ability of the Seljuks to respond effectively to the threat to Muslim Syria and Palestine presented by the First Christian Crusade in the Holy Land (1096–1099).

ALAN V. MURRAY

See also
Alp Arslan; Byzantine-Seljuk Wars; Crusades in the Holy Land, Christian; Fatimid Dynasty; Georgian-Seljuk Wars

References
Agadshanow, Sergei G. *Der Staat der Seldschukiden und Mittelasien im 11–12. Jahrhundert.* Berlin: Schletzer, 1994.
Boyle, J. A., ed. *The Cambridge History of Iran*, Vol. 5, *The Saljuk and Mongol Periods*. Cambridge: Cambridge University Press, 1968.
Cahen, Claude. "The Turkish Invasion: The Selchükids." In *A History of the Crusades*, Vol. 1, Kenneth M. Setton et al., 135–176. 2nd ed. Madison: University of Wisconsin Press, 1969.
Hillenbrand, Carole. "1092: A Murderous Year." *Arabist: Budapest Studies in Arabic* 15–16 (1995): 281–296.

Mamluk-Ilkhanid Wars (1260–1323)

Prolonged conflict between the Mamluk Sultanate of Egypt and the Mongol Ilkhanate. The wars began in 1260 when, two years after sacking Baghdad, Mongol leader Hulegu Khan invaded Syria, which the Mamluks claimed, and captured Aleppo. Hulegu left part of his army, about 12,000 men, in Syria under Ketbugha, one of his most trusted generals, while he himself marched with the remainder to northwestern Persia. Historians have traditionally explained Hulegu's sudden departure as a response to the news of the death of the Great Khan Mongke and the subsequent power struggle over the succession.

In leaving Ketbugha in Syria, however, Hulegu certainly underestimated his opponents in Egypt. On September 3, 1260, Mamluks led by Sultan Qutuz defeated Ketbugha's Mongol force at Ayn Jalut (Goliath's Well). This marked the first important defeat suffered by the Mongol armies. The Mamluks then reclaimed Aleppo and Damascus.

Hulegu was infuriated by this unprecedented setback and organized a punitive expedition under Baydar (some sources refer to Ilge Noyan or Koke-Ilge), who had been one of Ketbugha's officers and had escaped death at Ayn Jalut. The Mongols recaptured Aleppo and advanced into southern Syria. On December 11, 1260, they encountered the Muslim coalition of the lords of Aleppo, Hama, and Homs, under the overall command of al-Ashraf, near the tomb of the famous Arab commander Khalid ibn al-Walid at Homs. The battle, which pitted some 6,000 Mongols against about 1,400 Muslims, took place on the outskirts of Homs and resulted in a decisive Muslim victory, which some Mamluk chronicles consider greater than Ayn Jalut since the Muslims had numerical superiority at the latter.

For a variety of political and military reasons, for the next 21 years neither Hulegu nor his successor made any serious attempts to exact revenge on the Mamluks and their allies and reconquer Syria. The Mamluks used this period to reform their forces and establish political alliances (e.g., with the crusader states and the Golden Horde) to be better prepared for the future wars against the Ilkhan Mongols. Between 1261 and 1277, the Mamluks and the Mongols were engaged in prolonged border skirmishing, with neither side willing or able to undertake a major military effort.

In 1277, however, the Mamluk sultan Baybars became concerned by the Mongol expansion into the Sultanate of Rum and launched a preemptive invasion into Asia Minor, where he defeated the Mongols at Abulustayn. Informed of this setback, Abaka (Abagha) led a large army to Rum, where he executed its ruler, the perfidious Pervane Muin al-Din Sulayman, and sacked several cities, with large numbers of civilian population slain. Abaka initially wanted to pursue Baybars, but logistical difficulties prevented him from

A 14th-century miniature of the Mamluk victory over the Mongols in the December 22–23, 1299, battle of Wadi al-Khazandar during the Mamluk-Ilkhanid Wars (1260–1323). (Universal History Archive/UIG via Getty Images)

launching an invasion of Syria. He was, however, pleased to learn that Baybars did not live long to enjoy the glory of his victory at Abulustayn, as he died suddenly on July 1, 1277.

New Mamluk sultan Baraka Khan (al-Malik al-Said Berke Khan) proved to be incapable, and his reign was cut short in 1279 by senior officers led by Qalawun, Baybars's close associate. Qalawun, however, faced domestic challenges to his rule.

Informed of developments in Egypt and Syria, Abaka Khan sought to exploit the infighting among the Mamluks, and in the summer of 1280 he dispatched a large army into Syria. The Mongol force was divided into three groups: the first marched from Asia Minor under Samaghar, Tanji, and Taranji; the second proceeded from the east under Abaka's nephew Baidu; and the third group, which included the greater share of the army, was led by Mengu Temir. The Mongol army also included an Armenian contingent. In late 1280 the Mongols captured a number of Syrian fortresses, including that of Aleppo, and looted the entire region.

Learning of the Mongol invasion, Sultan Qalaqun left Cairo on November 2 at the head of the Mamluk forces but, upon reaching Gaza, learned that the Mongols had returned home for the winter. As the winter passed, Qalawun again mobilized his army once more and left Cairo for Syria on March 23, 1281. He reclaimed the cities that the Mongols took the previous fall and entered Damascus on May 10.

Informed by spies of the Mongol preparations for another invasion, Qalawun remained in Syria until August, when he learned about a Mongol force of some 40,000–50,000 men under Mengu Temur, Abaka's brother (actual command was, however, in the hands of experienced commanders Tukna and Dolabai), marching through Rum toward Syria. The Mongol force included large contingents from Georgia (led by King Demetre), Armenia (led by King Leon), and Rum. The Mongols avoided fortresses in northern Syria and advanced directly to Homs, where the Mamluks and their Arab allies had already carefully selected their positions. In the decisive Second Battle of Homs on October 29, 1281, the Mamluks scored yet another decisive victory against the Mongols.

Almost 20 years passed before another Ilkhan attempted to invade Syria. By then, the mighty Mamluk Army that Baybars forged was but a shadow of its former self, marked by divisions, command problems, and overconfidence. In 1299 Abaka's grandson, Ilkhan Ghazan, organized a third invasion of Syria. He crossed the Euphrates and captured Aleppo before proceeding south; as on previous occasions, the Mongol army featured contingents from Armenia and Georgia. Young sultan al-Malik al-Nasir Muhammad mobilized the Mamluk forces in southern Palestine, where floods swept away their supply trains, depriving the men of food and negatively affecting morale.

In early December, the sultan marched north of Damascus to the plains north of Homs. During this three-day long march the Mamluks wore full battle gear, which exhausted them and their mounts. The two sides met at Wadi al-Khaznadar at dawn on December 22, 1299, and this time the Mongols prevailed. The Mamluks then withdrew into Egypt, abandoning Syria and Palestine. After the battle Ghazan pushed southward to Damascus and, after sending raiding parties as far south as Gaza, returned home in 1300. Three years later, Ghazan dispatched Qutlugh-shah to reassert his authority in Syria. The Mamluks, led by Baybars al-Jashnakir and Sultan al-Nasir Muhammad, encountered the Mongols near Marj al-Saffar, south of Damascus on April 20 and were victorious in a hard-fought battle. This defeat marked the end of Mongol incursions into Syria.

ALEXANDER MIKABERIDZE

See also

Ayn Jalut, Battle of; Baybars I; Homs, First Battle of; Homs, Second Battle of; Homs, Third Battle of; Mamluk-Ilkhanid Wars; Mongol Invasion of the Middle East; Qalawun

References

Amitai-Preiss, Reuven. *Mongols and Mamluks: The Mamluk-Ilkhanid War, 1260–1281.* Cambridge: Cambridge University Press, 1995.

Amitai-Preiss, Reuven. "'Whither the Ilkhanid Armu?' Ghazan's First Campaign into Syria (1299–1300)." In *Inner Asian Warfare,* ed. N. DiCosmo, 221–264. Leiden: Brill, 2002.

Boyle, J. A. *The Mongol World Empire, 1206–1370.* London: Variorum, 1977.

Morgan, D. O. "The Mongols in Syria 1260–1300." In *Crusade and Settlement,* ed. Peter W. Edbury, 231–235. Cardiff: University College of Cardiff Press, 1985.

Nicolle, David. *The Mongol Warlords.* London: Brockhampton, 1990.

Mamluk-Ottoman Wars (1485–1491 and 1516–1517)

Relations between the Ottoman Empire and the Mamluk Sultanate of Egypt and Syria worsened in the mid-15th century as the Ottomans gradually expanded their influence throughout Asia Minor. During the Ottoman War of Succession in 1481–1482, Mamluks provided assistance to Jem against his older brother, Sultan Bayazid II, who later sought retribution against them. In 1485, the Ottomans and Mamluks became involved in a major war following a conflict over territory ruled by the Mamluk-backed Duldakir dynasty in Cappadocia. The war continued for six years and saw intermittent success on both sides. In the end, the two sides agreed on a peace treaty in which the Mamluks secured territorial concessions.

Following his victorious campaign against the rising Safavids, Sultan Selim I (1467–1520) turned his attention to the Mamluk Sultanate, ruled by the aged Sultan Kansu (Qansuh) al-Gauri. While conducting diplomatic negotiations with Selim, Kansur moved most of his army up to the north Syrian city of Aleppo. Learning of this Mamluk duplicity, Selim broke off negotiations, shaved the head and beard of the Mamluk negotiator before sending him home on a lame mule, and marched into Syria.

On August 24, 1516, the two sides met at Marj-Dabik (Dolbek). Taking advantage of his superior firearms and artillery, Selim placed his Janissaries in the center, flanked by batteries of artillery, while cavalry formed the wings. The Mamluks, who lacked firearms, were divided into three wings. Kansu commanded the center; Amir Sibay, the left wing; and Kha'irbay Mulbai, governor of Aleppo who had secretly gone over to the Ottomans, on the right. The battle began with the Mamluk charge that almost routed the Ottoman left flank. However, the Ottoman firearms played a decisive role in the center, and the Mamluks syffered heavy losses. Many of their commanders perished including Kansu, who died of a stroke while trying to rally his men. The Mamluks then withdrew to Egypt, giving up Syria.

In the fall of 1516 Selim seized Damascus, followed by the conquests of Beirut, Jerusalem, and Gaza, where Ottoman governors were installed. A Mamluk force under the renegade Janbardi al-Ghazali tried but failed to stop the Ottoman advance in Gaza. Selim offered peace to the new Mamluk sultan Tuman Bey (d. 1517) on the condition that he accept Ottoman suzerainty, but this was rejected. The Ottoman army then rapidly advanced to Cairo, where the Ottomans routed Tuman Bey's army at the Battle of Reydaniyya on January 22, 1517, and captured the Egyptian capital. Tuman Bey tried to organize guerrilla warfare (briefly reclaiming Cairo) but was defeated in a battle near the Pyramids at Giza, captured, and then executed.

ALEXANDER MIKABERIDZE

See also
Mamluk Sultanate; Marj Dabiq, Battle of; Selim I, Sultan

References
Ayalon, David. *Studies on the Mamluks of Egypt (1250–1517).* London: Variorum, 1977.
Holt, Peter M. *The Age of the Crusades: The Near East from the Eleventh Century to 1517.* London: Longman, 1986.

Mamluk Sultanate (1250–1517)

State ruled by slave-soldiers of predominantly Turkic and later Circassian origin from 1250 to 1517. The Mamluk Sultanate was originally established in Egypt but soon controlled Palestine and Syria. The sultanate was responsible for the attenuation of the Frankish presence in Outremer and its final elimination in 1291.

The Mamluk state emerged during the crusade of King Louis IX of France to the East (1248–1254). Ayyubid sultan As-Salih Ayyub died in late 1249 while the crusader army was opposite Mansurah (modern-day El-Mansûra, Egypt). An attack by the crusaders on the Egyptian camp was defeated, largely owing to the Bariyya, a regiment within the mamluk (slave-soldier, literally "owned") formation known as the *aliiyya*. Turan Shah, the son and heir of As-Salih Ayyub, quickly alienated his officers, including the Bariyya, and was assassinated on May 1, 1250.

The senior officers decided to dispense with a prince of the Ayyubid family and appointed Shajar al-Durr, the Turkic wife of the late sultan, but she was replaced by Aybak, a former mamluk although not a member of the Bariyya, who in turn married her. Egypt was now a Mamluk state, ruled by a Turkic military caste of slave origin.

Events of the 1250s were characterized by infighting among the various Mamluk factions, along with conflict with the Syrian Ayyubids, who sought to regain control of Egypt. The fledgling Mamluk state was little concerned with the Franks on the coast at this time. The arrival of the Mongols in northern Syria at the beginning of 1260 ended the infighting. Early that year Baybars, a Bariyya leader who had fled to Syria, returned to Cairo with his followers and reconciled with the new Mamluk ruler, Quuz. In the late winter Ayyubid rule collapsed in Damascus, and many soldiers and others fled to Egypt. Mongol raiders meanwhile were harrying the countryside as far south as Gaza and Hebron.

With the withdrawal from Syria of the Ilkhan Hulegu and most of his army in the late winter, the sultan, supported by Baybars, decided to attack the remaining Mongol troops in Egypt. This culminated in the decisive Mamluk victory in the Battle of Ayn Jalut in northern Palestine on September 3, 1260. The battle showed that the Mongols could be beaten, provided legitimacy for the nascent Mamluk state, and gave the Mamluks control over most of Muslim Syria up to the Euphrates and the foothills of the Taurus Mountains. Nonetheless, the Mamluks understood that they had defeated only part of Hulegu's army and that the real test was yet to come. Quuz was unable to savor his victory. Within a few weeks he had been assassinated on the order of Baybars, who now replaced him as sultan.

Sultan Baybars I (1260–1277) was the real architect of Mamluk power and the sultanate. He strengthened his position internally by consolidating the support of the Mamluk elite, particularly among his comrades in the *aliiyya/Bariyya*. Realizing that the greatest danger to the sultanate was from the Mongols, now seeking to revenge their defeat at Ayn Jalut, Baybars carried out a massive expansion of the army (perhaps as much as fourfold) and increased its readiness and training. A communication system, based on postal-horse relays (the famous *barid*), smoke signals, and carrier pigeons was established to bring quick word of threats to the citadel in Cairo. Baybars also established an extensive external intelligence service. It was active among the Mongols, the Armenians of Cilicia, and the Franks of the coast of Syria and Palestine.

Baybars also oversaw the strengthening of fortifications along the frontiers and inland and at places along the coast, as a crusdaer invasion of the Nile Delta region from the sea remained a real threat. It should be noted that the Mamluks were never particularly adept seamen and made only a half-hearted attempt to keep a navy, as a sorry performance at Cyprus in 1271 showed. It was this awareness of Mamluk weakness at sea that convinced Baybars to adopt a scorched-earth policy on most of the coast, which was followed by his successors. This included the razing of captured cities. The logic here was that the Franks, who enjoyed freedom of movement in the Mediterranean, would not be able to gain a significant foothold and fortify a coastal beachhead before mobile Mamluk forces could assemble and drive them off.

Baybars I also strengthened his hand politically, both internally and externally. He brought to Cairo a scion of the Abbasid family, who was declared caliph and given the title al-Mustanir. The latter's first act of "government" was to hand over effective power to the sultan, who would act in his name. Baybars also received a mandate to expand the state territorially. The caliph was soon sent across the border into Iraq with a small force and there was massacred by the local Mongol garrison. Either Baybars had wanted to get rid of him or there may have been a belief that the Mongols had withdrawn and that this region could be easily retaken.

Baybars's most important démarche was to establish close relations with the Mongols of the Golden Horde in the steppes north of the Black Sea. Word reached Baybars around 1262 that Berke, khan of the Golden Horde, was engaged in conflict with his cousin, the Ilkhan Hulegu. Baybars encouraged Berke (a Muslim) and his successor, Mongke Temur (a pagan) in this struggle, in order to ensure that his principal adversary was engaged militarily on another front. Baybars also secured approval from the Golden Horde for its merchants to continue exporting young mamluks (mostly Turkic but with a sprinkling of Mongols) from its territory. The main emporium for these young slaves was the Crimea; from there they were transported by Genoese ships via the Bosporus to the slave markets of Syria and Egypt.

Baybars I's initial attitude toward the Franks was not more aggressive than that of his Ayyubid predecessors. By the mid-1260s, however, matters had changed. In 1265, the Mamluks took Caesarea (modern-day Har Qesari, Israel) and Arsuf and the following year took Saphet (modern-day Zefat, Israel). Two years later they secured Jaffa (modern-day Tel Aviv–Yafo, Israel), and the following year they stormed Antioch (modern-day Antakya, Turkey). In 1271 they captured the important Hospitaller fortress of Krak des Chevaliers. They also took numerous smaller forts.

This policy vis-à-vis the Franks in Syria was largely centered in jihad (holy war) that pervaded the early Mamluk regime, largely as a result of the ongoing fight against the still pagan Mongols. Still, Baybars was aware that the Mongol Ilkhans in Persia were seeking to arrange an alliance with the Christians of the Levant and Europe itself, including the pope and the kings of France, England, and Aragon, against their common Mamluk enemy.

The perceived threat of fighting on two fronts and the possibility of a joint Mongol-Frankish force may well have convinced the Mamluk elite that the Frankish bridgehead in Syria and Palestine should be entirely eliminated. Even after the conquest of Acre in 1291 by Sultan al-Ashraf Khalil and the subsequent abandonment of the coast by the remaining Franks, there remained a fear among the Mamluk leadership of a possible alliance between the European powers and the Mongols of Persia. These fears were never realized, however. Apparently the closest the Franks ever came to military cooperation with the Mongols was during the campaign of Prince Edward of England in 1271, which saw some half-hearted and ineffective Mongol raids in Syria. Nonetheless, Mamluk leaders took seriously the threat of both renewed crusades and Frankish raids, even long after the peace with the Ilkhans (ca. 1320) and the breakup of their state (1335). This was not unjustified, as seen by the temporary capture of the port of Alexandria by Peter I, king of Cyprus, in 1365.

Throughout the reign of Baybars I there was an ongoing border war with the Mongols along the northern Euphrates and the frontier region north of Aleppo. The Ilkhans launched serious attacks against the border fortresses of Bira and al-Raba and several raids into the north of the country but did not attempt a determined campaign into Syria. None of these Mongol efforts were particularly successful, and all were met by immediate and forceful Mamluk response. In this fighting the Mamluks were assisted by the Bedouins of the Syrian Desert, who had been integrated into the Mamluk state by subsidies, land grants, and titles. The Mamluks themselves frequently carried the border war into Mongol territory, often using the border fortresses as staging areas, and they dispatched Bedouin and Turkoman raiders.

The kingdom of Lesser Armenia in Cilicia also suffered Mamluk depredations. In the early 1260s the Armenians, sure of the support of their Mongol overlords, had launched several raids into Syria, all of which were repulsed. The Mamluks responded by a series of devastating raids, thus weakening an important local ally of the Mongols and issuing a warning to the Armenian kings and barons about attempting ill-advised forays into Mamluk territory. Subsequent sultans continued raiding Cilicia until the Armenian kingdom was finally eliminated in 1375, and most of its lands were incorporated into the sultanate.

Baybars I's greatest success against the Mongols came in his campaign into Mongol-controlled Anatolia in 1276–1277, when he was able to take advantage of dissatisfaction among much of the local Seljuk elite. The campaign saw the complete defeat of a smaller Mongol, Seljuk, and Georgian army at Abulustayn (Elbistan). Informed of the approach of a large Mongol army, Baybars soon withdrew.

Baybars died soon afterward in Damascus and was succeeded by his son Baraka Khan, whose disastrous reign was ended in 1279 by a coterie of senior officers led by Qalawun, Baybars's close associate. For appearance's sake, another son of the late sultan, al-Adil Sülemish, was named ruler, but after a reign of only 100 days he was removed, and Qalawun gained the throne (1279–1290), taking the title al-Malik al-Manur.

Qalawun, an old and trusted comrade of Baybars I, continued his policies. During his reign, the institutions of the sultanate developed and crystallized. Early on he was faced with a large-scale Mongol invasion of Syria. This was the first serious attempt by the Mongols, now led by Abagha, to conquer Syria since 1260, and it was in a sense a test of all of the military preparations that Baybars had made to meet a major Mongol challenge. The two armies met on the plain to the north of Homs in October 29, 1281. This Second Battle of Homs hung in the balance throughout the day, but in the end the Mamluks were victorious.

During the remainder of Qalawun's reign, the frontier with the Mongols was to remain relatively quiet, and during the reign of the Ilkhan Tegüder Ahmad (1282–1284), envoys were even exchanged to discuss ending the war. Qalawun concluded a treaty with the Franks of Syria, but by the mid-1280s he was prepared to renew the offensive against them. He took the castle of Margat in 1285 and, more importantly, Tripoli (modern-day Trâblous, Syria) in 1289.

At his death in 1290, Qalawun was preparing a campaign to conquer Acre. Realization of this was left to his son and successor, al-Ashraf Khalil, in 1291. This sultan was evidently planning a campaign in Iraq when he was assassinated by a group of senior officers. His death initiated several years of political instability, which lasted until the reign of al-Nair Muhammad ibn Qalawun (1310–1340). This time of political confusion came too late, however, to help the Franks, whose presence in the Levant was now just a memory.

At the heart of the Mamluk Sultanate was the institution of military slavery developed in the Islamic world over several centuries. The mamluks were brought as young slaves (generally 8 to 12 years old) from pagan areas in the north (the steppe region north of the Black Sea and later the Caucasus). They were then converted to Islam and underwent religious and military training, which they completed around age 18, when they were officially manumitted and enrolled in the army or unit of their patron, either the sultan or an officer. In theory and generally in practice, they were loyal to both their patron (*ustadh*) and their comrades, mamluks of the same patron (known as *khushdashiyya*).

Mamluk society was a continually replicating, single-generational military caste. The sons of mamluks could not be enrolled as mamluks, although many, known as *awlad al-nas* (sons of the people [who matter]), served in inferior units. The Mamluk Army was therefore replenished by the constant import of young slave recruits. The Royal Mamluks were the mainstay of the army. Generally, Bedouins and Turkomans served as auxiliaries in time of war and also patrolled the northern frontier, occasionally raiding into enemy territory.

Compared to its Ayyubid predecessor, the Mamluk Sultanate was relatively centralized. Under normal circumstances, the sultan's authority reigned supreme throughout Syria, Palestine, and Egypt. The center of the government was the Citadel of the Mountain (Qal'at al-Jabal) in Cairo. The bulk of the Royal Mamluks were stationed there and in its environs; the senior officers and their contingents also resided in the city. The governors in Syria, which was divided into a number of provinces, were directly appointed by the sultan. The governors and officers in Syria also had their private contingents of mamluks, and there were other horsemen in their forces.

Provinces in the early sultanate included Damascus (which was responsible for Jerusalem, a subprovince until 1376, when it became a province, albeit of secondary rank), Homs, Hama (actually an Ayyubid puppet regime until the early 1330s), Aleppo, and Kerak. After their conquests, Saphet and Tripoli also became centers of provinces, as did Gaza later on. In some of the larger cities (most prominently Damascus and Aleppo), there was a separate commander of the local citadel who answered directly to the sultan and thus could help check any overly ambitious governors. The sultan resided in Cairo, but in the case of Baybars, much of his time was spent campaigning in Syria and Palestine.

The Mamluk sultans and senior officers were great patrons of Islamic architecture. This patronage resulted from the Mamluk elite's religiosity and spiritual needs and perhaps also from their need to prove their attachment to their new religion. The fact that these establishments were usually *waqfs* (endowments), which provided income for descendants in a volatile economic milieu (as well as circumvention of Muslim inheritance laws), was an added incentive. Finally, although this may not have been the original intention, the cultivation of religion won the Mamluk sultans and officers legitimacy in religious circles and among the population at large. Foremost among the institutions supported were madrassas (religious colleges focusing on legal studies), but mosques, *khanqahs* (Sufi lodges), and khans (hospices or caravanserai) also received extensive patronage.

The Mamluk elite saw itself as the defender of Sunni Islamic orthodoxy, which included moderate Sufism (mysticism), although individual Sufis of a more extreme variety could also enjoy the benefits of support from the military-political elite. Among various intellectual currents that flourished under the Mamluks, mention can be made of historiography, the extent and richness of which may be unsurpassed in premodern Muslim societies.

It is often thought that the height of the sultanate was the reign of al-Nair Muhammad ibn Qalawun, during which peace was concluded with the Mongols. It was certainly a time of massive urban and rural construction, encouraged by the sultan himself, as well as general luxurious living among the elite. Recent research has suggested that many of the subsequent political and economic problems may be attributed to the irresponsible fiscal policy of these years as well as to changes in the educational system of the young mamluks. In any event, after this ruler's death, the sultanate entered a 41-year period of political and economic instability, exacerbated by the arrival of the Black Death in 1348. In 1382 Barquq ascended the throne, providing a modicum of stability. He also inaugurated the succession of Circassian sultans known (incorrectly) as Burjis.

The 15th century was one of successive economic crises that made for smaller and less disciplined armies. Novice mamluks (now mostly imported from Circassia in the northern Caucasus) were bought at an older age and thus received less training. This period is often seen as one of gradual decline. With the demise of Frankish and Mongol power, the Mamluks had no serious external enemies (the excursion by Tamerlane [Timur] to Syria was short-lived), nor did they have any substantial internal opponents.

The appearance of the Ottoman Empire in the northern frontier region in the second half of the 15th century brought about a change for the Mamluks, who put up a spirited fight until their final defeat in 1517, which was aided by their unwillingness or inability to adopt gunpowder weapons.

Reuven Amitai

See also
Ayn Jalut, Battle of; Baybars I; Bedouins; Homs, First Battle of; Homs, Second Battle of; Homs, Third Battle of; Hulegu; Mamluk-Ilkhanid Wars; Mongol Invasion of the Middle East; Qalawun

References
Amitai-Preiss, Reuven. *Mongols and Mamluks: The Mamluk-Ilkhanid War, 1260–1281.* Cambridge: Cambridge University Press, 1995.
Ayalon, David. *The Mamluk Military Society: Collected Studies.* London: Variorum, 1979.
Ayalon, David. *Outsiders in the Land of Islam: Mamluks, Mongols and Eunuchs.* London: Ashgate, 1988.
Ayalon, David. *Studies on the Mamluks of Egypt (1250–1517).* London: Variorum, 1977.
Holt, Peter M. *The Age of the Crusades: The Near East from the Eleventh Century to 1517.* London: Longman, 1986.

Mandates, League of Nations

System of administration of the former German overseas colonies in Africa and Asia and territories of the Ottoman Empire in the Middle East after World War I (1914–1918). The mandates were established under the aegis of the new international organization of the League of Nations. By the end of war, British Empire and Allied Arab forces had driven the Ottoman Army from Mesopotamia, Palestine, and Syria.

U.S. president Woodrow Wilson, who held a strong bargaining position at the 1919 Paris Peace Conference after the war, refused to allow the distribution and outright annexation of colonial territory by the victorious powers. The peoples of the Middle East sought independence, but the leaders of Britain and France claimed that this was not feasible.

To resolve this matter, the conferees at Paris created the mandate system in Article 22 of the Covenant of the League of Nations. Colonial areas acquired from Germany and the Ottoman Empire would thus be in a transitional status until the people of these territories "could stand by themselves." These territories were entrusted to certain victor states until such time as they were deemed ready for independence.

Not surprisingly, problems arose from the creation of the mandate system. The question of whether the League of Nations or the mandate power held the final authority continued to bedevil officials throughout the existence of the mandate system. In addition, international law did not have a mechanism for temporary sovereignty over a particular area. The League of Nations did not have enforcement powers within the mandates, so mandate commission members could not visit a mandate to investigate problems. Issues of ascendant nationalism soon created tensions in Middle Eastern states, which ironically were supposed to be in the final stages of independence. Despite these problems, however, Article 22 helped change the face of colonialism and may have contributed to its ultimate demise after World War II.

Mandates were divided into three categories: Class-A mandates (the former Ottoman territories in the Middle East), Class-B mandates (mostly in Tropical Africa), and Class-C mandates (those territories of Southwest Africa and the Pacific). The local populations in Class-A mandates were to have a higher degree of autonomy, whereas those in Class-C would have the lowest. A Permanent Mandates Commission (PMC) was established within the League of Nations machinery to examine the annual administration reports submitted by the mandatory states and advise the League Council concerning them.

In the Class-A Middle East mandate system, France controlled Lebanon and Syria. Great Britain meanwhile took control of the Class-A territories Iraq and Palestine, the latter soon divided into Palestine and Transjordan (modern-day Jordan). In Iraq and Transjordan, the British allowed some autonomy early on by placing on the throne in Iraq Prince Faisal ibn Hussein, son of the sharif of Mecca; Faisal became King Faisal I in 1921. In Transjordan, Prince Abdullah, also a son of Sharif Hussein, became King Abdullah I, also in 1921. The Palestine mandate proved to be the most difficult administratively not only because of conflicting claims of interest by Arabs and Jews there but also because the British had sent conflicting signals to both groups over who would ultimately control the region.

Some accused the victorious imperial powers of an overt attempt to annex the conquered territories. Others saw it as a denial of the right of conquest and the forerunner of decolonization. The truth probably lies somewhere in between.

The British mandate of Iraq was terminated in 1932, when Iraq became an independent state (it joined the League of Nations the same year). However, Great Britain retained considerable influence there and intervened to crush a subsequent pro-Axis coup there during World War II.

Independence pledged to the Middle Eastern mandates was put off owing to World War II. Early in that conflict, the Axis powers sought to abet nationalist sentiment in the region. When Germany secured approval from the government of Vichy France to ship arms to the Iraqi rebels through Lebanon and Syria, British forces invaded and overran both Lebanon and Syria. At the end of the war there was some violence, but both Syria and Lebanon secured their independence.

Increased Jewish migration into Palestine meanwhile led to tensions and outright violence between Arabs and Jews in the 1930s. London soon found itself caught up in a three-way war between the British Army, Arabs, and Jews. The inability to work out a political arrangement satisfactory to the two sides led to a precipitous British termination of their mandate in Palestine in 1948. This brought a declaration of independence by the Jews of Palestine and the first Arab-Israeli war.

HARUO TOHMATSU AND DINO E. BUENVIAJE

See also
Iraq; Jordan; Lebanon; Palestine, British Mandate for; Syria

References
Crozier, Andrew J. *Appeasement and Germany's Last Bid for Colonies.* London: Macmillan, 1988.
Hall, H. Duncan. *Mandates, Dependencies, and Trusteeship.* New York: Carnegie Endowment for Peace, 1948.
Khoury, Philips S. *Syria and the French Mandate: The Politics of Arab Nationalism.* Princeton, NJ: Princeton University Press, 1989.
Smuts, Jan Christian. *The League of Nations: A Practical Suggestion.* London: Hodder and Stoughton, 1918.
Wright, Quincy. *Mandate under the League of Nations.* Chicago: Chicago University Press, 1930.

Mansurah, Battle of (February 8–11, 1250)

The town of Mansurah in Egypt was founded by Ayyubid sultan al-Kamil (r. 1218–1238) as a forward military base against the Fifth Christian Crusade in the Holy Land (1218–1221). Following a prolonged siege, the crusaders had in November 1219 seized the vital port of Damietta at the mouth of the eastern branch of the Nile.

After a long pause, largely caused by the divided leadership of King John of Jerusalem and Cardinal Pelagius, the crusader army advanced along the eastern bank of the Nile in July and August 1221, proceeding toward Cairo. It was, however, halted by the Ayyubid forces at Mansurah, a large fortified encampment of a type typical in Middle Eastern Islamic warfare. Its location dominated the eastern Nile and the Bahr al-Saghir, a strategic waterway linking the Nile and Lake Manzala. Al-Kamil ordered that the irrigation dikes be broken and the surrounding land flooded. The crusader army thus found itself caught on a small island between the eastern Nile and the Bahr al-Saghir and was obliged to negotiate a humiliating peace. However, in return for the surrender of Damietta, still held by the crusader garrison, the trapped army was permitted to withdraw safely at the end of August 1221.

In 1249 Damietta again fell to a crusade army, led by King Louis IX of France. Although he was dying, Sultan al-Salih (r. 1240–1249) assembled an army at Mansurah, supported by a river fleet. In November–December 1249, the crusaders advanced up the Nile toward Mansurah. The death of al-Salih on November 23 was kept a secret from his army, which skirmished with the crusaders outside Mansurah during December and January 1250. Eventually the crusaders crossed the Bahr al-Saghir to attack the town, but on February 11, 1250, the king's brother Robert, count of Artois, disobeyed orders and entered Mansurah, where he was defeated in street fighting. The Egyptians then counterattacked, and the crusaders were besieged in their camp, while the Egyptian river fleet won control of the Nile.

In March and April the crusaders retreated toward Damietta before being forced to surrender near Fariskur, where King Louis was taken prisoner. In May 1250 some senior crusader leaders were released after the payment of large ransoms, but much of their army was enslaved.

The 1250 Battle of Mansurah was one of the most important of the entire crusades in the Holy Land, confirming three strategic points: that Egypt was the center of Islamic power in the Middle East; that Frankish power in the Holy Land could only be preserved by dominating Egypt; and that the conquest of Egypt by a seaborne assault was probably impossible given the military technology of this period.

The Ayyubid sultanate collapsed during this campaign, replaced by a military regime, which evolved into the Mamluk Sultanate. Victory at Mansurah gave the Mamluks great prestige, helping them to inflict a major defeat on the invading Mongols a decade later.

DAVID NICOLLE

See also
Crusades in the Holy Land, Christian; Louis IX, King of France

References
Donovan, Joseph P. *Pelagius and the Fifth Crusade*. Philadelphia: University of Pennsylvania Press, 1950.
Irwin, Robert. *The Middle East in the Middle Ages: The Early Mamluk Sultanate, 1250–1382*. London: Longman, 1986.

Manuel I Komnenos, Emperor (1118–1180)

Byzantine emperor (r. 1143–1180). Manuel Komnenos was born on November 28, 1118, the fourth and youngest son of Emperor John II Komnenos. Manuel distinguished himself in John II's war against the Seljuk Turks, and in 1143 the emperor designated Manuel as his successor in place of Manuel's elder surviving brother Isaac. On John's death in Cilicia, on April 8, 1143, Manuel was acclaimed emperor by the Byzantine Army. His succession was not ensured, however, as Cilicia was distant from Constantinople (modern-day Istanbul), where Isaac was in the presidential palace with access to its treasury and imperial regalia. Manuel immediately dispatched an emissary to arrest Isaac before news of John's death could be known. This was accomplished, and after attending to his father's funeral and raising a monastery at place of death as required, Manuel himself arrived in Constantinople in August. Crowned emperor, he released his brother.

As emperor, Manuel welcomed Westerners to his court and fostered efforts to unify the Latin and Greek churches. His attempts to play the Italian maritime states against one another, however, led to the increasing alienation of Venice.

The arrival of the Second Christian Crusade in the Holy Land (1147–1149) on Byzantine territory provided an early challenge to Manuel's authority. He attempted, with little success, to revive the pacts that Alexios I Komnenos had established with the crusaders. The German contingent under King Conrad III refused to cross the Hellespont at Abydos and was suspected of planning to move against Constantinople itself. After its defeat in Asia Minor in 1147, Manuel received the ailing Conrad in Constantinople. Manuel then provided ships to take Conrad to Palestine and arranged the marriage of his niece Theodora to Conrad's nephew Henry Jasomirgott.

Manuel's relationship with the French contingent under King Louis VII was ambivalent, and even Byzantine chronicler Niketas Choniates believed that Manuel had failed to support the enterprise adequately. Manuel minted a debased coinage to be used in transactions with the crusaders and made a truce with the Seljuk sultan of Rum. Manuel did nothing to prevent attacks on the French by both Turks and Greeks, and the failure of the crusade left a legacy of bitterness in the West toward Byzantium.

In the East, Manuel had three major areas of concern: Jerusalem, Antioch, and Cilicia. He had cordial relations with the rulers of Jerusalem. Baldwin III and Amalric were both married to Byzantine princesses, and Manuel sent large gifts of money to maintain the defenses of the kingdom and to redecorate the Church of the Nativity in Bethlehem and the Church of the Holy Sepulchre in Jerusalem. In 1169, a force of 200 Byzantine ships joined King Amalric on his expedition to Egypt.

Manuel abandoned his father's aim of recovering the principality of Antioch but did manage to achieve the temporary return of a Greek patriarch there. Manuel's ceremonial entry into Antioch in 1159 emphasized his authority, and his second marriage, with Maria of Antioch in 1161, brought him further influence. In Cilicia, Manuel faced opposition from Armenian rulers, who had no scruples about allying with the neighboring Muslim and Christian powers against him. He was able to reconquer the coastal lands, but Byzantine authority was never fully reestablished.

Manuel attempted to assert his lordship over the Sultanate of Rum, which ruled much of central Anatolia. In a treaty in 1161, Sultan Qilij Arslan II agreed to hand over imperial cities and curb Turkoman raiders. However, Manuel's attempt to recapture the city of Ikonion (modern-day Konya, Turkey) ended in defeat at Myriokephalon (1176), and the situation in Asia Minor remained precarious. In general, however, Manuel succeeded in establishing a *pax byzantina* (Byzantine peace) whereby local potentates kept the peace while acknowledging the Byzantine emperor as their overlord. Emperor Manuel I Komnenos died on September 24, 1180, and was succeeded by his son Alexios II.

ROSEMARY MORRIS

See also
Amalric of Jerusalem; Baldwin III of Jerusalem; Conrad III, King of Germany; Crusades in the Holy Land, Christian; Myriokephalon, Battle of; Qilij Arslan II of Rum; Rum, Sultanate of

References
Angold, Michael. *The Byzantine Empire, 1025–1204: A Political History*. 2nd ed. London: Longman, 1997.
Cheynet, Jean-Claude. "Byzance et l'Orient latin: Le legs de Manuel Comnène." In *Chemins d'outre-mer: Etudes sur la Méditerranée médiévale offertes à Michel Balard*, Vol. 1, ed. Damien Coulon, Catherine Otten-Froux, Paul Pagès, and Dominique Valérian, 114–125. Paris: Publications de la Sorbonne, 2004.
Hamilton, Bernard. "Manuel I Comnenus and Baldwin IV of Jerusalem." In *Kathegetria: Essays Presented to Joan Hussey for Her 80th Birthday*, ed. Julian Chrysostomides, 353–375. Camberley, UK: Porphyrogenitus, 1988.
Lilie, Ralph-Johannes. *Byzantium and the Crusader States, 1096–1204*. Trans. J. C. Morris and Jean E. Ridings. Rev. ed. Oxford, UK: Clarendon, 1993.
Magdalino, Paul. *The Empire of Manuel I Komnenos, 1143–1180*. Cambridge: Cambridge University Press, 1993.

Manuel II Palaiologos, Emperor (1350–1425)

Byzantine emperor (r. 1391–1425). Born in Constantinople (modern-day Istanbul) on June 27, 1350, Manuel Palaiologos was the second son of Emperor John V Palaiologos and Helena Katakouzene and became heir to the throne on the death of his elder brother, Andronikos IV (1385). Manuel became emperor on February 16, 1391, on the death of John V.

As emperor, Manuel inherited his father's policy of accepting the position of vassal of the Ottoman sultan. In 1394, however, Sultan Bayezid I decided to abandon conciliation and laid siege to Constantinople, forcing Manuel to revert to the practice of seeking assistance from Western Europe. He sailed for Italy in 1399 with the aim of making a personal appeal. After touring the cities of northern Italy, the emperor and his retinue moved north, stopping at Paris and then arriving in London at the end of 1401. Manuel was warmly and sympathetically received wherever he went, and Pope Boniface IX ordered crusade preaching to encourage volunteers and donations of money.

Unsettled conditions of the time, however, made it impossible for large-scale assistance to be sent to Constantinople from either France or England, and salvation ultimately came from an entirely unexpected quarter. Following Bayezid's defeat and capture by Turkic khan Timur in the Battle of Ankara (July 20, 1402), the Ottoman threat to Constantinople evaporated, and Manuel was able to return. This was, however, only a stay of execution. By the time of Manuel's death in Constantinople on July 21, 1425, the Ottomans had recovered from their defeat and were once more making plans to capture Constantinople. Manuel was succeeded as emperor by his son John VIII Palaiologos.

JONATHAN HARRIS

See also

Ankara, Battle of; Bayezid I; Ottoman Empire

References

Barker, John W. *Manuel II Palaeologus (1391–1425): A Study in Late Byzantine Statesmanship.* New Brunswick, NJ: Rutgers University Press, 1969.

Carlson, David R. "Greeks in England, 1400." In *Interstices: Studies in Middle English and Anglo-Latin Texts in Honour of A. G. Rigg*, ed. Richard Firth Green and Linne R. Mooney, 74–98. Toronto: University of Toronto Press, 2004.

Nicol, Donald M. *Byzantium: Its Ecclesiastical History and Relations with the Western World.* London: Variorum, 1972.

Nicol, Donald M. *The Last Centuries of Byzantium, 1261–1453.* 2nd ed. Cambridge: Cambridge University Press, 1993.

Manzikert, Battle of (August 26, 1071)

Important battle in which Byzantine forces under Emperor Romanos IV Diogenes met a Seljuk army under Sultan Alp Arslan. It was fought near the fortress of Manzikert (modern-day Malazgirt, Turkey) on August 26, 1071.

In the summer of 1071, Emperor Romanos led a large force numbering some 40,000–70,000 men from Constantinople (modern-day Istanbul) in order to secure fortresses near Lake Van (modern-day Van Gölü) in Armenia against the threat posed by the Seljuks. The long march eastward across Anatolia proved difficult, with Romanos angering many of his men owing to his own large personal baggage train.

The expeditionary force arrived at Theodosiopolis (modern-day Erzurum) in June 1071. There some of his generals urged that they seize the moment and continue the march into Seljuk territory to catch Alp Arslan before he was fully prepared. Others suggested that they hold their present position and fortify. Romanos decided the issue in favor of continuing the advance. All this time Romanos had no idea of Alp Arslan's dispositions, while the latter was fully aware of the Byzantine movements through his scouts.

The Byzantines then moved on Lake Van, hoping to quickly take Manzikert as well as the nearby fortress of Khliat. Alp Arslan was already present, however, at the head of some 20,000–30,000 cavalry from Aleppo and Mosul and including provincial troops, contingents of Oghuz Turks, Rus mercenaries, and Armenian infantry. Unaware of this, Romanos ordered his subordinate Joseph Tarchaniotes to proceed with perhaps half the Byzantine army to Khliat (modern-day Ahlat), while Romanos and the remainder marched to Manzikert. It is unknown what happened to Tarchaniotes and his part of the army, although Islamic sources claim that it was defeated by Alp Arslan. In any case, Romanos was now left with only half his expeditionary force.

Romanos captured Manzikert on August 23. The next day Byzantine foraging parties discovered the Seljuk army and withdrew back on Manzikert. Romanos then sent out an Armenian cavalry force to reconnoiter, but it was promptly destroyed. On August 25, some of Romanos's Turkic mercenaries deserted. Romanos then rejected a Seljuk peace embassy and attempted to no avail to recall Tarchaniotes.

The battle occurred on August 26 when the Byzantine army marched on the Seljuk position, the latter organized in a great crescent-shaped formation some two and a half miles distant. The Seljuk archers opened up on the Byzantines when they were within range, with the center gradually withdrawing as their wings closed around the Byzantine flanks. Although that afternoon the Byzantines captured the Seljuk camp, the Byzantine left and right wings sustained casualties from the Seljuk bowmen, and when they charged the Seljuks, the latter simply disengaged. That evening Romanos was forced to order a withdrawal. However, the commander of the Byzantine right wing, Andronikos Doukas, a rival of Romanos, deliberately ignored the emperor's orders and marched back to the Byzantine camp outside Manzikert rather than covering the emperor's retreat. Taking advantage of the Byzantines disarray, the Seljuks attacked, routing the Byzantine right wing and then the Byzantine left. What remained of the Byzantine center, including Romanos and the imperial bodyguard, was encircled. Romanos was wounded and taken prisoner. Many in the Byzantine force escaped, although the professional soldiers in the army were largely wiped out. The total of those killed on the Byzantine side ranged between 2,000 and 8,000. Seljuk casualties are unknown.

Romanos was held prisoner for eight days. After his release he took refuge in Cilicia, where he was defeated by forces loyal to Doukas. Romanos was then blinded and forced to become a monk. Far more damaging to the Byzantines than the battle itself were the 10 years of civil war that followed the deposition of Romanos IV.

ROSEMARY MORRIS AND SPENCER C. TUCKER

See also

Alp Arslan; Seljuk Dynasty

References

Cahen, Claude. "La campagne de Manzikert d'après les sources Musulmanes." *Byzantion* 9 (1934): 628–642.

Cheynet, Jean-Claude. "Mantzikert: Un désastre militaire?" *Byzantion* 50 (1980): 410–438.

De Vries–Van Der Velden, Eva. "Psellos, Romain IV Diogénés et Mantzikert." *Byzantinoslavica* 58 (1997): 274–310.

Friendly, Albert. *The Dreadful Day: The Battle of Manzikert.* London: Hutchinson, 1981.

Hillenbrand, Carole. "Some Reflections on Seljuq Historiography." In *Eastern Approaches to Byzantium,* ed. Antony Eastmond, 73–88. Aldershot, UK: Ashgate, 2001.

Vryonis, Speros, Jr. "A Personal History of the Battle of Mantzikert." In *Byzantine Asia Minor,* ed. Stelios Lampakes, 225–244. Athens: Hestia, 1998.

Marcus, David (1901–1948)

U.S. Army colonel and Israeli general. David Daniel Marcus, known his whole life as "Mickey," was born in New York City on February 22, 1901. The fifth child of Jewish immigrants from Romania, he graduated from the United States Military Academy, West Point, in 1924. While serving as a lieutenant of infantry at Governors Island, he attended law school at night in New York City. Leaving active duty after his initial assignment, he became an assistant U.S. attorney in New York and, working with Thomas E. Dewey, helped to shut down a major crime ring. In 1934 Mayor Fiorello La Guardia appointed Marcus deputy commissioner and then later commissioner of corrections.

With an army reserve commission in the Judge Advocate General's Corps, Marcus returned to active duty in 1940. Although a military lawyer, he established and commanded the first Army Ranger school in Hawaii. In 1943 he was posted to the Pentagon as the chief of planning for the War Department's Civil Affairs Division. He played a key role in the negotiation and drafting of the Italian surrender and the Instrument of Unconditional Surrender of Germany.

In 1944 Marcus was sent to Britain to initiate the planning for the occupation and control of postwar Germany. On June 6, 1944, he managed to wrangle his way onto one of the troop carriers of the 101st Airborne Division and made the combat jump into Normandy, the first parachute jump he had made. He also served as a legal adviser to President Franklin D. Roosevelt at the Yalta Conference and to President Harry S. Truman at the Potsdam Conference. In 1946 Marcus headed the Pentagon's War Crimes Division, responsible for selecting judges and prosecutors for the war crimes trials in Germany and Japan.

Marcus left active duty in 1947, turning down a promotion to brigadier general, but later that year he accepted an invitation from the chairman of the Jewish Agency Executive, David Ben-Gurion, to come to the British Mandate for Palestine as his military adviser. As a reservist Marcus needed War Department permission to do that, which was

David Daniel "Mickey" Marcus (1901–1948) was a retired U.S. Army colonel who made a major contribution as a general and military adviser to the nascent Israeli army in the War of Independence (1948–1949) before he was killed by friendly fire on June 10, 1948. (Israeli Government Press Office)

granted with the proviso that he not use his American rank or real name. He arrived in Tel Aviv in January 1948 under the name Michael Stone.

More of an organizer and a trainer than a tactical commander, Marcus helped establish a new command structure for the Jewish self-defense organization Haganah and wrote training manuals based on memory from similar U.S. manuals. When Israel declared independence on May 14, two Egyptian brigades attacked into the southern Negev within hours, exactly where Marcus had predicted the first attack would come.

As the fighting ground on, the center of gravity shifted to Jerusalem, which was cut off and surrounded by the Arab Legion. With a cease-fire brokered by the United Nations (UN) scheduled to go into effect on June 11, the Israelis realized that they would lose all claim to the city unless they could establish a credible land bridge. After their May 25 attack at Latrun failed to break through, Ben-Gurion made the bold move of designating a single commander to control all combat operations to lift the siege. On May 28 Aluf (General) Michael Stone was appointed commander of the Jerusalem Front, with command over the Etzioni, Har-El, and 7th brigades. Marcus became the first Jewish soldier to hold the rank of general officer since Judas Maccabeus 2,100 years before.

Marcus launched another attack at Latrun on May 30. When that failed, he concluded that the only solution was to go around the Arab Legion. Sending engineers and construction crews into the wild Judaean hills south of Latrun, he oversaw the extension and improvement of a series of goat trails into a credible military road, which he wryly called the Burma Road. Despite the enormous obstacles, the land bridge was completed on June 9, lifting the siege of Jerusalem.

On the night of June 10 Marcus was at his command post in the village of Abu Gosh, a few miles outside of Jerusalem. At 3:50 a.m. on June 10 he was accidentally shot dead by one of his own jittery sentries. The cease-fire went into effect at 10:00 a.m. Marcus was the last casualty of that phase of the war.

Marcus was buried at the West Point post cemetery in July 1948. He is the only soldier buried there who died fighting under a foreign flag.

DAVID T. ZABECKI

See also
Ben-Gurion, David; Haganah; Latrun, Battles of

References
Berkman, Ted. *Cast a Giant Shadow*. Garden City, NY: Doubleday, 1962.
Collins, Larry, and Dominique Lapierre. *O Jerusalem!* New York: Simon and Schuster, 1972.

Marcus Aurelius, Emperor (121–180)

Roman emperor. Marcus Aurelius Antoninus Augustus, who ruled during 161–180, was the last of what Machiavelli described as the "Five Good Emperors." Marcus Aurelius was born on April 26, 121, and his reign overlapped with coemperors Lucius Verus and Marcus's son Commodus. Throughout this period Rome fought several wars, accompanied by revolts, plague, and famine. Consequently, Marcus's troubled reign foreshadowed the empire's eventual collapse.

Marcus Aurelius was originally named Marcus Catilius Severus. He was the son of praetor Marcus Annius Verus and the wealthy heiress Domitia Lucilla. Marcus Aurelius was also the nephew of the consul Marcus Annius Libo and Empress Annia Faustina Major (wife of Antoninus Pius). When Marcus was an infant his father died, and Marcus was adopted by his paternal grandfather, a former senator who shared the name Marcus Annius Verus. In February 138 Emperor Hadrian adopted Antoninus Pius as his successor, insisting that Antoninus adopt both Marcus Aurelius and Hadrian's adopted grandson, Lucius Verus.

Marcus was studious, and his adopted brother was carefree. During his youth, Marcus served as a priest of Mars and prefect during the Latin Festival. In contrast, at age 23, Lucius had never held public office. In 145 Marcus married Annia Faustina Minor, who was his biological cousin and adopted sister. Faustina would accompany him during campaigns. Together they would have 13 children.

In 140 at age 19, Marcus received the consulship, followed 6 years later by *tribunicia potestas* and proconsular imperium, powers of the emperor traditionally given to designated successors. Subsequently, in March 161 Antoninus Pius appointed Marcus as his sole successor. However, Marcus refused to serve as emperor unless Verus was appointed as coemperor. Following the death of Antoninus, the two new emperors were popular with the Senate. Unfortunately, the Tiber flooded, causing famine. Several months later the Arsacid Parthians invaded Armenia, and there were revolts in Britannia and Germania.

In 162, Marcus sent Lucius east to direct the Parthian war. Unfortunately, Lucius was a notorious playboy who wasted public funds and spent most of his time in taverns and brothels. However, under the command of Avidius Cassius, the legions occupied Ctesiphon in 165 and crossed the Tigris in 166.

During the winter of 166–167, 6,000 Germanic warriors crossed the Danube into Pannonia, while Rhine Celts crossed the Rhine and entered northern Italy. This sparked an increasingly genocidal conflict known as the Marcomannic Wars. Meanwhile, Lucius died in 169, probably of natural causes, although there are suggestions that he was plotting a coup.

When the legions returned from Persia during 166 and 167, they brought the plague to Europe. Scholars have suggested that this was the first known European outbreak of smallpox, though the disease is not certainly identified. The epidemic killed as much as 25 percent of the population and caused revolts across the empire. In 175 Avidius Cassius led an unsuccessful rebellion in the East, and three years later the North African Mauris (Moors) invaded Hispania.

In 177, Marcus appointed his son Commodus as coemperor. Together, they fought against the northerners until Marcus died on March 17, 180. Some sources suggest that the emperor was killed by the plague, but others insist that he was murdered by a physician loyal to Commodus. Shortly thereafter, the northern conflict ended because Commodus agreed to an unpopular armistice.

After his death, Marcus Aurelius became the model of a strong emperor: an excellent administrator who was merciful to his enemies and relentless against his foes. According to Roman historian Cassius Dio, Marcus lowered taxes, was generous with the imperial treasury, and forgave decades of debt. Marcus is best known for his meditations: "He who follows reason in all things is both tranquil and active at the same time, and also cheerful and collected.... Think of thy last hour. Let the wrong which is done [to you] stay there where the wrong was done." According to Machiavelli, modern leaders should learn from the "modest life" of Marcus "that one should avoid being despised and hated." However, despite the emperor's Stoic philosophy, his military policy was brutal and merciless. This paradox suggests the intense pressure on Marcus as the empire endured a growing crisis. Unfortunately, as Dio wrote, the golden era was followed by "an age of iron and rust."

ADAM RINKLEFF

See also
Hadrian, Emperor; Lucius Verus; Roman-Parthian Wars

References
Birley, Anthony. *Marcus Aurelius: A Biography*. Rev. ed. New York: Routledge, 2000.
McLynn, Frank. *Marcus Aurelius: A Life*. New York: Da Capo, 2010.

Marj Dabiq, Battle of (August 24, 1516)

Battle between the Ottomans and the Mamluks that led to the Ottoman conquest of Syria. After his victory at Chaldiran against the Safavids in 1514, Ottoman sultan Selim I learned that Mamluk sultan Qansuh al-Ghawri was massing forces against him. He then had to divert his forces to deal with the Mamluks. The Ottoman forces marched southward, and the two armies met on the plain of Marj Dabiq (Marj Dabik) in northern Syria on August 24, 1516.

The Ottoman infantry, armed with firearms and supported by artillery, deployed behind the protection of a defensive shield formed of 300 armored wagons chained together that the Mamluk cavalry could not breach. Furthermore, there was dissension within the ranks of the Mamluk army, and some units refused to fight. Also, Khayir Bey, governor of Aleppo, defected to the Ottomans. Sultan Qansuh died in the battle, which brought the Mamluk loss of Syria to the Ottomans.

ADAM ALI

See also
Mamluk-Ottoman Wars; Selim I, Sultan

References
Behrens-Abouseif, Doris. *Egypt's Adjustment to Ottoman Rule: Institutions, Waqf and Architecture in Cairo, 16th and 17th Centuries*. Leiden: New York: E. J. Brill, 1994.
Waterson, James. *The Knights of Islam: The Wars of the Mamluks*. London: Greenhill Books, 2007.

Maronites

The Maronites are a Christian group living mainly in modern Lebanon and the surrounding regions in the Levant. They derive their name either from a monastery named Mar Maron near Apamea (modern-day Afamiyah, Syria) or from Syriac Christian Saint Maron, whose followers migrated to the area of Mount Lebanon from around Antioch. The chief areas of Maronite settlement were the mountains and northern Lebanon.

The Maronites held to the beliefs of the Council of Chalcedon in 451, which held to the doctrine of monothelitism. This is the view that Jesus Christ had two natures but only one will. This is contrary to the dogma of Christology that holds that Christ had two wills (human and divine) corresponding to his two natures (dyothelitism). After the devastation wrought by the Byzantine-Sassanid War of 602–628, Emperor Heraclius propagated a new doctrine in an attempt to unify the various Eastern Empire Christian churches, which were divided over accepting monothelitism and its opponents, such as the Syrian Orthodox Christians or Jacobites. Although Pope Honorius I (r. 625–638) endorsed monothelitism, it was declared a heresy at the Sixth Ecumenical Council (680–681). Contemporary Greek and Arab sources claim that the Maronites rejected the decision of the Sixth Ecumenical Council and continued to believe in monothelitism and only moved away from it during the Christian crusades in order to avoid being classified as heretics by the crusaders. The modern Maronite Church, however, claims that Maronites were never monothelites.

The Maronites were able to retain their Christian religion and a degree of autonomy following the Islamic conquest.

Many Maronites aided the Franks during the crusades. Famine and confiscations under Ottoman rule during World War I may have claimed as many as half of the Maronite population, but they retained sufficient numbers to form the principal ethnoreligious component of Lebanon when it was established as a French mandate following the Allied victory in World War I. The Lebanese Civil War of 1975–1990 and a low birthrate have greatly decreased their numbers in the Levant, however. Today Maronite Christians constitute perhaps only 21 percent of the Lebanese population. With two exceptions, Lebanese presidents have all been Maronites as part of the constitutional arrangement that provides for a Maronite president, a Sunni Muslim prime minister, and a Shiite speaker of the National Assembly.

Although most Maronites reside in Lebanon, they also live in Syria, Palestine, Israel, and Cyprus. The Maronite diaspora sees Maronites living in North and South America, Western Europe, Australia, and Africa. The Maronite Church is headed by the patriarch of Antioch and is an Eastern particular church of the Catholic Church.

Spencer C. Tucker

See also
Byzantine-Sassanid War; Crusades in the Holy Land, Christian; Heraclius; Lebanon

References
Hamilton, Bernard. *The Latin Church in the Crusader States: The Secular Church*. London: Variorum, 1980.
Moosa, Matti. *The Maronites in History*. Syracuse, NY: Syracuse University Press, 1986.
Salibi, Kamal S. "The Maronites of Lebanon under Frankish and Mamluk Rule (1099–1516)." *Arabica* 4 (1957): 280–303.

Marsh Arabs

Indigenous peoples who have traditionally inhabited the marshlands in southern Iraq. The Marsh Arabs, also known as the Madan peoples, have a unique seminomadic 5,000-year-old waterborne culture derived from the ancient Sumerians and Babylonians. The Marsh Arabs are indigenous to the marshy lowlands of southern Iraq in the disputed border area near the Iranian border, an area also known as the Tigris-Euphrates alluvial salt marsh and Al-Hawizeh. They are ethnically Arab and religiously Shiite, the majority form of Islam in Iraq and Iran. Although the marshes provided a refuge from persecution by the Sunni Muslim Ottoman Empire, the Sunni Persians, the British, and the wetlands did not insulate the Marsh Arabs from the Iraq-Iran War (1980–1988), Iraqi president Saddam Hussein's wrath following his defeat in the 1991 Persian Gulf War, or the decades of United Nations economic sanctions that followed.

At the beginning of the Iraq-Iran War, there were 250,000–500,000 Marsh Arabs inhabiting approximately 7,700 square miles of wetlands. That conflict saw great pressure on the Marsh Arabs, and their numbers plummeted. The subsequent Persian Gulf War had removed Hussein's forces from Kuwait, but U.S. president George H. W. Bush also encouraged an internal revolt against Hussein. The Marsh Arabs joined the resultant short-lived Shiite uprising in southern Iraq that lasted for just a month, during March 1991.

After having brutally crushed the rebellion, Hussein instituted a program of draining the marshes by channeling the Tigris and the Euphrates Rivers directly into the Shatt al-Arab waterway, effectively converting the wetlands into a desert. The destruction of the wetlands' rich biodiversity drastically reduced the Marsh Arabs' primary food sources (rice, barley, wheat, pearl millet, fish, sheep, and cattle) as well as the reeds used to create their boats and homes. Their sources of income were also sharply curtailed, as the desertification decimated the Marsh Arabs' commercial fisheries.

Between 1991 and 2000 or so, many Marsh Arabs were killed, and most of those remaining fled to Iran or to Shiite strongholds within Iraq, leaving approximately 40,000 of the original population in their ancestral region. By 2001, the United Nations Environment Program (UNEP) estimated that Hussein's efforts had reduced the marshes to no more than 386 square miles. Hussein and his supporters asserted that the diversion was not intended to destroy the Madan people and culture. Rather, they argued that the draining of the marshes was intended to make rich oil reserves more accessible and to create new agricultural opportunities for an impoverished region.

The American- and British-led March 2003 invasion of Iraq that ousted Hussein and his Sunni-led Baathist government brought plans to restore the marshes. This was aided initially by the ending of a four-year drought in 2003 and the destruction of Hussein's diversion dams by the Marsh Arabs. By 2007, the marshes had been restored to approximately 50 percent of their area prior to the wars. The restoration of Madan culture and the resettlement of the region by the indigenous population has been slow and fitful, however, hindered by continuing conflict in Iraq, growing tensions with Iran, and the vastly reduced number of Marsh Arabs.

Richard M. Edwards

See also
Hussein, Saddam; Iraq; Iraq War; Persian Gulf War, Overview; Shatt al-Arab Waterway; Shia Islam; Sunni Islam

References
Coughlin, Con. *Saddam: His Rise and Fall.* New York: Harper Perennial, 2005.
Hiro, Dilip. *The Longest War: The Iran-Iraq Military Conflict.* London: Routledge, 1990.
Ochsenschlager, Edward L. *Iraq's Marsh Arabs in the Garden of Eden.* Philadelphia: University of Pennsylvania Museum Publication, 2004.
Thesiger, Wilfred. *The Marsh Arabs.* 2nd rev. ed. London: Harper.

Martyrdom

The act of dying for principles or a particular cause, usually religious. The term is derived from the Greek *martys*, meaning "witness," and was first used in a religious context in reference to the apostles of Jesus Christ, who were "witnesses" of the life and deeds of Jesus, although the idea of death and suffering for religious beliefs appear earlier in Egyptian, Hindu, and Mesopotamian religious beliefs.

Martyrdom acquired its current usage in the Western world in the early Christian period, when Christians were being persecuted by authorities of the Roman Empire. Those killed for upholding their beliefs were called martyrs, their acceptance of death being considered a testimony of their faith. Some Christian martyrs sought out and welcomed martyrdom as a means of emulating Jesus's willingness to be sacrificed on the cross. Judaism does not connect martyrdom to the idea of witnessing faith but rather refers to it as sanctification of the name of God, or *kiddush ha-Shem*. In both Christianity and Judaism, martyrdom refers to a case in which the believer accepts death rather than denies or changes his or her religious beliefs.

In Islam, martyrdom (*shuhada*), or becoming a martyr for the faith (*istishhad*) is connected to the concept of declaring or witnessing Islam and to jihad, which means struggle for the sake of Islam. The most important Quranic verse usually connected with martyrdom is 4:69; "Whosoever obeys Allah, and the Messenger—they are with those whom God has blessed, Prophets, just men, martyrs (*shuhada*), the righteous; good companions [are] they!" According to Islam, martyrs are not questioned after death by the two angels, Munkar and Nakir; bypass purgatory; and do not require the intercession of the prophet to proceed to Paradise as they are free of sin. Martyrs can serves as intercessors for others and are not washed after death and are buried in the clothes they die in.

In the early period of Islam, martyrdom referred to those Muslims killed in battle against the armies of Mecca and to 11 of the Shiite Imams. Today, the term also refers to suicide attackers who believe they are defending the cause of Islam. A true martyr (*shahid*) is, according to doctrine, one who does not seek his or her own death deliberately but accepts it and is granted religious legitimacy and assured a place in Heaven. However, suicide committed for personal reasons is prohibited by Islamic law and may be punished by an endless repetition of the same form of death in Hell.

Modern-day Islamic terrorist organizations alluded to the concept of martyrdom when they began using suicide attacks as a tactic. This was not a new phenomenon but was both a revival of an ancient tradition dating back to the early wars of Islam and an adaptation of the discourse of radical Islamic leaders who believed that martyrdom was inevitable for those struggling in the Islamic cause.

Suicide attacks provide two significant advantages over standard attacks. First, if successful, they are tactically and logistically easier to execute, because no escape route or retreat is needed, and they are therefore more efficient. Second, they provide a shock to the enemy that goes beyond the actual casualty figure, as they suggest great vulnerability and further probable use of this tactic. Third, they provide a martyr symbol that makes recruiting new members for the organization an easier task by strengthening the ideology behind a group's agenda. The fact that the martyr is willing to commit suicide is used by the group as "testimony" and "evidence" of the worthiness of its cause.

Terrorist suicide attacks in contemporary times began outside the Middle East in Sri Lanka by Tamil separatists. Much used there, they have no connection with Islamic ideology and demonstrated only the resolve of the attackers. Claims of martyrdom, however, were made for those killed in demonstrations against the Iranian government prior to the Islamic Revolution of 1979. Suicide attacks were not utilized in that revolution, however. Suicide attacks that involved claims of martyrdom did occur in Syria in the late 1970s and early 1980s in battles between Islamic groups and the Syrian government in Damascus, Hama, and Homs.

The term "martyr" was used in the Lebanon Civil War by both Christians and Muslims. The connection between martyrdom and suicide attacks came with the Islamic resistance that responded to the Israeli invasion and occupation of Lebanon in 1982. These actions were undertaken only by a few, but some of the large attacks launched in 1983, such as by Islamic Jihad against the U.S. marines and barracks and French forces, were truck bombings involving suicide.

Much of the present-day discussion of martyrdom comes out of the war on terror. This depends on one's point of view. Thus, Americans note suicide bomber attacks in Iraq, while some Iraqis style such events as martyrdom operations and part of the resistance against the occupation.

A long-standing discussion of martyrdom in acts of resistance also arose among Palestinians opposing Israeli occupation of what they perceive to be their homeland. Those killed in all stages of the resistance to Israel but particularly those active in political movements have been seen by most Palestinians as martyrs. Suicide attacks only began to be employed in the Palestinian-Israeli struggle in 1994 and were at the time very controversial among Palestinians. Were these necessary acts of desperation or a bona fide tactic in a war of the weak? That question led to discussions among religious leaders that only expanded after the 9/11 Al Qaeda terrorist attacks on the United States. Although these later were largely condemned by Muslim leaders, Palestinian suicide attacks were not because of the conditions of the Israeli occupation and collective punishment and other tactics employed by the Israeli government. Sheikh Qaradawi, a popular Egyptian preacher who now lives in Qatar, has pronounced those who engage in such attacks in Palestine to be acting under defensive jihad, justified by the Quran.

Some prominent Muslim religious leaders have given their public support for various types of martyrdom. Iranian leader Ayatollah Ruhollah Khomeini approved self-sacrifice by Iranian troops and citizens during the war against Iraq (1980–1988), when these forces that included civilian volunteers were forced to advance in human-wave assaults against Iraqi defensive fire in what would have to be classified as suicidal attacks. Other organizations that adopted the suicide/martyr method for attacks include Al Qaeda, groups such as Abu Sayyaf, and a Bedouin group called Tawhid wa-l Jihad by the Egyptian security services but also the non-Islamist al-Aqsa Martyrs Brigades. Even Al Qaeda leaders such as Sayf al-Adl indicate that they have sought to rein in the desire for suicide attacks by younger and less self-controlled members, for if such fervor was uncontrolled, there would be few operatives to run the movement.

Controversial aspects of the modern-day link between jihad and martyrdom include the deaths of innocent civilian victims who are not the primary targets of such attacks. Extremist groups employing suicide attacks excuse these victims away as simply additional martyrs. There is also the issue of motivation—whether the suicide bombers are impelled to act by the wrong intent, or *niyah*—because if so, then they are not true martyrs. According to the companion of the prophet and early caliph Umar, those waging jihad should not set out deliberately to die and become martyrs in an egotistical aim to be known as heroes. There is also a financial aspect to this, as those who engage in jihad (including those who are martyred or who live on) are enjoined not to leave their families without support or in debt. In contemporary times, would-be suicide martyrs sometimes ignore or reinterpret these rules, or organizations promise to provide for their widows and families.

All this has led to a serious effort to deradicalize by uncoupling the concepts of jihad and martyrdom within Muslim communities and by Muslim governments. While not uniform in approach and content, these generally stress moderation and peaceful efforts to change society rather than violence. This task is extremely difficult where foreign occupation and military campaigns are ongoing, as in Pakistan, Afghanistan, and Iraq but also in Saudi Arabia, where alliances with the United States are blamed for violence against Muslims.

Elliot Paul Chodoff and Sherifa Zuhur

See also

al-Aqsa Martyrs Brigades; Al Qaeda; Fatah, al-; Hamas; Hezbollah; Intifada, Second; Jihad; Khomeini, Ruhollah; Lebanon Civil War; Lebanon-Israeli War; Palestinian Islamic Jihad; Suicide Bombings

References

Ayoub, Mahmoud M. *Redemptive Suffering in Islam: A Study of the Devotional Aspects of 'Ashura' in Twelver Shi'ism.* The Hague: Brill, 1978.

Gambetta, Diego, ed. *Making Sense of Suicide Missions.* Oxford: Oxford University Press, 2005.

Oliver, Anne Marie, and Paul Steinberg. *The Road to Martyrs' Square: A Journey into the World of the Suicide Bomber.* Oxford: Oxford University Press, 2005.

Shay, Shaul. *The Shahids: Islam and Suicide Attacks.* New Brunswick, NJ: Transaction Publishers, 2004.

Smith, Jane I., and Yvonne Haddad. *The Islamic Understanding of Death and Resurrection.* Albany: State University of New York Press, 1981.

Masada

The term "masada" is a Latin transliteration of the Hebrew name "Metzada," meaning "fortress." Masada refers to a rock mesa overlooking the Dead Sea in the eastern Judaean Desert near Ein Gedi atop which Jewish Zealots stood against a Roman siege (72–73 CE) in the First Jewish-Roman War (66–73), also known as the Herodian Jewish Revolt and the Great Jewish Revolt.

Masada's eastern cliffs rise some 1,350 feet (150 feet above sea level) above the Dead Sea, with the more vertical western cliffs rising 300 feet above the floor of the Dead Sea Valley. The rhomboid-shaped flat plateau comprised an area some 1,200 feet by 900 feet. Access was limited to four very difficult and quite steep approaches: the Snake Path from the east, still used by some tourists today; the White Rock ascent from the west; and one approach each from the south and north. Three large cisterns hewn from the rock mesa collected rainwater. Numerous storehouses also dotted the site.

The Zealot defenders and their families were housed in barracks-like quarters and in the remains of a last century BCE Herodian palace. The plateau was ringed by a watchtower-studded stone casement wall 4,200 feet long and 12 feet thick that incorporated the walls of the living quarters and storehouses.

King Herod the Great was a pro-Roman ruler and appointed Pompey as regent of Palestine in 47 BCE. Herod first fled with his family to Masada in 40 when the Jews joined the Parthians in a rebellion against Rome. Herod then fled to Rome but was restored to his position in 37 after the Romans under Mark Antony crushed the rebellion. Fearing another Jewish rebellion and possible war with Cleopatra of Egypt, during 37–31 Herod fortified Masada to include an extensive and lavish palace.

Roman soldiers were garrisoned at Masada in 66 CE when it was captured at the beginning of the Great Jewish Revolt by Jewish Zealots led by Menahem ben Judah. Eleazar ben Ya'ir, nephew of Menahem, assumed command of Masada soon after rival Jews killed Menahem in Jerusalem that same year. Except for the Zealots at Masada, Jewish resistance ended when the Romans captured Jerusalem and destroyed its Temple in September 70.

Lucius Flavius Silva, the Roman governor of Palestine, laid siege to Masada in 73 with a force of 10,000–15,000 men consisting of the Roman Tenth Legion, its support troops, and Jewish prisoners of war who were used as construction slaves. The Jewish defenders and family members numbered between 1,000 and 1,500 people.

After surrounding the fortress with eight military camps and a three-foot-high wall, the Romans oversaw in a nine-month period the construction by Jewish slave labor of an assault ramp to the top of Masada. It was during this time that the Jewish defenders reinforced the stone wall with an earthen and wooden wall.

The Romans first used a battering ram to breach the stone wall and then succeeded in burning the wooden wall. As the Romans prepared to exploit the breach the next day, Eleazar exhorted the Zealot defenders and their families to a final act of defiance. They burned their personal belongings and selected by lot 10 defenders to kill the general population. These 10 then killed each other in turn, leaving only a final defender to commit suicide. The contents of the storehouses were not burned so as to demonstrate to the Romans that the defenders and their families chose to die rather than suffer defeat by siege and assault. These details and the personal exhortation of Eleazar to his followers were related to the Romans by 2 women and 5 children who survived by hiding in one of the cisterns. Their accounts were then recorded by the first-century Jewish historian Josephus.

Masada emerged as a symbol of Jewish and Zionist resolve and courage and became a widely visited pilgrimage site for many Zionist youth groups and Haganah in the years prior to the formation in 1948 of the State of Israel. The Star of David flag of Israel was raised over Masada following the end of the Israeli War of Independence in 1949, and the site continues to be used by various units of the Israel Defense Forces and contemporary youth movements for swearing-in ceremonies that conclude with the oath "Masada shall never fall again." Masada is accessible today both by foot on the arduous Snake Path and by aerial tramway.

RICHARD M. EDWARDS

See also
Haganah; Jewish-Roman War, First

References
Ben-Yehuda, Nachman. *Sacrificing Truth: Archaeology and the Myth of Masada*. Amherst, NY: Humanity Books, 2002.
Miklowitz, Gloria D. *Masada: The Last Fortress*. Grand Rapids, MI: Eerdmans, 1999.
Yadin, Yigael. *Masada: Herod's Fortress and the Zealots' Last Stand*. New York: Welcome Rain, 1998.

Mashal, Khaled (1956–)

Leader of the Islamic Palestinian organization Hamas. Khaled Mashal (Mashaal, Meshal) was born the son of a farmer on May 28, 1956, in the village of Silwad, north of Ramallah in the West Bank (then Jordan, now controlled by Israel). After the Six-Day War in 1967, Mashal moved with his family to Jordan. He then moved to Kuwait and earned a BS degree in physics from Kuwait University. While a student there, Mashal challenged the leadership of Yasser Arafat's Fatah organization in the General Union of Palestinian Students and helped form the Islamic Haqq bloc that competed with Fatah.

Mashal joined the Muslim Brotherhood in 1971. He taught school in Kuwait during 1978–1984. Mashal was one of the founders of the Palestinian Islamist organization known as Hamas in 1987 and was a member of its Political Bureau from the beginning. He first headed its Kuwaiti branch. Mashal lived in Kuwait until 1990, when with the Iraqi invasion of that country he moved to Jordan. He became the chairman of the Political Bureau, in effect head of Hamas, in 1996. Mashal survived an assassination attempt on September 25, 1997, believed to have been carried out by the Israeli Mossad special operations service and ordered by Prime Minister Benjamin Netanyahu. Mashal was poisoned, but the Israeli agents were caught, and a furious King Hussein of Jordan demanded that Israel supply an antidote, which was done.

With the expulsion from Jordan of the leadership of Hamas by King Abdullah in August 1999, Mashal relocated first to Qatar and then to Syria. Although not residing in the Palestinian territories, it was Mashal who directed Hamas strategy. Free of restraints, he was also the chief fund-raiser for the organization, which proved critical for Hamas after the United States and West European countries cut off aid to the Palestinian Authority in 2006. Charismatic with developed diplomatic skills, Mashal has met with Western diplomats as well as Arab leaders.

In May 2009 shortly after his reelection to a fourth four-year term as the leader of Hamas, Mashal gave an extensive two-day interview in Damascus to correspondents of the *New York Times*. In what may have been a gesture toward the Barack Obama administration in the United States and other Western governments, Mashal announced that Hamas was for the time suspending rocket attacks from the Gaza Strip against Israel and that the organization sought a Palestinian state only in the areas taken by Israel from Jordan in the 1967 war. Although he announced that Hamas sought to be "part of the solution," he stopped short of recognizing Israel. Indeed, Mashal declared that "There is only one enemy in the region, and that is Israel." Although he said that he would not seek to amend it, he urged outsiders to ignore the provision in the Hamas charter that calls for the obliteration of Israel through jihad. "We are shaped by our experiences," he said.

A resident of Damascus since 2001, in February 2012 with the Syrian Civil War continuing, Mashal distanced himself from the Syrian regime of President Bashar al-Assad and moved to Qatar. Hamas shut down its offices in Syria, and Mashal announced his support for the antigovernment opposition forces there. He has since divided his time between Doha and Cairo.

Mashal was involved in negotiating a prisoner exchange deal that saw captured Israeli soldier Gilad Shalit, who had been seized inside Israel and taken to Gaza, released in October 2011 in exchange for more than 1,000 Palestinian prisoners held by Israel.

In December 2012 following a truce between Israel and Hamas, Mashal made a four-day visit to Gaza on the occasion of the 25th anniversary of its funding. Addressing tens of thousands of Gaza residents in Gaza City's Katiba Square, Mashal stated that armed resistance was the correct path for Palestinians to gain their rights and "liberate" Palestine, reiterating Hamas's refusal to concede any part of historical Palestine. He did announce support for Palestinian president Mahmoud Abbas's initiative to secure international recognition of the State of Palestine at the United Nations but added that "resistance" was required as well as diplomacy.

In July 2014 after Israeli Operation PROTECTIVE EDGE (the 2014 Gaza War) and the recovery of documentation within Gaza, the Israeli press published stories of widespread corruption within the Hamas leadership. Mashal and Mousa Abu Marzuk, a senior member of Hamas, were said to have accumulated vast personal wealth estimated at as much as $2.5 billion each. In late 2017 Mashal stepped down as head of Hamas's politburo, although he remained leader of the organization. In recent years, Mashal and his associates have been accused of corruption and of appropriating large sums of money amounting to hundreds of millions of dollars to build their own personal fortunes. Mashal has vehemently denied such reports, however.

SPENCER C. TUCKER

See also
Abbas, Mahmoud; Arafat, Yasser; Assad, Bashar al-; Gaza War of 2014; Hamas; Netanyahu, Benjamin; Syria; Syrian Civil War

References
El-Khodary, Taghreed, and Ethan Bronner. "Addressing U.S., Hamas Says It Has Grounded Its Rockets to Israel." *New York Times*, May 5, 2009.

McGeough, Paul. *Kill Khalid: The Failed Mossad Assassination of Khalid Mishal and the Rise of Hamas.* New York: New Press, 2009.

Massacre at the Citadel (March 1, 1811)

Mamluk influence was drastically curtailed by the French invasion of Egypt (1798–1801). Despite centuries of power, their numbers and, more important, their prestige were dramatically reduced. This was evident in the appointment of Mehmed Ali as the new *wali* (governor) in 1805.

An Albanian adventurer who had charisma, political savvy, and a pinch of luck, Mehmed Ali spent much of 1805–1810 battling Mamluk grandees to further reduce their control. Although able to dominate Egypt's major urban centers, the governor faced a considerable challenge in his desire to extinguish Mamluk opposition. His opponents were mounted warriors par excellence, quite capable of speeding away from the *wali*'s infantry based army.

Mehmed Ali's solution was treachery. On the eve of his campaign to Arabia, he offered the Mamluk emirs safe conduct to attend a lavish ceremony in honor of his son, Tusun, to be held at Cairo's Citadel on March 1, 1811. Citadel parties were important social/political events in contemporary Cairo, and attendance was de rigueur for political hopefuls. Lured by offers of rich gifts, a sumptuous meal, and tradition, more than 400 emirs and their chief officers advanced up the narrow street leading to the Bab Al-Azab, the main gate to the Citadel. As they milled about, Mehmed Ali's Albanian mercenaries launched a near-perfect ambush, killing almost all the key leaders and many of their retainers. Although the Massacre at the Citadel did not wipe out the Mamluks, it did remove them as contenders for influence in Mehmed Ali's Egypt.

John P. Dunn

See also
Egyptian-Arab Wars; Mehmed Ali

Reference
Shaw, Stanford J., and Ezul Kural Shaw. *History of the Ottoman Empire and Modern Turkey*, Vol. 2, *Reform, Reaction and Republic: The Rise of Modern Turley, 1808–1975*. Cambridge: Cambridge University Press, 1977.

Maududi, Abul A'Ala (1903–1979)

Muslim scholar, author, and political activist. Abul A'Ala Maududi, often spelled "Mawdudi," who occupies an important place in the Islamic revival movement of the 20th century, was born on September 25, 1903, in the city of Aurangabad, Hyderabad Deccan, in central India. His father was a well-educated lawyer of the middle class. Maududi's education was a mix of home tutoring, education at a madrassa, and self-learning, which allowed him to pass the examinations required to become an Islamic teacher in India, known as a *maulvi*.

Maududi was also raised on the stories of the glory days of early Islam, which clearly impacted his own views later in life. When civil disturbances grew in India over British rule in the 1920s, Maududi participated in the Khilafat Movement, which called for the expulsion of the British and the creation of an Islamic state. He used his talents to write and edit Islamic newspapers to this end.

Growing weary of journalism, Maududi then decided to focus on writing religious-based books to promote Islam. He engaged in a serious study of the Quran, hadith literature, and the writings of such eminent Islamic scholars as Ibn Taymiyyah and Ibn Qayyim. In countering the Hindu majority in India, Maududi's writings noted that Muslims were to be missionaries to spread Islam, were not to assimilate into non-Muslim cultures, and should be in control of governmental affairs, while non-Muslims should be subordinate. He also stressed the need for an Islamic-based government to engage in jihad (holy war) to spread Islam to the rest of the world. Distressed over the lack of unity among Muslims in the region, Maududi worked to organize a united political front, which became a reality when he formed the Jama'at-i-Islam in 1941.

Maududi's principal concern was that any separate state created for Muslims had to be one that was based solely on Islamic law and that the movement should eventually spread internationally. To aid in this process, Muslims were not only to convert non-Muslims but were also to engage in a birth-rate revolution to increase their numbers. The creation of the Jama'at devoted itself to ensuring Islamic rule in what was soon to become Pakistan. Many supporters moved north into the Punjab region in anticipation of this event, and by 1947 Maududi had migrated to the newly created nation of Pakistan.

Maududi's conception of an Islamic state was one in which all aspects of life would be under the sway of Islamic law. Non-Muslims could continue to live in such a state but could not attempt to convert Muslims, as Islam was a public affair, and such conversion implied rebellion against the state, which merited the death penalty. Maududi advocated a threefold process for seizing power. Initially an invitation to Islam would be made, followed by efforts to gain power through peaceful and legal means. If this second stage failed, he discreetly advocated the use of revolutionary force to create the Islamic state.

The establishment of Pakistan in 1947 did not lead to the Islamic state that Maududi desired, and his political activism led to multiple arrests and the banning of some of his works by the Pakistani government. In the early 1950s he supported the violent Muslim suppression of the schismatic Qadianis, receiving a death sentence from the government that was later commuted. His struggle for an Islamic constitution for Pakistan was largely fulfilled in 1956. Later rulers scrapped this document, however, and beginning in 1958 Maududi and his followers had to endure four years of martial law under which the Jama'at was banned. It was restored in 1962 under a new constitution, which was seen as a departure from the nation's initial Islamic foundation.

While continuing his political work, Maududi focused on writing his *tafsir* (commentary) of the Quran, which he completed in 1972. Of particular importance were his introductions to each of its chapters. Traveling to the United States to seek medical treatment, Maududi died on September 22, 1979, in Buffalo, New York, from complications arising from stomach, kidney, and heart problems. He was buried in Lahore, Pakistan. Maududi, who wrote more than 120 books and pamphlets and gave close to 1,000 speeches, is considered one of the most prominent and important advocates of the modern Islamic revival movement. His works are still widely read by Muslims around the world, especially his introductions to the chapters of the Quran.

RUSSELL G. RODGERS

See also
Islamic Radicalism in the 20th and 21st Centuries; Quran; Shia Islam; Sunni Islam

References
Hasan, Masudul. *Sayyid Abul A'Ala Maududi and His Thought.* Lahore, Pakistan: Islamic Publications, 1984.
Maududi, Sayyid Abul A'la. *First Principles of the Islamic State.* Lahore, Pakistan: Islamic Publications, 1983.
Maududi, Sayyid Abul A'la. *Jihad in Islam.* Beirut, Lebanon: Holy Koran Publishing House, 1980.
Maududi, Sayyid Abul A'la. *Political Theory of Islam.* Lahore, Pakistan: Islamic Publications, 1980.

Mawdud (?–1113)

Mawdud ibn Altuntakin was the Seljuk Turkish lord of Mosul in Iraq during 1108–1113 who led three major military campaigns against the Franks of Outremer during the Christian crusades in the Holy Land.

In May 1110, at the request of the Seljuk sultan Muhammad Tapar, Mawdud attacked the city of Edessa (modern-day Sanliurfa, Turkey), assisted by two Turkoman leaders, Īlghāzī and Suqmān al-Qubī. They withdrew with the arrival of crusader relieving forces under King Baldwin I of Jerusalem and Tancred of Antioch but were able to defeat the Franks near the Euphrates. However, the Seljuk commanders lacked a strategy for further action and returned home.

In 1111 the inhabitants of Aleppo appealed to the Abbasid caliph in Baghdad for help against the encroachments of the Franks. Sultan Muhammad Tapar ordered Mawdud and other Turkish lords from Persia and Mesopotamia to undertake a jihad (holy war) and sent two of his sons on the campaign. This large army besieged Edessa and Turbessel (modern-day Tellbasar Kalesi, Turkey) without success, and when it moved on to Aleppo, the ruler of Aleppo, Riwan, closed the city to it, fearing the loss of his independence to the Seljuks. Although Mawdud and his allies were able to ward off a Frankish attack on the town of Shaizar (south of Aleppo), the army eventually dispersed.

Mawdud's last compaign was his most effective. In the spring of 1113 Tughtigin, *atabeg* of Damascus, asked Mawdud for military assistance against King Baldwin I of Jerusalem, who was plundering Damascene territory. Mawdud arrived with a large army in Syria in May 1113. Baldwin I, fearing the strength of the Muslim force, offered some territorial concessions to Tughtigin. Nonetheless, on June 28, 1113, the joint Muslim forces confronted the Army of Jerusalem at al-Sannabra, south of Lake Tiberias. According to William of Tyre and most Muslim chroniclers, the battle was disastrous for the Franks, and subsequently the Muslim forces plundered Palestine that summer, reaching as far as Jaffa (modern-day Tel Aviv–Yafo, Israel) and Acre (modern-day Akko, Israel). Fearing Mawdud's success, however, Tughtigin ended the campaign even though Jerusalem was then largely defenseless. When Mawdud withdrew to Damascus, he was murdered in September 1113 by Assassins hired by Tughtigin. As a result, Damascus and Jerusalem established peaceful relations and cooperated against the sultan.

TAEF EL-AZHARI

See also
al-Sannabra, Battle of; Baldwin I of Jerusalem; Crusades in the Holy Land, Christian

References
El-Azhari, Taef. *The Saljūqs of Syria during the Crusades, 463–459 A.H./1070–1154 A.D.* Berlin: Schwarz, 1997.
Fink, Harold. "Mawdud I of Mosul, Precursor of Saladin." *Muslim World* 43 (1953): 18–27.
Mouton, Jean-Michel. *Damas et sa principauté sous les Saljoukides et les Bourides, 1076–1154.* Le Caire: Institut Français d'Archéologie Orientale, 1994.

Maysalun, Battle of (July 24, 1920)

Battle between the forces of France and the Arab Kingdom of Syria. Also known as the Battle of Khan Maysalun, it was fought near Khan Maysalun in the Anti-Lebanon Mountains about 16 miles west of Damascus. In October 1918, Arab forces under Hashemite emir Faisal bin Hussein, leader of the forces of the Arab Revolt that had cooperated with the British against the Ottoman Empire during World War I, captured Damascus, Syria. Faisal attended the Paris Peace Conference in 1919, where he sought to secure recognition of an Arab kingdom under his rule. Despite the British having promised just this following an Allied victory over the Ottomans, the British and French governments had secretly agreed in the Sykes-Picot Agreement of May 1916 to divide the Ottoman Middle Eastern holdings between themselves, with the French securing Syria and Lebanon.

French forces, formed into the Army of the Levant under General Henri Gouraud, landed in Beirut, Lebanon, in November 1919. They then deployed to the Bekaa Valley between Beirut and Damascus, with the ultimate goal of bringing all Syria under their rule.

On March 8, 1920, the Syrian National Congress proclaimed establishment of the Arab Kingdom of Syria, with Faisal as king. A month later, however, the San Remo Conference led to an agreement by the World War I Allies that established Syria and Lebanon as French mandates under the League of Nations, an arrangement repudiated by both Faisal and the Syrian National Congress.

On July 14, 1920, Gouraud demanded that Faisal disband his Arab Army and submit to French authority by July 20 or face invasion. When Faisal refused, Gouraud set his army in motion toward Damascus. The French Army of the Levant numbered some 12,000 men. The Arab Army, under Faisal's minister of war General Ussuf al-Azma, which marched out to meet the French, numbered some 1,400–4,000 men as well as mounted Bedouin tribesmen and militia volunteers. The Arab forces were not only outnumbered; they were also at a great disadvantage in equipment. While both sides had artillery, the French had both tanks and aircraft.

French forces captured Aleppo without a fight on July 23, and on July 24 the two sides met near Khan Maysalun. The battle lasted some four hours and ended in a French victory. General al-Azma's death, probably from tank machine-gun fire, ended the battle. The withdrawing Arab forces then came under fire from French aircraft. According to the French, in the battle they lost 42 dead, 152 wounded, and 14 missing; the French put Arabs losses at some 150 killed and 1,500 wounded. Despite this easy French victory, the battle has been seen as a courageous example of Arab nationalism against foreign domination.

French forces entered Damascus the next day, and in short order they extended their control over all of Syria. Syria and Lebanon were officially recognized as French mandates by the League of Nations in 1923. The British agreed to make Faisal the king of their mandate of Iraq.

Spencer C. Tucker

See also
Faisal I, King of Iraq; San Remo Conference; Sykes-Picot Agreement; Syria

References
Allawi, Ali A. *Faisal I of Iraq*. New Haven, CT: Yale University Press, 2014.

Husri, Sati'. *The Day of Maysalun: A Page from the Modern History of the Arabs*. Washington, DC: Middle East Institute, 1966.

Khoury, Philip S. *Syria and the French Mandate: The Politics of Arab Nationalism, 1920–1945*. Princeton, NJ: Princeton University Press, 1987.

McHugo, John. *Syria: A Recent History*. London: Saqi, 2015.

Tauber, Eliezer. *The Formation of Modern Iraq and Syria*. New York: Routledge, 1995.

McMahon-Hussein Correspondence

Ten letters exchanged between British high commissioner for Egypt Sir A. Henry McMahon and Hussein ibn Ali, emir of the Arabian Hejaz and sharif of Mecca. Many Arabs have viewed the exchange as Britain's commitment to Arab autonomy and independence in the Middle East, including the entire area of Palestine. The exchange began with a letter from Hussein to McMahon, translated into English and read by McMahon on July 14, 1915. The last letter was one from McMahon to Hussein on March 10, 1916. The ambiguities in McMahon's proposals combined with subsequent British policies that flew in the face of the McMahon-Hussein correspondence have been a constant source of misunderstanding and frustration in the Middle East, and the issues that the letters raised continue to present obstacles to this very day.

Hussein's initial letter to McMahon outlined the conditions of Arab participation in the British struggle against the Ottoman Empire during World War I. Essentially, Hussein pledged Arab support for the fight against the Ottomans in exchange for British concessions, most specifically those relating to Arab independence. In an October 24, 1915, letter McMahon assured Hussein that Great Britain would recognize and support independence for Arabs residing in areas outlined by Hussein. The territories affected included the Arabian Peninsula, greater Syria, Palestine, Lebanon, and Transjordan. Thus, areas east of Hama, Homa, Aleppo, and Damascus would therefore be eligible for Arab statehood or the creation of a series of constituent Arab states. Quite naturally, many Arabs saw in this promise a British commitment to independence, either immediately or in the immediate wake of World War I (which would not end until November 1918).

At the same time, the British along with the French and Russians were drawing up the secret May 1916 Sykes-Picot Agreement, which would demonstrate that the British government had little intention of making good on the McMahon pledges. The Sykes-Picot Agreement was an arrangement whereby the powers would divide the Middle East into French, British, and Russian spheres of influence once the war was over. In 1917 Italy would also be added to that framework. These spheres incorporated much of the area that McMahon and Hussein had agreed would be subject to Arab autonomy. Not until December 1917 did Hussein learn the full details of the agreement, which had been leaked to him by the Ottoman government in hopes that it would drive a wedge in the Anglo-Arab alliance.

As if the Sykes-Picot Agreement had not been enough to give Hussein pause over British intentions, the November 1917 Balfour Declaration clearly seemed to show British duplicity. In the declaration, the British government made known its intention to support the creation of a Jewish homeland in Palestine. This, in the eyes of Hussein and other Arab leaders, was a patent violation of the promises McMahon had made to Hussein in 1915 and 1916.

The British claimed that the McMahon correspondence did not apply to Palestine. Therefore, the Balfour Declaration could not possibly be contradictory to any earlier pledges made to the Arabs. Indeed, McMahon's letter of October 25, 1915, had not explicitly mentioned Palestine. Nonetheless, Palestine had always been included in historic Syria. From the Arab perspective, because these areas were not specifically excluded from the Arab sphere, they were by understanding to come under Arab control. Furthermore, McMahon and Hussein had agreed that land not purely Arab in makeup was to be excluded from the understanding. The British argued that because Palestine was neither completely Arab nor Muslim, it was not part of the agreement. The Arabs, however, saw things differently. They argued that Palestine was overwhelmingly Arab and should therefore be part of Arab-controlled areas.

Of course, events not soon after the McMahon-Hussein correspondence ceased would make many of these discrepancies moot. The Balfour Declaration certainly seemed to fly in the face of Hussein's understanding of McMahon's agreement, but even that declaration contains a phrase that implies protection of the rights of the existing Arab inhabitants of Palestine. British prime minister David Lloyd George's insistence at the 1919 Paris Peace Conference that Great Britain maintain control of Palestine (and Iraq) further demonstrated the British unwillingness to honor the agreements that McMahon had made. The final insult, in the eyes of the Arabs, was the League of Nations mandate that granted the British de facto control over Palestine. It is certainly easy to see how the McMahon-Hussein correspondence buoyed the spirits of Arab nationalists and how its aftermath sowed the seeds of a deep-seated distrust and enmity toward the West.

PAUL G. PIERPAOLI JR.

See also
Balfour Declaration; Sykes-Picot Agreement; Zionism

References
Kent, Marian, ed. *The Great Powers and the End of the Ottoman Empire.* London: Routledge, 1996.

Smith, Charles D. *Palestine and the Arab-Israeli Conflict: A History with Documents.* 6th ed. New York: Bedford/St. Martin's, 2006.

Tauber, Eliezer. *The Arab Movements in World War I.* London: Frank Cass, 1993.

Medina, Siege of (1916–1919)

Significant event during the 1916–1918 Arab Revolt in World War I. One of the three holy cities of Islam and terminus of the Hejaz railroad, Medina was a natural target for the Arab insurgents in the Hejaz from the outset of the revolt. In fact, the standard of revolt was first raised on June 5, 1916, near the city, and a first attempt at capturing it failed the next day. While the forces of the grand sharif of Mecca Husayn ibn Ali, aided by Egyptian field artillery and British warships, were able to capture most important cities and ports in the Hejaz, among them Jidda, Mecca, Taif, and Yanbo, the Ottomans reinforced Medina and held it for almost three years.

In spite of a warning by their German allies that trying to defend both the Hejaz and Palestine in the face of the British buildup could result in losing both, the Ottoman leadership, fearing for its legitimacy when giving up the holy places, decided to hold the Hejaz. To this end, they turned Medina into an impregnable stronghold and reinforced its garrison. The Ottoman Army VIII Corps was tasked with defending the Hejaz railroad on its entire length of some 430 miles from Syria to the Hejaz. The principal component of this force, the Medina garrison itself that was called the Hejaz Expeditionary Force, numbered 14,000 men by the fall of 1916. The Ottoman commander at Medina Khairy Bey felt strong enough to stage repeated successful sorties against the weakly organized Arab forces that were more blockading than actually besieging the town, and he even planned a counteroffensive aimed at recapturing Mecca, though it never materialized.

In the summer of 1917 Prince Faisal's Arab Army, backed by British warships, moved north from al-Wejh, taking Aqaba and conducting raids on the Hejaz railroad, the sole artery of supply for the Medina garrison. When the British Egypt Expeditionary Force (EEF) and its Arab allies continued their advance into Palestine and Syria in late 1917 and 1918, the task of protecting the railroad increasingly imposed a heavy strain on the Ottoman forces. Including the Medina garrison, the Ottomans needed 22,000 troops in 1918 to keep the Hejaz railroad open. The men were distributed among some major garrisons and numerous small blockhouses along the track from which they usually dared not venture.

In April 1918 Arab forces finally cut the Hejaz railroad around Ma'an. Evacuation of the 12,000-man Ottoman garrison still in Medina, for a long time advocated by Ottoman officers but always refused by the government in Istanbul, was now out of the question. Fakhri Pasha refused to surrender well into January 1919, when his officers finally revolted and turned the influenza-plagued garrison over to the Arabs. Some 8,000 Ottoman soldiers were evacuated to Egypt, while many Arabs joined the victors' cause. Holding on to Medina may have been a political necessity for the Ottoman government, but the fall of the empire rendered it a vain sacrifice.

DIERK WALTER

See also
Arab Revolt of World War I; Faisal I, King of Iraq; Hejaz Railroad, Attacks on; Hussein ibn Ali ibn Mohammed

References
Bruce, Anthony P. C. *The Last Crusade: The Palestine Campaign in the First World War.* London: Murray, 2002.
Bullock, David L. *Allenby's War: The Palestinian-Arabian Campaigns, 1916–1918.* London: Blandford, 1988.
Erickson, Edward J. *Ordered to Die: A History of the Ottoman Army in the First World War.* Westport, CT: Greenwood, 2000.
Falls, Cyril. *Military Operations: Egypt and Palestine, from June 1917 to the End of the War.* London: HMSO, 1930.
McKale, Donald M. *War by Revolution: Germany and Great Britain in the Middle East in the Era of World War I.* Kent, OH: Kent State University Press, 1998.

Medina Ridge, Battle of (February 27, 1991)

The last major ground engagement of the 1991 Persian Gulf War and a decisive tank battle fought on February 27, 1991, near Basra, Iraq, between a brigade of the U.S. 1st Armored Division and the 2nd Brigade of the Iraqi Republican Guard (Medina Division).

The coalition plan for the liberation of Kuwait called for two U.S. Marine Corps divisions to attack directly into Kuwait to pin the Iraqi Army to its defenses. The main attack, however, would be carried out by the U.S. VII and XVIII Corps, which would execute a giant left hook through the western Iraqi desert, then encircle Iraqi forces in Kuwait. These two corps would also engage the Republican Guard divisions of the Iraqi Army, which were stationed in reserve north of Kuwait, and endeavor to cut them off.

The ground offensive began on February 24, 1991. On the morning of February 27, the U.S. VII Corps was preparing to complete the encirclement of Iraqi forces in Kuwait. The 2nd Brigade, 1st Armored Division, commanded by Colonel Montgomery Meigs, encountered an armored brigade of the Medina Republican Guard Division dug into the far side of a long, low ridge that ran north-south, known as the Medina Ridge.

The Iraqs planned to pick off American tanks and armored vehicles as they crested the ridge. The Iraqis were equipped with T-72 tanks mounting 125mm main guns and with BMP-1 armored vehicles and backed by an assortment of older T-55 and T-62 tanks. The Iraqi deployment line extended about six miles.

Meigs's brigade massed 200 vehicles for the engagement. The Americans were equipped with M1A1 Abrams tanks and Bradley Fighting Vehicles. The Abrams' 105mm main gun tank had a range of 4,375 yards and fired armor-piercing discarding sabot (APDS) ammunition, with a core projectile of depleted uranium. The Abrams tanks were also equipped with thermal sights that enabled them to fight in conditions of poor visibility. The T-72's main gun had an effective range of only about 2,000 yards, and its shells could not penetrate the Abrams' frontal armor. Only a very small proportion of Iraqi tanks, specifically the most advanced T-72 models, had laser rangefinders, and these were still outranged by the Abrams. Also, the Iraqi BMP vehicles were obsolete in comparison to the U.S. Bradley Fighting Vehicles.

Arriving on the ridge, the 2nd Brigade Abrams tank crews used their thermal sights to locate the Iraqi tanks and then commenced destroying them at long range. The Bradleys fired antitank missiles and engaged lighter Iraqi vehicles with 25mm cannon. The Iraqis aimed at the muzzle flashes of the Abrams tanks, but they were completely outranged and unable to respond adequately.

Multiple Launch Rocket System (MLRS) launchers provided artillery support for the 2nd Brigade, while A-10 Thunderbolt (Warthog) aircraft provided close air support. Additional assistance came from six AH-64 Apache helicopters firing Hellfire missiles. One U.S. aircraft was shot down by an Iraqi ZSU-23/4 antiaircraft gun.

Although the Iraqis knew that the Americans were coming, they failed to deploy observation teams and left many vehicles unmanned while the crews ate lunch. The Iraqis had also attempted to dig their tanks into hull-down positions, leaving only the turrets exposed. However, the procedure was improperly carried out. Instead of digging their tanks into the ground, the Iraqis simply pushed sand up against the sides and front of the tanks, which proved useless because American tank rounds easily penetrated this makeshift defense. Iraqi artillery fired only at preregistered positions and was unable to adjust to new targets. The Iraqi tank crews that did fight back mostly remained stationary. The one group of Iraqi tanks attempting a fighting withdrawal was promptly located and destroyed. The outcome of the battle, which lasted about three hours, was never in doubt.

The Battle of Medina Ridge was the largest armored engagement of the Persian Gulf War. It also marked the last really substantial opposition by the Iraqi Army in that conflict. Superiority in American equipment and technology was an important factor in the victory, but superior training and discipline enabled U.S. tank crews to fight successfully in conditions of extreme duress.

Estimates of Iraqi losses vary, but some 93 Iraqi tanks and 73 other vehicles were destroyed. The 2nd Brigade suffered 1 fatality, 30 wounded, and 4 Abrams tanks disabled but not destroyed. The Persian Gulf War ended in a cease-fire the following day.

PAUL WILLIAM DOERR

See also
Persian Gulf War, Overview

References
Biddle, Stephen. "Victory Misunderstood: What the Gulf War Tells Us about the Future of Conflict." *International Security* 21, no. 2 (Fall 1996): 139–179.
Bourque, Stephen Alan. *Jayhawk! The VII Corps in the Persian Gulf War.* Washington, DC: Center of Military History, 2002.
Gordon, Michael R., and General Bernard E. Trainor. *The Generals' War: The Inside Story of the Conflict in the Gulf.* New York: Little, Brown, 1995.

Pollack, Kenneth M. *Arabs at War: Military Effectiveness, 1948–1991.* Lincoln: University of Nebraska Press, 2002.
Scales, Robert H. *Certain Victory: The U.S. Army in the Gulf War.* Washington, DC: Brassey's, 1994.

Megiddo, Ancient Battle of (1479 BCE)

The first battle in history to be recorded by eyewitnesses, this engagement was fought near the city of Megiddo (Armageddon in Hebrew) in central Palestine in May 1479 BCE. Egyptian power was declining, and following the death of the Egyptian coregent Hatshepsut in 1482, the king of Kadesh led a revolt of cities of Palestine and Syria against Egyptian rule.

Pharaoh Thutmose III was anxious to assert his power and restore Egyptian authority in the Levant. After ordering the removal of Hatshepsut's name from all public buildings, Thutmose rebuilt the Egyptian Army, which had been dormant for decades, and led a rapid advance into Palestine. The size of his army has been estimated at 10,000–30,000 men; it is believed to have consisted largely of infantry, with some chariots. The infantrymen were armed with swords and axes and carried shields. The nobility fought from the chariots, probably as archers.

Thutmose's adversaries, who were similarly armed, were led by the king of Kadesh. He assembled a large force at the fortified city of Megiddo, north of Mount Carmel. Disregarding the advice of his generals, who feared an ambush, Thutmose chose the most direct route north to Megiddo, through a narrow pass. Apparently the king of Kadesh believed that the Egyptians would consider this route too risky, for he had deployed the bulk of his forces along another road to the east. Leading in person in a chariot, Thutmose pushed through Megiddo Pass, scattering its few defenders. He then consolidated his forces while the king of Kadesh withdrew his covering troops back on Megiddo.

Thutmose drew up his army in a concave formation of three main groups southwest of Megiddo and athwart the small Kina River. Both flanks were on high ground, with the left flank extending to the northwest of Megiddo to cut off any enemy escape along a road from the city. The rebel force was drawn up on high ground near Megiddo.

While the southern wing of his army held his adversary, Thutmose personally led the northern wing in an attack that sliced between the rebel left flank and Megiddo itself, enveloping the enemy force and winning the battle. The surviving enemy soldiers fled; they were saved by the fact that the Egyptian soldiers halted their pursuit to loot the enemy camp, something that greatly displeased Thutmose.

Thutmose then subjected Megiddo to a siege that lasted at least three months. On the surrender of Megiddo, Thutmose took most of the rebel kings prisoner, although the king of Kadesh escaped. Thutmose did capture the king's son and took him back to Egypt as a hostage, along with the sons of other captured kings. Among the spoils of war that the Egyptians recorded were more than 900 chariots and 2,200 horses as well as 200 suits of armor. Reportedly, in the entire campaign Thutmose acquired 426 pounds of gold and silver.

SPENCER C. TUCKER

See also
Egypt, Ancient; Thutmose III, Pharaoh

References
Benson, Douglas. *Ancient Egypt's Warfare*. Ashland, OH: Book Masters, 1995.

Gabriel, Richard, and Donald Boose. *The Great Battles of Antiquity*. Westport, CT: Greenwood, 1994.

Steindorff, George, and Keith Seele. *When Egypt Ruled the East*. Chicago: University of Chicago Press, 1957.

Megiddo, Battle of (September 19–21, 1918)

Opening stage of the final British offensive in the Palestinian Campaign. The Battle of Megiddo is also known as the Battle of Armageddon. After his Egyptian Expeditionary Force (EEF) had taken Jerusalem in December 1917, British lieutenant general Edmund Allenby planned to launch a final offensive to drive the remaining Ottoman-German forces from Palestine. The Allied Supreme War Council at Versailles assumed that victory on the Western Front would not be possible until 1919 and thus urged Allenby to proceed. Operations on this front also had the enthusiastic backing of British prime minister David Lloyd George.

Accordingly, in late February Allenby took Jericho in preparation for a Transjordan offensive. Prince Faisal's Arab Northern Army raided along the eastern and southern shores of the Dead Sea, and in March the EEF launched an unsuccessful attack across the Jordan River toward Amman. A second EEF attack in April was also unsuccessful. Meanwhile, fighting on the Western Front interceded. The massive German Ludendorff Offensives there began on March 21, 1918, and lasted until July 18. Desperate for manpower, London ordered Allenby to transfer two complete divisions to France plus separate battalions sufficient to constitute three more, a total of some 60,000 men. Two Indian divisions from Mesopotamia and fresh troops from India replaced them, but all of these men had to be trained, dashing hopes of an early offensive in Palestine. Allenby was thus limited to small operations east of the Jordan River in cooperation with Arab forces led by Faisal and Major T. E. Lawrence. By the time Allenby was ready to resume the offensive, he had at his disposal some 67,000 men: 56,000 infantry and 11,000 cavalry, along with 552 guns.

German general Otto Liman von Sanders, commander of Ottoman forces in Palestine known as Army Group Yildirim, was also experiencing difficulties. Tensions ran high between the Germans and Ottomans as Ottoman minister of war Enver Pasha siphoned off troops for the Caucasus front. Supplies were also difficult to obtain, and many Ottoman soldiers were deserting.

It was no secret that Allenby would soon resume offensive operations, so the British resorted to an elaborate deception. Allenby used his virtually total air superiority to screen his enemy's reconnaissance from the point of actual attack. This time he would feint inland and deliver the main blow along the left (Mediterranean) flank. In the meantime, he employed cavalry to patrol aggressively in the Jordan Valley and even staged two large cavalry raids toward the city of Amman, which was supporting Ottoman forces at Medina. This new threat forced Liman von Sanders to deploy a third of his troops east of the Jordan River.

Allenby then transferred substantial resources northward until he had three-quarters of his resources along only one-quarter of the front. His deception measures for the Jordan Valley included 15,000 stuffed canvas horses, a dummy headquarters, false radio traffic, sledges to kick up large clouds of dust, and even men marching about to give the false impression of large numbers.

Allenby brilliantly combined the principles of mass and surprise. Forward observers adjusted artillery fire, and armored cars operated with horse cavalry. All arms—infantry, cavalry, artillery, engineers, and the Royal Flying Corps—worked smoothly together, and irregular Arab forces, advised by Lawrence, provided useful support. Allenby planned to use fire and maneuver to secure key mountain passes and envelop the principal Ottoman units.

The ensuing battle began early on the morning of September 19 with an intense 15-minute artillery barrage. The infantry then attacked and created a lane for the cavalry, which drove north. By day's end one division controlled the pass near the small village of Megiddo, which gave its name to the campaign. The next morning another division hit Ottoman headquarters at Nazareth, nearly capturing Liman von Sanders. By September 21 the British had 25,000 prisoners. For all intents and purposes, the Ottoman Seventh and Eighth Armies now ceased to exist. Only part of the Ottoman Fourth Army managed to escape through Daraa. A large portion of the Ottomans surrendered at Amman on September 25, while the remainder surrendered with the fall of Damascus, occupied by the Desert Mounted Corps and the Arab Northern Army on October 1.

BRETT MILLS AND SPENCER C. TUCKER

See also
Allenby, Sir Edmund Henry Hynman; Amman Campaign; Enver Pasha; Faisal I, King of Iraq; Lawrence, Thomas Edward; Liman von Sanders, Otto; Medina, Siege of; Palestine and Syria Campaign, World War I; Transjordan Campaign

References
Bruce, Anthony P. C. *The Last Crusade: The Palestine Campaign in the First World War.* London: Murray, 2002.
Bullock, David. *Allenby's War: The Palestine-Arabian Campaigns, 1916–1918.* London: Blandford, 1988.
Falls, Cyril. *Armageddon, 1918: The Final Palestinian Campaign of World War I.* Philadelphia: University of Pennsylvania Press, 2003.
Falls, Cyril. *Military Operations: Egypt and Palestine, from June 1917 to the End of the War.* London: HMSO, 1930.
Hughes, Matthew. *Allenby and British Strategy in the Middle East, 1917–1919.* London: Frank Cass, 1999.
Liman von Sanders, Otto. *Five Years in Turkey.* Trans. Carl Reichmann. Annapolis, MD: Naval Institute Press.

Mehmed Ali (1769–1849)

Mehmed Ali (Muhammad Ali Pasha al-Mas'ud ibn Agha) played an important role in Egyptian history, dominating the affairs of that nation from 1805 to 1848, setting off a "military revolution" in the Middle East, and establishing a dynasty that survived until 1952. Although a self-described "Ottoman gentleman," Mehmed Ali was born of Albanian descent on March 4, 1769, in Kavala, Macedonia, then part of the Ottoman Empire and today in northeastern Greece. He worked as a sailor and merchant before becoming a soldier. Joining a battalion of Arnaut mercenaries, Mehmed Ali arrived in Egypt and took advantage of the turmoil following the 1798 French invasion, rapidly rising through the ranks. His charisma, innate ability, significant tactical skills, and political savvy brought him leadership of the Arnauts. He also arranged favorable connections with local notables. By 1805 a reluctant Ottoman government appointed Mehmed Ali the *wali* (viceroy), recognizing his de facto control of Egypt.

Mehmed Ali viewed centralized government and a powerful military machine as the twin pillars of the state. He strove to dramatically improve both and proved adroit both as copyist and innovator. He vigorously embraced fiscal and military programs already proposed by Ali Bey al-Kebir, who dominated Egypt during 1768–1772, plus Mehmed Ali's nominal overlord, Sultan Selim III (1761–1808). In addition, Mehmed Ali expanded the sultan's Nizam-i Cedid military reforms to incorporate conscription of the fellahin—Egyptian peasant farmers, the vast majority of the population but previously excluded from military service.

Military innovation was Mehmed Ali's strong suit. Hiring a motley array of Ottoman, European, and even American mercenaries helped him create a European-style army and navy. By 1811, these were potent enough for him to carry out the Ottoman Empire request to initiate what would be a seven-year campaign against the first Saudi state, ending in an Egyptian victory. A decade later Mehmed Ali's soldiers advanced southward, capturing significant portions of modern Sudan. The Porte then requested that Mehmed Ali intervene in Greece, where a revolt against Ottoman rule had begun in 1821. Egyptian military intervention in Greece during 1825–1827 would probably have been successful except for intervention on the side of the Greeks by Britain, France, and Russia.

Falling out with Sultan Mahmud II (r. 1808–1839) regarding terms of compensation for his Greek effort, Mehmed Ali started his largest military conflict, a nine-year struggle against the Ottoman Empire during 1831–1840. At first, all seemed possible. The Egyptians captured Acre (Akko), defeated several Ottoman armies, and were marching virtually unopposed on a weakly defended Istanbul (Constantinople) when Russia intervened in defense of the Ottomans. Forced to back down, Mehmed Ali agreed to the Convention of Kutahya (1833), which spared the Ottoman Empire from destruction but also allowed the largest Egyptian Empire in history. Between 1833 and 1840, Mehmed Ali dominated Greater Syria, Arabia, Crete, Cyprus, and much of the Sudan.

Kutahya was more of a truce than a peace treaty, however. Fighting between Egypt and the Ottoman Empire resumed in 1839 and saw a resounding Egyptian victory at Nezib. At this point Britain and Austria stepped in, forcing the Egyptians to disgorge all Middle Eastern territories gained at the expense of the Ottomans. Northeast Africa remained part of Mehmed Ali's Egyptian Empire. Here he directed forays as far apart as central Sudan and Eritrea. Although originally looking for gold, the Egyptian conquerors mainly generated revenues from the trade in slaves and ivory.

Mehmed Ali significantly altered the Middle Eastern status quo. Indeed, it can be argued that he started the "Eastern question," and his success on the battlefield forced neighboring states to embrace his military reforms. Under his direction, the Egyptian Army had evolved from a small antiquated collection of irregulars into a 100,000-man combined-arms force that smashed every local opponent. Islamic leaders as far away as Morocco attempted to copy this Egyptian model, and although the original rapidly atrophied after Mehmed Ali's death, it secured his family's hold on Egypt for the next century. Mehmed Ali Pasha died at age 80 on August 2, 1849, in Ras el-Tin Palace, Alexandria, Egypt. His son Ibrahim Pasha succeeded him.

JOHN P. DUNN

See also
Egyptian-Arab Wars; Egyptian-Ottoman Wars; Ibrahim Pasha; Kutahya Convention; London, 1840 Treaty of

References
Aharoni, Reuven. *Bedouin and State in the Egypt of Mehmed Ali, 1805–1848.* London: Routledge, 2006.
Fahmy, Khaled. *All the Pasha's Men: Mehmed Ali, His Army, and the Making of Modern Egypt.* Cambridge: Cambridge University Press, 1997.
Fahmy, Khaled. *Mehmed Ali: From Ottoman Governor to Ruler of Egypt.* Oxford, UK: Oneworld, 2009.
Sayyid-Marsot, Afaf Lufti, al-. *Egypt in the Reign of Muhammad Ali.* Cambridge: Cambridge University Press, 1984.

Mehmed II, Sultan (1432–1481)

Ottoman sultan. Born on March 30, 1432, at Edirne, Rumelia Eyalet (later Edirne, Turkey), at the time the capital of the Ottoman state, Mehmed II (Mohammed II) was the eldest son of Sultan Murad II. When Mehmed was 11, his father made him governor of Amasya so that he might gain experience in governing. Mehmed's strong Islamic education reinforced in him a determination to end what remained of the Byzantine Empire by conquering Constantinople. In August 1444, Murad II abdicated the throne in favor of his son, then only 12. Mehmed II's first reign lasted two years, until 1446, during which time the Christian crusade led by János Hunyadi of Hungary into Ottoman territory was defeated. Mehmed II had asked his father Murad II, who had taken up a contemplative life, to reclaim the throne, but Murad II refused. Mehmed II wrote to his father, saying "If you are the Sultan, come and lead your armies. If I am the Sultan I hereby order you to come and lead my armies." Murad II then led the victorious Ottoman forces in the Battle of Varna (November 10, 1444).

Grand Vizier Candarli Halil Pasha forced Murad II's return to the throne, but Mehmed became sultan for the second time on his father's death in February 1451. Determined to become a new Cyrus, Alexander, or Caesar, Mehmed spent most of his reign at war with neighboring states and became known as Fatih (Conqueror). Mehmed II began his campaign of conquest with an operation against Constantinople. He oversaw the construction of a large fortress outside the city during 1451–1453, then led a siege to Constantinople during April 3–May 29, 1453, using his large cannon to make a breach in the walls through which he sent his Janissaries.

The fall of Constantinople was an epic event in European history, ending the Byzantine Empire and opening Europe to further Ottoman invasion. Mehmed transferred his capital to Constantinople, renamed Istanbul, and then invaded the Balkans. Mehmed was stymied in July 1456 by Hungarian forces under János Hunyadi and failed to take Belgrade. Mehmed's armies did, however, occupy most of Serbia, southern Greece, and Bosnia during 1458–1463.

In 1463 Venice, Hungary, Albania, the Papacy, and Persia formed an alliance to contain the Ottomans, beginning 16 years of warfare. Nonetheless, Mehmed won a series of battles and the Venetian War (1463–1479), securing Albania, Bosnia, Dalmatia, southern Romania, and the Crimean Peninsula. In the Battle of Otlukbeli (August 11, 1473) he defeated an invading Persian army under Sultan Uzan Khan, resulting in Ottoman control of central Anatolia.

Mehmed then sent an expeditionary force to Italy, seizing Otranto in early 1480. He also sent forces to besiege the island of Rhodes (1480–1481), but the Knights of St. John held out against him. Mehmed died at Tekfur Cayiri near Gebze on May 3, 1481.

A careful planner and consummate strategist, Mehmed the Conqueror built a large Islamic empire that included much of Southeastern Europe. He was also a patron of the arts and wrote a book of law codes treating government practices. Mehmed is widely regarded as a hero in Turkey.

SPENCER C. TUCKER

See also
Constantinople, Ottoman Siege of; Otlukbeli, Battle of; Ottoman Empire; Ottoman-Hungarian Wars; Varna Crusade; Venetian-Ottoman Wars

References
Babinger, Franz. *Mehmed the Conqueror and His Time.* Princeton, NJ: Princeton University Press, 1978.

İnalcık, Halil. "Mehmed the Conqueror (1432–1481) and His Time." *Speculum* 35 (1960): 102–126.

Kritoboulous, Kritovoulos. *History of Mehmed the Conqueror*. Trans. Charles T. Riggs. Princeton, NJ: Princeton University Press, 1954.

Meir, Golda Mabovitch (1898–1978)

Israeli politician and prime minister (1969–1974). Born in Kiev, Russia, on May 3, 1898, Golda Mabovitch immigrated to Milwaukee, Wisconsin, in the United States with her family in 1903. Intent on becoming a teacher, she enrolled at the Wisconsin State Normal School in 1916 but never finished her degree. That same year she became an active member in the Zionist labor movement, where she met Morris Meyerson, whom she married in 1917.

Golda Meyerson and her husband immigrated to Palestine in 1921. They worked on a kibbutz, and Golda became active in the Histadrut, Israel's labor movement. She joined its executive community in 1934 and became the head of its political department in 1940, working to raise funds for Jewish settlement in Palestine.

Shortly before the 1948–1949 Israeli War of Independence, Meyerson twice met secretly with Jordan's King Abdullah. While she was not successful in averting a Jordanian invasion of the Jewish state, the contacts helped limit Jordanian participation in the war. Meyerson also traveled to the United States, where she raised substantial sums from private citizens. Following the war, Israel's first prime minister, David Ben-Gurion, sent Myerson to Moscow as Israel's ambassador. On his urging, she adopted the Hebrew surname Meir, which means "to burn brightly."

On Meir's election to the Knesset (Israeli parliament) in 1949 as a member of Mapai (Israel Workers' Party), Ben-Gurion appointed her minister of labor. Her greatest task was the resettlement of hundreds of thousands of Jewish refugees who had immigrated to Israel during these years. She soon gained a reputation as an aggressive politician, a powerful speaker, and a decisive manager.

In June 1956, Ben-Gurion appointed Meir foreign minister. She held that post until 1965. She supported Ben-Gurion's decision to go to war with Egypt in collusion with France and Britain in 1956, and she worked to strengthen Israel's relationship with the new nations of Africa. Meir also worked to improve U.S.-Israeli relations, which had been badly damaged by the Sinai Campaign. Along with Israeli ambassador Abba Eban, Meir convinced President John F. Kennedy to sell sophisticated Hawk antiaircraft missiles to Israel. This sale ended the U.S. embargo on arms sales to Israel and opened the door to further arms transfers.

Golda Meir was the fourth prime minister of Israel and the only woman to hold that post (1969–1974). Known for her bluntness, strong will, and determination, she resigned following revelations of the lack of Israeli military preparedness for the 1973 Yom Kippur War. (Library of Congress)

Due to worsening health, Meir resigned as foreign minister in 1965 but continued to serve in the Knesset, and the members of Mapai elected her the party's secretary-general. In that capacity she helped orchestrate the merger of Mapai with several smaller parties that created the new Labor Party, which dominated Israeli politics for the next decade.

On February 26, 1969, the ruling Labor Party elected Meir prime minister following the death of Levi Eshkol. Meir faced daunting challenges. Her efforts to trade recently conquered land for peace with Egypt, Syria, and Jordan failed, and terrorist attacks and cross-border raids into Israel increased.

Skirmishing with Egypt escalated into the War of Attrition, which lasted through August 1970. Meir insisted on Israeli retaliation for any attacks and apparently hoped that increasingly successful Israeli commando raids and air strikes would force Egyptian president Gamal Abdel Nasser into peace negotiations. Nasser, however, insisted on the return of all occupied territory as a prelude to any peace negotiations.

Meir increasingly coordinated Israel's foreign policy with the United States, and during her tenure as prime minister the special relationship between Israel and the United States blossomed. U.S. arms sales to Israel increased, while Israel shared important intelligence information with the United States and allowed U.S. technicians to examine sophisticated Soviet weapons systems captured by the Israeli Army. Despite the increasingly close relationship with the United States, Meir managed to convince the Soviet Union to allow some Russian Jews to immigrate to Israel.

Anwar Sadat, who assumed power following Nasser's death in September 1970, grew frustrated over Meir's refusal to withdraw from occupied territory as a prelude to negotiating a peace settlement. Tensions with Egypt and Syria increased steadily until the morning of October 6, 1973, when Israel's director of intelligence warned of an imminent attack. Concerned about Israel's international standing, Meir rejected a preemptive attack, as Israel had done in 1967. That afternoon, Egyptian and Syrian forces invaded the Sinai and the Golan Heights, driving back the surprised and outnumbered Israeli Army units. Meir overruled suggestions for deep withdrawals. Following early defeats, Israeli counteroffensives finally contained both Arab forces and left Israel in possession of additional Arab territory on the Syrian front and in Egypt. Israeli forces crossed the canal and had almost cut off two Egyptian divisions east of the canal. Neither the Soviet Union nor the United States wished to see Egypt completely defeated, and under their pressure a cease-fire went into effect on October 24.

Although the war was won, the early setbacks, surprise of the invasion, heavy casualties, and rumors that Meir had considered using nuclear weapons during the first days of the war tarnished her administration. A special investigating committee cleared Meir of responsibility for the near disaster, but she remained under constant attack from opposition politicians. Despite this, Meir led her party to another victory in the December 1973 elections, despite Labor's loss of six seats in the Knesset and the growing strength of the right-wing Likud Party.

In the following months, Meir negotiated cease-fire and disengagement agreements with Egypt and Syria. The complicated negotiations to extricate the trapped Egyptian Army paved the way for future negotiations that finally produced a lasting peace between Israel and Egypt. Meir resigned on June 3, 1974, and returned to private life. She died of leukemia in Jerusalem on December 8, 1978.

Stephen K. Stein

See also

Ben-Gurion, David; Israeli War of Independence; Nasser, Gamal Abdel; Sadat, Anwar; War of Attrition; Yom Kippur War

References

Klagsbrun, Francine. *Lioness: Golda Meir and the Nation of Israel.* New York: Schocken, 2017.

Martin, Ralph G. *Golda Meir: The Romantic Years.* New York: Scribner, 1988.

Meir, Golda. *My Life.* New York: Putnam, 1975.

Mersa Matruh, First Battle of (June 26, 1942)

Ground battle in which an Egyptian fortress was seized by Field Marshal Erwin Rommel's Panzerarmee Afrika. Mersa Matruh is located approximately 60 miles east of the Egyptian border with Libya. With Tobruk captured on June 21, 1942, Rommel decided on an immediate advance into Egypt. This abandoned the original Axis plan calling for a halt at the border to await the reduction of Malta, which would have ensured Axis supply lines on the drive toward the Suez Canal.

In spite of severe fuel shortages and mechanical breakdowns, Rommel's forces pushed eastward in hopes of enveloping and destroying the British Eighth Army. The Panzerarmee Afrika spearhead entered Egypt with fewer than 50 operational tanks, and its speedy advance outstripped fighter coverage, which brought vicious attacks by the Allied Desert Air Force. Nonetheless, on June 25 advanced Axis elements reached the outskirts of Mersa Matruh.

Eighth Army commander Lieutenant General Neil N. Ritchie hoped to make a stand at Mersa Matruh rather than withdraw farther east to El Alamein. On June 25, General Sir Claude Auchinleck relieved Ritchie and took personal command of the Eighth Army himself. Auchinleck decided to employ Ritchie's plan, with two strong wing elements of X and XIII Corps and a weakened center. He also instructed his corps commanders to withdraw rather than risk envelopment.

Rommel resumed his advance on June 26 by ordering his Italian infantry to fix X Corps inside Mersa Matruh's defenses while his armor swung east on the escarpments south of the city, hoping to envelop all British forces to his front. Rommel's forces now found themselves heavily engaged with the 2nd New Zealand and 1st Armoured Divisions of XIII Corps and unable to advance. Rommel's 90th Light Division, however, overran Auchinleck's weakened center and by the afternoon of June 27 was in striking distance of the coast behind Mersa Matruh.

Following Auchinleck's orders not to become decisively engaged, XIII Corps commander Lieutenant General William H. Gott broke off the battle and withdrew toward El Alamein, not realizing that he had the Afrika Korps in a precarious situation. Gott's withdrawal enabled the 90th Light Division to reach the coast at 7:00 p.m. on June 27. This cut off X Corps, which was unaware of the retirement of XIII Corps.

Rommel besieged Mersa Matruh on June 28. X Corps commander Lieutenant General William George Holmes ordered his units to break out of the city that night and escape to El Alamein. In spite of bitter fighting, much of the corps reached friendly lines because of the weakened condition of Rommel's forces. Axis troops entered Mersa Matruh on June 29, capturing 8,000 British personnel and quantities of weapons and supplies. Afrika Korps then continued its pursuit, reaching El Alamein on June 30.

The June 28, 1942, Battle of Mersa Matruh was Rommel's last victory in the Libyan-Egyptian theater. The battle exhausted much of what little strength was left in Rommel's dash into Egypt after the seizure of Tobruk, however. On the British side, the defeat at Mersa Matruh sent the Eighth Army to its final defensive barrier at El Alamein, but Auchinleck had preserved most of his command.

THOMAS D. VEVE

See also
Auchinleck, Sir Claude John Eyre; Rommel, Erwin Johannes Eugen; Suez Canal and Egypt, World War II Campaigns for Control of

References
Mellenthin, Friedrich Wilhelm von. *Panzer Battles*. Norman: University of Oklahoma Press, 1956.

Strawson, John. *The Battle for North Africa*. New York: Scribner, 1969.

Mersa Matruh, Second Battle of (November 7, 1942)

World War II battle in Egypt in which Field Marshal Erwin Rommel's Panzerarmee Afrika eluded capture by Lieutenant General Bernard Montgomery's pursuing Eighth Army. The battle followed shortly the Second Battle of El Alamein (October 23–November 4, 1942). Mersa Matruh is located about 60 miles east of the border with Libya.

Montgomery planned to pursue the beaten Rommel and envelop Axis forces before they could escape westward, but he had not allocated any particular forces for this effort prior to the Battle of Alamein. Rommel's temporary halt at Mersa Matruh offered the Eighth Army a chance to surround and destroy the Panzerarmee Afrika.

Rommel, who hoped to delay his retreat long enough to allow his infantry an opportunity to avoid capture, ordered his armored forces to fall back to Mersa Matruh on November 5. Montgomery sent the 1st Armoured Division on a wide sweep to the southwest to try to reach Mersa Matruh from the rear. Heavy rains impacted the movement of both armies, however. Despite poor road conditions and resupply problems, much of Rommel's remaining mechanized forces made it to Mersa Matruh. Both the 15th Panzer Division and the 90th Light Division reached there safely, but the 21st Panzer Division, short on fuel, was surrounded by the 22nd Armoured Brigade. The 21st Panzer Division then took up a hedgehog (circular) defense, eventually abandoning most of its remaining tanks.

Heavy rains, minefields, and undelivered fuel supplies prevented Montgomery's armor from advancing farther, saving the Panzerarmee Afrika from encirclement. Certainly, the poor weather also hampered air strikes by the Desert Air Force, which would had been virtually unchallenged by the Luftwaffe. On November 7 with three pursuing divisions halted, the 1st Armoured Division slowly moved forward along the coast road. But not until the evening of November 8 did the division's patrols enter Mersa Matruh, well after Rommel's departure.

Rommel believed that Montgomery's caution allowed him to escape at Mersa Matruh, whereas Montgomery blamed it on the heavy rains. Because the weather affected both sides equally, it was not the sole determinant. Montgomery had not prepared for a pursuit, and he failed to press his advantage by striking deeper into the desert behind Rommel. Further, the British victory in the Second Battle of El Alamein may have so exhausted the Eighth Army that an effective pursuit was impossible.

THOMAS D. VEVE

See also
El Alamein, Second Battle of; Montgomery, Bernard Law; Rommel, Erwin Johannes Eugen; Suez Canal and Egypt, World War II Campaigns for Control of

References

Montgomery, Bernard L. *The Memoirs of Field-Marshal the Viscount Montgomery of Alamein, K. G.* Cleveland, OH: World Publishing, 1958.

Playfair, I. S. O., and C. J. C. Molony. *The Mediterranean and the Middle East*, Vol. 4, *The Destruction of the Axis Forces in Africa*. London: HMSO, 1966.

Mesopotamia

Mesopotamia is the Middle Eastern region of the lands bordered by the Euphrates River to the west and the Tigris River to the east in what is now Iraq. Mesopotamia is a Greek term meaning "land between two rivers" and was generally used as a reference to the actual region and at times as a generic term for various civilizations that arose from or controlled that region. Both rivers originate in eastern Turkey and flow through Iraq; the Euphrates also runs through eastern Syria. Although parts of Turkey and Syria have also been historically associated with Mesopotamia, the term has primarily focused on the territory running about 200–250 miles northwest of Baghdad and southward to where the Tigris and Euphrates merge at the Shatt al-Arab (River of the Arabs), about 100 miles north of the Persian Gulf in far southeastern Iraq.

Physically, Mesopotamia is in general divided into two regions: lands north of Baghdad, referred to as Assyria, and those to the south known as Babylonia or Sumer. With only minor exceptions, most of Mesopotamia ranges in elevation from 0 to 1,500 feet in Iraq, with the highest area approximately 4,000 feet. Although some variations of climate exist between the north and the south, generally Mesopotamia's average temperatures, depending on the season, range from 68 to 95 degrees; however, during the hottest months (summer), temperatures can reach more than 120 degrees. Rainfall in northern Mesopotamia averages between 15.75 and 31.5 inches per year, while the south averages about 7.78 inches or less, primarily between December and February.

Mesopotamian land use in the northern area is somewhat varied, with arable land in the northeast, irrigated farming along the rivers and canals, and lands for grazing and pasturage. Although some wastelands, marshes, and swamps were in the southern region, irrigation allows areas along the rivers to be used for cultivation. Many of the marshes in the south were drained by order of Iraqi president Saddam Hussein during the early 1990s. Major crops include dates, cotton, barley, and rice. Although petroleum is a major natural resource in Mesopotamia, its importance was of limited value until the mid-1900s. In addition to being an important region on various trade routes for goods from Africa, Europe, and Asia, cities in Mesopotamia often served as important trading centers.

Mesopotamia demographics vary according to the particular era and/or particular area of Mesopotamia being discussed. Ethnically, several different groups have been represented in the region throughout history, including various Semitic groups such as the Assyrians and Arabs, Aryan groups such as the Kurds and Persians, and unknown ethnic groups such as the Sumerians and Turks during the Ottoman era. Prior to the Persian Empire's conquest of Mesopotamia during the mid-sixth century CE, the vast majority of civilizations and empires practiced either polytheism or pantheism. The Persians and their successors, the Parthians and the Sassanians, all established Zoroastrianism as their empires' official religion, though other religions were tolerated. Although the exile of Jews after the Assyrian and Babylonian conquests of the Kingdom of Israel and the Kingdom of Judah, respectively, introduced Judaism into parts of Mesopotamia, it was practiced exclusively by Jewish exiles.

Following the conquest of the region by the Arabs during the middle to late seventh century CE, Islam has been and remains the dominant religion in Mesopotamia. Although the majority of practitioners are Shiites, a significant number of Sunnis are also in the region. Furthermore, a small remnant of Jewish practitioners remain in Mesopotamia, as does a small Assyrian population in the north that practices Christianity.

The region can be broken into three major chronological divisions: ancient, Islamic, and modern. Although Mesopotamia has long been considered the "cradle of civilization," other cultures predating ancient Mesopotamia existed. Permanent civilizations in Mesopotamia arose circa 3500 BCE. Irrigation techniques developed by inhabitants in the region were responsible for the creation of agricultural surpluses, which led to the development of urban centers referred to as city-states. Kings with religious support or priest-kings ruled the various city-states. Urban development had a significant impact on a number of areas. The Sumerians created cuneiform, the world's first writing system, as a means to maintain written records; it would also be used by a number of Mesopotamian civilizations even after Sumer no longer existed. The world's first major piece of literature, the *Epic of Gilgamesh*, was also written during the period of Sumer's prominence. Laws were codified for the first time in

Mesopotamia. Hammurabi, an Amorite ruler, promulgated the most well-known early law code, Hammurabi's Code.

Sargon the Great, generally recognized as the first emperor in the world, ruled the Akkadian Empire, which ran from the Persian Gulf through Mesopotamia and onward to the Mediterranean Sea and the Taurus Mountains in Turkey. His grandson Naram-Sim also extended the empire. After the downfall of Akkad, the city-state Ur arose to prominence in the region, leading to the Ur III dynastic state, which established control over the region of Sumer. Amorites, a nomadic group, eventually conquered the region, leading to the establishment of several Amorite kingdoms, the most famous being the Amorite Kingdom of Babylon, ruled by Hammurabi. The Amorite Kingdom, also known as the Old Babylonian Kingdom, lasted for slightly over 100 years before the Hittite Empire defeated Babylonia. However, the Kassites occupied Babylonia for approximately 400 years, and other parts of Mesopotamia retained their independence.

In 934 BCE the Neo-Assyrians, commonly referred to as Assyrians, began to arise as a major power in Mesopotamia. During the reign of Tiglath-Pileser III, the Assyrians began to conquer large parts of Mesopotamia, areas south of Babylon, parts of the Kingdom of Israel, Turkey, and the Caucasus regions. Assyria's empire was further expanded by the Sargonid dynasty, which included Sargon II, Sennacherib, Esarhaddon, and Ashurbanipal. By 627 BCE Assyria's control over Mesopotamia and other regions began to decline. The Neo-Babylonians, also known as Babylonians or Chaldeans, joined with the Medes to overthrow the Assyrian Empire and reestablish control over Mesopotamia. Among them, Nabopolassar and his successor Nebuchadnezzar are the most well known. Both the Assyrians and the Chaldeans were responsible for deporting Jews from their homeland to Mesopotamia.

The Medes and Persians would dominate Mesopotamia for approximately 300 years. Cyrus the Great and his successors established and maintained the Persian Empire, which included Mesopotamia from 550 BCE through 330 BCE and was conquered by Alexander's the Great Macedonian armies. Seleucid rule in the region ran from 330 BCE to 238 BCE, followed by a relatively brief period of Parthian control. Mesopotamia fell under rule by the Sassanid Empire during from 265 CE, until Arab armies under Khalid ibn al-Walid conquered Mesopotamia during April 633–January 634. The region would thereafter remain as part of various Islamic empires, including the Umayyad and the Abbasid. Eventually, the Ottoman Empire during the reigns of Selim I and Suleiman the Magnificent conquered the region between 1512 and 1566. Mesopotamia was then divided into three provinces: Mosul, Baghdad, and Basra. Following World War I (1914–1918), Great Britain received the region as a League of Nations mandate. Eventually, the three provinces were merged into Mesopotamia, which eventually became the modern-day nation of Iraq on October 3, 1932.

Some of the most important historical cities in or near the Mesopotamian region included Nineveh, Babylon, and Baghdad. The first was destroyed by the Babylonians and their allies in 612 BCE, and the second was destroyed by Sennacherib in 689 BCE, rebuilt, and finally fell after 275 BCE, when the people were deported from the city. Baghdad was destroyed by the Mongols in the Battle of Baghdad (January 29–February 10, 1258 CE). Baghdad was rebuilt, only to be partially destroyed by Tamerlame in 1401 and then rebuilt to serve as a capital during the Ottoman Empire. Other cities of importance established during the Islamic period in the region include An Nasiriyah, An Najaf, Al Kut, Ar Ramadi, Karbala, Samarra, and Mosul. All were targeted during the Persian Gulf War (1991) and/or the Iraq War (2003–2011).

Because of Mesopotamia's physical location between Asia and the West along with the relatively flat terrain, it has often been the target of invasions from multiple civilizations. The Persians, Macedonians, Arabs, Mongols, and Ottomans are only some of the entities that have invaded the region over the centuries. In more recent times, Mesopotamia was invaded by the British in 1917, underwent missile attacks from Iran in 1987 during the Iraq-Iran War (1980–1988), and was attacked, invaded, and/or occupied in the 1990s and again after 2003 by U.S.-led coalition forces.

WYNDHAM E. WHYNOT

See also

Achaemenid Empire; Akkad; Ashurbanipal; Assyrian Empire; Babylonian Empire, Neo-; Babylonian Empire, Old; Cyrus II the Great; Hammurabi; Iraq; Iraq War; Mesopotamia; Mesopotamian Theater, World War I; Nebuchadnezzar II; Ottoman Empire; Persian Gulf War, Overview; Sargon of Akkad; Sennacherib; Sumer

References

Bertman, Stephen. *Handbook to Life in Ancient Mesopotamia.* New York: Oxford University Press, 2005.

Foster, Benjamin R. *The Age of Akkad: Inventing Empire in Ancient Mesopotamia.* London: Routledge, 2016.

Kramer, S. Noah. *History Begins at Sumer: Thirty-Nine "Firsts" in Recorded History.* Philadelphia: University of Pennsylvania Press, 1981.

Kramer, S. Noah. *The Sumerians: Their History, Culture and Character.* Chicago: University of Chicago Press, 2008.

Postgate, Nicholas. *Early Mesopotamia: Society and Economy at the Dawn of History.* London: Routledge, 2015.

Rawlinson, George. *The Five Great Monarchies of the Ancient Eastern World: Or, the History, Geography, and Antiquities of Chaldaea, Assyria, Babylon, Media, and Persia,* Vols. 1–3. Reprint ed. Elibron Classics series. Boston: Adamant Media Corporation, 2001.

Roux, Georges. *Ancient Iraq.* London: Penguin, 1980.

Van de Mieroop, Marc. *A History of the Ancient Near East, ca. 3000–323 BC.* Chichester, West Sussex, UK: Wiley, 2015.

Mesopotamian Theater, World War I

The October 29, 1914, entry of the Ottoman Empire into World War I on the side of the Central Powers threatened British interests in the Near East, especially the Suez Canal and the newly discovered oil fields in the area around Basra in Mesopotamia (present-day Iraq). At the end of September the British had discussed sending reinforcements to the area, and they now did so, seeking to protect these important assets and to encourage the Arabs to revolt against Ottoman rule. On November 7, a brigade of the Indian Army and 600 British troops landed at Fao at the head of the Persian Gulf. The initial British goal was to capture Basra.

The campaign began well. British and Indian forces captured Basra on November 22 and Qurna, at the confluence of the Tigris and Euphrates, on December 9. On April 12, 1915, however, the Ottoman Army attacked both Basra and Qurna in an effort to dislodge the British and Indians. On September 11–15 at Shaiba, southwest of Basra, 6,000 British and Indian defenders routed 10,000 Ottomans. The British sustained some 1,357 casualties, the Ottomans 2,435. The British were unable to follow up the victory, however, as they had no transport. The ease of the victory gave the British forces a false sense of Ottoman military inferiority.

Through 1915, Whitehall (the British Foreign Office) left much of the decision making for Mesopotamia to the government in India, which did not necessarily have the same interests as those in London. On April 9 General Sir John Nixon, commander of the Indian Northern Army, assumed command in Mesopotamia. Nixon's orders were to secure Basra and Lower Mesopotamia; protect the oil fields, the refinery at Abadan, and the pipeline; and prepare for an offensive against Baghdad.

To carry out these missions and expand the British defensive perimeter, Nixon called for drives up the Tigris and Euphrates Rivers. In May 1915 Major General Charles Townshend's 6th Indian Division proceeded up the Tigris, routing the Ottoman defenders and pursuing them in a series of quick, successful amphibious operations. The conclusion of the pursuit came at Amara (June 3), where an amphibious reconnaissance force of about 100 soldiers and sailors captured the town and its stores and garrison. The Ottoman troops there surrendered on the assumption that the main Anglo-Indian force was close on the heels of the reconnaissance force, when in reality it was nearly 100 miles away. Subsequently, Major General George Gorringe led the 12th Indian Division up the Euphrates and captured Nasiriyah, in another amphibious operation, during July 24–25. The Basra region and Lower Mesopotamia were now secure, and the oil fields were held safe from Ottoman attack.

These easy campaigns on the Tigris bred a sense of overconfidence among the British and convinced Nixon that he could capture Baghdad and bring a speedy close to the campaign. Despite Townshend's objections that his men were not prepared for such an effort in the heat of the summer and that he lacked sufficient logistical support, Nixon ordered the 6th Division to continue its advance up the Tigris. River towns fell in quick succession to Townshend's force as it drew closer to Baghdad. On September 28, 1915, following two days of fighting, the British occupied Kut, 90 miles from Baghdad. British supply lines now stretched 380 miles from Kut to the sea, and their transportation capacity was far from adequate.

Despite mixed opinion on the advisability of an advance on Baghdad, Townshend continued his push upriver on November 11. Eleven days later he was within 25 miles of Baghdad. At Ctesiphon during November 22–25, 1915, Townshend attacked an entrenched Ottoman force of 18,000 men and 52 guns commanded by German field marshal Colmar von der Goltz. The British lost 4,600 men, almost one-third of the force of three infantry brigades, without displacing the Ottomans. Although the Ottomans at Ctesiphon suffered 9,500 casualties, twice as many as Townshend's force, rather than breaking they counterattacked.

Lacking sufficient reserves and supplies, Townshend had little option but to retreat to Kut, sending his sick and wounded on a torturous 400-mile trek (13 days by boat) to the Persian Gulf. Townshend's exhausted troops needed a rest, and he halted at Kut to wait for reinforcements. From December 7, the Ottomans placed Kut under siege. The siege would endure until April 29, 1916. Townshend had 10,000 effectives; there were also 2,000 casualties and 3,500 Indian noncombatants.

In January 1916 Lieutenant General Sir Fenton Aylmer led a British effort to raise the siege. The main constraint in

British troops moving through the Jebel Hamrin (Jebel Mountains) during the Mesopotamian Campaign in 1917. The war ended with the Ottoman Empire defeated and Britain and France the dominant foreign powers in the Middle East. (National Archives)

Aylmer's attempt, as in all such British efforts in the campaign, was the supply situation. In January 1916 the rivers were the only viable means of transport open to the British. Although materials to build a narrow-gauge railway from Basra to the front lines at Ali Gharbi were available in India, no thought had been given to sending these to Mesopotamia, and by the time Ottoman forces had surrounded Townshend in Kut, it was too late. The British forces in Mesopotamia also faced a chronic shortage of boats for river transit. Aylmer faced the task of lifting a siege in an area that was a three-week round-trip boat journey from Basra. That port also left much to be desired. Its facilities were so inadequate that it could take up to six weeks for oceangoing transports to unload their cargo. Aylmer's relief force was therefore sent forward as troops arrived, and the maximum size of his force was set by the army's supply limitations rather than by the number of troops estimated to be necessary to lift the siege.

On January 3, 1916, Aylmer's force of 19,000 soldiers and 46 guns advanced up both banks of the Tigris toward Kut. On January 7–8 they failed to dislodge a Ottoman force at Sheikh Sa'ad, about 19 miles from Kut. The Ottomans, who had their own supply problems, soon withdrew. On January 9 Aylmer's force occupied Sheikh Sa'ad, but the fighting had claimed 4,000 of his men. Responding to pressure from Nixon, Aylmer continued to press the attack. On January 13 he engaged the Ottomans in the Battle of the Wadi, 12.5 miles from Kut, suffering another 1,600 casualties in the process.

Under pressure from Nixon and spurred on by reports from Townshend of dwindling supplies within Kut, Aylmer ordered his remaining forces to take the Hanna Defile in preparation for a final assault on Kut. Aylmer now had about 12,000 men, while the Ottomans had about 30,000 men between Aylmer and Kut. The attack on the Hanna Defile began with a British artillery barrage at midday on January 20 that continued until the next morning. It did little more than warn Ottoman commander Khalil Pasha where the attack was coming.

On January 21, 4,000 British soldiers set out across 600 yards of flooded terrain separating the two forces, only to be cut down by Ottoman machine-gun fire. Having sustained 2,700 casualties, Aylmer believed that his force was now inadequate to lift the siege. Nevertheless, Nixon ordered him to continue. With additional British reinforcements Aylmer tried again, and on March 8 he reached the Dujaila redoubt, two miles from Kut. The Ottoman Sixth Army, reinforced by 36,000 men, transferred from Gallipoli after the British evacuation there at the end of December, repulsed the British, leading Nixon to replace Aylmer with General Gorringe.

Gorringe made one last attempt to relieve Kut in the First Battle of Kut (April 5–22, 1916). His command was bolstered to 30,000 men by the arrival of Major General Sir Stanley Maude's 13th Division. Von der Goltz now drew on Ottoman reserves in Baghdad to match that number. Maude's division attacked the Hanna Defile at dawn on April 5, only to find the Ottoman frontline trenches unoccupied. Maude regrouped, attacked, and captured Fallahiyeh, while a diversionary attack on the other bank of the Tigris enjoyed similar success. Although these successes had cost 2,000 British casualties, Gorringe prepared to attack Sannaiyat the following day. The Ottomans fought off attacks on Sannaiyat on April 6, 7, and 9, inflicting further casualties on the British. On April 17, Gorringe switched targets to the other side of the river and took Bait Asia with light casualties. Ottoman counterattacks failed to dislodge the British and cost the Ottomans about 4,000 casualties. The loss of 1,600 men of the British and Indian force, however, made it impossible for Gorringe to continue in that sector on the bank of the river.

On April 22, Gorringe chose to resume his attack on Sannaiyat and failed, at a cost of 1,300 more casualties. This was the last effort to relieve Kut. In all, the British had suffered 23,000 casualties trying to rescue the 10,000 survivors at Kut.

Townshend surrendered unconditionally to Khalil Pasha on April 29, 1916. Goltz, who had masterminded the Ottoman siege, did not live to see the British surrender. He died of typhus on April 19, although rumors persisted that the Ottomans had poisoned him. The Ottoman victors forced some 8,000 British and Indian prisoners to march to camps in Anatolia without sufficient water or provisions. Through mistreatment and neglect, nearly 5,000 died before the end of the war.

In August 1916, General Sir Stanley Maude replaced Nixon as commander of British forces in Mesopotamia, having replaced Gorringe as commander of British forces on the Tigris the previous month. Maude reorganized the forces at his disposal, revamped the system of medical care, and improved the supply train. He then resumed the offensive up the Tigris on December 13 with some 59,000 British and 107,000 Indian soldiers. This force recaptured Kut on February 25, 1917, following the Second Battle of Kut (February 22–23).

After a brief rest and consolidation, Maude resumed his march on Baghdad on March 5, 1917. Khalil did not take effective advantage of the pause. He abandoned the construction of defenses around Ctesiphon, giving up on the idea of a forward defense, and ordered his 33,000 soldiers to dig in on both sides of the Tigris and along the Diyala River about 20 miles south of Baghdad. By March 10, Maude had forced a crossing of the Diyala. Khalil, ignoring German arguments for a counterattack, withdrew to the northwest to protect the Berlin-to-Baghdad railroad and then decided to evacuate Baghdad entirely. On March 11, Maude's forces entered Baghdad without a fight. This was a major propaganda coup at a time when the Allies needed any victory, although the capture of the city carried little strategic significance.

To consolidate his newly won position, Maude dispatched columns up the Tigris, Euphrates, and Diyala Rivers in an effort to destroy the Ottoman Army in the field. This renewed effort, which ultimately sought to capture the terminus of the Baghdad-Samarrah railway, began just two days after Maude's forces took Baghdad, pitting 45,000 British troops against 25,000 Ottomans. Although the Ottomans carried out a skillful fighting withdrawal, notable British successes, including the capture of the flood-control works at Falluja on March 19, prevented the Ottomans from flooding the plains between the Tigris and Euphrates. The British then took Samarrah on April 30. In the campaign, Maude's forces had sustained 58,000 casualties (40,000 from disease), and this forced a cessation of offensive action until the autumn.

On September 28, 1917, the British offensive resumed. Its most notable success was the capture of Tikrit during November 5–6. Maude died of cholera on November 18. His replacement, Lieutenant General Sir William Marshall, followed Maude's policy of advancing up the rivers to keep the pressure on Ottoman forces. Maude's death, however, gave General Sir William Robertson, chief of the Imperial General Staff, the opportunity to limit the resources earmarked for the Mesopotamian theater.

British efforts resumed in the spring of 1918 against dwindling Ottoman resistance. The capture of 5,000 Ottomans at Khan Baghdad on the Euphrates on March 26, 1918, showed that the Ottoman Army had lost its will to fight. In October a British force drove up the Tigris and captured the oil fields around Mosul shortly before the leaders of the Ottoman Empire asked for an armistice. The last battle in the Mesopotamian theater took place near the ancient Assyrian capital at Asshur. The Ottomans signed an armistice at Mudros on October 30, 1918. It went into effect the next day, ending Ottoman participation in the war.

Following the war, Mesopotamia received its modern name of Iraq and became a British mandate under the League of Nations. Fighting there during the war had cost the British and Indians 92,000 casualties, including 27,000 dead (13,000 of disease). In the same period, the Ottoman Army had sustained an estimated 325,000 casualties in what historian Michael Lyons has called "perhaps the most unnecessary campaign of the entire war."

JOHN LAVALLE

See also
Baghdad, Capture of; Ctesiphon, 1915 Battle of; Gallipoli Campaign; Goltz, Wilhelm Leopold Colmar von der; Kut al-Amara, Siege of; Nixon, Sir John Eccles; Townshend, Sir Charles Vere Ferrers

References
Barker, A. J. *The Bastard War: The Mesopotamian Campaign of 1914–1918.* New York: Dial, 1967.
Davis, Paul K. *Ends and Means: The British Mesopotamian Campaign and Commission.* Toronto: Associated University Presses, 1994.
Erickson, Edward J. *Ordered to Die: A History of the Ottoman Army in the First World War.* Westport, CT: Greenwood, 2000.
Moberly, F. J. *The Campaign in Mesopotamia, 1914–1918.* 3 vols. Nashville: Battery Press, 1997–1998.
Townshend, Charles. *Desert Hell: The British Invasion of Mesopotamia.* Cambridge, MA: Belknap Press of Harvard University Press, 2011.

Michael VIII Palaiologos (1223–1282)

Emperor of Nicaea (1259–1261) and then of the restored Byzantine Empire at Constantinople (1261–1282) and founder of the last reigning Byzantine dynasty. Born in 1223, Michael was the son of Grand Domestic Andronikos Palaiologos and the great-grandson of Byzantine emperor Alexios III Angelos. Michael had a distinguished military career, serving in the armies of the Empire of Nicaea and the Seljuk sultanate of Rum before he usurped the throne of Nicaea in 1259. In the same year in the valley of Pelagonia, in western Macedonia, he achieved a significant victory against a triple coalition consisting of Michael II of Epiros and his Western allies, King Manfred of Sicily and Prince William of Achaia, which paved the way for the liberation of Constantinople (modern-day Istanbul) from the Latins by the Nicaean Army in July 1261 and the restoration of the Byzantine Empire.

Throughout his reign, Michael was preoccupied with the plans of Western rulers to restore the Latin Empire of Constantinople and in particular with the ambitions of Charles I of Anjou, king of Sicily. In the 1260s and 1270s, Michael held negotiations with Popes Urban IV, Clement IV, and Gregory X concerning the reunification of the Latin and Greek Orthodox Churches, believing that the pope could and would prevent Charles of Anjou from attacking the Byzantine Empire if the Orthodox Church was subject to Rome. In 1274, Michael's representatives at the Second Council of Lyons agreed to reunification on the pope's terms, in spite of widespread and ardent opposition to this from among the Orthodox population of his empire. One of the outcomes of the agreement in Lyons was Michael's proposal to Pope Gregory X that a crusader army should pass through Constantinople on its way to the Holy Land, on condition that the crusaders would conquer and return Anatolia to the Byzantines. Before the details of the agreement were finalized, however, Pope Gregory died, and the new pope, Innocent V, abandoned plans for an overland crusade via Constantinople and Asia Minor.

In 1269 Michael promised King James I of Aragon aid for a crusade, and in 1269–1270 he made a similar offer to King Louis IX of France, with the proviso that Louis would mediate in restraining Charles of Anjou from attacking the Byzantine Empire. Between 1261 and 1277, taking advantage of the continuous enmity between Genoa and Venice over commercial supremacy in his territories, Michael signed treaties with the two Italian city-states, offering them commercial privileges in return for military aid or the promise of neutrality in the event of an attack against his empire from the West. In 1281, his army won a significant victory against the Angevin Army at the Battle of Berat, in Albania. The end of Charles of Anjou's ambitions to conquer Byzantium, however, came on Easter Monday 1282, when an anti-Angevin uprising, known as the Sicilian Vespers, took place in Palermo. Although Michael was not involved in the incident that sparked the uprising, the financial aid and encouragement he had previously offered to Charles's opponents contributed to the loss of Sicily and the consequent abandonment of Charles's plan to attack Byzantium. Michael was excommunicated once by Patriarch Arsenios of Constantinople for blinding the son and heir of Emperor Theodore II Laskaris and thrice by Pope Martin IV for failing to implement the reunification of the churches in the Byzantine Empire. Michael died on December 11, 1282. He was succeeded by his son Andronikos II.

APHRODITE PAPAYIANNI

See also
Louis IX, King of France

References

Chapman, Conrad. *Michel Paléologue, restaurateur de l' empire byzantin, 1261-1282.* Paris: Figuière, 1926.

Geanakoplos, Deno. *Emperor Michael Palaiologos and the West, 1958-1982.* Cambridge, MA: Harvard University Press, 1959.

Geanakoplos, Deno. "Greco-Latin Relations on the Eve of the Byzantine Restoration: The Battle of Pelagonia—1259." *Dumbarton Oaks Papers* 7 (1953): 107-141.

Geanakoplos, Deno. "Michael VIII Palaeologus and the Union of Lyons (1274)." *Harvard Theological Review* 46 (1953): 79-89.

Talbot, Alice Mary. "The Restoration of Constantinople under Michael VIII." *Dumbarton Oaks Papers* 47 (1993): 243-261.

Middle East Defense Organization

See Baghdad Pact

Miletus, Battle of (411 BCE)

Miletus was an ancient Greek city on the western coast of Anatolia near the mouth of the Maeander River in ancient Caria. Its ruins are near the modern-day village of Balat in Aydin Province, Turkey. The Battle of Miletus was an Athenian victory during the Greek Peloponnesian War (431-404 BCE). Before the Persian invasion of Anatolia in the midsixth century BCE, Miletus was thought to be the wealthiest of Greek cities.

An Athenian force under Phrynichus, Onomacles, and Scironides numbering 3,500 hoplites (including 1,000 allies and 1,500 Argives, 500 of whom were light troops provided with Athenian armor) was attempting to secure this strategic coastal city. The Milesian force consisted of 800 hoplites supported by an unknown number of Peloponnesian hoplites, mercenaries, and Persian cavalry under Tissaphernes. Alcibiades fought alongside the Milesians. The Argives, advancing overconfidently, were routed by the Milesians, losing around 300 men, but the Milesians withdrew when the Athenians drove back the Peloponnesians and Persians. The Athenians set up a trophy and began to besiege the city, but Phrynichus wisely withdrew his forces when he learned of an inbound Peloponnesian relief fleet.

IAIN SPENCE

See also
Achaemenid Empire

Reference
Tritle, Lawrence A. *A New History of the Peloponnesian War.* Malden, MA: Wiley-Blackwell, 2010.

Mithridates VI Eupator Dionysius (ca. 134-63 BCE)

Mithridates VI Eupator Dinoysius, also known as Mithridates the Great, was king of the partially Hellenized state of Pontus, located on the southern shores of the Black Sea in northern Anatolia. Certainly the greatest of the kings of Pontus and Rome's most formidable foe in the first century BCE, he greatly expanded the territory of his kingdom to encompass most of the coasts of the Black Sea and virtually all Anatolia.

Born of Persian and Greek ancestry (he claimed descent from Cyrus the Great and Alexander the Great) in the Pontic city of Sinope, probably in 134 BCE (sources vary widely on this), Mithridates reigned during circa 120-63 BCE. His Persian dynasty, having two centuries of ties with the Seleucids, had assumed some Greek cultural characteristics, including usage of the Greek language for official matters. His father, King Pharnaces II, had assisted Rome against Carthage in the Third Punic War (149-146) and against Aristonicus's revolt (132-129) and was given Phrygia as a reward. Pharnaces had married a Seleucid princess but was assassinated in 120, at which point Mithridates became king. He endured a number of murderous intrigues resulting in his killing his own mother and a brother.

Mithridates was determined to control the Black Sea and secure all of Asia Minor. He began the territorial expansion of his kingdom by conquering the Crimea and northern Euxine, ultimately securing most of the coastal areas of the Black Sea and considerable resources and manpower. He then secured Bithynia and Cappadocia in northeastern Anatolia while the Romans were engaged in the Social War (91-88) against their Italian allies. Rome was then expanding its own territorial holdings into the eastern Mediterranean and became alarmed. Rome sent special legates to force Mithridates to recognize Bithynia and Cappadocia's respective kings and to remove his armies from these places, then urged Bithynia's King Nicomedes III to invade Pontus and seize booty to compensate the Romans for their assistance. However, in 90 BCE Mithridates defeated Nicomedes, attacked Pergamum, and killed a Roman envoy.

The new ruler of Bithynia, Nicomedes IV, was largely a figurehead ruler controlled by Rome. Mithridates tried to overthrow him but failed, and under Roman pressure, Nicomedes IV declared war on Pontus. The years 89-85 BCE saw Mithridates battling Rome, but with Rome still occupied with the Social War, it had only two legions in Macedonia to commit to the effort against Mithridates. These legions combined with Nicomedes IV's army to invade Pontus in 89 BCE. Mithridates, however, defeated his enemies. Many cities welcomed Mithridates as *soter* (savior), and he secured all of Asia Minor and then built a fleet to attack Rhodes.

The following year, 88 BCE, Mithridates orchestrated a massacre of Roman and Italian settlers remaining in Anatolian cities. This included all Romans and Italians of both sexes and all ages, with the cities to share the victims' valuables with him. Slaves betraying or killing their masters were offered freedom; debtors killing their (presumably Italian) creditors were offered 50 percent debt remission. Atrocities are reported for Ephesus, Pergamum, Adramyttium, Caunus, and Tralles, among other cities. Later known as the Asiatic Vespers, the massacre is said to have claimed between 80,000 to 150,000 victims and essentially removed the Roman presence in the region. It also sparked a swift Roman military response. Support for Mithridates evidences a common anti-Roman attitude. Anti-Roman sentiment in the Greek East was aroused by usurious and extortive Roman tax collectors. This conclusion is supported by a proliferation of underground anti-Roman literature.

Mithridates even conquered Greece, but the Asiatic Vespers sparked a swift and heavy military response from Rome, now free of the Social War. Five Roman legions took the field against Mithridates and forced him back into Asia. Roman general Lucius Cornelius Sulla punished several Greek cities for supporting Mithridates, including looting Athens in 86. Sulla defeated Mithridates thoroughly in 85. The conclusion of peace that year saw Sulla confirmed to his Asian holdings. Mithridates was made *amicus* of Rome and forced to pay indemnities and surrender his warships. The Roman province of Asia was forced to pay ruinous indemnities.

Fighting resumed in 83–81 but was largely confined to skirmishes. Full-scale warfare was renewed in 73. In prolonged fighting, Roman general Lucius Cornelius Sulla forced Mithridates from Pontus and into exile in Armenia. Mithridates returned to Pontus in 68 but was defeated by Gnaeus Pompeius Magnus (Pompey the Great) in 65. Mithridates withdrew into his lands north of the Black Sea, hoping to gather resources there and resume the struggle, but strong opposition there to his heavy exactions for war led to revolt and his suicide in southern Russia in 63 BCE.

Timothy Doran and Spencer C. Tucker

See also
Pompeius Magnus, Gnaeus; Pontus

References
Duggan, Alfred. *He Died Old: Mithradates Eupator, King of Pontus.* London: Faber and Faber, 1958.

Ford, Michael Curtis. *The Last King: Rome's Greatest Enemy.* New York: Thomas Dunne Books, 2004.

Mayor, Adrienne. *The Poison King: The Life and Legend of Mithradates.* Princeton, NJ: Princeton University Press, 2010.

McGing, B. C. *The Foreign Policy of Mithridates VI Eupator, King of Pontus.* Leiden: Brill Academic Publishers, 1986.

Mithridatic Wars (89–84, 83–81, and 73–63 BCE)

Mithridates VI, ruler of the kingdom of Pontus on the southern shores of the Black Sea, opposed Rome's expansion into Asia Minor and triggered the three wars that carry his name. Often referred to as Mithridates the Great, he proved to be one of Rome's most determined and dangerous Hellenistic opponents. Mithridates VI spent virtually his entire reign either at war with Rome or preparing for it. Ruthless and vindictive in dealings with friends and foes alike, he fought all the major Roman commanders of his era from Sulla to Pompey the Great and made or sought alliances with nearly every one of Rome's enemies.

Mithridates triggered the first Mithridatic War (89–84 BCE) when in 89 BCE he attacked the Kingdom of Bithynia, a Roman client state in northwestern Anatolia. Several Greek city-states joined by rebelling against Roman authorities in Greece. Unfortunately for Mithridates, his Armenian and Parthian allies become bogged down in the civil conflict over the Parthian succession. Roman troops quickly captured Thrace and the province of Cappadocia in central Asia Minor. Mithridates recaptured Cappadocia in 88 BCE, slaughtering the Roman and Italian citizens in the areas he captured. His troops entered Greece that summer. Most Greek cities shifted allegiance back to Rome, however. Only Athens held out, but it fell to a Roman siege in February 86 BCE. Shortly thereafter, a Roman fleet defeated Mithridates's fleet at Tenedos. The Romans won two land battles at Chaeroneia and Orchomenus and restored their rule over Greece. With Greece lost and Roman troops in Asia Minor, Mithridates came to an agreement with Roman general Lucius Cornelius Sulla Felx, commonly known as Sulla, that left Mithridates in control of his Kingdom of Pontus but forced him to pay a large indemnity and saw the return to prewar territorial borders.

The Second Mithridatic War (83–81 BCE) began when Lucius Licinius Murena, Sulla's legate commanding two legions in Roman Asia Minor, claimed that Mithridates was rearming and posed a direct threat to Roman Asia Minor and on his own authority invaded Pontus. Mithridates inflicted a minor defeat on Murena and forced a Roman withdrawal, whereupon Sulla, now Roman dictator, insisted that Murena conclude peace.

Mithridates continued to make alliances and preparations to drive Rome out of the Hellenistic World. His alliance with the Cilician pirates alarmed Rome, as Roman forces had invaded the Cilician coast in order to end the piratic threat to Roman shipping. Thus, regional Roman officials seized the opportunity presented in 75 BCE when Bithynian king Nicomedes IV died without heirs, awarding his kingdom to Rome in his will. With Roman armies mobilizing along his western border and Rome heavily engaged in Gaul, Mithridates invaded Bithynia while his fleet blockaded the Roman naval bases in Asia Minor, launching the Third Mithridatic War of 73–63 BCE.

Five Roman legions under Lucius Lucullus drove Mithridates into lesser Armenia while Roman forces under Marcus Aurelius Cotta secured the coast. Lucullus then invaded Armenia, defeating King Tigranes the Great's army at Tigranocerta in October 69 BCE. Armenia's ally of Parthia was in no position to send aid, since its army was fighting off an invasion from Bactria. Lucullus again defeated the Armenian king in late 68, but a mutiny in the legions saved the kingdom from conquest. Mithridates and Tigranes used the respite to recapture some of their lost territories.

Fresh from his victories in Gaul, Pompey the Great gained command of the Roman legions and resumed the offensive in 65 BCE, defeating Mithridates and forcing him to flee to the Caucasus. Pompey forced Tigranes to become a Roman client and then pursued Mithridates through the Caucasus to Panticapaeum, where Mithridates murdered his own son to take the throne. The city's population rebelled, allowing the Roman troops to enter in the summer of 63 BCE. Learning that his son and designated successor Pharnaces planned to surrender him to the Romans, Mithridates ordered one of his own bodyguards to take his life with his sword.

The death of Mithridates VI marked the beginning of the end of Hellenistic domination of the Middle East. The remaining Hellenistic kingdoms there fell to Rome during the course of the next two decades. The wars also brought Asia Minor and all but a small portion of the Black Sea coast under Roman authority. Armenia would become a major source of Roman cavalry and heavy infantry for the next 400 years, but the territorial expansion came at a cost of extending the Roman border to Parthia's frontiers. With the former Hellenistic buffer states gone, Rome and later Byzantium would face almost continuous conflict along their eastern boundary until the Eastern Roman Empire fell to the Ottoman Turks in 1453.

Carl Otis Schuster

See also
Mithridates VI Eupator Dionysius; Pompeius Magnus, Gnaeus

References
Hojte, Jakob. *Mithridates VI and the Pontic Kingdom.* Aarhus, Denmark: Aarhus University Press, 2009.
Mayor, Adrienne. *The Poison King: The Life and Legend of Mithridates, Rome's Deadliest Enemy.* Princeton, NJ: Princeton University Press, 2010.
McGing, B. C. *The Foreign Policy of Mithridates VI Eupator, King of Pontus.* Leiden: Brill, 1997.
Waterfield, Robin. *Taken at the Flood.* Oxford: Oxford University Press, 2014.

Mitla Pass

A strategic pass in the west-central Sinai Peninsula, Egypt. Mitla Pass lies approximately 20 miles east of the Suez Canal near the city of Suez. The Sinai Peninsula features very rugged terrain in the south and extensive sand dunes in the north. Better transportation routes are available in central Sinai, which is dominated by the Tih Plateau. Giddi Mountain (Jabal al-Jiddi), a limestone massif with peaks rising to 2,750 feet, separates the Tih Plateau from the sand dunes. Mitla Pass traverses Giddi Mountain and is a critical link in the ancient Darb al-Hajj (pilgrimage route), now Highway 33, that provides a direct route between Suez and Aqaba. Steep ridges on either side of the pass are only 150–300 feet apart in places. Its narrow confines and its many caves make it a natural fortification. Approximately 20 miles east of the pass, Highway 33 intersects with the road leading northeast to Bir al-Thamiada, one of the traditional Sinai invasion routes. Mitla Pass was an objective for both the Ottoman Empire and British Empire forces during World War I and for Egyptian and Israeli forces in the 1956 Sinai Campaign, the 1967 Six-Day War, and the 1973 Yom Kippur War.

On October 29, 1956, a battalion of Major Ariel Sharon's 202nd Parachute Brigade landed 15 miles east of Mitla Pass on the first day of hostilities during the Suez Crisis. The remainder of the brigade arrived by land the following evening. The next day, Sharon received permission to send a patrol into the pass but instead sent a battalion, which was ambushed. Although Israelis captured the pass, the unplanned battle cost the lives of 38 Israeli paratroopers. More than 200 Egyptians died defending it. Following a cease-fire, Israel withdrew its forces in a phased withdrawal completed in January 1957.

During the 1967 Six-Day War, the Israeli Air Force repeatedly strafed retreating Egyptian units in and around Mitla Pass, turning it into a death trap. Israeli tanks arrived on June 7, 1967, and blocked the east side of the pass. The next day, Israeli forces secured the pass and trapped the remaining Egyptian soldiers in central Sinai. Thousands died from combat or the desert heat. Israel ultimately seized control of the entire Sinai Peninsula.

On October 6, 1973, Egyptian forces initiated the Yom Kippur War (Ramadan War) with a surprise crossing of the Suez Canal. Detailed planning and execution led to initial successes. On October 14, however, they launched a hastily planned assault on the Mitla and other passes. The poorly executed attacks failed and opened the door to effective Israeli counterattacks, which continued until a cease-fire was concluded on October 28.

Mitla Pass figured prominently in subsequent Egyptian-Israeli peace negotiations. The January 18, 1974, Sinai I Agreement involved the withdrawal of Israeli forces from the Suez Canal east to a defensive line that included Mitla Pass. Israeli forces withdrew from Mitla Pass as part of the September 4, 1975, Sinai II Agreement. That agreement included the stipulation that electronic sensors as well as human monitors would provide Israel with early warning of Egyptian military movements in the region. Successful international monitoring of Mitla Pass contributed to the signing of the Israel-Egypt Peace Treaty on March 26, 1979, the result of the Camp David Accords of the previous year.

CHUCK FAHRER

See also
Bar-Lev Line; Camp David Accords; Giddi Pass; Israel-Egypt Peace Treaty; Sharon, Ariel; Sinai Campaign of 1956; Sinai I and Sinai II Agreements; Sinai Peninsula; Six-Day War; Yom Kippur War

References
Greenwood, Ned H. *The Sinai: A Physical Geography*. Austin: University of Texas Press, 1997.
Herzog, Chaim. *The Arab-Israeli Wars: War and Peace in the Middle East from the War of Independence to Lebanon*. Westminster, MD: Random House, 1984.
Marshall, S. L. A. *Sinai Victory*. New York: William Morrow, 1967.
Pollack, Kenneth M. *Arabs at War: Military Effectiveness, 1948–1991*. Lincoln: University of Nebraska Press, 2002.

Mizrahi Judaism

Jews descended from the Jewish communities of North Africa and the Middle East, also known as Mizrahi Jews and Mizrahim (Easterner). The term "Mizrahi Judaism" has an ethnic meaning, a religious meaning, and a meaning that merges the two. The term "Mizrahi Jew" is a 20th-century Israeli designation acting as a substitute for the terms "Arab Jew" or "Oriental Jew." Mizrahi Jewry is subdivided into ethnic subsets based on individual countries of origin and their indigenous traditions and practices. Some examples include Iraqi Jews, Tunisian Jews, Persian Jews, Ethiopian Jews, and Yemenite Jews, among many others.

Mizrahi Jews comprise more than half of Israel's current population. The Mizrahim began immigrating to Israel from their countries of origin following the formation of the State of Israel in 1948. The refugee immigration was due in great part to the fleeing of virtually entire populations of Mizrahi Jews from the growing animosity and persecution of indigenous Jewish populations in Arab and Muslim countries. This began just prior to the formation of the State of Israel, accelerated after the Israeli War of Independence (1948–1949), and continued into the 1990s. For example, 25,000 Mizrahi Jews were expelled from Egypt after the 1956 Suez Crisis, and most went to Israel. And the number of Ethiopian Jews who fled their country via Israel's Operations MOSES (1984) and SOLOMON (1991) was so great that they now constitute approximately 1 percent of the contemporary Israeli population. More than 40,000 Mizrahim continue to reside in almost all of the Arab and Muslim states of North Africa and the Middle East, with large populations remaining in Uzbekistan, Iran, and Azerbaijan.

Although most Mizrahim arrived in Israel speaking the language of their countries of origin, all underwent intensive training in the Hebrew language. Most Mizrahim were craftsmen and merchants and remained so after immigration. Few had farming experience, and most either avoided settlement on *moshavim* (communal farms) or did not stay long once that option had been experienced. Mizrahi Judaism is not as doctrinally well developed or conservative in its understanding and regard to the Torah as Ashkenazic Judaism or even Sephardic Judaism. Mizrahi Judaism allows adherents wide latitude in the observance of the *mitzvoth* (commandments). The most conservative Mizrahim are regarded as observant, meaning that they closely follow or obey the commandments. The most liberal Mizrahim generally do not closely follow the commandments or consider obedience to them of prime concern. Many Mizrahim fall in between these extremes, but all Mizrahim regard mitzvoth observance as part of a progressive perfection. The observance of the mitzvoth for the Mizrahim is not a standard that one must meet or fail but rather a standard toward which one strives. In other words, total observance of the mitzvoth is the goal, but any observance is better than no observance and brings one closer to God.

RICHARD M. EDWARDS

See also
Ashkenazic Judaism; Hasidic Judaism; Sephardic Judaism

References
Biale, David. *Cultures of the Jews: A New History.* New York: Schocken, 2002.
Dimont, Max. *Jews, God and History.* New York: Simon and Schuster, 1962.
Robinson, George. *Essential Judaism: A Complete Guide to Beliefs, Customs & Rituals.* New York: Pocket Books/Simon and Schuster, 2001.
Seltzer, Robert. *Jewish People, Jewish Thought.* New York: Macmillan, 1980.
Zohar, Zion, ed. *Sephardic and Mizrahi Jewry: From the Golden Age of Spain to Modern Times.* New York: New York University Press, 2005.

Mongol Invasion of the Middle East (1256–1280)

By 1227, the Mongols under Genghis Khan had emerged from the steppes of Mongolia to spread their influence to Central Asia and parts of Persia and Afghanistan. The once mighty Khwarezm lay in ruins, as did various polities that lay in the path of the Mongol host. Genghis Khan's death in 1227 briefly halted the westward expansion of the Mongol Empire as the Mongols diverted their attention to consolidating their authority in China and the steppes. In the 1230s, however, the Mongols extended their control to Georgia, Armenia, and Azerbaijan as well as to Russian states and parts of Persia.

Mongol expansion into the Middle East was slow but steady until 1251, when the Great Khan Mongke resolved to extend his control to the Abbasid Caliphate. His brother, Hulegu, was given the title of Ilkhan (subordinate khan) and charged with extending Mongol authority over Western Asia. Hulegu left Mongolia in 1253 and began his campaign in earnest in the spring of 1256. He had a considerable army at his disposal. Persian historian Alaiddin Ata-Malik Juwayni's states in his chronicle that Hulegu's army was composed of 2 out of every 10 soldiers in the Mongol army, but scholars question whether this statement can be taken literally. Most studies suggest that Hulegu probably had an army of 15–17 *tumens* (each *tumen* equal to 10,000 men) of Mongol troops and additional forces of local auxiliaries (e.g., Georgians, Armenians, Chinese, etc.) who were ordered to provide contingents.

In January 1256, Hulegu crossed the Oxus River and entered Persia. As he advanced with his formidable war machine, a succession of rulers were made to pay homage to him. Hulegu initially directed his attention to the Elburz Mountains from where the sect of Ismaili Assassins had terrorized much of the Middle East since the 11th century. The Assassin's grand master Rukn ad-Din sought to negotiate with Hulegu but balked at the Mongol's steep demands. In the fall of 1256 the Ismaili domain was destroyed, its castles, including the impregnable Alamut, destroyed and its grand master captured and later executed.

Hulegu spent the year 1257 receiving submissions from the remaining princes in Persia before turning his army southwest to advance on Baghdad, the seat of the Abbasid caliph who had yet to submit to Mongol authority. The Abbasid Caliphate was then but a shadow of its former self, and the political authority of Abbasid caliph al-Mustasim (1242–1258) scarcely extended beyond Baghdad and its immediate territory. But the caliph still commanded religious and moral prestige and claimed universal sovereignty in the Islamic world. Hulegu was upset by the caliph's refusal to acknowledge Mongol authority (even though the caliph's envoys performed some expression of submission to the great khan in 1246) or to send troops to fight the Ismailis. As Hulegu advanced to Baghdad, he and al-Mustasim exchanged a number of letters in which the caliph castigated and insulted the Mongol leader. Yet, the caliph also failed to recognize the grave danger of confronting the Mongols and made no preparation to repel the invasion. Worse, he ignored his generals' warnings to strengthen the city's weakened walls and military.

In January 1258, the Mongols reached the Tigris River and approached Baghdad. Al-Mustasim tried to engage them, but his attack near the city failed abysmally when the Mongols broke the dikes and flooded the Muslim camp, drowning many of the Muslim troops and killing those who survived. By late January the Mongols took positions on both sides of the river, placing Baghdad under siege. The Chinese engineers constructed siege engines, and bombardment of the city commenced in early February. By February 10 Baghdad's walls had been breached, and the Mongol army launched its assault.

What followed remains one of the most tragic examples of wanton destruction of human lives and property.

Illumination from *Jami al-Tawarikh* by Rashid al-Din, about 1310, depicting the successful Mongol siege of Baghdad in 1258 led by Hulegu (grandson of Genghis Khan). The ruling Abbasid caliphate was effectively destroyed and probably some 100,000 residents of the city died. (DeAgostini/Getty Images)

Probably as many as 100,000 people died (some exaggerated accounts claim 800,000 to 1 million), while Baghdad's famous libraries, hospitals, palaces, and mosques were all destroyed. Never again would the city serve as the intellectual center of Islam. The sack of Baghdad played an important role in deteriorating relations between the offspring of Genghis Khan. Thus, Genghis's grandson Berke Khan of the Golden Horde had converted to Islam and was so incensed by Hulegu's action that he began negotiating an alliance with the Mamluks of Egypt against Hulegu.

Following the sack of Baghdad, Hulegu pushed northeast to Tabriz and then made preparations for a campaign into the Mediterranean littoral. Some scholars suggest that King Hetum of Cilicia or Lesser Armenia, who had recognized Mongol rule in 1243, may have played a role in provoking this invasion. During his stay at the great khan's camp in 1253–1256, he probably brought it to Mongke's attention. There is even a claim that Hetum desired to use the Mongols to liberate the Holy Land, which would then be given to the Christians. It is certain, however, that Hetum had a major influence on his son-in-law, Bohemund VI of Antioch, to enter into alliance with Hulegu.

On the eve of his campaign, Hulegu ordered the Seljuk sultans of Rum to participate in his invasion of Syria and Egypt and sent letters to al-Nasur Yusuf, the ruler of Syria, and Sultan Qutuz of Egypt requesting their submission. By the end of the summer of 1259 he finally departed from Tabriz, and after occupying the Jazira region in Upper Mesopotamia, the Mongol troops, accompanied by Georgian, Armenian, and Rum Seljuk contingents, entered Syria in early 1260.

Since 1250 Syria and Egypt were under control of the Mamluks, the slave-soldiers, mostly of Turkic origins, who had deposed the Ayyubid dynasty and consolidated their rule in the region. Al-Nasir Yusuf, the lord of Syria, initially sought to compromise with the Mongols and sent him gifts hoping to prevent the invasion. But Hulegu demanded that al-Nasir travel in person and submit to the "sultan of the world, supreme king of the face of the earth" or be destroyed. Al-Nasir then changed his position and adopted a defiant attitude toward the Mongols, sending a belligerent letter to Hulegu. Al-Nasir also requested military help from Egypt and mobilized his forces at a camp at Barza (near Damascus).

In January 1260 Hulegu besieged Aleppo, which surrendered on January 25 and was subjected to looting and slaughter. The Mongols then marched westward, receiving submissions from Hama and Homs. Hulegu dispatched part of his army, about 12,000 troops under one of his most trusted generals, Ketbugha, on a raid into southern syria while he himself left Syria to return to Tabriz. Historians have traditionally explained Hulegu's sudden departure as a response to the news of the death of the Great Khan Mongke and the issue of the succession. Some scholars also note that Hulegu left Syria because of the lack of adequate pastures for his army, which consisted predominantly of cavalry. Certainly Hulegu underestimated the number and quality of troops available to his opponents in Egypt.

In early February 1260 Ketbugha arrived in Damascus, which submitted to the Mongol authority. The Mongols then turned south and camped at Marj Barghuth on the road from Damascus to Jisr Yaqub. Ketbugha dispatched a reconnaissance force toward Palestine as he himself prepared for the campaign. These scouts raided Hebron, Ascalon, Nablus, and Jerusalem and reached as far as Gaza before returning to Damascus in April 1260. By then, Ketbugha was busy suppressing uprisings in Damascus and Baalbek, both of which he accomplished with ruthless efficiency, and then conquering the fortresses of al-Subayba and Ajlun in the Golan.

In Egypt, meanwhile, new Mamluk sultan Qutuz and his brilliant general Baybars had been preparing for battle. In late July 1260, taking advantage of Hulegu's withdrawal, Qutuz left Cairo for Salihiyya. There the Mamluks mobilized their forces and were joined by the refugee Syrian troops and assorted Turkmen, Bedouins (*al-urbani*), and Shahrazuriyya Kurds.

Although many of his emirs urged him to wait for the Mongols in Egypt, Qutuz decided to attack the Mongols in Syria. Advancing into Palestine, Baybars, at the head of the Mamluk advance guard, routed a Mongol forward force (*talia*) near Gaza. The surviving Christian crusader polities faced a difficult choice between siding with either the Mongols or the Mamluks but eventually chose to remain neutral, even though they sent supplies to the Muslim camp.

Ketbugha was in the Bekaa Valley when he received news of the Mamluk invasion of Palestine. He quickly gathered his forces, which included contingents from Georgia and Lesser Armenia, and marched to face the Mamluks. The two forces converged on the Plains of Esdraelon at the Battle of Ayn Jalut (Goliath's Well) on September 3, 1260. The outnumbered Mongols began the battle with a ferocious charge that drove the Mamluks back, but the tide of the battle turned after the defection of Syrian troops under al-Ashraf Musa. The Mamluk counterattack shattered the Mongol ranks and killed Ketbugha. Qutuz dispatched Baybars after the routed Mongols and the Mamluks chased them up through northern Syria.

Ayn Jalut was the first important defeat the Mongols had suffered, and it played a crucial role in the history of the Middle East. Ketbugha's defeat at Ayn Jalut, though a relatively small battle in itself, proved to be the Muslim version of the Christian victory at the Battle of Tours in 732. Just as Christian Europe had held back the forces of Islam, so too Muslim Egypt turned away the forces that could have had a devastating effect on the heart of the Islamic world. Instead, Egypt endured as one of the centers of Islam, and Syria became an integral part of the centralized Mamluk Sultanate. The myth of the Mongol invincibility was weakened, while the glory earned at Ayn Jalut allowed Baybars to assassinate Qutuz and assume leadership of the Mamluk Sultanate.

Hulegu was infuriated by this unprecedented Mongol defeat and prepared a major punitive expedition. However, a continued power struggle in the heart of the Mongol Empire prevented this plan from being carried out. Faced with the attacks from the Golden Horde, Hulegu campaigned against Berke Khan in the Caucasus in 1261–1263 but was unable to gain the upper hand. Hulegu was hoping to revive his alliance with the crusaders and invade the Mamluk realm when he died in 1264.

Hulegu's son Abaka continued his father's struggle against the Mamluks of Egypt and their allies. In 1266, Abaka built a fortified line in eastern Georgia to protect his territory from the attacks of the Golden Horde and campaigned against the north Caucasian tribes in 1270s. Abaka sought to establish diplomatic alliances with European nations against Egypt and sent embassies to France and the Papal States in 1274 and 1277. Although he had negotiated join operations with England, France, and the Papal States, the European states failed to organize any combined action, leaving Abaka alone to face the Mamluks, who attacked his territories throughout the 1270s and routed the Ilkhanate force near Albistan in 1277. Abaka responded with an invasion of Syria in 1280, and although he sacked Aleppo, his army suffered a major defeat in the Second Battle of Homs the next year.

ALEXANDER MIKABERIDZE

See also

Abbasid Caliphate; Assassins; Ayn Jalut, Battle of; Baghdad, 1258 Siege of; Baybars I; Homs, First Battle of; Mamluk-Ilkhanid Wars

References

Allsen, Thomas. *Mongol Imperialism: The Policies of the Grand Qan Mongke in China, Russia, and the Islamic Lands, 1251–1259.* Berkeley: University of California Press, 1987.

Chambers, James. *The Devil's Horsemen: The Mongol Invasion of Europe.* New York: Atheneum, 1979.

Christian, David. *A History of Russia, Central Asia, and Mongolia,* Vol. 1, *Inner Eurasia from Prehistory to the Mongol Empire.* Oxford, UK: Blackwell Publishers, 1998.

Grousset, René. *The Empire of the Steppes: A History of Central Asia.* Translated by Naomi Walford. New Brunswick, NJ: Rutgers University Press, 1970.

Morgan David. *The Mongols.* Oxford, UK: B. Blackwell, 1986.

Montenegrin-Ottoman Wars (1852–1913)

A series of three 19th- and early 20th-century conflicts between the Ottoman Empire and Montenegro, a small Balkan tributary state. Montenegro had come under Ottoman control in the 15th century but had been ruled by the prince-bishop (*vladika*) of Cetinje, who had jurisdiction over the entire region. In the early 1800s, Ottoman power in the Balkans was gravely undermined by successful revolts in Greece and Serbia that resulted in their independence. Montenegro, neighboring Serbia, also moved toward independence under the reign of its prince-bishop Danilo I (r. 1851–1860), who ended the existing system of government and sought closer ties with Russia, whose emperor Nicholas I recognized Danilo's claim as the prince of Montenegro.

Montenegrin-Ottoman War of 1852–1853

Danilo's proclamation of his princely power (supported by Austria as well as Russia), however, posed a direct challenge to Ottoman sovereignty in the region. The Ottomans refused to recognize Montenegro's new status and began to meddle in Montenegrin affairs. Danilo responded by seizing control of Žabljak Crnojevića, which gave the Ottomans a definitive pretext to invade. The Ottomans reasserted their authority by dispatching troops under Omar Pasha Latas, governor of the neighboring Bosnia, to Montenegro in 1852. A smaller Montenegrin army was unable to halt the Ottoman advance, but Austrian intervention persuaded the sultan to keep Danilo in power in 1853; Danilo's efforts to have the conference meeting in Paris to resolve the Crimean War and recognize Montenegrin independence led nowhere.

After the first Ottoman-Montenegrin war, the region experienced rising nationalism and tensions between Montenegrins and the Ottomans. Prince Danilo actively supported uprisings in Herzegovina, which, he believed, would erode Ottoman control in the entire Balkan region and lead to Montenegrin independence. Danilo's policies led to the Herzegovinan uprising of 1857 (supported and directed by the Montenegrins), which caused the Sublime Porte to dispatch Ottoman forces under Hussein Pasha to reign in the Montenegrin prince. In the spring of 1858 Hussein Pasha invaded Montenegro, but after occupying several settlements he suffered a major defeat at the hands of Grand Duke Mirko Petrović-Njegoš, "the Sword of Montenegro," at Grahovac during May 12–13, 1858.

The battle had major political and cultural influence. Proclaimed as the "Marathon of Montenegro," it quickly became a part of national folklore and mythology. More importantly, the Great Powers forced the Ottomans to accept a Conference of Ambassador at Constantinople, where border rectification of Montenegro took place. Thus, the border between Montenegro and the Porte was officially established, a significant step toward formal Montenegrin independence.

Montenegrin-Ottoman War of 1861–1862

Prince Danilo was assassinated in August 1860, but Montenegrin military successes against the Ottomans encouraged nationalistic sentiments in neighboring Herzegovina, where a major revolt against the Ottoman rule began in 1861. Montenegro did not directly intervene in this revolt due to the pressure from the Great Powers, but the Ottoman authorities accused Danilo's successor, Prince Nikola, of clandestine involvement and failing to contain Montenegrin groups that crossed into Herzegovina. In late November 1861 Omar Pasha, governor of Bosnia, suppressed the revolt in Herzegovina after routing the rebel forces (which included Montenegrins) at Piva.

When Montenegro mobilized its own forces and threatened to intervene under pretext of protecting fellow Slavs, Omar Pasha invaded during the winter of 1861. The campaign led to a rapid and decisive defeat for the Montenegrins, and the Great Powers had to again intervene to stop Ottoman troops entering the Montenegrin capital of Cetinje, which was invested. The subsequent Convention of Scutari (Shkodër in August 1862) left a status quo ante except that Montenegro agreed to cease helping the Herzegovinian rebels and agreed not to build forts on its borders or to import arms.

Montenegrin-Ottoman War of 1876–1878

The Montenegrins had to wait 14 years before exacting their revenge. In 1876, Prince Nikola forged an alliance with Serbia and supported the start of a revolt in Herzegovina. Declaring war on the Ottoman Empire, he dispatched some 11,000 troops to Herzegovina, where the Montenegrins scored early successes at Vučji Do (July) and Fundina (August). However, later that same year, the Ottoman offensive drove the Montenegrins deep into their own territory.

Only the start of the Russo-Ottoman War in 1877 saved Montenegro from another defeat. The Ottoman focus on the Danubian front against Russia allowed Montenegro to seize territories around Nikšić, Bar, and Ulcinj, which gave it leverage in the subsequent Congress of Berlin in 1878. The congress granted Montenegro formal recognition as an independent state and recognized its territorial enlargement, although it rejected the Treaty of San Stefano's territorial arrangement that would have doubled Montenegro in area.

First Balkan War of 1912–1913

Montenegro enjoyed a period of relative peace after 1878 but fought another war against the Ottoman Empire in 1912, when it joined Greece, Serbia, and Bulgaria against the Ottomans in the First Balkan War. During that conflict, the Montenegrin Army seized considerable territory in the Sandžak as well as Metohija (including the towns of Djakovica and Peć) and gained the towns of Bijelo Polje, Mojkovac, Berane, and Pljevlja, among others.

ALEXANDER MIKABERIDZE

See also
Balkan Wars; Russo-Ottoman Wars; San Stefano, Treaty of

References
Jelavich, Barbara. *History of the Balkans.* Cambridge: Cambridge University Press, 1983.
Morrison, Kenneth. *Montenegro: A Modern History.* London: I. B. Tauris, 2009.
Shaw, Stanford. *History of the Ottoman Empire and Modern Turkey,* Vol. 2. Cambridge: Cambridge University Press, 1977.

Mont Giscard, Battle of (November 25, 1177)

Battle fought between the forces of the Kingdom of Jerusalem led by King Baldwin IV and Reynald of Châtillon against an invasion force led by Egyptian sultan Saladin, who had launched a diversionary attack from Egypt soon after Raymond III of Tripoli and Philip of Flanders marched to besiege Hama in Syria. With a large proportion of the armed forces of Jerusalem and the military orders having proceeded to northward to lay siege to Hama, Baldwin summoned all remaining able-bodied men to muster at Ascalon (modern-day Tel Ashqelon, Israel). Saladin bypassed the city and moved inland toward Jerusalem, sending detachments to raid Ramla and Lydda and ambush Franks who were on their way to the muster.

On the afternoon of November 25, the Franks surprised and routed Saladin's main force at a hill known as Mont Gisard (modern-day Tell Jazar) some five miles southeast of Ramla, before the Muslims were able to form up in battle order. With most of his army dispersed and his base at El Arish overrun by Bedouins, Saladin withdrew to Egypt. A Benedictine priory dedicated to St. Catherine, the battle being on her feast day, was built on the battle site as an act of gratitude and commemoration.

ALAN V. MURRAY

See also
Baldwin IV of Jerusalem; Saladin

Reference
Hamilton, Bernard. *The Leper King and His Heirs: Baldwin IV and the Crusader Kingdom of Jerusalem.* Cambridge: Cambridge University Press, 2000.

Montgomery, Bernard Law (1887–1976)

British Army field marshal. Bernard Law Montgomery was born in London on November 17, 1887. His father was the Anglican bishop of Tasmania but the family returned to Britain when Montgomery was 13. Montgomery entered the Royal Military Academy of Sandhurst in 1907 and in 1908 was commissioned into the Royal Warwickshire Regiment. He served in India, and in World War I he fought on the Western Front and was wounded in the First Battle of Ypres in 1914. Posted to a training assignment in England, he returned to the front to fight as a major in the Battle of the Somme in 1916. Montgomery ended the war as a division staff officer.

Following occupation duty in Germany after the war, Montgomery graduated from the Staff College at Camberley in 1921 and returned as an instructor there in 1926. In 1929 he rewrote the infantry training manual. He then served in the Middle East, commanded a regiment, and was chief instructor at the Quetta Staff College (1934–1937). During 1937–1938 he commanded a brigade. He then took charge of the 3rd Infantry Division, which he led in France as part of the British Expeditionary Force after the start of World War II. Montgomery distinguished himself in the retreat to Dunkerque (Dunkirk, late May 1940). In July he took charge of V Corps in Britain protecting the English south coast against a possible German invasion.

In April 1941 Montgomery assumed command of the XII Corps, which held the Kent area. Montgomery established himself as a thorough professional soldier. He was also very much the maverick.

Montgomery helped plan the disastrous Dieppe raid (August 19, 1942) but left to command the First Army in the planned Allied invasion of North Africa. On August 13 following the death of General W. H. E. Gott, Montgomery assumed command of the British Eighth Army in Egypt, repulsing German field marshal Erwin Rommel's attack at Alam Halfa near El Alamein, Egypt (August 31–September 7).

Montgomery rebuilt the Eighth Army's morale. Known for his concern for his men's welfare, he was also deliberate as a commander. In the Battle of El Alamein (October 23–November 4, 1942), his superior forces defeated and drove west German and Italian forces under Rommel. Promoted to full general that November, Montgomery engaged in a less than rapid advance westward across North Africa that allowed the bulk of Axis forces to escape.

Following the Axis surrender in the Battle of Tunis (May 3–13, 1943), Montgomery played an active role in planning Operation HUSKY, the invasion of Sicily, and led the Eighth Army in the invasions of both Sicily (July 9) and Italy (September 3). He was again criticized for his slow advance, north from Reggio di Calabria. Returned to Britain to assist in planning Operation OVERLORD, the Allied invasion of Normandy (June 6, 1944), Montgomery insisted on changes that may well have saved the invasion from disaster. He temporarily commanded the land forces in the invasion until General Dwight Eisenhower moved his headquarters to France in September.

Elevated to field marshal on September 1, 1944, Montgomery commanded the British 21st Army Group on the Allied left flank. His failure to move beyond Antwerp, however, led to the escape of German forces on the Beveland peninsula. Montgomery rejected Eisenhower's broad front strategy and sought to secure a crossing over the lower Rhine at Arnhem. This plan, Operation MARKET-GARDEN, employed large numbers of airborne troops and came as a surprise from the conservative Montgomery. Eisenhower approved the plan, which, however, failed (September 17–25).

Montgomery's forces defended the north shoulder in the German Ardennes Offensive (Battle of the Bulge, December 16, 1944–January 16, 1945). His vanity came increasingly to the fore, and he never understood the necessity for cooperation in coalition warfare. Indeed, his insubordinate attitude almost brought his relief from command. At a press conference following the Battle of the Bulge, Montgomery gave the impression that he had saved the day in the Ardennes, infuriating the Americans. On May 4, 1945, Montgomery accepted the surrender of all German forces in northwest Germany, Denmark, and the Netherlands.

Following the war, Montgomery commanded British occupation troops in Germany during May 1945–June 1946. In January 1946 he was made Viscount Montgomery of Alamein. From 1946 to 1948 he was chief of the Imperial General Staff. He next served as chairman of the West European commanders in chief (1948–1951) and was commander of North Atlantic Treaty Organization (NATO) forces in Europe and deputy supreme commander (1951–1958). He retired in September 1958. A prolific writer, he personally drafted his memoirs in 1958. Montgomery died at Isington Mill, Hampshire, on March 24, 1976.

A latter-date Marlborough or Wellington, or "the most overrated general of World War II," Bernard Montgomery remains the best-known British general and most controversial senior Allied commander of World War II. His strengths lay in his meticulous organizing and planning. He easily grasped the essence of problems and insisted on effective, simple solutions to them. As a field commander, he was less successful. Deeply concerned for the welfare of his men, he was loath to take undue risks with them.

COLIN F. BAXTER AND SPENCER C. TUCKER

See also
El Alamein, Second Battle of

References
Baxter, Colin F. *Field Marshal Bernard Law Montgomery, 1887–1976.* Westport, CT: Greenwood, 1999.
Chalfont, Alun. *Montgomery of Alamein.* New York: Atheneum, 1976.
Hamilton, Nigel. *Monty.* 3 vols. New York: McGraw-Hill, 1981–1986.
Lewin, Ronald. *Montgomery as a Military Commander.* New York: Stein and Day, 1972.
Montgomery, Bernard L. *The Memoirs of Field-Marshal the Viscount Montgomery of Alamein, KG.* London: Collins, 1958.

Morrison-Grady Plan (July 31, 1946)

British proposal of July 1946 that called for a federal arrangement for Palestine under a British trusteeship. In the summer of 1946 both Jewish underground violence and the illegal immigration of Jews from Europe (Aliya Bet) began to impact British Palestinian policy. Arthur Creech-Jones, the somewhat pro-Zionist colonial secretary, succeeded in convincing Foreign Secretary Ernest Bevin that both the U.S. government and the Jews would insist on some restructuring of the British mandate.

Following the rejection by the British government of the Anglo-American Committee of Inquiry's report, U.S. president Harry S. Truman announced the appointment of a cabinet committee of the secretaries of state, war, and the treasury to advise him on Palestine policy and implementation of his proposal for the admission of 100,000 Jewish displaced persons (DPs) to Palestine. This committee in turn delegated a working body of three representatives headed by Assistant Secretary of State Henry F. Grady. This subcommittee then began discussions with a parallel British group headed by Herbert Morrison, deputy prime minister and leader of the House of Commons. Their goal was to develop a joint Anglo-American plan for Palestine. In late June the American group flew to Britain, and during the next five weeks the two groups of experts met under the chairmanship of Morrison. There was considerable pressure on the conferees to come up with a solution, for violence in Palestine was on the upswing, capped by the Irgun Tsvai Leumi (National Military Organization) bombing of the King David Hotel on July 22, 1946, when 91 people died.

On July 31, 1946, the joint committee presented its findings to the British Parliament. The report, which basically adhered to the British position, began by expressing the hope that the governments of occupied Germany would create a situation favorable to the resettlement in Europe of a majority of those displaced by the war. Other nations were also encouraged to take numbers of refugees.

Regarding Palestine, the Morrison-Grady Plan (also known as the Cantonization Plan) proposed a federative solution whereby the mandate would be transformed into a trusteeship divided into four areas: an Arab province, a Jewish province, the Negev, and Jerusalem, with the latter two areas under continued British administration. Both the Arab and Jewish provinces would elect their own legislatures, and from these the high commissioner would select two separate executive branches. The high commissioner would retain full authority over defense, foreign relations, customs, the police, and the court system. He would also have veto power over all legislation for the first five years.

The proposal was most disadvantageous to the Jews, who would be left with only about 17 percent of the land area of Palestine, the smallest amount allocated to them under any partition plan to that point and less than 60 percent of that allocated to them under the Peel Commission partition plan. The Jewish province would include about two-thirds of the coastal plain, the Jezreel Valley, and much of eastern Galilee. The sole advantage for the Jews was the proposal to admit 100,000 refugees in the first year after the plan went into effect. Thereafter, the high commissioner would control additional immigration into Palestine on the basis of the ability of the land to sustain it. Implementation of the plan, however, rested on acceptance of it by both the Arabs and Jews.

The British government greeted the Morrison-Grady Plan with approval. The plan clearly suited British requirements, for with Egypt demanding a British departure, control of the Negev would permit Britain bases just to the north of the Suez Canal. London announced its intention to invite both Arab and Jewish representatives to a conference in London in September 1946 to settle the Palestinian issue. The Zionist Executive, meeting in Paris in July, rejected that invitation outright, stating that it would participate only if the Jews were promised an adequate share of the land of Palestine. Meanwhile, President Truman informed the British government that because of intense opposition to the Morrison-Grady Plan in the United States, the U.S. government would not endorse it.

The Palestinian Arabs also rejected participation in the conference as long as the mufti of Jerusalem was denied participation. Thus, when the conference opened in September 1946 it was limited to the British government and to Arab representatives from states beyond Palestine. The Arabs, however, were uncompromising. They insisted on a unitary state with its own popularly elected legislature but were prepared to guarantee freedom of religion. There would be 3 Jewish ministers out of 10, and Hebrew could be a second official language in districts where Jews were the absolute majority. But naturalization would be extended only to those people who had lived in Palestine for 10 years, thus excluding DPs.

In an early October 1946 letter to Prime Minister Clement Attlee, Truman expressed his opposition to the plan and his interest in the earliest possible admission of the 100,000 Jewish refugees to Palestine.

SPENCER C. TUCKER

See also
Anglo-American Committee of Inquiry; Irgun Tsvai Leumi; Peel Commission

References
Sachar, Howard M. *A History of Israel: From the Rise of Zionism to Our Time*. 3rd ed. New York: Knopf, 2007.

Shepherd, Naomi. *Ploughing Sand: British Rule in Palestine, 1917–1948.* New Brunswick, NJ: Rutgers University Press, 1999.

Morsi, Mohamed (1951–2019)

Egyptian president during June 30, 2012–July 3, 2013. Mohamed Morsi was born in modest circumstances (his father was a farmer) on August 8, 1951, in the village of El Adwah in the Sharqia Governorate in northern Egypt. Moving to Cairo in the late 1960s, Morsi earned a BA in engineering from Cairo University in 1975. After fulfilling his military service in the Egyptian Army from 1975 to 1976, he resumed his studies and in 1978 earned an MS in metallurgical engineering, also from Cairo University. Obtaining an Egyptian government scholarship, he received a doctorate in materials science from the University of Southern California in 1982. During 1982–1985 Morsi was an assistant professor at the California State University, Northridge. He also worked with the U.S. National Aviation and Space Administration to develop engines for the space shuttle program.

Returning to Egypt in 1985, Morsi was a professor and head of the Engineering Department at Zagazig University until 2010. He also served in the Egyptian parliament during 2000–2005. A member of the Muslim Brotherhood, he rose in its hierarchy and gained a reputation as a competent and effective organizer but stood for election as an independent because President Hosni Mubarak had banned the Islamist Brotherhood from running candidates for office.

In 2011, however, Morsi became the president of the Muslim Brotherhood's new party, the Freedom and Justice Party, organized to give the Muslim Brotherhood a more pluralist veneer in order to contest in the postrevolutionary elections. Although condemning the 9/11 attacks on the United States, he voiced views shared by many Egyptians that Washington used this as an excuse to invade both Afghanistan and Iraq, that there was no evidence that the 9/11 attackers were Muslims, and that aircraft alone could not have brought down the Twin Towers of the World Trade Center towers.

The so-called Arab Spring, with its demand for democratic reforms, swept Egypt in January 2011. Protestors staged massive street demonstrations in Cairo against the repressive Mubarak government. When Egyptian government forces attempted to quash the rebellion, a number of civilians were killed. Morsi was one of two dozen leaders of the Islamist Muslim Brotherhood arrested on January 28,

Egyptian president Mohamed Morsi photographed during a meeting with U.S. secretary of defense Leon Panetta, at the Presidential Palace in Cairo, Egypt, on July 31, 2012. Morsi was removed from power in a coup led by General Abdel Fattah el-Sisi on July 3, 2013. Morsi was sentenced to death by an Egyptian court. The sentence was later overturned but Morsi remains in prison awaiting a new trial. (Mark Wilson/Getty Images)

although he escaped from prison in Cairo in a mass breakout two days later.

Mubarak's grasp on power quickly diminished. With spreading violence and the Egyptian president repudiated by a large part of the population and eventually even its chief backer, the United States, Mubarak reluctantly resigned on February 11, 2011. The Egyptian military then took effective control, suspending the constitution and parliament, but also pledging that democratic elections would occur in the near future.

Parliamentary elections indeed occurred during November 28, 2011–January 11, 2012. Then on June 24, 2012, Morsi was elected president of Egypt with an announced 51.73 percent of the vote. He was the nation's first democratically elected leader. Shortly after his election, Morsi resigned the presidency of the Freedom and Justice Party. On August 12, in a major purge of the country's military leadership, however, Morsi called on Generals Mohamad Hussein Tantawi, head of the country's armed forces, and Sami Hafez Anan, the army chief of staff, to resign. Other key security officials were also purged.

Morsi also announced the annulment of the constitutional amendments passed by the Supreme Council of the Armed Forces after the fall of Mubarak that had restricted presidential powers. Opposition leaders charged Morsi was planning to restore a totalitarian regime. Then in late August 2012, Morsi announced the appointment of 21 advisers and aides that included 3 women and 2 Christians as well as a number of Islamists. Morsi also appointed new governors for Egypt's 27 regions. The appointment of Islamists to key government positions raised alarm bells among secularists who greatly feared a takeover of Egyptian affairs by the Muslim Brotherhood. Many secular and liberal parliament members walked out of the assembly in protest, plunging Egypt into another government crisis.

On November 22, Morsi issued a declaration supposedly protecting the Constituent Assembly drafting a new constitution for Egypt, which, however, immunized his actions from any legal challenge until a new constitution was ratified. It also required new trials for those in the Mubarak era who had been arrested and tried for having attacked demonstrators but had been acquitted. It also authorized Morsi to take any measures necessary to protect the revolution. Upon the issuance of this declaration and with Morsi enjoying the full support of the Islamic Brotherhood, most liberal and secular members of the constitutional Constituent Assembly withdrew in the belief that it would impose strict Islamic practices.

Massive demonstrations now occurred in late November in Egyptian cities, most notably in Cairo's Tahrir Square, site of the protests that led to the resignation of Mubarak. Morsi defended the new constitution and declared his actions to be legal, charging that his critics were "reactionaries." This prompted more mass protests, which continued into the summer of 2013, virtually paralyzing both the nation and its economy. The protesters demanded the declaration be revoked and the Constituent Assembly dissolved. Then on December 1 the Constituent Assembly presented Morsi with its constitutional draft, and he announced that a constitutional referendum would be held on December 15, 2012. The new constitution was duly approved by a 64 percent vote but with only a third of voters participating.

Supposed slurs by Morsi against Jews and Israel also raised concerns abroad. Continued fears of rule by the Muslim Brotherhood led on June 30, 2013, to protests erupting across Egypt, with the demonstrators calling on Morsi to resign. The Egyptian military presented Morsi with a 48-hour ultimatum to meet their demands and resolve political differences or face their intervention. With Morsi defiant, on July 3 he was removed from power by a military coup council consisting of Defense Minister Abdel Fattah el-Sisi, opposition leader Mohamed ElBaradei, the grand imam of Al Azhar Ahmed el-Tayeb, and Coptic pope Tawadros II. The Egyptian military then suspended the constitution and established a new administration led by Sisi. The Muslim Brotherhood protested the military coup, but the pro-Morsi protests were crushed in the so-called Rabaa Massacre of August. It brought the deaths of 638 people (595 of them civilians and 43 police officers), while at least 3,994 people were injured.

In January 2014 a new constitution received overwhelming popular approval (although only some 39 percent of voters participated). The military now dominated Egyptian affairs, and new elections in May 2014 saw Sisi chosen president. He took office on June 8, 2014.

Sisi's government declared the Muslim Brotherhood a terrorist organization and imprisoned scores of Morsi supporters. Morsi himself was brought to trial and sentenced to death in connection with the mass prison break in 2011. This sentence was, however, overturned in late 2016, and a new trial was ordered. Still awaiting this, Morsi remains in prison, having received a sentence of 20 years without parole on charges arising from the killing of protesters in December 2012, 40 years on charges of spying for Qatar, and a life sentence on charges of spying for the Palestinian Islamist group Hamas. Morsi died during trial in Cairo on June 17, 2019.

Spencer C. Tucker

See also

Arab Spring; Egypt; Egyptian Revolution of 2011; Mubarak, Hosni; Sisi, Abdel Fattah el-

References

Fahim, Kareem, and David D. Kirkpatrick. "Clashes Break Out after Morsi Seizes New Power in Egypt." *New York Times,* November 24, 2012.

Hendrix, Steve, and Ernesto Londoño. "Egypt's Morsi Makes Bid to Reinstate Islamist Parliament." *Washington Post,* July 8, 2012.

Kirkpatrick, David D. "Morsi's Slurs against Jews Stir Concern." *New York Times,* January 15, 2013.

Kirkpatrick, David D. "President Mohamed Morsi of Egypt Said to Prepare Martial Law Decree." *New York Times,* April 26, 2012.

Malsin, Jared, and Owen Bowcott. "Egypt's Former President Mohamed Morsi Sentenced to 20 Years in Prison." *The Guardian,* April 21, 2015.

Mosul, First Battle of (November 8–16, 2004)

Iraq War (2003–2011) battle fought in the city of Mosul. Located in northern Iraq some 250 miles northwest of Baghdad, Mosul is Iraq's second-largest city, with an estimated 2004 population of more than 1.8 million. The 2004 Battle of Mosul was fought during November 8–16, 2004, and involved the U.S. Army 1st Battalion, 24th Infantry Regiment; Iraqi Security Forces (Iraqi police, Iraqi Army, Iraqi National Guard, and Iraqi Border Patrol); and Kurdish Peshmerga against Iraqi insurgents (former Baath Party members, fundamentalist factions with ties to the Al Qaeda organization, and fighters from other extremist groups). The battle was brought on as much by political expediency as by the need to protect civilians from harassment by the insurgents. It ended in a clear-cut victory for coalition forces.

The Battle of Mosul occurred simultaneously with another furious battle between coalition forces and insurgents in Fallujah. The Second Battle of Fallujah (November 7–23, 2004) drew insurgents and foreign fighters in droves. The coalition responded to the insurgent attacks with overwhelming force, which included recalling Major General David Petraeus and the 101st Airborne Division to Fallujah. The 101st had been maintaining a peaceful occupation of the primarily Sunni Mosul for the preceding year. Coalition troops took little time to rout the insurgency, and the surviving insurgents fled Fallujah. A number of them then went to Mosul.

The 25th Infantry Division was deployed to Mosul in mid-October 2004 to replace the 101st Airborne. This was approximately the same time that displaced insurgents began arriving from Fallujah. The insurgents announced their arrival with an enormous wave of kidnappings and beheadings that left more than 200 of Mosul's residents dead in the streets for resisting the insurgents.

On November 8, 2004, Iraqi insurgents began to carry out coordinated attacks within Mosul. This same day the 1st Battalion, 24th Infantry Regiment, reported the first major engagement of what would become the Battle of Mosul near the Yarmuk traffic circle in the western part of the city. Soldiers of the regiment were pinned down by coordinated mortar fire from the north and were being pounded from the other three directions by rocket-propelled grenades (RPGs) and machine-gun fire in a daylong firefight.

The insurgents also used this opening day of the battle to overrun two Iraqi police stations. The insurgents then cleaned out the station armories, taking weapons and flak jackets. They also killed a dozen Iraqi policemen, but the Western media reported that the majority of the policemen had deserted their posts after reporting attacks by "hundreds" of insurgents against their stations. When the Americans retook the stations, they estimated that only 20–30 insurgents had taken each station.

On November 9, insurgents successfully attacked a forward operating base in Mosul, killing two American army officers. By November 10 Iraqi insurgents were openly taking to the streets in defiance of coalition forces, and by November 11 they had taken another Iraqi police station and destroyed two others. The time had now come for a coalition counteroffensive.

Members of the U.S. 24th Infantry Regiment were dispatched in an effort to crush the insurgents between two companies. The blow was aimed, again, at the strategically critical Yarmuk traffic circle. The 24th encountered fierce resistance as it pushed from house to house in close-quarter urban fighting. Yet with air support, the 24th was able to regain control of four of the five bridges over the Tigris River.

In the meantime, the insurgents sacked nine more police stations, destroying eight and occupying the ninth. On November 12 additional insurgent reinforcements arrived, and despite U.S. Air Force attacks, by November 13 insurgent forces held as much as 70 percent of Mosul. The insurgents became so secure in their military superiority that they began seeking out members of the Iraqi Security Forces to behead.

Coalition reinforcements began to arrive by November 13, including a battalion of the U.S. 25th Infantry Regiment, a group of Peshmerga fighters, and elements of the Iraqi Special Forces and National Guard. On November 16 U.S. forces retook the fifth insurgent-held bridge over the Tigris and began to sweep through all of Mosul except for the western sector. The Americans met little resistance, but the insurgents burned many of the police stations they had occupied. By November 16, the major fighting was over. The western sector of Mosul, however, would remain in insurgent hands until another coalition surge involving an influx of 12,000 troops arrived in December and January 2005. This was timed to secure Mosul for Iraq's first democratic elections in January.

The coalition official casualty report for the Battle of Mosul was 4 U.S. soldiers, 9 Peshmerga fighters, and 116 Iraqi Security Forces troops killed (as many as 5,000 are believed to have deserted). Total losses for insurgents are unknown, although 71 were confirmed killed. Also, 5 civilians were reported killed, as were 2 contractors (1 British and 1 Turkish). Precise casualty figures, including the number of wounded, remain unknown, and some estimates claim much higher death tolls for both the civilians and insurgents.

The importance of the battle could be measured by the fact that although there were mass desertions of Iraqi police and security forces targeted by insurgents, a sense of esprit de corps and pride among Iraqi forces developed, which had been sorely lacking before the event. In turn, the police and the security forces became better equipped to handle the insurgency, and the Iraqi citizenry gained trust in them, which led to the citizenry providing more information to coalition forces regarding insurgent activity. The terrorist tactics employed by the insurgents in the battle backfired. However, Mosul remained one of the most violent places in Iraq.

B. KEITH MURPHY

See also
Fallujah, Second Battle of; Iraq Insurgency; Petraeus, David Howell

References
Allawi, Ali A. *The Occupation of Iraq: Winning the War, Losing the Peace*. New Haven, CT: Yale University Press, 2007.

Tucker, Mike. *Among Warriors in Iraq: True Grit, Special Ops, and Raiding in Mosul and Fallujah*. Guilford, CT: Lyons, 2005.

Mosul, Second Battle of (October 17, 2016–July 9, 2017)

In Operation WE ARE COMING, NINEVEH, during October 17, 2016–July 9, 2017, Iraqi forces, consisting of troops of the Iraqi Army, Shiite and Sunni militias, Kurdish Peshmerga fighters, and international forces, to include extensive coalition air support (largely from the United States, the United Kingdom, and France) as well as support from Iran and Hezbollah (based in Lebanon), battled to retake the city of Mosul from the Islamic State of Iraq and Syria (ISIS). The October 2016 offensive followed unsuccessful Iraqi attempts in 2015 and earlier in 2016 to retake the city. The battle is held to be the largest attack on a city in several generations.

During June 10–14, 2014, as sectarian violence raged largely unchecked in Iraq, ISIS militants mounted a lightning offensive that overran and seized control of Mosul, Iraq's second-largest city with a mostly Sunni population of some 1.5 million. ISIS also secured much of former president Saddam Hussein's hometown of Tikrit. Hundreds of thousands of Iraqi civilians fled the area, prompting a major refugee crisis. There were widespread reports of Iraqi security forces simply throwing down their weapons, shedding their uniforms, and fleeing or even rallying to the Islamists.

In Mosul, ISIS seized vast caches of weaponry and military supplies. There were fears, unrealized, that Baghdad would also fall.

ISIS then made Mosul its capital in Iraq. ISIS leader Abu Bakr al-Baghdadi addressed his followers and announced from inside the city's historic 12th-century Grand al-Nuri Mosque the establishment of an Islamic caliphate.

ISIS retained its firm grip on the city until the fall of 2016. Following the recapture of Fallujah in what was the third battle for that city during May 23–June 28, 2016, liberating Mosul became the Iraqi government's declared next goal. Mosul was near to major Iraqi oil fields as well as an oil pipeline that serviced Turkey. Securing these fields could bolster Iraq's economy and would certainly adversely affect ISIS finances in a meaningful way, as ISIS has sold oil illegally to fund its operations. Securing the safety of Mosul Dam, Iraq's largest and briefly held by ISIS, was also a vital goal. Certainly the ISIS capture of Mosul in 2014 had been a major embarrassment for the Iraqi government, one that it was anxious to reverse.

Iraqi lieutenant general Abdul Amir Rashid Yarallah had command of Operation WE ARE COMING, NINEVEH, in what was the largest Iraqi military operation since the end of the Iraq War in 2011. Coalition forces numbered as many as 108,000 men. In preparation for the offensive, U.S. forces in the country were increased in July 2016 to 4,647 personnel, although the vast majority of these remained in a training role rather than directly supporting the operation.

Haqqi Esmaeil Owaid (aka Abu Ahmed) was governor of Mosul, and Ahmad Khalaf al-Jabouri was military commander of Mosul. ISIS fighters defending Mosul numbered only 8,000–12,000 men, however, with ISIS air support limited to a few drones.

Before the offensive began, Iraqi and coalition forces endeavored to seal off Mosul in the Nineveh Governorate, preventing ISIS resupply and support. U.S. and British drones and manned aircraft struck identified ISIS targets in and around the city, including ammunition stockpiles, rocket launchers, artillery pieces, and mortar positions. Three days before the beginning of the ground offensive, leaflets dropped on the city called on noncombatants to try to leave and young males to rise up against ISIS.

Iraqi prime minister Haider al-Abadi announced the start of the offensive on October 16, 2016, although the first ground assaults of towns surrounding the city did not occur until the next day. The assaulting forces first focused on the eastern districts of the city before moving against the narrow streets of the Old City in the west.

On October 21, dozens of ISIS fighters attacked Kirkuk, targeting four police stations and Kurdish security offices in an apparent effort to divert Iraqi forces from the effort to retake Mosul, 109 miles to the northwest. ISIS militants also struck a government building in Dibis, a town some 25 miles northwest of Kirkuk.

During October 21–22, ISIS executed 284 men and boys as coalition forces closed in on Mosul. Those killed had reportedly been used as human shields in southern parts of the city. ISIS militants used a bulldozer to dump the corpses in a mass grave at the scene of the executions. ISIS fighters had reportedly taken more than 500 families from villages around Mosul as human shields.

With Mosul finally largely isolated, early on November 1, Iraqi Special Operations Forces entered the eastern part of the city. Heavy fighting ensued. Well aware of the oft-stated Iraqi determination to retake Mosul, ISIS fighters had made extensive preparations. The Iraqi Army advance was slowed by elaborate defenses, booby traps, tunnels that connected ISIS positions and also permitted escape, and the goal of trying to minimize civilian casualties. On January 24, 2017, the Iraqi government claimed that eastern Mosul had been liberated. Iraqi troops began their offensive to recapture western Mosul on February 19, 2017.

On June 29, 2017, al-Abadi announced that Iraqi forces had recaptured the Al Nuri Grand Mosque in Mosul, but only rubble remained, as the iconic structure as it had been blown up by ISIS on June 20 after having remained unscathed since the 12th century.

The campaign lasted far longer than expected and took a far heavier toll than predicted. After eight and a half months of combat, al-Abadi traveled to Mosul on July 9 and declared victory, although there was still some fighting in a small area in the city suburbs. Initially the Iraqi government set casualties in the battle at as many as 11,000 ISIS fighters killed, along with some 1,000 Iraqi soldiers killed and 6,100 wounded. Two U.S. military personnel were also killed, as were 3 Iranians. Civilian casualties were originally set at 1,266 killed. In mid-December, however, these figures were revised sharply upward, based on morgue count, to 9,606 civilians killed, with many more still buried in the rubble. Nearly a third of the deaths were attributed to air strikes by the U.S.-led coalition or shelling by Iraqi forces, another third died in ISIS's final frenzy of violence. The remainder of the dead could have been killed from actions by either side.

The physical destruction was also immense. At least six of western Mosul's 44 districts had been largely leveled, with air strikes, fierce house-to-house combat, and attacks by suicide bombers having obliterated crucial infrastructure such as roads, bridges, the waterworks, and the electricity net. Homes, schools, and hospitals were destroyed. United Nations officials estimated that $1 billion and more than a year would be required for the restoration of only basic services such as water, sewage, electricity, schools, and medical facilities. Long-term rebuilding would be much more costly and far longer. Certainly the level of destruction severely complicated the return of the Mosul residents who had fled the fighting, as more than 900,000 former residents had been displaced and were living with other family members or in refugee camps. For the vast majority a lengthy stay in a refugee camp lay ahead, and were this poorly managed, it could well feed radical sentiment.

Spencer C. Tucker

See also
Abadi, Haider al-; Baghdadi, Abu Bakr al-; Hezbollah; Iraq; Islamic State of Iraq and Syria; Peshmerga

References
Arango, Tim. "Tal Afar, West of Mosul, Becomes Center of Battle for Influence in Iraq." *New York Times,* October 29, 2016.

George, Susannah. "IS Attack Underscores Fragility of Iraqi Security Forces." *Washington Post,* July 6, 2017.

Hennessy-Fiske, Molly. "New Phase Begins in Offensive to Drive Islamic State Out of Key City of Mosul." *Los Angeles Times,* December 29, 2016.

Kesling, Ben. "ISIS Herds Civilians to Mosul as Human Shields." *Wall Street Journal,* October 28, 2016.

King, Laura. "Iraqi Forces Launch Assault on Mosul." *Los Angeles Times,* November 1, 2016.

Michaels, Jim. "U.S. Aircraft to Block ISIL Militants Fleeing Mosul in Iraq." *USA Today,* October 31, 2016.

Specia, Megan, and Rik Gladstone. "Iraq Recaptures Mosque in Mosul, but Only Rubble Remains." *New York Times,* June 30, 2017.

"Mother of All Battles"

Expression employed by Iraqi president Saddam Hussein to describe the impending 1991 Persian Gulf War. As early as September 1990, just weeks after he sent his forces into Kuwait, Hussein began preparing his people for potential war with the United States, exhorting them that "this battle will become the mother of all battles." On January 17, 1991, as U.S. bombers were about to begin the air campaign against Iraq, Hussein calmly informed his people that the "mother of all battles has begun."

In resorting to such terminology, Hussein was doing more than more posturing; he was appealing to Islamic archetypes in hopes of rallying his people to fight an endless war against an overwhelming enemy. The Arabic expression *umm al-ma'arik* (mother of all battles) is a metaphoric reference to the Battle of al-Qadisiyya (in modern-day Iraq) during November 16–19, 636, in which Islamic Arabs united to win their first decisive battle against the Sassanid Persian army. The phrase figuratively means "major" or "best." It is important to note that the Quran is also known as "the mother [metaphorically, origin] of all books (*umm al-Kitab*)."

Thus, Hussein's rallying cry called up powerful images from both religious and cultural history for the Iraqis. The term was quickly spread by the Iraqi government as a catch phrase, a grand propaganda scheme, which renamed the governmental-run radio station "The Mother of All Battles Radio."

After the rapid disintegration of the Iraqi military in February 1991, the United States was quick to turn the Iraqi ideological archetype into a symbol that served to reinforce the image of the overwhelming military might of the U.S.-led military coalition. In February 1991, Secretary of Defense Dick Cheney was quoted as saying that "it looks like what's happened is that the mother of all battles has turned into the mother of all retreats." The catch phrase entered American popular culture as well. U.S. general H. Norman Schwarzkopf's press conferences were known as "the mother of all press conferences," a 1991 war game based on the Persian Gulf War was titled "The Mother of All Battles," and in 2003 a three-quarter-ton bomb tested for the U.S. Air Force was nicknamed the "Mother of All Bombs," just in time for the Anglo-American–led war against Iraq.

Yet for Iraqis, this phrase continues to have meaning. In 2001 before his capture, Hussein unveiled his "Mother of All Battles" Mosque just outside Baghdad, which featured a Quran supposedly written with Hussein's own blood. *Umm al-ma'arik* is also said to be a battle cry among the Iraqi insurgents who continued to oppose the American forces in Iraq.

In July 2018 after the Donald Trump administration withdrew from the Iran Nuclear Deal and relations between Washington and Tehran plummeted, Iranian president Hassan Rouhani used a phrase similar to "Mother of all Battles," warning that a U.S. war of aggression against his country would be "the mother of all wars."

B. Keith Murphy

See also
Hussein, Saddam; Iraq; Iraq War; Persian Gulf War, Overview; Schwarzkopf, H. Norman, Jr.

References
Bengio, Ofra. *Saddam's Word: Political Discourse in Iraq.* New York: Oxford University Press, 1998.
Bin, Alberto, Richard Hill, and Archer Jones. *Desert Storm: A Forgotten War.* Westport, CT: Praeger, 1998.
Kent, Zachary. *The Persian Gulf War: "The Mother of All Battles."* Berkeley Heights, NJ: Enslow Publishers, 2000.
Williams, Paul L. *Al Qaeda: Brotherhood of Terror.* Upper Saddle River, NJ: Alpha (Pearson), 2002.

Moudros, Armistice of (October 30, 1918)

Armistice signed by the Ottoman Empire and the Allies on October 30, 1918, that ended fighting in the Middle Eastern theater at the end of World War I. In September 1918 the Bulgarian army in Macedonia collapsed, opening the way for an Allied advance on Istanbul (Constantinople), the Dardanelles, and the Bosporus. In Palestine, British forces had broken through Ottoman lines and quickly advanced toward Aleppo. With impending military disaster, poor army morale, and rising domestic discontent, the Ottoman government opted to leave the war. An Ottoman delegation, led by Minister of Marine Affairs Rauf Bey, traveled to Moudros on the Greek island of Lemnos to meet the Allied delegation headed by British admiral Somerset Arthur Gough-Calthorpe aboard the British battleship *Agamemnon*.

According to the armistice terms that ended the fighting, the remaining Ottoman garrisons outside Anatolia would surrender, and the Allies could occupy the forts controlling the straits and any territory in case of a security threat. The agreement also called for the Ottoman Army to demobilize, and Allied forces could use Ottoman ports, railways, and other strategic points as needed. Ottoman forces in the Caucasus also had to withdraw to the empire's prewar borders.

On August 10, 1920, Allied and Ottoman delegates signed the Treaty of Sèvres, which partitioned much of the Ottoman Empire among Greece, Italy, Britain, France, and Armenia and established an international zone around Istanbul and the straits. Turkish nationalists, led by former Ottoman Army brigadier general Mustafa Kemal (Ataturk), rejected the treaty and, after more than two years of fighting, established the Republic of Turkey, consisting of Turkish Anatolia and territory around Istanbul in Europe. On July 24, 1923, after eight months of negotiations, Turkey and the former Allies signed the Treaty of Lausanne, the only successful revision of the post–World War I treaties.

Robert B. Kane

See also
Ataturk, Mustafa Kemal; Lausanne, Second Treaty of; Ottoman Empire; Sèvres, Treaty of

References
Finkel, Caroline. *Osman's Dream The Story of the Ottoman Empire 1300–1923*. New York: Basic Books, 2005.
Shaw, Stanford J., and Ezul Kural Shaw. *Reform, Reaction and Republic: The Rise of Modern Turley, 1808–1975*, Vol. 2, *History of the Ottoman Empire and Modern Turkey*. Cambridge: Cambridge University Press, 1977.
Zuercher, Erik. *Turkey: A Modern History*. London: I. B. Tauris, 1994.

Mount Lebanon Civil War (1860)

In 1860, Lebanon witnessed a bloody conflict between the Druzes and the Maronite Christians. Known as the Mount Lebanon Civil War and the 1860 Civil War in Lebanon, the conflict stemmed from a long history of tensions between the Muslim and Christian populations of Mount Lebanon. Although this discord simmered under Ibrahim Pasha's rule in the early 19th century, it intensified under the governorship of Umar Pasha, who was appointed to Mount Lebanon in 1842. Foreign powers played an important role in this process, as they supported different groups, with France influencing Maronites and Britain supplying guns to the Druzes.

The events leading to the massacres began in 1858 when Maronite peasants of the Kasrawan region rebelled against heavy taxes and demanded abolition of feudal practices. As the violence spread, both sides established armed groups to protect themselves. On May 22, 1860, a minor incident near the entrance to Beirut provoked widespread clashes between the Druzes and Maronites, claiming several dozen lives. Events escalated very quickly between both sides, and the bloody attacks spread toward other areas of Mount Lebanon. By July, the violence had already reached Damascus in Syria.

The conflict led to the deaths of as many as 20,000 Christians, with some 380 Christian villages and 560 churches destroyed. The Druzes and Muslims also suffered heavy losses. This violence was not restricted to Lebanon, as Christians, including the American and Dutch consuls, were also slain in Syria.

The Ottoman government dispatched Foreign Minister Fuad Pasha to pacify the region, which he was able to accomplish by the fall of 1860. This, however, brought charges that the Ottomans were aiding the Islamists either directly or by disarming the Christians. Emperor Napoleon III, seeking to buttress French authority as protector of Christians in the Ottoman Empire, which had been established by treaty in 1523, prevailed on Istanbul to permit the distpatch to Lebanon of French forces. On August 3, 1860, the Porte agreed to accept 12,000 European troops to help keep order and protect the Druzes in Levanon. On September 5, the governments of Austria, Great Britain, France, Prussia, and Russia reached agreement on a European intervention force, with France to furnish half of that number.

In what has been called one of the first international humanitarian missions, on August 16, 1860, General Beaufort d'Hautpoul led the French expeditionary force ashore at Beirut. D'Hautpoul had experience in the region, as in the 1840s he had been chief of staff for Ibrahim Pasha in the Egyptian campaigns in southern Syria. Although Fuad Pasha had already restored calm, French forces remained in Syria longer than the agreed upon time of six months and did not depart until June 1861.

One consequence of the French presence was the conclusion of the Beyoglu Protocol of June 9, 1861, whereby the Porte recognized the autonomy of the Mount Lebanon Mutasarrifate from Ottoman Syria, with the sultan naming Dawd Pasha, an Armenian Christian, as its *mutassarif* (governor), to be assisted by the Administrative Council. This arrangement remained in effect until after World War I and the creation of Greater Lebanon in September 1920.

RAMI Y. SIKLAWI AND SPENCER C. TUCKER

See also
Lebanon

References
Boueiz-Kanaan, Claude. *Lebanon 1860–1960: A Century of Myth and Politics*. London: Saqi Books, 2005.
Farah, Caesar E. *The Politics of Interventionism in Ottoman Lebanon, 1830–1861*. London: I. B. Tauris, 2000.
Hitti, Philip K. *The Origins of the Druze People and Religion*. London: Saqi Books, 2007.

Muawiyah I (602–680)

First caliph of the Umayyad dynasty. Born in Mecca in Abria in 602, Abu Abd al-Rahman Muawiyah Ibn Abi Sufyan was a senior member of the Umayyad clan, long the rival of the Hashemite clan to which the fourth and final Rashidun "Rightly Guided" caliph Ali belonged. Rivalry between the Banu Umayyah and the Banu Hashim had existed long before the coming of Islam, despite the fact that both formed part of Prophet Muhammad's own tribe of the Quraysh. Muawiyah also commanded the Muslim army in Syria, the most prosperous of the Arab or Semitic provinces of the caliphal empire.

Although Ali, Prophet Muhammad's cousin, had been proclaimed caliph in the hope that he could heal rifts that were threatening the unity of the Muslim community, these problems became worse. Many provincial governors had been promoted by his predecessor, Caliph Uthman, and Ali now demanded that several step down. They included several members of the Banu Umayyah such as Muawiyah. After political and military clashes that highlighted Ali's ineffectiveness as a ruler, Muawiyah led his Syrian-based forces in open rebellion.

Following the inconclusive Battle of Siffin in 657, a compromise enabled Ali to remain caliph. He continued in that position until a puritanical zealot assassinated him in 661. This crime united the majority of Muslims for the first time in years, and Muawiyah was declared the new caliph. Muawiyah I ruled until 680. He pardoned those who had previously fought against him and tried where possible to rule by consensus. In fact, he became one of the most effective rulers in the early medieval period. The Umayyad caliphal dynasty that he founded endured for more than a century and consolidated Islamic power from the Atlantic Ocean to India.

Muawiyah also changed the caliphate from an almost republican or patriarchal state into an almost constitutional monarchy, with the "constitution" being the Quran and Islamic law. He similarly set about imposing the military discipline that had characterized his governorship of Syria, with field armies now normally commanded by members of the ruling Umayyad family.

Muawiyah made no special claim to religious insight and became renowned for his self-control and the careful consideration he gave before taking any important action, reputedly writing a book (now lost) on the subject. Furthermore, he sometimes placed men of remarkably humble origin in the highest positions of civil and military responsibility if they had proved themselves suited to the task.

Umayyad power rested on the army, in which Syrian units formed elites known as the *ahl al-sham,* or "People of Syria." Recruits came not only from Muslim tribes that had conquered Syria a generation earlier but also Syrian Arab tribes descended from Byzantine frontier forces and even local Christian Arab tribes. Furthermore, Muawiyah had a retinue of 3,000 non-Arab *mawali* (clients) attached to an Arab tribe. Also by moving the capital of the now vast caliphal empire from Arabia to Damascus in Syria, he shifted its power center to one of the most ancient, prosperous, and sophisticated cities in the Middle East. This decision would have profound cultural and military impact on the Islamic world for centuries. Muawiya died in Damascus on April 29 or May 1, 680.

David Nicolle

See also
Ali ibn Abi Talib; Siffin, Battle of; Umayyad Caliphate

References
Bewley, Aisha. *Mu'awiya: Restorer of the Muslim Faith.* London: Dar Al Taqwa, 2002.
Humphreys, Stephen. *Mu'awiya ibn Abi Sufyan: From Arabia to Empire.* Oxford: Onerworld, 2006.
Lammens, Henri. *Etudes sur le règne du Calife Omaijade Mo'awiya Ier.* Paris: Geuthner, 1908.

Mubarak, Hosni (1928–)

Egyptian Air Force marshal and president of Egypt (1981–2011). Muhammad Hosni Said Mubarak was born on May 4, 1928, in Kafr al-Musayliha in the Nile River delta, where his father was an inspector in the Ministry of Justice. Mubarak graduated from the Egyptian Military Academy in 1949 and the Egyptian Air Force Academy in 1950. He was briefly a fighter pilot, then taught at the Air Force Academy during 1952–1959. He continued his military training at the Soviet General Staff Academy in Moscow during 1964–1965, followed by advanced flight training at the Soviet air base at Frunze Bishkek in what was then Soviet Kyrgyzstan.

Mubarak advanced steadily in rank and position, from pilot to instructor to squadron leader and then to base commander. He was commandant of the Egyptian Air Force Academy (1967–1969), chief of staff of the Egyptian Air Force (1969–1972), and deputy minister of war (1972–1975). Mubarak received considerable credit for the early success of the Egyptian Air Force in the October 1973 Yom Kippur War (Ramadan War) and was promoted to air marshal in 1974.

In April 1975 Egyptian president Anwar Sadat appointed Mubarak vice president. On October 6, 1981, Sadat was assassinated by fundamentalist Muslim army officers, and Mubarak, who was injured—although not seriously—in the attack, succeeded Sadat as president. Mubarak was subsequently elected to four six-year presidential terms in 1987, 1993, 1999, and 2005. Only in the 2005 elections were other candidates allowed to run, and they were severely hampered by election rules.

As president, Mubarak mediated the dispute over Western (Spanish) Sahara and played a role in the bilateral

Egyptian president Hosni Mubarak arriving in the United States at Andrews Air Force Base, Maryland, on January 27, 1983. Mubarak held power in Egypt from 1981 to 2011 when massive protest demonstrations brought his resignation. (U.S. Department of Defense)

agreement between Israel and the Palestine Liberation Organization (PLO) in 1993 that emerged from the Oslo Accords. Although Mubarak supported Egypt's 1979 peace treaty with Israel, he was able to improve Egyptian relations with other Arab countries that had been strained by the peace accord. In 1989 Egypt was readmitted to the Arab League after having being expelled for making peace with the Israelis. The league headquarters, originally in Cairo and then moved, was also relocated to the Egyptian capital.

Mubarak played a key role in the 1991 Persian Gulf War. He supported the United Nations sanctions against Iraq for its August 1990 invasion and occupation of Kuwait. When the sanctions did not cause Iraq to withdraw, Mubarak led Arab League opposition to Iraq. Based largely on the decision of Saudi Arabia to allow the U.S.-led international military coalition to use that nation as a staging area, Mubarak contributed some 33,600 Egyptian troops, the fourth-largest commitment of coalition manpower, and Egyptian infantry were among the first coalition soldiers to enter Kuwait.

Mubarak certainly had no use for Iraqi president Saddam Hussein, whom he viewed as a threat and a potential source of regional destabilization, but he was also attracted to the Kuwaiti cause by Western incentives to join the fight, including pledges of significant economic assistance and debt forgiveness. After the war, Mubarak continued to support sanctions against Iraq to force compliance with UN mandates, including the disarmament and weapons of mass destruction (WMD). Mubarak opposed the 2003 U.S.-led invasion of Iraq, however.

Mubarak used the enormous power given the presidency under Egypt's 1971 constitution to continue some economic reform. Little progress was made in democratization, however, and Mubarak was overthrown by a popular revolution in the so-called Arab Spring of 2011, resigning after 18 days of violent demonstrations on February 11. Arrested and imprisoned, he was tried on corruption charges and sentenced to life in prison, after which he suffered a series of health crises. In January 2013, Egypt's Court of Cassation overturned Mubarak's sentence and ordered him retired. In May 2015, Mubarak and his sons were convicted of corruption and sentenced to prison. In October 2015, Mubarak's sons were freed. Mubarak, however, remained confined in a military hospital. On March 2, 2017, he was acquitted by an Egyptian appeals court and was released from custody on March 24.

RICHARD M. EDWARDS, PAUL G. PIERPAOLI JR.,
AND SHERIFA ZUHUR

See also
Arab League; Arab Spring; Egypt; Hussein, Saddam; Persian Gulf War, Overview; Sadat, Anwar; Yom Kippur War

References
Amin, Galal A. *Egypt in the Era of Hosni Mubarak, 1981–2011.* Cairo, Egypt: American University in Cairo Press, 2011.
Cox, Viki. *Hosni Mubarak.* Philadelphia: Chelsea House, 2002.
McDermott, Anthony. *Egypt from Nasser to Mubarak: A Flawed Revolution.* London: Routledge and Kegan Paul, 1998.
Tripp, Charles, and Roger Owen. *Egypt under Mubarak.* London: Routledge, 1990.

Müezzinzade Ali Pasha (?–1571)

Ottoman military official and grand admiral. Müezzinzade Ali Pasha's birth date is unknown but, as his nickname indicates, he was the son of a prayer caller (muezzin). He eventually became a favorite of Sultan Selim II, married one of his daughters, and enjoyed a successful career at the court. From 1563 to 1566, he was the Ottoman governor of Egypt. In September 1568 he undertook a reconnaissance raid on Cyprus, and in

1570 he supervised the Ottoman expedition to Cyprus. Commanding as many as 360 vessels, he prevented Christian relief fleets from reinforcing the besieged defenders of the island.

When the Holy League alliance of European states was proclaimed in 1571, Müezzinzade Ali Pasha served as the grand admiral of the Ottoman naval forces. He raided Crete in June, when he failed to capture Irakleio and Turluru but pillaged the islands of Kythira, Zakynthos, and Kefallonia before reaching Corfu. He attacked the Venetian garrison at Sopot, capturing it with heavy losses.

As the opposing navies gathered near southern Greece, the Ottomans held a war council on October 4 to discuss strategy. Knowing that the Ottoman Navy was undermanned and fatigued from the Cyprus campaign, Pertev Pasha, commander in chief of the 1571 campaign, and Uluç Ali Pasha, governor general of Algiers, urged that the Ottomans remain on the defensive inside the Gulf of Lepanto. However, Müezzinzade Ali Pasha overruled them and ordered his fleet of 205 galleys and up to 68 galliots (small galleys) to attack the Christian fleet of some 219 galleys and 6 galeasses commanded by Don Juan of Austria, half brother of King Philip II of Spain. During the ensuing Battle of Lepanto (October 7, 1571), a fierce melee developed in the center, where the two flagships, Don Juan's *Real* and Müezzinzade Ali Pasha's *Sultana,* clashed; although Müezzinzade Ali Pasha's men managed to board the *Real,* they were unable to overcome stiff resistance, and Müezzinzade Ali Pasha was killed in the action. Reportedly, he died at the hands of a Macedonian in the Venetian service who shot him in the head with a musket. As the admiral fell to the deck, he was beheaded by a zealous Spanish soldier, and his head was then displayed on a pike, which demoralized the Ottoman crews and contributed to the Ottoman defeat in this decisive battle.

ALEXANDER MIKABERIDZE

See also
Cezayirli Gazi Hasan Pasha; Venetian-Ottoman Wars

References
Bicheno, Hugh. *Crescent and Cross: The Battle of Lepanto, 1571.* London: Cassell, 2003.
Capponi, Niccolò. *Victory of the West: The Story of the Battle of Lepanto.* London: Macmillan, 2006.

Mughal-Safavid Wars (1622–1623 and 1648–1653)

A series of conflicts between the Safavid and Mughal Empires fought over possession of the strategic city-fortress of Kandahar in Afghanistan. In 1595 two Safavid princes defected to the Mughal court, surrendering the fortress to Emperor Akbar (1542–1605). In 1622 after consolidating his authority at home, Safavid Empire shah Abbas organized a major expedition to reclaim Kandahar.

Following a monthlong siege, the Mughal garrison surrendered. Mughal emperor Jahangir (1569–1627) initially planned to send a punitive expedition and charged his son Khurram (the future Shah Jahan) with leading it, but the expedition never materialized, since Jahangir soon fell seriously ill and died. The Mughal court then became embroiled in a bitter power struggle during the next few years.

Once Shah Jahan secured his authority, he turned his attention to Kandahar. The moment seemed opportune, since the death of Shah Abbas in 1629 had caused domestic instability in Persia. In 1638 as the Mughals made preparations for the campaign against Kandahar, Ali Mardan Khan, a Safavid commander of Kandahar who quarreled with Shah Safi (r. 1629–1642), defected to the Mughal side and surrendered the fortress to Shah Jahan.

A decade passed before the Safavids were able to turn their attention to Kandahar. Finally, in 1648 Shah Abbas II (r. 1642–1666) launched an expedition and, after a two-month siege, captured the fortress. The following year the Mughals counterattacked under the leadership of young Aurangzeb, the son of Shah Jahan, and laid siege to the fortress but could not take it before the onset of winter. The Mughals returned in late 1652 and once more in 1653 but failed to take the fortress on both occasions owing to bad weather and logistical difficulties as well as the tenacious defense by the Safavid garrison.

ALEXANDER MIKABERIDZE

See also
Abbas I the Great

References
Gommans, Jos J. *Mughal Warfare: Indian Frontiers and High Roads to Empire, 1500–1700.* London: Routledge, 2002.
Newman, Andrew. *Safavid Iran: Rebirth of a Persian Empire.* New York: I. B. Tauris, 2006.
Richards, John F. *The Mughal Empire.* Cambridge: Cambridge University Press, 1993.
Ward, Steven R. *Immortal: A Military History of Iran and Its Armed Forces.* Washington, DC: Georgetown University Press, 2009.

Muhammad, Campaigns of the Prophet (622–632)

Prophet Muhammad's military career began shortly after he moved to Medina with his followers in 622. Once settled, the prophet started to organize raids, an age-old Arab custom, against his Meccan enemies. The purpose behind these was to strategically and economically weaken Mecca and to secure much-needed provisions and booty for Medina.

The first clash occurred at Nakhla during the sacred month of Rajab in 624. A band of Muslims attacked a small Meccan caravan in which one Meccan was killed. There was outrage in Mecca at this attack during the holy month. However, unease of Muslims in Medina was alleviated when a revelation affirmed that while breaking the truce of the holy months was a grave matter, far graver was opposition to the true faith.

That same year Muhammad set out with a force of 317 men to attack a large Meccan caravan returning from Syria. However, the caravan, under the skillful leadership of Abu Sufyan, managed to avoid the would-be attackers. Instead, the Muslims found a force of 1,000 Meccans blocking their path at the wells of Badr. In the ensuing battle, the discipline and high morale of the Muslims and their control of the water source there won the day. Seventy Meccans lost their lives, and about the same number were taken prisoner.

In 625 Abu Sufyan led a punitive expedition against Medina. A Muslim force of 700 men met the Meccans and their allies numbering 3,000 at the hill of Uhud. Initially, the Muslims had the upper hand in the fight; however, the battle was lost when the Meccan cavalry, led by Khalid ibn al-Walid, attacked the Muslims from the rear. The prophet and his companions were driven onto the hill, but the Meccans failed to follow up their attack and retired from the field.

In 627, Mecca launched its last offensive against Muhammad. A force of 10,000 Meccans and allied Bedouins moved against Medina. Muhammad ordered a trench dug along the undefended northern section of the city. The Meccans set up an ineffective blockade of the city for several weeks but abandoned the siege after a few halfhearted skirmishes along the trench failed to breach its defenses.

In 628 Muhammad concluded a truce with Mecca at Hudaybiya. This treaty freed him up to conquer the fertile oasis of Khaybar. This conquest was carried out by a force of 1,600 men who managed to defeat the defenders piecemeal by isolating them in their fortresses and preventing them from assisting one another. In 630 Muhammad conquered Mecca after the truce of Hudaybiya was broken by tribes allied to Mecca. Muhammad's army of 10,000 men entered the city from four directions. Muhammad granted the populace of Mecca general amnesty, which resulted in a peaceful and bloodless conquest.

Shortly after conquering Mecca, Muhammad met and defeated a coalition of Bedouin tribes at the Battle of Hunayn. He also led 30,000 men to the borders of Syria in a show of force to the Bedouin tribes of the region. The prophet died in 632 while preparing another expedition against the Byzantine frontier.

ADAM ALI

See also

Badr, Battle of; Khalid ibn al-Walid; Khandaq, Battle of the; Ridda Wars

References

Gabrielli, Francesco. *Muhammad and the Conquests of Islam.* Trans. Virginia Luling and Rosamund Linell. London: World University Library, 1968.

Hodgson, Marshall G. S. *The Venture of Islam: Conscience and History in a World Civilization.* Chicago: University of Chicago Press, 1977.

Ibn Hisham, Abd al-Malik. *The Life of Muhammad: A Translation of Ishaq's Sirat Rasūl Allah, with Introd. and Notes by A. Guillaume.* Lahore: Oxford University Press, 1967.

Muhammad, Prophet of Islam (ca. 569–632)

The prophet of Islam who established the first community of Muslims in the Arabian Peninsula. Muhammad ibn Abdullah ibn Abd al-Mutallib, born in either 569 or 570 CE and always referred to by Muslims as Prophet Muhammad, was at once a military, political, and religious leader who effectively united the disparate tribes of the region into a single empire. As a prophet of Allah (God), he received a series of orally transmitted revelations that were eventually transcribed as the Quran (the Quran is therefore referred to as the Message, and he as the Messenger). Muslims refer to Muhammad as the Seal of Prophecy, which means that he, following the earlier prophets of the Bible and Jesus, was the last and final prophet. Unlike Jesus, Prophet Muhammad is not considered to be divine, but he is revered by Muslims as the Beautiful Model because his *sunna*, or way, provided the example for future generations of Muslims.

Muhammad was born into a branch of an important clan, the Banu Hashim of the Quraysh tribe, in Mecca, located in the western Arabian Peninsula area of the Hejaz. Prior to Muhammad's birth, his father died. Thus, Muhammad was, in the status of that era, an orphan. As an infant, he was sent to a wet nurse, Halima, a tribal woman. While in her care there were signs and portents of his future greatness.

Muhammad's mother died when he was six, and his grandfather died just two years later. Muhammad then passed under the guardianship of his uncle, Abi Talib, who was an influential merchant. Muhammad soon began accompanying his uncle on trading journeys during the pilgrimage season. On one journey to Bosra, Syria, he was greeted by a monk named Buhaira, who hailed Muhammad as a future prophet.

As an adult, Muhammad entered the employ of Khadija, a wealthy 40-year-old widow, managing her caravans and earning a reputation for honesty such that he was known as al-Amin (the faithful one). Khadija subsequently proposed to him. The two married in 595, and Muhammad remained devoted to her until her death in 619. The number of children born to the marriage remains in dispute. The pair had four daughters—Zaynab, Ruqayya, Umm Kulthum, and Fatima—and one or two sons who died. Only Fatima was still living after her father's death. Muhammad married other women after Khadija's death, and he had a son by one of these wives who also died before age 2.

According to Muslim tradition, Muhammad received his first revelation in the year 610 while fasting in the cave of Hira, near Mecca, during the month of Ramadan. It was the voice of the archangel Gabriel, who commanded him to recite verses of scripture that he spoke to Muhammad. At first Muhammad did not know how to respond, but Khadija regarded this as proof of a new revelation and thus became the first formal convert to Islam. For the remainder of his life, Muhammad continued to receive revelations.

Within a few years of his initial revelations, Muhammad began to preach to any who would listen to his message about the One God, creator and judge of the world. As the Meccans then worshipped a pantheon of gods and goddesses, they were increasingly hostile toward him.

As Muhammad's group of followers grew, they came to be seen as a threat by the leadership of Mecca, especially as some of the early converts to Islam came from the disaffected and disadvantaged segments of society. Most importantly, the new set of beliefs implicitly challenged the Meccans' and the Quraysh tribe's guardianship over the Kaaba, the holy site dedicated to the gods and goddesses of the area that hosted an annual pilgrimage. The leading merchants of Mecca attempted to persuade Muhammad to cease his preaching. When he refused, the city leadership persecuted Muhammad's followers, and many fled the city. One group of his followers immigrated to Abyssinia. In 619 Muhammad endured the loss of both Khadija and Abi Talib, while the mistreatment of his followers increased.

The following year Muhammad undertook two miraculous journeys with the archangel Gabriel. The first, called the Isra, took Muhammad from Mecca to Jerusalem, where he ascended to the site of today's Dome of the Rock in the al-Aqsa Compound in Jerusalem. The second, called the Miraj, included a visit to Heaven and Hell. During the Miraj, Muhammad also spoke with earlier monotheistic prophets, including Abraham, Moses, and Jesus, and saw Allah, "the Soul of Souls, the Face of Him who made the universe." Muhammad asked Allah for forgiveness for his *ummah*, the Muslim community, and Allah accepted his intercession (*shafa'*). Allah assigned Muhammad with the task of 50 daily prayers for Muslims, and Moses advised Muhammad to return to Allah and request the number of prayers be reduced (to 5), which he did. The Isra and Miraj were accomplished in a single night. Scholars have presented the travels as both a spiritual vision and an actual physical experience.

In 622 Muhammad decided to leave Mecca at the invitation of groups residing in the city of Yathrib (the future Madinat al-Nabi, or "City of the Prophet," today's Medina). Yathrib was located at a major oasis, and there Muhammad hoped to establish a new community of Muslims free from Meccan persecution. The immigration to Yathrib, called the Hijra, marks the beginning of the Muslim calendar.

When Muhammad arrived in Yathrib he found a city divided by the competing tribes of the Aws and the Khazraj. Both soon converted to Islam, uniting under Muhammad after a century of fighting. With the exception of a sizable Jewish community divided into three clans, the city was entirely under Muhammad's control by 624. There the rituals of Islam were established.

In March 624 Muhammad led an abortive raid on a Meccan caravan. In retaliation, 1,000 Meccans marched on Medina. Not content to await the attack, Muhammad led some 300 men to meet the attackers. The two sides clashed at Badr, and Muhammad's followers achieved a decisive victory, inflicting more than 100 casualties at a cost of only 14 on his side and driving off the Meccans.

In 625, 3,000 Meccans moved against Medina. Emboldened by the victory at Badr, Muhammad marched out of the city to face the enemy, only to lose the Battle of Uhud. But Meccan leader Abu Sufyan chose to withdraw. Two years later Abu Sufyan again moved against Medina but was forced to withdraw following the Battle of Khandaq (Battle of the Trench). In 628 Muhammad led 1,400 followers to Mecca, ostensibly as a pilgrimage (hajj). They were refused entry to the city, although differences between the Meccans and the Muslims were supposedly resolved in the Treaty of Hudhaybiyya. This truce lasted only two years, however.

Renewed skirmishing led Muhammad to attack Mecca directly. The conversion of other tribes now provided Muhammad with a force of more than 10,000 men, far too many for the Meccans to withstand. The polytheistic statues at the Kaaba in Mecca were destroyed, and the majority of the populace converted to Islam.

Muhammad did not live long after consolidating his power. In 632 he fell ill in Medina and died there several days later. His followers soon expanded his legacy, eventually conquering lands that stretched from Central Asia to the Iberian Peninsula. Islam is now the world's fastest-growing religion, with some 1.7 billion adherents.

Paul J. Springer and Sherifa Zuhur

See also
Badr, Battle of; Muhammad, Campaigns of the Prophet; Quran

References
Cook, M. A. *Muhammad.* New York: Oxford University Press, 1983.
Haykal, Muhammad Husayn. *The Life of Muhammad.* Translated by Isma'il R. al-Faruqi. Indianapolis: North American Trust Publications, 1976.
Schimmel, Annemarie. *And Muhammad Is His Messenger: The Veneration of the Prophet in Islamic Piety.* Chapel Hill: University of North Carolina Press, 1985.
Watt, W. Montgomery. *Muhammad at Mecca.* Oxford, UK: Clarendon, 1953.
Watt, W. *Muhammad at Medina.* Oxford, UK: Clarendon, 1962.
Weinberger, Eliot. *Muhammad.* New York: Verso, 2006.

Muhammad Ali Pasha al-Mas'ud ibn Agha

See Mehmed Ali

Multinational Force and Observers in the Sinai

Independent military force drawn from many nations and involved in a peacekeeping mission in the Sinai Peninsula. The Multinational Force and Observers (MFO) was first conceptualized in 1979 as a result of the 1978 Camp David Accords and the Israel-Egypt Peace Treaty of 1979. Following the conclusion of peace, the United States provided an interim monitoring force in its Sinai Field Mission while at the same time seeking to persuade the United Nations (UN) to establish a permanent force. When the UN refused, Egypt, Israel, and the United States began negotiations that led to a peacekeeping force apart from the UN. On August 3, 1981, a protocol to the peace treaty officially established the MFO. It first assumed its duties on April 26, 1982, the day that Israel turned over sovereignty of the Sinai to Egypt.

MFO headquarters is located in Rome, Italy, and has representatives in both Cairo and Tel Aviv. Most of the observers operate in the Sinai Peninsula, with their logistical and support base, North Camp, located at al-Gurah about 15 miles from the Israeli border. The smaller South Camp is located at Sharm El Sheikh on the southern tip of the Sinai Peninsula. Operating from these camps, the MFO maintains some 30 monitoring sites running the length of the peninsula. There is also one remote observation point on a small island that requires resupply by air.

The MFO base at al-Gurah has been twice hit by Islamist militants. The first occurrence was on August 15, 2005, with a remote-controlled bomb that wounded two MFO members. The second was on April 26, 2006, just after deadly attacks at the nearby seaside resort of Dahab, when two suicide bombers targeted the base but killed no one but themselves.

A number of different nations have provided personnel for the MFO since its formation. Twelve states—Australia, Canada, Colombia, the Czech Republic, Fiji, France, Italy, New Zealand, Norway, the United Kingdom, the United States, and Uruguay—currently provide the MFO with military personnel who constitute the force and perform specific and specialized tasks.

The United States provides the largest contingent, including a support unit and an infantry battalion on a rotational basis. Active army battalions were initially committed to the MFO mission, but in recent years National Guard units have been mobilized for duty with the MFO. At any given point, the U.S. Army contingent averages 600 troops. In addition to the equal funding provided by Egypt, Israel, and the United States, the MFO also presently receives contributions from the governments of Australia, Finland, Germany, Japan, the Netherlands, Norway, the Republic of Korea, Sweden, Switzerland, and the United Kingdom.

The basic mission of the MFO is to observe conditions in the Sinai and ensure that there are no violations of forces permitted to Egypt and Israel within certain zones. The MFO is also charged with ensuring freedom of navigation in the Strait of Tiran. To accomplish this mission, the MFO operates checkpoints and reconnaissance patrols along the international boundary between the two states.

Spencer C. Tucker

See also
Camp David Accords; Israel-Egypt Peace Treaty

References

Tabory, Mala. *The Multinational Force and Observers in the Sinai: Organization, Structure, and Function.* Westview Special Studies on the Middle East. Boulder, CO: Westview, 1986.

U.S. Congress, House Committee on Foreign Affairs. *Creation of the Multinational Force and Observers (MFO) for the Sinai.* Washington, DC: U.S. Government Printing Office, 1981.

Multi-National Force–Iraq (2004–2009)

U.S.-led military command of coalition forces in Iraq, established on May 15, 2004, and lasting through December 21, 2009. The Multi-National Force–Iraq (MNF-I) was created ostensibly to combat the growing Iraqi insurgency, which began in earnest in late 2003 and early 2004, and it replaced Combined Joint Task Force 7, which had been in operation from June 2003 to May 2004. On January 1, 2010, the MNF-I was reorganized and renamed United States Forces–Iraq. This followed the withdrawal of most coalition troops from Iraq between 2008 and 2010 and the signing of the U.S.-Iraq Status of Forces Agreement in December 2008. U.S. troops left Iraq in December 2011, ending the mission of the United States Forces–Iraq.

Commanders of the MNF-I were Lieutenant General Ricardo Sanchez (May–June 2004), General George W. Casey (June 2004–January 2007), General David Petraeus (January 2007–September 2008), and General Raymond Odierno (September 2008–January 2010). The MNF-I was tasked with bringing the growing Iraqi insurgency to an end but was largely unsuccessful in that effort until the George W. Bush administration placed General Petraeus in command and implemented a troop surge that placed as many as 30,000 additional U.S. troops on the ground in Iraq beginning in early 2007.

The troop-surge strategy seemed to have worked for a time, as violence fell off markedly beginning by early 2008; Petraeus was given much of the credit for this development. At the same time, the so-called Anbar Awakening groups in Iraq also helped to curb sectarian and insurgent violence. General Odierno, while acknowledging that the surge provided strengthened security forces, credited a change in counterinsurgency strategy more than the surge itself for reducing the level of violence. Referring to it as an "Anaconda strategy," Odierno explained it as a comprehensive approach that had success in, among other areas, cutting off insurgents from their support within the Iraqi population.

After its inception, the MNF-I was overwhelmingly composed of U.S. troops; the second-largest deployment was from Great Britain. The size of the MNF-I was fluid, but on average it contained around 150,000 combat-ready personnel, the vast majority of whom were American. The troop surge brought the total closer to 180,000 by early 2008, but that number dwindled steadily as troop withdrawals began that same year. Working with the MNF-I, but not falling under its direct command, was the United Nations (UN) Assistance Mission–Iraq, which provided humanitarian aid and observation, and the North Atlantic Treaty Organization (NATO) Training Mission–Iraq, whose goal was to train Iraqi security, police, and military personnel. The major component parts of the MNF-I were Multi-National Security Transition Command; Gulf Region Division, U.S. Corps of Engineers; Joint Base Balad; Multi-National Corps–Iraq; Multi-National Division–Baghdad; Multi-National Division–North; Multi-National Force–West; Multi-National Division Center; and Multi-National Division–Southeast.

In addition to battling the Iraqi insurgency and other indigenous violence, other goals of the MNF-I included support and aid to the Iraqi government, reconstruction efforts, specialized training of Iraqi military personnel, intelligence gathering, and border patrols. The December 2008 status of forces agreement between the U.S. and Iraqi governments stipulated that all U.S. troops be withdrawn by December 31, 2011. Under the terms of this arrangement, U.S. troops vacated Iraqi cities by July 31, 2009. The Iraqis concluded similar agreements with other coalition forces that still maintained a presence in Iraq. Numerous nations supplied troops to the MNF-I, many of whom were withdrawn by the end of December 2008. The participating members, along with the size of their deployments, included: United States (145,000 troops as of December 2008), Great Britain (4,000 as of December 2008), Romania (500 as of December 2008), Australia (350 as of December 2008), El Salvador (300 as of December 2008), and Estonia (40 as of December 2008).

Those nations that participated but were withdrawn prior to December 2008 included (figures in parentheses represent peak deployments) South Korea (3,600), Italy (3,200), Poland (2,500), Georgia (2,000), Ukraine (1,650), the Netherlands (1,345), Spain (1,300), Japan (600), Denmark (545), Bulgaria (458), Thailand (423), Honduras (368), Dominican Republic (302), the Czech Republic (300), Hungary (300), Azerbaijan (250), Albania (240), Nicaragua (230), Mongolia (180), Singapore (175), Norway (150), Latvia (136), Portugal (128), Lithuania (120), Slovakia (110), Bosnia-Herzegovina (85), Macedonia (77), New Zealand (61), Tonga (55), the Philippines (51), Armenia (46), Kazakhstan (29), Moldova (24), and Iceland (2).

To entice potential coalition partners to join the MNF-I effort, the U.S. government offered a plethora of financial aid and other incentives. Because the invasion of Iraq had not been sanctioned by the UN, the United States found it more difficult to convince other nations to become involved in the postwar stabilization effort in Iraq. Some nations and previously close allies, however, refused to take part in the mission despite U.S. promises of financial and other rewards. The United States reportedly offered Turkey up to $8.5 billion in loans if the country sent peacekeeping troops to Iraq; Turkey, which had forbade the use of its bases during the March 2003 invasion of Iraq, demurred. France and Germany refused any participation in Iraq. Some countries, such as Great Britain and Australia, were offered lucrative private-contractor business that would help fuel their economies. The Bush administration, however, refused to acknowledge that there were any quid pro quo arrangements in the assembling of international forces in Iraq.

PAUL G. PIERPAOLI JR.

See also
Iraq Insurgency; Petraeus, David Howell; Sanchez, Ricardo S.; Troop Surge, U.S., Iraq War

References
Cockburn, Patrick. *The Occupation: War and Resistance in Iraq.* New York: Verso, 2007.
Gordon, Michael R., and Bernard E. Trainor. *The Endgame: The Inside Story of the Struggle for Iraq, from George W. Bush to Barack Obama.* New York: Vintage, 2013.
Keegan, John. *The Iraq War: The Military Offensive, from Victory in 21 Days to the Insurgent Aftermath.* New York: Vintage, 2005.

Murad II, Sultan (1404–1451)

Ottoman sultan (1421–1444 and 1446–1451). Born in June 1404 at Amasya, Amasya Province, in the Ottoman Sultanate, Murad was the son of Sultan Mehmed I. On his father becoming sultan in 1413, Murad accompanied him to the capital of Adrianople (modern-day Edirne, Turkey). In order for his son to secure administrative experience, Mehmed appointed Murad governor of Amasya. Murad remained there until the death of Mehmed I in 1421, when he himself became sultan at age 16 on May 26.

Murad II faced two immediate challenges to his leadership: one from his uncle Düzme Mustafa and the other from his own brother, Mustafa. Having successfully defeated both rivals, Murad set about securing his position. He took to the field with success against the rival state of Karaman centered on Konya, and he dealt with enemies in Europe, notably the able John Hunyadi, *voivod* of Transylvania. Murad also endeavored to capture Constantinople (modern-day Istanbul), but after an unsuccessful siege of that city in 1422 Murad concluded a treaty in 1424 with the Byzantines.

By the 1440s Murad, reportedly a humane and liberal individual, appears to have tired of ruling and, possibly due to the death of his son Alaeddin, abdicated in 1444 in favor of his son Mehmed II. Before doing so, in 1444 Murad arranged the Treaty of Adrianople with Hungary and Serbia in 1444 and a treaty with Karaman in an attempt to ensure peaceful relations with his neighbors. Peace was, however, not achieved; on the accession of the young and inexperienced Mehmed II, John Hunyadi and King Vladislav I of Hungary promptly attacked. Mehmed II brought his father out of retirement to lead the Ottoman Army. In the Battle of Varna (1444), the Ottomans defeated the Hungarians; Vladislav was killed, and Hunyadi fled. For the next two years, Mehmed continued precariously on the throne, but he was toppled by a Janissary revolt in 1446. Brought back to the throne that September, Murad II reestablished Ottoman control firmly over the European territories, defeating Hunyadi at the Second Battle of Kosovo in 1448. Murad was less successful against George Kastrioti, known as Skanderbeg, who fought the Ottomans in Albania. Murad II died at Edirne at only age 46 on February 3, 1451, and was succeeded for a second time by his son Mehmed II.

KATE FLEET

See also
Adrianople, 1444 Treaty of; Mehmed II, Sultan; Ottoman Empire-Varna Crusade

References
Babinger, Franz. *Mehmed the Conqueror and His Time.* Princeton, NJ: Princeton University Press, 1978.
Imber, Colin. *The Ottoman Empire, 1300–1481.* Istanbul: Isis, 1990.
İnalcık, Halil. *The Ottoman Empire: The Classical Age, 1300–1600.* London: Weidenfeld and Nicolson, 1973.
Vatin, Nicolas. "L'ascension des Ottomans (1362–1429)." In *Histoire de l'empire Ottoman,* ed. Robert Mantran, 222–275. Paris: Fayard, 1989.

Murray, Sir Archibald James (1860–1945)

British Army general. Born on April 21, 1860, at Woodhouse, Hampshire, Archibald James Murray was educated at Cheltenham and the Royal Military College, Sandhurst. He joined the army in 1879 and served in the 1888 Zululand

Campaign and the 1899–1902 Second Boer War (South African War). He was promoted to colonel in October 1903 and to major general in July 1910. Appointed inspector of infantry in 1912, in early 1914 Murray was selected to command the 2nd Division.

Upon the mobilization of the British Expeditionary Force (BEF) at the beginning of World War I, Murray was appointed chief of the General Staff to BEF commander General Sir John French. Murray served in the Battle of Mons and the ensuing retreat as well as at the Marne, First Aisne, and First Ypres, all in 1914.

By January 1915 Murray had lost the confidence of French, who replaced him. Murray, however, retained the confidence of secretary of state for war Field Marshal Lord Kitchener, who appointed him deputy chief of the General Staff in February 1915 and chief of the Imperial General Staff in September 1915. Murray was promoted to lieutenant general in October 1915. His brief tenure as chief of the Imperial General Staff ended in December 1915 when he was dismissed by Prime Minister Sir Herbert Asquith, who considered Murray too weak to stand up to Kitchener, and Murray was once again replaced by General Robertson.

In January 1916, Murray was appointed commander of the Egyptian Expeditionary Force (EEF). Soon after his arrival in Egypt, his command was weakened by the transfer of several divisions to other theaters, yet Murray defeated an Ottoman attack on the Suez Canal in the Battle of Romani (August 4–9, 1916).

Late in 1916 Murray received permission to take the offensive on the Palestinian Front. The British soon cleared Ottoman forces from Rafah and Magheba and closed up the Palestine border. However, Murray's attempts to invade Palestine were defeated in the First Battle of Gaza (March 26–27, 1917) and the Second Battle of Gaza (April 17–19). These reverses cost Murray his command, and he was replaced by Lieutenant General Sir Edmund Allenby in June 1917.

Murray then headed Aldershot Command in Britain. He was promoted to full general in August 1919. He retired in 1922 and died at Makepeace, Reigate, England, on January 23, 1945.

BRADLEY P. TOLPPANEN

See also
Allenby, Sir Edmund Henry Hynman; Gaza, First Battle of; Gaza, Second Battle of; Palestine and Syria Campaign, World War I; Romani, Battle of; Sinai Campaign of 1916–1917

References
Bruce, A. P. C. *The Last Crusade: The Palestine Campaign in the First World War.* London: Murray, 2002.
Bullock, David L. *Allenby's War: The Palestinian-Arabian Campaigns, 1916–1918.* London: Blandford, 1988.
Murray, Sir Archibald. *Sir Archibald Murray's Despatches.* East Sussex, UK: Naval & Military Press, 2006.
Wavell, A. P. *The Palestine Campaigns.* London: Constable, 1928.

Muslim Brotherhood

The Muslim Brotherhood (Jami'at al-Ikhwan al-Muslimin, or Society of Muslim Brothers) is a Muslim fundamentalist (Islamist) organization that since 1928 has promoted the Islamic way of life and has been active in the political arena for many years. With separate and autonomous branches in more than 70 countries, the Muslim Brotherhood provides education, social services, and fellowship for religiously active Muslims. The secret military wing of the organization has been involved in assassinations and attempted assassinations throughout the 20th century and into the 21st century. The group has opposed the formation of Israel and has participated in Palestinian attempts to achieve independence from Israeli control. Supporters of the Muslim Brotherhood claim that it is extremely popular with the people of Arab nations, is more moderate than groups such as Al Qaeda, and has not in fact been involved in nearly as much violence as has been claimed. Opponents charge that the Muslim Brotherhood is a terrorist organization and is destructive to efforts to create peace in the Middle East.

The Muslim Brotherhood was founded in March 1928 in Egypt. Its founder, Hasan al-Banna, was a 22-year-old elementary school teacher. Al-Banna believed that Islam should be a way of life, not just a religion to be observed on ceremonial occasions, and that Wahhabism, or Islamism, was the proper form of Islam. He opposed Sufism and particularly wanted to create an organization that would revive Islamic rules of living and family values in the face of secularization and encroaching Westernization. He was motivated by the collapse of the Ottoman Empire and the establishment of a secular Turkish state, which he saw as a threat to the Islamic world. Al-Banna believed that Islamists should be involved in the government and encourage it to spread and defend Islam. The organization's motto was "Allah is our objective. The Prophet is our leader. Quran is our law. Jihad is our way. Dying in the way of Allah is our highest hope."

In its first years the Muslim Brotherhood sponsored social and educational programs for young people, preaching its

A child in Amman, Jordan, waves a toy gun during a Muslim Brotherhood demonstration on October 20, 2000, on the eve of an Arab summit in Cairo to discuss violence in the Palestinian territories and Israel. The protesters called for the severing of all ties with Israel in solidarity with the Palestinian people. (Jamal Nasrallah/AFP/Getty Images)

strict interpretation of the Quran. The organization quickly became extremely popular, partly because it emphasized fun activities such as sports and group trips. The group followed a set of eight tenets. These included rejecting anything that contradicted the Quran or *sunna*, working to spread the *sunna* into every part of life, loving Muslims, working to Islamize the government, engaging in regular physical exercise and preserving physical health, studying, economically supporting and sponsoring Islamist projects, and fostering social ties with other members of the Muslim Brotherhood. The group emphasized living as a conscientious Muslim, building a good Muslim family and educating children in Islam, and creating a Muslim society and state.

The Muslim Brotherhood became involved in politics in the late 1930s. Al-Banna formed branches of the organization in Syria (1935), Transjordan (1942), and Palestine (1942). By the end of World War II there were branches of the organization throughout the Middle East. The group was adamantly opposed to the creation of Israel, and many of its members fought in the Israeli War of Independence (1948–1949). The Muslim Brotherhood disapproved of what it considered the Egyptian government's failure to take action against Zionists and began performing acts of terrorism within Egypt. Egypt banned the group briefly, but it was legal again in 1948, though it was supposed to act only as a religious organization. On December 28, 1948, a member of the Muslim Brotherhood assassinated Egyptian prime minister Mahmud Fahmi Nokrashi. The Egyptian government retaliated by killing al-Banna in February 1949.

When Gamal Abdel Nasser came to power in 1954 the Muslim Brotherhood initially supported him, but the members were disappointed when he did not put Egypt under sharia law. A member of the organization attempted to assassinate Nasser on October 26, 1954, and Nasser responded by banning the Muslim Brotherhood and imprisoning more than 4,000 of its members. Other members moved to Syria,

Saudi Arabia, Lebanon, and Jordan. In Jordan, the group supported King Hussein when Nasser attempted to overthrow him. In 1957, King Hussein made the Muslim Brotherhood the only legal political party in Jordan. Syria joined Egypt in the United Arab Republic in 1958, and the Syrian Muslim Brotherhood went underground until Syria left that political entity in 1961. The Muslim Brotherhood won 10 seats in the next elections but had to go underground again after the Baath coup in 1963.

Nasser granted amnesty to the imprisoned members of the Muslim Brotherhood in 1964. Members of the group responded by trying to kill Nasser three more times in the next year. In 1966 Nasser ordered the execution of several Muslim Brotherhood leaders and imprisoned many more. All of this led to the radicalism expressed by Ikhwan member Sayyid Qutb, who had previously promoted societal change through education and reform but now called for jihad and martyrdom, which led to his subsequent arrest and execution.

Nasser's successor, Anwar Sadat (president of Egypt during 1970–1981), initially pleased the Muslim Brotherhood by promising to impose sharia law. Syria's new president, Hafez al-Assad, who held power during 1971–2000, however, upset the Muslim Brotherhood tremendously because he was an Alawite, so the group did not consider him a Muslim at all. The Muslim Brotherhood declared jihad against Assad and began a series of terrorist attacks. The group tried but failed to assassinate Assad in 1980, and in response Assad made membership in the Muslim Brotherhood a capital offense and had the army wipe out the entire organization. Many members were killed; those who survived fled to other Arab nations. The Egyptian Muslim Brotherhood was deeply angered by Sadat's 1979 peace treaty with Israel. Sadat was assassinated in 1981 by another Islamist group, the Islamic Jihad.

In Israel, Muslim Brotherhood member Ahmad Yassin spent the 1970s running welfare organizations for Palestinian Muslims, with the permission of the Israeli government. He became tremendously popular and in 1987 was one of the founding members of Hamas. The Muslim Brotherhood was once again permitted to operate in Egypt in 1984, though the government kept it under tight control and did not allow it to participate in elections. In 1993 the Muslim Brotherhood held the largest number of seats in Jordan's parliament. The organization was said to have been involved in the Afghan resistance and revolts in Chechnya. The Muslim Brotherhood generally supports democracy and free elections.

The Arab Spring, which began in 2010, initially looked promising for the Muslim Brotherhood. In 2011 the organization was legalized in Egypt, and it subsequently participated in parliamentary elections. In the 2012 Egyptian presidential election, the Muslim Brotherhood backed Mohammed Morsi, who was committed to aligning Egyptian laws with sharia law. He won the contest but soon overreached and was ousted by the Egyptian military in July 2013. This was a significant reversal in the Muslim Brotherhood's fortunes. Within weeks, Egypt's military-run government initiated a crackdown against the Muslim Brotherhood; in December 2013, the interim government declared it a terrorist organization. The group has reportedly been involved to some extent in the Syrian Civil War (2011–).

In March 2014 the Saudi government labeled the Muslim Brotherhood as a terrorist group. That same month, the Egyptian government sentenced 529 Muslim Brotherhood members to death for fomenting terrorism. An additional 183 members were given death sentences in February 2015. Morsi himself was sentenced to death in May 2015, although in November 2016 an Egyptian court overturned the sentence. Meanwhile, as of June 2016, some reports suggested that as many as 40,000–50,000 Muslim Brotherhood members had been arrested and imprisoned by Egyptian authorities. In April 2016 the Jordanian government shut down the Muslim Brotherhood headquarters in Amman after labeling the group a terrorist organization. Qatar's apparent refusal to crack down on terrorism, condemn the Muslim Brotherhood, and forbid its activities within its borders precipitated the 2017 Qatar Diplomatic Crisis, during which numerous Arab nations cut ties with Qatar, including Saudi Arabia, Bahrain, and Egypt. They then instituted an economic embargo against Qatar. The crisis had yet to be resolved.

AMY HACKNEY BLACKWELL

See also

Alawites; Al Qaeda; Assad, Hafez al-; Egypt; Hamas; Hussein ibn Talal, King of Jordan; Jihad; Jordan; Nasser, Gamal Abdel; Quran; Qutb, Sayyid Ibrahim Husayn Shadhili; Sadat, Anwar; Syria; Syrian Civil War; Wahhabism

References

Ayubi, Nazih N. *Political Islam: Religion and Politics in the Arab World.* New York: Routledge, 1993.

Baker, Raymond William. *Islam without Fear: Egypt and the New Islamists.* Cambridge, MA: Harvard University Press, 1993.

El-Ghobashy, Mona. "The Metamorphosis of the Egyptian Muslim Brothers." *International Journal of Middle East Studies* 37, no. 3 (August 2005): 373–395.

Mitchell, Richard P. *The Society of Muslim Brothers.* Oxford: Oxford University Press, 1993.

Muslim Wars of Expansion (623–732)

The wars of Muslim territorial expansion are traced to Prophet Muhammad and his desire and that of his followers to spread their new faith. Inspired by what he believed to have been a series of divine revelations beginning in 610, Muhammad began espousing a new monotheist and egalitarian religion known as Islam. In 622 he organized the tribes of Yathrib (now Medina) into a community under the will of God (Allah) as revealed in his teachings. As both prophet and military commander, Muhammad now sought to expand the faith by force of arms.

Muhammad's initial military campaign was against the prominent trading city of Mecca. Beginning in 623, Muhammad raided Meccan caravans, and on March 15, 624 in the Battle of Badr, he defeated a force sent out by Mecca to destroy him.

Many people in Arabia chose to see the victory of Muhammad's badly outnumbered and poorly armed and equipped force in the Battle of Badr as a sign from God. The outcome certainly added immensely to Muhammad's reputation, especially as a military leader. Defeat at Badr would probably have brought his death.

Muhammad's forces were, however, defeated in the Battle of Ohod in 625. Two years later in the Battle of the Khandaq (also known as the Battle of the Trench or Battle of the Confederates) during late April to early May 627, some 3,000 followers of Muhammad withstood a two-week siege of Medina by some 10,000 Meccan and allied forces. Following a period of truce, fighting resumed, and Muhammad and his followers captured Mecca by assault in 630. That city then converted to Islam.

Meanwhile, a long period of warfare between the Byzantine Empire and Persia during 602–628 had severely weakened both states and their ability to stand against a tide of Muslim conquest. In the initial Muslim raid into Byzantine Palestine in 629, however, the Byzantines turned back the Muslims in the Battle of Muta.

By the time of Muhammad's death from natural causes in June 632, he had, however, established control over most of Arabia and created there a theocratic state. Abu Bekr now became the first caliph, or successor to Muhammad. There was some initial resistance to his rule, but in the so-called Ridda Wars (632–633), assisted by his great general Khalid ibn al-Walid, Abu Bekr put down revolts by several "apostates," the last being Musaylima in the Battle of Akraba in 633. The Arab tribes were again united.

The new Arabian state now confronted the two great empires of Persia and Byzantium. With both of these states now seriously weakened, Islamic forces took the offensive, first expanding beyond Arabia in 632. Taking advantage of chaos in the Persian Sassanian Empire following the death of King Kavadh II, Khalid ibn al-Walid led an invasion of Persian Mesopotamia. Concurrently, Amr ibn al-As invaded Byzantine territory in Palestine and Syria. Byzantine forces replied with a counteroffensive. Khalid ibn al-Walid marched to Amr's relief and in the Battle of Ajnadain, between Gaza and Jerusalem, defeated Byzantine forces under General Theodore in July 634. Khalid pursued the Byzantines and again defeated them in the Battle of Fihl (Pella or Gilead) near Baisan in January 635. Continuing north, Muslim commander Abu Ubaidah ibn al-Jarrah and Khalid once more defeated Byzantine forces, under Baanes, in the Battle of Marjal-Saffar near Damascus. The Muslims then took Emesa (Homs) and Damascus.

Upon the departure of Muslim general Khalid ibn al-Walid for Palestine, Persian general Mihran defeated the remaining Muslim forces in the Battle of the Bridge (on the Euphrates River) in 634. However, reinforcing Muslim troops halted the Persian pursuit the next year in the Battle of Buwayb, south of Kufa.

In mid-August 636, Arab forces of the Rashidun Caliphate, led by Abu Ubaidah ibn al-Jarrah and Khalid ibn al-Walid, came together with Byzantine Empire forces under Mahan in Palestine next to the Yarmouk (Yarmuk, Yarmūk) River, the largest tributary of the Jordan. The battle was the culmination of Caliph Abu Bekr's order in 634 for Muslim forces to invade Syria that had seen the Arabs capture Damascus and most of Palestine. In the six-day Battle of the Yarmouk River, Khalid ibn al-Walid, who had taken direction of the Muslim forces, destroyed a far larger Byzantine force under Mahan. The battle gave the Muslims control of Syria and Palestine.

Caliph Umar (Omar) now dispatched Sa'd ibn Abi Waqqas and a new Arab 30,000-man army against Persia. Sa'd defeated a Sassanian Persian force of 50,000 men under Rustam in the Battle of al-Qādisiyyah during November 16–19, 636. This strategically significant encounter led to the Muslim capture of the Persian capital of Ctesiphon several months later. Sa'd and the Arabs defeated the Persians again in the Battle of Jalula in December 637.

During 637–645 the Arabs completed the conquest of Syria and Palestine. Among prominent places taken were Jerusalem and Antioch (638), Aleppo (639), Caesarea and Gaza (640), and Tripoli (645). Most fell after lengthy sieges. At the same time, during 639–641 the Arab forces conquered all of remaining Byzantine Mesopotamia.

Expansion of Islam, 814

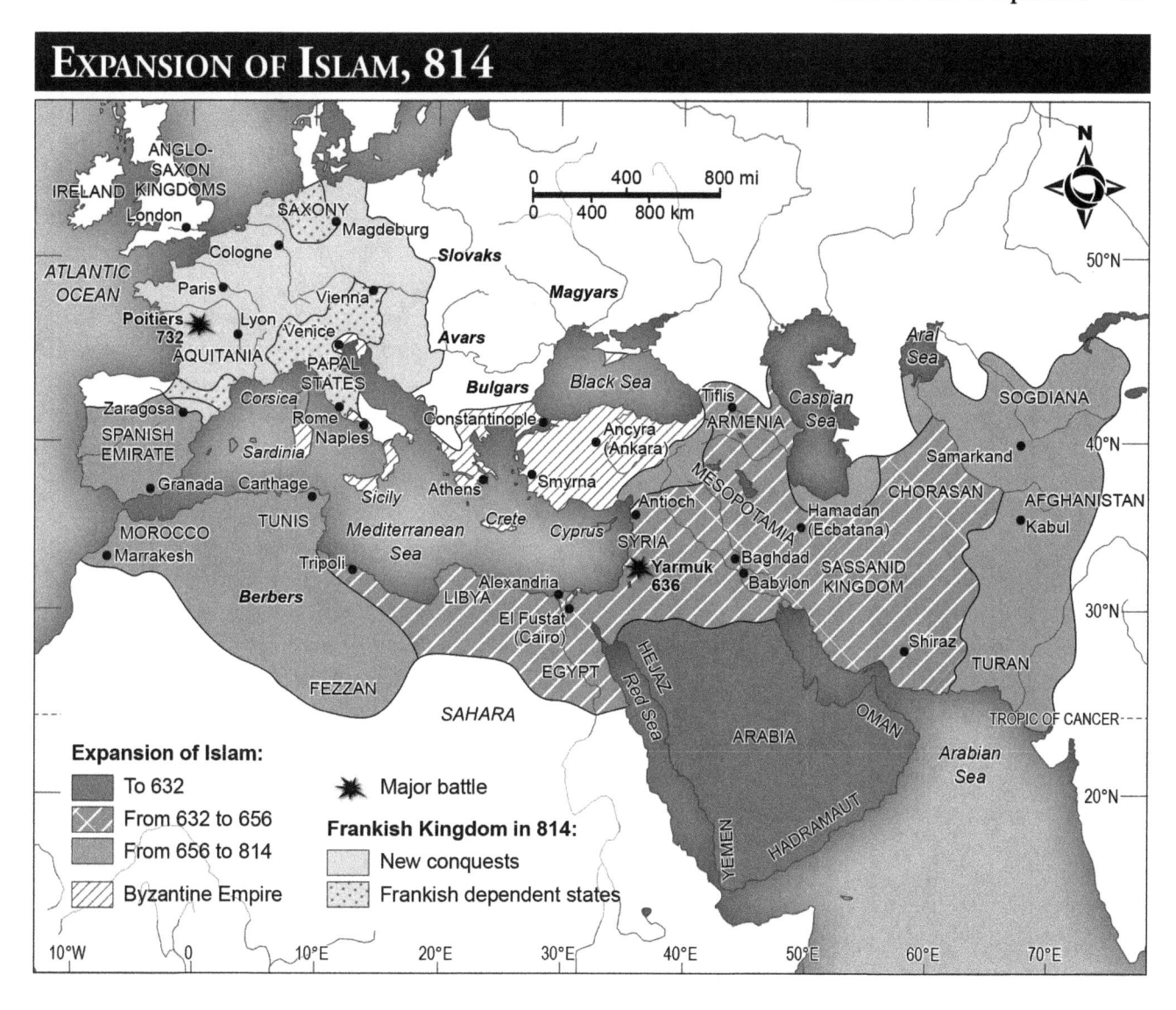

Egypt was the next Muslim target, beginning in 639. In July 640, General Amir ibn al-As was victorious over Byzantine forces in the Battle of Babylon, near Helliopolis. Following long sieges, he captured the fortified cities of Babylon in April 641 and Alexandria in September 642.

During 640–650 the Arab armies conquered what remained of Persian territory. Following decisive Muslim Arab victories in the Battle of Ram Hormuz in 640 and the Battle of Nahavend in 641, organized Persian resistance came to an end. During the next decade the Arabs solidified their control over what had been the Sassanid Persian Empire, with the Oxus River becoming the boundary between Arab and Turkish territory.

During 642–643 the Muslims expanded into North Africa from Egypt. Under Abdulla ibn Zubayr, their armies captured Cyrene and Tripoli, then raided farther west. In 645 Muslim forces under Amr turned back an ineffectual Byzantine effort to recapture Alexandria. A revolt within the city, however, forced Amr to retake Alexandria by storm.

At the same time, the Arabs took to the sea. The growing strength of their naval forces in the eastern Mediterranean was shown in their capture in 649 of the island of Cyprus. The Arabs also raided Sicily in 652 and captured Rhodes in 654. In 655 Byzantine emperor Constans II personally led a large fleet to attack the Arabs. Constans had perhaps 1,000 warships; the Arabs under Abdullah ibn Sa'd far fewer but won the two-day Battle of Lycia, or Battle of the Masts (Dhat al-sawari), at Phoinike (off the Lycian coast). Reportedly, some 500 Byzantine ships were destroyed. Emperor Constans was wounded but escaped.

During 657–661 a civil war occurred within the Rashidun Caliphate. The revolt of Talha and Zubayr, although suppressed in Basra with the Battle of the Camel in 657, sparked civil war and shelved Arab plans to attack Constantinople.

The civil war brought the division of Islam into the Sunni and Shia factions. Because of this, new caliph Mur'awiya concluded peace with the Byzantine Empire in 659, agreeing to pay an annual tribute. Mur'awiya founded the Umayyad dynasty, the rule of which traditionally dates from 661 to 750.

During 661–663, Ziyad ibn Abihi carried out the first Muslim raids against India. These penetrated Sind and the lower Indus River Valley. In 664, repeated Muslim invasions of Afghanistan from 652 brought the temporary capture of Kabul.

In 668 warfare was renewed between the Byzantine Empire and the Umayyad Caliphate. Muslim forces invaded Anatolia and reached Chalcedon on the Asian side of the Bosporus. They crossed the Bosporus to attack Constantinople itself but were repulsed in 669. The Byzantines then virtually destroyed the Arab army at Armorium and retook the city. The Byzantines also repulsed the Arab naval attack on Constantinople.

In 672 the Byzantines virtually destroyed an Arab fleet in the Battle of Cyzicus in the Sea of Marmora. The Byzantine use of a combustible mixture known as Greek fire, perhaps the first time it was employed in warfare at sea, was a major factor in the Byzantines' victory. Undeterred by this setback, the Arabs soon dispatched other forces and maintained an intermittent land and sea blockade of Constantinople during 673–677. The Byzantines were hard-pressed because the Arabs also raided Anatolia, and concurrently the Slavs attacked Thessalonika. This war was effectively ended by the Byzantine naval victory in the Sea of Marmora off Syllaeum. Again, Greek fire played a key role. The withdrawing Arab ships were caught in a storm, and nearly all were lost. The Byzantines also defeated the Arabs on land. Caliph Mur'awiya then agreed to peace terms; the Arabs agreed to evacuate Cyprus, pay an annual tribute to Constantinople, and maintain the peace for 30 years.

In 674 meanwhile, Arab forces invaded and conquered Transoxiana in Central Asia. The next year the Byzantines were forced to embark on a struggle in the Balkans. Taking advantage of war between the Byzantine Empire and the Umayyads, the Slavs invaded Thessalonika but were repulsed. Isperich, ruler of the Bulgars, led a large invasion force across the Danube and defeated Byzantine forces sent against him. In 680 he forced Emperor Constantine IV to cede the province of Moesia.

In 681 Arab forces reached Morocco. An Arab army led by Okba ibn Nafi gained the Atlantic before being driven back into Cyrene by the Berbers, who acted in alliance with the Byzantine forces at Carthage. Okba was killed during the withdrawal.

In 685 Justinian II become sole Byzantine emperor on his father's death. Only 16 years old, the young emperor took advantage of peace with the Arabs to recover the Balkans, which had come under the control of Slavic tribes. Defeating the Bulgars during 688–689, Justinian entered Thessalonika, the second most important Byzantine city in Europe. He then resettled the Bulgars in Anatolia and secured 30,000 of them for his army.

Emboldened by the additional manpower, Justinian renewed the war with the Arabs during 690–692. It did not go well for the Byzantines. Justinian was defeated by the Umayyads in the Battle of Sebastopolis (Sevastopol) on the western shore of the Black Sea in 692. The Byzantine loss resulted from the defection of upwards of 20,000 Slavs because of harsh treatment under Justinian and the influence of Arab bribes. Reportedly, in the aftermath of the battle the emperor ordered the deaths of every Slavic family in Bithynia. The Arabs then took all Armenia.

During 690–691 there was civil war within the Umayyad Caliphate. Forces under Caliph Abd ul-Malik (r. 685–705) reconquered Iraq and Arabia, taking Medina in 691 and Mecca in 692. By 698 Abd ul-Malik was again the undisputed ruler of all Muslim territory.

Arab operations continued in North Africa, where during 693–698 their forces conquered Tunisia. Byzantine influence in North Africa came to an end with the capture of Carthage in 698. Meanwhile, Justinian II's harsh rule led to his overthrow as emperor.

In 699 Ibn al-Ash'ath led an Arab army in revolt against al-Hajjaj ibn Yusuf, overall governor of the eastern Muslim territories. Marching to Iraq, ibn al-Ash'ath occupied Basra and then moved against Kufa, winning the indecisive Battle of Dair al-Jamajim against al-Hajjaj and forcing him into Kufa. After receiving reinforcements, al-Hajjaj defeated ibn al-Ash'ath in the Battle of Maskin on the Dujail River in 701, ending the rebellion.

In 703 the Berbers defeated an Arab army under Hassan ibn No'man near Mount Aurasius (Aures Mountains) in present-day Algeria but two years later concluded an alliance with the Arabs that allowed the latter to conquer all North Africa.

Deposed Byzantine emperor Justinian II escaped imprisonment and worked out a secret arrangement with the Bulgars. Thanks to their military support, he returned to power in Constantinople in 705 and began a six-year reign of terror there before his forces were defeated by 711 in intermittent wars with both his former ally Terbelis, ruler of the Bulgars, and the Arabs.

During 705–715 Caliph al-Walid, the son of Caliph Abd ul-Malik, pushed the caliphate to the greatest territorial extent of any Muslim empire under one ruler. Additions included Bokhara, Samarkand, Khwarizm (Kiva), Ferghana, and Tashkent. Muslim forces also raided into Sinkiang as far as Tashkent in 713. Kabul was taken in 708, and the Sind was secured during 708–712. Multan was taken after a long siege, and Umayyad raids extended into the Punjab. The Gujaras repulsed subsequent Arab raids into Rajputana and Gujrat, however. During 708–711, Arab forces under Musa ibn Nusair conquered Northwest Africa.

In 710 having reached the Strait of Gibraltar, Musa ibn Nusair launched raids across it into Spain. The following year Musa sent an army under Tarik ibn Ziyad across the straits to Gibraltar, which was then named for him (Gebel-al-Tarik, or the Rock of Tarik). Although his force was vastly outnumbered, Tarik met and defeated a Visigoth army in the Battle of the Guadalete (July 19, 711). He then won another victory at Ecija. Consolidating his hold over southern Spain, he captured the Visigothic capital of Toledo without opposition. The Muslims completed their conquest of Spain in 712.

In 710 also, Muslim forces invaded Anatolia, conquering Cilicia in 711 and securing partial control of Galatia in 714. The Bulgars reached Constantinople in 712, and the Arabs captured Cilicia and then invaded Pontus, taking Amasia (Amasya). Byzantine government weakness brought Leo the Isurian to the throne; he took the title Leo III. In 716 Muslim forces under Yeminite general Yazid ibn Mohallin invaded and conquered the Transcaspian region.

The chief Muslim goal throughout the seventh and eighth centuries remained the acquisition of Constantinople. This great Byzantine capital city controlled the Bosporus and thus access between the Mediterranean and Black Seas. Constantinople also guarded the entrance to south-central Europe. The Arabs had tried before in 655 and in 669. Several attempts in the 670s were turned back when the Byzantines defeated the attackers at sea.

The greatest threat to the city and to Byzantium came in 717 under Caliph Suleiman (r. 715–717). Leo III turned back large Muslim forces in the Siege of Constantinople during 717–718. Leo's victory at Constantinople was decisive. In 739 he also won a land victory that compelled the Muslims to withdraw from western Asia Minor. In the process he may have saved not only his empire but also West European civilization.

In 719 the Muslims in Spain took Narbonne in France, but two years later they met defeat at Toulouse. In 725 they occupied Carcassonne and Nîmes, and the next year they advanced up the Rhône River Valley and ravaged Burgundy.

In 732 Muslim governor of Spain Abd-ar-Rahmān launched a full-scale invasion of Aquitaine. Taking and sacking Bordeaux, he moved north but was met and defeated by Frankish leader Charles Martel in the Battle of Tours (October 25, 732). The Battle of Tours saw the deepest Muslim penetration into Europe, east and west. It may not have saved Western Europe from Arab rule but certainly made Charles supreme in Gaul and enabled him to establish the Carolingian dynasty, which reached its zenith under his grandson Charlemagne.

An Arab invasion of the Byzantine Empire in 739, at first successful, was halted by Byzantine forces under Emperor Leo III in the Battle of Akroinon (Afyon Karahisar). In 741 new Byzantine emperor Constantine V (r. 741–775) invaded Syria in renewed war with the Arabs but was almost immediately forced to withdraw on news of a revolt led by his brother-in-law, Artavasdus, and supported by those favoring the veneration of religious images. Returning to Constantinople, Constantine V crushed the revolt and then again invaded Syria, taking some border areas in 745. Constantine's fleet was also victorious at sea against the Arabs near Cyprus, and the Muslims were forced from that island in 746. Constantine then campaigned in Armenia, regaining part of it during 751–752. He was aided by considerable turmoil and outright fighting within the Umayyad Caliphate during 743–750, the result of dynastic struggles and religious strife.

In 750 Caliph Abu'l Abbas established the Abbasid Caliphate. The Abbasids moved the capital from Damascus to Baghdad. Recurring revolts in Syria and Mesopotamia in favor of the deposed Umayyad family allowed the Byzantines to raid deep into Arab territory. Although Umayyad leader Abd-ar-Rahmān established a separate state at Córdoba in Spain, sporadic warfare between Muslim and Christians there ultimately led to the Reconquista, or reconquest of the Iberian Peninsula by the Christian forces, that spanned 700 years. Although warfare continued, the Arabs made no major new conquests. The age of the great Arab conquests was at an end.

Spencer C. Tucker

See also
Badr, Battle of; Byzantine-Muslim Wars; Constantinople, Muslim Siege of; Khalid ibn al-Walid; Leo III the Isaurian; Muhammad, Prophet of Islam; Sassanid Empire; Shia Islam; Sunni Islam; Umayyad Caliphate; Yarmouk River, Battle of

References
Butler, A. J. *The Arab Conquests of Egypt*. 2nd ed. Brooklyn, NY: A&B Publishing, 1998.
Dixon, A. A. *The Umayyad Caliphate, 65–86/684–705*. London: Luzac, 1971.

Donner, Fred. *The Early Islamic Conquests.* Princeton, NJ: Princeton University Press, 1981.
Fregosi, Paul. *Jihad in the West: Muslim Conquests from the 7th to the 21st Centuries.* Amherst, NY: Prometheus Books, 1998.
Graham, Mark, and Akbar Ahmed. *How Islam Created the Modern World.* Beltsville, MD: Amana Publications, 2006.
Haldon, J. J. *Byzantium in the Seventh Century.* Cambridge: Cambridge University Press, 1990.
Jandora, John. *The March from Medina.* Clifton, NJ: Kingston Press, 1990.
Kaegi, Walter. *Byzantium and the Early Islamic Conquests.* Cambridge: Cambridge University Press, 1992.
Karsh, Efraim. *Islamic Imperialism: A History.* New Haven, CT: Yale University Press, 2007.
Kennedy, Hugh. *The Great Arab Conquests: How the Spread of Islam Changed the World We Live in.* Cambridge, MA: Da Capo, 2007.
McGraw, Donner F. *The Early Islamic Conquests.* Princeton, NJ: Princeton University Press, 1981.
Nicolle, David. *Armies of the Muslim Conquest.* London: Osprey, 1993.
Shoufani, E. *Al-Riaddah and the Muslim Conquest of Arabia.* Toronto: University of Toronto Press, 1973.

Mutla Ridge (February 25–27, 1991)

Mutla Ridge is the highest point in Kuwait, located just north and west of Kuwait City. The Jahrah Road, the major multilane highway from the city of Kuwait and southern Kuwait to the north, crosses Mutla Ridge. Steep ditches and slopes make the crossing at Mutla Ridge a natural choke point, where only a few vehicles at a time can pass. The sixth highway of the belt of roads circling the city of Kuwait also runs along the ridge and intersects the Jahrah Road near the Mutla police station.

Mutla Ridge caught the attention of coalition war planners in trying to develop the war plan to liberate Kuwait following its occupation by Iraqi forces in 1990. The war planners realized that seizing the ridge would effectively trap Iraqi forces in southern Kuwait. The task of seizing Multa Ridge was assigned to the U.S. 2nd Marine Division. To assist the marines in dealing with any Iraqi armor, they were augmented with the Tiger Brigade of the U.S. Army's 2nd Armored Division.

The ground campaign commenced on February 24, 1991. The marines quickly breached the Iraqi defenses on the Kuwaiti–Saudi Arabian border and moved north, capturing an entire Iraqi tank battalion and taking more than 5,000 prisoners. By the end of the first day of battle, the 2nd Marine Division was 20 miles into Kuwait. The marines quickly defeated an Iraqi counterattack the next morning, and the division continued north.

On the night of February 25, U.S. Marine Corps aircraft reported a large convoy of vehicles leaving Kuwait City on the Jahrah Road. Joint Surveillance and Target Reader System aircraft reported this as well. A flight of 12 F-15 Eagle attack aircraft was immediately dispatched to attack the convoy as it crossed Mutla Ridge. Using cluster bombs, the aircraft destroyed the leading vehicles. Air-dropped mines were also used to seal off the road so as to prevent the following vehicles from continuing around the destroyed leaders. Other vehicles were destroyed at the rear of the convoy to bottle up the fleeing Iraqis. U.S. Navy and Air Force planes continued to pound the Iraqis during the night. Some 1,400 to 1,500 vehicles were trapped there in what became known as the "Highway of Death."

On February 26, the marines and the Tiger Brigade continued their advance toward Mutla Ridge. The area was defended by a minefield through which the Americans had to clear lanes for their vehicles. They then encountered a number of Iraqi bunkers, which also had to be cleared and destroyed. Dug-in Iraqi tanks—almost all of them older T-55 models—were also defending the slopes of Mutla Ridge. During a three-hour battle, the Tiger Brigade destroyed 20 Iraqi tanks and took several hundred prisoners.

When the Tiger Brigade finally reached the crossroads on Mutla Ridge, the tankers saw 18 Iraqi tanks trying to pass through. The Americans opened fire and destroyed 3, and the crews of the other tanks quickly surrendered. The U.S. armored infantry then dismounted and began to clear the nearby Mutla police station. Fighting was fierce, as the Iraqis had to be cleared from each room. Forty Iraqis were killed. One American died when he was wounded and bled to death before he could be evacuated.

With the capture of Mutla Ridge, the Iraqi vehicles were trapped between the 2nd Marine Division and the 1st Marine Division approaching from the south. Coalition aircraft had bombed the convoy all day, and now the marine and army tanks began to fire on the vehicles below. The vehicles completely filled all six lanes of the highway for more than two miles as well as the available shoulders for several hundred yards on either side of the road. Most vehicles were civilian types taken from Kuwaiti citizens that were filled with looted goods. Most of the Iraqis realized that they would not now be able to drive north, and they abandoned the cars and trucks, walking across the desert for home.

Television crews soon arrived on Mutla Ridge, and the images they took were flashed around the world. On the stretch of highway below Mutla Ridge known as the "Highway of Death," the carnage was more apparent than real, however. Tiger Brigade officers who were the first U.S. personnel on the scene said that their troops found some 200 Iraqi bodies among the vehicle wreckage while capturing 2,000 Iraqis hiding nearby in the desert. But the scene of burned-out and bombed vehicles along with some charred bodies presented a gruesome spectacle. In Washington, D.C., President George H. W. Bush and his advisers feared that these would help turn opinion against the coalition effort, for it was patently obvious that the Iraqis had been defeated, and the images helped convince the president to order a cease-fire after only four days of ground operations.

Tim J. Watts

See also
Persian Gulf War, Overview

References
Gordon, Michael R., and Bernard E. Trainor. *The Generals' War: The Inside Story of the Conflict in the Gulf.* New York: Little, Brown, 1995.
Mroczkowski, Dennis P. *U.S. Marines in the Persian Gulf, 1990–1991: With the 2d Marine Division in Desert Shield and Desert Storm.* Washington, DC: History and Museums Division, U.S. Marine Corps, 1993.

Mwawi, Ahmad Ali al- (1897–ca. 1979)

Commander of the Egyptian forces that fought in Palestine during the 1948–1949 Israeli War of Independence. Ahmad Ali al-Mwawi (variously spelled Ahmed Ali el-Muawi, Ahmed Ah el-Mawawi, Ahmed Ali al-Muwawi, and Ahmed Ali al-Muaw) was born in 1897 in Egypt. Little is known about the circumstances of his birth, but he graduated from the Egyptian Military Academy in 1916. A career military officer, by the end of World War II he had risen to the rank of major. In 1945 he was promoted to brigadier general and appointed commander of Egypt's 4th Infantry Brigade.

On the evening of May 11, 1948, al-Mwawi attended a secret meeting of the Egyptian parliament. Before the parliamentary vote to declare war on Israel, he dismissed warnings that the Egyptian Army was unprepared, opining that there would be little real fighting. On May 12, now a major general, al-Mwawi was given command of Egyptian forces in the Sinai.

The Arab battle plan was still unclear, and worse yet, Egyptian war aims were vague, making al-Mwawi uncertain of his objectives. On May 15 he led the Egyptian Expeditionary Forces into Palestine. The Egyptians numbered between 7,000 and 10,000 men, divided into two brigades.

During May 16–24, the Egyptian forces attacked the Jewish settlements of Kibbutz Nirim and Kfar Darom but failed to capture either. Yad Mordechai was repeatedly attacked until its defenders departed on May 24. Before reaching Gaza, the Egyptian forces were split into two formations. The regular army units continued to move northward along the coast, while the irregulars of the Muslim Brotherhood pushed eastward toward Beersheba.

On May 24 the Egyptians reached Majdal. With supply lines stretched thin, al-Mwawi attempted to clear the area in front of his position. On June 3 the Egyptian 9th Rifle Battalion took Kibbutz Nitsanim, employing four tanks in a dawn assault following a nightlong artillery barrage.

On July 18 during the second truce, al-Mwawi sent a report to Cairo describing Egyptian shortages in armaments and matériel. He also reported that the Arab coalition was so divided by mistrust that Egypt must either face serious losses or find a political solution. On October 20, King Farouk I relieved al-Mwawi of his command. It is unclear what happened to al-Mwawi thereafter. He is believed to have died in 1979 in Egypt.

Andrew J. Waskey

See also
Egypt; Farouk I, King of Egypt; Israeli War of Independence

References
Gelber, Yoav. *Palestine 1948: War, Escape and the Emergence of the Palestinian Refugee Problem.* Portland, OR: Sussex Academic, 2001.
Tal, David. *War in Palestine, 1948: Strategy and Diplomacy.* New York: Routledge, 2004.

Mycale, Battle of (479)

The final major engagement of the Second Persian War (480–479 BCE). The battle occurred at Mycale, Ionia, in central coastal Anatolia (today Turkey). Greek tradition dated the battle to September 479, the same day as the Battle of Plataea, but this seems too coincidental to be true.

The Greek fleet under Spartan king Leotychidas II at Delos was invited to Samos by locals, who guaranteed an easy victory. The Greek historian Herodotus records 110 ships there in 480, but they may have been reinforced. The Persians withdrew, beached their ships at Mycale (a promontory on the mainland, on the north of the Bay of Miletus), built a stockade around them, and linked with a land force said to number 60,000 men under Tigranes.

Unless supplemented by rowers equipped as hoplites or troop transports, the hoplite force from the Greek marines at a maximum of 30 per ship (the usual complement was 14: 10 hoplites and 4 archers) can only at best have numbered between 3,300 and 7,500 and could not have faced a Persian army of this size. The Greeks landed and, encouraged by a rumor that the Persians had been defeated at Plataea that morning, routed the Persians. The Persians' Ionian Greek allies defected during the battle, joining in the slaughter of the Persian fugitives.

Herodotus emphasizes the Athenian role in the battle, while Diodorus has the Persians attacking the Greek landing force. Herodotus's account is probably to be preferred, but the most important aspect of the battle is its result.

Mycale confirmed Greek naval superiority in the Aegean and the Hellespont (Dardanelles), and many of the Aegean islands defected to the Hellenic League. This enabled the Greeks to conduct offensive naval and amphibious operations against the Persians and laid the foundations for the Delian League and the subsequent Athenian maritime empire.

IAIN SPENCE

See also
Greco-Persian Wars

References
Green, Peter. *The Greco-Persian Wars.* Rev. ed. Berkeley: University of California Press, 1996.
Lazenby, John F. *The Defence of Greece, 490–479 B.C.* Warminster, UK: Aris and Phillips, 1993.

Myriokephalon, Battle of (September 17, 1176)

Major battle between a Byzantine army under Emperor Manuel I Komnenos and forces of the Seljuk Sultanate of Rum fought on September 17, 1176. Although the battle has generally been named after the fortress of Myriokephalon, it actually took place in the pass of Tzivritze, north of Lake Eğirdir (modern-day Eğirdir Gölü, Turkey) in western Asia Minor.

In 1176, Manuel Komnenos marched eastward from Byzantine territory intending to capture the city of Ikonion (modern-day Konya) from the Seljuks of Rum and reopen the land route to Jerusalem. Seljuk sultan Qilij Arslan II was prepared to treat with Manuel, but Manuel rejected this and pressed on with a large force estimated at between 25,000 and 30,000 men accompanied by a large slow-moving baggage train. The distances were vast, and soon his army was suffering from shortages of food and water. Passing the deserted fortress of Myriokephalon, the Byzantine forces entered the pass of Tzivritze. Inadequate scouting had failed to reveal that the Seljuks controlled it. The Byzantine vanguard got through the pass with few casualties, however, as did most of the main body.

The Seljuks then descended from the heights, with the full weight of their attack falling on the Byzantine right wing, commanded by Baldwin of Antioch, Manuel's brother-in-law. The Byzantine right turned and fled, and Baldwin was killed. The emperor and his bodyguard, trapped behind the baggage train, could neither get information from the vanguard nor send orders forward. A violent sandstorm added further confusion. Qilij Arslan circled around behind the rear of the Byzantines, blocking their retreat.

Byzantine historian Niketas Choniates reports that Manuel contemplated flight but instead abandoned the baggage train and fought his way through to the vanguard, where he was eventually joined by elements of the rear guard and was able to withdraw. Byzantine casualties in the battle were heavy. According to Choniates, half of the army was lost in the battle, and he criticized "foreigners" on the right wing for cowardice. The Byzantine defeat, however, resulted from inadequate reconnaissance, faulty communication, and poor discipline. Many divisions were allowed to march into the pass in open order without deploying their archers effectively and without waiting for following groups and were thus defeated piecemeal.

Having escaped the battle, Manuel made peace with the Seljuks, promising to dismantle the fortifications of Soublaion and Dorylaion, an agreement that he subsequently broke. Manuel himself compared the defeat to that of Manzikert in 1071. In reality the situation in Asia Minor was little changed by it, although it marks the final effort by the Byzantines to recover the interior of Anatolia from the Seljuk Turks.

ROSEMARY MORRIS

See also
Rum, Sultanate of; Seljuk Dynasty

References
Angold, Michael. *The Byzantine Empire 1025–1204: A Political History.* London: Longman, 1997.
Birkenmeier, John W. *The Development of the Komnenian Army, 1081–1180.* Leiden: Brill, 2002.
Haldon, John F. *Warfare, State and Society in the Byzantine World, 565–1204.* London: UCL, 1999.

N

NACHSHON, Operation (April 5–20, 1948)

Israeli military operation undertaken in April 1948 during the Israeli War of Independence (1948–1949). By April 1948, Jerusalem was under siege by Arab forces and cut off from Tel Aviv as the Arabs attempted to prevent Jewish forces from taking the areas assigned to them before the departure of the British from their Palestine mandate. Jerusalem was divided into areas of Jewish and Arab control, and the Jewish enclave there had been deprived of both food supplies and support by mufti of Jerusalem Hasan Salamah's Army of Salvation. With supplies and medicine critically scarce, a link had to be established between the Jewish area of Jerusalem and the rest of the Jewish portions of Israel. Prime Minister David Ben-Gurion ordered a relief operation despite opposition from many members of his staff.

The Israelis conceived an operation, code-named Plan Dalet, to capture those areas mandated to the Jewish state by the United Nations (UN) or, according to other sources, to capture as many Arab-occupied villages and areas as possible. The first stage of this plan was to be Operation NACHSHON (NAKHSHON), the relief of Jerusalem, to be accomplished by opening the road between Tel Aviv and the besieged city. The operation was named for the biblical figure Nachshon ben Aminadav, heralded as the first Israelite to have entered the Red Sea during the exodus from Egypt.

For the operation, Haganah fielded a brigade of approximately 1,500 men, its largest tactical deployment to that point. The largest Haganah force in one operation had been a mere company. Not even a battalion operation had been attempted.

The force committed to NACHSHON was composed largely of the Givati Brigade under the overall command of Shimon Avidan, later a brigadier general. The plan called for the opening of a corridor that would be six miles wide in the coastal plain and some two miles wide in the mountains. Fortunately for the Israelis, a clandestine arms shipment of 200 rifles and 40 machine guns arrived by air on April 1.

To lay the groundwork for the operation, Haganah troops attacked and blew up the headquarters of the grand mufti's Army of Salvation in the town of Ramla. In the process many key staff members were killed, impeding the ability of the Army of Salvation to react to the Israeli moves. The Israelis also captured the village of Kastal, an Arab settlement to the west of Jerusalem, and this effectively blocked access to the city.

NACHSHON officially commenced on the evening of April 5. Two battalions were committed to the initial attack, with one held in reserve. Blocking units covered seven Arab villages, while larger units took and held the Arab villages of Hulda and Deir Mulheism. At the same time, Palmach forces attacked the Arab village of Bayt Machsir Mahsir near Bab al-Wad and cleared the mountain road to Jerusalem. This allowed 60 Palmach trucks carrying supplies to get through to the city.

As the operation moved into high gear, Haganah forces captured the strategic junction town of Latrun on the

Jerusalem Road, driving Arab units from the Wadi al-Sarrar military camp and routing Arab forces at Deir Mulheism and Arab Hulda. Arab units reacted by counterattacking the Haganah forces on April 7 and 8 near the town of Motza and began efforts to retake Kastal, which after six days of nearly continuous fighting they indeed accomplished. At Kastal the situation was dramatically reversed, however, when one of the best Arab commanders, Abd al-Qadir al-Husseini (aka Abu Musa), was killed when approaching an area held by the Israelis that he thought had already been taken. Arab forces then fell back in disarray. On April 11 a Palmach unit found Kastal unoccupied, and supplies then began moving into Jerusalem.

Considerable controversy surrounds the actions of the Irgun Tsvai Leumi (National Military Organization) detachment and the forces of Lehi during NACHSHON. These two units attacked the Arab village of Deir Yassin on the Jerusalem Road. According to some reports, at approximately 5:00 a.m. on April 9 an Israeli truck with a loudspeaker entered Deir Yassin and warned the inhabitants (mostly women and children) to evacuate because a battle was about to take place. Hundreds heeded the warning and departed, but many more stayed and came under tremendous danger as a pitched battle ensued. The battle raged for hours as Arab forces in the town put up a spirited resistance. When combat ceased, there were a number of civilian casualties. Israeli authorities place this figure at approximately 110, whereas Arab sources claim 250 civilians dead. The Arabs as well as the International Red Cross leveled allegations of Israeli bayoneting of pregnant women and other atrocities, including rape and mutilation. Recent historical research suggests that Irgun and Lehi did carry out executions by firing squad after the battle.

The results of the events at Deir Yassin, however, were profound. In retaliation for the attack, Arab forces massacred 70 injured and sick Israelis when they captured an evacuation convoy on the Mount Scopus Road outside Jerusalem on April 13. The subsequent broadcasting by Israeli officials of the atrocities also led to panic among many Palestinians and caused a large-scale flight into exile.

As part of NACHSHON on April 8, Haganah forces also attacked Palestinian militia in the town of Tiberias to relieve Jewish residents there under siege and to help secure a road link to Haganah forces in the northern part of the country. Fighting was intense, but Palmach forces moved in to assist Haganah, and the Arab forces were split. The Arabs called for British aid and, with their help, evacuated Tiberias on April 18.

The relief of Jerusalem was short-lived. Five convoys and the Palmach Harel Brigade made it into the city through April 20, but the relief effort ended that day when only part of an additional convoy got through. Arab forces again sealed off the city.

Operation NACHSHON was important not only because it was the first large military operation undertaken by Haganah, which would later become the nucleus of the Israel Defense Forces (IDF), but also because it was the first occasion in which the fractious and often hostile factions of Irgun, Lehi, Palmach, and Haganah were able to effectively work together in a joint operation. Although the success was only temporary, the relief of Jerusalem in the face of superior odds also demonstrated the élan and fighting abilities of the Israeli forces.

Operation NACHSHON, with the reports of Deir Yassin and the capture of Tiberias, also served to unify the Arab nations surrounding Palestine into support for the Palestinian cause. Arab forces from Egypt, Jordan, and other Arab nations invaded Israel in May 1948, widening the scope of the war. These attacks were largely in direct response to the Israeli successes in NACHSHON and related operations.

RODERICK VOSBURGH

See also
Deir Yassin Massacre; Expellees and Refugees, Palestinian; Haganah; Irgun Tsvai Leumi; Israeli War of Independence; Latrun, Battles of; Lohamei Herut Israel; Marcus, David; Palmach

References
Herzog, Chaim. *The Arab-Israeli Wars: War and Peace in the Middle East from the War of Independence to Lebanon.* Westminster, MD: Random House, 1984.
Karsh, Efraim. *The Palestine War, 1948.* London: Osprey, 2002.
Kurzman, Dan. *Genesis, 1948: The First Arab Israeli War.* New York: Da Capo, 1992.
Lorch, Netanel. *The Edge of the Sword: Israel's War of Independence, 1947–1949.* Norwalk, CT: Easton, 1991.
Milstein, Uri. *History of Israel's War of Independence.* 4 vols. Lanham, MD: University Press of America, 1996–1999.

Nadir Shah (1688–1747)

Shah of Persia and founder of the Afsharid dynasty. Nadir (Nader) Shah was born on August 6, 1688, at Dastgerd in Khorasan Province in the northeastern Persian Empire. He was a member of the Turkic Afshar tribe. His father was a shepherd who died when Nadir was young. According to tradition, Nadir and his mother were carried off as slaves by Uzbek or Turkmen raiders, but Nadir escaped and joined a band of brigands and rose to become their leader and a powerful military figure.

The Safavid dynasty that had ruled Persia since 1602 was then in collapse, enabling the Ottomans and Russians to carve off great chunks of the empire. Nadir rose to national prominence when he helped drive the Ghilzai Afghans out of Khorasan. Subsequently, Shah Tahmasp II (1729–1732) made Nadir commander of the Persian Army.

In late 1726 Nadir retook Mashhad in present-day northeastern Iran, which had rebelled against the shah. In May 1729 Nadir defeated the Abdai Afghans near Herat. He then defeated Ashraf, new shah of the Ghilzai Afghans, in the Battle of Damghnan (September 29–October 5, 1729) and again, decisively, at Murchakhort (November). Nadir then took Isfahan.

Tahmasp appointed Nadir governor of a number of eastern provinces, including Khorasan, and married him to Tahmasp's sister. In the spring of 1730 Nadir attacked the Ottomans, regaining much of the territory taken from Persia earlier. Forced by a revolt of the Abdali Afghans to suspend operations against the Ottomans, Nadir defeated them in a 14-month campaign during 1730–1731.

Shah Tahmasp meanwhile grew jealous of Nadir's success and, while Nadir was absent in the east, launched a campaign of his own to recapture Yerevan from the Ottomans. It ended in the loss of all of Nadir's recent gains and the cession of Georgia and Armenia in exchange for Tabriz. Furious at events, Nadir decided to take power himself. He denounced the treaty and in 1732 forced Tahmasp to abdicate in favor of his baby son, Abbas III, with Nadir as regent.

Nadir hoped to regain Armenia and Georgia by seizing Ottoman-held Baghdad and exchanging it for them. Invading Mesopotamia in 1733, he defeated one Ottoman army, then laid siege to Baghdad. But he turned with part of his force to do battle with a larger Ottoman relief force under Topal Osman and was defeated in the Battle of Kirkuk (July 19), whereupon the Ottoman garrison at Baghdad sortied and defeated the Persian troops there. Despite these disasters, Nadir rallied his remaining forces and held off Topal. With the arrival of reinforcements from Persia, Nadir again took the offensive and defeated Topal, who was killed, in the Battle of Leilan near Kirkuk. News of a revolt in Fars, however, led Nadir to break off his renewed siege of Baghdad and conclude the Treaty of Baghdad with Ahmed Pasha.

Nadir suppressed the revolt at Fars, then invaded Transcaucasia and won a great victory over a larger Ottoman force under Abdulla Koprula at Baghavard (June 8, 1735). By the summer of 1735 Nadir had secured Armenia and Georgia.

Portrait of Nadir Shah (1688–1747). The ruler of Persia and founder of the Afsharid dynasty, he conquered considerable territory and united the Persian Empire. One of the great military commanders in history, he was assassinated in 1747 at age 48 and Persia then reverted to chaos. (Los Angeles County Museum of Art)

Meanwhile, aware that Russia was preparing to go to war against the Ottoman Empire, he used the threat of joining the Ottomans to conclude the Treaty of Ganja (March 10, 1735), under the terms of which the Russians agreed to withdraw all of their troops from Persian territory. This completed the return of the Caspian provinces to Persia.

In January 1736, Nadir held a grand meeting of notables in the Mongol tradition and suggested that he be named shah in place of the five-year-old Abbas III. The representatives agreed, and Nadir was crowned on March 8, 1736.

Nadir now commanded the most powerful military force in Asia, if not the world of his day. He insisted on thorough training and based his campaigns on rapid movement over great distances. He favored cavalry attacks, which could come without warning from any direction. While his armies were weak in heavy artillery, his light artillery was excellent thanks in large part to French and Russian experts in his employ. Nadir also understood the value of naval power. Again assisted by European experts, he built up a naval force in the Persian Gulf and a small fleet on the Caspian Sea.

During 1737–1738 Nadir invaded Afghanistan. He took Kandahar in 1738 following a nine-month-long siege, during which he detached forces to secure the former Persian provinces of Balkh and Baluchistan. Nadir's lenient treatment of the Afghans caused many of them to join his army.

In 1738 seeking to punish Mogul (Mughal) emperor Mohammed Shah for supporting the Afghans, Nadir invaded India. He captured both Ghazni and Kabul (September), then bypassed a 50,000-man Mogul army guarding the Khyber Pass, crossing instead over the nearby Tsatsobi Pass, then circled around behind the Moguls and defeated them. Advancing into India, Nadir took Peshawar and Lahore, then crossed the Indus River. Mohammed Shah marched from Delhi with 80,000–150,000 men to meet Nadir Shah's army of 50,000 at Karmal, some 75 miles north of Delhi (February 14, 1738). Nadir was victorious and marched on Delhi and sacked it (March 9). He left Mohammed Shah on the throne but annexed Indian territory north and west of the Indus River. The Mogul Empire never recovered from this blow.

In 1740 Nadir conquered Bukhara (Bokhara, Boukhara) and Khiva in present-day Uzbekistan. Defeating the Uzbeks in the Battle of Charjul and the Battle of Khiva, he annexed the territory south of the Aral Sea. In 1741, Nadir attempted to put down an uprising of the Lesgians in Dagestan (Daghestan) on the Caspian Sea but was stymied by their resort to guerrilla warfare.

The invasion of India was the height of Nadir's rule. After it, increasingly troubled by poor health, he became ever more despotic. In 1743 the Ottomans invaded Persian territory seeking to exploit growing unrest in Persia over Nadir Shah's inept, cruel rule and his religious policies. Nadir blocked their larger army east of Kars, then defeated the Ottomans decisively in the Battle of Kars (August 19, 1745). Nadir went on to occupy most of Armenia.

Nadir's growing persecution of his own people and the heavy taxes he imposed to fight his many wars brought revolt in late 1745. On June 19, 1747, at age 48, Nadir was assassinated by his own officers, who feared that he planned to execute them. Persia then reverted to chaos.

The last great Asiatic conqueror, known as the Persian Napoleon, Nadir remained illiterate. A man of ruthless ambition and immense energy, he was certainly one of the great captains of military history. A master strategist, he was immensely successful in raising armies. He was also both cynical and cruel, and his reign was marked by violence and bloodshed. Nonetheless, he had taken Persia from near collapse to dominant power in the region.

Spencer C. Tucker

See also
Baghavard, First Battle of; Baghdad, 1733 Battle of; Ganja, Treaty of; Kars, Battle of; Leilan, Battle of; Ottoman-Persian Wars of the 18th and 19th Centuries

References
Axworthy, Michael. *The Sword of Persia: Nader Shah, from Tribal Warrior to Conquering Tyrant.* New York: Palgrave Macmillan, 2006.
Lockhart, Laurence. *Nadir Shah: A Critical Study Based Mainly upon Contemporary Sources.* New York: AMS Press, 1973.
Lockhart, Laurence. *The Navy of Nadir Shaw.* London: Iran Society, 1936.
Maynard, John, Sr. *Nadir Shah.* Oxford, UK: B. H. Blackwell, 1885.

Naguib, Mohammad (1901–1984)

Egyptian Army general and first president of the Republic of Egypt (1953–1954). Born in Khartoum on February 20, 1901, Mohammad Naguib (Najib) grew up in Sudan, which was then under de facto British control. Naguib's father was an Egyptian Army officer, and his mother was Sudanese. Naguib was educated at Gordon College and the Military Academy, from which he was commissioned as an artillery officer in 1918. He studied English, French, Italian, and German as well as political science and economics and earned a law degree in 1927.

Naguib soon came under suspicion for his strong nationalistic and anti-British political views. In 1934 he was transferred to the Coast Guard and posted to Sudan, where he was involved in efforts to prevent smuggling. In 1942, embittered regarding King Farouk's refusal to stand up to the British, Naguib submitted his resignation, which was rejected.

Naguib distinguished himself as a brigadier general and brigade commander in the 1948–1949 Israeli War of Independence and was considered one of the few Egyptian war heroes from that conflict. In 1950 he was promoted to major general. In 1951 he again unsuccessfully sought to resign to protest Farouk's policies.

In 1949 Naguib joined the Free Officers Movement. Led by Egyptian nationalist colonel Gamal Abdel Nasser and composed of young, relatively junior Egyptian Army officers, the Free Officers Movement sought to oust Farouk and reform the military due to its belief that it had been mismanaged in Palestine. The Free Officers Movement wanted to install a truly Egyptian government to the country (the royal family being Turko-Circassians) and put an end to all British interference. Naguib instead of King Farouk's preferred candidate was elected president of the Officer's Club, a signal that the king no longer enjoyed the army's loyalty.

Discontent against the government having increased, on January 19, 1952, rioting broke out at Ismailiyya. British troops then occupied the town, killing 40 of the local police and wounding 70. When the events at Ismailiyya became known in Cairo on January 26, mobs took to the streets, burning hundreds of well-known British- or other foreign-owned establishments. The human toll was 26 dead and 552 wounded. The government was slow to act, and a power vacuum existed. King Farouk and his ministers suspected trouble in the army and were planning to move against the Free Officers, but the latter acted first and seized power on July 23, 1952.

On July 26 the Revolutionary Command Council (RCC) demanded that King Farouk renounce the throne and leave Egypt. He departed the same day, abdicating in favor of his infant son as King Ahmed Fuad II. Ali Mahir served as prime minister, but Naguib soon replaced him.

The RCC of 13 army officers now held power, although the monarchy continued for one year with a regency council for the infant king. On June 18, 1953, the military junta ended the monarchy altogether and declared Egypt a republic. Naguib then became the unelected president.

The RCC did not cancel the liberal parliamentary form of government, but when the various political parties failed to come to agreement, the RCC took over the country's administration. Rural poverty and violence against large landowners had encouraged proposals for land reform in the Egyptian parliament, and discussion of the issue continued in the RCC. In 1952 Naguib announced the first Agrarian Reform Law, which sparked many panicked land sales.

Although Naguib was the nominal Egyptian leader, real authority remained in the hands of the RCC, which was split into two factions, one that urged a return to a parliamentary system and the other, under Nasser, that opposed handing over power to the existing political parties. The two factions had other differences as well, including policies regarding the Muslim Brotherhood and the fate of Sudan.

Nasser's faction of the RCC won the power struggle. On February 14, 1954, the RCC announced Naguib's resignation from his posts, saying that he had demanded absolute authority and that this was not acceptable. Following popular demonstrations in Sudan and then one in Cairo with the near mutiny of a cavalry corps, the RCC reversed itself and withdrew Naguib's resignation on February 26. On April 18, however, Nasser became the prime minister and RCC chairman, leaving Naguib as president only and in an increasingly isolated position. Finally, on November 14, 1954, Naguib was placed under house arrest. The RCC accused him of involvement in an assassination attempt on Nasser by the Muslim Brotherhood. A Sudanese delegation preempted Naguib from being tried for conspiracy but could not bring him back to power. The RCC offered the presidency to Ahmad Lutfi al-Sayyid, who turned it down, and Nasser then assumed that position as well.

Naguib was released from confinement in 1982 by order of Egyptian president Hosni Mubarak and died on August 29, 1984.

Spencer C. Tucker and Sherifa Zuhur

See also
Farouk I, King of Egypt; Israeli War of Independence; Mubarak, Hosni; Nasser, Gamal Abdel

References
Abdel-Malek, Anouar. *Egypt: Military Society, the Army Regime, the Left, and Social Change under Nasser.* New York: Random House, 1968.
Al-Sayyid Marsot, Afaf Lutfi. *A Short History of Modern Egypt.* Cambridge: Cambridge University Press, 1985.
Waterbury, John. *The Egypt of Nasser and Sadat: Political Economy of Two Regimes.* Princeton, NJ: Princeton University Press, 1983.

Nahr al-Bared Refugee Camp, Siege of (May 20–September 2, 2007)

Three-month siege by the Lebanese Army of militants in a refugee camp in northern Lebanon. The siege claimed more than 300 lives and captured widespread attention. On May 20, 2007, Fatah al-Islam, a radical group of some 360 Sunni Muslims inspired by the terrorist Al Qaeda organization, seized control of the Nahr al-Bared refugee camp northeast of Tripoli near the Syrian border and carried out a series of attacks on nearby Lebanese Army checkpoints, killing 22 soldiers.

Despite fears that fighting would spread to others of the 12 Palestinian refugee camps in Lebanon, the army responded by laying siege to and carrying out military operations against the camp. There was some fighting at Ain al-Hilwe refugee camp at Sidon in southern Lebanon in early June, as members of Nahr al-Bared there attacked an army checkpoint and demanded that the army halt its attacks on Nahr al-Bared in the north. A cease-fire was soon secured at Ain al-Hilwe, however.

Meanwhile, most of the estimated 30,000 inhabitants of Nahr al-Bared fled as the army brought up artillery and helicopters and shelled and rocketed the camp. Palestinian refugee camps in Lebanon had long been considered off limits to the army, but on this occasion army forces entered the camp in order to root out the insurgents.

At dawn on September 2, 2007, the remaining members of Nahr al-Bared attempted to flee the camp. In the ensuing firefight with Lebanese forces 31 of them were killed including their leader, Shakir al-Abassi. Another 32 were captured. Five Lebanese soldiers also died. The army then took control of Nahr al-Bared.

In all, the siege of Nahr al-Bared claimed the lives of an estimated 120 militants, at least 42 civilians, and 157 soldiers. During the siege the United States flew in substantial military aid to the Lebanese Army, and all major political factions in Lebanon, including Hezbollah, voiced strong support for the army, which was increasingly seen by the general population of a badly divided Lebanon as the one element in the country capable of holding it together. Events also greatly enhanced both the prestige and political clout of army commander General Michel Suleiman. Following the siege, Prime Minister Fuad Siniura pledged to rebuild the camp and secure the return of the refugees.

SPENCER C. TUCKER

See also
Al Qaeda; Lebanon; Siniura, Fuad

References
Bakri, Nada. "Lebanese Troops Seize Refugee Camp." *New York Times*, September 3, 2007.
Fisk, Robert. *Pity the Nation: The Abduction of Lebanon*. New York: Simon and Schuster, 1991.

Najaf, First Battle of (August 5–27, 2004)

Iraq War battle between U.S. forces and the Islamist Mahdi Army militia, controlled by Muqtada al-Sadr, during August 5–27, 2004. The Iraqi city of Najaf is located about 100 miles south of Baghdad and had a prewar population estimated at 585,000 people. Najaf is one of the holy cities of Shia Islam and a major center for Shia religious pilgrimages, education, and political power.

In March 1991 following the Persian Gulf War, the residents of Najaf rebelled against the regime of Iraqi dictator Saddam Hussein as part of a larger Shiite uprising against the government. Hussein's forces suppressed the uprising in the city with great brutality. Early in the Iraq War (Operation IRAQI FREEDOM) following two days of heavy fighting, Najaf was assaulted and then captured on April 1, 2003, by units of the U.S. 101st Airborne (Air Assault) Division, commanded by Major General David Petraeus.

Following the overthrow of Hussein's regime later that same month, Najaf witnessed the gradual emergence of the powerful cleric Muqtada al-Sadr, whose Mahdi Army militia was based in the city, as were the Badr Brigades. In April and May 2004 Sadr's militia led an uprising in Najaf that largely usurped control of the city from U.S. forces. Sadr's militia also took on U.S. and coalition military forces across the Shia-controlled areas of southern Iraq. On May 27 Sadr reached a deal with the Americans by which both sides agreed to withdraw their forces from Najaf. The Mahdi militia soon began rebuilding its forces in the city, however.

On July 31, 2004, the 11th Marine Expeditionary Unit, commanded by Colonel Anthony Haslam, took up positions around Najaf, relieving the army's Task Force Dragon. The marines first clashed with the Mahdi militia on August 2, when a marine patrol approached a house believed to be occupied by Sadr. Major fighting erupted on August 5 when the Mahdi militia attacked an Iraqi government police station and the marines responded in force. On August 9 three additional battalions of troops from the 1st Cavalry Division were sent from Baghdad to Najaf to reinforce the marines. Combat took the form of street fighting, with the Mahdi militia employing rocket-propelled grenades, mortars, and automatic rifles against U.S. Abrams tanks, Bradley Fighting Vehicles, attack helicopters, and infantry. A number of Abrams tanks and Bradley Fighting Vehicles were knocked out or heavily damaged by rocket-propelled grenades, and one U.S. helicopter was shot down.

After a few days, the scene of the fighting had approached the Imam Ali Mosque and a huge adjacent cemetery known as the Wadi of Peace. Because the mosque and cemetery represent some of the holiest sites in Shiite Islam, concerns were expressed throughout the Arab world for their safety, but the heavy fighting continued.

The turning point in the battle came on August 26, when two U.S. Air Force F-16 aircraft dropped four 2,000-pound Joint Direct Attack Munition (JDAM) bombs on hotels near the Imam Ali Mosque, then occupied by the Mahdi militia. The air strike prompted Sadr to negotiate a truce the next day. The Mahdi militia agreed to turn in its weapons and leave Najaf. In return, U.S. forces also left Najaf, and security was turned over to the Iraqi police. The Imam Ali Mosque did not suffer any significant damage during the Battle of Najaf.

Casualty figures remain in dispute. The Americans claimed that several hundred members of the Madhi Army were killed in the fight, but militia spokesmen claim that the toll was fewer than 30 dead. Eight U.S. service personnel were killed, and 30 more were wounded. The Battle of Najaf showcased not only the rise to prominence of such radical extremists as Sadr but also the general elevation of tensions between Shia, Sunnis, and Kurds in Iraq. By the end of 2004 U.S. and coalition forces found themselves locked in a deadly struggle with all the signs of a civil war, despite protestations to the contrary by both U.S. president George W. Bush and British prime minister Tony Blair. Indeed, the situation in Iraq continued to deteriorate until the summer of 2008, when some signs indicated that the Iraq insurgency violence had subsided a bit, a development that the British and Americans said was the result of the troop surge, implemented in 2007.

PAUL WILLIAM DOERR

See also
Hussein, Saddam; Iraq Insurgency; Petraeus, David Howell; Sadr, Muqtada al-; Shia Islam

References
Bremer, L. Paul, with Malcolm McConnell. *My Year in Iraq: The Struggle to Build a Future of Hope.* New York: Simon and Schuster, 2006.
Ricks, Thomas E. *Fiasco: The American Military Adventure in Iraq.* New York: Penguin, 2006.
Woodward, Bob. *State of Denial: Bush at War, Part III.* New York: Simon and Schuster, 2006.

Najaf, Second Battle of (January 28, 2007)

Fierce battle between the Iraqi Army and police, heavily aided by U.S. and British military units and airpower, and hundreds of well-armed followers of Ahmad al-Hassan al-Basri. The battle occurred on January 28, 2007, in the town of Zarqa, some 10 miles from the southern Iraqi Shia shrine city of Najaf. Details about Basri, his messianic religious movement known as the Soldiers of Heaven (Jund al-Samaa), and the battle itself are hotly debated.

According to some accounts, based on interviews with captured members of the group, Basri was the deputy to Dhia Abd al-Zahra Khadhim al-Krimawi (who died in 2007), a shadowy Iraqi Shia leader who claimed to be Imam Mahdi, the 12th in a line of religious and political leaders whom Shias believe will return at a time decided by God to usher in a period of absolute justice that will precede the Day of Judgment. The fate of Basri remains unknown, with some sources in the Shia religious establishment in southern Iraq claiming that he survived the battle and is living in seclusion, possibly in the southern shrine city of Karbala.

Following the suppression of the group, the Iraqi government and military spokespeople claimed that Basri, Krimawi, and their followers were really Sunnis and not Shias, although evidence of this is sketchy at best. The Iranian government, Al Qaeda, and remnants of the Iraqi Baath Party have all been accused of supporting the group. Initial Iraqi government reports claimed that foreign Sunnis from countries as far as Pakistan and Afghanistan were killed or captured fighting against Iraqi security forces. These reports were challenged, however, when dead and captured Jund fighters were identified as Iraqis instead of foreigners.

Anonymous sources in the Hawza Ilmiyya, the Shia seminary system in Najaf, have stated that Basri was a former student who left because of disagreements over religious theology with the seminary's religious scholars. Shia clerics loyal to Mahmoud Sarkhi al-Hassani, who heads another Shia messianic party in southern Iraq, denied that Basri and Krimawi were associated with their group. Hassani is a former student of Grand Ayatollah Sayyid Muhammad Sadiq al-Sadr, the father of Muqtada al-Sadr, and claims to be the representative of Imam Mahdi. His group broke with the larger Sadr Movement (Tayyar al-Sadr) over theological and political disputes, including a disagreement about who should assume command of the movement, Muqtada or Hassani. The latter has a relatively small but devoted following in southern Iraq. According to other sources, Basri was also a former student of Sadiq al-Sadr, a popular Shia religious opposition leader who was assassinated with two of his sons in 1999, probably by Baath Party operatives. These sources claim that the two had a falling out when the Iraqi Baathists attempted to split Sadiq al-Sadr's increasingly powerful sociopolitical network by sponsoring a rival splinter group, the Mehwadiya led by Basri.

Fighting began on January 28, 2007, when Iraqi police and a battalion of soldiers from the Iraqi 8th Army Division attempted to carry out a morning raid on an alleged safe house used by the Jund. They were acting on information that the group planned to assassinate Grand Ayatollah Sayyid Ali Husayn al-Sistani, Iraq's senior resident Shia religious authority, and other grand ayatollahs and senior religious leaders in Najaf. The assassinations allegedly were to be carried out during Ashura, the Shia period of mourning in commemoration for the martyrdom of Imam Hussein bin Ali and dozens of his companions and family members at Karbala in 680 by soldiers sent by the Umayyad caliph Yazid I. The Jund were reportedly acting on the orders of Basri to prepare for the return of Imam Mahdi and the establishment of a religious state governed with absolute justice, as foretold in Shia religious sources and traditions. Reportedly, group members planned to hide their weapons and use the sheer number of people, millions of Iraqis and foreign Shias who flood into the southern Iraqi shrine cities of Najaf, Karbala, and Kufa during Ashura, to their advantage, hiding in the crowds to get close to the grand ayatollahs' residences.

The Iraqi soldiers and police were soon overwhelmed by hundreds of armed Jund fighters and became pinned down by heavy gunfire, forcing them to call for U.S. and British air support, which came in the form of air strikes by F-16 aircraft and AH-64 Apache helicopter gunships along with a small contingent of British fighter jets. The aircraft dropped 500-pound bombs on Jund positions, including significant numbers of fighters in a grove of trees in Zarqa. In the early afternoon, the U.S. 25th Infantry Division and other units were sent from bases near Baghdad to aid the besieged Iraqi units.

During the 15 hours of fighting, one U.S. Apache helicopter was shot down, killing its 2 crew members, and 25 Iraqi soldiers and police were also killed. Iraqi government and U.S. military estimates place the number of Jund casualties at somewhere between 250 and 400, although the number was probably closer to 250–263, among them Krimawi. More than 450 Jund fighters were captured alive and later tried by Iraqi courts. Millions of dollars and a large cache of weapons, including antiaircraft guns, rockets, and automatic rifles, were seized from the Jund's well-equipped compound.

In September 2007 an Iraqi court sentenced 10 Jund leaders to death and 384 fighters to prison terms ranging from 15 years to life. It freed 54. Despite the trial and the apparent decimation of the Jund, the group is but one of several messianic Mahdist Shia groups active in post-Hussein Iraq. The largest is the party led by Mahmoud al-Hassani, who claims the rank of grand ayatollah despite the fact that his religious scholarly credentials do not support his claims and he is not recognized as such by Iraq's Shia religious establishment, the *marjaiyya*. Hassani's popularity is reportedly growing in southern Iraq as a greater number of the country's Shias become disenchanted with the *marjaiyya* traditionalists and the ruling Shia political parties such as the Islamic Dawa Party, the Sadr Movement, and the Supreme Islamic Iraqi Council.

CHRISTOPHER PAUL ANZALONE

See also

Najaf, First Battle of; Sadr, Muqtada al-; Sistani, Sayyid Ali Hisayn al-

References

Cave, Damien. "Mystery Arises over Identity of Militia Chief in Najaf Fight." *New York Times*, February 1, 2007.
Cave, Darien. "250 Are Killed in Major Iraq Battle." *New York Times*, January 29, 2007.
Cockburn, Patrick. "US 'Victory' against Cult Leader Was 'Massacre.'" *The Independent*, January 31, 2007.
Colvin, Ross. "US Military Still Probing Iraqi Cult Battle." *Reuters*, February 2, 2007.
Hardy, Roger. "Confusion Surrounds Najaf Battle." *BBC News*, January 31, 2007.
Jamail, Dahr, and Ali al-Fadhily. "Pilgrims Massacred in the 'Battle' of Najaf." *Asia Times*, February 2, 2007.
Santora, Marc. "Fierce Militia Fighters Catch Iraqi Army by Surprise." *International Herald Tribune*, January 30, 2007.
Visser, Reidar. *The Sadrists of Basra and the Far South of Iraq: The Most Unpredictable Political Force in the Gulf's Oil-Belt Region?* Oslo, Norway: Norwegian Institute of International Affairs, 2008.

Nasar, Mustafa bin Abd al-Qadir Setmariam (1958–)

One of militant Islam's most prolific strategic theorists in the past for decades and a member of the Al Qaeda terrorist organization. Mustafa bin Abd al-Qadir Setmariam Nasar (Abu Mus'ab al-Suri) was born in Aleppo, Syria, in 1958. He is widely known by his nom de guerre of Abu Mus'ab al-Suri.

Nasar experienced a religious awakening in 1980 after studying engineering at the University of Aleppo for four years. Joining a branch of the Syrian Muslim Brotherhood, he left Syria in 1980, never to return. Despite his self-imposed exile, he maintained his Syrian roots and connections, for the Syrian word "al-Suri" means "the Syrian," and he was considered the Syrian representative in Al Qaeda's highest leadership circles.

Nasar traveled widely after leaving Syria. He is known to have resided in Jordan, Saudi Arabia, Iraq, and France (mid-1980s), Afghanistan (1987–1992), Spain (1992–1997), and Afghanistan again from 1997 to 2002. While in Spain, he married a Spanish woman and secured Spanish citizenship. During his first visit to Afghanistan, he met both Abdallah Azzam and Osama bin Laden, founders of Al Qaeda. Nuri may have received sanctuary in Iran after the U.S.-led invasion of Afghanistan (Operation ENDURING FREEDOM) began in late 2001, and he reportedly traveled to Iraq to visit Ansar al-Islam's camp in Kurdistan prior to the U.S.-led invasion of Iraq in March 2003. In November 2004, the U.S. government offered a $5 million reward for information leading to his capture.

Nasar is best known for his prolific theoretical writing and speaking on jihad and the appropriate strategies for waging war against the West. His writings are notable for their systematic efforts to learn from past mistakes. His first book, *The Syrian Islamic Jihadist Revolution—Pains and Hopes,* was published around 1990 in Peshawar, Pakistan. In the 1990s, he established a media center called the Islamic Conflict Studies Bureau LTD and was able to create major media opportunities for bin Laden and the Al Qaeda leadership during 1996–1998. During this period he wrote a number of studies and analyses of jihadist efforts in the Middle East, Central Asia, and South Asia. His 160-page *Musharraf's Pakistan: The Problem and the Solution! And the Necessary Obligation* was published in late 2004. It called for the overthrow of the Pervez Musharraf regime, a call later echoed by Al Qaeda second-in-command Ayman al-Zawahiri. At about the same time, Nasar finally completed the 1,600-page *The Call for a Global Islamic Resistance,* a work he had begun in the early 1990s that articulates his ideas for a new global guerrilla warfare strategy based on a decentralized model of organization. He also hoped to write a book on jihad guerrilla strategy titled *The Fundamentals for Jihadi Guerrilla Warfare in Light of the Conditions of the Contemporary American Campaign* based on his lectures and research in Afghanistan, but he was arrested before the manuscript could be completed. Several transcripts of his lectures on this topic have been released on jihadi websites following his arrest.

Nasar apparently had strong reservations about the September 11 attacks on the United States. On the one hand, he recognized their mobilizing effect on the Islamic community. On the other hand, he also recognized that the attacks provided a justification for U.S. invasion, which shattered the jihadi movement. This recognition led to his publication of *The Call for a Global Islamic Resistance,* in which he argued that the old local and regional covert organizations (*tanzims*) were no longer an effective way of conducting revolution. Their large hierarchical organization, firmly rooted geographically, raised too many risks in an era of dominant American military and political influence and active opposition from many local governments. Nasar instead argued that a transnational structure based on small cells held together by common doctrine and ideology could carry out terror operations at lower risk. This also would create a deterritorialized jihadist war in which operations are carried out on a global scale, and resistance to occupation is not confined to the theater in question.

Nasar himself insisted in his writings that he was primarily a theorist and thinker, not an executor of operations. However, he is suspected of having had deep operational involvement in a variety of conflicts and, since 2001, attacks or attempted attacks on Western states. He fought with Al Qaeda and the Taliban in Afghanistan, where his experiences during American air strikes contributed strongly to his reassessment of proper resistance tactics. He is strongly suspected of involvement in the March 2004 Madrid bombing attacks and has been linked in some reports to attacks in London in July 2005. British authorities reportedly suspect that he had some involvement in the 1995 Paris Metro bombings, and he has significant ties with terrorist cells in both Europe and the Maghreb as well as a record of support for the Algerian terrorist organization Armed Islamic Group. Some reports also link him with Abu Mus'ab al-Zarqawi, as both men are associated with a virulent dislike of Shia Islam, and at least one account notes that the intellectually sophisticated and articulate Nasar must have had a strong ideological impact on the barely educated Zarqawi.

Nasar also ran a major training camp called Al Ghuraba (The Aliens) in Afghanistan from 2000 to 2001 that trained foreign fighters for Al Qaeda and the Taliban. Also, he is reported to have assisted in Al Qaeda's experiments with chemical weapons. Nasar almost certainly trained Al Qaeda operatives who went back to Europe and created sleeper cells.

Interestingly, Nasar was linked with a group of secessionists inside Al Qaeda who reportedly rejected bin Laden's leadership and pledged loyalty to the Taliban. Nasar had to take an oath of obedience to Mullah Mohammed Omar, leader of the Taliban, in order to run his training camp. Nasar himself denied rumors of a split, however, and emphasized his close links with Al Qaeda leadership, including his invitation to bin Laden's wedding in 2000. The nature of the connection to Al Qaeda is in some respects irrelevant, as Nasar's writings provide the basis for a school of jihadi strategic studies that have profoundly affected Al Qaeda and other transnational terrorist networks and raised significant concern for Western analysts and policy makers.

In late 2005, Pakistani security forces reportedly captured Nasar in Quetta. Believed to have been transferred to Syria, where he was a wanted man, he is believed to be held in a Syrian prison.

Timothy D. Hoyt

See also
Al Qaeda; Bin Laden, Osama; Terrorism

References
Lacey, Jim, ed. *A Terrorist's Call to Global Jihad: Deciphering Abu Musab al-Suri's Islamic Jihad Manifesto.* Annapolis, MD: Naval Institute Press, 2008.

Lia, Brynjar. *Architect of Global Jihad: The Life of Al-Qaeda Strategist Abu Mus'ab Al-Suri.* New York: Columbia University Press, 2008.

Nasiriyah, Battle of (March 23–29, 2003)

The Shiite-dominated town of Nasiriyah occupies an important location in southern Iraq. Situated some 225 miles southeast of the capital of Baghdad, Nasiriyah is the fourth most populous city of Iraq after Baghdad, Basra, and Mosul. In 2003 Nasiriyah had a population of some 560,000 people. It is also an important transportation hub, with key bridges spanning the Euphrates River on either side of the city. Located close to Tallil Airfield and the headquarters of the Iraqi Army III Corps of three divisions, Nasiriyah was thus a key objective in the first phases of the Iraq War. During the 1991 Persian Gulf War, Nasiriyah had been the most northerly point in Iraq for U.S. forces, with the 82nd Airborne having reached the city's outskirts.

In 2003 the task of taking Nasiriyah and the bridges over the Euphrates fell to U.S. Marine Corps Task Force Tarawa (TF Tarawa), commanded by Brigadier General Richard Natonski. TF Tarawa was the code name for the 2nd Marine Expeditionary Brigade, centered on the 2nd Marine Regiment, Marine Aircraft Group 29, Company A, the 8th Tank Battalion (with M-1 Abrams tanks) and Combat Service Support Battalion 22. TF Tarawa was the vanguard of the I Marine Expeditionary Force (I MEF), commanded by Lieutenant General James Conway, that was centered on the 1st Marine Division led by Major General James Mattis.

TF Tarawa's assignments were to first secure Jalibah Air Base and then secure the bridges across the Euphrates and the Saddam Canal. Taking and holding these crossing points were essential for enabling the 1st Marine Division to continue its drive northward on Highway 7 toward Kut. With this accomplished, TF Tarawa was to keep open the supply corridor that would enable the 1st Marine Division to continue north and engage and defeat the Republican Guard divisions defending the southern approaches to Baghdad.

In its drive north into Iraq from Kuwait, TF Tarawa was obliged to move through the desert to get to Jalibah Air Base because the supply vehicles of the U.S. Army's 3rd Infantry Division, which had movement priority, occupied the roads. Meanwhile, the 3rd Infantry Division also advanced toward Baghdad, taking a crossing over the Euphrates west of Nasiriyah. As the 3rd Infantry Division defeated Iraqi forces in and around Tallil Airfield and bypassed Nasiriyah to the west, TF Tarawa moved on that city.

TF Tarawa departed Jalibah Air Base for Nasiriyah early on March 23, but taking the city did not go according to plan. Natonski had planned for the 1st Battalion, 2nd Marine Regiment, to move through the eastern part of Nasiriyah and seize one of the northern bridges, after which another battalion was to secure the city, thereby allowing the three regimental combat teams of the I MEF to continue the drive north on Route 7.

The marines had anticipated fighting at Nasiriyah but not the level of resistance encountered. One thing did go according to plan: much of the Iraqi 11th Division simply deserted. What the marines had also expected did not occur, however: an uprising by the population of Nasiriyah against the regime. The inhabitants had done so in 1991, and many had been massacred by the Saddam Hussein regime. The survivors had learned their lesson. Indeed, they now prepared to defend the city. The composition of those fighting is still disputed, with some of the fighters certainly being members of the Fedayeen Saddam who began arriving in the city on March 22 in private vehicles and commandeered buses. Although poorly trained, they were fanatical fighters and willing to die in a jihad. Under the command of ruthless Iraqi general Al Hassan al-Majid, a relative of Hussein who had charge of the south, the defenders of Nasiriyah prepared to do battle with the marines.

Fighting began as soon as the leading marine element, the 1st Battalion, 2nd Marine Regiment, supported by some armor, arrived at the city outskirts. The marines quickly destroyed nine stationary T-72 tanks—a number of them bereft of engines—that had been dug in to defend a railroad bridge south of the river.

At about 7:30 a.m., marines of A Company were startled to make contact with an American military truck belonging to the army's 507th Maintenance Company. The men in it informed the marines that their 18 trucks had been part of a 3rd Infantry Division supply column. The 507th Maintenance Company, which included female soldiers Jessica Lynch and Lori Piestewa, had taken a wrong turn on Route 7 and proceeded into Nasiriyah, where it had been ambushed. In the ensuing fighting, 11 American soldiers had been killed, and 6 others, including Lynch and Piestewa, were taken prisoner. Piestewa died of her wounds shortly after capture, while the remaining 5 prisoners, including Lynch, were later rescued. Piestewa was a member of the Hopi tribe and is thus believed to have been the first Native American woman killed in combat in a foreign war. On learning of the plight of the 507th Maintenance Company, the marines immediately headed north and rescued a dozen wounded members of that unit.

Unfortunately for the marines, the appearance of the 507th Maintenance Company trucks had alerted the defenders of Nasiriyah to the imminent arrival of other American forces. The ensuing firefight and the desperate effort of the members of the maintenance company to escape also served to give the defenders a false sense of their ability to stop the Americans.

After a pause to refuel, the marines then drove to the Euphrates. The Iraqis had not blown the bridge, but a major firefight soon erupted. One company took a wrong approach to another bridge over the Saddam Canal, and a number of its vehicles became bogged down in soft sand. The marines resumed their advance to the canal down the city's main road, which they soon dubbed "Ambush Alley."

Supported by tank fire, the marines succeeded in getting across the canal, but one of their amphibious assault vehicles (AAV) took a hit from a rocket-propelled grenade (RPG) on the bridge. Four marines were wounded, and the AAV barely made it across the span. Worse, a Fairchild-Republic A-10 Warthog aircraft, supporting the marines, attacked marines on the north side of the bridge, mistaking them for Iraqis and killing six. Two other marine vehicles sent south of the river back down Ambush Alley as part of a convoy to remove wounded were struck and destroyed by RPG and small-arms fire that killed most of those inside. Heavy fighting for the bridgehead raged during the night, with the marines supported by Bell AH-1S Cobra attack helicopters. By the morning of March 24 the marines had control of both bridges and had suppressed some of the resistance along Ambush Alley. Determined to press on as quickly as possible in order to threaten Kut and thereby present the Iraqis with two threats to Baghdad, Conway, Mattis, and Natonski decided to push the 1st Marine Regiment up Ambush Alley through Nasiriyah and up Highway 7. At the same time, the 5th and 7th Marine Regiments were able to secure the bridge outside the urban area and reach Highway 1.

The 5th and 7th Marine Regiments had a relatively easy time of it, but it was a different story for the members of the 1st Marine Regiment, pushing up Highway 8 on the evening of March 24. They came under heavy small-arms fire including RPGs and mortar fire. Sustaining relatively few casualties, however, the 1st Marine Regiment passed through the city on the night of March 24–25 and was soon on its way to Kut.

TF Tarawa now was faced with the difficult task of clearing Nasiriyah in order to protect the marine supply line north to Routes 1 and 7. These efforts were severely impacted by the arrival of a *shamal*. This fierce sandstorm lasted several days and not only reduced air support available to the marines but also made the efforts to clear out snipers and fighters more difficult, complicating fighting conditions. Artillery proved to be the only all-weather continuous fire support asset for TF Tarawa. On March 26 high-explosive (HE) rounds with concrete-piercing fuses were fired against a hospital that was serving as a paramilitary strongpoint and that was then seized by the marines. A concentrated artillery fire mission against an estimated 2,000 fedayeen at a railroad station in the southern part of the city reported to be preparing to launch a counterattack not only ended that threat but also killed some 200 of the fedayeen.

A number of marine vehicles were lost to RPGs, but the situation was eased by a cordon around the city that cut off resupply to the Iraqi fighters. With the end of the *shamal* and the arrival of unmanned aerial vehicles over Nasiriyah, more accurate targeting information was soon available. Marine aircraft also took part. Also, some residents began to come forward to identify Iraqi sniper nests and command centers, and special forces units also assisted in the targeting.

Intelligence provided by friendly Iraqis also enabled a team of marines, navy SEALs, and army rangers to rescue Private Lynch and the other Americans who had been captured earlier. The fighting was largely over by March 29, but it was not until early April that Nasiriyah was completely secure. The fighting for the city claimed 18 marines killed and more than 150 wounded.

Spencer C. Tucker

See also
Fedayeen; Iraq War

References
Cordesman, Anthony H. *The Iraq War: Strategy, Tactics, and Military Lessons.* Westport, CT: Praeger, 2003.
Keegan, John. *The Iraq War: The Military Offensive, from Victory in 21 Days to the Insurgent Aftermath.* New York: Vintage, 2005.
Livingston, Gary. *An Nasiriyah: The Fight for the Bridges.* North Topsail Island, NC: Caisson, 2004.
Lowry, Richard S. *Marines in the Garden of Eden: The Battle for An Nasiriyah.* New York: Berkley, 2006.
Murray, Williamson, and Robert H. Scales Jr. *The Iraq War: A Military History.* Cambridge, MA: Belknap, 2005.
Pritchard, Tim. *Ambush Alley: The Most Extraordinary Battle of the Iraq War.* New York: Ballantine Books, 2007.

Nasser, Gamal Abdel (1918–1970)

Egyptian nationalist politician, vice president (1953–1954), premier (1954–1956), and president (1956–1970). Born in Beni Mor, Egypt, on January 16, 1918, the son of a civil servant, Gamal Abdel Nasser at an early age developed great antipathy toward Britain's rule over Egypt, setting the stage for his later championing of Egyptian nationalism and Pan-Arabism. Nasser graduated from the Egyptian Royal Military Academy in 1936 and was commissioned a second lieutenant. While stationed at a post in the Sudan, he met and became friends with future Egyptian president Anwar Sadat. Based on their mutual dislike of the British, they eventually laid the groundwork for a secret anti-British organization that came to be called the Free Officers.

The Free Officers movement recruited Egyptian military officers who wished to bring about an end to British colonial rule and oust King Farouk I. After months of painstaking planning, the organization fomented a revolt against Farouk's government on July 23, 1952. Three days later, the king abdicated and fled Egypt.

Upon Farouk's abdication, the Revolutionary Command Council was established under the leadership of Major General Mohammad Naguib, with Nasser working behind the scenes. When the council declared Egypt a republic in June 1953, Naguib became its first president, with Nasser as vice president. Beginning in the winter of 1954, a political power struggle ensued between Nasser and Naguib. Within months, Nasser took de facto control as president of the Revolutionary Command Council. Naguib was allowed to continue as president of Egypt, although this was in reality little more than a figurehead position.

Nasser and his faction consolidated their hold on power, and after the October 1954 attempt on his life, which he blamed on Naguib, Nasser ordered Naguib arrested. Using

Egyptian president Gamal Abdel Nasser shakes hands with Japanese chief delegate Tatsunosuke Takasaki at the 1960 Afro-Asian Conference. A highly influential yet controversial figure in the history of the Middle East, Nasser held power as Egyptian president from 1954 until his death in 1970. (Library of Congress)

the assassination attempt to solidify his power base, Nasser became premier of Egypt on February 25, 1955. Seven months later he also took the title of provisional president.

Nasser quickly moved to centralize his authority, creating a tightly controlled police state in which political opponents were imprisoned, intellectuals and elites were disenfranchised, and industries were nationalized. In June 1956 a national election saw Nasser as the sole candidate for the presidency, and he thus officially became Egypt's second president.

In addition to seeking land reform and following quasi-socialist economic policies, Nasser sought to modernize Egyptian infrastructure. His public works projects included the building of a massive dam at Aswan, for which he received promises of financial support from the United States and Great Britain. He also approached the United States about purchasing arms. When the United States refused this request for fear that the weapons would be used against Israel, Nasser turned to the Soviet Union.

The Soviets saw a chance to increase their influence in the region and negotiated an arms deal with Nasser, whereupon the United States and Britain withdrew their support for the Aswan Dam project in early July 1956. Seeing an additional opportunity to gain more influence with the Egyptians and to establish a foothold in the Middle East, the Soviet Union quickly offered to help Nasser with the construction of the dam.

Nasser used the loss of Western financial support as a pretext to nationalize the Suez Canal on July 26, 1956. This action provoked joint French, British, and Israeli military action against Egypt, beginning the Suez Crisis. On October 29, 1956, Israeli forces attacked Egypt, and two days later, having coordinated this with the Israelis, French and British forces attacked Egypt when Nasser rejected their demands to secure the Suez Canal. On November 5 French and British forces landed at Port Said, further escalating the conflict. The United States, not privy to the plans of its allies, applied great pressure on the Israelis, British, and French to withdraw, which they did.

Far from being defeated, Nasser was vindicated by the Suez Crisis, and he shrewdly used this victory to further consolidate his rule at home and to promote Pan-Arabism throughout the Middle East. The Suez Crisis turned him into a hero and chief spokesperson for Arab nationalism.

In pursuit of his Pan-Arab vision, Nasser established the United Arab Republic (UAR) on February 22, 1958. Consisting of only Egypt and Syria, however, the UAR fell apart when Syria withdrew on September 28, 1961, over the issue of Egyptian domination of the arrangement. Nevertheless, Nasser continued to promote Arab nationalism and his vision of a Pan-Arab union. He also sent substantial Egyptian forces into Yemen during the Yemen Civil War (1962–1970), which proved to be a major drain on the Egyptian economy and military.

Nasser's strong-arm rule began to work against him as the years progressed. Losing some of his popular appeal at home, he attempted to reform the government, which was corrupt and riddled with cronyism. Instead, he was forced to crack down on his opponents who tried to expand their power during the attempted reorganization. In foreign affairs, in an effort to play up Arab resentment toward Israel, Nasser signed a defense pact with Syria in November 1966. In early 1967 he began provoking the Israelis through a number of different actions, including insisting on the departure of United Nations (UN) peacekeepers from the Egyptian-Israeli border, blockading the Gulf of Aqaba, and moving troops into the Sinai.

In retaliation, on June 5, 1967, the Israelis attacked Egypt, Syria, and Jordan. The war lasted only until 9 June and proved to be a humiliating defeat for Nasser. His miscalculation further eroded his support in Egypt and blemished his reputation throughout the Middle East. In March 1969 he launched the War of Attrition against Israel, which resulted in many more Egyptian than Israeli casualties. In July 1970 he agreed to a cease-fire arrangement put forward by U.S. secretary of state William Rogers, ending the war. By then in deteriorating health, Nasser died on September 28, 1970, in Cairo.

DALLACE W. UNGER JR.

See also
Egypt; Sadat, Anwar; Six-Day War; Yemen, Civil War in the North

References
DuBius, Shirley Graham. *Gamal Abdel Nasser, Son of the Nile.* New York: Third Press, 1972.
Kerr, Malcolm. *The Arab Cold War: Gamal Abd al-Nasir and His Rivals.* New York: Oxford University Press, 1971.
Lacouture, Jean. *Nasser: A Biography.* New York: Knopf, 1973.

Nasuh Pasha, Treaty of (1612)

Treaty between the Safavid and Ottoman Empires signed on November 30, 1612, and named for Ottoman grand vizier Nasuh Pasha (Damat Nasuh Pasha). In 1590 following Ottoman victories and with considerable domestic discord and a simultaneous war with the Uzbeks, Shah Abbas I agreed to the Treaty of Constantinople with the Ottoman Empire.

It gave the Ottomans control of southern Caucasus, Tabriz, and northwestern Persia. Abbas also agreed to pay obeisance to Sunni Muslim religious leaders.

The treaty, however, allowed Abbas to reorganize his army and quell the domestic unrest. In 1603 a new sultan, 14-year-old Ahmet I, came to the Ottoman throne. The Ottoman regime was then also involved in war with the Byzantine Empire (the so-called Long War of 1593–1606) and dealing with considerable internal unrest (the Jelali revolts). Abbas took advantage of the situation to resume the war.

Following a series of Persian successes, the Ottomans agreed to the Treaty of Nasuh Pasha. Considered a great triumph for Abbas, the treaty called for the Ottomans to surrender to Persia all the territory secured in the Treaty of Constantinople of 1590, set the border between the two states as that drawn in the Peace of Amasya in 1555, provided that Persia would pay an annual tribute of 200 loads (59,000 kilograms) of silk, and changed the Persian religious pilgrimage route from through Iraq to through Syria.

When Abbas refused to pay the tribute called for in the treaty, however, war resumed between the two empires in 1615.

SPENCER C. TUCKER

See also
Abbas I the Great; Constantinople, 1590 Treaty of; Ottoman-Safavid Wars

References
Eskander Beg Monshi. *History of Shah Abbas the Great*. 2 vols. Trans. Roger M. Savory. Boulder, CO: Westview, 1978.
Nahavandi, H., and Y. Bomati. *Shah Abbas, empereur de Perse (1587–1629)*. Paris: Perrin, 1998.
Newman, Andrew J. *Safavid Iran: Rebirth of a Persian Empire*. London: I. B. Tauris, 2006.
Savory, Roger. *Iran under the Safavids*. Cambridge: Cambridge University Press, 2007.

Nebuchadnezzar II (ca. 634–562 BCE)

King of Babylon. Born circa 634 BCE, the son of Babylonian king Nabopolassar (r. ca. 626–605), and himself king from 605 to 562, Nebuchadnezzar was undoubtedly the greatest ruler and also had the longest reign of any monarch of the Neo-Babylonian (Chaldean) Empire of 626–539 BCE. King Nabopolassar paved the way for Nebuchadnezzar's success by leading a successful revolt against Assyrian control of Babylonia. He was greatly aided in this enterprise by an alliance worked out with Cyaxares, a vassal of Assyria but also king of the Iranian peoples of the Medes, Persians, Sagartians, and Parthians. The Scythians and Cimmerians from north of the Crimea and the Black Sea area also joined the alliance, as did regional Aramean tribes. The result of this enterprise was the defeat of the Assyrians and Babylonia again master of Mesopotamia.

In 607–606, Crown Prince Nebuchadnezzar campaigned with his father north of Assyria, then led independent military operations when his father returned to Babylon. Nebuchadnezzar became king on his father's death in 605. Babylonia's former allies of the Scythians and Cimmerians were now a threat, and Nebuchadnezzar led Babylonian forces into Anatolia and routed them. He also campaigned against the Egyptians who had taken advantage of the defeat of the Assyrians to advance eastward, defeating them and the Assyrians in the important Battle of Carchemish and forcing the Egyptians back across the Sinai.

During expeditions into Syria and Palestine in 604, Nebuchadnezzar received the submission of Judah and other states, and he captured the city of Ashkelon. He then undertook a series of campaigns in an effort to secure control of Palestine. In the last of these, during 601–600, Nebuchadnezzar's forces suffered heavy losses in a battle with the Egyptians. This brought the defection of the vassal states of Judah, the former kingdom of Ephraim, the Phoenicians of Caanan, and the Arameans in the Levant. Nebuchadnezzar mounted a series of campaigns there during 600–598 but also found time to subdue the Arab tribes of northwestern Arabia. He returned to Judah and besieged and took Jerusalem in 597, deposing King Jehoiachin and taking him back to Babylon. After a campaign in Syria during 596–595, Nebuchadnezzar acted to prevent a threatened invasion of eastern Babylon, probably by the Kingdom of Elam in present-day southwestern Iran. He also put down an insurrection involving elements of the Babylonian Army in late 595 and was sufficiently secure to campaign in Syria during 594.

Nebuchadnezzar undertook another siege of Jerusalem, this one lasting possibly as long as 30 months during 589–587, after which he razed much of the city, burning the Temple of Solomon and removing a large number of its people to Babylon in what became known as the Babylonian Captivity of the Jews. Nebuchadnezzar also took other cities, such as Tyre, Sidon, and Damascus. In 567 he again waged war against Egypt, attempting an invasion of that state. This marked the end of his expansionist policy, however.

Having now secured his realm, Nebuchadnezzar II employed the abundant slave labor available from his wars in building projects in an effort to make Babylon the most glorious city in the world. In this he enjoyed success. Dominating the city was the Tower of Babel, a ziggurat that rose to a height of some 300 feet. The high walls of Babylon were said to be so wide that chariot races could be held atop them, and they enclosed the city for some 56 miles. Tiles on his palace bore the inscription "I am Nebuchadnezzar, King of Babylon."

Nebuchadnezzar married Amytis, a princess of the royal house of Media, which secured that important alliance. Some sources say that he had the famous Hanging Gardens of Babylon constructed for her so she would not pine for her Persian homeland. The ancients dubbed these one of the Seven Wonders of the World.

Nebuchadnezzar died in 562. Babylonian's renaissance was to be brief. His son Amel-Marduk succeeded him as king, but he and most of his successors proved weak and in any case did not have long reigns. The Neo-Babylonian Empire was soon in decline, and in 539 the Persians under Cyrus II the Great arrived and easily captured the city.

Spencer C. Tucker

See also
Assyrian Empire; Babylonian Empire, Old; Cyrus II the Great

References
Bertman, Stephen. *Handbook to Life in Ancient Mesopotamia.* New York: Oxford University Press, 2005.
Foster, Benjamin Read, and Karen Polinger Foster. *Civilizations of Ancient Iraq.* Princeton, NJ: Princeton University Press, 2009.
Kriwaczek, Paul. *Babylon: Mesopotamia and the Birth of Civilization.* New York: St. Martin's Griffin, 2012.
Oates, Joan. *Babylon.* New York: Thames and Hudson, 2008.
Oates, Joan. *Babylon.* London: Thames and Hudson, 1979.
Oppenheim, A. Leo. *Ancient Mesopotamia: Portrait of a Dead Civilization.* Chicago: University of Chicago Press, 2013.
Pollock, Susan. *Ancient Mesopotamia: The Land That Never Was.* Cambridge: Cambridge University Press, 2008.
Saggs, H. W. F. *The Greatness That Was Babylon: A Survey of the Ancient Civilization of the Tigris-Euphrates Valley.* London: Sidgwick & Jackson, 1988.

Nelson, Horatio (1758–1805)

British admiral. Born the son of a clergyman at Burnham Thorpe in Norfolk on September 29, 1758, Horatio Nelson went to sea at age 12 with his maternal uncle Captain Maurice Suckling, who saw that his nephew's training included service as an ordinary sailor in a merchant ship and on an expedition to the Arctic during 1771–1774. Nelson rose swiftly in his profession and became a post captain at only age 20. During the American Revolutionary War (1775–1783) he saw much active service, mainly in the West Indies.

After five unhappy years ashore following a peacetime commission in the West Indies, on the outbreak of the war with revolutionary France in 1793, Nelson was appointed to command the ship of the line *Agamemnon*. He participated in the capture of Corsica in 1794, losing sight in his right eye in the process.

Nelson commanded a detached squadron off the coast of Italy as a commodore in 1796, hampering the advance of the victorious French armies under brilliant young general Napoleon Bonaparte. Fame came at last to Nelson when he played a decisive role in the British victory over the Spanish fleet in the Battle of Cape St. Vincent (February 14, 1797), capturing two ships. Promoted to rear admiral and knighted, Nelson suffered a serious setback on July 24 when, ordered to attack the Spanish town of Santa Cruz in Tenerife, one of the Canary Islands, his men were repulsed with heavy losses. Badly wounded, he lost his right arm.

Nelson returned to active service after only a few months' convalescence and received command of a detached squadron in the Mediterranean. He led it to a stunning victory over the French fleet in the Battle of Aboukir Bay (Battle of the Nile, August 1, 1798), in which his prebattle planning was crucial. Nelson was showered with praise and rewards, including a peerage from Britain, but the adulation went to his head, and he became embroiled in an ugly civil war in Naples, one of Britain's few remaining allies in the Mediterranean. He also fell very publicly in love with Emma, Lady Hamilton, wife of the British ambassador.

Recalled home in near disgrace in 1800, Nelson was promoted to vice admiral in January 1801 and sent back to sea again as second-in-command of a special fleet assembled to challenge the "Armed Neutrality of the North," which was threatening Britain's trade interests in the Baltic. In the ensuing Battle of Copenhagen (April 2, 1801) he again showed his leadership qualities, winning a very hard-fought victory against a determined and gallant foe.

Nelson's passionate love affair with Emma Hamilton continued, and when she bore him a daughter, he left his wife and set up home with Emma and her husband during the brief period of peace following the Treaty of Amiens in March 1802. When war began again with France in May 1803, Nelson received command in the Mediterranean.

In this challenging post, Nelson showed that he was far more than just a fighting admiral. He maintained his fleet at sea off the French port of Toulon for nearly two years during June 1803–April 1805 without once going into port, and he patiently trained his men, keeping them healthy and engaged. When Admiral Pierre Jean Pierre Baptiste Silvestre, comte de Villeneuve, and the French fleet escaped from Toulon in April 1805 and sailed to the West Indies, Nelson pursued relentlessly and drove them back into European waters. After a brief spell of leave with Emma and their daughter Horatia, he returned to take command of the British fleet off Cádiz and led it to a decisive victory over the combined French and Spanish fleets in the Battle of Trafalgar (October 21, 1805). At the height of the action, he was struck down by a musket ball while pacing the quarterdeck of his flagship, *Victory*. Carried below, he died about three hours later. His death was extravagantly mourned both in his own fleet and at home in England, where his body was given a lavish state funeral and buried in St. Paul's Cathedral, London.

An affectionate man with an endearing, almost boyish, enthusiasm, Nelson was loved by most of those who served with him. Although physically nondescript, he exuded energy and charisma and inspired his followers with his own extraordinary physical courage. But his administrative ability and his capacity for making meticulous plans were also important components of his success, as was his lifelong experience as a practical seaman. Traditionally portrayed as an isolated genius, it is now recognized that Nelson was in fact a member of one of the most gifted generations of officers the Royal Navy has ever produced. Nonetheless, Nelson still stood out then, and two centuries after his death he continues to fascinate and inspire.

Colin White

See also
Aboukir Bay, Battle of; Egypt, French Invasion and Occupation of

References
Bennett, Geoffrey. *Nelson, the Commander*. London: Batsford, 1972.
Oman, Carola. *Nelson*. London: Hodder and Stoughton, 1947.
Pocock, Tom. *Horatio Nelson*. London: Bodley Head, 1987.
White, Colin, ed. *The Nelson Companion*. Gloucester, UK: Suttons, 1995.

NEMESIS, Operation (1920–1922)

Code name given to a clandestine Armenian operation (1920–1922) to hunt down and assassinate key Young Turks and other leaders responsible for the 1915–1923 Armenian Genocide. Operation NEMESIS, named after the Greek god of retribution, was planned in October 1919 during the Ninth General Congress of the Armenian Revolutionary Federation (ARF), a political group within the Ottoman Empire whose chief goal was to achieve Armenian independence. As the horror of the Armenian Genocide became apparent, ARF leaders sought to retaliate against government officials who had unleashed the mass killings. The two principal plotters were Shahan Natalie and Soghomon Tehlirian, who were genocide survivors. Most of the other operatives who participated in NEMESIS were also survivors or those who had lost family members in the genocide. The majority of those targeted were Ottoman officials, but the individuals also included Armenian officials complicit in the genocide.

The first victim of Operation NEMESIS was Azerbaijani foreign minister Fatali Khan Khoyski, assassinated in Tiflis, Georgia, in June 1920. The next assassination was carried out against Mehmed Talaat Pasha, former interior minister in the Young Turk regime. He was gunned down in Berlin, Germany, on March 15, 1921. The ARF had considered him its primary target, as he had played a pivotal role in unleashing the genocide in 1915. ARF operatives also assassinated Azerbaijani interior minister Behbud Khan Janavshir (July 1921); Said Halam Pasha, a former Ottoman prime minister (December 1921); Behaeddin Shakir Bey, an Ottoman military adviser (April 1922); Jemal Azmi, a key player in the Armenian Genocide (April 1922); and Ahmed Djemal Pasha, a former Ottoman naval minister and governor of Syria (July 1922).

Natalie, who was the key figure behind Operation NEMESIS, personally assigned Tehlirian the task of killing Mehmed Talaat Pasha. Natalie instructed Tehlirian to shoot Talaat in the head but not to flee the scene. Instead Tehlirian was to remain, with his foot on the body, and surrender himself peaceably when the police arrived. In this way, the ARF would be assured that the entire world would know who was behind the deed and why it was carried out. The Germans placed Tehlirian on trial for murder, but he was ultimately acquitted by reason of insanity. During the trial, horrific details of the Armenian Genocide were made public. Armenian operatives killed other genocide perpetrators before, during, and after the two-year-long Operation NEMESIS, but they were not tied to the ARF's plan.

Paul G. Pierpaoli Jr.

See also
Armenians and the Armenian Genocide; Ottoman Empire; Ottoman Empire, Post–World War I Revolution in; Turkish-Armenian War; Young Turks

References
Akçam, Taner. *From Empire to Republic: Turkish Nationalism and the Armenian Genocide*. New York: Zed, 2004.

Derogy, Jacques. *Resistance and Revenge: The Armenian Assassination of the Turkish Leaders Responsible for the 1915 Massacres and Deportations.* New Brunswick, NJ: Transaction Publishers and Zoryan Institute, 1990.

Netanyahu, Benjamin (1949–)

Israeli soldier, diplomat, politician, prime minister (1996–1999 and March 2009–present), and probably the most dominant Israeli political leader since David Ben-Gurion. Born in Tel Aviv, Israel, on October 21, 1949, Benjamin (Binyamin) "Bibi" Netanyahu moved with his family from Jerusalem to Philadelphia, where his father, Benzion Netanyahu, taught history at the University of Pennsylvania. The younger Netanyahu returned to Israel in 1967 and entered the Israel Defense Forces (IDF) to serve as a soldier and officer in the antiterrorist Sayeret Matkal unit during 1967–1972. Netanyahu participated in the IDF's Operation GIFT during December 28–29, 1968, at Beirut Airport and was wounded during the rescue, led by Ehud Barak, of hijacked Sabena Airlines hostages at Ben-Gurion Airport on May 8, 1972.

Netanyahu's studies for a degree in architecture from the Massachusetts Institute of Technology (MIT) were interrupted by his service as a captain in the Yom Kippur War (Ramadan War) of October 1973, but he returned to receive his bachelor's degree in 1974. He then earned a master's of science degree in management studies from MIT in 1976 and pursued studies in political science both at MIT and Harvard University. He joined the international business consulting firm the Boston Consulting Group in 1976, but in 1978 he accepted a position in senior management at Rim Industries in Jerusalem.

Netanyahu created in Jerusalem the Jonathan Institute. Dedicated to the study of terrorism, the institute was named in memory of his brother, who was the commander and only IDF fatality of the successful raid to free the Jewish passengers and crew of an Air France commercial flight held captive at the airport in Entebbe, Uganda, in 1976. The institute sponsors international conferences and seminars on terrorism.

As the deputy chief of mission at the Israeli embassy in Washington during 1982–1984, Benjamin Netanyahu participated in initial discussions on strategic cooperation between the United States and Israel. As Israeli ambassador to the United Nations (UN) during 1984–1988, he was instrumental in opening the UN Nazi War Crimes Archives in 1987. A member of the conservative Likud Party, in 1988

Benjamin Netanyahu was prime minister of Israel during 1996–1999. A hardliner regarding peace with the Palestinians, Netanyahu again became prime minister in 2009 and is now the longest serving Israeli leader. (Israel Government Press Office)

he won election to the Knesset (Israeli parliament) and served as deputy foreign minister during 1988–1991, as a coalition deputy minister to Prime Minister Yitzhak Rabin during 1991–1992, and as the Israeli spokesman during the Persian Gulf War (1991). Netanyahu also participated in the Madrid Peace Conference of October 1991 that saw the first direct negotiations among Israel, Syria, Lebanon, and a joint Jordanian-Palestinian delegation.

Following Likud's defeat in the 1992 elections, Yitzhak Shamir stepped down as party leader. Netanyahu won election as party leader in 1993, in part because of his opposition to the 1993 peace accords between Israel and the Palestine Liberation Organization (PLO) that led to Israeli withdrawals from the West Bank and the Gaza Strip.

In the May 1996 national elections, for the first time Israelis elected their prime minister directly. Netanyahu hired an American campaign adviser and narrowly defeated Shimon Peres of the Labor Party, who had succeeded as prime minister after the 1995 assassination of Yitzhak Rabin. The election took place following a wave of Muslim suicide bombings that killed 32 Israeli citizens and that

Peres seemed powerless to halt. Netanyahu took office in June 1996, the youngest prime minister in Israeli history. He was also the first Israeli prime minister to be born after the establishment of the State of Israel.

Netanyahu's tenure as prime minister was marked by worsening relations with Syria that led to the occupation of Lebanon by the posting of Syrian troops in Lebanon; the troops were not withdrawn until 2005. Relations with the Palestinians also deteriorated when Netanyahu and Jerusalem mayor Ehud Olmert in September 1996 opened ancient tunnels under the Western (Wailing) Wall and the al-Aqsa Mosque complex. Netanyahu's position weakened within Likud when he ceased to oppose the Oslo Peace Accords of 1993 and withdrew troops from Hebron in the West Bank in 1997. His attempt to restore that support by increasing Israeli settlements in the West Bank, promoting Jewish housing in predominantly Arab East Jerusalem in March 1997, and decreasing the amount of land to be ceded to the Palestinians only served to provoke Palestinian violence and impede the peace process.

Netanyahu again angered the conservative wing of Likud when he agreed in the 1998 Wye River Accords to relinquish control of as much as 40 percent of the West Bank to the Palestinians. He again reversed himself and suspended the accords in December 1999. He resigned from the Knesset and the chairmanship of Likud after he was defeated by Barak in his bid for reelection in May 1999, stepping down as prime minister that July.

Netanyahu accepted the position of minister of foreign affairs in November 2002, and after the 2003 elections he became the finance minister under Prime Minister Ariel Sharon until August 2005. Netanyahu resigned to protest the Israeli pullout from the Gaza Strip. Following Sharon's departure from the Likud Party, Netanyahu was one of several candidates to replace him. In December 2005 Netanyahu retook the leadership of Likud. He has written or edited a number of books, among them *International Terrorism: Challenge and Response* (1979), *A Place among the Nations: Israel and the World* (1992), *Fighting Terrorism: How Democracies Can Defeat Domestic and International Terrorists* (1995), and *A Durable Peace: Israel and Its Place among the Nations* (2000).

Despite the fact that Netanyahu and his wife have been the subject of criminal investigations, he continued to lead Likud and again became Israeli prime minister on March 31, 2009. This followed an election in which his party had actually failed to win a majority and technically lost, but the opposing Labor Party was unable to build a coalition. The coalition that Netanyahu was able to form included right-winger Avigdor Lieberman as foreign minister.

Netanyahu's most recent tenure as prime minister was marked by confrontation with the Palestinians and a stalled peace process. Critics within the Israeli government charged that he did not really believe in a two-state solution. Sharply opposed to any nuclear deal with Iran and a hard-liner vis-à-vis Hamas, he took Israeli forces into a costly conflict war with Hamas in the Gaza Strip during July–August 2014, known to the Israelis as Operation PROTECTIVE EDGE. Angered by the April 2014 agreement between the Fatah-dominated Palestinian National Authority and Hamas to hold national elections in late 2014 and form a compromise unity government, Netanuahu's government increased Jewish housing construction in Arab areas. This brought sharp condemnation internationally, including from the European Community and the administration of U.S. president Barack Obama. At the end of 2014, Israeli-U.S. relations appeared to be at a new low, with name calling on both sides, including harsh Israeli criticism of U.S. secretary of state John Kerry.

On December 2, 2014, Netanyahu fired his cabinet and called for new elections to be held in March 2015, in advance of the date mandated by law. This occurred amid rising criticism of Israel from within the United States and Western Europe, with many observers believing that Netanyahu had rejected the two-state solution in favor of annexation of the West Bank.

In a stunning development, on December 23 in a speech at Tel Aviv University, Foreign Minister Lieberman denounced Netanyahu's Palestinian policy, accusing him of not doing anything to advance the peace process and warning that without an Israeli initiative, the country would face a "diplomatic tsunami." Lieberman referenced sanctions imposed by the European Union against Russia for its aggression in Ukraine and alluded that such action against Israel would greatly damage its economy, especially as the European Union is Israel's principal trading partner in both exports and imports.

On March 3, 2015, in an unprecedented interjection in U.S. politics, Netanyahu accepted an intervention by the Republican Party majority members in the U.S. Congress to address a joint session to voice his adamant opposition to the pending diplomatic agreement with Iran regarding that country's nuclear weapons program. The speech greatly angered the Obama administration and brought U.S.-Israeli relations to a historic low. On March 16, the day before Israeli national elections, in order to attract right-wing votes, Netanyahu announced his opposition to a two-state solution. His coalition narrowly won, whereupon he then publicly reversed his position on a two-state solution.

On August 22 only weeks after conclusion of the nuclear deal with Iran, U.S. and Israeli media outlets revealed that in 2009 and 2010 Israeli leaders, including Netanyahu, had drawn up plans to attack Iran, only to shelve this when it encountered stiff resistance from some Israeli cabinet members. In October 2015 Netanyahu created an international stir when he stated that Haj Amin al-Husseini, Jerusalem's grand mufti during World War II, had helped convince Nazi leaders to implement the Holocaust. This claim, which has long been debunked by scholars, created even more antipathy between Muslims and Israelis.

By March 2016, Netanyahu's coalition government showed considerable signs of strain as a number of Ultra-Orthodox members threatened to revolt over the government's plans to create a nonorthodox prayer space at the Western Wall in Jerusalem. On May 20 Israeli defense minister Moshe Yaalon resigned, claiming that the nation was being taken over by "extremist and dangerous elements" after Netanyahu moved to replace him with longtime Netanyahu rival and far-right politician Avigdor Lieberman to strengthen the governing coalition. As the Defense Ministry also runs civil affairs in the occupied West Bank, this did not bode well for the Palestinians there. A former chief of Israel's armed forces, Yaalon had shored up relations with the Pentagon that provided a counterweight to Netanyahu's policy feuds with President Obama regarding peace talks with the Palestinians and Iran's nuclear program. By contrast, Lieberman was inexperienced militarily and known for his past hawkish talk against Palestinians, Israel's Arab minority, and Egypt, an important Israeli regional security partner.

Meanwhile, ongoing construction of new Israeli settlements in the West Bank, undertaken in defiance of public opinion, makes a two-state solution far more difficult. In the late summer of 2018, peace among Israel, the Palestinians, and Israeli's Arab neighbors remained as elusive as ever. Nonetheless, the election of Donald Trump as U.S. president allowed Netanyahu to reset relations with the United States, as Trump had talked during the presidential campaign about the need to improve relations with Israel and had expressed his support for making Jerusalem the capital of the Jewish state. Indeed, Trump's first foreign visit abroad as U.S. president included a stop in Israel.

In February 2018, Trump made good on a campaign pledge and announced that the U.S. embassy in Israel would be relocated to Jerusalem. The move occurred in May 2018. Netanyahu and Israeli conservatives were jubilant, but many others criticized the move as counterproductive to the Israeli-Palestinian peace process. The Palestinians, unsurprisingly, loudly denounced the move. Also in May 2018, the Trump administration announced that it would no longer be a party to the 2015 Iran Nuclear Deal, another boon to Netanyahu and his supporters. Washington also announced that it would seek a "stronger, more comprehensive" agreement with Tehran and would seek to reimpose damaging economic sanctions on Iran. The Iranian government, however, made clear that it had no intention of renegotiating the 2015 deal.

In July 2018 the Israeli Knesset passed the so-call Basic Law, or Nation-State Law, which specifically categorizes Israel as a Jewish state for the Jewish people. Netanyahu strongly supported the declaration. The development, although largely symbolic, was heavily rebuked by Netanyahu's Israeli critics as well as by many foreign governments. Many Israelis who have eyed Netanyahu's coalition with increasing suspicion saw the law as yet another sign that the premier was bound and determined to impose a profoundly conservative agenda on Israel. The Palestinians also decried the move, as it appeared to only further marginalize them. Meanwhile, during 2017 and 2018 Netanyahu and members of his family were being investigated for alleged corruption and malfeasance. In February 2018, Israeli police recommended that Netanyahu be charged with corruption in office. Netanyahu has repeatedly denied all corruption claims and asserts that efforts to charge him with crimes are politically motivated. He won reelection in April 2019.

RICHARD M. EDWARDS AND SPENCER C. TUCKER

See also

Barak, Ehud; Ben-Gurion, David; Fatah, al-; Gaza War of 2014; Hamas; Husseini, Haj Amin al-; Iran Nuclear Deal; Israel; Madrid Conference; Olmert, Ehud; Oslo Accords; Palestine Liberation Organization; Palestinian National Authority; Rabin, Yitzhak; Sharon, Ariel; Wye River Agreement

References

Caspit, Ben, and Ilan Kfir. *Netanyahu: The Road to Power.* Translated by Ora Cummings. New York: Birch Lane, 1998.

Netanyahu, Benjamin. *Fighting Terrorism: How Democracies Can Defeat Domestic and International Terrorism.* New York: Farrar, Straus and Giroux, 1995.

Shindler, Colin. *Israel, Likud and the Zionist Dream: Power, Politics, and Ideology from Begin to Netanyahu.* New York: I. B. Tauris, 1995.

Nicaea, Empire of (1204–1261)

The largest of the three Greek successor states of the Byzantine Empire that emerged after the conquest of Constantinople by the Fourth Crusade (1202–1204) in April 1204. Byzantine successor states emerged in Epiros (in northern Greece), Trebizond (on the far northeastern coast of Anatolia and the southern Crimea), and Nicaea in northern and northwestern Anatolia.

The empire of Nicaea took its name from its capital, Nicaea (modern-day Iznik, Turkey), a city in the northwestern Anatolia. Nicaea, the venue of two ecumenical synods (325 and 787), had come under Turkish rule in the late 11th century and was the first capital of the Seljuk Sultanate of Rum until 1097, when it was captured by the First Crusade (1096–1099) and handed over to the Byzantine emperor.

The Empire of Nicaea was established by the first Byzantine emperor-in-exile, Theodore I Laskaris, who was recognized by the local Greeks in Asia Minor as "emperor of the Romans" in 1204 and ruled until 1222. Nicaea remained the capital until the recovery of Constantinople from the Latins in 1261, although the later emperors used Nymphaion (modern-day Kemalpafla, Turkey) as their principal residence.

Theodore I Laskaris died in 1222 and was succeeded by his son-in-law John III Vatatzes (r. 1222–1254), who was succeeded by his son Theodore II (r. 1254–1258). The last emperor, Michael VIII Palaiologos, usurped the throne in 1259 from Theodore II's son John IV (r. 1258–1261), then still a child, and ruled until 1261. At the peak of its power, the empire extended from the Black Sea coast to southwestern Asia Minor and from eastern Thrace to the Dalmatian coast in the Balkans.

The first conflicts between the Greeks of the Empire of Nicaea and the new Latin Empire of Constantinople took place in northwestern Asia Minor in the autumn of 1204. In December 1204 at Poimanenon, Nicaean forces suffered a crushing defeat at the hands of the Latins. In the spring of 1205 northwestern Asia Minor again came under fierce attack, but in April the Latin army was recalled to the European side of the Bosporus to repel the army of Bulgarian tsar Kalojan (Johannitsa). It was this diversion and the subsequent defeat of the Latins at the Battle of Adrianople (April 14–15, 1205) that saved the Greek towns in Asia Minor from falling to the Latins and offered the forces of Nicaea the opportunity to regroup. In the following years, the Latins captured a number of towns in Asia Minor, in spite of the resistance of the local Greeks under Theodore I. In 1212 after a successful expedition in Asia Minor, the Latin emperor Henry concluded a treaty with Theodore I at Nymphaion, offering him territories that had never previously been under Nicaean control. Until Theodore I's death (1222), it seems that there were no further conflicts between Nicaea and the Latin Empire.

In 1224 Emperor John III Vatatzes crushed the Latin forces at Poimanenon, and as a direct result of that victory almost all the Latin territories in Asia Minor came under Nicaean control. In the 1230s Emperor John of Brienne launched the final Latin military operation in Asia Minor, which resulted only in the brief recapture of the coastal town of Pegai. In 1234, John III crossed to Europe and captured Latin territories in Thrace and eastern Macedonia. In 1235–1236 the Nicaean emperor and his ally, the Bulgarian tsar Ivan Asen II, jointly besieged Constantinople by land and sea but to no avail. The main reasons for this failure lay with Ivan Asen's change of sides twice during the siege and with the subsequent defeats of the Nicaean fleet in sea battles against the Venetians, who had come to the aid of the Latin Empire in 1236.

Nicaea and Venice had further naval encounters in the 1230s over the lordship of the island of Crete, in which Nicaea failed to achieve long-term results. The significant military aid that reached Constantinople in the late 1230s interrupted the Nicaean advance against the Latin Empire, but only temporarily. Specifically, in 1241 the Thracian town of Tzouroulon came under Latin control when Western military reinforcements arrived in the area, but the city again came under Nicaean authority in 1247.

By the late 1250s, the Nicaean Empire had under its control all the former territories of the Latin Empire, apart from the city of Constantinople itself. In the autumn of 1259 in the valley of Pelagonia, the Nicaean forces achieved a significant victory against the triple military coalition of the principality of Epiros, the Angevin kingdom of Sicily, and the Frankish principality of Achaia, which threatened Nicaean plans to restore the Byzantine Empire.

The liberation of Constantinople by the Nicaeans took place by chance in July 1261. General Alexios Strategopoulos was passing outside Constantinople on his way to the Bulgarian borders with a small number of Nicaean soldiers when he found the city almost unguarded because most of its Latin garrison was absent besieging the castle of Daphnousion on the Black Sea coast. Encountering no resistance, the Nicaean troops entered Constantinople on July 25, 1261.

Emperor Michael VIII entered the city on August 15, and in September he was crowned "emperor of the Romans" for the second time (the first was in Nicaea in 1259) in the church of Hagia Sophia, according to Byzantine tradition. The Nicaean emperor had thus restored the Byzantine Empire.

During the Latin occupation of Constantinople, Nicaea attempted to establish diplomatic ties with the Latin Empire and Venice as well as with the Holy Roman Empire and with Genoa. In 1214 Theodore I Laskaris granted Venice commercial privileges for five years, although these were not renewed. In the late 1210s Theodore I Laskaris married Maria, the sister of Latin emperor Robert, and he proposed the marriage of one of his daughters to Robert himself. Most probably in 1244, John Vatatzes married Constanza, daughter of Frederick II, Holy Roman emperor and king of Sicily, thus sealing the good relations between Nicaea and the Western Empire, which had included military and financial help from the Nicaean emperor to Frederick II. On March 13, 1261, at Nymphaion, Emperor Michael VIII granted Genoa commercial privileges in exchange for military help against Venice.

The Latin Empire was only one of the enemies that the Empire of Nicaea had to face. The Seljuk Sultanate of Rum, with its capital at Ikonion (modern-day Konya, Turkey), signed a secret treaty with the Latin Empire in 1209 and laid claim to territories of the Empire of Nicaea during the first years of its existence. The Seljuk attacks ceased after the battle at Antioch in Pisidia (modern-day Yalvaç, Turkey), near the Meander River, in the spring of 1211, when the Nicaean forces defeated the Seljuk army and killed the sultan.

After 1204, another independent Greek state in Asia Minor, the Empire of Trebizond, under the brothers David and Alexios Komnenos, attacked the Empire of Nicaea, occasionally with the help of the Latin Empire of Constantinople. In 1214 Theodore I annexed Paphlagonia, the territory of David Komnenos, and extended his dominions to the southern coast of the Black Sea. The rivalry with the principality of Epiros, Nicaea's main Greek opponent in the contest for the throne of Constantinople, reached its peak in 1222, when the ruler of Epiros proclaimed himself "emperor of the Romans" at Didymoteichon in Thrace, and ended in 1259 with the Battle of Pelagonia. Interestingly, the first military engagements with the kingdom of Bulgaria, the only non-Greek contestant for the throne of Constantinople, took place during the reign of Theodore II Laskaris and ended with a peace treaty in 1256, which was sealed later with a match between the two royal families.

After 1204, Nicaea was recognized by the papal legates in Constantinople and later by the pope himself as the center of the Greek Orthodox East. Discussions occurred between Latins and Greeks regarding the ecclesiastical and dogmatic differences between their respective churches shortly after the Latin conquest of Constantinople and continued into the 1250s, but in the end no agreement regarding the reunification of the two churches could be reached, most probably because of disagreement over the lordship of Constantinople, which the Nicaeans demanded in exchange for acknowledgment of papal primacy.

Under John III Vatatzes and Theodore II Laskaris the economy of the empire flourished, enabling them to engage the services of mercenaries and also to make the empire the cultural center of the exiled Byzantines. The flourishing economy allowed the Nicaean emperors to establish hospitals, build churches, and fortify many towns on the borders of the empire. From the reign of John Vatatzes on, the Nicaean economy was much healthier than the Byzantine economy had been under the Angeloi, a prosperity that contributed significantly to the stability of the Byzantine Empire after 1261.

APHRODITE PAPAYIANNI

See also
Adrianople, Crusades Battle of; Antioch on the Meander, Battle of; Constantinople, Latin Empire of; Frederick II, Holy Roman Emperor; Rum, Sultanate of; Trebizond, Empire of

References
Ahrweiler, Helen. "L'expérience nicéenne." *Dumbarton Oaks Papers* 29 (1975): 23–40.
Angold, Michael. *A Byzantine Government in Exile: Government and Society under the Lascarids of Nicaea, 1204–1261*. Oxford: Oxford University Press, 1975.
Angold, Michael. "Byzantine 'Nationalism' and the Nicaean Empire." *Byzantine and Modern Greek Studies* 1 (1975): 49–75.
Foss, Clive. *Nicaea: A Byzantine Capital and Its Premises*. Brookline, MA: Hellenic College Press, 1996.
Geneakoplos, Deno J. "Greco-Latin Relations on the Eve of the Byzantine Restoration: The Battle of Pelagonia—1259." *Dumbarton Oaks Papers* 7 (1953): 99–141.
Janin, Robert. "Nicée: Etude historique et topographique." *Echos d'Orient* 24 (1925): 482–490.

Nika Uprising (January 13–18, 532)

The Nika Uprising, also known as the Nika Revolt and the Nika Riot, was a major event in the history of the Byzantine Empire. The most violent rioting in the history of Constantinople, it occurred during January 13–18, 532. Well-organized associations known as demes existed in both the Roman and Byzantine Empires. The demes supported certain sporting teams, especially in the immensely popular chariot racing. In chariot racing there were four major organizations, identified by the color of the uniform worn by the participants and their supporters. These were the Blues, Greens, Reds, and Whites. In the Byzantine era the Blues and the Greens were the dominant teams, with Emperor Justinian I the Great (r. 527–565) a staunch supporter of the Blues.

The demes were more than simple supporters of athletic contests, however. They were often little more than ruffians, street gangs out for a physical clash with opposing demes but at the same time often espousing political and theological points of view. The great aristocratic families of Constantinople sought to manipulate the demes to their own advantage, and some of these aristocrats believed that they had a better claim to the Byzantine throne than did Justinian.

In 531 some members of the Blues and Greens were arrested in connection with deaths that had occurred during rioting after a chariot race. While most of those arrested were hanged, two of the condemned—one a Blue and one a Green—managed to escape and seek refuge in a church, which was subsequently surrounded by an angry mob.

Justinian found himself in a difficult position, as he was then in the process of trying to reach a peace settlement with the Persians. Domestically, there was great unrest over high taxes occasioned by military expenditures. In order to try to calm the situation, Justinian announced that a chariot race would be held on January 13, 532, and he commuted to life in prison the death sentences of the two men who had escaped. Both the Blues and the Greens demanded that the two men be pardoned entirely, however.

On January 13, 532, a large and unruly crowd assembled at the Hippodrome for the chariot races. The Hippodrome was situated next to the emperor's palace complex, enabling the emperor to direct and watch the races from safety from the palace. From the very start, however, many in the crowd began shouting insults at Justinian. By race 22 and the end of the day, the crowd's partisan shouts in favor of one team or another had given way to one word: "Nika," meaning "win," "victory," or "conquer."

The crowd then spilled out of the Hippodrome and began to assault the palace. During the next five days the palace was under siege, and there was widespread destruction in the city. Fires started by the rioters spread quickly and caused immense damage, destroying as much as half of Constantinople, including the cathedral of Hagia Sophia.

Certainly some of the aristocrats in the Senate, who opposed the taxes and regarded Justinian as unsympathetic to their views, saw the rioting as an opportunity to overthrow Justinian. Manipulated by these individuals, the rioters, many of whom were now armed, demanded the dismissal of both the prefect John the Cappadocian, who had charge of tax collection, and the quaestor Tribonian, who was responsible for rewriting the legal code. Egged on by the disaffected senators, they also declared their support for the replacement of Justinian with Hypatius, the nephew of former emperor Anastasius I Dicorus (r. 491–518).

A distraught Justinian considered fleeing the city, and an escape route lay open from the palace by water across the Bosporus. Justinian had ordered his great general Belisarius to command an expedition to North Africa. Fortunately, he was still in Constantinople when the uprising occurred. Justinian was saved by the prompt action of Belisarius and Empress Theodoram, who is believed to have been the decisive factor in persuading Justinian to stand and fight.

A plan was then developed. Narses, a popular eunuch, was entrusted with a bag of gold and dispatched to the Hippodrome alone and unarmed to deal with the mob present there for Hypatius's coronation. Narses went directly to the Blues' section and reminded the leaders there of the emperor's past strong support for the Blues as well as the fact that Hypatius supported the Greens. He then distributed the gold he had with him to the Blues' leaders. They in turn convinced their followers, who left the Hippodrome. The Greens were stunned when, on the departure of the Blues, imperial troops under Belisarius and another general, Mundus, stormed into the Hippodrome, killing the remaining rebels and restoring order.

In addition to the destruction of half the city, the Nika Uprising may have cost as many as 30,000–40,000 lives. Justinian also had Hypatius executed and exiled those aristocrats who had abetted the riot. Constantinople, including Hagia Sophia, was rebuilt, and thanks to the crushing of the opposition, Justinian was now free to pursues his policies.

Spencer C. Tucker

See also
Belisarius; Byzantine Empire; Justinian I the Great, Emperor

References
Barker, John W. *Justinian and the Later Roman Empire.* Madison: University of Wisconsin Press, 1966.
Cesaretti, Paolo. *Theodora: Empress of Byzantium.* New York: Vendome, 2005.
Diehl, Charles. *Theodora, Empress of Byzantium.* Translated by S. R. Rosenbaum. New Yok: Frederick Ungar, 1972.
Evans, James Allan. *The Empress Theodora: Partner of Justinian.* Austin: University of Texas Press, 2003.
Moorhead, John. *Justinian.* London: Longman, 1994.

Nikopolis, Crusade in (1396)

Large Christian crusade against the Ottoman Empire, defeated by the forces of the latter at the frontier fortress of Nikopolis (modern-day Nikopol, Bulgaria) in 1396.

The Ottomans had penetrated the Balkan peninsula during the 1360s and demonstrated that they were a major military power when they vanquished the Serbs at Kosovo Polje in 1389. A struggle followed between Hungary and the Ottomans for the domination of the principalities on both sides of the Danube. The Ottomans had suzerainty over Serbia and the Bulgarian kingdom of Vidin, having annexed the other Bulgarian kingdom of Turnovo (including the stronghold of Nikopolis) in 1393. Vlad, *voivod* of Walacia, sought Ottoman help against his rival Mircea the Great, who turned to King Sigismund of Hungary. Sigismund (of Luxembourg), a German, had acceded to the Hungarian throne on his marriage to Maria, queen of Hungary, in 1387.

The Ottomans launched raids north of the Danube from 1391 onward. The Hungarians mounted a retaliatory expedition in 1393, recapturing Nikopolis Minor on the north side of the Danube. King Sigismund, well aware of the extent of the Ottoman threat, called on the leaders of Western Europe for assistance and sent an embassy there the same year. Dukes Louis of Orléans, Philip the Bold of Burgundy, and John of Gaunt of Lancaster all pledged their support, while King Charles VI of France dispatched a small force under the constable of France, Count Philip of Eu. The following year, the three dukes sent their own ambassadors to the king of Hungary. Farther east, the new Byzantine emperor, Manuel II Palaiologos, cast off his status as vassal of Ottoman sultan Bayezid I, leading to the siege of his capital of Constantinople (Istanbul) by the Ottomans.

Because the Ottoman advance constituted a threat to Italian navigation in the Black Sea, Venice joined the Christian coalition. In the spring of 1395, the ambassadors of Sigismund of Hungary and Manuel II Palaeologos came to Venice and Paris to plan the expedition, to which Charles VI promised to add a French corps. However, at the end of the year, the dukes of Lancaster and Orléans withdrew from the project, believing that they could not leave France even though a truce had been signed between England and France in 1392. Philip the Bold also decided that he could not leave France; his place was taken by his eldest son, John, count of Nevers. Venice, Genoa, and the Hospitallers agreed to participate in the expedition, while the rival popes at Rome and Avignon issued crusade bulls.

During the spring of 1396, individuals took the cross throughout much of Western Europe. Areas participating

The Battle of Nikopolis (September 25, 1396) depicted in a miniature from a 16th-century Ottoman manuscript in the Topkapi Museum Library, Istanbul. (DeAgostini/Getty Images)

included England, Germany, Savoy, Italy, and France. The unrealistic plan developed at the court of France was to expel the Ottomans from Europe, restore the Latin Empire of Constantinople, and go on to recover the Holy Land from the Mamluk Sultanate. The nominal head of the French army was John of Nevers. In July, the different Western forces assembled at Buda, where they joined the Hungarian army. The total Christian forces numbered between 15,000 and 20,000 men.

The plan of campaign called for the crusaders to march down the Danube accompanied by a supply fleet as far as Nikopolis, where the land forces were to meet a Genoese, Venetian, and Hospitaller naval force sailing upriver from the Black Sea. They would then proceed to Constantinople and raise the Ottoman siege. A small corps was diverted to Walacia to restore Mircea to the throne.

In early September the crusaders reached Ottoman territory at Vidin, held by the Bulgarian prince Ivan Stratsimir, who surrendered the town; the Ottoman garrison there was massacred. This was followed by an attack on Oryakhovo

(Rahova), where the French knights were the first to reach the walls. The Ottoman commander offered to surrender, but the French insisted on taking the place by storm. They then massacred not only the Ottomans but also the Orthodox population except for the richest citizens, who had to pay a ransom. The French then burned the town.

The crusaders arrived at Nikopolis, a nearly impregnable site protected by strong fortifications, around September 10, 1396, and immediately laid siege to it by land and from the river. The Genoese and Venetians (the Hospitaller fleet not having arrived) cut off communications by water. The French constructed ladders to be used in assaults, while the Hungarians dug two large mines up to the walls. However, siege machinery was in short supply, and there is no indication that the crusaders had artillery with them. Deluded by their early victories and the absence of any news of the sultan, the crusaders turned the siege into a blockade, spending their time in debauchery with little thought of security.

When the crusaders entered Ottoman territory, Sultan Bayezid I was occupied with the siege of Constantinople. After receiving news of the crusader arrival, he summoned troops from his Asian and European dominions and assembled these and his Christian allies at Philippopolis (modern-day Plovdiv, Bulgaria). Marching toward Nikopolis, he established his camp not far from the Danube on September 24. The same day, crusader forces carried out a raid to reconnoiter the Ottoman positions and were victorious in an encounter with a small Turkish force.

The battle occurred the next day, September 25. Bayezid chose the location. He disposed his light cavalry and foot archers on the slopes of a hill beyond a wooded ravine, while the Serbs and Sipahi cavalry remained hidden behind the hill. As had been decided in Paris, the French formed the vanguard. They foolishly rushed ahead of the Hungarian and allied troops against the Ottoman light cavalry; many impaled their horses on prepared stakes and were forced to dismount, which began to spread panic in the Hungarian ranks. Nevertheless, this force of mounted and unmounted men was able to defeat the Ottoman infantry and attacked the cavalry. They thought they had gained victory, but when they reached the top of the hill, exhausted, they discovered Bayezid's fresh forces. The battle now became a rout. The French were either killed or taken prisoner. The Hungarians had been attacked by the Serbs; Sigismund's fall in a desperate melee was the signal for a general flight. Sigismund was able to escape on a boat, however, and eventually made his way back to Hungary via Constantinople and Ragusa (modern-day Dubrovnik, Croatia).

The next day Bayezid took vengeance on his Christian prisoners for the killing of the Ottoman garrisons, although some were spared to be ransomed. Eventually the Ottomans tired of cutting off heads, and the survivors were enslaved.

The crusade of Nikopolis was a total failure, and the Ottomans were able to pursue their expansion in the Balkans.

JACQUES PAVIOT

See also
Balkans, Ottoman Conquest of the; Bayezid I

References
Atiya, Aziz S. *The Crusade of Nicopolis.* London: Methuen, 1934.
Imber, Colin. *The Ottoman Empire, 1300–1481.* Istanbul: Isis, 1990.
Nicolle, David. *Nicopolis 1396.* Oxford, UK: Osprey, 1999.
Rosetti, H. R. "Notes on the Battle of Nicopolis." *Slavonic Review* 15 (1936–1937): 629–638.

Nile, Battle of (47 BCE)
See Caesar's Campaign in Egypt

Nile, Battle of the (August 1, 1798)
See Aboukir Bay, Battle of

Nile River

The Nile River is located in Northeast Africa and flows through the countries of Sudan and Egypt. The Nile has several sources, notably the White Nile that originates from Lake Victoria in Uganda and the Blue Nile that originates from Lake Tana in Ethiopia. These contribute approximately 28 percent and 58 percent, respectively, of the Nile's waters in Egypt. A further 14 percent comes from the Atbarah River, which originates in Ethiopia.

The Nile is the world's longest river. It flows north for some 4,216 miles through 35 degrees of latitude ranging from the Sahara Desert to the Mediterranean Sea. It has a surface area of more than 1.86 million square miles and a discharge of about 829,000 gallons per second. Geographically, the Nile can be divided into three zones: the upstream region in which the tributaries coalesce (where the White and Blue Niles join) close to Khartoum in Sudan; the middle stretch between Cairo and Khartoum, which contains the Aswan Dam (Sadd al-Aali) and numerous waterfalls; and the delta region from north of Cairo where the river subdivides.

Abundant irrigation channels carry water beyond the fertile floodplain into the arid desert margins to create agricultural land, a major economic asset for Egypt, especially for cotton production. The delta region was once a wide estuary in which river-borne silt was deposited to produce a fan-shaped delta extending some 100 miles to the sea. The delta is about 150 miles wide and occupies some 13,600 square miles overall.

Historical documents indicate that the number of branches has changed in the last 2,000 years. Through natural silting and human engineering, seven branches have since been reduced to two, the Rosetta and Damietta Rivers. Numerous irrigation channels have also been constructed.

The Nile has always been important in the history of Sudan and Egypt. Its seasonal waters, dependent on rainfall in the headwater region, and fertile silt supported several great civilizations, including the Nubian and ancient Egyptian civilizations. So precious was the Nile floodplain that tombs and temples were constructed at the desert margins. Today more than 110 million people inhabit the Nile Valley, mostly in Egypt, and are mainly engaged in agriculture and tourism.

The construction of the Aswan High Dam, completed in 1971, altered the geography and economy of the Nile and its valley quite substantially. Not the least of these changes was the creation of the world's largest artificial lake, known as Lake Nasser. At the time of its construction, the Aswan High Dam was the world's largest dam. It has fulfilled its promise of regulated river flow and flood abatement as well as the provisioning of a large proportion of Egypt's electricity. Disadvantages include the loss of fertile silt deposition downstream and the consequent need for artificial fertilizers in agriculture as well as a decline in the fisheries industry in the eastern Mediterranean. Although the Aswan High Dam provided more water on a year-round basis instead of the annual flooding, a side effect of working in the fields irrigated by the river is infection by a small parasite, a blood fluke that spreads the debilitating bilharziasis (schistosomiasis) to large numbers of Egyptians, estimated to number in the 1960s at 40 percent of the entire population.

The Nile River and its discharge have been a constant source of political controversy between the Sudan and Egypt as well as the basis for numerous Nile political unity schemes. The Nile River and the Aswan High Dam project in particular were at the center of the 1956 Suez Crisis during which Israel, France, and Britain invaded Egypt to take back control of the Suez Canal. Egyptian president Gamal Abdel Nasser had nationalized the canal earlier that year with the stated aim of raising funds for the construction of the Aswan High Dam. He did so when the United States and Great Britain reneged on an earlier offer to help fund the project after Nasser had purchased armaments from the communist bloc. Nasser's decision ultimately led to a British, French, and Israeli invasion of Egypt.

As with other freshwater supplies in the generally parched Middle East, the Nile River is also at the center of ever-increasing concerns over potable water supplies in the face of growing populations and increased industry and agriculture.

ANTOINETTE MANNION

See also
Egypt; Nasser, Gamal Abdel; Suez Crisis

References
Holmes, Martha, Gavin Maxwell, and Tim Scoones. *Nile: Unveiling the Secrets of the World's Greatest River*. London: BBC Books, 2004.
Said, Rushdi. *The River Nile: Geology, Hydrology and Utilization*. Amsterdam: Elsevier, 1993.
Tvedt, Terje. *The River Nile in the Age of the British: Political Ecology and the Quest for Economic Power*. London: Tauris, 2004.
Waterbury, John. *Hydropolitics of the Nile Valley*. Syracuse: Syracuse University Press, 1979.

NIMBLE ARCHER, Operation (October 19, 1987)

U.S. Navy operation in which two Iranian oil platforms located in the Persian Gulf were destroyed on October 19, 1987. It was part of the larger Operation EARNEST WILL, which commenced in July 1987 and was designed to protect oil tankers navigating through the gulf during the Iran-Iraq War (1980–1988). EARNEST WILL was a reaction to the Tanker War that had erupted between Iran and Iraq during the war. For months, Iran had been preying on neutral shipping in the gulf and had taken a special interest in Kuwaiti oil tankers (at the time Kuwait was a major supporter of Iraq).

On October 16 Iran launched a Silkworm antiship missile, with the target being a Kuwaiti oil tanker off the coast of Kuwait. When the missile hit the *Sea Isle City,* the resulting explosion wounded 18 crew members and blinded the ship's captain, who was a U.S. citizen. The damage to the ship was extensive, but it remained afloat. Although the incident occurred after U.S. naval escorts had left the area, the Ronald Reagan administration was incensed by the unprovoked attack. Because this was the first major attack since EARNEST WILL was launched, the Americans believed that they had to retaliate promptly in order to demonstrate that they intended to support the tanker escorts by force if necessary.

Three days later on October 19, four U.S. Navy destroyers (the *Hoel, John Young, Kidd,* and *Leftwich*) attacked two Iranian oil platforms in the Persian Gulf's Rashadat Oil Field. Following considerable U.S. naval gunfire, the two platforms were both destroyed. Although the two platforms were no longer producing oil, the Americans targeted them because they believed that the Iranians were employing them as command posts from which to order shipping attacks. The Reagan administration also asserted that Iran had used the platforms to stage small-boat attacks against neutral shipping. Operation NIMBLE ARCHER set the precedent for future U.S. attacks in EARNEST WILL.

In 1992 Iran sued the U.S. government in the International Court of Justice (ICJ), claiming that the 1987 attack had been unprovoked and against international law. The United States subsequently brought its own counterclaims against Iran. In the end the ICJ refused to issue a ruling, citing fault on both sides of the issue.

PAUL G. PIERPAOLI JR.

See also
EARNEST WILL, Operation; Iran-Iraq War

References
Palmer, Michael A. *Guardians of the Gulf: A History of America's Expanding Role in the Persian Gulf, 1833–1992.* New York: Free Press, 1992.
Wise, Harold L. *Inside the Danger Zone: The U.S. Military in the Persian Gulf, 1987–1988.* Annapolis, MD: Naval Institute Press, 2007.

1956 War
See Suez Crisis

1967 War
See Six-Day War

Nineveh, Battle of (December 12, 627)

Key military engagement deciding the outcome of the Byzantine-Sassanid War of 602–628. Following Persian rejection of peace talks and in a daring move given previous Persian military successes, in March 624 Byzantine emperor Heraclius departed from Constantinople by sea with a force of no more than 40,000 men to attack the Persian heartland. Abandoning any attempt to secure his communications with the sea, he marched inland through Armenia and modern Azerbaijan to assault the heart of the Persian Empire in Media (today central Iran).

Sassanid shah Khosrau II then sought to force Heraclius to withdraw from Persian territory by ordering an all-out offensive against the Byzantine capital of Constantinople. Toward that end the Persians secured an alliance with the Avars to move against the city from the west. During June–August 626 the Persians and Avars then laid siege to Constantinople.

The city's defenses were strong, and Heraclius, trusting that Constantinople's land defenses and Byzantine naval strength would hold, refused to withdraw from Armenia. This strategy worked, with his opponents dissipating their strength in the futile effort to take the Byzantine capital. The Avars and Persians withdrew their greatly weakened forces from before Constantinople that fall. With Persian military strength now greatly reduced, Heraclius pursued the war in Anatolia, securing an alliance with the Khazars, a Turkish people in the Caucasus. The Byzantines and Khazars then laid siege to Tiflis.

In mid-September 627, with the Byzantine-Khazar siege of Tiflis continuing, Heraclius invaded Mesopotamia. Moving southwest with perhaps 25,000 men, he was pursued by Persian general Rhahzadh at the head of some 12,000 men. As they proceeded, Heraclius's forces ravaged the countryside of provisions, rendering it difficult for his pursuers, whose mounts suffered accordingly. On December 1, 627, Heraclius camped near the ruins of the former Assyrian capital of Nineveh. News that Persian reinforcements were arriving led Heraclius to cross the Tigris River, giving the appearance he was retreating. The Persians pursued.

On December 12, 627, the Persians attacked. Heraclius feigned flight, withdrawing to a great plain where, by prearranged plan, he turned and attacked, surprising the Persians. Fog obscured the battlefield and worked against the Persian advantage in missiles, the Byzantines having the advantage in lances. The battle reportedly lasted some eight hours, with the Persians finally withdrawing in the hills after having suffered some 6,000 killed, including Rhahzadh. The Persian reinforcements arrived after the battle.

The Battle of Nineveh proved decisive in the war. Heraclius went on to take Dastagird, securing significant treasure there and recovering a reported 300 Byzantine/Roman standards lost in previous warfare. Heraclius then raided in the vicinity of Ctesiphon, while a coup d'état ousted Shah Khosrow II, beginning a bloody Persian civil war. Persian general Shahrvaraz then struck a bargain with Heraclius in which Shahrvaraz agreed to return Egypt, Palestine, Syria, and the other conquered territories to Byzantium in return for permission to march on Ctesiphon and take power. By 630 Heraclius had recovered all of Egypt and western Asia Minor. The ancient Byzantine boundaries had been restored and the empire was at peace.

It was not to last. The long struggle between the Persians and Byzantines had exhausted both sides and rendered them susceptible to pressure from the new threat posed by Islam. By the time of Heraclius's death from illness in 641, the Arabs had taken the entire Middle East, which they held from that point forward.

SPENCER C. TUCKER

See also
Byzantine-Sassanid War; Heraclius

References
Haldon, J. F. *Byzantium in the Seventh Century.* Cambridge: Cambridge University Press, 1990.
Kaegi, Walter Emil. *Byzantium and the Early Islamic Conquests.* Cambridge: Cambridge University Press, 1995.
Kaegi, Walter Emil. *Heraclius, Emperor of Byzantium.* Cambridge: Cambridge University Press, 2003.
Pourshariati, Parvaneh. *The Sasanian Era.* London: I. B. Tauris, 2010.
Treadgold, Warren. *A History of the Byzantine State and Society.* Stanford, CA: Stanford University Press, 1997.

Nisibis, Battle of (217)

The Battle of Nisibis was fought between a Roman army, led by new emperor Macrinus (r. 217–218), and the Parthian army under King Artabanus IV (208–224). It occurred sometime in the spring of 217 near the Roman city of Nisibis (modern-day Nusaybin, Syria).

There had been a protracted period of warfare between Rome and the Persian Parthian Empire, during which Rome had undertaken several invasions of Parthian territory in the Middle East. In 208 a civil war began in the Parthian Empire in which Artabanus led a rebellion against his brother Vologases VI. Artabanus soon secured control of most of the western territories of the empire, although Vologases managed to maintain control of part of Babylon. In any case, Artabanus V now found himself in contact with the Roman Empire.

Roman emperor Caracalla (r. 188–217) had an exaggerated sense of his military abilities and sought to take advantage of the Parthian upheaval. He proposed an alliance to Artabanus, to include marriage with the Parthian king's daughter. Artabanus agreed, and Caracalla peacefully entered Mesopotamia with a large army, ostensibly to meet his ally and future father-in-law. But at the meeting with Artabanus and his court, the emperor treacherously attacked. Many of the Persians in the court were killed, although Artabanus managed to escape. This episode, however, gave the Romans free reign to plunder territory east of the Tigris before returning to Edessa in modern-day southeastern Turkey for the winter.

On April 8, 217, however, Caracalla was himself the victim of treachery, murdered by his Pretorian prefect Marcus Opellius Macrinus, who then became emperor. He now had to face Artabanus, who had put together a large force and was advancing on the Romans. Macrinus had scant military experience himself and sought to reach some accommodation with Artabanus that would avoid a military confrontation. The Persian ruler rejected the Roman offer to return all Persian prisoners taken, demanding that there also be financial compensation, that the Romans rebuild the towns they had pillaged and destroyed in Mesopotamia, and that they cede to the Parthians the Roman provinces of northern Mesopotamia that had recently been taken by Emperor Septimius Severus.

Marcrinus rejected the Parthian terms, with the situation to be resolved on the battlefield. The two armies came together near the Roman city of Nisibis. The size of the opposing forces is unknown, although sources give the Persians larger numbers.

The battle occurred during a three-day span. The Romans deployed in typical formation, with their infantry in the center and cavalry and light troops covering the flanks. The Parthians began the fray at sunrise, first with barrages of arrows, then with horses and camels attacking forward and engaging the Roman infantry at close quarters. While the Roman light infantry sustained casualties, many more mounted Persians fell. Several other Persian assaults that same day also failed, and both sides withdrew to their camps for the night. The second day saw a repeat of the first day's fighting. On the third day, the Parthians sought to take advantage of their greater numbers and mobility to outflank the Roman line. The Romans responded by abandoning their customary deep formation in order to extend their front. This enabled the Roman cavalry and light troops on the flanks to thwart the Parthian plan.

Both sides had by now suffered extensive casualties, and with the Roman situation in peril, Macrinus sent a message to Artabanus in which he informed the Parthian king of Caracalla's death and offered substantial compensation. With his own side having sustained heavy casualties and his army basically a feudal militia rather than a professional force like that of the Romans, Artabanus agreed to peace, for which he received 200 million sesterces.

In June 218, Macrinus was defeated outside Antioch (near modern-day Antakya, Turkey) by other Roman forces supporting a usurper, Elagabalus, who then became emperor and ruled until 222. At the same time, Artabanus faced a revolt by the Sassanid clan of Persia, led by Ardashir I, who defeated Artabanus I in 224 and became the first Sassanid emperor. Nisibis was thus the last major battle between Rome and Parthian Persia. It did not end warfare between Rome and Persia, however, as Ardashir and Roman emperor Alexander Severus (r. 222–235) soon were again at war over Mesopotamia.

SPENCER C. TUCKER

See also
Alexander Severus, Roman Emperor; Ardashir I; Parthian Empire; Roman-Parthian Wars; Septimius Severus, Emperor

References
Cowan, Ross. *Roman Battle Tactics, 109 BC-AD 313*. Oxford, UK: Osprey, 2009.

Herodian of Antioch's History of the Roman Empire: From the Death of Marcus Aurelius to the Accession of Gordian III. Translated by Edward C. Echols. Berkeley: University of California Press, 1961.

Rawlinson, George. *The Seven Great Monarchies of the Ancient Eastern World*, Vol 6, *A History of Parthia*. Charleston, SC: BiblioLife, 2007.

Nissa, Treaty of (October 3, 1739)

A peace treaty signed on October 3, 1739, at Nissa in Serbia between Russia and the Ottoman Empire that concluded the Russo-Ottoman War of 1736–1739. During this conflict Russia was supported by the Habsburgs, who, however, suffered defeats and were forced to accept the disadvantageous Treaty of Belgrade in September 1739. Although Russia continued the war for several more weeks, the Habsburg departure forced it to accept Ottoman conditions.

Russia restored portions of Moldavia and Bessarabia, including the city of Khotin, to the Ottomans and promised to dismantle the fortifications at Azov, which, however, Russia retained as a port. Russia also agreed not to maintain warships in the Black Sea. For their part, the Ottomans agreed to grant Russia certain trading privileges.

ALEXANDER MIKABERIDZE

See also
Ottoman-Habsburg Wars; Russo-Ottoman Wars

Reference
Shaw, Stanford. *History of the Ottoman Empire and Modern Turkey*. Cambridge: Cambridge University Press, 1977.

Nixon, Sir John Eccles (1857–1921)

British Army general. Born on August 16, 1857, at Brentford, England, John Eccles Nixon was educated at Wellington College and Sandhurst. He joined the army in 1875 and fought in the 1879–1880 Afghan War and the 1899–1902 Boer War, when he commanded a brigade. He then served in India. In 1904 he was promoted to major general and during 1906–1908 was inspector general of cavalry. He commanded the 7th (Meerut) Division during 1908–1910 and the 1st Peshawar Division during 1910–1912. Promoted to lieutenant general in 1909, in 1912 Nixon received command of the Indian Southern Army, and in 1914 he won promotion to full general. In 1915 he assumed command of the Indian Northern Army.

In April 1915 Nixon took command of the British Expeditionary Force in Mesopotamia. Policy makers in London favored a defensive strategy to protect the oil fields, but before Nixon left India, Indian Army commander in chief General Sir Beauchamp-Duff instructed him to advance on Baghdad. This was not known in London at the time.

Having received reinforcements, although not a requested cavalry brigade, Nixon ordered his field commander, Major General Charles Townshend, to take the offensive. In June 1915 Townshend captured Amara, followed by Kut al-Amara in September. London then authorized Nixon to move against Baghdad, promising two Indian divisions from France. Nixon was prepared to gamble to achieve success, and he underestimated the ability of Ottoman troops. Townshend was more realistic, opposing an advance on Baghdad without reinforcements.

After registering his objections, in late November Townshend moved toward Baghdad. Blocked by the Ottomans at Ctesiphon, he was forced back on Kut, where he was besieged by the Ottomans in December and forced to surrender in April 1916, the promised reinforcements not having arrived.

In January 1916 Nixon gave up his command, ostensibly for reasons of health. The Mesopotamia Commission, which during August 1916–April 1917 investigated the military failure, concluded that "the weightiest share of responsibility lies with Sir John Nixon," the general officer commanding in Mesopotamia, "whose confident optimism was the main cause of the decision to advance to Baghdad." Plans to bring Nixon before a special court of inquiry were overtaken by the end of the war, but his career was in tatters. Nixon died at St. Raphael, France, on December 15, 1921.

SPENCER C. TUCKER

See also
Ctesiphon, 1915 Battle of; Kut al-Amara, Siege of; Mesopotamian Theater, World War I; Townshend, Sir Charles Vere Ferrers

References
Barker, A. J. *The Bastard War: The Mesopotamian Campaign of 1914–1918*. New York: Dial, 1967.
Barker, A. J. *The First Iraq War, 1914–1918: Britain's Mesopotamian Campaign*. New York: Enigma Books, 2009.
Moberly, F. J. *The Campaign in Mesopotamia, 1914–1918*. 3 vols. Nashville: Battery Press, 1997–1998.

Nixon Doctrine (November 3, 1969)

Cold War (1947–1991) foreign policy doctrine of U.S. president Richard M. Nixon, first put forward in a press conference on Guam on July 25, 1969, and formally enunciated in an address to the nation on November 3. The Nixon Doctrine called for the United States to continue to meet all its current treaty commitments and to provide a nuclear shield for vital allies. But the doctrine backed away from the open-ended commitment that the United States had made to contain communism via the 1947 Truman Doctrine. As such, the United States promised only economic aid and military weaponry to developing world allies threatened by communist aggression, with the stipulation that such nations must enlist their own manpower to confront armed challenges to their security. In the wake of the politically unpopular deployment of hundreds of thousands of U.S. troops to Korea and then to Vietnam, the Nixon Doctrine warned that the United States would no longer bear the burden of directly confronting communist threats in the developing world. The Nixon Doctrine was born of the recognition that U.S. power had limits following the Vietnam debacle. No longer could the nation afford to "pay any price" or "bear any burden" as U.S. president John F. Kennedy had promised in his 1961 inaugural address.

The Sino-Soviet rift, France's 1967 withdrawal from the North Atlantic Treaty Organization (NATO) military command, Britain's retreat from the Persian Gulf region, and the rise of the developing world all influenced this change. The Nixon Doctrine also took into account the U.S. economy, with rising budget deficits, building inflation, and slow economic growth by 1970. The high costs of the Vietnam War, in conjunction with other U.S. commitments, had clearly influenced Nixon's posture.

Increasingly, the doctrine relied on regional strongmen assigned by Washington to guard U.S. interests. These U.S.-backed "deputy sheriffs" included shah of Iran Mohammad Reza Pahlavi, Egyptian president Anwar Sadat, Filipino president Ferdinand Marcos, Nicaragua's Anastasio Somoza, Zaire's Mobutu Sese Seko, and King Faisal of Saudi Arabia, among others. All were to safeguard U.S. interests in their respective regions while the United States provided them aid and arms. In the Middle East, Iran became the chief beneficiary of U.S. weaponry and military aid, as that nation became the linchpin of U.S. policy in the region.

Relying on the despotic rule of many of these "deputy sheriffs" elicited sharp criticism, however. Opponents viewed the Nixon Doctrine as a stratagem for U.S. hegemony on the cheap. Indeed, many of the rulers fell in the late 1970s and 1980s, and there were costly negative consequences to U.S. strategic interests. The 1979 collapse of the shah's regime in Iran offered a prime example of the Nixon Doctrine's distinct limitations.

The Nixon Doctrine prompted the 1980 Carter Doctrine, promulgated by President Jimmy Carter, which was actually a turn away from the Nixon Doctrine's more hands-off approach to American security in the Middle East. Carter promised direct military intervention in the region to protect vital American interests in the Persian Gulf—namely oil supplies and shipping lanes. This set the stage for a much stronger U.S. presence in the Middle East, including President Ronald Reagan's interventions in Lebanon and then American involvement in the 1991 Persian Gulf War as well as the Iraq War that began in 2003.

MICHAEL E. DONOGHUE

See also
Carter Doctrine; Iran; Iran, Islamic Revolution in; Lebanon, Second U.S. Intervention in; Reza Shah Pahlavi

References
Hoff, Joan. *Nixon Reconsidered* New York: Basic Books, 1994.
Kimball, J. "The Nixon Doctrine: A Saga of Misunderstanding." *Presidential Studies Quarterly* 36, no. 1 (2006): 59–74.
Litwak Robert S. *Détente and the Nixon Doctrine: American Foreign Policy and the Pursuit of Stability, 1969–1976*. Cambridge: Cambridge University Press, 1984.
Schurmann, Franz. *The Foreign Politics of Richard Nixon: The Grand Design*. Berkeley: Institute of International Studies, University of California, 1987.

Nizip, Battle of (June 24, 1839)

Decisive battl, fought on June 24, 1839, between Ottoman Empire forces and those of viceroy of Egypt Mehmed Ali. The battle was fought near present-day Nizip in southeastern Turkey. It is also known as the Battle of Nezib, the Battle of Nisib, and the Battle of Nizib.

In the early 1820s, faced with the Greek Revolt, Ottoman sultan Mahmud II asked Mehmed Ali for assistance in subduing the Greeks, promising to give in return additional provinces to the Egyptian ruler. An expedition commanded by Mehmed Ali's son Ibrahim Pasha landed in Greece in 1824 and subdued the Morea (Peloponnesus) but was eventually compelled to withdraw by the combined naval forces of Britain, France and Russia. After the war Mehmed Ali and Mahmud II disagreed over compensation promised to Egypt. The Egyptian-Ottoman War of 1831–1833 followed, with Ibrahim Pasha leading an Egyptian army through Palestine and Syria, defeating the Ottomans at Homs and Konya. The sultan was spared only by the intervention of the governments of Great Britain, Austria, Russia, and Prussia, which forced Mehmed Ali to accept the Convention of Kütahya (May 4, 1833) that granted Syria and Adana to Egypt.

These territorial concessions were not satisfactory to either party, however, and a new war occurred in 1839. An Ottoman army, led by Hafiz Pasha and advised by Prussian officers, among them Graf Helmuth Karl von Moltke, invaded Syria and met the Egyptians under Ibrahim Pasha at Nizip (Nezib).

The numbers of men on each side vary widely, depending on source. The Egyptians may have had 30,000–46,000 men, the Ottomans 30,000–80,000. The battle on June 24 was short but decisive. The Ottoman army was at Mezar, southwest of Nezib, with the Nezib River to its left. Ibrahim advanced his men under heavy Ottoman artillery fire, while the Egyptian artillery fired on the Ottomans. The latter proved particularly effective, with the Ottomans suffering such heavy casualties that by the time the Egyptian infantry reached the Ottoman line, the latter were in retreat. The Egyptians are believed to have sustained some 4,000 casualties, while Ottoman casualties are described as very heavy.

As the news of the defeat spread, Ottoman admiral Derya Ahmad Fewzi Pasha, dispatched to support the Ottoman army in Syria, led his fleet to Alexandria, where he handed it over to the Mehmed Ali.

The Egyptians, however, were unable to take advantage of these successes. The Great Powers again intervened on behalf of the Ottomans, forcing the Egyptians to evacuate Syria in 1840. Still, the Ottomans were compelled to compromise, and Sultan Abdulmecid I, who succeeded Mahmud II in July 1839, recognized Mehmed Ali as hereditary governor of Egypt in 1841.

ALEXANDER MIKABERIDZE

See also
Egyptian-Ottoman Wars; Ibrahim Pasha; Konya, Battle of; Mahmud II, Sultan; Mehmed Ali

References
Fahmy, Khaled. *All the Pasha's Men: Mehmed Ali, His Army, and the Making of Modern Egypt.* Cambridge: Cambridge University Press, 1997.
Farah, Caesar E. *The Politics of Interventionism in Ottoman Lebanon, 1830–1861.* London: Centre for Lebanese Studies in association with I. B. Tauris, 2000.
Shaw, Stanford. *History of the Ottoman Empire and Modern Turkey: Reform, Revolution and Republic: The Rise of Modern Turkey, 1808–1975,* Vol. 2. Cambridge: Cambridge University Press, 1977.

Norfolk, Battle of (February 26–27, 1991)

One of four engagements during the 1991 Persian Gulf War (Operation DESERT STORM) fought by Lieutenant General Frederick M. Franks Jr.'s VII U.S. Corps against the Tawakalna Mechanized Division in southeast Iraq. The four engagements were the 2nd Armored Cavalry Regiment's engagement with the Iraqi division during the Battle of 73-Easting; the 3rd Brigade, U.S. 1st Armored Division's envelopment of the northern portion of the Tawakalna's line; the 3rd Armored Division's attack toward Objective DORSET in the center; and the seizure by Major General Thomas G. Rhame's 1st Infantry Division (Mechanized) of Objective NORFOLK.

The Iraqi 18th Mechanized Brigade and the 37th Armored Brigade from the Iraqi 12th Armored Division defended this area, which was the southern portion of the Tawakalna's defensive line. These Iraqi forces defended a large collection of supply dumps and logistics areas that branched off from a high-speed road that ran along the Iraqi-Saudi Arabia strategic pipeline (IPSA) west of the Kuwaiti border. The forces had the task of blocking the coalition attack from the west, allowing units in Kuwait to withdraw to Iraq.

At 2:00 p.m. on February 26, General Rhame ordered Lieutenant Colonel Robert Wilson's 1st Squadron, 4th Cavalry, to contact the 2nd Cavalry's staff and coordinate the 1st Infantry Division's forward passage through its units engaging the Iraqi units. Moving with two brigades forward and one trailing, the division arrived behind the cavalry shortly before 10:00 p.m. Soon after, the lead brigades passed through the passage lanes and into the battle. In the distance, AH-64 Apache helicopters attacked the Iraqi brigade's second tactical echelon. The helicopter attack continued the pressure on the Iraqi commander and his artillery, preventing him from interfering with the 1st Infantry Division's approach.

At 10:30 p.m., Colonel Lon E. Maggart's 1st Brigade attacked in the north through a single passage lane. The lead battalion ran into elements of the Iraqi 18th Mechanized Brigade. Iraqi gunners destroyed two Bradley M3 Cavalry Scout vehicles silhouetted against the fires of burning Iraqi vehicles. The commander immediately pulled his scouts back and moved his tank companies forward. Unlike the division's experience in the first battle of the war along the border, the Iraqis here intended to fight. Two company teams of the 2nd Battalion of the 34th Armor Regiment strayed off their axis and began moving north rather than east. Lieutenant Colonel Gregory Fontenot, commander of the battalion, realized the error and soon had the two teams heading in the right direction.

At the same time, Colonel David Weisman's 3rd Brigade in the southern portion of the sector moved immediately into battle with his three battalions abreast, running into a T-55–equipped Iraqi tank battalion. Although the American assault caught many Iraqi tank crews on the ground in their shelters taking cover from the air attack, their scattered deployments made the night battle difficult. All night, bypassed Iraqi infantry squads and tanks tried to engage the American vehicles as they crossed their sector. In one instance, an M1 Abrams tank platoon passed by several Iraqi positions that appeared to contain only burning or destroyed vehicles. Hidden in this array were at least five operational T-55 tanks behind revetments and masked from the Americans' thermal sights. Iraqi infantry units, ranging in size from platoons to companies, also hid among the tanks. A slightly disoriented Bradley Fighting Vehicle platoon, attempting to follow the M1 tanks, moved across the front of these Iraqi positions, illuminated by burning vehicles behind them. The Iraqis took advantage and opened fire from three directions. The initial volley hit a Bradley, killing three American soldiers.

An American tank company trailing the lead units saw the engagement to their front and joined the melee, quickly destroying three T-55s before they could get off another shot. At the same time, several antitank missiles hit the Bradley platoon. From the perspective of the tank gunners looking through the thermal sights of the approaching M1 tanks, these Bradleys appeared to be T-55 tanks shooting at them. The young and exhausted American gunners, convinced that they were fighting against a determined enemy, opened fire, hitting three more American vehicles. When the confusion in the 3rd Brigade's sector was over, 1st Infantry Division crews had destroyed five of their own tanks and four infantry fighting vehicles. Six American soldiers perished in these attacks, and 30 others were wounded.

By 12:30 a.m on February 27, nine American battalions were on line and began methodically crossing the remaining six miles of Objective NORFOLK. As they advanced, M1A1 Abrams tank commanders acquired the thermal images of the Iraqi tanks or infantry fighting vehicles long before they were themselves spotted. Platoon leaders, team commanders, and even battalion commanders issued unit-wide fire commands. Before the defending Iraqis had any idea of what was happening, their entire line of vehicles exploded.

In the north of the 1st Infantry Division's sector, Colonel Wilson's 1st Squadron, 4th Cavalry, screened the division's flank with the 3rd Armored Division and ran into an Iraqi unit. With a mixture of both T-55 and T-72 tanks as well as many dismounted infantry, it was probably not an organized battalion. After the initial engagement, Wilson pulled his screen line back and consolidated his force. Attacking at 6:15 a.m., the squadron destroyed another 11 Iraqi tanks, many infantry vehicles, artillery batteries, and logistics bunkers.

By dawn on February 27, the 1st Infantry Division controlled Objective NORFOLK. The attack of the division and the 2nd Armored Cavalry Regiment killed approximately 5,000 Iraqi soldiers and destroyed two brigades of armored equipment. American casualties were 6 killed and fewer than 70 wounded. The way was now set for the 1st Infantry Division to clear northern Kuwait of Iraqi troops.

STEPHEN A. BOURQUE

See also
Persian Gulf War, Overview; 73 Easting, Battle of

References
Bourque, Stephen A. "Correcting Myths about the Persian Gulf War: The Last Stand of the Tawakalna." *Middle East Journal* 51, no. 4 (1997): 566–583.
Bourque, Stephen A. *Jayhawk! The VII Corps in the Persian Gulf War.* Washington, DC: U.S. Army Center of Military History, 2002.
Bourque, Stephen A., and John W. Burdan III. *The Road to Safwan: The 1st Squadron, 4th Cavalry in the 1991 Persian Gulf War.* Denton: University of North Texas Press, 2007.
Fontenot, Gregory. "Fright Night: Task Force 2/34 Armor." *Military Review* 73, no. 1 (1993): 38–52.

Scales, Robert H. *Certain Victory: The U.S. Army in the Gulf War.* Fort Leavenworth, KS: U.S. Army Command and General Staff College Press, 1994.

Staff, 1st Squadron, 4th Cavalry, 1st Infantry Division. "Riders on the Storm: A Narrative History of the 1–4 Cav's Campaign in Iraq and Kuwait—24 January–March 1991." *Armor* 100 (May–June 1991): 13–19.

Woods, Kevin M. *The Mother of All Battles: Saddam Hussein's Strategic Plan for the Persian Gulf War.* Annapolis, MD: Naval Institute Press, 2008.

NORTHERN WATCH Operation (January 1, 1997–March 17, 2003)

Surveillance and air policing operation of the U.S. European Command (EUCOM) that enforced the no-fly zone above the 36th parallel mandated by the United Nation (UN) to prevent Iraqi attacks against the Kurds in northern Iraq and to enforce Iraqi compliance with UN Security Council resolutions. Operation NORTHERN WATCH, carried out by the United States, Great Britain, and Turkey, began on January 1, 1997, and ended unofficially on March 17, 2003, and officially on May 1, 2003.

With the 1991 Persian Gulf War, the United States encouraged the Kurds in northern Iraq to revolt against the regime of President Saddam Hussein. Hussein retaliated by ordering devastating military attacks on the Kurds, and more than 1 million Kurds, remembering the Iraqi gas attacks on their settlements in 1988, fled northward toward Turkey. Turkey, which already had a substantial problem with its existing Kurdish population, would not allow the Iraqi Kurds to cross the border. As a result, the Kurds were left stranded in the mountains, starving, ill-prepared for severe weather winter, and at the mercy of Iraqi forces.

Thus, on April 6, 1991, U.S. president George H. W. Bush directed EUCOM to form a Joint Task Force (JTF) to protect the Kurds of northern Iraq. For this mission, called Operation PROVIDE COMFORT, coalition air forces flew more than 40,000 sorties, relocated more than 700,000 refugees, rebuilt more than 70 percent of the Kurdish villages destroyed in northern Iraq, delivered more than 17,000 tons of supplies, and prevented new Iraqi attacks on the Kurds. U.S. Air Force fighters from Incirlik Air Base, Turkey, patrolled the northern no-fly zone until PROVIDE COMFORT officially ended on December 31, 1996.

To continue policing the northern no-fly zone and to ensure Iraqi compliance with UN Security Council resolutions that called for UN inspection of Iraqi nuclear, biological, and chemical weapons facilities, EUCOM began Operation NORTHERN WATCH on January 1, 1997. The three coalition partners for this mission collectively provided approximately 45 aircraft and more than 1,400 personnel. Headquartered at Incirlik Air Base, the joint U.S. force numbered some 1,100 personnel from the U.S. Air Force, Army, Navy, and Marine Corps. The air force contingent consisted of active-duty, Air Force Reserve, and Air National Guard airmen on 14- to 180-day duty, depending on their status. With a 700 percent annual turnover rate in personnel, more than 9,000 personnel rotated through NORTHERN WATCH annually.

The Turkish government, which was opposed to a permanent U.S. military operation from its territory, originally permitted operations for six months and subsequently approved additional extensions at six-month intervals. Turkish prime minister Bulent Ecevit, who was critical of American policy in Iraq, placed major operational restrictions on the activities of NORTHERN WATCH forces, including the size of the operation, hours of flight operations, the types of aircraft deployed, and the types of munitions used. As a result, U.S. forces had to closely link U.S. responses to Iraqi provocations, and the Turkish military monitored American operations to see that these adhered to the restrictions. Turkish authorities also refused to allow coalition aircrews based at Incirlik Air Base to participate in Operation DESERT STRIKE in 1996 and Operation DESERT FOX in 1998, effectively grounding NORTHERN WATCH aircraft during those operations.

The coalition used a variety of fighters, tankers, and intelligence, surveillance, and reconnaissance aircraft, working as a team to enforce the no-fly zone. Typical missions required a mix of aircraft. Among the aircraft used were the EA-6B Prowler, the E-3 Sentry (AWACS), the F-15 Eagle, the F-16 Fighting Falcon, the HH-60 Jayhawk, the HC-130 Hercules, the KC-135 Stratotanker, the UH-60 Blackhawk, the EP-3 Aries, the C-12 Huron, the SEPECAT GR-3 Jaguar, the Nimrod, and the VC10 tanker.

British and U.S. aircraft flew patrol missions over Iraq an average of 18 days per month. In 2000, they flew 164 days; in 2001, 146 days; and by late November 2002, 106 days. For the first year of the operation, northern Iraq was quiet, with no incidents between coalition aircraft and Iraqi forces. However, Iraqi ground-based antiaircraft defenses engaged patrolling coalition aircraft during every subsequent mission.

Despite the coalition's enforcement of the no-fly zone for almost two years, Iraq continued to avoid compliance with UN resolutions, especially Security Council Resolution 687 requiring it to dispose of its weapons of mass destruction (WMD), ballistic missiles with a range over 93 miles, and

Armed with missiles and bombs, a U.S. Air Force F-16CJ Fighting Falcon of the Ohio Air National Guard flies over northern Iraq during Operation NORTHERN WATCH in 2002. (U.S. Department of Defense)

related production facilities and equipment. Iraq greatly interfered with the activities of the UN arms inspectors on three separate occasions. On November 13, 1997, Iraq expelled UN arms inspectors who returned one week later. On January 13, 1998, Iraq banned UN arms inspectors, who had been led by an American, and expelled the inspectors three days later. Finally, on October 31, 1998, the Iraqis stopped cooperating with UN inspectors, who were forced to withdraw on November 7, 1998.

These actions resulted in a flurry of diplomatic action by UN secretary-general Kofi Annan and a buildup of coalition military forces. The U.S. military then prepared units in the United States for deployment under Operations DESERT THUNDER I–II. However, Annan managed to convince Hussein to accept a tentative agreement that would allow UN arms inspectors full access to suspected Iraqi weapon sites. One month later, however, a report that summarized Iraq's continued history of uncooperative actions and violations of the weapons disposal requirements resulted in Operation DESERT FOX. During this operation (December 16–19, 1998), NORTHERN WATCH aircraft ceased operations for four days to allow aircraft designated for the contingency to reach their targets.

Shortly after DESERT FOX ended, Iraq announced that it would no longer recognize the northern and southern no-fly zones. When NORTHERN WATCH resumed, Iraqi air defenses shot at coalition aircraft with surface-to-air missiles (SAMs) on December 28, 1998. Up until March 1999, Iraqi SAM missile sites and antiaircraft guns, the most common threat, fired on U.S. and British aircraft over northern Iraq almost daily. Coalition forces retaliated by attacking Iraqi air defense systems, the first such action in northern Iraq since August 1993. Coalition aircraft employed a variety of weapons, including laser-guided bombs, the AGM-88 high-speed antiradiation missile, and the AGM-130 long-range air-to-surface missiles, against 225 targets. NORTHERN WATCH saw the first combat use of the AGM-130.

From June 1998 to June 1999, coalition aircraft flew patrols an average of 18 days per month, accumulating over 5,000 combat/combat-support sorties. These coalition air attacks severely degraded Iraq's integrated air defense systems without the loss of any coalition aircraft, despite Hussein having offered a $14,000 bounty to any Iraqi downing a coalition aircraft. During early 1999, coalition air activity over northern Iraq came to a temporary halt as aircraft transferred to Italy for Operation ALLIED FORCE.

The air policing and surveillance of northern Iraq had a number of critics. Some believed that coalition aircraft deliberately provoked Iraqi antiaircraft defenses to turn on their radars and/or fire SAMs or antiaircraft guns to draw a coalition attack. As this type of criticism mounted, Brigadier General Robert DuLaney, the American commander of Operation NORTHERN WATCH after October 1999, ordered coalition aircraft to be less confrontational and avoid known Iraqi air defense sites. Also, coalition planes stopped dropping cement-filled laser-guided bombs that had been used to attack SAM and radar sites located near sensitive buildings, such as mosques. Because of the length of the operation and the rules of engagement, some military strategists and even pilots who had flown missions for NORTHERN WATCH no longer saw any military objective in the ongoing operation.

The last flight for Operation NORTHERN WATCH occurred on March 17, 2003, two days before the start of Operation IRAQI FREEDOM. NORTHERN WATCH officially ended on May 1, 2003. Since its inception in 1997, more than 40,000 troops had rotated through Incirlik Air Base to support the mission, and assigned aircraft flew more than 36,000 sorties.

ROBERT B. KANE

See also
DESERT FOX, Operation; DESERT THUNDER I, Operation; DESERT THUNDER II, Operation; Hussein, Saddam; Iraq No-Fly Zones; Kurds; PROVIDE COMFORT, Operation; SOUTHERN WATCH, Operation

References
Boyne, Walter J. *Beyond the Wild Blue: A History of the U.S. Air Force, 1947–2007.* 2nd ed. New York: Macmillan, 2007.
Byman, Daniel L., and Matthew C. Waxman. *Confronting Iraq: U.S. Policy and the Use of Force since the Gulf War.* Santa Monica, CA: Rand Corporation, 2000.
Knights, Michael Andrew. *Cradle of Conflict: Iraq and the Birth of Modern U.S. Military Power.* Annapolis, MD: Naval Institute Press, 2005.
Rand Corporation. *Interoperability of U.S. and NATO Allied Air Forces: Supporting Data and Case Studies; Project Air Force.* Santa Monica, CA: Rand Corporation, 2003.

Nur al-Din (1118–1174)

Ottoman ruler of Aleppo and Damascus who united most of the Muslim Near East against the crusaders. Nur al-Din was the second son of Zangi, ruler of Mosul and Aleppo, who captured Edessa (modern-day Sanliurfa, Turkey) from the Franks in 1144. Mosul and the territories of upper Mesopotamia were inherited on Zangi's death in 1146 by his eldest son, Sayf al-Din Ghazi (d. 1149), while Nur al-Din received the western half, including Edessa and Aleppo. Relations between the two men were strained until Nur al-Din paid formal homage to his elder brother, who confirmed Nur al-Din's territories and charged him with jihad (holy war) against the Franks. The generally cordial relations between the two allowed Nur al-Din to devote his attention entirely to his Syrian interests without having to worry about his eastern borders.

When the Armenian populace of Edessa heard of Zangi's death, they neutralized the city's Muslim garrison and appealed to their former Frankish ruler, Count Joscelin II, for assistance. Nur al-Din arrived first, defeating the Franks and crushing the Armenians.

In May 1147 Nur al-Din and Mu'in al-Din of Damascus repelled the Franks from the Hauran plateau. Then in July 1148, the combined armies of the Second Crusade (1147–1149) and the Kingdom of Jerusalem attacked Damascus. Responding to appeals from Mu'in al-Din, Nur al-Din advanced on the city, and the Franks then withdrew. In June 1149 Nur al-Din attacked the region of Apamea in northern Syria and defeated the Franks near Inab. He then besieged Antioch (modern-day Antakya, Turkey), where a treaty was made after he had taken Apamea (modern-day Afamiyah, Syria) and Harenc (modern-day Arim, Syria).

In August, Mu'in al-Din died. Nur al-Din attempted to intervene in Damascus, appealing to the city's inhabitants for support against the Franks. They instead sought Frankish aid against him. Nur al-Din encamped near Damascus but, on hearing that Joscelin II of Edessa had been captured, returned to Aleppo.

In the summer of 1150 in cooperation with the Seljuk sultan of Rum, Mas'ud, Nur al-Din attacked territories around Antioch, and by autumn he held the region downstream of Bira (modern-day Birecik, Turkey). This moved the western border of Muslim lands from the Euphrates to the Orontes.

In 1151 Nur al-Din advanced on Damascus again but could not prevent its inhabitants from making terms with the Franks. However, he did secure their nominal recognition of his sovereignty. In 1152 he temporarily took Tortosa (modern-day Tartus, Syria), severing communications between the county of Tripoli and the principality of Antioch. To win Damascus to his side Nur al-Din cut off its supplies, while his agents engaged in propaganda. Damascus's ruler, Mujir al-Din Uvak, appealed to the Franks, but

Nur al-Din acted first. He entered Damascus in April 1154. There was some rioting, but he restored order and distributed provisions, and the city leadership capitulated. Muslim Syria was now united under Nur al-Din.

In 1155 Nur al-Din subdued Baalbek, made treaties with the Franks of Jerusalem and Antioch, and intervened in the inheritance struggle that broke out with the death of Mas'ud of Rum. As a result, Nur al-Din gained territories on the right bank of the Euphrates, including Bira. In the spring of 1156 he supported an attack by troops from Damascus on Harenc. Eventually a treaty was concluded. Harenc remained in Frankish hands, but its revenues were split between the Franks and Nur al-Din.

In February 1157, King Baldwin III of Jerusalem raided the Golan (Jawlan). In April Nur al-Din retaliated, sending troops to attack the town of Banyas. Its walls were breached, but hearing that Baldwin was marching to the rescue, Nur al-Din ordered a withdrawal. Baldwin followed the Muslims to Galilee, where they ambushed him. Most of the Frankish troops were captured, but Baldwin escaped. In July earthquakes struck the region, forcing Nur al-Din to return to Damascus to repair its damaged defenses. Then in October he fell seriously ill. He was transferred to Aleppo, where he recovered.

Nur al-Din returned to Damascus in April 1158. There he mustered an army to take revenge for recent Frankish raids. An inconclusive engagement occurred near the Jordan in July; then in December or January, Nur al-Din fell ill a second time. Again he recovered, and learning of a proposed Frankish-Byzantine coalition, he fortified Aleppo and set out to meet the allies.

Long negotiations followed, but in May 1159 Nur al-Din concluded an alliance with Byzantine emperor Manuel I Komnenos. This included an agreement to cooperate against Seljuk sultan of Rum Qilij-Arslan II. While the Byzantines attacked Eskişehir, Nur al-Din occupied a number of Seljuk territories and cities. In 1160 Qilij-Arslan negotiated a truce.

While Nur al-Din was campaigning to the north, Baldwin III of Jerusalem invaded Damascene territory. Najm al-Din Ayyub, Nur al-Din's lieutenant there (and the father of Saladin), negotiated a three-month truce. When it expired, the Franks invaded again. In the autumn of 1161, Nur al-Din returned and made a truce with Baldwin before performing the hajj (pilgrimage to Mecca). Upon his return in 1162 he again fought the Franks near Harenc, but bad weather cut the battle short. In the spring of 1163 Nur al-Din suffered a second setback when he was surprised by the Franks at the foot of Krak des Chevaliers and his army routed.

In early 1164 Nur al-Din received an appeal for aid from Shawar, who had been deposed as vizier of Fatimid Egypt. In exchange for promises of a third of the revenues of Egypt and other inducements, Nur al-Din sent troops under Asad al-Din Shirkuh, the brother of Ayyub, to restore Shawar to power. The new Egyptian vizier, Dirgham, appealed to the Franks, but harassed by Nur al-Din further north, they were unable to prevent Shirkuh and his army from entering the Nile Delta. Shawar was restored but refused to fulfill his promises, although he eventually paid the costs of the expedition. Meanwhile, in August Nur al-Din had defeated the Franks near Harenc and taken the city. Banyas followed in October.

In January 1167 Shirkuh set out for Egypt again. Meanwhile, Nur al-Din occupied Hunin, near Banyas. Shirkuh returned in September, having fought and then come to terms with both the Franks and Egyptians, and obtained a large payment from Cairo. Nur al-Din then took a number of fortresses on the coastal plain. He planned to take Beirut but was unable to do so because of dissension in his army.

In 1168, the Franks attacked Egypt. Fatimid caliph al-Aid appealed to Nur al-Din for aid, and in December Shirkuh set out with an army. The Franks withdrew, and Shirkuh entered Cairo in January 1169. Shawar was executed, and Shirkuh became the new vizier. He died shortly after and was succeeded by his nephew, Saladin.

In April 1170 Nur al-Din, apparently concerned about Saladin's ambitions, sent Ayyub to remind his son of his loyalties. In June another earthquake shook Syria. Nur al-Din spent time overseeing repairs and then in September, following the death of his brother Qub al-Din, who had succeeded Sayf al-Din at Mosul, intervened in the succession, confirming the authority of Qub al-Din's son Sayf al-Din Ghazi II.

In September 1171 Saladin suppressed the Fatimid caliphate of Egypt. He then attacked Kerak in Frankish Transjordan, while Nur al-Din attacked the county of Tripoli. However, when Kerak offered to surrender, Saladin withdrew, citing unrest in Cairo, although it seems more likely that he was reluctant to remove obstacles between his territory and that of Nur al-Din. An angry Nur al-Din announced his intention to depose his subordinate but relented when Saladin reaffirmed his loyalty.

In the autumn of 1172 Nur al-Din again repelled Frankish raids in the Hauran and intervened in northern Syria, where Qilij Arslan, obeying a warning from Manuel Komnenos, had refused Nur al-Din aid. Nur al-Din took several Seljuk territories on the right bank of the Euphrates, including

Marash (modern-day Karamanmaraﬂ, Turkey) in July 1173. Soon afterward Qilij Arslan sued for peace, and Nur al-Din instructed him to participate in the jihad. Meanwhile, Nur al-Din had instructed Saladin to attack Kerak again. Saladin obeyed in May 1173 but, upon hearing at the end of July that Nur al-Din had come south and was two days' march away, retired, claiming that his father was ill and that he was thus needed to keep order in Cairo. This time Nur al-Din accepted his excuse but also began to prepare an expedition to bring Saladin to heel. Setting out for Egypt in early May 1174 Nur al-Din soon again fell ill, dying on May 15, 1174.

It is not clear how far Nur al-Din's jihad against the Franks was motivated by genuine religious fervor. After his first two bouts of illness and his defeat at Krak des Chevaliers in 1163, he is said to have adopted a pious, ascetic lifestyle. However, he still spent much of his time campaigning against other Muslims as well as against the Franks. Nonetheless, many of his contemporaries saw him as a great *mujahid* (holy warrior), and his tomb in Damascus remains a site of popular veneration.

NIALL CHRISTIE

See also
Fatimid Dynasty; Saladin; Zangi, Imad ad-Din

References
Elisséeff, Nikita. *Nur ad-Din: Un grand prince musulman de Syrie au temps des croisades*. 3 vols. Damas: Institut Français de Damas, 1967.
Hillenbrand, Carole. *The Crusades: Islamic Perspectives*. Edinburgh, UK: Edinburgh University Press, 1999.
Holt, Peter M. *The Age of the Crusades*. London: Longman, 1986.
Lev, Yaacov. "The Social and Economic Policies of Nur al-Din (1146–1174): The Sultan of Syria." *Der Islam* 81 (2004): 218–242.
Sivan, Emmanuel. *L'Islam et la Croisade*. Paris: Maisonneuve, 1968.
Tabbaa, Yasser. "Monuments with a Message: Propagation of the Jihad under Nur al-Din." In *The Meeting of Two Worlds*, ed. Vladimir P. Goss, 223–240. Kalamazoo, MI: Medieval Institute Publications, 1986.

Nuri al-Said (1888–July 15, 1958)

Prominent pro-British Iraqi politician who served as prime minister 14 times between 1930 and 1958. Born in Baghdad in 1888, Nuri al-Said was the son of a minor Ottoman government official. Trained at the Staff College in Istanbul (Constantinople) as an officer in the Ottoman Army, Nuri al-Said helped wage guerrilla warfare against the Italian Army that had invaded and occupied Libya in the Italo-Libyan War of 1911–1912. Later taken prisoner by the British, he was held as a prisoner in Egypt.

Converted to the Arab nationalist cause, Nuri fought with British Army major T. E. Lawrence in the Arab Revolt (1916–1918) and served as an adviser to revolt leader Emir Faisal of Hejaz, who would later reign briefly as the king of Syria before becoming King Faisal I of Iraq. In 1918 Nuri commanded the Arab troops who took Damascus for Faisal and accompanied Faisal to the Paris Peace Conference following World War I.

Nuri secured his first cabinet position in 1922, as director-general of the police in Iraq. He used this post to staff the police with his own followers, a tactic he would repeat again and again. In 1924 he became deputy commander of the Iraqi Army, and in 1930 he became prime minister for the first time, signing the Anglo-Iraqi Treaty. The treaty provided for Iraqi independence in 1932 but was unpopular with many Iraqis because it also provided for a 25-year alliance between Britain and Iraq that included the leasing of bases to Britain. Nuri held numerous cabinet positions and served many times as prime minister.

Although he was dismissed from office in 1932, Nuri, who was a trusted ally of the British, was never far from the seat of power. In early 1941 he denounced Prime Minister Rashid Ali al-Gaylani's anti-British, pro-German policies, which were strongly influenced by Haj Amin al-Husseini, mufti of Jerusalem. At the end of January 1941 al-Gaylani fled into exile, only to return to power in April. It was then Nuri's turn to flee, to Jordan. When al-Gaylani attempted to align his government with the Axis side in World War II, fighting with the British occurred, and British forces, supported by Jordan's Arab Legion, deposed al-Gaylani and installed Nuri in his place. This time Nuri al-Said held the position of prime minister until June 1944.

Nuri was Iraqi prime minister for the 9th through 14th times during November 1946–March 1947, January–December 1949, September 1950–July 1952, August 1954–June 1957, and March–May 1958. In February 1955 he signed the Baghdad Pact with Iran, Turkey, Pakistan, and the United Kingdom, intended as a buffer against Soviet encroachments in the region.

Nuri's pro-Western position brought him into conflict with Egyptian leader Gamal Abdel Nasser, who opposed Western influence in the region. Nasser launched a media campaign that challenged the legitimacy of the Iraqi monarchy and called on the Iraqi military to overthrow it. In response to the Egyptian-Syrian union known as the United Arab Republic, on February 12, 1958, the Hashemite monarchies of Jordan and Iraq declared an Iraqi-Jordanian union known as the Arab Federation. In May 1958 Nuri resigned to become the first prime minister of the short-lived Arab Federation.

Nuri's pro-Western policies and his increasingly heavy-handed methods, from crushing a miners' strike in November 1946 to putting down demonstrations against the Baghdad Pact, made him very unpopular in Iraq. On July 14, 1958, a military coup led by Abdul Karim Qasim ended the Arab Federation, the Iraqi monarchy, and Nuri's life. King Faisal II and other members of the royal family were executed. Disguised as a veiled woman, Nuri al-Said escaped capture for a day but was caught on July 15 and promptly put to death. His body was buried but then dug up and reportedly tied to the back of a car and paraded through the streets of Baghdad until nothing remained but a portion of one leg.

MICHAEL R. HALL

See also

Arab Revolt of World War I; Baghdad Pact; Faisal I, King of Iraq; Faisal II, King of Iraq; Glubb, Sir John Bagot; Husseini, Haj Amin al-; Iraq; Lawrence, Thomas Edward

References

Birdwood, Lord. *Nuri as-Said.* London: Cassell, 1959.

Dodge, Toby. *Inventing Iraq: The Failure of Nation-Building and a History Denied.* New York: Columbia University Press, 2003.

Gallman, Waldemar J. *Iraq under General Nuri: My Recollection of Nuri Al-Said, 1954–1958.* Baltimore: Johns Hopkins University Press, 1964.